CurrentLaw

STATUTES

1995

VOLUME ONE

AUSTRALIA
The Law Book Company
Brisbane • Sydney • Melbourne • Perth

CANADA
Carswell
Ottawa • Toronto • Calgary • Montreal • Vancouver

Agents:
Steimatzky's Agency Ltd., Tel Aviv;
N. M. Tripathi (Private) Ltd., Bombay;
Eastern Law House (Private) Ltd., Calcutta;
M.P.P. House, Bangalore;
Universal Book Traders, Delhi;
Aditya Books, Delhi;
MacMillan Shuppan KK, Tokyo;
Pakistan Law House, Karachi

Current Law

STATUTES

1995

VOLUME ONE

SWEET & MAXWELL EDITORIAL TEAM
SARAH ANDREWS
MELANIE BHAGAT
ALA KUZMICKI
SOPHIE LOWE
CERI PICKERING

W. GREEN EDITORIAL TEAM
CHARLOTTE HALL
PETER NICHOLSON

LONDON

SWEET & MAXWELL

EDINBURGH

W. GREEN

1995

Published by
SWEET & MAXWELL LIMITED
of South Quay Plaza, 183 Marsh Wall, London,
and W. GREEN LIMITED
of Alva Street, Edinburgh,
Typeset by MFK Information Services Ltd., Hitchin, Herts.
and printed in Great Britain
by The Bath Press,
Bath, Avon.

ISBN This Volume only : 0 421 54760 X
As a set   : 0 421 54800 2

CONTENTS

CHRONOLOGICAL TABLE

VOLUME ONE

Annotators' names are in italic

VOLUME ONE

ALPHABETICAL INDEX OF SHORT TITLES

STATUTES 1995

(References are to chapter numbers of 1995)

EUROPEAN COMMUNITIES (FINANCE) ACT 1995

(1995 c. 1)

An Act to amend the definition of "the Treaties" and "the Community Treaties" in section 1(2) of the European Communities Act 1972 so as to include the decision of 31st October 1994 of the Council on the Communities' system of own resources and so as to remove a spent provision.

[16th January 1995]

PARLIAMENTARY DEBATES
  Hansard, H.C. Vol. 250, cols. 932, 1034; Vol. 251, cols. 327, 431; H.L. Vol. 559, col. 1088; Vol. 560, cols. 7, 112.

INTRODUCTION
  This Act extends the definition of "the Treaties" and "the Community Treaties" in the European Communities Act 1972 (c. 68), s.1(2)(e)(f).

Be it enacted by the Queen's most Excellent Majesty, by and with the advice and consent of the Lords Spiritual and Temporal, and Commons, in this present Parliament assembled, and by the authority of the same, as follows:—

Extended meaning of "the Treaties" and "the Community Treaties"

1. In section 1(2) of the European Communities Act 1972, in the definition of "the Treaties" and "the Community Treaties", for paragraphs (e) and (f) (Council decisions of 7th May 1985 and of 24th June 1988 on Communities' own resources, and undertaking of Member States confirmed on 24th June 1988 for financing the Communities' budget for 1988), and the word "and" immediately preceding them, there shall be substituted the words "and
    (e) the decisions of the Council of 7th May 1985, 24th June 1988, and 31st October 1994, on the Communities' system of own resources; and".

Short title and repeal

2.—(1) This Act may be cited as the European Communities (Finance) Act 1995.
  (2) The European Communities (Finance) Act 1988 (which is superseded by this Act) is hereby repealed.

INDEX

References are to sections

CONSOLIDATED FUND ACT 1995

(1995 c. 2)

An Act to apply certain sums out of the Consolidated Fund to the service of the years ending on 31st March 1994 and 1995.   [23rd March 1995]

PARLIAMENTARY DEBATES
Hansard, H.C. Vol. 256, col. 998, Vol. 257, col. 353; H.L. Vol. 562, cols. 1286, 1320.

INTRODUCTION
This Act makes provision for the allocation of £167,222,897.35 out of the Consolidated Fund for the service of the year ending March 31, 1994 and of £1,171,475,000 for the year ending March 31, 1995.

Issue out of the Consolidated Fund for the year ended 31st March 1994

1. The Treasury may issue out of the Consolidated Fund of the United Kingdom and apply towards making good the supply granted to Her Majesty for the service of the year ended on 31st March 1994 the sum of £167,222,897.35.

Issue out of the Consolidated Fund for the year ending 31st March 1995

2. The Treasury may issue out of the Consolidated Fund of the United Kingdom and apply towards making good the supply granted to Her Majesty for the service of the year ending on 31st March 1995 the sum of £1,171,475,000.

Short title

3. This Act may be cited as the Consolidated Fund Act 1995.

INDEX

References are to sections

SOUTH AFRICA ACT 1995

(1995 c. 3)

An Act to make provision in connection with the re-admission of South
Africa as a member of the Commonwealth.   [23rd March 1995]

PARLIAMENTARY DEBATES
Hansard, H.L. Vol. 561, cols. 440, 917; H.C. Vol. 256, col. 479.

INTRODUCTION
    This Act modifies certain U.K. enactments to take account of the re-admission of South
Africa as a member of the Commonwealth on June 1, 1994. Legislation relating to the Commonwealth Institute and the Imperial War Museum and to the services and visiting forces is modified. Repeal of certain provisions of the South Africa Act 1962 (c. 23) and the Maintenance
Orders (Reciprocal Enforcement) Act 1972 (c. 18) is also provided for.

Provisions relating to South Africa

1. The provisions in the Schedule to this Act, which are made in connection
with the re-admission of South Africa as a member of the Commonwealth,
shall have effect.

Short title

2. This Act may be cited as the South Africa Act 1995.

Section 1   SCHEDULE

PROVISIONS RELATING TO SOUTH AFRICA

Commonwealth Institute

1. In section 8(2) of the Imperial Institute Act 1925, as amended by the Commonwealth Institute Act 1958 (power to vary the provisions of the Act of 1925), after the words "New Zealand,"
there shall be inserted the words "South Africa,".

Imperial War Museum

2.—(1) In the Schedule to the Imperial War Museum Act 1920 (board of trustees), in paragraph (1)—
    (a) for the words "twenty other members" there shall be substituted the words "twenty-one
        other members"; and
    (b) in the first and second columns of the table after the entries relating to the Government of
        New Zealand there shall be inserted "1" and "The Government of South Africa"
        respectively.
    (2) The above amendments are without prejudice to the power to vary the said paragraph (1)
conferred by section 1 of the Imperial War Museum Act 1955.

The Services

3. In the definition of "Commonwealth force" in sections 225(1) of the Army Act 1955 and
223(1) of the Air Force Act 1955 (interpretation) and in the definition of "Commonwealth country" in section 135(1) of the Naval Discipline Act 1957 (interpretation), after the words "New
Zealand," there shall be inserted the words "South Africa,".

Visiting forces

4. In the Visiting Forces (British Commonwealth) Act 1933, section 4 (attachment of personnel and mutual powers of command) shall apply in relation to forces raised in South Africa as it
applies to forces raised in Dominions within the meaning of the Statute of Westminster 1931.
    5.—(1) In section 1(1)(a) of the Visiting Forces Act 1952 (countries to which Act applies),
after the words "New Zealand," there shall be inserted the words "South Africa,".

(2) Any Order in Council for the time being in force under section 8 of that Act (application to visiting forces of law relating to home forces) shall be deemed to apply to the visiting forces of South Africa until express provision with respect to that country is made under that section.

6. In section 84(2) of the Offices, Shops and Railway Premises Act 1963 and section 78(2) of the Office and Shop Premises Act (Northern Ireland) 1966 (exclusion of application of Act to visiting forces), after the word "Namibia" there shall be inserted the words ", South Africa".

South Africa Act 1962

7.—(1) The following provisions of the South Africa Act 1962 are hereby repealed:
    section 1(3) and (4) (nationality);
    section 2(3) (consequential amendments);
    in Schedule 2 (continuing operation of certain enactments in relation to South Africa),
        paragraphs 2 and 3 (maintenance orders);
    in Schedule 3 (transitional provisions), paragraph 5 (solicitors);
    Schedule 4 (consequential amendments).

(2) In section 22(2) of the Maintenance Orders (Reciprocal Enforcement) Act 1972 (amendments and repeals), paragraph (d) (South Africa Act) is hereby repealed.

INDEX

References are to sections and to the Schedule

FINANCE ACT 1995*

(1995 c. 4)

* Ian Ferrier, Barrister

Part I—Alcoholic liquor.
Part II—Road fuel gas.
Part III—Betting and gaming etc.
Part IV—Air passenger duty.
Part V—Vehicle excise and registration.
Part VI—Value added tax.
Part VII—Insurance premium tax.
Part VIII—Income tax, corporation tax and capital gains tax.
Part IX—Petroleum revenue tax.
Part X—Stamp duty.
Part XI—Inheritance tax: agricultural property.
Part XII—Ports levy.

An Act to grant certain duties, to alter other duties, and to amend the law relating to the National Debt and the Public Revenue, and to make further provision in connection with Finance. [1st May 1995]

PARLIAMENTARY DEBATES
Hansard, H.C. Vol. 252, col. 588, Vol. 253, cols. 38, 368, 692, Vol. 257, cols. 1405, 1537. H.L. Vol. 563, cols. 703, 1149.

INTRODUCTION AND GENERAL NOTE
This Act, resulting from Mr Kenneth Clarke's second Budget, is almost as long as its predecessor. Despite this length, it contains little innovation and reflects, rather, the ever-increasing complexity of fiscal legislation in detail.
The Government's defeat on December 6, 1994 over the increase in VAT on domestic fuel and power from eight per cent to 17.5 per cent as from April 1, 1995, necessitated the withdrawal of this measure and the introduction of a further package of increases in duty on alcohol, tobacco and petrol.
The following particular measures contributed to the length of the Act:
(1) a change in the system for vehicle excise duty (VED), moving from a charge by plated weight to a charge by revenue weight (s.19 and Sched. 4);
(2) the introduction of a tax relief for investment in venture capital trusts (ss.70–73 and Scheds. 14–16); and
(3) further refinements to the provisions for self-assessment and the change to a current year basis for charging taxpayers under Sched. D (ss.103–123 and Scheds. 20–22).
Much of the Act consisted of amendments to previous legislation, making comprehension even more difficult. A backbench demand for simplification of the law led to the carrying, over Government opposition, of a section requiring a report from the Inland Revenue on this topic (s.160).

ABBREVIATIONS
ACT	: Advance corporation tax
AMLD	: Amusement machine licence duty
BGDA 1981	: Betting and Gaming Duties Act 1981
BLAGAB	: Basic life assurance and general annuity business
CAA 1990	: Capital Allowances Act 1990
CGT	: Capital Gains Tax
DVLA	: Driver and Vehicle Licensing Agency
FA 1989	: Finance Act 1989
FA 1990	: Finance Act 1990
FA 1991	: Finance Act 1991
FA 1993	: Finance Act 1993
FA 1994	: Finance Act 1994
GMLD	: Gaming machine licence duty
ICTA 1988	: Income and Corporation Taxes Act 1988
IPT	: Insurance premium tax
OEIC	: Open-ended investment company
OTA 1975	: Oil Taxation Act 1975
PRT	: Petroleum Revenue Tax
TCGA 1992	: Taxation of Chargeable Gains Act 1992
TMA 1970	: Taxes Management Act 1970
VAT	: Value Added Tax

PART I

DUTIES OF EXCISE

Alcoholic liquor duties

Low-strength wine, made-wine and cider

1.—(1) The Alcoholic Liquor Duties Act 1979 shall be amended as follows.

(2) In section 1 (the alcoholic liquors dutiable under the Act) in subsections (4) and (5) (definitions of "wine" and "made-wine") after the words "any liquor" there shall in both cases be inserted "which is of a strength exceeding 1.2 per cent and which is".

(3) In section 1(6) (definition of "cider") after the word "strength" there shall be inserted "exceeding 1.2 per cent but".

(4) In section 59(1) (prohibition on rendering wine and made-wine sparkling) for paragraph (b) there shall be substituted the following paragraph—

"(b) is wine or made-wine of a strength exceeding 5.5 per cent.".

(5) Subsections (2) and (4) above—

(a) shall apply in relation to liquor imported into, or produced in, the United Kingdom on or after 1st January 1995, and

(b) as regards any provision about liquor removed to the United Kingdom from the Isle of Man, shall also apply in relation to liquor so removed on or after that date.

(6) Subsection (3) above shall apply in relation to liquor imported into, or made in, the United Kingdom on or after 1st January 1995.

GENERAL NOTE

A lower strength limit of 1.2 per cent is introduced into the definitions of wine, made-wine and cider, below which duty is not chargeable.

Wine and made-wine: rates

2.—(1) For the Table of rates of duty in Schedule 1 to the Alcoholic Liquor Duties Act 1979 (wine and made-wine) there shall be substituted the Table in Schedule 1 to this Act.

(2) This section shall be deemed to have come into force on 1st January 1995.

GENERAL NOTE

The section introduces Sched. 1, which changes the structure of the excise duty on wines and implements increases announced by the Chancellor on December 8, 1994 as a result of the Government's defeat over the increase in VAT on domestic fuel and power from eight per cent to 17.5 per cent.

See further the General Note to Sched. 1.

Spirits, beer and cider: rates

3.—(1) In section 5 of the Alcoholic Liquor Duties Act 1979 (spirits) for "£19.81" there shall be substituted "£20.60".

(2) In section 36(1) of that Act (beer) for "£10.45" there shall be substituted "£10.82".

(3) In section 62(1) of that Act (cider) for "£22.82" there shall be substituted "£23.78".

(4) This section shall be deemed to have come into force on 1st January 1995.

GENERAL NOTE

This implements the increase in duty on spirits, beer and cider announced by the Chancellor on December 8, 1994 following the Government's defeat over the increase in VAT on domestic fuel and power.

The increases are about four per cent, representing approximately 1p on a pint of beer, 1p on a litre bottle of cider and 26p on a bottle of spirits.

Alcoholic ingredients relief

4.—(1) Subject to the following provisions of this section, where any person proves to the satisfaction of the Commissioners that any dutiable alcoholic liquor on which duty has been paid has been—

(a) used as an ingredient in the production or manufacture of a product falling within subsection (2) below, or

(b) converted into vinegar,

he shall be entitled to obtain from the Commissioners the repayment of the duty paid thereon.

(2) The products falling within this subsection are—

(a) any beverage of an alcoholic strength not exceeding 1.2 per cent,

(b) chocolates for human consumption which contain alcohol such that 100 kilograms of the chocolates would not contain more than 8.5 litres of alcohol, or

(c) any other food for human consumption which contains alcohol such that 100 kilograms of the food would not contain more than 5 litres of alcohol.

(3) A repayment of duty shall not be made under this section in respect of any liquor except to a person who—

(a) is the person who used the liquor as an ingredient in a product falling within subsection (2) above or, as the case may be, who converted it into vinegar;

(b) carries on a business as a wholesale supplier of products of the applicable description falling within that subsection or, as the case may be, of vinegar;

(c) produced or manufactured the product or vinegar for the purposes of that business;

(d) makes a claim for the repayment in accordance with the following provisions of this section; and

(e) satisfies the Commissioners as to the matters mentioned in paragraphs (a) to (c) above and that the repayment claimed does not relate to any duty which has been repaid or drawn back prior to the making of the claim.

(4) A claim for repayment under this section shall take such form and be made in such manner, and shall contain such particulars, as the Commissioners may direct, either generally or in a particular case.

(5) Except so far as the Commissioners otherwise allow, a person shall not make a claim for a repayment under this section unless—

(a) the claim relates to duty paid on liquor used as an ingredient or, as the case may be, converted into vinegar in the course of a period of three months ending not more than one month before the making of the claim; and

(b) the amount of the repayment which is claimed is not less than £250.

(6) The Commissioners may by order made by statutory instrument increase the amount for the time being specified in subsection (5)(b) above; and a statutory instrument containing an order under this subsection shall be subject to annulment in pursuance of a resolution of the House of Commons.

(7) There may be remitted by the Commissioners any duty charged either—

(a) on any dutiable alcoholic liquor imported into the United Kingdom at a time when it is contained as an ingredient in any chocolates or food falling within subsection (2)(b) or (c) above; or

(b) on any dutiable alcoholic liquor used as an ingredient in the manufacture or production in an excise warehouse of any such chocolates or food.

(8) This section shall be construed as one with the Alcoholic Liquor Duties Act 1979, and references in this section to chocolates or food do not include references to any beverages.

GENERAL NOTE
There have previously been two separate systems of relief for the repayment of duty on alcohol used in preparing vinegar and certain food and beverage products—one relating to the duty on spirits and the other to the duty on beer, wine and cider. These are now unified.

Subs. (2)
The type of products covered include liqueur chocolates, whisky marmalade, fruit in brandy and particular flavours of ice cream and soft drinks which contain small amounts of alcohol.

Subss. (3)–(8)
These contain the administrative machinery for implementing the relief, including the conferment of regulation-making powers on the Customs and Excise. Claims for repayment of duty will normally cover a three-month period and be subject to a *de minimis* limit of £250.

Denatured alcohol

5.—(1) The liquors on which duty is charged under the Alcoholic Liquor Duties Act 1979 shall not include any denatured alcohol; and any duty so charged on liquor which has become denatured alcohol before the requirement to pay the duty takes effect shall be remitted.

(2) In this section—

"denatured alcohol" means any dutiable alcoholic liquor which has been subjected to the process of being mixed in the prescribed manner with a prescribed substance; and

"prescribed" means prescribed by the Commissioners by regulations made by statutory instrument.

(3) The power of the Commissioners to make regulations defining denatured alcohol for the purposes of this section shall include—

(a) power, in prescribing any substance or any manner of mixing a substance with a liquor, to do so by reference to such circumstances or other factors, or to the approval or opinion of such persons (including the authorities of another member State), as they may consider appropriate;

(b) power to make different provision for different cases; and

(c) power to make such supplemental, incidental, consequential and transitional provision as the Commissioners think fit;

and a statutory instrument containing any regulations under this section shall be subject to annulment in pursuance of a resolution of either House of Parliament.

(4) Sections 14 to 16 of the Finance Act 1994 (review and appeals) shall have effect in relation to any decision which—

(a) is made under or for the purposes of any regulations under this section, and

(b) is a decision given to any person as to whether a manner of mixing any substance with any liquor is to be, or to continue to be, approved in his case, or as to the conditions subject to which it is so approved,

as if that decision were a decision specified in Schedule 5 to that Act.

(5) Schedule 2 to this Act (which contains amendments for or in connection with the application to all denatured alcohol of provisions of the Alcoholic Liquor Duties Act 1979 relating to methylated spirits and also makes a consequential amendment of the Finance Act 1994) shall have effect.

(6) This section and Schedule 2 to this Act shall come into force on such day as the Commissioners may by order made by statutory instrument appoint, and different days may be appointed under this subsection for different purposes.

(7) An order under subsection (6) above may make such transitional provisions and savings as appear to the Commissioners to be appropriate in connection with the bringing into force by such an order of any provision for any purposes.

(8) This section shall be construed as one with the Alcoholic Liquor Duties Act 1979.

GENERAL NOTE

The previous system for relieving duty on denatured spirits (*i.e.* methylated spirits) is extended to the denaturing of beer, wine and cider. These are products used by industry for the manufacture of household cleaners, paints, inks, medicines etc. To discourage this alcohol being diverted to human consumption, it is made unsuitable for drinking ("denatured") prior to delivery.

For further provisions see the General Note to Sched. 2.

Hydrocarbon oil duties

Rates of duty

6.—(1) In section 6(1) of the Hydrocarbon Oil Duties Act 1979 for "£0.3314" (duty on light oil) and "£0.2770" (duty on heavy oil) there shall be substituted "£0.3526" and "£0.3044" respectively.

(2) In section 8 of that Act (duty on road fuel gas) the following subsection shall be substituted for subsections (3) to (5)—

"(3) The rate of the duty under this section shall be £0.3314 a kilogram."

(3) In section 11(1) of that Act (rebate on heavy oil) for "£0.0116" (fuel oil) and "£0.0164" (gas oil) there shall be substituted "£0.0166" and "£0.0214" respectively.

(4) In section 14(1) of that Act (rebate on light oil for use as furnace fuel) for "£0.0116" there shall be substituted "£0.0166".

(5) This section shall be deemed to have come into force at 6 o'clock in the evening of 29th November 1994.

GENERAL NOTE

The section implements the Budget increase in excise duty on hydrocarbon oils by 8.3 per cent on average. In the event, these rates were only in force for one month due to the further increase announced by the Chancellor on December 8, 1994 and implemented by the next section.

Rates of duty: further provisions

7.—(1) In section 6(1) of the Hydrocarbon Oil Duties Act 1979, as amended by section 6 above, for "£0.3526" (duty on light oil) and "£0.3044" (duty on heavy oil) there shall be substituted "£0.3614" and "£0.3132" respectively.

(2) This section shall be deemed to have come into force on 1st January 1995.

GENERAL NOTE

Following the Chancellor's announcement on December 8, 1994 the duty on road fuels is increased by a further 2.5 to three per cent, making a total increase of 9.5 to 13 per cent.

Hydrocarbon oil: "road vehicle"

8.—(1) In the definition of "road vehicle" in section 27(1) of the Hydrocarbon Oil Duties Act 1979 (road vehicle not to include vehicle of a kind specified in Schedule 1) for the words "of a kind specified in Schedule 1 to this Act" there shall be substituted "which is an excepted vehicle within the meaning given by Schedule 1 to this Act."

(2) The following Schedule shall be substituted for Schedule 1 to that Act—

"SCHEDULE 1

EXCEPTED VEHICLES

Unlicensed vehicles not used on public roads

1.—(1) A vehicle is an excepted vehicle while—

(a) it is not used on a public road, and

(b) no licence under the Vehicle Excise and Registration Act 1994 is in force in respect of it.

(2) A vehicle in respect of which there is current a certificate or document in the form of a licence issued under regulations under section 22(2) of the Vehicle Excise and Registration Act 1994 shall be treated for the purposes of sub-paragraph (1) above as a vehicle in respect of which a licence under that Act is in force.

Tractors

2.—(1) A vehicle is an excepted vehicle if it is—
(a) an agricultural tractor, or
(b) an off-road tractor.

(2) In sub-paragraph (1) above "agricultural tractor" means a tractor used on public roads solely for purposes relating to agriculture, horticulture, forestry or activities falling within sub-paragraph (3) below.

(3) The activities falling within this sub-paragraph are—
(a) cutting verges bordering public roads;
(b) cutting hedges or trees bordering public roads or bordering verges which border public roads.

(4) In sub-paragraph (1) above "off-road tractor" means a tractor which is not an agricultural tractor (within the meaning given by sub-paragraph (2) above) and which is—
(a) designed and constructed primarily for use otherwise than on roads, and
(b) incapable by reason of its construction of exceeding a speed of twenty-five miles per hour on the level under its own power.

Light agricultural vehicles

3.—(1) A vehicle is an excepted vehicle if it is a light agricultural vehicle.

(2) In sub-paragraph (1) above "light agricultural vehicle" means a vehicle which—
(a) has a revenue weight not exceeding 1,000 kilograms,
(b) is designed and constructed so as to seat only the driver,
(c) is designed and constructed primarily for use otherwise than on roads, and
(d) is used solely for purposes relating to agriculture, horticulture or forestry.

(3) In sub-paragraph (2)(a) above "revenue weight" has the meaning given by section 60A of the Vehicle Excise and Registration Act 1994.

Agricultural engines

4. An agricultural engine is an excepted vehicle.

Vehicles used between different parts of land

5. A vehicle is an excepted vehicle if—
(a) it is used only for purposes relating to agriculture, horticulture or forestry,
(b) it is used on public roads only in passing between different areas of land occupied by the same person, and

(c) the distance it travels on public roads in passing between any two such areas does not exceed 1.5 kilometres.

Mowing machines

6. A mowing machine is an excepted vehicle.

Snow clearing vehicles

7. A vehicle is an excepted vehicle when it is—
(a) being used, or
(b) going to or from the place where it is to be or has been used,
for the purpose of clearing snow from public roads by means of a snow plough or similar device (whether or not forming part of the vehicle).

Gritters

8. A vehicle is an excepted vehicle if it is constructed or adapted, and used, solely for the conveyance of machinery for spreading material on roads to deal with frost, ice or snow (with or without articles or material used for the purposes of the machinery).

Mobile cranes

9.—(1) A mobile crane is an excepted vehicle.
(2) In sub-paragraph (1) above "mobile crane" means a vehicle which is designed and constructed as a mobile crane and which—
(a) is used on public roads only as a crane in connection with work carried on at a site in the immediate vicinity or for the purpose of proceeding to and from a place where it is to be or has been used as a crane, and
(b) when so proceeding does not carry any load except such as is necessary for its propulsion or equipment.

Digging machines

10.—(1) A digging machine is an excepted vehicle.
(2) In sub-paragraph (1) above "digging machine" means a vehicle which is designed, constructed and used for the purpose of trench digging, or any kind of excavating or shovelling work, and which—
(a) is used on public roads only for that purpose or for the purpose of proceeding to and from the place where it is to be or has been used for that purpose, and
(b) when so proceeding does not carry any load except such as is necessary for its propulsion or equipment.

Works trucks

11.—(1) A works truck is an excepted vehicle.
(2) In sub-paragraph (1) above "works truck" means a goods vehicle which is designed for use in private premises and is used on public roads only—
(a) for carrying goods between private premises and a vehicle on a road within one kilometre of those premises,
(b) in passing from one part of private premises to another,
(c) in passing between private premises and other private premises in a case where the premises are within one kilometre of each other, or
(d) in connection with road works at the site of the works or within one kilometre of the site of the works.
(3) In sub-paragraph (2) above "goods vehicle" means a vehicle constructed or adapted for use and used for the conveyance of goods or burden of any description, whether in the course of trade or not.

Road construction vehicles

12.—(1) A vehicle is an excepted vehicle if it is—
(a) a road construction vehicle, and
(b) used or kept solely for the conveyance of built-in road construction machinery (with or without articles or material used for the purposes of the machinery).

(2) In sub-paragraph (1) above "road construction vehicle" means a vehicle—
(a) which is constructed or adapted for use for the conveyance of built-in road construction machinery, and
(b) which is not constructed or adapted for the conveyance of any other load except articles and material used for the purposes of such machinery.

(3) In sub-paragraphs (1) and (2) above "built-in road construction machinery", in relation to a vehicle, means road construction machinery built in as part of, or permanently attached to, the vehicle.

(4) In sub-paragraph (3) above "road construction machinery" means a machine or device suitable for use for the construction or repair of roads and used for no purpose other than the construction or repair of roads.

Road rollers

13. A road roller is an excepted vehicle.

Interpretation

14. In this Schedule "public road" means a road which is repairable at the public expense."
(3) This section shall come into force on 1st July 1995.

GENERAL NOTE
The section defines vehicles which are not to be classed as road vehicles and which are therefore entitled to use rebated heavy oil ("red diesel") when travelling on the public road. Existing entitlement depends on the vehicle excise duty category within which the vehicle falls. Under s.19 and Sched. 4 below, many of the categories which provided for entitlement are to be amended or abolished. This section provides for entitlement to be established by reference to the Hydrocarbon Oil Duties Act 1979, Sched. 1.
The new Sched. 1 includes vehicles not used on public roads, tractors (including machines for cutting hedges and roadside verges), all-terrain vehicles, agricultural engines (combine harvesters and the like), vehicles making journeys of up to 1.5 kilometres between parcels of agricultural land in the same ownership, mowing machines, snow ploughs, road gritters, mobile cranes used on roads at a site or going to and from the site, digging machines ("JCBs"), works trucks, road construction vehicles and road rollers.

Road fuel gas: old stock

9. In section 8 of the Hydrocarbon Oil Duties Act 1979 (road fuel gas) subsection (7) (no charge on use of gas if delivered or stocked before 3rd July 1972) shall be omitted.

GENERAL NOTE
An obsolete provision in the Hydrocarbon Oil Duties Act 1979 is repealed.

Tobacco products duty

Rates of duty

10.—(1) For the Table of rates of duty in Schedule 1 to the Tobacco Products Duty Act 1979 there shall be substituted—

"TABLE

1. Cigarettes	An amount equal to 20 per cent of the retail price plus £55.58 per thousand cigarettes.
2. Cigars	£82.56 per kilogram.
3. Hand-rolling tobacco.	£85.94 per kilogram.
4. Other smoking tobacco and chewing tobacco	£36.30 per kilogram."

(2) This section shall be deemed to have come into force at 6 o'clock in the evening of 29th November 1994.

GENERAL NOTE

This section implements the increases in duty on tobacco products, ranging from five per cent to 6.4 per cent, announced in the Budget.

Rates of duty: further provisions

11.—(1) For the Table of rates of duty in Schedule 1 to the Tobacco Products Duty Act 1979, as substituted by section 10 above, there shall be substituted—

"TABLE

1. Cigarettes	An amount equal to 20 per cent of the retail price plus £57.64 per thousand cigarettes.
2. Cigars	£85.61 per kilogram.
3. Hand-rolling tobacco	£85.94 per kilogram.
4. Other smoking tobacco and chewing tobacco	£37.64 per kilogram."

(2) This section shall be deemed to have come into force on 1st January 1995.

GENERAL NOTE

The further increases in tobacco duty announced on December 8, 1994 are implemented by this section. These amount to 3.7 per cent. However, the duty on hand-rolling tobacco, already subject to heavy smuggling, is left unchanged.

Pool betting duty

Pool betting duty

12.—(1) In section 7(1) of the Betting and Gaming Duties Act 1981 (which specifies 37.50 per cent. as the rate of pool betting duty) for "37.50 per cent." there shall be substituted "32.50 per cent."

(2) This section shall apply in relation to any pool betting duty the requirement to pay which takes effect on or after 6th May 1995.

GENERAL NOTE

The football pools companies have suffered a loss of revenue due to competition from the National Lottery. The reduction in pool betting duty from 37.5 per cent to 32.5 per cent is to compensate them for this.

Gaming machine licence duty

Rates of duty

13.—(1) In the Betting and Gaming Duties Act 1981 for the Table set out at the end of section 23 (amount of duty) there shall be substituted—

TABLE

(1) Period (in months) for which licence granted	*(2)* Small prize or five-penny machines	*(3)* Other machines
	£	£
1	60	150
2	105	275
3	155	400
4	205	520
5	250	645
6	295	755
7	340	880
8	390	1,005
9	435	1,115
10	480	1,235
11	510	1,305
12	535	1,375

(2) This section shall apply in relation to any gaming machine licence for which an application is made on or after 1st December 1994.

GENERAL NOTE

The rate of duty on gaming machine licences is increased by an average of 19 per cent.

Extension of duty to amusement machines

14.—(1) Schedule 3 to this Act (which contains amendments for or in connection with the application of the provisions of the Betting and Gaming Duties Act 1981 relating to gaming machine licence duty to amusement machines that are not gaming machines and also makes a consequential amendment of the Customs and Excise Management Act 1979) shall have effect.

(2) Schedule 3 to this Act shall have effect (subject to subsection (3) below) in relation only to the provision of a machine at a time on or after 1st November 1995 and to licences for periods beginning on or after that date and the duty on such licences.

(3) Where a gaming machine licence has been granted before 1st November 1995 for a period ending on or after that date, that licence shall have effect on and after that date, for so long as it remains in force, as an amusement machine licence authorising the provision, in accordance with the licence, of the machines the provision of which was authorised by the licence immediately before that date.

GENERAL NOTE

Gaming machine licence duty is extended to amusement machines, such as video and quiz machines. This proved one of the more contentious items in the Budget because of its possible effects on employment, particularly in seaside resorts, and the Government's original proposals were amended in order to reduce the impact on the entertainment industry.

In consequence of the change, gaming machine licence duty (GMLD) is renamed amusement machine licence duty (AMLD). The change takes effect for licences issued after November 1,

1995. Any gaming machine licence issued before that date but due to expire thereafter will have effect as an amusement machine licence.

See further the General Note to Sched. 3.

Air passenger duty

Rates of duty

15.—(1) Section 30 of the Finance Act 1994 (rate of air passenger duty) shall be deemed to have been enacted with the following modifications.

(2) The following subsection shall be substituted for subsection (2) (£5 if journey ends in member State or territory for whose external relations it is responsible)—

"(2) The rate is £5 if that place is in the area specified in subsection (3) below and in—
   (a) the United Kingdom or another EEA State, or
   (b) any territory for whose external relations the United Kingdom or another member State is responsible."

(3) The following subsection shall be inserted after subsection (8)—

"(9) In this section "EEA State" means a State which is a Contracting Party to the EEA Agreement but until the EEA Agreement comes into force in relation to Liechtenstein does not include the State of Liechtenstein; and "EEA Agreement" here means the Agreement on the European Economic Area signed at Oporto on 2nd May 1992 as adjusted by the Protocol signed at Brussels on 17th March 1993."

GENERAL NOTE

The £5 rate of air passenger duty, rather than £10, is extended from countries within the European Union to countries within the European Economic Area.

Assessment of interest on duty

16.—(1) In Schedule 6 to the Finance Act 1994 (air passenger duty: administration and enforcement) after paragraph 11 there shall be inserted—

"Assessment of interest

11A.—(1) Where by virtue of paragraph 7 above duty due from any person for an accounting period carries interest, the Commissioners may assess that person to an amount of interest in accordance with this paragraph.

(2) Notice of the assessment shall be given to the person liable for the interest or a representative of his.

(3) The amount of the interest shall be calculated by reference to a period ending on a date ("the due date") no later than the date of the notice.

(4) The notice shall specify—
   (a) the amount of the duty which carries the interest assessed ("the specified duty");
   (b) the amount of the interest assessed ("the specified interest");
   (c) the due date; and
   (d) a date by which that amount is required to be paid ("the payment date").

(5) Sub-paragraphs (6) and (7) below apply where the specified duty or any part of it is unpaid on the date of the notice.

(6) If the unpaid amount or any part of it is paid by the payment date, the payment shall be treated for the purposes of paragraph 7 above as made on the due date.

(7) To the extent that the unpaid amount is not paid by the payment date, an assessment may be made under this paragraph in respect of any interest on the unpaid amount which accrues after the due date.

(8) For the purposes of sub-paragraphs (6) and (7) above, a payment—

(a) which purports to be a payment of the unpaid amount or any part of it, but

(b) which is insufficient to discharge both the liability to pay the unpaid amount and the liability to pay the specified interest,

shall be treated as made in discharge (or partial discharge) of the liability to pay the specified interest before it is treated as discharging to any extent the liability to pay the unpaid amount.

(9) A notice of interest assessed under this paragraph may be combined in one document with notification of an assessment under section 12 of this Act which relates to the specified duty.

(10) A notice which is so combined must comply with the requirements of this paragraph which relate to a notice which is not so combined.

(11) The specified interest shall be recoverable as if it were duty due from the person assessed to that interest.

(12) For the purposes of this paragraph a person is a representative of another if—

(a) he is that other's personal representative;

(b) he is that other's trustee in bankruptcy or is a receiver or liquidator appointed in relation to that other or in relation to any of his property; or

(c) he is a person acting in some other representative capacity in relation to that other."

(2) In Schedule 5 to the 1994 Act (decisions subject to review and appeal) in paragraph 9 (decisions under Chapter IV of Part I of that Act) the word "and" immediately preceding sub-paragraph (d) shall be omitted and after that sub-paragraph there shall be inserted—

"(e) any decision with respect to the amount of any interest specified in an assessment under paragraph 11A of Schedule 6;".

(3) In section 16 of the 1994 Act (appeals to a tribunal) at the beginning of subsection (8) (meaning of "ancillary matter" for the purposes of that section) there shall be inserted "Subject to subsection (9) below" and after that subsection there shall be inserted—

"(9) References in this section to a decision as to an ancillary matter do not include a reference to a decision of a description specified in paragraph 9(e) of Schedule 5 to this Act.

(10) Nothing in this section shall be taken to confer on an appeal tribunal any power to vary an amount of interest specified in an assessment under paragraph 11A of Schedule 6 to this Act except in so far as it is necessary to reduce it to the amount which is appropriate under paragraph 7 of that Schedule."

(4) This section shall apply in relation to accounting periods ending on or after 1st January 1995.

General Note

The addition to FA 1994, Sched. 6 allows the Customs and Excise to raise assessments for interest due under para. 7 on unpaid air passenger duty. A decision to raise such an assessment is subject to appeal to the VAT and Duties Tribunal.

Preferential debts

17. In section 386(1) of the Insolvency Act 1986 (categories of preferential debts) and in Article 346(1) of the Insolvency (Northern Ireland) Order 1989 (equivalent provision for Northern Ireland) after "lottery duty" there shall be inserted ", air passenger duty".

<small>GENERAL NOTE</small>
Air passenger duty is added to the categories of preferential debts under the legislation cited.

Vehicle excise duty

Increased rates on 30th November 1994

18.—(1) Schedule 1 to the Vehicle Excise and Registration Act 1994 (annual rates of duty) shall be amended as follows.

(2) In paragraph 1(b) (rate for vehicle constructed after 1946 and for which no other rate is specified) for "£130" there shall be substituted "£135".

(3) In paragraph 3(1)(a) (rate for hackney carriage with seating capacity under nine) for "£130" there shall be substituted "£135".

(4) In paragraph 10 (trailer supplement)—
(a) in sub-paragraph (2) for "£130" there shall be substituted "£135";
(b) in sub-paragraph (3) for "£360" there shall be substituted "£370".

(5) This section shall apply in relation to licences taken out on or after 30th November 1994.

<small>GENERAL NOTE</small>
The rate of vehicle excise duty (VED) is increased from £130 to £135 for cars, small vans and taxis. VED is also increased by the same amount for trailers weighing between 4,000 kgs and 12,000 kgs, drawn by goods vehicles weighing more than 12,000 kgs. For trailers weighing more than 12,000 kgs, drawn by goods vehicles weighing more than 12,000 kgs, the increase is from £360 to £370.

Vehicle excise and registration: other provisions

19. Schedule 4 to this Act (which contains other provisions relating to vehicle excise and registration) shall have effect.

<small>GENERAL NOTE</small>
This section introduces Sched. 4, which makes considerable changes to the system relating to vehicle excise and registration, recently consolidated in the Vehicle Excise and Registration Act 1994. The purpose of the amendments is to update and simplify the provisions. The overall revenue effect is broadly neutral.
See further the General Note to Sched. 4.

Recovery of overpaid duty

Recovery of overpaid excise duty

20.—(1) In Part X of the Customs and Excise Management Act 1979, after section 137 (recovery of duties, &c.) insert—

"Recovery of overpaid excise duty
137A.—(1) Where a person pays to the Commissioners an amount by way of excise duty which is not due to them, the Commissioners are liable to repay that amount.

(2) The Commissioners shall not be required to make any such repayment unless a claim is made to them in such form, and supported by such documentary evidence, as may be prescribed by them by regulations; and regulations under this subsection may make different provision for different cases.

(3) It is a defence to a claim for repayment that the repayment would unjustly enrich the claimant.

(4) No claim for repayment may be made after the expiry of the period of six years beginning with the date of the payment or, if later, the date

on which the claimant (or, where the right to repayment has been assigned or otherwise transmitted, any predecessor in title of his) discovered, or could with reasonable diligence have discovered, that the amount was not due.

(5) Except as provided by this section the Commissioners are not liable to repay an amount paid to them by way of excise duty by reason of the fact that it was not due to them.".

(2) In section 17(5) of the Customs and Excise Management Act 1979, after paragraph (b) (restriction on repayment of sums overpaid in error) insert—

"Paragraph (b) above does not apply to a claim for repayment under section 137A below.".

(3) Section 29 of the Finance Act 1989 (recovery of overpaid excise duty and car tax) shall cease to have effect so far as it relates to excise duty.

(4) In section 14(1) of the Finance Act 1994 (decisions subject to review and appeal), after paragraph (b) insert—

"(bb) any decision of the Commissioners on a claim under section 137A of the Customs and Excise Management Act 1979 for repayment of excise duty;".

(5) The provisions of this section have effect in relation to payments made on or after such date as the Commissioners of Customs and Excise may appoint by order made by statutory instrument.

GENERAL NOTE

A statutory right of recovery from the Customs and Excise of excise duty paid which was not due is introduced. The new Customs and Excise Management Act 1979, s.137A follows generally the provisions regarding VAT in the Value Added Tax Act 1994, s.80 and replaces a more limited relief in the FA 1989, s.29. The Customs and Excise may be required to review a decision on a claim under this section, with appeal to the VAT and Duties Tribunal.

PART II

VALUE ADDED TAX AND INSURANCE PREMIUM TAX

Value added tax

Fuel and power for domestic or charity use

21.—(1) The Value Added Tax Act 1994 shall be amended as follows.

(2) In section 2 (rate of VAT) in subsection (1) the words "and paragraph 7 of Schedule 13" shall be omitted, and the following subsections shall be inserted after that subsection—

"(1A) VAT charged on—

(a) any supply for the time being falling within paragraph 1 of Schedule A1; or

(b) any equivalent acquisition or importation,

shall be charged at the rate of 8 per cent.

(1B) The reference in subsection (1A) above to an equivalent acquisition or importation, in relation to any supply for the time being falling within paragraph 1 of Schedule A1, is a reference (as the case may be) to—

(a) any acquisition from another member State of goods the supply of which would be such a supply; or

(b) any importation from a place outside the member States of any such goods.

(1C) The Treasury may by order vary Schedule A1 by adding to or deleting from it any description of supply for the time being specified in it or by varying any other provision for the time being contained in it."

(3) The following Schedule shall be inserted immediately before Schedule 1—

"SCHEDULE A1

CHARGE AT REDUCED RATE

The supplies

1.—(1) The supplies falling within this paragraph are supplies for qualifying use of—
   (a) coal, coke or other solid substances held out for sale solely as fuel;
   (b) coal gas, water gas, producer gases or similar gases;
   (c) petroleum gases, or other gaseous hydrocarbons, whether in a gaseous or liquid state;
   (d) fuel oil, gas oil or kerosene; or
   (e) electricity, heat or air-conditioning.
(2) In this paragraph "qualifying use" means—
   (a) domestic use; or
   (b) use by a charity otherwise than in the course or furtherance of a business.
(3) Where there is a supply of goods partly for qualifying use and partly not—
   (a) if at least 60 per cent. of the goods are supplied for qualifying use, the whole supply shall be treated as a supply for qualifying use; and
   (b) in any other case, an apportionment shall be made to determine the extent to which the supply is a supply for qualifying use.

Interpretation

2. For the purposes of this Schedule the following supplies are always for domestic use—
   (a) a supply of not more than one tonne of coal or coke held out for sale as domestic fuel;
   (b) a supply of wood, peat or charcoal not intended for sale by the recipient;
   (c) a supply to a person at any premises of piped gas (that is, gas within paragraph 1(1)(b) above, or petroleum gas in a gaseous state, provided through pipes) where the gas (together with any other piped gas provided to him at the premises by the same supplier) was not provided at a rate exceeding 150 therms a month or, if the supplier charges for the gas by reference to the number of kilowatt hours supplied, 4397 kilowatt hours a month;
   (d) a supply of petroleum gas in a liquid state where the gas is supplied in cylinders the net weight of each of which is less than 50 kilogrammes and either the number of cylinders supplied is 20 or fewer or the gas is not intended for sale by the recipient;
   (e) a supply of petroleum gas in a liquid state, otherwise than in cylinders, to a person at any premises at which he is not able to store more than two tonnes of such gas;
   (f) a supply of not more than 2,300 litres of fuel oil, gas oil or kerosene;
   (g) a supply of electricity to a person at any premises where the electricity (together with any other electricity provided to him at the premises by the same supplier) was not provided at a rate exceeding 1000 kilowatt hours a month.

3.—(1) For the purposes of this Schedule supplies not within paragraph 2 above are for domestic use if and only if the goods supplied are for use in—

(a) a building, or part of a building, which consists of a dwelling or number of dwellings;

(b) a building, or part of a building, used for a relevant residential purpose;

(c) self-catering holiday accommodation;

(d) a caravan; or

(e) a houseboat.

(2) For the purposes of this Schedule use for a relevant residential purpose means use as—

(a) a home or other institution providing residential accommodation for children;

(b) a home or other institution providing residential accommodation with personal care for persons in need of personal care by reason of old age, disablement, past or present dependence on alcohol or drugs or past or present mental disorder;

(c) a hospice;

(d) residential accommodation for students or school pupils;

(e) residential accommodation for members of any of the armed forces;

(f) a monastery, nunnery or similar establishment; or

(g) an institution which is the sole or main residence of at least 90 per cent. of its residents,

except use as a hospital, a prison or similar institution or an hotel or inn or similar establishment.

(3) For the purposes of this Schedule self-catering holiday accommodation includes any accommodation advertised or held out as such.

(4) In this Schedule "houseboat" means a boat or other floating decked structure designed or adapted for use solely as a place of permanent habitation and not having means of, or capable of being readily adapted for, self-propulsion.

4.—(1) Paragraph 1(1)(a) above shall be deemed to include combustible materials put up for sale for kindling fires but shall not include matches.

(2) Paragraph 1(1)(b) and (c) above shall not include any road fuel gas (within the meaning of the Hydrocarbon Oil Duties Act 1979) on which a duty of excise has been charged or is chargeable.

(3) Paragraph 1(1)(d) above shall not include hydrocarbon oil on which a duty of excise has been or is to be charged without relief from, or rebate of, such duty by virtue of the provisions of the Hydrocarbon Oil Duties Act 1979.

(4) In this Schedule "fuel oil" means heavy oil which contains in solution an amount of asphaltenes of not less than 0.5 per cent. or which contains less than 0.5 per cent. but not less than 0.1 per cent. of asphaltenes and has a closed flash point not exceeding 150°C.

(5) In this Schedule "gas oil" means heavy oil of which not more than 50 per cent. by volume distils at a temperature not exceeding 240°C and of which more than 50 per cent. by volume distils at a temperature not exceeding 340°C.

(6) In this Schedule "kerosene" means heavy oil of which more than 50 per cent. by volume distils at a temperature not exceeding 240°C.

(7) In this Schedule "heavy oil" shall have the same meaning as in the Hydrocarbon Oil Duties Act 1979."

(4) In section 97 (orders etc.) in subsection (4) (orders requiring approval) the following paragraph shall be inserted immediately before paragraph (a)—

"(aa) an order under section 2(1C);".

(5) In Schedule 13 (transitional provisions and savings) paragraph 7 (fuel and power) shall be omitted.

(6) This section shall apply in relation to any supply made on or after 1st April 1995 and any acquisition or importation taking place on or after that date.

GENERAL NOTE

This section was introduced following the Government's defeat on December 6, 1994 over the increase in VAT on domestic fuel and power from eight per cent to 17.5 per cent as from April 1, 1995. A two-stage imposition of VAT on domestic fuel and power was provided for by the FA 1993, s.42.

The new Value Added Tax Act 1994, Sched. A1 follows the provisions of the Value Added Tax Act 1993, Sched. 5, Group 7, which formerly zero-rated such supplies.

Imported works of art, antiques, etc.

22.—(1) In subsection (1) of section 21 of the Value Added Tax Act 1994 (value of imported goods), for "and (3)" there shall be substituted "to (4)"; and after subsection (3) there shall be inserted the following subsections—

"(4) For the purposes of this Act, the value of any goods falling within subsection (5) below which are imported from a place outside the member States shall be taken to be an amount equal to 14.29 per cent. of the amount which, apart from this subsection, would be their value for those purposes.

(5) The goods which fall within this subsection are—

(a) any work of art which was obtained by any person before 1st April 1973 otherwise than by his producing it himself or by succession on the death of the person who produced it;

(b) any work of art which was—

(i) exported from the United Kingdom before 1st April 1973,

(ii) exported from the United Kingdom on or after that date and before 1st January 1993 by a person who, had he supplied it in the United Kingdom at the date when it was exported, would not have had to account for VAT on the full value of the supply, or

(iii) exported from the United Kingdom on or after 1st January 1993 by such a person to a place which, at the time, was outside the member States,

being, in each case, a work of art which has not been imported between the time when it was exported and the importation in question;

(c) any antique more than one hundred years old, being neither a work of art nor pearls or loose gem stones; and

(d) collectors' pieces of zoological, botanical, mineralogical, anatomical, historical, archaeological, paleontological or ethnographic interest.

(6) In this section 'work of art' means goods falling within any of the following descriptions, that is to say—

(a) paintings, drawings and pastels executed by hand but not comprised in manufactured articles that have been hand-painted or hand-decorated;

(b) original engravings, lithographs and other prints;

(c) original sculptures and statuary, in any material.

(7) An order under section 2(2) may contain provision making such alteration of the percentage for the time being specified in subsection (4) above as the Treasury consider appropriate in consequence of any increase or decrease by that order of the rate of VAT."

(2) This section shall have effect in relation to goods imported at any time on or after the day on which this Act is passed.

GENERAL NOTE
A reduced valuation for VAT purposes is applied to the works of art, antiques and collectors' pieces specified in the section. The section implements the seventh VAT directive of the EEC (94/5/EC).

The rate of 14.29 per cent of the VAT rate of 17.5 per cent gives an effective rate of 2.5 per cent on the value of the imports in question.

The section replaces the Value Added Tax (Special Provisions) Order 1992 (S.I. 1992 No. 3129), art. 9.

Agents acting in their own names

23.—(1) In subsection (1) of section 47 of the Value Added Tax Act 1994 (agents etc.), for "the goods may" there shall be substituted "then, if the taxable person acts in relation to the supply in his own name, the goods shall".

(2) After subsection (2) of that section there shall be inserted the following subsection—

"(2A) Where, in the case of any supply of goods to which subsection (1) above does not apply, goods are supplied through an agent who acts in his own name, the supply shall be treated both as a supply to the agent and as a supply by the agent."

(3) In subsection (3) of that section, the words "goods or" shall be omitted.

(4) This section shall have effect—

(a) so far as it amends section 47(1) of that Act, in relation to goods acquired or imported on or after the day on which this Act is passed; and

(b) for other purposes, in relation to any supply taking place on or after that day.

GENERAL NOTE
The amendments to the Value Added Tax Act 1994 (c. 23), s.47 provide that goods supplied through an agent acting in his own name are treated for VAT purposes as supplied both to and by the agent.

This treatment previously applied on a discretionary basis and continues to apply on such a basis to services supplied through an agent acting in his own name.

Margin schemes

24.—(1) After section 50 of the Value Added Tax Act 1994 there shall be inserted the following section—

"Margin schemes

50A.—(1) The Treasury may by order provide, in relation to any such description of supplies to which this section applies as may be specified in the order, for a taxable person to be entitled to opt that, where he makes supplies of that description, VAT is to be charged by reference to the profit margin on the supplies, instead of by reference to their value.

(2) This section applies to the following supplies, that is to say—

(a) supplies of works of art, antiques or collectors' items;

(b) supplies of motor vehicles;

(c) supplies of second-hand goods; and

(d) any supply of goods through a person who acts as an agent, but in his own name, in relation to the supply.

(3) An option for the purposes of an order under this section shall be exercisable, and may be withdrawn, in such manner as may be required by such an order.

(4) Subject to subsection (7) below, the profit margin on a supply to which this section applies shall be taken, for the purposes of an order

under this section, to be equal to the amount (if any) by which the price at which the person making the supply obtained the goods in question is exceeded by the price at which he supplies them.

(5) For the purposes of this section the price at which a person has obtained any goods and the price at which he supplies them shall each be calculated in accordance with the provisions contained in an order under this section; and such an order may, in particular, make provision stipulating the extent to which any VAT charged on a supply, acquisition or importation of any goods is to be treated as included in the price at which those goods have been obtained or are supplied.

(6) An order under this section may provide that the consideration for any services supplied in connection with a supply of goods by a person who acts as an agent, but in his own name, in relation to the supply of the goods is to be treated for the purposes of any such order as an amount to be taken into account in computing the profit margin on the supply of the goods, instead of being separately chargeable to VAT as comprised in the value of the services supplied.

(7) An order under this section may provide for the total profit margin on all the goods of a particular description supplied by a person in any prescribed accounting period to be calculated by—

(a) aggregating all the prices at which that person obtained goods of that description in that period together with any amount carried forward to that period in pursuance of paragraph (d) below;

(b) aggregating all the prices at which he supplies goods of that description in that period;

(c) treating the total profit margin on goods supplied in that period as being equal to the amount (if any) by which, for that period, the aggregate calculated in pursuance of paragraph (a) above is exceeded by the aggregate calculated in pursuance of paragraph (b) above; and

(d) treating any amount by which, for that period, the aggregate calculated in pursuance of paragraph (b) above is exceeded by the aggregate calculated in pursuance of paragraph (a) above as an amount to be carried forward to the following prescribed accounting period so as to be included, for the period to which it is carried forward, in any aggregate falling to be calculated in pursuance of paragraph (a) above.

(8) An order under this section may—

(a) make different provision for different cases; and

(b) make provisions of the order subject to such general or special directions as may, in accordance with the order, be given by the Commissioners with respect to any matter to which the order relates."

(2) Section 32 of that Act (relief on supply of certain second-hand goods) shall cease to have effect on such day as the Commissioners of Customs and Excise may by order made by statutory instrument appoint.

GENERAL NOTE

The new Value Added Tax Act 1994, s.50A, which replaces *ibid.*, s.32, further implements the seventh VAT directive of the EEC (94/5/EC). The margin scheme of accounting for second-hand goods, by which VAT is charged on the difference between the purchase and sale price, is to be extended from a limited range of easily identifiable, high value items such as cars, boats and antiques, to all second-hand goods. The Government has given an assurance that charities will continue to enjoy zero-rating on the sale of donated goods (*Hansard*, Standing Committee D, col. 82).

Subs. (7)

This introduces a simplified method of accounting for VAT on margin schemes called global accounting. Businesses dealing in low value, bulk volume margin scheme goods will be able to account for VAT on the difference between the total purchases and sales of eligible goods in each tax period rather than on an item by item basis.

Groups of companies

25.—(1) Section 43 of the Value Added Tax Act 1994 (groups of companies) shall be amended as follows.

(2) After subsection (1) there shall be inserted the following subsection—

"(1A) Paragraph (a) of subsection (1) above shall not apply in relation to any supply of goods or services by one member of a group to another unless both the body making the supply and the body supplied continue to be members of that group until—

    (a) in the case of a supply of goods which are to be removed in pursuance of the supply, a time after the removal;

    (b) in the case of any other supply of goods, a time after the goods have been made available, in pursuance of the supply, to the body supplied; or

    (c) in the case of a supply of services, a time after the services have been performed.";

and in subsection (1)(b), for "other supply" there shall be substituted "supply which is a supply to which paragraph (a) above does not apply and is a supply".

(3) In subsection (5) (applications to be treated or to cease to be treated as members of a group etc.), for the words after paragraph (d) there shall be substituted—

"unless the Commissioners refuse the application under subsection (5A) below."

(4) After subsection (5) there shall be inserted the following subsection—

"(5A) If it appears to the Commissioners necessary to do so for the protection of the revenue, they may—

    (a) refuse any application made to the effect mentioned in paragraph (a) or (c) of subsection (5) above; or

    (b) refuse any application made to the effect mentioned in paragraph (b) or (d) of that subsection in a case that does not appear to them to fall within subsection (6) below."

(5) Subsection (2) above has effect in relation to—

    (a) any supply made on or after 1st March 1995, and

    (b) any supply made before that date in the case of which both the body making the supply and the body supplied continued to be members of the group in question until at least that date,

and subsections (3) and (4) above have effect in relation to applications made on or after the day on which this Act is passed.

GENERAL NOTE

The amendments to Value Added Tax Act 1994, s.43 are designed to prevent a tax avoidance scheme which was recently upheld by a tribunal (*Thorn v. Customs and Excise Commissioners* [1995] S.T.I. 477). The decision is being appealed, but in the meantime s.25 is enacted to protect the revenue.

The group concerned in the scheme, knowing that VAT paid on cars is not normally deductible, used two subsidiaries to purchase cars and other goods. Ninety per cent of the price was paid free of VAT in advance to the two companies. They promptly left the VAT group, purchased the cars and other goods and delivered them to a company that remained in the group. Apart from the VAT on the remaining 10 per cent of the price, which was paid later, the group had obtained the cars tax free.

The new s.43(1A), which applies to this particular scheme, is in force from March 1, 1995, when the new legislation was announced. The new s.43(5A), which applies from Royal Assent, gives the Customs and Excise a wide power to frustrate schemes involving de-grouping.

Co-owners etc. of buildings and land

26.—(1) After section 51 of the Value Added Tax Act 1994 there shall be inserted the following section—

"Co-owners etc. of buildings and land
51A.—(1) This section applies to a supply consisting in the grant, assignment or surrender of any interest in or right over land in a case where there is more than one person by whom the grant, assignment or surrender is made or treated as made; and for this purpose—
    (a) a licence to occupy land, and
    (b) in relation to land in Scotland, a personal right to call for or be granted any interest or right in or over land,
shall be taken to be a right over land.
(2) The persons who make or are treated as making a supply to which this section applies ('the grantors') shall be treated, in relation to that supply and in relation to any other such supply with respect to which the grantors are the same, as a single person ('the property-owner') who is distinct from each of the grantors individually.
(3) Registration under this Act of the property-owner shall be in the name of the grantors acting together as a property-owner.
(4) The grantors shall be jointly and severally liable in respect of the obligations falling by virtue of this section on the property-owner.
(5) Any notice, whether of assessment or otherwise, which is addressed to the property-owner by the name in which the property-owner is registered and is served on any of the grantors in accordance with this Act shall be treated for the purposes of this Act as served on the property-owner.
(6) Where there is any change in some, but not all, of the persons who are for the time being to be treated as the grantors in relation to any supply to which this section applies—
    (a) that change shall be disregarded for the purposes of this section in relation to any prescribed accounting period beginning before the change is notified in the prescribed manner to the Commissioners; and
    (b) any notice (whether of assessment or otherwise) which is served, at any time after such a notification, on the property-owner for the time being shall, so far as it relates to, or to any matter arising in, such a period, be treated for the purposes of this Act as served on whoever was the property-owner in that period."
(2) Paragraph 8 of Schedule 10 to that Act (persons to whom the benefit of consideration for the grant of an interest accrues to be treated as person making the grant) shall become sub-paragraph (1) of that paragraph, and after that sub-paragraph there shall be inserted the following sub-paragraphs—
    "(2) Where the consideration for the grant of an interest in, right over or licence to occupy land is such that its provision is enforceable primarily—
    (a) by the person who, as owner of an interest or right in or over that land, actually made the grant, or
    (b) by another person in his capacity as the owner for the time being of that interest or right or of any other interest or right in or over that land,
that person, and not any person (other than that person) to whom a benefit accrues by virtue of his being a beneficiary under a trust relating to the land, or the proceeds of sale of any land, shall be taken for the purposes of this paragraph to be the person to whom the benefit of the consideration accrues.

(3) Sub-paragraph (2) above shall not apply to the extent that the Commissioners, on an application made in the prescribed manner jointly by—

(a) the person who (apart from this sub-paragraph) would be taken under that sub-paragraph to be the person to whom the benefit of the consideration accrues, and

(b) all the persons for the time being in existence who, as beneficiaries under such a trust as is mentioned in that sub-paragraph, are persons who have or may become entitled to or to a share of the consideration, or for whose benefit any of it is to be or may be applied,

may direct that the benefit of the consideration is to be treated for the purposes of this paragraph as a benefit accruing to the persons falling within paragraph (b) above, and not (unless he also falls within paragraph (b) above) to the person falling within paragraph (a) above."

(3) This section shall come into force on such day as the Commissioners of Customs and Excise may by order made by statutory instrument appoint, and different days may be appointed under this subsection for different purposes.

GENERAL NOTE

At present co-owners of land—who are often trustees—are registered for VAT purposes as partnerships, but they are not usually partnerships in the legal sense. There may be significant direct tax disadvantages if they are so treated for fiscal purposes.

In response to representations to the Government, the new Value Added Tax Act 1994, s.51A, will register co-owners as a single taxable person without the quasi-legal tag of partnership. Joint and several liability for VAT is imposed on the co-owners. Where the legal and beneficial ownership of the land are not vested in the same person, the Customs and Excise may direct on a joint application that the beneficial owners are to be treated as being the persons to whom the benefit of the consideration for a grant in relation to the land accrues.

The new s.51A will come into force on a date to be appointed by the Customs and Excise following further consultation with those affected.

Set-off of credits

27.—(1) Section 81 of the Value Added Tax Act 1994 (which includes provision as to the setting off of credits) shall be amended as follows.

(2) For subsection (4) there shall be substituted the following subsections—

"(4A) Subsection (3) above shall not require any such amount as is mentioned in paragraph (a) of that subsection ('the credit') to be set against any such sum as is mentioned in paragraph (b) of that subsection ('the debit') in any case where—

(a) an insolvency procedure has been applied to the person entitled to the credit;

(b) the credit became due after that procedure was so applied; and

(c) the liability to pay the debit either arose before that procedure was so applied or (having arisen afterwards) relates to, or to matters occurring in the course of, the carrying on of any business at times before the procedure was so applied.

(4B) Subject to subsection (4C) below, the following are the times when an insolvency procedure is to be taken, for the purposes of this section, to be applied to any person, that is to say—

(a) when a bankruptcy order, winding-up order, administration order or award of sequestration is made in relation to that person;

(b) when that person is put into administrative receivership;

(c) when that person, being a corporation, passes a resolution for voluntary winding up;

(d) when any voluntary arrangement approved in accordance with Part I or VIII of the Insolvency Act 1986, or Part II or Chapter II of Part VIII of the Insolvency (Northern Ireland) Order 1989, comes into force in relation to that person;

(e) when a deed of arrangement registered in accordance with the Deeds of Arrangement Act 1914 or Chapter I of Part VIII of that Order of 1989 takes effect in relation to that person;

(f) when that person's estate becomes vested in any other person as that person's trustee under a trust deed.

(4C) In this section references, in relation to any person, to the application of an insolvency procedure to that person shall not include—

(a) the making of a bankruptcy order, winding-up order, administration order or award of sequestration at a time when any such arrangement or deed as is mentioned in subsection (4B)(d) to (f) above is in force in relation to that person;

(b) the making of a winding-up order at any of the following times, that is to say—

(i) immediately upon the discharge of an administration order made in relation to that person;

(ii) when that person is being wound up voluntarily;

(iii) when that person is in administrative receivership;

or

(c) the making of an administration order in relation to that person at any time when that person is in administrative receivership.

(4D) For the purposes of this section a person shall be regarded as being in administrative receivership throughout any continuous period for which (disregarding any temporary vacancy in the office of receiver) there is an administrative receiver of that person, and the reference in subsection (4B) above to a person being put into administrative receivership shall be construed accordingly."

(3) In subsection (5) (definitions), for "subsection (4) above" there shall be substituted "this section".

(4) This section shall have effect in relation to amounts becoming due from the Commissioners of Customs and Excise at times on or after the day on which this Act is passed.

GENERAL NOTE

The amendments to Value Added Tax Act 1994, s.81 introduced by this section extend and clarify the rules excluding insolvent traders from set-off of VAT credits arising during an insolvency administration.

The two main changes are:

(i) when companies trade under administrative orders and administrative receiverships, VAT credits arising after recovery will not be set off against debts remaining from the pre-insolvency period; and

(ii) the rules preventing set-off during the period for which a provisional liquidator is appointed in the winding-up of a company will also be applied during the period when an interim receiver is appointed in the bankruptcy of an individual.

It is also made clear that relief from VAT on bad debts is available only on supplies made on or after April 1, 1989.

Transactions treated as supplies for purposes of zero-rating etc.

28.—(1) In section 30 of the Value Added Tax Act 1994 (zero-rated supplies) for subsection (5) (transactions described in Schedule 8 to the Act to be treated as supplies) there shall be substituted—

"(5) The export of any goods by a charity to a place outside the member States shall for the purposes of this Act be treated as a supply made by the charity—

(a) in the United Kingdom, and

(b) in the course or furtherance of a business carried on by the charity."

(2) This section shall have effect in relation to transactions occurring on or after the day on which this Act is passed.

GENERAL NOTE

The new Value Added Tax Act 1994, s.30(5) removes a provision originally enacted to treat transfers of goods and services by U.K. subsidiaries to overseas parent companies as zero-rated exports. This is now covered by Sched. 1, para. 10.

An extra-statutory concession for charities exporting goods not in return for payment, allowing them to treat any VAT charged on the goods and related overheads as recoverable input tax, is given a statutory basis.

Goods removed from warehousing regime

29. In section 18 of the Value Added Tax Act 1994 (place and time of acquisition or supply of goods subject to warehousing regime) for subsection (5) (regulations about payment of VAT on supply of such goods) there shall be substituted the following subsections—

"(5) The Commissioners may by regulations make provision for enabling a taxable person to pay the VAT he is required to pay by virtue of paragraph (b) of subsection (4) above at a time later than that provided for by that paragraph.

(5A) Regulations under subsection (5) above may in particular make provision for either or both of the following—

(a) for the taxable person to pay the VAT together with the VAT chargeable on other supplies by him of goods and services;

(b) for the taxable person to pay the VAT together with any duty of excise deferment of which has been granted to him under section 127A of the Customs and Excise Management Act 1979;

and they may make different provision for different descriptions of taxable person and for different descriptions of goods."

GENERAL NOTE

The amendments to Value Added Tax Act 1994, s.18 are designed to place on a statutory basis a long-standing concession which allows the payment of VAT due when goods are removed from Excise warehouses to be deferred until the taxpayer's next VAT return or until the associated excise duty is paid.

Fuel supplied for private use

30.—(1) Section 57 of the Value Added Tax Act 1994 (determination of consideration for fuel supplied for private use) shall be amended as follows.

(2) The following subsection shall be inserted after subsection (1)—

"(1A) Where the prescribed accounting period is a period of 12 months, the consideration appropriate to any vehicle is that specified in relation to a vehicle of the appropriate description in the second column of Table A below."

(3) In subsection (2) (consideration where prescribed accounting period is period of 3 months) for "second" there shall be substituted "third".

(4) In subsection (3) (consideration where prescribed accounting period is period of one month) for "third" there shall be substituted "fourth".

(5) The following Table shall be substituted for Table A—

TABLE A

Description of vehicle (Type of engine and cylinder capacity in cubic centimetres)	12 month period £	3 month period £	1 month period £
Diesel engine			
2000 or less	605	151	50
More than 2000	780	195	65
Any other type of engine			
1400 or less	670	167	55
More than 1400 but not more than 2000	850	212	70
More than 2000	1260	315	105

(6) This section shall apply in relation to prescribed accounting periods beginning on or after 6th April 1995.

(7) Nothing in this section shall be taken to prejudice any practice by which the consideration appropriate to a vehicle is arrived at where a prescribed accounting period beginning before 6th April 1995 is a period of 12 months.

GENERAL NOTE
The VAT road fuel scales for taxing private use are increased by five per cent for petrol cars and four per cent for diesel cars, in line with the charge for income tax. A new 12-month scale is introduced for businesses using annual VAT accounting periods.

Appeals: payment of amounts shown in returns

31.—(1) In section 84(2) of the Value Added Tax Act 1994 (appeal not to be entertained unless amounts shown in returns paid, except in certain cases) the words ", except in the case of an appeal against a decision with respect to the matter mentioned in section 83(1)," shall be omitted.

(2) This section shall apply in relation to appeals brought after the day on which this Act is passed.

GENERAL NOTE
The right of appeal against a requirement to provide security is removed from businesses which have submitted but not paid their VAT returns which are due.

Penalties for failure to notify etc.

32.—(1) In section 67 of the Value Added Tax Act 1994 (failure to notify and unauthorised issue of invoices) in subsection (4) (the specified percentage)—

(a) in paragraph (a) for "10 per cent." there shall be substituted "5 per cent.";

(b) in paragraph (b) for "20 per cent." there shall be substituted "10 per cent."; and

(c) in paragraph (c) for "30 per cent." there shall be substituted "15 per cent."

(2) Section 15(3A) of the Finance Act 1985 (provision which is repealed by the 1994 Act and which corresponds to section 67(4)) shall have effect subject to the amendments made by subsection (1) above.

(3) Subject to subsection (4) below, subsections (1) and (2) above shall apply where a penalty is assessed on or after 1st January 1995.

(4) Subsections (1) and (2) above shall not apply in the case of a supplementary assessment if the original assessment was made before 1st January 1995.

GENERAL NOTE
The penalties for failure to notify liability to registration for VAT and associated offences are reduced by half, in line with the changes to other penalties made by FA 1993, Sched. 2.

Correction of consolidation errors

33.—(1) The Value Added Tax Act 1994 shall have effect, and be deemed always to have had effect, as if it had been enacted as follows.

(2) Section 35(1) (refund of VAT to persons constructing certain buildings) shall be deemed to have been enacted with the word "building" substituted for the word "dwelling" in each place where it occurs.

(3) Paragraph 5(5) and (6)(b) of Schedule 4 and paragraph 7(b) of Schedule 6 (which contain references to paragraph 5(3) of Schedule 4 which should

be references to paragraph 5(4) of that Schedule) shall be deemed to have been enacted—

(a) in the case of paragraph 5(5) and (6)(b), with "sub-paragraph (4) above" substituted for "sub-paragraph (3) above", in each case; and

(b) in the case of paragraph 7(b), with "paragraph 5(4)" substituted for "paragraph 5(3)".

(4) In paragraph 9 of Schedule 13 (which contains transitional provisions relating to bad debt relief), the following sub-paragraph shall be deemed to have been enacted instead of sub-paragraph (2) of that paragraph, that is to say—

"(2) Claims for refunds of VAT shall not be made in accordance with section 36 of this Act in relation to—

(a) any supply made before 1st April 1989; or

(b) any supply as respects which a claim is or has been made under section 22 of the 1983 Act."

(5) In paragraph 13 of Schedule 14 (consequential amendment of the Finance Act 1994), the following sub-paragraph shall be deemed to have been enacted instead of sub-paragraph (a) of that paragraph, that is to say—

"(a) in subsection (4) for '25 and 29 of the Finance Act 1985' and '40 of the Value Added Tax Act 1983' there shall be substituted, respectively, '85 and 87 of the Value Added Tax Act 1994' and '83 of that Act';".

GENERAL NOTE

A number of drafting errors in the Value Added Tax Act 1994 are corrected. The purpose of the amendments is to preserve the continuity of the application of the law as it existed before the consolidation.

Insurance premium tax

Insurance premium tax

34. Schedule 5 to this Act (which relates to insurance premium tax) shall have effect.

GENERAL NOTE

The section introduces Sched. 5, which makes minor amendments to the provisions regarding insurance premium tax (IPT) under FA 1994, Part III. The amendments are intended to enhance the management of IPT.

PART III

INCOME TAX, CORPORATION TAX AND CAPITAL GAINS TAX

Income tax: charge, rates and reliefs

Charge and rates of income tax for 1995–96

35.—(1) Income tax shall be charged for the year 1995–96, and for that year—

(a) the lower rate shall be 20 per cent.,

(b) the basic rate shall be 25 per cent., and

(c) the higher rate shall be 40 per cent.

(2) For the year 1995–96 section 1(2) of the Taxes Act 1988 shall apply as if the amount specified in paragraph (aa) were £3,200 (the lower rate limit); and accordingly section 1(4) of that Act (indexation) so far as relating to that paragraph shall not apply for the year 1995–96.

GENERAL NOTE

The rates of income tax for 1995/96 are the same as those for 1994/95. The lower rate limit is £3,200 and the basic rate limit increases by virtue of indexation to £24,300.

Personal allowance

36. Section 257 of the Taxes Act 1988 (personal allowance) shall apply for the year 1995–96 as if—
  (a) the amount specified in subsection (2) (persons of 65 or upwards) were £4,630, and
  (b) the amount specified in subsection (3) (persons of 75 or upwards) were £4,800;
and accordingly section 257C(1) of that Act (indexation) so far as relating to section 257(2) and (3) shall not apply for the year 1995–96.

GENERAL NOTE
  The personal allowance for 1995/96 is set at £4,630 for those aged 65 to 74, and at £4,800 for those aged 75 and above. By virtue of indexation the personal allowance for those aged under 65 increases to £3,525.

Corporation tax: charge and rate

Charge and rate of corporation tax for 1995

37. Corporation tax shall be charged for the financial year 1995 at the rate of 33 per cent.

GENERAL NOTE
  The rate of corporation tax remains at 33 per cent.

Small companies

38. For the financial year 1995—
  (a) the small companies' rate shall be 25 per cent., and
  (b) the fraction mentioned in section 13(2) of the Taxes Act 1988 (marginal relief for small companies) shall be one fiftieth.

GENERAL NOTE
  The small companies' rate, the limits for marginal relief and the marginal relief fraction remain unchanged.

Taxation of income from land

INTRODUCTION
  The purpose of the changes introduced to Schedule A is to assimilate so far as possible the income tax rules for that Schedule with Schedule D Case I. Also, income from furnished lettings, presently taxed under Schedule D Case VI, will be taxed under Schedule A. The effect, looking forward to self-assessment, will be to make the completion of tax returns simpler.
  Companies will continue to calculate their Schedule A income under the old rules. This will allow them to obtain relief through management expenses for expenditures not permissible under Schedule A.

Income chargeable under Schedule A

39.—(1) Section 15 of the Taxes Act 1988 (charge to Schedule A) shall have effect, except for the purpose of being applied by virtue of section 9 of that Act for the purposes of corporation tax, as if the following provisions were substituted for the Schedule A set out in subsection (1) of that section—

"SCHEDULE A

1.—(1) Tax under this Schedule shall be charged on the annual profits or gains arising from any business carried on for the exploitation, as a source of rents or other receipts, of any estate, interest or rights in or over any land in the United Kingdom.

(2) To the extent that any transaction entered into by any person is entered into for the exploitation, as a source of rents or other receipts, of any estate, interest or rights in or over any land in the United Kingdom that transaction shall be taken for the purposes of this Schedule to have been entered into in the course of such a business as is mentioned in sub-paragraph (1) above.

(3) In this paragraph 'receipts', in relation to any land, includes—

(a) any payment in respect of any licence to occupy or otherwise to use any land or in respect of the exercise of any other right over land; and

(b) rentcharges, ground annuals and feu duties and any other annual payments reserved in respect of, or charged on or issuing out of, that land.

2. Paragraph 1 above does not apply to—

(a) any profits or gains arising from any person's entitlement to receive any yearly interest;

(b) any profits or gains arising from a person's occupation of any woodlands which are managed on a commercial basis and with a view to the realisation of profits; or

(c) any profits or gains charged to tax under Schedule D by virtue of section 53 or 55 or arising from any person's entitlement to receive payments so charged under section 119 or 120;

and that paragraph has effect subject to the provisions of section 98 with respect to tied premises.

3.—(1) For the purposes of paragraph 1 above a right of any person to use a caravan or houseboat shall be deemed, where the use to which the caravan or houseboat may be put in pursuance of that right is confined to its use at only one location in the United Kingdom, to be a right the entitlement to confer which derives, in the case of the person conferring it, from an estate or interest in land in the United Kingdom.

(2) In sub-paragraph (1) above—

'caravan' has the meaning given by section 29(1) of the Caravan Sites and Control of Development Act 1960; and

'houseboat' means a boat or similar structure designed or adapted for use as a place of human habitation.

4.—(1) In any case where—

(a) a sum (whether rent or otherwise) is payable in respect of the use of any premises,

(b) the tenant or other person entitled to the use of the premises is also entitled to the use, in connection therewith, of furniture, and

(c) any part of the sum payable in respect of the use of the premises would fall to be taken into account as a receipt in computing the profits or gains chargeable to tax under this Schedule,

any amount payable as part of, or in connection with, the sums payable in respect of the use of the premises, in so far as it is payable for the use of the furniture, shall also be so taken into account.

(2) Sub-paragraph (1) above does not apply to any amount which, apart from that sub-paragraph, would fall to be taken into account as a

trading receipt in computing the profits or gains of any trade that consists in or involves the making available for use in any premises of any furniture.

(3) In sub-paragraph (1) above any reference to a sum shall be construed as including the value of any consideration, and references to a sum being payable shall be construed accordingly.

(4) In this paragraph 'premises' includes a caravan or houseboat within the meaning of paragraph 3 above."

(2) For section 21 of that Act (persons chargeable under Schedule A) there shall be substituted the following section—

"Persons chargeable and computation of amounts chargeable

21.—(1) Income tax under Schedule A shall be charged on and paid by the persons receiving or entitled to the income in respect of which the tax is directed by the Income Tax Acts to be charged.

(2) Income tax under Schedule A shall be computed on the full amount of the profits or gains arising in the year of assessment.

(3) Except in so far as express provision to the contrary is made by the Income Tax Acts, the profits or gains of a Schedule A business and the amount of any loss incurred in such a business shall be computed as if Chapter V of Part IV applied in relation to the business as it applies in relation to a trade the profits or gains of which are chargeable to tax under Case I of Schedule D.

(4) All the businesses and transactions carried on or entered into by any particular person or partnership, so far as they are businesses or transactions the profits or gains of which are chargeable to tax under Schedule A, shall be treated for the purposes of that Schedule as, or as entered into in the course of carrying on, the one business.

(5) Sections 103 to 106, 108, 109A and 110 shall apply in the case of the permanent discontinuance of a business the profits or gains of which are chargeable to income tax under Schedule A as they apply in the case of the permanent discontinuance of a trade.

(6) Section 111 shall apply in relation to a Schedule A business carried on in partnership as it applies in the case of a partnership whose business was set up and commenced on or after 6th April 1995.

(7) Subsections (1) and (2) of section 113 shall apply in relation to a change in the persons engaged in carrying on a Schedule A business as they apply in relation to a change in the persons carrying on a trade set up and commenced on or after 6th April 1995.

(8) The preceding provisions of this section do not apply for the purposes of the Corporation Tax Acts."

(3) That Act and the other enactments specified in Schedule 6 to this Act shall have effect with the further modifications set out in that Schedule; and, without prejudice to section 20(2) of the Interpretation Act 1978 (construction of references), a reference in any enactment to another enactment shall have effect, where the other enactment is applied or modified by virtue of this section or that Schedule, as including a reference to that other enactment as so applied or modified.

(4) This section and Schedule 6 to this Act shall have effect, subject to subsection (5) below—

(a) for the year 1995–96 and subsequent years of assessment, and

(b) so far as they make provision having effect for the purposes of corporation tax, in relation to accounting periods ending on or after 31st March 1995.

(5) This section and Schedule 6 to this Act shall not have effect for the year 1995–96 in relation to the profits or gains or losses arising or accruing from any source to any person where—

(a) that source is a source in respect of the profits or gains from which that person is chargeable to tax for the year 1994–95 under Schedule A or Case VI of Schedule D; and

(b) that source ceases, in the course of the year 1995–96, to be a source from which any such profits or gains arise to that or any other person as would be chargeable to tax under Schedule A or Case VI of Schedule D if the amendments for which this section and Schedule 6 to this Act provide were to be disregarded; and

(c) that person is not a person who sets up and commences a Schedule A business in the course of the year 1995–96;

and the provisions of that Schedule relating to the Capital Allowances Act 1990 shall not apply for the year 1995–96 in the case of any person who has a source of income for the whole or any part of that year which is a source falling within paragraphs (a) and (b) above and who is a person to whom paragraph (c) above applies.

GENERAL NOTE

Subs. (1)
The new ICTA 1988, s.15 extends the Schedule A charge to businesses and to casual lettings and to rents for the use of immobile caravans or permanently moored houseboats, together with payments for the use of furniture (except where these are trading receipts under Schedule D Case I).

Subs. (2)
The new ICTA 1988, s.21 adapts the provisions relating to chargeability to Schedule A to the new system.

Subss. (3)–(5)
These introduce Sched. 6 and provide for the introduction of the new rules, generally from the year 1995–96. See further the General Note to Sched. 6.

Non-residents and their representatives

40.—(1) The following section shall be inserted after section 42 of the Taxes Act 1988—

"Non-residents and their representatives

42A.—(1) The Board may by regulations make provision for the charging, assessment, collection and recovery on or from prescribed persons falling within subsection (2) below of prescribed amounts in respect of the tax which is or may become chargeable under Schedule A on the income of any person who has his usual place of abode outside the United Kingdom ('the non-resident').

(2) A person falls within this subsection if he is—

(a) a person by whom any such sums are payable to the non-resident as fall, or would fall, to be treated as receipts of a Schedule A business carried on by the non-resident; or

(b) a person who acts on behalf of the non-resident in connection with the management or administration of any such business.

(3) A person on whom any obligation to make payments to the Board is imposed by regulations under this section shall be entitled—

(a) to be indemnified by the non-resident for all such payments; and

(b) to retain, out of any sums otherwise due from him to the non-resident, or received by him on behalf of the non-resident, amounts sufficient for meeting any liabilities under the regulations to make payments to the Board which have been discharged by that person or to which he is subject.

(4) Without prejudice to the generality of the preceding provisions of this section, regulations under this section may include any or all of the following provisions, that is to say—

(a) provision for the amount of any payment to be made to the Board in respect of the tax on any income to be calculated by reference to such factors as may be prescribed;

(b) provision for the determination in accordance with any such regulations of the period for which, the circumstances in which and the times at which any payments are to be made to the Board;

(c) provision for requiring the payment of interest on amounts which are not paid to the Board at the times required under any such regulations;

(d) provision as to the certificates to be given in prescribed circumstances to the non-resident by a person falling within subsection (2) above, and as to the particulars to be included in any such certificate;

(e) provision for the making of repayments of tax to the non-resident and for such repayments to be made in prescribed cases to persons falling within subsection (2) above;

(f) provision for the payment of interest by the Board on sums repaid under any such regulations;

(g) provision for the rights and obligations arising under any such regulations to depend on the giving of such notices and the making of such claims and determinations as may be prescribed;

(h) provision for the making and determination of applications for requirements of any such regulations not to apply in certain cases, and for the variation or revocation, in prescribed cases, of the determinations made on such applications;

(i) provision for appeals with respect to questions arising under any such regulations;

(j) provision requiring prescribed persons falling within subsection (2)(b) above to register with the Board;

(k) provision requiring persons registered with the Board and other prescribed persons falling within subsection (2) above to make returns and supply prescribed information to the Board and to make available prescribed books, documents and other records for inspection on behalf of the Board;

(l) provision for the partnership, as such, to be treated as the person falling within subsection (2) above in a case where a liability to make any payment under the regulations arises from amounts payable or things done in the course of a business carried on by any persons in partnership;

(m) provision which, in relation to payments to be made by virtue of this section in respect of any tax or to any sums retained in respect of such payments, applies (with or without modifications) any enactment or subordinate legislation having effect apart from this section with respect to cases in which tax is or is treated as deducted from any income.

(5) Interest required to be paid by any regulations under this section shall be paid without deduction of tax and shall not be taken into account in computing any income, profits or losses for any tax purposes.

(6) Regulations under this section may—

(a) make different provision for different cases; and

(b) contain such supplementary, incidental, consequential and transitional provision as appears to the Board to be appropriate;

and the provision that may be made by virtue of paragraph (b) above may include provision which, in connection with any other provision made by any such regulations, modifies the operation in any case of section 59A of the Management Act or Schedule 21 to the Finance Act 1995 (payments on account of income tax).

(7) In this section—

'prescribed' means prescribed by, or determined by an officer of the
Board in accordance with, regulations made by the Board
under this section; and
'subordinate legislation' has the same meaning as in the Interpretation Act 1978.
(8) This section shall have effect—
(a) as if references in this section to a Schedule A business included
references to any activities which would be comprised in a Schedule A business if they were carried on by an individual, rather
than by a company; and
(b) in relation to companies that carry on such activities, as if the reference in subsection (1) above to tax which is or may become
chargeable under Schedule A included a reference to tax which is
or may become chargeable under Case VI of Schedule D."

(2) In the Table in section 98 of the Management Act (penalties in respect
of certain information provisions), after the entry in the first column relating
to section 42 of the Taxes Act 1988 and after the entry in the second column
relating to section 41(2) of the Taxes Act 1988, there shall, in each case, be
inserted the following entry—
"regulations under section 42A;".
(3) Section 43 of the Taxes Act 1988 (payments to non-residents of
amounts chargeable under Schedule A) shall not have effect in relation to
any payment made on or after 6th April 1996.

GENERAL NOTE
The new ICTA 1988, s.42A replaces the existing s.43, under which tenants are required to
deduct tax at source from payments to a landlord whose usual place of abode is outside the U.K.
The new system will be implemented by regulations to be made by the Revenue and will apply as
from April 6, 1996.

Section 42A(2)
The duty to deduct at source will continue to be laid on a tenant and also on an agent where the
landlord has his usual place of abode outside the U.K.

Section 42A(3)
The person making the deduction will be entitled to be indemnified by the landlord and to
recoup it out of amounts paid to the landlord.

Section 42A(4)–(7)
The regulations to be made by the Revenue will cover a wide range of ancillary matters in
relation to the administration of the charge.

Section 42A(8)
The new s.42A will apply to companies, for whom the previous Schedule A provisions remain
otherwise in force.

Income from overseas property

41.—(1) In section 65 of the Taxes Act 1988 (general provision about
Cases IV and V assessments), after subsection (2) there shall be inserted the
following subsections—
"(2A) Subject to section 65A and to the provisions of section 41(5) to
(9) of the Finance Act 1995 (which contain transitional provisions for
the years 1995–96 to 1997–98), income tax chargeable under Case V of
Schedule D on income which—
(a) arises from any business carried on for the exploitation, as a
source of rents or other receipts, of any estate, interest or rights in
or over any land outside the United Kingdom; and
(b) is not income immediately derived by any person from the carrying on by him of any trade, profession or vocation, either solely or
in partnership,

shall be computed in accordance with the rules which are applicable under the Income Tax Acts to the computation of the profits or gains of a Schedule A business.

(2B) The provisions of Schedule A shall apply for determining for the purposes of subsection (2A) above whether income falls within paragraph (a) of that subsection as they would apply if—

(a) the land in question were in the United Kingdom, or

(b) a caravan or houseboat which is to be used at a location outside the United Kingdom were to be used at a location in the United Kingdom;

and any provision of the Income Tax Acts in pursuance of which there is deemed in certain cases to be a Schedule A business in relation to any land in the United Kingdom shall have effect, where the corresponding circumstances arise with respect to land outside the United Kingdom, as if, for the purposes of that subsection, there were deemed to be a business such as is mentioned in that paragraph.";

and in subsection (4) of that section for "Subsections (1), (2) and (3)" there shall be substituted "Subsections (1) to (3)".

(2) After section 65 of that Act there shall be inserted the following section—

"Case V income from land overseas etc.

65A.—(1) Notwithstanding anything in section 21(4), subsection (2A) of section 65 shall require the rules referred to in that subsection to be applied separately in relation to—

(a) any business which is treated for the purposes of that subsection as if it were a Schedule A business, and

(b) any actual Schedule A business of the person chargeable,

as if, in each case, that business were the only Schedule A business carried on by that person.

(2) Section 21(3), so far as applied by virtue of section 65(2A) for the purposes of the computation of the amount of any income chargeable to tax under Case V of Schedule D, shall have effect as if it required sections 80 and 81 to be disregarded in the computation of the amount of any profits or gains, or losses, of a Schedule A business.

(3) Sections 503 and 504 of this Act and section 29 of the 1990 Act (furnished holiday accommodation) shall be disregarded in the computation in accordance with section 65(2A) of any income chargeable to tax under Case V of Schedule D.

(4) Section 65(2A) and this section shall not apply for the purposes of corporation tax."

(3) In section 161 of the Capital Allowances Act 1990 (interpretative provisions), after subsection (2) there shall be inserted the following subsection—

"(2A) This Act applies in accordance with subsection (2A) of section 65 of the principal Act in relation to cases where a person is treated for the purposes of that subsection as if any actual or deemed business of his were a Schedule A business as it applies in relation to cases where a person is carrying on a Schedule A business."

(4) In Schedule 8 to the Taxation of Chargeable Gains Act 1992 (which contains provision excluding from the charge to capital gains tax premiums taxed under Schedule A), after paragraph 7 there shall be inserted the following paragraph—

"7A. References in paragraphs 5 to 7 above to an amount brought into account as a receipt of a Schedule A business shall include references to any amount which, in accordance with section 65(2A) of the Taxes Act, is brought into account for the purposes of Case V of Schedule D as if it were such a receipt."

(5) Where any income falling within paragraphs (a) and (b) of subsection (2A) of section 65 of the Taxes Act 1988 which is chargeable to tax for any year of assessment under Case V of Schedule D would (apart from this section) be computed, wholly or partly, on an amount of income arising in the year preceding the year of assessment, that subsection shall have effect as if the income chargeable to tax for that year under Schedule A were to be computed, to the same extent, by reference to the year preceding the year of assessment (instead of being computed in accordance with the rule in section 21(2) of that Act), and as if the rules applied by section 65(2A) of that Act had effect accordingly.

(6) Notwithstanding anything in section 21(4) of the Taxes Act 1988, for the years 1995–96 and 1996–97 subsection (2A) of section 65 shall be treated as requiring the rules referred to in that subsection to be applied, in a case where a person is chargeable under Case V of Schedule D in respect of the rents or other receipts from more than one property situated outside the United Kingdom, separately in relation to each property outside the United Kingdom—

(a) as if a separate Schedule A business were carried on in relation to each property, and

(b) in the case of each such business, as if that business were the only Schedule A business carried on by the person chargeable.

(7) Where subsection (5) above applies for the computation of the income from any property for any year of assessment, then for that year no allowance or charge under the Capital Allowances Act 1990 shall be made on any person by virtue of this section for any purpose connected with the taxation of the income from that property.

(8) Section 379A of the Taxes Act 1988 (Schedule A losses) shall not apply by virtue of section 65(2A) of that Act for the computation of any income chargeable to tax under Case V of Schedule D for any year of assessment before the year 1998–99.

(9) Section 65(2A) of the Taxes Act 1988 shall not apply in any case which, if the land in question were in the United Kingdom, would be a case falling within section 39(5) above.

(10) Subject to subsections (5) to (9) above, this section has effect for the year 1995–96 and subsequent years of assessment.

GENERAL NOTE

The purpose of the amendments made by this section is to align the taxation of income from property situated outside the U.K. under Schedule D, Case V with the new rules for Schedule A under s.39.

Subs. (1)

The new ICTA 1988, s.65(2A) and (2B) provide that income tax on income from overseas property (other than trading income) will be computed in accordance with the rules applicable to a Schedule A business under s.39 above. As a result, taxpayers will be able to set-off Case V losses against Case V income and will, where appropriate, be able to deduct interest incurred in connection with the property (so reversing *Ockenden (Inspector of Taxes) v. Mackley* [1982] 1 W.L.R. 787). The system will not apply to non-domiciled individuals chargeable on the remittance basis.

Subs. (2)

The new s.65A requires Schedule A businesses carried on in the U.K. and abroad to be treated as separate, disapplies ICTA 1988, ss.80, 81, 503 and 504 and Capital Allowances Act 1990, s.29 and provides that the new rules shall not apply for corporation tax purposes.

Subss. (3) and (4)

These extend the relevant provisions of the Capital Allowances Act 1990 and the Taxation of Chargeable Gains Act 1992 to offshore Schedule A businesses.

Subss. (5)–(10)

These make transitional provisions for phasing-in the new system. This will in general apply from the year of assessment 1995–96, but for an existing business subject to the preceding year basis the new system will not be fully operative until 1998–99.

Abolition of interest relief for commercially let property

42.—(1) In section 355 of the Taxes Act 1988, paragraph (b) of subsection (1) (relief for property that is commercially let) shall cease to have effect.

(2) That Act shall be further amended as follows—

(a) in section 353(1B), in the words after paragraph (b), for "sections 237(5)(b) and 355(4)" there shall be substituted "section 237(5)(b)";

(b) in section 355, for the words "subsection (1)(a) above", wherever occurring, there shall be substituted "subsection (1) above";

(c) in sections 356(1) and 356B(5), for "355(1)(a)" there shall be substituted "355(1)";

(d) in sections 357A(7) and 357B(1)(c) and (6), for the words from "and is such" onwards there shall be substituted "by virtue of section 354"; and

(e) in section 357C—

(i) in subsection (1)(e), for the words from "and would have been" onwards, and

(ii) in subsection (2), for the words from "and was such" onwards, there shall, in each case, be substituted "by virtue of section 354".

(3) Subject to subsections (4) to (6) below, this section shall have effect in relation to any payment of interest made on or after 6th April 1995.

(4) Where—

(a) the profits or gains of any source of income that ceases in the course of the year 1995–96 are taxed, by virtue of section 39(5) or 41(9) above, without reference to the Schedule A that has effect by virtue of section 39(1) above, and

(b) that source of income includes any land, caravan or house-boat with respect to which the condition specified in section 355(1)(b) of the Taxes Act 1988 would be satisfied in the case of any loan,

this section shall not apply to any payment of interest on that loan which is made before the time in the year 1995–96 when that source of income ceases.

(5) Subject to paragraph 19(3) of Schedule 6 to this Act, no relief in respect of any payment of interest before 6th April 1995 shall be given under section 355(4) of the Taxes Act 1988 (income against which relief available) against any income for the year 1995–96 or any subsequent year of assessment except in a case where the income falls within subsection (4)(a) above.

(6) Schedule 7 to this Act (which makes amendments in relation to corporation tax which are consequential on this section) shall have effect in relation to accounting periods ending after 31st March 1995.

GENERAL NOTE

This section, together with Sched. 6, paras. 17 and 18, abolishes the present income tax relief for interest paid on a loan used to buy or improve property which is commercially let. Relief for such interest will instead be available as a deduction in computing the profits or gains of a Schedule A business under s.39. The amendments to ICTA 1988 disentangle the present rules from that Act. There are also transitional provisions dealing with cases where a source of income ceases, preventing excess relief.

Subs. (6)

This introduces Sched. 7, which deals with consequential amendments for corporation tax purposes. See further the General Note to Sched. 7.

Benefits in kind

Cars available for private use

43.—(1) After section 157 of the Taxes Act 1988 there shall be inserted—

"Cars available for private use: cash alternative, etc.
157A. Where, in any year in the case of a person employed in employment to which this Chapter applies—
(a) a car is made available as mentioned in section 157, and
(b) an alternative to the benefit of the car is offered,
the mere fact that the alternative is offered shall not make the benefit chargeable to tax under section 19(1)."

(2) In section 158 of the Taxes Act 1988 (car fuel) in subsection (1) for the words "which is made available as mentioned in section 157," there shall be substituted "the benefit of which is chargeable to tax under section 157 as his income,".

(3) In section 167 of the Taxes Act 1988 (employments to which Chapter II of Part V of that Act applies) at the beginning of subsection (2) (calculation of emoluments) there shall be inserted "Subject to subsection (2B) below" and after that subsection there shall be inserted—
"(2B) Where, in any relevant year—
(a) a car is made available as mentioned in section 157, and
(b) an alternative to the benefit of the car is offered,
subsection (2)(a) above shall have effect as if, in connection with the benefit of the car, the amount produced under subsection (2C) below together with any amounts falling within (2D) below were the amounts to be included in the emoluments.
(2C) The amount produced under this subsection is the higher of—
(a) the amount equal to the aggregate of—
(i) whatever is the cash equivalent (ascertained in accordance with Schedule 6) of the benefit of the car; and
(ii) whatever is the cash equivalent (ascertained in accordance with section 158) of the benefit of any fuel provided, by reason of the employee's employment, for the car; and
(b) the amount which would be chargeable to tax under section 19(1), if the benefit of the car were chargeable under that section by reference to the alternative offered to that benefit.
(2D) The amounts which fall within this subsection are those which would come into charge under section 141, 142 or 153 if the section in question applied in connection with the car."

(4) This section shall have effect for the year 1995–96 and subsequent years of assessment.

GENERAL NOTE
The new ICTA 1988, s.157A provides that where a car would otherwise be within the special income tax rules for company cars and an alternative to the benefit of that car is offered, the fact of the offer will not make the car benefit chargeable under, s.19(1). This frustrates schemes based on the assertions that where a cash alternative is offered, but not taken, tax should be charged on the amount of the cash alternative, which might be small, and that no employer's National Insurance contributions should be paid on the taxable value of the car.
The consequential amendments provide for the employee to pay tax and the employer to pay NICs on the higher of the car scale charges and the cash alternative. Car fuel scale charges apply only when the car is actually subject to a car benefit charge.

Cars: accessories for the disabled

44.—(1) At the end of section 168A(11) of the Taxes Act 1988 (mobile telephones not accessories for purpose of determining price of car) there shall be inserted "or equipment which falls within section 168AA".

(2) After section 168A of the Taxes Act 1988 there shall be inserted—

"Equipment to enable disabled person to use car

168AA.—(1) Equipment falls within this section if it is designed solely for use by a chronically sick or disabled person.

(2) Equipment also falls within this section if—

(a) at the time when the car is first made available to the employee, the employee holds a disabled person's badge, and

(b) the equipment is made available for use with the car because the equipment enables him to use the car in spite of the disability entitling him to hold the badge.

(3) In subsection (2) above "disabled person's badge" means a badge—

(a) which is issued to a disabled person under section 21 of the Chronically Sick and Disabled Persons Act 1970 or section 14 of the Chronically Sick and Disabled Persons (Northern Ireland) Act 1978 (or which has effect as if so issued), and

(b) which is not required to be returned to the issuing authority under or by virtue of the section in question.

(4) Subsection (12) of section 168A applies for the purposes of this section as it applies for the purposes of that."

(3) This section shall have effect for the year 1995–96 and subsequent years of assessment.

GENERAL NOTE

The new s.168AA exempts from the tax on benefits in kind, accessories fitted to a car in order to enable a disabled employee to use the car, where the employee is an orange badge holder because of his disability. The provision covers not only special accessories designed solely for use by a disabled person, but also optional accessories such as automatic transmission, power steering, electric windows, air conditioning or heated seats, which are fitted to a company car at extra cost in order to enable a disabled employee to use that car.

Beneficial loan arrangements: replacement loans

45.—(1) In Chapter II of Part V of the Taxes Act 1988 (benefits in kind, &c.), section 160 (beneficial loan arrangements) is amended as follows.

(2) In subsection (5) (interpretation), paragraph (b) (references to loan to include any replacement loan) shall cease to have effect.

(3) After subsection (3) (deemed continuance of employment to which that Chapter applies) insert—

"(3A) Where subsection (3) above applies, a loan which—

(a) is applied directly or indirectly to the replacement of any such loan as is mentioned in paragraph (a) of that subsection, and

(b) would, if the employment referred to in that subsection had not terminated or, as the case may be, ceased to be employment to which this Chapter applies, have been a loan the benefit of which was obtained by reason of that employment,

shall, unless it is a loan the benefit of which was obtained by reason of other employment, be treated as a loan the benefit of which was obtained by reason of that employment.".

(4) In paragraph 4 of Schedule 7 to the Taxes Act 1988 (loans obtained by reason of employment: normal method of calculation of benefit (averaging)), make the present provision sub-paragraph (1) and after it insert—

"(2) Where an employment-related loan is replaced, directly or indirectly—

(a) by a further employment-related loan, or

(b) by a non-employment-related loan which in turn is, in the same year of assessment or within 40 days thereafter, replaced, directly or indirectly, by a further employment-related loan,

sub-paragraph (1) above applies as if the replacement loan or, as the case may be, each of the replacement loans were the same loan as the first-mentioned employment-related loan.

(3) For the purposes of sub-paragraph (2) above "employment-related loan" means a loan the benefit of which is obtained by reason of a person's employment (and "non-employment-related loan" shall be construed accordingly).

(4) The references in sub-paragraph (2) above to a further employment-related loan are to an employment-related loan the benefit of which is obtained by reason of—

(a) the same or other employment with the person who is the employer in relation to the first-mentioned employment-related loan, or

(b) employment with a person who is connected (within the meaning of section 839) with that employer.".

(5) The above amendments have effect for the year 1995–96 and subsequent years of assessment and apply to loans whether made before or after the passing of this Act.

GENERAL NOTE

The purpose of this section is to remove a difficulty which presently occurs where an employer wishes to cease providing beneficial loans and transfers the portfolio to an outside lender who charges a commercial rate of interest. There could still be a charge on the employee because the official rate of interest may be higher than the commercial rate. Such replacement loans are taken out of charge.

Subs. (3)

This is an anti-avoidance measure, to ensure that a replacement loan waived by a former employer is charged to tax in the same way as it would be if the original loan was waived.

Subs. (4)

Where there is a switching of loans either by a new loan from the employer, or by a replacement loan followed by another loan from the employer, the loans are treated as if the original loan had continued for the purpose of calculating the taxable value.

Chargeable gains

Relief on re-investment: property companies etc.

46.—(1) Chapter IA of Part V of the Taxation of Chargeable Gains Act 1992 (roll-over relief on re-investment) shall be amended as follows.

(2) In section 164A (relief on re-investment for individuals) the following subsection shall be inserted after subsection (12)—

"(13) Where an acquisition is made on or after 29th November 1994 section 164H shall be ignored in deciding whether it is an acquisition of a qualifying investment for the purposes of this section."

(3) In section 164F (failure of conditions of relief) the following subsection shall be inserted after subsection (2)—

"(2A) In deciding for the purposes of subsection (2)(b) above whether a company is a qualifying company at a time falling on or after 29th November 1994 section 164H shall be ignored."

(4) In section 164I (qualifying trades) the following subsection shall be inserted after subsection (4)—

"(4A) In deciding whether a trade complies with this section at a time falling on or after 29th November 1994 paragraphs (g) and (h) of subsection (2) above shall be ignored."

GENERAL NOTE

The changes to TCGA 1992, Part V, Chapter 1A are as follows:

(i) The interest in land rule in s.164H is repealed as from November 29, 1994; and

(ii) Property development and farming are not excluded from relief on re-investment as from that date.

The purpose of the changes is to bring reinvestment relief more into line with the enterprise investment scheme (see FA 1994, Sched. 15).

Relief on re-investment: amount of relief, etc.

47.—(1) Chapter IA of Part V of the Taxation of Chargeable Gains Act 1992 (roll-over relief on re-investment) shall be amended as follows.

(2) In section 164A after subsection (13) (inserted by section 46 above) there shall be inserted—

"(14) This section is subject to sections 164FF and 164FG."

(3) In section 164F after subsection (10B) there shall be inserted—

"(10C) Subsection (10A) above is subject to sections 164FF and 164FG."

(4) After section 164F there shall be inserted—

"Qualifying investment acquired from husband or wife

164FF.—(1) This section applies where—

(a) a claim is made under subsection (2) of section 164A or subsection (10A) of section 164F; and

(b) the qualifying investment as respects which the claim is made is acquired by a disposal to which section 58 applies.

(2) The amounts by reference to which the reduction is determined shall be treated as including the amount of the consideration which the claimant would under this Act be treated as having given for the qualifying investment if he had, immediately upon acquiring the qualifying investment, disposed of it on a disposal which was not a no gain/no loss disposal.

(3) Where—

(a) the claimant makes a disposal, which is not a no gain/no loss disposal, of the qualifying investment, and

(b) any disposal after 31st March 1982 and before he acquired the qualifying investment was a no gain/no loss disposal,

nothing in paragraph 1 of Schedule 3, section 35 or section 55 shall operate to defeat the reduction falling to be made under section 164A(2)(b) or, as the case may be, section 164F(10A)(b) in the consideration for the acquisition of the qualifying investment.

(4) Where—

(a) the claimant makes a disposal of the qualifying investment and that disposal is a disposal to which section 58 applies, and

(b) any disposal after 31st March 1982 and before the claimant acquired the qualifying investment was a no gain/no loss disposal,

nothing in the application of paragraph 1 of Schedule 3, section 35 or section 55 to the person to whom the claimant makes the disposal of the qualifying investment shall operate to defeat the reduction made under section 164A(2)(b) or, as the case may be, section 164F(10A)(b).

(5) For the purposes of this section a no gain/no loss disposal is one on which by virtue of any of the enactments specified in section 35(3)(d) neither a gain nor a loss accrues."

(5) After section 164FF (inserted by subsection (4) above) there shall be inserted—

"**Multiple claims**
164FG.—(1) This section applies where—
(a) a reduction is claimed by a person as respects a qualifying investment under subsection (2) of section 164A or subsection (10A) of section 164F; and
(b) any other reduction has been or is being claimed by that person under either subsection as respects that investment.

(2) Subject to subsection (5) below, the reductions shall be treated as claimed separately in such sequence as the claimant elects or an officer of the Board in default of an election determines.

(3) In relation to a later claim as respects the qualifying investment under either subsection, the subsection shall have effect as if each of the relevant amounts were reduced by the aggregate of any reductions made in the amount or value of the consideration for the acquisition of that investment by virtue of any earlier claims as respects that investment.

(4) In subsection (3) above "the relevant amounts" means—
(a) if the claim is under section 164A(2), the amounts referred to in subsection (2)(a)(ii) and (iii) and any amount required to be included by virtue of section 164FF(2); and
(b) if the claim is under section 164F(10A), the amounts referred to in subsection (10A)(a)(i) and (ii) and any amount required to be included by virtue of section 164FF(2).

(5) A claim that has become final shall be treated as made earlier than any claim that has not become final.

(6) For the purposes of subsection (5) above, a claim becomes final when—
(a) it may no longer be amended, or
(b) it is finally determined,
whichever occurs first."

(6) Subsection (4) above (and subsections (1) to (3) above so far as relating to subsection (4) above) shall apply to a claim as respects a qualifying investment if—
(a) the qualifying investment is acquired on or after 20th June 1994; or
(b) the claim is under section 164A(2) and relates to a disposal on or after that day; or
(c) the claim is under subsection (10A) of section 164F and relates to a gain which (apart from that subsection) would accrue on or after that day.

(7) Subsection (5) above (and subsections (1) to (3) above so far as relating to subsection (5) above) shall apply to a claim as respects a qualifying investment if—
(a) the qualifying investment is acquired on or after 20th June 1994; or
(b) the claim is under section 164A(2) and relates to a disposal on or after that day; or
(c) the claim is under subsection (10A) of section 164F and relates to a gain which (apart from that subsection) would accrue on or after that day; or
(d) there is another claim as respects that qualifying investment which is under section 164A(2) and which relates to a disposal on or after that day; or
(e) there is another claim as respects that qualifying investment which is under subsection (10A) of section 164F and which relates to a gain which (apart from that subsection) would accrue on or after that day.

(8) Any such adjustment as is appropriate in consequence of this section may be made (whether by discharge or repayment of tax, the making of an assessment or otherwise).

GENERAL NOTE
The amendments to TCGA 1992, Part V, Chapter 1A are designed to close two loopholes:
 (i) The new s.164FF applies where a gain is rolled over against the acquisition cost of shares transferred between spouses and restricts the relief to the transferee's allowable acquisition cost of those shares;
 (ii) The new s.164FG applies where gains on more than one disposal are being rolled over against the acquisition cost of a single qualifying investment and ensures that the total gains which are rolled over cannot exceed the cost of the shares acquired.
The new sections take effect from June 20, 1994, when the changes in the law were announced.

Roll-over relief and groups of companies

48.—(1) In section 175 of the Taxation of Chargeable Gains Act 1992 (replacement of business assets by members of a group), after subsection (2) there shall be inserted the following subsections—
   "(2A) Section 152 shall apply where—
      (a) the disposal is by a company which, at the time of the disposal, is a member of a group of companies,
      (b) the acquisition is by another company which, at the time of the acquisition, is a member of the same group, and
      (c) the claim is made by both companies,
   as if both companies were the same person.
   (2B) Section 152 shall apply where a company which is a member of a group of companies but is not carrying on a trade—
      (a) disposes of assets (or an interest in assets) used, and used only, for the purposes of the trade which (in accordance with subsection (1) above) is treated as carried on by the members of the group which carry on a trade, or
      (b) acquires assets (or an interest in assets) taken into use, and used only, for those purposes,
   as if the first company were carrying on that trade.
   (2C) Section 152 shall not apply if the acquisition of, or of the interest in, the new assets—
      (a) is made by a company which is a member of a group of companies, and
      (b) is one to which any of the enactments specified in section 35(3)(d) applies."
(2) In section 247 of the Taxation of Chargeable Gains Act 1992 (roll-over relief on compulsory acquisition of land), after subsection (5) there shall be inserted the following subsection—
   "(5A) Subsections (2A) and (2C) of section 175 shall apply in relation to this section as they apply in relation to section 152 (but as if the reference in subsection (2C) to the new assets were a reference to the new land)."
(3) Subject to subsection (4) below—
   (a) the subsection inserted into section 175 of the Taxation of Chargeable Gains Act 1992 by subsection (1) above as subsection (2A) shall be deemed always to have had effect; and
   (b) the earlier enactments corresponding to that section shall be deemed to have contained provision to the same effect as that subsection (2A).
(4) Paragraph (c) of that subsection (2A) shall not apply unless the claim is made on or after 29th November 1994.
(5) The subsection inserted into section 175 of the Taxation of Chargeable Gains Act 1992 by subsection (1) above as subsection (2B) shall apply where

the disposal or the acquisition is on or after 29th November 1994; and the subsection so inserted as subsection (2C) shall apply where the acquisition is on or after that date.

(6) The subsection inserted into section 247 of the Taxation of Chargeable Gains Act 1992 by subsection (2) above shall apply—

    (a) so far as it relates to section 175(2A), where the disposal or the acquisition is on or after 29th November 1994; and

    (b) so far as it relates to section 175(2C), where the acquisition is on or after that date.

GENERAL NOTE

The amendments to TCGA 1992 effect the following changes in relation to roll-over relief as regards groups of companies:

    (i) a longstanding Revenue practice allowing roll-over relief where a qualifying asset is disposed of by one company in a group and a replacement asset is acquired by another group member is deemed always to have been valid. Doubt had been cast on its validity by the decision in *Campbell Connelly & Co. v. Barnett* (*H.M. Inspector of Taxes*) [1992] S.T.C. 316; [1993] S.T.C. 50;

    (ii) Roll-over relief is extended to cases where one company in a group disposes of land under a compulsory purchase order and another group member acquires replacement land;

    (iii) The device known as "roll around", whereby an asset transferred within a group can be treated as a replacement asset for roll-over relief purposes is prevented by disallowing the creation of qualifying expenditure from such transfers;

    (iv) Extra Statutory Concession D30, which allows assets held by a non-trading member of a group to qualify for roll-over relief where those assets are used for the purposes of a trade by other members of the group, is given statutory effect.

De-grouping charges

49.—(1) In section 179 of the Taxation of Chargeable Gains Act 1992 (de-grouping charges), after subsection (2) there shall be inserted the following subsections—

    "(2A) Where—

        (a) a company that has ceased to be a member of a group of companies ('the first group') acquired an asset from another company which was a member of that group at the time of the acquisition,

        (b) subsection (2) above applies in the case of that company's ceasing to be a member of the first group so that subsection (1) above does not have effect as respects the acquisition of that asset,

        (c) the company that made the acquisition subsequently ceases to be a member of another group of companies ('the second group'), and

        (d) there is a connection between the two groups,

subsection (1) above shall have effect in relation to the company's ceasing to be a member of the second group as if it had been the second group of which both companies had been members at the time of the acquisition.

    (2B) For the purposes of subsection (2A) above there is a connection between the first group and the second group if, at the time when the chargeable company ceases to be a member of the second group, the company which is the principal company of that group is under the control of—

        (a) the company which is the principal company of the first group or, if that group no longer exists, which was the principal company of that group when the chargeable company ceased to be a member of it;

        (b) any company which controls the company mentioned in paragraph (a) above or which has had it under its control at any time in the period since the chargeable company ceased to be a member of the first group; or

(c) any company which has, at any time in that period, had under its control either—
> (i) a company which would have fallen within paragraph (b) above if it had continued to exist, or
> (ii) a company which would have fallen within this paragraph (whether by reference to a company which would have fallen within that paragraph or to a company or series of companies falling within this sub-paragraph)."

(2) After subsection (9) of that section there shall be inserted the following subsection—

"(9A) Section 416(2) to (6) of the Taxes Act (meaning of control) shall have effect for the purposes of subsection (2B) above as it has effect for the purposes of Part XI of that Act; but a person carrying on a business of banking shall not for the purposes of that subsection be regarded as having control of any company by reason only of having, or of the consequences of having exercised, any rights of that person in respect of loan capital or debt issued or incurred by the company for money lent by that person to the company in the ordinary course of that business."

(3) This section has effect in relation to a company in any case in which the time of the company's ceasing to be a member of the second group is on or after 29th November 1994.

GENERAL NOTE

The amendments to TCGA 1992, s.179 are designed to prevent a device known as the "envelope trick". This sought to avoid the charge to tax on a company leaving a group within six years of acquiring an asset by an intra-group no gain/no loss transfer, by having both companies involved leave the group but in such a way that the group does not in fact lose economic ownership of the de-grouped companies. The amendments operate by effectively treating the original group and the group formed by the artificial de-grouping as one and the same when considering whether the de-grouping charge provisions apply. The artificial de-grouping can be achieved by having an outside financial institution subscribe for shares carrying negligible economic rights. The new s.179(9A) ensures that the anti-avoidance provision does not apply in connection with loans made in the ordinary course of business.

Corporate bonds

50. In section 117 of the Taxation of Chargeable Gains Act 1992 (qualifying corporate bonds) the following subsection shall be inserted after subsection (2)—

"(2A) Where it falls to be decided whether at any time on or after 29th November 1994 a security (whenever issued) is a corporate bond for the purposes of this section, a security which falls within paragraph 2(2)(c) of Schedule 11 to the Finance Act 1989 (quoted indexed securities) shall be treated as not being a corporate bond within the definition in subsection (1) above."

GENERAL NOTE

Securities linked to a share index attracted relief under TCGA 1992, s.115 as a qualifying corporate bond and also under FA 1989, Sched. 11, para. 2 as a qualifying indexed security in the provisions relating to deep gain securities. The resultant loss of tax and distortion in the investment market is remedied by the amendment to TCGA 1992, s.117, under which these securities will be treated as being within the charge to CGT like the underlying shares which determine their value.

Insurance companies and friendly societies

Companies carrying on life assurance business

51. Schedule 8 to this Act has effect in relation to companies carrying on life assurance business, as follows—

Part I contains general amendments,

Part II contains amendments of provisions relating to overseas life insurance companies, and

Part III contains supplementary provisions.

GENERAL NOTE

This section introduces Sched. 8, which makes a number of changes to the rules for taxing life assurance companies. The following are the more important:

(i) the scope of "overseas life assurance business" is expanded to include business written directly from the U.K. by a U.K. life insurance company or a U.K. branch of an overseas life insurance company with certain European policyholders, instead of being confined to policies with a non-U.K. resident written through a non-U.K. branch of a U.K. life insurance company;

(ii) the normal basis of taxing income from land in the U.K. is maintained where the land is used directly to support overseas life assurance business;

(iii) changes are made in the taxation of reinsurance (*i.e.* the insurance of insurance), to provide for a tax charge year by year on the investment return from the reinsurance;

(iv) a U.K. life insurance company will be taxed on the profits it makes and not on the investment return accruing for policyholders, in order to prevent double taxation of the same income and gains;

(v) life assurance business losses are quantified to prevent a loss being relieved more than once;

(vi) entitlement of a life assurance company to capital allowances is clarified;

(vii) improvements are made to the rules for allocating income and gains to the different types of business which a life assurance company may carry on and which are treated differently for tax purposes, *e.g.* "overseas life assurance business", "life reinsurance business", "pension business" and "basic life assurance and general annuity business". Investment income and gains accruing for policy holders are taxed in the hands of the insurance company year by year. The profit made from writing the other types of business is taxed but the investment return is not;

(viii) the general rules which apply when a company has elected to set-off management expenses against U.K. dividends so as to obtain payment of the tax credits are adapted for the special circumstances of life insurance companies;

(ix) life insurance companies are given an entitlement to interest on repayments of overpaid advance corporation tax;

(x) various provisions are adapted for U.K. branches of overseas life insurance companies, including those relating to foreign income dividends.

For further details, see the General Note to Sched. 8.

Meaning of "insurance company"

52.—(1) In section 431(2) of the Taxes Act 1988 (interpretation of provisions relating to insurance companies), for the definition of "insurance company" there shall be substituted the following definition—

" 'insurance company' means any company which is—

(a) a company to which Part II of the Insurance Companies Act 1982 applies, or

(b) an EC company carrying on insurance business through a branch or agency in the United Kingdom,

and in this definition 'EC company' and 'insurance business' have the same meanings as in that Act of 1982;".

(2) In section 168(7) of the Finance Act 1993 (meaning of "insurance company" for the purposes of provisions relating to exchange gains and losses), for the words from "a company" onwards there shall be substituted "any company which carries on any insurance business (within the meaning of the Insurance Companies Act 1982)."

(3) In section 177(1) of the Finance Act 1994 (interpretation of provisions relating to financial instruments), in the definition of "insurance company", for the words "to which Part II of the Insurance Companies Act 1982 applies" there shall be substituted "which carries on any insurance business (within the meaning of the Insurance Companies Act 1982);".

(4) In section 59(3)(b) of the Inheritance Tax Act 1984 (interests of insurance companies acquired before 14th March 1975 to be qualifying interests in possession), for the words from "if" onwards there shall be substituted "if the company is an insurance company (within the meaning of Chapter I of Part XII of the Taxes Act 1988) and either—

        (i) is authorised to carry on long term business under section 3 or 4 of the Insurance Companies Act 1982; or

        (ii) carries on through a branch or agency in the United Kingdom the whole or any part of any long term business which it is authorised to carry on by an authorisation granted outside the United Kingdom for the purposes of the first long term insurance Directive;

and in paragraph (b) above 'long term business' and 'the first long term insurance Directive' have the same meanings as in that Act of 1982."

(5) Subsections (1) to (3) above shall have effect in relation to any accounting period ending after 30th June 1994; and subsection (4) above shall have effect for the purposes of the making, on an anniversary or other occasion after that date, of any charge to tax under section 64 or 65 of the Inheritance Tax Act 1984.

GENERAL NOTE

The current definition of "insurance company" relates to operation in the U.K. on the basis of authorisation by the Department of Trade and Industry (DTI). This is no longer appropriate, since insurance companies that are based in other member states of the E.U., or in Iceland or Norway, no longer require DTI authorisation to operate through branches in the U.K. Accordingly, an amended definition is inserted in the various places in the Tax Acts where it appears.

The new definition, which was announced on June 24, 1994, applies for accounting periods ending after June 30, 1994 and for inheritance tax charges arising after that date.

Transfer of life insurance business

53.—(1) The amendments specified in Schedule 9 to this Act (which relate to enactments referring to the transfer of the whole or part of the long term business of an insurance company) shall have effect.

(2) This section and that Schedule shall have effect in relation to any transfers sanctioned or authorised after 30th June 1994.

GENERAL NOTE

This section introduces Sched. 9, which adapts the current provisions dealing with transfers of insurance business so as to comply with the European Community's Third Life Insurance and Third Non-Life Insurance Directives. Schedule 9 has effect for transfers sanctioned or authorised after June 30, 1994, the date when the Directives came into force.

See further the General Note to Sched. 9.

Friendly societies

54. Schedule 10 to this Act (which makes provision about friendly societies) shall have effect.

GENERAL NOTE

Various minor adjustments are made to the tax regime for friendly societies.
See the General Note to Sched. 10.

Insurance policies

Qualifying life insurance policies

55.—(1) Subject to subsections (2) and (3) below—

(a) paragraph 21 of Schedule 15 to the Taxes Act 1988 (certification of policies and of standard forms etc.) shall not apply, in relation to any time on or after 5th May 1996, for determining whether a policy is or would be a qualifying policy at that time; and

(b) no certificate may be issued under that paragraph at any time on or after that date except, in the case of a certificate under sub-paragraph (1)(a) of that paragraph, in relation to a time before that date.

(2) Subsection (1) above shall not affect the right of any person to bring or continue with an appeal under paragraph 21(3) of that Schedule against either a refusal before 5th May 1996 to certify any policy or a refusal on or after that date to certify any policy in relation to times before that date.

(3) A certificate issued—

(a) before 5th May 1996 in pursuance of paragraph 21(1)(a) of that Schedule, or

(b) in pursuance of a determination on an appeal determined after that date by virtue of subsection (2) above,

shall, in relation to any time on or after that date or, as the case may be, the date on which it is issued, be conclusive evidence that the policy to which it relates is (subject to any variation of the policy) a qualifying policy.

(4) Paragraph 22 of that Schedule (certificates from body issuing policy) shall cease to have effect in relation to any time on or after 5th May 1996.

(5) Paragraph 24 of that Schedule (policies issued by non-resident companies) shall have effect in relation to times on or after 5th May 1996—

(a) with the substitution of the following sub-paragraphs for sub-paragraph (2)—

"(2) Subject to section 55(3) of the Finance Act 1995 (transitional provision for the certification of certain policies), a new non-resident policy that falls outside sub-paragraph (2A) below shall not be a qualifying policy until such time as the conditions in sub-paragraph (3) are fulfilled with respect to it.

(2A) A policy falls outside this sub-paragraph unless, at the time immediately before 5th May 1996, it was a qualifying policy by virtue of sub-paragraphs (2)(b) and (4) of this paragraph, as they had effect in relation to that time.";

and

(b) with the omission, in sub-paragraph (3), of the word "first" and of sub-paragraph (4).

(6) In paragraph 25 of that Schedule (policies substituted for policies issued by non-resident companies), for sub-paragraph (2) there shall be substituted the following sub-paragraph—

"(2) The modifications are the following—

(a) if, apart from paragraph 24, the old policy or any related policy (within the meaning of paragraph 17(2)(b)) of which account falls to be taken would have been a qualifying policy, that policy shall be assumed to have been a qualifying policy for the purposes of paragraph 17(2); and

(b) if, apart from this paragraph, the new policy would be a qualifying policy, it shall not be such a policy unless the circumstances are as specified in paragraph 17(3); and

(c) in paragraph 17(3)(c) the words 'either by a branch or agency of theirs outside the United Kingdom or' shall be omitted;

and references in this sub-paragraph to being a qualifying policy shall have effect, in relation to any time before 5th May 1996, as including a reference to being capable of being certified as such a policy."

(7) In paragraph 27(1) of that Schedule, except so far as it has effect for the purposes of any case to which paragraph 21 of that Schedule applies by virtue of the preceding provisions of this section, for "paragraphs 21 and" there shall be substituted "paragraph".

(8) In section 553 of the Taxes Act 1988 (which contains provisions referring to paragraph 24(3) or (4) of Schedule 15 to that Act)—
  (a) in subsection (2), for the words from "neither" to "fulfilled" there shall
      be substituted "the conditions in paragraph 24(3) of Schedule 15 to
      this Act are not fulfilled"; and
  (b) in subsection (7), for "either sub-paragraph (3) or sub-paragraph (4)"
      there shall be substituted "sub-paragraph (3)";
but this subsection shall not affect the operation of Chapter II of Part XIII of
that Act in relation to any policy in relation to which the conditions in paragraph 24(4) of Schedule 15 to that Act, as it then had effect, were fulfilled at
times in accounting periods before those in relation to which section 103 of
the Finance Act 1993 (which repealed section 445 of the Taxes Act 1988) had
effect.

GENERAL NOTE
The section ends certification of qualifying policies of life insurance by the Revenue as from
May 5, 1996. In future, a policy will qualify if it meets certain conditions. The proceeds of such a
policy are generally exempt from income tax, while a non-qualifying policy may be subject to
tax. The main conditions required are that the policy must provide a significant amount on death
and must be for a term of at least 10 years with regular premiums.

Subs. (1)
This removes the requirement for certification as from May 5, 1996. Previously uncertified
policies made before that date will be certified where appropriate for prior periods.

Subs. (2)
The right of appeal against previous refusals to certify is preserved.

Subs. (3)
The qualifying status of a certified policy is maintained unless its terms are changed.

Subs. (4)
Insurers will no longer be obliged to provide a policyholder with a certificate confirming
certification.

Subs. (5)
A policy from a non-resident insurance company cannot be a qualifying policy unless it is with
a U.K. branch. This corresponds to the previous provision regarding certification of such
policies.

Subs. (6)
A non-resident policy which otherwise meets the qualifying conditions may, in certain circumstances, be replaced by a qualifying policy from a U.K. insurer. This again corresponds to
the previous provision.

Subs. (7)
A redundant reference is removed.

Subs. (8)
A provision for charging tax on gains under a policy of life insurance from a U.K. branch of a
non-resident insurer is removed. This became prospectively redundant when the basis for charging tax on such branches was changed by FA 1993, ss.97–103 and Scheds. 9–11.

Foreign life policies etc.

56.—(1) In section 547 of the Taxes Act 1988 (charging of certain gains arising in connection with insurance policies etc.), in subsection (5A), for "subsection (7)" there shall be substituted "subsection (6A) or (7)"; and after subsection (6) of that section there shall be inserted the following subsection—

"(6A) Subsection (6) above shall not apply in relation to a gain treated as arising in connection with a contract for a life annuity in any case where the Board are satisfied, on a claim made for the purpose—

(a) that the company liable to make payments under the contract ('the grantor') has not, at any time ('a relevant time') between the date on which it entered into the contract and the date on which the gain is treated as arising, been resident in the United Kingdom;

(b) that at all relevant times the grantor has—

(i) as a body deriving its status as a company from the laws of a territory outside the United Kingdom,

(ii) as a company with its place of management in such a territory, or

(iii) as a company falling, under the laws of such a territory, to be regarded, for any other reason, as resident or domiciled in that territory,

been within a charge to tax under the laws of that territory;

(c) that that territory is a territory within the European Economic Area when the gain is treated as arising;

(d) that the charge to tax mentioned in paragraph (b) above has at all relevant times been such a charge made otherwise than by reference to profits as (by disallowing their deduction in computing the amount chargeable) to require sums payable and other liabilities arising under contracts of the same class as the contract in question to be treated as sums or liabilities falling to be met out of amounts subject to tax in the hands of the grantor;

(e) that the rate of tax fixed for the purposes of that charge in relation to the amounts subject to tax in the hands of the grantor (not being amounts arising or accruing in respect of investments that are of a particular description for which a special relief or exemption is generally available) has at all relevant times been at least 20 per cent.; and

(f) that none of the grantor's obligations under the contract in question to pay any sum or to meet any other liability arising under that contract is or has been the subject, in whole or in part, of any reinsurance contract relating to anything other than the risk that the annuitant will die or will suffer any sickness or accident;

and subsection (6) above shall also not apply where the case would fall within paragraphs (a) to (f) above if references to a relevant time did not include references to any time when the contract fell to be regarded as forming part of so much of any basic life assurance and general annuity business the income and gains of which were subject to corporation tax as was being carried on through a branch or agency in the United Kingdom."

(2) In section 553 of that Act (non-resident policies and off-shore capital redemption policies), in subsection (6), for "subsection (7)" there shall be substituted "subsections (6A) and (7)"; and after that subsection there shall be inserted the following subsection—

"(6A) Paragraphs (a) and (b) of subsection (6) above do not apply to a gain in a case where the Board are satisfied, on a claim made for the purpose—

(a) that the insurer has not, at any time ('a relevant time') between the making of the insurance and the date on which the gain is treated as arising, been resident in the United Kingdom;

(b) that at all relevant times the insurer has—

(i) as a body deriving its status as a company from the laws of a territory outside the United Kingdom,

(ii) as a company with its place of management in such a territory, or

(iii) as a company falling, under the laws of such a territory, to be regarded, for any other reason, as resident or domiciled in that territory,

been within a charge to tax under the laws of that territory;

(c) that that territory is a territory within the European Economic Area when the gain is treated as arising;

(d) that the charge to tax mentioned in paragraph (b) above has at all relevant times been such a charge made otherwise than by reference to profits as (by disallowing their deduction in computing the amount chargeable) to require sums payable and other liabilities arising under policies of the same class as the policy in question to be treated as sums or liabilities falling to be met out of amounts subject to tax in the hands of the insurer;

(e) that the rate of tax fixed for the purposes of that charge in relation to the amounts subject to tax in the hands of the insurer (not being amounts arising or accruing in respect of investments that are of a particular description for which a special relief or exemption is generally available) has at all relevant times been at least 20 per cent.; and

(f) that none of the insurer's obligations under the policy in question to pay any sum or to meet any other liability arising under that policy is or has been the subject, in whole or in part, of any reinsurance contract relating to anything other than the risk that the person whose life is insured by the policy will die or will suffer any sickness or accident;

and paragraphs (a) and (b) of subsection (6) above shall also not apply where the case would fall within paragraphs (a) to (f) above if references to a relevant time did not include references to any time when the conditions required to be fulfilled in relation to that time for the purposes of subsection (7) below were fulfilled."

(3) For the purpose of securing that section 547(5) of the Taxes Act 1988 has effect in other cases (in addition to those specified in sections 547(6A) and 553(6A)) where it appears to the Board appropriate for section 547(6) or 553(6) to be disapplied by reference to tax chargeable under the laws of a territory outside the United Kingdom, the Board may by regulations provide that the cases described in subsection (6A) of each of sections 547 and 553 of that Act are to be treated as including cases, being cases which would not otherwise fall within the subsection, where the conditions specified in the regulations are fulfilled in relation to any time (including one before the making of the regulations).

(4) This section shall apply in relation to any gain arising on or after 29th November 1994 and in relation to any gain arising before that date the income tax on which has not been the subject of an assessment that became final and conclusive before that date.

GENERAL NOTE

The tax charge on gains on some foreign insurance policies is reduced. A notional basic tax credit is given when an insurance company has been taxed, as proxy for the policyholder, on the underlying income and gains accruing during the term of the policy.

Subs. (1)
Subs. (1)
The new ICTA 1988, s.547(6A) provides that on a claim gains on certain life annuity contracts issued by an insurance company resident in a country within the European Economic Area other than the U.K. will be treated, in the same way as U.K. life annuity gains are now treated, as having suffered tax at the basic rate. This is subject to provisions ensuring that the investment return under the contract has suffered tax at a rate of at least 20 per cent.

Subs. (2)
The new ICTA 1988, s.553(6A) makes provisions parallel to s.547(6A) in relation to life insurance and capital redemption policies issued by an insurance company resident in another country within the European Economic Area.

Subs. (3)
This gives the Revenue power to make regulations to give a notional basic rate credit in other circumstances, *e.g.* where a foreign company is subject to a tax regime which has substantially the same economic effect as a tax on the investment return, but takes a different form.

Subs. (4)
The changes take effect for all gains arising after Budget day and for all assessments which were still open at that time.

Duties of insurers in relation to life policies etc.

57.—(1) In section 552 of the Taxes Act 1988 (duties of insurers of life policies etc.), the following subsection shall be inserted after subsection (2) in relation to times on or after the day on which this Act is passed—

"(2A) Where the obligations under any policy or contract of the body that issued, entered into or effected it ('the original insurer') are at any time the obligations of another body ('the transferee') to whom there has been a transfer of the whole or any part of a business previously carried on by the original insurer, this section shall have effect in relation to that time, except where the chargeable event—

(a) happened before the transfer, and

(b) in the case of a death or assignment, is an event of which the notification mentioned in subsection (1) above was given before the transfer,

as if the policy or contract had been issued, entered into or effected by the transferee."

(2) In that section, the following subsections shall be inserted after subsection (4)—

"(4A) The Board may by regulations—

(a) make provision as to the form which is to be taken by certificates under this section (including provision enabling such a certificate to be delivered otherwise than in the form of a document); and

(b) make such provision as they think fit for securing that they are able to ascertain whether there has been or is likely to be any contravention of the requirements of this section and to verify any such certificate.

(4B) Regulations by virtue of subsection (4A)(b) above may include, in particular, provision requiring persons to whom premiums under any policy are or have at any time been payable to supply information to the Board and to make available books, documents and other records for inspection on behalf of the Board.

(4C) Regulations under subsection (4A) above may—

(a) make different provision for different cases; and

(b) contain such supplementary, incidental, consequential and transitional provision as appears to the Board to be appropriate."

(3) In the second column of the Table in section 98 of the Management Act (penalties in respect of certain information provisions), for the entry relating to section 552 of the Taxes Act 1988 there shall be substituted the following entries—

"section 552(1) to (4);
regulations under section 552(4A);".

GENERAL NOTE
The obligation which an insurer has to provide information about gains on life policies is extended to include business transferred to it. Provision is made for strengthening the Revenue's powers in this regard generally.

Subs. (1)
The obligation to provide information on transferred business will fall on the transferee rather than, as now, the transferor.

Subs. (2)
The Revenue is given power to make regulations to specify the form in which insurers are to provide information and to allow the audit of such information. This will be used to update the Revenue's audit and information capabilities in respect of gains under policies of life insurance and other insurances.

Subs. (3)
The penalty provisions of TMA 1970, s.98 are correspondingly extended.

Pensions

Personal pensions: income withdrawals

58. Schedule 11 to this Act has effect for the purpose of enabling income withdrawals to be made under a personal pension scheme where the purchase of an annuity is deferred.

GENERAL NOTE
The section introduces Sched. 11, which amends the provisions of ICTA 1988, Part XIV, Chapter IV (which deals with personal pension schemes) so as to allow members of such a scheme to defer buying an annuity to age 75 and to withdraw income from their pension fund broadly equivalent to the annuity which their fund could have provided.
See further the General Note to Sched. 11.

Pensions: meaning of insurance company etc.

59.—(1) Part XIV of the Taxes Act 1988 (pension schemes etc.) shall be amended as follows.
(2) In section 591 (discretionary approval of retirement benefits schemes) the following subsection shall be substituted for subsection (3)—
"(3) In subsection (2)(g) above "insurance company" has the meaning given by section 659B."
(3) In section 599 (charge to tax: commutation of entire pension in special circumstances) the following subsection shall be substituted for subsection (8)—
"(8) In subsection (7) above "insurance company" has the meaning given by section 659B."
(4) In section 630 (personal pension schemes: interpretation) the following definition shall be substituted for the definition of "authorised insurance company"—
" "authorised insurance company" has the meaning given by section 659B."
(5) The following sections shall be inserted after section 659A—

"**Definition of insurance company**
659B.—(1) In sections 591(2)(g) and 599(7) "insurance company" means one of the following—
(a) a person authorised under section 3 or 4 of the Insurance Companies Act 1982 (or any similar previous enactment) to carry on long term business;
(b) a friendly society carrying on long term business;

(c) an EC company falling within subsection (3) below.

(2) In Chapter IV of this Part "authorised insurance company" means a company that is an insurance company within the meaning given by subsection (1) above.

(3) An EC company falls within this subsection if it—

(a) lawfully carries on long term business, or lawfully provides long term insurance, in the United Kingdom, and

(b) fulfils the requirement under subsection (5) below or that under subsection (6) below or that under subsection (7) below.

(4) For the purposes of subsection (3) above an EC company—

(a) lawfully carries on long term business in the United Kingdom if it does so through a branch in respect of which such of the requirements of Part I of Schedule 2F to the Insurance Companies Act 1982 as are applicable have been complied with;

(b) lawfully provides long term insurance in the United Kingdom if such of those requirements as are applicable have been complied with in respect of the insurance.

(5) The requirement under this subsection is that—

(a) a person who falls within subsection (8) below is for the time being appointed by the company to be responsible for securing the discharge of the duties mentioned in subsection (9) below, and

(b) his identity and the fact of his appointment have been notified to the Board by the company.

(6) The requirement under this subsection is that there are for the time being other arrangements with the Board for a person other than the company to secure the discharge of those duties.

(7) The requirement under this subsection is that there are for the time being other arrangements with the Board designed to secure the discharge of those duties.

(8) A person falls within this subsection if—

(a) he is not an individual and has a business establishment in the United Kingdom, or

(b) he is an individual and is resident in the United Kingdom.

(9) The duties are the following duties that fall to be discharged by the company—

(a) any duty to pay by virtue of section 203 and regulations made under it tax charged under section 597(3);

(b) any duty to pay tax charged under section 599(3) and (7);

(c) any duty imposed by regulations made under section 605;

(d) any duty to pay by virtue of section 203 and regulations made under it tax charged under section 648A(1).

(10) For the purposes of this section—

(a) references to an EC company shall be construed in accordance with section 2(6) of the Insurance Companies Act 1982;

(b) references to long term business shall be construed in accordance with section 1(1) of that Act;

(c) references to the provision of long term insurance in the United Kingdom shall be construed in accordance with section 96A(3A) of that Act;

(d) a friendly society is a friendly society within the meaning of the Friendly Societies Act 1992 (including any society that by virtue of section 96(2) of that Act is to be treated as a registered friendly society within the meaning of that Act).

Effect of appointment or arrangements under section 659B

659C.—(1) This section shall have effect where—

(a) in accordance with section 659B(5) a person is for the time being appointed to be responsible for securing the discharge of duties, or

(b) in accordance with section 659B(6) there are for the time being arrangements for a person to secure the discharge of duties.

(2) In such a case the person concerned—

(a) shall be entitled to act on the company's behalf for any of the purposes of the provisions relating to the duties;

(b) shall secure (where appropriate by acting on the company's behalf) the company's compliance with and discharge of the duties;

(c) shall be personally liable in respect of any failure of the company to comply with or discharge any such duty as if the duties imposed on the company were imposed jointly and severally on the company and the person concerned."

GENERAL NOTE

The section provides a new and consistent definition of "insurance company" for the purposes of tax-approved pension arrangements. The new definition also includes certain insurance companies in the European Union and European Economic Area. It identifies the institutions from which the trustees or managers of tax-approved occupational and personal pension schemes may purchase annuities.

Subss. (2)–(4)

These replace the present definitions of an insurance company in ICTA 1988, ss.591, 599 and 630 with a cross-reference to the definition contained in the new s.659B.

Subs. (5)

This inserts new ss.659B and 659C. They provide a common definition of the term "insurance company" for the purposes of ICTA 1988, Part XIV (ss.590–659) which includes certain insurance companies established abroad. In particular, s.659B will permit the trustees or managers of tax-approved occupational and personal pension schemes to purchase annuities from insurance companies and friendly societies carrying on long-term business within the provisions of the Insurance Companies Act 1982 or the Friendly Societies Act 1992 and from E.C. companies (defined in accordance with the Insurance Companies Act 1982) which satisfy certain conditions. The conditions are that an E.C. company should be lawfully carrying on long-term business or providing long-term insurance in the U.K. and should either have appointed a U.K. resident person to be responsible for the duties arising under Part XIV or have entered into some other arrangement with the Revenue to secure the discharge of those duties. The duties are the same as those with which U.K. insurance companies must comply, *i.e.* deducting and accounting for income tax under the Pay As You Earn system in respect of annuity instalments paid, dealing with the special tax charges that can arise where annuities are commuted for a lump sum payment and providing information to the Revenue about the annuities.

Application of section 59

60.—(1) Section 59(2) above and the new section 659B, so far as relating to section 591(2)(g), shall apply in relation to a scheme not approved by virtue of section 591 before the day on which this Act is passed.

(2) Section 59(3) above and the new section 659B, so far as relating to section 599(7), shall apply where tax is charged under section 599 on or after the day on which this Act is passed.

(3) Section 59(4) above and the new section 659B, so far as relating to Chapter IV of Part XIV, shall apply in relation to a scheme not approved under that Chapter before the day on which this Act is passed.

(4) Subsection (5) below applies where—

(a) a scheme is approved under Chapter IV of Part XIV before the day on which this Act is passed,

(b) on or after that day the person who established the scheme proposes to amend it, and

(c) the scheme as proposed to be amended would make provision such that, if the scheme had not been approved before that day, section

59(4) above and the new section 659B (so far as relating to that Chapter) would allow the Board to approve it.

(5) The Board may at their discretion approve the amendment notwithstanding anything in Chapter IV of Part XIV, and if the amendment is made—

(a) section 59(4) above and the new section 659B, so far as relating to that Chapter, shall apply in relation to the scheme, and

(b) any question as to the validity of the Board's approval of the scheme shall be determined accordingly.

GENERAL NOTE

The section provides for the entry into force of s.59 in relation to the various sections of ICTA 1988 that are affected by the new definition of an insurance company in s.659B. This is generally the date of Royal Assent (May 1, 1995). Existing tax-approved personal pension schemes may amend their rules as from that date to adopt the new definition of insurance company contained in s.659B.

Cessation of approval of certain retirement benefits schemes

61.—(1) After section 591E of the Taxes Act 1988 there shall be inserted—

"Cessation of approval: tax on certain schemes

591C.—(1) Where an approval of a scheme to which this section applies ceases to have effect, tax shall be charged in accordance with this section.

(2) The tax shall be charged under Case VI of Schedule D at the rate of 40 per cent. on an amount equal to the value of the assets which immediately before the date of the cessation of the approval of the scheme are held for the purposes of the scheme (taking that value as it stands immediately before that date).

(3) Subject to section 591D(4), the person liable for the tax shall be the administrator of the scheme in his capacity as such.

(4) This section applies to a retirement benefits scheme in respect of which either of the conditions set out below is satisfied.

(5) The first condition is satisfied in respect of a scheme if, immediately before the date of the cessation of the approval of the scheme, the number of individuals who are members of the scheme is less than twelve.

(6) The second condition is satisfied in respect of a scheme if at any time within the period of one year ending with the date of the cessation of the approval of the scheme, a person who is or has been a controlling director of a company which has contributed to the scheme is a member of the scheme.

(7) For the purposes of subsection (6) above a person is a controlling director of a company if he is a director of it and within section 417(5)(b) in relation to it.

Section 591C: supplementary

591D.—(1) For the purposes of section 591C(2) the value of an asset is, subject to subsection (2) below, its market value, construing "market value" in accordance with section 272 of the 1992 Act.

(2) Where an asset held for the purposes of a scheme is a right or interest in respect of any money lent (directly or indirectly) to any person mentioned in subsection (3) below, the value of the asset shall be treated as being the amount owing (including any unpaid interest) on the money lent.

(3) The persons are—

(a) any employer who has at any time contributed to the scheme;

(b) any company connected with such an employer;

(c) any member of the scheme;

(d) any person connected with any member of the scheme.

(4) Where the administrator of the scheme is constituted by persons who include a person who is an approved independent trustee in relation to a scheme, that person shall not be liable for tax chargeable by virtue of section 591C.

(5) A person is an approved independent trustee in relation to a scheme only if he is—

(a) approved by the Board to act as a trustee of the scheme; and

(b) not connected with—

(i) a member of the scheme;

(ii) any other trustee of the scheme; or

(iii) an employer who has contributed to the scheme.

(6) For the purposes of section 596A(9) income and gains accruing to a scheme shall not be regarded as brought into charge to tax merely because tax is charged in relation to the scheme in accordance with section 591C.

(7) The reference in section 591C(1) to an approval of a scheme ceasing to have effect is a reference to—

(a) the scheme ceasing to be an approved scheme by virtue of section 591A(2);

(b) the approval of the scheme being withdrawn under section 591B(1); or

(c) the approval of the scheme no longer applying by virtue of section 591B(2);

and any reference in section 591C to the date of the cessation of the approval of the scheme shall be construed accordingly.

(8) For the purposes of section 591C and this section a person is a member of a scheme at a particular time if at that time a benefit—

(a) is being provided under the scheme, or

(b) may be so provided,

in respect of any past or present employment of his.

(9) Section 839 shall apply for the purposes of this section."

(2) After section 239 of the Taxation of Chargeable Gains Act 1992 there shall be inserted—

"Retirement benefits schemes

Cessation of approval of certain schemes

239A.—(1) This section applies where tax is charged in accordance with section 591C of the Taxes Act (tax on certain retirement benefits schemes whose approval ceases to have effect).

(2) For the purposes of this Act the assets which at the relevant time are held for the purposes of the scheme—

(a) shall be deemed to be acquired at that time for a consideration equal to the amount on which tax is charged by virtue of section 591C(2) of the Taxes Act by the person who would be chargeable in respect of a chargeable gain accruing on a disposal of the assets at that time; but

(b) shall not be deemed to be disposed of by any person at that time; and in this subsection "the relevant time" means the time immediately before the date of the cessation of the approval of the scheme.

(3) Expressions used in subsection (2) above and in section 591C of the Taxes Act have the same meanings in that subsection as in that section."

(3) This section shall apply in relation to any approval of a retirement benefits scheme which ceases to have effect on or after 2nd November 1994 other than an approval ceasing to have effect by virtue of a notice given before that day under section 591B(1) of the Taxes Act 1988.

The section introduces a tax charge under Case VI of Schedule D at 40 per cent on the value of the funds held by certain small occupational pension schemes (mainly those with less than 12 members) which cease to be approved on or after November 2, 1994. The object is to prevent exploitation of the system by obtaining the advantage of tax reliefs and subsequently making changes which are inconsistent with the purpose of the scheme.

Subs. (1)
The new s.591C imposes the charge to tax and makes the administrator liable. The schemes are identified as those with either less than 12 members or with a controlling director of a company which has contributed to the scheme. The definition of "controlling" follows the definition in s.417(5)(b), *i.e.* beneficial ownership or control of 20 per cent of the ordinary share capital.

The new s.591D provides that the value of the fund for the purposes of the charge to tax is market value as defined by TCGA 1992, s.272, except in the case of loans to connected persons (see ICTA 1988, s.839) where the value is treated as being the amount outstanding. An approved independent trustee is protected from liability where he has been acting as a joint administrator of the scheme. Schemes remain liable to charge under s.596A(9) notwithstanding the charge under s.591C. Cessation of approval is defined by reference to ss.591A(2), 591B(1) and 591B(2).

Subs. (2)
The new TCGA 1992, s.239A ensures that after a charge to income tax under ICTA 1988, s.591C, CGT on a future disposal of assets will be charged only on any growth in the value of the assets since the scheme ceased to be approved.

Subs. (3)
The section has effect where a scheme ceases to be approved after November 2, 1994, unless a notice withdrawing approval had been issued before that date.

Saving and investment: general

Follow-up TESSAs

62.—(1) The Taxes Act 1988 shall be amended as follows.
(2) After section 326B there shall be inserted—

"Follow-up TESSAs

326BB.—(1) Subsection (2) below applies where—
(a) an individual, within the period of six months from the day on which a tax-exempt special savings account held by him matured, opens another account ('a follow-up account') which is a tax-exempt special savings account at the time it is opened; and
(b) the total amount deposited in the matured account, before it matured, exceeded £3,000.

(2) In relation to the follow-up account section 326B(2)(a) shall apply as if the reference to £3,000 were a reference to the total amount so deposited.

(3) For the purposes of subsection (1) above a tax-exempt special savings account held by an individual matures when a period of five years throughout which the account was a tax-exempt special savings account comes to an end.

(4) An account is not connected with another account for the purposes of section 326A(8) merely because one of them is a follow-up account."

(3) In section 326C(1) (regulations about tax-exempt special savings accounts) after paragraph (c) there shall be inserted—
"(cc) providing that subsection (2) of section 326BB does not apply in relation to a follow-up account unless at such time as may be prescribed by the regulations the building society or institution with which the account is held has a document of a prescribed description containing such information as the regulations may prescribe;

(cd) requiring building societies and other institutions operating tax-exempt special savings accounts which mature to give to the individuals who have held them certificates containing such information as the regulations may prescribe;".

(4) In section 326C(1)(e) for "and 326B" there shall be substituted "326B and 326BB".

(5) In section 326C after subsection (1) there shall be inserted—

"(1A) In paragraph (cc) of subsection (1) above "document" includes a record kept by means of a computer; and regulations made by virtue of that paragraph may prescribe different documents for different cases.

(1B) Subsection (3) of section 326BB applies for the purposes of subsection (1) above as it applies for the purposes of subsection (1) of that section."

(6) In section 326C(2) for "section 326B" there shall be substituted "sections 326B and 326BB".

GENERAL NOTE

TESSAs (Tax Exempt Special Savings Accounts) were introduced by FA 1990, s.28 as from January 1, 1991. The scheme ran originally for a period of five years from the opening of the account.

New ICTA 1988, s.326BB enables investors who have held a TESSA for the full five-year term to open a new TESSA (a "follow-up account") with a maximum first year deposit equal to the full amount of the capital, but not the accumulated interest, which they had deposited in their first TESSA. To qualify for relief, the follow-up account must be opened within six years of maturity of the first TESSA.

The remainder of s.62 makes various consequential amendments to ICTA 1988, s.326C.

TESSAs: European institutions

63.—(1) Section 326A of the Taxes Act 1988 (tax-exempt special savings accounts) shall be amended as mentioned in subsections (2) and (3) below.

(2) In subsection (4) (account must be with building society or institution authorised under Banking Act 1987) after "1987" there shall be inserted "or a relevant European institution".

(3) The following subsection shall be inserted after subsection (9)—

"(10) In this section "relevant European institution" means an institution which—

(a) is a European authorised institution within the meaning of the Banking Co-ordination (Second Council Directive) Regulations 1992, and

(b) may accept deposits in the United Kingdom in accordance with those regulations."

(4) The following section shall be inserted after section 326C of the Taxes Act 1988 (regulations about tax-exempt special savings accounts etc.)—

"Tax-exempt special savings accounts: tax representatives

326D.—(1) Without prejudice to the generality of section 326C(1), the Board may make regulations providing that an account held with a relevant European institution shall not be a tax-exempt special savings account at the time it is opened, or shall cease to be a tax-exempt special savings account at a given time, unless at the time concerned one of the following three requirements is fulfilled.

(2) The first requirement is that—

(a) a person who falls within subsection (5) below is appointed by the institution to be responsible for securing the discharge of prescribed duties which fall to be discharged by the institution, and

(b) his identity and the fact of his appointment have been notified to the Board by the institution.

(3) The second requirement is that there are other arrangements with the Board for a person other than the institution to secure the discharge of such duties.

(4) The third requirement is that there are other arrangements with the Board designed to secure the discharge of such duties.

(5) A person falls within this subsection if—

(a) he is not an individual and has a business establishment in the United Kingdom, or

(b) he is an individual and is resident in the United Kingdom.

(6) Different duties may be prescribed as regards different institutions or different descriptions of institution.

(7) The regulations may provide that—

(a) the first requirement shall not be treated as fulfilled unless the person concerned is of a prescribed description;

(b) the appointment of a person in pursuance of that requirement shall be treated as terminated in prescribed circumstances.

(8) The regulations may provide that—

(a) the second requirement shall not be treated as fulfilled unless the person concerned is of a prescribed description;

(b) arrangements made in pursuance of that requirement shall be treated as terminated in prescribed circumstances.

(9) The regulations may provide as mentioned in subsection (10) below as regards a case where—

(a) in accordance with the first requirement a person is at any time appointed to be responsible for securing the discharge of duties, or

(b) in accordance with the second requirement there are at any time arrangements for a person to secure the discharge of duties.

(10) In such a case the regulations may provide that the person concerned—

(a) shall be entitled to act on the institution's behalf for any of the purposes of the provisions relating to the duties;

(b) shall secure (where appropriate by acting on the institution's behalf) the institution's compliance with and discharge of the duties;

(c) shall be personally liable in respect of any failure of the institution to comply with or discharge any such duty as if the duties imposed on the institution were imposed jointly and severally on the institution and the person concerned.

(11) Regulations under this section may include provision that section 326B(3) shall have effect as if the reference to subsection (1) included a reference to the regulations.

(12) In this section "prescribed" means prescribed by the regulations."

(5) Subsection (2) above shall apply in relation to accounts opened after such day as the Board may by order made by statutory instrument appoint.

GENERAL NOTE

The section extends the range of persons able to offer TESSAs (Tax Exempt Special Savings Accounts) so as to include "European Authorised Institutions". This reflects the Single Market in banking services introduced by the Second Banking Co-ordination Directive as applied by the Banking Co-ordination (Second Council Directive) Regulations 1992 (S.I. 1992 No. 3218).

The new ICTA 1988, s.326D empowers the Revenue to make regulations requiring European institutions wishing to offer TESSAs but which do not have a U.K. presence, to appoint a representative in the U.K. or to enter into other arrangements with the Revenue to secure the discharge of duties under the TESSA regulations (S.I. 1990 No. 2361).

The Revenue is given power to appoint by regulation the date from which this section takes effect.

Personal equity plans: tax representatives

64.—(1) The following section shall be inserted after section 333 of the Taxes Act 1988 (personal equity plans)—

> "**Personal equity plans: tax representatives**
>
> 333A.—(1) Regulations under section 333 may include provision that a European institution cannot be a plan manager unless one of the following three requirements is fulfilled.
>
> (2) The first requirement is that—
>
>   (a) a person who falls within subsection (5) below is for the time being appointed by the institution to be responsible for securing the discharge of prescribed duties which fall to be discharged by the institution, and
>
>   (b) his identity and the fact of his appointment have been notified to the Board by the institution.
>
> (3) The second requirement is that there are for the time being other arrangements with the Board for a person other than the institution to secure the discharge of such duties.
>
> (4) The third requirement is that there are for the time being other arrangements with the Board designed to secure the discharge of such duties.
>
> (5) A person falls within this subsection if—
>
>   (a) he is not an individual and has a business establishment in the United Kingdom, or
>
>   (b) he is an individual and is resident in the United Kingdom.
>
> (6) Different duties may be prescribed as regards different institutions or different descriptions of institution.
>
> (7) The regulations may provide that—
>
>   (a) the first requirement shall not be treated as fulfilled unless the person concerned is of a prescribed description;
>
>   (b) the appointment of a person in pursuance of that requirement shall be treated as terminated in prescribed circumstances.
>
> (8) The regulations may provide that—
>
>   (a) the second requirement shall not be treated as fulfilled unless the person concerned is of a prescribed description;
>
>   (b) arrangements made in pursuance of that requirement shall be treated as terminated in prescribed circumstances.
>
> (9) The regulations may provide as mentioned in subsection (10) below as regards a case where—
>
>   (a) in accordance with the first requirement a person is for the time being appointed to be responsible for securing the discharge of duties, or
>
>   (b) in accordance with the second requirement there are for the time being arrangements for a person to secure the discharge of duties.
>
> (10) In such a case the regulations may provide that the person concerned—
>
>   (a) shall be entitled to act on the institution's behalf for any of the purposes of the provisions relating to the duties;
>
>   (b) shall secure (where appropriate by acting on the institution's behalf) the institution's compliance with and discharge of the duties;
>
>   (c) shall be personally liable in respect of any failure of the institution to comply with or discharge any such duty as if the duties imposed on the institution were imposed jointly and severally on the institution and the person concerned.

(11) In this section—
(a) "European institution" has the same meaning as in the Banking Co-ordination (Second Council Directive) Regulations 1992;
(b) "prescribed" means prescribed by the regulations.
(12) The preceding provisions of this section shall apply in the case of a relevant authorised person as they apply in the case of a European institution; and "relevant authorised person" here means a person who is an authorised person for the purposes of the Financial Services Act 1986 by virtue of section 31 of that Act."

(2) In section 151 of the Taxation of Chargeable Gains Act 1992 (personal equity plans) the following subsection shall be inserted after subsection (2)—
"(2A) Section 333A of the Taxes Act (personal equity plans: tax representatives) shall apply in relation to regulations under subsection (1) above as it applies in relation to regulations under section 333 of that Act."

GENERAL NOTE
The section extends the Revenue's power to make regulations in respect of plan managers of Personal Equity Plans (PEPs) to managers of PEPs established in other E.C. states. The regulations may introduce a new compliance regime for European managers eligible for the scheme by virtue of authorisation under the Financial Services Act 1986. Under the Single Market in financial services, the same compliance regime will apply to European institutions (see S.I. 1992 No. 3218) when the regulations are in due course changed to admit them as PEP managers.
New ICTA 1988, s.333A authorises the making of regulations to ensure that European managers comply with their obligations under the scheme to a similar standard to that required of U.K. managers.
New TCGA 1992, s.151(2A) makes corresponding changes to the powers to make regulations for capital gains tax purposes.

Contractual savings schemes

65. Schedule 12 to this Act (which contains provisions about contractual savings schemes) shall have effect.

GENERAL NOTE
The section introduces Sched. 12, which makes four distinct changes to the statutory framework of Save As You Earn (SAYE):
(i) a Treasury model SAYE "Sharesave" scheme may be introduced in place of the current Department for National Savings model for banks and building societies;
(ii) individual institutions will be authorised by the Treasury to enter into Sharesave contracts;
(iii) certain European institutions which are able to accept deposits in the U.K. will be allowed to offer Sharesave contracts;
(iv) previous SAYE contracts not linked to employee share option schemes will only be eligible for tax relief if entered into before December 1, 1994.
See further the General Note to Sched. 12.

Enterprise investment scheme: ICTA amendments

66.—(1) Chapter III of Part VII of the Taxes Act 1988 as it has effect in relation to shares issued on or after 1st January 1994 (the enterprise investment scheme) shall be amended as follows.

(2) In section 292 (which denies relief where parallel trades are involved) the following subsection shall be inserted after subsection (4)—
"(5) This section shall not apply where the shares mentioned in subsection (1) above are issued on or after 29th November 1994."

(3) In section 293 (qualifying companies) the following subsection shall be inserted after subsection (8A) (which defines "the relevant period" for certain purposes)—
"(8B) In arriving at the relevant period for the purposes of sections 294 to 296 any time falling on or after 29th November 1994 shall be

ignored; and subsection (8A) above shall have effect subject to the preceding provisions of this subsection."

(4) In section 305 (reorganisation of share capital) the following subsections shall be inserted after subsection (4)—

"(5) Subsection (2) above shall not apply where the reorganisation occurs on or after 29th November 1994.

(6) Subsection (2) above shall not apply by virtue of subsection (3) above where the rights are disposed of on or after 29th November 1994."

GENERAL NOTE
The section abolishes three restrictions on the Enterprise Investment Scheme (EIS), which replaced the Business Expansion Scheme (BES), for shares issued since the beginning of 1994. The changes take effect from November 29, 1994.

Subs. (2)
This abolishes the parallel trades rule, which denied relief where an individual was involved in the control of two companies essentially in the same business.

Subs. (3)
Relief was denied where, during a period of three years from the issue of the shares, more than half of the value of the company's assets at any time was represented by land and buildings. This condition need no longer be satisfied after November 28, 1994.

Subs. (4)
Relief will no longer be reduced where a company makes a rights issue or where an individual disposes of such rights.

Enterprise investment scheme: TCGA amendments

67. Schedule 13 to this Act (which contains amendments relating to chargeable gains as regards the enterprise investment scheme) shall have effect.

GENERAL NOTE
The section introduces Sched. 13, which makes a number of changes to the capital gains provisions in relation to the Enterprise Investment Scheme (EIS).
See further the General Note to Sched. 13.

Business expansion scheme: ICTA amendments

68.—(1) Chapter III of Part VII of the Taxes Act 1988 as it has effect in relation to shares issued before 1st January 1994 (the business expansion scheme) shall be amended as follows.

(2) In section 289 (the relief) the following subsection shall be inserted after subsection (12) (which defines "the relevant period" for the purposes of the Chapter)—

"(12A) In arriving at the relevant period for the purposes of sections 294 to 296 any time falling on or after 29th November 1994 shall be ignored; and subsection (12) above shall have effect subject to the preceding provisions of this subsection."

(3) In section 305 (reorganisation of share capital) the following subsections shall be inserted after subsection (4)—

"(5) Subsection (2) above shall not apply where the reorganisation occurs on or after 29th November 1994.

(6) Subsection (2) above shall not apply by virtue of subsection (3) above where the rights are disposed of on or after 29th November 1994."

GENERAL NOTE
The abolition of the rules restricting interests in land and restricting relief where rights issues are made is extended from EIS companies (see s.66(3) and (4) above) to shares issued under the previous BES scheme.

Business expansion scheme: TCGA amendments

69. In section 150 of the Taxation of Chargeable Gains Act 1992 (business expansion schemes) the following subsections shall be inserted after subsection (8) (which disapplies provisions about exchanges, reconstructions or amalgamations in certain circumstances)—

"(8A) Subsection (8) above shall not have effect to disapply section 135 or 136 where—
> (a) the new holding consists of new ordinary shares carrying no present or future preferential right to dividends or to a company's assets on its winding up and no present or future preferential right to be redeemed,
> (b) the new shares are issued on or after 29th November 1994 and after the end of the relevant period, and
> (c) the condition in subsection (8B) below is fulfilled.

(8B) The condition is that at some time before the issue of the new shares—
> (a) the company issuing them issued eligible shares, and
> (b) a certificate in relation to those eligible shares was issued by the company for the purposes of subsection (2) of section 306 of the Taxes Act and in accordance with that section.

(8C) In subsection (8A) above—
> (a) "new holding" shall be construed in accordance with sections 126, 127, 135 and 136;
> (b) "relevant period" means the period found by applying section 289(12)(a) of the Taxes Act by reference to the company issuing the shares referred to in subsection (8) above and by reference to those shares."

GENERAL NOTE
The section provides the same exemption from CGT for holders of Business Expansion Scheme (BES) shares as is accorded to holders of Enterprise Investment Scheme (EIS) shares on a reconstruction or amalgamation of share capital (see Sched. 13, para. 2(4) below).

Venture capital trusts

Approval of companies as trusts

70.—(1) After section 842 of the Taxes Act 1988 (investment trusts) there shall be inserted the following section—

"Venture capital trusts

842AA.—(1) In the Tax Acts 'venture capital trust' means a company which is not a close company and which is for the time being approved for the purposes of this section by the Board; and an approval for the purposes of this section shall have effect as from such time as may be specified in the approval, being a time which, if it falls before the time when the approval is given, is no earlier than—
> (a) in the case of an approval given in the year 1995–96, 6th April 1995; or
> (b) in any other case, the time when the application for approval was made.

(2) Subject to the following provisions of this section, the Board shall not approve a company for the purposes of this section unless it is shown to their satisfaction in relation to the most recent complete accounting period of the company—

(a) that the company's income in that period has been derived wholly or mainly from shares or securities;

(b) that at least 70 per cent. by value of the company's investments has been represented throughout that period by shares or securities comprised in qualifying holdings of the company;

(c) that at least 30 per cent. by value of the company's qualifying holdings has been represented throughout that period by holdings of eligible shares;

(d) that no holding in any company, other than a venture capital trust or a company which would qualify as a venture capital trust but for paragraph (e) below, has at any time during that period represented more than 15 per cent. by value of the company's investments;

(e) that the shares making up the company's ordinary share capital (or, if there are such shares of more than one class, those of each class) have throughout that period been quoted on the Stock Exchange; and

(f) that the company has not retained more than 15 per cent. of the income it derived in that period from shares and securities.

(3) Where, in the case of any company, the Board are satisfied that the conditions specified in subsection (2) above are fulfilled in relation to the company's most recent complete accounting period, they shall not approve the company for the purposes of this section unless they are satisfied that the conditions will also be fulfilled in relation to the accounting period of the company which is current when the application for approval is made.

(4) The Board may approve a company for the purposes of this section notwithstanding that conditions specified in subsection (2) above are not fulfilled with respect to that company in relation to its most recent complete accounting period if they are satisfied—

(a) in the case of any of the conditions specified in paragraphs (a), (d), (e) and (f) of that subsection which are not fulfilled, that the conditions will be fulfilled in relation to the accounting period of the company which is current when the application for approval is made or in relation to its next accounting period;

(b) in the case of any of the conditions specified in paragraphs (b) and (c) of that subsection which are not fulfilled, that the conditions will be fulfilled in relation to an accounting period of the company beginning no more than three years after the time when they give their approval or, if earlier, when the approval takes effect; and

(c) in the case of every condition which is not fulfilled but with respect to which the Board are satisfied as mentioned in paragraph (a) or (b) above, that the condition will continue to be fulfilled in relation to accounting periods following the period in relation to which they are satisfied as so mentioned.

(5) For the purposes of subsection (2)(b) to (d) above the value of any holding of investments of any description shall be taken—

(a) unless—

(i) it is added to by a further holding of investments of the same description, or

(ii) any such payment is made in discharge, in whole or in part, of any obligation attached to the holding as (by discharging the whole or any part of that obligation) increases the value of the holding, to be its value when acquired, and

(b) where it is so added to or such a payment is made, to be its value immediately after the most recent addition or payment.

(6) The Board may withdraw their approval of a company for the purposes of this section wherever it at any time appears to them that there are reasonable grounds for believing—

(a) that the conditions for the approval of the company were not fulfilled at the time of the approval;

(b) in a case where the Board were satisfied for the purposes of subsection (3) or (4) above that a condition would be fulfilled in relation to any period, that that condition is one which will not be or, as the case may be, has not been fulfilled in relation to that period;

(c) in the case of a company approved in pursuance of subsection (4) above, that the company has not fulfilled such other conditions as may be prescribed by regulations made by the Board in relation to, or to any part of, the period of three years mentioned in subsection (4)(b) above; or

(d) that the company's most recent complete accounting period or its current one is a period in relation to which there has been or will be a failure of a condition specified in subsection (2) above to be fulfilled, not being a failure which, at the time of the approval, was allowed for in relation to that period by virtue of subsection (4) above.

(7) Subject to subsections (8) and (9) below, the withdrawal of the approval of any company for the purposes of this section shall have effect as from the time when the notice of the withdrawal is given to the company.

(8) If, in the case of a company approved for the purposes of this section in exercise of the power conferred by subsection (4) above, the approval is withdrawn at a time before all the conditions specified in subsection (2) above have been fulfilled with respect to that company in relation either—

(a) to a complete accounting period of twelve months, or

(b) to successive complete accounting periods constituting a continuous period of twelve months or more,

the withdrawal of the approval shall have the effect that the approval shall, for all purposes, be deemed never to have been given.

(9) A notice withdrawing the approval of a company for the purposes of this section may specify a time falling before the time mentioned in subsection (7) above as the time as from which the withdrawal is to be treated as having taken effect for the purposes of section 100 of the 1992 Act; but the time so specified shall be no earlier than the beginning of the accounting period in relation to which it appears to the Board that the condition by reference to which the approval is withdrawn has not been, or will not be, fulfilled.

(10) Notwithstanding any limitation on the time for making assessments, an assessment to any tax chargeable in consequence of the withdrawal of any approval given for the purposes of this section may be made at any time before the end of the period of three years beginning with the time when the notice of withdrawal is given.

(11) The following provisions of section 842 shall apply as follows for the purposes of this section as they apply for the purposes of that section, that is to say—

(a) subsections (1A) and (2) of that section shall apply in relation to subsection (2)(d) above (but with the omission of subsection (2)(a) of that section) as they apply in relation to subsection (1)(b) of that section;

(b) subsections (2A) to (2C) of that section shall apply in relation to subsection (2)(f) above as they apply in relation to subsection (1)(e) of that section; and

(c) without prejudice to their application in relation to provisions applied by paragraph (a) or (b) above, subsections (3) and (4) of that section shall apply in relation to any reference in this section to a holding or an addition to a holding as they apply in relation to any such reference in that section.

(12) In this section, and in the provisions of section 842 as applied for the purposes of this section, 'securities', in relation to any company—

(a) includes any liability of the company in respect of a loan (whether secured or not) which has been made to the company on terms that do not allow any person to require the loan to be repaid, or any stock or security relating to that loan to be re-purchased or redeemed, within the period of five years from the making of the loan or, as the case may be, the issue of the stock or security; but

(b) does not include any stock or security relating to a loan which has been made to the company on terms which allow any person to require the loan to be repaid, or the stock or security to be re-purchased or redeemed, within that period.

(13) Schedule 28B shall have effect for construing the references in this section to a qualifying holding.

(14) In this section 'eligible shares' means shares in a company which are comprised in the ordinary share capital of the company and carry no present or future preferential right to dividends or to the company's assets on its winding up and no present or future preferential right to be redeemed."

(2) Schedule 14 to this Act (meaning of "qualifying holdings") shall be inserted, before Schedule 29 to the Taxes Act 1988, as Schedule 28B to that Act, and shall be construed accordingly.

GENERAL NOTE

This section, together with ss.71–73 and Scheds. 14–16, introduces a new tax exemption for investment in a Venture Capital Trust (VCT). The Chancellor announced his intention to do so in his November 1993 Budget. The purpose of the scheme is to generate investment in the unquoted trading company sector, in particular among dynamic, innovative growing businesses. A VCT will be broadly similar to an investment trust.

The new ICTA 1988, s.842AA provides for approval of a VCT by the Revenue. The VCT must not be a close company (see *ibid.* s.414) and must meet the following conditions in relation to its most recent complete accounting period:

(i) its income has been derived wholly or mainly from shares or securities;

(ii) at least 70 per cent by value of its investments have been in qualifying holdings (see Sched. 14);

(iii) at least 30 per cent by value of its qualifying holdings have been in eligible shares, *i.e.* ordinary shares;

(iv) holdings outside the VCT area must not exceed 15 per cent of its investments;

(v) the VCT's ordinary share capital must be quoted on the Stock Exchange; and

(vi) it has not retained more than 15 per cent of its investment income.

The Revenue must be satisfied that the conditions for approval will also be met in the accounting period for which the application for approval is made. Approval may be given on a provisional basis where the Revenue are satisfied that, where conditions other than (ii) or (iii) are not met, they will be met within the current or next accounting period. For conditions (ii) or (iii), a three-year period of grace is allowed. Holdings are to be valued initially on cost of acquisition and at market value when they are added to.

Withdrawal of approval may take place on infringement of any of the above conditions or of others laid down by regulations in relation to provisional approval. Withdrawal is effective on notification and in the case of provisional approval takes effect as though the approval had never been given. For CGT, withdrawal may take effect from the beginning of the accounting period in which the VCT failed to fulfil the relevant condition.

Assessments to give effect to a withdrawal may be made within three years.

Certain of the conditions for approval of an investment trust under ICTA 1988, s.842 are adapted for a VCT. Medium term loans, *i.e.* loans carrying no right to repayment within five years, are allowable for a VCT.

Income tax relief

71.—(1) In Chapter IV of Part VII of the Taxes Act 1988 (special provisions), after section 332 there shall be inserted the following section—

"Venture capital trusts: relief
332A. Schedule 15B shall have effect for conferring relief from income tax in respect of investments in venture capital trusts and distributions by such trusts."

(2) Schedule 15 to this Act (relief in respect of holdings in a venture capital trust) shall be inserted, before Schedule 16 to the Taxes Act 1988, as Schedule 15B to that Act, and shall be construed accordingly.

(3) In the Table in section 98 of the Management Act (penalties in respect of certain information provisions)—

    (a) after the entry in the first column relating to paragraph 14(5) of Schedule 15 to the Taxes Act 1988 there shall be inserted the following entry—

"Schedule 15B, paragraph 5(2);"

and

    (b) after the entry in the second column relating to paragraph 14(4) of Schedule 15 to the Taxes Act 1988 there shall be inserted the following entry—

"Schedule 15B, paragraph 5(1);".

(4) This section has effect for the year 1995–96 and subsequent years of assessment.

GENERAL NOTE

The section introduces Sched. 15, which sets out the income tax relief available for investors in a VCT, through a new ICTA 1988, s.332A and Sched. 15B. The Taxes Management Act 1970, s.98 is also appropriately amended to provide for penalties in relation to certain information provisions.

See further the General Note to Sched. 15.

Capital gains

72.—(1) The Taxation of Chargeable Gains Act 1992 shall be amended as follows.

(2) In section 100(1) (exemption from charge for gains accruing to authorised unit trusts, investment trusts etc.), after "investment trust" there shall be inserted "a venture capital trust".

(3) In Chapter III of Part IV (miscellaneous provisions relating to securities), after section 151 there shall be inserted the following sections—

"Venture capital trusts: reliefs
151A.—(1) A gain or loss accruing to an individual on a qualifying disposal of any ordinary shares in a company which—

    (a) was a venture capital trust at the time when he acquired the shares, and

    (b) is still such a trust at the time of the disposal,

shall not be a chargeable gain or, as the case may be, an allowable loss.

(2) For the purposes of this section a disposal of shares is a qualifying disposal in so far as—

    (a) it is made by an individual who has attained the age of eighteen years;

    (b) the shares disposed of were not acquired in excess of the permitted maximum for any year of assessment; and

(c) that individual acquired those shares for bona fide commercial purposes and not as part of a scheme or arrangement the main purpose of which, or one of the main purposes of which, is the avoidance of tax.

(3) Schedule 5C shall have effect for providing relief in respect of gains invested in venture capital trusts.

(4) In determining for the purposes of this section whether a disposal by any person of shares in a venture capital trust relates to shares acquired in excess of the permitted maximum for any year of assessment, it shall be assumed (subject to subsection (5) below)—

(a) as between shares acquired by the same person on different days, that those acquired on an earlier day are disposed of by that person before those acquired on a later day; and

(b) as between shares acquired by the same person on the same day, that those acquired in excess of the permitted maximum are disposed of by that person before he disposes of any other shares acquired on that day.

(5) It shall be assumed for the purposes of subsection (1) above that a person who disposes of shares in a venture capital trust disposes of shares acquired at a time when it was not such a trust before he disposes of any other shares in that trust.

(6) References in this section to shares in a venture capital trust acquired in excess of the permitted maximum for any year of assessment shall be construed in accordance with the provisions of Part II of Schedule 15B to the Taxes Act; and the provisions of that Part of that Schedule shall apply (with subsections (4) and (5) above) for identifying the shares which are, in any case, to be treated as representing shares acquired in excess of the permitted maximum.

(7) In this section and section 151B 'ordinary shares', in relation to a company, means any shares forming part of the company's ordinary share capital (within the meaning of the Taxes Act).

Venture capital trusts: supplementary

151B.—(1) Sections 104, 105 and 107 shall not apply to any shares in a venture capital trust which are eligible for relief under section 151A(1).

(2) Subject to the following provisions of this section, where—

(a) an individual holds any ordinary shares in a venture capital trust,

(b) some of those shares fall within one of the paragraphs of subsection (3) below, and

(c) others of those shares fall within at least one other of those paragraphs,

then, if there is within the meaning of section 126 a reorganisation affecting those shares, section 127 shall apply separately in relation to the shares (if any) falling within each of the paragraphs of that subsection (so that shares of each kind are treated as a separate holding of original shares and identified with a separate new holding).

(3) The kinds of shares referred to in subsection (2) above are—

(a) any shares in a venture capital trust which are eligible for relief under section 151A(1) and by reference to which any person has been given or is entitled to claim relief under Part I of Schedule 15B to the Taxes Act;

(b) any shares in a venture capital trust which are eligible for relief under section 151A(1) but by reference to which no person has been given, or is entitled to claim, any relief under that Part of that Schedule;

(c) any shares in a venture capital trust by reference to which any person has been given, or is entitled to claim, any relief under that

Part of that Schedule but which are not shares that are eligible for relief under section 151A(1); and

(d) any shares in a venture capital trust that do not fall within any of paragraphs (a) to (c) above.

(4) Where—

(a) an individual holds ordinary shares in a company ('the existing holding'),

(b) there is, by virtue of any such allotment for payment as is mentioned in section 126(2)(a), a reorganisation affecting the existing holding, and

(c) immediately following the reorganisation, the shares or the allotted holding are shares falling within any of paragraphs (a) to (c) of subsection (3) above,

sections 127 to 130 shall not apply in relation to the existing holding.

(5) Sections 135 and 136 shall not apply where—

(a) the exchanged holding consists of shares falling within paragraph (a) or (b) of subsection (3) above; and

(b) that for which the exchanged holding is or is treated as exchanged does not consist of ordinary shares in a venture capital trust.

(6) Where—

(a) the approval of any company as a venture capital trust is withdrawn, and

(b) the withdrawal of the approval is not one to which section 842AA(8) of the Taxes Act applies,

any person who at the time when the withdrawal takes effect is holding shares in that company which (apart from the withdrawal) would be eligible for relief under section 151A(1) shall be deemed for the purposes of this Act, at that time, to have disposed of and immediately re-acquired those shares for a consideration equal to their market value at that time.

(7) The disposal that is deemed to take place by virtue of subsection (6) above shall be deemed for the purposes of section 151A to take place while the company is still a venture capital trust; but, for the purpose of applying sections 104, 105 and 107 to the shares that are deemed to be re-acquired, it shall be assumed that the re-acquisition for which that subsection provides takes place immediately after the company ceases to be such a trust.

(8) For the purposes of this section—

(a) shares are eligible for relief under section 151A(1) at any time when they are held by an individual whose disposal of the shares at that time would (on the assumption, where it is not the case, that the individual attained the age of eighteen years before that time) be a disposal to which section 151A(1) would apply; and

(b) shares shall not, in relation to any time, be treated as shares by reference to which relief has been given under Part I of Schedule 15B to the Taxes Act if that time falls after—

(i) any relief given by reference to those shares has been reduceu or withdrawn,

(ii) any chargeable event (within the meaning of Schedule 5C) has occurred in relation to those shares, or

(iii) the death of a person who held those shares immediately before his death;

and

(c) the references, in relation to sections 135 and 136, to the exchanged holding is a reference to the shares in company B or, as the case may be, to the shares or debentures in respect of which shares or debentures are issued under the arrangement in question."

(4) Schedule 16 to this Act (relief on re-investment in venture capital trusts) shall be inserted before Schedule 6, as Schedule 5C, and shall be construed accordingly.

(5) In section 257(1) (gifts to charities etc.), after paragraph (b) there shall be inserted—

> "and the disposal is not one in relation to which section 151A(1) has effect."

(6) In section 260, after the subsection (6A) inserted by Schedule 13 to this Act (no reduction in the case of a disposal which is a chargeable event for the purposes of Schedule 5B), there shall be inserted—

> "(6B) Subsection (3) above does not apply, so far as any gain accruing in accordance with paragraphs 4 and 5 of Schedule 5C is concerned, in relation to the disposal which constitutes the chargeable event by virtue of which that gain accrues."

(7) In section 288(1) (interpretation), after the definition of "trading stock" there shall be inserted the following definition—

> " 'venture capital trust' has the meaning given by section 842AA of the Taxes Act;".

(8) Subsection (2) above shall have effect in relation to gains accruing on or after 6th April 1995 and the other provisions of this section have effect for the year 1995–96 and subsequent years of assessment.

General Note

This section, together with Sched. 16, sets out the CGT relief available for investors in a venture capital trust (VCT). Individuals are exempt from CGT when they dispose of VCT shares where the original acquisition cost did not exceed £100,000 in any one year. Capital gains tax may also be rolled over on the disposal of any assets where the gain is reinvested in a VCT within a period of one year before to one year after the gain arises.

The main provisions are set out in new TCGA 1992, ss.151A and 151B. These are:

   (i) gains or losses accruing to an individual on shares in a VCT, which was a VCT at the time of acquisition, are neither chargeable gains nor allowable losses;

  (ii) the disposal must be made by an individual over 18 years who spent not more than £100,000 on the shares in a single year and acquired them for *bona fide* commercial purposes;

 (iii) similar rules to those in ICTA 1988, Sched. 15B (see Sched. 15, para. 8 below) are applied to determine whether a disposal was of shares acquired in excess of the £100,000 limit;

  (iv) the CGT pooling rules are not applicable to shares eligible for the VCT exemption;

   (v) where there is a reorganisation affecting VCT shares, these will be treated as separate holdings according to the tax reliefs they enjoy;

  (vi) the provisions relating to take-overs and reconstructions do not apply in situations involving a VCT acquiring another company, or being acquired itself, where a non-VCT company is involved;

 (vii) the share reorganisation rules do not apply for rights issues so that such an acquisition applies for relief in its own right; and

(viii) where approval of a VCT is withdrawn, there is a deemed disposal and reacquisition of the shares in the VCT at market value.

Further provisions contained in TCGA 1992, Sched. 5C (inserted by Sched. 16 below) allow a roll-over of gains on assets where the gain is reinvested in a VCT. See further the General Note to Sched. 16.

Regulations

73.—(1) The Treasury may by regulations make such provision as they may consider appropriate for—

> (a) giving effect to any relief for which provision is made by Schedule 15B to the Taxes Act 1988 or section 151A of, and Schedule 5C to, the Taxation of Chargeable Gains Act 1992; and
>
> (b) preventing such relief from being given except where a claim is made in accordance with the regulations and where such other requirements as may be imposed by the regulations have been complied with.

(2) Without prejudice to the generality of subsection (1) above, regulations under this section may make provision—

(a) as to the making of applications for approvals under section 842AA of the Taxes Act 1988 and otherwise as to the procedure in relation to any such applications and the giving of such approvals;

(b) as to the procedure to be followed in connection with the withdrawal of any such approval;

(c) as to the manner in which, and the persons by whom, relief is to be claimed;

(d) as to the obligations of a company which is a venture capital trust if it should appear to the company that the conditions for it to continue to be approved as such a trust are not satisfied;

(e) as to the accounts, records, returns and other information to be kept, and furnished or otherwise made available to the Board, by companies which are or have been venture capital trusts and by persons who hold or have held shares in such companies; and

(f) as to the persons liable to account for any tax becoming due where the approval of a company as a venture capital trust is withdrawn.

(3) Regulations under this section may make provision, in relation to tax credits to which any persons are entitled in respect of distributions of venture capital trusts—

(a) for the credits not to be set against income tax but to be claimed by and paid to the trusts; and

(b) for amounts equal to the credits to be paid by the trusts to the persons who receive or are entitled to receive the distributions;

and any such regulations may provide for sections 234 and 252 of the Taxes Act 1988 (information relating to distributions and rectification of excessive tax credit) to have effect, in relation to the distributions of venture capital trusts or, as the case may be, any provision made by virtue of paragraph (a) or (b) above, with such modifications as may be specified in the regulations.

(4) Regulations under this section may apply the following provisions of the Management Act, as they have effect in the case of repayments in respect of income tax, in relation to cases where amounts are paid to any person in pursuance of regulations made by virtue of subsection (3) above, that is to say—

(a) section 29(3)(c) (excessive relief);

(b) section 30 (tax repaid in error);

(c) section 88 (interest); and

(d) section 95 (incorrect return or accounts).

(5) In the Table in section 98 of the Management Act (penalties in respect of certain information provisions), at the end of the entries in the second column there shall be inserted the following entry—

"regulations under section 73 of the Finance Act 1995;".

(6) In this section "venture capital trust" has the meaning given by section 842AA of the Taxes Act 1988.

GENERAL NOTE

The Treasury is given the power to make regulations for the administration of the venture capital trust (VCT) scheme. Matters which may be covered in the regulations include:

(i) giving effect to the provision of income tax and CGT relief and specifying the requirements governing claims for relief;

(ii) the procedure for approval and withdrawal of approval of a VCT, the way in which tax relief may be claimed, the obligations of a VCT in relation to information, records and returns, and the liability to tax when approval is withdrawn;

(iii) arrangements for the payment of tax credits to a VCT on behalf of investors; and

(iv) excessive tax relief, repayment of tax in error, default interest and penalties for incorrect returns or accounts.

Provision is also made for penalties for failure to comply with information requirements.

Settlements and estates

Settlements: liability of settlor

74.—(1) Schedule 17 to this Act has effect with respect to settlement and the liability of the settlor, as follows—

Part I inserts new provisions in place of sections 660 to 676 and 683 to 685 of the Taxes Act 1988,

Part II makes minor and consequential amendments of that Act, and

Part III contains consequential amendments of other enactments.

(2) The amendments made by Schedule 17 have effect for the year 1995–96 and subsequent years of assessment and apply to every settlement, wherever and whenever it was made or entered into.

GENERAL NOTE

The section introduces Sched. 17, which is designed to simplify the law regarding the taxation of settlements. Originally it was intended to replace ICTA 1988, Part XV, Chapters I–IV (ss.660–685), but widespread concern was expressed about a proposal that the settlor should be taxed on the value of any loan between settlor and trustees that was interest free or at a beneficial rate of interest, which might have had a wider effect than intended. This was accordingly dropped at the committee stage, and ICTA 1988, ss.677–682, which deal with capital sums paid to settlors, were reinstated.

For the remaining provisions, see the General Note to Sched. 17.

Deceased persons' estates: taxation of beneficiaries

75. Part XVI of the Taxes Act 1988 (deceased persons' estates) shall have effect with the amendments specified in Schedule 18 to this Act.

GENERAL NOTE

The section introduces Sched. 18, which amends the provisions relating to the taxation of payments to residuary beneficiaries out of deceased persons' estates in ICTA 1988, Part XVI (ss.695–702). In future these will be taxed as income of the year of receipt rather than spread over the period of administration.

See further the General Note to Sched. 18.

Untaxed income of a deceased person's estate

76.—(1) In section 246D of the Taxes Act 1988 (foreign income dividends), after subsection (3) there shall be inserted the following subsection—

"(3A) Without prejudice to subsection (3) above, a foreign income dividend paid as mentioned in that subsection to personal representatives shall not be treated for the purposes of income tax as income of the personal representatives as such."

(2) In section 547 of that Act (method of charging certain gains to tax)—

(a) in subsection (1)(c) (case where rights vested in personal representatives), after "gain" there shall be inserted "(so far as it is not otherwise comprised in that income)"; and

(b) after subsection (7) there shall be inserted the following subsection—

"(7A) Where, in the case of any gain—

(a) this section has effect by virtue of subsection (5A) or (7) above with the omission of subsection (5) above, and

(b) the rights conferred by the contract or policy were vested immediately before the happening of the chargeable event in question in personal representatives within the meaning of Part XVI,

the gain shall be deemed for the purposes of income tax to be income of the personal representatives as such."

(3) In section 553 of that Act (non-resident policies), after subsection (7) there shall be inserted the following subsection—

"(7A) Where, in the case of a gain to which subsection (6)(a) and (b) above applies, the rights conferred by the policy were vested immediately before the happening of the chargeable event in question in personal representatives within the meaning of Part XVI, the gain shall be deemed for the purposes of income tax to be income of the personal representatives as such."

(4) After section 699 of that Act there shall be inserted the following section—

"Untaxed sums comprised in the income of the estate

699A.—(1) In this section 'a relevant amount' means so much of any amount which a person is deemed by virtue of this Part to receive or to have a right to receive as is or would be paid out of sums which—

(a) are included in the aggregate income of the estate of the deceased by virtue of any of sections 246D(3), 249(5), 421(2) and 547(1)(c); and

(b) are sums in respect of which the personal representatives are not directly assessable to United Kingdom income tax.

(2) In determining for the purposes of this Part whether any amount is a relevant amount—

(a) such apportionments of any sums to which subsection (1)(a) and (b) above applies shall be made between different persons with interests in the residue of the estate as are just and reasonable in relation to their different interests; and

(b) subject to paragraph (a) above, the assumption in section 701(3A)(b) shall apply, but (subject to that) it shall be assumed that payments are to be made out of other sums comprised in the aggregate income of the estate before they are made out of any sums to which subsection (1)(a) and (b) above applies.

(3) In the case of a foreign estate, and notwithstanding anything in section 695(4)(b) or 696(6), a relevant amount shall be deemed—

(a) to be income of such amount as would, after deduction of income tax for the year in which it is deemed to be paid, be equal to the relevant amount; and

(b) to be income that has borne tax at the applicable rate.

(4) Sums to which subsection (1)(a) and (b) above applies shall be assumed, for the purpose of determining the applicable rate in relation to any relevant amount, to bear tax—

(a) in the case of sums included by virtue of section 246D(3), 249(5) or 421(2), at the lower rate, and

(b) in the case of sums included by virtue of section 547(1)(c), at the basic rate.

(5) No repayment shall be made of any income tax which by virtue of this Part is treated as having been borne by the income that is represented by a relevant amount.

(6) For the purposes of sections 348 and 349(1) the income represented by a relevant amount shall be treated as not brought into charge to income tax."

(5) In section 701 of that Act (interpretation), after subsection (10), there shall be inserted the following subsection—

"(10A) Amounts to which section 699A(1)(a) and (b) applies shall be disregarded in determining whether an estate is a United Kingdom estate or a foreign estate, except that any estate the aggregate income of which comprises only such amounts shall be a United Kingdom estate."

(6) This section has effect for the year 1995–96 and subsequent years of assessment.

GENERAL NOTE

The section corrects technical defects in the legislation applying to foreign income dividends (FIDs) and deemed gains on life policies, stock dividends and loans to participators, as it relates to estates of deceased persons. At present FIDs and the gains in question are added to the aggregate income of estates without income tax being charged or treated as paid. In future, payments out of such income to residuary beneficiaries will be treated as made after deduction of tax at the basic or lower rate as appropriate.

Subs. (1)

FIDs are not to be treated as income of the personal representatives as such.

Subss. (2) and (3)

These provide that gains chargeable on life policies under ICTA 1988, ss.547 and 553 are charged on the personal representatives as they would be on an individual.

Subs. (4)

The new ICTA 1988, s.699A defines "a relevant amount" as any amount treated as income of a residuary beneficiary which is a FID, a gain on a life policy, a stock dividend (ICTA 1988, s.249) or a loan to a participator (ICTA 1988, s.421), which is not directly assessable on the personal representatives. Such amounts are to be apportioned among the beneficiaries and treated as made out of income taxed at the basic rate before the lower rate. However, payments to beneficiaries are to be treated as made out of other income first. Provision is also made for the treatment of amounts paid out of foreign estates. Payments out of FIDs, stock dividends or loans to participators written off are treated as having borne tax at the lower rate (20 per cent) and gains on life policies at the basic rate (25 per cent). Such tax is not repayable or usable to frank tax deducted from an annual payment.

Subs. (5)

Relevant amounts are disregarded in determining whether an estate is a U.K. estate or a foreign estate (see s.701(9), (10)), but where the aggregate income comprises only such amounts, it is to be treated as a U.K. estate.

Securities

Interest on gilt-edged securities payable without deduction of tax

77. After section 51 of the Taxes Act 1988 there shall be inserted the following section—

"Gilt-edged securities held under authorised arrangements

51A.—(1) Subject to the provisions of any regulations under section 51B, where gilt-edged securities of an eligible person are for the time being held under arrangements that satisfy the applicable requirements—

(a) those securities shall be deemed to have been issued subject to the condition that the interest on them is paid without deduction of income tax; and

(b) that interest shall be so paid accordingly, but shall be chargeable under Case III of Schedule D.

(2) For the purposes of this section gilt-edged securities are securities of an eligible person so long as—

(a) they are in the beneficial ownership of a company, local authority or local authority association or of any health service body (within the meaning of section 519A) and that company, authority, association or body is beneficially entitled to the interest on them;

(b) they are in the beneficial ownership of a person who does not fall within paragraph (a) above but is of any such description as may be prescribed by regulations made by the Treasury and that person is beneficially entitled to the interest on those securities;

(c) the circumstances in which they are held are such that any income from them is eligible for relief from tax by virtue of section 505(1)(c), or would be so eligible but for section 505(3);

(d) the circumstances in which they are held are such that any income from them is eligible for relief from tax by virtue of section 592(2), 608(2)(a), 613(4), 614(2), (3) or (4), 620(6) or 643(2);

(e) they are assets of any such trust fund as is referred to in section 83 of the Insurance Companies Act 1982 (premiums trust funds of members of Lloyd's); or

(f) the circumstances in which they are held are such that any income from them falls to be treated as the income of, or of the government of, a sovereign power or of an international organisation.

(3) For the purposes of this section the arrangements under which any gilt-edged securities are held shall be taken to satisfy the applicable requirements if—

(a) such conditions as may be imposed by or under any such regulations as may be made by the Treasury are satisfied in relation to those arrangements; and

(b) a declaration with respect to the satisfaction of those conditions has been made in accordance with any such regulations by such person having an entitlement to or in respect of the securities as may be determined under the regulations.

(4) The conditions that may, for the purposes of subsection (3)(a) above, be imposed by regulations under this section in relation to arrangements for the holding of any gilt-edged securities shall include—

(a) conditions as to the accounts in which the securities are to be held under the arrangements and as to the accounts into which interest on the securities is to be paid;

(b) conditions requiring persons holding the securities, or otherwise having functions under or in connection with the arrangements, to be persons of a description specified in the regulations or to be approved in accordance with the regulations;

(c) conditions requiring persons who, for purposes connected with the arrangements, act directly or indirectly—

(i) on behalf of the person beneficially entitled to the securities, or

(ii) on behalf of the person who holds them,

to be persons registered with the Board in accordance with the regulations; and

(d) conditions as to the provision about transfers of securities held under the arrangements that is to be contained in the arrangements.

(5) Regulations made by the Treasury for the purposes of this section may—

(a) impose requirements in relation to any such persons as are mentioned in subsection (4)(b) and (c) above with respect to the manner in which their functions under or in connection with the arrangements are exercised;

(b) require such persons—

     (i) to consider the accuracy of any declaration made for the purposes of subsection (3)(b) above; and

     (ii) themselves to make declarations as to the extent to which conditions or other requirements imposed for the purposes of this section appear to be, or to have been, satisfied or complied with;

  (c) make provision—

     (i) about the making of applications for approval or registration under any such regulations;

     (ii) for the circumstances in which any approval or registration is to be or may be given or refused;

     (iii) for the withdrawal or cancellation of any approval or registration;

     (iv) for appeals against any refusal to grant an approval or to register any person, or against the withdrawal or cancellation of any approval or registration;

  (d) make provision for the publication of information showing the effect of any determinations in pursuance of regulations made by virtue of paragraph (c) above;

  (e) make provision for notices to be issued by the Board to such persons as may be described in the regulations where the Board are satisfied that this section has effect, or does not have effect, in relation to any gilt-edged securities;

  (f) impose obligations—

     (i) on persons having any rights in relation to gilt-edged securities held under arrangements described in the regulations,

     (ii) on any such persons as are mentioned in subsection (4) (b) and (c) above, and

     (iii) on persons who are applying to be approved or registered for the purposes of this section,

as to the provision of information, and the production of documents, to the Board or, on request, to an officer of the Board;

and

  (g) impose requirements, framed wholly or partly by reference to the opinion of the Board, as to—

     (i) the contents of any declaration to be made in accordance with regulations under this section,

     (ii) the form and manner in which any declaration or information is to be made or provided in accordance with any such regulations, and

     (iii) the keeping and production to, or to an officer of, the Board of any document in which any such declaration or information is contained.

  (6) Any person who—

  (a) contravenes, or fails to comply with, any requirement imposed on him by or under any regulations under this section, or

  (b) fraudulently or negligently makes or produces any incorrect declaration, information or document in pursuance of any such requirement,

shall be liable to a penalty not exceeding £25,000.

  (7) In this section 'gilt-edged securities' means any securities which—

  (a) are gilt-edged securities for the purposes of the 1992 Act; or

  (b) will be such securities on the making of any order under paragraph 1 of Schedule 9 to that Act the making of which is anticipated in the prospectus under which they were issued.

  (8) In this section 'international organisation' means an organisation of which two or more sovereign powers, or the governments of two or

more sovereign powers, are members; and if, in any proceedings, any question arises whether a person is an international organisation for the purposes of this section a certificate issued by or under the authority of the Secretary of State stating any fact relevant to that question shall be conclusive evidence of that fact.

(9) Regulations made by the Treasury for the purposes of this section may—

(a) make different provision for different cases; and

(b) contain such supplementary, incidental, consequential and transitional provision as appears to the Treasury to be appropriate.

(10) This section shall not apply to any interest paid before such day as the Treasury may by order appoint, and different days may be appointed under this subsection for different purposes."

GENERAL NOTE

This section, together with ss.78, 80, 82, 83 and 84, which were all introduced at the Report stage, makes the tax changes necessary to facilitate the introduction of an open market in the sale and repurchase of Government securities ("the gilt repo market"). Interest on gilts will be payable gross in a much wider range of circumstances than before. The new market, which is anticipated to start in 1996, is expected to lower the cost of financing Government debt.

The new ICTA 1988, s.51A authorises the Treasury to make regulations enabling interest on gilt-edged securities, at present normally paid under deduction of tax, to be paid gross. The persons eligible to deal in the market include companies, local authorities, charities, pension schemes, Lloyd's, foreign governments, international organisations and others authorised by the Treasury. Satisfactory arrangements must be made for holding the securities, under conditions laid down by the Treasury. Ancillary matters such as the conferring and withdrawal of approval, the publication of information, the issue of notices and imposition of obligations and information requirements by the Revenue will also be covered in the regulations. A penalty of £25,000 may be imposed for breach of the regulations.

Periodic accounting for tax on interest on gilt-edged securities

78.—(1) After the section 51A of the Taxes Act 1988 inserted by section 77 above there shall be inserted the following section—

"Periodic accounting for tax on interest on gilt-edged securities

51B.—(1) The Treasury may by regulations provide for persons to whom payments of interest on relevant gilt-edged securities are made without deduction of tax to be required to make periodic returns to an officer of the Board of—

(a) amounts of any payments of such interest made to that person, and

(b) amounts of tax for which, assuming the payments to bear tax at the basic rate for the relevant year of assessment, that person is to be accountable under the regulations in respect of those payments;

and any such regulations may further provide for the amounts of tax required to be included in any such return to become due, at the time when the return is required to be made, from the person required to make it.

(2) Regulations made by the Treasury for the purposes of this section may—

(a) specify such periods as the Treasury may consider appropriate as the periods for which returns are to be made, and in respect of which any person is to account for tax, under the regulations;

(b) make provision for enabling returns under the regulations to be combined with returns under Schedule 16 and for requiring par-

ticulars of claims and calculations made for the purposes of the
regulations to be set out in the returns;
(c) provide, in respect of any period for which a return is to be made
by any person under the regulations, for that person to be
obliged, before the end of the period, to make a payment on
account of amounts that may become due from him in respect of
that period;
(d) impose a requirement for a special return to be made for the purposes of any obligation imposed by virtue of paragraph (c) above;
(e) provide for the amount which, under the regulations, is to be due
from any person in respect of any period to be reduced by reference to amounts which—
(i) are paid by or on behalf of that person under contracts or
arrangements relating to transfers of gilt-edged securities; and
(ii) are or fall to be treated as representative of interest on
those securities;
(f) authorise amounts in respect of which there is an obligation to
account for tax under the regulations to be treated for specified
purposes of the Tax Acts as payments on which a person has
borne income tax by deduction;
(g) make provision for the assessment of amounts due under the
regulations and for the repayment in specified circumstances of
amounts paid under the regulations;
(h) make provision for interest to be payable, at such rate as may be
determined by or under the regulations, on amounts that have
become due under the regulations but have not been paid;
(i) make provision, where payments of interest on any relevant gilt-
edged securities would be comprised in the income of a member
of Lloyd's, for obligations that may be imposed by regulations
under this section on the person to whom the interest is paid to be
imposed, instead, on such other person as may be described in the
regulations.
(3) Regulations made by the Treasury for the purposes of this section
may—
(a) include provision which for the purposes of the regulations makes
any provision corresponding, with or without modifications, to
any of the provisions of Schedule 16;
(b) make provision modifying the operation of Schedule 19AB in
relation to cases where payments of interest on relevant gilt-
edged securities are made without deduction of tax to companies
carrying on pension business;
(c) include provision which requires obligations and liabilities under
the regulations to be treated as obligations and liabilities to which
provisions of Schedule 23 to the Finance Act 1995 (UK representatives) apply; and
(d) include provision which, for any of the purposes of the regulations, applies provisions of sections 126 and 127 of, and Schedule 23 to, that Act in relation to times before those provisions
otherwise come into force.
(4) Regulations made by the Treasury for the purposes of this section
may—
(a) make different provision for different cases; and
(b) contain such supplementary, incidental, consequential and transitional provision as appears to the Treasury to be appropriate;
and subsection (3) of section 178 of the Finance Act 1989 (extent of
powers to set rates of interest) shall apply for the purposes of the power
conferred by virtue of subsection (2)(h) above as it applies for the purposes of the power to make regulations under that section.

(5) In this section 'relevant gilt-edged securities' means securities which are gilt-edged securities within the meaning of section 51A, other than any to which a direction of the Treasury under section 50 relates.

(6) In this section 'relevant year of assessment'—

    (a) in relation to a manufactured payment, means the year of assessment in which it is received by the person to whom it is paid; and

    (b) in relation to any other payment of interest, means the year of assessment in which the payment is made;

and in this subsection 'manufactured payment' means any payment which for the purposes of Schedule 23A is a payment of manufactured interest."

(2) In the Table in section 98 of the Management Act (penalties in respect of certain information provisions), immediately before the entry in the second column relating to section 124(3) of the Taxes Act 1988 there shall be inserted the following entry—

    "regulations under section 51B;".

GENERAL NOTE

The new ICTA 1988, s.51B enables regulations to be made to introduce a system of quarterly accounting for tax on gilt interest received gross. The system will be brought into effect on the same date as the gilt repo market (see s.77 above). It is necessary to contain the effect that paying gilt interest gross would otherwise have on the public sector borrowing requirement. The arrangements will reduce the cost from about £1.2 billion over two years to about £100 million in total.

The regulations will provide for quarterly returns to the Revenue including all relevant information. Provision will also be made for the assessment and collection of tax and for tying the returns in with those under ICTA 1988, Scheds. 16 and 19AB and FA 1995, Sched. 23.

Breach of the information requirements will attract a penalty under TMA 1970, s.98.

Sale and repurchase of securities: exclusion from accrued income scheme

79.—(1) In Chapter II of Part XVII of the Taxes Act 1988 (transfers of securities) after section 727 insert—

"Exception for sale and repurchase of securities

727A.—(1) Where securities are transferred under an agreement to sell them, and under the same or any related agreement the transferor or a person connected with him—

    (a) is required to buy back the securities, or

    (b) acquires an option, which he subsequently exercises, to buy back the securities,

section 713(2) and (3) and section 716 do not apply to the transfer by the transferor or the transfer back.

(2) For the purposes of this section agreements are related if they are entered into in pursuance of the same arrangement (regardless of the date on which either agreement is entered into).

(3) Section 839 (connected persons) applies for the purposes of this section.

(4) References in this section to buying back securities include buying similar securities.

For this purpose securities are similar if they entitle their holders—

    (a) to the same rights against the same persons as to capital and interest, and

    (b) to the same remedies for the enforcement of those rights,

notwithstanding any difference in the total nominal amounts of the respective securities or in the form in which they are held or the manner in which they can be transferred.

(5) For the purposes of this section—

(a) a person connected with the transferor who is required to buy securities sold by the transferor shall be treated as being required to buy the securities back, and

(b) a person connected with the transferor who acquires an option to buy securities sold by the transferor shall be treated as acquiring an option to buy the securities back,

notwithstanding that it was not he who sold them.".

(2) In section 728 of the Taxes Act 1988 (information) in subsections (1) and (5) for "sections 710 to 727" substitute "sections 710 to 727A".

(3) The above amendments have effect where the agreement to sell the securities is entered into on or after the date on which this Act is passed.

(4) If the appointed day for the purposes of section 737A of the Taxes Act 1988 in relation to any description of securities falls after the date on which this Act is passed, the reference in subsection (3) above to the date on which this Act is passed shall be construed in relation to an agreement relating to securities of that description and to which section 737A would apply if it were in force as a reference to that appointed day.

GENERAL NOTE

The new ICTA 1988, s.727A disapplies the accrued income scheme from transfers under certain sales and repurchase agreements ("repos"). Since the economic effect of a repo is to leave the benefit of the accruing interest with the original owner of the securities, there is no need to apportion the interest between the seller and the buyer for tax purposes.

The definition of repo agreements mirrors that in ICTA 1988, ss.737A–B.

Treatment of price differential on sale and repurchase of securities

80.—(1) After section 730 of the Taxes Act 1988 there shall be inserted the following sections—

"Treatment of price differential on sale and repurchase of securities

730A.—(1) Subject to subsection (8) below, this section applies where—

(a) a person ('the original owner') has transferred any securities to another person ('the interim holder') under an agreement to sell them;

(b) the original owner or a person connected with him is required to buy them back either—

(i) in pursuance of an obligation to do so imposed by that agreement or by any related agreement, or

(ii) in consequence of the exercise of an option acquired under that agreement or any related agreement;

and

(c) the sale price and the repurchase price are different.

(2) The difference between the sale price and the repurchase price shall be treated for the purposes of the Tax Acts—

(a) where the repurchase price is more than the sale price, as a payment of interest made by the repurchaser on a deemed loan from the interim holder of an amount equal to the sale price; and

(b) where the sale price is more than the repurchase price, as a payment of interest made by the interim holder on a deemed loan from the repurchaser of an amount equal to the repurchase price.

(3) Where any amount is deemed under subsection (2) above to be a payment of interest, that payment shall be deemed for the purposes of the Tax Acts to be one that becomes due at the time when the repur-

chase price becomes due and, accordingly, is treated as paid when that price is paid.

(4) Where any amount is deemed under subsection (2) above to be a payment of interest, the repurchase price shall be treated for the purposes of the Tax Acts (other than this section and sections 737A and 737C) and (in cases where section 263A of the 1992 Act does not apply) for the purposes of the 1992 Act—

(a) in a case falling within paragraph (a) of that subsection, as reduced by the amount of the deemed payment; and

(b) in a case falling within paragraph (b) of that subsection, as increased by the amount of the deemed payment.

(5) For the purposes of section 209(2)(d) and (da) any amount which is deemed under subsection (2)(a) above to be a payment of interest shall be deemed to be interest in respect of securities issued by the repurchaser and held by the interim holder.

(6) Any amount which—

(a) is deemed under subsection (2) above to be a payment of interest, and

(b) does not fall (apart from this subsection) to be treated as yearly interest,

shall be treated for the purposes of section 338 as if the reference to yearly interest in subsection (3)(a) of that section included a reference to that amount.

(7) The Treasury may by regulations provide for any amount which is deemed under subsection (2) above to be received as a payment of interest to be treated, in such circumstances and to such extent as may be described in the regulations, as comprised in income that is eligible for relief from tax by virtue of section 438, 592(2), 608(2)(a), 613(4), 614(2), (3) or (4), 620(6) or 643(2).

(8) Except where regulations under section 737E otherwise provide, this section does not apply if—

(a) the agreement or agreements under which provision is made for the sale and repurchase are not such as would be entered into by persons dealing with each other at arm's length; or

(b) all of the benefits or risks arising from fluctuations, before the repurchase takes place, in the market value of the securities sold accrue to, or fall on, the interim holder.

(9) In this section references to the repurchase price are to be construed—

(a) in cases where section 737A applies, and

(b) in cases where section 737A would apply if it were in force in relation to the securities in question,

as references to the repurchase price which is or, as the case may be, would be applicable by virtue of section 737C(3)(b), (9) or (11)(c).

Interpretation of section 730A

730B.—(1) For the purposes of section 730A agreements are related if they are entered into in pursuance of the same arrangement (regardless of the date on which either agreement is entered into).

(2) References in section 730A to buying back securities—

(a) shall include references to buying similar securities; and

(b) in relation to a person connected with the original owner, shall include references to buying securities sold by the original owner or similar securities,

notwithstanding (in each case) that the securities bought have not previously been held by the purchaser; and references in that section to repurchase or to a repurchaser shall be construed accordingly.

(3) In section 730A and this section 'securities' has the same meaning as in section 737A.

(4) For the purposes of this section securities are similar if they entitle their holders—

(a) to the same rights against the same persons as to capital, interest and dividends, and

(b) to the same remedies for the enforcement of those rights,

notwithstanding any difference in the total nominal amounts of the respective securities or in the form in which they are held or the manner in which they can be transferred.

(5) Section 839 (connected persons) applies for the purposes of section 730A."

(2) In section 729 of that Act (sale and repurchase of securities), after subsection (5) there shall be inserted the following subsection—

"(5A) This section shall not apply where section 737A applies; and this section shall be disregarded in determining whether the condition in subsection (2)(b) of that section is fulfilled in any case."

(3) In subsections (3)(b), (9) and (11)(c) of section 737C of that Act (adjustment of repurchase price), for "the Tax Acts other than section 737A and of the 1992 Act" there shall be substituted, in each case, "section 730A"; and after subsection (11) of that section there shall be inserted the following subsection—

"(11A) The deemed increase of the repurchase price which is made for the purposes of section 730A by subsection (3)(b), (9) or (11)(c) above shall also have effect—

(a) for all the purposes of the Tax Acts, other than section 737A, and

(b) in cases where section 263A of the 1992 Act does not apply, for the purposes of the 1992 Act,

wherever in consequence of that increase there is for the purposes of section 730A no difference between the sale price and the repurchase price."

(4) After section 263 of the Taxation of Chargeable Gains Act 1992 there shall be inserted the following section—

"Agreements for sale and repurchase of securities

263A.—(1) Subject to subsections (2) to (4) below, in any case falling within subsection (1) of section 730A of the Taxes Act (treatment of price differential on sale and repurchase of securities) and in any case which would fall within that subsection if the sale price and the repurchase price were different—

(a) the acquisition of the securities in question by the interim holder and the disposal of those securities by him to the repurchaser, and

(b) except where the repurchaser is or may be different from the original owner, the disposal of those securities by the original owner and any acquisition of those securities by the original owner as the repurchaser,

shall be disregarded for the purposes of capital gains tax.

(2) Subsection (1) above does not apply in any case where the repurchase price of the securities in question falls to be calculated for the purposes of section 730A of the Taxes Act by reference to provisions of section 737C of that Act that are not in force in relation to those securities when the repurchase price becomes due.

(3) Subsection (1) above does not apply if—

(a) the agreement or agreements under which provision is made for the sale and repurchase are not such as would be entered into by persons dealing with each other at arm's length; or

(b) any of the benefits or risks arising from fluctuations, before the repurchase takes place, in the market value of the securities sold accrues to, or falls on, the interim holder.

(4) Subsection (1) above does not apply in relation to any disposal or acquisition of qualifying corporate bonds in a case where the securities disposed of by the original owner or those acquired by him, or by any other person, as the repurchaser are not such bonds.

(5) Expressions used in this section and in section 730A of the Taxes Act have the same meanings in this section as in that section."

(5) This section shall have effect where the agreement to sell the securities is entered into on or after the date on which this Act is passed.

GENERAL NOTE

The section is designed to ensure that the tax rules for the treatment of repos reflect the underlying economic reality of the transaction and to prevent the risk of tax being lost by repos being used to turn income into capital. Because of this risk, the provisions will come into effect from Royal Assent, instead of awaiting the introduction of the gilt repo market in 1996.

The new ICTA 1988, s.730A treats the difference between the sale and repurchase price of securities (the price differential) as interest assessable under Case III of Schedule D. The payer can treat the difference as an interest expense for tax purposes. The normal rules governing interest apply except that short interest, if not otherwise deductible for tax purposes, will be treated as a charge on the income of the payer, so enabling investment companies which could not otherwise get relief for payment of price differential to treat it as a deduction for tax purposes.

The price differential is deemed to be interest on securities issued by the original holder for the purposes of ICTA 1988, s.209, but this will become relevant only if any of the interest paid by the repurchaser represents more than a reasonable return or would not have been paid but for the relationship between the parties to the repo. Even then, s.209 would only apply to the excessive element of the interest.

The new ICTA 1988, s.730B contains interpretative provisions for s.730A, widening the meaning of the terms in some cases.

Consequential amendments are also made to ICTA 1988, ss.729 and 737C.

The new TCGA 1992, s.263A provides that where all the risk of market fluctuations in the price of securities is borne by the original holder, transfers and re-transfers are ignored for CGT purposes. Correspondingly, disposals and reacquisitions of securities where any of the risks or benefits of market fluctuations are borne by the interim holder, are outside the scope of the price differential provisions for repos.

Manufactured interest payments: exclusion from bond-washing provisions

81.—(1) Section 731 of the Taxes Act 1988 (application of sections 732 to 734) is amended as follows.

(2) After subsection (2) insert—

"(2A) The relevant provisions do not apply where the first buyer is required under the arrangements for the purchase of the securities to make to the person from whom he purchased the securities, not later than the date on which he subsequently sells the securities, a payment of an amount representative of the interest, or is treated by virtue of section 737A(5) as required to make such a payment.".

(3) In consequence of the above amendment—

(a) in subsection (2) for "Subject to subsections (3) to (10) below" substitute "Subject to subsections (2A) to (10) below, and for "relate" substitute "apply";

(b) in subsection (3) for "relate to cases" substitute "apply".

(4) The above amendments have effect where the date on which the payment referred to in the inserted subsection (2A) is required to be made, or treated as required to be made, is after the passing of this Act.

GENERAL NOTE

The section disapplies the provisions of ICTA 1988, ss.732–734 in situations where a manufactured payment is made (or is treated as being paid) to the person from whom the securities were purchased. A manufactured payment occurs where securities are purchased and resold, with the result that interest becomes payable to the first purchaser. These provisions are unnecessary if the original holder of the security receives a manufactured payment, since such a holder still receives the benefit of the income arising on the security in the form of income rather than capital.

Manufactured interest on gilt-edged securities

82.—(1) In section 737 of the Taxes Act 1988 (manufactured dividends and interest)—

    (a) after subsection (1A) there shall be inserted the following subsection—

        "(1B) Subject to subsection (5AA) below, subsection (1) above shall not apply where the interest in question is interest on gilt-edged securities.";

    (b) at the beginning of subsections (2) and (5), there shall be inserted, in each case, "Subject to subsection (5AA) below,";

    (c) after subsection (5) there shall be inserted the following subsection—

        "(5AA) Regulations made by the Treasury may make provision in relation to any such case where the securities in question are gilt-edged securities as may be specified in the regulations—

            (a) for subsections (1B), (2) and (5) above to be disregarded in determining whether the case is one where subsection (1) above applies; or

            (b) for this section to have effect as if subsections (1B) and (2) above were omitted and the words in subsection (5) from 'unless' to the end of paragraph (b) were modified in such manner as may be set out in the regulations.";

    and

    (d) in subsection (6), after the definition of "foreign income dividend" there shall be inserted the following definition—

        " 'gilt-edged securities' has the same meaning as in section 51A;".

(2) In Schedule 23A to that Act, at the beginning of sub-paragraphs (2) and (3) of paragraph 3, there shall be inserted, in each case, "Subject to paragraph 3A below,"; and after that paragraph there shall be inserted the following paragraph—

    "3A.—(1) This paragraph applies, except in so far as dividend manufacturing regulations otherwise provide, in any case where paragraph 3 above applies and the United Kingdom securities in question are gilt-edged securities.

    (2) In a case where this paragraph applies, sub-paragraphs (2) and (3) of paragraph 3 above shall not have effect, but the gross amount of the manufactured interest shall be treated—

        (a) in relation to the interest manufacturer, for all the purposes of the Tax Acts except the determination of whether a deduction of tax is liable to be made on the making of the manufactured payment, and

        (b) in relation to the recipient and all persons claiming title through or under him, for all the purposes of those Acts,

    as if it were the gross amount of a periodical payment of interest on those gilt-edged securities, but made by the interest manufacturer.

    (3) Sub-paragraph (4) of paragraph 3 above shall apply for the purposes of this paragraph as it applies for the purposes of that paragraph.

    (4) In this paragraph 'gilt-edged securities' has the same meaning as in section 51A."

(3) In paragraph 5(6) of that Schedule (construction of references to securities in provisions relating to interest passing through the market), after "United Kingdom securities" there shall be inserted ", other than gilt-edged securities (within the meaning of section 51A),".

(4) This section shall have effect in relation to any payments made on or after such day as the Treasury may by order appoint, and different days may be appointed under this subsection for different purposes.

GENERAL NOTE

The necessary amendments to existing legislation are made in order to enable manufactured payments of gilt interest to be paid gross in all circumstances. This should assist the operation of the gilt repo market since participants will be able to make manufactured payments of gilt interest gross, regardless of the circumstances or identity of their counterpart. A manufactured payment occurs where securities are purchased and resold.

This treatment will apply in accordance with regulations made by the Treasury.

Power to make special provision for special cases

83.—(1) Immediately before section 738 of the Taxes Act 1988 there shall be inserted the following sections—

"Power to provide for manufactured payments to be eligible for relief

737D.—(1) The Treasury may by regulations provide for any manufactured payment made to any person to be treated, in such circumstances and to such extent as may be described in the regulations, as comprised in income of that person that is eligible for relief from tax by virtue of section 438, 592(2), 608(2)(a), 613(4), 614(2), (3) or (4), 620(6) or 643(2).

(2) In this section 'manufactured payment' means any manufactured dividend, manufactured interest or manufactured overseas dividend, within the meaning of Schedule 23A.

Power to modify sections 727A, 730A and 737A to 737C

737E.—(1) The Treasury may by regulations make provision for all or any of sections 727A, 730A and 737A to 737C to have effect with modifications in relation to cases involving any arrangement for the sale and repurchase of securities where—

(a) the obligation to make the repurchase is not performed or the option to repurchase is not exercised;

(b) provision is made by or under any agreement for different or additional securities to be treated as, or as included with, securities which, for the purposes of the repurchase, are to represent securities transferred in pursuance of the original sale;

(c) provision is made by or under any agreement for any securities to be treated as not included with securities which, for the purposes of the repurchase, are to represent securities transferred in pursuance of the original sale;

(d) provision is made by or under any agreement for the sale price or repurchase price to be determined or varied wholly or partly by reference to fluctuations, occurring in the period after the making of the agreement for the original sale, in the value of securities transferred in pursuance of that sale, or in the value of securities treated as representing those securities; or

(e) provision is made by or under any agreement for any person to be required, in a case where there are any such fluctuations, to make any payment in the course of that period and before the repurchase price becomes due.

(2) The Treasury may by regulations make provision for all or any of sections 727A, 730A and 737A to 737C to have effect with modifications in relation to cases where—

(a) arrangements, corresponding to those made in cases involving an arrangement for the sale and repurchase of securities, are made by any agreement, or by one or more related agreements, in relation to securities that are to be redeemed in the period after their sale; and

(b) those arrangements are such that the person making the sale or a person connected with him (instead of being required to repurchase the securities or acquiring an option to do so) is granted rights in respect of the benefits that will accrue from their redemption.

(3) The Treasury may by regulations provide that section 730A is to have effect with modifications in relation to cases involving any arrangement for the sale and repurchase of securities where there is an agreement relating to the sale or repurchase which is not such as would be entered into by persons dealing with each other at arm's length.

(4) The powers conferred by subsections (1) and (2) above shall be exercisable in relation to section 263A of the 1992 Act as they are exercisable in relation to section 730A of this Act.

(5) Regulations made for the purposes of this section may—

(a) make different provision for different cases; and

(b) contain such supplementary, incidental, consequential and transitional provision as appears to the Treasury to be appropriate.

(6) The supplementary, incidental and consequential provision that may be made by regulations under this section shall include—

(a) in the case of regulations relating to section 730A, provision modifying subsections (3)(b), (9), (11)(c) and (11A) of section 737C; and

(b) in the case of regulations relating to section 263A of the 1992 Act, provision modifying the operation of that Act in relation to cases where by virtue of the regulations any acquisition or disposal is excluded from those which are to be disregarded for the purposes of capital gains tax.

(7) In this section 'modifications' includes exceptions and omissions; and any power under this section to provide for an enactment to have effect with modifications in any case shall include power to provide for it not to apply (if it otherwise would do) in that case.

(8) References in this section to a case involving an arrangement for the sale and repurchase of securities are references to any case where—

(a) a person makes a sale of any securities under any agreement ('the original sale'); and

(b) that person or a person connected with him either—

(i) is required under that agreement or any related agreement to buy them back; or

(ii) acquires, under that agreement or any related agreement, an option to buy them back.

(9) Section 730B shall apply for the purposes of this section as it applies for the purposes of section 730A."

(2) In section 182(1) of the Finance Act 1993 and section 229 of the Finance Act 1994 (powers to modify provisions relating to Lloyd's), the following paragraph shall be inserted, in each case, after paragraph (c)—

"(ca) for modifying the application of this Chapter in relation to cases where assets forming part of a premiums trust fund are the subject of—

(i) any such arrangement as is mentioned in section 129(1), (2) or (2A) of the Taxes Act 1988 (stock lending etc.); or

(ii) any such arrangements or agreements as are mentioned in section 737E(2) and (8) of the Taxes Act 1988 (sale and repurchase of securities etc.);".

General Note
The new ICTA 1988, ss.737D and 737E provide the Treasury with power to make regulations to enable the operation of legislation affecting repos to take account of the detailed workings of the agreements under which these transactions are carried out. The purpose is to ensure the proper interaction of the new gilt repo market legislation with the existing anti-avoidance legislation governing repos.

Stock lending: power to modify rules

84.—(1) In subsection (1) of section 129 of the Taxes Act 1988 (description of stock lending arrangements)—
(a) for "subsection (4)" there shall be substituted "subsections (2B) and (4)"; and
(b) the words "has contracted to sell securities, and to enable him to fulfil the contract, he" shall be omitted.

(2) In subsection (2A) of that section, for "A to fulfil his contract" there shall be substituted "B to make the transfer to A or his nominee".

(3) After subsection (2A) of that section there shall be inserted the following subsection—

"(2B) Except in so far as the Treasury by regulations otherwise provide, this section applies only if A enters into the arrangement mentioned in subsection (1) above to enable him to fulfil a contract under which he is required to sell securities."

(4) After subsection (4) of that section there shall be inserted the following subsections—

"(4A) Regulations under subsection (4) above relating to section 271(9) of the 1992 Act may include provision modifying the operation of that Act in relation to cases where, by virtue of the regulations, any acquisition or disposal is excluded from those which are to be disregarded for the purposes of capital gains tax.

(4B) In such cases as the Treasury may by regulations provide, this section shall have effect as if references to a transfer of securities of the same kind and amount as those subject to a previous transfer included references to the grant of equivalent rights in respect of benefits accruing from the redemption of securities of the same kind and amount."

(5) For subsection (9) of section 271 of the Taxation of Chargeable Gains Act 1992 (exemption for arrangements to which section 129 applies) there shall be substituted the following subsection—

"(9) Subject to any regulations under subsection (4) of section 129 of the Taxes Act, any disposal and acquisition made in pursuance of an arrangement mentioned in subsection (1), (2) or (2A) of that section shall be disregarded for the purposes of capital gains tax unless it is one in the case of which subsection (2B) of that section has the effect of preventing that section from applying."

General Note
The Treasury is given power to make regulations modifying the circumstances in which transfers of securities under stock lending arrangements are disregarded for tax purposes in computing trading profits or capital gains. These are likely to remove constraints affecting stock lending, which has the same economic effect as a repo.

Stock lending: interest on cash collateral

85.—(1) In Chapter VIII of Part IV of the Taxes Act 1988 (provisions relating to the Schedule D charge: miscellaneous and supplementary provisions), after section 129 insert—

"Stock lending: interest on cash collateral
129A. The provisions of Schedule 5A have effect with respect to the tax treatment of interest earned on cash collateral provided in connection with certain stock lending arrangements.".

(2) In the Taxes Act 1988 insert as Schedule 5A the provisions set out in Schedule 19 to this Act.

(3) This section and that Schedule apply in relation to approved stock lending arrangements (within the meaning of that Schedule) entered into after the passing of this Act.

GENERAL NOTE

The new ICTA 1988, s.129A inserts Sched. 5A. The purpose of the changes is to enable lenders of stock who prefer cash as collateral to take a more active part in the market.

See further the General Note to Sched. 19.

Interest

Deduction of tax from interest on deposits

86.—(1) In section 481(4) of the Taxes Act 1988 (meaning of "relevant deposit" for the purposes of provisions relating to the deduction of tax), after paragraph (c) there shall be inserted "or

    (d) any interest in respect of the deposit is income arising to the trustees of a discretionary or accumulation trust in their capacity as such;"

and for "subsection (5)" there shall be substituted "any of subsections (5) to (5B)".

(2) After subsection (4) of section 481 of that Act there shall be inserted the following subsection—

    "(4A) For the purposes of the relevant provisions a trust is a discretionary or accumulation trust if it is such that some or all of any income arising to the trustees would fall (unless treated as income of the settlor or applied in defraying expenses of the trustees) to be comprised for the year of assessment in which it arises in income to which section 686 applies."

(3) In section 481(5)(k) of that Act (declaration by virtue of which deposit is not a relevant deposit)—

    (a) the word "that" before sub-paragraph (i) shall be omitted;

    (b) in sub-paragraph (i), at the beginning there shall be inserted "in a case falling within subsection (4)(a) or (b) above, that";

    (c) in sub-paragraph (ii), after "above" there shall be inserted ", that"; and

    (d) after sub-paragraph (ii) there shall be inserted the following sub-paragraph—

        "(iii) in a case falling within subsection (4)(d) above, that, at the time when the declaration is made, the trustees are not resident in the United Kingdom and do not have any reasonable grounds for believing that any of the beneficiaries of the trust is an individual who is ordinarily resident in the United Kingdom or a company which is resident in the United Kingdom."

(4) After subsection (5A) of section 481 of that Act there shall be inserted the following subsection—

    "(5B) In a case falling within subsection (4)(d) above, a deposit shall not be taken to be a relevant deposit in relation to a payment of interest in respect of that deposit if—

    (a) the deposit was made before 6th April 1995; and

    (b) the deposit-taker has not, at any time since that date but before the making of the payment, been given a notification by the Board or any of the trustees in question that interest in respect of that deposit is income arising to the trustees of a discretionary or accumulation trust."

(5) In section 482(2) of that Act (contents of declaration under section 481(5)(k)), for paragraph (a) there shall be substituted the following paragraph—

"(a) if made under sub-paragraph (i) or (iii), contain an undertaking by the person making it that where—

(i) the individual or any of the individuals in respect of whom it is made becomes ordinarily resident in the United Kingdom,

(ii) the trustees or any company in respect of whom it is made become or becomes resident in the United Kingdom, or

(iii) an individual who is ordinarily resident in the United Kingdom or a company which is resident in the United Kingdom becomes or is found to be a beneficiary of a trust to which the declaration relates,

the person giving the undertaking will notify the deposit-taker accordingly; and".

(6) After subsection (5) of section 482 of that Act there shall be inserted the following subsection—

"(5A) The persons who are to be taken for the purposes of section 481(5)(k)(iii) and subsection (2) above to be the beneficiaries of a discretionary or accumulation trust shall be every person who, as a person falling wholly or partly within any description of actual or potential beneficiaries, is either—

(a) a person who is, or will or may become, entitled under the trust to receive the whole or any part of any income under the trust; or

(b) a person to or for the benefit of whom the whole or any part of any such income may be paid or applied in exercise of any discretion conferred by the trust;

and for the purposes of this subsection references, in relation to a trust, to income under the trust shall include references to so much (if any) of any property falling to be treated as capital under the trust as represents amounts originally received by the trustees as income."

(7) In section 482(6) of that Act (definitions for the purposes of section 481(5)), in the definition of "appropriate person", for "as a personal representative in his capacity as such" there shall be substituted "in his capacity as a personal representative or as a trustee of a discretionary or accumulation trust".

(8) In section 482(11) of that Act (power to make regulations), after paragraph (aa) there shall be inserted the following paragraph—

"(ab) with respect to—

(i) the manner and form in which a notification for the purposes of section 481(5B) is to be given or may be withdrawn, and

(ii) the circumstances in which the deposit-taker is to be entitled to delay acting on such a notification,

and".

(9) In section 482A(1) of that Act (power to make regulations excluding audit requirements in certain cases), after "United Kingdom" there shall be inserted ", or investments of trustees who are not resident in the United Kingdom,".

(10) The preceding provisions of this section apply in relation to any payments made on or after 6th April 1996.

(11) Notwithstanding the repeal of section 67 of the Taxes Act 1988 by the Finance Act 1994 or anything contained in the transitional provisions relating to that repeal, where—

  (a) this section has effect so as to require any deposit made before 6th April 1996 to be treated in relation to payments made after a time falling before 6th April 1998 as a relevant deposit for the purposes of section 480A(1) of the Taxes Act 1988, and

  (b) section 67(2) of that Act does not otherwise apply in relation to the liability to deduction of tax that begins at that time,

section 67(1) of the Taxes Act 1988 shall apply in respect of payments made before that time as if the deposit were a source of income that the trustees in question ceased to possess at that time.

  (12) An officer of the Board may, by notice to any of the trustees of a trust, require the trustees to provide the Board with the following, that is to say—

  (a) information about any notification given by any of the trustees for the purposes of subsection (5B) of section 481 of the Taxes Act 1988; and

  (b) such information as the Board may reasonably require for the purposes of themselves giving a notification under that subsection with respect to any income arising to the trustees;

and section 98 of the Management Act (penalties in respect of special returns) shall have effect with a reference to this subsection inserted at the end of the first column of the Table.

  (13) Where a notice given by the Board before the passing of this Act requires any such information as is mentioned in subsection (12) above to be provided to the Board, and the period within which that information was required to be so provided does not expire until at least one month after the passing of this Act, that notice shall have effect as if given after the passing of this Act in accordance with that subsection.

  (14) Without prejudice to section 20(2) of the Interpretation Act 1978 (references to other enactments) and subject to any provision to the contrary made in exercise of any power to make, revoke or amend any subordinate legislation, the enactments and subordinate legislation having effect, apart from this section, in relation to any provisions of the Taxes Act 1988 amended by this section shall be assumed, in cases where this section applies, to have the corresponding effect in relation to those provisions as so amended.

  (15) In this section "subordinate legislation" has the same meaning as in the Interpretation Act 1978.

GENERAL NOTE

  The section extends the provisions relating to the deduction of tax at source from bank interest so as to cover deposits belonging to discretionary and accumulation trusts, as from the tax year 1996–97.

Subs. (1)

  The definition of "relevant deposit" is extended to cover discretionary and accumulation trusts.

Subs. (2)

  The new ICTA 1988, s.481(4A) applies the definition of discretionary or accumulation trust to ICTA 1988, s.686.

Subs. (3)

  The amendment of ICTA 1988, s.481(5)(k) provides for a declaration to be made by trustees that neither they nor any of the beneficiaries are resident in the U.K., so enabling them to receive interest gross.

Subs. (4)

  The new ICTA 1988, s.481(5B) disapplies the new provisions for deposits made before April 6, 1995, unless a notification has been given by the Revenue or a trustee that the deposit belongs to a discretionary or accumulation trust.

Subs. (5)

The requirements which a declaration has to fulfil are modified to include an undertaking by the trustees to notify the bank if the declaration ceases to be appropriate.

Subs. (6)

A wide definition of "beneficiary" is provided and includes possible recipients of capital as well as income.

Subs. (7)

Trustees of discretionary or accumulation trusts are added to the categories of persons who can make a declaration.

Subs. (8)

The Revenue are given the power to make regulations regarding notifications and their consequences (see subs. (4) above).

Subs. (9)

Provision is made for the extended exclusion of the Revenue's audit powers to the investments of non-resident trustees.

Subs. (10)

The new system operates from April 6, 1996.

Subs. (11)

For the purposes of the transition of interest from being taxed on the preceding year basis of assessment to being taxed on the current year basis, a deposit which becomes a relevant deposit by virtue of this section will be treated as ceasing to be a source of income within Schedule D Case III at that time.

Subs. (12)

The Revenue are empowered to obtain information from trustees about any notification given by them, or to enable the Revenue themselves to give a notification (see subs. (4) above), subject to penalties under TMA 1970, s.98.

Subs. (13)

This is a transitional provision covering information notices issued before the passing of the Act.

Subss. (14) and (15)

Existing legislation and regulations governing the deduction of tax from interest on deposits continue to apply, but as amended.

Interest payments deemed to be distributions

87.—(1) In subsection (2) of section 209 of the Taxes Act 1988 (meaning of "distribution" for the purposes of the Corporation Tax Acts), after paragraph (d) there shall be inserted the following paragraph—

"(da) any interest or other distribution out of assets of the company ('the issuing company') in respect of securities issued by that company which are held by another company where—

(i) the issuing company is a 75 per cent subsidiary of the other company or both are 75 per cent subsidiaries of a third company, and

(ii) the whole or any part of the distribution represents an amount which would not have fallen to be paid to the other company if the companies had been companies between whom there was (apart from in respect of the securities in question) no relationship, arrangements or other connection (whether formal or informal),

except so much, if any, of any such distribution as does not represent such an amount or as is a distribution by virtue of paragraph (d) above or an amount representing the principal secured by the securities;".

(2) In paragraph (e) of that subsection—

(a) for "paragraph (d)" there shall be substituted "paragraph (d) or (da)";
and

(b) sub-paragraphs (iv) and (v) (distribution in respect of securities of subsidiaries of non-resident companies etc.) shall be omitted;

and, in subsection (3) of that section, for "subsection (2)(d)" there shall be substituted "subsection (2)(d), (da)".

(3) After subsection (8) of that section there shall be inserted the following subsections—

"(8A) For the purposes of paragraph (da) of subsection (2) above subsections (2) to (4) of section 808A shall apply as they apply for the purposes of a special relationship provision such as is mentioned in that section but as if—

(a) the references in those subsections to the relationship in question were references to any relationship, arrangements or other connection between the issuing company and the other company mentioned in sub-paragraph (ii) of that paragraph; and

(b) the provision in question required no account to be taken, in the determination of any of the matters mentioned in subsection (8B) below, of (or of any inference capable of being drawn from) any other relationship, arrangements or connection (whether formal or informal) between the issuing company and any person, except where that person—

(i) has no relevant connection with the issuing company, or
(ii) is a company that is a member of the same UK grouping as the issuing company.

(8B) The matters mentioned in subsection (8A)(b) above are the following—

(a) the appropriate level or extent of the issuing company's overall indebtedness;

(b) whether it might be expected that the issuing company and a particular person would have become parties to a transaction involving the issue of a security by the issuing company or the making of a loan, or a loan of a particular amount, to that company; and

(c) the rate of interest and other terms that might be expected to be applicable in any particular case to such a transaction.

(8C) For the purposes of subsection (8A) above a person has a relevant connection with the issuing company if he is connected with it within the terms of section 839 or that person (without being so connected to the issuing company) is—

(a) an effective 51 per cent subsidiary of the issuing company; or

(b) a company of which the issuing company is an effective 51 per cent subsidiary.

(8D) For the purposes of subsection (8A) above any question as to what constitutes the UK grouping of which the issuing company is a member or as to the other members of that grouping shall be determined as follows—

(a) where the issuing company has no effective 51 per cent subsidiaries and is not an effective 51 per cent subsidiary of a company resident in the United Kingdom, the issuing company shall be taken to be a member of a UK grouping of which it is itself the only member;

(b) where the issuing company has one or more effective 51 per cent subsidiaries and is not an effective 51 per cent subsidiary of a company resident in the United Kingdom, the issuing company shall be taken to be a member of a UK grouping of which the only members are the issuing company and its effective 51 per cent subsidiaries; and

 (c) where the issuing company is an effective 51 per cent subsidiary of a company resident in the United Kingdom ('the UK holding company'), the issuing company shall be taken to be a member of a UK grouping of which the only members are—

  (i) the UK holding company or, if there is more than one company resident in the United Kingdom of which the issuing company is an effective 51 per cent subsidiary, such one of them as is not itself an effective 51 per cent subsidiary of any of the others, and

  (ii) the effective 51 per cent subsidiaries of the company which is a member of that grouping by virtue of sub-paragraph (i) above.

(8E) For the purposes of subsections (8C) and (8D) above section 170(7) of the 1992 Act shall apply for determining whether a company is an effective 51 per cent subsidiary of another company but shall so apply as if the question whether the effective 51 per cent subsidiaries of a company resident in the United Kingdom ('the putative holding company') include either—

 (a) the issuing company, or

 (b) a company of which the issuing company is an effective 51 per cent subsidiary,

were to be determined without regard to any beneficial entitlement of the putative holding company to any profits or assets of any company resident outside the United Kingdom.

(8F) References in subsections (8D) and (8E) above to a company that is resident in the United Kingdom shall not include references to a company which is a dual resident company for the purposes of section 404."

(4) In section 212 of that Act (exceptions from the definition of a "distribution" for certain interest and other payments)—

 (a) in subsection (1), in paragraph (b), after "within" there shall be inserted "paragraph (da) of section 209(2) or";

 (b) in subsection (3)—

  (i) at the beginning there shall be inserted "Without prejudice to subsection (4) below,"; and

  (ii) at the end there shall be inserted "and does not apply in relation to any interest or distribution falling within section 209(2) (da) if that interest or distribution is otherwise outside the matters in respect of which that company is within the charge to corporation tax."; and

 (c) after subsection (3) there shall be inserted the following subsection—

  "(4) Where any interest or other distribution is paid to a charity (within the meaning of section 506) or to any of the bodies mentioned in section 507, the interest or distribution so paid shall not be a distribution for the purposes of the Corporation Tax Acts if it would otherwise fall to be treated as such a distribution by virtue only of paragraph (da) of section 209(2)."

(5) In section 710(3)(a) of that Act (meaning of securities), for "section 209(2)(e)(iv) or (v)" there shall be substituted "section 209(2)(da)".

(6) In paragraph 5(5) of Schedule 4 to that Act (deep discount securities), for "section 209(2)(d)" there shall be substituted "section 209(2)(d), (da)".

(7) This section has effect, subject to subsection (8) below, in relation to any interest or other distribution paid on or after 29th November 1994.

(8) This section shall not have effect in relation to any interest or other distribution paid before 1st April 1995 in respect of any security if the security is one in the case of which a notice given before 29th November 1994 under Regulation 2(2) of the Double Taxation Relief (Taxes on Income) (General) Regulations 1970 was in force immediately before 29th November

1994 as regards payments of interest or other distributions made in respect of that security.

GENERAL NOTE
The section, which was heavily criticised in the Standing Committee for the obscurity of its drafting, amends the treatment of interest and similar payments made to associated companies. Previously, all such payments when made to certain non-resident associated companies were recharacterised as distributions. This recharacterisation is now restricted to amounts which are excessive. The section also removes the limitation to non-resident recipients and sets out the basis on which it is to be determined whether relevant payments are excessive.

Subs. (1)
The new ICTA 1988, s.209(2)(da) provides that interest etc. paid to a parent or fellow subsidiary company is to be treated as a distribution to the extent that it would not have been made had the companies been unconnected or is not already covered by ICTA 1988, s.209(2)(d), which deals with interest exceeding a reasonable commercial return.

Subs. (2)
Amendments and repeals are made to other provisions of ICTA 1988, s.209(2) (3) consequential on the introduction of ICTA 1988, s.209(2)(da).

Subs. (3)
The new ICTA 1988, s.209(8A)–(8F) establish the *modus operandi* of s.209(2)(da). In particular they:
  (i) set out what factors are to be taken into account in determining whether an excessive relevant payment has been made due to the relationship between the companies concerned and, if so, in determining the excessive amount;
  (ii) require the position to be examined from the perspective of the "U.K. grouping" of which the paying company is a member; and
  (iii) define "U.K. grouping" for this purpose.

Subs. (4)
The new ICTA 1988, s.209(2)(da) is disapplied in relation to payments on which the recipient is chargeable to corporation tax or is exempt as a charity.

Subss. (5) and (6)
Consequential amendments are made to ICTA 1988, s.710, which deals with the accrued income scheme; and to Sched. 4, which deals with deep discount securities, so that references to the repealed ICTA 1988, s.209(2)(e)(iv) and (v) are replaced by references to the new ICTA 1988, s.209(2)(da).

Subss. (7) and (8)
The new provisions apply from Budget Day, subject to a deferment to April 1, 1995 for payments made under certain Double Taxation Relief notices issued before Budget Day.

Debts

Generalisation of ss.63 to 66 of Finance Act 1993

88.—(1) In sections 63 to 66 of the Finance Act 1993 (deemed periodic disposal of certain debts), for "the resident company", wherever occurring, substitute "the creditor company".
  (2) After section 62 of that Act insert—

"Application of sections 63 to 66: supplementary
  62A. In sections 63 to 66 below as they apply by virtue of section 61 above—
      (a) 'the creditor company' means the company identified in subsection (1) of that section as the person entitled to the debt (referred to there as 'the resident company'); and
      (b) 'the commencement date' means 1st April 1993.".
  (3) In section 63 of that Act, omit subsection (12) (meaning of "commencement date").
  (4) The above amendments shall be deemed always to have had effect.
  (5) Anything done before the passing of this Act under or by reference to the provisions of sections 63 to 66 of the Finance Act 1993 as originally

enacted shall have effect as if done under or by reference to those provisions as amended by this section.

GENERAL NOTE
This paves the way for the following section (which extends the charge under FA 1993, ss.63–66 on certain cross-border transactions) by amending the phraseology of the existing legislation and rearranging its structure, so that it is appropriate to the extended future application.

Subs. (1)
"Resident company" is replaced by the more neutral term "creditor company" in defining a creditor.

Subs. (2)
The new FA 1993, s.62A links the reworded ss.63–66 with the introductory provisions in ss.61–62. In conjunction with subs. (3), it also moves the commencement date for the charge in existing law (April 1, 1993) away from the body of the charging provisions to the introductory provisions, so that, in future, distinct applications of the charging provisions can be given their own distinct commencement date.

Subss. (3) and (4)
These preserve the validity of the charges which have become due under the original wording of FA 1993, ss.63–66.

Application of ss.63 to 66 to debts held by associates of banks

89.—(1) A debt is a qualifying debt for the purposes of sections 63 to 66 of the Finance Act 1993 (deemed periodic disposal of certain debts) at any time if, at that time, the person entitled to the debt is a company which—
    (a) is resident in the United Kingdom, and
    (b) is an associated company of a company (whether or not itself resident in the United Kingdom) which carries on a banking business in the United Kingdom,
and the debt is not an exempted debt as defined by the following provisions.

(2) A debt is an exempted debt for those purposes at any time if at that time it is held by the company entitled to it for the purposes of long term insurance business.

(3) A debt is an exempted debt for those purposes at any time if each of the first, second and third conditions mentioned below—
    (a) is fulfilled at that time,
    (b) has been fulfilled throughout so much of the period of the debt as falls before that time, and
    (c) is likely to be fulfilled throughout so much of that period as falls after that time.

(4) The first condition is that the terms of the debt provide that any interest carried by it shall be at a rate which falls into one, and one only, of the following categories—
    (a) a fixed rate which is the same throughout the period of the debt,
    (b) a rate which bears to a standard published rate the same fixed relationship throughout that period, and
    (c) a rate which bears to a published index of prices the same fixed relationship throughout that period.

(5) The second condition is that those terms provide for any such interest to be payable as it accrues at intervals of 12 months or less.

(6) The third condition is that the terms of the debt are not such—
    (a) in the case of a debt on a security, that the security is a deep discount or deep gain security, or

(b) in any other case, that if the debt were a debt on a security it would be a deep discount or deep gain security.

In this subsection "deep discount security" has the same meaning as in Schedule 4 to the Taxes Act 1988 and "deep gain security" has the same meaning as in Schedule 11 to the Finance Act 1989, disregarding paragraph 1(4)(c) of that Schedule.

(7) In this section—

"associated company" shall be construed in accordance with section 416 of the Taxes Act 1988;

"long term insurance business" means insurance business of any of the classes specified in Schedule 1 to the Insurance Companies Act 1982; and

"published index of prices" means the retail prices index or any similar general index of prices which is published by, or by an agent of, the government of any territory outside the United Kingdom.

(8) In sections 63 to 66 of the Finance Act 1993 as they apply by virtue of this section "the creditor company" means the company identified in subsection (1) above as the person entitled to the debt.

(9) In sections 63 to 66 of the Finance Act 1993 as they apply by virtue of this section "the commencement date" means—

(a) in relation to a debt not falling within subsection (10) below, 29th November 1994; and

(b) in relation to a debt falling within that subsection, 1st April 1996.

(10) A debt falls within this subsection if the person liable for it is—

(a) an institution which is a higher education institution for the purposes of section 65 of the Further and Higher Education Act 1992 or Article 30 of the Education and Libraries (Northern Ireland) Order 1993,

(b) an institution which is an institution within the higher education sector for the purposes of the Further and Higher Education (Scotland) Act 1992, or

(c) a registered housing association within the meaning of the Housing Associations Act 1985 or Part II of the Housing (Northern Ireland) Order 1992,

and that person was so liable at the end of 28th November 1994.

GENERAL NOTE

The section extends the existing charge in FA 1993, ss.63–66 (as generalised by s.88 above), to certain debts offering a deferred return and held by associates of companies carrying on a U.K. banking business. Such returns are brought into charge each year as they accrue.

Subs. (1)

The charge treats the debts as disposed of and reacquired at the end of each accounting period. This brings accrued returns on the debt into charge to tax, subject to transitional provisions for debts entered into before Budget Day 1994.

Subs. (2)

Debts held for the purposes of long term insurance business (of which life insurance business is the predominant sub-category) are excluded.

Subss. (3)–(6)

These define what character of debts are covered by the new charge. Debts are excluded if:

(i) they carry interest at a fixed rate, at a rate which is tied to a benchmark rate, or at a rate tied to a price index;

(ii) the interest is payable at intervals of not more than a year; and

(iii) they are not on deep discount or deep gain terms, *i.e.* not redeemable for an amount significantly higher than the original consideration.

Subs. (7)
This provides definitions.

Subs. (8)
The section is linked to the existing charging provisions mentioned in subs. (1) above.

Subss. (9) and (10)
The new charge is brought into effect from Budget Day 1994. However, the charge is postponed to April 1, 1996 in the case of higher education institutions or registered housing associations. The latter concession was introduced by the Government in Standing Committee in response to concerns expressed on behalf of such organisations which had used this mode of financing.

Reliefs

Relief for post-cessation expenditure

90.—(1) In Chapter VI of Part IV of the Taxes Act 1988 (provisions relating to the Schedule D charge: discontinuance, &c.), after section 109 insert—

"Relief for post-cessation expenditure

Relief for post-cessation expenditure
109A.—(1) Where in connection with a trade, profession or vocation formerly carried on by him which has been permanently discontinued a person makes, within seven years of the discontinuance, a payment to which this section applies, he may, by notice given within twelve months from the 31st January next following the year of assessment in which the payment is made, claim relief from income tax on an amount of his income for that year equal to the amount of the payment.

(2) This section applies to payments made wholly and exclusively—
(a) in remedying defective work done, goods supplied or services rendered in the course of the former trade, profession or vocation or by way of damages (whether awarded or agreed) in respect of any such defective work, goods or services; or
(b) in defraying the expenses of legal or other professional services in connection with any claim that work done, goods supplied or services rendered in the course of the former trade, profession or vocation was or were defective;
(c) in insuring against any liabilities arising out of any such claim or against the incurring of such expenses; or
(d) for the purpose of collecting a debt taken into account in computing the profits or gains of the former trade, profession or vocation.

(3) Where a payment of any of the above descriptions is made in circumstances such that relief under this section is available, the following shall be treated as sums to which section 103 applies (whether or not they would be so treated apart from this subsection)—
(a) in the case of a payment within paragraph (a) or (b) of subsection (2) above, any sum received, by way of the proceeds of insurance or otherwise, for the purpose of enabling the payment to be made or by means of which it is reimbursed,
(b) in the case of a payment within paragraph (c) of that subsection, any sum (not falling within paragraph (a) above) received by way of refund of premium or otherwise in connection with the insurance, and
(c) in the case of a payment within paragraph (d) of that subsection, any sum received to meet the costs of collecting the debt;
and no deduction shall be made under section 105 in respect of any such sums.

Where such a sum is received in a year of assessment earlier than that in which the related payment is made, it shall be treated as having been received in that later year and not in the earlier year; and any such adjustment shall be made, by way of modification of any assessment or discharge or repayment of tax, as is required to give effect to this subsection.

(4) Where a trade, profession or vocation carried on by a person has been permanently discontinued and subsequently an unpaid debt which was taken into account in computing the profits or gains of that trade, profession or vocation and to the benefit of which he is entitled—

(a) is proved to be bad, or

(b) is released, in whole or in part, as part of a relevant arrangement or compromise (within the meaning of section 74),

he shall be treated as making a payment to which this section applies of an amount equal to the amount of the debt or, as the case may be, the amount released or, if he was entitled to only part of the benefit of the debt, to an appropriate proportion of that amount.

If any sum is subsequently received by him in payment of a debt for which relief has been given by virtue of this subsection, the sum shall be treated as one to which section 103 applies; and no deduction shall be made under section 105 in respect of any such sum.

(5) Where in the case of a trade, profession or vocation which has subsequently been permanently discontinued a deduction was made in computing the profits or losses of the trade, profession or vocation in respect of an expense not actually paid (an "unpaid expense"), then—

(a) if relief under this section in connection with that trade, profession or vocation is claimed in respect of any year of assessment, the amount of the relief shall be reduced by the amount of any unpaid expenses at the end of that year;

(b) for the purposes of the application of paragraph (a) above in relation to a subsequent year of assessment, any amount by which relief under this section has been reduced by virtue of that paragraph shall be treated as having been paid in respect of the expense in question; and

(c) if subsequently any amount is in fact paid in respect of an expense in respect of which a reduction has been made under paragraph (a), that amount (or, if less, the amount of the reduction) shall be treated as a payment to which this section applies.

(6) Relief shall not be given under this section in respect of an amount for which relief has been given or is available under any other provision of the Income Tax Acts.

In applying this subsection relief available under section 105 shall be treated as given in respect of other amounts before any amount in respect of which relief is available under this section.

(7) This section does not apply for the purposes of corporation tax.".

(2) Section 109A(1) of the Taxes Act 1988 (inserted by subsection (1) above) has effect as respects the years 1994–95 and 1995–96 with the substitution for the words "twelve months from 31st January next following" of the words "two years after".

(3) In section 110(1) of the Taxes Act 1988 (interpretation, &c.) for "sections 103 to 109" substitute "sections 103 to 109A".

(4) Where under section 109A of the Taxes Act 1988 (inserted by subsection (1) above) a person makes a claim for relief for a year of assessment in respect of an amount which is available for relief under that section, he may in the notice by which the claim is made make a claim to have so much of that amount as cannot be set off against his income for the year (the "excess relief") treated for the purposes of capital gains tax as an allowable loss accruing to him in that year.

(5) No relief shall be available by virtue of subsection (4) above in respect of so much of the excess relief as exceeds the amount on which the claimant

would be chargeable to capital gains tax for that year if the following (and the effect of that subsection) were disregarded—

    (a) any allowable losses falling to be carried forward to that year from a previous year for the purposes of section 2(2) of the Taxation of Chargeable Gains Act 1992;

    (b) section 3(1) of that Act (the annual exempt amount); and

    (c) any relief against capital gains tax under section 72 of the Finance Act 1991 (deduction of trading losses).

(6) In section 105(2) of the Taxes Act 1988 (deductions allowed against post-cessation receipts: exclusion of amounts allowed elsewhere), after "any other provision of the Tax Acts" insert "or by virtue of section 90(4) of the Finance Act 1995".

(7) This section has effect in relation to payments made or treated as made (see subsection (4) of section 109A of the Taxes Act 1988 inserted by subsection (1) above) on or after 29th November 1994.

GENERAL NOTE

The new ICTA 1988, s.109A provides relief for expenditure, such as professional indemnity insurance premiums, paid by individuals after a trade or profession has ceased. The relief is to be set against income and capital gains of the year in which the expenditure is paid.

Section 109A(1)

The payment must be made not more than seven years after the discontinuance and must be claimed within 12 months from January 31 following the year of assessment in which the payment is made.

Section 109A(2)

The relief is restricted to payments in respect of defective work etc., legal expenses in connection with claims in respect of such work, insuring against such claims or expenses, and debt collection.

Section 109A(3)

Payments in respect of proceeds or refund of insurance or the costs of debt collection are brought into charge under ICTA 1988, s.103.

Section 109A(4)

Bad debts are brought within the scope of the new relief, subject to recharge if they are later recovered.

Section 109A(5)

Where an unpaid expense has been allowed before discontinuance, relief under s.109A is reduced by the amount unpaid. If it is then subsequently paid, the payment will be treated as an expense within the new relief.

Section 109A(6)

Double relief is excluded and relief under s.105 takes priority over s.109A.

Section 109A(7)

Section 109A does not apply to companies.

Further provisions are made as follows:

    (i) claims for the new relief for 1994/95 and 1995/96 must be made within two years rather than 12 months;

    (ii) relief which cannot be set against income may be set against capital gains, provided that it cannot exceed the capital gains themselves, any losses brought forward, the annual exemption and any relief for trading losses;

    (iii) expenditure allowed under this section cannot be allowed under ICTA 1988, s.105;

    (iv) the changes take effect from Budget Day.

Employee liabilities and indemnity insurance

91.—(1) After section 201 of the Taxes Act 1988 there shall be inserted the following section—

"Employee liabilities and indemnity insurance
201AA.—(1) Subject to the provisions of this section, the following
may be deducted from the emoluments of any office or employment to
be assessed to tax, if defrayed out of those emoluments, that is to say—
- (a) any amount paid in or towards the discharge of a qualifying liability of the person who is the holder of the office or employment;
- (b) costs or expenses incurred in connection with any claim that that
person is subject to such a liability or with any proceedings relating to or arising out of such a claim; and
- (c) so much (if any) of any premium paid under a qualifying contract
of insurance as relates to the indemnification of that person
against a qualifying liability or to the payment of any such costs or
expenses.

(2) For the purposes of this section a liability is a qualifying liability, in
relation to any office or employment, if it is imposed either—
- (a) in respect of any acts or omissions of a person in his capacity as the
holder of that office or employment or in any other capacity in
which he acts in the performance of the duties of that office or
employment; or
- (b) in connection with any proceedings relating to or arising out of a
claim that a person is subject to a liability imposed in respect of
any such acts or omissions.

(3) For the purposes of this section a qualifying contract of insurance
is a contract of insurance which—
- (a) so far as the risks insured against are concerned, relates exclusively to one or more of the matters mentioned in subsection (4)
below;
- (b) is not connected with any other contract;
- (c) does not contain provision entitling the insured, in addition to
cover for the risks insured against and any right to renew the policy, to receive any payment or other benefit the entitlement to
which is something to which a significant part of the premium
under the contract is reasonably attributable; and
- (d) is a contract the period of insurance under which does not exceed
two years (except by virtue of one or more renewals each for a
period of two years or less) and is not a contract which the insured
is required to renew for any period.

(4) The matters referred to in subsection (3)(a) above in relation to
any contract of insurance are the following, that is to say—
- (a) the indemnification of any person holding any office or employment against any qualifying liability;
- (b) the indemnification of any person against any vicarious liability in
respect of acts or omissions giving rise, in the case of another, to
such a qualifying liability;
- (c) the payment of some or all of the costs or expenses incurred by or
on behalf of that or any other person in connection with any claim
that a person is subject to a liability to which the insurance relates
or with any proceedings relating to or arising out of such a claim;
and
- (d) the indemnification of any person against any loss from the payment by him (whether or not in discharge of any liability) to a
person holding an office or employment under him of any amount
in respect of a qualifying liability or of any such costs or expenses.

(5) For the purposes of this section a contract of insurance is connected with another contract at any time at or after the time when they have
both been entered into if—
- (a) either of them was entered into by reference to the other or with a
view to enabling the other to be entered into on particular terms

or to facilitating the other being entered into on particular terms; and

(b) the terms on which either of them was entered into would have been significantly different if it had not been entered into in anticipation of the other being entered into or if the other had not also been entered into.

(6) Two or more contracts of insurance shall not be prevented by virtue of paragraph (b) of subsection (3) above from being qualifying contracts if—

(a) they each satisfy the requirements of paragraphs (a), (c) and (d) of that subsection; and

(b) the only respects in which there is a significant difference between the terms on which any of those contracts is entered into and what would have been those terms if the other contract or contracts had not been entered into consist in such reductions of premium as are reasonably attributable to—

(i) the fact that, where different contracts have been entered into as part of a single transaction, the premium under each of the contracts has been fixed by reference to the appropriate proportion of what would have been the premium under a single contract relating to all the risks covered by the different contracts; or

(ii) the fact that the contract in question contains a right to renew or is entered into by way of renewal or in pursuance of such a right.

(7) For the purpose of determining the different parts of any premium under any contract of insurance which are to be treated for the purposes of this section as paid in respect of the different risks, different persons and different offices and employments to which the contract relates, such apportionment of that premium shall be made as may be reasonable.

(8) Where it would be unlawful for a person under whom any other person holds any office or employment to enter into a contract of insurance in respect of liabilities of any description or in respect of costs or expenses of any description, no deduction may be made under this section in respect of—

(a) the discharge of any liability of that other person which is a liability of that description; or

(b) any costs or expenses incurred by or on behalf of that other person which are costs or expenses of that description.

(9) References in this section to a premium, in relation to a contract of insurance, are references to any amount payable under the contract to the insurer."

(2) In sections 141(3), 142(2), 153(2) and 156(8) of that Act (which make provision, in relation to non-cash vouchers, credit-tokens, expenses and benefits in kind, about amounts which would have been deductible under certain provisions if paid out of a person's emoluments), after "201", in each case, there shall be inserted "201AA".

(3) This section has effect for the year 1995–96 and subsequent years of assessment.

GENERAL NOTE

The new ICTA 1988, s.201AA introduces a deduction for employees who incur expenditure on indemnity insurance or on certain liabilities such as legal costs relating to their work. It also permits an off-setting deduction against any charge on an employee where such expenditure is met by the employer.

Section 201AA(1)
This permits the deduction by the employee of amounts relating to a "qualifying liability".

Section 201AA(2)
"Qualifying liability" is defined. It relates to a liability in respect of acts or omissions or claims arising out of them incurred in the course of employment.

Section 201AA(3)
"Qualifying contract of insurance", which is covered under s.201AA(1), is defined. The insurance must not be connected with any other (see s.201AA(5)), must not provide for benefits other than the indemnity cover and must not exceed two years. The scope of the insurance is explained in s.201AA(4).

Section 201AA(4)
The risks which may be covered are indemnification for qualifying liabilities (see s.201AA (2)), and for vicarious liability, payments of costs and expenses in connection with claims and indemnification for losses incurred by an employer.

Section 201AA(5)
"Connected" is defined (see s.201AA(3)). Insurances are connected if, without the first, the second would not have been entered into on particular terms, or if the terms of either would have been significantly different without the other. The foregoing condition is modified by s.201AA(6).

Section 201AA(6)
Insurances are not prevented from qualifying if they satisfy the other conditions of s.201AA(3) and if the differences arising from the connection are a reduction in premium attributable to a proportionate distribution of risks or the existence of a right to renew.

Section 201AA(7)
Premiums may be apportioned where appropriate.

Section 201AA(8)
Unlawful expenditures, *e.g.* costs arising from criminal convictions, cannot be deducted.

Section 201AA(9)
"Premium" is any amount payable under the contract to the insurer.
Provision is also made, by means of amendment of ICTA 1988, to ensure a deduction from any liability to tax where expenditure allowable under the new s.201AA is met by the employer.

Post-employment deductions

92.—(1) Subject to the following provisions of this section, where any individual who has held any office or employment ("the former employee") defrays any amount to which this section applies, he shall be entitled, on making a claim for the purpose, to a deduction of that amount in computing, for income tax purposes, his total income for the year of assessment in which that amount is defrayed.

(2) This section applies to any amount defrayed by the former employee where that amount—
  (a) is defrayed by him in the period beginning when he ceased to hold the relevant office or employment and ending with the sixth year of assessment after that in which he ceased to hold it; and
  (b) is not deductible in pursuance of section 201AA of the Taxes Act 1988 from the emoluments of that office or employment to be assessed for tax but would be so deductible if—
      (i) the former employee had continued to hold that office or employment, and
      (ii) that amount had been defrayed out of the emoluments of that office or employment for the year of assessment in which it is in fact defrayed.

(3) In determining for the purposes of subsection (2) above whether any amount would be deductible as mentioned in paragraph (b) of that subsec-

tion, the assumption in sub-paragraph (i) of that paragraph shall be disregarded when identifying the liabilities which are to be regarded as qualifying liabilities within the meaning of section 201AA of the Taxes Act 1988.

(4) This section shall not apply to any amount defrayed by the former employee in so far as the cost of defraying that amount, without being met out of his relevant retirement benefits or post-employment emoluments, is borne—
  (a) by the person under whom he held the relevant office or employment;
  (b) by a person for the time being carrying on the whole or any part of the business or other undertaking for the purposes of which the former employee held that office or employment;
  (c) by a person who is for the time being subject to any of the liabilities with respect to that business or other undertaking of the person mentioned in paragraph (a) above;
  (d) by a person who within the terms of section 839 of the Taxes Act 1988 is connected with a person falling within any of paragraphs (a) to (c) above; or
  (e) out of the proceeds of any contract of insurance relating to the matters in respect of which the amount is defrayed.

(5) In so far as the amount of any expenditure which is either—
  (a) defrayed by any person mentioned in subsection (4)(a) to (d) above, or
  (b) borne as mentioned in subsection (4)(a) to (e) above,
is an amount which falls to be treated as a relevant retirement benefit or post-employment emolument of the former employee, that amount shall be deemed for the purposes of this section to be an amount defrayed by the former employee out of that benefit or emolument.

(6) Subject to subsection (7) below, if an amount to which this section applies exceeds by any amount ("the excess relief") the amount from which it is deductible in accordance with subsection (1) above, the former employee shall be entitled, on making a claim for the purpose, to have the amount of the excess relief treated for the purposes of capital gains tax as an allowable loss accruing to that person for that year of assessment.

(7) No relief shall be available by virtue of this section in respect of so much of the excess relief for any year of assessment as exceeds the maximum amount.

(8) For the purposes of subsection (7) above the maximum amount, in relation to the excess relief for any year of assessment, is the amount on which the claimant would be chargeable to capital gains tax for that year if the following (together with any relief available under this section) were disregarded, that is to say—
  (a) any allowable losses falling to be carried forward to that year from a previous year for the purposes of section 2(2) of the Taxation of Chargeable Gains Act 1992;
  (b) section 3(1) of that Act (the annual exempt amount); and
  (c) any relief against capital gains tax under section 72 of the Finance Act 1991 (deduction of trading losses) or under section 90(4) of this Act.

(9) In this section—
  "post-employment emolument", in relation to the former employee, means so much of any amount as, having been received when the relevant office or employment is no longer held by the former employee, is treated for the purposes of the Income Tax Acts as an emolument of that office or employment;
  "the relevant office or employment", in relation to the former employee, means the office or employment in respect of which he is the former employee; and
  "relevant retirement benefit", in relation to the former employee, means so much of any amount as, in accordance with section 596A

of the Taxes Act 1988, is chargeable to tax as a benefit received by him under a retirement benefits scheme of which he is a member in respect of the relevant office or employment.

(10) Tax shall not be charged under section 148 of the Taxes Act 1988 (payments on retirement or removal from office or employment) in respect of any payment made or treated as made to any individual, or to any individual's executors or administrators, in so far as the payment is made for meeting the cost of defraying any amount which, without being an amount to which this section applies in relation to that individual, would fall to be treated as such an amount if—

(a) subsection (4) of this section were omitted; and

(b) where that individual has died, he had not died but had himself defrayed any amounts defrayed by his executors or administrators;

and this subsection shall have effect in the case of any valuable consideration that is deemed under section 148(3) to be a payment as if the consideration were deemed, to the extent that it is or represents a benefit equivalent to meeting the cost of defraying such an amount, to be a payment made for meeting such a cost.

(11) This section applies for the year 1995–96 and subsequent years of assessment.

GENERAL NOTE

A deduction is allowed to former employees who bear the cost of indemnity insurance or certain liabilities such as legal costs relating to their former employment. The deduction is given in computing total income for the tax year in which the amount is paid.

Subs. (2)

The amount must be paid within six years after the end of the tax year in which the employment ceased and must have otherwise qualified for relief under ICTA 1988, s.201AA (see s.91 above).

Subs. (3)

Only liabilities arising when the employment actually existed may be taken into account.

Subs. (4)

A deduction is not allowed where the amount is not ultimately paid by the former employee but is borne instead by other specified persons, such as the former employer, or out of the proceeds of an insurance contract.

Subs. (5)

Where the amount is defrayed under subs. (4), a deduction is allowed to prevent a charge on the ex-employee.

Subss. (6)–(8)

Amounts not relieved against income may be relieved against capital gains in that year, subject to a maximum, defined as the chargeable gains for the year before deducting capital losses brought forward, the annual exempt amount, or relief under FA 1991, s.72 or under s.90(4) above.

Subs. (9)

Various definitions are provided.

Subs. (10)

The "golden handshake" provisions are disapplied for the purposes of this section.

Incidental overnight expenses etc.

93.—(1) In section 141 of the Taxes Act 1988 (non-cash vouchers), after subsection (6B) there shall be inserted the following subsections—

"(6C) Subsection (1) above shall not apply in relation to a non-cash voucher to the extent that it is used by the employee to obtain goods, services or money where—

(a) obtaining the goods or services is incidental to his being away from his usual place of abode during a qualifying absence from home or, as the case may be, the money is obtained for the purpose of being used to obtain goods or services which would be so incidental;

(b) the authorised maximum is not exceeded in relation to that qualifying absence; and

(c) the cost of obtaining the goods or services would not be deductible as mentioned in subsection (3) above if incurred by the employee out of his emoluments.

(6D) Subsections (3) to (5) of section 200A shall apply as they apply for the purposes of that section for construing the references in subsection (6C) above to a qualifying absence from home and for determining, for the purposes of that subsection, whether the authorised maximum is exceeded."

(2) In section 142 of that Act (credit-tokens), after subsection (3B) there shall be inserted the following subsections—

"(3C) Subsection (1) above shall not apply in relation to a credit-token to the extent that it is used by the employee to obtain goods, services or money where—

(a) obtaining the goods or services is incidental to his being away from his usual place of abode during a qualifying absence from home or, as the case may be, the money is obtained for the purpose of being used to obtain goods or services which would be so incidental;

(b) the authorised maximum is not exceeded in relation to that qualifying absence; and

(c) the cost of obtaining the goods or services would not be deductible as mentioned in subsection (2) above if incurred by the employee out of his emoluments.

(3D) Subsections (3) to (5) of section 200A shall apply as they apply for the purposes of that section for construing the references in subsection (3C) above to a qualifying absence from home and for determining, for the purposes of that subsection, whether the authorised maximum is exceeded."

(3) In section 155 of that Act (exceptions from general charge on benefits in kind for persons in director's or higher-paid employment), after subsection (1A) there shall be inserted the following subsections—

"(1B) Section 154 does not apply in the case of a benefit provided for the employee himself where—

(a) the provision of the benefit is incidental to the employee's being away from his usual place of abode during a qualifying absence from home;

(b) the authorised maximum is not exceeded in relation to that qualifying absence; and

(c) the cost of the benefit would not be deductible as mentioned in section 156(8) if incurred by the employee out of his emoluments.

(1C) Subsections (3) to (5) of section 200A shall apply as they apply for the purposes of that section for construing the references in subsection (1B) above to a qualifying absence from home and for determining, for the purposes of that subsection, whether the authorised maximum is exceeded."

(4) After section 200 of that Act there shall be inserted the following section—

"Incidental overnight expenses
200A.—(1) Subject to subsection (2) below, sums paid to or on behalf of any person holding an office or employment, to the extent that they

are paid wholly and exclusively for the purpose of defraying, or of being used for defraying, any expenses which—

    (a) are incidental to that person's being away from his usual place of abode during a qualifying absence from home, but

    (b) would not be deductible under section 193, 194, 195, 198 or 332 if incurred out of that person's emoluments,

shall not be regarded as emoluments of the office or employment for any purpose of Schedule E.

(2) Subsection (1) above shall not apply in the case of any qualifying absence in relation to which the authorised maximum is exceeded.

(3) For the purposes of this section a qualifying absence from home, in relation to a person holding an office or employment, is any continuous period throughout which that person is obliged to stay away from his usual place of abode and during which he—

    (a) has at least one overnight stay away from that place; but

    (b) does not on any occasion stay overnight at a place other than a place the expenses of travelling to which are either—

        (i) expenses incurred out of his emoluments and deductible, otherwise than by virtue of section 193(4), 194(2) or 195(6), under any of the provisions mentioned in subsection (1)(b) above, or

        (ii) expenses which would be so deductible if so incurred.

(4) In this section 'the authorised maximum', in relation to each qualifying absence from home by any person, means the aggregate amount equal to the sum of the following amounts—

    (a) £5 for every night (if any) during that absence which is a night the whole of which is spent by that person in the United Kingdom; and

    (b) £10 for every night (if any) during that absence which is a night the whole or any part of which is spent by that person outside the United Kingdom.

(5) For the purposes of this section the authorised maximum is exceeded in relation to a qualifying absence from home by any person if that maximum is exceeded by the amount which, in the absence of subsection (2) above and of the other requirements of this Act that that maximum is not exceeded, would fall by virtue of this section and sections 141(6C), 142(3C) and 155(1B) to be disregarded, in relation to that qualifying absence, in determining the amount of that person's emoluments.

(6) The Treasury may by order increase either or both of the sums for the time being specified in subsection (4)(a) and (b) above; and such an order shall have effect for determining what emoluments are received by any person on or after the date when the order comes into force."

(5) This section shall have effect for determining what emoluments are received by any person on or after 6th April 1995.

GENERAL NOTE

The section makes a minor concession by exempting from tax payments by employers for employees' incidental expenses when they stay away from home overnight on business, up to a limit of £5 per night in the U.K. and £10 per night overseas. The type of expenditure envisaged is telephone calls home.

Subs. (1)

The new ICTA 1988, s.141(6C) and (6D) take out of charge the use of non-cash vouchers to cover incidental expenses.

Subs. (2)

The new ICTA 1988, s.142(3C) and (3D) similarly exempt the use of credit-tokens, such as credit cards, to cover such expenses.

The new ICTA 1988, s.155(1B) and (1C) takes the incidental expenses out of charge under the benefit in kind provisions.

Subs. (4)
The new ICTA 1988, s.200A contains the substance of the exemption. The exemption applies to incidental expenses incurred during a business trip which includes at least one night away from home. The limit of £5 per night in the U.K. and £10 per night overseas applies to total payments by an employer, adding together cash, non-cash vouchers, credit-tokens and the value of benefits. The £5 and £10 limits may be increased by Treasury order.

Capital allowances: ships

Deferment of balancing charges in respect of ships

94. In Chapter II of Part II of the Capital Allowances Act 1990 (ships); after section 33 there shall be inserted the following sections—

"Balancing charges in respect of ship disposals etc.

Deferment of balancing charge

33A.—(1) This section applies in any case where—
(a) a balancing charge of any amount would, apart from this section, be made for any chargeable period ('the relevant period') on any person ('the shipowner') in respect of a trade carried on by him (his 'actual trade');
(b) there is, in the relevant period, an event falling within section 24(6)(c)(i) to (iii);
(c) that event is one occurring on or after 21st April 1994 with respect to a ship ('the old ship') provided by the shipowner for the purposes of his actual trade and belonging to him at some time in the relevant period;
(d) the old ship was a qualifying ship immediately before that event;
(e) the shipowner's expenditure on the provision of the old ship is not expenditure treated for any purposes by virtue of section 41(2), 61(1), 79(2) or 80(5) as expenditure incurred for the purposes of a trade carried on separately from his actual trade; and
(f) the old ship has not begun, and is not treated as having begun, before the event mentioned in paragraph (b) above, to be used partly, but not wholly, for purposes other than those of the shipowner's actual trade.

(2) If—
(a) the shipowner makes a claim in respect of the event mentioned in subsection (1)(b) above for the deferment under this section of the whole or part of the charge which would be made on him, and
(b) none of the amounts specified in subsection (3) below is nil,
the amount for which deferment is claimed, so far as it does not exceed the smallest of those amounts, shall for the purposes of sections 24, 25 and 26 be added to the shipowner's qualifying expenditure for the relevant period in respect of his actual trade.

(3) Subject to the following provisions of this section, those amounts are—
(a) the amount which, in accordance with section 33B, is treated as brought into account in respect of the old ship;
(b) the amount of expenditure which is or is to be incurred by the shipowner on new shipping in the period of six years beginning with the day on which the event mentioned in subsection (1)(b) above occurs;

(c) the amount of the balancing charge which, apart only from the claim in question, would be made on the shipowner for the relevant period in respect of his actual trade; and

(d) the amount which, on the assumption—

(i) that any other additions under this section to the shipowner's qualifying expenditure for the relevant period are taken into account, but

(ii) that amounts carried forward under section 385 or 393 of the principal Act (losses carried forward) are disregarded,

would have the effect of reducing to nil the amount (if any) falling to be taken into account, in computing the shipowner's total profits or total income for that period, as the trading income of that trade or, as the case may be, as profits or gains arising from that trade.

(4) If—

(a) an addition is made under this section to the shipowner's qualifying expenditure for the relevant period in respect of his actual trade, but

(b) the shipowner does not, in the period of six years mentioned in subsection (3)(b) above, incur expenditure on new shipping of an amount equal to or exceeding the addition,

the shipowner shall be assumed not to have been entitled to so much of the addition as exceeds the amount in fact incurred.

(5) Where an addition is made under this section to the shipowner's qualifying expenditure for the relevant period in respect of his actual trade, so much of the expenditure incurred or to be incurred by the shipowner on new shipping, being expenditure of an amount equal to the addition, as for the purposes of subsection (3)(b) or (4) above is (in accordance with section 33D(6)) either—

(a) identified by the shipowner in his claim or by notice to the inspector as the expenditure to which the addition is to be attributed, or

(b) in default of being so identified by the shipowner, determined by the inspector to be the expenditure to which that addition is to be attributed,

shall be disregarded for the purposes of subsections (3)(b) and (4) above in determining the shipowner's entitlement to any other addition under this section to his qualifying expenditure for any period.

(6) A balancing charge falling by virtue of section 41(2), 79(5) or 80(5) to be made for the relevant period in the case of the shipowner's actual trade shall be disregarded in determining the amount referred to in subsection (3)(c) above.

(7) In consequence of paragraph (d) of subsection (3) above, no addition shall be made under this section to the shipowner's qualifying expenditure for the relevant period in respect of his actual trade if—

(a) the amount falling (after disregarding any amounts carried forward under section 385 or 393 of the principal Act) to be taken into account as mentioned in that paragraph would have been nil even apart from this section, or

(b) he has, apart from this section, incurred a loss in that trade for the relevant period.

Amount brought into account in respect of the old ship

33B.—(1) For the purposes of section 33A where—

(a) the old ship is, by virtue of section 31(2), assumed for the purposes of sections 24, 25 and 26 to have been provided wholly and exclusively for the purposes of a single ship trade,

(b) in consequence of the event mentioned in section 33A(1)(b), a disposal value of the old ship falls for the purposes of section

31(7) to be brought into account for the chargeable period of the single ship trade which corresponds to the relevant period, and

(c) no notice has been given in relation to the single ship trade under section 33(1) or (4),

the amount treated as brought into account in respect of the old ship shall be the amount which under section 31(7)(b) falls to be brought into account for the relevant period of the shipowner's actual trade as an item of disposal value referable to machinery or plant.

(2) In any other case, the amount treated as brought into account in respect of the old ship shall be the amount equal to the amount which, on the assumptions specified in subsection (3) below, would have been the balancing charge for the relevant period in respect of the shipowner's actual trade.

(3) Those assumptions are—

(a) that section 31(2) did not apply with respect to expenditure on the provision of the old ship;

(b) that the old ship was the only item of machinery or plant in respect of which sections 24, 25 and 26 have effect for chargeable periods of the shipowner's actual trade; and

(c) that the allowances made to the shipowner in respect of the provision of the old ship are—

(i) the first-year allowance (if any) which was actually made to the shipowner;

(ii) any first-year allowance falling to be made to him that was postponed under section 30(1)(a) or (c); and

(iii) the maximum amount of any writing-down allowances which, on the preceding assumptions, could have been made for the chargeable periods of that trade ending with the relevant period.

(4) Where a notice under section 33(1) or (4) is given in the case of a single ship trade after the determination for the purposes of section 33A of the amount treated as brought into account in respect of the old ship, subsection (2) above, instead of subsection (1), shall apply, and be deemed always to have applied, in relation to that ship.

(5) In this section and the following provisions of this Chapter 'single ship trade' has the same meaning as in section 31."

GENERAL NOTE

The purpose of the amendments made to the Capital Allowances Act 1990 (CAA) by this section is to encourage the British shipping industry by deferring the balancing charge on the disposal of ships where the proceeds are reinvested within six years. The relief generally applies from April 21, 1994, when it was announced by the Chancellor.

Section 33A

The new CAA 1990, s.33A provides for the deferment.

Subs. (1)

A deferment may be claimed where a balancing charge arises as the result of the ship ceasing to belong to the shipowner, or of his losing possession of it permanently, or of its ceasing to exist on or after April 21, 1994, provided it belonged to him at some time in the relevant period and was used for the purposes of his trade. For the categories of ships which qualify, see the new CAA 1990, s.33E, inserted by s.96 below. The charge may not be deferred where the ship is leased for a non-qualifying purpose, is leased outside the U.K. or otherwise than by way of trade, is used partly for non-trade purposes, or receives a subsidy towards wear and tear.

Subs. (2)

Amounts deferred may be added to the shipowner's expenditure under the rules in CAA 1990, ss.24–26.

Subs. (3)

The charge which may be deferred is limited to the smallest of the following amounts:
(i) the balancing charge attributable to the old ship;
(ii) expenditure on new shipping in the next six years;
(iii) the balancing charge arising on the actual trade for that period; and
(iv) the amount needed to reduce the trading profit of the year to nil.

Subs. (4)

Relief is withdrawn if the shipowner does not in fact make the expenditure within the six-year period.

Subs. (5)

This provides a mechanism to prevent expenditure on a new ship from qualifying for capital allowances if it is needed to frank a deferred balancing charge.

Subs. (6)

A balancing charge arising from the disposal of the ship is to be disregarded in establishing the balancing charge referred to in subs. (3) above.

Subs. (7)

The relief may not be used to create or augment a trading loss.

Section 33B

The new CAA 1990, s.33B identifies the balancing charge attributable to the old ship.

Subs. (1)

Where the old ship has been dealt with separately from all other assets under the "single ship" rule in CAA 1990, s.31, the balancing charge attributable to the ship is the charge which arises in the separate single ship pool.

Subss. (2)–(3)

In other cases, the balancing charge is computed on the assumption that the ship was the only asset in the general pool, that any first-year allowance actually claimed was taken and that the maximum amount of writing-down allowance available was taken.

Subs. (4)

Where expenditure on a ship in the single ship pool is subsequently transferred to the general machinery and plant pool, the balancing charge attributable to the ship on a later disposal follows the rules in subss. (2)–(3) above.

Reimposition of deferred charge

95. In Chapter II of Part II of the Capital Allowances Act 1990 (ships), after the sections inserted by section 94 above there shall be inserted the following section—

"Reimposition of deferred charge

33C.—(1) Notwithstanding anything in section 31(2), the assumption specified in subsection (2) below shall apply, for the purposes of sections 24, 25 and 26 wherever—
(a) an addition is made under section 33A to the shipowner's qualifying expenditure for the relevant period;
(b) the shipowner incurs expenditure on new shipping within the period mentioned in section 33A(3)(b); and
(c) an identification or determination of the whole or any part of the expenditure on new shipping is made as mentioned in section 33A(5) in relation to the whole or any part of the addition.

(2) That assumption is that an amount equal to so much of the expenditure incurred on new shipping as is expenditure to which the whole or any part of the addition is to be attributed is to be brought into account—
(a) for the chargeable period in which that expenditure is incurred, and

(b) in respect of the single ship trade in respect of which that expenditure falls to be taken into account in determining qualifying expenditure of the shipowner,

as an item of disposal value referable to machinery or plant which in respect of that chargeable period and that trade falls within section 24(6)."

GENERAL NOTE
The new CAA 1990, s.33C details the method for reimposing the deferred charge.

Section 33C(1)
The circumstances under which the assumptions referred to in s.33C(2) will apply to reimpose the charge are detailed. These are that a balancing charge has been deferred, the shipowner has incurred expenditure on a new ship within six years and the shipowner has identified, or the inspector has determined, the expenditure as falling within the deferment provisions.

Section 33C(2)
The assumptions which will trigger s.33C(1) are that expenditure on new shipping attributable to the deferred charge is brought into account as disposal value of plant or machinery and, in the case of a single ship trade, is taken into account in determining the qualifying expenditure (see CAA, s.25).

Ships in respect of which charge may be deferred

96. In Chapter II of Part II of the Capital Allowances Act 1990 (ships), after the section inserted by section 95 above there shall be inserted the following sections—

"Expenditure to which deferments attributed

33D.—(1) Subject to the following provisions of this section, expenditure is expenditure on new shipping for the purposes of sections 33A to 33C in so far as it is both—

(a) capital expenditure incurred on the provision, wholly and exclusively for the purposes of the shipowner's actual trade, of a ship which it appears—
 (i) will be brought into use for the purposes of that trade as a qualifying ship, and
 (ii) will continue to be a qualifying ship throughout a period of at least three years after that; and

(b) expenditure falling, by virtue of section 31(2), to be taken into account for the purposes of sections 24, 25 and 26, in determining qualifying expenditure, as an amount of expenditure incurred by the shipowner wholly and exclusively for the purposes of a single ship trade.

(2) Expenditure on the provision of a ship shall not be, and shall be deemed never to have been, expenditure on new shipping if the ship—

(a) is brought into use for the purposes of any trade of the shipowner or (without having been so brought into use) for the purposes of any trade of a person connected with him;

(b) there is a time after it is first so brought into use when that ship is not a qualifying ship; and

(c) that time is before whichever is the earlier of—
 (i) the end of the period of three years beginning with the time when it is first so brought into use, and
 (ii) the first occasion after the beginning of that period when neither the shipowner nor any person connected with him is a person to whom the ship belongs.

(3) Where—
(a) a notice under section 33(1) or (4) has the effect, in relation to any expenditure which satisfies the conditions in subsection (1)(a)

and (b) above, of requiring any of that expenditure to be attributed for the purposes of sections 24, 25 and 26 to a trade which is not a single ship trade, or

(b) section 42 has effect with respect to expenditure on the provision of a ship in a case where the expenditure would have fallen to be taken into account as mentioned in subsection (1)(b) above if the ship had not been leased as mentioned in section 42(1),

the expenditure which falls to be so attributed or, as the case may be, with respect to which section 42 has effect shall not be, and shall be deemed never to have been, expenditure on new shipping.

(4) Expenditure on the provision of a ship is not expenditure on new shipping if—

(a) the ship had already belonged to the shipowner at some time in the period of six years ending with the time when it first belongs to him in consequence of his incurring that expenditure;

(b) the ship has at any time in that period belonged to a person who has, at a material time, been a person connected with the ship-owner; or

(c) the main object, or one of the main objects, of—

(i) the transaction by which the ship was provided for the purposes of the shipowner's actual trade,

(ii) any series of transactions of which that transaction was one, or

(iii) any transaction in such a series,

was to secure the deferment of a charge under section 33A.

(5) In subsection (4)(b) above 'a material time', in relation to any expenditure, means the time when the expenditure is incurred or any earlier time in the period of six years which is applicable in the case in question for the purposes of section 33A(3)(b).

(6) An addition made under section 33A to the shipowner's qualifying expenditure for any period shall not for the purposes of that section or section 33C be attributed to the whole or any part of any expenditure on new shipping if there is other expenditure incurred by the shipowner which—

(a) was incurred before that expenditure in the period of six years which is applicable, in the case of that addition, for the purposes of section 33A(3)(b), and

(b) is expenditure on new shipping or would fall to be treated as such expenditure but for any notice under section 33(1) or (4),

unless the whole amount of the other expenditure has been used for the purposes of attributions made in the case of that addition and of any other additions made under section 33A in respect of events occurring before the beginning of that period of six years.

(7) Notwithstanding any changes in the persons engaged in carrying on any trade previously carried on by the shipowner, expenditure shall be treated for the purposes of this Chapter as incurred by the shipowner if—

(a) it is incurred by the persons for the time being carrying on that trade, and

(b) the only changes in the persons so engaged, between the time when the trade was carried on by the shipowner and the time when the expenditure is incurred, are changes in respect of which that trade is to be treated by virtue of section 113(2) or 343(2) of the principal Act (continuity of trade) as not having been discontinued.

(8) For the purposes of this section a person is connected with the shipowner at any time if—

(a) at that time he is, within the terms of section 839 of the principal Act, connected either with the shipowner or with a person who is connected with the shipowner by virtue of paragraph (b) below, or

(b) any expenditure incurred by him at that time would fall, by virtue of subsection (7) above, to be; treated as expenditure incurred by the shipowner.

Qualifying ships

33E.—(1) Subject to the following provisions of this section, a ship is a qualifying ship for the purposes of sections 33A to 33D if it is a ship of a sea-going kind and is registered, in any register of shipping established and maintained under the law of the United Kingdom or of any other country or territory, as a ship with a gross tonnage of or in excess of 100 tons.

(2) In any case where the event mentioned in section 33A(1)(b) consists in or results from either—

(a) the total loss of the old ship, or

(b) damage to the old ship that puts it in a condition in which it is impossible, or not commercially worthwhile, for the repair required for restoring it to its previous use to be undertaken,

the references to a qualifying ship in section 33A(1)(d) and section 33D(1) and (2) shall have effect as if in subsection (1) above the words 'as a ship with a gross tonnage of or in excess of 100 tons' were omitted.

(3) A ship is not a qualifying ship if the primary use to which ships of the same kind as that ship are put by the persons to whom they belong or, where their use is made available to others, by those others is use for sport or recreation.

(4) A ship is not a qualifying ship at any time when—

(a) it is an offshore installation for the purposes of the Mineral Workings (Offshore Installations) Act 1971; or

(b) it would be such an installation if the activity for the carrying on of which it is or is to be established or maintained were carried on in or under controlled waters (within the meaning of that Act).

(5) Where, in the case of any ship which has been brought into use for the purposes of a trade of the shipowner or a person connected with him but was not so brought into use before 20th July 1994—

(a) there is a time in the qualifying period when the ship is not registered in a relevant register, and

(b) that time is more than three months after that period began,

the ship shall not, in relation to times after the time mentioned in paragraph (a) above, be a qualifying ship.

(6) In subsection (5) above 'the qualifying period' means the period between—

(a) the time when the ship is first brought into use for the purposes of any trade of the shipowner or (without having been so brought into use) for the purposes of any trade of a person connected with him; and

(b) whichever is the earlier of—

(i) the end of the period of three years beginning with that time, and

(ii) the first occasion after that time when neither the shipowner nor any person connected with him is a person to whom the ship belongs.

(7) In subsection (5) above 'relevant register', in relation to any ship, means any register of shipping established and maintained under the law of any part of the British Islands or of any country or territory which, at a time in the period which in the case of that ship is the qualifying

period for the purposes of that subsection, is a member State, another State within the European Economic Area or a colony.

(8) References in subsections (5) and (6) above to a person connected with the shipowner shall be construed in accordance with section 33D(8) but shall have effect in relation to the old ship as if a trade carried on at any time by any person were carried on at that time by a person so connected wherever—

    (a) it was subsequently carried on by the shipowner or a person connected with him; and

    (b) it underwent, between that time and the time when it was carried on by the shipowner or a person connected with him, only such changes in the persons engaged in carrying it on as are changes in respect of which it is to be treated by virtue of section 113(2) or 343(2) of the principal Act as not having been discontinued."

GENERAL NOTE

The new CAA 1990, ss.33D and 33E provide definitions of the expenditure to which the deferment of the balancing charge on ships is attributed and define a qualifying ship.

Section 33D

Subs. (1)

The expenditure must be incurred on a qualifying ship which will be used for the trade for at least three years and falls otherwise within CAA 1990, ss.24–26.

Subs. (2)

A new ship will not qualify if it previously belonged to the shipowner or a connected person, is not a qualifying ship during the three years from when it is brought into use or ceases to belong to the shipowner or a connected person.

Subs. (3)

Where expenditure satisfying the conditions in subs. (1) is attributed to a trade which is not a single ship trade or the ship is leased outside the U.K. such that the provisions of CAA 1990, s.42 apply, the expenditure shall be regarded as not being, and as never having been, expenditure on new shipping.

Subs. (4)

Relief is likewise denied where the ship had previously belonged to the shipowner or a connected person within the previous six years or where the main object of the acquisition is to secure a s.33A deferment.

Subs. (5)

The connected persons provision in subs. (4) bites within the six-year period.

Subs. (6)

A charge deferred under ss.33A or 33C may not be attributed to expenditure on new shipping where the shipowner has incurred earlier in the six-year period any expenditure on new shipping, or which would be such but for a notice under s.33(1) or (4), unless the earlier expenditure has already been attributed to that or an earlier deferred charge.

Subs. (7)

Expenditure is treated as having been incurred by the shipowner where it is incurred by the person carrying on the shipowner's trade and at the time of the expenditure the trade is not treated as having been discontinued.

Subs. (8)

The "connected persons" definition in ICTA 1988, s.839 applies.

Section 33E

The new CAA 1990, s.33E defines a qualifying ship.

Subs. (1)
A qualifying ship has a gross tonnage of at least 100 tons, is of a sea-going kind and is on a register of shipping.

Subs. (2)
The 100 ton limit does not apply where the old ship is lost or damaged beyond reasonable repair. This was inserted in Standing Committee to assist the fishing industry.

Subs. (3)
Ships of a type primarily used in sport or recreation are excluded.

Subs. (4)
Ships which are offshore installations are excluded.

Subs. (5)
The ship must be registered within three months from the start of the "qualifying period", as to which see subs. (6).

Subs. (6)
The qualifying period is the period between the time when the ship was first brought into use for the purposes of the trade and the earlier of the third anniversary of that date or the date when the ship ceases to belong to the shipowner or an associated person.

Subs. (7)
The register must be in the British Islands, the E.U., the European Economic Area or a colony (see the Interpretation Act 1978).

Subs. (8)
An extended definition of "connected person" is provided for the purposes of subss. (5) and (6).

Procedural provisions relating to deferred charges

97.—(1) In Chapter II of Part II of the Capital Allowances Act 1990 (ships), after the sections inserted by section 96 above there shall be inserted the following section—

"Procedural provisions relating to deferred charges
33F.—(1) Schedule A1 to this Act shall apply for the purposes of corporation tax in relation to the making of a claim under section 33A as it applies in relation to the making of a claim for an allowance.
(2) No claim under section 33A shall be allowed for the purposes of income tax unless it is made within twelve months from the 31st January next following the year of assessment in which the relevant period ends.
(3) No claim under section 33A may be made at any time before such date as the Treasury may by order appoint; and where by virtue of anything in subsection (1) or (2) above the period for making any such claim would have expired (but for this subsection) before the end of the period of twelve months beginning with that date, it shall expire, instead, at the end of that period of twelve months.
(4) An attribution made for the purposes of section 33A(5) or 33C may be varied by notice given by the shipowner to the inspector at any time before the end of the period for the making, by the person giving the notice, of claims under section 33A above in respect of events occurring in the earliest chargeable period affected; and for the purposes of this subsection a chargeable period is an affected chargeable period, in

relation to a variation, if it is one in which expenditure to which the variation relates was incurred.

(5) Where—

(a) a claim for the deferment of any charge has been made under section 33A, and

(b) circumstances subsequently arise that require the deferment claimed to be treated as one to which the shipowner was not entitled, either in whole or in part,

the shipowner shall, no later than three months after the end of the chargeable period in which those circumstances first arise, give notice of that fact, specifying the circumstances, to the inspector.

(6) All such assessments and adjustments shall be made as may be necessary to give effect to the provisions of sections 33A to 33C and subsection (4) above; and, notwithstanding any limitation on the time for making assessments, an assessment to tax chargeable in consequence of any such circumstances as are mentioned in subsection (5) above may be made at any time between—

(a) the time when those circumstances arise, and

(b) the time 12 months after notice of the circumstances is given to the inspector by the shipowner.

(7) In this section references to the shipowner, in relation to the giving of any notice, shall have effect where there have been any such changes as are mentioned in section 33D(7)(b) in the persons engaged in carrying on the shipowner's actual trade, as references to the persons who, in consequence of those changes, are carrying on that trade at the time of the giving of the notice or, as the case may be, when the notice is required to be given."

(2) In section 42(7)(c) of the Management Act (procedure for making claims under the Capital Allowances Act 1990 in the case of a partnership), so far as that section has effect as inserted by paragraph 13 of Schedule 19 to the Finance Act 1994 (self-assessment cases), after "33," there shall be inserted "33A,".

(3) In the second column of the Table in section 98 of the Management Act (penalties in respect of certain information provisions), in the entry relating to sections 23(2), 48 and 49(2) of the Capital Allowances Act 1990, after "23(2)," there shall be inserted "33F(5),".

GENERAL NOTE

The new CAA 1990, s.33F provides the procedure for making a claim for deferment of the tax on balancing charges.

Section 33F(1)

The procedures under CAA 1990, Sched. A1, apply to claims for corporation tax.

Section 33F(2)

Claims for income tax must be made within 12 months from January 31 following the year of assessment in which the relevant period ends.

Section 33F(3)

The procedure will be brought into operation by Treasury order. This is to allow time to obtain permission from Brussels for the deferment of charges.

Section 33F(4)

A shipowner may vary an attribution made under CAA 1990, ss.33A(5) or 33C by giving notice to the inspector within the period of time for making a claim under s.33A.

Section 33F(5)

The shipowner must advise the inspector within three months if he ceases to be entitled to the deferment.

Section 33F(6)

The provisions of CAA 1990, ss.33A–C and s.33F(4) have effect with all assessments and adjustments as are necessary. An assessment under s.33F(5) may be made within 12 months of notification to the inspector, irrespective of other time limits.

Section 33F(7)

Notice of a change in the persons carrying on a trade is given by the persons actually carrying it on.

The main section (s.97) also makes appropriate amendments to the TMA 1970, ss.42 (as prospectively substituted) and 98.

Deferred charges: commencement and transitional provisions

98.—(1) Sections 94 to 97 above shall have effect, subject to the following provisions of this section, in relation to every chargeable period ending on or after 21st April 1994.

(2) Those sections do not apply for the purposes of income tax in relation to a chargeable period if—

(a) that period is a year of assessment as respects which Chapter IV of Part IV of the Finance Act 1994 (changes for facilitating self-assessment) does not apply to the shipowner's actual trade ("a transitional year"); and

(b) the basis period for that chargeable period ended before 21st April 1994.

(3) Where the relevant period is a transitional year the references in paragraphs (b) and (c) of section 33A(1) of the Capital Allowances Act 1990 ("the 1990 Act") to the relevant period shall have effect for the purposes of income tax as if they were references to the basis period for the relevant period.

(4) Where the relevant period is a transitional year or any other year of assessment as respects which section 140 of the 1990 Act has effect without the substitution made by section 211 of the Finance Act 1994, section 33A(3)(d) and (7) of the 1990 Act shall have effect for the purposes of income tax—

(a) subject to the assumption for which subsection (5) below provides; and

(b) as if the reference to the shipowner incurring a loss in his actual trade for the relevant period were a reference to his incurring a loss in that trade for the period ("the assessment period") any profits or gains of which would have been the profits or gains on which income tax chargeable for the relevant period in respect of that trade would finally have fallen to be computed.

(5) That assumption is that in computing the profits or gains of the assessment period which arise from the shipowner's actual trade, and in computing whether he has incurred a loss in that trade for that period, all such deductions and additions were to be made as would have to be made if—

(a) allowances falling to be made under the 1990 Act for the relevant period in taxing that trade (excluding any allowances carried forward to the relevant period by virtue of section 140(4) of the 1990 Act) were trading expenses of the trade for the assessment period; and

(b) charges falling to be so made (apart from any allowances so carried forward) were charges on amounts falling to be treated as trading receipts of that trade for the assessment period.

(6) In relation to expenditure incurred in the basis period for a transitional year—
  (a) the reference in section 33C(2)(a) of the 1990 Act to the chargeable period in which the expenditure is incurred shall have effect as a reference to the chargeable period in the basis period for which it was incurred; and
  (b) the reference in section 33F(4) of the 1990 Act to a chargeable period shall include a reference to a basis period.

(7) Section 33F(2) of the 1990 Act shall not apply to any claim under section 33A for the deferment of the whole or any part of any charge for a transitional year, but no such claim shall be allowed for the purposes of income tax unless it is made—
  (a) within two years of the end of the relevant period; and
  (b) in a case where the shipowner's actual trade is carried on by two or more persons jointly, by the person required under section 9 of the Management Act (partnership return) to make a return for that period in respect of that trade.

(8) Expressions used in this section and in the provisions inserted by sections 94 to 97 above in the 1990 Act shall have the same meanings in this section as in those provisions.

GENERAL NOTE
The provisions for deferment of balancing charges apply in relation to periods ending on or after April 21, 1994, subject to transitional provisions.

Subss. (2) and (3)
These disapply ss.94–97 for income tax where the new self-assessment regime applies, in respect of a chargeable period if the chargeable period is a transitional year, and the basis period for the chargeable period ended before April 21, 1994. Where the relevant period is a transitional year, references in CAA 1990, s.33A(1) to the relevant period have effect as if they were references to the basis period for that period.

Subs. (4)
Where the relevant period is a transitional year of any other year to which the original CAA 1990, s.140 applies, s.33A(3)(d) and (7) of the 1990 Act applies subject to the assumption in subs. (5) below. It also applies as if a loss was incurred in the assessment period for which tax would finally have fallen to be computed.

Subs. (5)
The assumption is that all deductions and additions, with the exception of any allowances carried forward under CAA 1990, s.140(4), are to be made as if allowances due under the CAA 1990 and charges falling to be made were respectively trading expenses and receipts of the trade for the assessment period.

Subs. (6)
Where expenditure is incurred in the basis period for a transitional year, it is treated as having been incurred in the chargeable period for the purposes of CAA 1990, ss.33C(2)(a) and 33F(4).

Subs. (7)
For a transitional year not only will the provisions of CAA 1990, s.33F(2) not apply to any claim under s.33A, but no such claim will be allowed for the purposes of income tax unless it is made within two years of the end of the relevant period. Where the trade is carried on by two persons jointly the claim is to be made by the person required to make the partnership return under TMA 1970, s.9.

Subs. (8)
This provides for the same meaning to be applied to expressions in this section as in ss.94–97 above.

Capital allowances: other provisions

Highway concessions

99.—(1) The Capital Allowances Act 1990 shall be amended as follows.

(2) In section 3(5) (right to charge road tolls deemed to be interest in land for the purposes of writing-down allowance), for "charge tolls" there shall be substituted "a highway concession".

(3) In subsection (1) of section 4 (events giving rise to balancing allowances or charges), after paragraph (d) there shall be inserted the following paragraph—

"(da) that interest, being a highway concession, is brought to or comes to an end, or".

(4) After subsection (2) of section 4 there shall be inserted the following subsections—

"(2AA) No balancing allowance or balancing charge shall be made by reason of an event falling within paragraph (da) of subsection (1) above if the period for which the concession was granted is deemed for the purposes of this subsection to be extended to include any period after the end of the concession; and for the purposes of this subsection where in the case of any highway concession that period is or is deemed to be different in relation to different parts of the road in respect of which it has been granted such apportionment shall be made for the purposes of this subsection as may be just and reasonable.

(2AB) Where a highway concession in respect of any road ('the prior concession') is brought to or comes to an end in circumstances in which—

(a) the person entitled to that concession is afforded (whether or not in pursuance of any legally enforceable arrangements), and takes advantage of, an opportunity to be granted a renewal of the concession, on the same or modified terms, in respect of the whole or any part of that road, or

(b) that person, or a person who is connected with that person within the terms of section 839 of the principal Act, is so afforded, and takes advantage of, an opportunity to be granted a new concession, on the same or modified terms, in respect of, or of a road that includes, the whole or any part of that road,

then to the extent that the prior concession and the renewed or new concession relate to the same road, the period of the prior concession shall be deemed, for the purposes of subsection (2AA) above, to have been extended or further extended for the period of the renewed or new concession and any question for the purposes of this Part as to what constitutes the relevant interest at any time after the renewal, or (as the case may be) the grant of the new concession, shall be determined on the assumption that the renewed or new concession is a continuation of the prior concession."

(5) In section 18(1)(da) (definition of "industrial building or structure" to include structure in use for the purposes of a toll road undertaking), for "toll road" there shall be substituted "highway".

(6) In section 20 (meaning of "the relevant interest")—

(a) in subsection (5), for "a toll road, the right to charge tolls" there shall be substituted "any road, a highway concession"; and

(b) in subsection (6)—

(i) in the words before paragraph (a), for "toll road" there shall be substituted "road";

(ii) in paragraph (b), for "charge tolls" there shall be substituted "a highway concession"; and

   (iii) in the words after paragraph (b), for "right to charge tolls" there shall be substituted "highway concession".

 (7) After subsection (5) of section 21 (interpretation of Part I) there shall be inserted the following subsection—

  "(5AA) In this Part—

   'highway concession', in relation to any road, means—

    (a) any right, in respect of the fact that the road is or will be used by the general public, to receive sums from the Secretary of State or from the Department of the Environment for Northern Ireland, or

    (b) where that road is a toll road, the right to charge tolls in respect of the road,

   and

   'highway undertaking' means so much of any undertaking relating to the design, building, financing and operation of any roads as is carried on for the purposes of, or in connection with, the exploitation of highway concessions."

 (8) In subsections (5A) and (5B) of section 21, for the words "toll road undertaking", in each place where they occur, there shall be substituted "highway undertaking"; and in subsection (5B) for "toll road comprised in it" there shall be substituted "road in relation to which it is carried on".

 (9) In section 156 (meaning of sale, insurance, salvage or compensation moneys), after paragraph (d) there shall be inserted the following paragraph—

  "(e) where the event is the bringing or coming to an end of a highway concession (within the meaning of Part I), any insurance moneys or other compensation received by him in respect of any expenditure which is, or for the purposes of that Part is deemed to be, capital expenditure on the construction of the road in question, in so far as that compensation consists of capital sums."

 (10) This section has effect in relation to expenditure incurred on or after 6th April 1995.

GENERAL NOTE

 The amendments to the CAA 1990 extend the industrial buildings allowance to privately-financed public roads under the Design, Build, Finance and Operate (DBFO) initiative. Balancing adjustments are also introduced when a contract comes to an end in respect of these roads and also toll roads, which are collectively referred to as "highway concessions".

Subs. (2)

 A person entitled to a highway concession in respect of a road is treated as having an interest in it, even if he has no right to charge tolls.

Subs. (3)

 Where a highway concession ends, there will be a balancing adjustment.

Subs. (4)

 The new CAA 1990, s.4(2AA) and (2AB) ensure that no balancing allowance or balancing charge will arise where a highway concession is extended, with an apportionment being made where necessary; and that, where a concession is wholly or partially renewed, the termination of the old concession will not give rise to a balancing adjustment, in so far as it relates to the same piece of road as the new concession.

Subs. (5)

 In the definition of industrial buildings or structures "toll road undertaking" is replaced by "highway undertaking" (see subs. (7) below).

Subs. (6)

 The rules for determining the "relevant interest" in a highway undertaking are amended so that where a person incurring expenditure on a road does not otherwise have an interest in it, then the right to the concession is defined instead as being the relevant interest.

Subs. (7)

The definitions of "highway concession" and "highway undertaking" cover DBFO roads as well as toll roads, which were previously included.

Subs. (8)

Consequential amendments are made to CAA 1990, s.21(5A) and (5B).

Subs. (9)

The new CAA 1990, s.156(e) deals with capital sums which may be received on the bringing or coming to an end of a highway concession. These will be regarded as capital sums and brought into the capital allowances computation as taxable receipts.

Arrangements affecting the value of a relevant interest

100.—(1) After section 10C of the Capital Allowances Act 1990 there shall be inserted the following section—

"Arrangements affecting the value of the purchased interest

10D.—(1) This section has effect for determining the following amounts, that is to say—

(a) any amount which for the purposes of any of sections 10 to 10C is to be taken to be the sum paid on the sale of the relevant interest in any building or structure; and

(b) any amount which for the purposes of sections 1 to 8 is to be taken to be the amount of any sale, insurance, salvage or compensation moneys payable in respect of any building or structure where—

(i) a person is deemed, under any of sections 10 to 10C, to have incurred expenditure on the construction of the building or structure; and

(ii) the amount of the deemed expenditure is taken, under those sections, to have been equal to the price paid on a sale of the relevant interest in the building or structure;

and in this section 'the relevant amount' means the amount falling to be determined and 'the basic amount' means whatever would be the relevant amount for the purposes of this Part if the provisions of this section were disregarded.

(2) Where—

(a) arrangements falling within subsection (3) below have been entered into, and

(b) those arrangements contain any provision having an artificial effect on pricing,

the relevant amount shall be taken to be equal to the basic amount less so much of the basic amount as, on a just apportionment, represents the extent to which the sale price or, as the case may be, the amount of the sale, insurance, salvage or compensation moneys is more than it would have been if those arrangements had not contained that provision.

(3) The arrangements falling within this subsection are any arrangements relating to, or to any other arrangements made with respect to, any interest in or right over the building or structure in question (whether granted by the person entitled to the relevant interest or by somebody else), so far as they are arrangements which—

(a) were entered into between any two or more persons at or before the time mentioned in subsection (5) below; and

(b) had the effect at the time so mentioned of enhancing the value of the relevant interest in that building or structure.

(4) For the purposes of this section arrangements falling within subsection (3) above in relation to any building or structure shall be treated as containing a provision having an artificial effect on pricing to the extent that they go beyond what, at the time they were entered into, it was reasonable to regard as required, so far as transactions involving

interests in or rights over buildings or structures of the same or a similar description were concerned, by the market conditions then prevailing for persons dealing with each other at arm's length in the open market.

(5) The time mentioned in subsection (3)(a) above is—

   (a) in relation to the determination of an amount falling within subsection (1)(a) above, the time of the fixing of the sale price for the sale in question; and

   (b) in relation to the determination of an amount falling within subsection (1)(b) above, the time of the fixing of the sale price for the sale by reference to which the amount of the deemed expenditure on the construction of the building or structure fell to be determined in accordance with any of sections 10 to 10C."

(2) In section 151 of that Act (procedure on apportionments), after subsection (1) there shall be inserted the following subsection—

"(1A) This section applies in relation to so much of the determination of any price, or of any sale, insurance, salvage or compensation moneys, as is made in accordance with section 10D as it applies in relation to apportionments."

(3) This section has effect in relation to determinations on or after 29th November 1994 except where the time referred to in subsection (5) of the section 10D inserted in the Capital Allowances Act 1990 by this section would, in relation to the amount to be determined, be the time of the fixing of a sale price which either—

   (a) became payable before 29th November 1994; or

   (b) being an amount becoming payable before 6th April 1995, was fixed by a contract entered into before 29th November 1994.

GENERAL NOTE

The new CAA 1990, s.10D introduces provisions to determine the amount qualifying for industrial buildings allowances in the event that there are arrangements in place affecting the value of a relevant interest (see CAA 1990, s.20).

Section 10D(1)

This sets out the two main cases in which s.10D applies—*viz.*, to a buyer who qualifies for industrial buildings allowance (IBA) under ss.10–10C and to subsequent disposals by such a buyer. It also defines "relevant amount" and "basic amount".

Section 10D(2)

The sale price is reduced for IBA purposes by the amount attributable on a just apportionment to "arrangements" artificially increasing the price (see further s.10D(4)). The arrangements are further described in s.10D(3).

Section 10D(3)

The arrangements must be made between any two or more persons before the time mentioned in s.10D(5) and must enhance the value of the property at that time.

Section 10D(4)

Arrangements which have an artificial effect on price are those which go beyond what is reasonable. Comparison must be made with arm's length dealings in the open market.

Section 10D(5)

The time concerned is when a sale price was fixed for a buyer qualifying for an IBA.

The remainder of the main section (s.100) inserts a new CAA 1990, s.151(1A), providing for apportionments to be made. It also provides for the commencement of s.10D which generally applies from Budget Day, unless the price became payable before then or was payable before April 6, 1995 under a contract entered into before Budget Day.

Import warehouses etc.

101. Section 18(1)(f)(iv) of the Capital Allowances Act 1990 (industrial building or structure to include building or structure used for the storage of goods arriving by sea or air into the United Kingdom) shall have effect, and be deemed always to have had effect, as if for "by sea or air into any part of" there were substituted "in any part of the United Kingdom from a place outside".

GENERAL NOTE
   The section extends industrial buildings allowances to import warehouses which store goods or materials imported into the U.K. by any means of transportation (*e.g.* the Channel Tunnel) instead of restricting it only to those which store goods or materials imported into the U.K. by means of sea or air.

Commencement of certain provisions

   102.—(1) Chapter IV of Part IV of the Finance Act 1994 (changes for facilitating self-assessment) shall be deemed to have been enacted with the following modification.
   (2) In section 218 (commencement etc. of Chapter IV, sections 213(4) and (8) and 214(4) and (6) of which relate to capital allowances) the following subsection shall be inserted after subsection (1)—
      "(1A) In a case where—
      (a) a trade is set up and commenced by a company, and
      (b) it is not set up and commenced before 6th April 1994,
      sections 213(4) and (8) and 214(4) and (6) have effect only if it is set up and commenced on or after 6th April 1995."

GENERAL NOTE
   The new FA 1994, s.218(1A) provides that ss.213(4), (8) and 214(4), (6) only have effect for a company starting a trade after April 6, 1994 if it was started after April 6, 1995.

Management: self-assessment etc.

Liability of trustees

   103.—(1) In subsection (2) of section 7 of the Management Act (notice of liability)—
      (a) for the words "a person who is" there shall be substituted the words "persons who are"; and
      (b) for the words "a trustee" there shall be substituted the words "the relevant trustees".
   (2) After subsection (8) of that section there shall be inserted the following subsection—
      "(9) For the purposes of this Act the relevant trustees of a settlement are—
      (a) in relation to income, the persons who are trustees when the income arises and any persons who subsequently become trustees; and
      (b) in relation to chargeable gains, the persons who are trustees in the year of assessment in which the chargeable gains accrue and any persons who subsequently become trustees."
   (3) In subsection (1) of section 8A of that Act (trustee's return)—
      (a) for the words "a trustee" there shall be substituted the words "the relevant trustees"; and
      (b) for the words "the trustee", in the first place where they occur, there shall be substituted the words "any relevant trustee".
   (4) After subsection (4) of that section there shall be inserted the following subsection—
      "(5) The following references, namely—
      (a) references in section 9 or 28C of this Act to a person to whom a notice has been given under this section being chargeable to tax; and

    (b) references in section 29 of this Act to such a person being assessed
         to tax,
shall be construed as references to the relevant trustees of the settlement being so chargeable or, as the case may be, being so assessed."
    (5) At the beginning of Part XI of that Act (miscellaneous and supplemen-
tal) there shall be inserted the following section—

"Settlements

Relevant trustees
    107A.—(1) Subject to the following provisions of this section, any-
thing which for the purposes of this Act is done at any time by or in
relation to any one or more of the relevant trustees of a settlement shall
be treated for those purposes as done at that time by or in relation to the
other or others of those trustees.
    (2) Subject to subsection (3) below, where the relevant trustees of a
settlement are liable—
    (a) to a penalty under section 7, 12B, 93, 95 or 97AA of this Act or
         paragraph 2A of Schedule 1A to this Act, or to interest under
         section 103A of this Act on such a penalty;
    (b) to make a payment in accordance with an assessment under sec-
         tion 30 of this Act, or to make a payment under section 59A or
         59B of this Act;
    (c) to a surcharge under section 59C of this Act, or to interest under
         that section on such a surcharge; or
    (d) to interest under section 86 of this Act,
the penalty, interest, payment or surcharge may be recovered (but only
once) from any one or more of those trustees.
    (3) No amount may be recovered by virtue of subsection (2)(a) or (c)
above from a person who did not become a relevant trustee until after
the relevant time, that is to say—
    (a) in relation to so much of a penalty under section 93(3) or
         97AA(1)(b) of this Act as is payable in respect of any day, or to
         interest under section 103A of this Act on so much of such a pen-
         alty as is so payable, the beginning of that day;
    (b) in relation to a penalty under any other provision of this Act men-
         tioned in subsection (2)(a) above, or to interest under section
         103A of this Act on such a penalty, the time when the relevant act
         or omission occurred; and
    (c) in relation to a surcharge under subsection (2) or (3) of section
         59C of this Act, or to interest under that section on such a sur-
         charge, the beginning of the day mentioned in that subsection;
and in paragraph (b) above 'the relevant act or omission' means the act
or omission which caused the penalty to become payable.
    (4) In a case where—
    (a) subsection (2)(a) above applies in relation to a penalty under sec-
         tion 93 of this Act, or
    (b) subsection (2)(c) above applies in relation to a surcharge under
         section 59C of this Act,
subsection (8) of section 93 or, as the case may be, subsection (9) of
section 59C of this Act shall have effect as if the reference to the taxpayer were a reference to each of the relevant trustees."
    (6) In section 118 of that Act (interpretation), after the definition of "the
principal Act" there shall be inserted the following definition—
    " 'the relevant trustees', in relation to a settlement, shall be construed in
         accordance with section 7(9) of this Act."
    (7) Unless the contrary intention appears, this section, sections 104 to 115
below and Schedule 20 to this Act—

(a) so far as they relate to income tax and capital gains tax, have effect as respects the year 1996–97 and subsequent years of assessment, and

(b) so far as they relate to corporation tax, have effect as respects accounting periods ending on or after the appointed day for the purposes of Chapter III of Part IV of the Finance Act 1994.

GENERAL NOTE

The section deals with the liability of trustees under the new self-assessment regime, which comes into effect from 1996–97. It is linked with s.114, which deals with the liability of trustees for CGT.

Subs. (1)

The reference to trustees in the prospective TMA 1970, s.7(2) is replaced by a reference to "relevant trustees".

Subs. (2)

The new TMA 1970, s.7(9) defines relevant trustees as those to whom income or capital gains arise and their successors.

Subss. (3) and (4)

These make consequential amendments to TMA 1970, s.8A.

Subs. (5)

The new TMA 1970, s.107A provides that anything done by one or more relevant trustee is to be treated as done by them all, and that they are all liable for any penalties, payments, surcharges or interest, but not for any imposed before they became trustees. The provisions in TMA 1970, ss.59C and 93 dealing with surcharges and penalties are to be taken as referring to each of the relevant trustees.

Subs. (6)

The definition of relevant trustees is inserted in TMA 1970, s.118.

Subs. (7)

This section, ss.104–115 and Sched. 20 below take effect from 1996–97 as regards income tax and CGT and from the appointed date (which will not be earlier than April 1, 1996) as regards corporation tax.

Returns and self-assessments

104.—(1) In each of the following, namely—

(a) subsection (1A) of section 8 of the Management Act (personal return); and

(b) subsection (1A) of section 8A of that Act (trustee's return),

there shall be inserted at the end the words "and the amounts referred to in that subsection are net amounts, that is to say, amounts which take into account any relief, allowance or repayment of tax for which a claim is made and give credit for any income tax deducted at source and any tax credit to which section 231 of the principal Act applies".

(2) In subsection (1B) of section 8 of that Act, for the word "loss" there shall be substituted the words "loss, tax, credit".

(3) After subsection (4) of that section there shall be inserted the following subsection—

"(5) In this section and sections 8A, 9 and 12AA of this Act, any reference to income tax deducted at source is a reference to income tax deducted or treated as deducted from any income or treated as paid on any income."

(4) In subsection (1) of section 9 of that Act (returns to include self-assessment), for the words "on the basis of the information contained in the return" there shall be substituted the following paragraphs—

"(a) on the basis of the information contained in the return; and

(b) taking into account any relief, allowance or repayment of tax a claim for which is included in the return and giving credit for any income tax deducted at source and any tax credit to which section 231 of the principal Act applies,".

(5) In subsection (1) of section 11AA of that Act (return of profits to include self-assessment), for the words "on the basis of the information contained in the return" there shall be substituted the following paragraphs—

"(a) on the basis of the information contained in the return; and
(b) taking into account any relief, allowance or repayment of tax a claim for which is included in the return,".

(6) For subsection (1) of section 12AA of that Act (partnership return) there shall be substituted the following subsections—

"(1) Where a trade, profession or business is carried on by two or more persons in partnership, for the purpose of facilitating the establishment of the following amounts, namely—

(a) the amount in which each partner chargeable to income tax for any year of assessment is so chargeable, and
(b) the amount in which each partner chargeable to corporation tax for any period is so chargeable,

an officer of the Board may act under subsection (2) or (3) below (or both).

(1A) The amounts referred to in paragraphs (a) and (b) of subsection (1) above are net amounts, that is to say, amounts which—

(a) take into account any relief, allowance or repayment of tax for which a claim is made; and
(b) in the case of the amount referred to in paragraph (a) of that subsection, give credit for any income tax deducted at source and any tax credit to which section 231 of the principal Act applies."

(7) For subsection (1) of section 12AB of that Act (partnership return to include partnership statement) there shall be substituted the following subsection—

"(1) Every return under section 12AA of this Act shall include a statement (a partnership statement) of the following amounts, namely—

(a) in the case of each period of account ending within the period in respect of which the return is made—

(i) the amount of income or loss from each source which, on the basis of the information contained in the return and taking into account any relief or allowance a section 42(7) claim for which is included in the return, has accrued to or has been sustained by the partnership for that period,
(ii) each amount of income tax which, on that basis, has been deducted or treated as deducted from any income of the partnership, or treated as paid on any such income, for that period,
(iii) the amount of each tax credit which, on that basis, has accrued to the partnership for that period, and
(iv) the amount of each charge which, on that basis, was a charge on the income of the partnership for that period; and
(b) in the case of each such period and each of the partners, the amount which, on that basis and (where applicable) taking into account any such relief or allowance, is equal to his share of that income, loss, tax, credit or charge."

(8) In subsection (5) of that section, after the definition of "period of account" there shall be inserted the following definitions—

" 'section 42(7) claim' means a claim under any of the provisions mentioned in section 42(7) of this Act;
'tax credit' means a tax credit to which section 231 of the principal Act applies."

GENERAL NOTE
The provisions relating to returns, self-assessments and partnership statements are amended

to ensure that they all reflect the taxable position after claims to reliefs and allowances and after taking into account tax suffered on, and tax credits with, the items in the return. Information can be required about these items in the same way it can be about entries relating to income and gains.

Subs. (1)
The amendments to TMA 1970, ss.8 and 8A ensure that the object of the return is to ascertain the net tax position.

Subs. (2)
The amendment to TMA 1970, s.8 is consequential to the amendment made to TMA 1970, s.12AB (see subs. (7) below).

Subs. (3)
The new TMA 1970, s.8(5) inserts a definition of income tax deducted at source so that it includes amounts, such as sub-contractors' deductions, that are treated as tax and extends this definition to TMA 1970, ss.8A, 9 and 12AA.

Subs. (4)
The amendments to TMA 1970, s.9 follow those to TMA 1970, ss.8 and 8A (see subs. (1) above).

Subs. (5)
The amendments to TMA 1970, s.11AA, which deals with company self-assessment, ensure that the amount assessed is the net amount after claims to allowances and reliefs.

Subs. (6)
TMA 1970, s.12AA is amended to bring it into line with TMA 1970, ss.8 and 8A.

Subs. (7)
The amendments to TMA 1970, s.12AB ensure that the partnership statement includes amounts net of partnership claims and tax suffered on partnership income.

Subs. (8)
Definitions of partnership claims and tax credits are inserted into TMA 1970, s.12AB.

Records for purposes of returns

105.—(1) In subsection (1) of section 12B of the Management Act (records to be kept for purposes of returns), for paragraph (b) there shall be substituted the following paragraph—
"(b) preserve those records until the end of the relevant day, that is to say, the day mentioned in subsection (2) below or, where a return is required by a notice given on or before that day, whichever of that day and the following is the latest, namely—
(i) where enquiries into the return or any amendment of the return are made by an officer of the Board, the day on which, by virtue of section 28A(5) or 28B(5) of this Act, those enquiries are treated as completed; and
(ii) where no enquiries into the return or any amendment of the return are so made, the day on which such an officer no longer has power to make such enquiries."

(2) In subsection (2) of that section, the words from "or, where a return" to the end shall cease to have effect.

(3) After that subsection there shall be inserted the following subsection—

"(2A) Any person who—

(a) is required, by such a notice as is mentioned in subsection (1) above given at any time after the end of the day mentioned in subsection (2) above, to make and deliver a return for a year of assessment or other period; and

(b) has in his possession at that time any records which may be requisite for the purpose of enabling him to make and deliver a correct and complete return for the year or period,

shall preserve those records until the end of the relevant day, that is to say, the day which, if the notice had been given on or before the day mentioned in subsection (2) above, would have been the relevant day for the purposes of subsection (1) above."

(4) In subsection (3) of that section—

(a) in paragraph (a), after the words "subsection (1)" there shall be inserted the words "or (2A)"; and

(b) in paragraph (b), for the words "the day mentioned in subsection (2) above" there shall be substituted the words "the end of the relevant day".

(5) In subsection (4) of that section, after the words "subsection (1)" there shall be inserted the words "or (2A)".

(6) In subsection (5) of that section—

(a) at the beginning there shall be inserted the words "Subject to subsection (5A) below,"; and

(b) after the words "subsection (1)" there shall be inserted the words "or (2A)".

(7) After that subsection there shall be inserted the following subsection—

"(5A) Subsection (5) above does not apply where the records which the person fails to keep or preserve are records which might have been requisite only for the purposes of claims, elections or notices which are not included in the return."

GENERAL NOTE

The record-keeping requirements are amended and also expanded to deal with those needed for the purpose of making claims.

Subs. (1)

The substituted TMA 1970, s.12B(1)(b) requires that records are to be kept until enquiries by the Revenue can no longer be begun, or have been completed, whichever is later.

Subs. (2)

Section 12B(2) of TMA 1970 is simplified.

Subs. (3)

The new TMA 1970, s.12B(2A) provides that where a person receives a return after the normal record-keeping requirement has expired, he must keep the records he has until either no enquiries can be raised or they have been completed.

Subss. (4) and (5)

Consequential amendments are made to TMA 1970, s.12B(3) and (4).

Subs. (6)

The penalty provision in TMA 1970, s.12B(5) is made subject to s.12B(5A) (see subs. (7) below) and a further consequential amendment is made.

Subs. (7)

The new TMA 1970, s.12B(5A) disapplies the penalty provisions in relation to claims which could be made on their own.

Return of employees' emoluments etc.

106.—(1) For section 15 of the Management Act there shall be substituted the following section—

"Return of employees' emoluments etc.

15.—(1) Every employer, when required to do so by notice from an officer of the Board, shall, within the time limited by the notice, prepare and deliver to the officer a return relating to persons who are or have been employees of his, containing the information required under the following provisions of this section.

(2) An employer shall not be required to include in his return information relating to any year of assessment if the notice is given more than five years after the 31st January next following that year.

(3) A notice under subsection (1) above—

(a) shall specify the employees for whom a return is to be made and may, in particular, specify individuals (by name or otherwise) or all employees of an employer or all his employees who are or have been in employment to which Chapter II of Part V of the principal Act applies; and

(b) shall specify the years of assessment or other periods with respect to which the information is to be provided.

(4) A notice under subsection (1) above may require the return to state the name and place of residence of an employee to whom it relates.

(5) A notice under subsection (1) above may require the return to contain, in respect of an employee to whom it relates, the following particulars—

(a) in the case of relevant payments made by the employer, particulars of the payments;

(b) in the case of relevant payments not falling within paragraph (a) above the making of which by another person has been arranged by the employer—

(i) particulars of the payments; and

(ii) the name and business address of the other person; and

(c) in the case of relevant payments not falling within either of the preceding paragraphs, the name and business address of any person who has, to the employer's knowledge, made the payments.

(6) Any payments made to an employee in respect of his employment are relevant payments for the purposes of this section, including—

(a) payments to him in respect of expenses (including sums put at his disposal and paid away by him);

(b) payments made on his behalf and not repaid; and

(c) payments to him for services rendered in connection with a trade or business, whether the services were rendered in the course of his employment or not.

(7) Where, for the purposes of his return, an employer apportions expenses incurred partly in or in connection with a particular matter and partly in or in connection with other matters—

(a) the return shall contain a statement that the sum included in the return is the result of such an apportionment; and

(b) if required to do so by notice from an officer of the Board, the employer shall prepare and deliver to the officer, within the time limited by the notice, a return containing full particulars as to the amount apportioned and the manner in which, and the grounds on which, the apportionment has been made.

(8) A notice under subsection (1) above may require the return—

(a) to state in respect of an employee to whom it relates whether any benefits are or have been provided for him (or for any other person) by reason of his employment, such as may give rise to charges to tax under the relevant sections, that is to say, sections 141, 142, 143, 144A, 145, 146 and 154 to 165 of the principal Act (miscellaneous benefits in cash or in kind); and

(b) if such benefits are or have been provided, to contain such particulars of those benefits as may be specified in the notice.

(9) Where such benefits are provided the notice may, without prejudice to subsection (8)(b) above, require the return to contain the following particulars—

(a) in the case of benefits which are or have been provided by the employer, particulars of the amounts which may be chargeable to tax by virtue of the relevant sections;

(b) in the case of benefits not falling within paragraph (a) above the provision of which by another person is or has been arranged by the employer—

(i) particulars of the amounts which may be so chargeable; and

(ii) the name and business address of the other person; and

(c) in the case of benefits not falling within either of the preceding paragraphs, the name and business address of any person who has, to the employer's knowledge, provided the benefits.

(10) Where it appears to an officer of the Board that a person has, in any year of assessment, been concerned in making relevant payments to, or providing benefits to or in respect of, employees of another, the officer may at any time up to five years after the 31st January next following that year by notice require that person—

(a) to deliver to the officer, within the time limited by the notice, such particulars of those payments or benefits, or of the amounts which may be chargeable to tax in respect of the benefits, as may be specified in the notice (so far as known to him); and

(b) to include with those particulars the names and addresses (so far as known to him) of the employees concerned.

(11) In determining, in pursuance of a notice under subsection (1) or (10) above, amounts which may be chargeable to tax by virtue of the relevant sections, a person—

(a) shall not make—

(i) any deduction or other adjustment which he is unable to show, by reference to information in his possession or otherwise available to him, is authorised or required by the relevant sections; or

(ii) any deduction authorised by section 141(3), 142(2), 145(3) or 156(8) of the principal Act; but

(b) subject to that, shall make all such deductions and other adjustments as may be authorised or required by the relevant sections.

(12) Where the employer is a body of persons, the secretary of the body or other officer (by whatever name called) performing the duties of secretary shall be treated as the employer for the purposes of this section.

Where the employer is a body corporate, that body corporate, as well as the secretary or other officer, shall be liable to a penalty for failure to comply with this section.

(13) In this section—

'arranged' includes guaranteed and in any way facilitated;

'employee' means an office holder or employee whose emoluments fall to be assessed under Schedule E, and related expressions are to be construed accordingly;

'relevant payments' has the meaning given by subsection (6) above; and

'the relevant sections' has the meaning given by subsection (8)(a) above."
(2) This section has effect as respects payments made or benefits provided on or after 6th April 1996.

GENERAL NOTE
The new TMA 1970, s.15, applicable from April 6, 1996, enables the Revenue to make enquiries where it believes employers and others may be making payments to, or providing benefits for, employees.

Section 15(1)
An employer may be served with a notice requiring him to provide the information specified in s.15(2)–(9).

Section 15(2)
The normal time limit of five years 10 months applies as specified in TMA 1970, s.34 (as amended by FA 1994, Sched. 19, para. 10).

Section 15(3)
The notice may specify named employees, all employees or those earning more than £8,500 a year and must specify for what years or periods the information is required.

Section 15(4)
The notice may require the names and addresses of employees.

Section 15(5)
The notice may require details of "relevant payments" (see s.15(6)) made by the employer or any other person through whom he has arranged them, together with the name and address of that person and any other person who has to his knowledge been making such payments.

Section 15(6)
"Relevant payments" include payments for expenses, payments made on the employee's behalf and payments for services rendered.

Section 15(7)
Apportionments may be required where necessary.

Section 15(8)
The notice may require the employer to say whether benefits under the specified sections have been provided to any employee and, if so, to give further particulars.

Section 15(9)
The notice may also cover benefits provided otherwise than by the employer directly (*cf.* s.15(5) above).

Section 15(10)
A notice may be served within the normal time limit of five years 10 months requiring anyone who appears to have been making payments to, or providing benefits for, someone else's employees to make a return of these.

Section 15(11)
No adjustments may be made in respect of amounts chargeable to tax for benefits, unless the person concerned has the necessary information to justify these. Other permissible deductions will be made by the employee himself.

Section 15(12)
The existing right to issue notices to, and exact penalties from, the secretary of a company, is preserved.

Section 15(13)
Various definitions are specified. In particular, "arranged" (see s.15(5) and (9)) includes guaranteed and in any way facilitated.

Procedure for making claims etc.

107.—(1) After subsection (1) of section 42 of the Management Act (procedure for making claims etc.) there shall be inserted the following subsection—

"(1A) Subject to subsection (3) below, a claim for a relief, an allowance or a repayment of tax shall be for an amount which is quantified at the time when the claim is made."

(2) In subsection (2) of that section, for the words "subsection (3)" there shall be substituted the words "subsections (3) and (3A)".

(3) In subsection (3) of that section, for the words "Subsection (2)" there shall be substituted the words "Subsections (1A) and (2)".

(4) After subsection (3) of that section there shall be inserted the following subsections—

"(3A) Where a person makes a claim requiring relief for a loss incurred or treated as incurred, or a payment made, in one year of assessment ('the later year') to be given in an earlier year of assessment ('the earlier year')—

(a) subsection (2) above shall not apply in relation to the claim;
(b) the claim shall be made in relation to the later year;
(c) the claim shall be for an amount equal to the difference between—

(i) the amount in which he has been assessed to tax under section 9 of this Act for the earlier year; and
(ii) the amount in which he would have been so assessed if the claim could have been, and had been, included in a return made under section 8 or 8A of this Act for that year; and

(d) effect shall be given to the claim in relation to the later year, whether by repayment or set-off, or by an addition to the aggregate amount given by section 59B(1)(b) of this Act, or otherwise.

(3B) Where no notice under section 8 or 8A of this Act has been given to the person for the earlier year, subsection (3A)(c) above shall have effect as if—

(a) sub-paragraph (i) referred to the amount in which he would have been assessed to tax under section 9 of this Act for that year if such a notice had been so given; and
(b) sub-paragraph (ii) referred to the amount in which he would have been so assessed if such a notice had been so given and the claim could have been, and had been, included in a return made under section 8 or 8A of this Act for that year."

(5) In subsection (4) of that section, there shall be inserted at the beginning the words "Subject to subsection (4A) below,".

(6) After subsection (4) of that section there shall be inserted the following subsection—

"(4A) Subsection (4) above shall not apply where—

(a) the company is wholly exempt from corporation tax or is only not so exempt in respect of trading income; and
(b) the tax credit is not one in respect of which a payment on account may be claimed by the company under Schedule 19AB to the principal Act."

(7) In subsection (5) of that section, for the words "subsections (2) and (4) above" there shall be substituted the words "this section".

(8) In subsection (7)(a) of that section, for the words "sections 84" there shall be substituted the words "sections 62A, 84".

(9) In subsection (10) of that section, after the words "This section" there shall be inserted the words "(except subsection (1A) above)".

(10) In subsection (11) of that section, paragraph (b) and the word "and" immediately preceding that paragraph shall cease to have effect.

(11) Schedule 1A to that Act (claims etc. not included in returns) shall have effect subject to the amendments specified in Schedule 20 to this Act.

GENERAL NOTE

A number of changes are made to the procedure for making claims in order to facilitate self-assessment.

Subs. (1)

The new TMA 1970, s.42(1A) requires a claim to be quantified at the time it is made.

Subs. (2)

The amendment to TMA 1970, s.42(2) means that claims to carry back relief do not have to be made in a return.

Subs. (3)

The requirement to quantify a claim when it is made does not apply where the claim is reflected in a PAYE code number.

Subs. (4)

The new TMA 1970, s.42(3A) and (3B) provide that where reliefs are carried back to an earlier year, the relief is claimed in relation to the year the loss is incurred or the payment made, but is calculated in terms of tax in relation to the year in which the relief is taken.

Subss. (5) and (6)

Exempt companies, such as charities, can claim payment of tax credits on dividends without making a return.

Subs. (7)

A consequential amendment is made so that claims for carry back can be made by way of an amendment to a return.

Subs. (8)

The notice in ICTA 1988, s.62A (change of accounting date) is added to the list of provisions for which claims elections and notices have to be included in a partnership return.

Subs. (9)

The amendment to TMA 1970, s.42(10) disapplies it from s.42(1A), so that only claims, and not notices and elections, have to be quantified when they are made.

Subs. (10)

The qualification that prevents TMA 1970, Sched. 1A (claims *etc.* not included in returns) applying to claims, elections and notices that are taken into account in setting a PAYE code, is removed.

Subs. (11)

Amendments are made to TMA 1970, Sched. 1A. See further the General Note to Sched. 20.

Payments on account of income tax

108.—(1) In subsection (1) of section 59A of the Management Act (payments on account of income tax)—

(a) there shall be inserted at the beginning the words "Subject to subsection (9) below,"; and

(b) in paragraph (a), for the words "has been assessed" there shall be substituted the words "is assessed".

(2) In subsection (2) of that section, for the words "subsection (4)" there shall be substituted the words "subsections (4) and (4A)".

(3) After subsection (4) of that section there shall be inserted the following subsection—

"(4A) If as regards the year immediately preceding the year of assessment—

    (a) the taxpayer is assessed to income tax under section 9 of this Act after the date on or before which either payment on account is required to be made, or

    (b) his assessment to income tax under that section is amended after that date,

then, subject to subsections (3) and (4) above and to any subsequent application of this subsection, the amount of the payment on account shall be, and shall be deemed always to have been, equal to 50 per cent. of the relevant amount as determined on the basis of the assessment or, as the case may be, the assessment as amended."

(4) In subsection (5) of that section—

    (a) after the words "the taxpayer makes a claim under subsection (3) or (4) above" there shall be inserted the words "or subsection (4A) above applies"; and

    (b) after the words "whether by the repayment of amounts paid on account" there shall be inserted the words ", by the making of payments or further payments on account".

(5) For subsection (8) of that section there shall be substituted the following subsections—

"(8) In this section, in relation to a year of assessment, any reference to the amount of any income tax deducted at source is a reference to the amount by which the aggregate of the following, namely—

    (a) any income tax deducted or treated as deducted from any income, or treated as paid on any income, in respect of the year, and

    (b) any amounts which, in respect of the year, are to be deducted at source under section 203 of the principal Act in subsequent years, or are tax credits to which section 231 of that Act applies,

exceeds the aggregate of any amounts which, in the year, are deducted at source under the said section 203 in respect of previous years.

(9) If, at any time before the 31st January next following a year of assessment, an officer of the Board so directs—

    (a) this section shall not apply, and shall be deemed never to have applied, as regards that year to any person specified in the direction; and

    (b) there shall be made all such adjustments, whether by the repayment of amounts paid on account or otherwise, as may be required to give effect to the direction."

GENERAL NOTE

The rules for payments on account are amended to ensure that the amount that is deemed to be due for each of the payments on account is determined by the final tax liability for the previous year of assessment and that each of the two payments on account shall be regarded as half of the total. Also, an inspector can direct that payments on account are not due in any year of assessment.

Subs. (1)

A payment on account is due whether or not an assessment has actually been made.

Subs. (2)

It is made clear that TMA 1970, s.59A(2) is qualified by new TMA 1970, s.59A(4A).

Subs. (3)

New TMA 1970, s.59A(4A) provides that if an assessment is made or amended after the first date for a payment on account, any changes to the total liability reflected by the assessment shall be deemed to have had effect on each payment on account as if that liability had been shown in a self-assessment filed on time.

Subs. (4)
Amendments are made to TMA 1970, s.59A(5) so that it is qualified by the new s.59A(4A) and so as to make it clear that changes can be made by the making of payments or further payments on account, as well as by repayments.

Subs. (5)
Two new subsections are introduced into TMA 1970, s.59A. The first is a revised version of s.59A(8), which amends the current definition of "the amount of any income tax deducted at source" to exclude from it amounts deducted in a year which are deducted at source under ICTA 1988, s.203 (PAYE) in respect of a previous year. New TMA 1970, s.59A(9) allows an inspector to direct that payments on account are not required in respect of any year and to make all consequential adjustments. The direction must be made no later than January 31 following the year of assessment.

Surcharges on unpaid tax

109.—(1) In section 59C of the Management Act (surcharges on unpaid income tax and capital gains tax), in subsection (4) (exceptions to surcharge), for the words "or 95" there shall be substituted the words ", 95 or 95A".

(2) That section of that Act shall apply in relation to any income tax or capital gains tax which—
   (a) is charged by an assessment made on or after 6th April 1998; and
   (b) is for the year 1995–96 or an earlier year of assessment,
as it applies in relation to any income tax or capital gains tax which becomes payable in accordance with section 55 or 59B of that Act and is for the year 1996–97 or a subsequent year of assessment.

GENERAL NOTE
Two amendments are made to the provisions on surcharges.

Subs. (1)
A surcharge does not apply where there is a tax-geared penalty under TMA 1970, s.95A on an incorrect partnership return.

Subs. (2)
A surcharge applies where appropriate to all assessments made on or after April 6, 1998.

Interest on overdue tax

110.—(1) For section 86 of the Management Act there shall be substituted the following section—

"Interest on overdue income tax and capital gains tax
86.—(1) The following, namely—
   (a) any amount on account of income tax which becomes due and payable in accordance with section 59A(2) of this Act, and
   (b) any income tax or capital gains tax which becomes due and payable in accordance with section 55 or 59B of this Act,
shall carry interest at the rate applicable under section 178 of the Finance Act 1989 from the relevant date until payment.

(2) For the purposes of subsection (1)(a) above the relevant date is whichever of the dates mentioned in section 59A(2) of this Act is applicable; and for the purposes of subsection (1)(b) above the relevant date is—
   (a) in any such case as is mentioned in subsection (3) of section 59B of this Act, the last day of the period of three months mentioned in that subsection; and
   (b) in any other case, the date mentioned in subsection (4) of that section.

(3) Subsection (1) above applies even if the relevant date is a non-business day within the meaning of section 93 of the Bills of Exchange Act 1882.

(4) Subsection (5) below applies where as regards a year of assessment—

  (a) any person makes a claim under subsection (3) or (4) of section 59A of this Act in respect of the amounts (the section 59A amounts) payable by him in accordance with subsection (2) of that section, and

  (b) an amount (the section 59B amount) becomes payable by him in accordance with section 59B(3), (4) or (5) of this Act.

(5) Interest shall be payable under this section as if each of the section 59A amounts had been equal to—

  (a) the aggregate of that amount and 50 per cent. of the section 59B amount, or

  (b) the amount which would have been payable in accordance with subsection (2) of section 59A of this Act if the claim under subsection (3) or (4) of that section had not been made,

whichever is the less.

(6) In determining for the purposes of subsections (4) and (5) above what amount (if any) is payable by any person in accordance with section 59B(3), (4) or (5) of this Act—

  (a) it shall be assumed that both of the section 59A amounts have been paid, and

  (b) no account shall be taken of any amount which has been paid on account otherwise than under section 59A(2) of this Act or is payable by way of capital gains tax.

(7) Subsection (8) below applies where as regards any person and a year of assessment—

  (a) amounts (the section 59A amounts) become payable by him in accordance with section 59A(2) of this Act, and

  (b) an amount (the section 59B amount) becomes repayable to him in accordance with section 59B(3), (4) or (5) of this Act.

(8) So much of any interest payable under this section on either of the section 59A amounts as is not attributable to the amount by which that amount exceeds 50 per cent. of the section 59B amount shall be remitted.

(9) In determining for the purposes of subsections (7) and (8) above what amount (if any) is repayable to any person in accordance with section 59B(3), (4) or (5) of this Act, no account shall be taken of any amount which has been paid on account otherwise than under section 59A(2) of this Act or is payable by way of capital gains tax."

(2) That section of that Act shall apply in relation to any income tax or capital gains tax which—

  (a) is charged by an assessment made on or after 6th April 1998; and

  (b) is for the year 1995–96 or an earlier year of assessment,

as it applies in relation to any income tax or capital gains tax which becomes due and payable in accordance with section 55 or 59B of that Act and is for the year 1996–97 or a subsequent year of assessment.

(3) In that section of that Act as it so applies, "the relevant date" means the 31st January next following the year of assessment.

GENERAL NOTE

A new TMA 1970, s.86 is substituted in respect of interest on overdue income tax and CGT for assessments for the tax year 1996–97 onwards and for all assessments raised after April 5, 1998.

Subs. (1)

This introduces the new TMA 1970, s.86, which provides that any outstanding income tax due under s.59A or any outstanding income tax or capital gains tax due under ss.55 or 59B shall carry interest at the appropriate rate from the due date to the date of payment. The due dates, which are set out in the relevant sections, do not have to be a business day within the Bills of Exchange Act 1882.

Special rules are applied where a claim is made to reduce a payment on account and where an additional amount becomes payable under TMA 1970, s.59B on settlement of an enquiry. Interest is payable in the first case as if the payments on account had each been equal to half the previous year's liability, or half the current year's liability, as amended, whichever is the less. In determining the additional amount payable following an enquiry, it is assumed that both the payments on account had been made and no other payments of tax, for example capital gains tax, should be taken into account.

Any interest charged on payments on account under TMA 1970, s.59A will be remitted to the extent that it relates to amounts which have become repayable for that year of assessment.

Subs. (2)

The new s.86 is applied to any overdue income tax or CGT charged by an assessment made after April 5, 1998 for 1995–96 or an earlier year of assessment.

Subs. (3)

Unless otherwise specified, the due date is January 31 following the year of assessment.

Assessments in respect of income taken into account under PAYE

111.—(1) For section 205 of the Taxes Act 1988 there shall be substituted the following section—

"Assessments unnecessary in certain circumstances

205.—(1) Subject to the provisions of this section, no assessment need be made in respect of income assessable to income tax for any year of assessment if the income has been taken into account in the making of deductions or repayments of income tax by virtue of regulations made under section 203.

(2) Subsection (1) above does not apply if the total net tax deducted in the year in question from the income is not the same as it would have been if—

(a) all the relevant circumstances had been known to all parties throughout the year;

(b) deductions and repayments had throughout the year been made accordingly; and

(c) the deductions and repayments had been so made by reference to cumulative tax tables.

(3) Nothing in this section shall be construed as preventing an assessment (whether under section 9 of the Management Act or otherwise) being made in respect of income assessable to income tax for any year of assessment.

(4) A person as regards whose income for a year of assessment deductions or repayments have been made may by notice, given not later than five years after the 31st October next following that year, require an officer of the Board to give him notice under section 8 of that Act in respect of that year.

(5) In this section—

(a) 'cumulative tax tables' means tax tables prepared under section 203 which are so framed as to require the tax which is to be deducted or repaid on the occasion of each payment made in the year to be ascertained by reference to a total of emoluments paid in the year up to the time of making that payment; and

(b) any reference to the total net tax deducted shall be construed as a reference to the total income tax deducted during the year by virtue of regulations made under section 203, less any income tax repaid by virtue of any such regulations."

(2) In section 206 of that Act (additional provision for certain assessments) the words "under Schedule E" shall cease to have effect.

GENERAL NOTE

The new ICTA 1988, s.205 gives authority not to make assessments where the correct amount of tax has been deducted under Pay As You Earn (PAYE). This amount will be marginally less than the full legal liability because the PAYE tax tables are designed to under-deduct by a small amount over the full year.

Section 205(1)

No assessment need be made in respect of income assessable to income tax, if that income has been taken into account in making deductions and repayments through the PAYE system. No reference is made to Schedule E, because after 1996/97 assessments will generally be based on total income.

Section 205(2)

Section 205(1) does not apply if the total tax deducted differs from what it would have been had all relevant circumstances been known and had all deductions and repayments been made on that basis using the cumulative PAYE tables.

Section 205(3)

Notwithstanding s.205, an assessment, including a self-assessment, may be made for any year.

Section 205(4)

The taxpayer retains the right to require the Revenue to issue a return for any tax year so that he can make a self-assessment, within five years and seven months of the end of that year.

Section 205(5)

This contains necessary definitions.

A consequential amendment is also made to ICTA 1988, s.206, in order to remove the redundant reference to Schedule E.

Recovery of certain amounts deducted or paid under MIRAS

112.—(1) After section 374 of the Taxes Act 1988 there shall be inserted the following section—

"Interest which never has been relevant loan interest etc.

374A.—(1) This section applies where, in the case of any loan, interest on the loan never has been relevant loan interest or the borrower never has been a qualifying borrower.

(2) Without prejudice to subsection (3) below, in relation to a payment of interest—

(a) as respects which either of the conditions mentioned in paragraphs (a) and (b) of section 374(1) is fulfilled, and

(b) from which a deduction was made as mentioned in section 369(1),

section 369 shall have effect as if the payment of interest were a payment of relevant loan interest made by a qualifying borrower.

(3) Nothing in subsection (2) above shall be taken as regards the borrower as entitling him to make any deduction or to retain any amount deducted and, accordingly, where any amount has been deducted, he shall be liable to make good that amount and an officer of the Board may make such assessments as may in his judgment be required for recovering that amount.

(4) The Management Act shall apply to an assessment under subsection (3) above as if it were an assessment to income tax for the year of assessment in which the deduction was made and as if—

    (a) the assessment were among those specified in section 55(1) of that Act (recovery of tax not postponed);

    (b) the assessment were made for the purpose of making good to the Crown a loss of tax wholly attributable to such a failure or error as is mentioned in subsection (1) of section 88 of that Act (interest on tax recovered to make good loss due to taxpayer's fault); and

    (c) for the purposes of that section the date when the tax ought to have been paid were the 1st December following the year of assessment.

(5) If the borrower fraudulently or negligently makes any false statement or representation in connection with the making of any deduction, he shall be liable to a penalty not exceeding the amount deducted."

(2) In subsection (2) of section 375 of that Act (interest ceasing to be relevant loan interest etc.), after paragraph (a) there shall be inserted the following paragraph—

    "(aa) as respects which any of the conditions mentioned in section 374(1) is fulfilled, and".

(3) For subsection (4) of that section there shall be substituted the following subsections—

    "(4) The Management Act shall apply to an assessment under subsection (3) above as it applies, by virtue of subsection (4) of section 374A, to an assessment under subsection (3) of that section.

    (4A) If there is any unreasonable delay in the giving of a notice under subsection (1) above, the borrower shall be liable to a penalty not exceeding so much of the aggregate amount that he is liable to make good under subsection (3) above as is attributable to that delay."

(4) After subsection (8) of that section there shall be inserted the following subsection—

    "(8A) In any case where an amount to which a person is not entitled is paid to him by the Board in pursuance of regulations made by virtue of subsection (8) above, regulations may—

    (a) provide for an officer of the Board to make such assessments as may in his judgment be required for recovering that amount from that person; and

    (b) make provision corresponding to that made by subsection (4A) above and subsections (4) and (5) of section 374A."

(5) This section applies in relation to deductions made by borrowers, and payments made by the Board, after the passing of this Act.

GENERAL NOTE

The powers of the Revenue to recover from borrowers any excess relief obtained through the mortgage interest relief at source (MIRAS) scheme is clarified.

Subs. (1)

This inserts new ICTA 1988, s.374A, which sets out the Revenue's recovery powers relating to loans which should not have been dealt with under the MIRAS scheme, but nevertheless have been. A lender may claim reimbursement from the Revenue of amounts deducted, provided he applied the MIRAS scheme on the basis of a notice from either the borrower or the Revenue. The Revenue has the power to recover these amounts from the borrower, by means of an assessment. Payment of the assessment may be postponed if an appeal is made. The tax charged will carry interest from December 1 following the year of assessment until payment. A penalty, up to the amount deducted, is chargeable if the borrower makes a fraudulent or negligent misstatement.

Subss. (2)–(4)

These make amendments to ICTA 1988, s.375, which deals with the position where interest payments cease to qualify for relief under MIRAS. The lender's right to reimbursement only applies after the loan ceases to qualify if the loan was properly allowed into the MIRAS scheme by the lender. Recovery assessments under ICTA 1988, s.375(3) are subject to the same conditions as recovery assessments under the new ICTA 1988, s.374A. Penalties up to the amount deducted by the borrower may be charged if there is unreasonable delay by the borrower in notifying the lender in cases where MIRAS ceases to be applicable. Where amounts have been paid to a borrower by the Revenue under ICTA 1988, s.375(8), and it turns out that he was not entitled to them, they may be recovered by regulations under new ICTA 1988, s.375(8A). Assessments under these regulations will carry the same provisions regarding recovery and penalties as for other assessments under new ICTA 1988, s.374A and amended ICTA 1988, s.375.

Allowable losses: capital gains tax

113.—(1) After subsection (2) of section 16 of the Taxation of Chargeable Gains Act 1992 (computation of losses) there shall be inserted the following subsection—

"(2A) A loss accruing to a person in a year of assessment shall not be an allowable loss for the purposes of this Act unless, in relation to that year, he gives a notice to an officer of the Board quantifying the amount of that loss; and sections 42 and 43 of the Management Act shall apply in relation to such a notice as if it were a claim for relief."

(2) Deductions under that Act in respect of allowable losses shall be given preference as follows—

(a) a deduction in respect of a loss accruing to a person in the year 1996–97 or a subsequent year of assessment shall be preferred to a deduction in respect of a loss accruing to him in an earlier year of assessment; and

(b) a deduction in respect of a loss accruing to a company in an accounting period ending on or after the appointed day for the purposes of Chapter III of Part IV of the Finance Act 1994 shall be preferred to a deduction in respect of a loss accruing to the company in an accounting period ending before that day.

GENERAL NOTE

The amount of an allowable loss for CGT purposes has to be claimed in relation to the year in which it accrues. The loss can be included in the tax return and must be claimed by individuals within five years ten months of the end of the year of assessment, and by companies within six years of the end of the accounting period in which it accrued.

Subs. (1)

New TCGA 1992, s.16(2A) provides for notification of losses and for the notification to serve as a claim for relief.

Subs. (2)

Capital losses notified in this way will take precedence over losses which accrued earlier. The new provisions apply from 1996/97 for individuals and from an appointed day for companies.

Liability of trustees and personal representatives: capital gains tax

114.—(1) For subsection (1) of section 65 of the Taxation of Chargeable Gains Act 1992 (liability for tax of trustees and personal representatives) there shall be substituted the following subsection—

"(1) Subject to subsection (3) below, capital gains tax chargeable in respect of chargeable gains accruing to the trustees of a settlement or capital gains tax due from the personal representatives of a deceased person may be assessed and charged on and in the name of any one or more of the relevant trustees or the relevant personal representatives."

(2) After subsection (2) of that section there shall be inserted the following subsections—

"(3) Where section 80 applies as regards the trustees of a settlement ('the migrating trustees'), nothing in subsection (1) above shall enable any person—

(a) who ceased to be a trustee of the settlement before the end of the relevant period, and

(b) who shows that, when he ceased to be a trustee of the settlement, there was no proposal that the trustees might become neither resident nor ordinarily resident in the United Kingdom,

to be assessed and charged to any capital gains tax which is payable by the migrating trustees by virtue of section 80(2).

(4) In this section—

'the relevant period' has the same meaning as in section 82;

'the relevant trustees', in relation to any chargeable gains, means the trustees in the year of assessment in which the chargeable gains accrue and any subsequent trustees of the settlement, and 'the relevant personal representatives' has a corresponding meaning."

GENERAL NOTE

This section deals with the liability of trustees for CGT under the self-assessment regime and is linked with s.103 above, which deals with their liability for income tax. It also covers the CGT liability of personal representatives.

Subs. (1)

The substituted TCGA 1992, s.65(1) allows any relevant trustee or personal representative to be assessed and charged on chargeable gains accruing to a trust or estate of a deceased person.

Subs. (2)

A relevant trustee may not be charged under TCGA 1992, s.80, which imposes a CGT charge on trustees ceasing to be resident in the U.K., if he can show that there was no proposal that they cease to be so resident at the time he resigned.

Minor amendments and repeals

115.—(1) In subsection (7) of section 7 of the Management Act (notice of liability), for the words "income from which" there shall be substituted the words "income on which".

(2) In subsection (3) of section 9 of that Act (returns to include self-assessment), the words "the following provisions of" shall cease to have effect.

(3) Section 11A of that Act (notice of liability to capital gains tax) shall cease to have effect.

(4) In subsection (2) of section 12AA of that Act (partnership return), for the words "such accounts and statements" there shall be substituted the words "such accounts, statements and documents, relating to information contained in the return,".

(5) In subsection (1)(c) of section 30B of that Act (amendment of partnership statement where loss of tax discovered), after the word "relief" there shall be inserted the words "or allowance".

(6) In subsection (6) of section 59B of that Act (payment of income tax and capital gains tax), for the words "under section 29 of this Act shall" there shall be substituted the words "otherwise than under section 9 of this Act shall, unless otherwise provided,".

(7) In subsection (1) of section 100B of that Act (appeals against penalty determinations), after the words "95A of this Act" there shall be inserted the word "and".

(8) In section 103A of that Act (interest on penalties), for the words "Part II or VA" there shall be substituted the words "Part II, IV or VA".

(9) Section 73 of the Taxes Act 1988 (single assessments for purposes of Cases III, IV and V of Schedule D) shall cease to have effect.

(10) In sections 536 and 537B of that Act (taxation of royalties where owner abroad)—

    (a) in subsection (2) (exemption from requirement to deduct tax from royalties), the words "are shown on a claim to" shall cease to have effect; and

    (b) in subsection (4) (deduction of tax where agent's commission unknown), the words from "and in that case" to the end shall cease to have effect.

(11) In Schedule 3 to that Act (machinery for assessment, charge and payment of income tax under Schedule C and, in certain cases, Schedule D), in paragraph 6E, sub-paragraphs (1) and (3) shall cease to have effect.

(12) Section 7 of the Taxation of Chargeable Gains Act 1992 (time for payment of capital gains tax) shall cease to have effect.

(13) Subsection (3) above has effect as respects the year 1995–96 and subsequent years of assessment.

GENERAL NOTE
The section contains a number of minor amendments and repeals relating to self-assessment.

Transitional provisions

116.—(1) The provisions of the Management Act specified in Schedule 21 to this Act shall have effect subject to the transitional provisions contained in that Schedule.

(2) Section 198 of the Finance Act 1994 (which is superseded by this section) shall cease to have effect.

GENERAL NOTE
The section introduces Sched. 21, which provides transitional rules for notification of chargeability to tax in 1995–96 and for payments on account of income tax in 1996–97. FA 1994, s.198, which contained transitional provisions, is repealed.
See further the General Note to Sched. 21.

Changes for facilitating self-assessment

Treatment of partnerships

117.—(1) Section 215 of the Finance Act 1994 (treatment of partnerships) shall have effect, and shall be deemed always to have had effect, as if—

    (a) for the section set out in subsection (1) of that section there were substituted the section set out in subsection (2) below;

    (b) after the said subsection (1) there were inserted the subsection set out in subsection (3) below;

    (c) in subsection (2) of section 215, the word "and" were inserted immediately after paragraph (a), and paragraph (c) and the word "and" immediately preceding that paragraph were omitted; and

    (d) in subsection (3) of that section, in paragraph (a), for the words from "in subsection (3)" to the end there were substituted the words "subsections (3) and (4)".

(2) Subject to subsection (4) below, the section referred to in subsection (1)(a) above is as follows—

"Treatment of partnerships

    111.—(1) Where a trade or profession is carried on by persons in partnership, the partnership shall not, unless the contrary intention appears, be treated for the purposes of the Tax Acts as an entity which is separate and distinct from those persons.

(2) So long as a trade or profession is carried on by persons in partnership, and any of those persons is chargeable to income tax, the profits or gains or losses arising from the trade or profession ('the actual trade or profession') shall be computed for the purposes of income tax in like manner as if—

(a) the partnership were an individual; and

(b) that individual were an individual resident in the United Kingdom.

(3) A person's share in the profits or gains or losses arising from the actual trade or profession which for any period are computed in accordance with subsection (2) above shall be determined according to the interests of the partners during that period.

(4) Where a person's share in any profits or gains or losses is determined in accordance with subsection (3) above, sections 60 to 63A shall apply as if—

(a) that share of the profits or gains or losses derived from a trade or profession carried on by him alone;

(b) that trade or profession ('the deemed trade or profession') had been set up and commenced by him at the time when he became a partner or, where the actual trade or profession was previously carried on by him alone, the time when the actual trade or profession was set up and commenced;

(c) as regards each year of assessment, any accounting date or accounting change of the actual trade or profession were also an accounting date or accounting change of the deemed trade or profession;

(d) subsection (2) of section 62 applied in relation to any accounting change of the deemed trade or profession if, and only if, on the assumption that the partnership were an individual, that subsection would apply in relation to the corresponding accounting change of the actual trade or profession; and

(e) the deemed trade or profession were permanently discontinued by him at the time when he ceases to be a partner or, where the actual trade or profession is subsequently carried on by him alone, the time when the actual trade or profession is permanently discontinued.

(5) Where section 62(2) does not apply in relation to any accounting change of the deemed trade or profession which is made or treated as made in the year of assessment next following or next but one following the commencement year, sections 60(3)(a) and 61(2)(a) shall apply as if the old date in that year were the accounting date.

(6) For the purpose of determining whether, on the assumption that the partnership were an individual, section 62(2) would apply in relation to an accounting change of the actual trade or profession—

(a) a notice may be given under subsection (3) of section 62A; and

(b) an appeal may be brought under subsection (6) of that section,

by such one of the partners as may be nominated by them for the purposes of this subsection.

(7) Where—

(a) subsections (2) and (3) above apply in relation to the profits or gains or losses of a trade or profession carried on by persons in partnership; and

(b) other income or other relievable losses accrue to those persons by virtue of their being partners,

those subsections shall apply as if references to the profits or gains or losses arising from the trade or profession included references to that other income or those other relievable losses.

(8) Where a person's share in any untaxed income from one or more sources, or in any relievable losses, is determined in accordance with subsection (3) as applied by subsection (7) above, sections 60 to 63A shall apply as if—

(a) that share of that income or of those losses were profits or gains or losses of a trade or profession carried on by that person alone;

(b) that trade or profession ('the second deemed trade or profession') had been set up and commenced by him at the time when he became a partner;

(c) paragraphs (c) and (d) of subsection (4) and subsection (5) above applied in relation to the second deemed trade or profession as they apply in relation to the other deemed trade or profession;

(d) the second deemed trade or profession were permanently discontinued by him at the time when he ceases to be a partner; and

(e) each source of the income were treated as continuing until the second deemed trade or profession is treated as permanently discontinued.

(9) Where—

(a) the basis period for any year of assessment is given by section 62(2)(b) in the case of a person's second deemed trade or profession, or such a trade or profession is treated as permanently discontinued in any year of assessment; and

(b) the amount falling to be deducted under subsection (1) or (3) of section 63A exceeds that person's share, as determined in accordance with subsection (3) as applied by subsection (7) above, in any untaxed income,

the amount of the excess shall be deducted in computing that person's income for that year.

(10) Subsections (1) to (3) above apply in relation to persons in partnership by whom a business which is not a trade or profession is carried on as they apply in relation to persons in partnership by whom a trade or profession is carried on.

(11) In subsections (2) and (3) above as applied by subsection (10) above, references to the profits or gains or losses arising from the trade or profession shall have effect as references to any income or relievable losses arising from the business.

(12) In this section—

'accounting change' and 'the old date' have the meanings given by section 62(1);

'accounting date' has the meaning given by section 60(5);

'the commencement year', in relation to the deemed trade or profession or the second deemed trade or profession, means the year of assessment in which that trade or profession is deemed to have been set up and commenced;

'income' means any income (whether or not chargeable under Schedule D);

'untaxed income' means income which is not—

(a) income from which income tax has been deducted;

(b) income from or on which income tax is treated as having been deducted or paid; or

(c) income chargeable under Schedule F.

(13) In this section—

(a) any reference to sections 60 to 63A includes a reference to those sections as applied in relation to losses by section 382(3) and (4) and section 385(1); and

(b) any reference to a person becoming or ceasing to be a partner is a reference to his beginning or, as the case may be, ceasing to carry on the actual trade or profession in partnership with other persons."

(3) The subsection referred to in subsection (1)(b) above is as follows—

"(1A) In subsection (2) of section 110 of that Act (interpretation of sections 103 to 109A), for the words from 'any event' to the end there shall be substituted the following paragraphs—

'(a) any event which, under section 113 or 337(1), is to be treated as equivalent to the permanent discontinuance of a trade, profession or vocation; or

(b) in relation to a trade or profession carried on by a person in partnership with other persons, any event which, under subsection (4) of section 111, is to be treated as equivalent to the permanent discontinuance of his deemed trade or profession (within the meaning of that subsection)'."

(4) As respects the year 1994–95, the section set out in subsection (2) above shall have effect as if, in subsection (2) of that section, paragraph (b) and the word "and" immediately preceding that paragraph were omitted.

GENERAL NOTE

The section introduces an amended ICTA 1988, s.111 to clarify the rules introduced in FA 1994 governing the computation of income and of basis periods for partnerships.

Subs. (1)

This provides for changes to be made to FA 1994, s.215, which itself made changes to the treatment of partnerships.

Subs. (2)

This substitutes an amended ICTA 1988, s.111 for the s.111 contained in FA 1994, s.215(1).

Section 111(1). Where a trade or profession is carried on in partnership, the partnership will not be treated as a separate entity.

Section 111(2). Where at least one of the partners is subject to income tax, the profits will be computed as if the partnership were an individual resident in the U.K.

Section 111(3). A partner's share is to be computed in accordance with the interests of the partners during the basis period.

Section 111(4). The basis period rules in ICTA 1988, ss.60–63A are applied to each individual partner in accordance with the partner's own circumstances, as if each partner were the sole proprietor of a business whose profits equalled the partner's profit share. It aligns the accounting date of this notional business with that of the actual business carried on by the partnership and applies the change of accounting date rules in such a way as to maintain this alignment.

Section 111(5). A potential misalignment of accounting date is prevented when a new partner joins a firm.

Section 111(6). A notice of change of accounting date under ICTA 1988, s.62A(3) must be given at the partnership level, as does an appeal brought under s.62A(6).

Section 111(7). The rules in s.111(2) and (3) apply to all other income of a partnership, provided it carries on a trade or profession.

Section 111(8). This other income is assessed using the same basis periods as the trading or professional income, but is treated as accruing to a second deemed trade.

Section 111(9). Any income which is taxed as if it were from a second deemed trade but which cannot be relieved in that deemed trade, may be relieved against the total income of the partner for the year the relief falls to be given.

Section 111(10). The rules in s.111(1) to (3) apply to a partnership carrying on a business which is not a trade or profession.

Section 111(11). Similarly, references to the profits or gains of a trade or profession in s.111(2) and (3) apply to any business income.

Section 111(12). Various definitions are provided.

Section 111(13). Where losses arise to any of the sources of income in the second deemed trade, these are to be computed using the periods appropriate to trading losses. Ceasing to be a partner means cessation of carrying on the trade or profession in partnership.

Subs. (3)

This amends ICTA 1988, s.110(2), which provides the interpretation rules for ss.103–109A. These cover the taxation of post-cessation expenditure and receipts. The amendments ensure that all deemed cessations of a trade and deemed cessations of a deemed trade are treated as equivalent to a permanent discontinuance of a trade so that ss.103–109A will operate.

Subs. (4)

The rule requiring a partnership to be treated as an individual resident in the U.K. does not apply for the year 1994–95.

Loss relief: general

118. Section 209 of the Finance Act 1994 (loss relief: general) shall have effect, and shall be deemed always to have had effect, as if for subsection (7) (commencement of subsections (3) to (5)) there were substituted the following subsections—

"(7) Subsections (1), (2) and (6) above—

(a) except in their application to a trade set up and commenced on or after 6th April 1994, have effect in relation to losses sustained in the year 1996–97 and subsequent years of assessment; and

(b) in their application to a trade so set up and commenced, have effect in relation to losses sustained in the year 1994–95 and subsequent years of assessment.

(8) Subsections (3) to (5) above—

(a) except in their application to a trade set up and commenced on or after 6th April 1994, have effect in relation to losses sustained in the year 1997–98 and subsequent years of assessment; and

(b) in their application to a trade so set up and commenced, have effect in relation to losses sustained in the year 1994–95 and subsequent years of assessment.

(9) Any reference in subsection (7) or (8) above to a trade includes a reference to a profession, vocation or employment."

GENERAL NOTE

FA 1994, s.209 is amended to provide that trades, professions or vocations set up before April 6, 1994 may continue to set losses sustained in 1995–96 against other income for that year or for the year 1996–97.

FA 1994, s.209(7) is repealed and replaced by new s.209(7)–(9). The material change is that losses sustained in 1995–96 will be relievable against 1996–97 income under ICTA 1988, s.380(2). The new ICTA 1988, s.380(1) and (2), introduced by FA 1994, s.209(1) have effect for losses sustained in 1996–97. The original commencement date would have prevented the old s.380(2) giving relief for such losses.

Relief for losses on unquoted shares

119. Section 210 of the Finance Act 1994 (relief for losses on unquoted shares) shall have effect, and shall be deemed always to have had effect, as if, in subsection (2) (commencement), for the words "as respects" there were substituted the words "in relation to losses incurred in".

GENERAL NOTE

The amendment to FA 1994, s. 210 makes it clear that losses on unquoted shares sustained in 1993–94 can be relieved against income for 1993–94 or 1994–95. The previous wording would have prevented 1993–94 losses from being relieved against 1994–95 income.

Relief for pre-trading expenditure

120.—(1) In section 401 of the Taxes Act 1988 (relief for pre-trading expenditure)—

(a) in subsection (1), for the words from "treated" to the end there shall be substituted the words "treated as incurred on the day on which the trade, profession or vocation is first carried on by him"; and

(b) subsection (2) shall cease to have effect.

(2) This section has effect as respects trades, professions and vocations which are set up and commenced on or after 6th April 1995.

GENERAL NOTE
The amendment to ICTA 1988, s.401 makes the treatment of pre-trading expenditure the same for both companies subject to corporation tax and individuals and other persons subject to income tax. Separate treatment for the latter was necessary under the old preceding year basis of assessment.

Basis of apportionment for Cases I, II and VI of Schedule D

121. In section 72(2) of the Taxes Act 1988 (apportionments etc. for purposes of Cases I, II and VI of Schedule D) for the words "months, or fractions of months," there shall be substituted the word "days".

GENERAL NOTE
Apportionments needed for the purposes of Cases I, II and VI of Schedule D will be made in future by reference to days rather than months or fractions of months.

Amendments of transitional provisions

122.—(1) Schedule 20 to the Finance Act 1994 (changes for facilitating self-assessment: transitional provisions and savings) shall be amended as follows.

(2) In sub-paragraph (4) of paragraph 2 (Cases I and II of Schedule D), after the words "which arise" there shall be inserted the words "after the end of—

(a) the basis period for the year 1996–97; or

(b) in the case of a trade or profession carried on by a person in partnership with other persons, the basis period of the partnership for that year,

and (in either case)".

(3) After that sub-paragraph there shall be inserted the following sub-paragraphs—

"(4A) In calculating the amount of the profits or gains of the basis period for the year 1997–98 which arise as mentioned in sub-paragraph (4) above, any deduction of a capital allowance and any addition of a balancing charge shall be ignored.

(4B) Sub-paragraph (4A) above does not apply in the case of a trade or profession carried on by persons who include both an individual and a company."

(4) At the beginning of sub-paragraph (5) of paragraph 10 (double taxation relief) there shall be inserted the words "Subject to sub-paragraph (5A) below,".

(5) After that sub-paragraph there shall be inserted the following sub-paragraph—

"(5A) Where the period on the profits or gains of which income tax is chargeable under Case IV or V of Schedule D for the year 1995–96 is that year, sub-paragraph (5) above shall have effect as if for the words from '50 per cent.' to the end there were substituted the words 'the amount of foreign tax paid on income arising, or (as the case may require) received in the United Kingdom, in that year'."

GENERAL NOTE
Three amendments are made to the provisions in FA 1994, Sched. 20 covering the transition from the preceding year to the current year basis of assessment.

Subs. (2)
Transitional overlap relief under FA 1994, Sched. 20, para. 2(4) is prevented in respect of income which is also subject to an overlap relief under ICTA 1988, s.63A.

Subs. (3)
New FA 1994, Sched. 20, para. 2(4A) and (4B) provide that, in calculating the amount of transitional overlap relief, any deduction of a capital allowance and any addition of a balancing charge is ignored, except in the case of a partnership which includes both an individual and a company.

Subss. (4) and (5)
The rules for allowing foreign tax credit relief are amended to ensure that, where Case IV or Case V income is assessed for 1995–96 on the actual income of that year, the full amount of any foreign tax paid in respect of that income is eligible for credit relief.

Prevention of exploitation of transitional provisions

123. Schedule 22 to this Act shall have effect for preventing the exploitation of, and (in certain cases) penalising attempts to exploit, the transitional provisions set out in paragraphs 2(2) and (4), 4(2) and 6(2)(a) and (4) of Schedule 20 to the Finance Act 1994 (changes for facilitating self-assessment: transitional provisions and savings).

GENERAL NOTE
The section introduces Sched. 22, which contains measures designed to prevent and penalise attempts to use the transitional period between the preceding year basis and the current year basis for the artificial avoidance of tax.
See further the General Note to Sched. 22.

Change of residence and non-residents

Change of residence

124.—(1) In Chapter VI of Part IV of the Taxes Act 1988 (discontinuance and change of basis of computation), after section 110 there shall be inserted the following section—

"Change of residence

Change of residence
110A.—(1) Where there is a change of residence by an individual who is carrying on any trade, profession or vocation wholly or partly outside the United Kingdom and otherwise than in partnership with others, tax shall be chargeable, and loss relief may be claimed, as if the change—
    (a) constituted the permanent discontinuance of the trade, profession or vocation; and
    (b) was immediately followed, in so far as the trade, profession or vocation continues to be carried on by that individual, by the setting up and commencement of a new one;
but nothing in this subsection shall prevent any portion of a loss sustained before the change from being carried forward under section 385 and set against profits or gains arising or accruing after the change.
    (2) For the purposes of this section there is a change of residence by an individual if—
    (a) not being resident in the United Kingdom, he becomes so resident; or
    (b) being so resident, he ceases to be so resident."
    (2) This section shall have effect as respects the year 1997–98 and subsequent years of assessment and also, in relation only to a trade, profession or vocation set up and commenced on or after 6th April 1994, as respects the years 1995–96 and 1996–97.

GENERAL NOTE
New ICTA 1988, s.110A provides that where an individual who is carrying on a trade, profession or vocation wholly or partly outside the U.K. as a sole trader becomes or ceases to be

resident in the UK, he will be taxed as if the trade etc. had ceased and recommenced. This will ensure that the correct amount of profits are taxed under self-assessment, *i.e.* the worldwide profits for the period of residence, but only the profits earned in the U.K. for the period of non-residence. Notwithstanding the deemed cessation, trading losses can continue to be carried forward from before the change of residence and set against the profits of the continuing trade after the change.

The section applies generally from 1997–98 onwards and, where the trade commenced after April 5, 1994, for 1995–96 and 1996–97.

Non-resident partners

125.—(1) The provisions of the Taxes Act 1988 to which sections 215 and 216 of the Finance Act 1994 (partnerships and change of ownership of trade etc.) relate shall have effect as respects the year 1995–96 and subsequent years of assessment as if subsection (5)(b) of section 215 (amendments not to apply until the year 1997–98 to partnerships controlled abroad) were omitted; and the Taxes Act 1988 shall have effect—

(a) as respects the year 1997–98 and subsequent years of assessment, and
(b) in its application with the amendments made by those sections to partnerships whose trades, professions or businesses were set up and commenced on or after 6th April 1994, as respects the years 1995–96 and 1996–97,

with the further amendments specified in the following provisions of this section.

(2) For subsections (1) to (3) of section 112 (partnerships controlled abroad) there shall be substituted the following subsections—

"(1) So long as a trade, profession or business is carried on by persons in partnership and any of those persons is not resident in the United Kingdom, section 111 shall have effect for the purposes of income tax in relation to the partner who is not so resident as if—

(a) the reference in subsection (2)(b) to an individual resident in the United Kingdom were a reference to an individual who is not so resident; and
(b) in subsection (4)(a), after 'carried on' there were inserted 'in the United Kingdom'.

(1A) Where—

(a) any persons are carrying on a trade, profession or business in partnership,
(b) the trade, profession or business is carried on wholly or partly outside the United Kingdom,
(c) the control and management of the trade, profession or business is situated outside the United Kingdom, and
(d) any of the partners who is an individual resident in the United Kingdom satisfies the Board that he is not domiciled in the United Kingdom or that, being a Commonwealth citizen or a citizen of the Republic of Ireland, he is not ordinarily resident in the United Kingdom,

section 111 shall have effect in accordance with subsection (1) above as if that partner were not resident in the United Kingdom and, in addition (as respects that partner as an individual who is in fact resident in the United Kingdom), his interest as a partner, so far as it entitles him to a share of any profits or gains arising from the carrying on of the trade, profession or business otherwise than within the United Kingdom, shall be treated for the purposes of Case V of Schedule D as if it were a possession outside the United Kingdom.

(1B) Where any persons are carrying on a trade or profession in partnership, the trade or profession is carried on wholly or partly outside the United Kingdom and an individual who is one of the partners changes his residence (within the meaning of section 110A), it shall be assumed for income tax purposes—

    (a) that that individual ceased to be a partner at the time of the change and became one again immediately afterwards; and

    (b) in relation to matters arising after the change, that the time when he became a partner is the time immediately after the change;

but nothing in this subsection shall, in relation to that individual, prevent any portion of a loss sustained before the change from being carried forward under section 385 and set against profits or gains arising or accruing after the change."

(3) In that section—

(a) in subsection (4)(a), for "or is deemed to reside outside the United Kingdom" there shall be substituted "outside the United Kingdom or which carries on any trade, profession or business the control and management of which is situated outside the United Kingdom"; and

(b) in subsection (6), for "this section" there shall be substituted "subsections (4) and (5) above".

(4) In section 114(1) (partnerships including companies), after the word "company", in the second place where it occurs, there shall be inserted "and, subject to section 115(4), as if that company were resident in the United Kingdom".

(5) In section 115 (provisions supplementary to section 114), for subsections (4) and (5) there shall be substituted the following subsections—

    "(4) So long as a trade, profession or business is carried on by persons in partnership and any of those persons is a company which is not resident in the United Kingdom, section 114 shall have effect in relation to that company as if—

    (a) the reference in subsection (1) to a company resident in the United Kingdom were a reference to a company that is not so resident; and

    (b) in subsection (2), after 'carried on' there were inserted 'in the United Kingdom through a branch or agency'.

    (5) Where the partners in a partnership include a company, subsections (4) and (5) of section 112 shall apply for the purposes of corporation tax as well as for the purposes of income tax, and section 114 shall have effect accordingly."

GENERAL NOTE

The section makes explicit for self-assessment the rule that non-resident partners are only taxed on their share of the profits earned by the partnership in the U.K. It also confirms that where a trade *etc.* carried on in partnership is controlled and managed abroad and an individual partner is resident but not domiciled in the U.K., the partner's share of the profits earned by the partnership outside the U.K. will continue to be taxed on the remittance basis. It further provides that where an individual carrying on a trade *etc.* in partnership wholly or partly outside the U.K. becomes or ceases to be resident in the U.K., the individual will be taxed as if the trade had ceased and recommenced. This matches the provision in s.124 above for sole traders. The section applies from 1995–96 onwards wherever the basis rules for self-assessment also apply, *i.e.* for 1997–98 onwards generally and, where the trade commenced after April 5, 1994, for 1995–96 and 1996–97.

UK representatives of non-residents

126.—(1) Schedule 23 to this Act shall have effect for imposing obligations and liabilities in relation to income tax, corporation tax and capital gains tax on a branch or agency which, under this section, is the UK representative of a person who is not resident in the United Kingdom ("the non-resident").

(2) Subject to the following provisions of this section and to section 127 below, a branch or agency in the United Kingdom through which the non-resident carries on (whether solely or in partnership) any trade, profession or vocation shall, for the purposes of this section and Schedule 23 to this Act, be

the non-resident's UK representative in relation to the following amounts, that is to say—

    (a) the amount of any such income from the trade, profession or vocation as arises, directly or indirectly, through or from that branch or agency;

    (b) the amount of any income from property or rights which are used by, or held by or for, that branch or agency;

    (c) amounts which, by reference to that branch or agency, are chargeable to capital gains tax under section 10 of the Taxation of Chargeable Gains Act 1992 (non-residents) or fall under that section to be included in the chargeable profits of the non-resident; and

    (d) in a case where the non-resident is an overseas life insurance company, any other amounts which by virtue of paragraph 3 of Schedule 19AC to the Taxes Act 1988 fall by reference to that branch or agency to be included in the company's chargeable profits for the purposes of corporation tax.

(3) For the purposes of this section and Schedule 23 to this Act, the non-resident's UK representative in relation to any amount shall continue to be the non-resident's UK representative in relation to that amount even after ceasing to be a branch or agency through which the non-resident carries on the trade, profession or vocation in question.

(4) For the purposes of this section and Schedule 23 to this Act, the non-resident's UK representative in relation to any amount shall be treated, where he would not otherwise be so treated, as if he were a separate and distinct person from the non-resident.

(5) Where the branch or agency through which the non-resident carries on the trade, profession or vocation is one carried on by persons in partnership, the partnership, as such, shall be deemed for the purposes of this section and Schedule 23 to this Act to be the non-resident's UK representative in relation to the amounts mentioned in subsection (2) above.

(6) Where a trade or profession carried on by the non-resident through a branch or agency in the United Kingdom is one carried on by him in partnership, the trade or profession carried on through that branch or agency shall be deemed, for the purposes of this section and Schedule 23 to this Act, to include the deemed trade or profession from which the non-resident's share in the partnership's profits, gains or losses is treated for the purposes of section 111 or 114 of the Taxes Act 1988 as deriving.

(7) For the purposes of this section and Schedule 23 to this Act where—

    (a) a trade or profession carried on by the non-resident in the United Kingdom is one carried on by him in partnership, and

    (b) any member of that partnership is resident in the United Kingdom,

the deemed trade or profession from which the non-resident's share in the partnership's profits, gains or losses is treated for the purposes of section 111 or 114 of the Taxes Act 1988 as deriving shall be treated (in addition, where subsection (6) above also applies, to being treated as included in a trade or profession carried on through any such branch or agency as is mentioned in that subsection) as a trade carried on in the United Kingdom through the partnership as such.

(8) In this section "branch or agency" has the same meaning as in the Management Act.

(9) This section and Schedule 23 to this Act apply—

    (a) for the purposes of income tax and capital gains tax, in relation to the year 1996–97 and subsequent years of assessment; and

    (b) for the purposes of corporation tax, in relation to accounting periods beginning after 31st March 1996.

GENERAL NOTE

    This section, together with Sched. 23, establishes the obligations and liabilities of U.K. representatives of non-residents under self-assessment. The rules only apply where the non-resident is carrying on a trade, *etc.* in the U.K. through a branch or agent and they replace the present rules in the TMA 1970, ss.78–85. The branch or agent is made jointly responsible with the non-resident for all that needs to be done in connection with self-assessment of profits from or connected with the branch or agency and similarly for the charge on non-resident companies under Pay and File. The section comes into effect from 1996–97 for non-residents liable to income tax and for accounting periods beginning after March 31, 1996 for non-residents liable to corporation tax.

Subs. (1)
This introduces Sched. 23. See further the General Note to that Schedule.

Subs. (2)
The rules only apply where the non-resident is carrying on a trade *etc.* through a U.K. representative and in relation to the profits therefrom.

Subs. (3)
The representative does not cease to be liable for obligations accrued during his agency after it ceases.

Subs. (4)
The branch is treated as a separate entity from the non-resident.

Subs. (5)
A partnership can be the U.K. representative of a non-resident.

Subs. (6)
Where a partnership trades in the U.K. through a branch or agency, the branch or agent is also treated as the U.K. representative of any non-resident partner in relation to his share of the U.K. profits.

Subs. (7)
Where a partnership which trades in the U.K. includes both resident and non-resident members, the partnership is treated as the U.K. representative of any non-resident partner in relation to his share of the U.K. profits. This makes the partners jointly liable for tax on the non-resident partner's share of the U.K. profits.

Subs. (8)
For the definition of "branch or agency", see the TMA 1970, s.118(1).

Persons not treated as UK representatives

127.—(1) For the purposes of section 126 above and Schedule 23 to this Act, none of the following persons shall be capable of being the non-resident's UK representative in relation to income or other amounts falling within paragraphs (a) to (d) of section 126(2) above, that is to say—
    (a) where the income arises from, or the other amounts are chargeable by reference to, so much of any business as relates to transactions carried out through a person who (though an agent of the non-resident) does not act in relation to the transactions in the course of carrying on a regular agency for the non-resident, that agent;
    (b) where the income arises from, or the other amounts are chargeable by reference to, so much of any business as relates to transactions carried out through a broker and falling within subsection (2) below, that broker;
    (c) where the income arises from, or the other amounts are chargeable by reference to, so much of any business as relates to investment transactions carried out through an investment manager and falling within subsection (3) below, that manager; and
    (d) where the non-resident is a member of Lloyd's and the income arises from, or the other amounts are chargeable by reference to, his underwriting business, any person who, in relation to or to matters connected with that income or those amounts, has been the non-resident's members' agent or the managing agent of the syndicate in question.

(2) For the purposes of subsection (1)(b) above where any income arises from, or other amounts are chargeable by reference to, so much of any business as relates to any transaction carried out through a broker, that transaction shall be taken, in relation to the income or other amounts ("the taxable sums"), to fall within this subsection if—

(a) at the time of the transaction, the broker was carrying on the business of a broker;

(b) the transaction was carried out by the broker on behalf of the non-resident in the ordinary course of that business;

(c) the remuneration which the broker received for the provision of the services of a broker to the non-resident in respect of that transaction was at a rate not less than that which would have been customary for that class of business; and

(d) the non-resident does not fall (apart from this paragraph) to be treated as having the broker as his UK representative in relation to any income or other amounts not included in the taxable sums but chargeable to tax for the same chargeable period.

(3) For the purposes of subsection (1)(c) above where any income arises from, or other amounts are chargeable by reference to, so much of any business as relates to any investment transaction, that transaction shall be taken, in relation to that income or those amounts ("the taxable sums"), to have been carried out through an investment manager and to fall within this subsection if—

(a) the transaction was carried out on behalf of the non-resident by a person ("the manager") who at the time was carrying on a business of providing investment management services;

(b) the transaction was carried out in the ordinary course of that business;

(c) the manager, when he acted on behalf of the non-resident in relation to the transaction, did so in an independent capacity;

(d) the requirements of subsection (4) below are satisfied in relation to the transaction;

(e) the remuneration which the manager received for the provision to the non-resident of the investment management services in question was at a rate which was not less than that which would have been customary for that class of business; and

(f) the non-resident does not fall (apart from this paragraph) to be treated as having the manager as his UK representative in relation to any income or other amounts not included in the taxable sums but chargeable to tax for the same chargeable period.

(4) Subject to subsections (9) to (11) below, the requirements of this subsection are satisfied in relation to any transaction if—

(a) there is a qualifying period in relation to which it has been or is the intention of the manager and the persons connected with him that the non-resident's relevant excluded income should, as to at least 80 per cent., consist of amounts to which neither the manager nor any such person has a beneficial entitlement; and

(b) to the extent that there is a failure to fulfil that intention, that failure—

(i) is attributable (directly or indirectly) to matters outside the control of the manager and persons connected with him; and

(ii) does not result from a failure by the manager or any of those persons to take such steps as may be reasonable for mitigating the effect of those matters in relation to the fulfilment of that intention.

(5) For the purposes of this section any reference to the relevant excluded income of the non-resident for a qualifying period is a reference to the aggregate of such of the profits and gains of the non-resident for the chargeable periods comprised in the qualifying period as—

(a) derive from transactions carried out by the manager while acting on the non-resident's behalf; and

(b) for the purposes of section 128 or 129 below would fall (apart from the requirements of subsection (4) above) to be treated as excluded income for any of those chargeable periods.

(6) For the purposes of this section any reference to an amount of relevant excluded income to which a person has a beneficial entitlement is a reference to so much of any amount to which he has or may acquire a beneficial entitlement by virtue of—

(a) any interest of his (whether or not an interest giving a right to an immediate payment of a share in the profits or gains) in property in which the whole or any part of that income is represented, or

(b) any interest of his in or other rights in relation to the non-resident, as is or would be attributable to that income.

(7) For the purposes of subsections (4) to (6) above references to a qualifying period, in relation to any transaction, are references to any period consisting in or including the chargeable period for which the taxable sums are chargeable to tax, being, in a case where it is not that chargeable period, a period of not more than five years comprising two or more complete chargeable periods.

(8) Where there is a transaction which would fall within subsection (3) above but for its being a transaction in relation to which the requirements of subsection (4) above are not satisfied, this section shall have effect as if the transaction did fall within subsection (3) above but only in relation to so much of the amount of the taxable sums as does not represent any amount of the non-resident's relevant excluded income to which the manager or a person connected with him has or has had any beneficial entitlement.

(9) Subsections (10) and (11) below shall apply, where amounts arise or accrue to the non-resident as a participant in a collective investment scheme, for the purpose of determining whether a transaction carried out for the purposes of that scheme, in so far as it is a transaction in respect of which any such amounts arise or accrue to him, is one in relation to which the requirements of subsection (4) above are satisfied.

(10) Those requirements shall be deemed to be satisfied in relation to the transaction wherever the collective investment scheme is such that, if the following assumptions applied, namely—

(a) that all transactions carried out for the purposes of the scheme were carried out on behalf of a company constituted for the purposes of the scheme and resident outside the United Kingdom, and

(b) that the participants did not have any rights in respect of the amounts arising or accruing in respect of those transactions other than the rights which, if they held shares in the company on whose behalf the transactions are assumed to be carried out, would be their rights as shareholders,

the assumed company would not, in relation to the chargeable period in which the taxable sums are chargeable to tax, be regarded for tax purposes as a company carrying on a trade in the United Kingdom.

(11) Where, on those assumptions, the assumed company would be so regarded for tax purposes, subsections (4) to (8) above shall have effect in relation to the transaction as if, applying those assumptions—

(a) references to the non-resident were references to the assumed company; and

(b) the following subsection were substituted for subsection (5) above, namely—

"(5) In subsection (4) above the reference to the assumed company's relevant excluded income for a qualifying period is a reference to the aggregate of the amounts which would, for the chargeable periods comprised in the qualifying period, be chargeable to tax on that company as profits deriving from the transactions carried out by the manager and assumed to be carried out on the company's behalf."

(12) In this section "investment transactions" means—

(a) transactions in shares, stock, futures contracts, options contracts or securities of any description not mentioned in this paragraph, but excluding futures contracts or options contracts relating to land,

(b) transactions consisting in the buying or selling of any foreign currency or in the placing of money at interest, and

(c) such other transactions as the Treasury may by regulations designate for the purposes of this section;

and the power to make regulations for the purposes of paragraph (c) above shall be exercisable by statutory instrument subject to annulment in pursuance of a resolution of the House of Commons.

(13) For the purposes of subsection (12) above a contract is not prevented from being a futures contract or an options contract by the fact that any party is or may be entitled to receive or liable to make, or entitled to receive and liable to make, only a payment of a sum (as opposed to a transfer of assets other than money) in full settlement of all obligations.

(14) The preceding provisions of this section shall have effect in the case of a person who acts as a broker or provides investment management services as part only of a business as if that part were a separate business.

(15) For the purposes of this section—

(a) a person shall be taken to carry out a transaction on behalf of another where he undertakes the transaction himself, whether on behalf of or to the account of that other, and also where he gives instructions for it to be so carried out by another; and

(b) the references to the income arising from so much of a business as relates to transactions carried out through a branch or agency on behalf of the non-resident shall include references to income from property or rights which, as a result of the transactions, are used by, or held by or for, that branch or agency.

(16) In paragraph (d) of subsection (1) above—

(a) the reference to a member of Lloyd's is a reference to any person who is a member within the meaning of Chapter III of Part II of the Finance Act 1993 or a corporate member within the meaning of Chapter V of Part IV of the Finance Act 1994, and

(b) the references to a members' agent and to a managing agent shall also be construed in accordance with section 184 of that Act of 1993 or, as the case may be, section 230 of that Act of 1994.

(17) In this section—

"branch or agency" has the same meaning as in the Management Act;
"collective investment scheme" has the same meaning as in the Financial Services Act 1986; and
"participant", in relation to a collective investment scheme, shall be construed in accordance with section 75 of that Act of 1986;

and section 839 of the Taxes Act 1988 (connected persons) shall apply for the purposes of this section.

(18) For the purposes of this section a person shall not be regarded as acting in an independent capacity when acting on behalf of the non-resident unless, having regard to its legal, financial and commercial characteristics, the relationship between them is a relationship between persons carrying on independent businesses that deal with each other at arm's length.

(19) This section applies—

(a) for the purposes of income tax and capital gains tax, in relation to the year 1996–97 and subsequent years of assessment; and

(b) for the purposes of corporation tax, in relation to accounting periods beginning after 31st March 1996.

GENERAL NOTE

The section provides that agents, brokers, investment managers and members' agents or managing agents at Lloyd's, acting in the normal course of their business are not to be treated as the U.K. representative of the non-resident for the purposes of s.126. The present provisions are continued with some modifications.

Subs. (1)

Section 126, which imposes obligations and liabilities on an agent through whom a non-resident carries on a trade in the U.K., does not apply where the agent does not carry on a regular agency for the non-resident or is acting for him as a broker or investment manager or as a members' agent or managing agent at Lloyd's.

Subs. (2)

For the exemption in favour of brokers to apply, the transactions must be carried out in the ordinary course of the business and for the normal fee, and no other dealings can be carried on between the non-resident and the broker.

Subs. (3)

Corresponding conditions are imposed for the exemption in favour of investment managers. Additionally, the manager must act in an independent capacity (see subs. (18)) and satisfy further conditions set out in subss. (4) *et seq.*

Subs. (4)

The requirements of this subsection are met, subject to subss. (9)–(11), if there is a qualifying period (see subs. (7)) in respect of which the investment manager and persons connected with him intended that their beneficial interest in the total income for the period from transactions carried out through the investment manager would not exceed 20 per cent, provided that any failure to fulfil the intention is for reasons outside their control. What is aimed at is the position where a manager has an interest in the capital of a managed fund.

Subss. (5) and (6)

The income concerned is that deriving from transactions carried out through the manager and otherwise excluded from further tax by ss.128 and 129. Beneficial interest is further explained to include rights attributable to the income.

Subs. (7)

A qualifying period is a period, including the chargeable period, of not more than five years comprising two or more complete chargeable periods.

Subss. (8)–(11)

These were inserted in Standing Committee to meet concerns expressed by the fund management industry. Wherever the 20 per cent rule is not met, it is only that part of the non-resident's income to which the investment manager and connected persons are beneficially entitled that is excluded from the limitation of charge.

Special provision is also made where investment management services are provided to a collective investment scheme, as defined in the Financial Services Act 1986. In such a case, the 20 per cent rule is applied by looking at the scheme as a whole, and is treated as being satisfied by each participant where the scheme, if it were taxed as a separate entity, would not be regarded as carrying on a financial trade in the U.K., whatever the level of beneficial entitlement. Where the scheme, if it were taxed as a separate entity, would be regarded as carrying on a trade, the rule is satisfied provided it is met in respect of the beneficial entitlement of the investment manager and persons connected to the taxable income of the scheme.

Subss. (12) and (13)

The definition of "investment transactions" is imported from TMA 1970, s.78 with some rearrangement and the addition of transactions in foreign exchange. Further additions may be made by Treasury regulations.

Subss. (14)–(17)

These import other provisions from TMA 1970 and provide definitions.

Subs. (18)

This explains "independent capacity" and requires consideration to be given to the legal, financial and commercial characteristics of the relationship between the parties.

Subs. (19)
The commencement date corresponds with that for s.126 above.

Limit on income chargeable on non-residents: income tax

128.—(1) Subject to subsection (5) below, the income tax chargeable for any year of assessment on the total income of any person who is not resident in the United Kingdom shall not exceed the sum of the following amounts, that is to say—

(a) the amount of tax which, apart from this section, would be chargeable on that total income if—

(i) the amount of that income were reduced by the amount of any excluded income; and

(ii) there were disregarded any relief under Chapter I of Part VII of the Taxes Act 1988 to which that person is entitled for that year by virtue of section 278(2) of that Act or of any arrangements having effect by virtue of section 788 of that Act;
and

(b) the amount of tax deducted from so much of any excluded income as is income the tax on which is deducted at source.

(2) For the purposes of this section income arising for any year to a person who is not resident in the United Kingdom is excluded income in so far as it—

(a) falls within subsection (3) below; and

(b) is not income in relation to which that person has a UK representative for the purposes of section 126 above and Schedule 23 to this Act.

(3) Income falls within this subsection if—

(a) it is chargeable to tax under Schedule C, Case III of Schedule D or Schedule F;

(b) it is chargeable to tax under Case VI of Schedule D by virtue of section 56 of the Taxes Act 1988 (transactions in deposits);

(c) it is chargeable to tax under Schedule E by virtue of section 150 or 617(1) of the Taxes Act 1988 or section 139(1) of the Finance Act 1994 (social security benefits etc.);

(d) without being chargeable as mentioned in paragraphs (a) to (c) above or chargeable in accordance with section 171(2) of the Finance Act 1993 (profits of the underwriting business of a member of Lloyd's), it is income arising as mentioned in subsection (1)(b) or (c) of section 127 above; or

(e) it is income of such other description as the Treasury may by regulations designate for the purposes of this subsection;
and the power to make regulations for the purposes of paragraph (e) above shall be exercisable by statutory instrument subject to annulment in pursuance of a resolution of the House of Commons.

(4) In subsection (1)(b) above—

(a) the reference to excluded income the tax on which is deducted at source is a reference to excluded income from which an amount in respect of income tax is or is treated as deducted, on which any such amount is treated as paid or in respect of which there is a tax credit, and

(b) the reference, in relation to any such income, to the amount of income tax deducted shall be construed, accordingly, as a reference to the amount which is or is treated as deducted or which is treated as paid or, as the case may be, to the amount of that credit.

(5) This section shall not apply to the income tax chargeable for any year of assessment on the income of trustees not resident in the United Kingdom if there is a relevant beneficiary of the trust who is either—

(a) an individual ordinarily resident in the United Kingdom, or

(b) a company resident in the United Kingdom.

(6) In subsection (5) above, the reference to a relevant beneficiary, in relation to a trust, is a reference to any person who, as a person falling wholly or partly within any description of actual or potential beneficiaries, is either—

(a) a person who is, or will or may become, entitled under the trust to receive the whole or any part of any income under the trust; or

(b) a person to or for the benefit of whom the whole or any part of any such income may be paid or applied in exercise of any discretion conferred by the trust;

and for the purposes of this subsection references, in relation to a trust, to income under the trust shall include references to so much (if any) of any property falling to be treated as capital under the trust as represents amounts originally received by the trustees as income.

(7) This section shall apply, subject to subsections (8) and (9) below, in relation to the year 1995–96 and subsequent years of assessment.

(8) This section shall have effect in relation to the year 1995–96 as if the following paragraphs were substituted for paragraph (b) of subsection (2) above, that is to say—

"(aa) arises on or after 6th April 1995; and

(b) is not income in relation to which that person would have a UK representative for the purposes of section 126 above and Schedule 23 to this Act if sections 126 and 127 above and that Schedule applied for the year 1995–96."

(9) This section shall have effect in relation to the year 1995–96 as if—

(a) the income falling within paragraphs (a) and (b) of subsection (3) above did not include any income arising otherwise than from a transaction falling within subsection (10) below; and

(b) the reference in paragraph (d) of subsection (3) above to income arising as mentioned in subsection (1)(b) or (c) of section 127 above were a reference to any income which would be such income if that section applied in relation to the year 1995–96.

(10) A transaction falls within this subsection if—

(a) it is either—

(i) a transaction carried out on behalf of the non-resident by a person who, at the time of the transaction, was carrying on the business of a broker; or

(ii) an investment transaction carried out on behalf of the non-resident by a person ("the manager") who at the time was carrying on a business of providing investment management services;

(b) it was carried out by the broker or manager on behalf of the non-resident in the ordinary course of the business referred to in paragraph (a) above; and

(c) the remuneration which the broker or manager received in respect of that transaction for the provision to the non-resident of the services of a broker or, as the case may be, for the provision of the investment management services in question was at a rate not less than that which would have been customary for that class of business.

(11) In this section "investment transaction" has the same meaning as in section 127 above.

GENERAL NOTE

The income tax chargeable on non-residents in respect of income from investments (other than from property in the U.K.), or from trading in the U.K. through a broker or investment manager, is limited by this section to the tax, if any, which is deducted at source. The section replaces broadly similar limitations on charge under extra-statutory concessions ESC B13 (untaxed interest paid to non-residents) and B40 (U.K. investment managers acting for non-resident clients).

Subs. (1)

The income tax chargeable on the total income of a non-resident for a year of assessment shall not exceed the sum of the amount which would be chargeable on the total income if both excluded income (see subss. (2) and (3) below) and personal allowances were disregarded, plus the amount of tax deducted at source from the excluded income. This conforms with the rule in ESC B13.

Subs. (2)
Excluded income is income falling within subs. (3), other than income from or connected with a trade *etc.* carried on in the U.K. through a branch or agency which is not excluded from s.126 by s.127.

Subs. (3)
This provides that excluded income comprises:
(i) income chargeable under Schedule C, Case III of Schedule D or Schedule F (broadly, investment income other than that from land);
(ii) profits or gains from disposals of certificates of deposit;
(iii) certain social security benefits; or
(iv) income from transactions through investment managers or brokers which is excluded from s.126 by s.127, other than profits as a Lloyd's underwriter.
Further additions may be made by the Treasury by regulations.

Subs. (4)
Tax credits are included in tax deducted at source.

Subss. (5) and (6)
The limitation of charge does not apply to a non-resident trust if any beneficiary is either an individual ordinarily resident or a company resident in the U.K. For parallel provisions relating to income from banks and authorised unit trusts, see s.86 above and S.I. 1994 No. 2318.

Subss. (7)–(11)
The limitation on charge applies generally for 1996–97 and thereafter. It applies also for 1995–96 to any income from transactions carried out through brokers and investment managers which would be excluded income if all the provisions in ss.126 and 127 and this section were in force and to the social security benefits excluded from charge. ESC B13 will continue to apply for 1995–96 for investment income and gains on disposals of certificates of deposit.

Limit on income chargeable on non-residents: corporation tax

129.—(1) Subject to subsection (4) below, the corporation tax chargeable on the chargeable profits arising in any accounting period to a company which is not resident in the United Kingdom shall not exceed the sum of the following amounts, that is to say—
(a) the amount of tax deducted from so much of any excluded income as is income the tax on which is deducted at source; and
(b) the amount (if any) of corporation tax which would be chargeable on the chargeable profits arising to that company for that period if the excluded income of the company for that period were not included in those profits.

(2) For the purposes of this section income arising for any accounting period to any company is excluded income in so far as it—
(a) is income arising as mentioned in subsection (1)(b) or (c) of section 127 above; and
(b) is not income in relation to which that person has a UK representative for the purposes of section 126 above and Schedule 23 to this Act.

(3) In subsection (1)(a) above—
(a) the reference to excluded income the tax on which is deducted at source is a reference to excluded income from which an amount in respect of tax is or is treated as deducted, on which any such amount is treated as paid or in respect of which there is a tax credit, and
(b) the reference, in relation to any such income, to the amount of tax deducted shall be construed, accordingly, as a reference to the amount which is or is treated as deducted or which is treated as paid or, as the case may be, to the amount of that credit.

(4) This section does not apply in relation to the chargeable profits arising to a company which is a corporate member within the meaning of Chapter V of Part IV of the Finance Act 1994 (corporate Lloyd's underwriters etc.).

(5) This section applies, subject to subsection (6) below, in relation to any accounting period ending after 5th April 1995.

(6) This section shall have effect in relation to any accounting period beginning before 1st April 1996 as if the following paragraphs were substituted for paragraphs (a) and (b) of subsection (2) above, that is to say—

"(a) is income arising after 5th April 1995 which would be income arising as mentioned in subsection (1)(b) or (c) of section 127 above if that section applied in relation to accounting periods beginning before 1st April 1996; and

(b) is not income in relation to which that person would have a UK representative for the purposes of section 126 above and Schedule 23 to this Act if sections 126 and 127 above and that Schedule so applied."

GENERAL NOTE

The corporation tax chargeable on non-resident companies' income from trading in the U.K. through a broker or investment manager is limited to the tax, if any, deducted at source. This corresponds to the rules for income tax in s.128 and replaces broadly similar limitations on charge under extra-statutory concession B40.

Subs. (1)

The corporation tax chargeable on the chargeable profits of a non-resident company for an accounting period is not to exceed the sum of the amount chargeable if the excluded income were disregarded plus the amount of tax deducted at source from the excluded income.

Subs. (2)

Excluded income is defined as income from transactions carried out through brokers or investment managers which is excluded from s.126 by s.127, other than income in relation to which the non-resident has a U.K. representative. The latter is income from or connected with a trade carried on in the U.K. through a branch or agency which is not excluded from s.126 by s.127.

Subs. (3)

Tax credits are included in tax deducted at source.

Subs. (4)

The limitation on charge does not apply to corporate members of Lloyd's

Subss. (5) and (6)

The limitation on charge applies generally for accounting periods beginning on or after March 31, 1996 and also to any income which arises after April 5, 1995 from transactions carried out through brokers and investment managers which would be exempt income if all the provisions in ss.126 and 127 and this section were in force.

Exchange gains and losses and currency contracts

Exchange gains and losses: general

130. Schedule 24 to this Act (which amends the provisions of the Finance Act 1993 relating to exchange gains and losses and other provisions connected with exchange gains and losses) shall have effect.

GENERAL NOTE

The section introduces Sched. 24, which eliminates areas of overlap between the provisions of the FA 1993, Part II, Chapter II (the legislation dealing with exchange gains and losses from an appointed day which will be March 23, 1995) and the provisions dealing with charges on income and capital gains. It also ensures that in certain circumstances CGT charges are preserved and provides for amendments to the late payment interest and repayment interest rules relating to the consequences of a claim to carry back certain exchange losses, so that they tie in with the Pay and File provisions.

See further the General Note to Sched. 24.

Exchange gains and losses: transitional provision

131.—(1) The provisions specified in subsection (2) below, so far as they require a disposal to be treated, for the purposes of the Taxation of Chargeable Gains Act 1992, as a disposal on which neither a gain nor a loss accrues, shall not apply in relation to any disposal of a qualifying asset which is made—

(a) by one qualifying company to another such company; and

(b) at a time before the commencement day of the company making the disposal and on or after the commencement day of the company to which the disposal is made.

(2) The provisions referred to in subsection (1) above are—

(a) sections 139, 140A, 171, 172, 215, 216 and 217A of the Taxation of Chargeable Gains Act 1992; and

(b) section 486(8) of the Taxes Act 1988.

(3) In this section—

"commencement day", in relation to a qualifying company, means that company's commencement day for the purposes of section 165 of the Finance Act 1993;

"qualifying asset", in relation to a disposal, means anything which, after the disposal, is by virtue of section 153 of that Act a qualifying asset in relation to the company to which the disposal was made; and

"qualifying company" means any company which is a qualifying company within the meaning of section 152 of that Act.

(4) This section has effect in relation to any disposal of an asset taking place on or after 1st January 1995.

General Note

The section prevents loss of tax on companies' capital gains as a result of the interaction of the commencement provisions for the Foreign Exchange Gains and Losses (FOREX) regime with the provisions governing intra-group and other transfers of assets on a no gain/no loss basis.

Subs. (1)

This disapplies some of the provisions in TCGA 1992 and ICTA 1988 for intra-group and other transfers of assets on a no gain/no loss basis. It has effect where the transfer is made between qualifying companies (*i.e.* any two companies except charities, authorised unit trusts and investment trusts (see FA 1993, s.152)) at a time when the FOREX regime does not yet apply to the transferor company but does apply to the transferee.

Subss. (2)–(4)

These list the provisions to be disapplied, contain definitions and provide that s.131 applies to assets disposed of from January 1, 1995.

Currency contracts: transitional provisions

132.—(1) Section 175 of the Finance Act 1994 (currency contracts: transitional provisions) shall be deemed to have been enacted with the modifications set out below.

(2) In subsection (1) after paragraph (b) there shall be inserted "and

(c) the circumstances are such that if any profit or loss accrues (or were to accrue) to the company as regards the contract for an accounting period beginning before that time it falls (or would fall) to be taken into account as a profit or loss of the trade or part,".

(3) For subsection (2) there shall be substituted—

"(2) In a case where—

(a) at any time, a currency contract held by a qualifying company becomes a qualifying contract by virtue of section 147(2) above, and

(b) the circumstances are such that if any profit or loss accrues (or were to accrue) to the company as regards the contract for the accounting period beginning with that time it does not fall (or would not fall) to be taken into account as a profit or loss of a trade or part of a trade carried on by the company,
in applying section 158(2) and (4) above in relation to the contract and the period section 153(4) and (5) above shall be treated as omitted."

GENERAL NOTE
The section contains amendments to FA 1994, s.175 to ensure the correct operation of the transitional provisions relating to currency contracts entered into before a company's commencement day (see FA 1994, s.147(4)).

Subs. (2)
New FA 1994, s.175(1)(c) ensures that the transitional provision for currency contracts held for trading purposes applies only where a profit or loss on a currency contract entered into before a company's commencement day has been (or would have been) included as part of the company's trading profits.

Subs. (3)
The new s.175(2) substituted in the FA 1994 ensures that the transitional rule in that subsection applies to all qualifying currency contracts entered into before a company's commencement day, the profits or losses on which have not been (or would not have been) included as part of the company's trading profits. Its application is no longer restricted to contracts held otherwise than for the purposes of a company's trade. The application of the new s.175(2) is also restricted to forward premiums and discounts and does not apply to any other payments or receipts.

Provisions with a foreign element

Controlled foreign companies

133. Schedule 25 to this Act (which contains amendments of Chapter IV of Part XVII of the Taxes Act 1988 and connected amendments) shall have effect.

GENERAL NOTE
The section introduces Sched. 25, which contains amendments to ensure that where chargeable profits of a company need to be computed for the purposes of the controlled foreign companies legislation (see ICTA 1988, ss.747–756), they are expressed in the currency used in the company's accounts.
See further the General Note to Sched. 25.

Offshore funds

134.—(1) Section 759 of the Taxes Act 1988 (material interests in offshore funds) shall be amended as mentioned in subsections (2) and (3) below.
(2) In subsection (1)—
(a) for the words "of the following, namely" there shall be substituted "collective investment scheme which is constituted by";
(b) for the word "and" immediately preceding paragraph (c) there shall be substituted "or"; and
(c) for the words "company, unit trust scheme or arrangements" there shall be substituted "collective investment scheme".
(3) After subsection (1) there shall be inserted—

"(1A) In this section "collective investment scheme" has the same meaning as in the Financial Services Act 1986."

(4) In Schedule 27 to the Taxes Act 1988 (distributing funds) in Part I (the distribution test) in paragraph 1(2) for paragraphs (a) and (b) there shall be substituted—

"(a) there is no income of the fund and there are no United Kingdom equivalent profits of the fund, or

(b) the amount of the gross income of the fund does not exceed 1 per cent. of the average value of the fund's assets held during the account period,".

(5) Section 212 of the Taxation of Chargeable Gains Act 1992 (annual deemed disposal of certain holdings, including holdings consisting of a relevant interest in an offshore fund) shall be amended as mentioned in subsections (6) and (7) below.

(6) In subsection (5) (meaning of "relevant interest in an offshore fund") for paragraph (b) there shall be substituted—

"(b) it would be such an interest if either or both of the assumptions mentioned in subsection (6A) below were made."

(7) Immediately before subsection (7) there shall be inserted—

"(6A) The assumptions referred to in subsection (5)(b) above are—

(a) that the companies, unit trust schemes and arrangements referred to in paragraphs (a) to (c) of subsection (1) of section 759 of the Taxes Act are not limited to those which are also collective investment schemes;

(b) that the shares and interests excluded by subsections (6) and (8) of that section are limited to shares or interests in trading companies."

(8) Subsections (1) to (3) above shall apply where it falls to be decided—

(a) whether a material interest is, at any time on or after 29th November 1994, a material interest in an offshore fund;

(b) whether a company, unit trust scheme or arrangements in which any person has an interest which is a material interest is, at any time on or after that day, an offshore fund.

(9) Subsection (4) above shall apply in relation to account periods ending on or after 29th November 1994.

(10) Subsections (5) to (7) above shall apply where it falls to be decided whether an interest is, at any time on or after 29th November 1994, a relevant interest in an offshore fund.

GENERAL NOTE

The section makes two changes to the offshore funds legislation, under which gains arising on the disposal of an interest in an offshore fund are treated as income for tax purposes.

Subss. (1)–(3)

These amend the definition used for determining whether a person has a "material interest in an offshore fund." Such a fund must be a "collective investment scheme" within the definition in the Financial Services Act 1986. This is intended as a relaxation of the law to help promoters of bone fide arrangements to reduce their compliance costs.

Subs. (4)

A *de minimis* limit is introduced so that a fund is not required to distribute income if its gross income does not exceed one per cent of the average value of its assets for the year in question.

Subss. (5)–(7)

The amendments to TCGA 1992, s.212, which is concerned with the annual deemed disposal by insurance companies of certain holdings, including a "relevant interest in an offshore fund", have the effect that the revised definition of offshore fund in ICTA 1988, s.759 does not apply for the purpose of TCGA 1992, s.212.

Subss. (8)–(10)

The various changes come into effect as from Budget Day.

Miscellaneous

Change in ownership of investment company: deductions

135. Schedule 26 to this Act (which makes provision for the purposes of corporation tax about deductions following a change in the ownership of an investment company) shall have effect.

<small>GENERAL NOTE</small>
　The section introduces Sched. 26, which brings in provisions to prevent schemes involving the sale of shell companies with surplus management expenses.

Profit-related pay

136.—(1) In Schedule 8 to the Taxes Act 1988 (profit-related pay schemes) paragraph 19 (ascertainment of profits) shall be amended in accordance with subsections (2) to (4) below.

(2) In sub-paragraph (6) (cases where scheme may provide for departure from requirements applicable to profit and loss account) paragraphs (g) to (k) (extraordinary items) shall be omitted.

(3) After paragraph (ff) of sub-paragraph (6) there shall be inserted—
　　"(l)　any exceptional items which fall within sub-paragraph (6A) below and should in accordance with any accounting practices regarded as standard be shown separately on the face of the profit and loss account."

(4) After sub-paragraph (6) there shall be inserted—
　　"(6A) The items are—
　　(a)　profits or losses on the sale or termination of an operation;
　　(b)　costs of a fundamental reorganisation or restructuring having a material effect on the nature and focus of the employment unit's operations;
　　(c)　profits or losses on the disposal of fixed assets; and
　　(d)　the effect on tax of any of the items mentioned in paragraphs (a) to (c) above."

(5) Subject to subsections (6) to (10) below, subsections (2) to (4) above shall have effect in relation to the preparation, for the purposes of a scheme, of a profit and loss account in respect of a period beginning on or after the day on which this Act is passed.

(6) Subsections (2) to (4) above shall not have effect in relation to an existing scheme unless, before the end of the period of 6 months beginning with the day on which this Act is passed, the scheme is altered to take account of the amendments made by those subsections.

(7) Subsections (8) to (10) below apply where, before the end of the period mentioned in subsection (6) above, an existing scheme is altered as mentioned in that subsection.

(8) The provision made by the scheme in compliance with paragraph 20(1) of Schedule 8 to the Taxes Act 1988 shall not prevent a profit and loss account being prepared in accordance with the alteration.

(9) Where the distributable pool would but for this subsection be determined by reference—
　　(a)　to an amount shown in a profit and loss account prepared in accordance with the altered scheme, and
　　(b)　to an amount shown in a profit and loss account ("an earlier account") prepared in accordance with the scheme in a form in which it stood before the alteration,
then, for the purposes of the determination of the pool, the amount shown in the earlier account shall be recalculated using the same method as that used to calculate the amount mentioned in paragraph (a) above.

(10) The alteration of the existing scheme shall be treated as being within subsection (8) of section 177B of the Taxes Act 1988 (alterations which are registrable and which once registered cannot give rise to Board's power of cancellation).

(11) In subsections (6) to (10) above "an existing scheme" means a scheme which, immediately before the day on which this Act is passed, is registered under Chapter III of Part V of the Taxes Act 1988.

(12) After paragraph 19 of Schedule 8 to the Taxes Act 1988 there shall be inserted—

"19A.—(1) The Treasury may by order amend paragraph 19 above so as to add to, delete or vary any of the items mentioned in sub-paragraph (6) of that paragraph.

(2) In this paragraph references to an order are references to an order under sub-paragraph (1) above.

(3) Subject to sub-paragraphs (4) to (8) below, any amendment or amendments made by virtue of an order shall have effect in relation to the preparation, for the purposes of a scheme, of a profit and loss account in respect of a period beginning on or after the day on which the order comes into force.

(4) Any amendment or amendments made by virtue of an order shall not have effect in relation to an existing scheme unless, before the end of the period of 6 months beginning with the day on which the order comes into force, the scheme is altered to take account of the amendment or amendments.

(5) Sub-paragraphs (6) to (8) below apply where, before the end of the period mentioned in sub-paragraph (4) above, an existing scheme is altered as mentioned in that sub-paragraph.

(6) The provision made by the scheme in compliance with paragraph 20(1) below shall not prevent a profit and loss account being prepared in accordance with the alteration.

(7) Where the distributable pool would but for this sub-paragraph be determined by reference—

(a) to an amount shown in a profit and loss account prepared in accordance with the altered scheme, and

(b) to an amount shown in a profit and loss account ("an earlier account") prepared in accordance with the scheme in a form in which it stood before the alteration,

then, for the purposes of the determination of the pool, the amount shown in the earlier account shall be recalculated using the same method as that used to calculate the amount mentioned in paragraph (a) above.

(8) The alteration of the existing scheme shall be treated as being within subsection (8) of section 177B.

(9) An order may include such supplementary, incidental or consequential provisions as appear to the Treasury to be necessary or expedient.

(10) In this paragraph "an existing scheme", in relation to an order, means a scheme which, immediately before the day on which the order comes into force, is a registered scheme."

GENERAL NOTE

The amendments to the profit-related pay (PRP) scheme made by this section reflect the replacement of Statement of Standard Accounting Practice 6 (SSAP6) by Financial Reporting Standard 3 (FRS 3) and are designed to allow employers to continue to exclude unusual items when calculating PRP.

Subs. (2)

This removes the categories of extraordinary items from ICTA 1988, Sched. 8, para. 19(6).

Subss. (3)–(4)

New ICTA 1988, Sched. 8, para. 19(6A) inserts a new category of "exceptional items", which standard accounting practice requires to be shown separately on the face of the profit and loss account.

Subs. (5)

The new rules are effective for PRP profit periods from Royal Assent, subject to special rules for existing schemes—*i.e.* those registered before Royal Assent (see subs. (11)).

Subs. (6)

The changes will not apply to an existing scheme unless it alters its rules accordingly within six months of Royal Assent.

Subss. (7)–(10)

These deal with the effects of such an alteration to a scheme's rules. The alteration will not be treated as infringing the requirement for consistency in accounting policies, but previous accounts must be adjusted where necessary and the Revenue must be advised of the alteration.

Subs. (12)

New ICTA 1988, Sched. 8, para. 19A gives the Treasury power, for the future, to make changes to the list of items in sub-para. (6) of that para., by means of statutory instrument. Similar provisions to those in subss. (6)–(10) above apply to the procedures necessary to implement the changes in a PRP scheme.

Part-time workers: miscellaneous provisions

137.—(1) In Schedule 8 to the Taxes Act 1988 (profit-related pay schemes) paragraph 8(a) (employees working less than 20 hours a week excluded by scheme from receiving profit-related pay) shall be omitted.

(2) In Part III of Schedule 9 to the Taxes Act 1988 (savings-related share option schemes) in paragraph 26(1)(a) (certain full-time employees and directors must be eligible to participate in scheme) for the words "a full-time employee" there shall be substituted "an employee".

(3) In Part IV of Schedule 9 to the Taxes Act 1988 (share option schemes other than savings-related share option schemes) in paragraph 27(4) (qualifying employee defined as employee required to work at least 20 hours a week) the words from "who is required" to the end shall be omitted.

(4) In Part V of Schedule 9 to the Taxes Act 1988 (profit sharing schemes) in paragraph 36(1)(a) (certain full-time employees and directors must be eligible to participate in scheme on similar terms) for the words "a full-time employee" there shall be substituted "an employee".

(5) In Schedule 5 to the Finance Act 1989 (employee share ownership trusts) in paragraph 4(2)(c) (trust deed must provide that certain persons are beneficiaries if they work at rate of at least 20 hours a week) for the words "at that given time he worked as an employee or" there shall be substituted "in the case of a director, at that given time he worked as a".

(6) Subsection (1) above shall apply in relation to any scheme not registered before the day on which this Act is passed.

(7) Subsections (2) to (4) above shall apply in relation to any scheme not approved before the day on which this Act is passed.

(8) In a case where—

(a) a scheme is approved before the day on which this Act is passed, and

(b) on or after that day the scheme is altered in such a way that paragraph 27 of Schedule 9 to the Taxes Act 1988 would be fulfilled if subsection (3) above applied in relation to the scheme,

subsection (3) above shall apply in relation to the scheme with effect from the time the alteration is made.

(9) Subsection (5) above shall apply in relation to trusts established on or after the day on which this Act is passed; and for this purpose a trust is established when the deed under which it is established is executed.

GENERAL NOTE
This section, introduced in Standing Committee and amended on Report, is designed to comply with the decision of the House of Lords in *R.* v. *Secretary of State for Employment, ex p. Equal Opportunities Commission* [1995] 1 A.C. 1, that discrimination against part-time employees, *i.e.* those working less than 20 hours per week, infringed European Community Law. Accordingly, the benefits of the following tax provisions must be extended to part-time employees (but not to part-time directors):
(i) profit-related pay;
(ii) savings-related share option schemes;
(iii) other share option schemes;
(iv) profit sharing schemes; and
(v) employee share ownership trusts.
The section applies to schemes which are not registered, established, or approved before Royal Assent, as the case may be. The section also applies to share option schemes other than savings-related share option schemes which are altered in accordance with the section after Royal Assent.

Charities, etc.: lotteries

138.—(1) In section 505 of the Taxes Act 1988 (charities: general) in subsection (1) (exemptions) after paragraph (e) there shall be inserted—
> "(f) exemption from tax under Schedule D in respect of profits accruing to a charity from a lottery if—
>> (i) the lottery is promoted and conducted in accordance with section 3 or 5 of the Lotteries and Amusements Act 1976 or Article 133 or 135 of the Betting, Gaming, Lotteries and Amusements (Northern Ireland) Order 1985; and
>> (ii) the profits are applied solely to the charity's purposes."

(2) Subsection (1) above shall apply to chargeable periods beginning—
(a) in the case of a company, after 31st March 1995; and
(b) in any other case, after 5th April 1995.

GENERAL NOTE
The amendment to ICTA 1988, s.505 fills a lacuna in the law by exempting from tax income accruing to charities from lotteries which meet the conditions laid down in the Lotteries and Amusements Act 1976, ss.3 or 5 (or the corresponding Northern Ireland provisions), provided also that the income is applied solely for the purposes of the charity. In practice, the exemption will run from July 11, 1994, when a Government announcement was made.

Sub-contractors in the construction industry

139.—(1) Subsection (4) of section 559 of the Taxes Act 1988 (which requires deductions to be made from payments to certain sub-contractors in the construction industry) shall have effect in relation to payments made on or after the appointed day with the substitution for "25 per cent." of "the relevant percentage"; and after that subsection there shall be inserted the following subsection—
> "(4A) In subsection (4) above 'the relevant percentage', in relation to a payment, means such percentage (not exceeding the percentage which is the basic rate for the year of assessment in which the payment is made) as the Treasury may by order determine."

(2) Chapter IV of Part XIII of the Taxes Act 1988 (sub-contractors in the construction industry) shall be further amended in accordance with Schedule 27 to this Act.
(3) In this section and that Schedule "the appointed day" means such day, not being a day before 1st August 1998, as the Treasury may by order made by statutory instrument appoint; and different days may be appointed under this subsection for different purposes.

GENERAL NOTE
The section, together with Sched. 27, introduces various changes to the special tax scheme for labour-only sub-contractors in the construction industry, known as "the lump". The purpose of these changes is to cut down on evasion of the law.

Subs. (1)
The amendment to ICTA 1988, s.559 replaces the 25 per cent rate for deductions with a provision for the rate to be specified by Treasury order at not more than the basic rate (currently 25 per cent).

Subs. (2)
Schedule 27 is introduced. See further the General Note to that Schedule.

Subs. (3)
The changes may not be implemented any earlier than August 1, 1998.

Valuation of trading stock on discontinuance of trade

140.—(1) In section 100 of the Taxes Act 1988 (valuation of trading stock on discontinuance of trade), in paragraph (a) of subsection (1), for the words from "realised" to the end of the paragraph there shall be substituted "determined in accordance with subsections (1A) to (1C) below; and"; and after that subsection there shall be inserted the following subsections—

"(1A) Subject to subsections (1B) and (1C) below and to paragraph 2 of Schedule 12 to the Finance Act 1988 (gilt-edged securities and other financial trading stock), the value of any trading stock falling to be valued under paragraph (a) of subsection (1) above shall be taken—
  (a) except where the person to whom it is sold or transferred is connected with the person who makes the sale or transfer, to be the amount ('the price actually received for it') which is in fact realised on the sale or. as the case may be, which is in fact the value of the consideration given for the transfer; and
  (b) if those persons are connected with each other, to be what would have been the price actually received for it had the sale or transfer been a transaction between independent persons dealing at arm's length.
(1B) In a case falling within subsection (1)(a) above—
  (a) stock consisting of debts to which section 88A(2) applies shall have the value for which paragraph (a) of subsection (1A) above provides even where the persons in question are connected with each other; and
  (b) stock sold in circumstances in which the amount realised on the sale would be taken to be an amount determined in accordance with paragraph 5 of Schedule 5 shall be taken to have the value so determined, instead of the value for which subsection (1A)(a) or (b) above provides.
(1C) If—
  (a) trading stock is sold or transferred to a person in circumstances where paragraph (b) of subsection (1A) above would apply (apart from this subsection) for determining the value of the stock so sold or transferred,
  (b) the amount which would be taken in accordance with that paragraph to be the value of all of the stock sold or transferred to that person is more than the acquisition value of that stock and also more than the price actually received for it, and
  (c) both parties to the sale or transfer, by notice signed by them and sent to the inspector no later than two years after the end of the chargeable period in which the trade is discontinued, elect that this subsection shall apply,

then the stock sold or transferred to that person shall be taken to have a value equal to whichever is the greater (taking all the stock so sold or transferred together) of its acquisition value and the price actually received for it or, in a case where they are the same, to either of them.

(1D) In subsection (1C) above 'acquisition value', in relation to any trading stock, means the amount which, in computing for any tax purposes the profits or gains of the discontinued trade, would have been deductible as representing the acquisition value of that stock if—

(a) the stock had, immediately before the discontinuance, been sold in the course of the trade for a price equal to whatever would be its value in accordance with subsection (1A)(b) above; and

(b) the period for which those profits or gains were to be computed began immediately before the sale.

(1E) Where any trading stock falls to be valued under subsection (1)(a) above, the amount determined in accordance with subsections (1A) to (1C) above to be the amount to be brought into account as the value of that stock in computing profits or gains of the discontinued trade shall also be taken, for the purpose of making any deduction in computing the profits or gains of any trade carried on by the purchaser, to be the cost of that stock to the purchaser.

(1F) For the purposes of this section two persons are connected with each other if—

(a) they are connected with each other within the meaning of section 839;

(b) one of them is a partnership and the other has a right to a share in the partnership;

(c) one of them is a body corporate and the other has control over that body;

(d) both of them are partnerships and some other person has a right to a share in each of them; or

(e) both of them are bodies corporate or one of them is a partnership and the other is a body corporate and, in either case, some other person has control over both of them;

and in this subsection the references to a right to a share in a partnership are references to a right to a share of the assets or income of the partnership and 'control' has the meaning given by section 840.

(1G) In this section 'purchaser', in relation to a transfer otherwise than by sale, means the person to whom the transfer is made."

(2) This section applies in relation to any case in which a trade is discontinued at a time on or after 29th November 1994.

GENERAL NOTE

At present, when a business is discontinued and its stock is sold or transferred to another trader in the U.K., the price agreed between the parties is regarded as a trading receipt of one and a trading expense of the other. This price can be manipulated between connected parties so as to produce a favourable tax result. New provisions, effective from Budget Day, are inserted to negate this.

New ICTA 1988, s.100(1A)–(1G) provides that the existing rules will continue to apply between parties not connected with each other. If the parties are connected, the arm's length price will be substituted, although they may elect to use a lower figure—either the stock's acquisition value or, if more, the agreed sale price. "Acquisition value" is the cost which would have been deducted in computing the vendor's profits on a sale at arm's length immediately before the discontinuance. The definition of "connected persons" is in broad terms in order to cover any family or close business link. Other provisions ensure that the same stock value will be used in the purchaser's tax computation as is used in the vendor's, and extend "purchaser" to include any person to whom the transfer of stock is made.

The new ICTA 1988, s.100(1A)–(1G) provisions do not override specific provisions relating to gilt-edged securities and other financial trading stock of building societies, debts of overseas governments and state authorities, and farm animals.

Incapacity benefit

141.—(1) Section 139 of the Finance Act 1994 (taxation of incapacity benefit) shall have effect, and be deemed always to have had effect, with the following amendments.

(2) In subsection (5), for the definition of "initial period of incapacity" there shall be substituted—

" 'initial period of incapacity', in relation to incapacity benefit, means any period for which short-term incapacity benefit is payable otherwise than at the higher rate; and".

(3) After that subsection there shall be inserted the following subsection—

"(6) The reference in subsection (5) above to short-term incapacity benefit payable at the higher rate shall be construed in accordance with sections 30B(5), 40(8) and 41(7) of the Social Security Contributions and Benefits Act 1992 and the corresponding provisions of the Social Security Contributions and Benefits (Northern Ireland) Act 1992."

GENERAL NOTE

Under FA 1994, s.139 the new incapacity benefit was brought into charge to tax, save for short-term incapacity benefit paid during the first 28 weeks of incapacity. However, the legislation had the unintended effect of charging to tax short-term incapacity benefit paid to claimants who reach pensionable age during the first year of their incapacity. This anomaly is now corrected.

Annuities purchased where certain claims or actions are settled

142. The following sections shall be inserted after section 329 of the Taxes Act 1988—

"**Annuities purchased for certain persons**
329A.—(1) In a case where—
(a) an agreement is made settling a claim or action for damages for personal injury,
(b) under the agreement the damages are to consist wholly or partly of periodical payments, and
(c) under the agreement the person entitled to the payments is to receive them as the annuitant under one or more annuities purchased for him by the person against whom the claim or action is brought or, if he is insured against the claim concerned, by his insurer,
the agreement is for the purposes of this section a qualifying agreement.
(2) In a case where—
(a) an agreement is made settling a claim or action for damages for personal injury,
(b) under the agreement the damages are to consist wholly or partly of periodical payments, and
(c) a later agreement is made under which the person entitled to the payments is from a future date to receive them as the annuitant under one or more annuities purchased for him by the person against whom the claim or action is brought or, if he is insured against the claim concerned, by his insurer,
the agreement mentioned in paragraph (c) above is for the purposes of this section a qualifying agreement.
(3) Subsection (4) below applies where—
(a) a person receives a sum as the annuitant under an annuity purchased for him pursuant to a qualifying agreement, or

(b) a person receives a sum on behalf of the annuitant under an annuity purchased for the annuitant pursuant to a qualifying agreement.

(4) Where this subsection applies the sum shall not be regarded as the recipient's or annuitant's income for any purposes of income tax and accordingly shall be paid without any deduction under section 349(1).

(5) Subsections (6) to (10) below apply for the purposes of subsection (1) above.

(6) The periodical payments may be for the life of the claimant, for a specified period or of a specified number or minimum number or include payments of more than one of those descriptions.

(7) The amounts of the periodical payments (which need not be at a uniform rate or payable at uniform intervals) may be—

(a) specified in the agreement, with or without provision for increases of specified amounts or percentages,

(b) subject to adjustment in a specified manner so as to preserve their real value, or

(c) partly specified as mentioned in paragraph (a) and partly subject to adjustment as mentioned in paragraph (b) above.

(8) The annuity or annuities must be such as to provide sums which as to amount and time of payment correspond to the periodical payments described in the agreement.

(9) Personal injury includes any disease and any impairment of a person's physical or mental condition.

(10) A claim or action for personal injury includes—

(a) such a claim or action brought by virtue of the Law Reform (Miscellaneous Provisions) Act 1934;

(b) such a claim or action brought by virtue of the Law Reform (Miscellaneous Provisions) Act (Northern Ireland) 1937;

(c) such a claim or action brought by virtue of the Damages (Scotland) Act 1976;

(d) a claim or action brought by virtue of the Fatal Accidents Act 1976;

(e) a claim or action brought by virtue of the Fatal Accidents (Northern Ireland) Order 1977.

(11) For the purposes of subsection (2) above—

(a) subsections (6), (9) and (10) above apply;

(b) subsection (7) above applies as if the reference to the agreement were to that mentioned in subsection (2)(a) above;

(c) subsection (8) above applies as if the reference to periodical payments described in the agreement were to periodical payments described in the agreement mentioned in subsection (2)(a) above and falling to be made after the later agreement takes effect.

(12) This section does not apply unless the sum concerned is received after the day on which the Finance Act 1995 is passed, but it is immaterial when—

(a) the agreement mentioned in subsection (1) above is made or takes effect, or

(b) either of the agreements mentioned in subsection (2) above is made or takes effect.

Annuities assigned in favour of certain persons

329B.—(1) In a case where—

(a) an agreement is made settling a claim or action for damages for personal injury,

(b) under the agreement the damages are to consist wholly or partly of periodical payments,

   (c) the person against whom the claim or action is brought (or, if he is insured against the claim concerned, his insurer) purchases one or more annuities, and

   (d) a later agreement is made under which the annuity is, or the annuities are, assigned in favour of the person entitled to the payments so as to secure that from a future date he receives the payments as the annuitant under the annuity or annuities,

the agreement mentioned in paragraph (d) above is for the purposes of this section a qualifying agreement.

(2) Subsection (3) below applies where—

   (a) a person receives a sum as the annuitant under an annuity assigned in his favour pursuant to a qualifying agreement, or

   (b) a person receives a sum on behalf of the annuitant under an annuity assigned in the annuitant's favour pursuant to a qualifying agreement.

(3) Where this subsection applies the sum shall not be regarded as the recipient's or annuitant's income for any purposes of income tax and accordingly shall be paid without any deduction under section 349(1).

(4) For the purposes of subsection (1) above—

   (a) subsections (6), (9) and (10) of section 329A apply;

   (b) subsections (7) and (8) of section 329A apply as if references to the agreement were to that mentioned in subsection (1)(a) above.

(5) This section does not apply unless the sum concerned is received after the day on which the Finance Act 1995 is passed, but it is immaterial when either of the agreements mentioned in subsection (1) above is made or takes effect."

GENERAL NOTE

The section, introduced on Report following a discussion in Standing Committee, is designed to simplify the administration of the payment of agreed damages in cases of personal injury, where the damages are to be paid to the injured victim in instalments over a period or for life, *i.e.* in the form of a "structured settlement". It also represents a first step towards realising the Government's intention of implementing the recommendations made by the Law Commission in its report on Structured Settlements and Interim and Provisional Damages (1994, Law Com No. 224).

New ICTA 1988, s.329A provides for the victim of personal injury to receive his damages as an annuity directly from a life insurance company without turning a non-taxable capital sum into income chargeable to tax. At present, such payments have to be grossed up and paid by the defendant's insurers under deduction of tax. The annuitant will enjoy the advantage of protection under the Policyholders Protection Act 1975. It is also made possible for existing structured settlements to be re-negotiated so as to come within the new framework.

New ICTA 1988, s.329B accords similar treatment to cases where an annuity is assigned to the injured party.

Lloyd's underwriters: new-style special reserve funds

143.—(1) In Schedule 20 to the Finance Act 1993 (Lloyd's underwriters: special reserve funds) paragraph 2 (general requirements about special reserve funds) shall be deemed to have been enacted with the modification in subsection (2) below.

(2) For sub-paragraphs (2) and (3) there shall be substituted—

   "(2) The arrangements must be such as to secure that—

   (a) any income arising to the trustee or trustees of the special reserve fund shall be added to the capital of the fund and held on the same trusts as the fund; and

   (b) except as required or permitted by this Schedule, no payments shall be made into or out of the special reserve fund."

GENERAL NOTE
The amendment to FA 1993, Sched. 20, which governs the administration of special reserve funds set up by members of Lloyd's, ensures that the income of such funds will be retained and not distributed to the member.

Local government residuary body

144.—(1) In section 842A of the Taxes Act 1988 (meaning of "local authority" in the Tax Acts) in subsection (2) (England and Wales) after paragraph (g) insert—
"(h) a residuary body established by order under section 22(1) of the Local Government Act 1992;".

(2) This section shall be deemed to have come into force on 29th November 1994.

GENERAL NOTE
The amendment to ICTA 1988, s.842A adds residuary bodies established under the local government reorganisation in England and Wales to the definition of "local authority" for the purpose of the Tax Acts.

Payment of rent &c., under deduction of tax

145.—(1) In section 119(1) of the Taxes Act 1988 (rent, &c., payable in connection with mines, quarries and similar concerns), the words from "and, subject to subsection (2) below, shall be subject to deduction of income tax" to the end shall cease to have effect.

(2) In section 121 of that Act (management expenses of owner of mineral rights), for subsections (1) and (2) (right to repayment where tax paid by deduction, &c.) substitute—
"(1) Where for any year of assessment rights to work minerals in the United Kingdom are let, the lessor shall be entitled to deduct, in determining the amount chargeable to income tax in respect of the rents or royalties for that year, any sums wholly, exclusively and necessarily disbursed by him as expenses of management or supervision of those minerals in that year.".

(3) The provisions of this section have effect in relation to payments made after the passing of this Act.

GENERAL NOTE
The purpose of the amendments to ICTA 1988, ss.119 and 121 is to end the deduction at source of tax from rents in connection with mines, quarries and similar concerns. Such rents will in future be paid gross and taxed in the ordinary assessment cycle, like most other rental payments.

PART IV

PETROLEUM REVENUE TAX

Restriction of unrelievable field losses

146.—(1) In section 6 of the Oil Taxation Act 1975 (allowance of unrelievable loss from abandoned field), in subsection (1) after the words "Subject to" there shall be inserted "subsections (5) to (9) below and".

(2) After subsection (1) of that section there shall be inserted—
"(1A) In this section, in relation to an unrelievable field loss,—
(a) "the abandoned field" means the oil field from which the winning of oil has permanently ceased; and
(b) "the person to whom the loss accrued" means the person to whom, as a participator in the abandoned field, the loss accrued (whether or not he is the participator in another oil field who makes the claim for the allowance of the unrelievable field loss)."

(3) After subsection (4) of that section there shall be inserted—

"(5) Subsections (6) to (9) below apply if—

    (a) a claim is made for the allowance of an unrelievable field loss; and

    (b) the person to whom the loss accrued made a claim or election for the allowance of any expenditure unrelated to that field; and

    (c) that claim or election was received by the Board on or after 29th November 1994; and

    (d) the whole or a part of the expenditure to which the claim or election relates is allowed and, accordingly, falls to be taken into account under section 2(8)(a) of this Act for a chargeable period (whether beginning before or after 29th November 1994).

(6) Subject to subsection (7) below, where this subsection applies, from the amount which, apart from this subsection, would be the amount of the unrelievable field loss referred to in paragraph (a) of subsection (5) above there shall be deducted an amount equal to so much of any expenditure unrelated to the field as is allowed on a claim or election as mentioned in paragraph (d) of that subsection.

(7) If—

    (a) claims are made for the allowance of more than one unrelievable field loss derived from the same abandoned field, and

    (b) the person to whom the loss accrued is the same in respect of each of the unrelievable field losses,

subsection (6) above shall have effect as if the deduction referred to in that subsection fell to be made from the aggregate amount of those losses.

(8) Where subsection (7) above applies, the deduction shall be set against the unrelievable field losses in the order in which the claims for the allowance of each of those losses were received by the Board.

(9) In subsections (5) and (6) above, "expenditure unrelated to the field" means—

    (a) expenditure allowable under any of sections 5, 5A and 5B of this Act;

    (b) expenditure allowable under this section (derived from a different abandoned field); or

    (c) expenditure falling within section 65 of the Finance Act 1987 which is accepted by the Board as allowable in accordance with Schedule 14 to that Act;

and, in relation to expenditure falling within section 65 of the Finance Act 1987, "election" means an election under Part I of Schedule 14 to that Act."

GENERAL NOTE

The section restricts, in certain circumstances, the amount of any unrelievable field loss which can be used to reduce the Petroleum Revenue Tax (PRT) liability of another North Sea oil or gas field. Under existing legislation, an unrelievable field loss may include reliefs claimed for certain expenditure incurred outside the field. Such expenditure is now excluded from the unrelievable field loss for claims made from Budget Day.

This section, and ss.147 and 148, relate only to past expenditures, since PRT was abolished for fields with development consents from Budget Day 1994 by FA 1993, s.185.

The amendments to the Oil Taxation Act 1975 (OTA), s.6 implement the restriction. Where more than one unrelievable field loss is derived from the same field, the total restriction is taken from the aggregate of these losses, rather than from each one, but each will still be relieved individually. The reliefs arising outside the field which are affected by the new rules are:

    (i) abortive exploration expenditure (OTA 1975, s.5);

    (ii) exploration and appraisal expenditure (OTA 1975, s.5A);

    (iii) research expenditure (OTA 1975, s.5B);

    (iv) cross-field allowance (FA 1987, s.65); and

    (v) expenditure allowable under s.146 which is derived from a different abandoned field.

Removal of time limits for claims for unrelievable field losses

147.—(1) In Schedule 8 to the Oil Taxation Act 1975 (procedural provisions as to allowance of unrelievable field losses), in paragraph 4 (claims)—

(a) in sub-paragraph (1) (which requires a participator to make a claim to the Board within a time limit), for the words from "and must be made" to "that is to say" there shall be substituted "at any time after" and the words from "and the date" to the end of the sub-paragraph shall be omitted; and

(b) in sub-paragraph (2) the words "within the time allowed for making the original claim" shall be omitted.

(2) This section applies to claims made on or after the day on which this Act is passed.

GENERAL NOTE
    The current time limit of six years for claims for unrelievable field losses, which is too restrictive, is removed. This brings the rules governing claims for an unrelievable field loss into line with those governing claims for relief for exploration and appraisal expenditure.

Transfer of interests in fields: restriction of transferred losses

148.—(1) In Schedule 17 to the Finance Act 1980 (transfer of interests in oil fields) paragraph 7 (transfer of unused losses from the old to the new participator) shall be amended as follows.

(2) At the beginning of sub-paragraph (2) there shall be inserted "Subject to the following provisions of this paragraph".

(3) After sub-paragraph (2) there shall be inserted the following sub-paragraphs—

"(3) If, in the case of a transfer of the whole or part of an interest on or after 29th November 1994,—

(a) the old participator made a claim or election for the allowance of any expenditure unrelated to the field, and

(b) the claim or election was received by the Board on or after that date, and

(c) the expenditure allowed on the claim or election fell to be taken into account in computing the assessable profit or allowable loss of the old participator for the transfer period or any earlier chargeable period,

then, from the sum which, apart from this sub-paragraph, would be the aggregate of all the losses transferred to the new participator under this paragraph there shall be deducted (subject to sub-paragraphs (5) and (6) below) so much of the expenditure referred to in paragraph (a) above as is allowed on the claim or election (and, accordingly, the amount so deducted shall not fall to be transferred to the new participator under this paragraph).

(4) In this paragraph "expenditure unrelated to the field" means expenditure allowable under any of the following provisions—

(a) section 5 (abortive exploration expenditure);

(b) section 5A (exploration and appraisal expenditure);

(c) section 5B (research expenditure);

(d) section 6 (unrelievable loss from abandoned field); and

(e) section 65 of the Finance Act 1987 (cross-field allowance of certain expenditure incurred on new fields);

and, in relation to any such expenditure, "claim" means a claim under Schedule 7 or Schedule 8 and "election" means an election under Part I of Schedule 14 to the Finance Act 1987 and, in relation to such an election, expenditure shall be regarded as allowed if it is accepted by the Board as allowable in accordance with that Schedule.

(5) Where, in accordance with sub-paragraph (1) above, only a part of a loss (corresponding to the part of the interest transferred) falls to be

transferred under this paragraph, only a corresponding part of the expenditure referred to in sub-paragraph (3) above shall be deducted under that sub-paragraph.

(6) Where the amount of the deduction under sub-paragraph (3) above equals or exceeds the sum from which it is to be deducted, no part of any loss shall be transferred to the new participator under this paragraph."

GENERAL NOTE

The section restricts, in certain circumstances, the PRT losses which can be transferred when an interest in a North Sea oil or gas field is transferred from one company to another. Any reliefs arising from expenditure incurred outside the field which the vendor has claimed will be excluded from the losses transferred. This relates to transfers and claims from Budget Day. The categories of expenditure excluded correspond with those in s.146 above. Where there is a transfer of part of an interest, the relief is reduced proportionately. The deduction has a maximum effect of reducing any transferred losses to nil and has no effect on the PRT position of the company disposing of the field interest.

PART V

STAMP DUTY

Transfer: associated bodies

149.—(1) Section 42 of the Finance Act 1930 (relief from transfer stamp duty in case of transfer of property as between associated bodies corporate) shall be amended as mentioned in subsections (2) to (5) below.

(2) In subsection (2) (as substituted by section 27(2) of the Finance Act 1967) for the words from "that the effect" to the end of the subsection there shall be substituted "that—
  (a) the effect of the instrument is to convey or transfer a beneficial interest in property from one body corporate to another, and
  (b) the bodies in question are associated at the time the instrument is executed."

(3) The following subsections shall be inserted after subsection (2) (as so substituted)—

"(2A) For the purposes of this section bodies corporate are associated at a particular time if at that time one is the parent of the other or another body corporate is the parent of each.

(2B) For the purposes of this section one body corporate is the parent of another at a particular time if at that time the first body is beneficial owner of not less than 75 per cent. of the ordinary share capital of the second body."

(4) In subsection (3) (as so substituted) for "(2)" there shall be substituted "(2B)", and the words from "with the substitution" to the end shall be omitted.

(5) The following subsection shall be inserted after subsection (3) (as so substituted)—

"(4) In this section "ordinary share capital", in relation to a body corporate, means all the issued share capital (by whatever name called) of the body corporate, other than capital the holders of which have a right to a dividend at a fixed rate but have no other right to share in the profits of the body corporate."

(6) In section 27 of the Finance Act 1967 (which relates to section 42 of the Finance Act 1930) in subsection (3)(c) for the words from "a change" to "third body corporate" there shall be substituted "the transferor or a third body corporate ceasing to be the transferee's parent (within the meaning of the said section 42)".

(7) This section shall apply in relation to instruments executed on or after the day on which this Act is passed.

GENERAL NOTE

The group membership test for the stamp duty relief for transfers between companies in the same group is changed from 90 per cent of the issued share capital to 75 per cent of the ordinary share capital. This brings the test more into line with that for corporation tax purposes. The definition of "ordinary share capital" corresponds with that in ICTA 1988, s.832.

Northern Ireland transfer: associated bodies

150.—(1) Section 11 of the Finance Act (Northern Ireland) 1954 (relief from stamp duty in case of transfer of property between associated bodies corporate) shall be amended as follows.

(2) In subsection (2)(c)(iii) for the words from "a change" to "third body corporate" there shall be substituted "the transferor or a third body corporate ceasing to be the transferee's parent".

(3) The following subsections shall be substituted for subsection (3)—

"(3) For the purposes of this section a body corporate is associated with another body corporate at a particular time if at that time one is the parent of the other or another body corporate is the parent of each.

(3AA) For the purposes of this section one body corporate is the parent of another at a particular time if at that time the first body is beneficial owner of not less than 75 per cent. of the ordinary share capital of the second body."

(4) In subsection (3A) for the words "paragraphs (i) and (ii) of subsection (3)" there shall be substituted "subsection (3AA)", and the words from "with the substitution" to the end shall be omitted.

(5) The following subsection shall be inserted after subsection (3A)—

"(3AB) In this section "ordinary share capital", in relation to a body corporate, means all the issued share capital (by whatever name called) of the body corporate, other than capital the holders of which have a right to a dividend at a fixed rate but have no other right to share in the profits of the body corporate."

(6) This section shall apply in relation to instruments executed on or after the day on which this Act is passed.

GENERAL NOTE

The provisions in s.149 above are applied to the parallel legislation for Northern Ireland.

Lease or tack: associated bodies

151.—(1) Stamp duty under the heading "Lease or Tack" in Schedule 1 to the Stamp Act 1891 shall not be chargeable on an instrument which is—

(a) a lease or tack,

(b) an agreement for a lease or tack, or

(c) an agreement with respect to a letting,

as respects which the condition in subsection (2) below is satisfied.

(2) The condition is that it is shown to the satisfaction of the Commissioners of Inland Revenue that—

(a) the lessor is a body corporate and the lessee is another body corporate,

(b) those bodies are associated at the time the instrument is executed,

(c) in the case of an agreement, the agreement is for the lease or tack or letting to be granted to the lessee or to a body corporate which is associated with the lessee at the time the instrument is executed, and

(d) the instrument is not executed in pursuance of or in connection with an arrangement falling within subsection (3) below.

(3) An arrangement falls within this subsection if it is one under which—

(a) the consideration, or any part of the consideration, for the lease or tack or agreement was to be provided or received (directly or indirectly) by a person other than a body corporate which at the relevant time was associated with either the lessor or the lessee, or

(b) the lessor and the lessee were to cease to be associated by reason of the lessor or a third body corporate ceasing to be the lessee's parent;

and the relevant time is the time of the execution of the instrument.

(4) Without prejudice to the generality of paragraph (a) of subsection (3) above, an arrangement shall be treated as within that paragraph if it is one under which the lessor or the lessee or a body corporate associated with either at the relevant time was to be enabled to provide any of the consideration, or was to part with any of it, by or in consequence of the carrying out of a transaction which involved (or transactions any of which involved) a payment or other disposition by a person other than a body corporate associated with the lessor or the lessee at the relevant time.

(5) An instrument mentioned in subsection (1) above shall not be treated as duly stamped unless—

(a) it is duly stamped in accordance with the law that would apply but for that subsection, or

(b) it has, in accordance with section 12 of the Stamp Act 1891, been stamped with a particular stamp denoting either that it is not chargeable with any duty or that it is duly stamped.

(6) In this section—

(a) references to the lessor are to the person granting the lease or tack or (in the case of an agreement) agreeing to grant the lease or tack or letting;

(b) references to the lessee are to the person being granted the lease or tack or (in the case of an agreement) agreeing for the lease or tack or letting to be granted to him or another.

(7) For the purposes of this section bodies corporate are associated at a particular time if at that time one is the parent of the other or another body corporate is the parent of each.

(8) For the purposes of this section one body corporate is the parent of another at a particular time if at that time the first body is beneficial owner of not less than 75 per cent. of the ordinary share capital of the second body.

(9) In subsection (8) above "ordinary share capital", in relation to a body corporate, means all the issued share capital (by whatever name called) of the body corporate, other than capital the holders of which have a right to a dividend at a fixed rate but have no other right to share in the profits of the body corporate.

(10) The ownership referred to in subsection (8) above is ownership either directly or through another body corporate or other bodies corporate, or partly directly and partly through another body corporate or other bodies corporate; and Part I of Schedule 4 to the Finance Act 1938 (determination of amount of capital held through other bodies corporate) shall apply for the purposes of this section.

(11) This section shall apply in relation to instruments executed on or after the day on which this Act is passed.

GENERAL NOTE

A stamp duty relief is provided for the grant of a new lease by one company in a group to another such company, complementing the existing relief for sales and assignments of leases within a group. The same conditions apply as for the existing relief (see FA 1930, s.42 as amended by s.149 above, and FA 1967, s.27).

PART VI

MISCELLANEOUS AND GENERAL

Miscellaneous

Open-ended investment companies

152.—(1) The Treasury may, by regulations, make such provision as they consider appropriate for securing that the enactments specified in subsection (2) below have effect in relation to—

(a) open-ended investment companies of any such description as may be specified in the regulations,

(b) holdings in, and the assets of, such companies, and

(c) transactions involving such companies,

in a manner corresponding, subject to such modifications as the Treasury consider appropriate, to the manner in which they have effect in relation to unit trusts, to rights under, and the assets subject to, such trusts and to transactions for purposes connected with such trusts.

(2) The enactments referred to in subsection (1) above are—

(a) the Tax Acts and the Taxation of Chargeable Gains Act 1992; and

(b) the enactments relating to stamp duty and Part IV of the Finance Act 1986 (stamp duty reserve tax).

(3) The power of the Treasury to make regulations under this section in relation to any such enactments shall include power to make provision which does any one or more of the following, that is to say—

(a) identifies the payments which are or are not to be treated, for the purposes of any prescribed enactment, as the distributions of open-ended investment companies;

(b) modifies the operation of Chapters II, III and VA of Part VI of the Taxes Act 1988 in relation to open-ended investment companies or in relation to payments falling to be treated as the distributions of such companies;

(c) applies and adapts any of the provisions of Part IV of the Finance Act 1986 for the purpose of making in relation to transactions involving open-ended investment companies any provision corresponding (with or without modifications) to that which applies under the enactments relating to stamp duty in the case of equivalent transactions involving unit trusts;

(d) provides for any or all of the provisions of sections 75 to 77 of the Finance Act 1986 to have effect or not to have effect in relation to open-ended investment companies or the undertakings of, or any shares in, such companies;

(e) so modifies the operation of any prescribed enactment in relation to any such companies as to secure that arrangements for treating the assets of an open-ended investment company as assets comprised in separate pools are given an effect corresponding, in prescribed respects, to that of equivalent arrangements constituting the separate parts of an umbrella scheme;

(f) requires prescribed enactments to have effect in relation to an open-ended investment company as if it were, or were not, a member of the same group of companies as one or more other companies;

(g) identifies the holdings in open-ended investment companies which are, or are not, to be treated for the purposes of any prescribed enactment as comprised in the same class of holdings;

(h) preserves a continuity of tax treatment where, in connection with any scheme of re-organisation, assets of one or more unit trusts become assets of one or more open-ended investment companies, or vice versa;

(i) treats the separate parts of the undertaking of an open-ended investment company in relation to which provision is made by virtue of paragraph (e) above as distinct companies for the purposes of any regulations under this section;

(j) amends, adapts or applies the provisions of any subordinate legislation made under or by reference to any enactment modified by the regulations.

(4) The power to make regulations under this section shall be exercisable by statutory instrument and shall include power—

(a) to make different provision for different cases; and

(b) to make such incidental, supplemental, consequential and transitional provision as the Treasury may think fit.

(5) A statutory instrument containing regulations under this section shall be subject to annulment in pursuance of a resolution of the House of Commons.

(6) In this section—

"the enactments relating to stamp duty" means the Stamp Act 1891, and any enactment (including any Northern Ireland legislation) which amends or is required to be construed together with that Act;

"Northern Ireland legislation" shall have the meaning given by section 24(5) of the Interpretation Act 1978;

"open-ended investment company" has the same meaning as in the Financial Services Act 1986;

"prescribed" means prescribed by regulations under this section;

"subordinate legislation" means any subordinate legislation within the meaning of the Interpretation Act 1978 or any order or regulations made by statutory instrument under Northern Ireland legislation; and

"umbrella scheme" shall have the meaning given by section 468 of the Taxes Act 1988;

and references in this section to the enactments relating to stamp duty, or to any of them, or to Part IV of the Finance Act 1986 shall have effect as including references to enactments repealed by sections 107 to 110 of the Finance Act 1990.

(7) Any reference in this section to unit trusts has effect—

(a) for the purposes of so much of this section as confers power in relation to the enactments specified in paragraph (a) of subsection (2) above, as a reference to authorised unit trusts (within the meaning of section 468 of the Taxes Act 1988), and

(b) for the purposes of so much of this section as confers power in relation to the enactments specified in paragraph (b) of that subsection, as a reference to any unit trust scheme (within the meaning given by section 57 of the Finance Act 1946).

(8) For the purposes of this section the enactments which shall be taken to make provision in relation to companies that are members of the same group of companies shall include any enactments which make provision in relation to a case—

(a) where one company has, or in relation to another company is, a subsidiary, or a subsidiary of a particular description, or

(b) where one company controls another or two or more companies are under the same control.

GENERAL NOTE

The section paves the way for direct tax provision for open-ended investment companies and their shareholders. An open-ended investment company (OEIC) cannot currently be formed under U.K. company law, but it is commonly used elsewhere in the E.U. as a vehicle for collective investment. It is open-ended in the sense that its shares will be continuously created or redeemed, depending on the net demand by investors to acquire shares or to redeem their existing holdings. As with existing authorised unit trusts, these transactions will be undertaken at a price derived from the net asset value of the OEIC's underlying investments. The Government intends to proceed by means of secondary legislation under the European Communities Act 1972.

The Treasury is given power to make tax provisions for OEICs, for their shareholders and for transactions involving them, in a way which corresponds to the provisions in relation to unit trusts (and more specifically, authorised unit trusts). The power extends to income tax, CGT, corporation tax, stamp duty and stamp duty reserve tax.

Electronic lodgement of tax returns, etc.

153. Schedule 28 to this Act (which makes provision with respect to the electronic lodgement of certain tax returns and documents required in connection with tax returns) shall have effect.

GENERAL NOTE
The section introduces Sched. 28, which makes provision for the electronic lodgement of tax returns.
See further the General Note to Sched. 28.

Short rotation coppice

154.—(1) The cultivation of short rotation coppice shall be regarded for the purposes of the Tax Acts and the Taxation of Chargeable Gains Act 1992 as farming (and, where relevant, as husbandry or agriculture) and not as forestry; and land in the United Kingdom on which the activity is carried on shall accordingly be regarded for those purposes as farm land or agricultural land, as the case may be, and not as woodlands.

(2) For the purposes of the Inheritance Tax Act 1984 the cultivation of short rotation coppice shall be regarded as agriculture; and accordingly for those purposes—

(a) land on which short rotation coppice is cultivated shall be regarded as agricultural land, and

(b) buildings used in connection with the cultivation of short rotation coppice shall be regarded as farm buildings.

(3) In subsections (1) and (2) "short rotation coppice" means a perennial crop of tree species planted at high density, the stems of which are harvested above ground level at intervals of less than ten years.

(4) Subsection (1) and subsection (3) so far as relating to subsection (1) shall be deemed to have come into force on 29th November 1994.

(5) Subsection (2) and subsection (3) so far as relating to subsection (2) shall have effect in relation to transfers of value or other events occuring on or after 6th April 1995.

GENERAL NOTE
Short rotation coppice is a way of producing a renewable fuel for biomass-fed power stations. Willow or poplar cuttings are planted on farm land at a rate of 3,000 to 4,000 per acre. They are then cut back to ground level after a year. That causes them to throw up shoots, which are harvested every three years or so and turned into chips which are used as fuel.
Short rotation coppice has more in common with arable crops than with the production of timber and it will therefore be taxable as farming and excluded from the income tax and CGT exemption for commercial woodlands. It will also rank as agricultural property for inheritance tax purposes and qualify for agricultural property relief.

Inheritance tax: agricultural property

155.—(1) In section 116 of the Inheritance Tax Act 1984 (relief for transfers of agricultural property) in subsection (2) (rate of relief) the word "either" shall be omitted and at the end of paragraph (b) there shall be inserted "or

(c) the interest of the transferor in the property immediately before the transfer does not carry either of the rights mentioned in paragraph (a) above because the property is let on a tenancy beginning on or after 1st September 1995;".

(2) After subsection (2) of that section there shall be inserted the following subsection—

"(2A) In the application of this section as respects property in Scotland, the reference in subsection (2)(c) above to a tenancy beginning on or after 1st September 1995 includes a reference to its being acquired on or after that date by right of succession (the date of acquisition being taken to be the date on which the successor gives relevant notice under section 12 of the Agricultural Holdings (Scotland) Act 1991)."

(3) Subsections (1) and (2) above shall apply in relation to transfers of value made, and other events occurring, on or after 1st September 1995.

GENERAL NOTE

Total exemption from inheritance tax is extended to all agricultural property. This is in line with the policy of the Agricultural Tenancies Act 1995, which comes into force on September 1, 1995, and is intended to deregulate and stimulate the market for let farm land in England and Wales. Previously tenanted land attracted only a 50 per cent exemption.

As respects Scotland, the relief extends to tenancies acquired by right of succession.

Proceedings for tax in sheriff court

156.—(1) Section 67 of the Taxes Management Act 1970 (proceedings for tax in sheriff court) shall be amended as follows.

(2) In subsection (1) (tax not exceeding a specified sum recoverable in sheriff court) for the words from "where" to "the tax" there shall be substituted "tax due and payable under any assessment".

(3) The following subsection shall be inserted after subsection (1)—

"(1A) An officer of the Board who is authorised by the Board to do so may address the court in any proceedings under this section."

(4) This section shall apply in relation to proceedings commenced after the day on which this Act is passed.

GENERAL NOTE

The restriction whereby Collectors of Taxes in Scotland can sue in the sheriff court only up to a limit of £1,500 is removed.

Any authorised official of the Revenue may address the court in such proceedings.

Certificates of tax deposit

157.—(1) If, whether before or after the passing of this Act—
(a) any person ("the depositor") has received any sum on the making, on or after 6th April 1990, of a withdrawal for cash of a tax deposit made before that date,
(b) the whole or any part of any qualifying tax liability has been discharged by any payment made otherwise than by the application of a tax deposit, and
(c) that payment was made in the period beginning one month before the withdrawal and ending one month afterwards,
the depositor shall be entitled to receive compensation under this section from the Board.

(2) In this section "qualifying tax liability", in relation to a tax deposit, means so much of any liability as is—
(a) a liability of any person for any tax for the year 1990–91 or any subsequent year of assessment, or for interest on such tax;
(b) a liability that relates to tax for a year of assessment during the whole or any part of which that person was married to the depositor; and
(c) a liability of such a description that, if it had been a liability of the depositor (and the withdrawal were to be disregarded), the whole or any part of it could have been discharged, immediately before the time

of the payment mentioned in subsection (1)(b) above, by the application of that deposit and of accrued interest thereon.

(3) Subject to the following provisions of this section, the amount of the compensation to which the depositor is entitled under this section in the case of any deposit withdrawn for cash shall be equal to the difference between—

(a) the sum received as mentioned in subsection (1)(a) above on the withdrawal; and

(b) the sum that would have been received if interest had accrued on the relevant part of the sum received at the rate applicable under the relevant terms to sums applied in the payment of tax, instead of at the rate applicable to a withdrawal for cash.

(4) In subsection (3) above, the reference to the relevant part of the sum received on the withdrawal of a deposit is a reference to the following amount, that is to say—

(a) in a case where the sum received on the withdrawal is equal to or smaller than the amount of the liability discharged by the payment mentioned in subsection (1)(b) above, the amount equal to such part of the sum actually received as does not represent interest that has accrued under the relevant terms; and

(b) in any other case, to the amount which would have been the amount specified in paragraph (a) above if the sum actually received on the withdrawal had been equal to the amount of qualifying tax liability so discharged.

(5) The amount of compensation to which any person is entitled under this section shall also include an amount equal to interest, for the period from the withdrawal mentioned in subsection (1)(a) above until the payment of the compensation, on the amount determined in accordance with subsection (3) above; and a liability to compensation under this section shall not bear interest apart from in accordance with this subsection.

(6) Section 178 of the Finance Act 1989 (interest rates) shall apply to subsection (5) above for determining the rate of the interest treated, by virtue of that subsection, as included in any compensation under this section; and any regulations under that section which are in force at the passing of this Act shall be deemed, subject to the powers of the Treasury under that section, to have effect in relation to this section as they have effect in relation to the enactments specified in subsection (2)(f) of that section (interest on overdue tax).

(7) The part of any compensation under this section that represents interest under subsection (5) above shall not be treated as included in the income of the depositor for the purposes of income tax; but the remainder shall be chargeable to income tax under Case III of Schedule D.

(8) No compensation shall be paid under this section unless a claim for it has been made to the Board.

(9) Where any claim is made under this section with respect to any withdrawal for cash of a tax deposit—

(a) this section shall have effect if there is, in the period mentioned in subsection (1)(c) above, more than one such payment as is mentioned in subsection (1)(b) above as if (subject to paragraph (b) below) all the payments in that period were, for the purposes of that claim, to be aggregated and treated as one such payment; and

(b) the amount of compensation payable under this section on that claim shall be computed without regard to so much of any payment discharging a qualifying tax liability as, in pursuance of any claim under this section, has been or is to be so taken into account as to affect the amount of compensation payable in the case of any other withdrawal.

(10) Sums required by the Board for paying compensation under this section shall be issued to the Board by the Treasury out of the National Loans Fund.

(11) A withdrawal for cash of a tax deposit shall be taken for the purposes of this section to occur at the same time as, under the relevant terms, it is deemed to occur for the purposes of the calculation of interest on the amount withdrawn.

(12) This section shall be construed as one with the Tax Acts, and in this section—

(a) references to a tax deposit are references to the whole or any part of any deposit in respect of which a certificate of tax deposit has been issued by the Treasury under section 12 of the National Loans Act 1968; and

(b) references to the relevant terms, in relation to a tax deposit, are references to the terms applicable to that deposit and to the certificate issued in respect of it.

GENERAL NOTE

Holders of certificates of tax deposit, issued by the Treasury under the National Loans Act 1968, s.12 receive interest at one rate if they use them to pay their own tax bills, and at a lower rate if they surrender them for cash. This section compensates for loss of interest those who bought such certificates before the introduction of independent taxation of husbands and wives and subsequently could not set them against their spouses' tax bills. The cost is expected to be less than £1m.

The rate of interest payable on the compensation will be prescribed by Treasury regulation. It is intended to apply the formula prescribed for other interest payments in the tax system. The basic element of the compensation will be taxable, but not the interest on the compensation. Those eligible must claim the compensation from the Revenue. No certificate of tax deposit can be matched with more than one liability to produce compensation.

Amendment of the Exchequer and Audit Departments Acts 1866

158. Section 10 of the Exchequer and Audit Departments Act 1866 (Commissioners of Customs and Excise and of Inland Revenue to deduct repayments from gross revenues) shall have effect, and be deemed always to have had effect, as if the reference in that section to repayments included references to—

(a) payments in respect of any actual or deemed credits relating to any tax or duty; and

(b) payments of any interest on sums which are or are deemed to be repayments for the purposes of that section.

GENERAL NOTE

Section 10 of the Exchequer and Audit Departments Act 1866 allows the Customs and Excise and the Inland Revenue to deduct repayments of tax from the gross amounts which they pay into the Exchequer. Legal advice has recently been received that this does not strictly cover payments of VAT input tax to a trader, payments of tax credits attaching to dividends to exempt taxpayers (such as pension funds) and payments of interest on tax. The Act is retrospectively amended to validate these payments.

Ports levy

159.—(1) In Part I of the Ports Act 1991 (transfer of statutory port undertakings), after section 15 (duty to provide information for purposes of levy) insert—

"Notice of assessment: supplementary provisions

15A.—(1) Where a notice of assessment has been served under section 14(2) above on a former relevant port authority ("the authority"), the authority may, within the period mentioned in section 14(3) above, by notice in writing request the appropriate Minister to reconsider the amount of the assessment.

The request shall set out the grounds on which the authority allege that the amount assessed is incorrect.

(2) If it appears to the Minister that there are reasonable grounds for believing that the amount of the assessment may be excessive, he may direct that section 14(3) and (4) above shall not apply to the whole amount of the assessment but only to such lesser amount as he may specify.

(3) If a request for reconsideration is duly made, the appropriate Minister shall reconsider the amount of the assessment and may confirm or reduce it.

An appeal lies to the High Court or, in Scotland, to the Court of Session as the Court of Exchequer in Scotland from any decision of the Minister under this subsection.

(4) The appropriate Minister may reconsider the amount of an assessment under section 14(2) above in any other case, if he thinks fit, and may confirm or reduce it.

(5) When the amount of the assessment is finally determined—

    (a) if the amount of the assessment is less than the amount paid by the authority, the appropriate Minister shall make such payment to the authority as is required to put the authority in the same position as if the reduced amount had been specified in the original assessment;

    (b) if a further amount is payable by the authority, section 14(3) and (4) above shall apply in relation to that amount as if the reference to the date of issue of the notice of assessment were a reference to the date of the determination.

(6) Except as provided by this section a notice of assessment under section 14(2) above shall not be questioned in any legal proceedings whatsoever.".

(2) Sections 115 to 120 of the Finance Act 1990 (levy on privatisation of certain ports) shall cease to have effect.

(3) An Order in Council under paragraph 1(1)(b) of Schedule 1 to the Northern Ireland Act 1974 (legislation for Northern Ireland in the interim period) which states that it is made only for purposes corresponding to those of subsection (1) above—

    (a) shall not be subject to paragraph 1(4) and (5) of that Schedule (affirmative resolution of both Houses of Parliament), but

    (b) shall be subject to annulment in pursuance of a resolution of either House of Parliament.

GENERAL NOTE

The section inserts a new s.15A in the Ports Act 1991 and repeals ss.115–120 of the FA 1990. The original provisions in FA 1990 were enacted with a view to the possibility that certain ports might be privatised by private or local Acts. Privatisation under the Ports Act 1991 has superseded any possibility of privatisation under the FA 1990, and accordingly these provisions are repealed.

New Ports Act 1991, s.15A supplements the existing provisions for the assessment of ports levy on the disposal by certain port authorities of the securities of their successor companies. The appropriate Minister (see the Ports Act 1991, s.20) is empowered to reduce an assessment, either on his own initiative or on a request by the authority, and also to defer payment of part of the amount assessed, pending reconsideration or an appeal to the courts.

Tax simplification

160.—(1) The Inland Revenue shall prepare and present to Treasury Ministers a report on tax simplification.

(2) The report shall be laid before Parliament and published before 31st December 1995.

(3) The report shall give—

    (a) an account of recent tax legislation history;

    (b) full details of recent annual additions to both primary and secondary legislation;

(c) a summary of recent criticism of both the complexity of tax legislation and of parliamentary procedure; and

(d) the advantages and disadvantages of possible solutions including a Royal Commission on taxation and a tax law commission.

GENERAL NOTE

This section, introduced on the initiative of a Government backbencher, requires the Revenue to produce a report on tax simplification covering the matters set out in subs. (3). The proposal resulted from concern at the increasing complexity of fiscal legislation—this Finance Act and its predecessor are respectively the second longest and the longest in history. Unfortunately, previous attempts at simplification have usually resulted in greater complexity.

General

Interpretation

161.—(1) In this Act "the Taxes Act 1988" means the Income and Corporation Taxes Act 1988.

(2) In Part III of this Act "the Management Act" means the Taxes Management Act 1970.

(3) Part V of this Act shall be construed as one with the Stamp Act 1891.

Repeals

162. The provisions specified in Schedule 29 to this Act (which include provisions which are already spent) are hereby repealed to the extent specified in the third column of that Schedule, but subject to any provision of that Schedule.

Short title

163. This Act may be cited as the Finance Act 1995.

SCHEDULES

Section 2   SCHEDULE 1

TABLE OF RATES OF DUTY ON WINE AND MADE-WINE

PART I

WINE OR MADE-WINE OF A STRENGTH NOT EXCEEDING 22 PER CENT

Description of wine or made-wine	*Rates of duty per hectolitre*
	£
Wine or made-wine of a strength not exceeding 4 per cent	23.41
Wine or made-wine of a strength exceeding 4 per cent but not exceeding 5.5 per cent	42.14

Description of wine or made-wine	Rates of duty per hectolitre
	£
Wine or made-wine of a strength exceeding 5.5 per cent but not exceeding 15 per cent and not being sparkling	140.44
Sparkling wine or sparkling made-wine of a strength exceeding 5.5 per cent but not exceeding 15 per cent	200.64
Wine or made-wine of a strength exceeding 15 per cent but not exceeding 22 per cent	200.64

PART II

WINE OR MADE-WINE OF A STRENGTH EXCEEDING 22 PER CENT

Description of wine or made-wine	Rates of duty per litre of alcohol in the wine or made-wine
	£
Wine or made-wine of a strength exceeding 22 per cent	20.60

GENERAL NOTE

The previous five-band structure for duty on low-strength wines (*i.e.* wines not exceeding 5.5 per cent) is replaced by a two-band structure. The duty on sparkling wine and fortified wine is reduced to correct anomalies and to implement an agreement with Spain with respect to sherry.

It was originally intended not to increase the duty overall, but as a result of the Chancellor's announcement on December 8, 1994 the duty in each category was increased by about four per cent, representing approximately 5p on a bottle of table wine. However, taking the overall increase into account, the duty on sparkling wines is reduced by 10 per cent and that on fortified wines by three per cent.

Section 5   SCHEDULE 2

DENATURED ALCOHOL

The Alcoholic Liquor Duties Act 1979

1. In section 4(1) of the Alcoholic Liquor Duties Act 1979 (interpretation)—
(a) for the definition of "authorised methylator" there shall be substituted the following definition—
    " 'authorised denaturer' means a person authorised under section 75(1) below to denature dutiable alcoholic liquor;"
(b) in the definition of "British compounded spirits", for "methylated spirits" there shall be substituted "denatured alcohol";
(c) after the definition of "compounder" there shall be inserted the following definition—
    " 'denatured alcohol' means denatured alcohol within the meaning of section 5 of the Finance Act 1995, and references to denaturing a liquor are references to subjecting it to any process by which it becomes denatured alcohol;"
(d) for the definition of "licensed methylator" there shall be substituted the following definition—
    " 'licensed denaturer' means a person holding a licence under section 75(2) below;".
2. Section 9 of that Act (remission of duty on spirits for methylation) shall cease to have effect.
3. In section 10 of that Act (remission of duty on spirits), for "methylated spirits" there shall be substituted "denatured alcohol".
4. In section 24(1)(a) of that Act (restriction on distiller or rectifier carrying on other trades), for "methylated spirits" there shall be substituted "denatured alcohol".
5. In sections 75, 77, 79 and 80 of that Act (which contain provisions regulating methylation)—

  (a) for the words "methylate", "methylates", "methylator" and "methylators", wherever they occur, and for the word "methylated", where it occurs outside the expression "methylated spirits", there shall be substituted, respectively, "denature", "denatures", "denaturer", "denaturers" and "denatured";

  (b) for the words "methylation" and "methylating", wherever they occur, there shall be substituted, in each case, "denaturing";

  (c) for the word "spirits", wherever it occurs outside the expression "methylated spirits", there shall be substituted "dutiable alcoholic liquor";

  (d) for the words "methylated spirits", wherever they occur, there shall be substituted "denatured alcohol".

6. In section 77(2) of that Act (provisions supplemental to powers to make regulations), after paragraph (a) there shall be inserted the following paragraph—

  "(aa) frame any provision of the regulations with respect to the supply, receipt or use of denatured alcohol by reference to matters to be contained from time to time in a notice published in accordance with the regulations by the Commissioners and having effect until withdrawn in accordance with the regulations; and".

7. For section 78 of that Act (additional provisions relating to methylated spirits) there shall be substituted the following section—

"Defaults in respect of denatured alcohol

78.—(1) This subsection applies if, at any time when an account is taken and a balance struck of the quantity of any kind of denatured alcohol in the possession of an authorised or licensed denaturer, there is a difference between—

  (a) the quantity ('the actual amount') of the dutiable alcoholic liquor of any description in the denatured alcohol in his possession; and

  (b) the quantity ('the proper amount') of dutiable alcoholic liquor of that description which, according to any such accounts as are required to be kept by virtue of any regulations under section 77 above, ought to be in the denatured alcohol in his possession.

(2) Subsection (1) above shall not apply if the difference constitutes—

  (a) an excess of the actual amount over the proper amount of not more than 1 per cent. of the aggregate of—

    (i) the quantity of dutiable alcoholic liquor of the description in question in the balance of dutiable alcoholic liquor struck when an account was last taken; and

    (ii) the quantity of dutiable alcoholic liquor of that description which has since been lawfully added to the denaturer's stock;

    or

  (b) a deficiency such that the actual amount is less than the proper amount by not more than 2 per cent. of that aggregate.

(3) If, where subsection (1) above applies, the actual amount exceeds the proper amount, the relevant amount of any dutiable alcoholic liquor of the description in question which is in the possession of the denaturer shall be liable to forfeiture; and for this purpose the relevant amount is the amount corresponding to the amount of the excess or such part of that amount as the Commissioners consider appropriate.

(4) If, where subsection (1) above applies, the actual amount is less than the proper amount, the denaturer shall, on demand by the Commissioners, pay on the amount of the deficiency, or on such part of it as the Commissioners may specify in the demand, the duty payable on dutiable alcoholic liquor of the description comprised in the deficiency.

(5) If any person—

  (a) supplies to another, in contravention of any regulations under section 77 above, any denatured alcohol containing dutiable alcoholic liquor of any description, or

  (b) uses any such denatured alcohol in contravention of any such regulations,

that person shall, on demand by the Commissioners, pay on the amount of dutiable alcoholic liquor of that description comprised, at the time of its supply or use, in the denatured alcohol that is so supplied or used, or on such part of it as the Commissioners may specify, the duty payable on dutiable alcoholic liquor of that description.

(6) Any supply of denatured alcohol to a person who—

  (a) by virtue of any regulations under section 77 above is prohibited from receiving it unless authorised to do so by or under the regulations, and

  (b) is not so authorised in the case of the denatured alcohol supplied to him,

shall be taken for the purposes of subsection (5) above to be a supply in contravention of those regulations.

(7) A demand made for the purposes of subsection (4) or (5) above shall be combined, as if there had been a default such as is mentioned in that section, with an assessment and notification under section 12 of the Finance Act 1994 (assessments to excise duty) of the amount of duty due in consequence of the making of the demand."

The Finance Act 1994

8. In paragraph 3(1)(d) of Schedule 5 to the Finance Act 1994 (decisions under or for the purposes of section 9 or 10 of the Alcoholic Liquor Duties Act 1979 to be subject to review and appeal), for "section 9 or 10 (remission of duty on spirits for methylation or" there shall be substituted "section 10 (remission of duty on spirits".

GENERAL NOTE
This Schedule makes appropriate amendments to existing legislation in order to cover the extension of the relief for denatured spirits to denatured alcohol of all kinds.

Para. 7
The new Alcoholic Liquor Duties Act 1979, s.78 gives the Customs and Excise some further anti-avoidance powers. In future, they will be able to charge excise duty in cases where a user is unable to account satisfactorily for losses of denatured alcohol or has put the denatured alcohol to an unauthorised use. This is in addition to the penalty for using denatured alcohol as a beverage.

Section 14   SCHEDULE 3

AMUSEMENT MACHINE LICENCE DUTY

Introductory

1. The Betting and Gaming Duties Act 1981 shall be amended in accordance with paragraphs 2 to 11 below.

Amusement machine licences

2.—(1) In section 21 (gaming machine licences)—
(a) in subsection (1), for the words "gaming machine" and "for gaming" there shall be substituted, respectively, "amusement machine" and "for play";
(b) in subsection (2), for "a gaming machine licence" there shall be substituted "an amusement machine licence"; and
(c) in subsection (3), for "A gaming machine licence" there shall be substituted "An amusement machine licence".
(2) In subsection (3A) of that section (excepted machines), for paragraph (b) there shall be substituted the following paragraphs—
"(b) a five-penny machine which is a prize machine without being a gaming machine or which (if it is a gaming machine) is a small-prize machine, or
(c) a thirty-five-penny machine which is not a prize machine."

Amusement machine licence duty

3.—(1) In subsection (1) of section 22 (duty on gaming machine licences), for "gaming machine" there shall be substituted "amusement machine".
(2) In subsection (2) of that section (meaning of "small-prize machine"), for "a gaming machine is a small-prize machine if" there shall be substituted "an amusement machine is a small-prize machine if it is a prize machine and".

Rate of duty

4.—(1) In subsection (1) of section 23 (determination of rate of duty by reference to Table), for "a gaming machine licence" there shall be substituted "an amusement machine licence".
(2) In subsection (2) of that section—
(a) in paragraph (b), for "or column 3" there shall be substituted ", column 3 or column 4"; and
(b) in the words after that paragraph, for the words "gaming" and "or the rate in column 3" there shall be substituted, respectively, "amusement" and ", the rate in column 3 or the rate in column 4".
(3) For the Table in that subsection (as substituted by section 13 of this Act) there shall be substituted the following Table—

TABLE

(1) *Period (in months) for which licence granted*	*(2)* *Machines that are not gaming machines*	*(3)* *Gaming machines that are small- prize machines or are five-penny machines without being small- prize machines*	*(4)* *Other machines*
	£	£	£
1	30	60	150
2	50	105	275
3	75	155	400
4	95	205	520
5	120	250	645
6	140	295	755
7	160	340	880
8	185	390	1,005
9	205	435	1,115
10	225	480	1,235
11	240	510	1,305
12	250	535	1,375

Restrictions on provision of machines

5. In section 24 (restrictions on provision of gaming machines)—
   (a) for the words "Gaming machines", "gaming machines" and "gaming machine", wherever they occur, there shall be substituted, respectively, "Amusement machines", "amusement machines" and "amusement machine";
   (b) for the word "a", where it occurs before "gaming machine" in subsection (5)(f), there shall be substituted "an"; and
   (c) for the words "for gaming", wherever they occur, there shall be substituted "for play".

Meaning of "amusement machine"

6.—(1) For subsections (1) to (3) of section 25 (meaning of "gaming machine") there shall be substituted the following subsections—
   "(1) A machine is an amusement machine for the purposes of this Act if—
   (a) the machine is constructed or adapted for the playing of any game (whether a game of chance, a game of skill or a game of chance and skill combined);
   (b) the game is one played by means of the machine (whether automatically or by the operation of the machine by the player or players);
   (c) a player pays to play the game (except where he has an opportunity to play without payment as a result of having previously played successfully) either by inserting a coin or token into the machine or in some other way;
   (d) the machine automatically—
       (i) applies some or all of the rules of the game or displays or records scores in the game; and
       (ii) determines when a player who has paid to play a game by means of the machine can no longer play without paying again;
       and
   (e) the machine is a gaming machine, a video machine or a pinball machine.
   (1A) A machine constructed or adapted for the playing of a game is a gaming machine for the purposes of this Act if—
   (a) it is a prize machine;
   (b) the game which is played by means of the machine is a game of chance, a game of chance and skill combined or a pretended game of chance or of chance and skill combined; and
   (c) the outcome of the game is determined by the chances inherent in the action of the machine, whether or not provision is made for manipulation of the machine by a player;
   and for the purposes of this subsection a game in which the elements of chance can be overcome by skill shall be treated as a game of chance and skill combined if there is an element of chance in the game that cannot be overcome except by superlative skill.
   (1B) A machine constructed or adapted for the playing of a game is a video machine for the purposes of this Act if—
   (a) a micro-processor is used to control some or all of the machine's functions; and

(b) the playing of the game involves information or images being communicated or displayed to the player or players by means of any description of screen, other than one consisting only in a blank surface onto which light is projected.

(1C) For the purposes of this Act an amusement machine is a prize machine unless it is constructed or adapted so that a person playing it once and successfully either receives nothing or receives only—

(a) an opportunity, afforded by the automatic action of the machine, to play again (once or more often) without paying, or

(b) a prize, determined by the automatic action of the machine and consisting in either—

(i) money of an amount not exceeding the sum payable to play the machine once, or

(ii) a token which is, or two or more tokens which in the aggregate are, exchangeable for money of an amount not exceeding that sum."

(2) In subsection (4) of that section (machines playable by more than one person), for "a gaming machine" there shall be substituted "a machine of any description".

(3) For subsections (5) to (9) of that section there shall be substituted the following subsections—

"(5) For the purposes of sections 21 to 24 above a machine (the actual machine) in relation to which the number determined in accordance with subsection (5A) below is more than one shall be treated (instead of as one machine) as if it were a number of machines (accountable machines) equal to the number so determined.

(5A) That number is—

(a) except where paragraph (b) below applies, the number of individual playing positions provided on the machine for persons to play simultaneously (whether or not while participating in the same game); and

(b) where—

(i) that machine is a video machine but not a gaming machine, and

(ii) the number of such playing positions is more than the number of different screens used for the communication or display of information or images to any person or persons playing a game by means of the machine,

the number of such screens.

(6) Subsection (5) above does not apply in the case of any machine which is an excepted machine for the purposes of section 21 above or in the case of a pinball machine.

(7) Any question whether the accountable machines are, or are not, machines falling within any of the following descriptions, that is to say—

(a) gaming machines,

(b) prize machines,

(c) small-prize machines, or

(d) five-penny machines,

shall be determined according to whether or not the actual machine is a machine of that description, with the accountable machines being taken to be machines of the same description as the actual machine."

7. After section 25 there shall be inserted the following section—

"Power to modify definition of 'amusement machine'

25A.—(1) The Treasury may by order modify the provisions of section 25 above—

(a) by adding to the machines for the time being specified in subsection (1)(e) of that section any description of machines which it appears to them, having regard to the use to which the machines are put, to be appropriate for the protection of the revenue so to add to those machines; or

(b) by deleting any description of machines for the time being so specified.

(2) An order under this section may make such incidental, consequential or transitional provision as the Treasury think fit, including provision modifying section 21 or section 25(5A) above for the purpose of—

(a) specifying the circumstances (if any) in which a machine added to section 25(1)(e) above is to be an excepted machine for the purposes of section 21 above; or

(b) determining the number which, in the case of a machine so added, is to be taken into account for the purposes of section 25(5) above."

Supplementary provisions

8.—(1) In section 26 (supplementary provisions)—

(a) for the words "gaming machine licence duty" in subsection (1) there shall be substituted "amusement machine licence duty";

(b) for the words "a gaming machine" and "gaming machines", wherever they occur, there shall be substituted, respectively, "an amusement machine" and "amusement machines"; and

(c) for the words "for gaming", wherever they occur, there shall be substituted "for play".

(2) In subsection (2) of that section—

(a) after the definition of "United Kingdom" there shall be inserted the following definitions—

" 'video machine' has the meaning given by section 25(1B) above;

'prize machine' has the meaning given by section 25(1C) above;"

and

(b) after the definition of a "five-penny machine" there shall be inserted the following definition—

" 'thirty-five-penny machine' means an amusement machine which can only be played by the insertion into the machine of coins of an aggregate denomination not exceeding 35p;".

(3) After subsection (2) of that section there shall be inserted the following subsection—

"(2A) References in sections 21 to 25 above and in this section and Schedule 4 to this Act to a game, in relation to any machine, include references to a game in the nature of a quiz or puzzle and to a game which is played solely by way of a pastime or against the machine, as well as one played wholly or partly against one or more contemporaneous or previous players."

9.—(1) In sections 31 and 33(2) (protection of officers and savings for prohibitions of gaming etc.), for the words "gaming machine licences", in each case, there shall be substituted "amusement machine licences".

(2) In section 32(3) (orders subject to affirmative procedure), for "or 14(3)" there shall be substituted ", 14(3) or 25A".

(3) In section 33(1) (interpretation), in the definition of "gaming", the words "(except where it refers to a machine provided for gaming)" shall be omitted.

10. In Schedule 3 (bingo duty)—

(a) in paragraph 5(1)(b), for "a gaming machine licence" there shall be substituted "an amusement machine licence"; and

(b) in paragraph 6, for "a gaming machine" there shall be substituted "an amusement machine".

11.—(1) In Schedule 4 (supplementary provisions in relation to gaming machine licence duty)—

(a) for the words "gaming machine" and "gaming machines", wherever they occur, there shall be substituted, respectively, "amusement machine" and "amusement machines"; and

(b) for the indefinite article, wherever it occurs before an expression amended by paragraph (a) above, there shall be substituted "An" or "an", as the case may require.

(2) In paragraph 1(2) of that Schedule (conditions of exemption for charitable entertainments etc.)—

(a) in paragraph (a), for "of gaming by means of any machine" there shall be substituted "from any amusement machine"; and

(b) in paragraph (b), for "and any other provided for gaming" there shall be substituted "and any other amusement machines provided".

(3) In paragraph 2(2)(c) of that Schedule (conditions of exemption for pleasure fairs), for "and any other provided for gaming" there shall be substituted "and any other amusement machines provided".

(4) In paragraph 4 of that Schedule—

(a) for the words "small-prize machines", wherever they occur, there shall be substituted "relevant machines"; and

(b) after sub-paragraph (7) there shall be inserted the following sub-paragraph—

"(7A) An amusement machine is a relevant machine for the purposes of this paragraph unless it is a gaming machine which is not a small-prize machine.";

and in relation to the winter period beginning with November 1995, sub-paragraph (4) of that paragraph shall have effect as if the references by virtue of this paragraph to an amusement machine licence included references to a gaming machine licence.

(5) After paragraph 7 of that Schedule there shall be inserted the following paragraph—

"Payment of duty by instalments

7A.—(1) The Commissioners may make and publish arrangements setting out the circumstances in which, and the conditions subject to which, a person to whom an amusement machine licence is granted for a period of twelve months may, at his request and if the

Commissioners think fit, be permitted to pay the duty on that licence by regular instalments during the period of the licence, instead of at the time when it is granted.

(2) Arrangements under this paragraph shall provide for the amount of each instalment to be such that the aggregate amount of all the instalments to be paid in respect of any licence is an amount equal to 105 per cent of what would have been the duty on that licence apart from this paragraph.

(3) Sub-paragraph (4) below applies if a person who has been permitted, in accordance with arrangements under this paragraph, to pay the duty on any amusement machine licence by instalments—

(a) fails to pay any instalment at the time when it becomes due in accordance with the arrangements; and

(b) does not make good that failure within seven days of being required to do so by notice given by the Commissioners.

(4) Where this sub-paragraph applies—

(a) the licence shall be treated as having ceased to be in force as from the time when the instalment became due;

(b) the person to whom the licence was granted shall become liable to any unpaid duty to which he would have been liable under paragraph 11(1C) below if he had surrendered the licence at that time; and

(c) any amusement machines found on the premises to which the licence related shall be liable to forfeiture.

(5) Sections 14 to 16 of the Finance Act 1994 (review and appeals) shall have effect in relation to any decision of the Commissioners refusing an application for permission to pay duty by instalments in accordance with arrangements under this paragraph as if that decision were a decision of a description specified in Schedule 5 to that Act."

(6) In paragraph 11 of that Schedule (surrender), after sub-paragraph (1B) there shall be inserted the following sub-paragraph—

"(1C) Where, in a case where duty is being paid in accordance with arrangements made under paragraph 7A above, the amount of duty actually paid on a licence that is surrendered is less than the amount which would have been paid on that licence if the period for which it was granted had been reduced by the number of complete months in that period which have not expired when the licence is surrendered, the difference between those amounts shall be treated as unpaid duty."

(7) Paragraph 13 of that Schedule (labelling and marking of machines) shall cease to have effect.

(8) In paragraph 14 of that Schedule (power to enter premises), for the words "for gaming" there shall be substituted "for play".

(9) In paragraph 16 of that Schedule (enforcement), after sub-paragraph (1) there shall be inserted the following sub-paragraph—

"(1A) This paragraph does not apply to any contravention or failure to comply with arrangements under paragraph 7A above or to any failure or refusal to comply with a requirement made under or for the purposes of any such arrangements."

(10) In paragraph 17 of that Schedule (warrants etc.)—

(a) in sub-paragraph (1), for the words "for gaming" there shall be substituted "for play"; and

(b) in sub-paragraph (2)(a), for the words from "(including" to "by means of it)" there shall be substituted "(including any machine appearing to the officer to be an amusement machine or to be capable of being used as such)".

Consequential amendment of the Customs and Excise Management Act 1979

12. In section 102(3)(a) of the Customs and Excise Management Act 1979 (penalty for failure to deliver up a licence), for "a gaming machine licence" there shall be substituted "an amusement machine licence".

GENERAL NOTE

The Schedule implements amendments to the Betting and Gaming Duties Act 1981 (BGDA 1981), made necessary by the replacement of gaming machine licence duty (GMLD) by amusement machine licence duty (AMLD).

Para. 4

The maximum rate of duty on the machines now brought into charge to tax is £250.

Para. 6

This provides the definition of "amusement machine". The extension of the charge was restricted, by amendments made at Report Stage, to video machines, pinball machines and skill with prizes (quiz) machines. Non-prize machines costing 35p or less to play (including three plays for £1) are exempt. Duty is charged on the lower of the number of individual playing positions or screens in each machine.

Para. 7

The new BGDA 1981, 25A allows the Treasury to modify the definition in order to protect the revenue.

Para. 11

The new para. 7A to Sched. 4 of the BGDA 1981 provides for the payment of duty by instalments.

Section 19   SCHEDULE 4

VEHICLE EXCISE AND REGISTRATION

PART I

INTRODUCTION

1. In this Schedule "the 1994 Act" means the Vehicle Excise and Registration Act 1994.

PART II

EXEMPTIONS

Abolition of certain exemptions

2. The following paragraphs of Schedule 2 to the 1994 Act (exempt vehicles) shall be omitted—
   (a) paragraph 1 (electrically propelled vehicles);
   (b) paragraph 12 (road construction vehicles);
   (c) paragraph 13 (road rollers);
   (d) paragraph 14 (snow clearing vehicles);
   (e) paragraph 15 (gritting vehicles);
   (f) paragraph 16 (street cleansing vehicles);
   (g) paragraph 17 (tower wagons used solely in connection with street lighting);
   (h) paragraph 21 (vehicles used for short journeys between different parts of person's land).

Exemption for police vehicles

3. In Schedule 2 to the 1994 Act the following shall be inserted after paragraph 3—

"*Police vehicles*

3A. A vehicle is an exempt vehicle when it is being used for police purposes."

Exemption for vehicles used between different parts of land

4. In Schedule 2 to the 1994 Act the following shall be inserted after paragraph 20—

"*Vehicles used between different parts of land*

20A. A vehicle is an exempt vehicle if—
   (a) it is used only for purposes relating to agriculture, horticulture or forestry,
   (b) it is used on public roads only in passing between different areas of land occupied by the same person, and
   (c) the distance it travels on public roads in passing between any two such areas does not exceed 1.5 kilometres."

Commencement

5. This Part of this Schedule shall come into force on 1st July 1995.

PART III

RATES

General

6.—(1) In Schedule 1 to the 1994 Act (annual rates of duty) the following paragraph shall be substituted for paragraph 1 (annual rate of duty where no other rate specified)—

"1.—(1) The annual rate of vehicle excise duty applicable to a vehicle in respect of which no other annual rate is specified by this Schedule is—

(a) if it was constructed after 1946, the general rate;

(b) if it was constructed before 1947, the reduced rate.

(2) The general rate is £135.

(3) The reduced rate is 50 per cent of the general rate.

(4) Where an amount arrived at in accordance with sub-paragraph (3) is an amount—

(a) which is not a multiple of £5, and

(b) which on division by five does not produce a remainder of £2.50,

the rate is the amount arrived at rounded (either up or down) to the nearest amount which is a multiple of £5.

(5) Where an amount arrived at in accordance with sub-paragraph (3) is an amount which on division by five produces a remainder of £2.50, the rate is the amount arrived at increased by £2.50."

(2) The following amendments shall be made in consequence of sub-paragraph (1) above—

(a) in section 13 of the 1994 Act (trade licences) in subsection (3)(b) for "1(b)" there shall be substituted "1(1)(a)";

(b) in section 13 of the 1994 Act as substituted under paragraph 8 of Schedule 4 to that Act, in subsection (4)(b) for "1(b)" there shall be substituted "1(1)(a)";

(c) in section 36 of the 1994 Act (additional liability where cheque dishonoured) in subsection (3)(b) for "1(b)" there shall be substituted "1(1)(a)".

Motorcycles

7.—(1) Paragraph 2 of Schedule 1 to the 1994 Act (motorcycles) shall be amended as follows.

(2) In sub-paragraph (1) (rate for motorcycles not exceeding 450 kilograms) the following shall be substituted for paragraphs (a) to (c)—

"(a) if the cylinder capacity of the engine does not exceed 150 cubic centimetres, 10 per cent of the general rate specified in paragraph 1(2);

(b) if the vehicle is a motorbicycle and the cylinder capacity of the engine exceeds 150 cubic centimetres but does not exceed 250 cubic centimetres, 25 per cent of the general rate specified in paragraph 1(2);

(c) in any other case, 40 per cent of the general rate specified in paragraph 1(2)."

(3) The following sub-paragraphs shall be inserted after sub-paragraph (1)—

"(1A) Where an amount arrived at in accordance with sub-paragraph (1)(a), (b) or (c) is an amount—

(a) which is not a multiple of £5, and

(b) which on division by five does not produce a remainder of £2.50,

the rate is the amount arrived at rounded (either up or down) to the nearest amount which is a multiple of £5.

(1B) Where an amount arrived at in accordance with sub-paragraph (1)(a), (b) or (c) is an amount which on division by five produces a remainder of £2.50, the rate is the amount arrived at increased by £2.50."

Buses etc.

8. In Schedule 1 to the 1994 Act the following shall be substituted for Part III (hackney carriages)—

"PART III

BUSES

3.—(1) The annual rate of vehicle excise duty applicable to a bus is—

(a) if its seating capacity is nine to sixteen, the same as the basic goods vehicle rate;

(b) if its seating capacity is seventeen to thirty-five, 133 per cent of the basic goods vehicle rate;

(c) if its seating capacity is thirty-six to sixty, 200 per cent of the basic goods vehicle rate;

(d) if its seating capacity is over sixty, 300 per cent of the basic goods vehicle rate.

(2) In this paragraph "bus" means a vehicle which—
(a) is a public service vehicle (within the meaning given by section 1 of the Public Passenger Vehicles Act 1981), and
(b) is not an excepted vehicle.
(3) For the purposes of this paragraph an excepted vehicle is—
(a) a vehicle which has a seating capacity under nine,
(b) a vehicle which is a community bus,
(c) a vehicle used under a permit granted under section 19 of the Transport Act 1985 (educational and other bodies) and used in circumstances where the requirements mentioned in subsection (2) of that section are met, or
(d) a vehicle used under a permit granted under section 10B of the Transport Act (Northern Ireland) 1967 (educational and other bodies) and used in circumstances where the requirements mentioned in subsection (2) of that section are met.
(4) In sub-paragraph (3)(b) "community bus" means a vehicle—
(a) used on public roads solely in accordance with a community bus permit (within the meaning given by section 22 of the Transport Act 1985), and
(b) not used for providing a service under an agreement providing for service subsidies (within the meaning given by section 63(10)(b) of that Act).
(5) For the purposes of this paragraph the seating capacity of a vehicle shall be determined in accordance with regulations made by the Secretary of State.
(6) In sub-paragraph (1) references to the basic goods vehicle rate are to the rate applicable, by virtue of sub-paragraph (1) of paragraph 9, to a rigid goods vehicle which falls within column (3) of the table in that sub-paragraph and has a revenue weight exceeding 3,500 kilograms and not exceeding 7,500 kilograms.
(7) Where an amount arrived at in accordance with sub-paragraph (1)(b), (c) or (d) is an amount—
(a) which is not a multiple of £10, and
(b) which on division by ten does not produce a remainder of £5,
the rate is the amount arrived at rounded (either up or down) to the nearest amount which is a multiple of £10.
(8) Where an amount arrived at in accordance with sub-paragraph (1)(b), (c) or (d) is an amount which on division by ten produces a remainder of £5, the rate is the amount arrived at increased by £5."

Special vehicles

9.—(1) Part IV of Schedule 1 to the 1994 Act (special machines) shall be amended as follows.
(2) For the heading "SPECIAL MACHINES" there shall be substituted "SPECIAL VEHICLES".
(3) In paragraph 4(1) (annual rate of £35) for the words "special machine is £35" there shall be substituted "special vehicle is the same as the basic goods vehicle rate".
(4) In paragraph 4(2) (definition of "special machine")—
(a) for the words " "special machine" means" there shall be substituted " "special vehicle" means a vehicle which has a revenue weight exceeding 3,500 kilograms and is";
(b) paragraphs (a), (b) and (f) (tractors, agricultural engines and mowing machines) shall be omitted;
(c) after paragraph (e) there shall be inserted—
"(ee) a road roller."
(5) Paragraph 4(3) (definition of "tractor") shall be omitted.
(6) The following sub-paragraph shall be inserted after sub-paragraph (6) of paragraph 4—
"(7) In sub-paragraph (1) the reference to the basic goods vehicle rate is to the rate applicable, by virtue of sub-paragraph (1) of paragraph 9, to a rigid goods vehicle which falls within column (3) of the table in that sub-paragraph and has a revenue weight exceeding 3,500 kilograms and not exceeding 7,500 kilograms."

Special concessionary vehicles

10. In Schedule 1 to the 1994 Act the following shall be inserted after Part IV—

"PART IVA

SPECIAL CONCESSIONARY VEHICLES

4A.—(1) The annual rate of vehicle excise duty applicable to a special concessionary vehicle is 25 per cent of the general rate specified in paragraph 1(2).

(2) Where an amount arrived at in accordance with sub-paragraph (1) is an amount—

(a) which is not a multiple of £5, and

(b) which on division by five does not produce a remainder of £2.50,

the rate is the amount arrived at rounded (either up or down) to the nearest amount which is a multiple of £5.

(3) Where an amount arrived at in accordance with sub-paragraph (1) is an amount which on division by five produces a remainder of £2.50, the rate is the amount arrived at increased by £2.50.

4B.—(1) A vehicle is a special concessionary vehicle if it is—

(a) an agricultural tractor, or

(b) an off-road tractor.

(2) In sub-paragraph (1) "agricultural tractor" means a tractor used on public roads solely for purposes relating to agriculture, horticulture, forestry or activities falling within sub-paragraph (3).

(3) The activities falling within this sub-paragraph are—

(a) cutting verges bordering public roads;

(b) cutting hedges or trees bordering public roads or bordering verges which border public roads.

(4) In sub-paragraph (1) "off-road tractor" means a tractor which is not an agricultural tractor (within the meaning given by sub-paragraph (2)) and which is—

(a) designed and constructed primarily for use otherwise than on roads, and

(b) incapable by reason of its construction of exceeding a speed of twenty-five miles per hour on the level under its own power.

4C.—(1) A vehicle is a special concessionary vehicle if it is a light agricultural vehicle.

(2) In sub-paragraph (1) "light agricultural vehicle" means a vehicle which—

(a) has a revenue weight not exceeding 1,000 kilograms,

(b) is designed and constructed so as to seat only the driver,

(c) is designed and constructed primarily for use otherwise than on roads, and

(d) is used solely for purposes relating to agriculture, horticulture or forestry.

4D. An agricultural engine is a special concessionary vehicle.

4E. A mowing machine is a special concessionary vehicle.

4F.—(1) An electrically propelled vehicle is a special concessionary vehicle.

(2) A vehicle is not an electrically propelled vehicle for the purposes of sub-paragraph (1) unless the electrical motive power is derived from—

(a) a source external to the vehicle, or

(b) an electrical storage battery which is not connected to any source of power when the vehicle is in motion.

4G. A vehicle is a special concessionary vehicle when it is—

(a) being used,

(b) going to or from the place where it is to be or has been used, or

(c) being kept for use,

for the purpose of clearing snow from public roads by means of a snow plough or similar device (whether or not forming part of the vehicle).

4H. A vehicle is a special concessionary vehicle if it is constructed or adapted, and used, solely for the conveyance of machinery for spreading material on roads to deal with frost, ice or snow (with or without articles or material used for the purposes of the machinery)."

Recovery vehicles

11.—(1) Paragraph 5 of Schedule 1 to the 1994 Act (recovery vehicles) shall be amended as follows.

(2) In sub-paragraph (1) (annual rate of duty of £85) for the words "is £85" there shall be substituted "is—

(a) if it has a revenue weight exceeding 3,500 kilograms and not exceeding 12,000 kilograms, the same as the basic goods vehicle rate;

(b) if it has a revenue weight exceeding 12,000 kilograms and not exceeding 25,000 kilograms, 300 per cent of the basic goods vehicle rate;

(c) if it has a revenue weight exceeding 25,000 kilograms, 500 per cent of the basic goods vehicle rate."

(3) The following sub-paragraphs shall be inserted after sub-paragraph (5)—

"(6) In sub-paragraph (1) references to the basic goods vehicle rate are to the rate applicable, by virtue of sub-paragraph (1) of paragraph 9, to a rigid goods vehicle which falls within column (3) of the table in that sub-paragraph and has a revenue weight exceeding 3,500 kilograms and not exceeding 7,500 kilograms.

(7) Where an amount arrived at in accordance with sub-paragraph (1)(b) or (c) is an amount—

(a) which is not a multiple of £10, and

(b) which on division by ten does not produce a remainder of £5, the rate is the amount arrived at rounded (either up or down) to the nearest amount which is a multiple of £10.

(8) Where an amount arrived at in accordance with sub-paragraph (1)(b) or (c) is an amount which on division by ten produces a remainder of £5, the rate is the amount arrived at increased by £5."

Vehicles used for exceptional loads

12.—(1) Paragraph 6 of Schedule 1 to the 1994 Act (vehicles used for exceptional loads) shall be amended as follows.

(2) In sub-paragraph (2) (annual rate of duty) for "£5,000" there shall be substituted "the heavy tractive unit rate".

(3) The following sub-paragraph shall be inserted after sub-paragraph (3)—

"(3A) In sub-paragraph (2) the reference to the heavy tractive unit rate is to the rate applicable, by virtue of sub-paragraph (1) of paragraph 11, to a tractive unit which falls within column (3) of the table in that sub-paragraph and has a revenue weight exceeding 38,000 kilograms and not exceeding 44,000 kilograms."

Haulage vehicles

13.—(1) Paragraph 7 of Schedule 1 to the 1994 Act (haulage vehicles) shall be amended as follows.

(2) In sub-paragraph (1) for paragraphs (a) and (b) (rate of £100 for showmen's vehicles and of £330 for other haulage vehicles) there shall be substituted—

"(a) if it is a showman's vehicle, the same as the basic goods vehicle rate;

(b) in any other case, the general haulage vehicle rate."

(3) The following sub-paragraphs shall be inserted after sub-paragraph (2)—

"(3) In sub-paragraph (1) the reference to the basic goods vehicle rate is to the rate applicable, by virtue of sub-paragraph (1) of paragraph 9, to a rigid goods vehicle which falls within column (3) of the table in that sub-paragraph and has a revenue weight exceeding 3,500 kilograms and not exceeding 7,500 kilograms.

(4) In sub-paragraph (1) the reference to the general haulage vehicle rate is to 75 per cent of the rate applicable, by virtue of sub-paragraph (1) of paragraph 11, to a tractive unit which falls within column (3) of the table in that sub-paragraph and has a revenue weight exceeding 12,000 kilograms and not exceeding 16,000 kilograms.

(5) Where an amount arrived at in accordance with sub-paragraph (4) is an amount—

(a) which is not a multiple of £10, and

(b) which on division by ten does not produce a remainder of £5,

the rate is the amount arrived at rounded (either up or down) to the nearest amount which is a multiple of £10.

(6) Where an amount arrived at in accordance with sub-paragraph (4) is an amount which on division by ten produces a remainder of £5, the rate is the amount arrived at increased by £5."

Goods vehicles

14.—(1) Part VIII of Schedule 1 to the 1994 Act (goods vehicles) shall be amended as follows.

(2) Paragraph 8 (basic rate) shall be omitted.

(3) In paragraph 9(1) (rates of duty for rigid goods vehicles)—

(a) at the beginning there shall be inserted "Subject to sub-paragraphs (2) and (3),";

(b) for the words "a plated gross weight (or, in Northern Ireland, a relevant maximum weight) exceeding 7,500 kilograms" there shall be substituted "a revenue weight exceeding 3,500 kilograms";

(c) in paragraph (a) for the words "plated gross weight (or relevant maximum weight)" there shall be substituted "revenue weight".

(4) The following table shall be substituted for the table in paragraph 9(1)—

Revenue weight of vehicle		Rate		
(1) Exceeding	(2) Not Exceeding	(3) Two axle vehicle	(4) Three axle vehicle	(5) Four or more axle vehicle
kgs	kgs	£	£	£
3,500	7,500	150	150	150
7,500	12,000	290	290	290
12,000	13,000	450	470	340
13,000	14,000	630	470	340
14,000	15,000	810	470	340
15,000	17,000	1,280	470	340
17,000	19,000	1,280	820	340
19,000	21,000	1,280	990	340
21,000	23,000	1,280	1,420	490
23,000	25,000	1,280	2,160	800
25,000	27,000	1,280	2,260	1,420
27,000	29,000	1,280	2,260	2,240
29,000	31,000	1,280	2,260	3,250
31,000	44,000	1,280	2,260	4,250

(5) For sub-paragraph (2) of paragraph 9 there shall be substituted the following sub-paragraphs—

"(2) The annual rate of vehicle excise duty applicable—

(a) to any rigid goods vehicle which is a showman's goods vehicle with a revenue weight exceeding 3,500 kilograms but not exceeding 44,000 kilograms, and

(b) to any rigid goods vehicle which is an island goods vehicle with a revenue weight exceeding 3,500 kilograms,

shall be the basic goods vehicle rate.

(3) The annual rate of vehicle excise duty applicable to a rigid goods vehicle which has a revenue weight exceeding 44,000 kilograms and is not an island goods vehicle shall be the heavy tractive unit rate.

(4) In sub-paragraph (2) the reference to the basic goods vehicle rate is to the rate applicable, by virtue of sub-paragraph (1), to a rigid goods vehicle which falls within column (3) of the table in that sub-paragraph and has a revenue weight exceeding 3,500 kilograms and not exceeding 7,500 kilograms.

(5) In sub-paragraph (3) the reference to the heavy tractive unit rate is to the rate applicable, by virtue of sub-paragraph (1) of paragraph 11, to a tractive unit which falls within column (3) of the table in that sub-paragraph and has a revenue weight exceeding 38,000 kilograms and not exceeding 44,000 kilograms."

(6) In paragraph 10(1) (trailer supplement) for the words "plated gross weight (or relevant maximum weight)"—

(a) in the first place where they occur, there shall be substituted "revenue weight"; and

(b) in the second and third places where they occur, there shall be substituted "plated gross weight".

(7) In paragraph 10(2) (lower rate of trailer supplement)—

(a) the words "(or relevant maximum weight)" shall be omitted; and

(b) for "£135" there shall be substituted "an amount equal to the amount of the general rate specified in paragraph 1(2)".

(8) In paragraph 10(3) (higher rate of trailer supplement)—

(a) the words "(or relevant maximum weight)" shall be omitted; and

(b) for "£370" there shall be substituted "an amount equal to 275 per cent of the amount of the general rate specified in paragraph 1(2)".

(9) In paragraph 10 the following sub-paragraphs shall be inserted after sub-paragraph (3)—

"(3A) Where an amount arrived at in accordance with sub-paragraph (3) is an amount—

(a) which is not a multiple of £10, and

(b) which on division by ten does not produce a remainder of £5,

the amount of the trailer supplement is the amount arrived at rounded (either up or down) to the nearest amount which is a multiple of £10.

(3B) Where an amount arrived at in accordance with sub-paragraph (3) is an amount which on division by ten produces a remainder of £5, the amount of the trailer supplement is the amount arrived at increased by £5."

(10) Paragraph 10(4) (reference to paragraph 12) shall be omitted.

(11) In paragraph 11(1) (rates of duty for tractive units)—

(a) at the beginning there shall be inserted "Subject to sub-paragraphs (2) and (3),";

(b) for the words "a plated train weight (or, in Northern Ireland, a relevant maximum train weight) exceeding 7,500 kilograms" there shall be substituted "a revenue weight exceeding 3,500 kilograms";

(c) in paragraph (a) for the words "plated train weight (or relevant maximum train weight)" there shall be substituted "revenue weight".

(12) The following table shall be substituted for the table in paragraph 11(1)—

Revenue weight of tractive unit		Rate for tractive unit with two axles			Rate for tractive unit with three or more axles		
(1) Exceeding	(2) Not exceeding	(3) Any no. of semi-trailer axles	(4) 2 or more semi-trailer axles	(5) 3 or more semi-trailer axles	(6) Any no. of semi-trailer axles	(7) 2 or more semi-trailer axles	(8) 3 or more semi-trailer axles
kgs	kgs	£	£	£	£	£	£
3,500	7,500	150	150	150	150	150	150
7,500	12,000	290	290	290	290	290	290
12,000	16,000	440	440	440	440	440	440
16,000	20,000	500	440	440	440	440	440
20,000	23,000	780	440	440	440	440	440
23,000	26,000	1,150	570	440	570	440	440
26,000	28,000	1,150	1,090	440	1,090	440	440
28,000	31,000	1,680	1,680	1,050	1,680	640	440
31,000	33,000	2,450	2,450	1,680	2,450	970	440
33,000	34,000	5,000	5,000	1,680	2,450	1,420	550
34,000	36,000	5,000	5,000	2,750	2,450	2,030	830
36,000	38,000	5,000	5,000	3,100	2,730	2,730	1,240
38,000	44,000	5,000	5,000	3,100	2,730	2,730	1,240

(13) For sub-paragraph (2) of paragraph 11 there shall be substituted the following sub-paragraphs—

"(2) The annual rate of vehicle excise duty applicable—

(a) to any tractive unit which is a showman's goods vehicle with a revenue weight exceeding 3,500 kilograms but not exceeding 44,000 kilograms, and

(b) to any tractive unit which is an island goods vehicle with a revenue weight exceeding 3,500 kilograms,

shall be the basic goods vehicle rate.

(3) The annual rate of vehicle excise duty applicable to a tractive unit which has a revenue weight exceeding 44,000 kilograms and is not an island goods vehicle shall be the heavy tractive unit rate.

(4) In sub-paragraph (2) the reference to the basic goods vehicle rate is to the rate applicable, by virtue of sub-paragraph (1) of paragraph 9, to a rigid goods vehicle which falls within column (3) of the table in that sub-paragraph and has a revenue weight exceeding 3,500 kilograms and not exceeding 7,500 kilograms.

(5) In sub-paragraph (3) the reference to the heavy tractive unit rate is to the rate applicable, by virtue of sub-paragraph (1), to a tractive unit which falls within column (3) of the table in that sub-paragraph and has a revenue weight exceeding 38,000 kilograms and not exceeding 44,000 kilograms."

(14) Paragraph 12 (farmers' goods vehicles and showmen's goods vehicles) shall be omitted.

(15) In paragraph 13(1) (regulations for reducing plated weights) for the words from "its plated gross weight" to "weight specified" there shall be substituted "its revenue weight were such lower weight as may be specified".

(16) In paragraph 14 (vehicles for conveying machines) sub-paragraphs (b) and (c) shall be omitted.

(17) In paragraph 17(1) (meaning of "trailer")—

(a) at the end of paragraph (a) there shall be inserted "or";

(b) paragraphs (c) to (e) (road construction vehicles, certain farming implements drawn by farmer's goods vehicle, and certain trailers used to carry gas for propulsion, excluded from meaning of "trailer") shall be omitted.

(18) Paragraph 17(2) (interpretation of paragraph 17(1)(e)) shall be omitted.

(19) The following shall be inserted after paragraph 17—

"*Meaning of 'island goods vehicle'*

18.—(1) In this Part 'island goods vehicle' means any goods vehicle which—

(a) is kept for use wholly or partly on the roads of one or more small islands; and

(b) is not kept or used on any mainland road, except in a manner authorised by sub-paragraph (2) or (3).

(2) The keeping or use of a goods vehicle on a mainland road is authorised by this sub-paragraph if—

(a) the road is one used for travel between a landing place and premises where vehicles disembarked at that place are loaded or unloaded, or both;

(b) the length of the journey, using that road, from that landing place to those premises is not more than five kilometres;

(c) the vehicle in question is one which was disembarked at that landing place after a journey by sea which began on a small island; and

(d) the loading or unloading of that vehicle is to take place, or has taken place, at those premises.

(3) The keeping or use of a goods vehicle on a mainland road is authorised by this sub-paragraph if—

(a) that vehicle has a revenue weight not exceeding 17,000 kilograms;

(b) that vehicle is normally kept at a base or centre on a small island; and

(c) the only journeys for which that vehicle is used are ones that begin or end at that base or centre.

(4) References in this paragraph to a small island are references to any such island falling within sub-paragraph (5) as may be designated as a small island by an order made by the Secretary of State.

(5) An island falls within this sub-paragraph if—

(a) it has an area of 230,000 hectares or less; and

(b) the absence of a bridge, causeway, tunnel, ford or other way makes it at all times impracticable for road vehicles to be driven under their own power from that island as far as the mainland.

(6) The reference in sub-paragraph (5) to driving a road vehicle as far as the mainland is a reference to driving it as far as any public road in the United Kingdom which is not on an island with an area of 230,000 hectares or less and is not a road connecting two such islands.

(7) In this paragraph—

'island' includes anything that is an island only when the tide reaches a certain height;

'landing place' means any place at which vehicles are disembarked after sea journeys;

'mainland road' means any public road in the United Kingdom, other than one which is on a small island or which connects two such islands; and

'road vehicles' means vehicles which are designed or adapted primarily for being driven on roads and which do not have any special features for facilitating their being driven elsewhere;

and references in this paragraph to the loading or unloading of a vehicle include references to the loading or unloading of its trailer or semi-trailer."

Charge at higher rate

15. In section 17 of the 1994 Act (exceptions from charge at higher rate) the following provisions shall be omitted—

(a) subsections (3) to (5) (provisions about farmers' goods vehicles);

(b) subsections (6) and (7) (agricultural tractors and farmers' goods vehicles in Northern Ireland).

Commencement

16.—(1) This Part of this Schedule shall apply in relation to licences taken out on or after 1st July 1995.

(2) This Part of this Schedule shall also apply in relation to any use after 30th June 1995 of a vehicle which—

(a) had a plated gross weight or plated train weight (or, in Northern Ireland, a relevant maximum weight or relevant maximum train weight) on that date, and

(b) at the time when it is used has a confirmed maximum weight which, if that had been its plated gross weight or plated train weight (or relevant maximum weight or relevant maximum train weight) on that date, would have brought it within a description of vehicle to which a higher rate of duty was applicable on that date.

PART IV

Introduction

17. This Part of this Schedule (which supplements provisions of Part III of this Schedule) makes—

(a) provision for determining the revenue weight of a vehicle, and

(b) consequential amendments.

Issue of vehicle licences

18. In section 7(3) of the 1994 Act (matters that may be contained in declarations and particulars to be made or furnished by applicants for licences) for paragraph (b) there shall be substituted—

"(b) the vehicle's revenue weight,

(ba) the place where the vehicle has been or is normally kept, and".

Exchange of licences

19. In section 15(4) of the 1994 Act (exchange of licences where higher rate becomes chargeable) at the beginning there shall be inserted "Subject to section 7(5),".

Exceptions from charge at higher rate

20. In section 16 of the 1994 Act (exceptions from charge at higher rate) in each of subsections (2)(b)(i), (4)(b)(i) and (6)(b)(i) for the words "a plated train weight (or, in Northern Ireland, a relevant maximum train weight)" there shall be substituted "a revenue weight".

Combined road and rail transport

21. In section 20 of the 1994 Act (combined road and rail transport) for subsection (3) there shall be substituted the following subsection—

"(3) In this section 'relevant goods vehicle' means any vehicle the rate of duty applicable to which is provided for in Part VIII of Schedule 1 or which would be such a vehicle if Part VI of that Schedule did not apply to the vehicle."

Relevant higher rate used in calculating penalty

22. In section 39 of the 1994 Act (relevant higher rate used in calculating penalty)—

(a) in subsection (2)(a) for the words "plated gross weight or plated train weight (or, in Northern Ireland, a relevant maximum weight or relevant maximum train weight)" there shall be substituted "revenue weight";

(b) in each of subsections (4)(a) and (5)(a) for the words "plated gross weight or plated train weight (or, in Northern Ireland, relevant maximum weight or relevant maximum train weight)" there shall be substituted "revenue weight";

(c) in the words after paragraph (b) of each of subsections (4) and (5) for the words "plated gross weight or plated train weight (or relevant maximum weight or relevant maximum train weight)" there shall be substituted "revenue weight".

Relevant period used in calculating penalty

23. In section 40(2) of the 1994 Act (relevant period used in calculating penalty)—

(a) for the words "plated gross weight or a plated train weight (or, in Northern Ireland, a relevant maximum weight or relevant maximum train weight)" there shall be substituted "revenue weight";

(b) for the words "was plated with (or rated at) the higher weight" there shall be substituted "became a vehicle with a higher revenue weight".

False or misleading information etc.

24. In section 45 of the 1994 Act (false or misleading information) after subsection (3) there shall be inserted the following subsections—

"(3A) A person who, in supplying information or producing documents for the purposes of any regulations made under section 61A—

(a) makes a statement which to his knowledge is false or in any material respect misleading or recklessly makes a statement which is false or in any material respect misleading, or

(b) produces or otherwise makes use of a document which to his knowledge is false or in any material respect misleading,

is guilty of an offence.

(3B) A person who—
(a) with intent to deceive, forges, alters or uses a certificate issued by virtue of section 61A;
(b) knowing or believing that it will be used for deception lends such a certificate to another or allows another to alter or use it; or
(c) without reasonable excuse makes or has in his possession any document so closely resembling such a certificate as to be calculated to deceive,

is guilty of an offence."

25. In section 60(2) of the 1994 Act (orders subject to annulment), after "section 3(3)" there shall be inserted ", paragraph 18(4) of Schedule 1".

Meaning of "revenue weight"

26. Immediately before section 61 of the 1994 Act there shall be inserted the following section—

"Meaning of 'revenue weight'

60A.—(1) Any reference in this Act to the revenue weight of a vehicle is a reference—
(a) where it has a confirmed maximum weight, to that weight; and
(b) in any other case, to the weight determined in accordance with the following provisions of this section.

(2) For the purposes of this Act a vehicle which does not have a confirmed maximum weight shall have a revenue weight which, subject to the following provisions of this section, is equal to its design weight.

(3) Subject to subsection (4), the design weight of a vehicle is, for the purposes of this section—
(a) in the case of a tractive unit, the weight which is required, by the design and any subsequent adaptations of that vehicle, not to be exceeded by an articulated vehicle which—
(i) consists of the vehicle and any semi-trailer capable of being drawn by it, and
(ii) is in normal use and travelling on a road laden;
and
(b) in the case of any other vehicle, the weight which the vehicle itself is designed or adapted not to exceed when in normal use and travelling on a road laden.

(4) Where, at any time, a vehicle—
(a) does not have a confirmed maximum weight,
(b) has previously had such a weight, and
(c) has not acquired a different design weight by reason of any adaptation made since the most recent occasion on which it had a confirmed maximum weight,
the vehicle's design weight at that time shall be equal to its confirmed maximum weight on that occasion.

(5) An adaptation reducing the design weight of a vehicle shall be disregarded for the purposes of this section unless it is a permanent adaptation.

(6) For the purposes of this Act where—
(a) a vehicle which does not have a confirmed maximum weight is used on a public road in the United Kingdom, and
(b) at the time when it is so used—
(i) the weight of the vehicle, or
(ii) in the case of a tractive unit used as part of an articulated vehicle consisting of the vehicle and a semi-trailer, the weight of the articulated vehicle,
exceeds what, apart from this subsection, would be the vehicle's design weight,
it shall be conclusively presumed, as against the person using the vehicle, that the vehicle has been temporarily adapted so as to have a design weight while being so used equal to the actual weight of the vehicle or articulated vehicle at that time.

(7) For the purposes of this Act limitations on the space available on a vehicle for carrying a load shall be disregarded in determining the weight which the vehicle is designed or adapted not to exceed when in normal use and travelling on a road laden.

(8) A vehicle which does not have a confirmed maximum weight shall not at any time be taken to have a revenue weight which is greater than the maximum laden weight at which that vehicle or, as the case may be, an articulated vehicle consisting of that vehicle and a semi-trailer may lawfully be used in Great Britain.

(9) A vehicle has a confirmed maximum weight at any time if at that time—
(a) it has a plated gross weight or a plated train weight; and
(b) that weight is the maximum laden weight at which that vehicle or, as the case may be, an articulated vehicle consisting of that vehicle and a semi-trailer may lawfully be used in Great Britain;

and the confirmed maximum weight of a vehicle with such a weight shall be taken to be the weight referred to in paragraph (a).

(10) Where any vehicle has a special maximum weight in Northern Ireland which is greater than the maximum laden weight at which that vehicle or, as the case may be, an articulated vehicle consisting of that vehicle and a semi-trailer may lawfully be used in Great Britain, this section shall have effect, in relation to that vehicle, as if the references to Great Britain in subsections (8) and (9) were references to Northern Ireland.

(11) For the purposes of this section a vehicle has a special maximum weight in Northern Ireland if an order under Article 29(3) of the Road Traffic (Northern Ireland) Order 1981 (authorisation of use on roads of vehicles and trailers not complying with regulations) has effect in relation to that vehicle for determining the maximum laden weight at which it may lawfully be used in Northern Ireland or, as the case may be, for determining the maximum laden weight at which an articulated vehicle consisting of that vehicle and a semi-trailer may lawfully be used there."

Interpretation

27.—(1) In subsection (3) of section 61 of the 1994 Act (meaning of "appropriate plate")—
(a) the word "and" shall be inserted at the end of paragraph (a); and
(b) paragraph (c) (plated weight determined by reference to section 41 of the Road Traffic Act 1988) and the word "and" immediately preceding it shall be omitted.
(2) After subsection (3) of that section there shall be inserted the following subsection—
"(3A) Where it appears to the Secretary of State that there is a description of document which—
(a) falls to be treated for some or all of the purposes of the Road Traffic Act 1988 as if it were a plating certificate, or
(b) is issued under the law of any state in the European Economic Area for purposes which are or include purposes corresponding to those for which such a certificate is issued,
he may by regulations provide for references in this section to a plating certificate to have effect as if they included references to a document of that description."
(3) Subsections (4), (5) and (7) of that section (relevant weights in Northern Ireland and definition of "design weight") shall be omitted.

Certificates as to vehicle weight

28. After section 61 of the 1994 Act there shall be inserted the following section—

"Certificates etc. as to vehicle weight
61A.—(1) The Secretary of State may by regulations make provision—
(a) for the making of an application to the Secretary of State for the issue of a certificate stating the design weight of a vehicle;
(b) for the manner in which any determination of the design weight of any vehicle is to be made on such an application and for the issue of a certificate on the making of such a determination;
(c) for the examination, for the purposes of the determination of the design weight of a vehicle, of that vehicle by such persons, and in such manner, as may be prescribed by the regulations;
(d) for a certificate issued on the making of such a determination to be treated as having conclusive effect for the purposes of this Act as to such matters as may be prescribed by the regulations;
(e) for the Secretary of State to be entitled, in cases prescribed by the regulations, to require the production of such a certificate before making a determination for the purposes of section 7(5); and
(f) for appeals against determinations made in accordance with the regulations.
(2) Regulations under this section may provide for an adaptation of a vehicle—
(a) to be taken into account in determining the design weight of a vehicle in a case to which section 60A(6) does not apply, or
(b) to be treated as permanent for the purposes of section 60A(5),
if, and only if, it is an adaptation with respect to which a certificate has been issued under the regulations.
(3) Regulations under this section may provide that such documents purporting to be plating certificates (within the meaning of Part II of the Road Traffic Act 1988) as satisfy requirements prescribed by the regulations are to have effect, for some or all of the purposes of this Act, as if they were certificates issued under such regulations.

(4) Without prejudice to the generality of the preceding provisions of this section, regulations under this section may, in relation to—

(a) the examination of a vehicle on an application under the regulations, or

(b) any appeals against determinations made for the purposes of the issue of a certificate in accordance with the regulations,

make provision corresponding to, or applying (with or without modifications), any of the provisions having effect by virtue of so much of sections 49 to 51 of the Road Traffic Act 1988 as relates to examinations authorised by virtue of, or appeals under, any of those sections.

(5) In this section 'design weight' has the same meaning as in section 60A."

Commencement

29. Paragraph 16 above shall apply for the purposes of this Part of this Schedule as it applies for the purposes of Part III of this Schedule.

PART V

LICENCES

Applications for licences

30.—(1) In section 7 of the 1994 Act (issue of vehicle licences)—

(a) in subsection (1) (regulations about applications) for "prescribed by regulations made" there shall be substituted "specified";

(b) in subsection (2) for "prescribed" there shall be substituted "specified".

(2) In section 11 of the 1994 Act (issue of trade licences) in subsection (1) (regulations about applications)—

(a) for "prescribed by regulations made" there shall be substituted "specified";

(b) for "so prescribed" there shall be substituted "prescribed by regulations made by the Secretary of State".

(3) This paragraph shall apply in relation to applications made after the day on which this Act is passed.

Duration of trade licences

31.—(1) In section 13 of the 1994 Act (duration of trade licences) in subsection (1) at the end of paragraph (c) there shall be inserted "and ending no later than the relevant date."

(2) After subsection (1) of that section there shall be inserted—

"(1A) In subsection (1)(c) "the relevant date" means—

(a) in relation to a licence taken out for a period beginning with the first day of any of the months February to June in any year, 31st December of that year;

(b) in relation to a licence taken out for a period beginning with the first day of any of the months August to December in any year, 30th June of the following year."

(3) This paragraph shall apply in relation to licences taken out after the day on which this Act is passed.

Payment for licences by cheque

32.—(1) The following section shall be inserted after section 19 of the 1994 Act—

"Payment for licences by cheque

19A.—(1) The Secretary of State may, if he thinks fit, issue a vehicle licence or a trade licence on receipt of a cheque for the amount of the duty payable on it.

(2) In a case where—

(a) a vehicle licence or a trade licence is issued to a person on receipt of a cheque which is subsequently dishonoured, and

(b) the Secretary of State sends a notice by post to the person informing him that the licence is void as from the time when it was granted,

the licence shall be void as from the time when it was granted.

(3) In a case where—

(a) a vehicle licence or a trade licence is issued to a person on receipt of a cheque which is subsequently dishonoured,

(b) the Secretary of State sends a notice by post to the person requiring him to secure that the duty payable on the licence is paid within such reasonable period as is specified in the notice,

(c) the requirement in the notice is not complied with, and
(d) the Secretary of State sends a further notice by post to the person informing him that the licence is void as from the time when it was granted,
the licence shall be void as from the time when it was granted.
(4) Section 102 of the Customs and Excise Management Act 1979 (payment for excise licences by cheque) shall not apply in relation to a vehicle licence or a trade licence."
(2) The following section shall be inserted after section 35 of the 1994 Act—

"Dishonoured cheques
35A.—(1) In a case where—
(a) a notice sent as mentioned in section 19A(2)(b) or a further notice sent as mentioned in section 19A(3)(d) requires the person to deliver up the licence within such reasonable period as is specified in the notice, and
(b) the person fails to comply with the requirement within that period,
he shall be liable on summary conviction to a penalty of an amount found under subsection (2).
(2) The amount is whichever is the greater of—
(a) level 3 on the standard scale;
(b) an amount equal to five times the annual rate of duty that was payable on the grant of the licence or would have been so payable if it had been taken out for a period of twelve months."
(3) In section 36 of the 1994 Act (dishonoured cheques: additional liability) in subsection (1) for the words from "102" to "cheque)" there shall be substituted "35A".
(4) This paragraph shall apply in relation to licences taken out after the day on which this Act is passed.

PART VI

REGISTRATION

33. In section 21 of the 1994 Act (registration of vehicles) at the beginning of subsections (1) and (2) there shall be inserted "Subject to subsection (3)" and after subsection (2) there shall be inserted—
"(3) The Secretary of State may by regulations provide that in such circumstances as may be prescribed by the regulations a vehicle shall not be registered under this section until a fee of such amount as may be so prescribed is paid.
(4) The Secretary of State may by regulations make provision about repayment of any sum paid by way of a fee mentioned in subsection (3), and the regulations may in particular include provision—
(a) that repayment shall be made only if a specified person is satisfied that specified conditions are met or in other specified circumstances;
(b) that repayment shall be made in part only;
(c) that, in the case of partial repayment, the amount repaid shall be a specified sum or determined in a specified manner;
(d) for repayment of different amounts in different circumstances;
and "specified" here means specified in the regulations."
34.—(1) Section 22 of the 1994 Act (registration regulations) shall be amended as follows.
(2) In subsection (1) the following paragraph shall be inserted after paragraph (d)—
"(dd) require a person by whom any vehicle is sold or disposed of to furnish the person to whom it is sold or disposed of with such document relating to the vehicle's registration as may be prescribed by the regulations, and to do so at such time as may be so prescribed."
(3) The following subsections shall be inserted after subsection (1)—
"(1A) The Secretary of State may make regulations providing for the sale of information derived from particulars contained in the register—
(a) to such persons as the Secretary of State thinks fit, and
(b) for such price and on such other terms, and subject to such restrictions, as he thinks fit,
if the information does not identify any person or contain anything enabling any person to be identified.
(1B) Without prejudice to the generality of paragraph (d) of subsection (1) above, regulations under that paragraph may require—

(a) any person there mentioned to furnish particulars to the other person there mentioned or to the Secretary of State or to both;

(b) any person there mentioned who is furnished with particulars in pursuance of the regulations to furnish them to the Secretary of State."

PART VII

OFFENCES

35.—(1) In section 31 of the 1994 Act (relevant period for purposes of additional liability) in subsection (5)(b) (case where duty or amount equal to duty has been paid) the words "(or an amount equal to the duty due)" shall be omitted.

(2) This paragraph shall apply in relation to offences committed after the day on which this Act is passed.

36.—(1) The following section shall be inserted after section 32 of the 1994 Act—

"Immobilisation, removal and disposal of vehicles

32A. Schedule 2A (which relates to the immobilisation of vehicles as regards which it appears that an offence under section 29(1) is being committed and to their removal and disposal) shall have effect."

(2) The following Schedule shall be inserted after Schedule 2 to the 1994 Act—

"SCHEDULE 2A

IMMOBILISATION, REMOVAL AND DISPOSAL OF VEHICLES

Immobilisation

1.—(1) The Secretary of State may make regulations under this Schedule with respect to any case where an authorised person has reason to believe that, on or after such date as may be prescribed, an offence under section 29(1) is being committed as regards a vehicle which is stationary on a public road.

(2) The regulations may provide that the authorised person or a person acting under his direction may—

(a) fix an immobilisation device to the vehicle while it remains in the place where it is stationary, or

(b) move it from that place to another place on the same or another public road and fix an immobilisation device to it in that other place.

(3) The regulations may provide that on any occasion when an immobilisation device is fixed to a vehicle in accordance with the regulations the person fixing the device shall also fix to the vehicle a notice—

(a) indicating that the device has been fixed to the vehicle and warning that no attempt should be made to drive it or otherwise put it in motion until it has been released from the device;

(b) specifying the steps to be taken to secure its release;

(c) giving such other information as may be prescribed.

(4) The regulations may provide that—

(a) a vehicle to which an immobilisation device has been fixed in accordance with the regulations may only be released from the device by or under the direction of an authorised person;

(b) subject to that, such a vehicle shall be released from the device if the first and second requirements specified below are met.

(5) The first requirement is that such charge in respect of the release as may be prescribed is paid in any manner specified in the immobilisation notice.

(6) The second requirement is that—

(a) a vehicle licence is produced in accordance with instructions specified in the immobilisation notice, and the licence is one which is in force for the vehicle concerned at the time the licence is produced, or

(b) where such a licence is not produced, such sum as may be prescribed is paid in any manner specified in the immobilisation notice.

(7) The regulations may provide that they shall not apply in relation to a vehicle if—

(a) a current disabled person's badge is displayed on the vehicle, or

(b) such other conditions as may be prescribed are fulfilled;

and "disabled person's badge" here means a badge issued, or having effect as if issued, under any regulations for the time being in force under section 21 of the Chronically Sick

4–211

and Disabled Persons Act 1970 or any regulations for the time being in force under section 14 of the Chronically Sick and Disabled Persons (Northern Ireland) Act 1978.

(8) The regulations may provide that an immobilisation notice shall not be removed or interfered with except by or on the authority of a person falling within a prescribed description.

Offences connected with immobilisation

2.—(1) The regulations may provide that a person contravening provision made under paragraph 1(8) is guilty of an offence and liable on summary conviction to a fine not exceeding level 2 on the standard scale.

(2) The regulations may provide that a person who, without being authorised to do so in accordance with provision made under paragraph 1, removes or attempts to remove an immobilisation device fixed to a vehicle in accordance with the regulations is guilty of an offence and liable on summary conviction to a fine not exceeding level 3 on the standard scale.

(3) The regulations may provide that where they would apply in relation to a vehicle but for provision made under paragraph 1(7)(a) and the vehicle was not, at the time it was stationary, being used—

    (a) in accordance with regulations under section 21 of the Chronically Sick and Disabled Persons Act 1970 or regulations under section 14 of the Chronically Sick and Disabled Persons (Northern Ireland) Act 1978, and

    (b) in circumstances falling within section 117(1)(b) of the Road Traffic Regulation Act 1984 or Article 174A(2)(b) of the Road Traffic (Northern Ireland) Order 1981 (use where a disabled person's concession would be available),

the person in charge of the vehicle at that time is guilty of an offence and liable on summary conviction to a fine not exceeding level 3 on the standard scale.

(4) The regulations may provide that where—

    (a) a person makes a declaration with a view to securing the release of a vehicle from an immobilisation device purported to have been fixed in accordance with the regulations,

    (b) the declaration is that the vehicle is or was an exempt vehicle, and

    (c) the declaration is to the person's knowledge either false or in any material respect misleading,

he is guilty of an offence.

(5) The regulations may provide that a person guilty of an offence by virtue of provision made under sub-paragraph (4) is liable—

    (a) on summary conviction, to a fine not exceeding the statutory maximum, and

    (b) on conviction on indictment, to imprisonment for a term not exceeding two years or to a fine or (except in Scotland) to both.

Removal and disposal of vehicles

3.—(1) The regulations may make provision as regards a case where—

    (a) an immobilisation device is fixed to a vehicle in accordance with the regulations, and

    (b) such conditions as may be prescribed are fulfilled.

(2) The regulations may provide that an authorised person, or a person acting under the direction of an authorised person, may remove the vehicle and deliver it into the custody of a person—

    (a) who is identified in accordance with prescribed rules, and

    (b) who agrees to accept delivery in accordance with arrangements agreed between that person and the Secretary of State;

and the arrangements may include provision as to the payment of a sum to the person into whose custody the vehicle is delivered.

(3) The regulations may provide that the person into whose custody the vehicle is delivered may dispose of it, and in particular provision may be made as to—

    (a) the time at which the vehicle may be disposed of;

    (b) the manner in which it may be disposed of.

(4) The regulations may make provision allowing a person to take possession of the vehicle if—

    (a) he claims it before it is disposed of, and

    (b) any prescribed conditions are fulfilled.

(5) The regulations may provide for a sum of an amount arrived at under prescribed rules to be paid to a person if—

(a) he claims after the vehicle's disposal to be or to have been its owner,

(b) the claim is made within a prescribed time of the disposal, and

(c) any other prescribed conditions are fulfilled.

(6) The regulations may provide that—

(a) the Secretary of State, or

(b) a person into whose custody the vehicle is delivered under the regulations,

may recover from the vehicle's owner (whether or not a claim is made under provision made under sub-paragraph (4) or (5)) such charges as may be prescribed in respect of all or any of the following, namely, its release, removal, custody and disposal; and "owner" here means the person who was the owner when the immobilisation device was fixed.

(7) The conditions prescribed under sub-paragraph (4) may include conditions as to—

(a) satisfying the person with custody that the claimant is the vehicle's owner;

(b) the payment of prescribed charges in respect of the vehicle's release, removal and custody;

(c) the production of a vehicle licence;

(d) payment of a prescribed sum where a vehicle licence is not produced.

(8) Without prejudice to anything in the preceding provisions of this paragraph, the regulations may include provision for purposes corresponding to those of sections 101 and 102 of the Road Traffic Regulation Act 1984 (disposal and charges) subject to such additions, omissions or other modifications as the Secretary of State thinks fit.

Offences as to securing possession of vehicles

4.—(1) The regulations may provide that where—

(a) a person makes a declaration with a view to securing possession of a vehicle purported to have been delivered into the custody of a person in accordance with provision made under paragraph 3,

(b) the declaration is that the vehicle is or was an exempt vehicle, and

(c) the declaration is to the person's knowledge either false or in any material respect misleading,

he is guilty of an offence.

(2) The regulations may provide that a person guilty of such an offence is liable—

(a) on summary conviction, to a fine not exceeding the statutory maximum, and

(b) on conviction on indictment, to imprisonment for a term not exceeding two years or to a fine or (except in Scotland) to both.

Payment of sum where licence not produced

5.—(1) The regulations may make provision as regards a case where a person pays a prescribed sum in pursuance of provision made under—

(a) paragraph 1(6)(b), or

(b) paragraph 3(7)(d).

(2) The regulations may—

(a) provide for a voucher to be issued in respect of the sum;

(b) provide for setting the sum against the amount of any vehicle excise duty payable in respect of the vehicle concerned;

(c) provide for the refund of any sum;

(d) provide that where a voucher has been issued section 29(1) and any other prescribed provision of this Act shall not apply, as regards the vehicle concerned, in relation to events occurring in a prescribed period.

(3) The regulations may make provision—

(a) as to the information to be provided before a voucher is issued;

(b) as to the contents of vouchers;

(c) specifying conditions subject to which any provision under sub-paragraph (2)(b) to (d) is to have effect.

(4) The regulations may make provision as to any case where a voucher is issued on receipt of a cheque which is subsequently dishonoured, and in particular the regulations may—

(a) provide for a voucher to be void;

(b) provide that, where the sum concerned is set against the amount of any vehicle excise duty, the licence concerned shall be void;

(c) make provision under which a person is required to deliver up a void voucher or void licence.

Offences relating to vouchers

6.—(1) The regulations may provide that—
(a) a person is guilty of an offence if within such reasonable period as is found in accordance with prescribed rules he fails to deliver up a voucher that is void by virtue of provision made under paragraph 5(4);
(b) a person guilty of such an offence shall be liable on summary conviction to a fine not exceeding level 3 on the standard scale.

(2) The regulations may provide that a person is guilty of an offence if within such reasonable period as is found in accordance with prescribed rules he fails to deliver up a licence that is void by virtue of provision made under paragraph 5(4), and that a person guilty of such an offence shall be liable on summary conviction to a penalty of whichever is the greater of—
(a) level 3 on the standard scale;
(b) an amount equal to five times the annual rate of duty that was payable on the grant of the licence or would have been so payable if it had been taken out for a period of twelve months.

(3) The regulations may provide that where a person is convicted of an offence under provision made by virtue of sub-paragraph (2) he must pay, in addition to any penalty, an amount found in accordance with prescribed rules.

(4) The regulations may provide that if—
(a) a voucher is void by virtue of provision made under paragraph 5(4),
(b) a person seeks to set the sum concerned against the amount of any vehicle excise duty, and
(c) he knows the voucher is void,
he is guilty of an offence and liable on summary conviction to a fine not exceeding level 5 on the standard scale.

(5) The regulations may provide that a person who in connection with—
(a) obtaining a voucher for which provision is made under paragraph 5, or
(b) obtaining a refund of any sum in respect of which such a voucher is issued,
makes a declaration which to his knowledge is either false or in any material respect misleading is guilty of an offence.

(6) The regulations may provide that a person is guilty of an offence if he forges, fraudulently alters, fraudulently uses, fraudulently lends or fraudulently allows to be used by another person a voucher for which provision is made under paragraph 5.

(7) The regulations may provide that a person guilty of an offence under provision made under sub-paragraph (5) or (6) is liable—
(a) on summary conviction, to a fine not exceeding the statutory maximum, and
(b) on conviction on indictment, to imprisonment for a term not exceeding two years or to a fine or (except in Scotland) to both.

Vouchers: general

7. Without prejudice to anything in paragraphs 5(4) and 6 the regulations may include provision for purposes corresponding to those of sections 19A and 36 subject to such additions, omissions or other modifications as the Secretary of State thinks fit.

Disputes

8. The regulations may make provision about the proceedings to be followed where a dispute occurs as a result of the regulations, and in particular provision may be made—
(a) for an application to be made to a magistrates' court or (in Northern Ireland) a court of summary jurisdiction;
(b) for a court to order a sum to be paid by the Secretary of State.

Authorised persons

9. As regards anything falling to be done under the regulations (such as receiving payment of a charge or other sum or issuing a voucher) the regulations may provide that it may be done—

(a) by an authorised person, or

(b) by an authorised person or a person acting under his direction.

Application of provisions

10.—(1) The regulations may provide that they shall only apply where the authorised person has reason to believe that the offence mentioned in paragraph 1(1) is being committed before such date as may be prescribed.

(2) The regulations may provide that they shall only apply where the vehicle mentioned in paragraph 1(1) is in a prescribed area.

(3) Different dates may be prescribed under paragraph 1(1) or sub-paragraph (1) above in relation to different areas prescribed under sub-paragraph (2) above.

Interpretation

11.—(1) The regulations may make provision as to the meaning for the purposes of the regulations of "owner" as regards a vehicle.

(2) In particular, the regulations may provide that for the purposes of the regulations—

(a) the owner of a vehicle at a particular time shall be taken to be the person by whom it is then kept;

(b) the person by whom a vehicle is kept at a particular time shall be taken to be the person in whose name it is then registered by virtue of this Act.

12.—(1) The regulations may make provision as to the meaning in the regulations of "authorised person".

(2) In particular, the regulations may provide that—

(a) references to an authorised person are to a person authorised by the Secretary of State for the purposes of the regulations;

(b) an authorised person may be a local authority or an employee of a local authority or a member of a police force or some other person;

(c) different persons may be authorised for the purposes of different provisions of the regulations.

13. In this Schedule—

(a) references to an immobilisation device are to a device or appliance which is an immobilisation device for the purposes of section 104 of the Road Traffic Regulation Act 1984 (immobilisation of vehicles illegally parked);

(b) references to an immobilisation notice are to a notice fixed to a vehicle in accordance with the regulations;

(c) "prescribed" means prescribed by regulations made under this Schedule."

37.—(1) In section 37(2) of the 1994 Act (penalty where duty at higher rate is not paid) the following shall be omitted—

(a) the words "(or, in Scotland, on indictment or on summary conviction)", and

(b) the words "(or, in Scotland, the statutory maximum)".

(2) In section 41(1)(b) of the 1994 Act (order in Scotland in case of offence under section 37) the words "182 or" and "183 or" shall be omitted.

(3) This paragraph shall apply in relation to proceedings begun after the day on which this Act is passed.

PART VIII

PROCEEDINGS

38.—(1) In section 52 of the 1994 Act (records)—

(a) for the words "section 17(3) of the Law Reform (Miscellaneous Provisions) (Scotland) Act 1968" in subsection (3)(b) (meaning of "statement" and "document" in Scotland), and

(b) for the words "section 17(4) of the Law Reform (Miscellaneous Provisions) (Scotland) Act 1968" in subsection (4)(b) (construction of references to a copy of a document in Scotland),

there shall be substituted "Schedule 3 to the Prisoners and Criminal Proceedings (Scotland) Act 1993."

(2) This paragraph shall apply in relation to proceedings begun after the day on which this Act is passed.

PART IX

Higher rate not to apply

39.—(1) This paragraph applies where a vehicle licence is taken out—
(a) before 1st July 1995, and
(b) at the rate applicable (at the time it is taken out) under Schedule 1 to the 1994 Act or any provision re-enacted in that Schedule.
(2) While the licence is in force duty shall not, by virtue of any provision contained in Part III or IV of this Schedule other than paragraph 16(2) above, become chargeable under section 15 of the 1994 Act (vehicle used in manner attracting higher rate).

Regulations

40.—(1) This paragraph applies where regulations to determine the seating capacity of a hackney carriage are made, or have effect as if made, under sub-paragraph (2) of paragraph 3 of Schedule 1 to the 1994 Act (as that paragraph has effect apart from the substitution made by paragraph 8 above).
(2) The regulations shall have effect as if made under sub-paragraph (5) of paragraph 3 of that Schedule (as substituted by paragraph 8 above) to determine the seating capacity of a vehicle.
(3) This paragraph shall apply in relation to licences taken out on or after 1st July 1995.

PART X

Relief where exemption abolished

41.—(1) This paragraph applies where—
(a) a vehicle licence is taken out for a vehicle on or after 1st July 1995 and before 1st July 1996,
(b) the licence is the first vehicle licence to be taken out for the vehicle on or after 1st July 1995,
(c) the vehicle would be an exempt vehicle apart from paragraph 2 above, and
(d) the amount of vehicle excise duty to be paid on the licence would (apart from this paragraph) exceed £1,000.
(2) In such a case the amount of vehicle excise duty to be paid on the licence shall be £1,000.
(3) This paragraph shall be construed in accordance with the 1994 Act.

Relief where vehicle changes category

42.—(1) This paragraph applies where paragraph 41 above does not apply and—
(a) a vehicle licence is taken out for a vehicle on or after 1st July 1995 and before 1st July 1996,
(b) the licence is the first vehicle licence to be taken out for the vehicle on or after 1st July 1995,
(c) apart from Part III of this Schedule, the annual rate of vehicle excise duty applicable to the vehicle would be found under any of the provisions falling within sub-paragraph (3) below, and
(d) the new amount of duty exceeds the old amount of duty by more than £1,000.
(2) In such a case the amount of vehicle excise duty to be paid on the licence shall be an amount equal to £1,000 plus the old amount of duty.
(3) The provisions falling within this sub-paragraph are—
(a) paragraph 8(1) and (2)(b) of Schedule 1 to the 1994 Act;
(b) paragraph 8(1) and (2)(c) of that Schedule;
(c) paragraph 8(1) and (2)(d) of that Schedule;
(d) paragraph 12(2) of that Schedule;
(e) paragraph 12(3) to (5) of that Schedule.
(4) For the purposes of this paragraph—
(a) the new amount of duty is the amount of vehicle excise duty payable on the licence apart from this paragraph;
(b) the old amount of duty is the amount of vehicle excise duty that would be payable on the licence if Part III of this Schedule had not been enacted.
(5) This paragraph shall be construed in accordance with the 1994 Act.

GENERAL NOTE

The Schedule implements a new system for vehicle excise duty (VED) which reduces 132 classes of vehicle to four basic classes.

Para. 2

The classes of vehicle removed from exemption will attract either the very low rate of £35 (*e.g.* snow clearing or gritting vehicles) or the special low rate of £150 (*e.g.* road rollers).

Para. 6

The general rate for vehicles not otherwise covered is set at £135, with a reduced rate of 50 per cent for vehicles constructed before 1947. This does not represent an increase on the rate under the previous system. Provision is made for rounding up or down where necessary.

Para. 7

The rates for motorcycles are linked to the new general rate.

Para. 8

The hackney carriage class is replaced with a new "bus" class. The definition of "bus" is linked to that in the Public Passenger Vehicles Act 1981. The rate of duty is linked to that for basic goods vehicles, *i.e.* £150 (see para. 14(4) below). The existing exception for community buses is extended to vehicles used for educational purposes.

Para. 9

The previous category of special machines is divided into "special vehicles" and "special concessionary vehicles." The special vehicles class comprises works trucks, mobile cranes, digging machines and road rollers with a revenue weight exceeding 3500 kgs. These attract the basic goods vehicle rate, *i.e.* £150.

Para. 10

The class of special concessionary vehicles comprises tractors, agricultural machines, mowing machines, electrically powered vehicles, snow ploughs and gritting vehicles. The rate of VED applicable is 25 per cent of the general rate, *i.e.* £35.

Para. 11

The special rate for recovery vehicles is abolished.

Para. 12

The rate for vehicles used for exceptional loads is tied to the heavy tractive unit rate. This remains at £5,000.

Para. 13

The rate for showmen's haulage vehicles is set at £150, an increase of £50.

Para. 14

This deals with the rationalisation of taxation for goods vehicles between 3,500 kgs and 44,000 kgs, so that VED is chargeable by revenue weight as set out in the substituted tables. Showmen's goods vehicles in this category are charged at the basic goods vehicles rate of £150. Vehicles exceeding 44,000 kgs pay a rate of £5,000. The special rate for an "island goods vehicle" maintains an existing concession for small islands.

Para. 15

Consequential repeals are made following the abolition of farmers' goods vehicles concessions.

Para. 18

This amendment is made as a consequence of the introduction of the concept of revenue weight (see para. 26 below).

Para. 19

The right to exchange a licence is made subject to the Secretary of State being satisfied that the licence applied for is appropriate to the vehicle and its use.

Paras. 20–23
These make amendments consequential on the introduction of the concept of revenue weight.

Para. 24
A new offence is created covering the provision of false or misleading information when applying for a design weight certificate (see para. 28 below). Offences are also created regarding forgery and misuse of such a certificate.

Para. 26
"Revenue weight" means either the plated gross weight, the plated train weight (see the Vehicle Excise and Registration Act 1994, s.61) or the design weight of the vehicle or the maximum weight at which it can lawfully operate in the U.K., whichever is less.

Para. 27
Regulations may be made which provide for documents issued or recognised pursuant to the EEC Treaty and the EEA Agreement to be treated as if they were plating certificates for VED purposes.

Para. 28
Provision is made for the issue of design weight certificates. Such certificates are to be conclusive evidence of a vehicle's design weight.

Para. 30
The particulars given in a licence application are to be specified by the Secretary of State rather than prescribed by regulations.

Para. 31
Trade licences taken out for periods of between six and 12 months must expire on either June 30 or December 31.

Para. 32
Where a licence is paid for by a cheque which is dishonoured, the defaulter may be given a second chance to pay before the licence is declared void.

Para. 33
A fee may be charged for new registrations (in practice this will be charged for registrations not notified to the DVLA under the automated registration scheme). The fee may be repaid in certain circumstances, *e.g.* if a vehicle is de-registered.

Para. 34
Regulations may be made requiring the vendor of a vehicle to provide the purchaser with documentation relating to the vehicle's registration. This is to reinforce the move to joint notification. Non-identifying information derived from particulars held in the vehicle register may be sold.

Para. 35
Convicted VED evaders will be required to take out a licence for the period covered by any back-duty paid.

Para. 36
The new Sched. 2A which is inserted in the Vehicle Excise and Registration Act 1994 confers enabling powers to set up a scheme for wheelclamping unlicensed vehicles on public roads. The regulations to be made will cover the immobilisation, removal and disposal of vehicles, the payment of declamping fees and unpaid duty and will create a range of new offences.

Para. 37
The penalties for VED underlicensing in Scotland are brought into line with those in England and Wales.

Para. 38
Minor amendments are made to certain definitions relating to evidence in proceedings taken in Scotland.

Para. 39

Vehicles with current licences for concessionary classes which are to be abolished from July 1, 1995, may be used under the old licences until these expire.

Para. 40

Regulations for calculating the seating capacity of hackney carriages will apply to the new "bus" class (see para. 8 above).

Para. 41

The VED on the first licence taken out for a previously exempt vehicle between July 1, 1995 and July 1, 1996 is restricted to a maximum of £1,000.

Para. 42

A similar maximum is applied where a vehicle moves into a higher category of charge as a result of the changes. The increase in charge is restricted to £1,000 for the first licence.

Section 34   SCHEDULE 5

INSURANCE PREMIUM TAX

1. Part III of the Finance Act 1994 (insurance premium tax) shall be amended as provided by this Schedule.

2.—(1) Section 53 (registration of insurers) shall be amended as follows.

(2) In subsection (5) (Commissioners to cancel registration of person who ceases to receive premiums)—

  (a) the word "and" shall be inserted after paragraph (a);
  (b) paragraph (c) (person to satisfy Commissioners that no tax is unpaid) and the word "and" immediately preceding it shall be omitted.

(3) The following subsection shall be inserted after subsection (5)—

  "(5A) In a case where—
    (a) the Commissioners are satisfied that a person has ceased to receive, as insurer, premiums in the course of any taxable business, but
    (b) he has not notified them under subsection (3) above,
they may cancel his registration with effect from the earliest practicable time after he so ceased."

(4) Sub-paragraph (2) above shall apply in relation to notifications made under section 53(3) on or after the day on which this Act is passed.

3. Section 53 shall be further amended by inserting the following subsection after subsection (1)—

  "(1A) The register kept under this section may contain such information as the Commissioners think is required for the purposes of the care and management of the tax."

4. The following section shall be inserted after section 53—

"Information required to keep register up to date

  53A.—(1) Regulations may make provision requiring a registrable person to notify the Commissioners of particulars which—

    (a) are of changes in circumstances relating to the registrable person or any business carried on by him,
    (b) appear to the Commissioners to be required for the purpose of keeping the register kept under section 53 above up to date, and
    (c) are of a prescribed description.

  (2) Regulations may make provision—

    (a) as to the time within which a notification is to be made;
    (b) as to the form and manner in which a notification is to be made;
    (c) requiring a person who has made a notification to notify the Commissioners if any information contained in it is inaccurate."

5.—(1) Section 59 (review of Commissioners' decisions) shall be amended as follows.

(2) In subsection (1)(d) (review of decision with respect to assessment) for the words "under section 56 above" there shall be substituted "falling within subsection (1A) below".

(3) The following subsection shall be inserted after subsection (1)—

  "(1A) An assessment falls within this subsection if it is an assessment under section 56 above in respect of an accounting period in relation to which a return required to be made by virtue of regulations under section 54 above has been made."

(4) This paragraph shall apply in relation to assessments made on or after the day on which this Act is passed.

6. In section 73(1) (interpretation) after the entry relating to "conduct" there shall be inserted—

" "insurance business" means a business which consists of or includes the provision of insurance;".

7.—(1) In Schedule 7 (information, powers, etc.) paragraphs 2(1) to (3) and 3(1) to (3) (duty to furnish information and produce documents) shall be amended as follows—

(a) for the words "a taxable business" (in each place where they occur) there shall be substituted "an insurance business";

(b) for the words "taxable insurance contracts" (in each place where they occur) there shall be substituted "contracts of insurance";

(c) for the words "taxable insurance contract" (in each place where they occur) there shall be substituted "contract of insurance.".

(2) This paragraph shall apply in relation to contracts whether entered into before or after the passing of this Act.

8.—(1) In Schedule 7 the following shall be inserted after paragraph 4—

"Order for access to recorded information etc.

4A.—(1) Where, on an application by an authorised person, a justice of the peace or, in Scotland, a justice (within the meaning of section 462 of the Criminal Procedure (Scotland) Act 1975) is satisfied that there are reasonable grounds for believing—

(a) that an offence in connection with tax is being, has been or is about to be committed, and

(b) that any recorded information (including any document of any nature whatsoever) which may be required as evidence for the purpose of any proceedings in respect of such an offence is in the possession of any person,

he may make an order under this paragraph.

(2) An order under this paragraph is an order that the person who appears to the justice to be in possession of the recorded information to which the application relates shall—

(a) give an authorised person access to it, and

(b) permit an authorised person to remove and take away any of it which he reasonably considers necessary,

not later than the end of the period of 7 days beginning on the date of the order or the end of such longer period as the order may specify.

(3) The reference in sub-paragraph (2)(a) above to giving an authorised person access to the recorded information to which the application relates includes a reference to permitting the authorised person to take copies of it or to make extracts from it.

(4) Where the recorded information consists of information contained in a computer, an order under this paragraph shall have effect as an order to produce the information in a form in which it is visible and legible and, if the authorised person wishes to remove it, in a form in which it can be removed.

(5) This paragraph is without prejudice to paragraphs 3 and 4 above."

(2) In paragraph 5(1) of Schedule 7 (duty to provide record of anything removed in exercise of power) after the words "paragraph 4" there shall be inserted "or 4A".

9. In paragraph 7 of Schedule 7 (recovery of tax etc.) the following sub-paragraphs shall be substituted for sub-paragraph (8)—

"(8) In respect of Scotland, where any tax or any amount recoverable as if it were tax is due and has not been paid, the sheriff, on an application by the Commissioners accompanied by a certificate by the Commissioners—

(a) stating that none of the persons specified in the application has paid the tax or other sum due from him,

(b) stating that payment of the amount due from each such person has been demanded from him, and

(c) specifying the amount due from and unpaid by each such person,

shall grant a summary warrant in a form prescribed by act of sederunt authorising the recovery, by any of the diligences mentioned in sub-paragraph (9) below, of the amount remaining due and unpaid.

(9) The diligences referred to in sub-paragraph (8) above are—

(a) a poinding and sale in accordance with Schedule 5 to the Debtors (Scotland) Act 1987;

(b) an earnings arrestment;

(c) an arrestment and action of furthcoming or sale.

(10) Subject to sub-paragraph (11) below and without prejudice to paragraphs 25 to 34 of Schedule 5 to the Debtors (Scotland) Act 1987 (expenses of poinding and sale) the sheriff officer's fees, together with the outlays necessarily incurred by him, in connection with the execution of a summary warrant shall be chargeable against the debtor.

(11) No fee shall be chargeable by the sheriff officer against the debtor for collecting, and accounting to the Commissioners for, sums paid to him by the debtor in respect of the amount owing.

(12) Regulations may make provision for anything which the Commissioners may do under sub-paragraphs (8) to (11) above to be done by an officer of the Commissioners holding such rank as the regulations may specify."

GENERAL NOTE

The amendments made by this Schedule to insurance premium tax (IPT) are intended to enhance its management.

Para. 2

This removes the requirement that an insurer who is no longer liable to be registered must first satisfy the Customs and Excise that no IPT is unpaid before his registration may be cancelled. It also provides that, where Customs and Excise are satisfied that an insurer is no longer liable to be registered, they may cancel the registration without requiring formal notification from the insurer.

Para. 3

The Customs and Excise are given power to determine what information is required for the IPT register.

Para. 4

The new FA 1994, s.53A provides for regulations to be made specifying the information which is required in order to keep the IPT register up to date and detailing when and how such information should be notified.

Para. 5

The power to require Customs and Excise to review an assessment of tax due only applies if the return for the relevant accounting period has been made.

Para. 6

The definition of "insurance business" is linked to the following paragraph, which extends the powers of Customs and Excise to obtain information concerning insurance contracts.

Para. 7

Customs and Excise are given access to all contracts of insurance, not merely those which are liable to IPT.

Para. 8

The new FA 1994, Sched. 7, para. 4A provides for the Customs and Excise to be given access in fraud investigations to recorded information held by a third party.

Para. 9

This paragraph replaces a regulation-making power by inserting the relevant provisions in FA 1994. It also harmonises the recovery of debts in Scotland associated with IPT with that for other taxes.

Section 39   SCHEDULE 6

AMENDMENTS IN CONNECTION WITH CHARGE UNDER SCHEDULE A

The Taxes Act 1988

1. Subsection (2) of section 15 of the Taxes Act 1988 (election under paragraph 4 of Schedule A) shall cease to have effect except for the purpose of being applied by virtue of section 9 of that Act for the purposes of corporation tax.

2. In section 18(3) of that Act (Cases under Schedule D), in Case I, at the end there shall be inserted "but not contained in Schedule A".

3. Sections 22 and 23 of that Act (assessments to income tax under Schedule A and collection from lessees and agents) shall cease to have effect.

4. The following provisions of Part II of that Act shall cease to have effect except for the purpose of being applied by virtue of section 9 of that Act for the purposes of corporation tax, that is to say—

(a) sections 25 and 28 (deductions from rent);
(b) section 29 (sporting rights);
(c) section 31 (supplementary provisions);
(d) section 33 (allowance for excess expenditure in relation to agricultural land);
(e) sections 33A and 33B (rents and receipts received by connected persons and payments made by connected persons);
(f) subsection (5) of section 40 (application of Schedule A rules as to receipts and outgoings on sale of land); and
(g) section 41 (relief for rent not paid).

5.—(1) Section 26 of that Act (land managed as one estate), except where it is applied for the purposes of corporation tax, shall have effect with the following modifications.

(2) Subsection (1) shall have effect as if—
(a) in paragraph (a), the words "at a full rent (not being a tenant's repairing lease)" were omitted; and
(b) for the words from "not being" in paragraph (b) to the end of the subsection there were substituted "as if the rent, so far as it relates to that part and would otherwise be treated as being at a lower rate, were at a rate per annum equal to the relevant annual value."

(3) Subsection (2) shall have effect as if paragraph (a) were omitted.

(4) The following subsection shall be deemed to be inserted after subsection (2)—

"(2A) Where subsection (1) above applies, the following rules shall apply in computing the profits or gains on which the owner is charged under Schedule A—
(a) disbursements and expenses relating to any of that part of the estate which comprises land the rent in respect of which is determined under that subsection ('the relevant part of the estate') shall not be deductible from any receipts which are not so determined except to the extent that—
(i) the amount of the disbursements and expenses exceeds the amount of the rent so determined; and
(ii) the receipts against which the remainder is set are receipts in respect of land comprised in the estate;
(b) any excess for any chargeable period of the disbursements and expenses relating to the relevant part of the estate (including any excess carried forward under this paragraph) over the receipts for that period from which they are deductible in accordance with paragraph (a) above—
(i) shall be disregarded in computing any loss in respect of which relief may be given under section 379A, but
(ii) may be carried forward to the following chargeable period and treated in relation to the later period as if it were a disbursement or expense relating to the relevant part of the estate;
(c) disbursements and expenses relating to any land not comprised in the relevant part of the estate shall be deductible from the deemed receipts in respect of the land which is so comprised to the extent only that the deemed receipts exceed the aggregate of—
(i) the actual disbursements and expenses for that period relating to the relevant part of the estate, and
(ii) any amounts carried forward to that period under paragraph (b) above; and
(d) any excess of the disbursements and expenses for that period relating to land not comprised in the relevant part of the estate over the amounts from which they are deductible shall be treated for the purposes of section 379A as a loss for that period in the Schedule A business in question."

6.—(1) Subsection (3)(a) of section 27 of that Act (maintenance funds for historic buildings), except where it is applied for the purposes of corporation tax, shall be construed subject to subsection (2A) of section 26 (as deemed to be inserted by paragraph 5 above) and shall have effect as if—
(a) in the words before sub-paragraph (i), for "rents" there were substituted "receipts";
(b) in sub-paragraph (i), for the words from "payments" to "section 25" there were substituted "disbursements or expenses of the trustees of the settlement which relate to the other part of the estate and which would be so deductible"; and
(c) for sub-paragraph (ii) there were substituted the following sub-paragraph—
"(ii) any disbursements or expenses of the owner of the other part of the estate to the extent to which they cannot be deducted by him in the chargeable period in which they are incurred because of an insufficiency of any receipts for that period from which they are deductible apart from this sub-paragraph."

(2) Subsection (3)(b) of that section shall have effect, except where it is so applied, as if for "under section 33" there were substituted "by virtue of section 379A(2)(b)".

7. Section 30(1) of that Act (expenditure on sea walls), except where it is applied for the purposes of corporation tax, shall have effect as if—

(a) for "for the purposes of sections 25, 28 and 31" there were substituted "for the purpose of computing the profits or gains, or losses, of any Schedule A business carried on in relation to those premises"; and

(b) for "in respect of dilapidation attributable to the year" there were substituted "as an expense of the business for that year".

8.—(1) Section 32 of that Act (capital allowances for machinery and plant used in estate management), except where it is applied for the purposes of corporation tax, shall have effect with the following modifications.

(2) Subsection (1) shall have effect as if—

(a) for the words from "entitled" to "arise" there were substituted "for the purposes of a Schedule A business"; and

(b) at the end there were inserted "set up and commenced on or after 6th April 1995 and as if that business were that person's trade".

(3) The following subsections shall be deemed to be inserted after that subsection—

"(1A) Subsection (1) above and the 1990 Act shall have effect, subject to subsections (1B) and (1C) below—

(a) as if the purposes for which a Schedule A business is to be treated as a trade did not include the purposes of so much of sections 61 and 67(2) of that Act (leased plant or machinery and expenditure on thermal insulation) as makes provision in relation to cases where machinery or plant or, as the case may be, an industrial building or structure has been let otherwise than in the course of a trade; and

(b) as if expenditure which for the purposes of section 61 of that Act is or falls to be treated as expenditure on the provision of machinery or plant first let otherwise than in the course of a trade were to be treated in all cases as expenditure on the provision of machinery or plant which, at the time when it is let or treated as let, is used for purposes which are other than those of a Schedule A business.

(1B) Section 73(2) and (3) of the 1990 Act shall not apply in the case of any allowance or charge by virtue of section 61(1) of that Act where the letting of the machinery or plant is in connection with anything done in the course of the carrying on of a Schedule A business; and in such a case, the allowance or charge shall be made in taxing the business as if the business were the trade of the person carrying on the business and were a trade set up and commenced on or after 6th April 1995.

(1C) Any allowance made by virtue of section 61(1) of the 1990 Act in a case where it applies by virtue of section 67(2) of that Act shall be made as mentioned in subsection (1B) above as if (in so far as it is not otherwise the case)—

(a) the person to whom the allowance is made were carrying on a Schedule A business; and

(b) the letting of the machinery or plant which is deemed under section 67(2) of that Act to have taken place had been a letting in connection with the carrying on of the Schedule A business which is carried on, or treated as carried on, by that person."

(4) Subsections (2) to (6), and in subsection (7), the words from "and, on any assessment" onwards shall be deemed to be omitted.

9.—(1) Section 34 of that Act (premiums), except where it is applied for the purposes of corporation tax, shall have effect with the following modifications.

(2) Subsection (3) shall have effect as if for the words from "from the rent" onwards there were substituted "as an expense of any Schedule A business carried on by the landlord".

(3) Subsection (4) shall have effect as if in paragraph (a), for the words from "in computing" to "in lieu of rent" there were substituted "in computing the profits or gains, or losses, of the Schedule A business of which the sum payable in lieu of rent is by virtue of this subsection to be treated as a receipt".

(4) Subsection (5) shall have effect as if in paragraph (a), for "tax chargeable by virtue of this subsection" there were substituted "the profits or gains, or losses, of the Schedule A business of which that sum is by virtue of this subsection to be treated as a receipt".

(5) Subsection (6) shall have effect as if for the words from "no charge" onwards there were substituted "no amount shall fall under that subsection to be treated as a receipt of any Schedule A business carried on by the landlord; but that other person shall be taken to have received as income an amount equal to the amount which would otherwise fall to be treated as rent and to be chargeable to tax as if he had received it in consequence of having, on his own account, entered into a transaction falling to be treated as mentioned in paragraph 1(2) of Schedule A."

10. Section 35(2) of that Act (charge on assignment of lease granted at an undervalue), except where it is applied for the purposes of corporation tax, shall have effect as if for the words from

"treated as profits or gains" onwards there were substituted "deemed to have been received as income by the assignor and to have been received by him in consequence of his having entered into a transaction falling to be treated as mentioned in paragraph 1(2) of Schedule A."

11. Section 36(1) of that Act (charge on sale of land with a right to a reconveyance), except where it is applied for the purposes of corporation tax, shall have effect as if—

(a) for "the vendor shall be chargeable to tax under Case VI of Schedule D on" there were substituted "the following amount shall be deemed to have been received as income by the vendor and to have been received by him in consequence of his having entered into a transaction falling to be treated as mentioned in paragraph 1(2) of Schedule A, that is to say"; and

(b) for "on that excess" there were substituted "the amount of the excess".

12.—(1) Section 37 of that Act (deductions from premiums and rents received), except where it is applied for the purposes of corporation tax, shall have effect with the following modifications.

(2) Subsection (1) shall have effect as if for paragraphs (a) and (b) there were substituted the following paragraphs—

"(a) any amount falls to be treated as a receipt of a Schedule A business by virtue of section 34 or 35; or

(b) any amount would fall to be so treated but for the operation of subsection (2) or (3) below;".

(3) Subsection (2) shall have effect as if—

(a) in paragraph (b), for the words from "be" to "any amount" there were substituted "be treated by virtue of section 34 or 35 as receiving any amount as income in the course of carrying on a Schedule A business"; and

(b) for "on which he is so chargeable" there were substituted "which he shall be treated as having so received".

(4) Subsection (3) shall have effect as if—

(a) for "chargeable under section 34 or 35" there were substituted "treated by virtue of section 34 or 35 as having received any amount as income in the course of carrying on a Schedule A business and falls to be so treated"; and

(b) for "on which he is so chargeable" there were substituted "which he shall be treated as having so received".

(5) Subsection (4) shall have effect as if for the words from "purposes" to "other premises" there were substituted "purpose, in computing the profits or gains, or losses, of a Schedule A business, of making deductions in respect of the disbursements and expenses of that business".

13. In subsection (6) of section 82 of that Act (rules as to interest paid to non-residents not to apply for the purposes of corporation tax), at the end there shall be inserted "and shall be treated as excluded from the provisions that have effect by virtue of section 21(3) for the computation of the profits or gains, or losses, of a Schedule A business."

14.—(1) Subsection (1) of section 87 of that Act (taxable premiums), except where it is applied for the purposes of corporation tax, shall have effect as if for paragraphs (a) and (b) there were substituted the following paragraphs—

"(a) any amount falls to be treated as a receipt of a Schedule A business by virtue of section 34 or 35; or

(b) any amount would fall to be so treated but for the operation of section 37(2) or (3);".

(2) After subsection (9) of that section there shall be inserted the following subsection—

"(10) This section shall not apply for the computation in accordance with section 21(3) of the amount of any profits or gains to be charged to tax under Schedule A."

15. In section 96(11) of that Act (relief for fluctuating profits of farming or market gardening not to apply for corporation tax purposes), after "corporation tax" there shall be inserted "or to any profits or gains chargeable to income tax under Schedule A."

16.—(1) In subsection (5) of section 98 of that Act (tied premises)—

(a) in paragraph (a), for "in respect of the rent" there shall be substituted "to tax chargeable under that Schedule"; and

(b) in paragraph (b), for "his total liability (so computed) in respect of the rent" there shall be substituted "the liability so computed".

(2) After subsection (8) of that section there shall be inserted the following subsection—

"(9) The references in this section to a trade shall not by virtue of section 21(3) have effect, for the purposes of the computation of profits or gains chargeable to tax under Schedule A, as including a Schedule A business."

17. In section 368(3) and (4) of that Act (exclusion of double relief for interest), after "for the purposes of", in each case, there shall be inserted "Schedule A or".

18. After section 375 of that Act there shall be inserted the following section—

"Option to deduct interest for the purposes of Schedule A

375A.—(1) If an individual who is a qualifying borrower with respect to any interest on a loan which is relevant loan interest—

(a) is carrying on or proposing to carry on a Schedule A business, and

(b) gives notice to the Board that deductions are to be made in respect of payments of interest on that loan in computing the profits or gains of that business,

then (subject to the following provisions of this section) section 369 shall not apply to any payment of interest on that loan which becomes due or is made on or after such date as may be specified for the purposes of this subsection in the notice.

(2) A notice specifying a date for the purposes of subsection (1) above—

(a) may be given at any time before the end of the period of twenty-two months beginning with the end of the year of assessment in which that date falls, but

(b) once given, shall not be withdrawn.

(3) Where notice is given to the Board under subsection (1) above, the Board shall give notice to the lender and the borrower specifying a date, not being a date before either—

(a) the date specified for the purposes of that subsection, or

(b) the date on which the notice under this subsection is given to the lender,

as the date on or after which payments of interest on the loan are to be treated in relation to the lender as payments of interest to which section 369 does not apply.

(4) Subsections (2) and (3) of section 375 shall have effect in relation to any period between—

(a) the beginning of any date specified for the purposes of subsection (1) above, and

(b) the date specified in that case in the notice given under subsection (3) above,

as they apply, in the case of any relevant loan interest, in relation to the period between the time when the borrower ceases to be a qualifying borrower and the date on which he gives notice of that fact to the lender.

(5) Where a notice under subsection (1) above has taken effect in relation to payments of interest on any loan, section 369 shall not again apply to payments of interest on that loan except where they become due after such time as may be specified in a further notice given by the Board for the purposes of this subsection to the lender and the borrower.

(6) A notice under subsection (5) above shall not specify a time for the purposes of that subsection which falls before the time when the Schedule A business in question is permanently discontinued or, as the case may be, when the proposal to carry it on is finally abandoned."

19.—(1) In Chapter I of Part X of that Act (loss relief for the purposes of income tax), before section 380, there shall be inserted the following section—

"Schedule A losses

Schedule A losses

379A.—(1) Subject to the following provisions of this section, where for any year of assessment any person sustains any loss in a Schedule A business carried on by him either solely or in partnership—

(a) the loss shall be carried forward to the following year of assessment and, to the extent that it does not exceed them, set against any profits or gains of that business for the year to which it is carried forward; and

(b) where there are no profits or gains for the following year or the profits or gains for that year are exceeded by the amount of the loss, the loss or, as the case may be, the remainder of it shall be so carried forward to the next following year, and so on.

(2) Subsection (3) below shall apply where a loss is sustained in a Schedule A business for any year of assessment ('the year of the loss') and one or both of the following conditions is satisfied, that is to say—

(a) the amount of the relevant capital allowances treated as expenses of that business in computing that loss exceeds, by any amount ('the net capital allowances'), the amount of any charges under the 1990 Act which are treated as receipts of that business in computing that loss;

(b) the Schedule A business has been carried on in relation to land that consists of or includes an agricultural estate to which allowable agricultural expenses deducted in computing that loss are attributable;

and the relevant capital allowances for the purposes of this subsection are allowances under the 1990 Act other than the whole or, as the case may be, a proportionate part of any allowances made in accordance with section 32(1B) of this Act in respect of expenditure on the provision of machinery or plant which is let, for the whole or a part of the year in question, to a person who does not use it or uses it for purposes other than those of a trade.

(3) Where the person carrying on the Schedule A business in a case to which this subsection applies makes a claim, in relation to the year of the loss or the year following that year, for relief under this subsection in respect of the loss—

    (a) relief from income tax may be given, for the year to which the claim relates, on an amount of that person's income for that year which is equal to the amount of relief available for that year in respect of the loss; and

    (b) the loss which is to be or has been carried forward under subsection (1) above shall be treated as reduced (if necessary to nil) by an amount equal to the amount on which relief is given;

but a claim for relief under this subsection shall not be made after the end of twelve months from the 31st January next following the end of the year to which it relates and shall be accompanied by all such amendments as may be required by virtue of paragraph (b) above of any self-assessment previously made by the claimant under section 9 of the Management Act.

(4) Subject to subsection (5) below, the reference in subsection (3) above to the amount of the relief available for any year in respect of a loss is a reference to whichever is the smallest of the following amounts, that is to say—

    (a) the amount of the relievable income for the year to which the claim relates;

    (b) the loss sustained in the Schedule A business in the year of the loss; and

    (c) the amount which, according to whether one or both of the conditions mentioned in subsection (2) above is satisfied in relation to the year of the loss, is equal—

        (i) to the net capital allowances,

        (ii) to the amount of the allowable agricultural expenses for the year of the loss,

    or

        (iii) to the sum of the net capital allowances and the amount of those expenses.

(5) Where relief under subsection (3) above is given in respect of a loss in relation to either of the years in relation to which relief may be claimed in respect of that loss, relief shall not be available in respect of the same loss for the other year except, in a case where the relief already given is of an amount determined in accordance with subsection (4)(a) above, to the extent that the smaller of the amounts applicable by virtue of subsection (4)(b) and (c) above exceeds the amount of relief already given.

(6) For the purposes of subsection (4)(a) above the amount of relievable income for any year, in relation to any person, shall be equal to the amount of his income for that year—

    (a) after effect has been given to subsection (1) above in relation to any amount carried forward to that year in respect of a loss sustained in any year before the year of the loss, and

    (b) in the case of a claim under subsection (3) above in relation to the year of the loss, after effect has been given to any claim under that subsection in respect of a loss sustained in the preceding year.

(7) For the purposes of this section the loss sustained in any Schedule A business shall be computed in like manner as the profits or gains arising or accruing from such a business are computed under the provisions of the Income Tax Acts applicable to Schedule A.

(8) In this section 'allowable agricultural expenses', in relation to an agricultural estate, means any disbursements or expenses attributable to the estate which are deductible in respect of maintenance, repairs, insurance or management of the estate and otherwise than in respect of the interest payable on any loan.

(9) For the purposes of this section the amount of any disbursements or expenses attributable to an agricultural estate shall be determined as if—

    (a) disbursements and expenses were to be disregarded to the extent that they would not have been attributable to the estate if it did not include the parts of it used wholly for purposes other than purposes of husbandry, and

    (b) disbursements and expenses in respect of parts of the estate used partly for purposes of husbandry and partly for other purposes were to be reduced to an extent corresponding to the extent to which those parts were used for other purposes.

(10) In this section—

    'agricultural estate' means any land (including any houses or other buildings) which is managed as one estate and which consists of or includes any agricultural land; and

    'agricultural land' means land, houses or other buildings in the United Kingdom occupied wholly or mainly for the purposes of husbandry."

(2) Where apart from this Act any person who carries on a Schedule A business in the year 1995–96 would have been entitled—

(a) by virtue of Part II of the Taxes Act 1988, to deduct any amount that became due before the beginning of that year from rent received in that year, being rent which is in fact brought into account in computing the profits or gains of that business, or

(b) by virtue of section 392 of that Act, to carry forward to that year the amount of any portion of a loss sustained in any transaction, being a transaction of such a nature that if it occurred in that year it would be treated as a transaction in the course of that Schedule A business,

that amount shall be treated for the purposes of income tax as if it were a loss falling, in accordance with section 379A(1) of that Act, to be carried forward from the previous year to the year 1995–96 and (in so far as not used in giving relief for that year) to subsequent years.

(3) Where—

(a) any person carrying on a Schedule A business in the year 1995–96 would, by virtue of section 355(4) of the Taxes Act 1988 (power to carry forward excess interest), have been entitled, in respect of an amount of interest representing an excess of interest over the income against which relief was available for any previous year, to be given relief against an equivalent amount of income for the year 1995–96 from the letting of any land, caravan or house-boat, and

(b) that business relates to any land, caravan or house-boat in relation to which the condition specified in section 355(1)(b) of that Act would have been fulfilled for the year 1995–96,

that amount shall be treated for the purposes of income tax as if it were a loss falling, in accordance with section 379A(1) of that Act, to be carried forward from the previous year to the year 1995–96 and (in so far as not used in giving relief for that year) to subsequent years.

(4) Section 379A(3) of that Act shall have effect for the purposes of the making of a claim in a case where the year to which the claim relates is the year 1995–96 as if the period for making such a claim ended two years after the end of that year.

20. In section 401 of that Act (relief for pre-trading expenditure), after subsection (1A) there shall be inserted the following subsection—

"(1B) Except for the purposes of corporation tax, subsection (1) above shall apply in relation to expenditure for the purposes of a Schedule A business as it applies in relation to expenditure for the purposes of a trade; and, accordingly, that subsection shall have effect in relation to expenditure for the purposes of a Schedule A business as if the reference to the computation of the profits or gains for the purposes of Case I or II of Schedule D were a reference to the computation of profits or gains for the purposes of Schedule A."

21.—(1) Section 503 of that Act (letting of furnished holiday accommodation), except so far as it applies for the purposes of corporation tax, shall have effect with the following modifications.

(2) Subsection (1) shall have effect as if for "380 to 390, 393, 393A(1), 401" there were substituted "379A to 390" and as if the following paragraph were substituted for paragraph (a)—

"(a) any Schedule A business, so far as it consists in the commercial letting of furnished holiday accommodation in the United Kingdom, shall be treated as a trade the profits or gains of which are chargeable to tax under Case I of Schedule D; and".

(3) The following subsection shall be deemed to be substituted for subsection (2)—

"(2) In its application by virtue of subsection (1) above section 390 shall have effect as if the reference to the trade the profits of which are chargeable to tax under Case I or II of Schedule D were a reference to the Schedule A business so far as it is treated as a trade."

(4) Subsection (5) shall be deemed to be omitted.

22. In section 577(9) of that Act (exception in relation to business entertaining expenses for gifts to bodies established for charitable purposes), after "under" there shall be inserted "Schedule A or".

23. Section 579 of that Act (statutory redundancy payments), except so far as it applies for the purposes of corporation tax, shall have effect as if the following subsection were substituted for subsection (4)—

"(4) Where a redundancy payment or other employer's payment is made in respect of employment wholly in a Schedule A business carried on by the employer—

(a) the amount of the redundancy payment or the corresponding amount of the other employer's payment shall (if not otherwise so allowable) be allowable as a deduction in computing for the purposes of Schedule A the profits or gains or losses of the business; but

(b) if the employer's payment was made after the discontinuance of the business, the net amount so deductible shall be treated as if it were a payment made on the last day on which the business was carried on."

24. Section 588 of that Act (training courses for employees), except so far as it applies for the purposes of corporation tax, shall have effect as if the following subsection were inserted after subsection (4)—

"(4A) Subsection (3) above shall have effect where the employee is or was employed for the purposes of a Schedule A business carried on by the employer as if the references to computing for the purposes of Schedule D the profits or gains of a trade, profession or vocation mentioned in that subsection were references to computing for the purposes of Schedule A the profits or gains of that business."

25. Section 589A of that Act (counselling services for employees), except so far as it applies for the purposes of corporation tax, shall have effect as if the following subsection were inserted after subsection (9)—

"(9A) Subsection (8) above shall have effect where the employee is or was employed for the purposes of a Schedule A business carried on by the employer as if the references to computing for the purposes of Schedule D the profits or gains of the trade, profession or vocation mentioned in that subsection were references to computing for the purposes of Schedule A the profits or gains of that business."

26. In section 692(1) of that Act (reimbursement of settlor), for the words from "the profits" onwards there shall be substituted "either the profits of a trade carried on by the settlor or the profits of a Schedule A business so carried on".

27. In section 779(13)(a) of that Act (definition of relevant tax relief for the purposes of anti-avoidance provisions), the words "allowable by virtue of sections 25, 26 and 28 to 31 and Schedule 1" shall be omitted.

28. In section 832(1) of that Act (interpretation of the Tax Acts), after the definition of "recognised clearing system" there shall be inserted the following definition—

" 'Schedule A business' means any business the profits or gains of which are chargeable to income tax under Schedule A, including the business in the course of which any transaction is by virtue of paragraph 1(2) of that Schedule to be treated as entered into;".

The Capital Allowances Act 1990 (c. 1)

29.—(1) In section 9 of the Capital Allowances Act 1990 (manner of making industrial buildings allowance), in subsection (1), for "mentioned in subsections (2) to (7) below" there shall be substituted "where subsections (2) to (7) below apply".

(2) After that subsection there shall be inserted the following subsections—

"(1A) In the case of an allowance or charge made to or on a person whose interest in the building or structure is subject to a lease at the relevant time, subsection (1) above shall have effect for the purposes of income tax—

(a) as if any Schedule A business carried on by that person at any time in the chargeable period for which the allowance or charge is made were the trade in the taxing of which the allowance or charge were to be made; or

(b) where that person is not carrying on such a business at any time in that period, as if he were carrying on such a business and the business were the trade in the taxing of which the allowance or charge is to be made;

and this Act shall have effect in each case as if the Schedule A business which is deemed to be a trade for the purposes of this subsection were a trade set up and commenced on or after 6th April 1995.

(1B) In subsection (1A) above 'the relevant time'—

(a) in relation to an initial allowance, means the time when the expenditure is incurred or any subsequent time before the building or structure is used for any purpose;

(b) in relation to a writing-down allowance, means the end of the chargeable period for which the allowance is made; and

(c) in relation to a balancing allowance or charge, means the time immediately before the event giving rise to the allowance or charge."

(3) At the beginning of subsections (2), (3), (4) and (6) of that section there shall be inserted, in each case, the words "For the purposes of corporation tax"; and in subsection (6), paragraph (a) and, in paragraph (b), the words "if it is a charge to corporation tax" shall be omitted.

30. In subsection (2) of section 15 of that Act of 1990 (method of making allowances and charges in the case of buildings falling temporarily out of use), at the beginning there shall be inserted "For the purposes of corporation tax" and after that subsection there shall be inserted the following subsection—

"(2A) For the purposes of income tax any allowance or charge falling to be made to any person in respect of a building or structure during a period while the building or structure—

(a) is temporarily out of use, but

(b) is deemed by virtue of subsection (1) above still to be an industrial building or structure,

shall be made, in a case falling within subsection (2)(a) or (b) above, in accordance with section 9(1A) as if (where section 9(1A) does not otherwise apply) the building or structure were subject to a lease at the relevant time."

31. Section 29(1) of that Act of 1990 (commercial letting of furnished holiday accommodation to be treated as trade for the purposes of Part II), except so far as it applies for the purposes of

corporation tax, shall have effect as if the following paragraph were substituted for paragraph (a)—

"(a) any Schedule A business consisting in the commercial letting of furnished holiday accommodation in the United Kingdom shall be treated as a trade; and".

32. In section 67(3) of that Act of 1990 (manner of making allowance in certain cases in respect of expenditure on thermal insulation), for "shall (notwithstanding section 73(2)), be available" there shall be substituted "shall be made to any person for the purposes of income tax in accordance with section 32(1B) and (1C) of the principal Act and, for the purposes of corporation tax, shall be available (notwithstanding section 73(2))".

33. In section 73 of that Act of 1990 (manner of making allowances and charges in respect of machinery and plant), after subsection (3) there shall be inserted the following subsection—

"(4) Subsections (2) and (3) above apply subject to the provisions of section 32(1B) of the principal Act."

34.—(1) In section 92 of that Act of 1990 (manner of making assured tenancy allowances and related charges), at the beginning there shall be inserted the following subsection—

"(A1) For the purposes of income tax any allowance or charge made to or on any person under this Part shall be made to or on him in taxing his trade—

(a) as if any Schedule A business carried on by that person were the trade in the taxing of which the allowance or charge were to be made; or

(b) where that person is not carrying on such a business, as if he were carrying on such a business and that business were the trade in the taxing of which the allowance or charge is to be made;

and this Act shall have effect in each case as if the Schedule A business which is deemed to be a trade for the purposes of this subsection were a trade set up and commenced on or after 6th April 1995."

(2) In subsections (1) and (2) of that section, at the beginning there shall be inserted, in each case, the words "For the purposes of corporation tax"; and in subsection (2), paragraph (a) and, in paragraph (b), the words "if it is a charge to corporation tax" shall be omitted.

35.—(1) After subsection (2) of section 132 of that Act of 1990 (manner of making agricultural buildings allowances and related charges), there shall be inserted the following subsection—

"(2A) In the case of an allowance or charge which falls to be made to a person for a chargeable period in which he is not carrying on a trade, subsection (2) above shall have effect for the purposes of income tax—

(a) as if any Schedule A business carried on by that person at that time were the trade in the taxing of which the allowance or charge were to be made; or

(b) where that person is not carrying on such a business at that time, as if he were carrying on such a business and the business were the trade in the taxing of which the allowance or charge is to be made;

and this Act shall have effect in each case as if the Schedule A business which is deemed to be a trade for the purposes of this subsection were a trade set up and commenced on or after 6th April 1995."

(2) In subsections (3) and (4) of that section, at the beginning there shall be inserted, in each case, the words "For the purposes of corporation tax"; and in subsection (4), paragraph (a) and, in paragraph (b), the words "if it is a charge to corporation tax" shall be omitted.

The Taxation of Chargeable Gains Act 1992 (c. 12)

36. Section 241(3) of the Taxation of Chargeable Gains Act 1992 (commercial letting of furnished holiday accommodation to be treated as trade for certain purposes), except so far as it applies for the purposes of corporation tax, shall have effect as if the following paragraph were substituted for paragraph (a)—

"(a) any Schedule A business (within the meaning of the Taxes Act) which consists in the commercial letting of furnished holiday accommodation in the United Kingdom shall be treated as a trade; and".

37.—(1) Schedule 8 to that Act of 1992 (which includes provision excluding from the charge to capital gains tax premiums taxed under Schedule A), except so far as it applies in accordance with section 8 of that Act for the purposes of corporation tax, shall have effect as follows.

(2) In paragraph 5—

(a) in sub-paragraphs (1) and (2), for the words "income tax has become chargeable under section 34 of the Taxes Act on any amount" there shall, in each case, be deemed to be substituted "any amount is brought into account by virtue of section 34 of the Taxes Act as a receipt of a Schedule A business (within the meaning of that Act)"; and

(b) in sub-paragraph (3), for "income tax has become chargeable under section 36 of the Taxes Act (sale of land with right of re-conveyance) on any amount" there shall be deemed to be substituted "any amount is brought into account by virtue of section 36 of the Taxes Act (sale of land with right of re-conveyance) as a receipt of a Schedule A business (within the meaning of that Act)".

(3) In paragraph 6(2), for the words from "on which tax is paid" onwards there shall be deemed to be substituted "brought into account by virtue of section 35 of the Taxes Act (charge on assignment of a lease granted at an undervalue) as a receipt of a Schedule A business (within the meaning of that Act)".

(4) In paragraph 7, for the words from "income tax" to "so chargeable" there shall be deemed to be substituted "any amount is brought into account by virtue of section 34(2) and (3) of the Taxes Act as a receipt of a Schedule A business (within the meaning of that Act) which is or is treated as carried on by any person, that person".

The Finance (No. 2) Act 1992 (c. 48)

38. In paragraph 2(1) of Schedule 10 to the Finance (No. 2) Act 1992 (furnished accommodation), for "under Case I or Case VI of Schedule D (or both those Cases)" there shall be substituted "under Schedule A or Case I of Schedule D (or under both together)".

GENERAL NOTE

The Schedule contains the necessary amendments to previous legislation in order to accommodate the new system for charging tax under Schedule A on persons other than companies.

Paras. 1–4

These adapt the specified sections of ICTA 1988 to the new system.

Para. 5

This modifies ICTA 1988, s.26. The new subs. (2A) restricts the set-off of losses under new ICTA 1988, s.379A (see para. 19 below) to those incurred on land leased at a rent higher than its annual value.

Paras. 6–8

These make further necessary amendments to ICTA 1988, ss.27, 30 and 32. The new s.32 (1A)–(1C) permit relief for machinery and plant which qualifies for capital allowances under the Capital Allowances Act 1990, ss.61 and 67, to operate within the context of a Schedule A business.

Para. 9

A premium chargeable to tax under ICTA 1988, s.34 will in future be treated as income in the computation of the profits or losses of a Schedule A business.

Paras. 10–17

These make further consequential amendments to ICTA 1988, ss.35–37, 82, 87, 96, 98 and 368.

Para. 18

The new ICTA 1988, s.375A takes account of the abolition of the present income tax relief for interest paid on a loan used to buy or improve property which is commercially let. Relief for such interest will instead be available as a deduction in computing the gains of a Schedule A business (see ss.39 and 42 above).

Para. 19

The new ICTA 1988, s.379A provides for the treatment of income tax Schedule A losses. Losses may generally be carried forward and set-off against future Schedule A profits. They may also be set-off against other income within prescribed limits and conditions.

Paras. 20–28

Further consequential amendments are made to ICTA 1988.

Paras. 29–35

Consequential amendments are also made to the Capital Allowances Act 1990.

Paras. 36–37

The relevant provisions of the TCGA 1992 will continue to operate in the context of a Schedule A business.

Para. 38
The "rent a room" provisions in the F (No2) A 1992 will continue to operate when furnished residential accommodation previously charged under Schedule D, Case VI becomes chargeable under Schedule A.

Section 42   SCHEDULE 7

COMMERCIALLY LET PROPERTY: CORPORATION TAX

1. In subsection (6) of section 338 of the Taxes Act 1988 (charges on income), for paragraph (d) and the words after that paragraph (allowance of interest as a charge on income in a case where it would be eligible for relief in the case of an individual) there shall be substituted the following paragraph—
    "(d) the interest qualifies under section 338A for treatment in accordance with this paragraph as a charge on income."
2. After section 338 of that Act there shall be inserted the following section—

"Charges on income: loans to buy land
338A.—(1) Subject to the following provisions of this section, interest shall qualify for treatment in accordance with section 338(6)(d) as a charge on income if—
    (a) at the time when the interest is paid the company in question owns an estate or interest in land, or the property in a caravan or house-boat, in the United Kingdom or the Republic of Ireland;
    (b) the interest is paid on a loan to defray money applied—
            (i) in purchasing that estate, interest or property, or another estate, interest or property absorbed into, or given up to obtain, that estate, interest or property;
            (ii) in improving or developing the land, or buildings on the land; or
            (iii) in paying off another loan in a case in which interest on that other loan would have qualified under this section for treatment as a charge on income had the loan not been paid off (and on the assumption, if the loan was free of interest, that it carried interest);
    (c) the land, caravan or house-boat—
            (i) is occupied by the company and used as the only or main residence of an individual;
            (ii) is occupied by the company and used otherwise than as a residence; or
            (iii) is, in any period of 52 weeks comprising the time at which the interest is payable, let at a commercial rent for more than 26 weeks and, when not so let, either available for letting at such a rent or occupied and used as mentioned in sub-paragraph (i) or (ii) above;
        and
    (d) the interest is not interest incurred by overdrawing an account or by debiting the account of any person as the holder of a credit card or under similar arrangements.
    (2) Subsections (2) and (7) of section 354 shall have effect in relation to subsection (1) above as they have effect in relation to subsection (1) of that section.
    (3) Interest shall qualify under this section for treatment as a charge on income by reference to any land, caravan or house-boat which is being used as the only or main residence of an individual to the extent only that the amount on which it is payable does not exceed the following limit, that is to say, the qualifying maximum for the year of assessment in which the payment is made reduced by the amount on which interest is payable by the company under any earlier loans so far as they—
    (a) are loans the interest on which qualifies under this section for treatment as a charge on income; and
    (b) fall within subsection (1)(b) above in respect of the same land, caravan or house-boat.
    (4) Accordingly—
    (a) if the amount on which interest is payable under any loan exceeds the limit specified in subsection (3) above, so much only of the interest that would otherwise qualify under this section shall so qualify as bears to the whole of that interest the same proportion as that part of that amount that does not exceed the limit bears to the whole of that amount; and
    (b) if the amount on which interest is payable under the earlier loans mentioned in that subsection is equal to or exceeds the qualifying maximum for the year of assessment

in which the interest is paid, none of the interest on the later loan shall qualify under this section for treatment as a charge on income.

(5) Subsections (1A) and (2) of section 355 shall have effect for the purposes of this section in relation to the condition in paragraph (c) of subsection (1) above as they have effect in relation to the condition referred to in section 355(1A)(a).

(6) Interest shall not qualify under this section for treatment as a charge on income by reference to any case in which—

(a) the land, caravan or house-boat is used as the only or main residence of an individual, and

(b) the interest is paid on a home improvement loan,

unless the loan was made before 6th April 1988; and subsections (2B) and (2C) of section 355 shall apply for the purposes of this subsection as they apply for the purposes of subsection (2A) of that section.

(7) Interest shall not qualify by virtue of subsection (1)(b)(i) above for treatment as a charge on income—

(a) where the purchaser has, since 15th April 1969, disposed of an estate or interest in the land, or the property in the caravan or house-boat, in question and it appears that the main purpose of the disposal and purchase was to obtain relief in respect of interest on the loan or to allow interest on the loan to be treated as a charge on income; or

(b) where the purchaser is directly or indirectly purchasing from a person who is connected with him and the price substantially exceeds the value of what is acquired;

and interest shall not qualify by virtue of subsection (1)(b)(ii) above for such treatment where the money spent is received directly or indirectly by a person connected with the person spending it and substantially exceeds the value of the work done.

(8) For the purposes of subsection (7) above one person is connected with another if he is so connected within the terms of section 839.

(9) In this section—

'caravan' and 'house-boat' have the same meanings as are given to them for the purposes of sections 354 to 366 by subsection (1) of section 367; and

'the qualifying maximum' has the same meaning as is given to it for the purposes of sections 356A to 357 by subsection (5) of that section;

and subsections (2) to (4) of section 367 shall apply with the necessary modifications for the determination of any question whether interest qualifies under this section for treatment as a charge on income as they apply for the determination of any question whether interest is eligible for relief under section 353 by virtue of section 354.

(10) References in this section to an estate or interest do not include references—

(a) to a rentcharge or, in Scotland, a superiority or the interest of a creditor in a contract of ground annual; or

(b) to the interest of a chargee or mortgagee or, in Scotland, the interest of a creditor in a charge or security of any kind over land."

GENERAL NOTE

This Schedule provides interest relief for corporation tax purposes on loans used to buy or improve property which is commercially let. It replaces the present form of relief which is given by reference to the current income tax rules.

Para. 1

This repeals the existing relief and introduces the new relief.

Para. 2

The new ICTA 1988, s.338A reproduces the interest relief for companies which was previously given by reference to the income tax rules. Where the relief applies, the interest is relieved as a charge on income.

Section 51   SCHEDULE 8

LIFE ASSURANCE BUSINESS

PART I

GENERAL AMENDMENTS

Classes of life assurance business

1. In section 431(2) of the Taxes Act 1988 (interpretative provisions relating to insurance companies), insert the following at the appropriate places in alphabetical order—

"pension business" has the meaning given by section 431B;
"life reinsurance business" has the meaning given by section 431C;
"overseas life assurance business" has the meaning given by section 431D;
"basic life assurance and general annuity business" has the meaning given by section 431F;
"reinsurance business" includes retrocession business.
2. After section 431A of the Taxes Act 1988 insert—

"Classes of life assurance business

Meaning of 'pension business'
431B.—(1) In this Chapter 'pension business' means so much of a company's life assurance business as is referable to contracts of the following descriptions or to the reinsurance of liabilities under such contracts.
(2) The descriptions of contracts are—
 (a) any contract with an individual who is, or would but for an insufficiency of profits or gains be, chargeable to income tax in respect of relevant earnings (as defined in section 623(1) and (2)) from a trade, profession, vocation, office or employment carried on or held by him, being a contract approved by the Board under section 620 or a substituted contract within the meaning of section 622(3);
 (b) any contract (including a contract of insurance) entered into for the purposes of, and made with the persons having the management of, an exempt approved scheme as defined in Chapter I of Part XIV, being a contract so framed that the liabilities undertaken by the insurance company under the contract correspond with liabilities against which the contract is intended to secure the scheme;
 (c) any contract made under approved personal pension arrangements within the meaning of Chapter IV of Part XIV;
 (d) any annuity contract entered into for the purposes of—
     (i) a scheme which is approved or is being considered for approval under Chapter I of Part XIV;
     (ii) a scheme which is a relevant statutory scheme for the purposes of Chapter I of Part XIV; or
     (iii) a fund to which section 608 applies,
  being a contract which is made with the persons having the management of the scheme or fund, or those persons and a member of or contributor to the scheme or fund, and by means of which relevant benefits (see subsections (3) and (4) below), and no other benefits, are secured;
 (e) any annuity contract which is entered into in substitution for a contract within paragraph (d) above and by means of which relevant benefits (see subsections (3) and (4) below), and no other benefits, are secured;
 (f) any contract with the trustees or other persons having the management of a scheme approved under section 620 or, subject to subsection (5) below, of a superannuation fund which was approved under section 208 of the 1970 Act, being a contract which—
     (i) was entered into for the purposes only of that scheme or fund or, in the case of a fund part only of which was approved under section 208, for the purposes only of that part of that fund, and
     (ii) (in the case of a contract entered into or varied after 1st August 1956) is so framed that the liabilities undertaken by the insurance company under the contract correspond with liabilities against which the contract is intended to secure the scheme or fund (or the relevant part of the fund).
(3) For the purposes of subsection (2)(d) and (e) above 'relevant benefits' means relevant benefits as defined by section 612(1) which correspond—
 (a) where subsection (2)(d)(i) above applies, or subsection (2)(e) above applies and the contract within subsection (2)(d) was entered into for the purposes of a scheme falling within subsection (2)(d)(i), with benefits that could be provided by a scheme approved under Chapter I of Part XIV;
 (b) where subsection (2)(d)(ii) above applies, or subsection (2)(e) above applies and the contract within subsection (2)(d) was entered into for the purposes of a scheme falling within subsection (2)(d)(ii), with benefits that could be provided by a scheme which is a relevant statutory scheme for the purposes of Chapter I of Part XIV;
 (c) where subsection (2)(d)(iii) above applies, or subsection (2)(e) above applies and the contract within subsection (2)(d) was entered into for the purposes of a fund falling within subsection (2)(d)(iii), with benefits that could be provided by a fund to which section 608 applies.

(4) For the purposes of subsection (3)(a), (b) or (c) above a hypothetical scheme or fund (rather than any particular scheme or fund), and benefits provided by a scheme or fund directly (rather than by means of an annuity contract), shall be taken.

(5) Subsection (2)(f) above shall not apply to a contract where the fund in question was approved under section 208 of the 1970 Act unless—

(a) immediately before 6th April 1980 premiums paid under the contract with the trustees or other persons having the management of the fund fell within section 323(4) of that Act (premiums referable to pension business); and

(b) the terms on which benefits are payable from the fund have not been altered since that time; and

(c) section 608 applies to the fund.

(6) In subsection (5) above 'premium' includes any consideration for an annuity.

Meaning of 'life reinsurance business'

431C.—(1) In this Chapter 'life reinsurance business' means reinsurance of life assurance business other than pension business or business of any description excluded from this section by regulations made by the Board.

(2) Regulations under subsection (1) above may describe the excluded business by reference to any circumstances appearing to the Board to be relevant.

Meaning of 'overseas life assurance business'

431D.—(1) In this Chapter 'overseas life assurance business' means life assurance business, other than pension business or life reinsurance business, which—

(a) in the case of life assurance business other than reinsurance business, is business with a policy holder or annuitant not residing in the United Kingdom, and

(b) in the case of reinsurance business, is—

(i) reinsurance of life assurance business with a policy holder or annuitant not residing in the United Kingdom, or

(ii) reinsurance of business within sub-paragraph (i) above or this sub-paragraph.

(2) Subject to subsections (5) and (7) below, in subsection (1) above the references to life assurance business with a policy holder or annuitant do not include life assurance business with a person who is an individual if—

(a) the policy holder or annuitant is not beneficially entitled to the rights conferred by the policy or contract for the business, or

(b) any benefits under the policy or contract for the business are or will be payable to a person other than the policy holder or annuitant (or his personal representatives) or to a number of persons not including him (or them).

(3) For the purposes of subsection (2) above any nomination by a policy holder or annuitant of an individual or individuals as the recipient or recipients of benefits payable on death shall be disregarded.

(4) Subject to subsections (5) and (7) below, in subsection (1) above the references to life assurance business with a policy holder or annuitant do not include life assurance business with a person who is not an individual.

(5) Subsections (2) and (4) above do not apply if—

(a) the rights conferred by the policy or contract for the business are held subject to a trust,

(b) the settlor does not reside in the United Kingdom, and

(c) each beneficiary is either an individual not residing in the United Kingdom or a charity.

(6) In subsection (5) above—

(a) 'settlor' means the person, or (where more than one) each of the persons, by whom the trust was directly or indirectly created (and for this purpose a person shall, in particular, be regarded as having created the trust if he provided or undertook to provide funds directly or indirectly for the purposes of the trust or made with any other person a reciprocal arrangement for that other person to create the trust),

(b) 'beneficiary' means any person who is, or will or may become, entitled to any benefit under the trust (including any person who may become so entitled on the exercise of a discretion by the trustees of the trust), and

(c) 'charity' means a person or body of persons established for charitable purposes only; and for the purpose of that subsection an individual who is a trustee (of any trust) shall not be regarded as an individual.

(7) Subsections (2) and (4) above do not apply if the policy or contract for the business was effected solely to provide benefits for or in respect of—
   (a) persons all, or all but an insignificant number, of whom are relevant overseas employees, or
   (b) spouses, widows, widowers, children or dependants of such persons.
(8) In subsection (7) above 'relevant overseas employees' means persons who are not residing in the United Kingdom and are—
   (a) employees of the policy holder or annuitant,
   (b) employees of a person connected with the policy holder or annuitant, or
   (c) employees in respect of whose employment there is established a superannuation fund to which section 615(3) applies;
and section 839 applies for the purposes of this subsection.

Overseas life assurance business: regulations

431E.—(1) The Board may by regulations make provision for giving effect to section 431D.
(2) Such regulations may, in particular—
   (a) provide that, in such circumstances as may be prescribed, any prescribed issue as to whether business is or is not overseas life assurance business (or overseas life assurance business of a particular kind) shall be determined by reference to such matters (including the giving of certificates or undertakings, the giving or possession of information or the making of declarations) as may be prescribed,
   (b) require companies to obtain certificates, undertakings, information or declarations from policy holders or annuitants, or from trustees or other companies, for the purposes of the regulations,
   (c) make provision for dealing with cases where any issue such as is mentioned in paragraph (a) above is (for any reason) wrongly determined, including provision allowing for the imposition of charges to tax (with or without limits on time) on the insurance company concerned or on the policy holders or annuitants concerned,
   (d) require companies to supply information and make available books, documents and other records for inspection on behalf of the Board, and
   (e) make provision (including provision imposing penalties) for contravention of, or non-compliance with, the regulations.
(3) The regulations may—
   (a) make different provision for different cases, and
   (b) contain such supplementary, incidental, consequential or transitional provision as appears to the Board to be appropriate.

Meaning of 'basic life assurance and general annuity business'

431F. In this Chapter 'basic life assurance and general annuity business' means life assurance business (including reinsurance business) other than pension business, life reinsurance business or overseas life assurance business.".
3. In section 432C(2) of the Taxes Act 1988 after "assets of the overseas life assurance fund" insert "or land in the United Kingdom linked to overseas life assurance business".
4.—(1) Section 438 of the Taxes Act 1988 is amended as follows.
(2) In subsection (1) for "life assurance fund and separate annuity fund, if any" substitute "long term business fund".
(3) In subsection (8) for "431(4)(c)" substitute "431B(2)(c)".
5.—(1) Section 440 of the Taxes Act 1988 is amended as follows.
(2) In subsection (3) for "paragraphs (a) to (d)" substitute "paragraphs (a) to (e)".
(3) For subsection (4) substitute—
   "(4) The categories referred to in subsections (1) to (3) above are—
   (a) assets linked solely to pension business;
   (b) assets linked solely to life reinsurance business;
   (c) assets of the overseas life assurance fund;
   (d) assets linked solely to basic life assurance and general annuity business;
   (e) assets of the long term business fund not within any of the preceding paragraphs;
   (f) other assets.".
6. In section 440A of the Taxes Act 1988, in subsection (2) for paragraphs (a) and (b) substitute—
   "(a) so many of the securities as are identified in the company's records as securities by reference to the value of which there are to be determined benefits provided for under

policies or contracts the effecting of all (or all but an insignificant proportion) of which constitutes the carrying on of—
    (i) pension business, or
    (ii) life reinsurance business, or
    (iii) basic life assurance and general annuity business,
shall be treated for the purposes of corporation tax as a separate holding linked solely to that business,".

7. In section 76(1)(d) of the Taxes Act 1988 after "pension business" insert ", life reinsurance business".

8. In Schedule 19AA to the Taxes Act 1988, in the closing words of paragraph 5(5) for "pension business or basic life assurance business" substitute "pension business, life reinsurance business or basic life assurance and general annuity business".

9.—(1) The Taxation of Chargeable Gains Act 1992 is amended as follows.

(2) In section 212(2) after "pension business" insert "or life reinsurance business".

(3) In section 214A(11)(a) for "any pension business or" substitute "any pension business or life reinsurance business of that company or to".

10.—(1) Schedule 18 to the Finance Act 1994 is amended as follows.

(2) In paragraph 1(5) for "life assurance fund and separate annuity fund, if any," substitute "long term business fund".

(3) In paragraph 1(6) after "pension business" insert ", life reinsurance business".

(4) In paragraph 4 omit the definition of "life assurance business" and after the definition of "non-life mutual business" insert—
    "and other expressions have the same meaning as in Chapter I of Part XII of the Taxes Act 1988.".

Linked assets

11.—(1) In section 431(2) of the Taxes Act 1988, for the definition of "linked assets" substitute—
    "linked assets", and related expressions, shall be construed in accordance with section 432ZA;".

(2) After section 432 of the Taxes Act 1988 insert—

"Linked assets
    432ZA.—(1) In this Chapter 'linked assets' means assets of an insurance company which are identified in its records as assets by reference to the value of which benefits provided for under a policy or contract are to be determined.

(2) Linked assets shall be taken—
    (a) to be linked to long term business of a particular category if the policies or contracts providing for the benefits concerned are policies or contracts the effecting of which constitutes the carrying on of business of that category; and
    (b) to be linked solely to long term business of a particular category if all (or all but an insignificant proportion) of the policies or contracts providing for the benefits concerned are policies or contracts the effecting of which constitutes the carrying on of business of that category.

(3) Where an asset is linked to more than one category of long term business, a part of the asset shall be taken to be linked to each category; and references in this Chapter to assets linked (but not solely linked) to any category of business shall be construed accordingly.

(4) Where subsection (3) above applies, the part of the asset linked to any category of business shall be a proportion determined as follows—
    (a) where in the records of the company values are shown for the asset in funds referable to particular categories of business, the proportion shall be determined by reference to those values;
    (b) in any other case the proportion shall be equal to the proportion which the total of the linked liabilities of the company referable to that category of business bears to the total of the linked liabilities of the company referable to all the categories of business to which the asset is linked.

(5) For the purposes of sections 432A to 432F—
    (a) income arising in any period from assets linked but not solely linked to a category of business,
    (b) gains arising in any period from the disposal of such assets, and
    (c) increases and decreases in the value of such assets,
shall be treated as arising to that category of business in the proportion which is the mean of the proportions determined under subsection (4) above at the beginning and end of the period.

(6) In this section 'linked liabilities' means liabilities in respect of benefits to be determined by reference to the value of linked assets.

(7) In the case of a policy or contract the effecting of which constitutes a class of life assurance business the fact that it also constitutes long term business other than life assurance business shall be disregarded for the purposes of this section unless the benefits to be provided which constitute long term business other than life assurance business are to be determined by reference to the value of assets.".

12.—(1) In the following provisions for "linked solely" substitute "linked"—

(a) section 432C(1), section 432D(1) (twice) and section 432E(3)(a) and (b) and (6)(a) of the Taxes Act 1988;

(b) paragraph 1(5)(b)(i) of Schedule 19AB to the Taxes Act 1988;

(c) paragraph 1(4)(b) of Schedule 18 to the Finance Act 1994.

(2) The amendments made by paragraph 11 above do not affect the meaning of "linked assets", and related expressions, in sections 214 and 214A of the Taxation of Chargeable Gains Act 1992 (transitional provisions relating to changes made in 1990 and 1991).

(3) In section 432 of the Taxes Act 1988 for "class" in each place where it occurs substitute "category".

13.—(1) Section 432A of the Taxes Act 1988 is amended as follows.

(2) For subsections (1) to (3) substitute—

"(1) This section has effect where in any period an insurance company carries on more than one category of business and it is necessary for the purposes of the Corporation Tax Acts to determine in relation to the period what parts of—

(a) income arising from the assets of the company's long term business fund, or

(b) gains or losses accruing on the disposal of such assets,

are referable to any category of business.

(2) The categories of business referred to in subsection (1) above are—

(a) pension business;

(b) life reinsurance business;

(c) overseas life assurance business;

(d) basic life assurance and general annuity business which is ordinary life assurance business;

(e) basic life assurance and general annuity business which is industrial assurance business; and

(f) long term business other than life assurance business.

(3) Income arising from, and gains or losses accruing on the disposal of, assets linked to any category of business (apart from overseas life assurance business) shall be referable to that category of business.".

(3) In subsections (5) and (6)(b)(i) for "any of the appropriate categories" substitute "any category".

(4) For subsection (7) substitute—

"(7) For the purposes of subsections (5) and (6) above—

(a) income, gains or losses are directly referable to a category of business if referable to that category by virtue of subsection (3) or (4) above, and

(b) assets are directly referable to a category of business if income arising from the assets is, and gains or losses accruing on the disposal of the assets are, so referable by virtue of subsection (3) above.".

(5) For subsection (9) substitute—

"(9) Where a company carries on overseas life assurance business—

(a) references in this section to liabilities do not include liabilities of that business, and

(b) the appropriate part of the investment reserve as defined by paragraph 4(2)(a) of Schedule 19AA shall be left out of account in determining that reserve for the purposes of this section.".

14.—(1) Section 432C of the Taxes Act 1988 is amended as follows.

(2) In subsection (1) for the words from "life assurance business" to "general annuity business" substitute "pension business, life reinsurance business, basic life assurance and general annuity business or long term business other than life assurance business".

(3) In subsection (3) for "any of the appropriate categories of business" substitute "any category of business".

(4) In subsection (4)(b) for "any of the appropriate categories of business" substitute "any category of business".

(5) In subsection (5), omit paragraph (a).

(6) For subsection (6) substitute—

"(6) For the purposes of this section, where a company carries on overseas life assurance business "liabilities" does not include liabilities of that business.".

15.—(1) Section 432D of the Taxes Act 1988 is amended as follows.

(2) In subsection (1) for the words from "life assurance business" to "general annuity business" substitute "pension business, life reinsurance business, basic life assurance and general annuity business or long term business other than life assurance business".

(3) In subsection (2) for "any of the appropriate categories of business" substitute "any category of business".

(4) For subsection (3) substitute—

"(3) For the purposes of subsection (2) above "the relevant fraction", in relation to a category of business, is the fraction of which—

(a) the numerator is the mean of the opening and closing liabilities of the relevant business so far as referable to the category, reduced by the mean of the opening and closing values of any assets of the relevant business directly referable to the category; and

(b) the denominator is the mean of the opening and closing liabilities of the relevant business, reduced by the mean of the opening and closing values of any assets of the relevant business directly referable to any category of business.

(4) For the purposes of subsections (2) and (3) above, the part of the amount brought into account as the increase or decrease in the value of assets which is directly referable to a category of business is the part referable to the category by virtue of subsection (1) above and assets are directly referable to a category of business if such part of the amount brought into account as the increase or decrease in the value of assets as is attributable to them is so referable.".

Receipts to be brought into account

16.—(1) For section 83 of the Finance Act 1989 substitute—

"Receipts to be brought into account

83.—(1) The following provisions of this section have effect where the profits of an insurance company in respect of its life assurance business are, for the purposes of the Taxes Act 1988, computed in accordance with the provisions of that Act applicable to Case I of Schedule D.

(2) So far as referable to that business, the following items, as brought into account for a period of account (and not otherwise), shall be taken into account as receipts of the period—

(a) the company's investment income from the assets of its long term business fund, and

(b) any increase in value (whether realised or not) of those assets.

If for any period of account there is a reduction in the value referred to in paragraph (b) above (as brought into account for the period), that reduction shall be taken into account as an expense of that period.

(3) In ascertaining whether or to what extent a company has incurred a loss in respect of that business any amount transferred into the company's long term business fund from other assets of the company, or otherwise added to that fund, shall be taken into account, in the period in which it is brought into account, as an increase in value of the assets of that fund within subsection (2)(b) above.

This subsection does not apply where, or to the extent that, the amount concerned—

(a) would fall to be taken into account as a receipt apart from this section,

(b) is otherwise taken into account under subsection (2) above, or

(c) is specifically exempted from tax.

Meaning of 'brought into account'

83A.—(1) In section 83 'brought into account' means brought into account in an account which is recognised for the purposes of that section.

(2) Subject to the following provisions of this section and to any regulations made by the Treasury, the accounts recognised for the purposes of that section are—

(a) a revenue account prepared for the purposes of the Insurance Companies Act 1982 in respect of the whole of the company's long term business;

(b) any separate revenue account required to be prepared under that Act in respect of a part of that business.

Paragraph (b) above does not include accounts required in respect of internal linked funds.

(3) Where there are prepared any such separate accounts as are mentioned in subsection (2)(b) above, reference shall be made to those accounts rather than to the account for the whole of the business.

(4) If in any such case the total of the items brought into account in the separate accounts is not equal to the total amount brought into account in the account prepared for the whole business, there shall be treated as having been required and prepared a further separate revenue account covering the balance.

(5) Where a company carries on both ordinary long term business and industrial assurance business, the references above to the company's long term business shall be construed as references to either or both of those businesses, as the case may require.".

(2) In section 432B of the Taxes Act 1988—

(a) in subsection (1) for the words from "brought into account" to "1982" substitute "brought into account, within the meaning of that section,"; and

(b) for subsection (2) substitute—

"(2) Where for that purpose reference falls to be made to more than one account recognised for the purposes of that section, the provisions of sections 432C to 432F apply separately in relation to each account.".

(3) In section 432E(1) of the Taxes Act 1988 for the words from "of the items referred to in subsection (1)" to "paragraph (b))" substitute "to be taken into account in accordance with section 83(2) of the Finance Act 1989 (that is to say, the aggregate amount to be taken into account as receipts reduced by the aggregate amount to be taken into account as expenses)".

(4) In section 436(3) of the Taxes Act 1988, after paragraph (a) insert—

"(aa) section 83(3) of that Act shall not apply;".

(5) In section 441(4) of the Taxes Act 1988, after paragraph (a) (and before the word "and" following that paragraph) insert—

"(aa) section 83(3) of that Act shall not apply,".

(6) In section 65(2) of the Finance (No.2) Act 1992 for paragraph (d) substitute—

"(d) section 83(2) of the Finance Act 1989 (amounts to be taken into account as receipts or expenses);".

Supplementary provisions as to apportionment

17.—(1) In section 432B of the Taxes Act 1988 (apportionment of receipts brought into account)—

(a) in subsections (1) and (2) for "sections 432C to 432E" substitute "sections 432C to 432F", and

(b) in subsection (3) for "section 432E applies" substitute "sections 432E and 432F apply".

(2) In section 432E of the Taxes Act 1988 (section 432B apportionment: participating funds)—

(a) in subsection (1), for the words from "shall be" to the end substitute "shall be the amount determined in accordance with subsection (2) below or, if greater, the amount determined in accordance with subsection (3) below."; and

(b) in subsection (5) at the end insert—

"References in this subsection to the amount determined in accordance with subsection (3) above are to that amount after making any deduction required by section 432F.".

(3) After section 432E of the Taxes Act 1988 insert—

"Section 432B apportionment: supplementary provisions

432F.—(1) The provisions of this section provide for the reduction of the amount determined in accordance with section 432E(3) ('the subsection (3) figure') for an accounting period in which that amount exceeds, or would otherwise exceed, the amount determined in accordance with section 432E(2) ('the subsection (2) figure').

(2) For each category of business in relation to which section 432E falls to be applied there shall be determined for each accounting period the amount (if any) by which the subsection (2) figure, after making any reduction required by section 432E(5), exceeds the subsection (3) figure ('the subsection (2) excess').

(3) Where there is a subsection (2) excess, the amount shall be carried forward and if in any subsequent accounting period the subsection (3) figure exceeds, or would otherwise exceed, the subsection (2) figure, it shall be reduced by the amount or cumulative amount of subsection (2) excesses so far as not previously used under this subsection.

(4) Where in an accounting period that amount is greater than is required to bring the subsection (3) figure down to the subsection (2) figure, the balance shall be carried forward and aggregated with any subsequent subsection (2) excess for use in subsequent accounting periods.".

(4) In section 444A of the Taxes Act 1988 (transfers of business) after subsection (3) insert—

"(3A) Any subsection (2) excess (within the meaning of section 432F(2)) which (assuming the transferor had continued to carry on the business transferred after the transfer) would have been available under section 432F(3) or (4) to reduce a subsection (3) figure (within the meaning of section 432F(1)) of the transferor in an accounting period following that which ends with the day on which transfer takes place—

(a) shall, instead, be treated as a subsection (2) excess of the transferee, and

(b) shall be taken into account in the first accounting period of the transferee ending after the date of the transfer (to reduce the subsection (3) figure or, as the case may be, to produce or increase a subsection (2) excess for that period),

in relation to the revenue account of the transferee dealing with or including the business transferred.".

(5) In section 444A(5) of the Taxes Act 1988 for "subsection (2) or (3)" substitute "subsection (2), (3) or (3A)".

Franked investment income: supplementary provisions

18.—(1) Chapter V of Part VI of the Taxes Act 1988 is amended as follows.

(2) In section 238(1) for the definition of "surplus of franked investment income" substitute—

" 'surplus of franked investment income' shall be construed in accordance with subsection (1A) below;".

(3) After that subsection insert—

"(1A) For the purposes of this Chapter, a company has a surplus of franked investment income in an accounting period if the amount of the franked investment income of the company in that period exceeds the amount of the franked payments made by it in that period.

For the purposes of determining whether a company has such a surplus, or the amount of the surplus, franked investment income that cannot be used to frank distributions of the company shall be disregarded.".

(4) For section 238(3) substitute—

"(3) References in this Chapter to using franked investment income to frank distributions of a company are to using the income in accordance with section 241(1) and Schedule 13 so as to relieve the company from, or obtain repayment of, advance corporation tax for which the company would otherwise be liable.".

(5) In section 241(3) for the words from the beginning to "the excess" substitute "Where a company has a surplus of franked investment income for any accounting period, the surplus".

(6) In section 241(5) omit the words from "(that is to say,"to "otherwise be liable)".

(7) In section 242(1)(b) omit "for purposes of section 241(3)".

(8) In section 242(9)—

(a) omit "by virtue of section 241(5)", and

(b) for "a company" substitute "the company".

19.—(1) Section 434 of the Taxes Act 1988 is amended as follows.

(2) For subsection (1) substitute—

"(1) Nothing in section 208 shall prevent franked investment income or foreign income dividends from being taken into account—

(a) in any computation of profits for the purposes of section 89(7) of the Finance Act 1989, or

(b) in any computation for the purposes of section 76(2) of the tax that would have been paid if the company had been charged to tax under Case I of Schedule D in respect of its life assurance business.".

(3) For subsection (3) substitute—

"(3) The policy holders' share of the franked investment income from investments held in connection with a company's life assurance business shall not be used under Chapter V of Part VI to frank distributions made by the company; but it may be the subject of a claim under section 242 and shall be treated for that purpose as a surplus of franked investment income additional to any surplus under section 238(1A).

For the purpose of ascertaining whether any surplus or what amount of surplus franked investment income falls to be carried forward under section 241(3), relief under section 242 shall be treated as given against the policy holders' share before other franked investment income.".

Computation of losses

20.—(1) For section 434A of the Taxes Act 1988 substitute—

"Computation of losses and limitation on relief
434A.—(1) In ascertaining whether or to what extent a company has incurred a loss on its life assurance business profits derived from investments held for the purposes of that business (including franked investment income of, and foreign income dividends arising to, a company resident in the United Kingdom) shall be treated as part of the profits of that business.

(2) Where for any accounting period the loss arising to an insurance company from its life assurance business falls to be computed in accordance with the provisions of this Act applicable to Case I of Schedule D, any loss resulting from the computation shall be reduced (but not below nil) by the aggregate of—

(a) any losses for that period under section 436, 441 or 439B, and

(b) the amount of interest and annuities treated as charges on income in computing for the period otherwise than in accordance with the provisions of this Act applicable to Case I of Schedule D the profits or losses of the company's life assurance business.

(3) In the case of a company carrying on life assurance business, no relief shall be allowable under—

(a) Chapter II (loss relief) or Chapter IV (group relief) of Part X, or

(b) Chapter II of Part II of the Finance Act 1993 so far as it has effect in relation to losses treated as non-trading losses for the purposes of section 160 of the Finance Act 1994,

against the policy holders' share of the relevant profits for any accounting period.

For the purposes of this subsection 'the policy holders' share of the relevant profits' has the same meaning as in section 88 of the Finance Act 1989.".

(2) In section 65(2) of the Finance (No. 2) Act 1992, for paragraph (a) substitute—

"(a) section 434A(1) of the Taxes Act 1988 (profits derived from investments held for purposes of life assurance business treated as profits of that business in ascertaining loss);".

Treatment of interest and annuities

21.—(1) After section 434A of the Taxes Act 1988 insert—

"Treatment of interest and annuities
434B.—(1) Where the profits or losses arising to an insurance company from its life assurance business, or any class of life assurance business, fall to be computed for any purpose in accordance with the provisions of this Act applicable to Case I of Schedule D, section 337(2)(b) shall not prevent the deduction of any interest or annuity payable by the company under a liability of its long term business so far as referable to its life assurance business or any class of that business.

(2) Nothing in subsection (1) above or in section 338(2) shall be construed as preventing any such interest or annuity as is mentioned in subsection (1) above, so far as referable to the company's basic life assurance and general annuity business, from being treated as a charge on income for the purposes of the computation of the profits or losses of that business otherwise than in accordance with Case I of Schedule D.".

(2) In section 88 of the Finance Act 1989, for subsection (3) substitute—

"(3) For the purposes of subsection (1) above, the relevant profits of a company for an accounting period are the income and gains of the company's life assurance business reduced by the aggregate amount of—

(a) expenses of management falling to be deducted under section 76 of the Taxes Act 1988, and

(b) charges on income,

so far as referable to the company's life assurance business.".

Interest on repayment of advance corporation tax

22. After section 434B of the Taxes Act 1988 (inserted by paragraph 21 above) insert—

"Interest on repayment of advance corporation tax
434C. Section 826(1) applies in a case where a repayment falls to be made of advance corporation tax paid by a company carrying on life assurance business in respect of distributions made by it.

In relation to such a case the material date for the purposes of that section is that specified in subsection (2A) of that section.".

Capital allowances

23.—(1) After section 434C of the Taxes Act 1988 (inserted by paragraph 22 above) insert—

"**Capital allowances: management assets**

434D.—(1) This section has effect with respect to the allowances and charges to be made under the 1990 Act in respect of 'management assets', that is, assets provided for use or used for the management of life assurance business carried on by a company.

(2) No allowances or charges shall be made under that Act in respect of expenditure on management assets except under Part II (machinery and plant).

(3) Where the company is charged to tax under section 441 in respect of the profits of its overseas life assurance business for an accounting period—

(a) any allowance falling to be made under Part II of the 1990 Act in respect of expenditure on the provision outside the United Kingdom of machinery or plant for use for the management of that business shall be given effect by treating it as an expense of the business for that period; and

(b) any charge in respect of such expenditure falling to be so made shall be given effect by treating it as a receipt of the business for that period;

and sections 73, 144 and 145 of the 1990 Act do not apply.

(4) Allowances and charges falling to be made under Part II of the 1990 Act in respect of expenditure in respect of management assets not falling within subsection (3) above shall be apportioned between the different classes of life assurance business carried on by the company.

The amount referable to any class of life assurance business shall be the relevant fraction of the amount of the allowance or charge, that is, the fraction of which—

(a) the numerator is the mean of the opening and closing liabilities of the class of life assurance concerned, and

(b) the denominator is the mean of the opening and closing liabilities of all the classes of life assurance business carried on by the company.

(5) Where the company is charged to tax under section 436, 439B or 441 in respect of the profits of its pension business, life reinsurance business or overseas life assurance business for an accounting period—

(a) any allowance falling to be made under Part II of the 1990 Act in respect of expenditure on the provision of machinery or plant for use for the management of that business shall be given effect by treating the relevant proportion of the allowance as an expense of that business for the purpose of calculating the Case VI profit for that period; and

(b) any charge in respect of such expenditure falling to be so made shall be given effect by treating the relevant proportion of the charge as a receipt of that business for that purpose.

(6) Where a company carries on basic life assurance and general annuity business and the profits arising from that business do not fall to be charged to tax in accordance with the provisions applicable to Case I of Schedule D—

(a) allowances falling to be given under Part II of the 1990 Act in respect of expenditure on management assets shall be treated as additional expenses of management within section 76; and

(b) any charge falling to be made under that Part in respect of such assets shall be chargeable to tax under Case VI of Schedule D.

(7) For the purposes of this section the purposes of the management of a business shall be taken to be those purposes expenditure on which would be treated as expenses of management within section 76.

(8) Expenditure to which this section applies shall not be taken into account otherwise than in accordance with this section.

This shall not be construed as preventing any allowance under Part II of the 1990 Act which falls to be given by virtue of this section from being taken into account—

(a) in any computation of profits for the purposes of section 89(7) of the Finance Act 1989, or

(b) in any computation for the purposes of section 76(2) of the tax that would have been paid if the company had been charged to tax under Case I of Schedule D in respect of its life assurance business.

Capital allowances: investment assets

434E.—(1) In this section 'investment asset' means an asset held by a company for the purposes of its life assurance business otherwise than for the management of that business.

(2) The letting by a company of an investment asset shall be treated for the purposes of section 61 of the 1990 Act (machinery and plant on lease) as a letting otherwise than in the course of a trade.

(3) Any allowance under Part V of the 1990 Act (agricultural buildings, &c.) in respect of an investment asset shall be made by way of discharge or repayment of tax and shall be available primarily against agricultural income and income which is the subject of a balancing charge.

Effect shall be given to any balancing charge under that Part in respect of an investment asset by treating the amount on which the charge is to be made as agricultural income.

(4) Any allowance under the 1990 Act in respect of an investment asset shall be treated as referable to the category or categories of business to which income arising from the asset is or would be referable and shall be apportioned in accordance with section 432A in the same way as such income.

(5) No allowance under the 1990 Act in respect of an investment asset shall be taken into account—

(a) in computing the profits of any class of life assurance business under section 436, 439B or 441, or

(b) where the company is charged to tax in respect of its life assurance business under Case I of Schedule D, in computing the profits of that business.

(6) Where any allowance under the 1990 Act in respect of an investment asset falls to be taken into account (having regard to subsection (5) above), only such allowances as are referable to the company's basic life assurance and general annuity business shall be given effect under section 145(1) of that Act, and then only against income referable to that business; and section 145(3) shall not apply.".

(2) In section 75(4) of the Taxes Act 1988 omit the words "and insurance".

(3) In section 86 of the Finance Act 1989 (spreading of relief for acquisition expenses), after subsection (5) insert—

"(5A) References in this section to expenses of management do not include any amounts treated as additional expenses of management by virtue of section 434D(6)(a) of the Taxes Act 1988 (capital allowances in respect of expenditure on management assets).".

24. In Chapter I of Part II of the Capital Allowances Act 1990 (machinery and plant), for section 28 (investment companies and life assurance companies) substitute—

"Investment companies

28.—(1) This Part and the other provisions of the Corporation Tax Acts relating to allowances or charges under this Part apply with the necessary adaptations in relation to machinery and plant provided for use or used for the purposes of the management of the business of an investment company (as defined in section 130 of the principal Act) as they apply in relation to machinery and plant provided for use or used for the purposes of a trade.

(2) Effect shall be given to allowances and charges falling to be made by virtue of this section as follows—

(a) any allowance falling to be made for any accounting period shall, as far as may be, be given effect by deducting the amount of the allowance from any income for the period of the business, and in so far as effect cannot be so given section 75(4) of the principal Act shall apply; and

(b) effect shall be given to any charge falling to be made under this section by treating the amount on which the charge is to be made as income of the business;

and sections 73, 144 and 145 do not apply.

(3) Except as provided by subsection (2) above, the Corporation Tax Acts apply in relation to allowances or charges falling to be made by virtue of this section as if they were to be made in taxing a trade.

(4) For the purposes of this section the purposes of the management of a business shall be taken to be those purposes expenditure on which would be treated as expenses of management within section 75 of the principal Act.

(5) Corresponding allowances or charges in the case of the same machinery or plant shall not be made under this Part both under this section and in some other way.

(6) Expenditure to which this section applies shall not be taken into account otherwise than under this Part or as provided by section 75(4) of the principal Act.".

Treatment of tax-free income

25.—(1) In the Taxes Act 1988 omit—

(a) section 474(1)(b); and

(b) in section 475(2)(a), the words from "or," to "life assurance business".

(2) In section 474 of the Taxes Act 1988, at the end insert—

"(3) In this section any reference to insurance business includes a reference to insurance business of any category.".

Taxation of pure reinsurance business

26. After section 439 of the Taxes Act 1988 insert—

"Taxation of pure reinsurance business

439A. If a company does not carry on life assurance business other than reinsurance business, and none of that business is of a type excluded from this section by regulations made by the Board, the profits of that business shall be charged to tax in accordance with Case I of Schedule D and not otherwise.".

Life reinsurance business: separate charge on profits

27.—(1) After section 439A of the Taxes Act 1988 (inserted by paragraph 26 above) insert—

"Life reinsurance business: separate charge on profits

439B.—(1) Where a company carries on life reinsurance business and the profits arising from that business are not charged to tax in accordance with the provisions applicable to Case I of Schedule D, then, subject as follows, those profits shall be treated as income within Schedule D and be chargeable to tax under Case VI of that Schedule, and for that purpose—

    (a) that business shall be treated separately, and

    (b) subject to paragraph (a) above, the profits from it shall be computed in accordance with the provisions of this Act applicable to Case I of Schedule D.

(2) Subsection (1) above does not apply to so much of reinsurance business of any description excluded from that subsection by regulations made by the Board.

Regulations under this subsection may describe the excluded business by reference to any circumstances appearing to the Board to be relevant.

(3) In making the computation referred to in subsection (1) above—

    (a) sections 82(1), (2) and (4) and 83 of the Finance Act 1989 shall apply with the necessary modifications and in particular with the omission of the words "tax or" in section 82(1)(a),

    (b) section 83(3) of that Act shall not apply, and

    (c) there may be set off against the profits any loss, to be computed on the same basis as the profits, which has arisen from life reinsurance business in any previous accounting period beginning on or after 1st January 1995.

(4) Section 396 shall not be taken to apply to a loss incurred by a company on life reinsurance business.

(5) Nothing in section 128 or 399(1) shall affect the operation of this section.

(6) Gains accruing to a company which are referable to its life reinsurance business shall not be chargeable gains.

(7) In ascertaining whether or to what extent a company has incurred a loss on its life reinsurance business, franked investment income and foreign income dividends shall be taken into account (notwithstanding anything in section 208) as part of the profits of that business.".

(2) In section 444A(3)(a) of the Taxes Act 1988 after "section 436(3)(c)" insert "or 439B(3)(c)".

(3) In section 724(3) and (4) of the Taxes Act 1988 after "section 436" insert ", 439B".

Provisions applicable to charge under Case I of Schedule D

28.—(1) After section 440A of the Taxes Act 1988 insert—

"Modifications where tax charged under Case I of Schedule D

440B.—(1) The following provisions apply where the profits of a company's life assurance business are charged to tax in accordance with Case I of Schedule D.

(2) Section 438 applies as if in subsections (6), (6B) and (6E) for the reference to any profit arising to the company and computed under section 436 there were substituted a reference to the profit that would arise on a computation under section 436 if the profits of the company's life assurance business were not charged to tax under Case I of Schedule D.

(3) Section 440(1) and (2) apply as if the only categories set out in subsection (4) of that section were—

    (a) assets of the long term business fund, and

    (b) other assets.

(4) Section 440A applies as if for paragraphs (a) to (e) of subsection (2) there were substituted—

'(a) so many of the securities as are identified in the company's records as securities by reference to the value of which there are to be determined benefits provided for under policies or contracts the effecting of all (or all but an insignificant proportion) of which constitutes the carrying on of long term business, shall be treated for the purposes of corporation tax as a separate holding linked solely to that business, and

(b) any remaining securities shall be treated for those purposes as a separate holding which is not of the description mentioned in the preceding paragraph.'.

(5) Section 212(1) of the 1992 Act does not apply, but without prejudice to the bringing into account of any amounts deferred under section 213(1) or 214A(2) of that Act from any accounting period beginning before 1st January 1995.".

(2) In section 438 of the Taxes Act 1988, after subsection (8) insert—

"(9) In a case where the profits of a company's life assurance business are charged to tax in accordance with Case I of Schedule D this section has effect with the modification specified in section 440B(2).".

(3) In section 440 of the Taxes Act 1988, after subsection (5) insert—

"(6) In a case where the profits of a company's life assurance business are charged to tax in accordance with Case I of Schedule D this section has effect with the modification specified in section 440B(3).".

(4) In section 440A of the Taxes Act 1988, after subsection (6) insert—

"(7) In a case where the profits of a company's life assurance business are charged to tax in accordance with Case I of Schedule D this section has effect with the modification specified in section 440B(4).".

(5) In section 212 of the Taxation of Chargeable Gains Act 1992, after subsection (7) insert—

"(7A) In a case where the profits of a company's life assurance business are charged to tax in accordance with Case I of Schedule D subsection (1) above has effect subject to section 440B(5) of the Taxes Act.".

29. In section 438(3) and (3AA) of the Taxes Act 1988 after "taken into account" insert "—(a)" and after "pension business" insert—

", or

(b) where the company is charged to tax in respect of its life assurance business under Case I of Schedule D, in computing the profits of that business.".

Overseas life assurance business

30. In section 441(1) of the Taxes Act 1988 omit the words "resident in the United Kingdom".

31. In section 441A of the Taxes Act 1988 for subsections (3) to (6) substitute—

"(3) A company shall be entitled to such a tax credit if and to the extent that regulations made by the Board so provide.

(4) Regulations under subsection (3) above may, in particular, provide for the entitlement of a company to a tax credit, and the amount to which the company is entitled, to be determined by reference to—

(a) the residence of any description of policy holders or annuitants prescribed by the regulations, or

(b) the location of any branch or agency at or through which the policy or contract for any business is effected.

(5) Subsections (2) and (3) of section 431E apply in relation to regulations under subsection (3) above as they apply in relation to regulations under subsection (1) of that section but as if any issue which falls to be decided for the purposes of the regulations under subsection (3) above were an issue such as is mentioned in subsection (2)(a) of that section.".

32. After section 441A of the Taxes Act 1988 insert—

"Treatment of UK land

441B.—(1) This section applies to land in the United Kingdom which—

(a) is held by a company as an asset linked to the company's overseas life assurance business, or

(b) is held by a company which is charged to tax under Case I of Schedule D in respect of its life assurance business as an asset by reference to the value of which benefits under any policy or contract are to be determined, where the policy or contract (or, in the case of a reinsurance contract, the underlying policy or contract) is held by a person not residing in the United Kingdom.

(2) Income arising from land to which this section applies shall be treated for the purposes of this Chapter as referable to basic life assurance and general annuity business.

(3) Where (apart from this subsection) an insurance company would not be carrying on basic life assurance and general annuity business it shall be treated as carrying on such business if any income of the company is treated as referable to such business by subsection (2) above.

(4) A company may be charged to tax by virtue of this section—

(a) notwithstanding section 439A, and

(b) whether or not the income to which subsection (2) above relates is taken into account in computing the profits of the company for the purposes of any charge to tax in accordance with Case I of Schedule D.

(5) In this section 'land' has the same meaning as in Schedule 19AA.".

33. In paragraph 1(2) of Schedule 19AA to the Taxes Act 1988, at the end insert "(including any modification of any of those provisions made by paragraph 14A of Schedule 19AC)".

Taxation of investment return where risk reinsured

34. After section 442 of the Taxes Act 1988 insert—

"Taxation of investment return where risk reinsured

442A.—(1) Where an insurance company reinsures any risk in respect of a policy or contract attributable to its basic life assurance and general annuity business, the investment return on the policy or contract shall be treated as accruing to the company over the period of the reinsurance arrangement and shall be charged to tax under Case VI of Schedule D.

(2) The Board may make provision by regulations as to the amount of investment return to be treated as accruing in each accounting period during which the reinsurance arrangement is in force.

(3) The regulations may, in particular, provide that the investment return to be treated as accruing to the company in respect of a policy or contract in any accounting period shall be calculated by reference to—

(a) the aggregate of the sums paid by the company to the reinsurer during that accounting period and any earlier accounting periods by way of premium or otherwise;

(b) the aggregate of the sums paid by the reinsurer to the company during that accounting period and any earlier accounting periods by way of commission or otherwise;

(c) the aggregate amount of the net investment return treated as accruing to the company in any earlier accounting periods, that is to say, net of tax at such rate as may be prescribed; and

(d) such percentage rate of return as may be prescribed.

(4) The regulations shall provide that the amount of investment return to be treated as accruing to the company in respect of a policy or contract in the final accounting period during which the policy or contract is in force is the amount, ascertained in accordance with regulations, by which the profit over the whole period during which the policy or contract, and the reinsurance arrangement, were in force exceeds the aggregate of the amounts treated as accruing in earlier accounting periods.

If that profit is less than the aggregate of the amounts treated as accruing in earlier accounting periods, the difference shall go to reduce the amounts treated by virtue of this section as arising in that accounting period from other policies or contracts, and if not fully so relieved may be carried forward and set against any such amounts in subsequent accounting periods.

(5) Regulations under this section—

(a) may exclude from the operation of this section such descriptions of insurance company, such descriptions of policies or contracts and such descriptions of reinsurance arrangements as may be prescribed;

(b) may make such supplementary provision as to the ascertainment of the investment return to be treated as accruing to the company as appears to the Board to be appropriate, including provision requiring payments made during an accounting period to be treated as made on such date or dates as may be prescribed; and

(c) may make different provision for different cases or descriptions of case.

(6) In this section 'prescribed' means prescribed by regulations under this section.".

PART II

APPLICATION OF PROVISIONS TO OVERSEAS LIFE INSURANCE COMPANIES

35.—(1) After paragraph 5 of Schedule 19AC to the Taxes Act 1988 insert—

"5A.—(1) Where an overseas life insurance company receives a qualifying distribution made by a company resident in the United Kingdom and the distribution (or part of the distribution)—

(a) would fall within paragraph (a), (aa) or (ab) of section 11(2) but for the exclusion contained in that paragraph, and

(b) is referable to life assurance business, but not to overseas life assurance business,

then the recipient shall be treated for the purposes of the Corporation Tax Acts as entitled to such a tax credit in respect of the distribution (or part of the distribution) as it would be entitled to under section 231 if it were resident in the United Kingdom.

(2) Where part only of a qualifying distribution would fall within paragraph (ab) of section 11(2) but for the exclusion contained in that paragraph, the tax credit to which the recipient shall be treated as entitled by virtue of sub-paragraph (1) above is the proportionate part of the tax credit to which the recipient would be so treated as entitled in respect of the whole of the distribution.

5B.—(1) An overseas life insurance company may, on making a claim for the purpose, require that any UK distribution income for an accounting period shall for all or any of the purposes mentioned in sub-paragraph (2) below be treated as if it were a like amount of profits chargeable to corporation tax; and where it does so—

(a) the provisions mentioned in that sub-paragraph shall apply to reduce the amount of the UK distribution income, and

(b) the company shall be entitled to have paid to it the amount of the tax credits comprised in the amount of UK distribution income which is so reduced.

(2) The purposes for which a claim may be made under this paragraph are those of—

(a) the setting of trading losses against total profits under section 393A(1);

(b) the deduction of charges on income under section 338 or paragraph 5 of Schedule 4;

(c) the deduction of expenses of management under section 76;

(d) the setting of certain capital allowances against total profits under section 145(3) of the 1990 Act.

(3) Subsections (3), (4) and (8) of section 242 shall apply for the purposes of a claim under this paragraph as they apply for the purposes of a claim under that section.

(4) In this paragraph 'UK distribution income' means income of an overseas life insurance company which consists of a distribution (or part of a distribution) in respect of which the company is entitled to a tax credit (and which accordingly represents income equal to the aggregate of the amount or value of the distribution (or part) and the amount of that credit).

5C.—(1) This paragraph applies to income from the investments of an overseas life insurance company attributable to the basic life assurance and general annuity business of the branch or agency in the United Kingdom through which the company carries on life assurance business.

(2) Where, in computing the income to which this paragraph applies, any interest on any securities issued by the Treasury is excluded by virtue of a condition of the issue of those securities regulating the treatment of the interest on them for tax purposes, the relief under section 76 shall be reduced so that it bears to the amount of relief which would be granted apart from this sub-paragraph the same proportion as the amount of that income excluding that interest bears to the amount of that income including that interest.".

(2) In paragraph 2(1) of Schedule 19AC to the Taxes Act 1988, for "section 444D" substitute "paragraph 5B of Schedule 19AC".

(3) After paragraph 6(4) of that Schedule insert—

"(4A) In that subsection the following definition shall be inserted at the appropriate place—

'UK distribution income' has the meaning given by paragraph 5B(4) of Schedule 19AC;".

(4) In section 475(6) of the Taxes Act 1988 for "section 444E(2)" (twice) substitute "paragraph 5C(2) of Schedule 19AC".

(5) In paragraph 2(2) of Schedule 8A to the Finance Act 1989 for "section 444D(4) of the Taxes Act 1988" substitute "paragraph 5B(4) of that Schedule".

36. In paragraph 5(1) of Schedule 19AC to the Taxes Act 1988, in the notionally inserted subsection (6B)—

(a) for "242" substitute "section 242", and

(b) for "444D" substitute "paragraph 5B of Schedule 19AC".

37. In paragraph 6 of Schedule 19AC to the Taxes Act 1988, omit sub-paragraphs (3) and (4).

38. After paragraph 6 of Schedule 19AC to the Taxes Act 1988 insert—

"6A. In section 431D(1), the words 'carried on through a branch or agency in the United Kingdom by an overseas life insurance company' shall be treated as inserted after the words 'means life assurance business'.".

39. For paragraph 7 of Schedule 19AC to the Taxes Act 1988 substitute—

"7.—(1) Section 432A has effect as if the references in subsections (3), (6) and (8) to assets were to such of the assets concerned as are—

(a) section 11(2)(b) assets,

(b) section 11(2)(c) assets, or

(c) assets which by virtue of section 11B are attributed to the branch or agency in the United Kingdom through which the company carries on life assurance business;

and as if the references in subsections (6) and (8) to liabilities were to such of the liabilities concerned as are attributable to the branch or agency.

Expressions used in this sub-paragraph to which a meaning is given by section 11A have that meaning.

(2) For the purposes of section 432A as it applies in relation to an overseas life insurance company, income which falls within section 11(2)(aa) or (ab), and chargeable gains or allowable losses which fall within section 11(2)(d) or (e)—

(a) shall not be referable to long term business other than life assurance business; and

(b) shall be apportioned under subsections (5) and (6) of that section separately from other income, gains and losses.

(3) For the purposes of the application of section 432A(6) in relation to such income, gains or losses as are mentioned in sub-paragraph (2) above—

(a) 'liabilities' does not include liabilities of the long term business other than life assurance business;

(b) the value of assets directly referable to any category of business does not include assets directly referable to long term business other than life assurance business; and

(c) the reference in section 432A(6)(b)(ii) to the investment reserve shall be construed as a reference to so much of the investment reserve as is not referable to long term business other than life assurance business.".

40.—(1) Paragraph 8 of Schedule 19AC to the Taxes Act 1988 is amended as follows.

(2) In sub-paragraph (1)—

(a) for "paragraph 1" substitute "paragraph 1C"; and

(b) for "the word '1982' " substitute "the words 'brought into account, within the meaning of that section,' ".

(3) In sub-paragraph (2) for "paragraph 1(6), (7) or (8)" substitute "any provision of paragraph 1C".

(4) For sub-paragraph (3) substitute—

"(3) Subsection (3) of section 432B shall have effect as if after the words 'with which an account is concerned' there were inserted the words 'or in respect of which items are treated as brought into account by virtue of paragraph 1C of Schedule 8A to the Finance Act 1989'; and that subsection and sections 432C to 432E shall have effect as if the reference to relevant business were to relevant business of the branch or agency in the United Kingdom through which the company carries on life assurance business.".

41. In paragraph 9(1) of Schedule 19AC to the Taxes Act 1988 in the notionally inserted section 434(1A)—

(a) after "UK distribution income of" insert ", or foreign income dividends arising to,"; and

(b) for the words from "as part of the profit" to the end substitute—

"—

(a) in any computation of profits for the purposes of section 89(7) of the Finance Act 1989, or

(b) in any computation for the purposes of section 76(2) of the tax that would have been paid if the company had been charged to tax under Case I of Schedule D in respect of its life assurance business.".

42. After paragraph 9 of Schedule 19AC to the Taxes Act 1988 insert—

"9A. In section 434A(1)—

(a) the words 'UK distribution income' shall be treated as substituted for 'franked investment income', and

(b) the words 'an overseas life insurance company' shall be treated as substituted for 'a company resident in the United Kingdom'.

9B. In section 434B the following subsection shall be treated as inserted after subsection (2)—

"(3) An overseas life insurance company shall not be entitled to treat as paid out of profits or gains brought into charge to income tax any part of the annuities paid by the company which is referable to its life assurance business.".

9C. In its application to an overseas life insurance company section 434D(4) shall have effect as if the references to liabilities were only to such liabilities as are attributable to the branch or agency in the United Kingdom through which the company carries on the business concerned.".

43.—(1) In paragraph 10(1) of Schedule 19AC to the Taxes Act 1988, in the notionally inserted section 438(3A)—
(a) for "subsection (6)" substitute "subsections (6) and (6B)";
(b) after "UK distribution income of" insert ", or foreign income dividends arising to,";
(c) after "taken into account" insert "—(a)"; and
(d) after "pension business" insert—
", or
(b) where the company is charged to tax in respect of its life assurance business under Case I of Schedule D, in computing the profits of that business.".
(2) In paragraph 10(2) for "subsections (6) and (6A)" substitute "subsections (6), (6A), (6D) and (6E)".
44. After paragraph 10 of Schedule 19AC to the Taxes Act 1988 insert—
"10A. In section 439B the following subsection shall be treated as inserted after subsection (7) of that section—
"(7A) In ascertaining whether or to what extent the company has incurred a loss on its life reinsurance business, UK distribution income of an overseas life insurance company shall be taken into account (notwithstanding anything in paragraph (a), (aa) or (ab) of section 11(2)) as part of the profits of that business.".
10B.—(1) Where the company mentioned in section 440(1) is an overseas life insurance company, section 440 has effect with the following modifications.
(2) Subsection (4) shall be treated as if—
(a) in paragraphs (a), (b), (d), (e) and (f) the words 'UK assets' were substituted for the words 'assets'; and
(b) at the end there were inserted—
"(g) section 11C assets;
(h) non-UK assets.".
(3) The following subsection shall be treated as inserted at the end of the section—
"(7) For the purposes of this section—
(a) UK assets are—
(i) section 11(2)(b) assets;
(ii) section 11(2)(c) assets; or
(iii) assets which by virtue of section 11B are attributed to the branch or agency in the United Kingdom through which the company carries on life assurance business;
(b) section 11C assets are assets—
(i) (in a case where section 11C (other than subsection (9)) applies) of the relevant fund, other than UK assets; or
(ii) (in a case where that section including that subsection applies) of the relevant funds, other than UK assets;
(c) non-UK assets are assets which are not UK assets or section 11C assets;
and any expression used in this subsection to which a meaning is given by section 11A has that meaning.".
(4) Where one of the companies mentioned in section 440(2) is an overseas life insurance company, section 440(2)(b) shall have effect as if for the words 'is within another of those categories' there were substituted 'is not within the corresponding category'.
(5) Where the transferor company mentioned in section 440(2) is an overseas life insurance company, section 440 shall have effect, as regards the time immediately before the acquisition, with the modifications in sub-paragraphs (2) and (3) above.
(6) Where the acquiring company mentioned in section 440(2) is an overseas life insurance company, section 440 shall have effect, as regards the time immediately after the acquisition, with the modifications in sub-paragraphs (2) and (3) above.
10C.—(1) In section 440B the following subsection shall be treated as substituted for subsection (3)—
"(3) Section 440(1) and (2) have effect as if the only categories specified in subsection (4) of that section were—
(a) UK assets of the long term business fund,
(b) other UK assets,
(c) section 11C assets, and
(d) non-UK assets,
(those expressions having the meanings given by section 440(7)).".
(2) The following subsection shall be treated as substituted for subsection (4) of that section—
"(4) Section 440A applies as if for paragraphs (a) to (e) of subsection (2) there were substituted—

"(a) so many of the UK securities as are identified in the company's records as securities by reference to the value of which there are to be determined benefits provided for under policies or contracts the effecting of all (or all but an insignificant proportion) of which constitutes the carrying on of long term business, shall be treated for the purposes of corporation tax as a separate holding linked solely to that business,

(b) any remaining UK securities shall be treated for those purposes as a separate holding which is not of the description mentioned in the preceding paragraph,

(c) the section 11C securities shall be treated for those purposes as a separate holding which is not of any of the descriptions mentioned in the preceding paragraphs, and

(d) the non-UK securities shall be treated for those purposes as a separate holding which is not of any of the descriptions mentioned in the preceding paragraphs." ".

45.—(1) Paragraph 11 of Schedule 19AC to the Taxes Act 1988 is amended as follows.

(2) For sub-paragraph (1) substitute—

"(1) In section 440A(2), in paragraph (a) the words "UK securities" shall be treated as substituted for the word "securities" in the first place where it occurs.".

(3) Omit sub-paragraph (2).

(4) In sub-paragraph (5) renumber the notionally inserted subsection as (6A).

46. After paragraph 11 of Schedule 19AC to the Taxes Act 1988 insert—

"11A.—(1) In section 441A, the following subsection shall be treated as inserted after subsection (1)—

"(1A) The exclusion from section 11(2)(a), (aa) and (ab) of distributions received from companies resident in the United Kingdom shall not apply in relation to a distribution in respect of any asset of the overseas life assurance fund of an overseas life insurance company.".

(2) The following subsection shall be treated as substituted for subsections (2) and (3) of that section—

"(3) An overseas life insurance company shall be entitled to a tax credit in respect of a distribution which—

(a) is a distribution in respect of an asset of the company's overseas life assurance fund, and

(b) is received from a company resident in the United Kingdom,

if and to the extent that regulations made by the Board so provide.".

11B. In section 442A the following subsection shall be treated as inserted after subsection (6)—

"(7) In the case of an overseas life insurance company, the investment return treated as accruing under this section in any accounting period in relation to a policy or contract shall be treated as chargeable profits within section 11(2) of the Taxes Act 1988 where the policy or contract is one which in that accounting period gives rise, or but for the reinsurance arrangement would give rise, to such profits.".""

47. In paragraph 12(1) of Schedule 19AC to the Taxes Act 1988, for "section 444D" substitute "paragraph 5B of Schedule 19AC".

48. After paragraph 14 of Schedule 19AC to the Taxes Act 1988 insert—

"14A.—(1) In Schedule 19AA, paragraph 5(5)(c) (and the reference to it in paragraph 2(3) of that Schedule) shall be treated as omitted.

(2) The following paragraph shall be treated as inserted at the end of that Schedule—

"6. In its application to an overseas life insurance company this Schedule shall have effect as if—

(a) the references in paragraphs 2 and 3 to assets of the long term business fund were to such of the assets as are—

(i) section 11(2)(b) assets;

(ii) section 11(2)(c) assets; or

(iii) assets which by virtue of section 11B are attributed to the branch or agency in the United Kingdom through which the company carries on life assurance business; and

(b) the references in paragraphs 2 and 4 to the liabilities of the company's long term business were to such of those liabilities as are attributable to the branch or agency;

and any expression used in this paragraph to which a meaning is given by section 11A has that meaning.".".

49.—(1) Schedule 8A to the Finance Act 1989 is amended as follows.

(2) For paragraph 1 substitute—

"1.—(1) In their application to an overseas life insurance company sections 83 and 83A of this Act shall have effect with the modifications specified in paragraphs 1A to 1C below.

(2) In those paragraphs—

(a) any reference to the Taxes Act 1988 is a reference to that Act as it has effect in relation to such a company by virtue of Schedule 19AC to that Act; and

(b) any expression to which a meaning is given by section 11A of that Act has that meaning.

1A.—(1) The reference in section 83(2)(a) to investment income shall be construed as a reference to such of the income concerned as is attributable to the branch or agency in the United Kingdom through which the company carries on life assurance business.

(2) The reference to assets in section 83(2)(b) (as it applies apart from subsection (3) of that section) shall be construed as a reference to such of the assets concerned—

(a) as are—

(i) section 11(2)(b) assets;

(ii) section 11(2)(c) assets; or

(iii) assets which by virtue of section 11B of the Taxes Act 1988 are attributed to the branch or agency; or

(b) as are assets—

(i) (in a case where section 11C of that Act (other than subsection (9)) applies) of the relevant fund, or

(ii) (in a case where that section including that subsection applies) of the relevant funds,

other than assets which fall within paragraph (a) above.

(3) In determining for the purposes of section 83(2) (as it applies apart from subsection (3) of that section) whether there has been any increase or reduction in the value (whether realised or not) of assets—

(a) no regard shall be had to any period of time during which an asset held by the company does not fall within paragraph (a) or (b) of sub-paragraph (2) above; and

(b) in the case of an asset which falls within paragraph (b) of that sub-paragraph, only the specified portion of any increase or reduction in the value of the asset shall be taken into account.

For the purposes of paragraph (b) above the specified portion of any increase or reduction in the value of an asset is found by applying to that increase or reduction the same fraction as would, by virtue of section 11C of the Taxes Act 1988, be applied to any relevant gain accruing to the company on the disposal of the asset.

(4) For the reference in section 83(3) to any amount being transferred into the company's long term business fund from other assets of the company, or otherwise added to that fund, there shall be substituted a reference to assets becoming assets of the long term business fund used or held for the purposes of the company's United Kingdom branch or agency, having immediately previously been held by the company otherwise than as assets of that fund or used or held otherwise than for those purposes.

The amount of the increase in value under section 83(2)(b), as it applies in relation to such a transfer, shall be taken to be an amount equal to the value of the assets transferred.

1B. The references in section 83A to the company's long term business shall be construed as references to the whole of that business or to the whole of that business other than business in respect of which preparation of a revenue account for the purposes of the Insurance Companies Act 1982 is not required.

1C.—(1) Where for a period of account any investment income referred to in section 83(2)(a) is not otherwise brought into account within the meaning of that section, it shall be treated as brought into account for the period if it arises in the period.

(2) Where for a period of account any increase in value referred to in section 83(2)(b) (as it applies apart from subsection (3) of that section) is not otherwise brought into account within the meaning of that section, it shall be treated as brought into account for the period if it is shown in the company's records as available to fund one or both of the following for the period, namely, bonuses to policy holders and dividends to shareholders.

(3) Where for a period of account any reduction in value referred to in section 83(2) (as it applies apart from subsection (3) of that section) is not otherwise brought into account within the meaning of that section, it shall be treated as brought into account for the period if it is shown in the company's records as reducing sums available to fund one or both of the following for the period, namely, bonuses to policy holders and dividends to shareholders.

(4) Where in any period of account any such transfer is made as is mentioned in section 83(3) which is not otherwise brought into account within the meaning of that section, it shall be treated as brought into account for the period in which it is made.".

(3) In paragraph 2(7) for the words following paragraph (b) substitute—
"and in paragraph (b) above "the specified portion" has the same meaning as in paragraph 1A(3)(b) above.".

(4) After paragraph 2(7) insert—
"(7A) For the purposes of this paragraph any expression to which a meaning is given by section 11A of the Taxes Act 1988 has that meaning.".

PART III

SUPPLEMENTARY PROVISIONS

Penalties

50. In the Table in section 98 of the Taxes Management Act 1970 (penalties for failure to comply with notice or to furnish information etc.), the entry "regulations under section 431E(1) or 441A(3);" shall be inserted—
(a) in the first column after the entry relating to regulations under section 333 of the Taxes Act 1988, and
(b) in the second column after the entry relating to section 375(5) of that Act.

Miscellaneous

51.—(1) The Taxes Act 1988 is amended as follows.
(2) Before section 432 insert the heading "*Separation of different categories of business*".
(3) In the sidenote to section 432 for "classes" substitute "categories".
(4) Before section 434 insert the heading "*Miscellaneous provisions relating to life assurance business*".
(5) In the sidenote to section 436 for "Annuity business and pension business" substitute "Pension business".

Commencement

52. The amendment made by paragraph 43(2) above shall be deemed always to have had effect.

53.—(1) The amendments made by paragraph 17 above have effect in relation to accounting periods ending on or after 1st January 1994.

(2) In the first accounting period of a company ending on or after 1st January 1994 in which the subsection (3) figure for any category of business exceeds the subsection (2) figure, the subsection (2) figure shall be treated as increased by an amount not exceeding the amount or aggregate amount of any subsection (2) excesses in relation to that category of business for accounting periods beginning on or after 1st January 1990 and ending before 1st January 1994, but not so as to produce a subsection (2) excess for that period.

For this purpose the subsection (2) excess for an accounting period beginning on or after 1st January 1990 and ending before 1st January 1994 shall be determined without regard to the fact that in any other such accounting period the subsection (3) figure exceeded the subsection (2) figure.

Expressions used in this sub-paragraph have the same meaning as in section 432F of the Taxes Act 1988.

(3) Where a transfer mentioned in section 444A of the Taxes Act 1988 took place at the end of an accounting period of the transferor beginning on or after 1st January 1990 and ending before 1st January 1994, section 444A(3A) shall have effect in relation to the transfer as if it read—
"(3A) Any subsection (2) excess (within the meaning of section 432F(2)) of the transferor for an accounting period beginning on or after 1st January 1990 and ending before 1st January 1994 which (assuming the transferor had continued to carry on the business transferred after the transfer) would have been available to increase the subsection (2) figure (within the meaning of section 432F(1)) of the transferor in the first accounting period ending on or after 1st January 1994 in which the subsection (3) figure exceeded the subsection (2) figure—
(a) shall, instead, be treated as a subsection (2) excess of the transferee, and
(b) shall be taken into account to increase the subsection (2) figure of the transferee in its first accounting period ending on or after 1st January 1994 in which the subsection (3) figure exceeds the subsection (2) figure, but not so as to produce a subsection (2) excess for that period,
in relation to the revenue account of the transferee dealing with or including the business transferred.

For this purpose the subsection (2) excess for an accounting period beginning on or after 1st January 1990 and ending before 1st January 1994 shall be determined without regard to the fact that in any other such accounting period the subsection (3) figure exceeded the subsection (2) figure.".

54. The amendment made by paragraph 22 above applies in relation to distributions made by an insurance company in any accounting period ending after 30th September 1993.

55.—(1) Subject to sub-paragraphs (2) and (3) below, the amendments made by the following provisions of this Schedule have effect in relation to accounting periods beginning on or after 1st November 1994—

    paragraph 1 so far as relating to the definition of "overseas life assurance business",

    paragraph 2 so far as relating to sections 431D and 431E of the Taxes Act 1988,

    paragraphs 3, 25, 30 to 33, 37, 38 and 45(1) and (3),

    paragraph 46 so far as relating to paragraph 11A of Schedule 19AC to the Taxes Act 1988, and

    paragraphs 48 and 50.

(2) Where the policy or contract for any life assurance business was made before 1st November 1994, the amendments made by this Schedule (and the repeals consequential on those amendments) shall not have effect for determining whether the business is overseas life assurance business.

(3) Where the policy or contract for any life assurance business effected by a company resident in the United Kingdom at or through a branch or agency outside the United Kingdom was made before 29th November 1994, subsections (2) to (8) of section 431D of the Taxes Act 1988 shall not have effect for determining whether the business is overseas life assurance business.

56. The amendments made by paragraphs 41(a) and 43(1) above have effect in relation to foreign income dividends paid after 29th November 1994.

57.—(1) Except as provided by paragraphs 52 to 56 above, and subject to sub-paragraph (2) below, the amendments made by provisions of this Schedule have effect in relation to accounting periods beginning on or after 1st January 1995.

(2) Section 442A of the Taxes Act 1988 does not apply in relation to the reinsurance of a policy or contract where the policy or contract was made, and the reinsurance arrangement effected, before 29th November 1994.

58. Any power to make regulations exercisable by virtue of an amendment made by any provision of this Schedule may be exercised so as to make provision having effect in relation to any accounting period in relation to which that provision has effect in accordance with paragraph 55 or 57 above.

GENERAL NOTE

This implements a number of changes to the rules for taxing life assurance companies.

Para. 1

The list of different types of life assurance business is amended.

Para. 2

This contains detailed descriptions of the four types of life assurance business listed in para. 1, inserting them as ICTA 1988, ss.431B, 431C, 431D and 431F. One new type is included (life reinsurance business—see para. 27 below). The existing definition of overseas life assurance business in s.431D is extended to include certain business written directly from the U.K. for the benefit of an individual resident in another state in the European Economic Area (EEA) and also certain insurances entered into by European employers for the benefit of their employees. The other definitions are otherwise unchanged except from some structural improvements. New s.431E authorises the Revenue to make regulations regarding the administration of overseas life assurance business.

Para. 3

The amendment of ICTA 1988, s.432C(2) is consequent on a new rule introduced by para. 32 below concerning income from land in the U.K. linked to overseas life assurance business.

Para. 4

This makes a change arising from the restructuring of the definition of pension business and updates a reference.

Paras. 5–10

These make consequential amendments to existing legislation, to take account of the introduction of life reinsurance business.

Para. 11

The new ICTA 1988, s.432ZA extends the current rule for allocating income and gains in respect of investment-linked life assurance business where the benefits due to the policyholder are determined by reference to linked assets. The new section provides that income and gains from assets which are partly linked to one type of business and partly to another will be allocated on a pro-rata basis, instead of following a general rule for allocating income and gains from non-linked assets. It also determines how income and gains arising from the assets are to be split between the different categories of business and allows certain non-linked benefits to be ignored when determining whether an asset is a linked asset.

Para. 12

This makes consequential amendments arising from the extended definition of linked assets in para. 11.

Para. 13

The amendments to ICTA 1988, s.432A, which deals with apportionment of income and gains, take account of the new category of life reinsurance business and of the new provisions regarding linked assets in para. 11. They also make simplifications and structural improvements. In particular, it will no longer be necessary to calculate the capital gains of overseas life assurance business, which are exempt from tax.

Para. 14

This makes similar changes to existing provisions for identifying the investment income which is to be included in a computation of the profits of different types of life assurance business where that is written wholly on a without-profits basis, *i.e.* the policyholder does not participate in the profits of the business by way of bonuses.

Para. 15

This makes changes and structural improvements, similar to those in para. 14 above, to the provisions for identifying the investment appreciation (or depreciation) to be included in a computation of the profits of different types of life assurance business written wholly on a without-profits basis.

Para. 16

The new FA 1989, ss.83 and 83A are designed to prevent tax relief being given for a loss when additional assets are introduced into an insurance company's long-term business fund to match an increase in the company's liabilities to its policyholders. Previously, no account was taken of the funds introduced, but the increase in the liabilities to policyholders was relievable for tax. The Treasury is given power to make regulations further defining which accounts are recognised for the purposes of s.83. Consequential amendments are made to other legislation.

Para. 17

The new ICTA 1988, s.432F modifies the existing provisions for dividing out the investment return from assets in computing the profits of types of life assurance business where some business is with-profits, *i.e.* where policyholders participate in the profits of the business by way of bonuses. This has been done by comparing the bonuses allocated to with-profits policyholders with the lower of the investment return on the fund as a whole or the yield on 15-year gilts—known as the "floor" calculation. The higher amount determined the tax liability and the lower amount was ignored. From 1994 accounting periods onwards, where the first calculation gives a higher amount than the second "floor" calculation for a particular class of business, any excess may be carried forward and used to reduce the allocation of investment return in any later year in which the second "floor" calculation would otherwise determine the tax liability for that class.

The new ICTA 1988, S.444A(3A) ensures that any s.432F excess may be carried forward when a transfer of business between insurance companies takes place.

Paras. 18 and 19

These make minor changes to the provisions regarding payment of tax credits attaching to dividends received ("franked investment income"). A claim may be made if a company has management expenses or other reliefs in excess of its profits. This may be reversed in a subsequent year in which a company makes dividend payments in excess of the dividends which it receives. This reversing mechanism can cause distortions for life assurance companies which are not allowed to set-off all the dividends they received when calculating the advance corporation tax (ACT) they have to pay, since dividends are split between those relevant to shareholders and those relevant to policyholders. The amendments restore the expenses where there is an ACT restriction. They also make a clearer divide between policyholders' and shareholders' dividends and tax credits and clarify the operation of the rules applying to life assurance companies when dividends are paid.

Para. 20
    The substituted ICTA 1988, s.434A reduces any overall loss from life assurance business by losses specifically related to pension business, overseas life assurance business and life reinsurance business and by interest and annuities deducted from income otherwise chargeable to tax. This will prevent a company from obtaining relief twice for the same loss.

Para. 21
    The new ICTA 1988, s.434B provides that annuities (and interest) payable under a liability deriving from life assurance business are to be deducted in arriving at the trading profit, instead of being treated exclusively as charges on income, which are a final deduction made from the total profits of the company. The previous provision could result in a larger than intended proportion of profits being charged at the normal corporation tax rate of 33 per cent rather than the special 25 per cent rate applicable to the profits accruing to policyholders, or vice versa.
    The amendment to FA 1989, s.88 makes a consequential clarification of the existing rule regarding the measurement of the policyholders' share of the profits that are charged at the lower rate of tax.

Para. 22
    Interest on overpaid tax will be allowed where a life assurance company has overpaid advance corporation tax (ACT). Uniquely, life assurance companies may be unable to determine accurately the amount of ACT which they should pay until some time after the end of their accounting period.

Para. 23
    The new ICTA 1988, s.434D provides that capital allowances on assets used in the management of a life assurance company's business are to be apportioned between the different types of business and allowed, as appropriate, in computing, *e.g.*, the profits of pension business, overseas life assurance business or life reinsurance business, or as an expense of management of basic life assurance and general annuity business.
    The new s.434E gives a clear entitlement to capital allowances on investment assets. It also contains provisions regarding the allocation of allowances between the different types of life assurance business. An amount allocated to basic life assurance and general annuity business will obtain relief against the separately taxable income and gains of that business, but there will be no relief generally where an amount is allocated to other types of business, such as pension business.

Para. 24
    The substituted Capital Allowances Act 1990, s.28, which formerly dealt with both investment companies and life assurance companies, reflects the removal of the provisions regarding the latter to para. 23 above, and updates the way in which capital allowances for investment companies are granted.

Para. 25
    The amendments to ICTA 1988, ss.474 and 475 adjust the provisions relating to foreign dividends, foreign state dividends and free of tax securities issued by the Treasury where these are held by non-resident life assurance companies, to reflect the creation of the new category of life reinsurance business and the fact that such companies will now be able to write overseas life assurance business.

Para. 26
    The new ICTA 1988, s.439A provides that a company carrying on nothing but reinsurance business will pay tax on its trading profits only, subject to regulations made by the Revenue.

Para. 27
    The new ICTA 1988, s.439B deals with the situation where a company carries on life reinsurance business as well as any other type of life assurance business. It will be charged to tax on the trading profits from life reinsurance business in a similar way to that which applies to pension business and overseas life assurance business profits. The investment income and gains will not be charged to tax. This result reflects that for a pure reinsurer under para. 26 above. Losses from life reinsurance business may be carried forward and will be available to the transferee if there is a transfer of life reinsurance business. As with para. 26, the Revenue retains a power to exclude certain types of business from the provisions by regulation.

Para. 28
The modifications and amendments made by this paragraph are the result of the new basis for taxing a pure reinsurance company under Case I of Schedule D. The amendments ensure that such companies are taxed on their trading profits and eliminate inappropriate charges to corporation tax on chargeable gains.

Para. 29
Franked investment income and foreign income dividends are brought into charge in computing Case I profits.

Para. 30
This is a consequential change for overseas life assurance business arising from the extension to include business written directly from the U.K. in the case of U.K. branches of overseas insurance companies (see ICTA 1988, s.431D, inserted by para. 2 above).

Para. 31
The Revenue is given the power to make regulations concerning entitlement to tax credits for overseas life assurance business. The existing provision, under which entitlement is determined by reference to the location of the branch which has written the business, is not suitable for business written directly from the U.K.

Para. 32
The new ICTA 1988, s.441B deals with the consequences of changes made to the type of assets which can be treated as included in the fund used to back overseas life assurance business. In future, land in the U.K. will largely be excluded from this fund. The new section ensures that income from land in the U.K. which is contractually linked to overseas life assurance business will be taxed in full on the normal basis.

Para. 33
This makes another consequential amendment resulting from the extension of overseas life assurance business to U.K. branches of an overseas insurance company.

Para. 34
The new ICTA 1988, s.442A introduces a charge to tax where a company buys reinsurance of its basic life assurance and general annuity business (BLAGAB). Any investment return derived from the reinsurance is brought into charge in order to preserve the normal tax charge on the investment income and gains accruing under a BLAGAB. The Revenue is given the power to make regulations determining the amount of the investment return that is to be treated as accruing in each year. In the accounting period during which the reinsurance ends, there will be a sweep-up calculation and the amounts charged year by year will be compared with the total return to ensure that the correct total amount is charged.

Paras. 35–49
This Part, comprising paras. 35–49, makes changes, with similar effect to those detailed in previous paragraphs, to the existing special provisions in ICTA 1988, Sched. 19AC for U.K. branches of overseas life insurance companies and also further adapts the provisions relating to foreign income dividends.

Paras. 35–40
These provide that a U.K. branch of an overseas life insurance company may undertake certain overseas life assurance business with individuals and employers resident in other European Economic Area (EEA) states (see para. 2 above for the corresponding provisions relating to U.K. insurance companies). Other consequential changes are made to the existing provisions regarding the taxation of these overseas companies.

Paras. 41 and 43
These correct a minor technical defect in the legislation in FA 1994 for foreign income dividends. The change will allow these dividends to be taken into account as part of the company's trading profits and, where these are separately calculated, as part of the pension business profits. The provisions under which a company can elect for part of the franked investment income and foreign income dividends it receives to be excluded from its pension business or Case I profit are adapted to fit the circumstances of an overseas company.

Para. 42

This adapts, for overseas life insurance companies, the provisions in para. 20 regarding a life assurance business loss and those in para. 23 concerning the way capital allowances are apportioned between different classes of life assurance business. It also re-enacts existing provisions which prevent an overseas company from treating annuities and pensions which it pays as paid out of profits on which it bears income tax, but widens these provisions to cover all types of life assurance business.

Paras. 44 and 45

These make various adaptations for overseas life insurance companies in the new provisions in paras. 27 and 28 concerning the tax treatment of pure reinsurers and life reinsurance business.

Para. 46

The provisions dealing with overseas life assurance business in paras. 2 and 31 and for the tax charge in respect of reinsured basic life assurance and general annuity business in para. 34 are adapted for overseas life insurance companies.

Para. 47

This makes a consequential change as a result of the restructuring of the rules dealing with the tax credits of an overseas life insurance company (see para. 35).

Para. 48

This adapts the provisions for identifying the assets of the overseas life assurance fund.

Para. 49

The new FA 1989, ss.83 and 83A (see para. 16) are adapted for the circumstances of overseas life insurance companies by appropriate amendments to Sched. 8A of that Act.

Para. 50

Penalties may be imposed for failure to provide information required under the regulations concerning overseas life assurance business which may be made under new ICTA 1988, s.431E (see para. 2) and the substituted ICTA 1988, s.441A (see para. 31).

Para. 51

This contains some consequential retitling.

Paras. 52–57

These contain the commencement provisions. The amendment to ICTA 1988, Sched. 19AC, para. 10(2) (see para. 43 above) is given retrospective effect. The provisions in para. 17 regarding the apportionment of income between different types of business apply for accounting periods ending on or after January 1, 1994, subject to transitional provisions relating to the period 1990–94. Interest on overpaid ACT (see para. 22) will apply for accounting periods ending after September 30, 1993 to coincide with the introduction of the "Pay and File" system for corporation tax. The new provisions regarding overseas life assurance business take effect generally from November 1, 1994, subject to the exclusion of ICTA 1988, s.431D(2)–(8) (see para. 2) in relation to business written by a U.K. resident company through a non-resident branch or agency before November 29, 1994. Foreign income dividends paid after November 29, 1994 will be brought into the computation of pension business profits made by an overseas life insurance company. The other changes take effect in the first accounting period of a company beginning on or after January 1, 1995, save that the imputation of income under a reinsurance contract (see para. 34) only applies to business written on or after November 29, 1994.

Para. 58

The same commencement rule applies to regulations made under the provisions to which they relate.

Section 53   SCHEDULE 9

TRANSFER OF LIFE INSURANCE BUSINESS

Consequential amendment of references to sanctioned transfers

1.—(1) In the enactments specified in sub-paragraph (2) below, for the words "section 49 of the Insurance Companies Act 1982", in each place where they occur, there shall be substituted "Part I of Schedule 2C to the Insurance Companies Act 1982".

(2) The enactments mentioned in sub-paragraph (1) above are—
(a) section 12(7A) of the Taxes Act 1988 (accounting periods);
(b) sections 440(2)(a) and 444A(1) of that Act (transfer of assets or business of insurance company);
(c) section 460(10A) of that Act (transfer of business to friendly society); and
(d) sections 211(1), 213(5), 214(11) and 214A(7) of the Taxation of Chargeable Gains Act 1992 (transfers of business).
(3) In section 444A(3)(b) of the Taxes Act 1988 (losses treated as losses of transferee)—
(a) after "where" there shall be inserted "the transfer relates to any overseas life assurance business or"; and
(b) for "overseas life assurance" there shall be substituted "such".

Modification of the Taxes Act 1988 in relation to overseas life insurance companies

2.—(1) Schedule 19AC to the Taxes Act 1988 (modification of Act in relation to overseas life insurance company) shall be amended as follows.
(2) After paragraph 4 there shall be inserted the following paragraph—
"4A.—(1) In section 12(7A), the reference to a transfer of the whole or part of a company's long term business in accordance with a scheme sanctioned by a court under Part I of Schedule 2C to the Insurance Companies Act 1982 shall be treated as including a reference to a qualifying overseas transfer.
(2) In this paragraph 'a qualifying overseas transfer' means so much of any transfer of the whole or any part of the business of an overseas life insurance company carried on through a branch or agency in the United Kingdom as takes place in accordance with any authorisation granted outside the United Kingdom for the purposes of Article 11 of the third long term insurance Directive.
(3) In sub-paragraph (2) above 'the third long term insurance Directive' has the same meaning as in that Act of 1982."
(3) After the paragraph 10A inserted by Schedule 8 to this Act there shall be inserted the following paragraph—
"10AA. In section 440(2)(a), the reference to a transfer of the whole or part of a company's long term business in accordance with a scheme sanctioned by a court under Part I of Schedule 2C to the Insurance Companies Act 1982 shall be treated as including a reference to a qualifying overseas transfer (within the meaning of paragraph 4A above)."
(4) Before paragraph 12 there shall be inserted the following paragraph—
"11C. In sections 444A(1) and 460(10A), the references to a transfer of the whole or part of a company's long term business in accordance with a scheme sanctioned by a court under Part I of Schedule 2C to the Insurance Companies Act 1982 shall be treated as including references to a qualifying overseas transfer (within the meaning of paragraph 4A above)."

Modification of the Capital Allowances Act 1990

3. For subsection (1) of section 152A of the Capital Allowances Act 1990 (transfer of insurance company business), there shall be substituted the following subsections—
"(1) Subject to subsection (1A) below, this section applies where assets are transferred as part of, or in connection with, the transfer ('a relevant transfer') of the whole or part of the business of an insurance company ('the transferor') to another company ('the transferee') if the relevant transfer is—
(a) a transfer, in accordance with a scheme sanctioned by a court under Part I of Schedule 2C to the Insurance Companies Act 1982, of the whole or part of any long term business of the transferor; or
(b) a qualifying overseas transfer (within the meaning of paragraph 4A of Schedule 19AC to the principal Act).
(1A) This section does not apply in relation to any asset transferred to a company resident outside the United Kingdom unless the asset would fall to be treated, immediately after the relevant transfer, as either—
(a) an asset held for use for the purposes of the management of the whole or any part of so much of any business carried on by that company as is carried on through a branch or agency in the United Kingdom; or
(b) an asset which is otherwise held for the purposes of the whole or any part of so much of any business carried on by that company as is carried on through such a branch or agency.

(1B) In subsection (1) above 'insurance company' has the same meaning as in Chapter I of Part XII of the principal Act; and in subsection (1A) above, the reference to the purposes of the management of any business is to be taken as a reference to those purposes expenditure on which falls, in relation to that business, to be treated for the purposes of sections 75 and 76 of the principal Act as expenses of management."

Modification of the Taxation of Chargeable Gains Act 1992

4. In subsection (5) of section 213 of the Taxation of Chargeable Gains Act 1992 (spreading of gains and losses under section 212 where there is a transfer of long term business), at the beginning there shall be inserted "Subject to subsections (5A) to (7) below"; and after that subsection there shall be inserted the following subsection—

"(5A) Subsection (5) above shall not apply where the transferee is resident outside the United Kingdom unless the business to which the transfer relates is carried on by the transferee, for a period beginning with the time when the transfer takes effect, through a branch or agency in the United Kingdom."

5. In subsection (7) of section 214A of that Act of 1992 (application of transitional provisions where there is a transfer of long term business), at the beginning there shall be inserted "Subject to subsections (7A) and (8) below"; and after that subsection there shall be inserted the following subsection—

"(7A) Paragraph (b) of subsection (7) above shall not apply where the transferee is resident outside the United Kingdom unless the business to which the transfer relates is carried on by the transferee, for a period beginning with the time when the transfer takes effect, through a branch or agency in the United Kingdom."

6.—(1) Schedule 7B to that Act of 1992 (modification of Act in application to overseas life insurance companies) shall be amended as follows.

(2) After paragraph 9 there shall be inserted the following paragraph—

"9A. In section 211(1), the reference to a transfer of the whole or part of a company's long term business in accordance with a scheme sanctioned by a court under Part I of Schedule 2C to the Insurance Companies Act 1982 shall be treated as including a reference to any qualifying overseas transfer (within the meaning of paragraph 4A of Schedule 19AC to the Taxes Act)."

(3) In paragraph 11, after sub-paragraph (1) there shall be inserted the following sub-paragraph—

"(1A) In section 213(5), the reference to a transfer of the whole or part of a company's long term business in accordance with a scheme sanctioned by a court under Part I of Schedule 2C to the Insurance Companies Act 1982 shall be treated as including a reference to any qualifying overseas transfer (within the meaning of paragraph 4A of Schedule 19AC to the Taxes Act)."

(4) In sub-paragraph (1) of paragraph 12, after paragraph (b) of the subsection (12) which, for the purpose of modifying section 214, is set out in that sub-paragraph, there shall be inserted the following paragraph—

"(c) the reference in subsection (11) to a transfer of the whole or part of a company's long term business in accordance with a scheme sanctioned by a court under Part I of Schedule 2C to the Insurance Companies Act 1982 were to be treated as including a reference to any qualifying overseas transfer (within the meaning of paragraph 4A of Schedule 19AC to the Taxes Act), and the references in that subsection to the business to which the transfer relates were to be construed accordingly;".

(5) In paragraph 13, after sub-paragraph (2) there shall be inserted the following sub-paragraph—

"(2A) In subsection (7) of that section, the reference to a transfer of the whole or part of a company's long term business in accordance with a scheme sanctioned by a court under Part I of Schedule 2C to the Insurance Companies Act 1982 shall be treated as including a reference to any qualifying overseas transfer (within the meaning of paragraph 4A of Schedule 19AC to the Taxes Act); and the references in that subsection and in subsection (8) of that section to the business to which the transfer relates shall be construed accordingly."

GENERAL NOTE

The Schedule makes various changes to the provisions relating to transfer of life insurance business.

Para. 1

The references to the Insurance Companies Act 1982 are amended to bring them in line with changes made for the Single Market in insurance.

Para. 2

The various special provisions that apply on a transfer of U.K. business authorised by a U.K. court are made available on a transfer of business carried on in the U.K. by a branch of an E.C. company which is authorised in that company's home state.

Para. 3

Capital allowances will continue to be available on transfers authorised in another member state, as they are on transfers authorised by a U.K. court, unless the assets concerned are not to be used for the purposes of a business within the charge to U.K. tax.

Para. 4

Tax charges which would otherwise arise on a deemed disposal of unit trust holdings after the transfer of business are instead crystallised if the transfer is to a company which will not carry on the transferred business through a branch in the U.K.

Para. 5

This contains a similar provision to para. 4 to crystallise tax charges on a transfer of business outside the U.K. which are otherwise defined under a transitional provision for deemed disposals of unit trust holdings.

Para. 6

Modifications to CGT legislation, similar to those for income tax in para. 2, are made to cater for transfers of business by a branch of an E.C. company authorised in that company's home state.

Section 54   SCHEDULE 10

FRIENDLY SOCIETIES

Tax exempt life or endowment business

1.—(1) Section 460 of the Taxes Act 1988 (exemption from tax in respect of life or endowment business) shall be amended as follows.

(2) In paragraph (c) of subsection (2), before sub-paragraph (ai) there shall be inserted the following sub-paragraph—

"(zai) where the profits relate to contracts made on or after the day on which the Finance Act 1995 was passed, of the assurance of gross sums under contracts under which the total premiums payable in any period of 12 months exceed £270 or of the granting of annuities of annual amounts exceeding £156;".

(3) In sub-paragraph (ai) of that paragraph, after "passed" there shall be inserted "but before the day on which the Finance Act 1995 was passed".

(4) In subsection (3), for the words "subsection (2)(c)(ai)," in each place where they occur, there shall be substituted "subsection (2)(c)(zai), (ai),".

(5) In subsection (4A), for "the Finance Act 1991" there shall be substituted "the Finance Act 1995".

(6) In subsection (4B), for the words from "variation made" onwards there shall be substituted "variation made—

(a) in the period beginning with 25th July 1991 and ending with 31st July 1992, or

(b) in the period beginning with the day on which the Finance Act 1995 was passed and ending with 31st March 1996,

the contract shall, for the purposes of subsection (2)(c) above, be treated, in relation to any profits relating to it as varied, as made at the time of the variation."

Maximum benefits payable to members

2.—(1) Section 464 of that Act (maximum benefits payable to members) shall be amended as follows.

(2) In subsection (3), before paragraph (za) there shall be inserted the following paragraph—

"(zza) contracts under which the total premiums payable in any period of 12 months exceed £270; or".

(3) In paragraph (za) of that subsection, after "contracts" there shall be inserted "made before the day on which the Finance Act 1995 was passed and".

(4) In subsection (4A), for "the Finance Act 1991" there shall be substituted "the Finance Act 1995".

(5) In subsection (4B), for the words from "variation made" onwards there shall be substituted "variation made—

(a) in the period beginning with 25th July 1991 and ending with 31st July 1992, or

(b) in the period beginning with the day on which the Finance Act 1995 was passed and ending with 31st March 1996,

the contract shall, for the purposes of subsection (3) above, be treated, in relation to times when the contract has effect as varied, as made at the time of the variation."

Qualifying policies

3. In paragraph 3 of Schedule 15 to that Act (friendly society policies that are qualifying policies), sub-paragraph (2)(c) (condition limiting consideration for early surrender) shall cease to have effect.

4.—(1) This paragraph applies to any policy which—

(a) was issued by a friendly society, or a branch of a friendly society, in the course of tax exempt life or endowment business (as defined in section 466 of the Taxes Act 1988); and

(b) was effected by a contract made after 31st August 1987 and before the day on which this Act is passed.

(2) Where—

(a) the amount payable by way of premium under a policy to which this paragraph applies is increased by virtue of a variation made in the period beginning with the day on which this Act is passed and ending with 31st March 1996, and

(b) the variation is not such as to cause a person to become in breach of the limits in section 464 of the Taxes Act 1988,

Schedule 15 to that Act, in its application to the policy, shall have effect, in relation to that variation, with the omission of paragraph 4(3)(a) and the insertion at the end of paragraph 18(2) of the words set out in sub-paragraph (3) below.

(3) Those words are as follows, that is to say, "and as if for paragraph 3(2)(b) above there were substituted—

'(b) subject to sub-paragraph (4) below, the premiums payable under the policy shall be premiums of equal or rateable amounts payable at yearly or shorter intervals—

(i) over the whole of the term of the policy as from the variation, or

(ii) where premiums are not payable for any period after the person liable to pay them or whose life is insured has attained a specified age, being an age attained at a time not less than ten years after the beginning of the term of the policy, over the whole of the remainder of the period for which premiums are payable.' "

GENERAL NOTE

Para. 1

The maximum annual premium allowed under a life assurance policy insured by a friendly society in the course of its tax exempt life or endowment business is increased from £200 to £270 as from May 1, 1995, The new maximum will also apply to a contract made before that date if its terms are varied before March 31, 1996.

Para. 2

A matching adjustment is made to the limit on an individual's entitlement to hold totally tax-exempt policies issued by one or more friendly societies.

Para. 3

The restriction on the surrender value of a policy which is to be a qualifying policy is removed.

Para. 4

If the premiums payable under an existing qualifying tax-exempt policy are increased to a level within the new limit on the policies that can be held by an individual, that increase will not cause the policy to lose its qualifying status, This provision applies to policies made after August 31, 1987, the terms of which are varied before March 31, 1996 so as to increase the premium.

Section 58   SCHEDULE 11

PERSONAL PENSIONS: INCOME WITHDRAWALS

Introductory

1.—(1) Chapter IV of Part XIV of the Taxes Act 1988 (personal pension schemes) is amended as follows.

(2) The amendments have effect in relation to approvals, of schemes or amendments, given under that Chapter after the passing of this Act.

(3) They do not affect any approval previously given.

Interpretation

2.—(1) Section 630 (interpretation) is amended as follows.

(2) Make the present provision subsection (1) and insert the following definitions at the appropriate places—

"income withdrawal" means a payment of income, under arrangements made in accordance with a personal pension scheme, otherwise than by way of an annuity;

"pension date", in relation to any personal pension arrangements, means the date determined in accordance with the arrangements on which—

(a) an annuity such as is mentioned in section 634 is first payable, or

(b) the member elects to defer the purchase of such an annuity and to make income withdrawals in accordance with section 634A;

and in the definition of "personal pension scheme" after "annuities" insert ", income withdrawals".

(3) After that subsection insert—

"(2) For the purposes of this Chapter the annual amount of the annuity which would have been purchasable by a person on any date shall be calculated by reference to—

(a) the value on that date, determined by or on behalf of the scheme administrator, of the fund from which income withdrawals are to be or have been made by him under the arrangements in question, and

(b) the current published tables of rates of annuities prepared for the purposes of this Chapter by the Government Actuary.

(3) The reference in subsection (2)(a) above to the value of the fund from which income withdrawals are to be or have been made under any personal pension arrangements is to the value of the accrued rights to which the person concerned is entitled conferring prospective entitlement to benefits under those arrangements.

Where a lump sum falls to be paid on the date in question, the reference is to the value of the fund after allowing for that payment.

(4) The Board may make provision by regulations as to the basis on which the tables mentioned in subsection (2)(b) above are to be prepared and the manner in which they are to be applied.".

Conditions of approval: benefits that may be provided

3.—(1) Section 633(1) (conditions of approval: benefits that may be provided) is amended as follows.

(2) In paragraph (a) (annuity to member) after "section 634" insert "or income withdrawals with respect to which the conditions in section 634A are satisfied".

(3) In paragraph (c) (annuity after death of member) after "section 636" insert "or income withdrawals with respect to which the conditions in section 636A are satisfied".

(4) In paragraph (d) (lump sum on death of member) for the words from "either" to the end substitute "the conditions in section 637 (death benefit);".

(5) After that paragraph insert—

"(e) the payment on or after the death of a member of a lump sum satisfying the conditions in section 637A (return of contributions).".

Income withdrawals

4. After section 634 (annuity to member) insert—

"Income withdrawals by member
634A.—(1) Where a member elects to defer the purchase of an annuity such as is mentioned in section 634, income withdrawals may be made by him during the period of deferral, subject as follows.
(2) Income withdrawals must not be made before the member attains the age of 50, unless—
    (a) they are available on his becoming incapable through infirmity of body or mind of carrying on his own occupation or any occupation of a similar nature for which he is trained or fitted, or
    (b) the Board are satisfied that his occupation is one in which persons customarily retire before that age.
(3) Income withdrawals must not be made after the member attains the age of 75.
(4) The aggregate amount of income withdrawals by a member in each successive period of twelve months beginning with his pension date must be not less than 35 per cent or more than 100 per cent of the annual amount of the annuity which would have been purchasable by him on the relevant reference date.
(5) For the purposes of this section the relevant reference date for the first three years is the member's pension date, and for each succeeding period of three years is the first day of that period.
(6) The right to income withdrawals must not be capable of assignment or surrender.".

Lump sum to member

5.—(1) Section 635 (lump sum to member) is amended as follows.
(2) In subsection (1) (date of election for lump sum), for the words from "the date on which" to the end substitute "his pension date under the arrangements in question".
(3) In subsection (2) (date of payment of lump sum), for the words "when that annuity is first payable" substitute "on the date which is his pension date under the arrangements in question".
(4) In subsection (3) (limit on amount of lump sum)—
    (a) in paragraph (a) for "the arrangements made by the member in accordance with the scheme" substitute "the arrangements in question"; and
    (b) in paragraph (b) for "under the scheme" substitute "under those arrangements".

Annuity after death of member

6. In section 636 (annuity after death of member), in subsection (3) (limit on aggregate annual amount), for "vested" substitute "been purchased".

Income withdrawals after death of member

7. After section 636 (annuity after death of member) insert—

"Income withdrawals after death of member
636A.—(1) Where a person entitled to such an annuity as is mentioned in section 636 elects to defer the purchase of the annuity, income withdrawals may be made by him during the period of deferral, subject as follows.
(2) No such deferral may be made, and accordingly income withdrawals may not be made, if the person concerned elects in accordance with section 636(5)(a) to defer the purchase of an annuity.
(3) Income withdrawals must not be made after the person concerned if he had purchased such an annuity as is mentioned in section 636 would have ceased to be entitled to payments under it.

(4) Income withdrawals must not in any event be made after the member would have attained the age of 75 or, if earlier, after the person concerned attains the age of 75.

(5) The aggregate amount of income withdrawals by a person in each successive period of twelve months beginning with the date of the member's death must be not less than 35 per cent or more than 100 per cent of the annual amount of the annuity which would have been purchasable by him on the relevant reference date.

(6) For the purposes of this section the relevant reference date for the first three years is the date of the member's death, and for each succeeding period of three years is the first day of that period.

(7) The right to income withdrawals must not be capable of assignment or surrender.".

Lump sum on death of member

8. For section 637 (lump sum on death of member) substitute—

"Death benefit

637. The lump sum—

(a) must be payable on the death of the member before he attains the age of 75, and

(b) must be payable by an authorised insurance company.

Return of contributions on or after death of member

637A.—(1) The lump sum must be payable on or after the death of the member and represent no more than the return of contributions together with reasonable interest on contributions or bonuses out of profits, after allowing for any income withdrawals.

To the extent that contributions are invested in units under a unit trust scheme, the lump sum may represent the sale or redemption price of the units.

(2) The lump sum must be payable only if—

(a) no annuity has been purchased by the member under the arrangements in question,

(b) no such annuity as is mentioned in section 636 has been purchased by the person to whom the payment is made, and

(c) the person to whom the payment is made has not elected in accordance with subsection (5)(a) of section 636 to defer the purchase of such an annuity as is mentioned in that section.

(3) Where the member's death occurs after the date which is his pension date in relation to the arrangements in question, the lump sum must be payable not later than two years after the death.".

Other restrictions on approval

9. In section 638 (other restrictions on approval), after subsection (7) insert—

"(7A) The Board shall not approve a personal pension scheme unless it prohibits, except in such cases as may be prescribed by regulations made by the Board—

(a) the acceptance of further contributions, and

(b) the making of transfer payments,

after the date which is the member's pension date in relation to the arrangements in question.".

Maximum amount of deductions

10. In section 640 (maximum amount of deductions), in subsection (3) (maximum amount to secure death benefit) for "section 637(1)" substitute "section 637".

Treatment of personal pension income

11. In section 643 (employer's contributions and personal pension income, &c.), after subsection (4) insert—

"(5) Income withdrawals under approved personal pension arrangements shall be assessable to tax under Schedule E (and section 203 shall apply accordingly) and shall be treated as earned income of the recipient.".

Tax charge on return of contributions after pension date

12. Omit the heading before section 648A and after that section insert—

"Return of contributions after pension date

648B.—(1) Tax shall be charged under this section on any payment to a person under approved personal pension arrangements of such a lump sum as is mentioned in section

637A in a case where the member's death occurred after his pension date in relation to the arrangement in question.

(2) Where a payment is chargeable to tax under this section, the scheme administrator shall be charged to income tax under Case VI of Schedule D and, subject to subsection (3) below, the rate of tax shall be 35 per cent.

(3) The Treasury may by order from time to time increase or decrease the rate of tax under subsection (2) above.

(4) The tax shall be charged on the amount paid or, if the rules of the scheme permit the scheme administrator to deduct the tax before payment, on the amount before deduction of tax; and the amount so charged to tax shall not be treated as income for any other purpose of the Tax Acts.".

GENERAL NOTE

Para. 1
This introduces the Schedule which amends the provisions relating to personal pension schemes and stipulates that the amendments do not affect approvals previously granted.

Para. 2
The amendments to ICTA 1988, s.630 add new definitions of "income withdrawal" and "pension date" and provide for the use of tables prepared by the Government Actuary for the purpose of calculating the annual amount of the annuity which would have been purchasable by a person on any date. Amended ICTA 1988, s.630(3) explains the term "value of the fund."

Para. 3
The benefits which may be provided are extended to include income withdrawals by the member (see para. 4 below) or by a person who, following the member's death, satisfies certain conditions (see para. 7 below).

Para. 4
New ICTA 1988, s.634A sets out the provisions governing income withdrawals. A member may normally begin to make income withdrawals at the age of 50, provided an annuity has not already been purchased under the arrangement in question. Withdrawals may continue until the age of 75, when an annuity must be purchased. The annual amount withdrawn may not exceed the amount which an annuity could have provided and must be at least 35 per cent of that amount. The withdrawal amounts are to be reviewed at intervals of three years.

Para. 5
The payment of a lump sum is related to the members' pension date (see para. 2 above), rather than the date when an annuity is first payable.

Para. 6
This makes a consequential amendment to ICTA 1988, s.636.

Para. 7
The new ICTA 1988, s.636A sets out the provisions governing the withdrawal of income after the death of a member. Withdrawals may be made by a person entitled to an annuity under ICTA 1988, s.636, provided no annuity had become payable to the member before his death and provided also that the person concerned has not elected to defer purchase of an annuity in accordance with ICTA 1988, s.636(5)(a). Income withdrawals continue until the person entitled to make them either purchases an annuity or takes a lump sum under new ICTA 1988, s.637A (see para. 8 below), but not after the member would have reached the age of 75 or, if earlier, the person concerned reaches that age. The provisions regarding amounts of withdrawal follow those in new ICTA 1988, s.634A (see para. 4 above).

Para. 8
This substitutes ss.637 and 637A for the existing ICTA 1988, s.637. New s.637 corresponds with existing s.637(1). New s.637A adds two provisos to the existing s.637(1):
  (i) the lump sum must be taken within two years of the member's death; and
  (ii) the person to whom it is made has not elected to defer the purchase of an annuity in accordance with s.636(5)(a).

Para. 9
The new ICTA 1988, s.638(7A) provides that approval will not be given to a personal pension scheme (except under regulations made by the Revenue) unless the scheme prohibits the

acceptance of further contributions to, and the making of transfer payments from, an arrangement under which income withdrawals have been made.

Para. 10

A consequential amendment is made to ICTA 1988, s.640.

Para. 11

The new ICTA 1988, s.643(5) provides that income withdrawals under approved personal pension schemes will be assessable to tax under Schedule E and will be treated as earned income.

Para. 12

The new ICTA 1988, s.648B introduces a tax charge on any payment of a lump sum under ICTA 1988, s.637A when it is paid following the death of a member and after the member's pension date. The tax is chargeable on the scheme administrator under Schedule D, Case VI at a rate of 35 per cent (subject to alteration by Treasury order).

Section 65   SCHEDULE 12

CONTRACTUAL SAVINGS SCHEMES

Introduction

1. In this Schedule references to section 326 are to section 326 of the Taxes Act 1988 (contractual savings schemes).

Curtailment of schemes

2.—(1) The following provisions of section 326, namely—

(a) subsection (2) (schemes governed by regulations made under section 11 of National Debt Act 1972),

(b) subsection (3) (schemes with building societies), and

(c) subsection (4) (schemes with institutions authorised under Banking Act 1987),

shall be amended as mentioned in sub-paragraph (2) below.

(2) In each subsection for the words "a scheme" (where they first occur) there shall be substituted "a share option linked scheme".

(3) This paragraph shall apply in relation to schemes not certified as mentioned in section 326(2)(c), (3)(b) or (4)(b) before 1st December 1994.

European institutions

3.—(1) Section 326 shall be further amended as follows.

(2) In subsection (1) (relief for sums payable in respect of bank deposits etc.) after paragraph (c) there shall be inserted "or

(d) in respect of money paid to a relevant European institution,".

(3) In subsection (2) (meaning of certified scheme except in relation to institutions authorised under Banking Act 1987 etc.) after "1987" there shall be inserted "or a relevant European institution".

(4) The following subsection shall be inserted after subsection (4)—

"(5) In this section "certified contractual savings scheme" means, in relation to a relevant European institution, a share option linked scheme—

(a) providing for periodical contributions by individuals for a specified period, and

(b) certified by the Treasury as corresponding to a scheme certified under subsection (2) above, and as qualifying for exemption under this section."

(5) Sub-paragraph (2) above shall apply in relation to schemes established after the day on which this Act is passed.

Certification: Treasury specifications

4.—(1) Section 326 shall be further amended as follows.

(2) In each of the following provisions, namely—

(a) subsection (3)(b) (Treasury certification of schemes with building societies),

(b) subsection (4)(b) (Treasury certification of schemes with institutions authorised under Banking Act 1987), and

(c) subsection (5)(b) (inserted by paragraph 3 above),

for the words "corresponding to a scheme certified under subsection (2) above" there shall be substituted "fulfilling such requirements as the Treasury may specify for the purposes of this section".

(3) This paragraph shall apply in relation to schemes not certified as mentioned in section 326(3)(b), (4)(b) or (5)(b) before such day as the Treasury may by order made by statutory instrument appoint.

Treasury authorisation

5.—(1) Section 326 shall be further amended by inserting the following subsections after subsection (5) (inserted by paragraph 3 above)—

"(6) Any terminal bonus, interest or other sum payable under a scheme shall not be treated as payable under a certified contractual savings scheme for the purposes of this section if—

(a) the contract under which the sum is payable provides for contributions to be made by way of investment in a building society or to be made to an institution authorised under the Banking Act 1987 or to a relevant European institution, and

(b) neither the requirement under subsection (7) below nor that under subsection (8) below is fulfilled.

(7) The requirement under this subsection is that—

(a) when the contract is entered into there is Treasury authorisation for the society or institution concerned to enter into contracts under the scheme, and

(b) the authorisation was given without any conditions being imposed.

(8) The requirement under this subsection is that—

(a) when the contract is entered into there is Treasury authorisation for the society or institution concerned to enter into contracts under the scheme,

(b) the authorisation was given subject to conditions being met, and

(c) the conditions are met when the contract is entered into."

(2) This paragraph shall apply in relation to schemes not certified as mentioned in section 326(3)(b), (4)(b) or (5)(b) before the day appointed under paragraph 4(3) above.

Section 326: supplementary

6.—(1) Section 326 shall be further amended by inserting the following subsection after subsection (8) (inserted by paragraph 5 above)—

"(9) Schedule 15A to this Act (which contains provisions supplementing this section) shall have effect."

(2) The following Schedule shall be inserted after Schedule 15 to the Taxes Act 1988—

"SCHEDULE 15A

CONTRACTUAL SAVINGS SCHEMES

Introduction

1. This Schedule shall have effect for the purposes of section 326.

Share option linked schemes

2.—(1) A share option linked scheme is a scheme under which periodical contributions are to be made by an individual—

(a) who is eligible to participate in (that is, to obtain and exercise rights under) an approved savings-related share option scheme, and

(b) who is to make the contributions for the purpose of enabling him to participate in that approved scheme.

(2) In sub-paragraph (1) above—

(a) "savings-related share option scheme" has the meaning given by paragraph 1 of Schedule 9, and

(b) "approved" means approved under that Schedule.

Relevant European institutions

3. A relevant European institution is an institution which—

(a) is a European authorised institution within the meaning of the Banking Co-ordination (Second Council Directive) Regulations 1992, and

(b) may accept deposits in the United Kingdom in accordance with those regulations.

Treasury specifications

4.—(1) The requirements which may be specified under section 326(3)(b), (4)(b) or (5)(b) are such requirements as the Treasury think fit.

(2) In particular, the requirements may relate to—

(a) the descriptions of individuals who may enter into contracts under a scheme;

(b) the contributions to be paid by individuals;

(c) the sums to be paid or repaid to individuals.

(3) The requirements which may be specified under any of the relevant provisions may be different from those specified under any of the other relevant provisions; and the relevant provisions are section 326(3)(b), (4)(b) and (5)(b).

5.—(1) Where a specification has been made under section 326(3)(b), (4)(b) or (5)(b) the Treasury may—

(a) withdraw the specification and any certification made by reference to the specification, and

(b) stipulate the date on which the withdrawal is to become effective.

(2) No withdrawal under this paragraph shall affect—

(a) the operation of the scheme before the stipulated date, or

(b) any contract entered into before that date.

(3) No withdrawal under this paragraph shall be effective unless the Treasury—

(a) send a notice by post to each relevant body informing it of the withdrawal, and

(b) do so not less than 28 days before the stipulated date;

and a relevant body is a society or institution authorised (whether unconditionally or subject to conditions being met) to enter into contracts under the scheme concerned.

6.—(1) Where a specification has been made under section 326(3)(b), (4)(b) or (5)(b) the Treasury may—

(a) vary the specification,

(b) withdraw any certification made by reference to the specification obtaining before the variation, and

(c) stipulate the date on which the variation and withdrawal are to become effective;

and the Treasury may at any time certify a scheme as fulfilling the requirements obtaining after the variation.

(2) No variation and withdrawal under this paragraph shall affect—

(a) the operation of the scheme before the stipulated date, or

(b) any contract entered into before that date.

(3) No variation and withdrawal under this paragraph shall be effective unless the Treasury—

(a) send a notice by post to each relevant body informing it of the variation and withdrawal, and

(b) do so not less than 28 days before the stipulated date;

and a relevant body is a society or institution authorised (whether unconditionally or subject to conditions being met) to enter into contracts under the scheme concerned.

Treasury authorisation

7.—(1) The Treasury may authorise a society or institution under section 326(7) or (8) as regards schemes generally or as regards a particular scheme or particular schemes.

(2) More than one authorisation may be given to the same society or institution.

8.—(1) Where an authorisation has been given under section 326(7) or (8) the Treasury may withdraw the authorisation and stipulate the date on which the withdrawal is to become effective; and the withdrawal shall have effect as regards any contract not entered into before the stipulated date.

(2) No withdrawal under this paragraph shall be effective unless the Treasury—

(a) send a notice by post to the society or institution concerned informing it of the withdrawal, and

(b) do so not less than 28 days before the stipulated date.

(3) A withdrawal of an authorisation shall not affect the Treasury's power to give another authorisation or other authorisations.

9.—(1) Where an authorisation has been given under section 326(7) the Treasury may—

(a) stipulate that the authorisation is to be varied by being treated as given subject to specified conditions being met, and

(b) stipulate the date on which the variation is to become effective.

(2) As regards any contract entered into on or after the stipulated date the authorisation shall be treated as having been given under section 326(8) subject to the conditions being met.

(3) No variation under this paragraph shall be effective unless the Treasury—

(a) send a notice by post to the society or institution concerned informing it of the variation, and

(b) do so not less than 28 days before the stipulated date.

10.—(1) Where an authorisation has been given under section 326(8) the Treasury may withdraw the conditions and stipulate the date on which the withdrawal is to become effective.

(2) As regards any contract entered into on or after the stipulated date the authorisation shall be treated as having been given under section 326(7) without any conditions being imposed.

11.—(1) Where an authorisation has been given under section 326(8) the Treasury may vary the conditions and stipulate the date on which the variation is to become effective, and the variation shall have effect as regards any contract entered into on or after the stipulated date.

(2) No variation under this paragraph shall be effective unless the Treasury—

(a) send a notice by post to the society or institution concerned informing it of the variation, and

(b) do so not less than 28 days before the stipulated date.

12.—(1) If the Treasury act as regards an authorisation under a relevant paragraph, the paragraph concerned shall have effect subject to their power to act later, as regards the same authorisation, under the same or (as the case may be) another relevant paragraph.

(2) If the Treasury act later as mentioned in sub-paragraph (1) above that sub-paragraph shall apply again, and so on however many times they act as regards an authorisation.

(3) If the Treasury act as regards an authorisation under a relevant paragraph the paragraph concerned shall have effect subject to their power to act later, as regards the same authorisation, under paragraph 8 above.

(4) For the purposes of this paragraph the relevant paragraphs are paragraphs 9 to 11 above."

Payments under certain contracts

7.—(1) Any terminal bonus, interest or other sum payable under a scheme shall not be treated as payable under a certified contractual savings scheme for the purposes of section 326 if—

(a) the scheme is not a share option linked scheme, and

(b) the contract under which the sum is payable is not entered into before 1st December 1994.

(2) Any terminal bonus, interest or other sum payable under a scheme shall not be treated as payable under a certified contractual savings scheme for the purposes of section 326 if—

(a) the contract under which the sum is payable provides for contributions to be made by way of investment in a building society or to be made to an institution authorised under the Banking Act 1987 or to a relevant European institution,

(b) the scheme is certified as mentioned in section 326(3)(b), (4)(b) or (5)(b) before the day appointed under paragraph 4(3) above, and

(c) the contract is not entered into before that day.

(3) In this paragraph "share option linked scheme" and "relevant European institution" have the same meanings as in section 326.

Transitional

8.—(1) The Treasury may by regulations provide that at the beginning of the day appointed under paragraph 4(3) above Treasury authorisation shall be treated as given under section 326(7) to any specified relevant body without any conditions being imposed.

(2) The Treasury may by regulations provide that—

(a) at the beginning of the day appointed under paragraph 4(3) above Treasury authorisation shall be treated as given under section 326(8) to any specified relevant body subject to conditions being met;

(b) the conditions as regards a body shall be such as are specified in, or identified by provision contained in, the regulations as regards that body.

(3) Any authorisation treated as given as mentioned in sub-paragraph (1) or (2) above shall be treated as given as regards schemes generally; but this is subject to any provision to the contrary in the regulations.

(4) For the purposes of this paragraph the following are relevant bodies—

(a) any building society;

(b) any institution authorised under the Banking Act 1987;

(c) any relevant European institution.

(5) In this paragraph—

(a) "relevant European institution" has the same meaning as in section 326;

(b) "specified" means specified in the regulations.

(6) Regulations under this paragraph shall be made by statutory instrument subject to annulment in pursuance of a resolution of the House of Commons.

GENERAL NOTE

The Schedule implements changes to Save As You Earn (SAYE).

Para. 2

Unless an SAYE scheme was certified before December 1, 1994, it must be linked to an approved share option scheme (a 'Sharesave' scheme) to obtain relief.

Para. 3

"Relevant European institutions" (see para. 6 below) will be allowed to offer Sharesave contracts after May 1, 1995.

Para. 4

The Treasury, rather than the Department of National Savings, will be authorised after an appointed day to provide a model Sharesave scheme.

Para. 5

Sharesave schemes after the appointed day will require Treasury authorisation.

Para. 6

The new ICTA 1988, Sched. 15A defines share option linked schemes and European institutions. It allows the Treasury to specify the requirements which may be imposed in respect of model share option linked schemes and to withdraw or vary such specifications on notice given. The Treasury may grant, withdraw or vary an authorisation to participate in Sharesave schemes. Conditions under a conditional authorisation may be withdrawn or varied. An authorisation so varied by the imposition, withdrawal or variation of conditions may be subsequently varied or withdrawn.

Para. 7

Tax relief is removed from SAYE contracts not linked to an approved share option scheme as from December 1, 1994 and, with effect from the appointed day, from Sharesave schemes certified under the old procedure.

Para. 8

The Treasury is empowered to make regulations introducing the new system.

Section 67   SCHEDULE 13

ENTERPRISE INVESTMENT SCHEME

Introduction

1. The Taxation of Chargeable Gains Act 1992 shall be amended as mentioned in this Schedule.

Amendments of section 150A

2.—(1) Section 150A (enterprise investment scheme) shall be amended as mentioned in sub-paragraphs (2) to (4) below; and the amendments made by sub-paragraphs (2) and (3) below shall apply in relation to shares issued on or after 1st January 1994.

(2) The following subsection shall be inserted after subsection (2)—

"(2A) Notwithstanding anything in section 16(2), subsection (2) above shall not apply to a disposal on which a loss accrues."

(3) In subsection (3) (reduction of relief) the following paragraph shall be inserted after paragraph (a)—

"(aa) the amount of the reduction is not found under section 289A(2)(b) of that Act, and".

(4) The following subsections shall be inserted after subsection (8) (which disapplies provisions about exchanges, reconstructions or amalgamations in certain circumstances)—

"(8A) Subsection (8) above shall not have effect to disapply section 135 or 136 where—

(a) the new holding consists of new ordinary shares carrying no present or future preferential right to dividends or to a company's assets on its winding up and no present or future preferential right to be redeemed,

(b) the new shares are issued on or after 29th November 1994 and after the end of the relevant period, and

(c) the condition in subsection (8B) below is satisfied.

(8B) The condition is that at some time before the issue of the new shares—

(a) the company issuing them issued eligible shares, and

(b) a certificate in relation to those eligible shares was issued by the company for the purposes of subsection (2) of section 306 of the Taxes Act and in accordance with that section.

(8C) In subsection (8A) above—

(a) "new holding" shall be construed in accordance with sections 126, 127, 135 and 136;

(b) "relevant period" means the period found by applying section 312(1A)(a) of the Taxes Act by reference to the company issuing the shares referred to in subsection (8) above and by reference to those shares."

Reduction of relief

3. The following section shall be inserted after section 150A—

"Enterprise investment scheme: reduction of relief

150B.—(1) This section has effect where section 150A(2) applies on a disposal of eligible shares, and before the disposal but on or after 29th November 1994—

(a) value is received in circumstances where relief attributable to the shares is reduced by an amount under section 300(1A)(a) of the Taxes Act,

(b) there is a repayment, redemption, repurchase or payment in circumstances where relief attributable to the shares is reduced by an amount under section 303(1A)(a) of that Act, or

(c) paragraphs (a) and (b) above apply.

(2) If section 150A(2) applies on the disposal but section 150A(3) does not, section 150A(2) shall apply only to so much of the gain as remains after deducting so much of it as is found by multiplying it by the fraction—

(a) whose numerator is equal to the amount by which the relief attributable to the shares is reduced as mentioned in subsection (1) above, and

(b) whose denominator is equal to the amount of the relief attributable to the shares.

(3) If section 150A(2) and (3) apply on the disposal, section 150A(2) shall apply only to so much of the gain as is found by—

(a) taking the part of the gain found under section 150A(3), and

(b) deducting from that part so much of it as is found by multiplying it by the fraction mentioned in subsection (2) above.

(4) Where the relief attributable to the shares is reduced as mentioned in subsection (1) above by more than one amount, the numerator mentioned in subsection (2) above shall be taken to be equal to the aggregate of the amounts.

(5) The denominator mentioned in subsection (2) above shall be found without regard to any reduction mentioned in subsection (1) above.

(6) Subsections (11) and (12) of section 150A apply for the purposes of this section as they apply for the purposes of that section."

Re-investment

4.—(1) The following section shall be inserted after section 150B—

"Enterprise investment scheme: re-investment

150C. Schedule 5B to this Act (which provides relief in respect of re-investment under the enterprise investment scheme) shall have effect."

(2) In section 260, after subsection (6) (no reduction in the case of certain disposals in respect of held-over gains), there shall be inserted the following subsection—

"(6A) Subsection (3) above does not apply, so far as any gain accruing in accordance with paragraphs 4 and 5 of Schedule 5B is concerned, in relation to the disposal which constitutes the chargeable event by virtue of which that gain accrues."

(3) The following Schedule shall be inserted after Schedule 5A—

"SCHEDULE 5B

ENTERPRISE INVESTMENT SCHEME: RE-INVESTMENT

Application of Schedule

1.—(1) This Schedule applies where—
- (a) there would (apart from paragraph 2(2)(a) below) be a chargeable gain ("the original gain") accruing to an individual ("the investor") at any time ("the accrual time") on or after 29th November 1994;
- (b) the gain is one accruing either on the disposal by the investor of any asset or in accordance with paragraphs 4 and 5 below or paragraphs 4 and 5 of Schedule 5C;
- (c) the investor makes a qualifying investment; and
- (d) the investor is resident or ordinarily resident in the United Kingdom at the accrual time and the time when he makes the qualifying investment and is not, in relation to the qualifying investment, a person to whom sub-paragraph (4) below applies.

(2) The investor makes a qualifying investment for the purposes of this Schedule if—
- (a) he subscribes for any shares to which any relief given to him under Chapter III of Part VII of the Taxes Act is attributable;
- (b) those shares are issued at a qualifying time; and
- (c) where that time is before the accrual time, those shares are still held by the investor at the accrual time;

and in this Schedule "relevant shares", in relation to a case to which this Schedule applies, means any of the shares which are acquired by the investor in making the qualifying investment.

(3) In this Schedule "a qualifying time", in relation to any shares subscribed for by the investor, means—
- (a) any time in the period beginning one year before and ending three years after the accrual time, or
- (b) any such time before the beginning of that period or after it ends as the Board may by notice allow.

(4) This sub-paragraph applies to the investor in relation to a qualifying investment if—
- (a) though resident or ordinarily resident in the United Kingdom at the time when he makes the investment, he is regarded for the purposes of any double taxation relief arrangements as resident in a territory outside the United Kingdom, and
- (b) were section 150A to be disregarded, the arrangements would have the effect that he would not be liable in the United Kingdom to tax on a gain arising on a disposal, immediately after their acquisition, of the shares acquired in making that investment.

Postponement of original gain

2.—(1) On the making of a claim by the investor for the purposes of this Schedule, so much of the investor's unused qualifying expenditure on relevant shares as—
- (a) is specified in the claim, and
- (b) does not exceed so much of the original gain as is unmatched,

shall be set against a corresponding amount of the original gain.

(2) Where an amount of qualifying expenditure on any relevant shares is set under this Schedule against the whole or part of the original gain—
- (a) so much of that gain as is equal to that amount shall be treated as not having accrued at the accrual time; but
- (b) paragraphs 4 and 5 below shall apply for determining the gain that is to be treated as accruing on the occurrence of any chargeable event in relation to any of those relevant shares.

(3) For the purposes of this Schedule—
- (a) the investor's qualifying expenditure on any relevant shares is so much of the amount subscribed by him for the shares as represents the amount in respect of which there is given the relief under section 289A of the Taxes Act which is attributable to those shares; and

(b) that expenditure is unused to the extent that it has not already been set under this Schedule against the whole or any part of a chargeable gain.

(4) For the purposes of this paragraph the original gain is unmatched, in relation to any qualifying expenditure on relevant shares, to the extent that it has not had any other expenditure set against it under this Schedule or Schedule 5C.

Chargeable events

3.—(1) Subject to the following provisions of this paragraph, there is for the purposes of this Schedule a chargeable event in relation to any relevant shares if, after the making of the qualifying investment—

(a) the investor disposes of those shares otherwise than by way of a disposal within marriage;

(b) those shares are disposed of, otherwise than by way of a disposal to the investor, by a person who acquired them on a disposal made by the investor within marriage;

(c) the investor becomes a non-resident while holding those shares and within the first relevant period;

(d) a person who acquired those shares on a disposal within marriage becomes a non-resident while holding those shares and within the first relevant period;

(e) the company that issued those shares ceases to be a qualifying company within the second relevant period; or

(f) the relief given under section 289A of the Taxes Act in respect of the amount subscribed for those shares is withdrawn or reduced in circumstances not falling within any of paragraphs (a) to (e) above.

(2) For the purposes of sub-paragraph (1) above—

(a) the first relevant period in the case of any relevant shares is the period found by applying section 312(1A)(a) of the Taxes Act by reference to the company that issued the shares and by reference to the shares;

(b) the second relevant period in the case of any shares is the period found by applying section 312(1A)(b) of that Act by reference to the company that issued the shares and by reference to the shares; and

(c) whether a company is a qualifying company at any given time shall be determined in accordance with section 293 of that Act.

(3) For the purposes of this Schedule there shall not be a chargeable event by virtue of sub-paragraph (1)(c) or (d) above in relation to any shares if—

(a) the reason why the person in question becomes a non-resident is that he works in an employment or office all the duties of which are performed outside the United Kingdom, and

(b) he again becomes resident or ordinarily resident in the United Kingdom within the period of three years from the time when he became a non-resident, without having meanwhile disposed of any of those shares;

and accordingly no assessment shall be made by virtue of sub-paragraph (1)(c) or (d) above before the end of that period in a case where the condition in paragraph (a) above is satisfied and the condition in paragraph (b) above may be satisfied.

(4) For the purposes of sub-paragraph (3) above a person shall be taken to have disposed of any shares if and only if there has been such a disposal as would have been a chargeable event in relation to those shares if the person making the disposal had been resident in the United Kingdom.

(5) Where in any case—

(a) the investor or a person who has acquired any relevant shares on a disposal within marriage dies, and

(b) an event occurs at or after the time of the death which (apart from this sub-paragraph) would be a chargeable event in relation to any relevant shares held by the deceased immediately before his death,

that event shall not be a chargeable event in relation to the shares so held.

Gain accruing on chargeable event

4.—(1) On the occurrence of a chargeable event in relation to any relevant shares in relation to which there has not been a previous chargeable event—

(a) a chargeable gain shall be treated as accruing at the time of the event; and

(b) the amount of the gain shall be equal to so much of the original gain as is an amount against which there has under this Schedule been set any expenditure on those shares.

(2) Any question for the purposes of this Schedule as to whether any relevant shares to which a chargeable event relates are shares the expenditure on which has under this Schedule been set against the whole or any part of any gain shall be determined in accordance with the assumptions for which sub-paragraph (3) below provides.

(3) For the purposes of sub-paragraph (2) above it shall be assumed, in relation to any disposal of shares (including a disposal within marriage) that—

(a) as between qualifying shares acquired by the same person on different days, those acquired on an earlier day are disposed of by that person before those acquired on a later day; and

(b) as between qualifying shares acquired by the same person on the same day, those the expenditure on which has been set under this Schedule against the whole or any part of any gain are disposed of by that person only after he has disposed of any other qualifying shares acquired by him on that day.

(4) In sub-paragraph (3) above "qualifying shares" means any shares which—

(a) were subscribed for by a person eligible for relief in respect of those shares under Chapter III of Part VII of the Taxes Act (the enterprise investment scheme), and

(b) are shares in respect of which relief is given under section 289A of that Act in respect of the whole or any part of the amount subscribed.

(5) Where at the time of a chargeable event any relevant shares are treated for the purposes of this Act as represented by assets which consist of or include assets other than those shares—

(a) the expenditure on those shares which was set against the gain in question shall be treated, in determining for the purposes of this paragraph the amount of expenditure on each of those assets which is to be treated as having been set against that gain, as apportioned in such manner as may be just and reasonable between those assets; and

(b) as between different assets treated as representing the same relevant shares, the assumptions for which sub-paragraph (3) above provides shall apply with the necessary modifications in relation to those assets as they would apply in relation to the shares.

Person to whom gain accrues

5.—(1) The chargeable gain which accrues, in accordance with paragraph 4 above, on the occurrence in relation to any relevant shares of a chargeable event shall be treated as accruing, as the case may be—

(a) to the person who makes the disposal,

(b) to the person who becomes a non-resident,

(c) to the person who holds the shares in question when the company ceases to be a qualifying company, or

(d) to the person who holds the shares in question when the circumstances arise in respect of which the relief is withdrawn or reduced.

(2) Where—

(a) sub-paragraph (1) above provides for the holding of shares at a particular time to be what identifies the person to whom any chargeable gain accrues, and

(b) at that time, some of those shares are held by the investor and others are held by a person to whom the investor has transferred them by a disposal within marriage,

the amount of the chargeable gain accruing by virtue of paragraph 4 above shall be computed separately in relation to the investor and that person without reference to the shares held by the other.

Interpretation

6.—(1) In this Schedule "non-resident" means a person who is neither resident nor ordinarily resident in the United Kingdom.

(2) In this Schedule references to a disposal within marriage are references to any disposal to which section 58 applies.

(3) Notwithstanding anything in section 288(5), shares shall not for the purposes of this Schedule be treated as issued by reason only of being comprised in a letter of allotment or similar instrument.

(4) Chapter III of Part VII of the Taxes Act shall apply for the purposes of this Schedule to determine whether and to what extent any relief under that Chapter is attributable to any shares.

(5) References in this Schedule to Chapter III of Part VII of the Taxes Act or any provision of that Chapter are to that Chapter or provision as it applies in relation to shares issued on or after 1st January 1994."

(4) This paragraph has effect in relation to gains accruing and events occurring on or after 29th November 1994.

GENERAL NOTE
The Schedule makes a number of changes to the CGT provisions relating to the Enterprise Investment Scheme (EIS), which replaced the Business Expansion Scheme (BES) from the beginning of 1994.

Para. 2
This provides various additional reliefs, backdated to the introduction of the EIS. These are:
  (i) a loss on a disposal of EIS shares held for five years is allowable for CGT;
  (ii) the CGT exemption will not be restricted where an investor's income tax relief is restricted under ICTA 1988, s.289A(2)(b) because he had insufficient income tax liability to claim full relief; and
  (iii) the CGT exemption for EIS shares may be carried forward into new shares in a reconstruction or amalgamation, where the new shares are ordinary shares, the reconstruction takes place more than five years after the issue of the original shares, and the company issuing the new shares has issued shares under the BES or the EIS.

Para. 3
The new TCGA 1992, s.150B restricts the CGT exemption where the investor has had his income tax relief withdrawn under ICTA 1988, ss.300 or 303 because he has received value from the company, or the company has purchased another holder's shares. In such a case, the CGT relief is reduced in proportion to the amount of income tax relief withdrawn.

Para. 4
The new TCGA 1992, Sched. 5B provides a new relief which allows a U.K. resident investor to roll over the chargeable gain arising on any disposal where be subscribes for shares under the EIS. The relief applies from November 29, 1994. The gain is brought back into charge when shares are transferred as a gift on which inheritance tax is chargeable.

The reinvestment must normally be made within the period of one year before and three years after the disposal, subject to extension by the Revenue. The gain may be deferred on a claim being made up to the amount on which income tax relief has been given under the EIS. The gain is brought back into charge on a disposal of the shares other than to a spouse; on cessation of residence in the U.K. (except in the case of overseas employment, where the investor returns within three years without having disposed of the shares); on the company ceasing to qualify for EIS purposes within three years; or on the investor ceasing to qualify for income tax relief. Events occurring after the death of an investor, or of a spouse to whom shares are transferred, are ignored for this purpose. Where EIS shares in the same company are acquired at different times, gains are charged on a first in, first out basis. Where they are acquired at the same time, the shares to which the deferred gain does not relate are deemed to be disposed of before those to which it does relate. These rules apply, *mutatis mutandis*, to new EIS shares acquired on a reconstruction. Tax may be charged on an investor or a spouse to whom shares have been transferred.

Section 70   SCHEDULE 14

VENTURE CAPITAL TRUSTS: MEANING OF "QUALIFYING HOLDINGS"

Introductory

1.—(1) This Schedule applies, where any shares in or securities of any company ("the relevant company") are at any time held by another company ("the trust company"), for determining whether and to what extent those shares or securities ("the relevant holding") are, for the purposes of section 842AA, to be regarded as at that time comprised in the trust company's qualifying holdings.

(2) The relevant holding shall be regarded as comprised in the trust company's qualifying holdings at any time if—
  (a) all the requirements of the following provisions of this Schedule are satisfied at that time in relation to the relevant company and the relevant holding; and
  (b) the relevant holding consists of shares or securities which were first issued by the relevant company to the trust company and have been held by the trust company ever since.

(3) Subject to paragraph 6(3) below, where the requirements of paragraph 6 or 7 below would be satisfied as to only part of the money raised by the issue of the relevant holding and that

holding is not otherwise capable of being treated as comprising separate holdings, this Schedule shall have effect in relation to that holding as if it were two holdings consisting of—

(a) a holding from which that part of the money was raised; and

(b) a holding from which the remainder was raised;

and section 842AA shall have effect as if the value of the holding were to be apportioned accordingly between the two holdings which are deemed to exist in pursuance of this sub-paragraph.

Requirement that company must be unquoted company

2.—(1) The requirement of this paragraph is that the relevant company (whether or not it is resident in the United Kingdom) must be an unquoted company.

(2) In this paragraph "unquoted company" means a company none of whose shares, stocks, debentures or other securities is marketed to the general public.

(3) For the purposes of this paragraph shares, stocks, debentures or other securities are marketed to the general public if they are—

(a) listed on a recognised stock exchange,

(b) listed on a designated exchange in a country outside the United Kingdom, or

(c) dealt in on the Unlisted Securities Market or dealt in outside the United Kingdom by such means as may be designated.

(4) In sub-paragraph (3) above "designated" means designated by an order made by the Board for the purposes of that sub-paragraph; and an order made for the purposes of paragraph (b) of that sub-paragraph may designate an exchange by name, or by reference to any class or description of exchanges, including a class or description framed by reference to any authority or approval given in a country outside the United Kingdom.

(5) Section 828(1) does not apply to an order made for the purposes of sub-paragraph (3) above.

(6) Where a company any shares in or securities of which are included in the qualifying holdings of the trust company ceases at any time while the trust company is approved as a venture capital trust to be an unquoted company, the requirements of this paragraph shall be deemed, in relation to shares or securities acquired by the trust company before that time, to continue to be satisfied for a period of five years after that time.

Requirements as to company's business

3.—(1) The requirements of this paragraph are as follows.

(2) The relevant company must be one of the following, that is to say—

(a) a company which exists wholly for the purpose of carrying on one or more qualifying trades or which so exists apart from purposes capable of having no significant effect (other than in relation to incidental matters) on the extent of the company's activities;

(b) a company whose business consists entirely in the holding of shares in or securities of, or the making of loans to, one or more qualifying subsidiaries of that company; or

(c) a company whose business consists entirely in—

(i) the holding of such shares or securities, or the making of such loans; and

(ii) the carrying on of one or more qualifying trades.

(3) Subject to sub-paragraph (4) below, the relevant company or a qualifying subsidiary of that company must, when the relevant holding was issued and at all times since, have been either—

(a) carrying on a qualifying trade wholly or mainly in the United Kingdom; or

(b) preparing to carry on a qualifying trade which at the time when the relevant holding was issued it intended to carry on wholly or mainly in the United Kingdom.

(4) The requirements of sub-paragraph (3) above shall not be capable of being satisfied by virtue of paragraph (b) of that sub-paragraph at any time after the end of the period of two years beginning with the issue of the relevant holding unless—

(a) the relevant company or the subsidiary in question began to carry on the intended trade before the end of that period, and

(b) that company or subsidiary has, at all times since the end of that period, been carrying on a qualifying trade wholly or mainly in the United Kingdom.

(5) The requirements of that sub-paragraph shall also be incapable of being so satisfied at any time after the abandonment, within the period mentioned in sub-paragraph (4) above, of the intention in question.

Meaning of "qualifying trade"

4.—(1) For the purposes of this Schedule—

(a) a trade is a qualifying trade if it is a trade complying with this paragraph; and

(b) the carrying on of any activities of research and development from which it is intended that there will be derived a trade that—

    (i) will comply with this paragraph, and

    (ii) will be carried on wholly or mainly in the United Kingdom,

shall be treated as the carrying on of a qualifying trade.

(2) Subject to sub-paragraphs (3) to (9) below, a trade complies with this paragraph if neither that trade nor a substantial part of it consists in one or more of the following activities, that is to say—

(a) dealing in land, in commodities or futures or in shares, securities or other financial instruments;

(b) dealing in goods otherwise than in the course of an ordinary trade of wholesale or retail distribution;

(c) banking, insurance, money-lending, debt-factoring, hire-purchase financing or other financial activities;

(d) leasing (including letting ships on charter or other assets on hire) or receiving royalties or licence fees;

(e) providing legal or accountancy services;

(f) providing services or facilities for any such trade carried on by another person (not being a company of which the company providing the services or facilities is a subsidiary) as—

    (i) consists, to a substantial extent, in activities within any of paragraphs (a) to (e) above; and

    (ii) is a trade in which a controlling interest is held by a person who also has a controlling interest in the trade carried on by the company providing the services or facilities.

(3) For the purposes of sub-paragraph (2)(b) above—

(a) a trade of wholesale distribution is one in which the goods are offered for sale and sold to persons for resale by them, or for processing and resale by them, to members of the general public for their use or consumption;

(b) a trade of retail distribution is one in which the goods are offered for sale and sold to members of the general public for their use or consumption; and

(c) a trade is not an ordinary trade of wholesale or retail distribution if—

    (i) it consists, to a substantial extent, in dealing in goods of a kind which are collected or held as an investment, or in that activity and any other activity of a kind falling within sub-paragraph (2)(a) to (f) above, taken together; and

    (ii) a substantial proportion of those goods are held by the company for a period which is significantly longer than the period for which a vendor would reasonably be expected to hold them while endeavouring to dispose of them at their market value.

(4) In determining for the purposes of this paragraph whether a trade carried on by any person is an ordinary trade of wholesale or retail distribution, regard shall be had to the extent to which it has the following features, that is to say—

(a) the goods are bought by that person in quantities larger than those in which he sells them;

(b) the goods are bought and sold by that person in different markets;

(c) that person employs staff and incurs expenses in the trade in addition to the cost of the goods and, in the case of a trade carried on by a company, to any remuneration paid to any person connected with it;

(d) there are purchases or sales from or to persons who are connected with that person;

(e) purchases are matched with forward sales or vice versa;

(f) the goods are held by that person for longer than is normal for goods of the kind in question;

(g) the trade is carried on otherwise than at a place or places commonly used for wholesale or retail trade;

(h) that person does not take physical possession of the goods;

and for the purposes of this sub-paragraph the features specified in paragraphs (a) to (c) above shall be regarded as indications that the trade is such an ordinary trade and those in paragraphs (d) to (h) above shall be regarded as indications of the contrary.

(5) A trade shall not be treated as failing to comply with this paragraph by reason only of its consisting, to a substantial extent, in the receiving of royalties or licence fees if—

(a) the company carrying on the trade is engaged in—

    (i) the production of films; or

    (ii) the production of films and the distribution of films produced by it since the issue of the relevant holding;

    and

(b) all royalties and licence fees received by it are in respect of films produced by it since the issue of the relevant holding, in respect of sound recordings in relation to such films or in respect of other products arising from such films.

(6) A trade shall not be treated as failing to comply with this paragraph by reason only of its consisting, to a substantial extent, in the receiving of royalties or licence fees if—

(a) the company carrying on the trade is engaged in research and development; and

(b) all royalties and licence fees received by it are attributable to research and development which it has carried out.

(7) A trade shall not be treated as failing to comply with this paragraph by reason only of its consisting in letting ships, other than oil rigs or pleasure craft, on charter if—

(a) every ship let on charter by the company carrying on the trade is beneficially owned by the company;

(b) every ship beneficially owned by the company is registered in the United Kingdom;

(c) the company is solely responsible for arranging the marketing of the services of its ships; and

(d) the conditions mentioned in sub-paragraph (8) below are satisfied in relation to every letting of a ship on charter by the company;

but where any of the requirements mentioned in paragraphs (a) to (d) above are not satisfied in relation to any lettings, the trade shall not thereby be treated as failing to comply with this paragraph if those lettings and any other activity of a kind falling within sub-paragraph (2) above do not, when taken together, amount to a substantial part of the trade.

(8) The conditions are that—

(a) the letting is for a period not exceeding 12 months and no provision is made at any time (whether in the charterparty or otherwise) for extending it beyond that period otherwise than at the option of the charterer;

(b) during the period of the letting there is no provision in force (whether by virtue of being contained in the charterparty or otherwise) for the grant of a new letting to end, otherwise than at the option of the charterer, more than 12 months after that provision is made;

(c) the letting is by way of a bargain made at arm's length between the company and a person who is not connected with it;

(d) under the terms of the charter the company is responsible as principal—

(i) for taking, throughout the period of the charter, management decisions in relation to the ship, other than those of a kind generally regarded by persons engaged in trade of the kind in question as matters of husbandry; and

(ii) for defraying all expenses in connection with the ship throughout that period, or substantially all such expenses, other than those directly incidental to a particular voyage or to the employment of the ship during that period; and

(e) no arrangements exist by virtue of which a person other than the company may be appointed to be responsible for the matters mentioned in paragraph (d) above on behalf of the company;

but this sub-paragraph shall have effect, in relation to any letting between one company and another where one of those companies is the relevant company and the other is a qualifying subsidiary of that company, or where both companies are qualifying subsidiaries of the relevant company, as if paragraph (c) were omitted.

(9) A trade shall not comply with this paragraph unless it is conducted on a commercial basis and with a view to the realisation of profits.

Provisions supplemental to paragraph 4

5.—(1) In paragraph 4 above—

"film" means an original master negative of a film, an original master film disc or an original master film tape;

"oil rig" means any ship which is an offshore installation for the purposes of the Mineral Workings (Offshore Installations) Act 1971;

"pleasure craft" means any ship of a kind primarily used for sport or recreation;

"research and development" means any activity which is intended to result in a patentable invention (within the meaning of the Patents Act 1977) or in a computer program; and

"sound recording", in relation to a film, means its sound track, original master audio disc or original master audio tape.

(2) For the purposes of paragraph 4 above, in the case of a trade carried on by a company, a person has a controlling interest in that trade if—

(a) he controls the company;

(b) the company is a close company and he or an associate of his, being a director of the company, either—

(i) is the beneficial owner of more than 30 per cent of the ordinary share capital of the company, or

(ii) is able, directly or through the medium of other companies or by any other indirect means, to control more than 30 per cent of that share capital;

or

(c) not less than half of the trade could, in accordance with section 344(2), be regarded as belonging to him for the purposes of section 343;

and, in any other case, a person has a controlling interest in a trade if he is entitled to not less than half of the assets used for, or of the income arising from, the trade.

(3) For the purposes of sub-paragraph (2) above there shall be attributed to any person any rights or powers of any other person who is an associate of his.

(4) References in paragraph 4 above or this paragraph to a trade, except the references in paragraph 4(2)(f) to the trade for which services or facilities are provided, shall be construed without reference to so much of the definition of trade in section 832(1) as relates to adventures or concerns in the nature of trade; and those references in paragraph 4(2)(f) above to a trade shall have effect, in relation to cases in which what is carried on is carried on by a person other than a company, as including references to any business, profession or vocation.

(5) In this paragraph—

"associate" has the meaning given in subsections (3) and (4) of section 417, except that in those subsections, as applied for the purposes of this paragraph, "relative" shall not include a brother or sister; and

"director" shall be construed in accordance with subsection (5) of that section.

Requirements as to the money raised by the investment in question

6.—(1) The requirements of this paragraph are that the money raised by the issue of the relevant holding must—

(a) have been employed wholly for the purposes of the trade by reference to which the requirements of paragraph 3(3) above are satisfied; or

(b) be money which the relevant company or a qualifying subsidiary of that company is intending to employ wholly for the purposes of that trade.

(2) The requirements of sub-paragraph (1) above shall not be capable of being satisfied by virtue of paragraph (b) of that sub-paragraph at any time after twelve months have expired from whichever is applicable of the following, that is to say—

(a) in a case where the requirements of sub-paragraph (3) of paragraph 3 above were satisfied in relation to the time when the relevant holding was issued by virtue of paragraph (a) of that sub-paragraph, that time; and

(b) in a case where they were satisfied in relation to that time by virtue of paragraph (b) of that sub-paragraph, the time when the relevant company or, as the case may be, the subsidiary in question began to carry on the intended trade.

(3) For the purposes of this paragraph money shall not be treated as employed otherwise than wholly for the purposes of a trade if the only amount employed for other purposes is an amount which is not a significant amount; and nothing in paragraph 1(3) above shall require any money whose use is disregarded by virtue of this sub-paragraph to be treated as raised by a different holding.

(4) References in this paragraph to employing money for the purposes of a trade shall include references to employing it for the purpose of preparing for the carrying on of the trade.

Requirement imposing a maximum on qualifying investments in the relevant company

7.—(1) The requirement of this paragraph is that the relevant holding did not, when it was issued, represent an investment in excess of the maximum qualifying investment for the relevant period.

(2) Subject to sub-paragraph (4) below, the maximum qualifying investment for any period is exceeded to the extent that the aggregate amount of money raised in that period by the issue to the trust company during that period of shares in or securities of the relevant company exceeds £1 million.

(3) Any question for the purposes of this paragraph as to whether any shares in or securities of the relevant company which are for the time being held by the trust company represent an investment in excess of the maximum qualifying investment for any period shall be determined on the assumption, in relation to disposals by the trust company, that, as between shares or securities of the same description, those representing the whole or any part of the excess are disposed of before those which do not.

(4) Where—

(a) at the time of the issue of the relevant holding the relevant company or any of its qualifying subsidiaries was a member of a partnership or a party to a joint venture,

(b) the trade by virtue of which the requirements of paragraph 3(3) above are satisfied was at that time being carried on, or to be carried on, by those partners in partnership or by the parties to the joint venture as such, and

(c) the other partners or parties to the joint venture include at least one other company,

this paragraph shall have effect in relation to the relevant company as if the sum of money for the time being specified in sub-paragraph (2) above were to be divided by the number of companies (including the relevant company) which, at the time when the relevant holding was issued, were members of the partnership or, as the case may be, parties to the joint venture.

(5) For the purposes of this paragraph the relevant period is the period beginning with whichever is the earlier of—

(a) the time six months before the issue of the relevant holding; and

(b) the beginning of the year of assessment in which the issue of that holding took place.

Requirement as to the assets of the relevant company

8.—(1) The requirement of this paragraph is that the value of the relevant assets—

(a) did not exceed £10 million immediately before the issue of the relevant holding; and

(b) did not exceed £11 million immediately afterwards.

(2) Subject to sub-paragraph (3) below, the reference in sub-paragraph (1) above to the value of the relevant assets is a reference—

(a) in relation to a time when the relevant company did not have any qualifying subsidiaries, to the value of the gross assets of that company at that time; and

(b) in relation to any other time, to the aggregate value at that time of the gross assets of all the companies in the relevant company's group.

(3) For the purposes of this paragraph assets of any member of the relevant company's group that consist in rights against, or in shares in or securities of, another member of the group shall be disregarded.

(4) In this paragraph references, in relation to any time, to the relevant company's group are references to the relevant company and its qualifying subsidiaries at that time.

Requirements as to the subsidiaries etc. of the relevant company

9.—(1) The requirements of this paragraph are that, subject to sub-paragraph (2) below, the relevant company must not be—

(a) a company which controls (whether on its own or together with any person connected with it) any company that is not a qualifying subsidiary of the relevant company; or

(b) a company which is under the control of another company (or of another company and a person connected with the other company);

and arrangements must not be in existence by virtue of which the relevant company could fall within paragraph (a) or (b) above.

(2) A company shall not fall within sub-paragraph (1)(b) above where—

(a) the other company is the trust company or a venture capital trust which is not the trust company; and

(b) the fact that the relevant company is under the control of the other is attributable primarily to a change in the value of any shares in or securities of the relevant company.

Meaning of "qualifying subsidiary"

10.—(1) Subject to the following provisions of this paragraph, a company is a qualifying subsidiary of the relevant company for the purposes of this Schedule if—

(a) the company in question ("the subsidiary"), and

(b) where the relevant company has more than one subsidiary, every other subsidiary of the relevant company,

is a company falling within each of sub-paragraphs (2) and (3) below.

(2) The subsidiary falls within this sub-paragraph if—

(a) it is a company in relation to which the requirements of paragraph 3(2)(a) above are satisfied;

(b) it exists wholly for the purpose of holding and managing property used by the relevant company or any of the relevant company's other subsidiaries for the purposes of—

(i) research and development from which it is intended that a qualifying trade to be carried on by the relevant company or any of its qualifying subsidiaries will be derived, or

(ii) one or more qualifying trades so carried on;

(c) it would exist wholly for such a purpose apart from purposes capable of having no significant effect (other than in relation to incidental matters) on the extent of the company's
activities; or

(d) it has no profits for the purposes of corporation tax and no part of its business consists in
the making of investments.

(3) The subsidiary falls within this sub-paragraph if—

(a) the relevant company, or another of its subsidiaries, possesses not less than 90 per cent of
the issued share capital of, and not less than 90 per cent of the voting power in, the
subsidiary;

(b) the relevant company, or another of its subsidiaries, would in the event of a winding up of
the subsidiary or in any other circumstances be beneficially entitled to receive not less
than 90 per cent of the assets of the subsidiary which would then be available for distribution to the equity holders of the subsidiary;

(c) the relevant company, or another of its subsidiaries, is beneficially entitled to not less than
90 per cent of any profits of the subsidiary which are available for distribution to the equity
holders of the subsidiary;

(d) no person other than the relevant company or another of its subsidiaries has control of the
subsidiary within the meaning of section 840; and

(e) no arrangements are in existence by virtue of which the relevant company could cease to
fall within this sub-paragraph.

(4) The subsidiary shall not be regarded, at a time when it is being wound up, as having ceased
on that account to be a company falling within sub-paragraphs (2) and (3) above if it is shown—

(a) that it would fall within those sub-paragraphs apart from the winding up; and

(b) that the winding up is for bona fide commercial reasons and not part of a scheme or
arrangement the main purpose of which, or one of the main purposes of which, is the
avoidance of tax.

(5) The subsidiary shall not be regarded, at any time when arrangements are in existence for
the disposal by the relevant company, or (as the case may be) by another subsidiary of that
company, of all its interest in the subsidiary in question, as having ceased on that account to be a
company falling within sub-paragraphs (2) and (3) above if it is shown that the disposal is to be
for bona fide commercial reasons and not part of a scheme or arrangement the main purpose of
which, or one of the main purposes of which, is the avoidance of tax.

(6) For the purposes of this paragraph the persons who are equity holders of the subsidiary
and the percentage of the assets of the subsidiary to which an equity holder would be entitled
shall be determined in accordance with paragraphs 1 and 3 of Schedule 18, taking references in
paragraph 3 to the first company as references to an equity holder, and references to a winding
up as including references to any other circumstances in which assets of the subsidiary are available for distribution to its equity holders.

Winding up of the relevant company

11. None of the requirements of this Schedule shall be regarded, at a time when the relevant
company is being wound up, as being, on that account, a requirement that is not satisfied in
relation to that company if it is shown—

(a) that the requirements of this Schedule would be satisfied in relation to that company apart
from the winding up; and

(b) that the winding up is for bona fide commercial reasons and not part of a scheme or
arrangement the main purpose of which, or one of the main purposes of which, is the
avoidance of tax.

Power to amend Schedule

12. The Treasury may by order amend this Schedule for any or all of the following purposes,
that is to say—

(a) to make such modifications of paragraphs 4 and 5 above as they may consider expedient;

(b) to substitute different sums for the sums of money for the time being specified in paragraphs 7(2) and 8(1) above.

General interpretation

13.—(1) In this Schedule—

"debenture" has the meaning given by section 744 of the Companies Act 1985; and

"securities" has the same meaning as in section 842AA;

and references in this Schedule to the issue of any securities, in relation to any security consisting
in a liability in respect of an unsecured loan, shall have effect as references to the making of the
loan.

(2) Section 839 applies for the purposes of this Schedule.

(3) For the purposes of paragraphs 5(2) and 9 above a person shall be taken to have control of a company if he would be so taken for the purposes of Part XI by virtue of section 416(2) to (6).

GENERAL NOTE

The Schedule defines the meaning of "qualifying holding" for a Venture Capital Trust (VCT). At least 70 per cent of a VCT's assets must be in qualifying holdings.

Para. 1

The holding must have been first issued to the VCT and retained by it ever since.

Para. 2

The holding must be in an unquoted company. However, where such a company becomes quoted, the holding may be retained by the VCT for a further five years.

Para. 3

The relevant company must carry on a "qualifying trade" (see para. 4 below), or its business must consist entirely of investment in "qualifying subsidiaries" (see para. 10 below) or a combination of the two. A trade must be carried on wholly or mainly in the U.K. or within two years of the issue of the relevant holding.

Para. 4

This lays down the conditions governing a qualifying trade. Research and development from which it is intended such a trade will be carried on is included. Sub-paragraph (2) sets out a range of trades which do not qualify and sub-paras. (3) and (4) explain what is an ordinary trade of wholesale or retail distribution (which does qualify). Sub-paragraphs (5)–(8) set out special provisions relating to the production and distribution of films, royalties or licence fees and the circumstances in which ship chartering is a qualifying trade.

Para. 5

This provides definitions for the purposes of para. 4.

Para. 6

Money raised by the investment in question must be employed in the company's trade within 12 months.

Para. 7

A £1 million limit applies to investment in a qualifying company in any year. Where a company is part of a joint venture, the limit is proportionally reduced. Investments made in different tax years which are less than six months apart are counted together for the purposes of the limit.

Para. 8

The gross assets of the relevant company should not exceed £10 million before the investment or £11 million thereafter. This includes assets of subsidiaries, but excludes assets consisting of claims against other members of the group.

Para. 9

A company cannot be controlled by another company nor itself control a company other than a 90 per cent subsidiary. However, where a VCT unintentionally acquires control of the company, this fact can be ignored.

Para. 10

A company may not have a subsidiary other than a 90 per cent subsidiary, which itself carries on a qualifying trade or is a property-managing or dormant company.

Para. 11

The *bona fide* winding-up of a company does not prevent it from counting towards the qualifying holdings of a VCT.

Para. 12

The Treasury are empowered to vary by regulation the definition of a qualifying trade and the investment limits.

Para. 13
This defines various terms referred to in the Schedule.

Section 71   SCHEDULE 15

VENTURE CAPITAL TRUSTS: RELIEF FROM INCOME TAX

PART I

RELIEF ON INVESTMENT

Entitlement to claim relief

1.—(1) Subject to the following provisions of this Schedule, an individual shall, for any year of assessment, be entitled under this Part of this Schedule to claim relief in respect of an amount equal to the aggregate of the amounts (if any) which, by reference to eligible shares issued to him by venture capital trusts in the course of that year, are amounts on which he is eligible for relief in accordance with sub-paragraph (2) below.

(2) The amounts on which an individual shall be taken for the purposes of sub-paragraph (1) above to be eligible for relief shall be any amounts subscribed by him on his own behalf for eligible shares issued by a venture capital trust for raising money.

(3) An individual shall not be entitled under this Part of this Schedule to claim relief for any given year of assessment in respect of an amount of more than £100,000.

(4) An individual shall not be entitled under this Schedule to claim any relief to which he is eligible by reference to any shares unless he had attained the age of eighteen years before those shares were issued.

(5) Where an individual makes a claim for any relief to which he is entitled under this Part of this Schedule for any year of assessment, the amount of his liability for that year to income tax on his total income shall be equal to the amount to which he would be so liable apart from this Part of this Schedule less whichever is the smaller of—

   (a) an amount equal to tax at the lower rate for that year on the amount in respect of which he is entitled to claim relief for that year, and
   (b) the amount which reduces his liability to nil.

(6) In determining for the purposes of sub-paragraph (5) above the amount of income tax to which a person would be liable apart from this Part of this Schedule, no account shall be taken of—

   (a) any income tax reduction under section 289A,
   (b) any income tax reduction under Chapter I of Part VII or under section 347B,
   (c) any income tax reduction under section 353(1A),
   (d) any income tax reduction under section 54(3A) of the Finance Act 1989,
   (e) any relief by way of a reduction of liability to tax which is given in accordance with any arrangements having effect by virtue of section 788 or by way of a credit under section 790(1), or
   (f) any tax at the basic rate on so much of that person's income as is income the income tax on which he is entitled to charge against any other person or to deduct, retain or satisfy out of any payment.

(7) Where, in the case of any claim for relief under this Part of this Schedule in respect of any shares issued in any year of assessment, effect is given to the claim by repayment of tax, section 824 shall have effect in relation to the repayment as if the time from which the twelve months mentioned in subsections (1)(a) and (3)(a) of that section are to be calculated were the end of the year of assessment in which the shares were issued.

(8) A person shall not be entitled to be given any relief under this Part of this Schedule by reference to any shares if circumstances have arisen which would have resulted, had that relief already been given, in the withdrawal or reduction of the relief.

(9) A person shall not under this Part of this Schedule be eligible for any relief on any amount by reference to any shares unless the shares are both subscribed for and issued for bona fide commercial purposes and not as part of a scheme or arrangement the main purpose of which, or one of the main purposes of which, is the avoidance of tax.

Loan-linked investments

2.—(1) An individual shall not be entitled to relief under this Part of this Schedule in respect of any shares if—

   (a) there is a loan made by any person, at any time in the relevant period, to that individual or any associate of his; and

   (b) the loan is one which would not have been made, or would not have been made on the same terms, if that individual had not subscribed for those shares or had not been proposing to do so.

(2) References in this paragraph to the making by any person of a loan to any individual or an associate of his include references—

   (a) to the giving by that person of any credit to that individual or any associate of his; and

   (b) to the assignment or assignation to that person of any debt due from that individual or any associate of his.

(3) In this paragraph—

     "associate" has the meaning given in subsections (3) and (4) of section 417, except that in those subsections (as applied for the purposes of this paragraph) "relative" shall not include a brother or sister; and

     "the relevant period", in relation to relief under this Part of this Schedule in respect of any shares in a company which is a venture capital trust, means the period beginning with the incorporation of the company (or, if the company was incorporated more than two years before the date on which the shares were issued, beginning two years before that date) and ending five years after the issue of the shares.

Loss of investment relief

3.—(1) This paragraph applies, subject to sub-paragraph (5) below, where—

   (a) an individual who has made any claim for relief under this Part of this Schedule makes any disposal of eligible shares in a venture capital trust, and

   (b) that disposal takes place before the end of the period of five years beginning with the issue of those shares to that individual.

(2) If the disposal is made otherwise than by way of a bargain made at arm's length, any relief given under this Part of this Schedule by reference to the shares which are disposed of shall be withdrawn.

(3) Where the disposal was made by way of a bargain made at arm's length—

   (a) if, apart from this sub-paragraph, the relief given by reference to the shares that are disposed of is greater than the amount mentioned in sub-paragraph (4) below, it shall be reduced by that amount, and

   (b) if paragraph (a) above does not apply, any relief given by reference to those shares shall be withdrawn.

(4) The amount referred to in sub-paragraph (3) above is an amount equal to tax at the lower rate for the year of assessment for which the relief was given on the amount or value of the consideration which the individual receives for the shares.

(5) This paragraph shall not apply in the case of any disposal of shares which is made by a married man to his wife or by a married woman to her husband if it is made, in either case, at a time when they are living together.

(6) Where any eligible shares issued to any individual ("the transferor"), being shares by reference to which any amount of relief under this Part of this Schedule has been given, are transferred to the transferor's spouse ("the transferee") by a disposal such as is mentioned in sub-paragraph (5) above, this paragraph shall have effect, in relation to any subsequent disposal or other event, as if—

   (a) the transferee were the person who had subscribed for the shares,

   (b) the shares had been issued to the transferee at the time when they were issued to the transferor,

   (c) there had been, in respect of the transferred shares, such a reduction under this Part of this Schedule in the transferee's liability to income tax as is equal to the actual reduction in respect of those shares of the transferor's liability, and

   (d) that deemed reduction were (notwithstanding the transfer) to be treated for the purposes of this paragraph as an amount of relief given by reference to the shares transferred.

(7) Any assessment for withdrawing or reducing relief by reason of a disposal or other event falling within sub-paragraph (6) above shall be made on the transferee.

(8) In determining for the purposes of this paragraph any question whether any disposal relates to shares by reference to which any relief under this Part of this Schedule has been given, it shall be assumed, in relation to any disposal by any person of any eligible shares in a venture capital trust, that—

   (a) as between eligible shares acquired by the same person on different days, those acquired on an earlier day are disposed of by that person before those acquired on a later day; and

(b) as between eligible shares acquired by the same person on the same day, those by reference to which relief under this Part of this Schedule has been given are disposed of by that person only after he has disposed of any other eligible shares acquired by him on that day.

(9) Where—

(a) the approval of any company as a venture capital trust is withdrawn, and

(b) the withdrawal of the approval is not one to which section 842AA(8) applies,

any person who, at the time when the withdrawal takes effect, is holding any shares by reference to which relief under this Part of this Schedule has been given shall be deemed for the purposes of this paragraph to have disposed of those shares immediately before that time and otherwise than by way of a bargain made at arm's length.

Assessment on withdrawal or reduction of relief

4.—(1) Any relief given under this Part of this Schedule which is subsequently found not to have been due shall be withdrawn by the making of an assessment to tax under Case VI of Schedule D for the year of assessment for which the relief was given.

(2) An assessment for withdrawing or reducing relief in pursuance of paragraph 3 above shall also be made as an assessment to tax under Case VI of Schedule D for the year of assessment for which the relief was given.

(3) No assessment for withdrawing or reducing relief given by reference to shares issued to any person shall be made by reason of any event occurring after his death.

Provision of information

5.—(1) Where an event occurs by reason of which any relief under this Part of this Schedule falls to be withdrawn or reduced, the individual to whom the relief was given shall, within 60 days of his coming to know of the event, give a notice to the inspector containing particulars of the event.

(2) If the inspector has reason to believe that a person has not given a notice which he is required to give under sub-paragraph (1) above in respect of any event, the inspector may by notice require that person to furnish him within such time (not being less than 60 days) as may be specified in the notice with such information relating to the event as the inspector may reasonably require for the purposes of this Part of this Schedule.

(3) No obligation as to secrecy imposed by statute or otherwise shall preclude the inspector from disclosing to a venture capital trust that relief given by reference to a particular number or proportion of its shares has been given or claimed under this Part of this Schedule.

Interpretation of Part I

6.—(1) In this Part of this Schedule "eligible shares", in relation to a company which is a venture capital trust, means new ordinary shares in that trust which, throughout the period of five years beginning with the date on which they are issued, carry no present or future preferential right to dividends or to a company's assets on its winding up and no present or future preferential right to be redeemed.

(2) In this Part of this Schedule "ordinary shares", in relation to a company, means shares forming part of a company's ordinary share capital.

(3) In this Part of this Schedule references to a disposal of shares shall include references to a disposal of an interest or right in or over the shares.

PART II

RELIEF ON DISTRIBUTIONS

7.—(1) A relevant distribution of a venture capital trust shall not be regarded as income for any income tax purposes if the person beneficially entitled to it is a qualifying investor.

(2) For the purposes of this paragraph a person is a qualifying investor, in relation to any distribution, if he is an individual who has attained the age of eighteen years and is beneficially entitled to the distribution—

(a) as the person who himself holds the shares in respect of which the distribution is made, or

(b) as a person with such a beneficial entitlement to the shares as derives from their being held for him, or for his benefit, by a nominee of his.

(3) In this paragraph "relevant distribution", in relation to a company which is a venture capital trust, means any distribution which—

(a) consists in a dividend (including a capital dividend) which is paid in respect of any ordinary shares in that company which—

(i) were acquired by the person to whom the distribution is made at a time when the company was such a trust, and

(ii) are not shares acquired in excess of the permitted maximum for any year of assessment;

and

(b) is not a dividend paid in respect of profits or gains arising or accruing in any accounting period ending at a time when the company was not such a trust.

Meaning of "permitted maximum"

8.—(1) For the purposes of this Part of this Schedule shares in a venture capital trust shall be treated, in relation to any individual, as acquired in excess of the permitted maximum for any year of assessment to the extent that the value of the shares comprised in the relevant acquisitions of that individual for that year exceeds £100,000.

(2) The reference in sub-paragraph (1) above to the relevant acquisitions of an individual for a year of assessment is a reference to all shares which—

(a) are acquired in that year of assessment by that individual or any nominee of his;

(b) are ordinary shares in a company which is a venture capital trust at the time of their acquisition; and

(c) are shares so acquired for bona fide commercial purposes and not as part of a scheme or arrangement the main purpose of which, or one of the main purposes of which, is the avoidance of tax.

(3) Sub-paragraph (4) below applies where—

(a) any ordinary shares in a venture capital trust ("the new shares") are acquired by any individual in circumstances in which they are required for the purposes of the 1992 Act to be treated as the same assets as any other shares; and

(b) the other shares consist of or include any ordinary shares in a venture capital trust that were, or are treated as, acquired otherwise than in excess of the permitted maximum for any year of assessment.

(4) Where this sub-paragraph applies—

(a) the value of the new shares shall be disregarded in determining whether any other shares acquired in the same year of assessment as the new shares are acquired in excess of the permitted maximum for that year; and

(b) the new shares or, as the case may be, an appropriate proportion of them shall be treated as themselves acquired otherwise than in excess of the permitted maximum.

(5) For the purposes of this paragraph the value of any shares acquired by or on behalf of any individual shall be taken to be t︣ eir market value (within the meaning of the 1992 Act) at the time of their acquisition.

(6) Where any shares in a venture capital trust are acquired in excess of the permitted maximum for any year of assessment, the shares representing the excess shall be identified for the purposes of this Part of this Schedule—

(a) by treating shares acquired later in the year as comprised in the excess before those acquired earlier in the year;

(b) by treating shares of different descriptions acquired on the same day as acquired within the permitted maximum in the same proportions as are borne by the respective values of the shares comprised in the acquisitions of each description to the total value of all the shares in the trust acquired on that day; and

(c) by applying the rules in section 151A(4) and (5) of the 1992 Act for determining the shares to which any disposal of shares in the trust relates (even one which is not a disposal for the purposes of that Act).

Interpretation of Part II

9.—(1) In this Part of this Schedule "ordinary shares", in relation to a company, means shares forming part of the company's ordinary share capital.

(2) In this Part of this Schedule "nominee", in relation to any individual, includes the trustees of a bare trust of which that individual is the only beneficiary.

GENERAL NOTE

The income tax reliefs provided by this Schedule for investors in a VCT fall into two categories. Part I of the Schedule deals with relief on investment and Part II with relief on distributions.

Part I: relief on investment

Para. 1

An individual aged at least 18 years may claim relief on a subscription for eligible shares (see para. 6) issued by a VCT in order to raise money. Relief may be given on subscriptions up to

£100,000 in any given year. Relief is given by way of reduction in the investor's tax liability for the year in which the shares are issued. The reduction is an amount equivalent to the lower rate of income tax (20 per cent for 1995–96) multiplied by the amount subscribed for eligible shares or the amount, if smaller, which reduces the investor's income tax liability to nil. The relief is given before all other reliefs by means of an income tax reduction. There is a general provision denying relief in cases of tax avoidance.

Para. 2

Where there is a loan linked in some way to the investment, relief is denied. This is aimed at an arrangement which became popular in the later years of the Business Expansion Scheme.

Para. 3

The shares in the VCT must be retained for at least five years. The relief is wholly withdrawn if the shares are disposed of otherwise than by way of an arm's length bargain or at a gain; and wholly or partly withdrawn if the investor sells the shares at arm's length for less than the purchase price. The amount of relief withdrawn cannot exceed an amount equivalent to tax at the lower rate for the year in which the relief was given multiplied by the proceeds or valuable consideration received on disposal.

Para. 4

Withdrawal of relief is effected by way of an assessment under Case VI of Schedule D for the year of assessment in which the relief was given. No assessment will be raised on an event occurring after the death of the investors (or spouse, if there has been a transfer).

Para. 5

The investor should notify his inspector within 60 days of an event necessitating the withdrawal of any relief. Likewise, the inspector has the right to demand information and to communicate with the VCT.

Para. 6

This provides certain definitions. "Eligible shares" are new ordinary shares which for a period of five years carry no preferential rights to dividends or assets.

Part II: relief on distributions

Para. 7

Dividends in respect of ordinary shares in a VCT are exempt from income tax, provided that the holding is within the permitted maximum (see para. 8).

Para. 8

The permitted maximum for any one year of assessment is £100,000. Where shares are acquired in excess of the maximum, relief is given on the first £100,000 worth acquired in any year, whether or not they are new shares qualifying for relief on investment under para. 1 above. Where VCT shares, on which the investor already has tax relief on distributions, are exchanged for ordinary shares in another VCT, the new shares do not count towards the permitted maximum, but may themselves qualify in whole or part for distribution relief.

Para. 9

This contains interpretation provisions.

Section 72   SCHEDULE 16

Venture Capital Trusts: Deferred charge on re-investment

Application of Schedule

1.—(1) This Schedule applies where—
- (a) there would (apart from paragraph 2(2)(a) below) be a chargeable gain ("the original gain") accruing to an individual ("the investor") at any time ("the accrual time") on or after 6th April 1995;
- (b) that gain is one accruing on the disposal by the investor of any asset or in accordance with paragraphs 4 and 5 of Schedule 5B or paragraphs 4 and 5 below;
- (c) the investor makes a qualifying investment; and
- (d) the investor is resident or ordinarily resident in the United Kingdom at the accrual time and the time when he makes the qualifying investment and is not, in relation to the qualifying investment, a person to whom sub-paragraph (4) below applies.

(2) The investor makes a qualifying investment for the purposes of this Schedule if—

(a) he subscribes for any shares by reference to which he is given relief under Part I of Schedule 15B to the Taxes Act on any amount;

(b) those shares are issued at a qualifying time; and

(c) where that time is before the accrual time, those shares are still held by the investor at the accrual time;

and in this Schedule "relevant shares", in relation to a case to which this Schedule applies, means any of the shares in a venture capital trust which are acquired by the investor in making the qualifying investment.

(3) In this Schedule "a qualifying time", in relation to any shares subscribed for by the investor, means—

(a) any time in the period beginning twelve months before the accrual time and ending twelve months after the accrual time, or

(b) any such time before the beginning of that period or after it ends as the Board may by notice allow.

(4) This sub-paragraph applies to an individual in relation to a qualifying investment if—

(a) though resident or ordinarily resident in the United Kingdom at the time when he makes the investment, he is regarded for the purposes of any double taxation relief arrangements as resident in a territory outside the United Kingdom; and

(b) were section 151A(1) to be disregarded, the arrangements would have the effect that he would not be liable in the United Kingdom to tax on a gain arising on a disposal, immediately after their acquisition, of the shares acquired in making that investment.

The postponement of the original gain

2.—(1) On the making of a claim by the investor for the purposes of this Schedule, so much of the investor's unused qualifying expenditure on relevant shares as—

(a) is specified in the claim, and

(b) does not exceed so much of the original gain as is unmatched,

shall be set against a corresponding amount of the original gain.

(2) Where the amount of any qualifying expenditure on any relevant shares is set under this Schedule against the whole or any part of the original gain—

(a) so much of that gain as is equal to that amount shall be treated as not having accrued at the accrual time; but

(b) paragraphs 4 and 5 below shall apply for determining the gain that is to be treated as accruing on the occurrence of any chargeable event in relation to any of those relevant shares.

(3) For the purposes of this Schedule, but subject to the following provisions of this paragraph—

(a) the investor's qualifying expenditure on any relevant shares is the sum equal to the amount on which he is given relief under Part I of Schedule 15B to the Taxes Act by reference to those shares; and

(b) that expenditure is unused to the extent that it has not already been set under this Schedule against the whole or any part of a chargeable gain.

(4) For the purposes of this paragraph the original gain is unmatched, in relation to any qualifying expenditure on relevant shares, to the extent that it has not had any other amount set against it under this Schedule or Schedule 5B.

Chargeable events

3.—(1) Subject to the following provisions of this paragraph, there is for the purposes of this Schedule a chargeable event in relation to any relevant shares if, after the making of the qualifying investment—

(a) the investor disposes of those shares otherwise than by way of a disposal within marriage;

(b) those shares are disposed of, otherwise than by way of a disposal to the investor, by a person who acquired them on a disposal made by the investor within marriage;

(c) there is, in a case where those shares fall within section 151B(3)(c), such an actual or deemed exchange of those shares for any non-qualifying holdings as, under section 135 or 136, requires, or but for section 116 would require, those holdings to be treated for the purposes of this Act as the same assets as those shares;

(d) the investor becomes a non-resident while holding those shares and within the relevant period;

   (e) a person who acquired those shares on a disposal within marriage becomes a non-resident while holding those shares and within the relevant period;

   (f) the company in which those shares are shares has its approval as a venture capital trust withdrawn in a case to which section 842AA(8) of the Taxes Act does not apply; or

   (g) the relief given under Part I of Schedule 15B to the Taxes Act by reference to those shares is withdrawn or reduced in circumstances not falling within any of paragraphs (a) to (f) above.

(2) In sub-paragraph (1) above—

   "non-qualifying holdings" means any shares or securities other than any ordinary shares (within the meaning of section 151A) in a venture capital trust; and

   "the relevant period", in relation to any relevant shares, means the period of five years beginning with the time when the investor made the qualifying investment by virtue of which he acquired those shares.

(3) For the purposes of sub-paragraph (1) above there shall not be a chargeable event by virtue of sub-paragraph (1)(d) or (e) above in relation to any shares if—

   (a) the reason why the person in question becomes a non-resident is that he works in an employment or office all the duties of which are performed outside the United Kingdom, and

   (b) he again becomes resident or ordinarily resident in the United Kingdom within the period of three years from the time when he became a non-resident, without having meanwhile disposed of any of those shares;

and, accordingly, no assessment shall be made by virtue of sub-paragraph (1)(d) or (e) above before the end of that period in any case where the condition in paragraph (a) above is satisfied and the condition in paragraph (b) above may be satisfied.

(4) For the purposes of sub-paragraph (3) above a person shall be taken to have disposed of any shares if and only if there has been such a disposal as would, if the person making the disposal had been resident in the United Kingdom, have been a chargeable event in relation to those shares.

(5) Where in any case—

   (a) the investor or a person who has acquired any relevant shares on a disposal within marriage dies, and

   (b) an event occurs at or after the time of the death which (apart from this sub-paragraph) would be a chargeable event in relation to any relevant shares held by the deceased immediately before his death,

that event shall not be chargeable event in relation to the shares so held.

(6) Without prejudice to the operation of paragraphs 4 and 5 below in a case falling within sub-paragraph (1)(f) above, the references in this paragraph to a disposal shall not include references to the disposal which by virtue of section 151B(6) is deemed to take place in such a case.

Gain accruing on chargeable event

4.—(1) On the occurrence of a chargeable event in relation to any relevant shares in relation to which there has not been a previous chargeable event—

   (a) a chargeable gain shall be treated as accruing at the time of the event; and

   (b) the amount of the gain shall be equal to so much of the original gain as is an amount against which there has under this Schedule been set any expenditure on those shares.

(2) In determining for the purposes of this Schedule any question whether any shares to which a chargeable event relates are shares the expenditure on which has under this Schedule been set against the whole or any part of any gain, the assumptions in sub-paragraph (3) below shall apply and, in a case where the shares are not (within the meaning of section 151B) eligible for relief under section 151A(1), shall apply notwithstanding anything in any of sections 104, 105 and 107.

(3) Those assumptions are that—

   (a) as between shares acquired by the same person on different days, those acquired on an earlier day are disposed of by that person before those acquired on a later day; and

   (b) as between shares in a company that were acquired on the same day, those the expenditure on which has been set under this Schedule against the whole or any part of any gain are disposed of by that person only after he has disposed of any other shares in that company that were acquired by him on that day.

(4) Where at the time of a chargeable event any relevant shares are treated for the purposes of this Act as represented by assets which consist of or include assets other than the relevant shares—

   (a) the expenditure on those shares which was set against the gain in question shall be treated, in determining for the purposes of this paragraph the amount of expenditure on each of those assets which is to be treated as having been set against that gain, as apportioned in such manner as may be just and reasonable between those assets; and

(b) as between different assets treated as representing the same relevant shares, the assumptions mentioned in sub-paragraph (3) above shall apply with the necessary modifications in relation to those assets as they would apply in relation to the shares.

Persons to whom gain accrues

5.—(1) The chargeable gain which accrues in accordance with paragraph 4 above on the occurrence in relation to any relevant shares of a chargeable event shall be treated as accruing, as the case may be—

(a) to the person who makes the disposal,

(b) to the person who holds the shares in question at the time of the exchange or deemed exchange,

(c) to the person who becomes a non-resident,

(d) to the person who holds the shares in question when the withdrawal of the approval takes effect, or

(e) to the person who holds the shares in question when the circumstances arise in respect of which the relief is withdrawn or reduced.

(2) Where—

(a) sub-paragraph (1) above provides for the holding of shares at a particular time to be what identifies the person to whom any chargeable gain accrues, and

(b) at that time, some of those shares are held by the investor and others are held by a person to whom the investor has transferred them by a disposal within marriage,

the amount of the chargeable gain accruing by virtue of paragraph 4 above shall be computed separately in relation to the investor and that person without reference to the shares held by the other.

Interpretation

6.—(1) In this Schedule "non-resident" means a person who is neither resident nor ordinarily resident in the United Kingdom.

(2) In this Schedule references to a disposal within marriage are references to any disposal to which section 58 applies.

(3) Notwithstanding anything in section 288(5), shares shall not for the purposes of this Schedule be treated as issued by reason only of being comprised in a letter of allotment or similar instrument.

GENERAL NOTE

This provides a roll-over relief on gains arising on the disposal of assets where these are reinvested in a VCT (for general provisions defining a VCT see s.70 above). The Schedule takes effect as a new TCGA 1992, Sched. 5C (see s.72(4) above).

Para. 1

U.K. resident individuals who subscribe for new ordinary shares in a VCT can defer CGT on a gain arising from the disposal of any assets where the gain is reinvested, up to the £100,000 income tax relief limit, within the period of a year before and a year after the accrual of the gain.

Para. 2

Roll-over is provided on a claim by setting off the expenditure on the subscription in the VCT against a corresponding amount of the chargeable gain.

Para. 3

This lists the circumstances in which a rolled-over gain is brought into charge ("the chargeable event"). The most likely of these is when the investor disposes of his shares. Others include the investor ceasing to be resident in the U.K.; loss of approval by the VCT, or other event leading to the withdrawal of income tax relief; or the take-over of a VCT by a non-VCT. However, a charge is not triggered by the death of the investor or his departure from the U.K. for work-related reasons, provided he becomes resident again within three years.

Para. 4

The gain accruing on a chargeable event is equal to the original gain which obtained roll-over relief when the investment in VCT shares was made. The shares acquired are ranked in a first-in, first-out order for the purpose of calculating the charge. Where some of the gain is chargeable and some not, an apportionment may be made on a just and reasonable basis.

Para. 5

This identifies the person to whom the gain accrues, essentially the person who makes the disposal or who holds the shares at the time of the chargeable event.

Para. 6

Various terms are defined.

Section 74   SCHEDULE 17

SETTLEMENTS: LIABILITY OF SETTLOR

PART I

THE NEW PROVISIONS

1. In Part XV of the Taxes Act 1988 (settlements) the following provisions are inserted (in place of sections 660 to 676 and 683 to 685) as Chapter IA—

"CHAPTER IA

LIABILITY OF SETTLOR

Main provisions

Income arising under settlement where settlor retains an interest

660A.—(1) Income arising under a settlement during the life of the settlor shall be treated for all purposes of the Income Tax Acts as the income of the settlor and not as the income of any other person unless the income arises from property in which the settlor has no interest.

(2) Subject to the following provisions of this section, a settlor shall be regarded as having an interest in property if that property or any derived property is, or will or may become, payable to or applicable for the benefit of the settlor or his spouse in any circumstances whatsoever.

(3) The reference in subsection (2) above to the spouse of the settlor does not include—

(a) a person to whom the settlor is not for the time being married but may later marry, or

(b) a spouse from whom the settlor is separated under an order of a court, or under a separation agreement or in such circumstances that the separation is likely to be permanent, or

(c) the widow or widower of the settlor.

(4) A settlor shall not be regarded as having an interest in property by virtue of subsection (2) above if and so long as none of that property, and no derived property, can become payable or applicable as mentioned in that subsection except in the event of—

(a) the bankruptcy of some person who is or may become beneficially entitled to the property or any derived property, or

(b) an assignment of or charge on the property or any derived property being made or given by some such person, or

(c) in the case of a marriage settlement, the death of both parties to the marriage and of all or any of the children of the marriage, or

(d) the death of a child of the settlor who had become beneficially entitled to the property or any derived property at an age not exceeding 25.

(5) A settlor shall not be regarded as having an interest in property by virtue of subsection (2) above if and so long as some person is alive and under the age of 25 during whose life that property, or any derived property, cannot become payable or applicable as mentioned in that subsection except in the event of that person becoming bankrupt or assigning or charging his interest in the property or any derived property.

(6) The reference in subsection (1) above to a settlement does not include an outright gift by one spouse to the other of property from which income arises, unless—

(a) the gift does not carry a right to the whole of that income, or

(b) the property given is wholly or substantially a right to income.

For this purpose a gift is not an outright gift if it is subject to conditions, or if the property given or any derived property is or will or may become, in any circumstances whatsoever, payable to or applicable for the benefit of the donor.

(7) The reference in subsection (1) above to a settlement does not include an irrevocable allocation of pension rights by one spouse to the other in accordance with the terms of a relevant statutory scheme (within the meaning of Chapter I of Part XIV).

(8) Subsection (1) above does not apply to income arising under a settlement made by one party to a marriage by way of provision for the other—

    (a) after the dissolution or annulment of the marriage, or

    (b) while they are separated under an order of a court, or under a separation agreement or in such circumstances that the separation is likely to be permanent,

being income payable to or applicable for the benefit of that other party.

(9) Subsection (1) above does not apply to income consisting of—

    (a) annual payments made by an individual for bona fide commercial reasons in connection with his trade, profession or vocation; or

    (b) covenanted payments to charity (as defined by section 347A(7)).

(10) In this section "derived property", in relation to any property, means income from that property or any other property directly or indirectly representing proceeds of, or of income from, that property or income therefrom.

Payments to unmarried minor children of settlor

660B.—(1) Income arising under a settlement which does not fall to be treated as income of the settlor under section 660A but which during the life of the settlor is paid to or for the benefit of an unmarried minor child of the settlor in any year of assessment shall be treated for all the purposes of the Income Tax Acts as the income of the settlor for that year and not as the income of any other person.

(2) Where income arising under a settlement is retained or accumulated by the trustees, any payment whatsoever made thereafter by virtue or in consequence of the settlement, or any enactment relating thereto, to or for the benefit of an unmarried minor child of the settlor shall be deemed for the purposes of subsection (1) above to be a payment of income if or to the extent that there is available retained or accumulated income.

(3) There shall be taken to be available retained or accumulated income at any time when the aggregate amount of the income which has arisen under the settlement since it was made or entered into exceeds the aggregate amount of income so arising which has been—

    (a) treated as income of the settlor or a beneficiary, or

    (b) paid (whether as income or capital) to or for the benefit of a beneficiary other than an unmarried minor child of the settlor, or

    (c) applied in defraying expenses of the trustees which were properly chargeable to income (or would have been so chargeable but for any express provisions of the trust).

(4) Where an offshore income gain (within the meaning of Chapter V of Part XVII) accrues in respect of a disposal of assets made by a trustee holding them for a person who would be absolutely entitled as against the trustee but for being a minor, the income which by virtue of section 761(1) is treated as arising by reference to that gain shall for the purposes of this section be deemed to be paid to that person.

(5) Income paid to or for the benefit of a child of a settlor shall not be treated as provided in subsection (1) above for a year of assessment in which the aggregate amount paid to or for the benefit of that child which but for this subsection would be so treated does not exceed £100.

(6) In this section—

    (a) "child" includes a stepchild and an illegitimate child;

    (b) "minor" means a person under the age of 18 years, and "minor child" shall be construed accordingly; and

    (c) references to payments include payments in money or money's worth.

Nature of charge on settlor

660C.—(1) Tax chargeable by virtue of this Chapter shall be charged under Case VI of Schedule D.

(2) In computing the liability to income tax of a settlor chargeable by virtue of this Chapter the same deductions and reliefs shall be allowed as would have been allowed if the income treated as his by virtue of this Chapter had been received by him.

(3) Subject to section 833(3), income which is treated by virtue of this Chapter as income of a settlor shall be deemed for the purposes of this section to be the highest part of his income.

Adjustments between settlor and trustees, &c.

660D.—(1) Where by virtue of this Chapter income tax becomes chargeable on and is paid by a settlor, he is entitled—

(a) to recover from any trustee, or any other person to whom the income is payable by virtue or in consequence of the settlement, the amount of the tax so paid; and

(b) for that purpose to require an officer of the Board to furnish to him a certificate specifying the amount of income in respect of which he has so paid tax and the amount of tax so paid.

A certificate so furnished is conclusive evidence of the facts stated therein.

(2) Where a person obtains, in respect of an allowance or relief, a repayment of income tax in excess of the amount of the repayment to which he would, but for this Chapter, have been entitled, an amount equal to the excess shall be paid by him to the trustee, or other person to whom the income is payable by virtue or in consequence of the settlement, or, where there are two or more such persons, shall be apportioned among those persons as the case may require.

If any question arises as to the amount of a payment or as to an apportionment to be made under this subsection, that question shall be decided by the General Commissioners whose decision shall be final.

(3) Nothing in this Chapter shall be construed as excluding a charge to tax on the trustees as persons by whom any income is received.

Supplementary provisions

Application to settlements by two or more settlors

660E.—(1) In the case of a settlement where there is more than one settlor, this Chapter shall have effect in relation to each settlor as if he were the only settlor, as follows.

(2) In this Chapter, in relation to a settlor—

(a) references to the property comprised in a settlement include only property originating from that settlor, and

(b) references to income arising under the settlement include only income originating from that settlor.

(3) For the purposes of section 660B there shall be taken into account, in relation to a settlor, as income paid to or for the benefit of a child of the settlor only—

(a) income originating from that settlor, and

(b) in a case in which section 660B(2) applies, payments which are under that provision (as adapted by subsection (4) below) to be deemed to be payments of income.

(4) In applying section 660B(2) to a settlor—

(a) the reference to income arising under the settlement includes only income originating from that settlor; and

(b) the reference to any payment made by virtue or in consequence of the settlement or any enactment relating thereto includes only a payment made out of property originating from that settlor or income originating from that settlor.

(5) References in this section to property originating from a settlor are references to—

(a) property which that settlor has provided directly or indirectly for the purposes of the settlement; and

(b) property representing that property; and

(c) so much of any property which represents both property so provided and other property as, on a just apportionment, represents the property so provided.

(6) References in this section to income originating from a settlor are references to—

(a) income from property originating from that settlor; and

(b) income provided directly or indirectly by that settlor.

(7) In subsections (5) and (6) above—

(a) references to property or income which a settlor has provided directly or indirectly include references to property or income which has been provided directly or indirectly by another person in pursuance of reciprocal arrangements with that settlor, but do not include references to property or income which that settlor has provided directly or indirectly in pursuance of reciprocal arrangements with another person; and

(b) references to property which represents other property include references to property which represents accumulated income from that other property.

Power to obtain information

660F. An officer of the Board may by notice require any party to a settlement to furnish him within such time as he may direct (not being less than 28 days) with such particulars as he thinks necessary for the purposes of this Chapter.

Meaning of "settlement" and related expressions

660G.—(1) In this Chapter—

"settlement" includes any disposition, trust, covenant, agreement, arrangement or transfer of assets, and

"settlor", in relation to a settlement, means any person by whom the settlement was made.

(2) A person shall be deemed for the purposes of this Chapter to have made a settlement if he has made or entered into the settlement directly or indirectly, and, in particular, but without prejudice to the generality of the preceding words, if he has provided or undertaken to provide funds directly or indirectly for the purpose of the settlement, or has made with any other person a reciprocal arrangement for that other person to make or enter into the settlement.

(3) References in this Chapter to income arising under a settlement include, subject to subsection (4) below, any income chargeable to income tax by deduction or otherwise, and any income which would have been so chargeable if it had been received in the United Kingdom by a person domiciled, resident and ordinarily resident in the United Kingdom.

(4) Where the settlor is not domiciled, or not resident, or not ordinarily resident, in the United Kingdom in a year of assessment, references in this Chapter to income arising under a settlement do not include income arising under the settlement in that year in respect of which the settlor, if he were actually entitled thereto, would not be chargeable to income tax by deduction or otherwise by reason of his not being so domiciled, resident or ordinarily resident.

But where such income is remitted to the United Kingdom in circumstances such that, if the settlor were actually entitled to that income when remitted, he would be chargeable to income tax by reason of his residence in the United Kingdom, it shall be treated for the purposes of this Chapter as arising under the settlement in the year in which it is remitted.".

PART II

MINOR AND CONSEQUENTIAL AMENDMENTS OF THE TAXES ACT 1988

2. In section 125(3)(a) of the Taxes Act 1988, for the words from "subsection (1)(a)" to the end substitute "section 660A(8) or (9)(a)".

3. In section 339(1)(a) of the Taxes Act 1988, for "section 660(3)" substitute "section 347A(7)".

4.—(1) Section 347A of the Taxes Act 1988 (annual payments not a charge on the income of the payer) applies to a payment which is treated by virtue of Chapter IA of Part XV of the Taxes Act 1988 as income of the payer notwithstanding that it is made in pursuance of an obligation which is an existing obligation within the meaning of section 36(3) of the Finance Act 1988.

(2) In section 347A of the Taxes Act 1988, after subsection (6) add—

"(7) In subsection (25)(b) above 'a covenanted payment to charity' means a payment made under a covenant made otherwise than for consideration in money or money's worth in favour of a body of persons or trust established for charitable purposes only whereby the like annual payments (of which the payment in question is one) become payable for a period which may exceed three years and is not capable of earlier termination under any power exercisable without the consent of the persons for the time being entitled to the payments.

(8) For the purposes of subsection (7) above the bodies mentioned in section 507 shall each be treated as a body of persons established for charitable purposes only."

5. In section 360A(2)(b) of the Taxes Act 1988, for "section 681(4)" substitute "Chapter IA of Part XV (see section 660G(1) and (2))".

6. In section 417(3)(b) of the Taxes Act 1988, for "section 681(4)" substitute "Chapter IA of Part XV (see section 660G(1) and (2))".

7. In section 505(6) of the Taxes Act 1988, for "section 660(3)" substitute "section 347A(7)".

8. Before section 677 of the Taxes Act 1988 insert the heading—

"CHAPTER IB

PROVISIONS AS TO CAPITAL SUMS PAID TO SETTLOR".

9.—(1) Section 677 of the Taxes Act 1988 is amended as follows.

(2) In subsection (2)(b) after "the amount of" insert "that income taken into account under that subsection in relation to".

(3) After subsection (2)(f) insert—

"(fa) any income arising under the settlement in that year or any previous year which has been treated as income of the settlor by virtue of section 660A or 660B; and".

(4) In subsection (9) after "one of the events specified in section 673(3)" insert "or, in the case of a sum paid on or after 6th April 1995, in one of the events specified in section 660A(4) or on the death under the age of 25 of any such person as is mentioned in section 660A(5)".

10. In section 678 of the Taxes Act 1988, omit subsection (7).

11. After section 682 of the Taxes Act 1988 insert—

"Supplementary provisions

682A.—(1) The provisions of sections 660E to 660G apply for the purposes of this Chapter as they apply for the purposes of Chapter IA.

(2) For the purposes of this Chapter, a body corporate shall be deemed to be connected with a settlement in any year of assessment if at any time in that year—

(a) it is a close company (or only not a close company because it is not resident in the United Kingdom) and the participators then include the trustees of the settlement; or

(b) it is controlled (within the meaning of section 840) by a company falling within paragraph (a) above."

12. For the heading before section 686 of the Taxes Act 1988 substitute—

"Chapter IC

Liability of trustees".

13. In section 686 of the Taxes Act 1988 (liability to income tax at rate applicable to trusts), in subsection (2) (income to which the section applies) for paragraph (b) substitute—

"(b) is not, before being distributed, either—

(i) the income of any person other than the trustees, or

(ii) treated for any of the purposes of the Income Tax Acts as the income of a settlor; and".

14.—(1) Section 687 of the Taxes Act 1988 (payments under discretionary trusts) is amended as follows.

(2) For subsection (1) (cases in which the section applies) substitute—

"(1) Where in any year of assessment trustees make a payment to any person in the exercise of a discretion, whether a discretion exercisable by them or by any other person, then if the payment—

(a) is for all the purposes of the Income Tax Acts income of the person to whom it is made (but would not be his income if it were not made to him), or

(b) is treated for those purposes as the income of the settlor by virtue of section 660B,

the following provisions of this section apply with respect to the payment in lieu of section 348 or 349(1).".

(3) In subsection (2)(a) (person credited with having paid tax) after "to whom the payment is made" insert "or, as the case may be, the settlor".

(4) After subsection (4) add—

"(5) References in this section to payments include payments in money or money's worth.".

15. Omit section 689 of the Taxes Act 1988 (recovery from trustees of discretionary trusts of higher rate tax due from beneficiaries).

16. In section 694(3) of the Taxes Act 1988, for "Chapters I to IV" substitute "Chapter IA".

17.—(1) Section 720 of the Taxes Act 1988 is amended as follows.

(2) In subsection (6)—

(a) for "Chapters II to IV" substitute "Chapters IA, IB and IC"; and

(b) for the words from "(within Chapter II)" to the end substitute "arising under the settlement".

(3) In subsection (7) for "Chapters II to IV" substitute "Chapters IA, IB and IC".

(4) In subsection (8)(a) for "Chapter II, III or IV of Part XV (as the case may be)" substitute "Chapter IA of Part XV (see section 660G(1) and (2))".

18. In section 745(6) of the Taxes Act 1988, for "section 681(4)" substitute "section 660G(1) and (2)".

19. In section 783(10)(b) of the Taxes Act 1988, for "section 670(2)" substitute "section 660G(1) and (2)".

20. In section 839(3) of the Taxes Act 1988, for subsection (3) substitute—

"(3) A person, in his capacity as trustee of a settlement, is connected with—

(a) any individual who in relation to the settlement is a settlor,

(b) any person who is connected with such an individual, and

(c) any body corporate which is connected with that settlement.

In this subsection "settlement" and "settlor" have the same meaning as in Chapter IA of Part XV (see section 660G(1) and (2)).

(3A) For the purpose of subsection (3) above a body corporate is connected with a settlement if—

    (a) it is a close company (or only not a close company because it is not resident in the United Kingdom) and the participators include the trustees of the settlement; or

    (b) it is controlled (within the meaning of section 840) by a company falling within paragraph (a) above.".

PART III

CONSEQUENTIAL AMENDMENTS OF OTHER ENACTMENTS

Taxes Management Act 1970 (c.9)

21. In section 27(2) of the Taxes Management Act 1970, for "section 681(4)" substitute "section 660G(1) and (2)".

22. In section 31(3) of the Taxes Management Act 1970 (including that provision as proposed to be substituted by paragraph 7 of Schedule 19 to the Finance Act 1994), for "sections 660 to 685" substitute "sections 660A to 660G or 677 to 682A".

23. In column 1 of the Table in section 98 of the Taxes Management Act 1970, for the references to section 669 and 680 of the Taxes Act 1988 substitute "section 660F".

Finance Act 1989 (c.26)

24. In section 59(1)(c) of the Finance Act 1989, for "section 660(3)" substitute "section 347A(7)".

25. In section 60 of the Finance Act 1989, omit subsection (3) and in subsection (4) for "subsections (2) and (3)" substitute "subsection (2)".

Finance Act 1990 (c.29)

26. In section 25(12)(b) of the Finance Act 1990, for "section 660(3)" substitute "section 347A(7)".

Taxation of Chargeable Gains Act 1992 (c.12)

27. For section 77 of the Taxation of Chargeable Gains Act 1992 (charge on settlor with interest in settlement), substitute—

"Charge on settlor with interest in settlement

77.—(1) Where in a year of assessment—

    (a) chargeable gains accrue to the trustees of a settlement from the disposal of any or all of the settled property,

    (b) after making any deduction provided for by section 2(2) in respect of disposals of the settled property there remains an amount on which the trustees would, disregarding section 3, be chargeable to tax for the year in respect of those gains, and

    (c) at any time during the year the settlor has an interest in the settlement,

the trustees shall not be chargeable to tax in respect of those but instead chargeable gains of an amount equal to that referred to in paragraph (b) shall be treated as accruing to the settlor in that year.

(2) Subject to the following provisions of this section, a settlor shall be regarded as having an interest in a settlement if—

    (a) any property which may at any time be comprised in the settlement, or any derived property is, or will or may become, payable to or applicable for the benefit of the settlor or his spouse in any circumstances whatsoever, or

    (b) the settlor or his spouse enjoys a benefit deriving directly or indirectly from any property which is comprised in the settlement or any derived property.

(3) The references in subsection (2)(a) and (b) above to the spouse of the settlor do not include—

    (a) a person to whom the settlor is not for the time being married but may later marry, or

    (b) a spouse from whom the settlor is separated under an order of a court, or under a separation agreement or in such circumstances that the separation is likely to be permanent, or

    (c) the widow or widower of the settlor.

(4) A settlor shall not be regarded as having an interest in a settlement by virtue of subsection (2)(a) above if and so long as none of the property which may at any time be comprised in the settlement, and no derived property, can become payable or applicable as mentioned in that provision except in the event of—

4–296

(a) the bankruptcy of some person who is or may become beneficially entitled to the property or any derived property, or

(b) an assignment of or charge on the property or any derived property being made or given by some such person, or

(c) in the case of a marriage settlement, the death of both parties to the marriage and of all or any of the children of the marriage, or

(d) the death of a child of the settlor who had become beneficially entitled to the property or any derived property at an age not exceeding 25.

(5) A settlor shall not be regarded as having an interest in a settlement by virtue of subsection (2)(a) above if and so long as some person is alive and under the age of 25 during whose life the property or any derived property cannot become payable or applicable as mentioned in that provision except in the event of that person becoming bankrupt or assigning or charging his interest in that property.

(6) This section does not apply—

(a) where the settlor dies during the year; or

(b) in a case where the settlor is regarded as having an interest in the settlement by reason only of—

(i) the fact that property is, or will or may become, payable to or applicable for the benefit of his spouse, or

(ii) the fact that a benefit is enjoyed by his spouse,

where the spouse dies, or the settlor and the spouse cease to be married, during the year.

(7) This section does not apply unless the settlor is, and the trustees are, either resident in the United Kingdom during any part of the year or ordinarily resident in the United Kingdom during the year.

(8) In this section "derived property", in relation to any property, means income from that property or any other property directly or indirectly representing proceeds of, or of income from, that property or income therefrom.".

28. In section 78 of the Taxation of Chargeable Gains Act 1992, in subsections (1), (2) and (3), for "section 77(2)" substitute "section 77".

29.—(1) Section 79 of the Taxation of Chargeable Gains Act 1992 is amended as follows.

(2) In subsection (2) omit paragraph (b) and the word "and" preceding it.

(3) Omit subsection (4).

(4) In subsection (5)—

(a) for "subsections (3) and (4)" substitute "subsection (3)"; and

(b) in paragraph (a), omit the words "or income" wherever occurring.

30. In section 97 of the Taxation of Chargeable Gains Act 1992, in subsection (7) for "section 681(4)" substitute "section 660G(1) and (2)".

31. In section 286 of the Taxation of Chargeable Gains Act 1992, for subsection (3) substitute—

"(3) A person, in his capacity as trustee of a settlement, is connected with—

(a) any individual who in relation to the settlement is a settlor,

(b) any person who is connected with such an individual, and

(c) any body corporate which is connected with that settlement.

In this subsection "settlement" and "settlor" have the same meaning as in Chapter IA of Part XV of the Taxes Act (see section 660G(1) and (2) of that Act).

(3A) For the purpose of subsection (3) above a body corporate is connected with a settlement if—

(a) it is a close company (or only not a close company because it is not resident in the United Kingdom) and the participators include the trustees of the settlement; or

(b) it is controlled (within the meaning of section 840 of the Taxes Act) by a company falling within paragraph (a) above.".

32. In Schedule 1 to the Taxation of Chargeable Gains Act 1992, in paragraph 2(7), for "section 681(4)" substitute "section 660G(1) and (2)".

GENERAL NOTE

The Schedule introduces new provisions to replace ICTA 1988, ss.660 to 676 and 683 to 685. These deal with the circumstances in which the income of settlements is to be treated as that of the settlor. The old provisions had been enacted over a long period of years and contained a certain overlapping and duplication. The new provisions are designed to simplify the law in this area.

Para. 1

This contains the new substantive provisions.

New s.660A. This lays down the main principle that, subject to certain exceptions, income arising under a settlement is to be treated as the income of the settlor for tax purposes, unless it arises from property in which the settlor has no interest. A settlor retains an interest if there is any possibility of the property being applied for the benefit of the settlor or a spouse. "Spouse" does not include a future spouse, a separated spouse or a widow or widower. There are four improbable contingencies upon which a settlor may provide that the property should revert to him without triggering a charge:

(i) the bankruptcy of any beneficiary;
(ii) the assignment of or charge on the property by any beneficiary;
(iii) the death of all the beneficiaries under a marriage settlement; or
(iv) the death of a child under the age of 25 who had become beneficially entitled to the property.

If the property cannot be applied for the benefit of a settlor or spouse while someone else is alive, the settlor will not be regarded as having an interest while that other person is under 25.

Outright gifts between spouses, the irrevocable allocation of pension rights between spouses, settlements made by one party to a marriage to provide for the other after the marriage has broken up, annual payments made by an individual for bona fide commercial reasons and covenanted payments are excluded from the scope of the section.

Under the general law, a settlement requires an element of bounty: *Bulmer* v. *I.R.C.*; *Same* v. *Same*; *Kennedy* v. *Same*; *Oates* v. *Same*; *Oates and Others* v. *Same*; *Macaulay* v. *Same* [1967] Ch. 145.

New s.660B. Income arising under a settlement which is paid to, or applied for the benefit of, an unmarried minor child of the settlor is treated as the settlor's income. Any other related payments to the child are also treated as the settlor's income, where the payments can be matched against available, retained or accumulated income of the settlement. Amounts already treated as the settlor's income, payments to non-minor beneficiaries and administrative expenses are not treated as available. A charge under ICTA 1988, s.761 on the income gains of an offshore fund is treated as income paid to a child, where he would have been absolutely entitled to the assets but for his minority. There is a *de minimis* limit of £100 a year below which no tax is charged on the settlor.

New s.660C. Tax is charged on the settlor under Case VI of Schedule D, but with the benefit of any reliefs or deductions to which he would have been entitled had he actually received the income. It is treated as the highest part of his income (ignoring termination payments and certain gains on insurance policies).

New s.660D. The settlor is allowed to recover from the trustees any tax paid by him on the income of the settlement and is entitled to obtain from the Revenue a certificate stating the amount paid. Any excess repayment obtained by virtue of the operation of the provisions must be paid to the trustee or beneficiary concerned, with apportionment where necessary. The General Commissioners adjudicate any dispute.

New s.660E. This adapts the provisions for cases where there is more than one settlor.

New s.660F. The Revenue are given the usual powers to obtain information.

New s.660G. Various definitions are provided. The definition of "settlement" is extraordinarily wide, but is limited in practice by the requirement that there must be an element of bounty: *Bulmer* v. *I.R.C.*; *Same* v. *Same*; *Kennedy* v. *Same*; *Oates* v. *Same*; *Oates* v. *Same*; *Macaulay* v. *Same* [1967] Ch. 145. Income which, had the settlor been entitled to it, would not have been chargeable, because he was not domiciled, resident or ordinarily resident in the U.K., is excluded. Where it is subsequently remitted to the U.K. in a year when the settlor is resident here, it is treated as arising in that year.

Paras. 2 and 3

These replace references to sections containing the old provisions with the section numbers of the new provisions.

Para. 4

ICTA 1988, s.347A is applied to annual payments under existing obligations (as defined by FA 1988, s.36(4)) which are within the provisions of the new Chapter IA. Thus, payments under non-charitable covenants made before March 15, 1988 will no longer be allowed as a charge on the income of the person making them. The definition of "a covenanted payment to charity", which is repealed with s.660, is inserted in s.347A.

Paras. 5–7

These also update references within the legislation.

Para. 8

This inserts a new heading for the retained ss.677–682.

Para. 9
Necessary amendments are made to s.677 so that it ties in with the new Chapter IA.

Para. 10
The redundant s.678(7) is now covered by the new provisions imported by para. 11.

Para. 11
The new s.682A imports the provisions of ss.660E–G for the purposes of ss.677–682 and provides the criteria for connecting a company with a settlement.

Para. 12
A new Chapter heading is inserted for ss.686–689.

Para. 13
This clarifies the application of s.686(2)(b).

Para. 14
Section 687 is amended so that the settlor can be given credit against his liability under s.660B for tax already paid by the trustees where they make a payment to the settlor's minor unmarried child.

Para. 15
Section 689, which gave the Revenue power to collect tax from discretionary trustees in certain circumstances where it could not be collected from a beneficiary, is removed. This is now covered elsewhere.

Paras. 16–19
These amend statutory references to the old Chapter and section number in ICTA 1988, Part XV.

Para. 20
Section 839(3) is reworded in the light of the repeal of s.681.

Paras. 21–26
These amend or remove statutory references to the old Chapter and section numbers in Part XV.

Paras. 27–29
TCGA 1992, ss.77–79 are revised in line with the new income tax provisions in para. 1 above.

Paras. 30–33
Updated references are inserted in TCGA 1992, ss.97 and 286 and Sched. 1.

Section 75   SCHEDULE 18

DECEASED PERSONS' ESTATES

Introductory

1. Part XVI of the Taxes Act 1988 shall be amended as follows.

Limited interests in residue

2.—(1) In section 695 (limited interests in residue), the words "subject to subsection (3) below" in subsection (2) shall be omitted, and the following subsection shall be substituted for subsection (3)—

"(3) Where, on the completion of the administration of the estate, there is an amount which remains payable in respect of that limited interest, that amount shall be deemed for all tax purposes to have been paid to that person as income for the year of assessment in which the administration period ends or, in the case of a sum which is deemed to be paid in respect of an interest that ceased before the end of that period, for the last year of assessment in which that interest was subsisting."

(2) This paragraph has effect in relation to any estate the administration of which is completed on or after 6th April 1995.

Absolute interests in residue

3.—(1) In section 696 (absolute interests in residue), for subsection (3) there shall be substituted the following subsections—

"(3) When any sum has been paid during the administration period in respect of that absolute interest, that sum, except so far as it is excluded from the operation of this subsection, shall be deemed for all tax purposes to have been paid to that person as income for the year of assessment in which it was actually paid.

(3A) A payment shall be excluded from the operation of subsection (3) above to the extent (if any) that the aggregate of that sum and all the sums which—

(a) have been paid previously during the administration period in respect of that absolute interest, and

(b) fall under this section to be treated as paid to that person as income,

exceeds the aggregated income entitlement of that person for the year of assessment in which the sum is paid.

(3B) For the purposes of this section the aggregated income entitlement of that person for any year of assessment is the amount which would be the aggregate of the amounts received for that year of assessment and all previous years of assessment in respect of the interest if that person had a right in each year to receive, and had received—

(a) in the case of a United Kingdom estate, his residuary income for that year less income tax at the applicable rate for that year; and

(b) in the case of a foreign estate, his residuary income for that year."

(2) For subsection (5) of that section there shall be substituted the following subsection—

"(5) Where, on the completion of the administration of the estate, the aggregate of all the sums which, apart from this subsection—

(a) have been paid during the administration period in respect of that absolute interest, and

(b) fall under this section to be treated as paid to that person as income,

is exceeded by the aggregated income entitlement of that person for the year of assessment in which the administration of the estate is completed, then an amount equal to the amount of the excess shall be treated for the purposes of subsections (3) to (4) above as having been actually paid, immediately before the end of the administration period, in respect of that interest."

(3) Sub-paragraph (1) above has effect, subject to sub-paragraph (4) below, in relation to any payment made on or after 6th April 1995; and sub-paragraph (2) above shall have effect in relation to any estate the administration of which is completed on or after 6th April 1995.

(4) Where any sum is deemed by virtue of subsection (3) of section 696 of the Taxes Act 1988 (as it has effect apart from this Schedule) to have been paid to any person as income for the year 1994–95 or any previous year of assessment, that sum shall be treated for the purposes of subsections (3A) and (5) of that section (as they have effect by virtue of this Schedule) as a sum actually paid in respect of that person's absolute interest in that year of assessment.

Supplemental provisions relating to section 696

4.—(1) After subsection (1) of section 697 (calculation of residuary income) there shall be inserted the following subsection—

"(1A) For the purpose of ascertaining under subsection (1) above the residuary income of an estate for any year, where the amount of the deductions falling to be made from the aggregate income of the estate for that year (including any falling to be made by virtue of this subsection) exceeds the amount of that income, the excess shall be carried forward and treated for that purpose as an amount falling to be deducted from the aggregate income of the estate for the following year."

(2) In subsection (2) of that section (reduction of residuary income where benefits received are less than aggregate of residuary income), for the words from "his residuary income for" onwards there shall be substituted "section 696 shall have effect as if the amount of the deficiency were to be applied in reducing the amount taken to be his residuary income for the year in which the administration of the estate is completed and, in so far as the deficiency exceeds that income, in reducing the amount taken to be his residuary income for the previous year, and so on."

(3) Sub-paragraph (1) above has effect for ascertaining the residuary income of an estate for the year 1995–96 or any subsequent year of assessment; and sub-paragraph (2) above has effect in relation to any estate the administration of which is completed on or after 6th April 1995.

Special provisions as to successive interests in residue

5.—(1) For subsection (2) of section 698 (special provisions as to successive interests in residue) there shall be substituted the following subsections—

"(1A) Subsection (1B) below applies where—

(a) successively during the administration period there are different persons with interests in the residue of the estate of a deceased person or in parts of such a residue;

(b) the later interest or, as the case may be, each of the later interests arises or is created on the cessation otherwise than by death of the interest that precedes it; and

(c) the earlier or, as the case may be, earliest interest is a limited interest.

(1B) Where this subsection applies, this Part shall have effect in relation to any payment made in respect of any of the interests referred to in subsection (1A) above—

(a) as if all those interests were the same interest so that none of them is to be treated as having ceased on being succeeded by any of the others;

(b) as if (subject to paragraph (c) below) the interest which is deemed to exist by virtue of paragraph (a) above ('the deemed single interest') were an interest of—

(i) except in a case to which sub-paragraph (ii) below applies, the person in respect of whose interest or previous interest the payment is made;

(ii) in a case where the person entitled to receive the payment is any other person who has or has had an interest which is deemed to be comprised in the deemed single interest, that other person;

and

(c) in so far as any of the later interests is an absolute interest as if, for the purposes of section 696(3A) to (5)—

(i) the earlier interest or interests had never existed and the absolute interest had always existed;

(ii) the sums (if any) which were deemed in relation to the earlier interest or interests to have been paid as income for any year of assessment to any of the persons entitled thereto were sums previously paid during the administration period in respect of the absolute interest; and

(iii) those sums were sums falling to be treated as sums paid as income to the person entitled to the absolute interest.

(2) Where successively during the administration period there are different persons with absolute interests in the residue of the estate of a deceased person or in parts of such a residue, the aggregate payments and aggregated income entitlement referred to in subsections (3A) and (3B) of section 696 shall be computed for the purposes of that section in relation to an absolute interest subsisting at any time ('the subsequent interest')—

(a) as if the subsequent interest and any previous absolute interest corresponding to the subsequent interest, or relating to any part of the residue to which the subsequent interest relates, were the same interest; and

(b) as if the residuary income for any year of the person entitled to the previous interest were residuary income of the person entitled to the subsequent interest and any amount deemed to be paid as income to the person entitled to the previous interest were an amount deemed to have been paid to the person entitled to the subsequent interest."

(2) This paragraph has effect in relation to any payment made on or after 6th April 1995 and, so far as it relates to the operation of section 695(3) or 696(5) of the Taxes Act 1988, in relation to any estate the administration of which is completed on or after that date.

Adjustments and information

6. After subsection (4) of section 700 (adjustments and information) there shall be inserted the following subsections—

"(5) It shall be the duty of a personal representative of a deceased person, if a request to do so is made in writing by a person who has, or has had, an absolute or limited interest in the residue of the estate of the deceased or by a person to whom any of the income of the residue of that estate has been paid in the exercise of any discretion, to furnish the person making the request with a statement in writing setting out—

(a) in respect of every amount which has been, or is treated as having been, actually paid to that person in respect of that interest or in the exercise of that discretion, the amount (if any) deemed under this Part to have been paid to him as income for a year of assessment; and

  (b) the amount of any tax at the applicable rate which any amount falling within paragraph (a) above is deemed to have borne;
and, where an amount deemed to have been paid as income to any person for any year of assessment is deemed for any of the purposes of this Part to have borne tax on different parts of it at different applicable rates, the matters to be set out in pursuance of paragraphs (a) and (b) above shall be set out separately as respects each part of that amount.
  (6) The duty imposed by subsection (5) above shall be enforceable at the suit or instance of the person making the request."

Interpretation

  7. Subsection (14) of section 701 (cases where residuary income has borne income tax at the additional rate) shall cease to have effect.

GENERAL NOTE
  The Schedule implements changes in the system for the taxation of the estates of deceased persons which are in the course of administration.

Para. 2
  Where a beneficiary has an interest only in the income of the residuary estate, any amount to which he is entitled which remains unpaid on completion of the administration is deemed to be paid to him in that year. If he himself has died, it is deemed to be his income for the year in which he died.

Para. 3
  This deals with the position where a beneficiary has an interest in both the income and the capital of the estate. Any sum paid during the administration is deemed to be income of the tax year in which it is paid. However, any amount by which the aggregate of the payment and any previous amounts deemed to be paid as income exceed the "aggregated income entitlement" of the beneficiary is excluded. "Aggregated income entitlement" is defined as the aggregate of the amounts which would have been received by the beneficiary had he received, in the case of a U.K. estate (see s.701(9)) his residuary income for each year less tax at the basic rate (or the lower rate in the case of dividends), or in the case of a foreign estate his residuary income. Where, on the completion of the administration of the estate, the aggregated income entitlement exceeds the aggregate of the sums paid, the excess is treated as paid immediately before completion. The new system is applied to payments or deemed payments before and after April 6, 1995.

Para. 4
  The new s.697(1A) provides that, in computing the residuary income of any year, any excess of deductions over the aggregate income for the year is to be carried forward and deducted in the following year (see previously, extra-statutory concession A13). Where the benefits which a beneficiary receives from an estate amount to less than his total residuary income, relief is given by reducing his residuary income by the shortfall, working back from the year in which the administration of the estate is completed.

Para. 5
  This deals with the situation where there are successive interests in residue through the disclaimer or assignment of an interest. Successive limited interests are treated as the same interest and as held by the beneficiary to whom a payment is made. If a subsequent interest is an absolute interest, it is treated as having always existed. Any payments made to the beneficiary having the earlier limited interest are taken into account, for the purposes of applying s.696, as if they had been made to the beneficiary who acquires the absolute interest. The result is that each beneficiary is charged on the income he receives.
  Successive absolute interests in residue are treated as if they were the same interest for the purpose of computing and charging income under s.696.

Para. 6
  Personal representatives are obliged to supply, at a beneficiary's request, a statement of amounts deemed to be paid as income and the amount of tax deemed to have been deducted, with amounts bearing tax at the basic and lower rates shown separately.

Para. 7
  The obsolete s.701(14) is repealed.

SCHEDULE 19

STOCK LENDING: INTEREST ON CASH COLLATERAL

Introductory

1.—(1) In this Schedule—
(a) "approved stock lending arrangement" means an arrangement such as is mentioned in subsection (1), (2) or (2A) of section 129 and in relation to which that section and section 271(9) of the 1992 Act apply;
(b) "the borrower", in relation to such an arrangement, means the person to whom the securities are transferred under the arrangement; and
(c) "the lender" means the person making that transfer and to whom, in return, securities of the same kind and amount are to be transferred.
(2) References in this Schedule to the borrower or lender under an approved stock lending arrangement include any person acting as the nominee of the borrower or lender.

Treatment of interest earned on cash collateral

2.—(1) This paragraph applies where in connection with an approved stock lending arrangement—
(a) the borrower pays to the lender an amount ("cash collateral") by way of security for the performance of the obligation to transfer to the lender securities of the same kind and amount as those transferred by him;
(b) interest is earned by the lender on the whole of the cash collateral in respect of the period for which he holds it, and is paid to him without deduction of tax; and
(c) the lender pays to the borrower an amount ("rebate interest") equal to the amount of interest earned by him on the cash collateral.
(2) Where this paragraph applies—
(a) the interest earned by the lender on the cash collateral shall be treated for all purposes of the Tax Acts as the income of the borrower and not as the income of the lender;
(b) the lender shall not be required to deduct from the payment of rebate interest any sum representing income tax thereon;
(c) no relief shall be given to the lender in respect of the payment under any provision of the Tax Acts; and
(d) the rebate interest shall not be regarded as the income of the borrower.
(3) This paragraph does not apply unless the amount of the rebate interest is identified as such by the parties separately from any fee or other amount payable in connection with the arrangement.

Application of paragraph 2 in case of chain of arrangements

3.—(1) Where the lender under one or more approved stock lending arrangements ("the lending arrangements") is also the borrower under one or more other such arrangements ("the borrowing arrangements") entered into to enable him to fulfil his obligations under the former arrangements, the interest which by virtue of paragraph 2(2)(a) above as it applies in relation to the borrowing arrangements is treated as his (the "attributed interest") shall be treated for the purposes of that paragraph as it applies in relation to the lending arrangements as interest earned by him on the cash collateral provided under those arrangements, as follows.
(2) Where the aggregate amount of the cash collateral provided under the borrowing arrangements equals that provided under the lending arrangements, the whole of the attributed interest shall be so treated.
(3) Where the aggregate amount of the cash collateral provided under the borrowing arrangements exceeds that provided under the lending arrangements, a part of the attributed interest shall be so treated.
That part shall be the proportion of the attributed interest which the aggregate amount of the cash collateral provided under the lending arrangements bears to that provided under the borrowing arrangements.
(4) Where the aggregate amount of the cash collateral provided under the borrowing arrangements is less than that provided under the lending arrangements, the attributed interest shall

be treated as earned by him on a part of the cash collateral provided under the lending arrangements.

That part shall be an amount equal to the aggregate amount of the cash collateral provided under the borrowing arrangements.

Interpretation

4. In this Schedule—
  "relief" means relief by way of—
      (i) deduction in computing profits or gains, or
      (ii) deduction or set off against income or total profits; and
  "securities" includes stocks and shares.

GENERAL NOTE

The Schedule allows stock lenders to pay interest on cash collateral to the borrower without deduction of tax.

Para. 1

This provides definitions.

Para. 2

Where interest on cash collateral is received gross by the lender and paid to the borrower it is treated as income of the borrower rather than of the lender. The interest rebated must be identified separately from any fee which is payable.

Para. 3

This applies the provisions in para. 2 to cases where the securities loaned have themselves been borrowed. The interest on any cash collateral provided by an intermediary (when acting as borrower) is treated as the income of the person who provided the intermediary with the cash collateral (the intermediary's borrower). This is adapted to cover cases where the amount of cash collateral the intermediary provides is the same, greater or less than the amount of cash collateral the intermediary receives.

Para. 4

This provides further definitions.

Section 107(11) SCHEDULE 20

CLAIMS ETC. NOT INCLUDED IN RETURNS

Making of claims

1. In Schedule 1A to the Management Act (claims etc. not included in returns), in sub-paragraph (5) of paragraph 2 (making of claims), for paragraph (b) there shall be substituted the following paragraphs—
  "(b) such information as is reasonably required for the purpose of determining whether and, if so, the extent to which the claim is correct;
  (bb) the delivery with the claim of such accounts, statements and documents, relating to information contained in the claim, as are reasonably required for the purpose mentioned in paragraph (b) above;".

Keeping and preserving of records

2. After paragraph 2 of that Schedule there shall be inserted the following paragraph—

"Keeping and preserving of records

2A.—(1) Any person who may wish to make a claim in relation to a year of assessment or other period shall—

(a) keep all such records as may be requisite for the purpose of enabling him to make a correct and complete claim; and

(b) shall preserve those records until the end of the relevant day.

(2) In relation to a claim, the relevant day for the purposes of sub-paragraph (1) above is whichever of the following is the latest, namely—

(a) where enquiries into the claim or any amendment of the claim are made by an officer of the Board, the day on which, by virtue of paragraph 7(4) below, those enquiries are treated as completed; and

(b) where no enquiries into the claim or any amendment of the claim are so made, the day on which such an officer no longer has power to make such enquiries.

(3) The duty under sub-paragraph (1) above to preserve records may be discharged by the preservation of the information contained in them; and where the information is so preserved a copy of any document forming part of the records shall be admissible in evidence in any proceedings before the Commissioners to the same extent as the records themselves.

(4) Any person who fails to comply with sub-paragraph (1) above in relation to any claim which is made for a year of assessment or accounting period shall be liable to a penalty not exceeding £3,000."

Amendments of claims

3. In paragraph 3 of that Schedule (amendments of claims), in sub-paragraph (1)(a), for the word "return" there shall be substituted the word "claim".

Giving effect to claims and amendments

4.—(1) At the beginning of sub-paragraph (1) of paragraph 4 of that Schedule (giving effect to claims and amendments) there shall be inserted the words "Subject to sub-paragraphs (1A) and (3) below and to any other provision in the Taxes Acts which otherwise provides,".

(2) After that sub-paragraph there shall be inserted the following sub-paragraph—

"(1A) In relation to a claim which would otherwise fall to be taken into account in the making of deductions or repayments of tax under section 203 of the principal Act, sub-paragraph (1) above shall apply as if for the word 'shall' there were substituted the word 'may'."

(3) At the beginning of sub-paragraph (2) of that paragraph there shall be inserted the words "Subject to sub-paragraph (3) below,".

(4) After the said sub-paragraph (2) there shall be inserted the following sub-paragraph—

"(3) Where any such claim or amendment as is mentioned in sub-paragraph (1) or (2) above is enquired into by an officer of the Board—

(a) that sub-paragraph shall not apply until the day on which, by virtue of paragraph 7(4) below, the officer's enquiries are treated as completed; but

(b) the officer may at any time before that day give effect to the claim or amendment, on a provisional basis, to such extent as he thinks fit."

Power to enquire into claims

5. In paragraph 5 of that Schedule (power to enquire into claims), for sub-paragraphs (2) and (3) there shall be substituted the following sub-paragraphs—

"(2) The period referred to in sub-paragraph (1) above is whichever of the following ends the latest, namely—

(a) the period ending with the quarter day next following the first anniversary of the day on which the claim or amendment was made;

(b) where the claim or amendment relates to a year of assessment, the period ending with the first anniversary of the 31st January next following that year; and

(c) where the claim or amendment relates to a period other than a year of assessment, the period ending with the first anniversary of the end of that period;

and the quarter days for the purposes of this sub-paragraph are 31st January, 30th April, 31st July and 31st October.

(3) A claim or amendment which has been enquired into under sub-paragraph (1) above shall not be the subject of—

(a) a further notice under that sub-paragraph; or

(b) if it is subsequently included in a return, a notice under section 9A(1), 11AB(1) or 12AC(1) of this Act."

GENERAL NOTE

The Schedule makes a number of amendments to the prospective TMA 1970, Sched. 1A, which deals with claims which are not included in returns.

Para. 1

This expands the provision detailing the back-up information which may be required in support of a claim.

Para. 2

The new para. 2A introduces a requirement to keep records for the purpose of making claims. It mirrors generally the requirement to keep records for the purpose of making a return (see new s.12B), save that the penalty is only applicable if a claim is made.

Para. 3

A minor error in Sched. 1A, para. 3(1)(a) is corrected.

Para. 4

The provisions for giving effect to claims and amendments are amended so that claims which fall to be taken into account in determining a PAYE code can continue to be dealt with outside the machinery for self-assessment and claims that are being enquired into can be given partial effect on a provisional basis.

Para. 5

The period within which enquiries into a claim can be begun is amended to bring it into line with the period for beginning enquiries into a return. Claims may not be enquired into twice.

Section 116(1)   SCHEDULE 21

SELF-ASSESSMENT ETC: TRANSITIONAL PROVISIONS

Notice of liability

1. Section 7 of the Management Act (notice of liability) shall have effect as respects the year 1995–96 as if the reference in subsection (7) to a self-assessment made under section 9 of that Act in respect of that year were a reference to assessments made more than six months after the end of that year.

Payments on account of income tax

2.—(1) Section 59A of that Act (payments on account of income tax) shall have effect as respects the year 1996–97 with the modifications made by sub-paragraphs (2) to (7) below.

(2) The references in subsections (1)(a) and (4A) to a person being assessed to income tax under section 9 of that Act shall be construed as references to his being assessed to income tax under section 29 of that Act.

(3) The reference in subsection (1)(b) to the assessed amount shall be construed as a reference to the difference between that amount and the aggregate of the following, namely—

(a) so much of any income tax charged at a higher rate on any income—

(i) from which tax has been deducted otherwise than under section 203 of the Taxes Act 1988, or

(ii) from or on which income tax is treated as having been deducted or paid,

as is attributable to the difference between that rate and the basic rate; and

(b) so much of any income tax charged at a higher rate on any income chargeable under Schedule F as is attributable to the difference between that rate and the lower rate.

(4) The reference in subsection (1)(c) to the relevant amount shall be construed as a reference to the difference between that amount and the amount of any income tax charged under Schedule E which—

(a) has not been deducted under section 203 of the Taxes Act 1988; and

(b) is not charged by an assessment made under regulation 103 of the Income Tax (Employments) Regulations 1993.

(5) Subsection (2) shall have effect as if it required—

(a) the first payment on account to be of an amount equal to the aggregate of—

(i) such part of the relevant amount as represents tax charged under Schedule A or any of Cases III to VI of Schedule D; and

(ii) 50 per cent of the remaining part of the relevant amount, and

(b) the second payment on account to be of an amount equal to 50 per cent of that remaining part.

(6) Subsection (4) shall have effect as if it provided that, in the circumstances there mentioned—

(a) the amount of the first payment on account should be, and should be deemed always to have been, equal to the aggregate of—

(i) such part of the stated amount as represents tax charged under Schedule A or any of Cases III to VI of Schedule D; and

(ii) 50 per cent of the remaining part of the stated amount, and

(b) the amount of the second payment on account should be, and should be deemed always to have been, equal to 50 per cent of that remaining part.

(7) Subsection (4A) shall have effect as if it provided that, in the circumstances and subject as there mentioned—

(a) the amount of the first payment on account should be, and should be deemed always to have been, equal to the aggregate of—

(i) such part of the relevant amount (as determined on the basis of the assessment or, as the case may be, the assessment as amended) as represents tax charged under Schedule A or any of Cases III to VI of Schedule D; and

(ii) 50 per cent of the remaining part of the relevant amount, as so determined, and

(b) the amount of the second payment on account should be, and should be deemed always to have been, equal to 50 per cent of that remaining part.

(8) In this paragraph "higher rate" means a rate other than the basic rate or the lower rate.

Partnerships

3.—(1) This paragraph applies in the case of a partnership whose trade, profession or business is set up and commenced before 6th April 1994.

(2) Section 32 of the Management Act (relief for double assessments to tax) shall have effect, as respects each partner and the year 1996–97, as if the partnership had not been assessed to income tax for that year.

(3) Section 59B of that Act (payment of income tax and capital gains tax) shall have effect, as respects each partner and that year, as if his share of any income tax to which the partnership is assessed for that year were income tax which in respect of that year had been deducted at source.

GENERAL NOTE

The Schedule, which replaces FA 1994, s.198, provides special rules for notification of chargeability to tax in 1995–96 and for payments on account of income tax in 1996–97.

Para. 1

Notification of liability to tax for 1995–96 must be made within six months of the end of the tax year, unless a return has been issued or the income or capital gains has been assessed.

Para. 2

Taxes Management Act 1970, s.59A is amended with respect to the year 1996–97. The amendments provide that payments on account in respect of tax under Schedule A and Cases III–VI of Schedule D, shall be payable on January 31, 1997; and in respect of tax under Cases I and II of Schedule D, half on January 31, 1997 and half on July 31, 1997. Any subsequent change to the 1995/96 assessed amounts will affect the payments on account accordingly. For that year only, higher rate tax in respect of any income that has had tax deducted at source will not be included in payments on account.

Para. 3

Special rules are applied for partnerships which commenced before April 6, 1994. Any tax paid by the partnership in respect of a partner's share of partnership income in that year is treated as tax deducted at source for the purposes of the partner's self-assessment. No claim for relief under TMA 1970, s.32 is allowed in respect of that income for that year.

Section 123 SCHEDULE 22

PREVENTION OF EXPLOITATION OF SCHEDULE 20 TO FINANCE ACT 1994

CASES I AND II OF SCHEDULE D

Increase of profits or gains of transitional period

1.—(1) This paragraph applies where, in the case of a trade, profession or vocation carried on by any person—
(a) paragraph 2(2) of Schedule 20 to the Finance Act 1994 applies without the modification made by paragraph 2(3) of that Schedule; and
(b) any amount which is included in the profits or gains of the transitional period would not have been so included if—
(i) any relevant change made by that person had not been made; or
(ii) any relevant transaction entered into by that person had not been entered into.
(2) Subject to sub-paragraph (3) below, the said paragraph 2(2) shall have effect as if the reference to the appropriate percentage of the aggregate of the amounts there mentioned were a reference to the aggregate of—
(a) that percentage of each of those amounts; and
(b) 1.25 times the complementary percentage of each of the amounts falling within sub-paragraph (1)(b) above.
(3) Sub-paragraph (2) above does not apply where—
(a) the aggregate of the amounts falling within sub-paragraph (1)(b) above is less than such amount as may be prescribed by regulations made by the Board;
(b) the proportion which the aggregate of those amounts bears to the aggregate of the amounts mentioned in the said paragraph 2(2) is less than such proportion as may be so prescribed; or
(c) the appropriate percentage of the turnover for the transitional period is less than such amount as may be so prescribed;
and regulations under this sub-paragraph may make as respects trades or professions carried on by persons in partnership provision different from that made as respects trades, professions or vocations carried on by individuals.
(4) In this paragraph—
"the appropriate percentage" means the following expressed as a percentage, that is, 365 divided by the number of days in the transitional period;
"the complementary percentage" means the difference between 100 per cent and the appropriate percentage;
"the transitional period" means the basis period for the year 1996–97 and the relevant period (within the meaning of paragraph 2 of Schedule 20 to the Finance Act 1994) taken together.
2.—(1) This paragraph applies where, in the case of a trade or profession carried on by persons in partnership—
(a) paragraph 2(2) of Schedule 20 to the Finance Act 1994 applies without the modification made by paragraph 2(3) of that Schedule;
(b) a claim is made under section 353 of the Taxes Act 1988 (relief for interest: general provision) in respect of interest on a loan to defray money contributed or advanced by a partner to the partnership; and
(c) sub-paragraph (2) below applies to any of the money so contributed or advanced.
(2) This sub-paragraph applies to money so contributed or advanced unless it was contributed or advanced wholly or mainly—
(a) for bona fide commercial reasons; or
(b) for a purpose other than the reduction of the partnership's borrowings for a relevant period.
(3) Subject to sub-paragraph (4) below, the amount eligible for relief under the said section 353 in respect of interest paid by the partner in respect of the transitional period on money to which sub-paragraph (2) above applies shall not exceed the appropriate percentage of that interest.
(4) Sub-paragraph (3) above does not apply where—
(a) the loan was made before 1st April 1994; or
(b) the aggregate amount of interest paid as mentioned in that sub-paragraph is less than such amount as may be prescribed by regulations made by the Board.

(5) Where relief under the said section 353 in respect of interest on any loan ("the original loan") is restricted by sub-paragraph (3) above, relief under that section in respect of interest on any other loan used to defray money applied in paying off the original loan shall be restricted to the same extent as if that other loan were the original loan.

(6) In this paragraph—

"the appropriate percentage" and "the transitional period" have the same meanings as in paragraph 1 above;

"relevant period" means a period the whole or part of which falls within the transitional period.

Increase of profits or gains of transitional overlap period

3.—(1) This paragraph applies where, in the case of a trade, profession or vocation carried on by any person—

(a) paragraph 2(4) of Schedule 20 to the Finance Act 1994 applies; and

(b) any amount which is included in the transitional overlap profit would not have been so included if—

(i) any relevant change made by that person had not been made; or

(ii) any relevant transaction entered into by that person had not been entered into.

(2) Subject to sub-paragraph (3) below, the said paragraph 2(4) shall have effect as if the reference to the transitional overlap profit were a reference to the amount (if any) by which that profit exceeds 1.25 times the aggregate of the amounts falling within sub-paragraph (1)(b) above.

(3) Sub-paragraph (3) of paragraph 1 above shall apply for the purposes of this paragraph as it applies for the purposes of that paragraph but subject to the following modifications, namely—

(a) the reference to the aggregate of the amounts mentioned in the said paragraph 2(2) shall have effect as a reference to the transitional overlap profit; and

(b) the reference to the appropriate percentage of the turnover for the transitional period shall have effect as a reference to the appropriate percentage of the turnover for the transitional overlap period.

(4) In this paragraph—

"the appropriate percentage" means the following expressed as a percentage, that is, 365 divided by the number of days in the transitional overlap period;

"the transitional overlap period" means the period beginning immediately after the end of—

(a) the basis period for the year 1996–97; or

(b) in the case of a trade or profession carried on by any person in partnership with other persons, the basis period of the partnership for that year,

and (in either case) ending with 5th April 1997;

"the transitional overlap profit" means the amount mentioned in the said paragraph 2(4).

4.—(1) This paragraph applies where, in the case of a trade or profession carried on by any person in partnership with other persons—

(a) that person ("the retiring partner") ceases to carry on the trade or profession at any time in the transitional overlap period; and

(b) if he had not so ceased, paragraph 3(2) above would have applied in relation to him.

(2) The retiring partner shall for the year 1996–97 be chargeable to income tax under Case I or II of Schedule D on 1.25 times the aggregate of the amounts which would have fallen within paragraph 3(1)(b) above.

(3) In this paragraph "the transitional overlap period" has the same meaning as in paragraph 3 above.

5.—(1) This paragraph applies where, in the case of a trade or profession carried on by any person in partnership with other persons—

(a) paragraph 2(4) of Schedule 20 to the Finance Act 1994 applies with or without the modification made by paragraph 3(2) above;

(b) a claim is made under section 353 of the Taxes Act 1988 (relief for interest: general provision) in respect of interest on a loan to defray money contributed or advanced by him ("the partner") to the partnership; and

(c) sub-paragraph (2) below applies to any of the money so contributed or advanced.

(2) This sub-paragraph applies to money so contributed or advanced unless it was contributed or advanced wholly or mainly—

(a) for bona fide commercial reasons; or

(b) for a purpose other than the reduction of the partnership's borrowings for a relevant period.

(3) Subject to sub-paragraph (4) below, the said paragraph 2(4) shall have effect as if the reference to the transitional overlap profit were a reference to the difference between that profit

and the amount of interest paid by the partner in respect of the transitional overlap period on money to which sub-paragraph (2) above applies.

(4) Sub-paragraph (3) above does not apply where—

(a) the loan was made before 1st April 1994; or

(b) the aggregate amount of interest paid as mentioned in that sub-paragraph is less than such amount as may be prescribed by regulations made by the Board.

(5) In this paragraph—

"relevant period" means a period the whole or part of which falls within the transitional overlap period;

"the transitional overlap period" has the same meaning as in paragraph 3 above;

"the transitional overlap profit" means the amount mentioned in the said paragraph 2(4) (whether having effect with or without the modification made by paragraph 3(2) above).

PART II

CASES III, IV AND V OF SCHEDULE D

Increase of trade etc. profits or gains arising in 1995–96 and 1996–97

6.—(1) This paragraph applies where, in the case of any income derived by any person from the carrying on by him of a trade, profession or vocation—

(a) paragraph 6(2)(a) of Schedule 20 to the Finance Act 1994 applies; and

(b) any amount which is included in the income arising within the years 1995–96 and 1996–97 would not have been so included if—

(i) any relevant change made by that person had not been made; or

(ii) any relevant transaction entered into by that person had not been entered into.

(2) Subject to sub-paragraph (3) below, the said paragraph 6(2)(a) shall have effect as if the reference to 50 per cent of the aggregate of the amounts there mentioned were a reference to the aggregate of—

(a) 50 per cent of each of those amounts; and

(b) 62.5 per cent of each of the amounts falling within sub-paragraph (1)(b) above.

(3) Sub-paragraph (3) of paragraph 1 above shall apply for the purposes of this paragraph as it applies for the purposes of that paragraph but subject to the following modifications, namely—

(a) the reference to the said paragraph 2(2) shall have effect as a reference to the said paragraph 6(2)(a); and

(b) the reference to the appropriate percentage of the turnover of the transitional period shall have effect as a reference to 50 per cent of the turnover of the years 1995–96 and 1996–97.

Increase of trade etc. profits or gains arising in transitional overlap period

7.—(1) This paragraph applies where, in the case of any income derived by any person from the carrying on by him of a trade, profession or vocation—

(a) paragraph 6(4) of Schedule 20 to the Finance Act 1994 applies; and

(b) any amount which is included in the transitional overlap profit would not have been so included if—

(i) any relevant change made by that person had not been made; or

(ii) any relevant transaction entered into by that person had not been entered into.

(2) Subject to sub-paragraph (3) below, the said paragraph 6(4) shall have effect as if the reference to the transitional overlap profit were a reference to the amount (if any) by which that profit exceeds 1.25 times the aggregate of the amounts falling within sub-paragraph (1)(b) above.

(3) Sub-paragraph (3) of paragraph 1 above shall apply for the purposes of this paragraph as it applies for the purposes of that paragraph but subject to the following modifications, namely—

(a) the reference to the aggregate of the amounts mentioned in the said paragraph 2(2) shall have effect as a reference to the transitional overlap profit; and

(b) the reference to the appropriate percentage of the turnover for the transitional period shall have effect as a reference to the appropriate percentage of the turnover for the transitional overlap period.

(4) In this paragraph—

"the appropriate percentage" means the following expressed as a percentage, that is, 365 divided by the number of days in the transitional overlap period;

"the transitional overlap period" means the period beginning immediately after the end of—

(a) the basis period for the year 1996–97; or

(b) in the case of any income derived by any person from the carrying on by him of a trade or profession in partnership with other persons, the basis period of the partnership for that year,

and (in either case) ending with 5th April 1997;

"the transitional overlap profit" means the amount mentioned in the said paragraph 6(4).

8.—(1) This paragraph applies where, in the case of any income derived by any person from the carrying on by him of a trade or profession in partnership with other persons—

(a) that person ("the retiring partner") ceases to carry on the trade or profession at any time in the transitional overlap period; and

(b) if he had not so ceased, paragraph 7(2) above would have applied in relation to him.

(2) The retiring partner shall for the year 1996–97 be chargeable to income tax under Case IV or V of Schedule D on 1.25 times the aggregate of the amounts which would have fallen within paragraph 7(1)(b) above.

(3) In this paragraph "the transitional overlap period" has the same meaning as in paragraph 7 above.

Increase of interest arising in 1995–96 and 1996–97

9.—(1) This paragraph applies where, in the case of any interest arising to any person from any source—

(a) paragraph 4(2) or 6(2)(a) of Schedule 20 to the Finance Act 1994 applies; and

(b) any amount which is included in the interest arising within the years 1995–96 and 1996–97 would not have been so included if any relevant arrangements made between that person and another had not been made.

(2) Subject to sub-paragraph (3) below, the said paragraph 4(2) or 6(2)(a) shall have effect as if the reference to 50 per cent of the aggregate of the amounts there mentioned were a reference to the aggregate of—

(a) 50 per cent of each of those amounts; and

(b) 62.5 per cent of each of the amounts falling within sub-paragraph (1)(b) above.

(3) Sub-paragraph (2) above does not apply where—

(a) the aggregate of the amounts falling within sub-paragraph (1)(b) above is less than such amount as may be prescribed by regulations made by the Board; or

(b) the proportion which the aggregate of those amounts bears to the aggregate of the amounts mentioned in the said paragraph 4(2) or 6(2)(a) is less than such proportion as may be so prescribed.

Increase of other income arising in 1995–96 and 1996–97

10.—(1) This paragraph applies where, in the case of any income (other than income falling within paragraph 6 or 9 above) arising to any person from any source—

(a) paragraph 4(2) or 6(2)(a) of Schedule 20 to the Finance Act 1994 applies; and

(b) any amount which is included in the income arising within the years 1995–96 and 1996–97 would not have been so included if—

(i) any relevant arrangements made between that person and another had not been made; or

(ii) any relevant transaction entered into by that person had not been entered into.

(2) Subject to sub-paragraph (3) below, the said paragraph 4(2) or 6(2)(a) shall have effect as if the reference to 50 per cent of the aggregate of the amounts there mentioned were a reference to the aggregate of—

(a) 50 per cent of each of those amounts; and

(b) 62.5 per cent of each of the amounts falling within sub-paragraph (1)(b) above.

(3) Sub-paragraph (3) of paragraph 9 above shall apply for the purposes of this paragraph as it applies for the purposes of that paragraph.

PART III

PROCEDURAL AND OTHER PROVISIONS

Time limits for purposes of paragraphs 1, 2, 4, 6 and 8 to 10

11.—(1) Nothing in subsection (2) or (3) of section 29 of the Management Act (as substituted by section 191 of the Finance Act 1994) shall prevent an assessment being made under subsection (1) of that section in any case where—

(a) the loss of tax there mentioned is attributable to any failure to give effect to any of paragraphs 1, 2, 4, 6 and 8 to 10 above; and

(b) at the time when the assessment is made, the condition mentioned in sub-paragraph (3) below is fulfilled.

(2) Nothing in subsection (3) or (4) of section 30B of the Management Act (amendment of partnership statement where loss of tax discovered) shall prevent an amendment being made under subsection (1) of that section in any case where—

(a) the omission, deficiency or excess there mentioned is attributable to any failure to give effect to any of paragraphs 1, 2, 4, 6 and 8 to 10 above; and

(b) at the time when the amendment is made, the condition mentioned in sub-paragraph (3) below is fulfilled.

(3) The condition referred to in sub-paragraphs (1) and (2) above is that either—

(a) an assessment under section 9 of the Management Act or, as the case may require, a partnership statement under section 12AB of that Act has been made for the year 1997–98 and that assessment or statement is still capable of being amended; or

(b) no such assessment or, as the case may require, statement has been so made.

Advance notice for purposes of paragraphs 3, 5 and 7

12.—(1) An officer of the Board shall not so amend an assessment made under section 9 of the Management Act (returns to include self-assessment) as to give effect to paragraph 3, 5 or 7 above unless a notice stating—

(a) in the case of paragraph 3 or 7 above, the aggregate of the amounts falling within sub-paragraph (1)(b) of that paragraph; and

(b) in the case of paragraph 5 above, the aggregate amount of interest paid as mentioned in sub-paragraph (3) of that paragraph,

is given by such an officer at a time when the condition mentioned in sub-paragraph (2) below is fulfilled.

(2) The condition referred to in sub-paragraph (1) above is that either—

(a) an assessment under section 9 of the Management Act has been made for the year 1998–99 and that assessment is still capable of being amended; or

(b) no such assessment has been so made.

(3) Subject to sub-paragraph (4) below, a notice under sub-paragraph (1) above shall be conclusive of the matters stated in it.

(4) An appeal may be brought against a notice under sub-paragraph (1) above at any time within the period, of 30 days beginning with the date on which the notice is given.

(5) Subject to sub-paragraph (6) below, the provisions of the Management Act relating to appeals shall have effect in relation to an appeal under sub-paragraph (4) above as they have effect in relation to an appeal against an assessment to tax.

(6) On an appeal under sub-paragraph (4) above, section 50(6) to (8) of the Management Act (procedure on appeals) shall not apply but the Commissioners may—

(a) if it appears to them that the matters stated in the notice under sub-paragraph (1) above are correct, confirm the notice; or

(b) if it does not so appear to them, set aside or modify the notice accordingly.

Penalties not to apply in certain cases

13.—(1) Where a relevant return (as originally made) states—

(a) that paragraph 1, 3 or 4 above applies in the case of a trade, profession or vocation carried on by any person; or

(b) that paragraph 7 or 8 above applies in the case of any income derived by any person from the carrying on by him of a trade, profession or vocation,

sub-paragraph (2) of that paragraph shall have effect, in its application to any amounts stated in the return (as so made) to fall within sub-paragraph (1)(b) of that paragraph or, in the case of paragraph 4 or 8 above, to be amounts which would have fallen within sub-paragraph (1)(b) of the preceding paragraph, as if the words "1.25 times" were omitted.

(2) Where a relevant return (as originally made) states—

(a) that paragraph 6 above applies in the case of any income derived by any person from the carrying on by him of a trade, profession or vocation; or

(b) that paragraph 9 or 10 above applies in the case of any income arising to any person from any source,

sub-paragraph (2) of that paragraph shall have effect, in its application to any amounts stated in the return (as so made) to fall within sub-paragraph (1)(b) of that paragraph, as if for the words "62.5 per cent" there were substituted the words "50 per cent".

(3) In this paragraph—

"relevant return" means a return which, for the relevant year, is made under section 8, 8A or 12AA of the Management Act in respect of the trade, profession or vocation or, as the case may be, the source of the income;

"the relevant year" means—
> (a) in relation to paragraph 1, 6, 9 or 10 above, the year 1996–97;
> (b) in relation to paragraph 3, 4, 7 or 8 above, the year 1997–98.

PART IV

INTERPRETATION

Relevant changes for purposes of paragraphs 1, 3, 6 and 7

14.—(1) Any accounting change or change of business practice is a relevant change for the purposes of paragraphs 1, 3, 6 and 7 above unless—
> (a) the change is made exclusively for bona fide commercial reasons; or
> (b) the obtaining of a tax advantage is not the main benefit that could reasonably be expected to arise from the making of the change.

(2) In this paragraph "accounting change"—
> (a) does not include any change of accounting date which brings the end of the basis period for the year 1996–97 closer to 5th April 1997; but
> (b) subject to that, means any change of accounting date or other modification of an accounting policy or any substitution of one such policy for another.

(3) In this paragraph "change of business practice" means any change in an established practice of trade, profession or vocation carried on by any person—
> (a) as to the timing of any of the following, namely—
>> (i) the supply of goods or services, the invoicing of customers or clients and the collection of outstanding debts; and
>> (ii) the obtaining of goods or services, the incurring of business expenses and the settlement of outstanding debts; or
> (b) as to the obtaining or making of payments in advance or payments on account.

Relevant transactions for purposes of paragraphs 1, 3, 6 and 7

15. Any self-cancelling transaction or transaction with a connected person is a relevant transaction for the purposes of paragraphs 1, 3, 6 and 7 above unless—
> (a) the transaction is entered into exclusively for bona fide commercial reasons; or
> (b) the obtaining of a tax advantage is not the main benefit that could reasonably be expected to arise from the entering into of the transaction.

16.—(1) An agreement by which the person by whom a trade, profession or vocation is carried on agrees to sell or transfer trading stock or work in progress is a self-cancelling transaction for the purposes of paragraph 15 above if by the same or any collateral agreement that person—
> (a) agrees to buy back or re-acquire the trading stock or work in progress; or
> (b) acquires or grants an option, which is subsequently exercised, for him to buy back or re-acquire the trading stock or work in progress.

(2) In sub-paragraph (1) above—
"trading stock" has the same meaning as in section 100 of the Taxes Act 1988;
"work in progress", in relation to a profession or vocation, means—
>> (a) any services performed in the ordinary course of the profession or vocation, the performance of which is wholly or partly completed at the time of the sale or transfer and for which it would be reasonable to expect that a charge would have been made on their completion if the sale or transfer had not been effected; and
>> (b) any article produced, and any such material as is used, in the performance of any such services,

and references in that sub-paragraph to the sale or transfer of work in progress shall include references to the sale or transfer of any benefits and rights which accrue, or might reasonably be expected to accrue, from the carrying out of the work.

17.—(1) For the purposes of paragraph 15 above, any question whether the person by whom a trade, profession or vocation is carried on is connected with another person shall be determined in accordance with sub-paragraphs (2) to (5) below.

(2) An individual carrying on a trade, profession or vocation is connected with another person if they are connected with each other within the meaning of section 839 of the Taxes Act 1988 (disregarding for this purpose the exception in subsection (4) of that section).

(3) Persons carrying on a trade or profession in partnership are connected with an individual if he controls the partnership.

(4) Persons carrying on a trade or profession in partnership are connected with a company if the company controls the partnership or the same person controls both the company and the partnership.

(5) Persons carrying on a trade or profession in partnership are connected with persons carrying on another trade or profession in partnership if the same person controls both partnerships.

(6) In this paragraph—

(a) "control" shall be construed—

(i) in relation to a company, in accordance with section 416 of the Taxes Act 1988;

(ii) in relation to a partnership, in accordance with section 840 of that Act; and

(b) any reference to a person controlling a company or partnership is a reference to his doing so either alone or with one or more persons connected with him.

Relevant arrangements for purposes of paragraph 9

18.—(1) Any arrangements under which—

(a) interest arises at irregular intervals during the years 1994–95 to 1997–98, or

(b) there are artificial variations in the rate of interest applicable during those years,

are relevant arrangements for the purposes of paragraph 9 above unless the obtaining of a tax advantage is not the main benefit that could reasonably be expected to arise from the making of the arrangements.

(2) Any variations in the rate of interest applicable during the years 1994–95 to 1997–98 are artificial variations for the purposes of this paragraph unless they are based on variations in a variable rate of interest the values of which from time to time are regularly published.

Relevant arrangements for purposes of paragraph 10

19. Any arrangements under which income arises at irregular intervals during the years 1994–95 to 1997–98 are relevant arrangements for the purposes of paragraph 10 above unless—

(a) the arrangements are made exclusively for bona fide commercial reasons; or

(b) the obtaining of a tax advantage is not the main benefit that could reasonably be expected to arise from the making of the arrangements.

Relevant transactions for purposes of paragraph 10

20.—(1) Any transaction with a connected person is a relevant transaction for the purposes of paragraph 10 above unless—

(a) the transaction is entered into exclusively for bona fide commercial reasons; or

(b) the obtaining of a tax advantage is not the main benefit that could reasonably be expected to arise from the entering into of the transaction.

(2) A person is connected with another person for the purposes of this paragraph if they are connected with each other within the meaning of section 839 of the Taxes Act 1988.

General

21.—(1) In this Schedule "turnover", in relation to a trade, profession or vocation, means the amounts derived from the provision of goods or services falling within its ordinary activities, after deduction of trade discounts and value added tax.

(2) Obtaining a tax advantage shall not be regarded as a bona fide commercial reason for the purposes of this Schedule.

GENERAL NOTE

The Schedule contains provisions designed to prevent and, in some cases, penalise attempts to exploit the transitional period from the preceding year basis to the current year basis of assessment.

Para. 1

The purpose of this paragraph is to counter avoidance of tax by shifting profits artificially into the periods which will be averaged down in arriving at the 1996–97 assessment. Profits are shifted artificially by a "relevant change" or a "relevant transaction" (see paras. 14 and 15 below). In such a case, the 1996/97 assessment is increased to include the profit which would have escaped tax plus a 25 per cent penalty element. *De minimis* limits covering amounts and proportions of profit and turnover will be set later by regulation.

Para. 2

This deals with an avoidance device whereby partnership borrowing is switched from the partnership itself to individual partners, in order to obtain a full deduction for loan interest paid. The provision applies where a partner takes on partnership borrowing and claims relief against general income for the interest. There is an exclusion for bona fide commercial transactions. To counteract the device, the partner's relief on the interest is reduced by the same fraction to be used in setting the partnership's assessment for 1996/97. Loans taken out before April 1, 1994, or on which the interest is below a *de minimis* level to be set by the Revenue, are also excluded. The restriction also applies to a further loan taken out to repay an original loan which is within para. 2.

Para. 3
This counters avoidance by shifting profits artificially into the accounting period ending in the 1997/98 tax year in order to increase the profits of the part prior to April 6, 1997, which qualify for transitional relief. Artificiality is again defined by reference to a "relevant change" or a "relevant transaction" (see paras. 14 and 15 below) and the transitional relief is reduced 1.25 times the amount by which the profit shifting would otherwise have increased it. *De minimis* limits will again be set.

Para. 4
In the case of a partner retiring during the period beginning immediately after the end of the 1996/97 basis period and ending on April 5, 1997, whose relief would otherwise have been restricted under para. 3, an assessment will be raised to cover the restriction.

Para. 5
This complements para. 2, covering cases where partnership borrowing is switched to an individual partner and interest is paid by the partner in respect of the period (or a part of the period) beginning immediately after the end of the 1996/97 basis period and ending on April 5, 1997 (the transitional overlap period). The other provisions of para. 2 apply *mutatis mutandis*.

Para. 6
Similar anti-avoidance provisions to those in para. 1 for Case I or Case II income are introduced here for Case IV or Case V income in respect of foreign businesses. See further the Note to para. 1 above.

Para. 7
The anti-avoidance provisions in para. 3 for Case I or Case II income are extended to Case IV and Case V income. See further the Note to para. 3 above.

Para. 8
This extends the anti-avoidance provisions in para. 4 for Case I or Case II income to Case IV or Case V income. See further the Note to para. 4 above.

Para. 9
This is designed to prevent avoidance involving interest assessable under Cases III, IV or V. The target is interest shifted artificially by means of "relevant arrangements" (see para. 18 below) into the years 1995/96 or 1996/97, which will be halved in arriving at the amount of the 1996/97 assessment. In such a case the 1996/97 assessment is increased by 50 per cent to include that part of the interest shift plus a penalty element of 12.5 per cent (25 per cent of the amount shifted). *De minimis* limits will be prescribed.

Para. 10
This paragraph relates to income assessable under Case III, other than interest, and Cases IV and V, other than interest and business profits, which is shifted artificially into the years 1995/96 and 1996/97 by means of "relevant arrangements" or "relevant transactions" (see paras. 19 and 20 below). The counteraction follows that in para. 9.

Para. 11
The time limit for making an assessment to give effect to the counteraction (other than those which involve restricting transitional relief, dealt with in para. 12) is the time at which the 1997/98 assessment becomes final, subject to extension in cases of fraud, negligence or incomplete disclosure. The normal conditions to be satisfied before a discovery assessment or a discovery amendment to a partnership statement can be made are disapplied for this purpose.

Para. 12
A mechanism and time limit is provided for determining any adjustments under the provisions of this Schedule to a person's transitional relief. Except in cases of fraud, negligence or incomplete disclosure, the inspector is required to issue a notice of restriction of transitional relief before the 1998/99 self-assessment has become final. Normal appeal procedures apply to the notice.

Para. 13

Introduced in Standing Committee, this is a mitigating provision disapplying the penalties where the taxpayer discloses on the relevant tax return that the provisions of the Schedule apply to relevant changes, transactions or arrangements that he has carried out.

Para. 14

A "relevant change" is any "accounting change" or "change of business practice". Changes of accounting date bringing the end of the basis period for the year 1996/97 nearer to April 5, 1997 are specifically excluded, as are bona fide commercial changes without a tax avoidance motive.

Para. 15

A "relevant transaction" is a "self-cancelling transaction" (see para. 16) or a "transaction with a connected person" (see para. 17). The exclusion for bona fide commercial transactions without a tax avoidance motive applies.

Para. 16

A "self-cancelling transaction" is an agreement involving sale and buy-back of stock or work in progress.

Para. 17

"Connected person" is defined for the purposes of para. 15. The rule in ICTA 1988, s.839 applies (excluding the exception in subs. (4) for transactions relating to acquisitions or disposals of partnership assets pursuant to bona fide commercial arrangements). Further provisions bring within the net partnerships controlled by the same person or by a company controlled by him.

Para. 18

"Relevant arrangements" for the purposes of para. 9 are non-commercial arrangements varying interest rates other than in accordance with published figures, or causing interest to arise at irregular intervals during 1994/95 to 1997/98.

Para. 19

Any arrangements under which income arises at irregular intervals during 1994/95 to 1997/98 are "relevant arrangements" for the purposes of para. 10, unless the commerciality defence applies.

Para. 20

"Relevant transaction" is defined for the purposes of para. 10. The definition covers any transaction with a connected person within the meaning of ICTA 1988, s.839, unless the commerciality defence applies.

Para. 21

"Turnover" is defined for the purposes of the *de minimis* limit (see para. 1(3)(c) above). Also, a tax advantage is not a commercial purpose.

Section 126   SCHEDULE 23

OBLIGATIONS ETC. IMPOSED ON UK REPRESENTATIVES

General imposition of obligations etc.

1.—(1) Subject to the following provisions of this Schedule, the provisions of the Tax Acts, of the Taxation of Chargeable Gains Act 1992 and of any subordinate legislation made under the Tax Acts or that Act of 1992, so far as they—

  (a) make provision for or in connection with the assessment, collection and recovery of tax, or of interest on any tax, and

  (b) apply in any case for purposes connected with the taxation of any amounts in relation to which the non-resident has a UK representative,

shall have effect in that case with respect to tax chargeable on, and interest payable by, the non-resident as if the obligations and liabilities of the non-resident by virtue of those provisions were also obligations and liabilities of the UK representative.

(2) In this paragraph "subordinate legislation" has the same meaning as in the Interpretation Act 1978.

Discharge of obligations and liabilities

2. Subject to the following provisions of this Schedule—

  (a) the discharge by the non-resident's UK representative or by the non-resident himself of an obligation or liability which is or corresponds to one to which that representative is subject under this Schedule shall be treated as discharging the corresponding obligation or liability to which the other is subject; and

(b) the non-resident shall be bound, as if they were his own, by any acts or omissions of his UK representative in the discharge of the obligations and liabilities imposed on that representative by this Schedule.

Obligations and liabilities requiring notice

3. Where any obligation or liability such as is mentioned in paragraph 2 above arises only if the person on whom it is imposed has been given or served with a notice or other document or has received a request or demand, that obligation or liability shall not by virtue of this Schedule be treated as having been imposed on the non-resident's UK representative unless the notice or document, or a copy of it, was given to or served on that representative, or he was notified of the request or demand.

Information requirements

4.—(1) The obligations relating to the furnishing of information which are imposed by this Schedule on the non-resident's UK representative in a case where that representative is his independent agent shall not require that representative to do anything except so far as it is practicable for the representative to do so by acting to the best of his knowledge and belief after having taken all reasonable steps to obtain the necessary information.

(2) Paragraph 2 above shall not have the effect—

(a) of discharging the non-resident from any obligation to furnish information in a case where that obligation has been discharged by his UK representative by virtue only of sub-paragraph (1) above; or

(b) of requiring the non-resident to be bound by any error or mistake contained, otherwise than as a result of—

(i) any act or omission of the non-resident himself, or

(ii) any act or omission to which he consented or in which he connived,

in information furnished by his UK representative in compliance, so far as required by sub-paragraph (1) above, with any obligation imposed by virtue of this Schedule on that representative.

(3) In this paragraph "information" includes anything contained in any return, self-assessment, account, statement or report that is required to be provided to the Board or any officer of the Board, and references to furnishing information shall be construed accordingly.

Criminal offences and penalties etc

5.—(1) A person shall not by virtue of this Schedule be guilty of a criminal offence except where he committed the offence himself or consented to, or connived in, its commission.

(2) An independent agent of the non-resident shall not by virtue of this Schedule be liable, in respect of any act or omission, to any civil penalty or surcharge if—

(a) the act or omission is neither an act or omission of the agent himself nor an act or omission to which he consented or in which he connived, and

(b) he is able to show that he will not, after being indemnified for his other liabilities by virtue of this Schedule, be able to recover the amount of the penalty or surcharge out of any such sums as are mentioned in paragraph 6 below.

Indemnities

6. An independent agent of the non-resident shall be entitled—

(a) to be indemnified in respect of the amount of any liability of the non-resident which is discharged by that agent by virtue of paragraph 2 above; and

(b) to retain, out of any sums otherwise due from that agent to the non-resident, or received by that agent on behalf of the non-resident, amounts sufficient for meeting any liabilities by virtue of that paragraph which have been discharged by the agent, or to which he is subject.

Meaning of "independent agent"

7.—(1) In this Schedule "independent agent", in relation to the non-resident, means any person who is the non-resident's UK representative in respect of any agency from the non-resident in which he was acting on the non-resident's behalf in an independent capacity.

(2) For the purposes of this paragraph a person shall not be regarded as acting in an independent capacity on behalf of the non-resident unless, having regard to its legal, financial and com-

mercial characteristics, the relationship between them is a relationship between persons carrying on independent businesses that deal with each other at arm's length.

GENERAL NOTE

This defines the responsibilities of a U.K. representative of a non-resident taxpayer carrying on a trade in the U.K. through a branch or agency.

Para. 1

The representative is jointly liable with the non-resident for tax obligations in relation to the trade.

Para. 2

The obligations can be discharged by either, but the acts and omissions of the representative are treated as those of the non-resident.

Para. 3

Obligations which depend on the service of a notice are not imposed on the representative unless he has been served with the notice or a copy of it.

Para. 4

Where the representative is an independent agent (see para. 7 below), he discharges his obligation to provide information where he acts to the best of his knowledge and belief after taking all reasonable steps to obtain the necessary information. The non-resident is then responsible for completing the information and may correct errors made by the agent to which he was not privy.

Para. 5

An agent is not guilty of a criminal offence as a result of something done by the non-resident unless it was done with his consent or connivance, and vice versa. An independent agent (see para. 7 below) is only liable for civil penalties as a result of acts or omissions made without his connivance to the extent of amounts which he can recover out of monies of the non-resident.

Para. 6

The independent agent is entitled to indemnify himself out of monies of the non-resident for amounts paid or due to the Revenue. This corresponds to the similar right in favour of persons required to deduct tax at source from income deriving from property of overseas landlords under ICTA 1988, s.42A(3) (see s.40 above).

Para. 7

An independent agent must deal at arm's length with his principal, having regard to the legal, financial and commercial characteristics of their relationship.

Section 130   SCHEDULE 24

EXCHANGE GAINS AND LOSSES

PART I

AMENDMENTS OF FINANCE ACT 1993

Introduction

1. Chapter II of Part II of the Finance Act 1993 (exchange gains and losses) shall be deemed to have been enacted with the modifications set out in paragraphs 2 to 6 below.

Trading gains and losses

2. In section 128 (trading gains and losses) the following subsections shall be inserted after subsection (10)—

"(10A) In a case where—
(a) an exchange gain of a trade or part of a trade or an exchange loss of a trade or part of a trade would (apart from this subsection) accrue to a company as regards a liability consisting of a duty to settle under a qualifying debt, and
(b) a charge is allowed to the company in respect of the debt under section 338 of the Taxes Act 1988 (allowance of charges on income and capital),

the exchange gain or loss shall be treated as not accruing.

(10B) A charge shall be treated as allowed as mentioned in subsection (10A) above if—

(a) it would be so allowed if the company's total profits were sufficient,

(b) it would be so allowed if the duty mentioned in that subsection were settled, and if in settling it payment were made out of the company's profits brought into charge to corporation tax, or

(c) it would be so allowed if the facts were as mentioned in both paragraph (a) and paragraph (b) above."

Non-trading gains and losses

3.—(1) Section 129 (non-trading gains and losses) shall be amended as follows.

(2) In subsection (8) (no non-trading exchange gain or loss where a charge is allowed) in paragraph (b) the words "or the circumstances are such that a charge would be so allowed if the duty were settled" shall be omitted.

(3) The following subsection shall be inserted after subsection (8)—

"(8A) A charge shall be treated as allowed as mentioned in subsection (8) above if—

(a) it would be so allowed if the company's total profits were sufficient,

(b) it would be so allowed if the duty mentioned in that subsection were settled, and if in settling it payment were made out of the company's profits brought into charge to corporation tax, or

(c) it would be so allowed if the facts were as mentioned in both paragraph (a) and paragraph (b) above."

Assets and liabilities

4.—(1) Section 153 (qualifying assets and liabilities) shall be amended as follows.

(2) In subsection (4) (certain convertible securities excluded from qualifying assets) for the words from "which" to "shares" there shall be substituted "and did not represent a normal commercial loan when it was created".

(3) In subsection (6) (certain convertible securities excluded from qualifying liabilities) for the words from "which" to "shares" there shall be substituted "and did not represent a normal commercial loan when it was created".

(4) The following subsection shall be inserted after subsection (11)—

"(11A) In subsections (4) and (6) above "normal commercial loan" has the meaning which would be given by sub-paragraph (5) of paragraph 1 of Schedule 18 to the Taxes Act 1988 if—

(a) for paragraph (a)(i) to (iii) of that sub-paragraph there were substituted the words "corporate bonds (within the meaning of section 117 of the Taxation of Chargeable Gains Act 1992)", and

(b) paragraphs (b) and (c) of that sub-paragraph were omitted."

Chargeable gains

5. In Schedule 17 (chargeable gains) in paragraph 4 (no chargeable gain or allowable loss on disposal of certain debts other than debts on securities) the following sub-paragraph shall be inserted after sub-paragraph (2)—

"(2A) In sub-paragraph (1)(e) above "security" includes a debenture that is deemed to be a security for the purposes of section 251 of the 1992 Act by virtue of subsection (6) of that section (debentures issued on reorganisation etc.)".

6. In Schedule 17, the following paragraph shall be substituted for paragraph 5—

"5.—(1) This paragraph applies where—

(a) a right to settlement under a debt on a security is a qualifying asset,

(b) there occurs in relation to the security an event which is a disposal of it for the purposes of the 1992 Act by a qualifying company or which would be such a disposal but for section 127 of that Act (reorganisations),

(c) the event occurs on or after the company's commencement day, and

(d) immediately before the occurrence of the event the company did not hold the right in exempt circumstances.

(2) In applying section 117 of that Act (qualifying corporate bonds) in relation to the event mentioned in sub-paragraph (1) above or to a transaction (if any) falling within sub-paragraph (4) below, that section shall be construed as if subsection (1)(b) (corporate bond must be in sterling) were omitted.

(3) Where the settlement currency of the debt is a currency other than sterling, then, in applying section 117 of the 1992 Act in relation to the event mentioned in sub-paragraph (1) above or to a transaction (if any) falling within sub-paragraph (4) below—

(a) the definition of normal commercial loan for the purposes of section 117(1)(a) shall have effect, and be treated as always having had effect, as if paragraphs (b) and (c) of paragraph 1(5) of Schedule 18 to the Taxes Act 1988 had always been omitted;

(b) section 117 shall be construed as if subsection (10) (securities issued within group) were omitted.

(4) A transaction falls within this sub-paragraph if—

(a) it is a transaction in relation to which sections 127 to 130 of the 1992 Act apply by virtue of any provision of Chapter II of Part IV of that Act, or would apply apart from section 116 of that Act,

(b) it is a transaction under which the qualifying company becomes entitled to the right,

(c) it occurs on or after the company's commencement day but before the event mentioned in sub-paragraph (1) above, and

(d) the company holds the right at all times following the time when it becomes entitled to it and preceding the event mentioned in sub-paragraph (1) above.

(5) Paragraph 3 above applies for the purposes of this paragraph as if references to currency were references to a right."

PART II

AMENDMENTS OF OTHER PROVISIONS

Introduction

7. Paragraphs 8 to 12 below shall be deemed to have come into force on the day appointed under section 165(7)(b) of the Finance Act 1993 (which relates to exchange gains and losses).

Interest on overdue tax

8. In section 87A of the Taxes Management Act 1970 (interest on overdue tax) in subsection (4A) (claims under section 131(5) or (6) of the Finance Act 1993)—

(a) for paragraph (c) there shall be substituted—

"(c) if the claim had not been made, there would be an amount or, as the case may be, an additional amount of corporation tax for the earlier period which would carry interest in accordance with this section,", and

(b) for the words from "then" to the end there shall be substituted "then, for the purposes of the determination at any time of whether any interest is payable under this section or of the amount of interest so payable, the amount mentioned in paragraph (c) above shall be taken to be an amount of unpaid corporation tax for the earlier period except so far as concerns interest for any time after the date on which any corporation tax for the later period became (or, as the case may be, would have become) due and payable as mentioned in subsection (1) above."

9.—(1) In subsection (4) of that section (amounts of surplus advance corporation tax) for the words "subsection (7)" there shall be substituted "subsections (4B) and (7)".

(2) After subsection (4A) of that section there shall be inserted—

"(4B) Where, in a case falling within subsection (4A)(a) and (b) above—

(a) there is in the earlier period, as a result of the claim under section 131(5) or (6) of the Finance Act 1993, an amount of surplus advance corporation tax, as defined in section 239(3) of the principal Act, and

(b) pursuant to a claim under the said section 239(3), the whole or any part of that amount is to be treated for the purposes of section 239 of the principal Act as discharging liability for an amount of corporation tax for an accounting period before the earlier period,

the claim under the said section 239(3) shall be disregarded for the purposes of subsection (4A) above but subsection (4) above shall have effect in relation to that claim as if the reference in the words after paragraph (c) to the later period within the meaning of subsection (4) above were a reference to the period which, in relation to the claim under section 131(5) or (6) of the Finance Act 1993, would be the later period for the purposes of subsection (4A) above."

10. In section 91 of the Taxes Management Act 1970 (effect on interest of reliefs) in subsection (1B) (provisions to which section 91(1A) is subject) after the words "section 87A(4)" there shall be inserted ", (4A), (4B),".

Interest on tax overpaid

11. In section 826 of the Taxes Act 1988 (interest on tax overpaid) in subsection (7C) (claims under section 131(5) or (6) of the Finance Act 1993)—

(a) at the end of paragraph (c) there shall be inserted "or of income tax in respect of a payment received by the company in that accounting period", and

(b) for the words from "repayment of corporation tax" to "resulting from" there shall be substituted "repayment referred to in paragraph (c) above, no account shall be taken of so much of the amount of the repayment as falls to be made as a result of".

12.—(1) In subsection (7) of that section (amounts of surplus advance corporation tax) for the words "subsection (7AA)" there shall be substituted "subsections (7AA) and (7CA)".

(2) After subsection (7C) of that section there shall be inserted—

"(7CA) Where, in a case falling within subsection (7C)(a) and (b) above—

(a) there is in the earlier period, as a result of the claim under section 131(5) or (6) of the Finance Act 1993, an amount of surplus advance corporation tax, as defined in section 239(3), and

(b) pursuant to a claim under section 239(3), the whole or any part of that amount is to be treated for the purposes of section 239 as discharging liability for an amount of corporation tax for an accounting period before the earlier period,

then subsection (7) above shall have effect in relation to the claim under section 239(3) as if the reference in the words after paragraph (c) to the later period within the meaning of subsection (7) above were a reference to the period which, in relation to the claim under section 131(5) or (6) of the Finance Act 1993, would be the later period for the purposes of subsection (7C) above."

(3) In section 102 of the Finance Act 1989 (surrender of company tax refund etc. within group) in subsection (4A) (cases where any of subsections (7) to (7C) of section 826 of the Taxes Act 1988 applies) for "(7C)" there shall be substituted "(7CA)".

(4) Subject to sub-paragraph (5) below, section 826(7CA) of the Taxes Act 1988 (inserted by sub-paragraph (2) above) shall apply in relation to any claim under section 131(5) or (6) of the Finance Act 1993 as a result of which there is an amount of surplus advance corporation tax in an accounting period ending after 30th September 1993.

(5) Where there is a claim in relation to which section 826(7CA) would, but for this sub-paragraph, apply, and—

(a) the case is one falling within section 826(7CA)(a) and (b), but

(b) the period mentioned in section 826(7CA)(b) ended on or before 30th September 1993, section 826(7CA) shall not apply but section 825(4)(a) of the Taxes Act 1988 shall have effect as if the reference to the accounting period in the case of which the amount of surplus advance corporation tax arose were a reference to the period which, in relation to the claim, would be the later period for the purposes of section 826(7C) of that Act.

GENERAL NOTE

The Schedule introduces amendments into FA 1993, Part II, Chapter II and other provisions for the elimination of areas of overlap. It also makes further changes relating to administration.

Para. 2

New FA 1993, s.128(10A) and (10B) prevent double counting of trading exchange gains and losses which have been taken into account as charges on income, or would have been but for either an insufficiency of income in the accounting period or their non-payment in that period.

Para. 3

FA 1993, s.129(8) is amended and a new s.129(8A) is inserted. The effect is to widen the existing provisions which ensure that non-trading exchange gains or losses taken into account as charges on income are not double counted, by providing that non-trading exchange differences which would have been taken into account as charges if there had been sufficient income in the accounting period are treated as taken into account.

Para. 4

FA 1993, s.153(4) and (6) are amended and a new s.153(11A) is inserted. These amendments ensure that convertible securities which are chargeable assets for CGT purposes are excluded from the charge under FA 1993, Part II, Chapter II.

Para. 5

New FA 1993, Sched. 17, para. 4(2A) ensures that para. 4 does not remove from the charge to CGT foreign currency debentures issued on a reorganisation or other transaction and treated as securities for the purposes of the TCGA 1992, s.251.

Para. 6

A new para. 5 is substituted for the existing FA 1993, Sched. 17, para. 5. The new paragraph clarifies the circumstances in which foreign currency securities are treated as qualifying corporate bonds for capital gains purposes. In particular, it ensures that, whilst foreign currency securities are excluded from CGT if they are derived from an earlier holding of shares or other chargeable assets, gains or losses in respect of this earlier holding which crystallise on the disposal of the securities are still taken into account.

Para. 7
The rest of the Schedule is deemed to have come into force on the appointed day (March 23, 1995).

Para. 8
The amendments to the TMA 1970, s.87A(4A), which governs the interest charge on overdue tax for an earlier period to which non-trading exchange losses are carried back, mirror amendments made to TMA 1970, s.87(6) for the carry-back of trading losses, introduced by FA 1993 as part of the Pay and File provisions.

Para. 9
A new TMA 1970, s.87A(4B) is inserted, with a consequential amendment to s.87A(4). Where non-trading exchange losses are carried back to an earlier period, they can displace advance corporation tax already set off against the corporation tax charged on the profits of that earlier period. The new subsection deals with the interest consequences of this surplus advance corporation tax then being carried back to an even earlier period.

Para. 10
A consequential amendment is made to TMA 1970, s.91.

Para. 11
ICTA 1988, s.826(7C) is amended to reflect parallel amendments made to s.826(7) as a consequence of the introduction of the new Pay and File provisions.

Para. 12
Sub-paragraphs (1) and (2) amend ICTA 1988, s.826(7) and insert a new s.826(7CA). The new provisions deal with the consequences for repayment interest on overpaid tax, where advance corporation tax is carried back to an earlier period as a result of its displacement from an intervening period due to the carry-back of non-trading exchange losses from a later period. Sub-paragraph (3) makes a consequential amendment to FA 1989, s.102. Sub-paragraph (4) provides for new s.826(7CA) to apply where advance corporation tax is displaced from an earlier period ending after September 30, 1993, the appointed day for the Pay and File provisions, by the carry-back of non-trading exchange losses from a later period. Sub-paragraph (5) disapplies s.826(7CA) where the accounting period to which the displaced advance corporation tax is carried back ends on or before September 30, 1993; and provides that repayment supplement under the pre-Pay and File rules is to be calculated on similar lines.

Section 133   SCHEDULE 25

CONTROLLED FOREIGN COMPANIES

Introduction

1. In this Schedule—
(a) paragraph 2 contains an amendment designed to secure that in certain cases the chargeable profits of a company resident outside the United Kingdom are to be computed and expressed in the currency used in its accounts;
(b) the other paragraphs contain amendments connected with that amendment.

The principal amendment

2. The following section shall be inserted after section 747 of the Taxes Act 1988—

"Special rule for computing chargeable profits
747A.—(1) Subsection (2) below applies where for the purposes of this Chapter a company's chargeable profits fall to be determined for—
(a) the first relevant accounting period of the company, or
(b) any subsequent accounting period of the company.
(2) Notwithstanding any other rule (whether statutory or otherwise) the chargeable profits for any such period shall be computed and expressed in the currency used in the accounts of the company for its first relevant accounting period.

(3) Subsection (4) below applies where for the purposes of this Chapter a company's chargeable profits fall to be determined for any accounting period of the company which—

(a) begins on or after the appointed day, and

(b) falls before the company's first relevant accounting period.

(4) Notwithstanding any other rule (whether statutory or otherwise) the chargeable profits for any such period shall be computed and expressed in the currency used in the accounts of the company for the accounting period concerned.

(5) For the purposes of this section the first relevant accounting period of the company shall be found in accordance with subsections (6) to (8) below.

(6) Where a direction has been given under section 747 as regards an accounting period of the company which begins before its commencement day, its first relevant accounting period is its accounting period which begins on its commencement day.

(7) Where the company is a trading company and subsection (6) above does not apply, its first relevant accounting period is its first accounting period which begins on or after its commencement day and as regards which a direction has been given under section 747.

(8) Where the company is not a trading company and subsection (6) above does not apply, its first relevant accounting period is its first accounting period which begins on or after its commencement day and as regards which—

(a) a direction has been given under section 747, or

(b) it can reasonably be assumed that a direction would have been given under section 747 but for the fact that it pursued, within the meaning of Part I of Schedule 25, an acceptable distribution policy.

(9) For the purposes of this section—

(a) a company's commencement day is the first day of its first accounting period to begin after the day preceding the appointed day;

(b) the appointed day is such day as may be appointed under section 165(7)(b) of the Finance Act 1993 (which relates to exchange gains and losses).

(10) References in this section to the accounts of a company—

(a) are to the accounts which the company is required by the law of its home State to keep, or

(b) if the company is not required by the law of its home State to keep accounts, are to the accounts of the company which most closely correspond to the individual accounts which companies formed and registered under the Companies Act 1985 are required by that Act to keep;

and for the purposes of this subsection the home State of a company is the country or territory under whose law the company is incorporated or formed."

Connected amendments

3. In section 747 of the Taxes Act 1988 (imputation of chargeable profits and creditable tax of controlled foreign companies) the following subsections shall be inserted after subsection (4)—

"(4A) Where by virtue of section 747A a company's chargeable profits for an accounting period are to be computed and expressed in a currency other than sterling, for the purposes of subsection (4)(a) above the apportioned amount shall be taken to be the sterling equivalent of the apportioned amount found in the currency other than sterling.

(4B) The translation required by subsection (4A) above shall be made by reference to the London closing exchange rate for the two currencies concerned for the last day of the accounting period concerned."

4. In section 748 of the Taxes Act 1988 (limitations on direction-making power) the following subsections shall be inserted after subsection (3)—

"(4) Where by virtue of section 747A a company's chargeable profits for an accounting period are to be computed and expressed in a currency other than sterling, for the purposes of subsection (1)(d) above its chargeable profits for the period shall be taken to be the sterling equivalent of its chargeable profits found in the currency other than sterling.

(5) The translation required by subsection (4) above shall be made by reference to the London closing exchange rate for the two currencies concerned for the last day of the accounting period concerned."

5. In section 750 of the Taxes Act 1988 (territories with a lower level of taxation) the following subsections shall be inserted after subsection (4)—

"(5) Subsections (6) and (7) below apply where by virtue of section 747A a company's chargeable profits for an accounting period are to be computed and expressed in a currency other than sterling.

(6) For the purposes of subsection (2) above the company's chargeable profits for the period shall be taken to be the sterling equivalent of its chargeable profits found in the currency other than sterling.

(7) In applying section 13 for the purposes of making the determination mentioned in subsection (3) above, any reference in section 13 to the amount of the company's profits for the period on which corporation tax falls finally to be borne shall be construed as a reference to the sterling sum found under subsection (6) above.

(8) Any translation required by subsection (6) above shall be made by reference to the London closing exchange rate for the two currencies concerned for the last day of the accounting period concerned."

6.—(1) Schedule 24 to the Taxes Act 1988 (assumptions for calculating chargeable profits etc.) shall be amended as mentioned in sub-paragraphs (2) to (5) below; and—

(a) the amendment made by sub-paragraph (2) below shall be deemed always to have had effect, and

(b) paragraph 1(4) of Schedule 16 to the Finance Act 1984 shall be deemed always to have had effect subject to the same amendment.

(2) In paragraph 1 (general assumptions for calculating chargeable profits etc.) in sub-paragraph (4) (assumption for certain purposes that a direction has been given) before the words "it shall be assumed" there shall be inserted "in determining the chargeable profits of the company for the accounting period mentioned in paragraph (a) above".

(3) Paragraph 4A (computation of basic profits or losses of a trade) shall be deemed never to have been inserted.

(4) The following paragraph shall be inserted after paragraph 11—

"11A.—(1) This paragraph applies where by virtue of section 747A the company's chargeable profits for an accounting period (the period in question) are to be computed and expressed in a currency (the relevant foreign currency) other than sterling.

(2) For the purposes of making in relation to the period in question any calculation which—

(a) falls to be made under the enactments relating to capital allowances, and

(b) takes account of amounts arrived at under those enactments in relation to accounting periods falling before the company's commencement day (within the meaning given by section 747A(9)),

it shall be assumed that any such amount is the equivalent, expressed in the relevant foreign currency, of the amount expressed in sterling.

(3) For the purposes of the application in relation to the period in question of paragraph 11(1)(c) above, it shall be assumed that the company's chargeable profits for the period are the sterling equivalent of its chargeable profits found in the relevant foreign currency.

(4) For the purposes of the application of section 34, 35 or 96 of the 1990 Act (motor cars and dwelling-houses) in relation to expenditure incurred in the period in question, it shall be assumed that any sterling sum mentioned in any of those sections is the equivalent, expressed in the relevant foreign currency, of the amount expressed in sterling.

(5) The translation required by sub-paragraph (2) above shall be made by reference to the London closing exchange rate for the two currencies concerned for the first day of the period in question.

(6) The translation required by sub-paragraph (3) above shall be made by reference to the London closing exchange rate for the two currencies concerned for the last day of the period in question.

(7) The translation required by sub-paragraph (4) above shall be made by reference to the London closing exchange rate for the two currencies concerned for the day on which the expenditure concerned was incurred."

(5) The following shall be inserted after paragraph 12—

"*Exchange gains and losses*

13. Paragraphs 14 to 19 below apply for the purposes of the application of Chapter II of Part II of the Finance Act 1993.

14.—(1) This paragraph applies where—

(a) by virtue of section 747A the company's chargeable profits for an accounting period are to be computed and expressed in a particular currency (the relevant currency),

(b) in an accrual period an asset or contract was held, or a liability was owed, by the company, and

(c) the accrual period falls within or constitutes the accounting period concerned.

(2) It shall be assumed that—

(a) the local currency for the purposes of sections 125 to 127 of the Finance Act 1993 is the relevant currency, and

(b) section 149 of that Act (local currency to be used) does not apply as regards the accrual period concerned.

15. Where the accounting period mentioned in section 139(1) of the Finance Act 1993 is one for which, by virtue of section 747A, the company's chargeable profits are to be computed and expressed in a currency other than sterling—

(a) section 142(1) to (4) of that Act shall be assumed not to apply as regards that period;

(b) section 142(5) and (6) of that Act shall be assumed not to apply as regards the next accounting period of the company.

16.—(1) This paragraph applies where the last relevant accounting period for the purposes of section 146 of the Finance Act 1993 is one for which by virtue of section 747A the company's chargeable profits are to be computed and expressed in a particular currency (the relevant currency).

(2) Subsections (10), (11) and (14) of section 146 of the Finance Act 1993 shall be assumed not to apply.

17. Where by virtue of section 747A the company's chargeable profits for an accounting period are to be computed and expressed in a particular currency, the references in section 148(9) of the Finance Act 1993 to sterling shall be assumed to be references to that particular currency.

18.—(1) This paragraph applies where the accounting period mentioned in paragraph (b) of subsection (11) of section 153 of the Finance Act 1993 is one for which, by virtue of section 747A, the company's chargeable profits are to be computed and expressed in a particular currency (the relevant currency).

(2) That subsection shall have effect as if the reference to the local currency of the trade for the accounting period were a reference to the relevant currency.

19.—(1) This paragraph applies where—

(a) Chapter II of Part II of the Finance Act 1993 falls to be applied as regards an accounting period of the company;

(b) under that Chapter, an exchange gain or an exchange loss accrued to the company for an accrual period constituting or falling within an earlier accounting period of the company, and

(c) the accounting period mentioned in paragraph (b) above falls before the company's first relevant accounting period.

(2) It shall be assumed, for the purposes of applying Chapter II of Part II of the Finance Act 1993 as respects the accounting period mentioned in sub-paragraph (1)(a) above, that the exchange gain or loss mentioned in sub-paragraph (1)(b) above never existed.

(3) In sub-paragraph (1) above—

(a) references to an exchange gain are to an exchange gain of a trade or an exchange gain of part of a trade or a non-trading exchange gain;

(b) references to an exchange loss are to an exchange loss of a trade or an exchange loss of part of a trade or a non-trading exchange loss;

(c) the reference in sub-paragraph (1)(b) to an exchange gain or an exchange loss accruing is to the gain or loss accruing before the application of any of sections 131, 136, 137 and 140 of the Finance Act 1993 in relation to the accounting period mentioned in sub-paragraph (1)(b);

(d) references to the first relevant accounting period of the company shall be construed in accordance with section 747A."

7. The following section shall be inserted after section 168 of the Finance Act 1993—

"Application of Chapter to certain companies becoming resident in the United Kingdom
168A.—(1) In a case where—

(a) by virtue of section 751 of the Taxes Act 1988, an exchange gain or an exchange loss accrues to a company for an accrual period constituting or falling within an accounting period during which the company is resident outside the United Kingdom, and

(b) the company subsequently becomes resident in the United Kingdom,

the company shall be treated, for the purposes of applying this Chapter to accounting periods beginning on or after the date when the company becomes resident in the United Kingdom, as if the exchange gain or loss mentioned in paragraph (a) above never existed.

(2) In this section—

(a) references to an exchange gain are to an exchange gain of a trade or an exchange gain of part of a trade or a non-trading exchange gain;

(b) references to an exchange loss are to an exchange loss of a trade or an exchange loss of part of a trade or a non-trading exchange loss;

(c) the reference in paragraph (a) of subsection (1) above to an exchange gain or an exchange loss accruing is to the gain or loss accruing before the application of any of sections 131, 136, 137 and 140 above in relation to the accounting period mentioned in that paragraph."

GENERAL NOTE

The amendments to the controlled foreign companies legislation are designed to allow such a company to compute its chargeable profits, including both its trading and non-trading income, in the currency of its accounts when the calculation is required for U.K. tax purposes.

Para. 2

New ICTA 1988, s.747A provides that where a company's chargeable profits have to be calculated for its first relevant accounting period (see new subs. (6)–(8)), for any subsequent accounting period or for any prior accounting period, they are to be computed in the currency used in the account of the company for that period.

Paras. 3–5

These make amendments to ICTA 1988, ss.747–750 so as to adapt them for the situation where chargeable profits are computed in a currency other than sterling.

Para. 6

This contains a number of amendments to ICTA 1988, Sched. 24. The amendment made to para. 1(4) of Sched. 16 to the FA 1984 is confirmatory of the generally accepted interpretation and is therefore retrospective. Paragraph 4A of Sched. 24 to ICTA 1988 (which was inserted by FA 1993, s.96 to deal with the situation where a controlled foreign company kept its accounts in a currency other than sterling) is deleted. New para. 11A adapts the capital allowances computation when a currency other than sterling is being used. New paras. 13–19 contain further provisions consequent upon permitting a controlled foreign company to compute its profits in a currency other than sterling. In particular, new para. 19 prevents exchange gains and losses accruing prior to a company's first relevant accounting period (see para. 2 above) from being taken into account in computing the chargeable profits of a later accounting period.

Para. 7

New FA 1993, s.168A prevents exchange gains or losses accruing to a controlled foreign company prior to its migration to the U.K. from being taken into account in calculating its exchange gains or losses once it is resident in the U.K.

Section 135　　　　　　　　　SCHEDULE 26

CHANGE IN OWNERSHIP OF INVESTMENT COMPANY: DEDUCTIONS

Introductory

1. The Taxes Act 1988 shall have effect subject to the amendments in paragraphs 2 to 4 below.

Main provisions

2. After section 768A there shall be inserted the following sections—

"Change in ownership of investment company: deductions generally

768B.—(1) This section applies where there is a change in the ownership of an investment company and—

    (a)　after the change there is a significant increase in the amount of the company's capital; or

    (b)　within the period of six years beginning three years before the change there is a major change in the nature or conduct of the business carried on by the company; or

    (c)　the change in the ownership occurs at any time after the scale of the activities in the business carried on by the company has become small or negligible and before any considerable revival of the business.

(2) For the purposes of subsection (1)(a) above, whether there is a significant increase in the amount of a company's capital after a change in the ownership of the company shall be determined in accordance with the provisions of Part I of Schedule 28A.

(3) In paragraph (b) of subsection (1) above 'major change in the nature or conduct of a business' includes a major change in the nature of the investments held by the company, even if the change is the result of a gradual process which began before the period of six years mentioned in that paragraph.

(4) For the purposes of this section—

    (a)　the accounting period of the company in which the change in the ownership occurs shall be divided into two parts, the first the part ending with the change, the second the part after;

(b) those parts shall be treated as two separate accounting periods; and

(c) the amounts in issue for the accounting period being divided shall be apportioned to those parts.

(5) In Schedule 28A—

(a) Part II shall have effect for identifying the amounts in issue for the accounting period being divided; and

(b) Part III shall have effect for the purpose of apportioning those amounts to the parts of that accounting period.

(6) Any sums which—

(a) are disbursed or treated as disbursed as expenses of management in the accounting period being divided, and

(b) under Part III of Schedule 28A are apportioned to either part of that period,

shall be treated for the purposes of section 75 as disbursed in that part.

(7) Any charges which under Part III of Schedule 28A are apportioned to either part of the accounting period being divided shall be treated for the purposes of sections 338 and 75 as paid in that part.

(8) Any allowances which under Part III of Schedule 28A are apportioned to either part of the accounting period being divided shall be treated for the purposes of section 28 of the 1990 Act and section 75(4) as falling to be made in that part.

(9) In computing the total profits of the company for an accounting period ending after the change in the ownership, no deduction shall be made under section 75 by reference to—

(a) sums disbursed or allowances falling to be made for an accounting period beginning before the change; or

(b) charges paid in such an accounting period.

(10) To the extent that a payment of interest made by the company represents excess overdue interest, the payment shall not be deductible under section 338(1) from the total profits for the accounting period in which it is made.

(11) Whether a payment of interest made by the company represents excess overdue interest, and if so to what extent, shall be determined in accordance with the provisions of Part IV of Schedule 28A.

(12) Subject to the modification in subsection (13) below, subsections (6) to (9) of section 768 shall apply for the purposes of this section as they apply for the purposes of that section.

(13) The modification is that in subsection (6) of section 768 for the words 'relief in respect of a company's losses has been restricted' there shall be substituted 'deductions from a company's total profits have been restricted'.

(14) In this section 'investment company' has the same meaning as in Part IV.

Deductions: asset transferred within group

768C.—(1) This section applies where—

(a) there is a change in the ownership of an investment company ('the relevant company');

(b) none of paragraphs (a) to (c) of section 768B(1) applies;

(c) after the change in the ownership the relevant company acquires an asset from another company in circumstances such that section 171(1) of the 1992 Act applies to the acquisition; and

(d) a chargeable gain ('a relevant gain') accrues to the relevant company on a disposal of the asset within the period of three years beginning with the change in the ownership.

(2) For the purposes of subsection (1)(d) above an asset acquired by the relevant company as mentioned in subsection (1)(c) above shall be treated as the same as an asset owned at a later time by that company if the value of the second asset is derived in whole or in part from the first asset, and in particular where the second asset is a freehold and the first asset was a leasehold and the lessee has acquired the reversion.

(3) For the purposes of this section—

(a) the accounting period of the relevant company in which the change in the ownership occurs shall be divided into two parts, the first the part ending with the change, the second the part after;

(b) those parts shall be treated as two separate accounting periods; and

(c) the amounts in issue for the accounting period being divided shall be apportioned to those parts.

(4) In Schedule 28A—

(a) Part V shall have effect for identifying the amounts in issue for the accounting period being divided; and

(b) Part VI shall have effect for the purpose of apportioning those amounts to the parts of that accounting period.

(5) Subsections (6) to (8) of section 768B shall apply in relation to the relevant company as they apply in relation to the company mentioned in subsection (1) of that section except that any reference in those subsections to Part III of Schedule 28A shall be read as a reference to Part VI of that Schedule.

(6) Subsections (7) and (9) below apply only where, in accordance with the relevant provisions of the 1992 Act and Part VI of Schedule 28A, an amount is included in respect of chargeable gains in the total profits for the accounting period of the relevant company in which the relevant gain accrues.

(7) In computing the total profits of the relevant company for the accounting period in which the relevant gain accrues, no deduction shall be made under section 75 by reference to—

(a) sums disbursed or allowances falling to be made for an accounting period of the relevant company beginning before the change in ownership, or

(b) charges paid in such an accounting period,

from an amount of the total profits equal to the amount which represents the relevant gain.

(8) For the purposes of this section, the amount of the total profits for an accounting period which represents the relevant gain is—

(a) where the amount of the relevant gain does not exceed the amount which is included in respect of chargeable gains for that period, an amount equal to the amount of the relevant gain;

(b) where the amount of the relevant gain exceeds the amount which is included in respect of chargeable gains for that period, the amount so included.

(9) To the extent that a payment of interest made by the relevant company in the accounting period in which the relevant gain accrues represents excess overdue interest, the payment shall not be deductible under section 338(1) from such part of the total profits for that accounting period as represents the relevant gain.

(10) Whether a payment of interest made by the relevant company represents excess overdue interest, and if so to what extent, shall be determined in accordance with the provisions of Part IV of Schedule 28A.

(11) Subsections (8) and (9) of section 768 shall apply for the purposes of this section as they apply for the purposes of that section.

(12) In this section—

'the relevant provisions of the 1992 Act' means section 8(1) of and Schedule 7A to that Act; and

'investment company' has the same meaning as in Part IV."

Supplementary provisions

3. After Schedule 28 there shall be inserted—

"SCHEDULE 28A

CHANGE IN OWNERSHIP OF INVESTMENT COMPANY: DEDUCTIONS

PART I

SIGNIFICANT INCREASE IN COMPANY CAPITAL

General

1. The provisions referred to in section 768B(2) for determining whether there is a significant increase in the amount of a company's capital after a change in the ownership of the company are as follows.

The basic rule

2. There is a significant increase in the amount of a company's capital if amount B—

(a) exceeds amount A by at least £1 million; or

(b) is at least twice amount A.

Amount A

3.—(1) Amount A is the lower of—

(a) the amount of the company's capital immediately before the change in the ownership; and

(b) the highest 60 day minimum amount for the pre-change year, found in accordance with sub-paragraphs (2) to (6) below.

(2) Find the daily amounts of the company's capital over the pre-change year.

(3) Take the highest of the daily amounts.

(4) Find out whether there was in the pre-change year a period of 60 days or more in which there was no daily amount lower than the amount taken.

(5) If there was, the amount taken is the highest 60 day minimum amount for the pre-change year.

(6) If there was not, take the next highest of the daily amounts and repeat the process in sub-paragraph (4) above; and so on, until the highest 60 day minimum amount for the pre-change year is found.

(7) In this Part of this Schedule 'the pre-change year' means the period of one year ending immediately before the change in the ownership of the company in question.

Amount B

4.—(1) Amount B is the highest 60 day minimum amount for the post-change period (finding that amount for that period in the same way as the highest 60 day minimum amount for the pre-change year is found).

(2) In this paragraph 'the post-change period' means the period of three years beginning with the change in the ownership of the company in question.

Capital and amounts of capital

5.—(1) The capital of a company consists of the aggregate of—

(a) the amount of the paid up share capital of the company;

(b) the amount outstanding of any debts incurred by the company which are of a description mentioned in any of paragraphs (a) to (c) of section 417(7); and

(c) the amount outstanding of any redeemable loan capital issued by the company.

(2) For the purposes of sub-paragraph (1) above—

(a) the amount of the paid up share capital includes any amount in the share premium account of the company (construing 'share premium account' in the same way as in section 130 of the Companies Act 1985); and

(b) the amount outstanding of any debts includes any interest due on the debts.

(3) Amounts of capital shall be expressed in sterling and rounded up to the nearest pound.

PART II

AMOUNTS IN ISSUE FOR PURPOSES OF SECTION 768B

6. The amounts in issue referred to in section 768B(4)(c) are—

(a) the amount of any sums (including commissions) actually disbursed as expenses of management for the accounting period being divided, except any such expenses as would (apart from section 768B) be deductible in computing profits otherwise than under section 75;

(b) the amount of any charges which are paid in that accounting period wholly and exclusively for the purposes of the company's business;

(c) the amount of any excess carried forward under section 75(3) to the accounting period being divided;

(d) the amount of any allowances falling to be made for that accounting period by virtue of section 28 of the 1990 Act which would (apart from section 768B) be added to the expenses of management for that accounting period by virtue of section 75(4);

(e) any other amounts by reference to which the profits or losses of that accounting period would (apart from section 768B) be calculated.

PART III

APPORTIONMENT FOR PURPOSES OF SECTION 768B

7.—(1) Subject to paragraph 8 below, the apportionment required by section 768B(4)(c) shall be made—

(a) in the case of the sums and charges mentioned in paragraph 6(a) and (b) above, by reference to the time when the sum or charge is due to be paid;

(b) in the case of the excess mentioned in paragraph 6(c) above, by apportioning the whole amount of the excess to the first part of the accounting period being divided;

(c) in the case of the amounts mentioned in paragraph 6(d) and (e) above, by reference to the respective lengths of the parts of the accounting period being divided.

(2) For the purposes of sub-paragraph (1)(a) above, in the case of any charge consisting of interest, the interest shall be assumed to become due on a day to day basis as it arises.

8. If it appears that any method of apportionment given by paragraph 7 above would work unreasonably or unjustly for any case for which it is given, such other method shall be used for that case as appears just and reasonable.

PART IV

EXCESS OVERDUE INTEREST

Introductory

9.—(1) The provisions referred to in sections 768B(11) and 768C(10) for determining whether a payment of interest made by the company or, as the case may be, the relevant company represents excess overdue interest, and if so to what extent, are set out in paragraphs 10 to 12 below.

(2) In those paragraphs—

(a) 'overdue interest' means interest due to be paid by the company or, as the case may be, the relevant company before the change in the ownership and still unpaid at the end of the actual accounting period in which the change occurs;

(b) 'amount C' means the amount of all the overdue interest; and

(c) 'amount P' means the amount of the profits for the accounting period ending with the change in the ownership.

(3) For the purposes of sub-paragraph (2) above—

(a) interest shall be assumed to become due on a day to day basis as it arises;

(b) the reference to the profits is a reference to the profits after making all deductions and giving all reliefs that for the purposes of corporation tax are made or given against the profits, including deductions and reliefs which under any provision are treated as reducing them for those purposes.

The rules

10.—(1) A payment of interest does not represent excess overdue interest except to the extent that it discharges a liability to pay overdue interest.

(2) For the purposes of this Part of this Schedule, a payment of interest on a debt shall be treated as discharging any liability to pay overdue interest before it is treated to any extent as discharging a liability to pay interest which is not overdue interest.

11. Where amount C does not exceed amount P, no payment of interest represents excess overdue interest.

12.—(1) Where amount C exceeds amount P—

(a) find the amount by which amount C exceeds amount P (amount X);

(b) take all the payments and parts of payments which discharge any liability to pay overdue interest;

(c) treat those payments and parts of payments as cancelling out amount X before any other part of amount C.

(2) A payment of interest represents excess overdue interest to the extent that, in accordance with sub-paragraph (1) above, it is treated as cancelling out amount X.

PART V

AMOUNTS IN ISSUE FOR PURPOSES OF SECTION 768C

13.—(1) The amounts in issue referred to in section 768C(3)(c) are—

(a) the amount which would in accordance with the relevant provisions of the 1992 Act (and apart from section 768C) be included in respect of chargeable gains in the total profits for the accounting period being divided;

(b) the amount of any sums (including commissions) actually disbursed as expenses of management for the accounting period being divided except any such expenses as would (apart from section 768C) be deductible in computing total profits otherwise than under section 75;

(c) the amount of any charges which are paid in that accounting period wholly and exclusively for the purposes of the company's business;

(d) the amount of any excess carried forward under section 75(3) to the accounting period being divided;

(e) the amount of any allowances falling to be made for that accounting period by virtue of section 28 of the 1990 Act which would (apart from section 768C) be added to the expenses of management for that accounting period by virtue of section 75(4); and

4–330

(f) any other amounts by reference to which the profits or losses of the accounting period being divided would (apart from section 768C) be calculated.

(2) In sub-paragraph (1)(a) above 'the relevant provisions of the 1992 Act' means section 8(1) of and Schedule 7A to that Act.

PART VI

APPORTIONMENT FOR PURPOSES OF SECTION 768C

14. The apportionment required by section 768C(3)(c) shall be made as follows.

15. In the case of the amount mentioned in paragraph 13(1)(a) above—

(a) if it does not exceed the amount of the relevant gain, the whole of it shall be apportioned to the second part of the accounting period being divided;

(b) if it exceeds the amount of the relevant gain, the excess shall be apportioned to the first part of the accounting period being divided and the relevant gain shall be apportioned to the second part.

16.—(1) Subject to paragraph 17 below, the apportionment shall be made—

(a) in the case of the sums and charges mentioned in paragraph 13(1)(b) and (c) above, by reference to the time when the sum or charge is due to be paid;

(b) in the case of the excess mentioned in paragraph 13(1)(d) above, by apportioning the whole amount of the excess to the first part of the accounting period being divided;

(c) in the case of the amounts mentioned in paragraph 13(1)(e) and (f) above, by reference to the respective lengths of the parts of the accounting period being divided.

(2) For the purposes of sub-paragraph (1)(a) above, in the case of any charge consisting of interest, the interest shall be assumed to become due on a day to day basis as it arises.

17. If it appears that any method of apportionment given by paragraph 16 above would work unreasonably or unjustly for any case for which it is given, such other method shall be used for that case as appears just and reasonable."

Consequential amendments

4.—(1) Section 769 (rules for ascertaining change in ownership of company) shall be amended in accordance with sub-paragraphs (2) to (4) below.

(2) In subsections (1), (2)(d) and (5) for "sections 767A, 768 and 768A" there shall in each case be substituted "sections 767A, 768, 768A, 768B and 768C".

(3) After subsection (3) there shall be inserted—

"(3A) Subsection (3) above shall apply for the purposes of sections 768B and 768C as if the reference to the benefit of losses were a reference to the benefit of deductions."

(4) In subsection (4) for "section 768 or 768A" there shall be substituted "section 768, 768A, 768B or 768C".

Application of Schedule

5. This Schedule shall apply in relation to a change in ownership occurring on or after 29th November 1994 other than a change occurring in pursuance of a contract entered into before that date.

GENERAL NOTE

Restrictions are introduced on the use of reliefs for management expenses and charges carried forward when the ownership of an investment company changes. Depending on the circumstances, relief is either withdrawn or the profits against which the reliefs can be set are restricted.

Para. 2

New ICTA 1988, ss.768B and 768C respectively withdraw relief for management expenses and charges carried forward in certain circumstances, and restrict the profits against which such expenses and charges carried forward can be set, when there is a change in ownership of an investment company.

New s.768B(1). This sets out the three different circumstances, combined with a change of ownership, in which the section applies.

New s.768B(2). The question whether a significant increase in capital has taken place is to be determined in accordance with Sched. 28A, Part I (see para. 3 below).

New s.768B(3). A "major change in the nature or conduct of a business" includes a major change in the nature of the investments held even as the result of a gradual process beginning before the six-year period.

New s.768B(4). Where a change of ownership takes place during an accounting period, the periods before and after the change are treated as separate accounting periods.

New s.768B(5). The rules for apportioning amounts to the two accounting periods are set out in Sched. 28A, Parts II and III (see para. 3 below).

New s.768B(6)–(8). Expenses, charges and allowances apportioned to the separate accounting periods are treated as if they belonged to those periods.

New s.768B(9). No relief is given for accounting periods ending after the change of ownership in respect of amounts of excess management expenses, or excess charges, from periods before the change.

New s.768B(10)–(11). Relief is similarly denied in the case of "excess overdue interest", as defined in Sched. 28A, Part IV (see para. 3 below).

New s.768B(12)–(13). The rules in s.768(6)–(9) concerning the application of balancing charges are applied with an appropriate modification.

New s.768B(14). The definition of "investment company" in ICTA 1988, Part IV applies (see s.130).

New s.768C(1). This section applies where there is a change in ownership of an investment company and within three years a company acquires and then disposes of an asset acquired on an intra-group transfer. It does not apply where s.768B applies.

New s.768C(2). This provides for cases where the value of an asset disposed of is derived from the asset acquired, *e.g.* where a lessee acquires the reversion and then sells the freehold.

New s.768C(3)–(5). The rules in s.768B(4)–(8) apply for the purposes of s.768C. The provisions regarding apportionment are in Sched. 28A, Parts V and VI.

New s.768C(6). The section only applies where there are chargeable gains, after deducting allowable losses, in profits for a period ending after the change in ownership.

New s.768C(7)–(8). No relief is given against profits equal to the lesser of the gain under new subs. (1), or the net chargeable gains in respect of amounts of excess management expenses or excess charges from periods before the change in ownership.

New s.768C(9)–(10). A similar restriction applies in relation to "excess overdue interest", as defined in Sched. 28A, Part IV (see para. 3 below).

New s.768C(11)–(12). The relevant administration and definition provisions are applied.

Para. 3

This inserts the new ICTA 1988, Sched. 28A.

New Sched. 28A, Part I. This provides rules for determining what constitutes a significant increase in capital for the purposes of s.768B(2). There is a significant increase if, during the three years after the change, the capital doubles or increases by at least £1 million. Capital includes share capital, share premium account, loans outstanding including interest and redeemable loan capital. Increase in capital is measured by reference to minimum amounts over 60-day periods.

New Sched. 28A, Part II. The amounts to be apportioned under s.768B(4)(c) are the amount of any sums disbursed as expenses of management, other than those deductible under s.75, plus charges paid wholly and exclusively for the purposes of the company's business, plus management expenses carried forward under s.75(3), plus capital allowances under the Capital Allowances Act 1990, s.28 plus any other amounts by reference to which the profits or losses of the accounting period would be calculated.

New Sched. 28A, Part III. Expenses and charges are to be apportioned by reference to their due date; losses carried forward to the first period; and capital allowances and other amounts in proportion to the respective lengths of the parts of the period being divided. Interest accrues on a day-to-day basis. If this method of apportionment works unreasonably or unjustly, another just and reasonable basis may be used.

New Sched. 28A, Part IV. This defines "excess overdue interest" for the purposes of ss.768B(11) and 768C(10). Where overdue interest does not exceed profits in the period ending with the change of ownership, none of it is treated as excess. Where it does, the excess is treated as excess overdue interest and payments of interest are treated as applying to it before any other interest.

New Sched. 28A, Part V. The amounts to be apportioned for s.768C(3)(c) correspond with those in Part II for s.768(4)(c), with the addition of chargeable gains for the period.

New Sched. 28A, Part VI. The apportionment works generally in accordance with that in Part III. Where the gain to be apportioned does not exceed the gain mentioned in s.768C(1)(d) it is apportioned to the second half of the accounting period being divided. Where it does, the excess is apportioned to the first half.

Para. 4

Some consequential amendments are made. In particular, the rules in s.769 are applied for ascertaining whether there has been a change in ownership of a company.

Para. 5

The new provisions apply to changes in ownership from Budget Day, save in pursuance of a contract entered into before that date.

Section 139   SCHEDULE 27

<small>SUB-CONTRACTORS IN THE CONSTRUCTION INDUSTRY</small>

Payments to which provision for deductions applies

1.—(1) In subsection (1) of section 559 of the Taxes Act 1988 (payments from which deductions are made), for "subsection (2) below" there shall be substituted "subsections (2) and (3A) below".

(2) Subsection (3) of that section (limit on payments exempted where a guarantee has been given or the recipient is a school leaver) shall not apply in relation to payments made to a person in any case where that person's certificate under section 561 of that Act is one issued or renewed with respect to a period beginning on or after the appointed day.

(3) Before subsection (4) of that section there shall be inserted the following subsection—

"(3A) Subsection (1) above shall not apply to a payment made under any contract if such conditions as may be prescribed in regulations made by the Board are satisfied in relation to the payment and the person making it."

(4) Sub-paragraphs (1) and (3) above shall have effect in relation to payments made on or after the appointed day.

Persons who are contractors and sub-contractors

2.—(1) In subsection (2) of section 560 of that Act (persons who are contractors)—

(a) after paragraph (a) there shall be inserted the following paragraph—
   "(aa) any public office or department of the Crown (including any Northern Ireland department);";

   and

(b) after paragraph (e) there shall be inserted the following paragraph—
   "(ea) any such body, being a body (in addition to those falling within paragraphs (aa) to (e) above) which has been established for the purpose of carrying out functions conferred on it by or under any enactment, as may be designated as a body to which this subsection applies in regulations made by the Board;".

(2) In paragraph (f) of that subsection and in subsection (3) of that section (persons to be contractors where average annual expenditure on construction exceeds £250,000), for "£250,000", wherever it occurs, there shall be substituted "£1,000,000".

(3) This paragraph applies in relation to any payments made on or after the appointed day.

Individual partners and liabilities for certain contraventions

3.—(1) In subsection (2)(b) of section 561 of that Act (condition of certificate for a member of a firm), for "563" there shall be substituted "562".

(2) In subsection (10) of that section (offence in connection with obtaining certificate), for "on summary conviction to a fine not exceeding £5,000" there shall be substituted "to a penalty not exceeding £3,000".

(3) In subsection (11) of that section (offences in connection with certificates, vouchers etc.)—

(a) after "section 566(2)(j)" there shall be inserted "or who is in possession of any form or other document supplied to him by the Board for use in connection with any regulations under this Chapter"; and

(b) for "on summary conviction to a fine not exceeding £5,000" there shall be substituted "to a penalty not exceeding £3,000".

Turnover test etc.

4.—(1) Section 562 of that Act (conditions for grant of exemption certificate to be satisfied by individuals) shall be amended as follows.

(2) In subsection (1) (applications to which section applies)—

(a) the words "(otherwise than as a partner in a firm)" shall be omitted; and

(b) at the end there shall be inserted "except that, where the application is for the issue of that certificate to that individual as a partner in a firm, this section shall have effect with the omission of subsections (2) to (2B)."

(3) After subsection (2) there shall be inserted the following subsections—

"(2A) The applicant must satisfy the Board, by such evidence as may be prescribed in regulations made by the Board, that the carrying on of the business mentioned in subsection

(2) above is likely to involve the receipt, annually in the period to which the certificate would relate, of an aggregate amount by way of relevant payments which is not less than the amount specified in regulations made by the Board as the minimum turnover for the purposes of this subsection.

(2B) In subsection (2A) above 'relevant payments' means the following payments, other than so much of them as would fall, as representing the direct cost to any person of any materials, to be disregarded in calculating the amount of any deductions under subsection (4) of section 559, that is to say—

    (a) payments from which such deductions would fall to be made if the certificate is not granted; and

    (b) payments which would be such payments but for any regulations under subsection (3A) of that section."

(4) Subsections (3) to (7) (which relate to the period for which an individual has carried on his business) shall cease to have effect.

(5) In subsection (9) (compliance by companies of which the applicant has had control), for "has the meaning given by section 840" there shall be substituted "shall be construed in accordance with section 416(2) to (6)".

(6) In subsection (11) (persons who have been out of the United Kingdom), for the words from the beginning to the word "Board", in the second place where it occurs, there shall be substituted—

"(11) Where the applicant states, for the purpose of showing that he has complied with all obligations imposed on him as mentioned in subsection (8) above, that he was not subject to any of one or more obligations in respect of any period ending within the qualifying period—

    (a) he must satisfy the Board of that fact by such evidence as may be prescribed in regulations made by the Board; and

    (b) if for that purpose he states that he has been outside the United Kingdom for the whole or any part of the qualifying period, he must also satisfy them, by such evidence as may be so prescribed,".

(7) For subsection (14) (meaning of "qualifying period") there shall be substituted the following subsections—

"(13A) Subject to subsection (10) above, a person shall not be taken for the purposes of this section to have complied with any such obligation or request as is referred to in subsections (8) to (11) above if there has been a contravention of a requirement as to the time at which, or the period within which, the obligation or request was to be complied with.

(14) In this section 'the qualifying period', in relation to an application for the issue of a certificate under section 561, means the period of three years ending with the date of the application."

5. Section 563 of that Act (conditions to be satisfied by individuals who are partners) shall cease to have effect.

6. For subsections (3) to (5) of section 564 of that Act there shall be substituted the following subsections—

"(2A) The partners must satisfy the Board, by such evidence as may be prescribed in regulations made by the Board, that the carrying on of the firm's business is likely to involve the receipt, annually in the period to which the certificate would relate, of an aggregate amount by way of relevant payments which is not less than whichever is the smaller of—

    (a) the sum specified in subsection (2B) below; and

    (b) the amount specified for the purposes of this paragraph in regulations made by the Board;

and in this subsection 'relevant payments' has the meaning given by section 562(2B).

(2B) The sum referred to in subsection (2A)(a) above is the sum of the following amounts, that is to say—

    (a) the amount obtained by multiplying the number of partners in the firm who are individuals by the amount specified in regulations as the minimum turnover for the purposes of section 562(2A); and

    (b) in respect of each partner in the firm who is a company (other than one to which section 565(2A)(b) would apply), the amount equal to what would have been the minimum turnover for the purposes of section 565(2A) if the application had been for the issue of a certificate to that company.

(3) Subject to subsection (4) below, each of the persons who are partners at the time of the application must have complied, so far as any such charge to income tax or corporation tax is concerned as falls to be computed by reference to the profits or gains of the firm's business—

    (a) with all obligations imposed on him by or under the Tax Acts or the Management Act in respect of periods ending within the qualifying period; and

    (b) with all requests to him as such a partner to supply to an inspector accounts of, or other information about, the firm's business or his share of the profits or gains of that business.

  (4) Where a person has failed to comply with such an obligation or request as is referred to in subsection (3) above the firm shall nevertheless be treated, in relation to that partner, as satisfying that condition as regards that obligation or request if the Board are of the opinion that the failure is minor and technical and does not give reason to doubt that the condition mentioned in subsection (5) below will be satisfied.

  (5) There must be reason to expect that each of the persons who are from time to time partners in the firm will, in respect of periods ending after the end of the qualifying period, comply with such obligations and requests as are referred to in subsection (3) above.

  (6) Subject to subsection (4) above, a person shall not be taken for the purposes of this section to have complied with any such obligation or request as is referred to in subsection (3) above if there has been a contravention of a requirement as to the time at which, or the period within which, the obligation or request was to be complied with.

  (7) In this section 'the qualifying period', in relation to an application for the issue of a certificate under section 561, means the period of three years ending with the date of the application."

7.—(1) After subsection (2) of section 565 of that Act there shall be inserted the following subsections—

  "(2A) The company must either—

    (a) satisfy the Board, by such evidence as may be prescribed in regulations made by them, that the carrying on of its business is likely to involve the receipt, annually in the period to which the certificate would relate, of an aggregate amount by way of relevant payments which is not less than the amount which is the minimum turnover for the purposes of this subsection; or

    (b) satisfy the Board that the only persons with shares in the company are companies which are limited by shares and themselves excepted from section 559 by virtue of a certificate which is in force under section 561;

and in this subsection 'relevant payments' has the meaning given by section 562(2B).

  (2B) The minimum turnover for the purposes of subsection (2A) above is whichever is the smaller of—

    (a) the amount obtained by multiplying the amount specified in regulations as the minimum turnover for the purposes of section 562(2A) by the number of persons who are relevant persons in relation to the company; and

    (b) the amount specified for the purposes of this paragraph in regulations made by the Board.

  (2C) For the purposes of subsection (2B) above a person is a relevant person in relation to the company—

    (a) where the company is a close company, if he is a director of the company (within the meaning of Chapter II of Part V) or a beneficial owner of shares in the company; and

    (b) in any other case, if he is such a director of the company."

  (2) After subsection (8) of that section there shall be inserted the following subsection—

  "(8A) Subject to subsection (4) above, a company shall not be taken for the purposes of this section to have complied with any such obligation or request as is referred to in subsections (3) to (7) above if there has been a contravention of a requirement as to the time at which, or the period within which, the obligation or request was to be complied with."

Commencement of paragraphs 3 to 7

8.—(1) Except in the case of paragraph 3(2) and (3) above, paragraphs 3 to 7 above shall have effect in relation to any application for the issue or renewal of a certificate under section 561 of the Taxes Act 1988 which is made with respect to any period beginning on or after the appointed day.

  (2) Paragraph 3(2) and (3)(b) above shall have effect in relation to contraventions of section 561(10) or (11) occurring on or after the appointed day; and paragraph 3(3)(a) above shall have effect in relation to forms and other documents in a person's possession at any time after the passing of this Act.

Powers to make regulations

9. In section 566 of that Act (general powers to make regulations), after subsection (2) there shall be inserted the following subsection—

"(3) Any power under this Chapter to make regulations prescribing the evidence required for establishing what is likely to happen at any time shall include power to provide for such matters to be presumed (whether conclusively or unless the contrary is shown in the manner provided for in the regulations) from evidence of what has previously happened."

GENERAL NOTE

In conjunction with s.139, the Schedule makes prospective changes to the system for sub-contractors in the construction industry which are designed to reduce the opportunity for tax evasion. The "appointed day" will not be before August 1, 1998.

Para. 1

A long-standing extra-statutory concession excepting certain small payments from the scheme may be incorporated into regulations, but the limited exemption from deduction conferred by special certificates, issued to school leavers or those who have obtained bank guarantees, will be abolished.

Para. 2

The definition of "contractor" is extended to include government departments and any other body carrying out public functions and designated in regulations made by the Revenue, but the annual expenditure on construction work which a non-construction business must incur before being required to operate the scheme is raised from £250,000 to £1 million.

Para. 3

The issue of business partners' certificates is made subject to the same rules that apply to certificates for sole traders. The specific criminal sanction of summary prosecution and a maximum fine of £5,000 for a fraudulent or negligent application for a certificate, or for misuse of a certificate or voucher, is replaced by a tax penalty of up to £3,000.

Para. 4

The amendments to ICTA 1988, s.562 introduce, firstly, a new certificate eligibility test for sole traders, requiring that they produce evidence that their annual business turnover, net of the direct cost of materials, is likely to reach a certain amount. The evidence required and the amount may be specified by the Revenue in regulations. Secondly, the requirement to have worked in the U.K. for a certain period before becoming eligible for a certificate is abolished, but the Revenue may make regulations, prescribing what evidence must be given by applicants to show that they have not been working or have been out of the U.K. Thirdly, the definition of "control" is amended to bring it into line with the more comprehensive tests in ICTA 1988, s.416. Finally, applicants who have complied with obligations or requests must have done so within the stipulated times and the "qualifying period", considered for the purposes of an individual's application for a certificate, is re-defined as the three years up to the date of the application.

Para. 5

The redundant ICTA 1988, s.563, dealing with partnership applications, is removed.

Para. 6

The requirements for partners to have met the tax liability of a partnership are replaced with new requirements:
  (i) entitlement to a partner's certificate is made dependent on evidence that the firm's turnover is likely to reach the amount specified for a sole trader multiplied by the number of partners (except for a corporate partner (see para. 7)), or an amount specified by the Revenue, whichever is smaller;
 (ii) all the partners must have complied with their tax obligations and complied with requests for information. Minor and technical breaches may be disregarded for this purpose;
(iii) there must be reason to expect that each of the partners will comply with his tax obligations in the future.

Para. 7

The requirements for entitlement to a company certificate are similarly adjusted. The turnover test is the amount specified for a sole trader multiplied by the number of directors (together with beneficial shareholders in the case of a close company) or, if smaller, an amount specified by the Revenue, unless the only shareholders are other companies which qualify for certificates in their own right. Applicant companies that have complied with obligations or requests must have done so within the stipulated times.

Para. 8

The new conditions for applications and the new penalties apply from the appointed day, *i.e.* not before August 1, 1998. However, a new requirement to ensure the safety of any form or document used in connection with the scheme (see para. 3(3)(a)) applies from Royal Assent.

Para. 9

The Revenue are empowered, when making regulations, to provide for the manner in which presumptions may be made from the evidence of past events.

Section 153   SCHEDULE 28

ELECTRONIC LODGEMENT OF TAX RETURNS, ETC.

1. In the Taxes Management Act 1970 after section 115 there shall be inserted—

"Electronic lodgement of tax returns, etc.

115A. Schedule 3A to this Act (which makes provision with respect to the electronic lodgement of tax returns and documents required in connection with tax returns) shall have effect."

2. After Schedule 3 to that Act there shall be inserted—

"SCHEDULE 3A

ELECTRONIC LODGEMENT OF TAX RETURNS, ETC.

PART I

TAX RETURNS: GENERAL

The basic rule

1.—(1) Sub-paragraph (2) below applies where a person is—

(a) required by a notice to which this Schedule applies, or

(b) subject to any other requirement to which this Schedule applies,

to deliver or make a return to an officer of the Board or to the Board.

(2) The requirement to deliver or make the return shall be treated as fulfilled by the person subject to the requirement if—

(a) information is transmitted electronically in response to that requirement; and

(b) each of the conditions in Part III of this Schedule is met with respect to that transmission.

(3) Sub-paragraphs (4) and (5) below apply where the requirement to deliver or make the return is fulfilled by virtue of sub-paragraph (2) above.

(4) Any requirement—

(a) under any provision of Part II of this Act that the return include a declaration by the person making the return to the effect that the return is to the best of his knowledge correct and complete, or

(b) under or by virtue of any other provision of the Taxes Acts that the return be signed or include any description of declaration or certificate,

shall not apply.

(5) The time at which the requirement to deliver or make the return is fulfilled is the end of the day during which the last of the conditions in Part III of this Schedule to be met with respect to the transmission is met.

(6) In sub-paragraph (2)(a) above "information" includes any self-assessment, partnership statement, particulars or claim.

Returns to which Schedule applies

2.—(1) This Schedule applies to a notice requiring a return to be delivered or made if—

(a) the notice is given under any provision of the Taxes Acts or of regulations made under the Taxes Acts;

(b) the provision is specified for the purposes of this Schedule by an order made by the Treasury; and

(c) the notice is given after the day appointed by the order in relation to notices under the provision so specified.

(2) This Schedule applies to any other requirement to deliver or make a return if—

(a) the requirement is imposed by any provision of the Taxes Acts or of regulations made under the Taxes Acts;

(b) the provision is specified for the purposes of this Schedule by an order made by the Treasury; and

(c) the requirement is required to be fulfilled within a period beginning after the day appointed by the order in relation to the specified provision.

(3) The power to make an order under this paragraph shall be exercisable by statutory instrument which shall be subject to annulment in pursuance of a resolution of the House of Commons.

(4) For the purposes of this Schedule, any reference to a requirement to deliver a return includes, in relation to regulations made under the principal Act, a reference to a requirement to render a return.

PART II

DOCUMENTS SUPPORTING CERTAIN TAX RETURNS

3.—(1) This paragraph applies where—

(a) a person is required by a notice to which this Schedule applies to deliver a return to an officer of the Board;

(b) the notice also requires any document other than the return ('a supporting document') to be delivered;

(c) the provision under which the notice is given requires the supporting document to be delivered with the return;

(d) the notice states that the supporting document may be transmitted electronically; and

(e) the requirement to deliver the return is fulfilled by virtue of paragraph 1(2) of this Schedule.

(2) The requirement to deliver the supporting document shall be treated as fulfilled by the person subject to the requirement if—

(a) information is transmitted electronically in response to that requirement; and

(b) each of the conditions in Part III of this Schedule is met with respect to that transmission.

(3) If information is not transmitted electronically in response to the requirement to deliver the supporting document, that requirement shall have effect as a requirement to deliver the document on or before the day which is the last day for the delivery of the return.

(4) For the purposes of sub-paragraph (1)(b) above the reference to a document includes in particular a reference to any accounts, statements or reports.

(5) Where the requirement to deliver the supporting document is fulfilled by virtue of sub-paragraph (2) above, the time at which it is fulfilled is the end of the day during which the last of the conditions in Part III of this Schedule to be met with respect to the transmission is met.

PART III

THE CONDITIONS

Approved persons

4.—(1) The first condition is that the transmission must be made by a person approved by the Board.

(2) A person seeking approval under this paragraph shall be given notice of the grant or refusal of approval.

(3) A person may be approved for the purpose of transmitting the information—

(a) on behalf of another person or other persons; or

(b) on his own behalf.

(4) An approval under this paragraph may be withdrawn by notice with effect from such date as may be specified in the notice.

(5) A notice refusing or withdrawing an approval shall state the grounds for the refusal or withdrawal.

(6) A person who is refused approval or whose approval is withdrawn may appeal to the Special Commissioners against the refusal or withdrawal.

(7) The appeal shall be made by notice given to the Board before the end of the period of 30 days beginning with the day on which notice of the refusal or withdrawal was given to the appellant.

(8) The Special Commissioners shall not allow the appeal unless it appears to them that, having regard to all the circumstances, it is unreasonable for the approval to be refused or (as the case may be) withdrawn.

(9) If the Special Commissioners allow an appeal by a person who has been refused approval, they shall specify the date from which the approval is to have effect.

Approved manner of transmission

5.—(1) The second condition applies if the person who makes the transmission is notified by the Board of any requirements for the time being applicable to him as to the manner in which transmissions are to be made by him or as to the manner in which any description of transmission is to be made by him.

(2) The second condition is that the transmission must comply with the requirements so notified.

(3) The requirements referred to include in particular requirements as to—

(a) the hardware or type of hardware, or

(b) the software or type of software,

to be used to make transmissions or a description of transmissions.

Content of transmission

6. The third condition is that the transmission must signify, in a manner approved by the Board, that before the transmission was made a hard copy of the information proposed to be transmitted was made and authenticated in accordance with Part IV of this Schedule.

Procedure for accepting electronic transmissions

7.—(1) The fourth condition is that the information transmitted must be accepted for electronic lodgement.

(2) For the purposes of this Schedule, information is accepted for electronic lodgement if it is accepted under a procedure selected by the Board for the purposes of this Schedule.

(3) The selected procedure may in particular consist of or include the use of specially designed software.

PART IV

HARD COPIES OF INFORMATION TRANSMITTED

Provisions about making of hard copies

8.—(1) A hard copy is made in accordance with this Part of this Schedule if it is made under arrangements designed to ensure that the information contained in the hard copy is the information in fact transmitted.

(2) A hard copy is authenticated in accordance with this Part of this Schedule if—

(a) where the transmission is made in response to a requirement imposed by a notice under Part II of this Act to deliver a return, the hard copy is endorsed with a declaration by the relevant person that the hard copy is to the best of his knowledge correct and complete; and

(b) in any other case, if the hard copy is signed by the relevant person.

(3) In sub-paragraph (2) above "the relevant person" means—

(a) where the transmission is made as mentioned in sub-paragraph (2)(a) above, the person who, but for paragraph 1(4)(a) of this Schedule, would have been required to make the declaration there mentioned;

(b) in any other case, the person subject to the requirement to deliver or make the return or, in the case of a document other than a return, deliver the document.

Meaning of 'hard copy'

9. In this Part of this Schedule 'hard copy', in relation to information held electronically, means a printed out version of that information.

PART V

STATUS OF INFORMATION

Exercise of powers

10.—(1) Sub-paragraphs (2) to (5) below apply where information transmitted in response to a requirement to deliver or make a return is accepted for electronic lodgement.

(2) An officer of the Board shall have all the powers that he would have had if the information accepted had been contained in a return delivered by post.

(3) The Board shall have all the powers that they would have had if the information accepted had been contained in a return delivered by post.

(4) Where the information is transmitted in response to a notice given under any provision of Part II of this Act, any power which, if the information had been contained in a return delivered by post, a person would have had under this Act to amend the return—

(a) by delivering a document, or

(b) by notifying amendments,

to an officer of the Board, shall have effect as if the power enabled that person to deliver a statement of amended information to the officer.

(5) Any right that a person would have had, if the information transmitted had been contained in a return delivered by post, to claim that tax charged under an assessment was excessive by reason of some mistake or error in the return shall have effect as far as the claimant is concerned as if the information transmitted had been contained in a return delivered by post.

(6) Where information transmitted in response to a requirement to deliver a document other than a return is accepted for electronic lodgement, an officer of the Board shall have all the powers that he would have had if the information had been contained in a document delivered by post.

(7) This paragraph is subject to paragraph 11 of this Schedule.

Proceedings

11.—(1) Sub-paragraphs (2) to (4) below apply where—

(a) a person is required by a notice to which this Schedule applies, or subject to any other requirement to which this Schedule applies, to deliver or make a return; and

(b) that requirement is fulfilled by virtue of paragraph 1(2) of this Schedule.

(2) A hard copy shown to have been made and authenticated in accordance with Part IV of this Schedule for the purposes of the transmission in question shall be treated for the purposes of any proceedings as if it were a return delivered or made in response to the requirement.

(3) Sub-paragraph (4) below applies if no hard copy is shown to have been made and authenticated in accordance with Part IV of this Schedule for the purposes of the transmission in question.

(4) A hard copy certified by an officer of the Board to be a true copy of the information transmitted shall be treated for the purposes of any proceedings in relation to which the certificate is given as if it—

(a) were a return delivered or made in response to the requirement in question, and

(b) contained any declaration or signature which would have appeared on a hard copy made and authenticated in accordance with Part IV of this Schedule for the purposes of the transmission.

(5) Where—

(a) a person is required by a notice to which this Schedule applies to deliver any document other than a return, and

(b) that requirement is fulfilled by virtue of paragraph 3(2) of this Schedule,

sub-paragraphs (2) to (4) above shall apply as if any reference to a return delivered in response to the requirement were a reference to a document delivered in response to the requirement.

(6) In this paragraph—

'hard copy' has the same meaning as in Part IV of this Schedule; and

'proceedings' includes proceedings before the General or Special Commissioners or any tribunal having jurisdiction by virtue of any provision of the Taxes Acts."

GENERAL NOTE

The Schedule inserts a new TMA 1970, s.115A, which itself introduces a new Sched. 3A to that Act. This provides for certain tax returns and documents to be lodged with the Revenue by electronic transmission.

New Sched. 3A

Para. 1. The requirement to send a return to the Revenue may be fulfilled when the information is transmitted electronically and the conditions in paras. 4–7 are met.

Para. 2. The returns which may be sent by electronic transmission include those required by a notice or any other type of return, in respect of which an order is made by the Treasury.

Para. 3. Where supporting documents are required, they may be sent electronically but must in any case arrive within the time limit for the return. "Document" includes accounts, statements or reports.

Paras. 4–7. The conditions to be satisfied for acceptance by the Revenue of electronic lodgement are:

  (i) the Revenue must approve the person making the transmission, who may be the taxpayer or his agent. This is to minimise the possibility of the system being used for fraud. There is a right of appeal to the Special Commissioners against the refusal or withdrawal of approval;

 (ii) the Revenue must also approve the mode of transmission (including specifications as to the hardware and software used);

(iii) the transmission must include confirmation that a hard copy has been made and authenticated (see paras. 8 and 9);

 (iv) the Revenue must accept the transmission, the procedure for which may include specially designed software.

Paras. 8 and 9. The hard copy, *i.e.* a print-out, must conform with the information transmitted and must contain the usual statutory declaration or signature.

Paras. 10 and 11. An electronically lodged return has the same status as a return delivered by post and may be amended or corrected in the same way. Where a hard copy is proved to have been made in accordance with para. 8, it is treated as if it were the return. If not, a hard copy of the information transmitted, certified as such by the Revenue, will be treated as the return and as if it included the statutory declaration or signature.

Section 162   SCHEDULE 29

REPEALS

PART I

ALCOHOLIC LIQUOR

(1) LOW-STRENGTH LIQUOR

Chapter	Short Title	Extent of repeal
1979 c. 4.	The Alcoholic Liquor Duties Act 1979.	In section 55A(1), the words "exceeding 1.2 per cent, but". Section 60(1A). Section 63(2).
1988 c. 39.	The Finance Act 1988.	In Schedule 1, in Part II, paragraph 8 and in paragraph 9 the words from "and after" to the end.

These repeals have effect in accordance with section 1 of this Act.

(2) ALCOHOLIC INGREDIENTS RELIEF

Chapter or Number	Citation	Extent of repeal
1979 c. 4.	The Alcoholic Liquor Duties Act 1979.	Section 6A. Section 45. Section 60(1) and (2). Section 63(1).
1988 c. 39.	The Finance Act 1988.	In Schedule 1, paragraph 2.
1991 c. 31.	The Finance Act 1991.	In Schedule 2, paragraph 12.
SI 1992/3158.	The Excise Duty (Amendment of the Alcoholic Liquor Duties Act 1979 and the Hydrocarbon Oil Duties Act 1979) Regulations 1992.	Regulation 2(4).

(3) Denatured Alcohol

Chapter	Short Title	Extent of repeal
1979 c. 4.	The Alcoholic Liquor Duties Act 1979.	In section 1(2), the words "but does not include methylated spirits". In section 2— (a) in subsection (1), the words "methylated spirits"; (b) in subsection (7), the words "or in any methylated spirits" and the words "or methylated spirits"; and (c) in subsection (8), the words "methylated spirits". In section 4(1), the definition of "methylated spirits". Section 9. Section 77(1)(b).
1979 c. 5.	The Hydrocarbon Oil Duties Act 1979.	In section 27(3), in the Table, the words "'methylated spirits'".
1990 c. 29.	The Finance Act 1990.	Section 8.
1993 c. 34.	The Finance Act 1993.	Section 8.
1994 c. 9.	The Finance Act 1994.	In Schedule 4, paragraph 47. In Schedule 5, in paragraph 3— (a) in sub-paragraph (1)(o), the words "methylated spirits and"; and (b) in sub-paragraph (2), the words "methylated spirits".

The powers in section 5(6) and (7) of this Act shall apply in relation to these repeals as they apply in relation to the provisions of that section and Schedule 2 to this Act.

PART II

Road Fuel Gas

Chapter	Short Title	Extent of repeal
1979 c. 5.	The Hydrocarbon Oil Duties Act 1979.	Section 8(7).

PART III

Betting and Gaming etc.

Chapter	Short Title	Extent of repeal
1981 c. 63.	The Betting and Gaming Duties Act 1981.	Sections 28(4) and 29(4). In section 33(1), in the definition of "gaming", the words "(except where it refers to a machine provided for gaming)". In Schedule 4, paragraph 13.
1993 c. 34.	The Finance Act 1993.	Section 16(8).
1994 c. 9.	The Finance Act 1994.	In Schedule 3, paragraph 3(8).

1. These repeals, except the repeals of sections 28(4) and 29(4) of the Betting and Gaming Duties Act 1981, have effect in accordance with section 14 of this Act.

2. The repeals of sections 28(4) and 29(4) of that Act come into force with the passing of this Act.

PART IV

AIR PASSENGER DUTY

Chapter	Short Title	Extent of repeal
1994 c. 9.	The Finance Act 1994.	In Schedule 5, in paragraph 9, the word "and" immediately preceding sub-paragraph (d).

This repeal has effect in accordance with section 16 of this Act.

PART V

VEHICLE EXCISE AND REGISTRATION

(1) EXEMPTIONS

Chapter	Short Title	Extent of repeal
1994 c. 22.	The Vehicle Excise and Registration Act 1994.	In Schedule 2, paragraphs 1, 12, 13, 14, 15, 16, 17 and 21.
1968 c. xxxii.	The Port of London Act 1968.	In section 199, paragraph (a) of the proviso to each of subsections (3) and (5).

These repeals come into force on 1st July 1995.

(2) RATES

Chapter	Short Title	Extent of repeal
1994 c. 22.	The Vehicle Excise and Registration Act 1994.	Section 17(3) to (7). In section 61, in subsection (3), paragraph (c) and the word "and" immediately preceding it, and subsections (4), (5) and (7). In section 62(1) the definitions of "built-in road construction machinery", "farmer's goods vehicle", "road construction machinery" and "road construction vehicle". In Schedule 1— (a) paragraph 4(2)(a), (b) and (f) and (3); (b) paragraph 8; (c) in paragraph 10, in each of sub-paragraphs (2) and (3), the words "(or relevant maximum weight)", and sub-paragraph (4); (d) paragraphs 12, 14(b) and (c) and 17(1)(c) to (e) and (2).

These repeals have effect in accordance with Parts III, IV and IX of Schedule 4 to this Act.

(3) OTHER REPEALS

Chapter	Short Title	Extent of repeal
1994 c. 22.	The Vehicle Excise and Registration Act 1994.	In section 31(5)(b) the words "(or an amount equal to the duty due)". In section 37(2) the words "(or, in Scotland, on indictment or on summary conviction)" and "(or, in Scotland, the statutory maximum)". In section 41(1)(b) the words "182 or" and "183 or".

1. The repeal in section 31(5)(b) applies in relation to offences committed after the day on which this Act is passed.

2. The repeals in sections 37(2) and 41(1)(b) apply in relation to proceedings begun after the day on which this Act is passed.

PART VI

VALUE ADDED TAX

(1) FUEL AND POWER

Chapter	Short Title	Extent of repeal
1994 c. 23.	The Value Added Tax Act 1994.	In Schedule 13, paragraph 7.

This repeal has effect in accordance with section 21 of this Act.

(2) AGENTS

Chapter	Short Title	Extent of repeal
1994 c. 23.	The Value Added Tax Act 1994.	In section 47(3), the words "goods or".

This repeal has effect in accordance with section 23(4)(b) of this Act.

(3) MARGIN SCHEMES

Chapter	Short Title	Extent of repeal
1994 c. 23.	The Value Added Tax Act 1994.	Section 32.

This repeal comes into force on the day appointed by an order under section 24(2) of this Act.

(4) APPEALS

Chapter	Short Title	Extent of repeal
1994 c. 23.	The Value Added Tax Act 1994.	In section 84(2) the words ", except in the case of an appeal against a decision with respect to the matter mentioned in section 83(1),".

This repeal has effect in accordance with section 31 of this Act.

PART VII

INSURANCE PREMIUM TAX

Chapter	Short Title	Extent of repeal
1994 c. 9.	The Finance Act 1994.	In section 53(5), paragraph (c) and the word "and" immediately preceding it.

This repeal has effect in accordance with paragraph 2 of Schedule 5 to this Act.

PART VIII

INCOME TAX, CORPORATION TAX AND CAPITAL GAINS TAX

(1) SCHEDULE A

Chapter	Short Title	Extent of repeal
1988 c. 1.	The Income and Corporation Taxes Act 1988.	Sections 22 and 23. Section 34(9). In section 354(2)(a), the words "or any of the other payments mentioned in section 25(1)". In section 779(13)(a), the words "allowable by virtue of sections 25, 26 and 28 to 31 and Schedule 1".
1989 c. 26.	The Finance Act 1989.	Section 170(1).
1990 c. 1.	The Capital Allowances Act 1990.	In section 9(6), paragraph (a) and, in paragraph (b), the words "if it is a charge to corporation tax". In section 92(2), paragraph (a) and, in paragraph (b), the words "if it is a charge to corporation tax". In section 132(4), paragraph (a) and, in paragraph (b), the words "if it is a charge to corporation tax".
1991 c. 31.	The Finance Act 1991.	In Schedule 15, paragraph 18.

These repeals come into force in accordance with section 39(4) and (5) of this Act.

(2) Interest Relief for Commercially Let Property

Chapter	Short Title	Extent of repeal
1988 c. 1.	The Income and Corporation Taxes Act 1988.	In section 353— (a) in subsection (1A), paragraph (b) and the word "and" immediately preceding that paragraph; (b) in subsection (1B), paragraph (b) and the word "or" immediately preceding that paragraph; (c) subsections (1C) and (1D); and (d) in subsection (1E), the words "the following factors, that is to say", and paragraph (b) and the word "and" immediately preceding that paragraph. Section 354(4). In section 355— (a) in subsection (1), the words from "or" at the end of paragraph (a) to the end of the subsection; and (b) subsection (4). In section 356A(3), the words "or but for section 353(1C)(a) would be". In section 356D(1), the words from "in a case" to "358". In section 357(1), the words from "in a case" to "358". Section 358(4A). In section 366(1)(c), the words "355(4) or". In section 370— (a) in subsection (6), in paragraph (a), the words "in paragraph (a)", and paragraph (b) and the word "and" immediately preceding it; (b) subsection (6A); and (c) in subsection (7), in paragraph (a), the words from "and paragraph (b)" to "omitted", and in paragraph (aa), sub-paragraph (ii).
1994 c. 9.	The Finance Act 1994.	In Schedule 9, paragraphs 4 to 6, 7(2) to (4) and 8.

These repeals come into force in accordance with section 42(3) to (5) of this Act.

(3) Beneficial Loans: Replacement Loans

Chapter	Short Title	Extent of repeal
1988 c. 1.	The Income and Corporation Taxes Act 1988.	Section 160(5)(b).

This repeal has effect in accordance with section 45(5) of this Act.

(4) Roll-over Relief: Groups

Chapter	Short Title	Extent of repeal
1992 c. 12.	The Taxation of Chargeable Gains Act 1992.	In section 175(1), the words from "(unless" to the end.

This repeal has effect where the acquisition of, or of the interest in, the new assets is on or after 29th November 1994.

(5) LIFE ASSURANCE BUSINESS

Chapter	Short Title	Extent of repeal
1988 c. 1.	The Income and Corporation Taxes Act 1988.	In section 75(4), the words "and insurance". In section 241(5), the words from "(that is to say," to "otherwise be liable)". In section 242(1)(b), the words "for purposes of section 241(3)". In section 242(9), the words "by virtue of section 241(5)". In section 431(2), the definitions of "general annuity business" and "pension business", "annuity fund", "basic life assurance business", "basic life assurance and general annuity business", "offshore income gain" and "overseas life assurance business", the word "and" following the definition of "overseas life insurance company" and the definition of "UK distribution income". Section 431(2A) to (6). Section 431AA. Section 432C(5)(a). Section 434(2) and (7). In section 436(3)(d), from the word "and" following sub-paragraph (i) to the end of the paragraph. Section 437(6). In section 441, in subsection (1), the words "resident in the United Kingdom" and subsection (7). Sections 444C to 444E. In section 474(1), paragraph (b) and the word "and" immediately preceding it. In section 475(2)(a), the words from "or," to "life assurance business". In Schedule 19AC, paragraphs 2(2), 3(4), 4(2), 5(2), 6(3), (4) and (6), 7(3), 8(4), 9(2) and (3), 10(3), 11(2) and (6), 12(2), 13(3), 14(3) and 15(2). In Schedule 28, in Part I, paragraph 3(4).
1989 c. 26.	The Finance Act 1989.	In Schedule 6, paragraph 2. In Schedule 8, paragraph 4. In Schedule 8A, paragraph 2(11).
1990 c. 29.	The Finance Act 1990.	Section 45(8). In Schedule 6— (a) paragraph 1(2)(a); (b) in paragraph 1(2)(b), the definitions of "basic life assurance business", "linked assets" and "overseas life assurance business"; and (c) paragraph 1(3) and (4). In Schedule 7, paragraph 7.
1991 c. 31.	The Finance Act 1991.	In Schedule 7, paragraphs 2, 3, 6 and 10.
1992 c. 12.	The Taxation of Chargeable Gains Act 1992.	In Schedule 10, paragraph 14(63)(b)(iv).
1993 c. 34.	The Finance Act 1993.	Section 99. Section 100(1) and (2)(a).
1994 c. 9.	The Finance Act 1994.	Section 143. Section 176(1). In Schedule 16, paragraph 5(2) and (3). In Schedule 17, paragraph 4.

1. The following repeals have effect in accordance with paragraph 55 of Schedule 8 to this Act—

the repeal of the definitions of "offshore income gain" and "overseas life assurance business" in section 431(2) of the Taxes Act 1988,

the repeal in section 441(1) of that Act,

the repeal of section 444C of that Act so far as it relates to subsection (2)(a) of that section,

the repeals in sections 474 and 475 of that Act,

the repeals of paragraphs 6(3) and (4) and 11(2) of Schedule 19AC to that Act,

the repeal in Schedule 28 to that Act,

the repeal of the definition of "overseas life assurance business" in paragraph 1(2)(b) of Schedule 6 to the Finance Act 1990 and the repeal in Schedule 7 to that Act,

the repeal of paragraph 10 of Schedule 7 to the Finance Act 1991, and

the repeal in the Taxation of Chargeable Gains Act 1992.

2. The repeals other than those listed above have effect in accordance with paragraph 57 of Schedule 8 to this Act.

3. The repeal of the definitions of "general annuity business" and "basic life assurance business" in Chapter I of Part XII of the Taxes Act 1988 does not affect the meaning of those expressions in paragraph 16 or 17 of Schedule 7 to the Finance Act 1991 or section 214 of the Taxation of Chargeable Gains Act 1992 (transitional provisions relating to changes in 1991).

(6) FRIENDLY SOCIETIES

Chapter	Short Title	Extent of repeal
1988 c. 1.	The Income and Corporation Taxes Act 1988.	In Schedule 15, paragraph 3(2)(c).
1992 c. 48.	The Finance (No. 2) Act 1992.	In Schedule 9, paragraph 19(3).

(7) QUALIFYING LIFE INSURANCE POLICIES

Chapter	Short Title	Extent of repeal
1988 c. 1.	The Income and Corporation Taxes Act 1988.	In Schedule 14, in paragraph 7(1), the words "and paragraphs 9 and 10 of Schedule 15". In Schedule 15, paragraphs 21, 22 and, in paragraph 24, in sub-paragraph (3), the word "first" and sub-paragraph (4).

These repeals come into force, in accordance with section 55(1) to (5) of this Act, on 5th May 1996.

(8) SETTLEMENTS: LIABILITY OF SETTLOR

Chapter	Short Title	Extent of repeal
1988 c. 1.	The Income and Corporation Taxes Act 1988.	In section 347A(2)(b), the words "within the meaning given by section 660(3)". Sections 660 to 676. Section 678(7). Sections 679 to 681. Sections 683 to 685. Section 689. In Schedule 29, in paragraph 32, the entry relating to section 27(2) of the Taxes Management Act 1970. In Schedule 30, paragraphs 10 to 12.
1988 c. 39.	The Finance Act 1988.	In Schedule 3, paragraph 20.
1989 c. 26.	The Finance Act 1989.	Section 60(3).

Chapter	Short Title	Extent of repeal
		Sections 108 and 109(1) to (3).
1990 c. 29.	The Finance Act 1990.	Section 82.
1991 c. 50.	The Age of Legal Capacity (Scotland) Act 1991.	In Schedule 1, paragraph 48.
1992 c. 12.	The Taxation of Chargeable Gains Act 1992.	Section 6(1) and (2)(b).
		In section 79(2), paragraph (b) and the word "and" preceding it.
		Section 79(4).
		In section 79(5)(a), the words "or income" wherever occurring.
1992 c. 48.	The Finance (No. 2) Act 1992.	In section 19(3), the words "683(2), 684(2), 689(2)".
		Section 23(2).
		Section 27.
1993 c. 34.	The Finance Act 1993.	In Schedule 6—
		(a) in paragraph 1, the words "683(2), 684(2)";
		(b) in paragraph 6, the word "689(2)";
		(c) paragraph 24.

These repeals have effect for the year 1995–96 and subsequent years of assessment.

(9) Stock lending

Chapter	Short Title	Extent of repeal
1988 c. 1.	The Income and Corporation Taxes Act 1988.	In section 129(1), the words "has contracted to sell securities, and to enable him to fulfil the contract, he".

(10) Deceased Persons' Estates

Chapter	Short Title	Extent of repeal
1988 c. 1.	The Income and Corporation Taxes Act 1988.	In section 695, in subsection (2), the words "subject to subsection (3) below". In section 701, subsection (14).

(11) Deduction of Tax from Interest on Deposits

Chapter	Short Title	Extent of repeal
1988 c. 1.	The Income and Corporation Taxes Act 1988.	In section 481(5)(k), the word "that" before sub-paragraph (i).

This repeal comes into force in accordance with section 86 of this Act.

(12) Meaning of "distribution"

Chapter	Short Title	Extent of repeal
1988 c. 1.	The Income and Corporation Taxes Act 1988.	In section 209(2)(e), sub-paragraphs (iv) and (v).

These repeals come into force in accordance with section 87(7) and (8) of this Act.

(13) GENERALISATION OF SS.63 TO 66 OF FINANCE ACT 1993

Chapter	Short Title	Extent of repeal
1993 c. 34.	The Finance Act 1993.	Section 63(12).

This repeal has effect in accordance with section 88(4) and (5) of this Act.

(14) MANAGEMENT: SELF-ASSESSMENT ETC.

Chapter	Short Title	Extent of repeal
1970 c. 9.	The Taxes Management Act 1970.	In section 9(3), the words "the following provisions of". Section 11A. In section 12B(2), the words from "or, where a return" to the end. In section 42(11), paragraph (b) and the word "and" immediately preceding that paragraph.
1988 c. 1.	The Income and Corporation Taxes Act 1988.	In section 73. In section 206, the words "under Schedule E". In section 536, in subsection (2), the words "are shown on a claim to" and, in subsection (4), the words from "and in that case" to the end. In section 537B, in subsection (2), the words "are shown on a claim to" and, in subsection (4), the words from "and in that case" to the end. In Schedule 3, in paragraph 6E, sub-paragraphs (1) and (3).
1992 c. 12.	The Taxation of Chargeable Gains Act 1992.	Section 7.
1994 c. 9.	The Finance Act 1994.	Section 198.

1. The repeal of section 11A of the Taxes Management Act 1970 has effect in accordance with section 115(13) of this Act.

2. The other repeals, except that in the Finance Act 1994, have effect in accordance with section 103(7) of this Act.

(15) CHANGES FOR FACILITATING SELF-ASSESSMENT

Chapter	Short Title	Extent of repeal
1988 c. 1.	The Income and Corporation Taxes Act 1988.	Section 114(3). Section 401(2).

1. The repeal of section 114(3) has effect in accordance with section 218(1) of the Finance Act 1994.

2. The other repeal has effect in accordance with section 120(2) of this Act.

(16) Non-residents

Chapter	Short Title	Extent of repeal
1970 c. 9.	The Taxes Management Act 1970.	Sections 78 to 85.
1985 c. 54.	The Finance Act 1985.	Section 50.
1987 c. 51.	The Finance (No. 2) Act 1987.	In Schedule 6, paragraph 7.
1988 c. 1.	The Income and Corporation Taxes Act 1988.	Section 43.
		In section 115(7), the words "this section and".
		In section 510A, in subsection (6), the words "Subject to subsection (7) below", and subsections (7) and (8).
		In Schedule 29, in the Table in paragraph 32, the entries relating to section 78(1) and (5) of the Taxes Management Act 1970.
1989 c. 26.	The Finance Act 1989.	In section 182(3)(c), the words "for the purposes of section 80(3) of the Taxes Management Act 1970 or".
1991 c. 31.	The Finance Act 1991.	Section 81.
1992 c. 12.	The Taxation of Chargeable Gains Act 1992.	In section 59, paragraph (c) and the word "and" immediately preceding it.
		In Schedule 10, paragraph 2(2), the words "78(3)(b)".
1994 c. 9.	The Finance Act 1994.	In section 215(5), paragraph (b), and the word "and" immediately preceding it.

1. The repeal of section 43 of the Taxes Act 1988 comes into force in accordance with section 40(3) of this Act.

2. The repeals in sections 115(7) of the Taxes Act 1988 and of section 59(c) of the Taxation of Chargeable Gains Act 1992 shall have effect in relation to any cases in relation to which section 112 of the Taxes Act 1988 has effect as amended by section 125 of this Act.

3. The repeals in section 510A of the Taxes Act 1988 have effect as respects the year 1997–98 and subsequent years of assessment and also, in relation to groupings whose trades or professions were set up and commenced on or after 6th April 1994, as respects the years 1995–96 and 1996–97.

4. The repeal of section 215(5)(b) of the Finance Act 1994 has effect in accordance with section 125(1) of this Act for the year 1995–96 and subsequent years of assessment.

5. The other repeals come into force—
   (a) for the purposes of income tax and capital gains tax, in relation to the year 1996–97 and subsequent years of assessment, and
   (b) for the purposes of corporation tax, in relation to accounting periods beginning after 31st March 1996.

(17) Exchange Gains and Losses

Chapter	Short Title	Extent of repeal
1993 c. 34.	The Finance Act 1993.	In section 129(8)(b) the words "or the circumstances are such that a charge would be so allowed if the duty were settled".

This repeal has effect in accordance with Schedule 24 to this Act.

(18) CONTROLLED FOREIGN COMPANIES

Chapter	Short Title	Extent of repeal
1988 c. 1.	The Income and Corporation Taxes Act 1988.	In Schedule 24, paragraph 4A.
1993 c. 34.	The Finance Act 1993.	Section 96.

Paragraph 4A of Schedule 24 to the Taxes Act 1988 is deemed never to have been inserted, and section 96 of the Finance Act 1993 is deemed never to have been enacted.

(19) PROFIT-RELATED PAY

Chapter	Short Title	Extent of repeal
1988 c. 1.	The Income and Corporation Taxes Act 1988.	In Schedule 8, in paragraph 19(6), paragraphs (g) to (k).

This repeal has effect in accordance with section 136 of this Act.

(20) PART-TIME WORKERS

Chapter	Short Title	Extent of repeal
1988 c. 1.	The Income and Corporation Taxes Act 1988.	In Schedule 8, paragraph 8(a). In Schedule 9, in paragraph 27(4) the words from "who is required" to the end.

These repeals have effect in accordance with section 137 of this Act.

(21) SUB-CONTRACTORS IN THE CONSTRUCTION INDUSTRY

Chapter	Short Title	Extent of repeal

1988 c. 1.	The Income and Corporation Taxes Act 1988.	Section 559(3).
		In section 561—
		  (a) in subsection (1), the words "subsection (5) below or";
		  (b) in subsection (3), the words "563";
		  (c) subsections (4) and (5);
		  (d) in subsection (6), the words from "(not being" to "apply)."; and
		  (e) subsection (12).
		In section 562—
		  (a) in subsection (1), the words "(otherwise than as a partner in a firm)"; and
		  (b) subsections (3) to (7).
		Section 563.

1988 c. 39.	The Finance Act 1988.	Section 28.

1. The repeal of sections 559(3) and 561(4) and (5) of the Taxes Act 1988, and the repeal in section 561(1) of that Act, have effect in relation to payments made to a person in any case where that person's certificate under section 561 of that Act is one issued or renewed with respect to a period beginning on or after the appointed day.

2. The repeal of section 561(12) of the Taxes Act 1988 comes into force in accordance with paragraph 8(2) of Schedule 27 to this Act.

3. The other repeals in the Taxes Act 1988 have effect in relation to any application for the issue or renewal of a certificate under section 561 of that Act which is made with respect to a period beginning on or after the appointed day.

4. The repeal of section 28 of the Finance Act 1988 has effect in relation to payments made on or after the appointed day.

5. In Notes 1, 3 and 4 above, "the appointed day" has the same meaning as in section 139 of this Act.

(22) PAYMENT OF RENT, &C UNDER DEDUCTION OF TAX

Chapter	*Short Title*	*Extent of repeal*
1988 c. 1.	Income and Corporation Taxes Act 1988.	In section 3(1)(c), the words "119 or". In section 74(1)(q), the words "119 or". In section 119(1), the words from "and, subject to subsection (2) below, shall be subject to deduction of income tax" to the end. In section 119(2), the words from "instead of" to "subsection (1) above". In section 122(1), the words from "but without prejudice" to the end. In section 348(2)(b), the words "119 or". In section 349(1)(c), the words "119 or". In section 821(3)(c), the words "119 or".
1992 c. 12.	Taxation of Chargeable Gains Act 1992.	In section 201(2), the words from "but without prejudice" to the end.

These repeals have effect in relation to payments made after the passing of this Act.

PART IX

PETROLEUM REVENUE TAX

Chapter	*Short Title*	*Extent of repeal*
1975 c. 22.	The Oil Taxation Act 1975.	In Schedule 8, in paragraph 4, in sub-paragraph (1), the words from "and the date" to the end of the sub-paragraph and, in sub-paragraph (2), the words "within the time allowed for making the original claim".

These repeals have effect in accordance with section 147 of this Act.

PART X

STAMP DUTY

Chapter	*Short Title*	*Extent of repeal*
1930 c. 28.	The Finance Act 1930.	In section 42(3) the words from "with the substitution" to the end.
1954 c. 23 (N.I.).	The Finance Act (Northern Ireland) 1954.	In section 11(3A) the words from "with the substitution" to the end.

These repeals have effect in accordance with sections 149 and 150 of this Act.

PART XI

INHERITANCE TAX: AGRICULTURAL PROPERTY

Chapter	Short Title	Extent of repeal
1984 c. 51.	The Inheritance Tax Act 1984.	In section 116(2) the word "either".

This repeal has effect in accordance with section 155 of this Act.

PART XII

PORTS LEVY

Chapter	Short Title	Extent of repeal
1989 c. 26.	The Finance Act 1989.	Section 178(2)(n).
1990 c. 29.	The Finance Act 1990.	Sections 115 to 120.
1991 c. 52.	The Ports Act 1991.	Section 41(3).

INDEX

BUILDING SOCIETIES (JOINT ACCOUNT HOLDERS) ACT 1995

(1995 c. 5)

An Act to secure the rights of second-named account holders in building society joint accounts; and for connected purposes. [1st May 1995]

PARLIAMENTARY DEBATES
Hansard, H.C. Vol. 254, col. 636; Vol. 258, col. 1087. H.L. Vol. 561, col. 1357; Vol. 562, cols. 914, 1691; Vol. 563, col. 389.

INTRODUCTION

This Act amends the Building Societies Act 1986 (c. 53) by inserting s.102A into that Act. This new section secures the rights of second-named account holders in building society joint accounts. Schedule 2, para. 7 of the 1986 Act is also amended. The Act came into force on May 1, 1995.

Rights of second-named joint shareholders

1.—(1) After section 102 of the Building Societies Act 1986 there shall be inserted the following section—

"Rights of second-named joint shareholders

102A.—(1) This section applies where the terms of a transfer of business by a building society to the company which is to be its successor include such provision as is mentioned in section 100(1).

(2) If—

(a) a person ('A') held shares in the society throughout the requisite period;

(b) any shares in the society held by A were jointly held for any period ('the joint ownership period') constituting the whole or part of the requisite period;

(c) A was the second-named holder of the jointly held shares for the whole or part of the joint ownership period; and

(d) no person who has priority over A for the purposes of this section held shares in the society throughout the requisite period,

the jointly held shares shall be treated for the purposes of subsections (8) and (9) of section 100 as having been held by A alone.

(3) The following persons shall have priority over A for the purposes of this section, namely—

(a) where A was not the first-named holder of the jointly held shares for any part of the joint ownership period—

(i) any person who was the first-named holder of those shares for the whole or part of that period; and

(ii) where A was the second-named holder of those shares for part only of that period, any person who was the second-named holder of those shares for a later part of that period; and

(b) where A was the first-named holder of the jointly held shares for part of the joint ownership period, any person who was the first-named holder of those shares for a later part of that period.

(4) If a person dies during the requisite period at a time when he is named in the records of the society as a joint holder of any shares jointly held, this section shall have effect in relation to any later time as if he had never been so named.

(5) In this section—

'the first-named holder', in relation to any shares jointly held, means that one of the joint holders who is named first in the records of the society, that is to say, the person by whom alone, apart from this section, those shares would, by virtue of paragraph 7(5) of Schedule 2, be treated as held for the purposes of section 100;

'qualifying day' has the same meaning as in subsections (8) and (9) of section 100;

'the requisite period' means the period beginning two years before the end of the qualifying day and ending immediately before the vesting date;

'the second-named holder', in relation to any shares jointly held, means that one of the joint holders who is named second in the records of the society;

'the vesting date' has the same meaning as in section 100."

(2) In paragraph 7 (joint shareholders) of Schedule 2 to that Act (establishment, incorporation and constitution of building societies), after sub-paragraph (5) there shall be inserted the following sub-paragraph—

"(5A) In its application to section 100, sub-paragraph (5) above shall have effect subject to the provisions of section 102A."

Citation and application

2.—(1) This Act may be cited as the Building Societies (Joint Account Holders) Act 1995.

(2) This Act shall apply in any case where the vesting date (within the meaning of section 100 of the Building Societies Act 1986) falls after the passing of this Act.

INDEX

References are to sections

CIVIL EVIDENCE (FAMILY MEDIATION) (SCOTLAND) ACT 1995*

(1995 c. 6)

An Act to make provision for the inadmissibility as evidence in civil proceedings in Scotland of information as to what occurred during family mediation. [1st May 1995]

PARLIAMENTARY DEBATES
Hansard, H.L. Vol. 560, col. 1643; Vol. 561, col. 1097; Vol. 562, cols. 794, 1438.

INTRODUCTION AND GENERAL NOTE

This Act establishes in Scots Law the principle that whatever occurs during family mediation should not be admissible as evidence in a civil court, subject to certain defined exceptions. The purpose is to enable those participating in mediation to talk freely and frankly in the knowledge that what is said cannot be used against them in later civil proceedings.

With an increasing number of couples deciding to split up it is only too clear that for those involved this can be an extremely painful, traumatic and often bitter process. Through the years it has emerged that divorcing or separating couples can be greatly helped in coming to mutually acceptable arrangements if they can meet in a neutral place with an impartial third person who has the knowledge and skills to provide information to assist in looking at the practical options and, if possible, in obtaining some agreement.

During the past decade a network of affiliated local voluntary organisations has developed family mediation services across Scotland. They work under the umbrella body known as Family Mediation Scotland which, among other functions, sets standards, trains and accredits people to act as mediators. Mediation is used increasingly. In 1994–95 3,644 families contacted Family Mediation Scotland. In addition the Law Society of Scotland has its own separate system for accrediting solicitor mediators, most of whom are members of an organisation known as Comprehensive Accredited Lawyer Mediators (CALM).

Family mediation is not a formal part of the legal system but it is now widely recognised as an extremely useful tool. In 1990 a Rule of Court was introduced enabling a Sheriff to require parties in any family actions in which custody or access is in dispute to go to a specified mediation service for an information session and thereafter to seek mediation or otherwise return to the court (see the Act of Sederunt (Sheriff Court) (Ordinary Cause Rules) 1993 (S.I. 1993 No. 1956 (s.223)), r.33.22). In the Court of Session the judge must obtain both parties' consent before referring them to the Mediation Service (Rules of the Court of Session, r.49.23).

The need for this legislation arises from the fact that, as the law stood, it was uncertain whether participants in mediation sessions could decline to give evidence in court about what occurred during mediation. The uncertainty of the law was regarded as having an inhibiting influence on family mediation which, to be effective, requires those participating to discuss the disputed issues frankly, without fear of what they say being used against them later in court.

In 1990, because of the increasing importance of mediation and the dubiety in the law, Family Mediation Scotland asked the Scottish Law Commission to look at the problem. In 1991 the Scottish Law Commission published Discussion Paper No. 92, *Confidentiality in Family Mediation*. That was followed in 1992 by Report No. 136, *Report of Evidence. Protection of Family Mediation*. The Commission took the view that to await adequate clarification through Scots case law might take some time and that legislation was the preferable route. A suggested draft Bill was appended to the report.

The Bill was read for the first time in the House of Lords on January 17, 1995 upon being introduced by the Baroness Carnegy of Lour. The Bill received cross-bench support, with considerable technical drafting assistance from the Government. The purpose of the Act is limited to assisting the process of mediation.

---

* Annotations by Hugh R. Donald WS, Partner, Shepherd & Wedderburn WS, Edinburgh.

The scheme of the Act

Section 1 sets out the general rule that information as to what occurred during family mediation to which the Act applies is not admissible as evidence in any civil proceedings. The Act does not extend to criminal proceedings. This section defines family mediation to which the Act applies by reference to the parties involved and the subject-matter of the mediation. The Act applies to family mediation between two or more individuals concerning matters generally relating to a child's welfare, or between couples, whether married or not, concerning matters arising from the breakdown of their relationship, or of such other description as the Secretary of State may determine. A mediator must be accredited by an organisation approved for the purposes of the Act by the Lord President of the Court of Session, who may specify the period for which approval is granted and may, if he thinks fit, withdraw that approval at any time.

Section 2 sets out the exceptions to the general rule of inadmissibility provided for in s.1. Information is admissible as to any contract entered into during family mediation or of the fact that no contract was entered into. This section also allows information from family mediation to be admissible in legal proceedings relating to a child's care and protection involving a local authority or a voluntary organisation, including a children's hearing or adoption proceedings.

Information from family mediation is to be admitted in civil proceedings if all the participants (other than the mediator) agree that this should be done. Section 2(2) defines who shall be regarded as a participant in family mediation for the purpose of these exceptions. In certain circumstances a child shall be regarded as a participant in family mediation and shall have the legal capacity to agree to information being admitted in evidence if, at the time of the mediation, that child is capable of understanding the nature and significance of the information in question.

Section 3 sets out the title of the Act, its provisions for regulations and its commencement. The Act applies only to Scotland.

Inadmissibility in civil proceedings of information as to what occurred during family mediation

1.—(1) Subject to section 2 of this Act, no information as to what occurred during family mediation to which this Act applies shall be admissible as evidence in any civil proceedings.

(2) This Act applies to family mediation—

(a) between two or more individuals relating to—

    (i) the residence of a child;

    (ii) the regulation of personal relations and direct contact between a child and any other person;

    (iii) the control, direction or guidance of a child's upbringing;

    (iv) the guardianship or legal representation of a child; or

    (v) any other matter relating to a child's welfare;

(b) between spouses or former spouses concerning matters arising out of the breakdown or termination of their marriage;

(c) between parties to a purported marriage concerning matters arising out of the breakdown or annulment of their purported marriage;

(d) between co-habitants or former co-habitants concerning matters arising out of the breakdown or termination of their relationship; or

(e) of such other description as the Secretary of State may prescribe,

which is conducted by a person accredited as a mediator in family mediation to an organisation which is concerned with such mediation and which is approved for the purposes of this Act by the Lord President of the Court of Session.

(3) The Lord President of the Court of Session may—

(a) in approving an organisation under subsection (2) above, specify the period for which the approval is granted;

(b) if he thinks fit, withdraw the approval at any time.

(4) A certificate by the Lord President approving an organisation under subsection (2) above shall be—

(a) in such form as may be prescribed by Act of Sederunt; and

(b) admissible as evidence in any civil proceedings and sufficient evidence of the matters contained therein.

(5) A document purporting to be a certificate by the Lord President for the purposes of this Act shall be accepted by the court as such unless the contrary is proved.

(6) The Lord President may, in connection with the performance of any of his functions under this Act, require an organisation which is seeking, or has been granted, approval under subsection (2) above to provide him with such information as he thinks fit.

(7) For the purposes of subsection (2)(d) above, "co-habitants" means a man and a woman who are not married to each other but who are living together as if they were husband and wife.

(8) In this Act, "civil proceedings" does not include an arbitration or proceedings before a tribunal or inquiry.

(9) In this section and section 2 of this Act, any reference to what occurred during family mediation shall include a reference to what was said, written or observed during such mediation.

GENERAL NOTE

This section sets out the general rule that information as to what occurred during family mediation to which this Act applies is not admissible as evidence in any civil proceedings. Only mediation conducted by mediators accredited to an approved organisation is protected by the Act. Approval is conferred on the organisation by the Lord President of the Court of Session.

Subs. (1)

This subsection provides that information as to what occurred during family mediation to which the Act applies is not admissible as evidence in any civil proceedings. However, information as to when and where the family mediation took place, who was present and any contract which was entered into during the family mediation is admissible by virtue of subs. (9) and s.2.

Subs. (2)

This subsection defines the family mediation to which the Act applies by reference to the parties in attendance and the subject-matter of the mediation. The list of parties whose presence may suffice to bring a mediation within the scope of the Act includes the parties to a purported marriage, this being a supposed or apparent marriage, which is not a marriage in law, such as a bigamous marriage. It is provided that family mediation must be conducted by an accredited mediator for the Act to apply. Such a mediator must be accredited to an organisation which is concerned with family mediation and approved by the Lord President of the Court of Session. This reflects the concern of the Scottish Law Commission that, because the rule making mediation information inadmissible applies to civil proceedings in any Scottish Court, a central legal authority should be involved in the approval process. The Scottish Law Commission had recommended that because admissibility of evidence is a matter for the courts, this authority should be the Lord President of the Court of Session.

Subss. (4) and (5)

The Lord President of the Court of Session is enabled to issue a certificate approving an organisation under subs. (2) in a form to be prescribed by Act of Sederunt, which certificate will be admissible as evidence in any civil proceedings and sufficient evidence of the matters contained therein. This avoids any unnecessary challenge to the Lord President's approval to the extent that a document purporting to be a certificate will be accepted as such unless the contrary is proved.

Subs. (6)

This subsection enables the Lord President to have a certain degree of flexibility in the form of approval of the organisation and the means by which approval may be withdrawn. Requiring the Lord President to be satisfied with any organisation seeking approval was seen to be important, in view of the evidential immunity attracting to family mediation. It was considered inappropriate to rely upon information being produced voluntarily. The Lord President will decide if an organisation can be approved or if any approval given should be withdrawn based upon his investigations of the organisation, its aims, methods, training practices and arrangements. The Lord President is not to act as an overall guardian of the standards of mediation organisations, his power is restricted to the purposes of the Act.

Exceptions to general rule of inadmissibility

2.—(1) Nothing in section 1 of this Act shall prevent the admissibility as evidence in civil proceedings—

(a) of information as to any contract entered into during family mediation or of the fact that no contract was entered into during such mediation;

(b) where any contract entered into as a result of family mediation is challenged in those civil proceedings, of information as to what occurred during family mediation which relates to the subject matter of that challenge;

(c) of information as to what occurred during family mediation if every participant (other than the mediator) in that mediation agrees that the information should be admitted as evidence; or

(d) of information as to what occurred during family mediation if those civil proceedings are proceedings—

(i) (whether under any enactment or otherwise) relating to a child's care or protection to which a local authority or a voluntary organisation is a party;

(ii) under Part III of the Social Work (Scotland) Act 1968 before, or relating to, a children's hearing;

(iii) for an adoption order under section 12 of the Adoption (Scotland) Act 1978;

(iv) for an order under section 18 of the said Act of 1978 declaring a child free for adoption;

(v) against one of the participants, or the mediator, in a family mediation in respect of damage to property, or personal injury, alleged to have been caused by that participant or, as the case may be, mediator during family mediation; or

(vi) arising from the family mediation and to which the mediator is a party.

(2) For the purposes of this section—

(a) an individual, spouse, former spouse, party to a purported marriage, or co-habitant referred to in section 1(2) of this Act; and

(b) insofar as the family mediation includes any of the matters mentioned in section 1(2)(a) of this Act, a child who—

(i) is the subject of such a family mediation; and

(ii) at the time the family mediation took place was capable of understanding the nature and significance of the matters to which the information which is sought to be admitted as evidence relates,

shall be regarded as a participant in the family mediation.

(3) Notwithstanding anything in the Age of Legal Capacity (Scotland) Act 1991, any child who is regarded as a participant in family mediation by virtue of subsection (2) above shall have legal capacity to agree that information should be admitted as evidence.

(4) The Secretary of State may prescribe other persons or classes of person who shall be regarded for the purposes of this section as participants in a family mediation.

GENERAL NOTE

Subs. (1)

Subsection (1) sets out the exceptions to the general rule of inadmissibility provided for in s.1. Inadmissibility is confined to matters which are essential to the effectiveness of mediation. In particular, the inadmissibility rule does not apply in children's hearings, adoption proceedings and certain other proceedings involving children and local authorities or voluntary organisations. This reflects the view of the Scottish Law Commission Report that in such proceedings the public interest in the protection and future well-being of children should rank above public interest in the promotion of family mediation.

In subs. (1)(a), reference is made to the admissibility of evidence of information as to any contract entered into during family mediation or of the fact that no contract was entered into during such mediation. When the Bill was presented reference was made to agreement (whether written or oral) as opposed to contract. However, it was considered that this term might be too wide, and the term contract was introduced to draw a distinction between an agreement intended to be binding and other kinds of informal arrangements which often emerge during family mediation. If a contract, legal and binding, is entered into, evidence regarding that contract is admissible. Most mediation conducted aims to achieve practical solutions for the families and not binding contracts.

As a result of subs. (1)(c), information as to what occurs during family mediation may be admissible if every participant agrees. The consent of the mediator is not required. It is recognised that this agreement may be given in advance by the participants, particularly in regard to the exchange of financial information.

Subss. (2) and (3)

These subsections provide the definition of a participant in family mediation and in particular the circumstances in which a child will be regarded as a participant. It extends to a child who is the subject of mediation, regardless of whether or not the other participants are the mother and father and requires that the child's agreement be obtained if at the time the mediation took place the child was capable of understanding the nature and significance of the matters to which the information which is sought to be admitted as evidence relates. This will require some determination to be made as to the child's ability at that time to understand the nature and significance of the matters to which the information relates, which may concern with whom the child should reside, the maintenance of personal relationships and direct contact with parents. It would not extend to any child too young to understand the nature and significance of the matters involved. This provision is not to be overridden by any provision of the Age of Legal Capacity (Scotland) Act 1991 (c.50) which provides that generally children under the age of 16 have no legal capacity.

Short title, construction, commencement and extent

3.—(1) This Act may be cited as the Civil Evidence (Family Mediation) (Scotland) Act 1995.

(2) In this Act, "prescribe", except in relation to an Act of Sederunt, means prescribe by regulations made by statutory instrument subject to annulment in pursuance of a resolution of either House of Parliament.

(3) This Act shall come into force on such day as the Lord Advocate may by order made by statutory instrument appoint; and such order may include such transitional or incidental provisions as appear to him to be necessary or expedient.

(4) This Act extends to Scotland only.

General Note

Subs. (3)

The Lord Advocate is permitted flexibility in bringing the Act into force, the purpose of which is to enable any cross-reference to be made to the Children (Scotland) Act 1995 and any consequent amendments arising from the passage of that Act, in particular in regard to the status of the child. Transitional provisions allow the Lord Advocate to apply the Act to cases where family mediation has commenced but in which proof has not yet taken place.

INDEX

References are to sections

REQUIREMENTS OF WRITING (SCOTLAND) ACT 1995*

(1995 c. 7)

ARRANGEMENT OF SECTIONS

An Act to reform the law of Scotland with regard to the requirement of writing for certain matters and the formal validity of contractual and other documents and presumptions relating thereto; to abolish any rule of law restricting the proof of any matter to writ or oath and to abolish the procedure of reference to oath; and for connected purposes. [1st May 1995]

PARLIAMENTARY DEBATES
Hansard, H.L. Vol. 561, col. 1367, Vol. 562, cols. 1320, 1712.

INTRODUCTION AND GENERAL NOTE

This Act implements most of the recommendations of the Scottish Law Commission's Report on Requirements of Writing, which was published in July 1988 (Scot. Law Com. No. 112). A previous Requirements of Writing Bill was introduced to the House of Commons on April 26, 1989 by a Private Member but did not proceed beyond its first reading. The Act substantially follows the text of this earlier Bill and, less directly, of the draft bill attached to the Scottish Law Commission's Report.

The Act sweeps away a great deal of archaic and obscure law, much of it based on statutes of the pre-Union Scots Parliament, and presents in its place a coherent and systematic scheme for the execution of deeds and other documents under the law of Scotland.

The Act deals with six main topics.

(1) The requirement for writing

Section 1 of the Act simplifies and re-states in modern language the rule of the common law that formally executed writing is required (a) for the constitution of certain types of contracts

---

* Annotations by Kenneth G.C. Reid, M.A., LL.B., Solicitor, Professor of Property Law at the University of Edinburgh.

and other obligations (the so-called *obligationes literis*), (b) for the performance of certain juristic acts in relation to land, and (c) for the making of a will or other testamentary disposition. At the same time s.11(1) abolishes the rule whereby certain other obligations, although capable of constitution without writing, could only be proved by writ or oath. Homologation is also abolished, and the principles of *rei interventus* are re-stated in modern language.

(2) Execution of deeds: the minimum formalities

Before the 1995 Act there were three methods by which a deed or other document could be formally executed: either (a) the deed was subscribed by the granter and attested by two witnesses (attested writing); or (b) it was in the handwriting of and subscribed by the granter (holograph writing); or (c) it was subscribed by the granter with the addition of the holograph docquet (adopted as holograph). The 1995 Act abolishes all three methods. In their place there is now only one method of formal execution: s.2 provides that a deed is formally valid if it is subscribed by the granter. Witnesses are not required. This new method of execution is mandatory in all cases where s.1(2) requires writing and it is optional in the case of any other obligation or juristic act.

The Act also contains provisions defining the meaning of signature (s.7), and allowing for notarial execution on behalf of a person who is blind or unable to write (s.9).

(3) Execution of deeds: presumption of valid execution

A deed which is merely subscribed under s.2 is not self-evidencing (or "probative", in traditional vocabulary). This means that the onus of proving that such a deed truly was subscribed by the granter would rest on any person who wished to rely on its terms. However, a deed may be made self-evidencing by attestation by a single witness. Section 3(1) provides that a deed which bears to be subscribed by the granter and attested by the signature of one witness is presumed to have been subscribed by the granter. Similarly if the deed or testing clause contains information as to date and place of execution, the deed is presumed to have been executed on that date and at that place (s.3(8)). There is continuity here with the previous law which conferred similar presumptions in relation to attested writings (although under that law two witnesses were required for attestation).

A deed which has not been attested can nevertheless be made self-evidencing by application to the sheriff court (s.4). If the court is satisfied, usually by affidavit evidence, that the deed was subscribed by the granter, it will cause a docquet to that effect to be endorsed on the deed.

It is likely that attestation will continue to be used in the future for much the same categories of deed as in the past. Indeed the Act expressly provides that conveyancing deeds must be attested (or contain a court docquet under s.4) before they can be registered (s.6).

(4) Annexations and alterations

Special provision is made for the authentication, both of annexations (such as schedules or plans) attached to deeds (s.8), and also of alterations ("vitiations" in traditional terminology) made to deeds (s.5). In both cases separate provision is made depending upon whether the deed is subscribed only or attested.

(5) Companies and other special categories of granter

Schedule 2 makes provision for the execution of deeds by (a) partnerships, (b) companies, (c) local authorities, (d) other bodies corporate, and (e) Ministers of the Crown and other office-holders. In all cases there are dual provisions depending on whether the deed is subscribed only or is self-evidencing ("probative"). In the case of some of the categories dealt with in Sched. 2, attestation is not the only method by which a deed can be made self-evidencing.

Since a juristic person cannot sign personally, a question arises as to the authority of the person who signs on their behalf. Schedule 2 approaches this issue differently in respect of different granters. In some cases (*e.g.* local authorities) the presumption arising from attestation (or equivalent) is a double presumption, namely (i) that the deed is presumed to have been subscribed by the signatory and (ii) that the signatory is presumed to have had authority to sign on behalf of the granter. In other cases (*e.g.* companies) the presumption stops with (i), and the deed is not self-evidencing in relation to authority to sign.

(6) Wills and other testamentary dispositions

In general the Act treats wills in the same way as other deeds. However, three special rules deserve mention.

First, even where a will is attested by a witness, it is not self-evidencing unless it has been signed by the granter on every sheet (s.3(2)). This simply re-enacts the previous law. By contrast, a will which is subscribed only and not witnessed need not be signed on every sheet.

Secondly, the date and place of execution given in a will are presumed to be correct in all cases, even where the will is not attested (s.3(10)).

Finally, confirmation of executors cannot be issued in respect of a will which is not self-evidencing: see Sched. 4, para. 39, which inserts a new s.21A into the Succession (Scotland) Act 1964 (c. 41). Accordingly a will which has not been attested requires to be set up by affidavit evidence under s.4, although in practice this can be done as part of the application for confirmation. This corresponds to the previous rule in relation to the setting up of holograph wills (s.21 of the 1964 Act).

COMMENCEMENT
    The Act received Royal Assent on May 1, 1995. It comes into force on August 1, 1995 (see s.15(2)).

EXTENT
    The Act applies to Scotland only (see s.15(3)).

Writing required for certain contracts, obligations, trusts, conveyances and wills

    1.—(1) Subject to subsection (2) below and any other enactment, writing shall not be required for the constitution of a contract, unilateral obligation or trust.
    (2) Subject to subsection (3) below, a written document complying with section 2 of this Act shall be required for—
    (a) the constitution of—
            (i) a contract or unilateral obligation for the creation, transfer, variation or extinction of an interest in land;
            (ii) a gratuitous unilateral obligation except an obligation undertaken in the course of business; and
            (iii) a trust whereby a person declares himself to be sole trustee of his own property or any property which he may acquire;
    (b) the creation, transfer, variation or extinction of an interest in land otherwise than by the operation of a court decree, enactment or rule of law; and
    (c) the making of any will, testamentary trust disposition and settlement or codicil.
    (3) Where a contract, obligation or trust mentioned in subsection (2)(a) above is not constituted in a written document complying with section 2 of this Act, but one of the parties to the contract, a creditor in the obligation or a beneficiary under the trust ("the first person") has acted or refrained from acting in reliance on the contract, obligation or trust with the knowledge and acquiescence of the other party to the contract, the debtor in the obligation or the truster ("the second person")—
    (a) the second person shall not be entitled to withdraw from the contract, obligation or trust; and
    (b) the contract, obligation or trust shall not be regarded as invalid,
on the ground that it is not so constituted, if the condition set out in subsection (4) below is satisfied.
    (4) The condition referred to in subsection (3) above is that the position of the first person—
    (a) as a result of acting or refraining from acting as mentioned in that subsection has been affected to a material extent; and
    (b) as a result of such a withdrawal as is mentioned in that subsection would be adversely affected to a material extent.
    (5) In relation to the constitution of any contract, obligation or trust mentioned in subsection (2)(a) above, subsections (3) and (4) above replace the rules of law known as *rei interventus* and homologation.
    (6) This section shall apply to the variation of a contract, obligation or trust as it applies to the constitution thereof but as if in subsections (3) and (4) for the references to acting or refraining from acting in reliance on the contract, obligation or trust and withdrawing therefrom there were substituted respectively references to acting or refraining from acting in reliance on the

variation of the contract, obligation or trust and withdrawing from the variation.

(7) In this section "interest in land" means any estate, interest or right in or over land, including any right to occupy or to use land or to restrict the occupation or use of land, but does not include—

(a) a tenancy;
(b) a right to occupy or use land; or
(c) a right to restrict the occupation or use of land,

if the tenancy or right is not granted for more than one year, unless the tenancy or right is for a recurring period or recurring periods and there is a gap of more than one year between the beginning of the first, and the end of the last, such period.

(8) For the purposes of subsection (7) above "land" does not include—

(a) growing crops; or
(b) a moveable building or other moveable structure.

DEFINITIONS
   "decree": s.12(1).
   "document": s.12(1).
   "enactment": s.12(1).
   "land": Sched. 1 to the Interpretation Act 1978.
   "writing": Sched. 1 to the Interpretation Act 1978.

GENERAL NOTE
   This section makes far-reaching alterations to the law relating to the use of writing in the constitution and variation of contracts and other voluntary obligations. It also makes provision for the use of writing for conveyances and other dealings in relation to land, and for the making of wills. The section should be read together with s.11 which abolishes the rule by which certain voluntary obligations, though capable of oral constitution, may be proved only by writ or oath.

Subs. (1)
   This reaffirms the basic rule of the common law that voluntary obligations may be constituted without writing. The common law exceptions to that rule – known collectively as the *obligationes literis* – are abolished by s.11(3)(a) and are replaced by the new statutory list set out in subs. (2)(a).

   Any other enactment. For example, the Consumer Credit Act 1974 (c. 39), s.60, provides that regulated consumer credit agreements and consumer hire agreements shall be constituted in a prescribed written form and with a prescribed content.

   Unilateral obligation. Section 1 distinguishes unilateral obligations from contracts. The only unilateral obligation recognised in Scots law is a promise.

Subs. (2)
   Where subs. (2) applies, not only must there be writing but the writing must be in a form which complies with s.2. A written document complies with s.2 if it is subscribed by the granter.

Para. (a). Under the previous law certain voluntary obligations, known collectively as *obligationes literis*, could be constituted only in formal writing (that is to say, in writing which was attested, holograph of the granter, or adopted as holograph). These included obligations relating to land, contracts of service for more than a year, submissions to arbitration, and possibly (although the law was open to doubt) contracts of insurance and cautionary obligations. The previous law is abolished by s.11(3)(a), and this paragraph provides in replacement a much abbreviated list of obligations which must continue to be constituted in (formal) writing. The list is exhaustive: obligations which do not appear on the list fall within subs. (1) and do not require written constitution (except in the rare cases where some other statute or statutory instrument provides otherwise). Where writing is required for initial constitution it is also, by subs. (6), required for any subsequent variation of the obligation. The requirement of writing may be displaced in certain circumstances where there have been appropriate actings: see subs. (3).
   Subparagraph (i) is narrower than the common law rule it replaces, which required formal writing for *all* obligations relating to heritable property. Paragraph (b) of subs. (2) (see below)

provides for writing in the case of the creation, transfer, variation or extinction of an interest in land, and para. (a)(i) simply extends the same rule to any preliminary contract or promise. Common examples of such preliminary obligations are missives for the sale of land, missives of let, and undertakings to grant servitudes. While an offer forming part of a contract requires to be in writing (see also s.2(2)), no corresponding provision is made about the withdrawal of such an offer before it has been accepted and the common law rule that a withdrawal may be made orally continues to apply. See *McMillan v. Caldwell* 1991 S.L.T. 325.

Under the previous law a gratuitous promise could be constituted orally but could be proved only by writ or oath. Proof by writ or oath is abolished by s.11(1), but it is provided by subpara. (ii) that gratuitous unilateral obligations (*i.e.* promises) must be constituted in writing subscribed by the obligant. This includes (gratuitous) cautionary obligations, so replacing the former, and unclear, rule contained in s.6 of the Mercantile Law Amendment Act 1856 (c. 97) (which is repealed by Sched. 5). It appears that the rule is not extended to gratuitous *contracts* (see *e.g. Morton's Tr. v. Aged Christian Friend Society of Scotland* (1899) 2 F. 82), and such contracts may therefore be constituted without writing. In practice the majority of unilateral obligations are likely to be gratuitous. Two which may be argued not to be so are (a) where the obligant enters into the obligation only in virtue of payment by the obligee or by some third party (*e.g.* a personal bond to repay a loan), and (b) where the obligation is entered into gratuitously but the obligee, while not bound to make payment, cannot enforce the obligation without such payment being made (*e.g.* an option to buy property). The exception for obligations undertaken in the course of business is because businessmen are regarded as less prone to rash and impulsive promises. It is also a shadowy survival of the former privilege (abolished by s.11(3)(b)(ii)) which was accorded to writs *in re mercatoria*. For the arguments in favour of this exception see H.L. MacQueen *Constitution and Proof of Gratuitous Obligations* 1986 S.L.T. (News) 1. It is thought that only the obligant need act in the course of business.

Subparagraph (iii) is, in effect, confined to *inter vivos* trusts. (All *mortis causa* trusts are required to be in writing by para. (c) of subs. (2).) Under the former law an *inter vivos* trust could be declared orally in most, or perhaps even in all, cases, but proof of trust was sometimes restricted to writ or oath in virtue of the Blank Bonds and Trusts Act 1696. The 1696 Act was not only "unprincipled and arbitrary" in effect (see Scot. Law Com. No. 112, para. 2.36) but also very difficult to interpret. It is now repealed by Sched. 5. As a general rule there is no restriction under the 1995 Act on either the constitution or the proof of trusts. However, subpara. (iii) requires writing for the constitution of trusts where the truster is also the sole trustee. Trusts of this kind were first recognised in *Allan's Trs v. Lord Advocate* 1971 S.C. (H.L.) 45 and in recent years they have become quite common, especially in the commercial world where they are valuable as surrogate rights in security (see *e.g. Tay Valley Joinery v. C.F. Financial Services* 1987 S.L.T. 207). Only the declaration of trust need be in writing, and intimation of the declaration to a beneficiary, which is a further requirement for trusts of this kind, may thus be oral. Other *inter vivos* trusts (*i.e.* where truster and trustee are *different* people) may continue to be constituted orally. The fact that ownership has to be transferred from truster to trustee (usually in writing) was felt to supply a sufficient degree of formality. In practice it is anticipated that declarations of trust will continue to be in writing except in the most unusual cases.

There is probably no common ground between subparas. (ii) and (iii). The scheme of the section suggests that declarations of trust, although in practice usually gratuitous, are not regarded as gratuitous unilateral obligations within subpara. (ii).

Para. (b). If a right falls within para. (a) of subs. (2), writing is required for its constitution and also for its variation (see subs. (6)). By contrast a para. (b) right requires writing, not only for constitution and variation but for transfer and extinction also. It probably follows from this, although the Act does not expressly say so (compare here s.1(1)), that writing is *not* required for the transfer or extinction of a para. (a) right. Indeed s.11(3)(a) abolishes the rule of common law (if it was a rule) that writing is needed for the assignation of incorporeal moveables; and, while nothing is said in the Act about assignation of incorporeal heritable property, such as trusts of land, it is thought that the rule here is probably the same. Thus it appears that while a para. (a) right, such as the right of a purchaser under missives of sale of land, must be constituted and varied in writing, it may be assigned or extinguished orally. Some may find the idea of oral assignation surprising, although in practice writing will no doubt continue to be used in almost every case.

Paragraph (b) applies to interests in land. This expression is defined in subs. (7). Essentially it means a real right in land such as *dominium* (both *utile* and *directum*), standard security, lease for more than a year, proper liferent, and servitude. Paragraph (b) does not change the law, except in relation to the type of writing required. At common law, writing has always been required for the creation, transfer, variation or extinction of real rights in land, and in the case of some real rights the common law requirement was repeated in statutory provisions which are now modified (Sched. 4), but not repealed, by the new Act. Examples are the provisions for standard securities in Pt. II of the Conveyancing and Feudal Reform (Scotland) Act 1970 (c. 35).

"Variation" of an interest in land should be contrasted with an "alteration", such as an interlineation or deletion, made on the deed of constitution itself. In practice the difference is that variation is effected by a later and separate deed. Alterations to deeds are regulated by s.5 of the Act.

The final words of para. (b) are intended to confine the rule requiring writing to voluntary acts. In fact there are many occasions in which interests in land are created, transferred, varied or extinguished by court decree, enactment, or by rule of law. Thus both a positive servitude and the occupancy right of a non-entitled spouse are or may be created by enactment (respectively s.3(2) of the Prescription and Limitation (Scotland) Act 1973 (c. 52) and s.1 of the Matrimonial Homes (Family Protection) (Scotland) Act 1981 (c. 59)). Real rights in land are transferred by court decree on the appointment of a trustee in sequestration or an executor. They are transferred by enactment by s.15 of the Local Government *etc.* (Scotland) Act 1994 (c. 39). They are transferred by rule of law whenever a survivorship destination is triggered by death. The variation of a servitude by the Lands Tribunal under s.1 of the Conveyancing and Feudal Reform (Scotland) Act 1970 is an example of an interest in land being varied by court decree. Finally, a real right in land may be extinguished by prescription by s.8 of the Prescription and Limitation (Scotland) Act 1973. Note should be taken of the precise wording used by para. (b): it is restricted to court decrees, enactments, and rules of law which of their own force effect the juristic acts in question (as distinct from decrees, enactments and rules which merely make provision for others to effect the juristic acts).

A difficulty with para. (b) is that it does not cover all possible cases. It has the character of a residual category, dealing with those juristic acts which are not dealt with in paras. (a) and (c); but it contains no provision (as s.1(1) does for para. (a)) to the effect that any juristic act not specially mentioned in para. (b) may be carried out without writing. This leaves a gap in the law. What other juristic acts might there be? One example, the assignation of incorporeal moveables, is expressly said in s.11(3)(a) not to require writing. The creation of a floating charge, a second example, was formerly required to be in writing by s.462(2) of the Companies Act 1985; but s.462(2) was repealed by the Law Reform (Miscellaneous Provisions) (Scotland) Act 1990 (c. 40), Sched. 8, para. 33(6), and there is no replacement provision in the 1995 Act. However, the references to "instrument" in s.462 and the immediately succeeding sections of the 1985 Act might be thought to create a requirement of writing by implication. A third example is the granting of a power of attorney which, unlike mandate, seems not to be a contract and hence not to fall within s.1(1). There are probably other examples also. In the case of juristic acts which are untouched by the 1995 Act or other legislation, the position is probably (i) that they may be constituted without writing (except, arguably, floating charges, for reasons already mentioned), but (ii) that in practice granters will always opt to use writing executed in accordance with the 1995 Act, as they are entitled to do. The only alternative view, namely that certain juristic acts require writing as a matter of common law, runs into the serious practical difficulty that the methods which were provided by the law for executing such deeds have now all been repealed by the 1995 Act.

Para. (c). At common law formal writing (*i.e.* writing which was attested by two witnesses, or holograph, or adopted as holograph) was required for wills and other testamentary dispositions, except for bequests of moveables not exceeding £100 Scots (£8.33), which could be made orally. Paragraph (c) removes the exception but otherwise re-enacts the common law. Thus formal writing continues to be required for wills and other testamentary dispositions, and also for any later will or codicil which varies the terms of the original deed. Manuscript alterations to the words in the original deed are provided for separately, by s.5.

Formal validity under the Act is achieved by the testator's subscription at the end of the last page: see s.2. While a will in this form is valid, it is not sufficient to obtain confirmation of the executor. By s.21A of the Succession (Scotland) Act 1964 (c. 41) (inserted by Sched. 4 to the Act) confirmation may not be granted unless the will is presumed under either s.3 or s.4 of the 1995 Act to have been subscribed by the testator.

The previous law allowed a testator to provide in his will for the validity of future informal testamentary writings. It is unclear whether such "enfranchising" clauses are now effective. This is because a future informal writing may be classified either as a will or as a codicil, and so would itself require to be in formal writing by para. (c). However, even if this is correct, the change is of limited practical importance: although in theory a clause in a will could enfranchise a future writing which had not been signed (see *e.g. Crosbie v. Wilson* (1865) 3 M. 870), the usual practice has been for the clause to require the later writing to be "under my hand", which means subscribed by the testator (see *Waterson's Trs. v. St. Giles Boys' Club* 1943 S.C. 369). Under the 1995 Act an informal writing which has been subscribed by the testator will be perfectly valid on its own account without the help of an enfranchising clause.

Subss. (3)–(5)

These three subsections apply only to the rights set out in para. (a) of subs. (2) (*i.e.* certain contracts, promises and trusts). In relation to these rights the personal bar doctrines of *rei interventus* and homologation are abolished by subs. (5) and replaced by a statutory version of *rei interventus*, set out in subss. (3) and (4). There is no statutory counterpart of homologation, which thus disappears as a legal doctrine. In general the need for personal bar will be lessened by the reduction in the formalities in execution effected by s.2 of the Act.

Subsections (3) and (4) re-enact the common law rules of *rei interventus*, but in a simplified form. Under the new rules a contract, promise or trust will not fail for lack of formal validity where it has been followed by significant actings. More specifically, a party is personally barred from withdrawing from an informal contract (or promise or trust) if (i) the other party has acted or refrained from acting in reliance on the contract, (ii) to the knowledge of and with the acquiescence of the party now seeking to withdraw, and (iii) the actings (or absence of actings) have been material such that the other party would be prejudiced by such withdrawal. The new wording follows quite closely the personal bar provisions in relation to rectification of defectively expressed documents contained in s.9(2) of the Law Reform (Miscellaneous Provisions) (Scotland) Act 1985 (c. 73). The most important change in the law is the removal, by s.11(1), of the need to prove the informal contract by writ or oath. Now there is no restriction as to proof and in many cases the actings which evidence personal bar are likely to be used to evidence also the fact of agreement. Under the new law the oral promise in *Smith v. Oliver* 1911 S.C. 103 (to make a will bequeathing money to pay for improvements to a church, which was then followed by actings) would have been perfectly enforceable.

The new personal bar provisions are confined to the rights listed in para. (a) of subs. (2), and so do not apply to para. (b) and para. (c) rights. At common law personal bar was also available in respect of para. (b) rights (*i.e.* real rights in land). See *e.g. Clark's Exr. v. Cameron* 1982 S.L.T. 68. The Act's silence on this subject may give rise to the argument that the common law of *rei interventus* and homologation is preserved in relation to para. (b) rights, so that for example a lease could continue to be set up by homologation. In support of this argument it might be pointed out that the abolition of *rei interventus* and homologation in subs. (5) is expressly confined to para. (a) rights. The alternative and, it is submitted, the better view is that the bald and unqualified statement in subs. (2) that writing is required for para. (b) rights has the effect of excluding the common law of personal bar. That was certainly the intention of the Scottish Law Commission: see Scot. Law Com. No. 112, para. 2.50. If that is correct, it is possible to question the policy assumptions on which the change in the law is based. The Commission argued that if a deed intended to create a real right failed for lack of formality, the grantee would be able to rely on the antecedent contract, which could itself, if necessary, be set up by personal bar. There are two difficulties with this argument. One is that in some cases where real rights are being created there is no such antecedent contract (as in the case of a lease constituted only by missives of let and without a preliminary contract). The other is that there may have been supervening insolvency of the granter which would prevent the enforcement of any contract.

Subs. (6)

Writing formally executed under s.2 of the Act is required for the variation of the contracts, obligations and trusts listed in para. (a) of subs. (2). Writing is not required for their extinction. The absence of proper formalities can be cured by *rei interventus* in accordance with subss. (3) and (4). It is thought that parties are not able to contract out of these rules (for example, by providing in missives of sale that a new date of entry can be agreed informally).

Subs. (7)

For "land" see subs. (8). "Interest in land" is a mysterious expression much favoured by parliamentary draftsmen in recent years in preference to more traditional terminology: see *e.g.* the Conveyancing and Feudal Reform (Scotland) Act 1970 (c. 35), s.9, the Prescription and Limitation (Scotland) Act 1973 (c. 52), s.1, and the Land Registration (Scotland) Act 1979 (c. 33), s.1. As is now customary, the definition given here is largely circular in nature (an interest in land is an estate, interest or right in or over land). This is unfortunate. In the scheme of the Act the precise meaning of "interest in land" is important as setting the limits for when writing is and is not required.

Despite the coyness of the drafting, it is thought that as a general proposition "interest in land" means real right in land. Certainly most personal rights are excluded. For example, the view has been expressed that the (personal) right of a purchaser under missives of sale is not an interest in land (see *Margrie Holdings v. Commissioners of Customs and Excise* 1991 S.L.T. 38 *per* Lord

President Hope at p. 42B); and since s.1 distinguishes, on the one hand contracts and unilateral obligations relating to interests in land (subs. (2)(a)(i)) and trusts (subs. (2)(a)(iii)), and on the other hand interests in land themselves (subs. (2)(b)), it appears to follow that the former (all of which are personal rights) are not to be treated as examples of the latter.

The real rights in land are listed in *The Law of Scotland: Stair Memorial Encyclopaedia* (Butterworths, 1993) vol. 18, para. 5. The main examples are: *dominium* (ownership), both *utile* and *directum*; proper liferent; lease; standard security; and servitude. In addition two personal rights are expressly included in the definition in subs. (6), namely (i) a right to occupy or to use land (*e.g.* a contractual licence), and (ii) a right to restrict the occupation or use of land (*e.g.* a contractual right, falling short of a servitude, to prevent a neighbour from making some use of his land).

Whether other examples of interest in land exist is a matter of speculation. An attached floating charge is presumably an interest in land, at least to the extent that the property attached consists of land.

Granted for more than one year. The test is the period of grant and not the period of endurance. Thus a lease for a year which in fact continues for a number of years by tacit relocation is not a lease granted for more than one year (and hence does not require to be in writing).

Recurring periods. The reference to "recurring periods" envisages two main situations, namely (i) consecutive recurring periods, as in a lease with a break clause, and (ii) non-consecutive recurring periods, as in a shooting lease or a time share, where the right is to a certain number of weeks every year for a series of years.

Subs. (8)

Land includes things which are part of the land by nature, such as soil, rock and minerals, as well as things, such as buildings and fixtures within buildings, which have become part by accession. However, because "land" is defined in Sched. 1 to the Interpretation Act 1978 (c. 30) as including "buildings and other structures" without qualification, subs. (8) takes the precaution of making an express exclusion of moveable buildings and structures. Also excluded are growing crops. This is directed at natural crops such as trees and grass. Industrial growing crops (*i.e.* crops which require annual seed and labour) are already moveable at common law. The main practical effect of the exclusion is that contracts for the sale of growing crops may be made orally.

A by-product of the exclusion of growing crops is to clarify a difficulty arising out of the Sale of Goods Act 1979 (c. 54). In terms of that Act writing is required neither for the constitution of the contract of sale of goods (s.4) nor for the transfer of ownership (s.17). In view of the fact that "goods" are defined (see s.61(1)) as including "things attached to or forming part of the land which are agreed to be severed before sale or under the contract of sale", the argument arose that growing crops and other like things escaped the requirement of writing which applied to the sale of land. See J.J. Gow *When are Trees "Timber"?* 1962 S.L.T.(News) 13, and T.B. Smith *A Short Commentary on the Law of Scotland* at pp. 499–500. By excluding growing crops but not other cases of "things attached to or forming part of the land", subs. (8) makes clear that writing is required for the sale of the latter but not of the former.

Type of writing required for formal validity of certain documents

2.—(1) No document required by section 1(2) of this Act shall be valid in respect of the formalities of execution unless it is subscribed by the granter of it or, if there is more than one granter, by each granter, but nothing apart from such subscription shall be required for the document to be valid as aforesaid.

(2) A contract mentioned in section 1(2)(a)(i) of this Act may be regarded as constituted or varied (as the case may be) if the offer is contained in one or more documents and the acceptance is contained in another document or other documents, and each document is subscribed by the granter or granters thereof.

(3) Nothing in this section shall prevent a document which has not been subscribed by the granter or granters of it from being used as evidence in relation to any right or obligation to which the document relates.

(4) This section is without prejudice to any other enactment which makes different provision in respect of the formalities of execution of a document to which this section applies.

DEFINITIONS
   "document": s.12(1).
   "enactment": s.12(1).
   "subscription": s.7(1).

GENERAL NOTE
   This provision effects a radical change in, and simplification of, the previous law. Under that law a document was formally valid if it was either (i) subscribed by the granter and by two witnesses, or (ii) holograph of and subscribed by the granter, or (iii) subscribed by the granter who was also required to write the words "adopted as holograph". In addition, writs *in re mercatoria*, an obscure and uncertain category, were formally valid if they were subscribed by the granter (only).
   This whole complicated structure is swept away by the 1995 Act. Section 11(3)(b) abolishes the special status attached to documents which are holograph or adopted as holograph or *in re mercatoria*; and s.3 re-casts the rules for attestation by witnesses. Section 2 introduces a single type of formally valid document to replace the three types of document mentioned above. Under s.2 a document is formally valid if it is subscribed by the granter. No further steps are required. However, the addition of a witness, although not improving on the formal validity of a document, will confer the benefit of a presumption under s.3 that the document was indeed subscribed by the granter.

Subs. (1)
   This sets out a universal rule for formal validity. The rule is mandatory only in relation to the documents required to be in writing by s.1(2), but even in other cases parties may elect – or be taken to have elected – that their agreement should be reduced to a document subscribed in accordance with this subsection. The rule in subs. (1) makes no distinction between cases where the granter is a natural person and cases where the granter is a juristic person, although the actual mechanics of subscription (see s.7) are necessarily different in the two cases. The previous law is preserved by which a granter who is blind or unable to write may subscribe through the agency of a solicitor or certain other categories of authorised person (see s.9), while s.12(2) continues the common law rule by which an agent acting under a power of attorney may subscribe on behalf of his principal.

Subs. (2)
   Subsection (1) takes as its model a single document, for example a will or a declaration of trust. However, in practice contracts often comprise a series of letters or documents; an offer, a qualified acceptance, a further qualified acceptance, and so on until the final acceptance is given. Subsection (2) makes clear that such a contract is formally valid provided that each constituent letter or document is subscribed by the "granter", *i.e.* by the person issuing that letter or document. This does no more than re-state the existing law.

Subs. (3)
   This provision is inserted for the avoidance of doubt. In practice an unsubscribed document might be useful evidence of the terms of an agreement or other juristic act conferring rights. In the small number of cases where the right fell within s.1(2) and required subscribed writing, the absence of the proper formalities might then be cured by actings under s.1(3).

Subs. (4)
   In particular cases statute may make more, or less, onerous the rules of formal validity. An example of the former is the general provision in para. 1(1) of Sched. 4 in terms of which any reference in any enactment to a probative document is to be construed as a reference to a document in conformity with s.6(2). A document is not in conformity with s.6(2) where it has merely been subscribed by the granter.

Presumption as to granter's subscription or date or place of subscription

   3.—(1) Subject to subsections (2) to (7) below, where—
   (a) a document bears to have been subscribed by a granter of it;

(b) the document bears to have been signed by a person as a witness of that granter's subscription and the document, or the testing clause or its equivalent, bears to state the name and address of the witness; and

(c) nothing in the document, or in the testing clause or its equivalent, indicates—

(i) that it was not subscribed by that granter as it bears to have been so subscribed; or

(ii) that it was not validly witnessed for any reason specified in paragraphs (a) to (e) of subsection (4) below,

the document shall be presumed to have been subscribed by that granter.

(2) Where a testamentary document consists of more than one sheet, it shall not be presumed to have been subscribed by a granter as mentioned in subsection (1) above unless, in addition to it bearing to have been subscribed by him and otherwise complying with that subsection, it bears to have been signed by him on every sheet.

(3) For the purposes of subsection (1)(b) above—

(a) the name and address of a witness may be added at any time before the document is—

(i) founded on in legal proceedings; or

(ii) registered for preservation in the Books of Council and Session or in sheriff court books; and

(b) the name and address of a witness need not be written by the witness himself.

(4) Where, in any proceedings relating to a document in which a question arises as to a granter's subscription, it is established—

(a) that a signature bearing to be the signature of the witness of that granter's subscription is not such a signature, whether by reason of forgery or otherwise;

(b) that the person who signed the document as the witness of that granter's subscription is a person who is named in the document as a granter of it;

(c) that the person who signed the document as the witness of that granter's subscription, at the time of signing—

(i) did not know the granter;

(ii) was under the age of 16 years; or

(iii) was mentally incapable of acting as a witness;

(d) that the person who signed the document, purporting to be the witness of that granter's subscription, did not witness such subscription;

(e) that the person who signed the document as the witness of that granter's subscription did not sign the document after him or that the granter's subscription or, as the case may be, acknowledgement of his subscription and the person's signature as witness of that subscription were not one continuous process;

(f) that the name or address of the witness of that granter's subscription was added after the document was founded on or registered as mentioned in subsection (3)(a) above or is erroneous in any material respect; or

(g) in the case of a testamentary document consisting of more than one sheet, that a signature on any sheet bearing to be the signature of the granter is not such a signature, whether by reason of forgery or otherwise,

then, for the purposes of those proceedings, there shall be no presumption that the document has been subscribed by that granter.

(5) For the purposes of subsection (4)(c)(i) above, the witness shall be regarded as having known the person whose subscription he has witnessed at the time of witnessing if he had credible information at that time of his identity.

(6) For the purposes of subsection (4)(e) above, where—

(a)　a document is granted by more than one granter; and

(b)　a person is the witness to the subscription of more than one granter,

the subscription or acknowledgement of any such granter and the signature of the person witnessing that granter's subscription shall not be regarded as not being one continuous process by reason only that, between the time of that subscription or acknowledgement and that signature, another granter has subscribed the document or acknowledged his subscription.

(7) For the purposes of the foregoing provisions of this section a person witnesses a granter's subscription of a document—

(a)　if he sees the granter subscribe it; or

(b)　if the granter acknowledges his subscription to that person.

(8) Where—

(a)　by virtue of subsection (1) above a document to which this subsection applies is presumed to have been subscribed by a granter of it;

(b)　the document, or the testing clause or its equivalent, bears to state the date or place of subscription of the document by that granter; and

(c)　nothing in the document, or in the testing clause or its equivalent, indicates that that statement as to date or place is incorrect,

there shall be a presumption that the document was subscribed by that granter on the date or at the place as stated.

(9) Subsection (8) above applies to any document other than a testamentary document.

(10) Where—

(a)　a testamentary document bears to have been subscribed and the document, or the testing clause or its equivalent, bears to state the date or place of subscription (whether or not it is presumed under subsections (1) to (7) above to have been subscribed by a granter of it); and

(b)　nothing in the document, or in the testing clause or its equivalent, indicates that that statement as to date or place is incorrect,

there shall be a presumption that the statement as to date or place is correct.

DEFINITIONS

"document": s.12(1).

"signed by a witness": s.7(5).

"subscription": s.7(1).

"writing": Sched. 1 to the Interpretation Act 1978.

GENERAL NOTE

This section provides for the attestation of documents by witnesses. By contrast to the previous law (where two witnesses were necessary) only a single witness is required, thus bringing the rules for instrumentary witnesses into line with the Civil Evidence (Scotland) Act 1988 (c. 32), s.1, which abolished the requirement of corroboration in civil proceedings. In most other respects the rules of attestation are unchanged, and much of s.3 is a statutory restatement of rules originally introduced by the Subscription of Deeds Act 1681 and later developed by the common law.

The main difference between the new law and the old law lies in function rather than in form. Under the old law attestation by witnesses had two distinct functions. In the first place it made the document formally valid. In the second place it made the deed self-evidencing or "probative", that is to say, it gave rise to an evidential presumption of formal validity such that a person founding on a deed which appeared to have been validly attested was relieved of having to lead evidence as to that validity. Under the new law only the second function remains. By s.2 a document is already formally valid from the moment that it is subscribed by the granter. Attestation adds nothing to formal validity. However, once a document has been attested by a witness it carries an evidential presumption under s.3(1) that it was subscribed by the granter.

A significant advantage of the new law is that a defect in attestation does not affect the formal validity of the deed. As long as the granter has subscribed, the deed is valid. By contrast, the old law was obliged to grade defects in execution as either "informalities of execution" (which could be cured by s.39 of the Conveyancing (Scotland) Act 1874 (c. 94)) or as more serious defects (which could not be cured and which therefore rendered the deed invalid). Section 39 of the 1874 Act is now repealed and there is no direct equivalent in the new law.

At first sight, s.3 may seem to be set out in a strange and unhelpful way. The key to understanding the section is the realisation that it is concerned exclusively with matters evidential. The question of whether a deed has *in fact* been properly executed is a question for s.2. The question of whether a deed is *presumed* to have been properly executed is a question for s.3. The presumption is activated (as under the former law) if the deed appears to have been validly attested. The requirements as to appearance which have to be satisfied are set out in subss. (1)–(3). Once activated, the presumption is rebuttable by establishing in court proceedings that the deed was not validly attested due to some latent factor not apparent on the face of the deed. An exhaustive list of possible latent factors is given in subss. (4)–(7). As already noted, invalid attestation does not of itself mean invalid execution. A deed is invalid only if it was not in fact subscribed by the granter. The effect of establishing that the attestation was invalid is simply to alter the onus of proof by extinguishing the presumption of valid execution. Thereafter the onus of showing formal validity rests on the person seeking to found on the deed.

The final three subsections (subss. (8)–(10)) are concerned with ancillary presumptions in relation to date and place of execution.

Subss. (1)–(3)

These subsections set out what must appear on the face of a document (including the testing clause) in order to trigger the presumption of valid execution. The provisions apply to all deeds which satisfy its terms, including cases where formal writing is used electively by the parties despite not being required by s.1(2).

The following must appear from the face of the deed: (i) that the granter or granters subscribed; (ii) that a witness signed; (iii) that the name and address of the witness (which need not be written by the witness himself) are given in the deed or testing clause; (iv) that the name and address were added before the deed was founded on in legal proceedings or registered for preservation; and (v) that nothing in the deed or testing clause indicates that the deed was not subscribed by the granter or granters, or was not validly witnessed for the (latent) reasons specified in paras. (a)–(e) of subs. (4). In addition, in the case of a testamentary document extending to more than one sheet, there is the further requirement (vi) that the granter signed on every sheet. Note that (following the previous law) this final requirement refers to sheet and not to page. So a will written on a single sheet which is then folded up to form four pages requires to be signed only at the end of the last page. See *e.g. Baird's Trs. v. Baird* 1955 S.C. 286.

On the whole the above requirements merely re-state the law previously in force. Requirement (i) should be read together with s.7(2), which provides that a granter of an attested deed may sign either with the full name by which he is identified in the deed or with his surname preceded by at least one forename or initial.

On (ii) it may be noted that witnesses need only sign and not subscribe. That is a change in the law. Presumably a witness may sign anywhere at all on the deed. Further rules about witnesses' signatures are given in s.7(5). It may be noted in particular that where a person witnesses the signature of more than one granter, he need sign only once.

Requirement (iii) refers to designation by name and address of the witness. It is thought that the full name is not required. The address could be a home address or a business address. Presumably both name and address must be legible. Perhaps unwisely, the test previously in use, namely that the witness must be capable of identification, is abandoned. Thus it appears that the designation "Donald Macdonald, 4 Braes Road, Portree, Isle of Skye" would be a valid designation notwithstanding that three generations of Donald Macdonalds live at 4 Braes Road and that it is impossible to say which one is being referred to. The requirement to state the witness's name is additional to the requirement that the witness sign, and for this reason it appears not to be enough to append the witness's address beneath his signature without at the same time repeating his name.

In requirement (iv) the expression "legal proceedings" is sufficiently wide to cover arbitration proceedings and also proceedings before tribunals.

A slightly puzzling feature of requirement (v) is that it excludes paras. (f) and (g) of subs. (4). It will be noted that the requirement is confined to evidence from the deed or from the testing clause. Thus the fact that attestation could be shown by extrinsic evidence to have been defective would not (except in court proceedings under subs. (4)) remove the presumption of valid execution.

Requirement (vi), for testamentary writings, prescribes signature rather than subscription (although of course the final page must be subscribed, under (i)). Moreover, the signature need only be on each sheet, although in practice testators are likely to continue to sign on each page. An oddity of the new provisions is that while the final subscription must be witnessed (subs. (1)(b)), there is no corresponding requirement in relation to the signature of the intermediate pages. Thus there seems no reason why a testator should not sign the intermediate pages at some different time, perhaps even years later than the original (witnessed) subscription.

If the various requirements set out above are duly complied with, the result is that the deed is presumed to have been subscribed by the granter, and hence to be formally valid under s.2. (Section 3 avoids here the slippery word "probative", the proper meaning of which was disputed under the old law.) If there is more than one granter then each is treated separately by the legislation, and it is possible in theory, if unlikely in practice, for a deed with multiple granters to have witnesses in respect of some of the granters only.

It is not clear whether a signature by a consenter would also benefit from the presumption of valid subscription: subs. (1) refers to "granter" only.

There is no equivalent presumption that a deed which has been witnessed is validly *attested* (attestation not being required for formal validity), but the effect of subs. (4) is to place the onus of showing invalid attestation on the person who alleges it.

Subss. (4)–(7)

A deed may appear to have been attested, and yet the attestation may not in fact have been carried out properly due to some factor which is not apparent from the face of the deed. The fact that the deed appears to have been properly attested gives rise to a presumption of valid execution under subs. (1); while the fact that there was a latent error – if that fact can be established in court proceedings – leads to the displacement of that presumption under subs. (4). In effect a person who believes that a deed has not been validly executed has a choice as to how to proceed. Either he can attack the deed directly by seeking to show that it was not subscribed by the granter. If he is successful the deed will be a nullity. Alternatively, he can attack the deed indirectly by seeking to show that there was a latent error in the attestation by the witness. If he is successful, the deed will not be a nullity but the onus of proof will shift and it will be for the person founding on the deed to establish that it really was subscribed by the granter. Subsection (4) is exclusively concerned with this second, indirect approach. A limitation of the subsection is that its effect is confined to the proceedings in which it is actually pled. Thus a deed in respect of which the attestation can be shown to be defective continues to carry the presumption of validity except in relation to the particular court proceedings in which the defect is established.

Subsection (4) comprises of a list of defects in attestation which are, or at any rate which may be, latent. If any of defects (a)–(e) are in fact patent on the face of the deed – a likely example is defect (b) – the position is then governed by subs. (1)(c)(ii), with the consequence that there is no initial triggering of the presumption of valid execution and hence no need for evidence to be led under subs. (4). The structure of s.3 requires that the list is expressed negatively, *i.e.* in the form of defects of attestation; but from the point of view of a person seeking guidance on how attestation may validly be effected, the list should be treated as a list of positive rules of execution which require to be complied with.

To a large extent the list simply re-enacts the rules of attestation which were in force under the previous law. Only a brief commentary is required here.

Defect (a). Two situations are distinguished here. The first is where the signature is not actually written by the witness, *i.e.* where it is forged. The other is where the signature is written by the witness but does not conform with the rules for a valid signature set out in s.7(5).

Defect (b). This reaffirms the rule of the previous law that a granter may not witness the signature of a fellow granter. In almost every case where this occurs, the error will be obvious from the face of the deed, with the result that the attestation will fail under subs. (1)(c)(ii). However, there may be unusual cases, *e.g.* where the granter/witness uses different names.

Defect (c). This reaffirms the rule introduced by the Age of Legal Capacity (Scotland) Act 1991 (c. 50), ss.1(1) and 9 (definition of "transaction") that an instrumentary witness must be 16 or over. The requirement that the witness must "know" the granter reflects the traditional view that the witness attests to the granter's identity and not merely to the fact that the deed was subscribed by some person unknown. However, case law had reduced the requirement of knowledge to something quite perfunctory, such as an introduction by a third party, and continuity with that previous law is emphasised by the definition of knowledge given in subs. (5), which repeats the formula ("credible information") which is found in the case law. See *Walker v. Adamson* (1716) Mor. 16,896 and *Brock v. Brock* 1908 S.C. 964 at p. 967 *per* Lord Low.

Defect (d). By subs. (7) a person witnesses a granter's subscription either if he sees the granter subscribe or if the granter acknowledges his subscription. This is the traditional formula, familiar from the Subscription of Deeds Act 1681.

Acknowledgement can be non-verbal: see, most recently, *Lindsay v. Milne* 1995 S.L.T. 487.

It should be noticed that the witnessing is confined to the granter's "subscription". Thus the witness is not required to attest to the signature of any plan or other annexation which may be attached to the deed under s.8(2), or, in the case of a will, to the signature on every sheet, and in both cases such signature can be added by the granter on his own at some later date.

Defect (e). There are two separate requirements here. The first is concerned with chronology. The witness must sign later in time than the granter. The second is concerned with continuity. Signature of granter and witness must be one continuous process. This is to avoid the danger that the deed which the witness signs is not the same as the deed on which he saw the granter subscribe.

Subsection (6) deals with the position where multiple signatures are attested by a single witness. In practice the witness will wait until all the granters have subscribed (for otherwise he would have to sign separately for each granter); and the mere fact that he waits will not in itself be regarded as disturbing the continuity of execution. However, it is plain from the words "by reason only that" in subs. (6) that the existence of multiple granters will not be accepted as an excuse for unreasonable delay in the witness signing.

The meaning of "continuous process" has been litigated on a number of occasions in the past. See *e.g. Thomson v. Clarkson's Trs.* (1892) 20 R. 59. Prudence suggests that the witness should normally sign at once. In the view of the Scottish Law Commission (Scot. Law Com. No. 112, para. 5.15) the new statutory wording displaces the rule invented by the House of Lords in *Walker v. Whitwell* 1916 S.C.(H.L.) 75 to the effect that a witness cannot sign after the granter's death.

Defect (f). The meaning of "erroneous in any material respect" is not clear. There is no express adoption either here or in subs. (1)(b) of the rule of the former law that a designation was valid provided that the witness could be identified. In practice it is possible to imagine cases where a designation is badly flawed and yet it is still possible to identify the witness. In the event of a designation being found erroneous in the sense meant here, it cannot thereafter be cured because *ex hypothesi* the deed has been founded on in legal proceedings (see subs. (3)(a)).

Defect (g). The remarks made in the context of defect (a) apply here also.

Subss. (8)–(10)

Under the Act, as under the previous law, there is no formal requirement that a document give the date and place of execution. However, subs. (8) is drafted on the assumption that in the future, as in the past, the testing clause of an attested deed will usually give information on both date and place.

Different regimes are provided for testamentary and for non-testamentary documents. See subs. (9).

In the case of testamentary documents, if the deed or testing clause states the date and/or place of execution, there is a presumption that the statement is correct. See subs. (10). This repeats and extends the existing rule in relation to holograph wills enacted by s.40 of the Conveyancing (Scotland) Act 1874 (c. 94) (which is now repealed). The main reason for the presumption is the practical problem of dating a sequence of wills after a testator's death. The precise terms of the presumption should be noted: in order to cover the case of a will which has been subscribed only and not attested, the presumption does not extend to the fact of the testator's subscription. Compare here the equivalent presumption in subs. (8). In effect the presumption states that if the will was subscribed by the testator, then it is presumed to have been subscribed on the date and at the place mentioned.

In the case of non-testamentary documents, the presumption is confined (as under the previous law) to attested deeds. Documents which are merely subscribed by the granter do not prove their own date and place any more than they prove the fact of subscription itself. By subs. (8), if a deed appears to be attested and hence benefits from the presumption of valid execution under subs. (1), any date or place of execution given in the deed or (as usually in practice) in the testing clause is presumed to be correct.

In both cases the presumption is excluded if there is anything in the deed or testing clause which indicates that the statement as to date or place is incorrect. A standard example would be a disposition in which the date given in the testing clause was later than the date of registration. Further, the presumption can be rebutted by extrinsic evidence.

It should be noticed that the presumption is confined to the date and place of subscription (*i.e.* by the granter). There is no parallel presumption that the witness counter-signed at that date or place. From this it follows that it would not of itself disturb the presumption as to date and place of subscription if it could be shown that the witness was somewhere else on the relevant day and so could not have acted as a witness. The granter may have subscribed on one day and acknowledged his subscription to a witness on another day.

Presumption as to granter's subscription or date or place of subscription when established in court proceedings

4.—(1) Where a document bears to have been subscribed by a granter of it, but there is no presumption under section 3 of this Act that the document has been subscribed by that granter, then, if the court, on an application being made to it by any person who has an interest in the document, is satisfied that the document was subscribed by that granter, it shall—

(a) cause the document to be endorsed with a certificate to that effect; or

(b) where the document has already been registered in the Books of Council and Session or in sheriff court books, grant decree to that effect.

(2) Where a document bears to have been subscribed by a granter of it, but there is no presumption under section 3 of this Act as to the date or place of subscription, then, if the court, on an application being made to it by any person who has an interest in the document, is satisfied as to the date or place of subscription, it shall—

(a) cause the document to be endorsed with a certificate to that effect; or

(b) where the document has already been registered in the Books of Council and Session or in sheriff court books, grant decree to that effect.

(3) On an application under subsection (1) or (2) above evidence shall, unless the court otherwise directs, be given by affidavit.

(4) An application under subsection (1) or (2) above may be made either as a summary application or as incidental to and in the course of other proceedings.

(5) The effect of a certificate or decree—

(a) under subsection (1) above shall be to establish a presumption that the document has been subscribed by the granter concerned;

(b) under subsection (2) above shall be to establish a presumption that the statement in the certificate or decree as to date or place is correct.

(6) In this section "the court" means—

(a) in the case of a summary application—

(i) the sheriff in whose sheriffdom the applicant resides; or

(ii) if the applicant does not reside in Scotland, the sheriff at Edinburgh; and

(b) in the case of an application made in the course of other proceedings, the court before which those proceedings are pending.

DEFINITIONS

"decree": s.12(1).
"document": s.12(1).
"subscription": s.7(1).

GENERAL NOTE

Under s.2 of the Act a document is formally valid if it is subscribed by the granter. However, a document which carries or bears to carry only such a subscription is not self-evidencing ("probative"), in the sense of being presumed to be validly executed. Often this does not matter: after all, many documents have a short time-span and are very unlikely to be subject to a challenge as to authenticity. However, sometimes it may matter. Furthermore, there are two cases where the Act positively requires documents that are presumed to be validly executed. One (under s.6) is where the document is to be registered in the Register of Sasines, Books of Council and Session, or sheriff court books. The other (under Sched. 4, adding a new s.21A to the Succession (Scotland) Act 1964 (c. 41)) is where a testamentary document is to be used as the basis of an application for confirmation of executors.

The question then arises as to how a document which has merely been subscribed can be converted into one which is presumed to be validly executed. The simplest method of proceeding is to have the document promptly countersigned by a witness under s.3 of the Act. However, this requires that the granter acknowledge his signature to the witness under s.3(7), which for various reasons may not always be possible. For instance the granter may be dead (as in the case of wills), or incapax, or unwilling, or otherwise unavailable. It is for these situations that s.4 will be of use. In practice it seems likely that s.4 will be used mainly for wills, particularly in the context of confirmation of executors.

Section 4(1) empowers the court (usually the sheriff court, see subs. (6)) to cause a document to be endorsed with a docquet ("certificate") stating that the court is satisfied that the granter did duly subscribe. The court will usually be satisfied by affidavit evidence alone (subs. (3)). The effect of the docquet is to establish a presumption that the document has indeed been subscribed by the granter (subs. (5)): a s.4 deed is thus of equivalent weight to a s.3 deed. There is a parallel provision (subs. (2)) in relation to the date and place of execution. It is envisaged that further guidance will be given in the form of rules of court.

Subs. (1)

This is the judicial counterpart of s.3(1). A court application is possible only where "there is no presumption under s.3". Tactical difficulties, though not perhaps insuperable ones, may arise in the case of a document which is found not to have been properly attested under one of the heads in s.3(4), but which nonetheless continues to carry the s.3 presumption for all purposes other than the particular proceedings in which the fact of non-attestation was established.

The normal outcome of a successful application will be the endorsing of a docquet on the document. It is only when the document has been registered for preservation and so is physically unavailable that the alternative of a decree will be used.

Subs. (2)

This is the judicial counterpart of s.3(8). In practice it is very unlikely to be used except in conjunction with an application under subs. (1).

Subs. (3)

The procedure here seems modelled on s.21 of the Succession (Scotland) Act 1964 (which provides for affidavits to establish the authenticity of holograph wills). The court is entitled, but not bound, to be satisfied on the basis of a single affidavit: see the Civil Evidence (Scotland) Act 1988 (c. 32), s.1(1).

Subs. (4)

The "other proceedings" most likely to be encountered in practice are applications for confirmation of executors. See s.21A of the Succession (Scotland) Act 1964 (as inserted by Sched. 4, para. 39 of this Act).

Subs. (5)

In view of the role played by uncorroborated affidavit evidence, there is no reason to suppose that the (judicial) presumption established under s.4 is stronger than the (extra-judicial) presumption established under s.3.

Alterations to documents: formal validity and presumptions

5.—(1) An alteration made to a document required by section 1(2) of this Act—

(a) before the document is subscribed by the granter or, if there is more than one granter, by the granter first subscribing it, shall form part of the document as so subscribed;

(b) after the document is so subscribed shall, if the alteration has been signed by the granter or (as the case may be) by all the granters, have effect as a formally valid alteration of the document as so subscribed,

but an alteration made to such a document otherwise than as mentioned in paragraphs (a) and (b) above shall not be formally valid.

(2) Subsection (1) above is without prejudice to—

(a) any rule of law enabling any provision in a testamentary document to be revoked by deletion or erasure without authentication of the deletion or erasure by the testator;

(b) the Erasures in Deeds (Scotland) Act 1836 and section 54 of the Conveyancing (Scotland) Act 1874.

(3) The fact that an alteration to a document was made before the document was subscribed by the granter of it, or by the granter first subscribing it, may be established by all relevant evidence, whether written or oral.

(4) Where a document bears to have been subscribed by the granter or, if there is more than one granter, by all the granters of it, then, if subsection (5) or (6) below applies, an alteration made to the document shall be presumed to have been made before the document was subscribed by the granter or, if there is more than one granter, by the granter first subscribing it, and to form part of the document as so subscribed.

(5) This subsection applies where—

(a) the document is presumed under section 3 of this Act to have been subscribed by the granter or granters (as the case may be);

(b) it is stated in the document, or in the testing clause or its equivalent, that the alteration was made before the document was subscribed; and

(c) nothing in the document, or in the testing clause or its equivalent, indicates that the alteration was made after the document was subscribed.

(6) This subsection applies where subsection (5) above does not apply, but the court is satisfied, on an application being made to it, that the alteration was made before the document was subscribed by the granter or, if there is more than one granter, by the granter first subscribing it, and causes the document to be endorsed with a certificate to that effect or, where the document has already been registered in the Books of Council and Session or in sheriff court books, grants decree to that effect.

(7) Subsections (3), (4) and (6) of section 4 of this Act shall apply in relation to an application under subsection (6) above as they apply in relation to an application under subsection (1) of that section.

(8) Where an alteration is made to a document after the document has been subscribed by a granter, Schedule 1 to this Act (presumptions as to granter's signature and date and place of signing in relation to such alterations) shall have effect.

DEFINITIONS
   "alteration": s.12(1).
   "document": s.12(1).
   "signing": s.7(2).
   "subscription": s.7(1).

GENERAL NOTE
   Section 5 deals with alterations or (in more traditional language) vitiations. Alterations are very much less common than they once were due to the widespread use of word processors in the preparation of legal documents.
   The structure of the previous law is preserved by s.5. The fundamental distinction to be made (see subs. (1)) is between pre-subscription and post-subscription alterations.
   A *pre-subscription* alteration is one which is already in place at the time when the granter or granters subscribe. Accordingly, as subs. (1)(a) confirms, the alteration is given effect to as part of the deed. While the legal position is straightforward, there remains the difficult evidential question of how it is to be demonstrated that the alteration did indeed precede subscription. This question occupies the bulk of s.5 (more precisely, subss. (3)–(7)). Roughly speaking, s.5 distinguishes between documents which are attested and documents which are merely subscribed by the granter. Subsection (5) preserves the previous law in terms of which a vitiation in an attested deed (or equivalent) is "authenticated" by being declared in the testing clause. The effect of such authentication (subs. (4)) is that the vitiation is then presumed to have preceded subscription and so to be part of the deed. Conversely, where the deed is subscribed only and not attested, the onus rests on the person wishing to found on the deed to show that the alteration forms part of the deed. One way of discharging this onus is to apply for a court docquet under subs. (6).
   A *post-subscription* alteration is one which was not in place at the time when the deed was subscribed. Thus as matters stand it is not legally effective. However, it can be made part of the deed if it is separately executed: see subs. (1)(b). In effect, a post-subscription alteration is in the same position as a codicil or an endorsed minute of variation. For the purposes of authentication it is treated as a completely separate document. Thus, in order to be formally valid it requires to be signed by the granter; and attestation by a witness gives rise to the usual presumption of valid execution (see subs. (8) and Sched. 1, para. 1).
   "Alteration" is defined in s.12(1) to include interlineation, marginal addition, deletion, substitution, erasure or anything written on erasure. A more precise definition involves focusing on what it is that has been "altered". Here pre- and post-subscription alterations are different. A pre-subscription alteration is any alteration of the deed as originally *written*, other than (see Scot. Law Com. No. 112, para. 5.22) alterations written in blanks deliberately left for that purpose. Hence such an alteration is obvious from a physical inspection of the deed. By contrast, a

post-subscription alteration is any alteration of the deed as originally *executed*. That is a wider definition, and it cannot be assumed that such alterations will always be obvious on the face of the deed.

It is suggested that the difference between a post-subscription alteration and, say, a codicil (which requires to be formally executed under s.1(2)(c)), is that while the latter is usually written beneath the original subscription, the former is always written above the subscription, as if it were part of the original deed.

Subs. (1)

This subsection is expressed as applying only to documents required by s.1(2); but since the rule given in subs. (1) is little more than declaratory of the common law, it is thought that the rule would apply also in cases where the parties, not being bound by s.1(2), nonetheless elect to use a document which is subscribed or attested.

Signed by the granter. A post-subscription alteration is authenticated by signature and not by subscription. This concession is made necessary by the fact that there may not be room on the deed for subscription. Signature is permitted by any of the methods set out in s.7(2), including by initials. Thus it is competent for the deed itself to be signed by one method and an alteration to the deed by a different method.

Subs. (2)

This is a saving provision.

Para. (a). The deletion or erasure of a will, or part of a will, after the will has been executed may raise issues both of the law of execution of deeds and of the substantive law of succession. The issue from the point of view of the law of execution of deeds is, is the deletion part of the deed? The issue from the point of view of the law of succession is, does the deletion revoke the will (or part thereof)? The effect of para. (a) is to preserve the rule of succession law that a will can be revoked by deletion by the testator *animo revocandi*. See *e.g. Pattison's Trs. v. University of Edinburgh* (1888) 16 R. 73. In fact para. (a) is expressed rather narrowly: the rule of revocation by deletion probably applies to *any* executed deed which has not yet taken effect (*e.g.* because it has not been delivered).

Para. (b). These are minor provisions, of little practical importance today. The Erasures in Deeds (Scotland) Act 1836 (c. 33) (as extended by the Titles to Land Consolidation (Scotland) Act 1868, s.144 and the Conveyancing (Scotland) Act 1924 (c. 27), s.6) provides that a (notarial) instrument or instrument of sasine or notice of title may not be challenged on the ground that it is written on erasure except where fraud is involved. This is a special privilege which is restricted to certain classes of deed executed by notaries public. For the background see Bell *Principles* s.875. Section 54 of the Conveyancing (Scotland) Act 1874 makes an equivalent provision for cases where the copy of a deed made for the purposes of the Register of Sasines is written on erasure. The advent, first of the photocopy and then of the microfiche, has made this provision obsolete and it is difficult to see why it was thought worth preserving.

Subs. (3)

This provision is included for the avoidance of doubt. It confirms that the special rule allowing alterations to be authenticated in the testing clause of an attested writing (subs. (5)) is without prejudice to other methods of establishing that an alteration was in place prior to subscription.

Subs. (4)

Compliance with subs. (5) (authentication in the testing clause) or subs. (6) (court docquet) gives rise only to a presumption, which could be overcome by contrary evidence. In traditional vocabulary, the alteration is "probative" (or self-evidencing).

Subs. (5)

This preserves the common law rule for attested deeds by which a vitiation can be authenticated by being declared in the deed itself or in the testing clause. It therefore perpetuates what some have seen as a defect in the law, arising from the fact that the testing clause is usually added *after* execution. Thus there is nothing to stop a party (typically the grantee or his agent) from making an alteration to a deed after subscription and then declaring in the testing clause, falsely, that the alteration was made prior to subscription. The resulting presumption would make it difficult to uncover the falsehood.

The provision is confined to deeds falling within s.3(1) (*i.e.* to deeds which are attested, or the equivalent). In some cases it may be worth converting a subscribed deed into an attested deed by the expedient of having the granter acknowledge his signature to a witness. A testing clause can then be added containing an appropriate declaration in relation to the alteration, thus avoiding the judicial procedure laid down in subs. (6).

The declaration must state, not merely that the alteration was made (as is sometimes found in testing clauses) but that it was made prior to subscription. The relevant date is subscription by the granter and not attestation by the witness (which may sometimes have occurred much later). There is no rule, either of common law or under the Act, which requires that a testing clause be added within a special time scale; and since a testing clause is not part of the deed itself (being usually added after subscription) it may freely be altered at a later date. Accordingly, a testing clause which in its original version failed to authenticate an alteration may later be adjusted to include an appropriate form of words. Nothing more is required than a declaration in the testing clause. Thus the practice sometimes employed under the former law of signing certain vitiations, in particular marginal additions, is unnecessary and does not add to the validity of the alteration.

The presumption arising from authentication, namely that the alteration was made before subscription, will not apply (para. (c)) if it can be shown from the deed itself that the alteration was made after subscription. An example would be a reference in the deed to a recording date for another deed which was later than the date on which the principal deed was executed.

Subs. (6)

This provides for a court docquet ("certificate") that an alteration was made before subscription. The provision has some parallels with s.39 of the Conveyancing (Scotland) Act 1874 (which is now repealed), and like s.39 it will probably be used mainly for wills. In the case of *inter vivos* deeds the granter is often still available and so it will usually be possible to have the deed counter-signed by a witness and then to make use of subs. (5).

Often alterations are minor in nature and it would not affect the sense or validity of the deed if they were to be treated as *pro non scripto*. Where that is the case the expense of an application under subs. (6) will hardly be justified, unless it is incidental to some other court proceedings.

Subs. (7)

This imports the procedural rules set out in s.4 in the context of the court docquet that a deed was subscribed by the granter.

Subs. (8)

This re-enacts s.3 and s.4 of the Act, with the necessary modifications for post-subscription alterations. The effect is that an alteration is presumed to have been signed by the granter (and hence to be valid under subs. (1)(b)) if the alteration is counter-signed by a witness, or if a court docquet is obtained.

Registration of documents

6.—(1) Subject to subsection (3) below, it shall not be competent—
  (a) to record a document in the Register of Sasines; or
  (b) to register a document for execution or preservation in the Books of Council and Session or in sheriff court books,
unless subsection (2) below applies in relation to the document.
  (2) This subsection applies where—
  (a) the document is presumed under section 3 or 4 of this Act to have been subscribed by the granter; or
  (b) if there is more than one granter, the document is presumed under section 3 or 4 or partly under the one section and partly under the other to have been subscribed by at least one of the granters.
  (3) Subsection (1) above shall not apply in relation to—
  (a) the recording of a document in the Register of Sasines or the registration of a document in the Books of Council and Session or in sheriff court books, if such recording or registration is required or expressly permitted under any enactment;
  (b) the recording of a court decree in the Register of Sasines;
  (c) the registration in the Books of Council and Session or in sheriff court books of—
        (i) a testamentary document;
        (ii) a document which is directed by the Court of Session or (as the case may be) the sheriff to be so registered;

(iii) a document whose formal validity is governed by a law other than Scots law, if the Keeper of the Registers of Scotland or (as the case may be) the sheriff clerk is satisfied that the document is formally valid according to the law governing such validity;

(iv) a court decree granted under section 4 or 5 of this Act in relation to a document already registered in the Books of Council and Session or in sheriff court books (as the case may be); or

(d) the registration of a court decree in a separate register maintained for that purpose.

(4) A document may be registered for preservation in the Books of Council and Session or in sheriff court books without a clause of consent to registration.

DEFINITIONS
"decree": s.12(1).
"document": s.12(1).
"enactment": s.12(1).

GENERAL NOTE
Subject to the exceptions listed in subs. (3), a document will be accepted for registration in the Register of Sasines or in the Books of Council and Session or sheriff court books only if it is attested (or the equivalent) or if, failing attestation, it bears a court docquet under s.4 of the Act. This rule will catch a certain number of documents which do not fall within s.1(2) of the Act and which, but for the rule, would not require to be attested – for example, affidavits sworn under s.6(3)(e) and s.8(2A) of the Matrimonial Homes (Family Protection) (Scotland) Act 1981 (c. 59). The rule applies only to documents executed on or after August 1, 1995: see s.14(3)(a).

To a considerable extent this provision reinforces existing practice as to which documents should or should not be attested. All deeds destined for the listed registers were in fact attested, although this was probably mandatory only in the case of the Books of Council and Session. The Registration Act 1698, c. 4 (now repealed by Sched. 5) provided for the registration for preservation of "Probative Writs".

Section 6 makes no mention of the Land Register, and indeed, strictly, what is registered there is not the deed itself but rather the right or rights flowing from the deed. By s.4(1) of the Land Registration (Scotland) Act 1979 (c. 33) the Keeper has a discretion to refuse applications for registration in the Land Register if they are not accompanied by such documents as he may require, and it is understood that the Keeper intends to use this power to apply the same rules to the Land Register as are now, by s.6 of the 1995 Act, applied to the Register of Sasines. The practical effect is that all conveyancing deeds will require to be attested (or the equivalent under Sched. 2). In cases where a conveyancing deed has a prescribed statutory form (for example, a long lease or a standard security), there is now added to that form by Sched. 4 the following, rather cryptic, note: "Subscription of the document by the granter of it will be sufficient for the document to be formally valid, but witnessing of it may be necessary or desirable for other purposes (see the Requirements of Writing (Scotland) Act 1995)".

Subs. (2)
Where a deed has a number of granters, the effect of para. (b) is that registration is permitted if the subscription of just one of the granters has been witnessed. However, it is difficult to see how a document can be presumed to be subscribed by a *single* granter partly under s.3 and partly under s.4. Indeed the two sections seem mutually exclusive: see s.4(1). The wording here has been carried over from cl. 11(1) of the draft bill annexed to Scot. Law Com. No. 112 where it was used (appropriately) in the context of subscription by two or more granters.

Subs. (3)
This lists the cases where attestation (or court docquet) is not required. Paragraphs (a) and (b) overlap. See *e.g.* the Conveyancing (Scotland) Act 1924, s.46(1), which empowers the recording of an extract decree of reduction. An example of an enactment under para. (a) which does not deal with the recording of a court decree is the Bills of Exchange Act 1681 (registration of protests of bills of exchange).

Subs. (4)
This repeats the rule enacted by the Registration Act 1698 (c. 4) (which is now repealed by Sched. 5). A clause of consent continues to be required in respect of registration for execution

(*i.e.* for the purposes of summary diligence): see the Titles to Land Consolidation (Scotland) Act 1868, s.138.

Subscription and signing

7.—(1) Except where an enactment expressly provides otherwise, a document is subscribed by a granter of it if it is signed by him at the end of the last page (excluding any annexation, whether or not incorporated in the document as provided for in section 8 of this Act).

(2) Subject to paragraph 2(2) of Schedule 2 to this Act, a document, or an alteration to a document, is signed by an individual natural person as a granter or on behalf of a granter of it if it is signed by him—

  (a) with the full name by which he is identified in the document or in any testing clause or its equivalent; or

  (b) with his surname, preceded by at least one forename (or an initial or abbreviation or familiar form of a forename); or

  (c) except for the purposes of section 3(1) to (7) of this Act, with a name (not in accordance with paragraph (a) or (b) above) or description or an initial or mark if it is established that the name, description, initial or mark—

      (i) was his usual method of signing, or his usual method of signing documents or alterations of the type in question; or

      (ii) was intended by him as his signature of the document or alteration.

(3) Where there is more than one granter, the requirement under subsection (1) above of signing at the end of the last page of a document shall be regarded as complied with if at least one granter signs at the end of the last page and any other granter signs on an additional page.

(4) Where a person grants a document in more than one capacity, one subscription of the document by him shall be sufficient to bind him in all such capacities.

(5) A document, or an alteration to a document, is signed by a witness if it is signed by him—

  (a) with the full name by which he is identified in the document or in any testing clause or its equivalent; or

  (b) with his surname, preceded by at least one forename (or an initial or abbreviation or familiar form of a forename),

and if the witness is witnessing the signature of more than one granter, it shall be unnecessary for him to sign the document or alteration more than once.

(6) This section is without prejudice to any rule of law relating to the subscription or signing of documents by members of the Royal Family, by peers or by the wives or the eldest sons of peers.

(7) Schedule 2 to this Act (special rules relating to subscription and signing of documents etc by partnerships, companies, local authorities, other bodies corporate and Ministers) shall have effect.

DEFINITIONS
  "alteration": s.12(1).
  "annexation": s.12(1).
  "company": s.12(1) (incorporating the Companies Act 1985, s.735(1)).
  "document": s.12(1).
  "enactment": s.12(1).
  "local authority": s.12(1).
  "Minister": s.12(1) (incorporating the Ministers of the Crown Act 1975, s.8).

GENERAL NOTE
  Section 7 begins by defining subscription as the signature of a document at the end of the last page. Thereafter the section is mainly concerned with prescribing the methods by

which a natural person may sign. Parallel provision for signatures by juristic persons and by Ministers of the Crown is made in Sched. 2. The new rules as to signature are welcome as introducing relative certainty into an area of law where the existing rules were very far from clear.

Section 7 applies to all documents and not merely to those which are "required" by s.1(2). It is thought that the rules as to signature are intended to be exhaustive and that a signature made in some other way would not be legally effective. If that were not so there would have been no need for the saving provision in subs. (6) for peers and members of the Royal Family. However, the methods of signature permitted by subs. (2) are so wide that this result is unlikely to cause hardship in practice.

Subs. (1)

This provision defines how a granter subscribes. It is concerned with the physical act only and does not touch on the issue of capacity. Compare here s.3(4)(c). It should be borne in mind that a document which was properly subscribed by the granter under s.7 would still fail if the granter was incapax.

Subscribed by a granter. By s.12(1) this phrase is extended to include execution by an agent for the granter acting under a power of attorney. No express provision is made here, or elsewhere in s.7, for subscription by a consenter; but a consenter grants something, if only his consent to the deed, and it is thought that in this context "granter" is sufficiently wide to include consenter.

At the end of the last page. This is rather vaguely expressed, possibly intentionally. It seems broad enough to encompass (i) a signature immediately following the deed proper (*i.e.* excluding the testing clause or equivalent), (ii) a signature separated from the deed proper by a space which is later used for a testing clause, and (iii) a signature at the very foot of the last page. A more difficult case is where a testing clause straddles two pages. Where is the granter to sign? The common law rule was that he could sign on either page. See *Ferguson* 1959 S.C. 56 and *McNeill v. McNeill* 1973 S.L.T. (Sh. Ct.) 16. However, that rule could only be adopted into the new law if it were accepted that there could be two "last pages", and it may be that a choice will have to be made as to whether a document "ends" with the deed proper or with the testing clause.

In the case of missives of sale and other contracts comprising two or more documents, the rule is that each separate document must be subscribed: see s.2(2).

Subs. (2)

Three possible methods of signature by a granter are set out. Separate provision is made in subs. (5) for signature by a witness. Subsection (2) is subject to para. 2(2) of Sched. 2 which allows a person signing on behalf of a partnership to do so in the firm name. The granter must "sign", which presumably means by the application of a pen, pencil, or other writing implement to the document. It is thought that a signature must be in handwriting, so that for example it would not be sufficient if the granter were to type his name. The granter should not normally be aided in writing his signature, although a signature has been accepted in circumstances where the granter's wrist was supported but without his hand actually being led (see *Noble v. Noble* (1875) 3 R. 74). If the granter cannot write, whether due to physical infirmity or to illiteracy, the proper course is to have the deed executed by a solicitor or other authorised person under s.9 of the Act. There is, however, no objection to a signature by a blind granter: see s.9(7).

Of the three alternative methods of signing set out in subs. (2), alternative (b) is the one most commonly employed in current practice. The alternative is quite widely expressed. Thus Donald Ramsay Macdonald could sign as "D. Macdonald" or as "R. Macdonald" or as "Donnie Macdonald", although not merely as "Macdonald". On signature by surname only, compare *American Express Europe v. Royal Bank of Scotland (No. 2)* 1989 S.L.T. 650.

In most cases alternative (a) will be subsumed within alternative (b). However, there will be rare cases where the "full name" in the deed comprises only a surname or a forename or some kind of informal name. In that case a signature is valid if it repeats the name used in the deed.

Alternative (c) authorises certain types of less formal signature, but subject to the rider that they cannot be used for attested deeds (which attract the presumption of valid execution under s.3). More specifically, alternative (c) authorises signature by a name which does not fall within either of the other two alternatives, and also signature by something less than a name, *viz* by a description (*e.g.* "Mum": see *Rhodes v. Peterson* 1971 S.C. 56) or by initial or even by mark. In practice an informal signature is likely to be used either because the document is itself informal in nature (*e.g.* a letter) or because the granter has difficulty in writing his name. However, an informal signature is not automatically sufficient. A person seeking to found on such a signature will have to show not only that the deed was actually signed by the granter (which is the normal evidential burden imposed in relation to deeds not falling within s.3) but also that the signature was the granter's usual method of signing or that it was intended by him as his signature. The issue is likely to arise most often in practice with informal wills when confirmation of executors requires to be obtained.

A signature can be validated as falling within one of the permitted alternatives only if it is at least to some extent legible. The standard is probably not very high: see Scot. Law Com. No. 112, para. 6.18. There seems no reason why a signature should be in Roman script, so that a Russian in Moscow (or indeed in Edinburgh) executing a disposition of Scottish heritage could do so using the cyrillic alphabet.

The rules just described do not prevent a person from adding to his signature a territorial designation (*e.g.* "of Bogmyrtle"): see s.14(5).

Subs. (3)

This is a useful provision for cases where the granters are too numerous to sign on a single page. There is no requirement that granters sign on the same additional page, and thus it seems permissible to have more than one additional page containing the signatures of granters. See Scot. Law Com. No. 112, para. 6.4.

Under the Act witnesses are required to sign and not to subscribe (see s.3(1)(b)), and hence it is immaterial whether witnesses sign on the first page of a deed or on the last page proper or on one of the additional pages.

Subs. (4)

This re-states, for the avoidance of doubt, the rule which was thought to exist at common law. Its effect is that a person who executes in two capacities, for example as executor and as an individual, need sign the document only once.

Subs. (5)

This makes available to witnesses two of the three methods of signing which are available to granters under subs. (2). The informal method is excluded, so that a witness may not sign by initials or by mark. The subsection also confirms existing practice to the effect that a person witnessing the signatures of several granters need sign only once. However, this provision must be read together with s.3(4)(e) and (6) (requirement of one continuous process). Thus unless all the granters sign (or acknowledge their signatures) together, the witness will require to sign separately in respect of each granter.

Subs. (6)

Peers sign by their title alone. Wives of peers sign their husband's title prefixed by their own forename. Eldest sons of peers may sign by their courtesy title. See J. M. Halliday *Conveyancing Law and Practice* (W. Green & Son, 1985) vol. I, p. 80. So far as the Queen is concerned, subs. (6) should be read together with s.13(1)(a) which preserves the existing practice of superscription.

Annexations to documents

8.—(1) Subject to subsection (2) below and except where an enactment expressly otherwise provides, any annexation to a document shall be regarded as incorporated in the document if it is—

   (a) referred to in the document; and

   (b) identified on its face as being the annexation referred to in the document,

without the annexation having to be signed or subscribed.

(2) Where a document relates to land and an annexation to it describes or shows all or any part of the land to which the document relates, the annexation shall be regarded as incorporated in the document if and only if—

   (a) it is referred to in the document; and

   (b) it is identified on its face as being the annexation referred to in the document; and

   (c) it is signed on—

        (i) each page, where it is a plan, drawing, photograph or other representation; or

        (ii) the last page, where it is an inventory, appendix, schedule or other writing.

(3) Any annexation referred to in subsection (2) above which bears to have been signed by a granter of the document shall be presumed to have been signed by the person who subscribed the document as that granter.

(4) Section 7(2) of this Act shall apply in relation to any annexation referred to in subsection (2) above as it applies in relation to a document as if for any reference to a document (except the reference in paragraph (a)) there were substituted a reference to an annexation.

(5) It shall be competent to sign any annexation to a document at any time before the document is—

(a) founded on in legal proceedings;

(b) registered for preservation in the Books of Council and Session or in sheriff court books;

(c) recorded in the Register of Sasines;

(d) registered in the Land Register of Scotland.

(6) Where there is more than one granter, the requirement under subsection (2)(c)(ii) above of signing on the last page shall be regarded as complied with (provided that at least one granter signs at the end of the last page) if any other granter signs on an additional page.

DEFINITIONS

"annexation": s.12(1).
"document": s.12(1).
"enactment": s.12(1).
"land": Sched. 1 to the Interpretation Act 1978.

GENERAL NOTE

Section 8 deals with annexations, which are defined in s.12(1) as including any inventory, appendix, schedule, other writing, plan, drawing, photograph or other representation annexed to a document. At the margins this definition is perhaps not very clear. For instance, there may be doubt as to the precise difference between (i) an annexation and (ii) any other document (or part of a document) which is incorporated into the principal document. A standard example of the latter is a description of land contained in an earlier deed and incorporated into a later deed. The earlier deed would presumably not be classified as an annexation, although it performs the same function as an annexation. It is suggested that the distinguishing features of an annexation may be that it is contemporaneous in time with the principal document, and that it is physically attached to, or at least intended to be kept with, that document.

Another difficulty arising from the definition is the distinction between an annexation on the one hand and the document proper on the other. Indeed for many purposes the two are treated together by the Act. ("Document" is defined in s.12(1) to include any annexation incorporated under s.8.) Conveyancers at least will usually be clear as to the distinction. In some cases it may be artificial to say that, for example, pages 1–12 of a deed comprise the document proper and pages 13–17 the annexation. The rules of execution require the granter to make a decision on this issue, because subscription is defined in s.7(1) as signature at the end of the last page excluding any annexation; and it may be that, for practical purposes, the true definition of an annexation is any part of a document occurring after the granter's subscription.

Section 8 applies to all documents and not merely to those "required" by s.1(2). Subsection (1) lays down the basic rule that an annexation is incorporated into a document if it is referred to in the document and if it is identified on its face as being the annexation in question. The remainder of the section is taken up with special rules for plans (or the equivalent) annexed to documents relating to land.

Subs. (1)

It is not clear whether this provision is permissive or mandatory. A cautious view would be that it is mandatory. However, some may regard it as significant that the wording departs from the wording employed in subs. (2), which is clearly mandatory ("... shall be regarded as incorporated in the document *if and only if ...*").

Subsection (1) requires that the fact of incorporation should be manifest both from the document itself and from the annexation. Thus (i) the document must refer to the annexation (*e.g.* "the Schedule annexed as relative hereto"); and (ii) the annexation must in turn be identified on its face as the thing which has been incorporated. It is probably enough to satisfy (ii) if the annexation is simply headed with the appropriate name (*e.g.* "Schedule"), but it is preferable to add some kind of identifying docquet (*e.g.* "this is the Schedule referred to in the foregoing Disposition by Donald Ramsay Macdonald in favour of Lucy Anne Robertson").

In practice annexations are often signed, which greatly assists in their identification; and signature is usually anticipated in the reference contained in the document proper (*e.g.* "the Schedule annexed *and signed* as relative hereto"). However, signature is not a formal requirement for annexations (except in relation to plans *etc.* falling under subs. (2)); and it seems an open question whether incorporation will fail if a signature of the annexation is promised in the document but does not in the end materialise in the annexation.

Subs. (2)

This introduces a special rule for plans *etc.* annexed to missives of sale, dispositions, and other documents relating to land. In addition to compliance with the usual rules set out in subs. (1), the plan or other annexation must also be signed. Unhelpfully, the subsection does not say who must sign, but it is not perhaps difficult to guess the answer. Indeed subs. (3) refers expressly to signature by the granter. The permissible methods of signature are set out in subs. (4). It will be noted that (except where the signatures spill over on to a new page: see subs. (6)) the requirement is for signature and not for subscription.

Subs. (3)

Three mandatory requirements for the annexation of plans *etc.* are prescribed by subs. (2). Of the three only the last (signature by the granter) depends to some extent on latent factors, with the result that compliance cannot be wholly verified from an inspection of the deed. Hence the presumption in subs. (3). The terms of this presumption should be noted carefully. It is not that the annexation has been signed by the granter. Rather it is that it has been signed by the person who subscribed the document as that granter. This is a presumption at one remove. The "person who subscribed" may, or may not, be the real granter. (It could also be a forger of signatures.) However, if the document itself is attested (as in the case of dispositions), the person who subscribed that document will in turn be presumed to be the granter under s.3(1). Hence, in effect, the presumption becomes that the annexation was signed by the granter. Conversely, if the document is subscribed only and not attested (as, usually, in the case of missives of sale), there is no further presumption that the person who subscribed was in fact the granter and that fact, if disputed, would have to be established by anyone seeking to rely on the document.

The presumption is limited to annexations "referred to in subsection (2)", that is to say, to plans and their equivalents. Thus in other cases it seems that granters have nothing to gain from signing annexations. Indeed to do so may act to the disadvantage of the grantee: if the method chosen to identify an annexation under subs. (1) is to sign it, the grantee may at some time in the future have need to establish the authenticity of that signature without the benefit of any presumption. This prompts the difficult question of whether an annexation could ever be regarded as a "document" under s.3(1), with the result that an annexation which was subscribed and witnessed would be presumed to have been subscribed by the granter.

Subs. (4)

This incorporates the three methods of signing permitted by s.7(2). It is noteworthy that the use of initials or other informal signature under s.7(2)(c) will not disqualify the annexation from the benefit of the presumption conferred by subs. (3).

Subs. (5)

An annexation does not require to be signed at the same time as the principal document. This may have odd consequences. For instance, if a plan or other annexation falling within subs. (2) is not signed until, say, two years after the document itself is executed, the document will have existed in two different forms. For the first two years it will take effect without the annexation. Thereafter it will take effect with the annexation.

Subs. (6)

This echoes the equivalent provision (s.7(3)) in relation to the execution of the document itself. It is confined to subs. (2)(c)(ii). It is not clear how multiple granters are to sign plans or photographs under subs. (2)(c)(i).

Subscription on behalf of blind granter or granter unable to write

9.—(1) Where a granter of a document makes a declaration to a relevant person that he is blind or unable to write, the relevant person—

(a) having read the document to that granter; or

(b) if the granter makes a declaration that he does not wish him to do so, without having read it to the granter,

shall, if authorised by the granter, be entitled to subscribe it and, if it is a testamentary document, sign it as mentioned in section 3(2) of this Act, on the granter's behalf.

(2) Subscription or signing by a relevant person under subsection (1) above shall take place in the presence of the granter.

(3) This Act shall have effect in relation to subscription or signing by a relevant person under subsection (1) above subject to the modifications set out in Schedule 3 to this Act.

(4) A document subscribed by a relevant person under subsection (1) above which confers on the relevant person or his spouse, son or daughter a benefit in money or money's worth (whether directly or indirectly) shall be invalid to the extent, but only to the extent, that it confers such benefit.

(5) This section and Schedule 3 to this Act apply in relation to the signing of—

(a) an annexation to a document as mentioned in section 8(2) of this Act;

(b) an alteration made to a document or to any such annexation to a document,

as they apply in relation to the subscription of a document; and for that purpose, any reference to reading a document includes a reference to describing a plan, drawing, photograph or other representation in such an annexation or in an alteration to such an annexation.

(6) In this Act "relevant person" means a solicitor who has in force a practising certificate as defined in section 4(c) of the Solicitors (Scotland) Act 1980, an advocate, a justice of the peace or a sheriff clerk and, in relation to the execution of documents outwith Scotland, includes a notary public or any other person with official authority under the law of the place of execution to execute documents on behalf of persons who are blind or unable to write.

(7) Nothing in this section shall prevent the granter of a document who is blind from subscribing or signing the document as mentioned in section 7 of this Act.

DEFINITIONS
  "alteration": s.12(1).
  "annexation": s.12(1).
  "authorised": s.12(1).
  "document": s.12(1).
  "subscription": s.7(1).

GENERAL NOTE
  Section 9 re-casts and simplifies the rules in relation to notarial execution, *i.e.* execution by a notary or other authorised person on behalf of a person who is blind or unable to write. Even under the previous law the category of persons who could execute deeds in this way was much wider than notaries public. Accordingly s.9 now abandons the word "notary" in favour of what some may regard as a colourless alternative, "relevant person". It is anticipated that members of the legal profession (who will be the main users of s.9) will cling defiantly to the word "notary", and these annotations are happy to do likewise.
  Like other documents executed under the Act, a notarial document may be executed either with or without witnesses. It is anticipated that a witness will normally be used, so that the deed is self-evidencing ("probative") under s.3. In cases where the execution is to be witnessed, the procedure prescribed by s.9 and by Sched. 3 is as follows. (i) The granter, notary and witness assemble. (ii) The granter declares that he is blind or that he is unable to write. (iii) The notary reads the document to the granter, unless the granter declares that he does not wish him to do so. If there is a plan (or equivalent) the notary must describe it unless, again, this is dispensed with. (iv) The granter authorises the notary to subscribe, expressly or by implication. (v) The notary subscribes. If the document is a will he also signs on every sheet. (vi) The witness signs immediately. (vii) The document or, more usually, the testing clause contains a statement that the document was read (or as the case may be, not read) and that the granter gave authority to the notary to sign.

Stages (i)–(vi) must be carried out in the presence of all three persons and, arguably, must be one continuous process. (That was the rule under the former law: see *e.g. Hynd's Tr. v. Hynd's Trs.* 1955 S.C. (H.L.) 1. However, the 1995 Act expressly requires continuity only in respect of stages (v) and (vi): see s.3(4)(e), as substituted by Sched. 3, para. 4.) The final stage (adding the testing clause or equivalent) can be carried out at any time, and in practice will usually be done by the grantee or his agent. Section 9 removes the requirement of the previous law (contained in s.18 of the Conveyancing (Scotland) Act 1924) that the notary write a holograph docquet on the deed.

An important but unexplored issue is the relationship between notarial execution and execution by an attorney or other authorised person. At common law a granter is always free to authorise a person to sign on his behalf, at least in the case of *inter vivos* deeds, and this practice is expressly recognised by s.12(2) of the Act. Furthermore there is probably no requirement that such authorisation be in writing. Accordingly, in the case of *inter vivos* deeds a person who is blind or unable to write has a choice. On the one hand he could authorise a notary under s.9. On the other hand he could grant a verbal power of attorney to any person, whether a "notary" or not. Which should he choose? The disadvantage of using a notary is that the procedure set out in s.9 is detailed and prescriptive. Hence a procedural error could invalidate the execution altogether. The advantage of using a notary is largely the practical one that solicitors, while perfectly accustomed to oral authorisations of notaries, are not accustomed to oral authorisations of mere attorneys and might be reluctant to accept deeds executed in this way, at least without further inquiry. There may also be a second advantage. With both methods of execution the effect of using a witness is that the deed is presumed by s.3(1) to have been subscribed by the notary (or, as the case may be, by the attorney). However, in the case of notaries (only) there is an argument, though perhaps not a very strong one, that the effect of s.3(1) (as substituted by Sched. 3, para. 2) is to create the useful additional presumption that the notary had authority to subscribe on behalf of the granter.

Subs. (1)

Notarial execution is about physical and not mental incapacity. A person who cannot write because of *mental* incapacity almost certainly lacks the mental capacity necessary to grant deeds in the first place. A person who is blind or unable to write is not obliged to use a notary or other agent. It is expressly provided in subs. (7) that a blind person may subscribe; and the relaxation in the rules as to signatures contained in s.7(2) mean that in many cases a person who is unable to write would nonetheless succeed in signing. Thus notarial execution may be less common in the future than it has been in the past.

As with documents executed by the granter personally, mere subscription, without witnesses, is all that is required for formal validity. Under the previous law two witnesses were always required for notarial execution. In practice it is likely that a witness will be used under the new law in order to attract the presumption of valid execution under s.3(1).

The granter is required to make a declaration that he is blind or unable to write; but there is no requirement that the declaration be true, or even that it is believed to be true by the notary. Thus a notary need take no steps to verify the supposed infirmity of the granter.

The power to dispense with reading the document is a welcome reform. A granter who is unable to write, perhaps because of an illness or accident, may be perfectly able to read the document for himself. However, the power to dispense is not limited to cases where the granter is able to read.

"Relevant person" is defined in subs. (6). "Authorised" is defined in s.12(1) to include cases of implied authorisation.

Subs. (2)

If a witness is used, subscription of the document (but not, strictly, signing of the additional sheets of a will) must also take place in the witness's presence. It is not competent for a notary to acknowledge his subscription to a witness. See s.3(4)(d) (as substituted by Sched. 3, para. 4).

If notarial execution fails due to a failure to comply with the procedures set out in this section, but nonetheless the notary subscribed with the granter's authority, it is arguable that the execution is valid at common law as execution by an agent (or attorney) on behalf of his principal.

Subs. (3)

Schedule 3 re-enacts ss.3 and 4 of the Act with a number of important modifications to take account of the fact that the execution is taking place notarially.

Subs. (4)

Under the previous law the whole document (typically a will) was invalid if the notary stood to benefit from its provisions. The restriction to the part of the document which benefits the notary is a welcome reform. The common law rules on the meaning of benefit will by and large continue to apply. For a review of the case law, see A.G.M. Duncan *The Notarially Executed Will* 1979 S.L.T. (News) 173. Under subs. (4), as at common law, the offending benefit may be "indirect", as for example where a will appoints a person who is in partnership with the notary as executor with power to charge professional remuneration. It will be noted that grandchildren and cohabitees can take benefit from the document, although in some cases this may be treated as an indirect benefit to the notary.

Subs. (5)

Notaries may sign annexations to documents, and also alterations. Schedule 3 re-states, with appropriate modifications, the provisions of Sched. 1 in relation to post-subscription alterations (Sched. 1 being itself a restatement with modifications of ss.3 and 4).

Not all notaries may feel confident as to their ability to describe a plan or photograph, and it may be that the standard applied by the courts will not be very exacting.

Subs. (6)

The "relevant person" replaces the notary public. Since in practice the "relevant person" most commonly used will be a solicitor, and since very many solicitors are notaries, the principle of "notarial" execution in the strict sense has not been entirely lost. The list of relevant persons is different and slightly wider than under the previous law (for which see s.18 of the Conveyancing (Scotland) Act 1924, now repealed). One change is that a parish minister acting in his own parish is now an irrelevant person.

Subs. (7)

The fact that the granter cannot see that which he is subscribing does not of itself affect the validity of his signature. As the Scottish Law Commission observed (see Scot. Law Com. No. 112, para. 6.28): "There is no rule that documents have to be read by the granter before being subscribed: if there were, many documents would be invalidated". Nonetheless a signature written by a blind person is open to challenge on the ground that the granter was misled as to what he was signing: see *Royal Bank of Scotland v. Purvis* 1990 S.L.T. 262. Prudence suggests that notarial execution will usually be the wiser course.

Forms of testing clause

10.—(1) Without prejudice to the effectiveness of any other means of providing information relating to the execution of a document, this information may be provided in such form of testing clause as may be prescribed in regulations made by the Secretary of State.

(2) Regulations under subsection (1) above shall be made by statutory instrument which shall be subject to annulment in pursuance of a resolution of either House of Parliament and may prescribe different forms for different cases or classes of case.

DEFINITIONS
"document": s.12(1).

GENERAL NOTE
This empowers the Secretary of State to prescribe model testing clauses. Any testing clauses so prescribed would be purely permissive. No firm decision has been reached as to whether this power will be exercised, but it is understood that if regulations are to be made they will come into force at the same time as the Act. Any regulations are likely to prescribe testing clauses along the lines of those proposed by the Scottish Law Commission: see Scot. Law Com. No. 112, pp. 192–196. The Commission's styles are designed to be typed on the document in advance, thus preventing the testing clause from being used to alter the deed after execution, notably by a false declaration that an alteration to the deed was in place prior to subscription: see s.5(5)(b). There is of course no reason why the Commission's styles should not be used without regulations having been made under this section.

Abolition of proof by writ or oath, reference to oath and other common law rules

11.—(1) Any rule of law and any enactment whereby the proof of any matter is restricted to proof by writ or by reference to oath shall cease to have effect.

(2) The procedure of proving any matter in any civil proceedings by reference to oath is hereby abolished.

(3) The following rules of law shall cease to have effect—

(a) any rule whereby certain contracts and obligations and any variations of those contracts and obligations, and assignations of incorporeal moveables, are required to be in writing; and

(b) any rule which confers any privilege—

(i) on a document which is holograph or adopted as holograph; or

(ii) on a writ *in re mercatoria.*

(4) Subsections (1) and (2) above shall not apply in relation to proceedings commenced before the commencement of this Act.

DEFINITIONS
"document": s.12(1).
"enactment": s.12(1).
"writing": Sched. 1 to the Interpretation Act 1978.

GENERAL NOTE
Section 11 comprises a veritable bonfire of archaisms, thus emphasising the far-reaching nature of the changes introduced by the Act.

Subs. (1)
At common law a number of obligations which could be constituted without writing could only be proved by writ or oath. These included gratuitous obligations, innominate and unusual contracts, payments of money under an antecedent contract, and certain loans. The idea that an obligation existed but could not be proved, and hence not be enforced, was not perhaps a happy one. The policy of the Act is to remove all restrictions as to proof and to confine formalities to constitution only: see s.1. Subsection (1) abolishes proof by writ or oath and allows proof by all competent evidence, including parole evidence.

Subs. (2)
In the words of the Scottish Law Commission (Scot. Law Com. No. 112, para. 3.16), the procedure of reference to oath "is an anachronism which originated at a time when the parties to an action were not competent witnesses. Although still resorted to by desperate litigants on rare occasions, with little apparent success, it is widely regarded as absurd and archaic". As a result of subs. (2) desperate litigants will now have to look elsewhere for assistance.

Subs. (3)
This provision is consequential on the new rules on the requirements of writing, and on the type of writing thereby required, which are introduced by ss.1 and 2. It abolishes the common law category of *obligationes literis*, as well as the types of privileged formal writing recognised by the common law. The statutory type of formal writing is abolished by Sched. 5.

Some may be surprised that incorporeal moveables are assignable without writing, especially as writing still appears to be required for intimation. No doubt writing will continue to be used in practice. Subsection (3) abolishes only the common law rule ("rule of law") and so is without prejudice to any statutory provision which requires written assignations, *e.g.* the Policies of Assurance Act 1867, s.5 (life assurance policies), and the Patents Act 1977, s.31(6) (as now amended by the Sched. 4, para. 49 of this Act) (patents).

Subs. (4)
This is a transitional provision.

Interpretation

12.—(1) In this Act, except where the context otherwise requires—

"alteration" includes interlineation, marginal addition, deletion, substitution, erasure or anything written on erasure;

"annexation" includes any inventory, appendix, schedule, other writing, plan, drawing, photograph or other representation annexed to a document;

"authorised" means expressly or impliedly authorised and any reference to a person authorised to sign includes a reference to a person authorised to sign generally or in relation to a particular document;

"company" has the same meaning as in section 735(1) of the Companies Act 1985;

"decree" includes a judgment or order, or an official certified copy, abbreviate or extract of a decree;

"director" includes any person occupying the position of director, by whatever name he is called;

"document" includes any annexation which is incorporated in it under section 8 of this Act and any reference, however expressed, to the signing of a document includes a reference to the signing of an annexation;

"enactment" includes an enactment contained in a statutory instrument;

"governing board", in relation to a body corporate to which paragraph 5 of Schedule 2 to this Act applies, means any governing body, however described;

"local authority" means a local authority within the meaning of section 235(1) of the Local Government (Scotland) Act 1973 and a council constituted under section 2 of the Local Government etc. (Scotland) Act 1994;

"Minister" has the same meaning as "Minister of the Crown" has in section 8 of the Ministers of the Crown Act 1975;

"office-holder" does not include a Minister but, subject to that, means—

(a) the holder of an office created or continued in existence by a public general Act of Parliament;

(b) the holder of an office the remuneration in respect of which is paid out of money provided by Parliament; and

(c) the registrar of companies within the meaning of the Companies Act 1985;

"officer"—

(a) in relation to a Minister, means any person in the civil service of the Crown who is serving in his Department;

(b) in relation an office-holder, means any member of his staff, or any person in the civil service of the Crown who has been assigned or appointed to assist him in the exercise of his functions;

"proper officer", in relation to a local authority, has the same meaning as in section 235(3) of the Local Government (Scotland) Act 1973; and

"secretary" means, if there are two or more joint secretaries, any one of them.

(2) Any reference in this Act to subscription or signing by a granter of a document or an alteration made to a document, in a case where a person is subscribing or signing under a power of attorney on behalf of the granter, shall be construed as a reference to subscription or signing by that person of the document or alteration.

GENERAL NOTE

Subs. (2)

At common law a granter is always free to appoint an attorney or other agent to sign on his behalf, at least in the case of *inter vivos* deeds. It is not, perhaps, clear how formal the appointment need be. In normal conveyancing practice there will be an attested power of attorney, but it seems likely that an attorney could also be appointed orally. Unfortunately, this question seems not to be covered by the 1995 Act. (Mandate is a contract and so is free from any requirement of writing under s.1(1); but, unlike mandate in the strict sense, a power of attorney confers powers rather than imposes obligations and appears not to be a contract.)

Subsection (2) makes the necessary modifications to the Act for cases where signature is by an attorney. Where a deed subscribed by an attorney on behalf of a granter is attested, s.3(1) (as modified by subs. (2)) provides that the deed is presumed to have been subscribed by the attorney (only). There is no further presumption that the attorney had authority to sign for the granter, and it is for the grantee or other person relying on the deed to satisfy himself on this point.

Application of Act to Crown

13.—(1) Nothing in this Act shall—
(a) prevent Her Majesty from authenticating—
    (i) a document by superscription; or
    (ii) a document relating to her private estates situated or arising in Scotland in accordance with section 6 of the Crown Private Estates Act 1862;
(b) prevent authentication under the Writs Act 1672 of a document passing the seal appointed by the Treaty of Union to be kept and used in Scotland in place of the Great Seal of Scotland formerly in use; or
(c) prevent any document mentioned in paragraph (a) or (b) above authenticated as aforesaid from being recorded in the Register of Sasines or registered for execution or preservation in the Books of Council and Session or in sheriff court books.

(2) Nothing in this Act shall prevent a Crown writ from being authenticated or recorded in Chancery under section 78 of the Titles to Land Consolidation (Scotland) Act 1868.

(3) Subject to subsections (1) and (2) above, this Act binds the Crown.

DEFINITIONS
"document": s.12(1).

GENERAL NOTE
The Act applies to the Crown, with the consequence that deeds may be executed by the Queen according to its provisions. However, certain existing methods of execution are preserved and may continue to be used in place of the provisions of the 1995 Act.

Subs. (1)
By custom the Queen authenticates documents by superscription (*i.e.* by signature at the top) and not by subscription. Section 6 of the Crown Private Estates Act 1862 (c. 37) provides for conveyances of the private estates of Her Majesty to be executed under the sign manual and attested by two witnesses. The meaning of private estates is given in s.1 of the 1862 Act.
The Writs Act 1672, narrating the unsuitability of deeds passing the Great Seal which are written "in one broad parchment of soe great lenth and largenes that they can hardly be read", permits such deeds to be written on more than one page, "book-wise".
Paragraph (c) is necessary because otherwise such registration would be prevented by s.6.

Subs. (2)
A Crown writ means a charter, precept or writ from Her Majesty or from the Prince and Steward of Scotland: see the Titles to Land Consolidation (Scotland) Act 1868, s.3. A substantial part of the 1868 Act (ss.63–90) is taken up with the subject of Crown writs. Section 78 makes provision for the execution of such writs.

Minor and consequential amendments, repeals, transitional provisions and savings

14.—(1) The enactments mentioned in Schedule 4 to this Act shall have effect subject to the minor and consequential amendments specified in that Schedule.

(2) The enactments mentioned in Schedule 5 to this Act are hereby repealed to the extent specified in the third column of that Schedule.

(3) Subject to subsection (4) below and without prejudice to subsection (5) below and section 11(4) of this Act, nothing in this Act shall—
(a) apply to any document executed or anything done before the commencement of this Act; or
(b) affect the operation, in relation to any document executed before such commencement, of any procedure for establishing the authenticity of such a document.

(4) In the repeal of the Blank Bonds and Trusts Act 1696 (provided for in Schedule 5 to this Act), the repeal of the words from "And farder" to the end—
  (a) shall have effect in relation to a deed of trust, whether executed before or after the commencement of this Act; but
  (b) notwithstanding paragraph (a) above, shall not have effect in relation to proceedings commenced before the commencement of this Act in which a question arises as to the deed of trust.

(5) The repeal of certain provisions of the Lyon King of Arms Act 1672 (provided for in Schedule 5 to this Act) shall not affect any right of a person to add a territorial designation to his signature or the jurisdiction of the Lord Lyon King of Arms in relation to any such designation.

(6) For the purposes of this Act, if it cannot be ascertained whether a document was executed before or after the commencement of this Act, there shall be a presumption that it was executed after such commencement.

DEFINITIONS
  "document": s.12(1).
  "enactment": s.12(1).

GENERAL NOTE

Subs. (1)
  See notes to Sched. 4 to this Act.

Subs. (2)
  Schedule 5 repeals the various authentication statutes on which the previous law of execution of deeds rested, and makes a number of consequential repeals: See Scot. Law Com. No. 112, pp. 189–191.

Subs. (3)
  The Act applies only to documents executed on or after the date of commencement (August 1, 1995). The date of delivery – which in the case of unilateral documents is the date on which the document actually becomes effective – is not relevant for this purpose. In the case of documents which are undated and apparently undatable, subs. (6) creates a presumption that they were executed after the commencement of the Act.
  For many years to come lawyers especially will have to deal with deeds executed prior to August 1, 1995. The formal validity of such deeds and (para. (b)) the procedure for establishing their authenticity will be governed by the now-repealed former law.

Subs. (4)
  The part of the Blank Bonds and Trusts Act 1696 which is referred to provides that certain trusts may be proved only by writ or oath. In conformity with s.11(1) and (4), the abolition of proof by writ or oath applies to all trusts regardless of date except in cases where proceedings commenced prior to August 1, 1995.

Subs. (5)
  The new rules as to signature set out in s.7(2) and (5) do not prevent a person adding after his signature a territorial designation (*e.g.* "of Bogmyrtle"). The right to add such a designation was previously provided for in the part of the Lyon King of Arms Act 1672 which is now repealed by Sched. 5.

Short title, commencement and extent

15.—(1) This Act may be cited as the Requirements of Writing (Scotland) Act 1995.

(2) This Act shall come into force at the end of the period of three months beginning with the date on which it is passed.

(3) This Act extends to Scotland only.

GENERAL NOTE

The Act received Royal Assent on May 1, 1995 and comes into force on August 1, 1995.

SCHEDULES

Section 5(8)   SCHEDULE 1

ALTERATIONS MADE TO A DOCUMENT AFTER IT HAS BEEN SUBSCRIBED

Presumption as to granter's signature or date or place of signing

1.—(1) Subject to sub-paragraphs (2) to (7) below, where—

(a) an alteration to a document bears to have been signed by a granter of the document;

(b) the alteration bears to have been signed by a person as a witness of that granter's signature and the alteration, or the testing clause or its equivalent, bears to state the name and address of the witness; and

(c) nothing in the document or alteration, or in the testing clause or its equivalent, indicates—

(i) that the alteration was not signed by that granter as it bears to have been so signed; or

(ii) that it was not validly witnessed for any reason specified in paragraphs (a) to (e) of sub-paragraph (4) below,

the alteration shall be presumed to have been signed by that granter.

(2) Where an alteration to a testamentary document consists of more than one sheet, the alteration shall not be presumed to have been signed by a granter as mentioned in sub-paragraph (1) above unless, in addition to it bearing to have been signed by him on the last sheet and otherwise complying with that sub-paragraph, it bears to have been signed by him on every other sheet.

(3) For the purposes of sub-paragraph (1)(b) above—

(a) the name and address of a witness may be added at any time before the alteration is—

(i) founded on in legal proceedings; or

(ii) registered for preservation in the Books of Council and Session or in sheriff court books; and

(b) the name and address of a witness need not be written by the witness himself.

(4) Where, in any proceedings relating to an alteration to a document in which a question arises as to a granter's signature, it is established—

(a) that a signature bearing to be the signature of the witness of that granter's signature is not such a signature, whether by reason of forgery or otherwise;

(b) that the person who signed the alteration as the witness of that granter's signature is a person who is named in the document as a granter of the document;

(c) that the person who signed the alteration as the witness of that granter's signature, at the time of signing—

(i) did not know the granter;

(ii) was under the age of 16 years; or

(iii) was mentally incapable of acting as a witness;

(d) that the person who signed the alteration, purporting to be the witness of that granter's signature, did not witness such signature;

(e) that the person who signed the alteration as the witness of that granter's signature did not sign the alteration after him or that the signing of the alteration by the granter or, as the case may be, the granter's acknowledgement of his signature and the signing by the person as witness were not one continuous process;

(f) that the name or address of the witness of that granter's signature was added after the alteration was founded on or registered as mentioned in sub-paragraph (3)(a) above or is erroneous in any material respect; or

(g) in the case of an alteration to a testamentary document consisting of more than one sheet, that a signature on any sheet of the alteration bearing to be the signature of the granter is not such a signature, whether by reason of forgery or otherwise,

then, for the purposes of those proceedings, there shall be no presumption that the alteration has been signed by that granter.

(5) For the purposes of sub-paragraph (4)(c)(i) above, the witness shall be regarded as having known the person whose signature he has witnessed at the time of witnessing if he had credible information at that time of his identity.

(6) For the purposes of sub-paragraph (4)(e) above, where—

(a) an alteration to a document is made by more than one granter; and

(b) a person is the witness to the signature of more than one granter,

the signing of the alteration by any such granter or the acknowledgement of his signature and the signing by the person witnessing that granter's signature shall not be regarded as not being one continuous process by reason only that, between the time of signing or acknowledgement by that granter and of signing by that witness, another granter has signed the alteration or acknowledged his signature.

(7) For the purposes of the foregoing provisions of this paragraph a person witnesses a granter's signature of an alteration—

(a) if he sees the granter sign it; or

(b) if the granter acknowledges his signature to that person.

(8) Where—

(a) by virtue of sub-paragraph (1) above an alteration to a document to which this sub-paragraph applies is presumed to have been signed by a granter of the document;

(b) the alteration, or the testing clause or its equivalent, bears to state the date or place of signing of the alteration by that granter; and

(c) nothing in the document or alteration, or in the testing clause or its equivalent, indicates that that statement as to date or place is incorrect,

there shall be a presumption that the alteration was signed by that granter on the date or at the place as stated.

(9) Sub-paragraph (8) above applies to any document other than a testamentary document.

(10) Where—

(a) an alteration to a testamentary document bears to have been signed and the alteration, or the testing clause or its equivalent, bears to state the date or place of signing (whether or not it is presumed under sub-paragraphs (1) to (7) above to have been signed by a granter of the document); and

(b) nothing in the document or alteration, or in the testing clause or its equivalent, indicates that that statement as to date or place is incorrect,

there shall be a presumption that the statement as to date or place is correct.

Presumption as to granter's signature or date or place of signing when established in court proceedings

2.—(1) Where an alteration to a document bears to have been signed by a granter of the document, but there is no presumption under paragraph 1 above that the alteration has been signed by that granter, then, if the court, on an application being made to it by any person having an interest in the document, is satisfied that the alteration was signed by that granter, it shall—

(a) cause the document to be endorsed with a certificate to that effect; or

(b) where the document has already been registered in the Books of Council and Session or in sheriff court books, grant decree to that effect.

(2) Where an alteration to a document bears to have been signed by a granter of the document, but there is no presumption under paragraph 1 above as to the date or place of signing, then, if the court, on an application being made to it by any person having an interest in the document, is satisfied as to the date or place of signing, it shall—

(a) cause the document to be endorsed with a certificate to that effect; or

(b) where the document has already been registered in the Books of Council and Session or in sheriff court books, grant decree to that effect.

(3) In relation to an application under sub-paragraph (1) or (2) above evidence shall, unless the court otherwise directs, be given by affidavit.

(4) An application under sub-paragraph (1) or (2) above may be made either as a summary application or as incidental to and in the course of other proceedings.

(5) The effect of a certificate or decree—

(a) under sub-paragraph (1) above shall be to establish a presumption that the alteration has been signed by the granter concerned;

(b) under sub-paragraph (2) above shall be to establish a presumption that the statement in the certificate or decree as to date or place is correct.

(6) In this paragraph "the court" means—

(a) in the case of a summary application—

(i) the sheriff in whose sheriffdom the applicant resides; or

(ii) if the applicant does not reside in Scotland, the sheriff at Edinburgh; and

(b) in the case of an application made in the course of other proceedings, the court before which those proceedings are pending.

DEFINITIONS
"decree": s.12(1).
"document": s.12(1).
"signed by a granter": s.7(2).
"signed by a witness": s.7(5).

GENERAL NOTE
Paragraph 1 re-states s.3 of the Act and para. 2 re-states s.4, with the minor modifications necessary for the provisions to apply to the authentication of alterations made after subscription. There are two main substantive changes. First, and following s.5(1)(b), the alteration requires only to be signed by the granter and not to be subscribed. Secondly, the granter may sign by any of the three methods set out in s.7(2). That includes method (c) (signature by initials or mark), which is excluded for s.3 proper. Method (c) is not available for the witness: see s.7(5).

Section 7(7)   SCHEDULE 2

SUBSCRIPTION AND SIGNING: SPECIAL CASES

General

1. Any reference in this Act to subscription or signing by a granter of a document or an alteration to a document, in a case where the granter is a person to whom any of paragraphs 2 to 6 of this Schedule applies shall, unless the context otherwise requires, be construed as a reference to subscription or, as the case may be, signing of the document or alteration by a person in accordance with that paragraph.

DEFINITIONS
"alteration": s.12(1).
"authorised": s.12(1).
"company": s.12(1) (incorporating the Companies Act 1985, s.735(1)).
"director": s.12(1).
"document": s.12(1).
"enactment": s.12(1).
"governing body": s.12(1).
"local authority": s.12(1).
"Minister": s.12(1) (incorporating the Ministers of the Crown Act 1975, s.8).
"office-holder": s.12(1).
"officer": s.12(1).
"proper officer": s.12(1) (incorporating the Local Government (Scotland) Act 1973, s.235(3)).
"secretary": s.12(1).
"subscription": s.7(1).

GENERAL NOTE
By s.2(1) a document is formally valid if it is subscribed by the granter; and by s.7(1) a document is subscribed if it is signed at the end of the last page. Schedule 2 prescribes the methods by which documents are signed by the following classes of person: (i) partnerships (para. 2), (ii) companies (para. 3), (iii) local authorities (para. 4), (v) other bodies corporate (para. 5), and (vi) Ministers of the Crown and office-holders (para. 6). It is thus the counterpart in respect of these persons of s.7(2) of the Act (which prescribes the method of signature for natural persons). In all cases apart from partnership, there are also consequential amendments to s.3, both in its original form and as adapted by Sched. 1, para. 1, to apply to post-subscription alterations.
Paragraph 1 sets out the general principle that, for the purposes of the Act, the classes of person listed in Sched. 2 are to sign in accordance with the rules set out in that Schedule. By s.12(1), "document" includes any annexation to a document which is incorporated under s.8.

Partnerships

2.—(1) Except where an enactment expressly provides otherwise, where a granter of a document is a partnership, the document is signed by the partnership if it is signed on its behalf by a partner or by a person authorised to sign the document on its behalf.

(2) A person signing on behalf of a partnership under this paragraph may use his own name or the firm name.

(3) Sub-paragraphs (1) and (2) of this paragraph apply in relation to the signing of an alteration made to a document as they apply in relation to the signing of a document.

(4) In this paragraph "partnership" has the same meaning as in section 1 of the Partnership Act 1890.

GENERAL NOTE

This paragraph clarifies the rules for signature by a partnership. Two alternative methods of signature are provided. Either (i) the document is signed by one of the partners, or (ii) it is signed by a person who is authorised to sign on behalf of the partnership. No witnesses are required for formal validity (see s.2(1)), but if a witness is used the document will benefit from the presumption of valid execution under s.3(1) of the Act.

It is clear from the definition of "authorised" in s.12(1), (a) that authorisation to sign may be implied, and (b) that the authorisation may either be a general authorisation to sign all documents (or all documents of a particular type) or a specific authorisation to sign a particular document. A partner or other person signing on behalf of a partnership may use either his own name or the firm name. In conveyancing practice the firm name is always used for missives of sale and for letters of obligation.

Method (ii) was probably not available at common law: see *Littlejohn v. MacKay* 1974 S.L.T. (Sh. Ct.) 82. The new provisions open the way for *e.g.* missives of sale being signed by assistant solicitors rather than (as under the former law) by partners only.

Paragraph 2 is concerned solely with the formal validity of documents and does not touch on the broader question of whether the signatory was entitled to bind the partnership in relation to the transaction in question. That broader question is regulated by ss.5 and 6 of the Partnership Act 1890. Accordingly, a document which is executed in accordance with para. 2 is valid and effective unless or until reduced; but one possible ground of reduction would be that the partner who signed the document was acting beyond his authority in entering into the particular transaction.

Under para. 2 a document is formally valid only if it is signed by a partner or by an authorised person. This raises the practical problem of how a person wishing to rely on the document can be assured that the signatory was indeed a partner or, as the case may be, an authorised person. The problem is particularly difficult if some years have elapsed since the date of execution. The solution proposed by the Scottish Law Commission was for there to be a presumption that the signatory was a partner or authorised person: see cl. 15(3) of the draft bill included in Scot. Law Com. No. 112. This solution has not been used directly by para. 2. However, if the signature has been attested by a witness, s.3(1) creates a presumption that the document has been subscribed by the granter, that is to say (para. 1 of Sched. 2) *by the partnership*. The precise meaning of this presumption is perhaps open to doubt. Unlike the presumption standardly created by s.3(1), which is a presumption of fact, this is a presumption as to legal result (since, as a matter of fact, a juristic person cannot wield a pen and subscribe a deed). It is not clear in what sense a legal result can be *presumed* to have occurred, and indeed in what manner such a presumption could be rebutted. (The point arises again in respect of execution by companies and by the other special categories dealt with in Sched. 2.) However, be that as it may, a presumption that the partnership has subscribed necessarily includes within it a presumption (of fact) that the signatory was a proper person to sign the document. Hence in effect his authority is presumed. It will be noted that there is no equivalent for partnerships of s.3(1C) (as substituted by para. 3(5) of Sched. 2).

Companies

3.—(1) Except where an enactment expressly provides otherwise, where a granter of a document is a company, the document is signed by the company if it is signed on its behalf by a director, or by the secretary, of the company or by a person authorised to sign the document on its behalf.

(2) This Act is without prejudice to—

(a) section 283(3) of the Companies Act 1985; and

(b) paragraph 9 of Schedule 1, paragraph 9 of Schedule 2, and paragraph 7 of Schedule 4, to the Insolvency Act 1986.

(3) Sub-paragraphs (1) and (2) of this paragraph apply in relation to the signing of an alteration made to a document as they apply in relation to the signing of a document.

(4) Where a granter of a document is a company, section 3 of and Schedule 1 to this Act shall have effect subject to the modifications set out in sub-paragraphs (5) and (6) below.

(5) In section 3—

(a) for subsection (1) there shall be substituted the following subsections—

"(1) Subject to subsections (1A) to (7) below, where—

(a) a document bears to have been subscribed on behalf of a company by a director, or by the secretary, of the company or by a person bearing to have been authorised to subscribe the document on its behalf;

(b) the document bears to have been signed by a person as a witness of the subscription of the director, secretary or other person subscribing on behalf of the company and to state the name and address of the witness; and

(c) nothing in the document, or in the testing clause or its equivalent, indicates—

(i) that it was not subscribed on behalf of the company as it bears to have been so subscribed; or

(ii) that it was not validly witnessed for any reason specified in paragraphs (a) to (e) of subsection (4) below,

the document shall be presumed to have been subscribed by the company.

(1A) Where a document does not bear to have been signed by a person as a witness of the subscription of the director, secretary or other person subscribing on behalf of the company it shall be presumed to have been subscribed by the company if it bears to have been subscribed on behalf of the company by—

(a) two directors of the company; or

(b) a director and secretary of the company; or

(c) two persons bearing to have been authorised to subscribe the document on its behalf.

(1B) For the purposes of subsection (1)(b) above, the name and address of the witness may bear to be stated in the document itself or in the testing clause or its equivalent.

(1C) A presumption under subsection (1) or (1A) above as to subscription of a document does not include a presumption—

(a) that a person bearing to subscribe the document as a director or the secretary of the company was such director or secretary; or

(b) that a person subscribing the document on behalf of the company bearing to have been authorised to do so was authorised to do so.";

(b) in subsection (4) after paragraph (g) there shall be inserted the following paragraph—

"(h) if the document does not bear to have been witnessed, but bears to have been subscribed on behalf of the company by two of the directors of the company, or by a director and secretary of the company, or by two authorised persons, that a signature bearing to be the signature of a director, secretary or authorised person is not such a signature, whether by reason of forgery or otherwise;".

(6) In paragraph 1 of Schedule 1—

(a) for sub-paragraph (1) there shall be substituted the following sub-paragraphs—

"(1) Subject to sub-paragraphs (1A) to (7) below, where—

(a) an alteration to a document bears to have been signed on behalf of a company by a director, or by the secretary, of the company or by a person bearing to have been authorised to sign the alteration on its behalf;

(b) the alteration bears to have been signed by a person as a witness of the signature of the director, secretary or other person signing on behalf of the company and to state the name and address of the witness; and

(c) nothing in the document or alteration, or in the testing clause or its equivalent, indicates—

(i) that the alteration was not signed on behalf of the company as it bears to have been so signed; or

(ii) that the alteration was not validly witnessed for any reason specified in paragraphs (a) to (e) of sub-paragraph (4) below,

the alteration shall be presumed to have been signed by the company.

(1A) Where an alteration does not bear to have been signed by a person as a witness of the signature of the director, secretary or other person signing on behalf of the company it shall be presumed to have been signed by the company if it bears to have been signed on behalf of the company by—

(a) two directors of the company; or

(b) a director and secretary of the company; or

(c) two persons bearing to have been authorised to sign the alteration on its behalf.

(1B) For the purposes of sub-paragraph (1)(b) above, the name and address of the witness may bear to be stated in the alteration itself or in the testing clause or its equivalent.

(1C) A presumption under sub-paragraph (1) or (1A) above as to signing of an alteration to a document does not include a presumption—

(a) that a person bearing to sign the alteration as a director or the secretary of the company was such director or secretary; or

(b) that a person signing the alteration on behalf of the company bearing to have been authorised to do so was authorised to do so.";

(b) in sub-paragraph (4) after paragraph (g) there shall be inserted the following paragraph—
     "(h) if the alteration does not bear to have been witnessed, but bears to have been signed
          on behalf of the company by two of the directors of the company, or by a director and
          secretary of the company, or by two authorised persons, that a signature bearing to
          be the signature of a director, secretary or authorised person is not such a signature,
          whether by reason of forgery or otherwise;".

GENERAL NOTE

This provision has a long and unusual legislative history. Section 36(3) of the Companies Act
1985 (as originally enacted) provided that companies execute deeds by seal accompanied by the
signatures of two directors or a director and a secretary. This did not make new law but simply
repeated the rule from previous Companies Acts. However, with effect from July 31, 1990,
s.36(3) was repealed by s.130 of the Companies Act 1989 and replaced by a new s.36B which was
modelled on the proposals for companies contained in Scot. Law Com. No. 112. Unfortunately
doubts rapidly grew as to whether the new provisions were adequately drafted and could safely
be relied upon. See K.G.C. Reid *Execution of Deeds by Companies* 1990 S.L.T. (News) 241. As a
result they were withdrawn, retrospectively, by s.72 of the Law Reform (Miscellaneous Provisions) (Scotland) Act 1990. In their place s.72 substituted a new s.36B, which also took effect
from July 31, 1990. Under the new provisions a company executed deeds by the subscriptions of
(i) two directors, or (ii) a director and the secretary, or (iii) two authorised persons. This new
version of s.36B is now repealed by the 1995 Act with effect from August 1, 1995. (In fact there is
now a third version of s.36B – see Sched. 4, para. 51 of this Act – but it deals only tangentially with
the execution of deeds.) From that date the execution of deeds by companies is governed by the
paragraph currently under consideration. Although the rules are altered once again, para. 3
acknowledges the uncertainty created by recent legislative changes by, in effect, permitting
companies to continue to execute deeds in the manner which they used immediately prior to
August 1, 1995 (*i.e.* under the version of s.36B of the 1985 Act which was substituted by s.72 of
the 1990 Act).

As usual in the 1995 Act, separate provision is made for formal validity and for self-evidencing
status (or "probativity"). The requirements for formal validity are set out in subpara. (1) (as read
together with ss.2(1) and 7(1)). They are very straightforward. A document is formally valid if it
is subscribed on behalf of the company, (i) by a director, or (ii) by the secretary, or (iii) by a
person authorised to sign the document on its behalf. In cases where there are two or more joint
secretaries, (ii) is satisfied by the signature of any one of them (s.12(1) (definition of "secretary")). In relation to (iii), a person may be authorised expressly or impliedly, and the authorisation may be a general one or it may be confined to a particular deed: see s.12(1) (definition of
"authorised"). There appears to be no requirement that the authorisation be in writing, but in
practice the grantee of a deed executed on behalf of a company is likely to require written evidence of authorisation, for example a board minute.

Self-evidencing (or "probativity") is regulated by s.3, but with the modifications contained in
subpara. (5). There are two possible routes to probativity, one new and one old. The new route is
the one adopted elsewhere in the 1995 Act: attestation by a single witness. See s.3(1) and (1B).
Under this method a deed is subscribed by a director or the secretary or an authorised person,
and signed by a single witness. There is no requirement that the director *etc.* be named or
designed. Compare here the rule for the witness, in s.3(1)(b); but it seems that the deed or testing
clause must indicate whether the signatory is a director or secretary or authorised person.

The old route to probativity is the method of execution which was in force immediately prior
to the 1995 Act. Under this method the deed is subscribed by two directors or by a director and
the secretary, or by two authorised persons: see s.3(1A). In effect (if not in law) the second
signatory is taking the place of the witness. It should be noted that the categories in s.3(1A)
cannot be mixed. Thus a deed executed by, say, a director and an authorised person, would not
be executed in accordance with s.3(1A). However, there might be an argument that the
execution fell within s.3(1), on the basis that the second signatory could be treated as a witness;
and in any event the deed would be formally valid under subpara. (1).

The presumption of valid execution conferred by s.3(1) is displaced if any of the latent factors
listed in s.3(4) can be established. Although augmented to some degree by subpara. (5)(b), the
latent factors are almost entirely directed at attestation. An important practical consequence is
that, in the case of the second method of execution, there is no requirement that the two signatures should be made as part of one continuous process, and it appears to be perfectly competent
for one director to subscribe on one day (whereupon the deed will become formally valid) and
for a second director to subscribe on a different day, perhaps many years later (whereupon the
deed will become self-evidencing under s.3(1A)).

The effect of attestation, or of the introduction of a second signatory, is that the document
"shall be presumed to have been subscribed by the company". However, some of the effect of

this presumption is then removed by s.3(1C) which declares that the presumption does not extend to a presumption that the signatory was indeed a director, or the secretary or an authorised person (as the case may be). This qualification is not entirely easy to interpret; but it appears to be a clumsy way of reformulating the original presumption as a presumption that the document was executed, not by the company (as is stated by s.3(1)) but by the actual signatory. The link between signatory and company then falls to be proved. The purpose behind s.3(1C) is to prevent deeds being granted by unscrupulous company employees masquerading as permitted signatories: see D.J. Cusine *Execution of Deeds by Companies* (1989) 34 J.L.S. 135. The practical consequence is that a grantee or other person seeking to rely on a deed executed by a company will require evidence of the signatory's status or authorisation. (In fact even without s.3(1C) it is doubtful whether in relation to directors and secretaries a presumption so easily rebutted by reference to the company file could have been relied upon without further inquiry.)

Subparagraph (6) inserts equivalent modifications into para. 1 of Sched. 1, which is itself largely a re-statement of s.3 in the context of post-subscription alterations.

Finally, it may be noted that subpara. (2) states that the Act is without prejudice to s.283(3) of the Companies Act 1985 and to various provisions of the Insolvency Act 1986. The Insolvency Act provisions authorise the execution of deeds on behalf of a company by administrators, receivers and liquidators. Section 283(3) of the Companies Act makes provision for an assistant or deputy secretary to act where the office of secretary is vacant.

Local authorities

4.—(1) Except where an enactment expressly provides otherwise, where a granter of a document is a local authority, the document is signed by the authority if it is signed on their behalf by the proper officer of the authority.

(2) For the purposes of the signing of a document under this paragraph, a person purporting to sign on behalf of a local authority as an officer of the authority shall be presumed to be the proper officer of the authority.

(3) Sub-paragraphs (1) and (2) of this paragraph apply in relation to the signing of an alteration made to a document as they apply in relation to the signing of a document.

(4) Where a granter of a document is a local authority, section 3 of and Schedule 1 to this Act shall have effect subject to the modifications set out in sub-paragraphs (5) to (8) below.

(5) For section 3(1) there shall be substituted the following subsections—

"(1) Subject to subsections (1A) to (7) below, where—

(a) a document bears to have been subscribed on behalf of a local authority by the proper officer of the authority;

(b) the document bears—

(i) to have been signed by a person as a witness of the proper officer's subscription and to state the name and address of the witness; or

(ii) (if the subscription is not so witnessed), to have been sealed with the common seal of the authority; and

(c) nothing in the document, or in the testing clause or its equivalent, indicates—

(i) that it was not subscribed on behalf of the authority as it bears to have been so subscribed; or

(ii) that it was not validly witnessed for any reason specified in paragraphs (a) to (e) of subsection (4) below or that it was not sealed as it bears to have been sealed or that it was not validly sealed for the reason specified in subsection (4)(h) below,

the document shall be presumed to have been subscribed by the proper officer and by the authority.

(1A) For the purposes of subsection (1)(b)(i) above, the name and address of the witness may bear to be stated in the document itself or in the testing clause or its equivalent.".

(6) In section 3(4) after paragraph (g) there shall be inserted the following paragraph—

"(h) if the document does not bear to have been witnessed, but bears to have been sealed with the common seal of the authority, that it was sealed by a person without authority to do so or was not sealed on the date on which it was subscribed on behalf of the authority;".

(7) For paragraph 1(1) of Schedule 1 there shall be substituted the following sub-paragraphs—

"(1) Subject to sub-paragraphs (1A) to (7) below, where—

(a) an alteration to a document bears to have been signed on behalf of a local authority by the proper officer of the authority;

(b) the alteration bears—

(i) to have been signed by a person as a witness of the proper officer's signature and to state the name and address of the witness; or

(ii) (if the signature is not so witnessed), to have been sealed with the common seal of the authority; and

(c) nothing in the document or alteration, or in the testing clause or its equivalent, indicates—

(i) that the alteration was not signed on behalf of the authority as it bears to have been so signed; or

(ii) that the alteration was not validly witnessed for any reason specified in paragraphs (a) to (e) of sub-paragraph (4) below or that it was not sealed as it bears to have been sealed or that it was not validly sealed for the reason specified in sub-paragraph (4)(h) below,

the alteration shall be presumed to have been signed by the proper officer and by the authority.

(1A) For the purposes of sub-paragraph (1)(b)(i) above, the name and address of the witness may bear to be stated in the alteration itself or in the testing clause or its equivalent.".

(8) In paragraph 1(4) of Schedule 1 after paragraph (g) there shall be inserted the following paragraph—

"(h) if the alteration does not bear to have been witnessed, but bears to have been sealed with the common seal of the authority, that it was sealed by a person without authority to do so or was not sealed on the date on which it was signed on behalf of the authority;".

GENERAL NOTE

This makes provision for execution of deeds by local authorities. Until April 1, 1996 this means district, regional and islands councils. Thereafter it means the new unitary councils established by the Local Government *etc.* (Scotland) Act 1994.

The previous rules on execution by local authorities were cumbersome, requiring (i) subscription by the proper officer, (ii) subscription by two councillors, and (iii) sealing with the common seal. See the Local Government (Scotland) Act 1973, s.194(1). The new law is much simpler. As is usual in the 1995 Act, separate provision is made for formal validity and for self-evidencing status (or "probativity").

For formal validity all that is required (subpara. (1), read together with ss.2(1) and 7(1)) is subscription by the proper officer of the authority. The proper officer is an officer of the local authority appointed for the purpose of execution of deeds: see the Local Government (Scotland) Act 1973, s.235(3) (imported by s.12(i)). Contrary to the usual rule for juristic persons in Sched. 2, there is a presumption of authority to act, subpara. (2) providing that a person purporting to sign on behalf of a local authority is presumed to be the proper officer. In practice this relieves a grantee or other person relying on a deed by a local authority of the need to enquire into authority to act.

Self-evidencing (or "probativity") is regulated by s.3, but with the modifications contained in subparas. (5) and (6). There are two possible routes to probativity. Either the document is sealed with the common seal, or the subscription of the proper officer is attested by a single witness: see s.3(1) and (1A). The rules on attestation are the standard ones set out in s.3. The rules on sealing are (i) that the document is sealed by a person with authority to do so, and (ii) that it is sealed on the date on which it is subscribed by the proper officer: see s.3(4)(h), and, on authority to seal, s.194(2) of the Local Government (Scotland) Act 1973.

Subparagraphs (7) and (8) insert equivalent modifications into para. 1 of Sched. 1, which is itself largely a re-statement of s.3 in the context of post-subscription alterations.

Other bodies corporate

5.—(1) This paragraph applies to any body corporate other than a company or a local authority.

(2) Except where an enactment expressly provides otherwise, where a granter of a document is a body corporate to which this paragraph applies, the document is signed by the body if it is signed on its behalf by—

(a) a member of the body's governing board or, if there is no governing board, a member of the body;

(b) the secretary of the body by whatever name he is called; or

(c) a person authorised to sign the document on behalf of the body.

(3) Sub-paragraphs (1) and (2) of this paragraph apply in relation to the signing of an alteration made to a document as they apply in relation to the signing of a document.

(4) Where a granter of a document is a body corporate to which this paragraph applies, section 3 of and Schedule 1 to this Act shall have effect subject to the modifications set out in sub-paragraphs (5) to (8) below.

(5) For section 3(1) there shall be substituted the following subsections—

"(1) Subject to subsections (1A) to (7) below, where—

(a) a document bears to have been subscribed on behalf of a body corporate to which paragraph 5 of Schedule 2 to this Act applies by—

(i) a member of the body's governing board or, if there is no governing board, a member of the body;

(ii) the secretary of the body; or

(iii) a person bearing to have been authorised to subscribe the document on its behalf;

(b) the document bears—

(i) to have been signed by a person as a witness of the subscription of the member, secretary or other person signing on behalf of the body and to state the name and address of the witness; or

(ii) (if the subscription is not so witnessed), to have been sealed with the common seal of the body; and

(c) nothing in the document, or in the testing clause or its equivalent, indicates—

(i) that it was not subscribed on behalf of the body as it bears to have been so subscribed; or

(ii) that it was not validly witnessed for any reason specified in paragraphs (a) to (e) of subsection (4) below or that it was not sealed as it bears to have been sealed or that it was not validly sealed for the reason specified in subsection (4)(h) below,

the document shall be presumed to have been subscribed by the member, secretary or authorised person (as the case may be) and by the body.

(1A) For the purposes of subsection (1)(b)(i) above, the name and address of the witness may bear to be stated in the document itself or in the testing clause or its equivalent.

(1B) A presumption under subsection (1) above as to subscription of a document does not include a presumption—

(a) that a person bearing to subscribe the document as a member of the body's governing board, a member of the body or the secretary of the body was such member or secretary; or

(b) that a person subscribing the document on behalf of the body bearing to have been authorised to do so was authorised to do so.".

(6) In section 3(4) after paragraph (g) there shall be inserted the following paragraph—

"(h) if the document does not bear to have been witnessed, but bears to have been sealed with the common seal of the body, that it was sealed by a person without authority to do so or was not sealed on the date on which it was subscribed on behalf of the body;".

(7) For paragraph 1(1) of Schedule 1 there shall be substituted the following sub-paragraphs—

"(1) Subject to sub-paragraphs (1A) to (7) below, where—

(a) an alteration to a document bears to have been signed on behalf of a body corporate to which paragraph 5 of Schedule 2 to this Act applies by—

(i) a member of the body's governing board or, if there is no governing board, a member of the body;

(ii) the secretary of the body; or

(iii) a person bearing to have been authorised to sign the alteration on its behalf;

(b) the alteration bears—

(i) to have been signed by a person as a witness of the signature of the member, secretary or other person signing on behalf of the body and to state the name and address of the witness; or

(ii) (if the signature is not so witnessed), to have been sealed with the common seal of the body; and

(c) nothing in the document or alteration, or in the testing clause or its equivalent, indicates—

(i) that the alteration was not signed on behalf of the body as it bears to have been so signed; or

(ii) that the alteration was not validly witnessed for any reason specified in paragraphs (a) to (e) of sub-paragraph (4) below or that it was not sealed as it bears to have been sealed or that it was not validly sealed for the reason specified in sub-paragraph (4)(h) below,

the alteration shall be presumed to have been signed by the member, secretary or authorised person (as the case may be) and by the body.

(1A) For the purposes of sub-paragraph (1)(b)(i) above, the name and address of the witness may bear to be stated in the alteration itself or in the testing clause or its equivalent.

(1B) A presumption under sub-paragraph (1) above as to signing of an alteration to a document does not include a presumption—

    (a) that a person bearing to sign the alteration as a member of the body's governing board, a member of the body or the secretary of the body was such member or secretary; or

    (b) that a person signing the alteration on behalf of the body bearing to have been authorised to do so was authorised to do so.".

(8) In paragraph 1(4) of Schedule 1 after paragraph (g) there shall be inserted the following paragraph—

    "(h) if the alteration does not bear to have been witnessed, but bears to have been sealed with the common seal of the body, that it was sealed by a person without authority to do so or was not sealed on the date on which it was signed on behalf of the body;".

GENERAL NOTE

This provides for the first time a uniform regime of execution of documents for bodies corporate (other than companies and local authorities, for which special provision is made in paras. 3 and 4 respectively). This welcome reform is subject to any enactments which expressly provide otherwise (subpara. (2)), but the opportunity has been taken by the Act (Scheds. 4 and 5) to amend or repeal substantial numbers of enactments which formerly provided otherwise in relation to a very varied series of bodies corporate. These range from the Red Deer Commission (Deer (Scotland) Act 1959, Sched. 1, paras. 12 and 13, repealed by Sched. 5) to industrial and provident societies (Industrial and Provident Societies Act 1965, s.36, repealed by Sched. 5) to the Law Society of Scotland (Solicitors (Scotland) Act 1980, Sched. 1, para. 12, repealed by Sched. 5). Of those enactments that remain on the statute book, many are concerned with the narrow issue of authenticating the common seal and so do not prevent the operation of the new rules introduced by para. 5. See Scot. Law Com. No. 112, para. 6.62. Mention should also be made of the small number of bodies corporate – for example, the ancient Universities, or building societies – for which no statutory provisions previously existed. They too will now be governed by para. 5.

Foreign bodies corporate sometimes have to execute documents under the law of Scotland. From May 16, 1994 onwards the execution of deeds by foreign companies was regulated by the Foreign Companies (Execution of Documents) Regulations 1994 (S.I. 1994 No. 950). (The position prior to this date was obscure and uncertain.) The Regulations operated by applying to foreign companies the rules for British companies contained in s.36B of the Companies Act 1985, but with certain modifications. However, now that the relevant parts of s.36B are repealed by the 1995 Act (Sched. 4, para. 51), it is thought that the Regulations must fall with them. It is understood that a formal amendment to the 1994 Regulations will be brought forward in due course. Accordingly, with effect from August 1, 1995, foreign companies and other bodies corporate will execute deeds under the law of Scotland in accordance with para. 5 of Sched. 2.

As is usual in the 1995 Act, para. 5 makes separate provision for formal validity and for self-evidencing status (or "probativity"). The requirements for formal validity are modelled on the equivalent provisions for companies. By subpara. (2) (read together with ss.2(1) and 7(1)) a document is formally valid if it is subscribed (i) by a member of the body's governing board or, if there is no board, a member of the body, or (ii) by the secretary, or (iii) by an authorised person. By (i) is meant a director or the equivalent. "Governing board" is defined in s.12(1) to mean any governing body, however described. In relation to (iii), a person may be authorised expressly or impliedly, and the authorisation may be a general one or it may be confined to a particular deed: see s.12(1) (definition of "authorised"). There appears to be no requirement that the authorisation be in writing, but in practice the grantee of a deed executed by a body corporate will usually wish to be reassured by some appropriate written evidence.

Self-evidencing (or "probativity") is regulated by s.3, but with the modifications contained in subparas. (5) and (6). There are two possible routes to probativity. Either the subscription of the authorised signatory is attested by the signature of a single witness, or the deed is sealed with the common seal: see s.3(1) and (1A). The rules on attestation are the standard ones set out in s.3. The rules on sealing are (i) that the document is sealed by a person with authority to do so, and (ii) that it is sealed on the date on which it was subscribed by the authorised signatory: see s.3(4)(h). The presumption of valid execution conferred by s.3(1) is qualified, as in the case of companies, by a declaration (s.3(1B)) that there is no presumption as to the authority of the signatory to sign. See further the discussion of this issue in the context of para. 3 (above). This has the important implication for practice that a grantee or other person relying on a deed executed by a body corporate is likely to require evidence as to authority. A drafting point is that the presumption is stated as being one of subscription by the authorised signatory *and* by the body corporate, and not just (as in the case of the parallel provision for companies in para. 3) by the body corporate.

Subparagraphs (7) and (8) insert equivalent modifications into para. 1 of Sched. 1, which is itself largely a re-statement of s.3 in the context of post-subscription alterations.

Ministers of the Crown and office-holders

6.—(1) Except where an enactment expressly provides otherwise, where a granter of a document is a Minister or an office-holder, the document is signed by the Minister or office-holder if it is signed—

(a) by him personally; or

(b) in a case where by virtue of any enactment or rule of law a document by a Minister may be signed by an officer of his or by any other Minister, by that officer or by that other Minister as the case may be; or

(c) in a case where by virtue of any enactment or rule of law a document by an office-holder may be signed by an officer of his, by that officer; or

(d) by any other person authorised to sign the document on his behalf.

(2) For the purposes of the signing of a document under this paragraph, a person purporting to sign—

(a) as an officer as mentioned in sub-paragraph (1)(b) or (1)(c) above;

(b) as another Minister as mentioned in sub-paragraph (1)(b) above;

(c) as a person authorised as mentioned in sub-paragraph (1)(d) above,

shall be presumed to be the officer, other Minister or authorised person, as the case may be.

(3) Sub-paragraphs (1) and (2) of this paragraph are without prejudice to section 3 of and Schedule 1 to the Ministers of the Crown Act 1975.

(4) Sub-paragraphs (1) to (3) of this paragraph apply in relation to the signing of an alteration made to a document as they apply in relation to the signing of a document.

(5) Where a granter of a document is a Minister or office-holder, section 3 of and Schedule 1 to this Act shall have effect subject to the modifications set out in sub-paragraphs (6) and (7) below.

(6) For section 3(1) there shall be substituted the following subsections—

"(1) Subject to subsections (1A) to (7) below, where—

(a) a document bears to have been subscribed—

(i) by a Minister or, in a case where by virtue of any enactment or rule of law a document by a Minister may be signed by an officer of his or by any other Minister, by that officer or by that other Minister; or

(ii) by an office-holder or, in a case where by virtue of any enactment or rule of law a document by an office-holder may be signed by an officer of his, by that officer; or

(iii) by any other person bearing to have been authorised to subscribe the document on behalf of the Minister or office-holder;

(b) the document bears to have been signed by a person as a witness of the subscription mentioned in paragraph (a) above and to state the name and address of the witness; and

(c) nothing in the document, or in the testing clause or its equivalent, indicates—

(i) that it was not subscribed as it bears to have been subscribed; or

(ii) that it was not validly witnessed for any reason specified in paragraphs (a) to (e) of subsection (4) below,

the document shall be presumed to have been subscribed by the officer, other Minister or authorised person and by the Minister or office-holder, as the case may be.

(1A) For the purposes of subsection (1)(b) above, the name and address of the witness may bear to be stated in the document itself or in the testing clause or its equivalent.".

(7) For paragraph 1(1) of Schedule 1 there shall be substituted the following sub-paragraphs—

"(1) Subject to sub-paragraphs (1A) to (7) below, where—

(a) an alteration to a document bears to have been signed by—

(i) a Minister or, in a case where by virtue of any enactment or rule of law a document by a Minister may be signed by an officer of his or by any other Minister, by that officer or by that other Minister; or

(ii) an office-holder or, in a case where by virtue of any enactment or rule of law a document by an office-holder may be signed by an officer of his, by that officer; or

(iii) any other person bearing to have been authorised to sign the alteration on behalf of the Minister or office-holder;

(b) the alteration bears to have been signed by a person as a witness of the signature mentioned in paragraph (a) above and to state the name and address of the witness; and

(c) nothing in the document or alteration, or in the testing clause or its equivalent, indicates—

(i) that the alteration was not signed as it bears to have been signed; or

(ii) that the alteration was not validly witnessed for any reason specified in paragraphs (a) to (e) of sub-paragraph (4) below,

the alteration shall be presumed to have been signed by the officer, other Minister or authorised person and by the Minister or office-holder, as the case may be.

(1A) For the purposes of sub-paragraph (1)(b) above, the name and address of the witness may bear to be stated in the alteration itself or in the testing clause or its equivalent.".

GENERAL NOTE

The final paragraph of Sched. 2 provides for execution by Ministers of the Crown and office-holders. A Minister of the Crown is a holder of an office in Her Majesty's Government in the U.K. (Ministers of the Crown Act 1975, s.8(1), incorporated by s.12(1)), for example the Secretary of State for Scotland or the Lord Advocate. An office-holder (s.12(1)) includes the registrar of companies and is the holder of an office created or continued in existence by a Public General Act of Parliament, or the holder of an office the remuneration in respect of which is paid out of money provided by Parliament, for example the Chairman of the Scottish Law Commission.

The previous rules as to execution, where they were not actually uncertain, were drafted with English law in mind and were difficult to interpret for Scotland. See Scot. Law Com. No. 112, paras. 6.72 ff. Paragraph 6 now provides a uniform and simple set of rules which fit into the wider framework of the 1995 Act.

Separate provision is made for formal validity and for self-evidencing status (or "probativity"). The requirements for formal validity (subpara. (1), read together with ss.2(1) and 7(1)) are subscription either by the Minister or office-holder in person or by a person authorised to sign on his behalf (including an officer authorised by statute or common law). A person who signs on behalf of a Minister or office-holder is presumed to have authority to do so (subpara. (2)). The practical effect of the presumption is to relieve a grantee or other person relying on a deed of the need to inquire into authority to act.

Self-evidencing ("or probativity") is regulated by s.3, but with the modifications contained in subpara. (6). As usual, probativity is achieved by the attestation of a single witness (s.3(1)(b)); but, unlike some of the other cases provided for in Sched. 2, sealing is not available as an alternative. The terms of s.3(1)(a)(i) and (ii) should be noted: a deed purportedly executed by an officer acting under the authority of statute or common law cannot be relied upon as probative without first verifying the existence of the statute or the rule of common law.

Subparagraph (7) inserts equivalent modifications into para. 1 of Sched. 1, which is itself largely a re-statement of s.3 as modified for post-subscription alterations.

Section 9(3)   SCHEDULE 3

MODIFICATIONS OF THIS ACT IN RELATION TO SUBSCRIPTION OR SIGNING BY RELEVANT PERSON UNDER SECTION 9

1. For any reference to the subscription or signing of a document by a granter there shall be substituted a reference to such subscription or signing by a relevant person under section 9(1).

2. For section 3(1) there shall be substituted the following subsection—

"(1) Subject to subsections (2) to (6) below, where—

(a) a document bears to have been subscribed by a relevant person with the authority of a granter of it;

(b) the document, or the testing clause or its equivalent, states that the document was read to that granter by the relevant person before such subscription or states that it was not so read because the granter made a declaration that he did not wish him to do so;

(c) the document bears to have been signed by a person as a witness of the relevant person's subscription and the document, or the testing clause or its equivalent, bears to state the name and address of the witness; and

(d) nothing in the document, or in the testing clause or its equivalent, indicates—
　　　　(i) that it was not subscribed by the relevant person as it bears to have been so subscribed;
　　　　(ii) that the statement mentioned in paragraph (b) above is incorrect; or
　　　　(iii) that it was not validly witnessed for any reason specified in paragraphs (a) to (e) of subsection (4) below (as modified by paragraph 4 of Schedule 3 to this Act),
the document shall be presumed to have been subscribed by the relevant person and the statement so mentioned shall be presumed to be correct.".

3. In section 3(3) for the words "subsection (1)(b)" there shall be substituted the words "subsection (1)(c)".

4. For section 3(4) there shall be substituted the following subsection—
"(4) Where, in any proceedings relating to a document in which a question arises as to a relevant person's subscription on behalf of a granter under section 9(1) of this Act, it is established—
(a) that a signature bearing to be the signature of the witness of the relevant person's subscription is not such a signature, whether by reason of forgery or otherwise;
(b) that the person who signed the document as the witness of the relevant person's subscription is a person who is named in the document as a granter of it;
(c) that the person who signed the document as the witness of the relevant person's subscription, at the time of signing—
　　　　(i) did not know the granter on whose behalf the relevant person had so subscribed;
　　　　(ii) was under the age of 16 years; or
　　　　(iii) was mentally incapable of acting as a witness;
(d) that the person who signed the document, purporting to be the witness of the relevant person's subscription, did not see him subscribe it;
(dd) that the person who signed the document as the witness of the relevant person's subscription did not witness the granting of authority by the granter concerned to the relevant person to subscribe the document on his behalf or did not witness the reading of the document to the granter by the relevant person or the declaration that the granter did not wish him to do so;
(e) that the person who signed the document as the witness of the relevant person's subscription did not sign the document after him or that such subscription and signature were not one continuous process;
(f) that the name or address of such a witness was added after the document was founded on or registered as mentioned in subsection (3)(a) above or is erroneous in any material respect; or
(g) in the case of a testamentary document consisting of more than one sheet, that a signature on any sheet bearing to be the signature of the relevant person is not such a signature, whether by reason of forgery or otherwise,
then, for the purposes of those proceedings, there shall be no presumption that the document has been subscribed by the relevant person on behalf of the granter concerned.".

5. In section 3(6) the words "or acknowledgement" in both places where they occur shall be omitted.

6. Section 3(7) shall be omitted.

7. For section 4(1) there shall be substituted the following subsection—
"(1) Where—
(a) a document bears to have been subscribed by a relevant person under section 9(1) of this Act on behalf of a granter of it; but
(b) there is no presumption under section 3 of this Act (as modified by paragraph 2 of Schedule 3 to this Act) that the document has been subscribed by that person or that the procedure referred to section 3(1)(b) of this Act as so modified was followed,
then, if the court, on an application being made to it by any person who has an interest in the document, is satisfied that the document was so subscribed by the relevant person with the authority of the granter and that the relevant person read the document to the granter before subscription or did not so read it because the granter declared that he did not wish him to do so, it shall—
　　　　(i) cause the document to be endorsed with a certificate to that effect; or
　　　　(ii) where the document has already been registered in the Books of Council and Session or in sheriff court books, grant decree to that effect.".

8. At the end of section 4(5)(a) there shall be added the following words—
"and that the procedure referred to in section 3(1)(b) of this Act as modified by paragraph 2 of Schedule 3 to this Act was followed.".

9. For paragraph 1(1) of Schedule 1 there shall be substituted the following sub-paragraph—

"(1) Subject to sub-paragraphs (2) to (6) below, where—

(a) an alteration to a document bears to have been signed by a relevant person with the authority of a granter of the document;

(b) the document or alteration, or the testing clause or its equivalent, states that the alteration was read to that granter by the relevant person before such signature or states that the alteration was not so read because the granter made a declaration that he did not wish him to do so;

(c) the alteration bears to have been signed by a person as a witness of the relevant person's signature and the alteration, or the testing clause or its equivalent, bears to state the name and address of the witness; and

(d) nothing in the document or alteration, or in the testing clause or its equivalent, indicates—

(i) that the alteration was not signed by the relevant person as it bears to have been so signed;

(ii) that the statement mentioned in paragraph (b) above is incorrect; or

(iii) that the alteration was not validly witnessed for any reason specified in paragraphs (a) to (e) of sub-paragraph (4) below (as modified by paragraph 11 of Schedule 3 to this Act),

the alteration shall be presumed to have been signed by the relevant person and the statement so mentioned shall be presumed to be correct.". ·

10. In paragraph 1(3) of Schedule 1 for the words "sub-paragraph (1)(b)" there shall be substituted the words "sub-paragraph (1)(c)".

11. For paragraph 1(4) of Schedule 1 there shall be substituted the following sub-paragraph—

"(4) Where, in any proceedings relating to an alteration to a document in which a question arises as to a relevant person's signature on behalf of a granter under section 9(1) of this Act, it is established—

(a) that a signature bearing to be the signature of the witness of the relevant person's signature is not such a signature, whether by reason of forgery or otherwise;

(b) that the person who signed the alteration as the witness of the relevant person's signature is a person who is named in the document as a granter of it;

(c) that the person who signed the alteration as the witness of the relevant person's signature, at the time of signing—

(i) did not know ⸱he granter on whose behalf the relevant person had so signed;

(ii) was under the age of 16 years; or

(iii) was mentally incapable of acting as a witness;

(d) that the person who signed the alteration, purporting to be the witness of the relevant person's signature, did not see him sign it;

(dd) that the person who signed the alteration as the witness of the relevant person's signature did not witness the granting of authority by the granter concerned to the relevant person to sign the alteration on his behalf or did not witness the reading of the alteration to the granter by the relevant person or the declaration that the granter did not wish him to do so;

(e) that the person who signed the alteration as the witness of the relevant person's signature did not sign the alteration after him or that the signing of the alteration by the granter and the witness was not one continuous process;

(f) that the name or address of such a witness was added after the alteration was founded on or registered as mentioned in sub-paragraph (3)(a) above or is erroneous in any material respect; or

(g) in the case of an alteration to a testamentary document consisting of more than one sheet, that a signature on any sheet of the alteration bearing to be the signature of the relevant person is not such a signature, whether by reason of forgery or otherwise,

then, for the purposes of those proceedings, there shall be no presumption that the alteration has been signed by the relevant person on behalf of the granter concerned.".

12. In paragraph 1(6) of Schedule 1 the words "or the acknowledgement of his signature" and the words "or acknowledgement" shall be omitted.

13. Paragraph 1(7) of Schedule 1 shall be omitted.

14. For paragraph 2(1) of Schedule 1 there shall be substituted the following sub-paragraph—

"(1) Where—

(a) an alteration to a document bears to have been signed by a relevant person under section 9(1) of this Act on behalf of a granter of the document; but

(b) there is no presumption under paragraph 1 of Schedule 1 to this Act (as modified by paragraph 9 of Schedule 3 to this Act) that the alteration has been signed by that

person or that the procedure referred to in paragraph 1(1)(b) of Schedule 1 to this Act as so modified was followed,
then, if the court, on an application being made to it by any person who has an interest in the document, is satisfied that the alteration was so signed by the relevant person with the authority of the granter and that the relevant person read the alteration to the granter before signing or did not so read it because the granter declared that he did not wish him to do so, it shall—
>   (i) cause the document to be endorsed with a certificate to that effect; or
>   (ii) where the document has already been registered in the Books of Council and Session or in sheriff court books, grant decree to that effect.".
15. At the end of paragraph 2(5)(a) of Schedule 1 there shall be added the following words—
"and that the procedure referred to in paragraph 1(1)(b) of Schedule 1 to this Act as modified by paragraph 9 of Schedule 3 to this Act was followed.".

DEFINITIONS
"alteration": s.12(1).
"authorised": s.12(1).
"decree": s.12(1).
"document": s.12(1).
"relevant person": s.9(6).
"signed by a witness": s.7(5).
"subscription": s.7(1).

GENERAL NOTE
Schedule 3 re-enacts, with modifications appropriate to notarial execution, the following provisions of the Act, namely (i) s.3 (paras. 2–6), (ii) s.4 (paras. 7 and 8), and (iii) Sched. 1 (paras. 9–15).

Para. 1
A "relevant person" is a notary or other person signing on behalf of a granter under s.9 of the Act. This is a general substitution of notary for granter, comparable to the equivalent provision for attorneys (s.12(2)). It has the merit of allowing the remaining paragraphs of Sched. 3 to be less extensive than would otherwise have been necessary.

Paras. 2–6
These paragraphs re-enact s.3 (presumption of valid execution by attestation) with modifications for the purposes of notarial execution. The main changes are as follows.
So far as patent factors are concerned, there are two additional requirements to be met. First, the document must bear to be subscribed by a notary with the authority of a granter of it (s.3(1)(a)). Secondly, the document or its testing clause must contain a statement that the document was read to the granter or that such reading was dispensed with (s.3(1)(b)). It is not clear whether the first requirement is satisfied merely by the fact of a notary appearing to have subscribed, or whether the document or testing clause must contain some firm statement of his authority to do so. It will be noted that, in contrast to the second requirement, no reference is made to the need for a statement. However, prudence suggests that the testing clause should state that the notary acted with the granter's authority, and this is the formulation adopted in the model testing clause suggested by the Scottish Law Commission (Scot. Law Com. No. 112, p. 194).
The changes in the latent factors are concerned with the event which is being witnessed. A notary is not permitted merely to acknowledge his subscription to the witness. Instead the witness must attest to three distinct events, namely (i) the giving of authority by the granter to the notary, (ii) the reading of the document or the dispensing with such a reading, and (iii) the subscription by the notary: see s.3(4)(d) and (dd).
It is not clear that all three of the witnessed events are covered by presumption which is earned by the use of the witness. Section 3(1) states that "the document shall be presumed to have been subscribed by the relevant person and the statement so mentioned [*i.e.* as to the document having been read or the reading dispensed with] shall be presumed to be correct". That is two presumptions and not three. The second presumption is the equivalent of witnessed event (ii). The first presumption clearly covers witnessed event (iii). However, it is far from clear that it covers event (i) also, even in the slightly extended form in which the presumption is found in s.3(4) ("subscribed by the relevant person *on behalf of the granter concerned*"). If event (i) is not covered, then there is no presumption as to the authority of the notary to act, and a person seeking to rely on a notarially executed document would bear the onus of establishing the existence of such authority.

Paras. 7 and 8

These paragraphs re-enact s.4 (presumption of valid execution by court docquet) with such modifications as are necessary for the purposes of notarial execution. The modifications follow the same pattern as the modifications to s.3, just discussed. Thus the court in s.4 (like the witness in s.3) has to be satisfied as to three events, namely (i) the giving of authority by the granter to the notary, (ii) the reading of the document or the dispensing with such a reading, and (iii) the subscription by the notary: see s.4(1). However, despite the fact that the court is then directed to endorse a certificate "to that effect", the actual presumption conferred by the certificate (s.4(5)(a)) is in similar terms to the presumption achieved by attestation under s.3(1) and does not make clear whether or not it extends to the notary's authority to act (*i.e.* to event (i)).

Paras. 9–15

These paragraphs re-enact Sched. 1 (presumptions of valid execution in relation to post-subscription alterations) with modifications for the purposes of notarial execution. Schedule 1 is itself a re-enactment of ss.3 and 4 of the Act with modifications for the purposes of the execution of post-subscription alterations.

More specifically, paras. 9–13 of Sched. 3 re-enact para. 1 of Sched. 1, which in turn re-enacts s.3; and paras. 14 and 15 of Sched. 3 re-enact para. 2 of Sched. 1, which in turn re-enacts s.4. The modifications made by these paragraphs are substantially the same as the modifications made (directly) to ss.3 and 4 by paras. 2–8 of Sched. 3.

SCHEDULE 4

MINOR AND CONSEQUENTIAL AMENDMENTS

General adaptation

1.—(1) Any reference in any other enactment to a probative document shall, in relation to a document executed after the commencement of this Act, be construed as a reference to a document in relation to which section 6(2) of this Act applies.

(2) For the purposes of any enactment—

(a) providing for a document to be executed by a body corporate by affixing its common seal; or

(b) referring (in whatever terms) to a document so executed,

a document signed or subscribed by or on behalf of the body corporate in accordance with the provisions of the Requirements of Writing (Scotland) Act 1995 shall have effect as if so executed.

Specific enactments

Lands Clauses Consolidation (Scotland) Act 1845

2. In Schedules (A) and (B) to the Lands Clauses Consolidation (Scotland) Act 1845 at the end of each of the forms there shall be added—

"Note - Subscription of the document by the granter of it will be sufficient for the document to be formally valid, but witnessing of it may be necessary or desirable for other purposes (see the Requirements of Writing (Scotland) Act 1995).".

Infeftment Act 1845

3. In Schedules (A) and (B) to the Infeftment Act 1845 for the words from "In witness" to the end there shall be substituted the words "Testing clause+

+Note - Subscription of the document by the granter of it will be sufficient for the document to be formally valid, but witnessing of it may be necessary or desirable for other purposes (see the Requirements of Writing (Scotland) Act 1995).".

Commissioners Clauses Act 1847

4. At the end of section 59 of the Commissioners Clauses Act 1847 there shall be added the following subsection—

"(2) This section shall apply to Scotland as if—

(a) for the words from "by deed under" to "recorded" there were substituted the words—

"by a document—
(a) if they are a corporation, subscribed in accordance with section 7 of, and paragraph 5 of Schedule 2 to, the Requirements of Writing (Scotland) Act 1995;
(b) if they are not a corporation, subscribed in accordance with the said section 7 by the commissioners or any two of them acting by the authority of and on behalf of the commissioners;
and a document so subscribed, followed by infeftment duly recorded,";
(b) for the words from "under such" to "acting" there were substituted the word "subscribed".".

5. At the end of section 75 of that Act there shall be added the following subsection—
"(2) This section shall apply to Scotland as if for the words "by deed" to "five of them" there were substituted the words—
"in a document—
(a) which is duly stamped;
(b) in which the consideration is truly stated; and
(c) which is subscribed, if the commissioners—
(i) are a corporation, in accordance with section 7 of, and paragraph 5 of Schedule 2 to, the Requirements of Writing (Scotland) Act 1995;
(ii) are not a corporation, in accordance with the said section 7 by the commissioners or any five of them,".".

6. At the end of section 77 of that Act there shall be added the following subsection—
"(2) This section shall apply to Scotland as if for the words "by deed duly stamped" there were substituted the words "in a document which is duly stamped and which is subscribed in accordance with the Requirements of Writing (Scotland) Act 1995.".".

7. In Schedule (B) to that Act—
(a) the words from "or, if the deed" to "case may be," are hereby repealed;
(b) at the end there shall be added the words "[or, if the document is granted under Scots law, insert testing clause+]
+Note - As regards a document granted under Scots law, subscription of it by the granter will be sufficient for the document to be formally valid, but witnessing of it may be necessary or desirable for other purposes (see the Requirements of Writing (Scotland) Act 1995).".

8. In Schedule (C) to that Act—
(a) the words from "[or, if the deed" to "Scotland,]" are hereby repealed;
(b) at the end there shall be added the words "[or, if the document is granted under Scots law, insert testing clause+]
+Note - As regards a document granted under Scots law, subscription of it by the granter will be sufficient for the document to be formally valid, but witnessing of it may be necessary or desirable for other purposes (see the Requirements of Writing (Scotland) Act 1995).".

Entail Amendment Act 1848

9. In section 50 of the Entail Amendment Act 1848 for the word "tested" there shall be substituted the word "subscribed".

10. In the Schedule to that Act—
(a) the words "and of the witnesses subscribing," are hereby repealed;
(b) for the words from "In witness whereof" to the end there shall be substituted the words "Testing clause+
+Note - Subscription of the document by the heir of entail in possession and the notary public will be sufficient for the document to be formally valid, but witnessing of it may be necessary or desirable for other purposes (see the Requirements of Writing (Scotland) Act 1995).".

Ordnance Board Transfer Act 1855

11. At the end of section 5 of the Ordnance Board Transfer Act 1855 there shall be added the following subsection—
"(2) This section shall apply to Scotland as if for the words from "signing" to "his deed" there were substituted the words "subscribing it in accordance with the Requirements of Writing (Scotland) Act 1995".

Registration of Leases (Scotland) Act 1857

12. In Schedule (A) to the Registration of Leases (Scotland) Act 1857 for the words "in common form" there shall be substituted—
"+
+Note - Subscription of the document by the granter of it will be sufficient for the docu-

ment to be formally valid, but witnessing of it may be necessary or desirable for other purposes (see the Requirements of Writing (Scotland) Act 1995).".

13. In each of Schedules (B), (C), (D), (F), (G) and (H) to that Act after the words "Testing clause" there shall be inserted "+

+Note - Subscription of the document by the granter of it will be sufficient for the document to be formally valid, but witnessing of it may be necessary or desirable for other purposes (see the Requirements of Writing (Scotland) Act 1995).".

Transmission of Moveable Property (Scotland) Act 1862

14. In each of Schedules A and B to the Transmission of Moveable Property (Scotland) Act 1862 for the words from "In witness whereof" to the end there shall be substituted the words "Testing clause+

+Note - Subscription of the document by the granter of it will be sufficient for the document to be formally valid, but witnessing of it may be necessary or desirable for other purposes (see the Requirements of Writing (Scotland) Act 1995).".

15. In Schedule C to that Act for the words from "and D" to the end there shall be substituted the words "Testing clause".

Titles to Land Consolidation (Scotland) Act 1868

16. In Schedule (B) nos. 1 and 2 and (AA) no. 3 to the Titles to Land Consolidation (Scotland) Act 1868 for the words from "In witness whereof" to "usual form]" there shall be substituted the words "Testing clause+

+Note - Subscription of the document by the granter of it will be sufficient for the document to be formally valid, but witnessing of it may be necessary or desirable for other purposes (see the Requirements of Writing (Scotland) Act 1995).".

17. In Schedules (J), (BB) no. 1, (CC) nos. 1 and 2 and (OO) to that Act for the words from "In witness whereof" to the end there shall be substituted the words "Testing clause+

+Note - Subscription of the document by the granter of it will be sufficient for the document to be formally valid, but witnessing of it may be necessary or desirable for other purposes (see the Requirements of Writing (Scotland) Act 1995).".

18. In Schedule (FF) no. 1 to that Act—
(a) for the words from "In witness whereof" to "usual form]" there shall be substituted the words "Testing clause+";
(b) at the end there shall be added "+ Subscription of the document by the granter of it will be sufficient for the document to be formally valid, but witnessing of it may be necessary or desirable for other purposes (see the Requirements of Writing (Scotland) Act 1995).".

19. In Schedule (GG) to that Act—
(a) for the words from "In witness whereof" to "I K Witness" there shall be substituted the words "Testing clause+";
(b) after Note (b) there shall be inserted—
"+ (c) Subscription of the document by the granter of it will be sufficient for the document to be formally valid, but witnessing of it may be necessary or desirable for other purposes (see the Requirements of Writing (Scotland) Act 1995).".

20. In Schedule (NN) to that Act—
(a) for the words from "In witness whereof" to "G H Witness" there shall be substituted the words "Testing clause+";
(b) at the end there shall be added—
"+Subscription of the document by the granter if it will be sufficient for the document to be formally valid, but witnessing of it may be necessary or desirable for other purposes (see the Requirements of Writing (Scotland) Act 1995).".

Conveyancing (Scotland) Act 1874

21. In Schedules C, F, L nos. 1 and 2 and N to the Conveyancing (Scotland) Act 1874 for the words "In witness whereof [testing clause]" there shall be substituted the words "Testing clause+

+Note - Subscription of the document by the granter of it will be sufficient for the document to be formally valid, but witnessing of it may be necessary or desirable for other purposes (see the Requirements of Writing (Scotland) Act 1995).".

22. In Schedule G to that Act—

(a) for the words "In witness whereof [testing clause]" there shall be substituted the words "Testing clause+";

(b) at the end of the Note there shall be added—

"+Subscription of the document by the granter of it will be sufficient for the document to be formally valid, but witnessing of it may be necessary or desirable for other purposes (see the Requirements of Writing (Scotland) Act 1995).".

23. In Schedule M to that Act for the words "and add testing clause]" there shall be substituted the words "Testing clause+]

+Note - Subscription of the document by the granter of it will be sufficient for the document to be formally valid, but witnessing of it may be necessary or desirable for other purposes (see the Requirements of Writing (Scotland) Act 1995).".

Colonial Stock Act 1877

24. At the end of subsection (1) of section 4 of the Colonial Stock Act 1877 there shall be added the words "or, in relation to Scotland, subscribed in accordance with section 7 of the Requirements of Writing (Scotland) Act 1995.".

25. At the end of section 6 of that Act there shall be added the following subsection—

"(2) This section shall have effect in relation to Scotland as if for the words from "given" to "attested" there were substituted the words "subscribed by the person not under disability in accordance with section 7 of the Requirements of Writing (Scotland) Act 1995.".".

Colonial Stock Act 1892

26. After subsection (2) of the Colonial Stock Act 1892 there shall be added the following subsection—

"(2A) This section shall have effect in relation to Scotland as if—

(a) in subsection (1) for the words from "deed according" to "parties" there were substituted the words "a document in the form set out in the Schedule to this Act or to the like effect and the document as executed";

(b) in subsection (2) for the words "by deed" there were substituted the words "under this section"."

27. At the end of the Schedule to that Act there shall be added the words "[If the document is granted under the law of Scotland, for the words from "Witness our hands" to the end substitute "[Testing clause+

+Note - Subscription of the document by the granter of it will be sufficient for the document to be formally valid, but witnessing of it may be necessary or desirable for other purposes (see the Requirements of Writing (Scotland) Act 1995).]"]".

Feudal Casualties (Scotland) Act 1914

28. In each of Schedules B and C to the Feudal Casualties (Scotland) Act 1914—

(a) for the words "In witness whereof" there shall be substituted the words "Testing clause"; and

(b) at the end of the Note there shall be added the words "Subscription of the document by the granter of it will be sufficient for the document to be formally valid, but witnessing of it may be necessary or desirable for other purposes (see the Requirements of Writing (Scotland) Act 1995).".

Trusts (Scotland) Act 1921

29. In Schedule A to the Trusts (Scotland) Act 1921—

(a) for the words "(To be attested)" there shall be substituted the words "Testing clause+";

(b) at the end there shall be added—

"+Note - Subscription of the document by the granter of it will be sufficient for the document to be formally valid, but witnessing of it may be necessary or desirable for other purposes (see the Requirements of Writing (Scotland) Act 1995).".

30. In Schedule B to that Act for the words "(To be attested)" there shall be substituted the words "Testing clause+

+Note - Subscription of the document by the granter or granters of it will be sufficient for the document to be formally valid, but witnessing of it may be necessary or desirable for other purposes (see the Requirements of Writing (Scotland) Act 1995).".

Conveyancing (Scotland) Act 1924

31. In Schedule B to the Conveyancing (Scotland) Act 1924—
(a) in forms nos. 1 to 6 for the words "[To be attested]" there shall be substituted the words "Testing clause+";
(b) at the end of the Notes there shall be added—
"+Note 8 - Subscription of the document by the notary public (or law agent) on behalf of the granter of it will be sufficient for the document to be formally valid, but witnessing of it may be necessary or desirable for other purposes (see the Requirements of Writing (Scotland) Act 1995).".

32. In Schedule E to that Act for the words "[To be attested]" there shall be substituted the words "Testing clause+
+Note - Subscription of the document by the granter of it will be sufficient for the document to be formally valid, but witnessing of it may be necessary or desirable for other purposes (see the Requirements of Writing (Scotland) Act 1995).".

33. In Schedules G and H to that Act for the words "[to be attested]" there shall be substituted the words "Testing clause+
+Note - Subscription of the document by the granter of it will be sufficient for the document to be formally valid, but witnessing of it may be necessary or desirable for other purposes (see the Requirements of Writing (Scotland) Act 1995)".

34. In Schedule K to that Act—
(a) in forms nos 1 to 7 for the words "[To be attested]" there shall be substituted the words "Testing clause+";
(b) at the end of the notes there shall be added—
"+Note 5 - Subscription of the document by the granter of it will be sufficient for the document to be formally valid, but witnessing of it may be necessary or desirable for other purposes (see the Requirements of Writing (Scotland) Act 1995).".

35. In Schedule L to that Act, in form 4, for the words "[To be attested]" there shall be substituted the words "Testing clause+
+Note - Subscription of the document by the notary public or law agent on behalf of the granter of it will be sufficient for the document to be formally valid, but witnessing of it may be necessary or desirable for other purposes (see the Requirements of Writing (Scotland) Act 1995).".

36. In Schedule N to that Act for the words "[To be attested]" there shall be substituted the words "Testing clause+
+Note - Subscription of the document by the granter of it will be sufficient for the document to be formally valid, but witnessing of it may be necessary or desirable for other purposes (see the Requirements of Writing (Scotland) Act 1995).".

Long Leases (Scotland) Act 1954

37. In the Fourth Schedule to the Long Leases (Scotland) Act 1954—
(a) for the words "[To be attested]" there shall be substituted the words - "Testing clause+";
(b) at the end of the Notes there shall be added—
"+4 Subscription of the feu contract by the parties to it will be sufficient for the contract to be formally valid, but witnessing of it may be necessary or desirable for other purposes (see the Requirements of Writing (Scotland) Act 1995).".

Succession (Scotland) Act 1964

38. At the end of section 21 of the Succession (Scotland) Act 1964 there shall be added the following subsection—
"(2) This section shall not apply to a testamentary document executed after the commencement of the Requirements of Writing (Scotland) Act 1995.".

39. After section 21 of that Act there shall be inserted the following section—

"Evidence as to testamentary documents in commissary proceedings
21A. Confirmation of an executor to property disposed of in a testamentary document executed after the commencement of the Requirements of Writing (Scotland) Act 1995 shall not be granted unless the formal validity of the document is governed—
(a) by Scots law and the document is presumed under section 3 or 4 of that Act to have been subscribed by the granter so disposing of that property; or

    (b) by a law other than Scots law and the court is satisfied that the document is formally valid according to the law governing such validity.".

40. For section 32 of that Act there shall be substituted the following section—

"Certain testamentary dispositions to be formally valid

32.—(1) For the purpose of any question arising as to entitlement, by virtue of a testamentary disposition, to any relevant property or to any interest therein, the disposition shall be treated as valid in respect of the formalities of execution.

(2) Subsection (1) above is without prejudice to any right to challenge the validity of the testamentary disposition on the ground of forgery or on any other ground of essential invalidity.

(3) In this section "relevant property" means property disposed of in the testamentary disposition in respect of which—

    (a) confirmation has been granted; or

    (b) probate, letters of administration or other grant of representation—

        (i) has been issued, and has noted the domicile of the deceased to be, in England and Wales or Northern Ireland; or

        (ii) has been issued outwith the United Kingdom and had been sealed in Scotland under section 2 of the Colonial Probates Act 1892.".

41. In Schedule 1 to that Act for the words "[To be attested by two witnesses] [Signature of A B]" there shall be substituted the words "Testing clause+

    +Note - Subscription of the document by the granter of it will be sufficient for the document to be formally valid, but witnessing of it may be necessary or desirable for other purposes (see the Requirements of Writing (Scotland) Act 1995).".

Industrial and Provident Societies Act 1965

42. In Schedule 3 to the Industrial and Provident Societies Act 1965 in each of Forms C, D and E for the words from "Signed" to the end there shall be substituted the words "Testing clause+

    +Note - Subscription of the document by the granter of it will be sufficient for the document to be formally valid, but witnessing of it may be necessary or desirable for other purposes (see the Requirements of Writing (Scotland) Act 1995).".

43. In Schedule 4 to that Act, in Form C for the words from "Signed" to the end there shall be substituted the words "Testing clause+

    +Note - Subscription of the document by the cautioner will be sufficient for the document to be formally valid, but witnessing of it may be necessary or desirable for other purposes (see the Requirements of Writing (Scotland) Act 1995).".

Conveyancing and Feudal Reform (Scotland) Act 1970

44. In Schedule 2 to the Conveyancing and Feudal Reform (Scotland) Act 1970—

    (a) in forms A and B for the words "[To be attested]" there shall be substituted the words "Testing clause+";

    (b) at the end of the Notes there shall be added—

        "+Note 8 - Subscription of the document by the granter of it will be sufficient for the document to be formally valid, but witnessing of it may be necessary or desirable for other purposes (see the Requirements of Writing (Scotland) Act 1995).".

45. In Schedule 4 to that Act—

    (a) in form A and forms C to F for the words "[To be attested]" there shall be substituted the words "Testing clause+";

    (b) at the end of the Notes there shall be added—

        "+Note 7 - Subscription of the document by the granter of it, or in the case of form E the granter and the consenter to the variation, will be sufficient for the document to be formally valid, but witnessing of it may be necessary or desirable for other purposes (see the Requirements of Writing (Scotland) Act 1995).".

46. In Schedule 5 to that Act, in form D—

    (a) in nos 1 and 2 for the words "[To be attested]" there shall be substituted the words "Testing clause+";

    (b) at the end there shall be added—

        "+Note - Subscription of the document by the granter of it will be sufficient for the document to be formally valid, but witnessing of it may be necessary or desirable for other purposes (see the Requirements of Writing (Scotland) Act 1995).".

47. In Schedule 9 to that Act—

    (a) for the words "[To be attested]" there shall be substituted the words "Testing clause+";

    (b) at the end of the Notes there shall be added—

"+Note 4 - Subscription of the document by the granter of it will be sufficient for the document to be formally valid, but witnessing of it may be necessary or desirable for other purposes (see the Requirements of Writing (Scotland) Act 1995).".

Petroleum and Submarine Pipe-lines Act 1975

48. At the end of section 18(5)(b) of the Petroleum and Submarine Pipelines Act 1975 there shall be added the words "or, as respects Scotland, by an instrument subscribed by the Secretary of State and the licensee in accordance with the Requirements of Writing (Scotland) Act 1995.".

Patents Act 1977

49. In section 31(6) of the Patents Act 1977 for the words from "probative" to the end there shall be substituted the words "subscribed in accordance with the Requirements of Writing (Scotland) Act 1995.".

Oil and Gas (Enterprise) Act 1982

50. At the end of section 19(2) of the Oil and Gas (Enterprise) Act 1982 there shall be added the words "or, as respects Scotland, by an instrument subscribed by the Secretary of State and the licensee in accordance with the Requirements of Writing (Scotland) Act 1995.".

Companies Act 1985

51. For section 36B of the Companies Act 1985 there shall be substituted the following section—

"**Execution of documents by companies**
36B.—(1) Notwithstanding the provisions of any enactment, a company need not have a company seal.
(2) For the purposes of any enactment—
(a) providing for a document to be executed by a company by affixing its common seal; or
(b) referring (in whatever terms) to a document so executed,
a document signed or subscribed by or on behalf of the company in accordance with the provisions of the Requirements of Writing (Scotland) Act 1995 shall have effect as if so executed.
(3) In this section "enactment" includes an enactment contained in a statutory instrument.".
52. At the end of section 38 of that Act there shall be added the following subsection—
"(3) This section does not extend to Scotland.".
53. In section 39 of that Act—
(a) after subsection (2) there shall be inserted the following subsection—
"(2A) Subsection (2) does not extend to Scotland.";
(b) in subsection (3) after the words "common seal" there shall be inserted the words "or as respects Scotland by writing subscribed in accordance with the Requirements of Writing (Scotland) Act 1995".
54. Section 40 of that Act shall become subsection (1) of that section and at the end there shall be added the following subsection—
"(2) Nothing in this section shall affect the right of a company registered in Scotland to subscribe such securities and documents in accordance with the Requirements of Writing (Scotland) Act 1995.".
55. Section 186 of that Act shall become subsection (1) of that section and at the end there shall be added the following subsection—
"(2) Without prejudice to subsection (1), as respects Scotland a certificate specifying any shares held by a member and subscribed by the company in accordance with the Requirements of Writing (Scotland) Act 1995 is, unless the contrary is shown, sufficient evidence of his title to the shares.".
56. In section 188 of that Act in subsection (2) after the words "common seal" there shall be inserted the words "(or, in the case of a company registered in Scotland, subscribed in accordance with the Requirements of Writing (Scotland) Act 1995)".

Companies Consolidation (Consequential Provisions) Act 1985

57. At the end of section 11 of the Companies Consolidation (Consequential Provisions) Act 1985 there shall be added the following subsection—

"(3) The foregoing provisions of this section are without prejudice to the right of a company to subscribe such securities and documents in accordance with the Requirements of Writing (Scotland) Act 1995.".

Insolvency Act 1986

58. In section 53 of the Insolvency Act 1986—
(a) in subsection (1) for the words "a validly executed instrument in writing" there shall be substituted the words "an instrument subscribed in accordance with the Requirements of Writing (Scotland) Act 1995";
(b) for subsection (4) there shall be substituted the following subsection—
"(4) If the receiver is to be appointed by the holders of a series of secured debentures, the instrument of appointment may be executed on behalf of the holders of the floating charge by any person authorised by resolution of the debenture-holders to execute the instrument.".

Housing (Scotland) Act 1987

59. In section 53(1) of the Housing (Scotland) Act 1987 for the words from "probative" to the end there shall be substituted the words "subscribed by the parties in accordance with the Requirements of Writing (Scotland) Act 1995.".
60. In section 54(6) of that Act for the words "probative or holograph of the parties" there shall be substituted the words "subscribed by the parties in accordance with the Requirements of Writing (Scotland) Act 1995,".

GENERAL NOTE
Schedule 4 makes a number of consequential amendments to existing statutes. A very large number of these amendments fall into one of two categories.
The first of these is the alteration of statutory styles of conveyancing deeds (*e.g.* notices of title and standard securities) in order to conform with the methods of execution introduced by the Act. This involves (i) the substitution of "Testing clause" for the words "[to be attested]" or, in earlier deeds, "in witness whereof"; and (ii) the addition of a note in the following, perhaps rather laconic, terms: "Subscription of the document by the granter of it will be sufficient for the document to be formally valid, but witnessing of it may be necessary or desirable for other purposes (see the Requirements of Writing (Scotland) Act 1995.)". So far as (i) is concerned the deletion of the expression "in witness whereof" is designed partly to facilitate the new form of testing clause suggested by the Scottish Law Commission (see Scot. Law Com. No. 112, pp. 192–196) which eschews the traditional phrase in favour of "This document is signed and witnessed by …".
The second category of amendment is the replacement in particular cases of statutory provisions about execution of deeds with a reference to execution in terms of the 1995 Act. Usually this has the effect of reducing the level of formality required. The following paragraphs of Sched. 4 come into this category: paras. 4–8; 11; 24–5; 48–50; and 53–60. In a few cases, such as the Merchant Shipping Act 1894, s.24(2) (bill of sale of a registered ship), the decision was taken not to amend: see Scot. Law Com. No. 112, para. 7.16.
A small number of provisions do not fall within either general category and require separate comment.

Para. 1
This makes two general adaptations of existing enactments. (By s.12(1) an "enactment" includes a statutory instrument.)
First, "probative" is to mean the 1995 Act equivalent, which is a document presumed to be valid under either s.3 (attestation) or s.4 (court docquet). In the particular case of the Prescription and Limitation (Scotland) Act 1973, Sched. 5 repeals the references to "probative" in Sched. 1 to that Act, with the consequence that a deed will no longer fall under the 20-year negative prescription merely because it is attested.
Secondly, any provision requiring a document to be executed by a body corporate by affixing its common seal is to be satisfied by execution in accordance with the 1995 Act (which (see Sched. 2, para. 5(2)) does not require the use of a seal). A parallel provision in relation to companies is contained in para. 51 of this Schedule.

Paras. 38–40
These provisions make two important amendments to the Succession (Scotland) Act 1964 in relation to the formal validity of wills.
Paragraph 39 inserts into the 1964 Act a new s.21A, which makes it a precondition of confirmation of an executor that the will is presumed validly executed under either s.3 or s.4. In prac-

tice if the will is not attested (and so does not fall under s.3), the "setting up" of the will by affidavit evidence under s.4 will be carried out as part of the confirmation process itself. Parallel provision is made in respect of foreign wills. The new s.21A applies only to wills executed on or after August 1, 1995. For wills executed prior to that date, s.21 of the 1964 Act (on which s.21A is modelled) continues to apply (see para. 38).

Paragraph 40 inserts a new version of s.32 into the 1964 Act. Its effect is to allow wills on which confirmation (or certain foreign equivalents) has been obtained to be "treated as valid in respect of the formalities of execution", but subject to any right to challenge their validity on the ground of forgery or other essential invalidity. Given the qualification in relation to forgery, it is difficult to see how this provision confers more than is already conferred by s.3 or s.4 of the 1995 Act. After all, the principal ground on which a will, presumed to be validly subscribed under these sections, could be challenged would also be that the signature of the testator was forged. As a result of s.21A of the 1964 Act (inserted by para. 39) wills on which confirmation has been obtained already benefit from the presumption conferred by s.3 or s.4. If this analysis is correct, then the main role for s.32 will be in relation to the foreign equivalents of confirmation listed in subs. (3)(b).

Paras. 51–56

These make a number of consequential amendments to the Companies Act 1985. Most do no more than provide for execution of particular documents in accordance with the 1995 Act (but with the notable omission of the floating charge). Three are worthy of special mention.

Section 36B previously contained the rules for the execution of deeds by companies. The whole of s.36B is now repealed by para. 51 (and replaced by Sched. 2, para. 3 of the 1995 Act), except for subss. (5) and (6) which are retained in slightly modified form and re-numbered.

Paragraph 52 disapplies s.38 of the 1985 Act to Scotland. This is an issue on which minds have been changed more than once before. As originally enacted in 1985 it applied to Scotland. It was then disapplied as from July 31, 1990 by the Companies Act 1989, Sched. 17, para. 1(1) and (2), but promptly re-applied with effect from December 1, 1990 by the Law Reform (Miscellaneous Provisions) (Scotland) Act 1990, Sched. 8, para. 33(2). It is now disapplied once more with effect from August 1, 1995. However, the contents of s.38 are not as controversial as this turbulent legislative history might suggest. The section permits a company to appoint a person as attorney to execute deeds outside the U.K. Presumably the view has now been taken that such special provision is unnecessary having regard to the wide terms of the 1995 Act.

Finally, para. 54 amends s.40 of the 1985 Act to the effect of allowing a company registered in Scotland to subscribe share certificates in accordance with the 1995 Act.

Section 14(2)   SCHEDULE 5

Repeals

Chapter	Short title	Extent of repeal
1540 c. 37 (S.).	The Subscription of Deeds Act 1540.	The whole Act.
1579 c. 18 (S.).	The Subscription of Deeds Act 1579.	The whole Act.
1672 c. 47 (S.).	The Lyon King of Arms Act 1672.	The words from "And his Maiestie with consent" to "contraveiners heirof".
1681 c. 5 (S.).	The Subscription of Deeds Act 1681.	The whole Act.
1696 c. 15 (S.).	The Deeds Act 1696.	The whole Act.
1696 c. 25 (S.).	The Blank Bonds and Trusts Act 1696.	The whole Act.
1698 c. 4 (S.).	The Registration Act 1698.	The whole Act.
10 & 11 Vict. c. 16.	The Commissioners Clauses Act 1847.	In section 56, the words from "(that is to say,)" to "discharge the same" where they first occur. In Schedule (B), the words from "or, if the deed" to "case may be,". In Schedule (C), the words from "[or, if the deed" to "Scotland,]".

Chapter	Short title	Extent of repeal
11 & 12 Vict. c. 36.	The Entail Amendment Act 1848.	In the Schedule the words "and of the witnesses subscribing,".
19 & 20 Vict. c. 60.	The Mercantile Law Amendment Act, Scotland 1856.	Section 6.
31 & 32 Vict. c. 101.	The Titles to Land Consolidation (Scotland) Act 1868.	Sections 139 and 149.
37 & 38 Vict. c. 94.	The Conveyancing (Scotland) Act 1874.	Sections 38 to 41. Schedule I.
7 Edw. 7 c. 51.	The Sheriff Courts (Scotland) Act 1907.	In section 35 the words "either holograph or attested by one witness". In Schedule 1, paragraph 67 and in the Appendix in Form M the words from "If not holograph" to the end of the form.
4 & 5 Geo. 5 c. 48.	The Feudal Casualties (Scotland) Act 1914.	In section 8 the words "which need not be tested or holograph".
14 & 15 Geo. 5 c. 27.	The Conveyancing (Scotland) Act 1924.	Section 18. Schedule I.
23 & 24 Geo. 5 c. 44.	The Church of Scotland (Property and Endowments) (Amendment) Act 1933.	Section 13.
2 & 3 Geo. 6 c. 20.	The Reorganisation of Offices (Scotland) Act 1939.	In section 1(8) the words from "and any such" to the end.
1959 c. 40.	The Deer (Scotland) Act 1959.	In Schedule 1, paragraphs 12 and 13.
1963 c. 18.	The Stock Transfer Act 1963.	Section 2(4).
1965 c. 12.	The Industrial and Provident Societies Act 1965.	In section 34(5)(a), in the definition of "receipt" the words from "signed by two members" to "as such". Section 36.
1967 c. 10.	The Forestry Act 1967.	Section 39(5).
1968 c. 16.	The New Towns (Scotland) Act 1968.	In Schedule 2, paragraphs 10 and 11.
1970 c. 35.	The Conveyancing and Feudal Reform (Scotland) Act 1970.	Section 44.
1973 c. 52.	The Prescription and Limitation (Scotland) Act 1973.	Section 5(2). In Schedule 1, paragraphs 2(c), 3 and 4(b).
1973 c. 65.	The Local Government (Scotland) Act 1973.	Section 194, other than subsection (2). In Schedule 8, paragraph 5.
1978 c. 29.	The National Health Service (Scotland) Act 1978.	In section 79(1A) the words from "and where" to the end of the subsection. In Schedule 1, paragraphs 9 and 10. In Schedule 5, paragraphs 10 and 11.
1980 c. 46.	The Solicitors (Scotland) Act 1980.	In Schedule 1, paragraph 12.
1985 c. 6.	The Companies Act 1985.	In section 2(6) the words from "and that" to the end. In section 7(3)(c) the words from "(which attestation" to the end. Section 462(3).
1985 c. 16.	The National Heritage (Scotland) Act 1985.	In Schedule 1, paragraphs 8 and 19.
1986 c. 47.	The Legal Aid (Scotland) Act 1986.	In Schedule 1, paragraph 14.

Chapter	Short title	Extent of repeal
1988 c. 43.	The Housing (Scotland) Act 1988.	In Schedule 1, paragraphs 18 and 19.
1990 c. 40.	The Law Reform (Miscellaneous Provisions) (Scotland) Act 1990.	Section 72. Section 75(6). In Schedule 8, paragraph 33.
1990 c. 35.	The Enterprise and New Towns (Scotland) Act 1990.	In Schedule 1, paragraph 23.
1991 c. 28.	The Natural Heritage (Scotland) Act 1991.	In Schedule 1, paragraph 18.
1993 c. 44.	The Crofters (Scotland) Act 1993.	In Schedule 1, paragraphs 14 and 15.
1994 c. 39.	The Local Government etc. (Scotland) Act 1994.	In section 172(4), paragraph (h). In Schedule 3, paragraph 11. In Schedule 5, in Part II, paragraph 8. In Schedule 7, paragraph 17. In Schedule 12, paragraph 13. In Schedule 13, paragraph 92(60).

INDEX

References are to sections and Schedules

AGRICULTURAL TENANCIES ACT 1995*

(1995 c. 8)

Arrangement of Sections

Part I

General Provisions

Farm business tenancies

Part II

Rent Review Under Farm Business Tenancy

Part III

Compensation on Termination of Farm Business Tenancy

Tenant's entitlement to compensation

---

* Annotations by Della Evans, Partner, Burges Salmon, Solicitors, Bristol

An Act to make further provision with respect to tenancies which include agricultural land.   [9th May 1995]

PARLIAMENTARY DEBATES
   Hansard, H.L. Vol. 559, cols. 25, 485, 1089, 1112, 1166, 1205, Vol. 560, cols. 862, 884, 1258, 1279, Vol. 563, col. 1348. H.C. Vol. 254, col. 23, Vol. 258, col. 230.

INTRODUCTION AND GENERAL NOTE
   This Act reforms the law relating to the letting of agricultural land, providing an entirely new framework for the agricultural landlord and tenant relationship for lettings in England and Wales. The Act is not retrospective and will only apply to new lettings beginning (within the meaning of the Act) on or after September 1, 1995 when the Act comes into force.

Background
   Since 1875 there has been legislation regulating the relationship between landlords and tenants of agricultural land culminating in legislation which provided the tenant with, effectively, lifetime security of tenure. The high watermark of statutory interference with freedom of contract came in 1976 with the retrospective introduction of succession rights upon the death of a tenant of an agricultural holding (the Agriculture (Miscellaneous Provisions) Act 1976 (c. 55)), although automatic rights of succession were abolished in the Agricultural Holdings Act 1984 (c. 41) for lettings after July 12, 1984.
   The current agricultural holdings legislation, which will continue to apply to all existing lettings and to new lettings beginning before September 1, 1995, is the Agricultural Holdings Act 1986 (c. 5) which is an Act consolidating 10 previous Acts and following the scheme, so far as security of tenure is concerned, of the Agricultural Holdings Act 1948 (c. 63).
   Security of tenure under the 1986 Act is afforded by controls over both the length of, and the operation of, notices to quit served by the landlord in relation to annual periodic tenancies and the conversion of other types of tenancy and contractual licences conferring exclusive possession into annual periodic tenancies. If a 1986 Act tenant objects to the notice to quit and complies with the statutory requirements, the consent of the Agricultural Land Tribunal is necessary before a landlord can rely on the notice to quit save in very limited circumstances set out in Sched. 3 to the 1986 Act. In very many cases, in the absence of default by the tenant, the controls upon the operation of notices to quit have led to lifetime security of tenure for the tenant with a consequent depreciation in the value of the landlord's land by up to 50 per cent.

Whilst the security of tenure of the 1986 Act and its statutory predecessors achieved a great deal for tenants, there has been increasing reluctance on the part of landowners to let under the 1986 Act regime as a result of the lack of flexibility and their inability to regain vacant possession of the land. The figures set out in the Ministry of Agriculture, Food and Fisheries (MAFF) Consultation Paper on the Reform of Agricultural Tenancy Law (1991) show that whilst in 1910, 90 per cent of agricultural land was tenanted, that figure had fallen to 36 per cent by 1991 (see also *Agricultural Land Tenure in England and Wales*, Winter, Richardson, Short and Watkins, research by the Centre for Rural Studies, Cirencester (published by the RICS in 1990)).

A variety of alternative devices have been utilised by land owners and farmers to achieve the farming of agricultural land without security of tenure either utilising exceptions within the 1986 Act (for example short-term grazing agreements of less than one year), exploiting loopholes within the 1986 Act (for example *Gladstone v. Bower* ([1960] 2 Q.B. 383) agreements of more than one but less than two years' duration which do not convert to annual periodic tenancies) or by avoiding a landlord and tenant relationship altogether by creating sharefarming, partnership or contracting arrangements (for further details see *Scammell & Densham's Law of Agricultural Holdings* (7th Edition, Butterworths) or Muir Watt, *Agricultural Holdings* (13th Edition, Sweet & Maxwell)). This was clearly an unsatisfactory state of affairs: short-term arrangements are not conducive to good husbandry and trying to force structures, such as partnerships, to work where essentially the parties wanted to be in a landlord and tenant relationship has resulted in difficulties.

The solution to the problem was perceived to be the deregulation of the landlord and tenant relationship leaving the parties free to negotiate their own letting arrangements. The road which led to the 1995 Act started with the 1991 consultation paper referred to above, where the objectives of the reform were stated to be to deregulate and simplify the existing legislation, to encourage the letting of land, and to provide an enduring framework of legislation which could accommodate change within the industry. In this initial consultation paper, it was envisaged that there would be almost no statutory interference with freedom of contract: there was to be no statutory provision for notices to quit or rent review or for dispute resolution, and compensation for improvements was only to be available as a fall back if the tenancy agreement was silent on the issue.

By the time of the MAFF detailed proposals paper in September 1992 (*Reform of Agricultural Holdings Legislation: Detailed Proposals*), the compromise between regulation and freedom of contract had already begun. It was recognised that the common law notice period for annual periodic tenancies (six months terminating on the term date) was too short in the context of the agricultural year and that there was some benefit in requiring fixed-term tenancies of a certain duration to be brought to an end by notice rather than simply by effluxion of time. There was to be compensation for tenants' improvements and a right for the parties to have the rent reviewed on the basis of an open market rent unless the parties chose their own basis in the tenancy agreement or stated that there was not to be a rent review. The emphasis had shifted away from leaving the parties to the court system for dispute resolution and towards encouraging alternative dispute resolution with a fall back of statutory arbitration. Industry agreement was sought to the proposals and a compromise was achieved which was set out in an industry agreement of 1993 backed by the Country Landowners' Association, Tenant Farmers' Association, the National Farmers' Union and the National Federation of Young Farmers' Clubs. The industry agreement is largely reflected in the provisions of the Act itself.

Main features of the Act

(1) The parties are free to negotiate the term of their tenancy. There is no minimum term. The hope is that long fixed-term tenancies will result from this legislation which will to an extent compensate the tenant for the lack of security of tenure but will allow the landlord to know exactly when he can get the land back.

(2) There is minimal security of tenure linked only to a length of notice requirement reflecting the need to allow the tenant time in the context of the farming year to vacate the land. If a landlord complies with the length of notice requirements set out in the Act, the tenant has no response that he can make to that notice provided that it is valid in accordance with the common law requirements and leaves the average tenant in no doubt as to what is required of him. A landlord does not have to wait until the tenant defaults before he can serve a notice to quit. However, there are disadvantages for a landlord letting on a fixed-term tenancy who would have let on an annual tenancy under the 1986 Act. Under the 1986 Act, for example, if the tenant fails to pay his rent, the landlord can serve a notice to pay under Case D of Sched. 3 to the 1986 Act requiring the tenant to pay that rent within two months. If the tenant fails to pay the rent within two months, the landlord can serve a notice to quit to which the tenant has no answer. Under the new Act, if a tenant under a fixed-term tenancy fails to pay his rent, the landlord is dependent upon the common law remedies. He can sue or distrain or he can make the tenant bankrupt.

However, if he wishes to regain possession of the farm as a result of the non-payment of rent, he must (if he can) forfeit the lease. As the tenant is then able to apply for relief from forfeiture, this does not guarantee, in the way that the 1986 Act guaranteed, that the landlord will regain possession of the farm (for a detailed analysis of forfeiture see Woodfall, *Landlord and Tenant*, Vol. 1, Chap. 17 (Sweet & Maxwell)).

(3) In recognition of the realities of life in the rural community, the Act provides for the possibility of substantial diversification into non-agricultural activities without the danger of the tenancy slipping out of the farm business tenancy regime and into the Landlord and Tenant Act 1954 (c. 56), Part II, as a general commercial letting.

(4) The landlord and tenant have a limited number of options available to them as far as rent review is concerned. If they fail to choose one of those options, the Act provides for the rent to be reviewed on an open market basis. The parties are free to choose the frequency of reviews but, if they fail to do so, the reviews will be every three years.

(5) The tenant is free in most cases to remove fixtures.

(6) The tenant will be compensated for tenants' improvements (as defined in s.15) where the landlord's written consent has been obtained to those improvements or, in certain cases, the approval of an arbitrator has been obtained.

(7) The emphasis, so far as dispute resolution is concerned, is on encouraging the parties to choose their own alternative dispute resolution mechanism but with the fall back of statutory arbitration should the parties either not choose their own mechanism or should one of the parties not wish to use that mechanism in connection with any particular dispute. Arbitrations are under the Arbitration Acts 1950–1979 and there is no discrete arbitration regime as there is in Sched. 11 to the 1986 Act.

(8) The Act makes no provisions for repairs or for dilapidation claims or for compensation other than in relation to tenants' improvements as defined by s.15. Much more is left for negotiation between the parties.

As the Act passed through first the House of Lords, and then the House of Commons, it was clear that there were two stumbling blocks in the way of its success, despite survey reports from the RICS that the farm business tenancy regime would lead to a significant increase in agricultural land available for letting (see *Farm Business Tenancies New Farms and Land 1995 to 1997*, RICS, October 1994). First, there was the lack of commitment from the Labour Party that, should they get into power, they would not introduce retrospective legislation conferring security of tenure upon tenants under farm business tenancies and, secondly, the inheritance tax treatment of let land was still less advantageous. Both of those stumbling blocks have been removed. The Labour Party has given a commitment that it will not introduce legislation which will retrospectively confer security of tenure on tenants holding under farm business tenancies (see *Hansard*, H.C. Vol. 258, cols. 256–257). In addition, an amendment has been made in the Finance Act 1995 (c. 4) (s.155) so that 100 per cent agricultural property relief will be allowed in respect of land let on or after September 1, 1995.

The Act was given Royal Assent on May 9, 1995 and comes into force on September 1, 1995.

ABBREVIATIONS
MAFF: Ministry of Agriculture, Fisheries and Food.
The 1986 Act: The Agricultural Holdings Act 1986.
WOAD: Welsh Office Agriculture Department.

PART I

GENERAL PROVISIONS

Farm business tenancies

Meaning of "farm business tenancy"

1.—(1) A tenancy is a "farm business tenancy" for the purposes of this Act if—

(a) it meets the business conditions together with either the agriculture condition or the notice conditions, and

(b) it is not a tenancy which, by virtue of section 2 of this Act, cannot be a farm business tenancy.

(2) The business conditions are—

(a) that all or part of the land comprised in the tenancy is farmed for the purposes of a trade or business, and

(b) that, since the beginning of the tenancy, all or part of the land so comprised has been so farmed.

(3) The agriculture condition is that, having regard to—

(a) the terms of the tenancy,

(b) the use of the land comprised in the tenancy,

(c) the nature of any commercial activities carried on on that land, and

(d) any other relevant circumstances,

the character of the tenancy is primarily or wholly agricultural.

(4) The notice conditions are—

(a) that, on or before the relevant day, the landlord and the tenant each gave the other a written notice—

(i) identifying (by name or otherwise) the land to be comprised in the tenancy or proposed tenancy, and

(ii) containing a statement to the effect that the person giving the notice intends that the tenancy or proposed tenancy is to be, and remain, a farm business tenancy, and

(b) that, at the beginning of the tenancy, having regard to the terms of the tenancy and any other relevant circumstances, the character of the tenancy was primarily or wholly agricultural.

(5) In subsection (4) above "the relevant day" means whichever is the earlier of the following—

(a) the day on which the parties enter into any instrument creating the tenancy, other than an agreement to enter into a tenancy on a future date, or

(b) the beginning of the tenancy.

(6) The written notice referred to in subsection (4) above must not be included in any instrument creating the tenancy.

(7) If in any proceedings—

(a) any question arises as to whether a tenancy was a farm business tenancy at any time, and

(b) it is proved that all or part of the land comprised in the tenancy was farmed for the purposes of a trade or business at that time,

it shall be presumed, unless the contrary is proved, that all or part of the land so comprised has been so farmed since the beginning of the tenancy.

(8) Any use of land in breach of the terms of the tenancy, any commercial activities carried on in breach of those terms, and any cessation of such activities in breach of those terms, shall be disregarded in determining whether at any time the tenancy meets the business conditions or the agriculture condition, unless the landlord or his predecessor in title has consented to the breach or the landlord has acquiesced in the breach.

DEFINITIONS

"agriculture": s.38(1).
"agricultural": s.38(1).
"agricultural condition": subs. (3).
"beginning of the tenancy": s.38(4).
"business conditions": subs. (2).
"farm business tenancy": ss.1, 2.
"farmed": s.38(2).
"gave": s.36.
"landlord": s.38(1), (5).
"notice conditions": subs. (4).
"relevant day": subs. (5).
"tenancy": s.38(1).
"tenant": s.38(1), (5).

GENERAL NOTE

The provisions of this Act apply only to farm business tenancies. Section 1 defines a "farm business tenancy" and the definition is by reference to compliance with the conditions set out in s.1. Proof of compliance is assisted by a presumption (see subs. (7)) and by a disregard for unlawful uses (see subs. (8)).

The first note of importance is that the Act applies only to *tenancies* which comply with the s.1 conditions: there is no equivalent to s.2 of the 1986 Act which converts informal licence arrangements into tenancies. There is no requirement that a farm business tenancy be in writing and the tenancy can, therefore, be oral, written or by deed, provided that the general formalities required by property law are complied with in relation to the particular term granted. Leases for a term exceeding three years and other leases not taking effect in possession and/or not at the best rent must be contained in a deed (see s.52 of the Law of Property Act 1925 (c. 20)). There is no minimum term for which a farm business tenancy must be granted. It can, therefore, be for a fixed term of anything from, for example, one day to 999 years or a periodic tenancy of any period. "Tenancy" is defined by s.38(1) (see below) to include a sub-tenancy or an agreement for a tenancy or a sub-tenancy.

Under the 1986 Act, as we have already seen (see the Introduction above) many short-term letting arrangements were designed to avoid the lifetime security of tenure of that Act. Either as a result of specific exceptions in the Act (for example, certain grazing lets) or because of loopholes (for example, *Gladstone v. Bower* ([1960] 2 Q.B. 384) tenancies for more than one but less than two years) a short-term arrangement could be made which would simply expire on its term date. The farm business tenancy is capable of replacing all of those short-term arrangements. Grazing agreements for a specified period of the year can now be by farm business tenancy as can a letting equivalent to the length of the letting under a *Gladstone v. Bower* arrangement. The landowner will be no worse off in respect of such short-term lettings than he was before this Act: short-term farm business tenancies for two years or less, will simply expire by effluxion of time (see s.5 below).

As this Act applies only to tenancies, it will still be possible to grant licences for grass keep without falling within the farm business tenancy regime, provided that the grant is properly a licence and does not confer exclusive possession on the grazier.

Subs. (1)

All farm business tenancies must meet the business conditions (see subs. (2) below). There is then a choice which is in the hands of the parties at the beginning of the tenancy. If the parties choose not to serve the notices required by the notice conditions (see subs. (4) below) before the "relevant day" (see subs. (5) below), the tenancy will have to comply with the agriculture condition to be a farm business tenancy. The combination of the business conditions and the notice conditions allow the farmer to diversify substantially after the tenancy has been set up, to a point where commercial farming is a very minor part of the activities being carried on on the land. However, the legislation is designed to allow diversification of *farming* businesses and not to enable landlords to force a predominantly non-farming enterprise into this regime to avoid the greater security of tenure of the Landlord and Tenant Act 1954 (c. 56), Pt. II, which applies to general commercial lettings. This is prevented by a minimum requirement that all farm business tenancies must be primarily or wholly agricultural at the beginning of the tenancy. As any commercial enterprise which fails to comply with the s.1 conditions is likely to fall within the Landlord and Tenant Act 1954, Pt. II, landlords ought to be careful to ensure continuing compliance. This is not as difficult as it appears. For fixed-term leases, it may be possible as a "belt and braces" exercise to exclude, by an agreement approved by the court, the security of tenure provisions of the 1954 Act (see s.38 of that Act). It is not yet clear to what extent the courts would be prepared to do this, because if the tenancy is a farm business tenancy at the outset, it is specifically excluded from the provisions of Pt. II of the 1954 Act (see para. 10 of the Schedule to this Act). Control is also possible through the user covenants in the tenancy itself (see subs. (8) below).

Subs. (2)

All farm business tenancies must comply with the business conditions. The business conditions require commercial farming on part of the land let on the farm business tenancy at all times from the beginning of the tenancy. The beginning of the tenancy is defined by reference to the date upon which the tenant is entitled to go into possession under the terms of the tenancy (see s.38(4)) and is not, therefore, necessarily the date the tenancy agreement was entered into. The reason is obvious: whilst the business conditions do not require the tenant personally to farm (although there may be constraints in the tenancy agreement itself), the tenant cannot be in control of the activities on a holding until he is entitled to go into possession.

There is a positive requirement in subs. (2)(b) that there be no break in compliance at any time during the life of the tenancy (*cf.* the agriculture condition in subs. (3) below). If there is a period when there is no commercial farming on the holding, however short and whatever the reasons and however far in the past, the status of the tenancy as a farm business tenancy will be at an end (although see the presumption in subs. (7) in relation to historic non-compliance). If there is still non-farming commercial activity on the holding, the letting is likely to fall within the security of tenure of the Landlord and Tenant Act 1954, Pt. II.

This section requires only *part* of the land to be farmed with no stated or specified percentage requirement. It is possible that the courts will impose a *de minimis* test but there is no requirement that the part farmed be a self-sufficient business or, indeed, that the business which the farming supports needs to be agricultural in nature (see below for the meaning of "farmed" and "agriculture"). There is no requirement that the part of the land being farmed remain the same throughout the term of the tenancy and it is possible to move the farming activity around the holding. Care will need to be taken to ensure that there is no period of non-compliance when no part of the land is being farmed whilst the farming activity is moved to another area of land.

The requirement that all or part of the land be *farmed*, as opposed to used for agriculture is new. There is no definition of "farmed", save that s.38(2) provides that it includes the carrying on in relation to land of any agricultural activity and "agriculture" is defined in s.38(1) by importing the definition found in s.96 of the 1986 Act (save for a change in relation to the definition of livestock). The choice of such a wide term is deliberate: it is sufficiently flexible to grow with changes and developments within the industry and does not (as yet) suffer from many years of judicial scrutiny as "agriculture" does.

There may be circumstances where an activity could be regarded as farming although it would not be agricultural. For example, growing crops for the purpose of testing pesticides has been held not to be "agriculture" (see *Dow Agrochemicals v. Lane (E.A.) (North Lynn)* (1965) 192 E.G. 737) although it could possibly be farming as could the rearing of livestock for research purposes. No assistance is given in the Act as to whether set-aside land can be said to be farmed.

As the definition of agriculture remains the same, grazing remains as an independent agricultural activity. As with the 1986 Act (see *Rutherford v. Maurer* [1962] 1 Q.B. 16) there does not appear to be any requirement that the trade or business which the farming activity supports be itself farming or agricultural in nature. Where the predominant use of land within a farm business tenancy is grazing, it does not matter that the business supported by that grazing is, for example, a riding school or a stud farm (see the cases on horses and grazing cited in *Scammell & Densham's Law of Agricultural Holdings*, pp. 27–29 (7th edition, Butterworths) and also see *The Agricultural Holdings Act 1986* by James Muir Watt, Current Law Statutes Annotated Reprints, at pp. 5–124 and 5–125 (Sweet & Maxwell)).

The word "farmed" is used *only* in the business conditions and not in the notice conditions or the agriculture condition where the word used is agriculture. Those farming activities which are not agricultural are therefore regarded as diversification activities under the Act and the tenancy must be primarily agricultural at the outset. If there is "farming" at the outset but no agricultural activity the tenancy cannot be a farm business tenancy.

"*For the purposes of a trade or business*". The requirement that the farming be commercial in nature is not new in concept. Hobby farming or the use of the land for recreation or amenity was also excluded from the 1986 Act. Essentially, the idea is to cut out non-commercial activities. In *Hickson and Welch v. Cann* (1977) 40 P. & C.R. 218, Bridge LJ said "There is all the difference in the world between what hundreds and hundreds of people all over the country do, that is, add a small amount to their earnings by buying or selling animals of one sort or another, and the carrying on of a trade or business of an agricultural nature". Growing vegetables primarily for own use, even if the surplus is sold or keeping a few sheep as pets, even if they are eventually sold, will not amount to using the land for a trade or business. Although grazing is farming, the use of land as a pony paddock or to keep horses used for hunting will not comply with the business conditions because the farming is not for the purposes or a trade or business.

Subs. (3)

If the parties do not choose to rely on the notice conditions in subs. (4) the agriculture condition must be complied with together with the business conditions.

There are two things to note about the agriculture condition. First, substantial diversification is not catered for as the requirement is that the character of the tenancy must be primarily or wholly agricultural. Secondly, non-compliance with the agriculture condition does not have the same consequences as non-compliance with the business conditions. Non-compliance with the agriculture condition will take the tenancy out of the farm business tenancy regime, but later compliance may bring it back in again. It is only really, therefore, at the time of testing the status of the tenancy as a farm business tenancy that the agriculture condition becomes relevant. If, at the time of testing, the tenancy is not primarily or wholly agricultural but is commercial in nature, the tenant may have the greater security of tenure of the business tenancy regime in the Landlord and Tenant Act 1954, Pt. II. In most cases therefore it is likely that professional advice would be to opt for the greater certainty and flexibility of the notice conditions. The agriculture condition is likely to be relied upon primarily where professional advice has not been sought and where, therefore, notices have not been exchanged or where defective notices or defective service of notices means that reliance cannot be placed on the notice conditions. If, however, the parties intend a relatively short-term agreement and are prepared to agree to very restrictive user covenants limiting use to an agricultural use, they may choose not to serve notices. Subsection (8) (see below) means that unlawful uses outside of the scope of the user covenants can be ignored in assessing compliance with the agriculture condition save where the landlord consents or acquiesces in the breach. In circumstances, for example, where grass keep is being auctioned and, therefore, the service of notices is not feasible, tight user covenants to grazing and/or mowing only, will suffice to ensure compliance with the agriculture condition.

"Primarily or wholly agricultural" is a new phrase. Under the 1986 Act, to establish that a contract of tenancy was for an agricultural tenancy it was necessary to show that the whole of the land subject to such exceptions as did not substantially affect the character of the tenancy was let for use as agricultural land. Whilst the wording in the new Act is different, the concept is familiar. Factors such as the percentage area of the holding used for agriculture; the percentage that agricultural and non-agricultural activities contribute to turnover and profit; the amount of time and labour which each activity takes up, will all be relevant and, at the end of the day, it will be a matter of overall impression. A non-agricultural activity which is insubstantial in terms of acreage but is predominant in terms of income may well mean in some cases that the tenancy is not primarily agricultural.

"Agriculture" is defined in s.38(1) and is the same definition as found in s.96 of the 1986 Act save for the fact that livestock is now differently defined. It should be noted that unlike the business conditions, the agriculture condition does not use the word "farmed". It is possible, therefore, for the entire holding to be farmed but not to be a farm business tenancy if the use is not agricultural.

Subs. (4)

An exchange of notices between landlord and tenant in the form set out in this subsection will allow substantial diversification away from agricultural activities without the danger of the tenancy losing its status as a farm business tenancy. Whilst the character of the tenancy must be primarily or wholly agricultural at the beginning of the tenancy (*i.e.* when the tenant is entitled to go into possession—see s.38), diversification thereafter into non-agricultural use will not breach the notice conditions. The notice conditions require matters to be looked at only at the beginning of the tenancy. Provided, therefore, that part of the land is always farmed for the purposes of a trade or business in compliance with the business conditions, the tenancy will remain a farm business tenancy despite possibly predominantly non-agricultural activity on the land.

The notice conditions are likely to be relied upon where diversification is intended by the tenant or to ensure certainty where diversification could happen unlawfully and where a landlord is concerned about consent or acquiescence in breach of the user covenants in longer term tenancies (see subs. (8) below), or where diversification, whilst not intended by the tenant, is permissible under the terms of user covenants which have been drafted widely in order not to impact adversely on the rent. The notice conditions still require the letting to be primarily or wholly agricultural at the outset to ensure that businesses which are intended to be predominantly non-agricultural cannot be farm business tenancies, thereby avoiding the security of tenure provisions of the Landlord and Tenant Act 1954, Pt. II. The purpose of this regime is to allow diversification of essentially farming businesses.

The phrase "primarily or wholly agricultural" has been discussed in connection with the agriculture condition (see subs. (3) above), the only difference is that here, as a snapshot picture is being taken at the beginning of the tenancy, greater emphasis will be placed, of necessity, on the terms of the tenancy itself.

There is no prescribed form for the notice to be served under this section although, as can be seen, there is prescribed information which must be included in the notice. For evidential purposes each notice should be signed, dated and acknowledged by the recipient. Care must be taken with service of the notice and reference should be made to s.36 and the General Note to that section. Section 36 sets out prescribed methods of service for any notice or document required or authorised to be given under the Act.

Failure to serve notices, the service of defective notices or defective service of notices does not necessarily mean that the tenancy will not be a farm business tenancy. If the agriculture condition is complied with, that will act as a safety net for most lettings.

Subs. (5)

This subsection defines the date by which the notices referred to above must be exchanged. Notices must be exchanged by the earlier of the date of a written tenancy agreement and the date upon which the tenant is entitled to go into possession. There is no requirement that notices be exchanged first on that day, before the tenancy is entered into.

Subs. (6)

The requirement for a separate notice not within the body of the tenancy agreement mirrors that for assured shorthold tenancies under the Housing Act 1988 (c. 50). It is considered more likely that a tenant will understand the importance of such a notice, read it thoroughly and obtain proper advice upon it if it is not just one of many clauses in a tenancy agreement.

Subs. (7)

Proof of compliance with the business conditions at the time when the tenancy's status as a farm business tenancy is challenged raises a presumption of historical compliance since the date upon which the tenant was entitled to go into possession. The burden of proof is therefore on the party trying to show historical non-compliance to prove that there has been a period, however short, when there was no commercial farming on the holding.

Subs. (8)

It is not possible for the tenant unilaterally to bring himself into or out of the farm business tenancy regime in breach of the terms of his tenancy agreement. Unlawful uses, prohibited by the terms of the tenancy, or failure to comply with positive obligations in the tenancy agreement in connection with user, can therefore be ignored when investigating ongoing compliance with the business conditions or the agriculture condition. A similar provision exists in s.1(3) of the 1986 Act.

Appropriately drawn user covenants, limiting the use of the holding to a specific agricultural use, to a use which is for agriculture in general or to a use which simply requires part of the land to be farmed commercially, will assist in ensuring compliance. However, restrictive user clauses may have an adverse impact on the rent achievable for the holding. In addition, in longer fixed-term tenancies, the risk of the landlord consenting to or acquiescing in the unlawful use means that controls through the user covenants alone are not enough to guarantee compliance.

A landlord will be taken to have acquiesced in a use in breach of covenant if from his conduct it can be inferred that he has waived his rights in relation to the breach. For example, if the tenant opens a garden centre from which the landlord regularly purchases plants. In many cases, the amount of time which has elapsed since the initial breach will be important, but there may be acquiescence without any delay at all.

Tenancies which cannot be farm business tenancies

2.—(1) A tenancy cannot be a farm business tenancy for the purposes of this Act if—

  (a) the tenancy begins before 1st September 1995, or

  (b) it is a tenancy of an agricultural holding beginning on or after that date with respect to which, by virtue of section 4 of this Act, the Agricultural Holdings Act 1986 applies.

  (2) In this section "agricultural holding" has the same meaning as in the Agricultural Holdings Act 1986.

DEFINITIONS

  "agricultural holding": subs. (2) and the 1986 Act, s.1.
  "begins": s.38(4).
  "farm business tenancy": ss.1, 2.
  "tenancy": s.38(1).

GENERAL NOTE

  The cut-off date between the farm business tenancy regime and the 1986 Act is the date of the coming into force of this Act on September 1, 1995. The legislation is not retrospective in any respect. It is by reference to the beginning of the tenancy, *i.e.* the date upon which the tenant is entitled to go into possession (see s.38) that the tenancy will fall either to be considered under the 1986 Act or to be considered under this Act. However, there are exceptions set out in s.4 (see below) which will allow certain tenancies created on or after September 1, 1995 to be protected under the 1986 Act.

Compliance with notice conditions in cases of surrender and re-grant

3.—(1) This section applies where—
  (a) a tenancy ("the new tenancy") is granted to a person who, immediately before the grant, was the tenant under a farm business tenancy ("the old tenancy") which met the notice conditions specified in section 1(4) of this Act,
  (b) the condition in subsection (2) below or the condition in subsection (3) below is met, and
  (c) except as respects the matters mentioned in subsections (2) and (3) below and matters consequential on them, the terms of the new tenancy are substantially the same as the terms of the old tenancy.

(2) The first condition referred to in subsection (1)(b) above is that the land comprised in the new tenancy is the same as the land comprised in the old tenancy, apart from any changes in area which are small in relation to the size of the holding and do not affect the character of the holding.

(3) The second condition referred to in subsection (1)(b) above is that the old tenancy and the new tenancy are both fixed term tenancies, but the term date under the new tenancy is earlier than the term date under the old tenancy.

(4) Where this section applies, the new tenancy shall be taken for the purposes of this Act to meet the notice conditions specified in section 1(4) of this Act.

(5) In subsection (3) above, "the term date", in relation to a fixed term tenancy, means the date fixed for the expiry of the term.

DEFINITIONS
  "farm business tenancy": ss.1, 2.
  "fixed term tenancy": s.38(1).
  "granted": s.38(3).
  "holding": s.38(1).
  "new tenancy, the": subs. (1)(a).
  "notice conditions": s.1(4).
  "old tenancy, the": subs. (1)(a).
  "tenancy": s.38(1).
  "tenant": s.38(1), (5).
  "term date, the": s.5(2).

GENERAL NOTE
  Where a farm business tenancy is granted with reliance being placed on the notice conditions, compliance with the notice conditions will have to be considered afresh in all cases of surrender and regrant. This is so whether what is intended by the parties is in fact a surrender and regrant or whether the parties are purporting to vary the terms of an existing farm business tenancy but where, in law, this amounts to a surrender and regrant. Without s.3, in all cases of surrender and regrant, whether express or inadvertent, new notices would have to be served and the parties would have to be able to show, in accordance with the second notice condition, that at the time of the regrant the character of the tenancy was primarily or wholly agricultural. With farms which have become highly diversified, the second condition could not be fulfilled and, where the surrender and regrant is inadvertent, the parties are unlikely to have considered the service of fresh notices.
  Section 3 prevents these problems from arising in two common situations: small changes in the area of land let and moving forward the term date in a fixed-term tenancy. In both cases, provided that the old tenancy met the notice conditions, and the new tenancy, apart from changes in the area of land or the term date, is on substantially the same terms, the fulfilment of the notice conditions at the outset of the old tenancy will stand for the new. No new notices need be served and no investigation is necessary into the primary use of the holding at the time of the new

grant. For all other situations of surrender and regrant, either the notice conditions must be complied with again or the parties will have to rely on the fallback of the agriculture condition. Care will need to be taken in agreeing variations which may amount to a surrender and regrant, particularly in relation to highly diversified estates.

Exclusion of Agricultural Holdings Act 1986

Agricultural Holdings Act 1986 not to apply in relation to new tenancies except in special cases

4.—(1) The Agricultural Holdings Act 1986 (in this section referred to as "the 1986 Act") shall not apply in relation to any tenancy beginning on or after 1st September 1995 (including any agreement to which section 2 of that Act would otherwise apply beginning on or after that date), except any tenancy of an agricultural holding which—

(a) is granted by a written contract of tenancy entered into before 1st September 1995 and indicating (in whatever terms) that the 1986 Act is to apply in relation to the tenancy,

(b) is obtained by virtue of a direction of an Agricultural Land Tribunal under section 39 or 53 of the 1986 Act,

(c) is granted (following a direction under section 39 of that Act) in circumstances falling within section 45(6) of that Act,

(d) is granted on an agreed succession by a written contract of tenancy indicating (in whatever terms) that Part IV of the 1986 Act is to apply in relation to the tenancy,

(e) is created by the acceptance of a tenant, in accordance with the provisions as to compensation known as the "Evesham custom" and set out in subsections (3) to (5) of section 80 of the 1986 Act, on the terms and conditions of the previous tenancy, or

(f) is granted to a person who, immediately before the grant of the tenancy, was the tenant of the holding, or of any agricultural holding which comprised the whole or a substantial part of the land comprised in the holding, under a tenancy in relation to which the 1986 Act applied ("the previous tenancy") and is so granted merely because a purported variation of the previous tenancy (not being an agreement expressed to take efect as a new tenancy between the parties) has effect as an implied surrender followed by the grant of the tenancy.

(2) For the purposes of subsection (1)(d) above, a tenancy ("the current tenancy") is granted on an agreed succession if, and only if,—

(a) the previous tenancy of the holding or a related holding was a tenancy in relation to which Part IV of the 1986 Act applied, and

(b) the current tenancy is granted otherwise than as mentioned in paragraph (b) or (c) of subsection (1) above but in such circumstances that if—

(i) Part IV of the 1986 Act applied in relation to the current tenancy, and

(ii) a sole (or sole surviving) tenant under the current tenancy were to die and be survived by a close relative of his,

the occasion on which the current tenancy is granted would for the purposes of subsection (1) of section 37 of the 1986 Act be taken to be an occasion falling within paragraph (a) or (b) of that subsection.

(3) In this section—

(a) "agricultural holding" and "contract of tenancy" have the same meaning as in the 1986 Act, and

(b) "close relative" and "related holding" have the meaning given by section 35(2) of that Act.

<small>DEFINITIONS</small>
"agreed succession": subs. (2).
"agricultural holding": subs. (3) and the 1986 Act, s.1.

"beginning": s.38(4).
"close relative": subs. (3) and the 1986 Act, s.35(2).
"contract of tenancy": subs. (3) and the 1986 Act, s.1(5).
"current tenancy, the": subs. (2).
"Evesham custom": 1986 Act, s.80(3)–(5).
"holding": s.38(1).
"previous tenancy, the": subs. (1)(f).
"related holding": subs. (3) and the 1986 Act, s.35(2).
"tenancy": s.38(1).
"tenant": s.38(1), (5).

GENERAL NOTE
This section makes it clear that, subject to the limited exceptions set out below, the 1986 Act will not apply to tenancies which begin on or after September 1, 1995 or to informal licence arrangements which begin on or after that date which would otherwise be converted into tenancies by s.2 of the 1986 Act. A tenancy begins on the date upon which the tenant is entitled to go into possession (see s.38). This is not necessarily the date on the tenancy agreement.

With one exception (see subs. (1)(a)), the s.4 exceptions cover circumstances where, for various reasons, it can reasonably be said that the legitimate expectations of the tenant would be that he or his successors would have 1986 Act security and therefore the exceptions are within the spirit of the government's stated intention that this Act will not be retrospective.

There is no general ability (apart from subs. (1)(a)) to contract back into 1986 Act security, although this did appear, almost certainly inadvertently, in an earlier draft of the Bill. The exceptions in s.4 are limited and the idea is that 1986 Act tenancies should disappear as soon as possible, with as few new lettings on or after September 1, 1995 under that regime as accords with the new Act not being retrospective. It is recognised that this could cause difficulties, for example, where a landlord and a tenant wish the tenant to move farms on or after September 1, 1995. Whilst, to an extent, the lack of security of tenure can be compensated for by the grant of a long fixed-term, other constraints, such as a limited range of options in respect of rent review mechanisms (see s.9 *et seq*), make it extremely difficult to replicate a 1986 Act tenancy.

Subs. (1)(a)
This exception does allow a limited ability to contract back into 1986 Act security. It recognises that, in the run up to the coming into force of the legislation on September 1, 1995, parties may wish to take an opportunity to reorganise estates – moving tenants between farms – or to promise 1986 Act security to new tenants or effect express surrenders and regrants not covered by subs. (1)(e) below. However, the exception also recognises that it may not be convenient in terms of the farming year to move such tenants before September 1, 1995 which would create difficulties without this exception, as the cut-off date between the two Acts is by reference to the date upon which the tenant is entitled to go into possession.

This exception provides that if a written contract of tenancy (as defined by the 1986 Act) is entered into before September 1, 1995 stating that the 1986 Act is to apply to that tenancy, then it will apply regardless of the fact that the tenancy is not to begin within the meaning of the Act (*i.e.* the tenant is not to be entitled to go into possession) until on or after September 1. It will enable reorganisation plans to be put in place before September 1 with the tenants moved, say, at Michaelmas.

Subs. (1)(b)–(d)
This group of exceptions is designed to ensure that what might loosely be called succession tenancies, succeeding to tenancies currently governed by the 1986 Act, will themselves fall under the 1986 Act regime, to accord with the legitimate expectations of the parties. The Agriculture (Miscellaneous Provisions) Act 1976 (c. 55) first introduced a statutory entitlement to succession on the death of a tenant by a defined class of close relatives who satisfied certain eligibility tests. The Agricultural Holdings Act 1984 (c. 41) extended succession to retirement and altered the eligibility tests. The Agricultural Holdings Act 1986 (c. 5), which is the current legislation, now contains the succession rules. The basic position is that all 1986 Act tenancies carry the right to succession, save for those granted after July 12, 1984, which will only carry the right to succession if the tenancy itself is a succession tenancy or if the parties have contracted back into succession rights or if there is a new tenancy of substantially the same holding granted to an existing tenant whose original tenancy carried succession rights.

Subsection (1)(b) relates to succession tenancies obtained as a result of the direction of the Agricultural Lands Tribunal to an eligible person (s.39 of the 1986 Act) or to a nominated successor (s.53 of the 1986 Act).

Subsection (1)(c) relates to circumstances where the landlord has actually granted a tenancy to a successor following a direction but before the time when the direction would, in accordance with the provisions of s.45 and s.46 of the 1986 Act, entitle the successor to the new tenancy.

Subsection (1)(d) is the most problematic of this group of exceptions. Subsection (1)(d) recognises that there will be circumstances where a successor tenant is agreed between the parties and the matter never goes before the Agricultural Lands Tribunal. However, it was recognised by the drafters of the Act that simply to refer to an agreed succession without further definition could create an opportunity for contracting back into 1986 Act security simply by calling the new tenancy an agreed succession. There are two controls: the first is in subs. (1)(d) itself: the tenancy must state that Pt. IV of the 1986 Act (succession provisions) is to apply to the new tenancy. The second control is in the definition of an agreed succession set out in subs. (2) below.

Subs. (1)(e)

This exception is to encourage the ongoing working of the Evesham Custom. The custom, set out in the 1986 Act, allows investment by tenants in market gardens predominantly, though not exclusively, in and around Evesham in such a way as to enable a landlord not to have to pay compensation for the improvements in certain circumstances where the tenant quits the holding. Again, it is an exception to reflect the legitimate expectations of the parties and to ensure that this Act does not put tenants of market gardens in a position of not being able to obtain recompense for their investment on quitting the holding. The Evesham Custom is set out in s.80(3)–(5) of the 1986 Act. In brief, where the Agricultural Lands Tribunal is satisfied that a holding is suitable for the purposes of market gardening, it may direct that s.79(2)–(5) of the 1986 Act shall apply. Section 79(2)–(5) gives additional rights to tenants of market gardens in respect of improvements consisting of the planting of trees, bushes and certain plants or the erection, alteration or enlargement of buildings for the purposes of the trade or business of a market garden. If such a direction is made and a notice to quit is served by the tenant or the tenant becomes insolvent, the tenant will not obtain compensation from the landlord for the improvements unless he produces an offer in writing from a suitable person: (a) to accept a tenancy on the same terms and conditions; and (b) to pay all compensation due under the Act or the tenancy to the outgoing tenant; and the landlord has failed to accept that offer within three months.

Unless a new tenant were to obtain security of tenure under the 1986 Act, it is unlikely that one could be found who would be prepared to pay the outgoing tenant for the improvements. In those circumstances, the outgoing tenant would be left with a condition for obtaining compensation which he could not fulfil.

Subs. (1)(f)

This exception recognises that there are circumstances where parties will believe that they are merely varying the terms of a 1986 Act tenancy but where, as a matter of law, they have effected a surrender and regrant. If such a purported variation of a tenancy protected under the 1986 Act takes effect as a surrender, the grant of a new tenancy beginning on or after September 1, 1995 would, without this exception, put the tenant in a position of having lost his security of tenure without realising that that is what has happened. This exception goes some way to alleviating the problem. It is, however, limited in its scope and will not give 1986 Act protection to a new grant where: (1) there is an additional tenant on the new grant; (2) the land in the new grant is not the whole or a substantial part of the land in the old tenancy; (3) the arrangement is an express surrender and regrant and not an inadvertent surrender and regrant arising from a purported variation.

For circumstances which fall outside of this exception, care will need to be taken when advising tenants whether or not to accept variations to a 1986 Act tenancy after the coming into force of this Act. Ultimately, whether a purported variation operates as a surrender and regrant depends upon the intention of the parties. The addition of a new tenant is not necessarily a surrender and regrant (see *Saunders Trustees v. Ralph* [1993] 28 E.G. 127) and whilst the addition of extra land will often amount to a surrender and regrant, this is not invariably the case. In *Fredco Estates v. Bryant* [1961] 1 All E.R. 34, in the context of residential property, it was implied that if the regrant offered less security than the original grant, it could be said that the tenant would not have intended to put himself in that position and would not therefore have intended a surrender.

Subs. (2)

Reference should be made also to the commentary to subs. (1)(d) above. The intention of subs. (2) is to define "an agreed succession" in such a way as to ensure that it is not open to parties to use the exception in subs. (1)(d) as an indirect method of contracting back into 1986 Act security of tenure simply by calling the tenancy an agreed succession. The method by which subs. (2) attempts to achieve this is not straightforward. First, the tenancy to which the exception is to apply must be succeeding to a tenancy which does actually carry succession rights. The second condition is extremely convoluted and based on the application of hypotheses to the tenancy. What it amounts to is that a tenancy will only be treated as granted on an agreed succession for the purposes of this exception if the grant of the tenancy is in such circumstances that it would count as one of the two successions allowed by law under the 1986 Act.

Part of the reason for the complexity is the terms of the succession provisions in the 1986 Act. Instead of saying, in terms, that there shall be two successions, s.37 of the 1986 Act provides that there shall be no entitlement to apply to succeed if on two previous occasions when a sole or sole surviving tenant died, there had been a succession by direction or grant following direction or there had been an agreed succession by a close relative. This exception attempts to mirror that provision.

Whilst directions of the Agricultural Lands Tribunal and grants following directions are specifically excluded from falling within the definition of agreed succession having already been dealt with by other exceptions within s.4 (see subs. (1)(b) and (c) above), care has to be taken. The two circumstances which will count as a succession under the 1986 Act are set out in s.37(1)(a) and s.37(1)(b) of that Act. Reference is made to those provisions in s.4(2). While s.37(1)(a) refers to directions of the Agricultural Lands Tribunal and grants following directions, as a result of s.37(2) there are certain factual circumstances which will be deemed to fall within s.37(1)(a) which will not fall within subs. (1)(b) or (c) above. For example, s.37(2) provides that agreements prior to the date of the death of the tenant where a new tenant would be a close relative, if the old tenant died immediately before the grant, will be deemed to fall within s.37(1)(a) and be treated as a direction of the Agricultural Lands Tribunal. Section 37(1)(b) covers the situation where a new tenancy was granted to a close relative of a tenant who had died and who had become the sole remaining applicant for succession.

In determining eligibility for succession, the 1986 Act will still apply. However, in the Schedule to this Act, (para. 32), the 1986 Act is amended so that a potential successor does not have counted against him any land which he holds on a farm business tenancy of less than five years when assessing whether he is the occupier of a commercial unit of agricultural land which would disqualify him from being a person eligible for succession.

Termination of the tenancy

Tenancies for more than two years to continue from year to year unless terminated by notice

5.—(1) A farm business tenancy for a term of more than two years shall, instead of terminating on the term date, continue (as from that date) as a tenancy from year to year, but otherwise on the terms of the original tenancy so far as applicable, unless at least twelve months but less than twenty-four months before the term date a written notice has been given by either party to the other of his intention to terminate the tenancy.

(2) In subsection (1) above "the term date", in relation to a fixed term tenancy, means the date fixed for the expiry of the term.

(3) For the purposes of section 140 of the Law of Property Act 1925 (apportionment of conditions on severance of reversion), a notice under subsection (1) above shall be taken to be a notice to quit.

(4) This section has effect notwithstanding any agreement to the contrary.

DEFINITIONS
  "farm business tenancy": s.1.
  "fixed term tenancy": s.38(1).
  "given": s.36.
  "tenancy": s.38(1).

"term date, the": subs. (2).
"termination": s.38(1).

GENERAL NOTE

This section provides limited security of tenure to a tenant under a fixed-term farm business tenancy of more than two years by requiring positive action on the part of either the landlord or tenant to bring it to an end. Such a tenancy will not expire by effluxion of time. It can only be brought to an end on its term date by the service of a written notice in advance of the term date giving at least 12 but less than 24 months' notice. If such a notice is not served, the tenancy will continue as an annual periodic tenancy until brought to an end in accordance with the provisions of s.6 below.

It is possible that the courts will find such a continuation tenancy to be contractual in nature. Cases under the Landlord and Tenant Act 1954, Pt. II, where commercial business tenancies continue after the expiry of the fixed term, have concluded that the continuation tenancy is an extension of the contractual term with a variation as to the method of termination. See, for example, *Weinbergs Weatherproofs v. Radcliffe Paper Mill Co.* [1958] Ch 437 and *City of London Corp. v. Fell* [1993] QB 589 (C.A.) and [1994] 1 AC 458 (H.L.). This means that the tenant has an estate in land rather than simply a personal right to occupy. There is, however, a distinction between the two Acts: the 1954 Act does not refer to the tenancy continuing as an annual period tenancy. Section 5 of this Act, on the other hand, specifically provides that the farm business tenancy continues as a tenancy from year to year.

No contracting out is permitted from this section. Any provisions in the tenancy agreement for no notice or for a short notice will therefore be ineffective, although an agreed surrender between landlord and tenant remains a possibility.

Fixed-term tenancies with a duration of two years or less are not governed by the Act and will simply come to an end by effluxion of time on their term date. These tenancies (see the General Note to s.1 above) will replace the short-term grazing agreements, *Gladstone v. Bower* agreements and Ministry consent tenancies currently used to avoid the security of tenure of the 1986 Act.

Service of all notices and documents authorised or required to be served under this Act must be served in accordance with the provisions of s.36 (see below). There is, however, no prescribed form for the notice, although it must comply with the common law requirements.

Subs. (3)

Section 140 of the Law of Property Act 1925 deals with the apportionment of conditions upon the severance of a reversionary estate in land. The section provides for conditions and rights of re-entry, following a severance of the reversionary estate, to be apportioned to remain annexed to the severed parts of the reversionary estate. By s.140(2) a right of re-entry is defined to include a right to determine the lease by notice to quit, and by this subsection a notice served under this section to terminate the farm business tenancy on its term date is deemed to be a notice to quit.

This subsection ensures that the right of a tenant under s.140(2) of the Law of Property Act 1925 to choose to give a counter-notice to bring the entire tenancy to an end on the date upon which the original notice takes effect where he receives a notice to quit from the owner of one part of the severed reversionary estate, is preserved.

Length of notice to quit

6.—(1) Where a farm business tenancy is a tenancy from year to year, a notice to quit the holding or part of the holding shall (notwithstanding any provision to the contrary in the tenancy) be invalid unless—

  (a) it is in writing,
  (b) it is to take effect at the end of a year of the tenancy, and
  (c) it is given at least twelve months but less than twenty-four months before the date on which it is to take effect.

(2) Where, by virtue of section 5(1) of this Act, a farm business tenancy for a term of more than two years is to continue (as from the term date) as a tenancy from year to year, a notice to quit which complies with subsection (1) above and which is to take effect on the first anniversary of the term date shall not be invalid merely because it is given before the term date; and in this subsection "the term date" has the meaning given by section 5(2) of this Act.

(3) Subsection (1) above does not apply in relation to a counter-notice given by the tenant by virtue of subsection (2) of section 140 of the Law of Property Act 1925 (apportionment of conditions on severance of reversion).

DEFINITIONS
   "farm business tenancy": s.1.
   "given": s.36.
   "holding": s.38(1).
   "tenancy": s.38(1).
   "tenant": s.38(1), (5).
   "term date, the": s.5(2).

GENERAL NOTE
   At common law, a notice to quit in respect of an annual periodic tenancy must be of at least six months' duration and take effect at the end of a year of the tenancy. This section overrides the common law position and provides for an extended notice period to be given by either landlord or tenant with no ability to contract out of its provisions. There is nothing in the Act, however, which interferes with the parties' ability to agree a surrender of the tenancy. There is no pre-scribed form for the notice and the common law rules must be complied with. Service of all notices and documents authorised or required to be served under this Act must be served in accordance with the provisions of s.36.
   This section applies to tenancies which are annual periodic tenancies from the outset or those which were originally fixed-term tenancies of more than two years' duration which have not been terminated but which are continuing by reason of the provisions of s.5 above. There are no restrictions other than the length of notice requirement of this section and the service require-ments in s.36, on the circumstances in which a landlord or a tenant can serve a notice to quit an annual periodic tenancy. This is a major change from the position under the 1986 Act where the landlord either had to have a ground set out in Sched. 3 to that Act which enabled him to serve an incontestable notice to quit or had to obtain the consent of the Agricultural Lands Tribunal to the operation of his notice to quit. Under this Act, once a tenant receives a notice to quit, pro-vided that it complies with the common law rules as to validity, the length of notice requirements of this section and the service requirements of s.36, there is nothing that he can do to prevent it taking effect. Other periodic tenancies, weekly, monthly or quarterly, are not governed by the Act and the common law rules as to notice period will apply.

Subs. (2)
   This subsection provides for the situation which falls between s.5 and s.6. Section 5 envisages the service of a notice to bring a fixed-term tenancy to an end on its term date; s.6(1) provides for the service of a notice to quit an annual periodic tenancy. A notice given in the final year of a fixed-term tenancy to expire on the first anniversary of the end of the fixed-term is neither a notice under s.5 or a notice under s.6 as the tenancy is not yet a tenancy from year to year. The validity of such a notice is preserved by this subsection.

Subs. (3)
   The counter-notice referred to is that mentioned in the notes to s.5(3) above.

Notice required for exercise of option to terminate tenancy or resume possession of part

   7.—(1) Where a farm business tenancy is a tenancy for a term of more than two years, any notice to quit the holding or part of the holding given in pursu-ance of any provision of the tenancy shall (notwithstanding any provision to the contrary in the tenancy) be invalid unless it is in writing and is given at least twelve months but less than twenty-four months before the date on which it is to take effect.
   (2) Subsection (1) above does not apply in relation to a counter-notice given by the tenant by virtue of subsection (2) of section 140 of the Law of Property Act 1925 (apportionment of conditions on severance of reversion).
   (3) Subsection (1) above does not apply to a tenancy which, by virtue of subsection (6) of section 149 of the Law of Property Act 1925 (lease for life or lives or for a term determinable with life or lives or on the marriage of the lessee), takes effect as such a term of years as is mentioned in that subsection.

DEFINITIONS
   "farm business tenancy": s.1.
   "given": s.36.
   "holding": s.38(1).

"tenancy": s.38(1).
"tenant": s.38(1), (5).

GENERAL NOTE

This section controls break clauses in fixed-term tenancies of more than two years by imposing a statutory restriction on the length of notice to be given to operate a contractual option to break. As a result of this length of notice requirement, care should be taken in advising landlords who may need to be able to resume possession quickly, for example, for the purposes of redevelopment. It may be necessary (if practical in the particular circumstances of the case) to have a separate tenancy of any parts where this is likely to be an issue. Such a tenancy could either be a periodic (say, quarterly) farm business tenancy where only one period's notice would need to be given or, if the primary use of that part is not agricultural, a fixed-term tenancy under the Landlord and Tenant Act 1954, Pt. II, excluded by an agreement approved by the courts from the security of tenure provisions of that Act (see s.38 of the 1954 Act). Break clauses in such an excluded 1954 Act tenancy would not be subject to this length of notice requirement.

Contracting out of this provision is not permitted, although a consensual surrender between the parties is always a possibility. A break clause which allows for a shorter period of notice will probably not be void, but the notice requirements will be overridden by the statute.

Subs. (2)

The counter-notice referred to is that mentioned in the notes to s.5(3) above.

Subs. (3)

Section 149(6) of the Law of Property Act 1925 converts certain leases which are for life or determinable upon the tenant's marriage into 90-year terms determinable after death or marriage (as the case may be) by one month's notice expiring on a quarter day applicable to the tenancy or, if none, on a usual quarter day. The provisions of s.7 relating to break clauses do not apply to such leases and, therefore, they continue to be determinable by one quarter's notice as stated above.

Tenant's right to remove fixtures and buildings

Tenant's right to remove fixtures and buildings

8.—(1) Subject to the provision of this section—
(a) any fixture (of whatever description) affixed, whether for the purposes of agriculture or not, to the holding by the tenant under a farm business tenancy, and
(b) any building erected by him on the holding,
may be removed by the tenant at any time during the continuance of the tenancy or at any time after the termination of the tenancy when he remains in possession as tenant (whether or not under a new tenancy), and shall remain his property so long as he may remove it by virtue of this subsection.

(2) Subsection (1) above shall not apply—
(a) to a fixture affixed or a building erected in pursuance of some obligation,
(b) to a fixture affixed or a building erected instead of some fixture or building belonging to the landlord,
(c) to a fixture or building in respect of which the tenant has obtained compensation under section 16 of this Act or otherwise, or
(d) to a fixture or building in respect of which the landlord has given his consent under section 17 of this Act on condition that the tenant agrees not to remove it and which the tenant has agreed not to remove.

(3) In the removal of a fixture or building by virtue of subsection (1) above, the tenant shall not do any avoidable damage to the holding.

(4) Immediately after removing a fixture or building by virtue of subsection (1) above, the tenant shall make good all damage to the holding that is occasioned by the removal.

(5) This section applies to a fixture or building acquired by a tenant as it applies to a fixture or building affixed or erected by him.

(6) Except as provided by subsection (2)(d) above, this section has effect notwithstanding any agreement or custom to the contrary.

(7) No right to remove fixtures that subsists otherwise than by virtue of this section shall be exercisable by the tenant under a farm business tenancy.

DEFINITIONS
"agriculture": s.38(1).
"building": s.38(1).
"farm business tenancy": s.1.
"holding": s.38(1).
"landlord": s.38(1), (5).
"tenancy": s.38(1).
"tenant": s.38(1), (5).
"termination": s.38(1).

GENERAL NOTE
At common law, whether a particular object on land is a fixture or a chattel depends to an extent upon the degree of annexation of the object to the land, the ease with which it can be removed and, more importantly, whether the purpose for which it was originally attached was for the permanent improvement of the land or for some temporary purpose. It is beyond the scope of this commentary to go into detail (see Woodfall, *Landlord and Tenant*, Sweet & Maxwell, volume 1, paras. 13.131 *et seq*). Chattel assets can always be removed by a tenant at any time. Fixtures can be removed in certain circumstances although at common law they become attached to the land and the property of the freehold owner. The common law was relaxed in relation to trade fixtures (*Pooles case* (1703) 1 SALK 368) but this did not extend to general agricultural fixtures not of a specialised nature (see *Elwes v. Maw* [1802] 3 East 38).

Under s.10 of the 1986 Act, the tenant is given a right to remove certain fixtures provided that two conditions are fulfilled. The first is that the tenant must have paid all of the rent and complied with all of the terms and conditions of his tenancy. Should a landlord wish to take the point, compliance with this condition is extremely difficult in the context of, particularly, a tenant's repairing obligation. The second condition requires a notice to be served on the landlord stating the tenant's intention to remove the fixture. Where a tenant serves such a notice the landlord can elect to purchase the fixture and hence override the tenant's right to remove.

By this new section the tenant's position is greatly improved: there is no requirement that he must have complied with the terms and conditions of his tenancy and there is no obligation to serve a notice of intention to remove. The landlord cannot elect to purchase the fixture and override the tenant's right to remove although, as can be seen below (subs. (2)(d)), there are circumstances in which the landlord can indirectly force the tenant to treat the fixture as an improvement and take compensation instead of removing it at the end of the tenancy.

If the tenant chooses not to remove the fixture, it may in certain circumstances be treated as an improvement for which the tenant will be paid compensation (see the General Notes to Pt. III below).

Subs. (1)
The right to remove is not confined to general agricultural fixtures but extends to other trade fixtures or, indeed, to those affixed merely for domestic or ornamental purposes and to buildings provided, in all cases, that they were affixed by the tenant. The tenant may remove, without notice being given to the landlord, during the tenancy or after termination provided that he remains in possession "as a tenant". By s.38(5) the designations of landlord and tenant continue to apply until the conclusion of any proceedings under the Act relating to compensation, but that does not, of course, mean that the tenant remains in possession as tenant. The tenant will remain in possession as tenant if he is holding over or if he takes a new tenancy but if he fails to leave after the expiry of a notice to quit or after forfeiture has been effected, he will not be in possession as a tenant but as a trespasser.

For so long as the tenant has a right to remove in accordance with this section, the common law position as to title to the fixture is altered. At common law, regardless of any rights of removal, title to the fixture vests in the landlord at the moment that the fixture is affixed. Under this subsection, property remains in the tenant and is therefore vulnerable to any remedies or enforcement methods which can be taken against the tenant's property.

Subs. (2)
This subsection circumscribes the tenant's right to remove set out in subs. (1) above.

Paragraphs (a) and (b) also appear as restrictions in the 1986 Act. The obligation referred to in para. (a) may be an obligation imposed by the tenancy but may equally be a statutory obligation. In cases falling within para. (a), the tenant may nevertheless be entitled to compensation for the item as an improvement (see the General Notes to Pt. III below).

Paragraph (c) effectively presents the tenant, in some cases, with an option. Some improvements which would fall to be compensated under s.16 of the Act will fall within the definition of fixture. Under the 1986 Act, if a fixture could be compensated as an improvement, the tenant could not choose to remove it as a fixture at the end of the tenancy but had to rely on his compensation claim. Under this paragraph, it is only if the tenant has actually obtained compensation for the fixture as an improvement that he is prevented from removing it. At the end of his farm business tenancy, therefore, where the tenant has a right to compensation, subject to para. (d) below, he can choose to remove the improvement as a fixture. In many cases, this will be far more straightforward for a tenant than going through arbitration to obtain compensation where he cannot reach agreement as to the amount of compensation with the landlord. Care needs to be taken, however, to ensure that the time taken up in attempting to negotiate compensation does not put the tenant out of time for removing as a fixture.

Paragraph (d) refers to s.17. Section 17 sets out the conditions of eligibility for compensation for tenants' improvements. Before a tenant is entitled to compensation, he must have obtained the landlord's written consent to the improvement. That consent may be conditional provided that the condition imposed relates to the improvement itself. If a condition is that the tenant shall not be entitled to treat the improvement as a fixture, the tenant must rely on his right to compensation and may not rely on the right to remove set out in subs. (1) above.

Subss. (3) and (4)

There is a positive obligation not to do avoidable damage and an obligation to make good all damage whether avoidable or otherwise. The need for subs. (3) in addition to subs. (4) is to enable the landlord to obtain an injunction if necessary and not to have to get into a position of "suffering" the damage and seeking damages from a tenant who may not be in a position to pay.

Subs. (5)

This subsection may apply, for example, where the fixture was acquired from a previous tenant.

Subs. (6)

No contracting out of this section is permitted save insofar as a landlord, when giving written consent to an improvement, may impose a condition that the tenant may not remove the improvement as a fixture. This prohibition on contracting out can be compared with the uncertain position in connection with s.10 of the 1986 Act where it was at least arguable that the parties could contract out (see *Premier Dairies v. Garlick* [1920] 2 Ch. 17 although this was doubted in *Johnson v. Moreton* [1980] AC 37).

Whilst contracting out of the right to remove is not permitted, there is nothing to prevent the parties agreeing to a clause in the tenancy agreement saying that a tenant cannot erect fixtures or cannot erect fixtures of a particular type. However, if such a fixture would amount to an improvement under the definition contained in s.15 below such a clause could, it is submitted, be overridden by arbitration such as to allow the improvement to be made (see the General Note to s.19 below). If such a clause is overridden, it is not clear whether that entitles the tenant to take the improvement, put up after the arbitrator's consent, as a fixture or whether he is confined to his compensation claim. Whilst a landlord can, as a condition of giving consent to the improvement, prevent the tenant from removing it as a fixture, an arbitrator is not entitled to impose conditions upon his consent to an improvement (see s.19) and, should he choose to override a prohibition on the erection of fixtures, he might thereby be giving the tenant a free choice contrary to the terms of the tenancy agreement.

Subs. (7)

This subsection can be compared with the 1986 Act where the common law rules allowing removal of trade fixtures still apply in relation to a 1986 Act tenancy. However, s.10 of the 1986 Act was drafted much more tightly and there were far greater conditions upon the ability of a tenant to remove fixtures.

Part II

Rent Review Under Farm Business Tenancy

INTRODUCTION

In the initial Consultation Paper produced by MAFF and WOAD in February 1991, it was proposed that there should be no regulation at all in relation to rent or rent reviews in the new tenancies regime. By the time of the detailed proposals paper in September 1992, fallback provisions relating to the timing of rent reviews and to the basis for determining the new rent were envisaged, but the emphasis was still very much on complete freedom of contract with the new legislation filling in where the parties had not turned their minds to it. What has ended up in the Act is a more complicated compromise between freedom of contract and regulation such that, in broad terms: (1) the initial rent set can be any amount agreed between the parties; (2) the parties can choose any basis for rent review that they wish; (3) if the basis chosen is one of the options set out in s.9, the parties have to abide by it and cannot opt back into the statutory open market basis; (4) if the basis chosen is not one of the options set out in s.9, it will operate only for so long as both parties are content for it to operate, but either party may opt back into the statutory basis on any of the rent reviews (s.12(b) below); (5) if the parties say nothing about the basis of the rent reviews in their agreement, the statutory open market formula set out in s.13 will apply; (6) in any case, the parties can choose the frequency of their rent reviews.

Application of Part II

9. This Part of this Act applies in relation to a farm business tenancy (notwithstanding any agreement to the contrary) unless the tenancy is created by an instrument which—
  (a) expressly states that the rent is not to be reviewed during the tenancy, or
  (b) provides that the rent is to be varied, at a specified time or times during the tenancy—
      (i) by or to a specified amount, or
      (ii) in accordance with a specified formula which does not preclude a reduction and which does not require or permit the exercise by any person of any judgment or discretion in relation to the determination of the rent of the holding,
  but otherwise is to remain fixed.

DEFINITIONS
  "farm business tenancy": s.1.
  "holding": s.38(1).
  "tenancy": s.38(1).

GENERAL NOTE
  Section 9 provides for the statutory rent review mechanism to apply unless the parties have agreed to one of the other options set out in s.9. Save for these options, contracting out of the statutory mechanism is not permitted although arbitration on the statutory *formula* is a last resort in the absence of agreement or some form of mediation (see s.12(b)). The options in s.9 are designed to avoid the long express rent review clauses found in commercial leases. However, where the parties do agree a formula which is not permitted by the statute, recognition is given to this in s.12(b) (see below). Evidential problems of showing the rent review agreement between the parties have been avoided by only permitting these options where they are set out in a written contract of tenancy between the parties. With oral lettings, the statutory mechanisms will, therefore, apply regardless of any agreement between the parties.
  Option (a). This may be attractive in short-term agreements which would nevertheless be long enough for the statutory mechanism to trigger a rent review in the absence of an express clause, for example, a five-year agreement. There may also be circumstances where both parties wish to avoid risk and where the tenant is prepared to pay more by way of an initial rent to avoid a statutory rent review. As a result of s.10(4) below, it is possible for the parties to agree that there should be no reviews for the early part of the term and then to commence reviews thereafter either under one of the two options set out in s.9(b) below or under the statutory rent review mechanism. This is because it is possible for the parties to choose the frequency of their reviews.
  Option (b)(i). It is important if this option is chosen that the tenancy agreement makes it clear that, other than the stated increases or decreases, the rent is to remain fixed. If not, the parties' choice will not prevail over the statutory mechanism. The circumstances in which this option is chosen are likely to be special: neither landlord nor tenant in a long fixed-term lease are likely to want to second guess the market at the outset. It may be something which the parties will want if, for example, the length of the agreement is such that there will only be one review or the length of the agreement is such that they would have agreed no rent review but either (a) the tenant is

required to do works on the holding such that a lower than usual rent is negotiated for the early part of the term or (b) a higher than usual rent is negotiated by way of a rentalised premium for the early part of the term and the arrangement, in either case, is that an appropriate increase or decrease in the rent will take place part way through the term.

Option (b)(ii). The formula chosen under this option must be objective, require no judgement or discretion to be exercised and cannot be upwards only. Effectively, the formula must be one which leads to a mathematical and certain calculation with no room for dispute between the parties. Indexation of some kind is the most obvious example of such a formula although care would have to be taken in identifying the relevant index, particularly in a long-term lease where changes to indices are possible, and in choosing the index: movements in the Retail Prices Index, for example, may bear little relation to farm profitability or rental levels.

Initial concerns were expressed that where the compilation of an index itself required the exercise of judgement or discretion, for example in the choice of commodities to be included in the index, such exercise would fall foul of the limits of this option. It is submitted that the exercise of judgement or discretion in the compilation of the index does not present a problem: it is only in connection with the application of the index to the rent that pure objectivity is necessary. The section makes it clear that judgement or discretion is outlawed "... in relation to the determination of the rent of the holding".

Alternative formulations may be linked to commodity prices, whether one particular commodity or a basket of commodities, although careful drafting will be needed to ensure complete clarity as to the method of determination of the price, or to a turnover rent in particular circumstances.

As in relation to option (b)(i) above, this option, if chosen, must provide for the rent to remain fixed other than for changes in relation to the application of the formula. If not, the statutory rent review mechanisms will prevail, not as additional reviews but as the only method by which the rent can be reviewed as a result of the fact that the option will not be in accordance with those permitted under s.9 (subject to s.12(b) below).

Such are the strictures of the formula under s.9(b)(ii) that achieving the equivalent to a sitting tenant rent under s.12 of and Sched. 2 to the 1986 Act would be difficult if not impossible. This will create stumbling blocks for landlords and tenants who wish to effect deals, either by an express surrender and regrant, or by moving a 1986 Act protected tenant to another farm on the estate on or after September 1, 1995. The loss of security of tenure for such a tenant may, to an extent, be compensated by a long fixed term, but the inability of the landlord to guarantee 1986 Act level rents may be difficult to overcome.

In respect of the above options, the timing of reviews is a matter for agreement between the parties. As the rest of this Part of the Act only applies where one of the options is not chosen, the parties will also have to be specific on trigger mechanisms for instigating reviews if that is what they want.

Notice requiring statutory rent review

10.—(1) The landlord or tenant under a farm business tenancy in relation to which this Part of this Act applies may by notice in writing given to the other (in this Part of this Act referred to as a "statutory review notice") require that the rent to be payable in respect of the holding as from the review date shall be referred to arbitration in accordance with this Act.

(2) In this Part of this Act "the review date", in relation to a statutory review notice, means a date which—

(a) is specified in the notice, and

(b) complies with subsections (3) to (6) below.

(3) The review date must be at least twelve months but less than twenty-four months after the day on which the statutory review notice is given.

(4) If the parties have agreed in writing that the rent is to be, or may be, varied as from a specified date or dates, or at specified intervals, the review date must be a date as from which the rent could be varied under the agreement.

(5) If the parties have agreed in writing that the review date for the purposes of this Part of this Act is to be a specified date or dates, the review date must be that date or one of those dates.

(6) If the parties have not agreed as mentioned in subsection (4) or (5) above, the review date—

(a) must be an anniversary of the beginning of the tenancy or, where the landlord and the tenant have agreed in writing that the review date for the purposes of this Act is to be some other day of the year, that day of the year, and

(b) must not fall before the end of the period of three years beginning with the latest of any of the following dates—

(i) the beginning of the tenancy,

(ii) any date as from which there took effect a previous direction of an arbitrator as to the amount of the rent,

(iii) any date as from which there took effect a previous determination as to the amount of the rent made, otherwise than as arbitrator, by a person appointed under an agreement between the landlord and the tenant, and

(iv) any date as from which there took effect a previous agreement in writing between the landlord and the tenant, entered into since the grant of the tenancy, as to the amount of the rent.

DEFINITIONS

"beginning of the tenancy": s.38(4).
"farm business tenancy": s.1.
"given": s.36.
"holding": s.38(1).
"landlord": s.38(1), (5).
"review date, the": subs. (2), s.14.
"Statutory review notice": subs. (1), s.14.
"tenancy": s.38(1).
"tenant": s.38(1), (5).

GENERAL NOTE

This section only applies if the parties have not agreed one of the options in s.9 above. It does three things: (1) sets out the mechanism by which a rent review is triggered; (2) provides that the review is by way of arbitration; and (3) enables the review date to be determined.

Either landlord or tenant can instigate the review.

The notice is similar to that under s.12 of the 1986 Act. Under that Act it has been held that the notice, once given, cannot unilaterally be withdrawn by the giver: if the other party wishes the rent review to go ahead then it must go ahead. The notice is a trigger for the statutory procedure (see *Buckinghamshire County Council v. Gordon* (1986) 279 E.G. 853). The trigger notice has no prescribed form but must be in writing and it must specify the review date. See s.36 for service methods.

The review date is defined in such a way that the parties can choose the frequency of their reviews and/or the actual date in any particular year from which a review will take effect even if they are content to rely on the rent being reviewed in accordance with the s.13 open market formula and have not chosen their own basis for review. If the parties do not choose the frequency of reviews, basically there is a three-yearly rent review cycle.

Subss. (4) to (6)

It is these subsections which effectively define the review date. The parties can agree: (1) when reviews are to commence; and/or (2) the intervals between reviews; and/or (3) the actual review date itself.

Any arrangement must be in writing. If it is not agreed in writing, the review date will be as defined in subs. (6). Unlike the options in s.9, the agreement in writing defining the review date does not need to be in a written tenancy agreement and these options are therefore available where the letting is oral or where the parties reach a separate agreement. In the absence of agreement on the actual date of the review, the review date will be the anniversary of the date upon which the tenant is entitled to go into possession (which is the definition of the beginning of the tenancy – see s.38) and not necessarily the anniversary of the date of the tenancy agreement or the commencement of the term itself. This will apply where the parties have made no provision or where they have made provision for the intervals between reviews but have not specified the date itself.

The parties may, of course, agree a review date but be content with the statutory three-yearly intervals and may wish to do so where, for some reason, the beginning of the tenancy (when the tenant is entitled to go into possession) does not coincide with the usual rent day.

The net effect of subs. (6) is that the earliest date possible for the first rent review under the statutory fall back provisions is three years after the date upon which the tenant is entitled to go into possession. Thereafter rent reviews will take place at three-yearly intervals from the date of the last review, regardless of whether that review was by arbitration or by some other person appointed by the parties (s.12(b)) or by agreement and, more importantly, whether or not the last review was comprehensive or not. The Act does not deal with the problem highlighted in *Mann v. Gardner* (1990) 61 P. & C.R. 1 where the Court of Appeal held that a rent reduction of £100 on surrender of the farmhouse out of a total rent of over £21,000 was sufficient to prevent a comprehensive review of the rent for three years thereafter. Other minor alterations in rent which would not have triggered the review period under the 1986 Act will trigger the period under this Act; there is no equivalent to the provisions in Sched. 2, para. 4(2) to the 1986 Act which allow certain changes in the rent to be disregarded for the purposes of ascertaining whether or not the review period has been triggered. These small alterations are as a result of specific provisions in the 1986 Act which are not replicated in the 1995 Act.

Three-yearly reviews are familiar from the 1986 Act. However, there is a difference. Under the 1986 Act, the three years from the date of an agreement between the parties as to the rent only begins to run if the agreement was to increase or decrease the rent not if there was an agreement that the rent should stay at the same level (although a direction of the arbitrator that the rent should remain unchanged does start time running). Under this Act, any agreement as to the amount of the rent between the parties will start time running.

Review date where new tenancy of severed part of reversion

11.—(1) This section applies in any case where a farm business tenancy ("the new tenancy") arises between—

    (a) a person who immediately before the date of the beginning of the tenancy was entitled to a severed part of the reversionary estate in the land comprised in a farm business tenancy ("the original tenancy") in which the land to which the new tenancy relates was then comprised, and

    (b) the person who immediately before that date was the tenant under the original tenancy,

and the rent payable under the new tenancy at its beginning represents merely the appropriate portion of the rent payable under the original tenancy immediately before the beginning of the new tenancy.

    (2) In any case where this section applies—

    (a) references to the beginning of the tenancy in subsection (6) of section 10 of this Act shall be taken to be references to the beginning of the original tenancy, and

    (b) references to rent in that subsection shall be taken to be references to the rent payable under the original tenancy,

until the first occasion following the beginning of the new tenancy on which any such direction, determination or agreement with respect to the rent of the new holding as is mentioned in that subsection takes effect.

DEFINITIONS
    "beginning of the tenancy": s.38(4).
    "farm business tenancy": s.1.
    "holding": s.38(1).
    "new tenancy, the": subs. (1).
    "original tenancy, the": subs. (1)(a).
    "tenancy": s.38(1).
    "tenant": s.38(1), (5).

GENERAL NOTE
Since the Court of Appeal decision in *Jelley v. Buckman* [1974] Q.B. 488 (see also the later county court decisions of *Styles v. Farrow* [1977] 241 E.G. 623 and *Greenway v. Tempest* (1983) unreported) it has been clear that a severance of the landlord's reversionary estate does not bring about separate tenancies on those severed parts: the original tenancy continues, simply now with more than one landlord. Section 140 of the Law of Property Act 1925 then provides that each landlord may enforce covenants and may exercise rights of re-entry and notices to quit independently of one another. As a result of the decision in *Jelley v. Buckman*, there are only limited circumstances in which this section could bite. The first is where, following the severance of the reversion, there is an express agreement with the tenant to enter into new tenancies of each severed part. The second is where the tenant is a party to the deed of severance and agrees the apportionment of the rents between the severed parts where new tenancies of each part may

be implied. The section will, however, only bite where the rent under each new tenancy is merely the appropriate portion of the original rent. There is nothing to prevent the parties agreeing some other rent or basis for apportioning the rent at that stage.

There may actually be good reason for landlords on a severed reversion to have new tenancies. Whilst it is clear that s.140 of the Law of Property Act 1925 (see above) enables each landlord to enforce covenants and serve notices to quit, rent reviews are more difficult. In *Styles v. Farrow* (above) it was held that following a severance of the reversion, the rent could only be reviewed as to the whole holding and that separate demands for rent from each reversioner were invalid: s.140 of the Law of Property Act 1925 does not extend to apportion statutory procedures as opposed to contractual arrangements between the parties and, therefore, all landlords of a severed estate must join in the service of a statutory review notice. Where, however, the parties have chosen a s.9 option and there is a contractual trigger notice, s.140 may operate to apportion that contractual right to each and every reversioner.

Where s.11 bites, it continues the rent review timetable through to the new tenancies to ensure a continuation of the three-year cycle. If, for example, the rent was reviewed (whether by arbitration, determination or agreement) 12 months prior to the beginning of the new tenancies, the first rent review that can take place under the new tenancies is two years later and not three years later.

Appointment of arbitrator

12. Where a statutory review notice has been given in relation to a farm business tenancy, but—
  (a) no arbitrator has been appointed under an agreement made since the notice was given, and
  (b) no person has been appointed under such an agreement to determine the question of the rent (otherwise than as arbitrator) on a basis agreed by the parties,
either party may, at any time during the period of six months ending with the review date, apply to the President of the Royal Institution of Chartered Surveyors (in this Act referred to as "the RICS") for the appointment of an arbitrator by him.

DEFINITIONS
  "farm business tenancy": s.1.
  "given": s.36.
  "review date, the": ss.10(2), 14.
  "RICS, the": ss.12, 37(1).
  "statutory review notice": ss.10(1), 14.

GENERAL NOTE
Section 12 must be read together with s.30 which sets out general provisions dealing with the appointment of an arbitrator under the Act. Section 28, which sets out the timetable for general arbitrations, does not apply to a rent arbitration (see s.28(5)), although any arbitration in respect of the rent will still be under the Arbitration Acts 1950 to 1979. If no arbitrator is appointed by agreement, application can be made by either party to the President of the RICS in the final six-month run up to the review date. The application need not be made by the person who served the statutory review notice.

This section makes it clear that the ability of either party to apply to the President ends on the review date and, therefore, if agreement has not been reached as the review date nears, a protective application should be made by the party wanting the rent to be reviewed to preserve the position.

If the parties agree a basis for reviewing the rent which is either: (a) one of the options set out in s.9 but not contained in a written tenancy agreement; or (b) some other basis for reviewing the rent, whether contained in a written tenancy agreement or not, s.12(b) provides a mechanism for allowing the rent to be determined on that basis with the assistance of a third party, provided that (a) that third party is not appointed as arbitrator and (b) the parties both still want the rent to be determined on that basis. The difference between the circumstances set out in (a) and (b) above and the s.9 options is that, in this case, neither party can be forced to follow through the agreed basis but can opt back into arbitration and the statutory basis for review.

If a s.10 notice is given the parties may agree any basis for reviewing the rent or agree to follow through such a basis as set out in their tenancy agreement and appoint their third party to determine the rent on that agreed basis. Each party is, by the appointment of that third party (likely in most cases to be an expert), then disabled from opting for arbitration because s.12 does not then permit an application to be made to the President of the RICS. If the parties do not agree the appointment of their expert or their third party, application can be made for an arbitrator to be appointed but the arbitrator can only review the rent in accordance with s.13 and not in accordance with the agreement between the parties. Each party will make an assessment as to whether the open market formula or the chosen basis is likely to provide a better result for them and will act accordingly.

The upshot of the interrelationship between s.9 and s.12(b) is that the parties can choose any rent review mechanism they wish but they will only be bound to follow a rent review formula which is not the statutory formula or one of the options set out in s.9 if they have reached the point of agreeing the appointment of their expert. Either party can opt out up to that point. This fits with the interrelationship between s.28 and s.29 for other arbitrations and alternative dispute resolution mechanisms under the Act.

Mention was made earlier of the difficulty in re-organising estates after September 1, 1995 for tenancies with existing 1986 Act security of tenure. Whilst if a tenant is moved to another farm and put on to a farm business tenancy a long fixed-term tenancy can, to an extent, compensate for the lack of security of tenure of the 1986 Act, a sticking point may well be the inability of the parties to guarantee a s.12, Sched. 2 rent equivalent for the new tenancy. It is clear that the parties can, in their tenancy agreement, put in that the rent should be reviewed in accordance with s.12 of and Sched. 2 to the 1986 Act by an expert but it is equally clear that, on any particular review, the landlord or the tenant can revert to the open market rent formula in s.13 below by simply refusing to agree the appointment of the necessary expert to deal with the review on the basis of s.12 and Sched. 2.

Amount of rent

13.—(1) On any reference made in pursuance of a statutory review notice, the arbitrator shall determine the rent properly payable in respect of the holding at the review date and accordingly shall, with effect from that date, increase or reduce the rent previously payable or direct that it shall continue unchanged.

(2) For the purposes of subsection (1) above, the rent properly payable in respect of a holding is the rent at which the holding might reasonably be expected to be let on the open market by a willing landlord to a willing tenant, taking into account (subject to subsections (3) and (4) below) all relevant factors, including (in every case) the terms of the tenancy (including those which are relevant for the purposes of section 10(4) to (6) of this Act, but not those relating to the criteria by reference to which any new rent is to be determined).

(3) The arbitrator shall disregard any increase in the rental value of the holding which is due to tenant's improvements other than—

(a) any tenant's improvement provided under an obligation which was imposed on the tenant by the terms of his tenancy or any previous tenancy and which arose on or before the beginning of the tenancy in question,

(b) any tenant's improvement to the extent that any allowance or benefit has been made or given by the landlord in consideration of its provision, and

(c) any tenant's improvement to the extent that the tenant has received any compensation from the landlord in respect of it.

(4) The arbitrator—

(a) shall disregard any effect on the rent of the fact that the tenant who is a party to the arbitration is in occupation of the holding, and

(b) shall not fix the rent at a lower amount by reason of any dilapidation or deterioration of, or damage to, buildings or land caused or permitted by the tenant.

(5) In this section "tenant's improvement", and references to the provision of such an improvement, have the meaning given by section 15 of this Act.

DEFINITIONS
    "beginning of the tenancy": s.38(4).
    "holding": s.38(1).

"landlord": s.38(1), (5).
"rent properly payable": subs. (2).
"review date, the": ss.10(2), 14.
"statutory review notice": ss.10(1), 14.
"tenancy": s.38(1).
"tenant": s.38(1), (5).
"tenant's improvement": subs. (5), s.15.

GENERAL NOTE

This section sets out the arbitrator's task on an appointment following a statutory review notice. The arbitrator must determine the rent properly payable as at the review date (not the date of reference to arbitration as under the 1986 Act) and the section sets out how that figure is to be found.

Subs. (2)

In a departure from the sitting tenant approach of s.12 of and Sched. 2 to the 1986 Act, the rent payable under the statutory review mechanism is the open market rent with minimal disregards. In comparison with the 1986 Act, the arbitrator no longer has to consider the productive capacity or related earning capacity of the holding and the arbitrator does not have to assume that the parties are "prudent" but simply "willing".

The arbitrator must look at all of the relevant factors but the open market formula is based on a hypothetical landlord and a hypothetical tenant. This is confirmed by subs. (4)(a) where the fact that the tenant is in occupation of the holding is to be disregarded. Circumstances personal to the parties can therefore be ignored. The terms of the tenancy, including the length of the unexpired term, the user covenants, the repairing obligations *etc.* and expressly the rent review intervals and dates (but not any references in the tenancy to a rent review formula) must be considered.

Tenants' improvements, insofar as they would otherwise lead to a rental increase, are to be ignored save in those circumstances set out in s.13(3)(a)–(c). Grant aid provided to either landlord or tenant to assist in the provision of the improvement does not feature so that where grant aid has been provided to a tenant the improvement may still be disregarded, although the definition of tenant's improvement must be considered as it is only those improvements which are provided by the tenant by his own effort or wholly or partly at his own expense which are tenants' improvements within the meaning of the Act (see s.15 below).

Scarcity can be taken into account as can marriage value save insofar as it arises from the tenant's occupation of the holding which is a specific disregard.

Subs. (3)(a)

Subsection (3)(a) disposes of one problem which arose from a similar provision in the 1986 Act. Under the 1986 Act tenants' improvements were brought into account if provided under an obligation imposed on the tenant by the terms of his contract of tenancy. It was unclear whether an improvement resulting from the landlord's conditional consent during the tenancy, which led to a variation of the tenancy agreement, would be caught. Under this subsection it is clear that such improvements would be taken into account on a rent review and that the disregard only relates to improvements provided pursuant to an obligation which arose before or at the time of the tenant becoming entitled to possession under the terms of his tenancy agreement.

Under the 1986 Act, the arbitrator was directed to consider (see Sched. 2 to that Act) the level of rents on comparable holdings, and other arbitrators' awards could be submitted in evidence. Under the 1995 Act, other arbitrators' awards may be inadmissible (see *Land Securities v. Westminster City Council* [1993] 1 W.L.R. 286).

Subs. (3)(b)

An improvement may still be a tenant's improvement within the meaning of s.15 if the landlord has assisted in paying for it, whether directly or whether by a rent reduction or other indirect benefit.

Subs. (3)(c)

This would cover, for example, an improvement provided by the tenant under a previous tenancy in respect of which he has received compensation.

Interpretation of Part II

14. In this Part of this Act, unless the context otherwise requires—
    "the review date", in relation to a statutory review notice, has the meaning given by section 10(2) of this Act;

"statutory review notice" has the meaning given by section 10(1) of this Act.

DEFINITIONS
"the review date": ss.10(2), 14.
"statutory review notice": ss.10(1), 14.

PART III

COMPENSATION ON TERMINATION OF FARM BUSINESS TENANCY

Tenant's entitlement to compensation

INTRODUCTION
Under the 1995 Act the only compensation payable on termination is for tenants' improvements as defined by s.15. Any other matter, whether for a landlord or for a tenant, will be a matter of contract between the parties. This Part sets out a new and wide-ranging definition of tenants' improvements and a discrete regime for establishing eligibility and the amount of compensation to be paid.

Meaning of "tenant's improvement"

15. For the purposes of this Part of this Act a "tenant's improvement", in relation to any farm business tenancy, means—
(a) any physical improvement which is made on the holding by the tenant by his own effort or wholly or partly at his own expense, or
(b) any intangible advantage which—
(i) is obtained for the holding by the tenant by his own effort or wholly or partly at his own expense, and
(ii) becomes attached to the holding,
and references to the provision of a tenant's improvement are references to the making by the tenant of any physical improvement falling within paragraph (a) above or the obtaining by the tenant of any intangible advantage falling within paragraph (b) above.

DEFINITIONS
"farm business tenancy": s.1.
"holding": s.38(1).
"tenant": s.38(1), (5).
"tenant's improvement": s.15.

GENERAL NOTE
This section, and its wide definition of tenants' improvements, can be compared with the extensive lists of different types of improvement all with their own rules under the 1986 Act. The idea of the new definition is to avoid lists which can go out of date and need amendment and to choose a definition which can grow with the changes in the industry.
There are basically two classes of improvement: physical improvement and intangible advantages. As will be seen below, for some purposes, those two classes have been further broken down. Certain types of physical improvements, called "routine improvements" (see below) have different rules so far as references to arbitration are concerned and certain types of intangible advantages, namely planning permissions, have their own rules for eligibility and amount of compensation payable. Physical improvements may now also be fixtures (see s.8 above). This can be compared with the position under the 1986 Act where if a particular item was capable of attracting compensation as an improvement, it could not be treated as a fixture by the tenant. Here, it is only where compensation has actually been paid to the tenant that that restriction applies.
The Act allows compensation not only where a tenant has paid in whole or in part for the provision of the improvement but also where the improvement is made by the tenant's own effort, for example, his own labour. This is a change from the position under the 1986 Act and may be wide enough to cover not only the position where no costs other than the tenant's own efforts are involved but also to compensate the tenant where the landlord has provided the materials and the tenant the labour. As we shall see, the compensation payable to a tenant may

be reduced where the landlord has paid for the provision of the improvement, but only if there is an agreement in writing to that effect (see s.20(2)) and there may be cases therefore where the landlord has paid for the materials and the tenant has provided the labour but where the tenant reaps the entire benefit on termination.

During the passage of the Bill, attempts were made to try to ensure that express provisions were included to provide for compensation to a tenant on quitting for tenant-right matters. The Bill always provided for compensation on quitting for physical improvements and there is no doubt that certain tenant-right matters, such as ploughing, liming, fertilizing, *etc.* would fall within that definition. During the final stages of the Bill in the House of Commons, however, a sub-category of physical improvements, called routine improvements was introduced. Routine improvements are defined in s.19(10) below and cover some, although not all, of those matters which would be tenant-right matters in the 1986 Act (see s.65 of and Sched. 8 to the 1986 Act). The only purpose of the subcategory (see s.19(2)) is to enable the Act to provide that the tenant may, in the case of a routine improvement but not otherwise, go to arbitration following a landlord's refusal to consent to the improvement, even where the tenant has begun the improvement in question.

Intangible advantages are a new concept and recognise that value may be added to a holding other than by the provision of physical improvements. It is only those intangible advantages which become attached to the holding and which remain on the holding at the termination of the tenancy in respect of which compensation may be paid.

Specifically provided for in the Act are planning permissions where the specified physical improvement has not been completed or the change of use effected. It is clear that milk quota is also intended to be compensated for as an intangible advantage and most would accept that, since the decision of Chadwick J in *Faulks v. Faulks* [1992] 1 E.G.L.R. 9, milk quota is attached to the holding despite the fact that in certain very limited circumstances a transfer of milk quota can now take place without a transfer of land (see reg. 13 of the Dairy Produce Quotas Regulations 1994 (S.I. 1994 No. 672)). Other quotas, subsidies and premiums payable are, at the moment, personal rights of the farmer but there is a certain amount of pressure to alter this position and to attach other subsidy payments to the land.

In addition to planning permissions and quotas, it is possible that goodwill and licences or designations, particularly of an environmental nature, may well fall to be treated as intangible advantages.

Tenant's right to compensation for tenant's improvement

16.—(1) The tenant under a farm business tenancy shall, subject to the provisions of this Part of this Act, be entitled on the termination of the tenancy, on quitting the holding, to obtain from his landlord compensation in respect of any tenant's improvement.

(2) A tenant shall not be entitled to compensation under this section in respect of—

(a) any physical improvement which is removed from the holding, or

(b) any intangible advantage which does not remain attached to the holding.

(3) Section 13 of, and Schedule 1 to, the Agriculture Act 1986 (compensation to outgoing tenants for milk quota) shall not apply in relation to a farm business tenancy.

DEFINITIONS

"farm business tenancy": s.1.
"holding": s.38(1).
"landlord": s.38(1), (5).
"tenant": s.38(1), (5).
"tenant's improvement": s.15.
"termination of the tenancy": s.38(1).

GENERAL NOTE

Subsections (1) and (2) set out the entitlement to compensation and make it clear (if it were not already) that it is effectively only where the benefit of the improvement remains with the holding that the tenant is entitled to compensation. Furthermore, two things have to coincide before the tenant is entitled to compensation; (1) the tenancy must be terminated, and (2) the tenant must be quitting the holding. If the tenant remains on the holding, for example, under a new tenancy, there is no *entitlement* at the termination of the earlier tenancy to compensation. Reference should be made to the General Note to s.23 below.

Subsection (3) ensures that the compensation provisions for outgoing tenants in relation to milk quotas set out in the Agriculture Act 1986 (c. 49) cannot apply to farm business tenancies and that the amount of compensation is by reference to s.20 of this Act. This is designed to prevent a tenant from claiming twice. Any tenant moving from a 1986 Act tenancy carrying with it the right to compensation for milk quota in accordance with the provisions of the Agriculture Act 1986 is, therefore, advised to make his claim for compensation before moving, and to reach agreement as to the amount of compensation due under the 1986 Act to fix entitlement at the termination of the 1986 tenancy. A tenant may, of course, be prepared for the landlord to delay actual payment.

Conditions of eligibility

Consent of landlord as condition of compensation for tenant's improvement

17.—(1) A tenant shall not be entitled to compensation under section 16 of this Act in respect of any tenant's improvement unless the landlord has given his consent in writing to the provision of the tenant's improvement.

(2) Any such consent may be given in the instrument creating the tenancy or elsewhere.

(3) Any such consent may be given either unconditionally or on condition that the tenant agrees to a specified variation in the terms of the tenancy.

(4) The variation referred to in subsection (3) above must be related to the tenant's improvement in question.

(5) This section does not apply in any case where the tenant's improvement consists of planning permission.

DEFINITIONS
   "given": s.36.
   "landlord": s.38(1), (5).
   "planning permission": s.27 and the Town and Country Planning Act 1990, s.336(1).
   "tenancy": s.38(1).
   "tenant": s.38(1), (5).
   "tenant's improvement": s.15.

GENERAL NOTE

Subs. (1)
   Consent may be given after the improvement has been effected but the tenant runs a risk: if consent is refused then, save in the case of routine improvements (see s.19(2), (8) and (10) below), the tenant cannot then go to arbitration to obtain the approval of the arbitrator to the provision of the improvement. The requirement for consent is particularly important in the context of milk quota where the tenant may inadvertently transfer milk quota off another holding which he occupies (whether as owner-occupier or as tenant) on to the farm business tenancy land simply by using the land for milk production (within the wide meaning of *Puncknowle Farms v. Kane* [1985] 3 All E.R. 790). The moment that the tenant begins to use the farm business tenancy land in connection with his dairy business the improvement has begun, as the milk quota will begin to attach to the farm business tenancy land and it is then too late to go to arbitration should the landlord subsequently refuse consent. Careful drafting of tenancies for tenants or owners of dairy enterprises taking additional land on farm business tenancies is required to avoid this problem.

Subs. (2)
   It is likely that consent will be given in the tenancy agreement to routine improvements. If consent is not given directly, but the tenant is placed under a positive obligation to effect the improvement, such an obligation will imply the consent of the landlord. For example, if a tenant is obliged to farm to a certain standard and husbandry rules are laid down in the tenancy agreement, the consent to routine improvements to farm to that standard will have been impliedly given.

Subss. (3) and (4)

Examples of permitted variations will be an alteration to the repairing covenant or (and this can be seen by s.8(2)(d)) a condition that the tenant will treat the improvement as an improvement and not remove it as a fixture on the termination of the tenancy.

Conditions in relation to compensation for planning permission

18.—(1) A tenant shall not be entitled to compensation under section 16 of this Act in respect of a tenant's improvement which consists of planning permission unless—

   (a) the landlord has given his consent in writing to the making of the application for planning permission,

   (b) that consent is expressed to be given for the purpose—

        (i) of enabling a specified physical improvement falling within paragraph (a) of section 15 of this Act lawfully to be provided by the tenant, or

        (ii) of enabling the tenant lawfully to effect a specified change of use, and

   (c) on the termination of the tenancy, the specified physical improvement has not been completed or the specified change of use has not been effected.

(2) Any such consent may be given either unconditionally or on condition that the tenant agrees to a specified variation in the terms of the tenancy.

(3) The variation referred to in subsection (2) above must be related to the physical improvement or change of use in question.

DEFINITIONS

   "given": s.36.
   "landlord": s.38(1), (5).
   "planning permission": s.27 and the Town and Country Planning Act 1990, s.336(1).
   "tenancy": s.38(1).
   "tenant": s.38(1), (5).
   "tenant's improvement": s.15.
   "termination of the tenancy": s.38(1).

GENERAL NOTE

Subs. (1)

This section sets out a separate, although similar, set of conditions of eligibility for planning permissions than for other improvements. Planning permissions are a species of intangible advantage. Compensation will only be available for planning permissions if the landlord's written consent has been obtained: there is no fall back of arbitration (see s.19(1)(a)).

The regime for compensating for planning permissions is to ensure that a tenant who, with consent, has applied for planning permission as a first stage of effecting a physical improvement or change of use (see subs. (1)(b)) but who has not completed the improvement or effected the change of use (see subs. (1)(c)) on the termination of the tenancy, is compensated. The compensation provisions are most likely to be relevant where a landlord forfeits the lease or exercises a break clause or where the tenant is on a continuing annual periodic tenancy and the landlord serves 12 months notice to quit: in other words, in circumstances where, from the tenant's point of view, the tenancy unexpectedly comes to an end before he has implemented the permission.

If planning permission is likely to improve the value of the holding (see s.20 below) and particularly if the application is going to cost the tenant a substantial amount of money, it would be wise to seek the landlord's consent specifically to the application for planning permission itself as well as to the improvement to cover the unexpected termination situation. If the landlord refuses consent to the planning permission and to the improvements, the tenant can still apply for planning permission and can go to arbitration in respect of the improvement (see below) but the planning permission would not be compensatable in those circumstances if the tenancy were to end before the physical improvement or change of use had been effected.

Of course, the landlord can himself apply for planning permission but it will be at his cost. Whether he does so or gives the tenant permission to do so will depend on the circumstances, including the costs of the planning permission against the likely cost of compensating the tenant for an unimplemented permission and the landlord's ability to terminate the lease and the like-lihood that he will do so.

Subss. (2) and (3)
The conditions which may be imposed must relate to the physical improvement or change of use and not to the planning permission itself.

Reference to arbitration of refusal or failure to give consent or of condition attached to consent

19.—(1) Where, in relation to any tenant's improvement, the tenant under a farm business tenancy is aggrieved by—
 (a) the refusal of his landlord to give his consent under section 17(1) of this Act,
 (b) the failure of his landlord to give such consent within two months of a written request by the tenant for such consent, or
 (c) any variation in the terms of the tenancy required by the landlord as a condition of giving such consent,
the tenant may by notice in writing given to the landlord demand that the question shall be referred to arbitration under this section; but this sub-section has effect subject to subsections (2) and (3) below.

(2) No notice under subsection (1) above may be given in relation to any tenant's improvement which the tenant has already provided or begun to provide, unless that improvement is a routine improvement.

(3) No notice under subsection (1) above may be given—
 (a) in a case falling within paragraph (a) or (c) of that subsection, after the end of the period of two months beginning with the day on which notice of the refusal or variation referred to in that paragraph was given to the tenant, or
 (b) in a case falling within paragraph (b) of that subsection, after the end of the period of four months beginning with the day on which the writ-ten request referred to in that paragraph was given to the landlord.

(4) Where the tenant has given notice under subsection (1) above but no arbitrator has been appointed under an agreement made since the notice was given, the tenant or the landlord may apply to the President of the RICS, subject to subsection (9) below, for the appointment of an arbitrator by him.

(5) The arbitrator shall consider whether, having regard to the terms of the tenancy and any other relevant circumstances (including the circumstances of the tenant and the landlord), it is reasonable for the tenant to provide the tenant's improvement.

(6) Subject to subsection (9) below, the arbitrator may unconditionally approve the provision of the tenant's improvement or may withhold his approval, but may not give his approval subject to any condition or vary any condition required by the landlord under section 17(3) of this Act.

(7) If the arbitrator gives his approval, that approval shall have effect for the purposes of this Part of this Act and for the purposes of the terms of the farm business tenancy as if it were the consent of the landlord.

(8) In a case falling within subsection (1)(c) above, the withholding by the arbitrator of his approval shall not affect the validity of the landlord's con-sent or of the condition subject to which it was given.

(9) Where, at any time after giving a notice under subsection (1) above in relation to any tenant's improvement which is not a routine improvement, the tenant begins to provide the improvement—
 (a) no application may be made under subsection (4) above after that time,

(b) where such an application has been made but no arbitrator has been appointed before that time, the application shall be ineffective, and

(c) no award may be made by virtue of subsection (6) above after that time except as to the costs of the reference and award in a case where the arbitrator was appointed before that time.

(10) For the purposes of this section—

"fixed equipment" includes any building or structure affixed to land and any works constructed on, in, over or under land, and also includes anything grown on land for a purpose other than use after severance from the land, consumption of the thing grown or its produce, or amenity;

"routine improvement", in relation to a farm business tenancy, means any tenant's improvement which—

(a) is a physical improvement made in the normal course of farming the holding or any part of the holding, and

(b) does not consist of fixed equipment or an improvement to fixed equipment,

but does not include any improvement whose provision is prohibited by the terms of the tenancy.

DEFINITIONS

"farm business tenancy": s.1.
"fixed equipment": subs. (10).
"given": s.36.
"landlord": s.38(1), (5).
"RICS": s.38(1).
"routine improvement": subs. (10).
"tenancy": s.38(1).
"tenant": s.38(1), (5).
"tenant's improvement": s.15.

GENERAL NOTE

Subs. (1)

The ability of the tenant to refer the matter of consent to an improvement to arbitration, is confined to the refusal to give consent under s.17. Section 17 does not apply to planning permissions and therefore it is not possible to apply to an arbitrator to override a landlord's refusal to grant consent to obtain planning permission. This means that where a landlord refuses consent to planning permission and to the improvement and the tenant obtains the consent of the arbitrator to the improvement, he must run the risk of obtaining planning permission and it not being implemented by the time of the termination of the tenancy.

In order to start time running against a landlord who does not respond, the tenant must make his request in writing (see s.19(1)(b)). In all cases, therefore, in order to save time, all requests for consent should be made in writing. The tenant can apply not only following a refusal or no response from the landlord but also if he feels "aggrieved" by the conditions which the landlord wishes to impose. If the tenant refers the matter to arbitration for this reason, he obviously runs the risk of a refusal of approval. However, that refusal would not put him in any worse a position (see subss. (7) and (8) below).

Section 28 of this Act does not apply to arbitrations under this section (s.28(5)) although s.30 does and s.29 (alternative dispute resolution) is not available as it only disapplies s.28 when s.28 would otherwise apply.

The arbitration is under the Arbitration Acts 1950 to 1979.

Subs. (2)

See the General Note to s.17(1) above and the commentary to subs. (9) below.

Subs. (3)(b)

In effect the landlord is deemed to have refused after two months and this timetable brings it into line with (3)(a) above. The tenant cannot let matters drift. Notice has to be given demanding arbitration within a set time period. However, there is nothing to stop a tenant starting again by making a fresh request for consent.

Subs. (4)

There is no time-limit within which the tenant or the landlord must apply for the appointment of an arbitrator, although by subs. (9) below no application may be made after the tenant begins to provide the improvements. If an agreement between the parties as to the identity of the arbitrator is to oust the ability of the parties to apply to the President, it must be an agreement reached after notice is given under subs. (1) above. The identity of an arbitrator cannot, therefore, be by way of a standing agreement in the tenancy agreement itself.

Subs. (5)

The arbitrator is specifically directed to take into account the circumstances of the tenant and the landlord, and this may include their financial and personal circumstances. If the landlord is able to show that he will not be able to afford to pay compensation on the termination of the tenancy, this will be a consideration which the arbitrator may take into account. The arbitrator must also have regard to the terms of the tenancy and this will obviously include the length of the unexpired term and the ability of either party to bring it to an end before that date. It will also include any clause in the tenancy agreement prohibiting the improvement in question. However, it is submitted that the arbitrator is able to override such a prohibition, otherwise a refusal by the landlord in advance in the tenancy agreement could achieve what a refusal at the time of a request could not. It may be, however, that a refusal in the tenancy agreement would carry more weight: the tenant has known from the outset of the prohibition and that prohibition together with the other terms of the tenancy will have determined the rent payable.

Other considerations for the arbitrator will be the need for the improvement and the impact on the tenant's business if it is not provided, the likely life of the improvement against the unexpired term of the tenancy and whether the improvement is needed to comply with statutory obligations, for example relating to pollution control. The question for the arbitrator is whether it is reasonable for a tenant to provide the improvement not whether it is necessary.

Subss. (6)–(8)

The arbitrator is limited in what he can do: he can grant permission for the improvement or he can refuse it. He cannot impose conditions or, for example, state that the tenant may not remove the improvement as a fixture at the termination of the tenancy. If the arbitrator refuses consent and the tenant commenced arbitration because he did not like the landlord's qualified consent, subs. (8) ensures that the tenant is no worse off and can return and take the conditions imposed by that qualified consent. The landlord is not able to withdraw his consent once it has been given.

Subs. (9)

This subsection extends subs. (2) above effectively to prevent a tenant from obtaining compensation for an improvement which he begins to implement before the arbitration award has been made, by ensuring that he is not entitled to continue the arbitration process if he begins the improvement.

Subs. (10)

Routine improvements are essentially certain tenant-right matters, being physical improvements made in the normal course of farming. A wide definition, avoiding lists, has been chosen and many traditional tenant-right matters will be caught; for example, growing crops, cultivations, liming, fertilising *etc.* and many other matters set out as tenant-right matters in Sched. 8 to the 1986 Act.

Where there are tenant-right matters which do not fall within the definition of routine improvements, the parties will have to make specific provision in the tenancy agreement if the tenant is to obtain compensation on quitting. The only difference between routine improvements and other physical improvements is the tenant's right to apply for arbitrator's approval retrospectively after the improvement has begun (see subs. (2)) and to enable the tenant to begin to provide the improvement during the arbitration process (see subs. (9)) which he may have to do by virtue of the nature of the improvement concerned which may have to be effected at a certain time of the year.

At first sight, requiring the landlord's written consent to tenant-right matters seems unworkable. However, it will be relevant in most cases only in the final year of the tenancy and such consents will often be in the tenancy agreement itself, either expressly or impliedly as a result of the user covenants or the husbandry obligations placed on the tenant (see the General Note to s.17(2) above).

Amount of compensation

Amount of compensation for tenant's improvement not consisting of planning permission

20.—(1) The amount of compensation payable to the tenant under section 16 of this Act in respect of any tenant's improvement shall be an amount equal to the increase attributable to the improvement in the value of the holding at the termination of the tenancy as land comprised in a tenancy.

(2) Where the landlord and the tenant have entered into an agreement in writing whereby any benefit is given or allowed to the tenant in consideration of the provision of a tenant's improvement, the amount of compensation otherwise payable in respect of that improvement shall be reduced by the proportion which the value of the benefit bears to the amount of the total cost of providing the improvement.

(3) Where a grant has been or will be made to the tenant out of public money in respect of a tenant's improvement, the amount of compensation otherwise payable in respect of that improvement shall be reduced by the proportion which the amount of the grant bears to the amount of the total cost of providing the improvement.

(4) Where a physical improvement which has been completed or a change of use which has been effected is authorised by any planning permission granted on an application made by the tenant, section 18 of this Act does not prevent any value attributable to the fact that the physical improvement or change of use is so authorised from being taken into account under this section in determining the amount of compensation payable in respect of the physical improvement or in respect of any intangible advantage obtained as a result of the change of use.

(5) This section does not apply where the tenant's improvement consists of planning permission.

DEFINITIONS
"holding": s.38(1).
"landlord": s.38(1), (5).
"planning permission": s.27 and the Town and Country Planning Act 1990, s.336(1).
"tenancy": s.38(1).
"tenant": s.38(1), (5).
"tenant's improvement": s.15.
"termination of the tenancy": s.38(1).

GENERAL NOTE

Subs. (1)
The idea of the compensation provisions is not to compensate the tenant for the cost of the improvement but to be restitutionary in nature and they are designed to ensure that the landlord is not unjustly enriched at the tenant's expense. This section works on the assumption that in many cases the benefit that the landlord would obtain from the improvement (if any) is by way of an increased rent from the holding. The landlord would obviously receive that increased rent for the length of the life of the improvement and it is that benefit or assumed benefit which must be passed to the tenant. The amount of compensation which the tenant receives, therefore, is in most cases the capitalised increase in the rental value of the holding as a result of the improvement for the length of the life of the improvement. Capitalised rental values as a basis for valuation will not be needed in the case of tenant-right matters where a clear value (for example, of the standing crop) can be seen.

The valuation takes place at the termination of the tenancy and, therefore, the tenant takes the risk of the improvement becoming unfashionable, in breach of regulations or overtaken by new technology. This also reflects the restitutionary nature of the provisions.

Subs. (2)
Reference should be made to the General Note to s.15(1) above. Unlike the position under the 1986 Act, a tenant may be compensated for improvements where he has not paid for the improvement but where it has been provided by the tenant's own efforts. This may be wide enough to compensate a tenant where the costs of materials have been met by the landlord but the labour has been put in by the tenant himself. If so, care will have to be taken by landlords to ensure that the arrangement is reduced into writing to enable them to take advantage of this subsection.

Subs. (3)
Note that for the purposes of rent review (see s.13(3) above) the grant-aided elements of the tenant's improvements still fall to be disregarded.

Subs. (4)
Unimplemented planning permissions where the physical improvement has not been completed or the change of use effected are compensated as separate items (see s.18 above). This section recognises, however, that the increase in the value of the holding attributable to an improvement may be greater where that improvement has been authorised by a valid planning consent and makes it clear that such additional value is not factored out by s.18.

Amount of compensation for planning permission

21.—(1) The amount of compensation payable to the tenant under section 16 of this Act in respect of a tenant's improvement which consists of planning permission shall be an amount equal to the increase attributable to the fact that the relevant development is authorised by the planning permission in the value of the holding at the termination of the tenancy as land comprised in a tenancy.

(2) In subsection (1) above, "the relevant development" means the physical improvement or change of use specified in the landlord's consent under section 18 of this Act in accordance with subsection (1)(b) of that section.

(3) Where the landlord and the tenant have entered into an agreement in writing whereby any benefit is given or allowed to the tenant in consideration of the obtaining of planning permission by the tenant, the amount of compensation otherwise payable in respect of that permission shall be reduced by the proportion which the value of the benefit bears to the amount of the total cost of obtaining the permission.

DEFINITIONS
"landlord": s.38(1), (5).
"planning permission": s.27 and the Town and Country Planning Act 1990, s.336(1).
"relevant development, the": subs. (2).
"tenancy": s.38(1).
"tenant": s.38(1), (5).
"tenant's improvement": s.15.
"termination of the tenancy": s.38(1).

GENERAL NOTE

Subs. (1)
Subsection (1) provides a similar method of calculating compensation to that for physical improvements and for intangible advantages other than planning permissions.

Subs. (2)
The limit in subs. (2) must be noted. The planning permission obtained may be wide enough to permit development other than the specific physical improvement or change of use authorised by the landlord's consent, but it is by reference to the consented improvement or change of use and not the planning permission itself that the increase in value is determined. Also, it is not the increase in value of the freehold as a result of the planning permission which the tenant obtains, but the increase in value of the land as land comprised in a tenancy. Landlords should ensure that their consent is narrowly drafted to the specific physical improvement or change of use required by the tenant.

Subs. (3)
See the General Note to s.20(2) above.

Settlement of claims for compensation

22.—(1) Any claim by the tenant under a farm business tenancy for compensation under section 16 of this Act shall, subject to the provisions of this section, be determined by arbitration under this section.

(2) No such claim for compensation shall be enforceable unless before the end of the period of two months beginning with the date of the termination of the tenancy the tenant has given notice in writing to his landlord of his intention to make the claim and of the nature of the claim.

(3) Where—
   (a) the landlord and the tenant have not settled the claim by agreement in writing, and
   (b) no arbitrator has been appointed under an agreement made since the notice under subsection (2) above was given,
either party may, after the end of the period of four months beginning with the date of the termination of the tenancy, apply to the President of the RICS for the appointment of an arbitrator by him.

(4) Where—
   (a) an application under subsection (3) above relates wholly or partly to compensation in respect of a routine improvement (within the meaning of section 19 of this Act) which the tenant has provided or has begun to provide, and
   (b) that application is made at the same time as an application under section 19(4) of this Act relating to the provision of that improvement,
the President of the RICS shall appoint the same arbitrator on both applications and, if both applications are made by the same person, only one fee shall be payable by virtue of section 30(2) of this Act in respect of them.

(5) Where a tenant lawfully remains in occupation of part of the holding after the termination of a farm business tenancy, references in subsections (2) and (3) above to the termination of the tenancy shall, in the case of a claim relating to that part of the holding, be construed as references to the termination of the occupation.

DEFINITIONS
   "farm business tenancy": s.1.
   "given": s.36.
   "holding": s.38(1).
   "landlord": s.38(1), (5).
   "RICS, the": s.38(1).
   "tenant": s.38(1), (5).
   "termination of the tenancy": subs. (4), s.38(1).

GENERAL NOTE
   Section 28 of the Act does not apply to arbitrations under this section (see s.28(5)), although s.30 does, and s.29 (alternative dispute resolution) is not available as s.29 only applies to disapply s.28 in circumstances where that section would otherwise apply. However, the arbitration under this section is under the Arbitration Acts 1950 to 1979.
   This section provides for mandatory reference to arbitration as to the amount of compensation in the absence of agreement between the parties. Subsection (1) sets up a discrete arbitration timetable for the determination of compensation claims and is self-explanatory. This section applies to all physical improvements including routine improvements (although note subs. (4)) and to all intangible advantages including planning permissions.

Subss. (2) and (3)
   The service of a notice to make a claim and the appointment of an arbitrator are familiar from the 1986 Act. There is no prescribed form for the notice although it must set out the information specified in subs. (2). Both relevant dates, for the service of the notice and for the appointment of an arbitrator in default of agreement, run from the date of the termination of the tenancy (see subs. (5) below).

Subs. (4)
. This cuts down on the bureaucracy and costs where a tenant is applying at the same time for consent to routine improvements already made or started and for compensation in respect of improvements generally. In practical terms, an arbitrator will take first the question of consent for routine improvements and will then go on to deal with all questions of compensation.

Subs. (5)
This extends the period for claiming compensation in the event of the tenant holding over, for example, in the buildings until sale of the grain or on the land to take a late harvested crop.

Supplementary provisions with respect to compensation

Successive tenancies

23.—(1) Where the tenant under a farm business tenancy has remained in the holding during two or more such tenancies, he shall not be deprived of his right to compensation under section 16 of this Act by reason only that any tenant's improvement was provided during a tenancy other than the one at the termination of which he quits the holding.

(2) The landlord and tenant under a farm business tenancy may agree that the tenant is to be entitled to compensation under section 16 of this Act on the termination of the tenancy even though at that termination the tenant remains in the holding under a new tenancy.

(3) Where the landlord and the tenant have agreed as mentioned in subsection (2) above in relation to any tenancy ("the earlier tenancy"), the tenant shall not be entitled to compensation at the end of any subsequent tenancy in respect of any tenant's improvement provided during the earlier tenancy in relation to the land comprised in the earlier tenancy.

DEFINITIONS
"earlier tenancy, the": subs. (3).
"farm business tenancy": s.1.
"holding": s.38(1).
"landlord": s.38(1), (5).
"tenancy": s.38(1).
"tenant": s.38(1), (5).
"tenant's improvement": s.15.
"termination": s.38(1).
"termination of the tenancy": s.38(1).

GENERAL NOTE

Subs. (1)
Unless the tenant quits the holding on the termination of the tenancy there is no entitlement to compensation at that time (see s.16).
This provision allows the tenant to "roll over" his claim for compensation for improvements where he remains on the holding under a new tenancy. It is an important provision if, in the early days of this Act, fixed-term tenancies granted are initially going to be relatively short but may be renewed. However, as the roll over only applies between farm business tenancies, a tenant should be careful to ensure that the later tenancies are farm business tenancies and have not, for example, slipped into the Landlord and Tenant Act 1954, Pt. II, by reason of the fact that they are diversified estates in respect of which it can no longer be said that they are primarily or wholly agricultural at the outset (see the General Note to s.1 above).
"Holding" (see s.38(1)) means the aggregate of land comprised in the tenancy, and this subsection will only, therefore, apply where the land in the two or more tenancies is the same, although a *de minimis* rule may apply. It is the land which must be the same and not the terms of the subsequent tenancies. This subsection preserves the tenant's claim not only where there has been a technical surrender and regrant but also where he continues to occupy under the terms of a new tenancy and where he cannot obtain the landlord's agreement or does not wish to obtain the landlord's agreement under subs. (2) below.

Subss. (2) and (3)
By virtue of s.16 above, a tenant's right to compensation only arises on the termination of the tenancy upon the tenant quitting the holding. If he remains, therefore, the entitlement does not

arise. The route by which the tenant can take his compensation at the end of the earlier tenancy is by obtaining the agreement of the landlord in accordance with this subsection. If the landlord refuses to agree, the tenant's only option is to refuse the new tenancy and quit the holding to obtain compensation. There is no fallback of arbitration for the refusal of agreement under subs. (2). Where there is a risk that the increase in value of the holding as a result of the improvement will be significantly less at the end of a later tenancy when the tenant actually quits, whether as a result of the age of the improvement, technological advances or changes in a relevant regulatory framework, a tenant should seek the agreement of the landlord to take compensation early. In circumstances where it is likely, however, to be in the interests of a tenant to want to take his compensation early, it is unlikely to be in the interests of the landlord. However, this issue will not be treated in isolation but as part and parcel of the negotiations for the new tenancy.

Subs. (3)
Subsection (3) makes it clear that the tenant is not entitled to be compensated twice for the same improvement.

Resumption of possession of part of holding

24.—(1) Where—
  (a) the landlord under a farm business tenancy resumes possession of part of the holding in pursuance of any provision of the tenancy, or
  (b) a person entitled to a severed part of the reversionary estate in a holding held under a farm business tenancy resumes possession of part of the holding by virtue of a notice to quit that part given to the tenant by virtue of section 140 of the Law of Property Act 1925,
the provisions of this Part of this Act shall, subject to subsections (2) and (3) below, apply to that part of the holding (in this section referred to as "the relevant part") as if it were a separate holding which the tenant had quitted in consequence of a notice to quit and, in a case falling within paragraph (b) above, as if the person resuming possession were the landlord of that separate holding.

(2) The amount of compensation payable to the tenant under section 16 of this Act in respect of any tenant's improvement provided for the relevant part by the tenant and not consisting of planning permission shall, subject to section 20(2) to (4) of this Act, be an amount equal to the increase attributable to the tenant's improvement in the value of the original holding on the termination date as land comprised in a tenancy.

(3) The amount of compensation payable to the tenant under section 16 of this Act in respect of any tenant's improvement which consists of planning permission relating to the relevant part shall, subject to section 21(3) of this Act, be an amount equal to the increase attributable to the fact that the relevant development is authorised by the planning permission in the value of the original holding on the termination date as land comprised in a tenancy.

(4) In a case falling within paragraph (a) or (b) of subsection (1) above, sections 20 and 21 of this Act shall apply on the termination of the tenancy, in relation to the land then comprised in the tenancy, as if the reference in subsection (1) of each of those sections to the holding were a reference to the original holding.

(5) In subsections (2) to (4) above—
   "the original holding" means the land comprised in the farm business tenancy—
      (a) on the date when the landlord gave his consent under section 17 or 18 of this Act in relation to the tenant's improvement, or
      (b) where approval in relation to the tenant's improvement was given by an arbitrator, on the date on which that approval was given,
   "the relevant development", in relation to any tenant's improvement which consists of planning permission, has the meaning given by section 21(2) of this Act, and

"the termination date" means the date on which possession of the relevant part was resumed.

DEFINITIONS
  "farm business tenancy": s.1.
  "holding": s.38(1).
  "landlord": s.38(1), (5).
  "original holding, the": subs. (5).
  "planning permission": s.27 and the Town and Country Planning Act 1990, s.336(1).
  "relevant development, the": subs. (5), s.21(2).
  "relevant part, the": subs. (1).
  "tenancy": s.38(1).
  "tenant": s.38(1), (5).
  "tenant's improvement": s.15.
  "termination date, the": subs. (5).
  "termination of the tenancy": s.38(1).

GENERAL NOTE
Section 74 of the 1986 Act contains similar provisions as found in this section but does not require the assessment of compensation by reference to the original holding (see below).

Subs. (1)
This subsection only applies where a landlord has instigated the resumption of part of the holding either as a result of the exercise of a break clause or by service of a notice to quit under s.140(2) of the Law of Property Act 1925 by reason of being the owner of a severed reversionary estate. On s.140(2) see the General Note to s.5 above.
This subsection ensures that the tenant's entitlement to compensation arises when the landlord resumes possession of that part.

Subs. (2)
The entitlement to compensation is in respect of improvements "provided for" the part of the holding being taken back. This may cover improvements on adjoining land which serve only the part taken back, for example, storage facilities. The compensation is assessed not by reference to the increase in value of the part taken back, which could give a distorted picture, but by reference to the land which was within the tenancy at the date that the consent or arbitrator's approval was given for the improvement.

Subs. (3)
This provides a similar provision for planning permission save that the planning permission must relate to the part taken back.

Subs. (4)
This ensures that on the termination of the tenancy (which will then only include the balance of the land) compensation is assessed by reference to the land which was in the tenancy at the date that the consent or arbitrator's approval was given for the improvement.

Compensation where reversionary estate in holding is severed

25.—(1) Where the reversionary estate in the holding comprised in a farm business tenancy is for the time being vested in more than one person in several parts, the tenant shall be entitled, on quitting the entire holding, to require that any compensation payable to him under section 16 of this Act shall be determined as if the reversionary estate were not so severed.

(2) Where subsection (1) applies, the arbitrator shall, where necessary, apportion the amount awarded between the persons who for the purposes of this Part of this Act together constitute the landlord of the holding, and any additional costs of the award caused by the apportionment shall be directed by the arbitrator to be paid by those persons in such proportions as he shall determine.

DEFINITIONS
  "farm business tenancy": s.1.
  "holding": s.38(1).

"landlord": s.38(1), (5).
"tenant": s.38(1), (5).

GENERAL NOTE
This provision replicates s.75 of the 1986 Act.

Subs. (1)
This is an enabling provision. The tenant can, if it suits him to do so, have his compensation claim separately assessed for each severed part of the reversion as a tenant can under s.75 of the 1986 Act. However, if the assessment is under the provisions of s.24, above, the improvement will nevertheless be assessed by reference to the holding as it was at the time of the consent or the arbitrator's approval to the improvement. Section 24 will not apply in all cases as it only operates if the landlord exercises a break clause or if the owner of a severed part of a reversionary estate serves a notice to quit under s.140(2) of the Law of Property Act 1925. Where the tenant serves a notice to quit on an estate with a severed reversion, he can choose to treat each severed part as a separate holding and have the improvement assessed by reference to the increase in value of that part (and not the whole) if it is advantageous to him to do so.

Subs. (2)
There is no guidance for arbitrators on how such an apportionment should be made.

Extent to which compensation recoverable under agreements

26.—(1) In any case for which apart from this section the provisions of this Part of this Act provide for compensation, a tenant shall be entitled to compensation in accordance with those provisions and not otherwise, and shall be so entitled notwithstanding any agreement to the contrary.

(2) Nothing in the provisions of this Part of this Act, apart from this section, shall be construed as disentitling a tenant to compensation in any case for which those provisions do not provide for compensation.

DEFINITIONS
"tenant": s.38(1), (5).

GENERAL NOTE
This section prevents contracting out of Pt. III of the Act if the Act provides for compensation for the particular item or matter. The parties are unable to provide in the tenancy agreement for no compensation and cannot provide for a different basis of assessment or, for example, that the improvement be written down over a number of years. There is nothing to prevent the parties from agreeing compensation for items or matters not covered by the Act, for example, in connection with items of tenant-right which do not fall within the definition of routine improvements.

Interpretation of Part III

27. In this Part of this Act, unless the context otherwise requires—
   "planning permission" has the meaning given by section 336(1) of the Town and Country Planning Act 1990;
   "tenant's improvement", and references to the provision of such an improvement, have the meaning given by section 15 of this Act.

PART IV

MISCELLANEOUS AND SUPPLEMENTAL

Resolution of disputes

Resolution of disputes

28.—(1) Subject to subsections (4) and (5) below and to section 29 of this Act, any dispute between the landlord and the tenant under a farm business tenancy, being a dispute concerning their rights and obligations under this Act, under the terms of the tenancy or under any custom, shall be determined by arbitration.

(2) Where such a dispute has arisen, the landlord or the tenant may give notice in writing to the other specifying the dispute and stating that, unless before the end of the period of two months beginning with the day on which the notice is given the parties have appointed an arbitrator by agreement, he proposes to apply to the President of the RICS for the appointment of an arbitrator by him.

(3) Where a notice has been given under subsection (2) above, but no arbitrator has been appointed by agreement, either party may, after the end of the period of two months referred to in that subsection, apply to the President of the RICS for the appointment of an arbitrator by him.

(4) Subsection (1) above does not affect the jurisdiction of the courts, except to the extent provided by section 4(1) of the Arbitration Act 1950 (staying of court proceedings where there is submission to arbitration), as applied to statutory arbitrations by section 31 of that Act.

(5) Subsections (1) to (3) above do not apply in relation to—

(a) the determination of rent in pursuance of a statutory review notice (as defined in section 10(1) of this Act),

(b) any case falling within section 19(1) of this Act, or

(c) any claim for compensation under Part III of this Act.

DEFINITIONS
"farm business tenancy": s.1.
"give/given": s.36.
"landlord": s.38(1), (5).
"RICS, the": s.38(1).
"statutory review notice": s.10(1).
"tenancy": s.38(1).
"tenant": s.38(1), (5).

GENERAL NOTE

Subs. (1)
Section 28 applies to arbitrations for disputes other than in connection with rent review, consent to improvements or compensation for improvements each of which have their own procedure set out in the Act (see subs. (5) below). Section 28 arbitrations are a fallback for parties who have not agreed an alternative dispute resolution mechanism or, if they have agreed one, have not agreed on the particular occasion of the dispute in question that it will be used (see s.29 below). Arbitrations under this section will be under the Arbitration Acts 1950 to 1979 and not under any discrete code. This is a departure from the position under the 1986 Act where all arbitrations are carried out under the provisions of a discrete statutory code set out in the Act itself (see s.84 and Sched. 11). Schedule 11 to the 1986 Act provides a highly regulated code, specific procedures and mandatory time-limits, and the change over to the Arbitration Acts procedure, which leaves far more in the hands of the parties and the arbitrator, will be a significant change for those involved in agricultural arbitrations to adapt to.

Apart from the provisions of the Arbitration Acts themselves and case law decided under those Acts, the only regulation of arbitrations under s.28 or under the specific arbitrations relating to rent reviews, consent to improvements and compensation for improvements is contained in s.30.

Discussion of the Arbitration Acts procedures is beyond the scope of this annotation and reference should be made to the standard books on commercial arbitrations (for example, *Handbook of Arbitration Practice*, Bernstein & Wood (1993, Sweet & Maxwell); *Commercial Arbitration*, Mustill & Boyd (2nd edition, Butterworths)). However, one or two points showing the difference between 1986 Act arbitrations and Arbitration Acts arbitrations are worth mentioning.

(1) Under the 1986 Act the parties are required to deliver a statement of their case, with all of the necessary particulars, to the arbitrator within 35 days from the date of his appointment (Sched. 11, para. 7). The time-limit is mandatory and inflexible. Under the Arbitration Acts, how the case is pleaded out is entirely in the hands of the arbitrator, not only in terms of whether he requires pleadings or statements of case but also in terms of whether those documents are to be exchanged or produced sequentially and in terms of the timetable for the pleadings. Furthermore, failure to comply with the timetable set by an arbitrator under the Arbitration Acts can only effectively be dealt with by the arbitrator if an application is made by one of the parties

under s.5 of the Arbitration Act 1979 (c. 42) to the High Court to allow the arbitrator to extend his powers to those of a High Court Judge. Whilst the arbitrator may himself apply under s.5, it is rare and it is more likely that the party not in default will make the application.

(2) The method by which the arbitrator deals with points of law is different. Under the 1986 Act, the case stated procedure enabled an arbitrator, at any stage of the proceedings, to state a case for the opinion of the county court on any question of law or any question relating to the arbitrator's jurisdiction (see s.84(1) of and Sched. 11, para. 26 to the 1986 Act). Under the Arbitration Acts, however, the case stated procedure does not exist. In the MAFF & WOAD consultation document of September 1992, which set out detailed proposals for this legislation, the suggestion was that, whilst the discrete arbitration code of the 1986 Act would be disposed of, the ability of the arbitrator to refer points of law to the courts would be preserved.

Under the Arbitration Acts, the High Court may determine any question of law arising in the course of the reference on the application of any of the parties with the consent of the arbitrator or on the application of any of the parties with the consent of all of the other parties (see s.2 of the Arbitration Act 1979). The ability of the arbitrator to consent without the consent of all other parties is limited (see s.2(2) of the Arbitration Act 1979).

(3) The requirement under the 1986 Act that an award be delivered within 56 days of the date of the appointment of an arbitrator (Sched. 11, para. 14) is not repeated in this Act and does not appear in the Arbitration Acts. The award under the 1986 Act is in a prescribed form. Under the Arbitration Acts, there are no legal requirements as to the form of the award and the absence of reasons does not invalidate the award. However, if a reasoned award is requested by both parties, the arbitrator must give reasons.

Subs. (2)

There is no prescribed form for the Notice, although the prescribed information set out in the subsection must be contained in the Notice.

Subs. (3)

The application must be in writing (see s.30(2) and (3)). In making the appointment of the arbitrator, the President of the RICS is acting in an administrative and not a judicial capacity (see *Ramsey v. McClaren* [1936] S.L.T. 35). Accordingly if either party disputes the validity of the arbitrator's appointment, the matter should be raised with the arbitrator himself and not with the President of the RICS.

Subs. (4)

This subsection makes it clear that the use of the mandatory "shall" in subs. (1) above does not operate so as to oust the jurisdiction of the courts save to the extent set out in that subsection. Section 4(1) of the Arbitration Act 1950 (c. 27) provides that a court may stay any proceedings commenced in the court in respect of any matter which falls within the scope of an arbitration agreement or (by s.31 of the Arbitration Act 1950) within the scope of a statutory arbitration. The courts will stay the proceedings if satisfied that there is no sufficient reason why the matter should not be referred to arbitration and that the applicant who is attempting to stay the court proceedings was and is ready, willing and able to do all things necessary for the proper conduct of the arbitration. If neither party applies for a stay of the proceedings commenced in the court, the hearing will go ahead and hence the parties can agree to go to court rather than to arbitration.

Subs. (5)

This sets out the three specific references to arbitration for rent review, approval of the arbitrator to an improvement where a landlord has refused or failed to give consent, and a claim for compensation for tenant's improvements on quitting the holding.

Those specific arbitrations will still be under the Arbitration Acts 1950 to 1979 but have their own timetables set out in the relevant sections of this Act.

Cases where right to refer claim to arbitration under section 28 does not apply

29.—(1) Section 28 of this Act does not apply in relation to any dispute if—
(a) the tenancy is created by an instrument which includes provision for disputes to be resolved by any person other than—

     (i) the landlord or the tenant, or
     (ii) a third party appointed by either of them without the consent
    or concurrence of the other, and
  (b) either of the following has occurred—
     (i) the landlord and the tenant have jointly referred the dispute to
    the third party under the provision, or
     (ii) the landlord or the tenant has referred the dispute to the third
    party under the provision and notified the other in writing of the
    making of the reference, the period of four weeks beginning with
    the date on which the other was so notified has expired and the
    other has not given a notice under section 28(2) of this Act in
    relation to the dispute before the end of that period.

(2) For the purposes of subsection (1) above, a term of the tenancy does not provide for disputes to be "resolved" by any person unless that person (whether or not acting as arbitrator) is enabled under the terms of the tenancy to give a decision which is binding in law on both parties.

Definitions
 "given": s.36.
 "landlord": s.38(1), (5).
 "tenancy": s.38(1).
 "tenant": s.38(1), (5).

General Note

Subs. (1)

The arbitration provisions set out in s.28 above are designed as a fallback in the absence of some other agreed mechanism for dispute resolution.

This section allows the parties to choose an alternative dispute resolution mechanism but provides either party with the ability to opt back into arbitration for any particular dispute despite an agreement for an alternative procedure. The alternative dispute resolution procedure only applies to oust s.28 of the Act and, therefore, does not apply to oust arbitration in connection with the rent review arbitration, the consent to improvement arbitration or the compensation for tenant's improvement arbitration referred to in s.28(5). However, so far as rent review is concerned, the ability of the parties to follow through their own rent review formula not within s.9, by reference to an expert, has already been discussed (see s.12(b) above).

The ability to avoid arbitration only arises where the alternative dispute mechanism is contained in the tenancy agreement itself and where that tenancy agreement is in writing. Unlike the position in connection with the rent review procedure in s.12, this section does not prohibit the parties from agreeing to a contractual arbitration. An express arbitration clause can, of course, circumscribe the jurisdiction of the arbitrator and it may be advantageous in particular circumstances for the parties to do that.

Even where the parties choose to insert into their tenancy agreement an alternative dispute resolution mechanism, the parties must agree in connection with each and every dispute that that mechanism will be utilised. It is open to either party in connection with any dispute, to opt out and to force the matter back into the statutory arbitration framework. The method by which a party does that is set out in subs. (1)(b)(ii): he gives a notice within the timetable set out in that subsection that he wishes the matter to be referred to arbitration.

Subs. (2)

As this "opt out" is only available where the person to be appointed is able to give a decision which is binding in law on both parties, the position is that where the parties have jointly appointed a third party to determine the dispute or where the timetable as set out in subs. (1)(b)(ii) has expired, the award made by that third party will be binding on the parties. Whether or not the parties can abandon the alternative dispute mechanism at a stage before the award is given depends upon the terms of the contractual reference itself. However, the parties will then be left in some difficulty in the determination of that dispute as they cannot opt back into s.28 once their agreed third party has been appointed. Any form of alternative dispute resolution mechanism or mediation which does not specifically have the power to bind the parties can be utilised as the arbitration provisions are only a fallback in the absence of agreement. However, such facilities do not have the power to bind the parties and do not fall within s.29 so as to prevent the parties from ignoring any decision and then referring the matter to arbitration.

General provisions applying to arbitrations under Act

30.—(1) Any matter which is required to be determined by arbitration under this Act shall be determined by the arbitration of a sole arbitrator.

(2) Any application under this Act to the President of the RICS for the appointment of an arbitrator by him must be made in writing and must be accompanied by such reasonable fee as the President may determine in respect of the costs of making the appointment.

(3) Where an arbitrator appointed for the purposes of this Act dies or is incapable of acting and no new arbitrator has been appointed by agreement, either party may apply to the President of the RICS for the appointment of a new arbitrator by him.

DEFINITIONS
  "RICS, the": s.37(1).

GENERAL NOTE

Subs. (2)
  See the General Note to s.28(3) above.

Miscellaneous

Mortgages of agricultural land

31.—(1) Section 99 of the Law of Property Act 1925 (leasing powers of mortgagor and mortgagee in possession) shall be amended in accordance with subsections (2) and (3) below.

(2) At the beginning of subsection (13), there shall be inserted "Subject to subsection (13A) below,".

(3) After that subsection, there shall be inserted—
  "(13A) Subsection (13) of this section—
  (a) shall not enable the application of any provision of this section to be excluded or restricted in relation to any mortgage of agricultural land made after 1st March 1948 but before 1st September 1995, and
  (b) shall not enable the power to grant a lease of an agricultural holding to which, by virtue of section 4 of the Agricultural Tenancies Act 1995, the Agricultural Holdings Act 1986 will apply, to be excluded or restricted in relation to any mortgage of agricultural land made on or after 1st September 1995.
  (13B) In subsection (13A) of this section—
  'agricultural holding' has the same meaning as in the Agricultural Holdings Act 1986; and
  'agricultural land' has the same meaning as in the Agriculture Act 1947."

(4) Paragraph 12 of Schedule 14 to the Agricultural Holdings Act 1986 (which excludes the application of subsection (13) of section 99 of the Law of Property Act 1925 in relation to a mortgage of agricultural land and is super-

seded by the amendments made by subsections (1) to (3) above) shall cease to have effect.

DEFINITIONS
    "agricultural holding": subs. (3).
    "agricultural land": subs. (3).

GENERAL NOTE

Section 99 of the Law of Property Act 1925 confers upon a mortgagor in possession the power to make such leases as are authorised by the section in such a way as bind a prior mortgagee. Authorised leases include agricultural or occupation leases not exceeding 50 years (see s.99(3)(i)).

Such a lease must satisfy the requirements of s.99(5)–(7) namely: it must take effect in possession within 12 months; it must reserve the best rent reasonably obtainable, regard being had to the circumstances of the case but without any fine being taken; and it must contain a covenant for the payment of rent and a condition for re-entry if the rent is unpaid for a period specified not exceeding 30 days.

The section authorises agreements for leases and oral lettings and, in such cases, the absence of a condition for re-entry and the failure to comply with the requirement for the delivery of a counterpart lease to the mortgagee (see s.99(8)) will not affect the validity of the lease or its ability to bind the mortgagee (*Rhodes v. Dalby* [1971] 1 W.L.R. 1325).

Section 99(13) provides that the s.99 powers of leasing shall not apply if there is a clause in the mortgage document excluding those powers. All standard mortgage documentation excludes the powers conferred on the mortgagor by s.99. However, for mortgages of agricultural land made after March 1, 1948, Sched. 14, para. 12 to the Agricultural Holdings Act 1986 provides that the powers given to the mortgagor cannot be excluded.

As a tenancy granted under the 1986 Act could devalue the land by as much as 50 per cent, the impact of such a grant on the mortgagee's security, where the mortgagee has lent against the freehold vacant possession value of the land, is acute. The grant of a long fixed-term farm business tenancy would also have a devaluing effect on the land and, it should be noted, that tenancies with residential security of tenure or under the business tenancy regime in the Landlord and Tenant Act 1954, Pt. II, could also be granted. It is the nature of the mortgage and not the tenancy which brings Sched. 14, para. 12 to the 1986 Act into play.

In circumstances where a tenancy is granted where the mortgagor is already in financial difficulties, whilst the tenancy may bind the mortgagee, it may be set aside by an application under s.423 of the Insolvency Act 1986 (c. 45) as a transaction at an undervalue even where the best rent is being paid (see the Court of Appeal decision in *Agricultural Mortgage Corp. v. Woodward* [1995] 04 E.G. 155).

Section 31 introduces an amendment to s.99 of the Law of Property Act 1925 which replaces Sched. 14, para 12, to the 1986 Act which, on September 1, 1995, shall cease to have effect. The new s.99(13A) which is introduced to the 1925 Act means that, in relation to any mortgage of agricultural land made between March 1, 1948 and September 1, 1995, the powers in s.99 still cannot be excluded. This fits with the government's stated policy that the Act should not be retrospective in any respect. Any mortgage made on or after September 1, 1995 can validly contain a prohibition on leasing, regardless of whether or not it is a mortgage of agricultural land.

The cut off date is in relation to the date of the mortgage and not the date of the tenancy agreement. If a mortgage of agricultural land is already in existence at the time of the coming into force of the Act, the mortgagee still cannot contract out of the s.99 powers of leasing. What may happen is that lending institutions will review their agricultural lending portfolios and insist on new security being taken on or after September 1, 1995. Whether or not these moves will be attacked by the courts as being against public policy remains to be seen and probably depends as much on the circumstances surrounding the grant of the tenancy as the motives of the mortgagee.

Power of limited owners to give consents etc.

32. The landlord under a farm business tenancy, whatever his estate or interest in the holding, may, for the purposes of this Act, give any consent, make any agreement or do or have done to him any other act which he might give, make, do or have done to him if he were owner in fee simple or, if his interest is an interest in a leasehold, were absolutely entitled to that leasehold.

DEFINITIONS
"farm business tenancy": s.1.
"holding": s.38(1).
"landlord": s.38(1), (5).

GENERAL NOTE
This replicates s.88 of the 1986 Act.

Power to apply and raise capital money

33.—(1) The purposes authorised by section 73 of the Settled Land Act 1925 (either as originally enacted or as applied in relation to trusts for sale by section 28 of the Law of Property Act 1925) or section 26 of the Universities and College Estates Act 1925 for the application of capital money shall include—

(a) the payment of expenses incurred by a landlord under a farm business tenancy in, or in connection with, the making of any physical improvement on the holding,

(b) the payment of compensation under section 16 of this Act, and

(c) the payment of the costs, charges and expenses incurred by him on a reference to arbitration under section 19 or 22 of this Act.

(2) The purposes authorised by section 71 of the Settled Land Act 1925 (either as originally enacted or as applied in relation to trusts for sale by section 28 of the Law of Property Act 1925) as purposes for which money may be raised by mortgage shall include the payment of compensation under section 16 of this Act.

(3) Where the landlord under a farm business tenancy—

(a) is a tenant for life or in a fiduciary position, and

(b) is liable to pay compensation under section 16 of this Act,

he may require the sum payable as compensation and any costs, charges and expenses incurred by him in connection with the tenant's claim under that section to be paid out of any capital money held on the same trusts as the settled land.

(4) In subsection (3) above—

"capital money" includes any personal estate held on the same trusts as the land; and

"settled land" includes land held on trust for sale or vested in a personal representative.

DEFINITIONS
"capital money": subs. (4).
"farm business tenancy": s.1.
"holding": s.38(1).
"landlord": s.38(1), (5).
"settled land": subs. (4).
"tenant": s.38(1), (5).

GENERAL NOTE
Section 89 of the 1986 Act contains similar provisions. Certain problems with the provisions in s.89 have been avoided in s.33. The provisions of the Settled Land Act 1925 (c. 18) on the permitted uses of capital money and on the repayment of capital money spent on certain improvements by instalments out of income, are designed to maintain the correct balance between the interest of those persons entitled for life (and hence to income) and those persons entitled in remainder (and hence to capital). Section 89 of the 1986 Act specifically provided for improvements listed in Sched. 7 to the 1986 Act, when paid for out of capital monies, not to have to be replaced out of income. As Sched. 7 includes repairs to fixed equipment, the remaindermen essentially end up paying for repairs which does not accord with the spirit of the Settled Land Act 1925 provisions.

A further problem with s.89 is that a tenant for life or a trustee for sale who paid out compensation for improvements himself had no right of recompense directly from the settlement or trust funds (see *Duke of Wellington's Parliamentary Estates, Re; King v. Wellesley* [1972] Ch. 374).

Subs. (1)

This subsection extends s.73 of the Settled Land Act 1925 to enable capital monies to be spent on the matters set out in subs. (1)(a) to (c) but makes no mention of repayment out of income. Reference is therefore now made direct to the provisions of the Settled Land Act 1925 itself (ss.83 to 89 and Sched. 3) which set out those improvements in respect of which instalment payments out of income do not need to be made, where they must and where the trustees or the court have a discretion. However, s.84 and Sched. 3 deal with the provision of money "... in or towards payment for any improvement" and it is arguable whether that would cover a payment of compensation to the tenant for the provision of such an improvement. It is submitted that it does.

Subs. (2)

This allows the monies to be paid in compensation to a tenant to be raised on mortgage.

Subs. (3)

This deals with the problem identified in the *Duke of Wellington's Parliamentary Estates* (see above) and enables the tenant for life or the trustee to obtain repayment direct from the relevant fund.

Estimation of best rent for purposes of Acts and other instruments

34.—(1) In estimating the best rent or reservation in the nature of rent of land comprised in a farm business tenancy for the purposes of a relevant instrument, it shall not be necessary to take into account against the tenant any increase in the value of that land arising from any tenant's improvements.

(2) In subsection (1) above—

"a relevant instrument" means any Act of Parliament, deed or other instrument which authorises a lease to be made on the condition that the best rent or reservation in the nature of rent is reserved;

"tenant's improvement" has the meaning given by section 15 of this Act.

DEFINITIONS

"farm business tenancy": s.1.
"relevant instrument, a": subs. (2).
"tenant": s.38(1), (5).
"tenant's improvement": subs. (2), s.15.

GENERAL NOTE

There are several provisions which require best rent to be taken in respect of a lease. See, for example, the following provisions.

(1) Section 42 of the Settled Land Act 1925 confers powers on a tenant for life to grant leases provided that such leases reserve the best rent. By s.28 of the Law of Property Act 1925, this power is also conferred on trustees for sale.

(2) Section 54 of the Law of Property Act 1925 provides that leases which do not exceed three years can be oral or in writing provided that they are at the best rent. Otherwise, such leases would have to be executed by deed in accordance with s.52 of the Law of Property Act 1925.

(3) Section 99 of the Law of Property Act 1925 confers upon a mortgagor in possession powers of leasing so as to bind a mortgagee where the lease reserves the best rent (see the General Note to s.31 above).

As all of the examples set out above require the lease simply to reserve the best rent or be at the best rent, this section can only be relevant where a new tenancy has been granted to a tenant who is already in place as the question of best rent is only relevant at the commencement of the tenancy.

Preparation of documents etc. by valuers and surveyors

35.—(1) Section 22 of the Solicitors Act 1974 (unqualified person not to prepare certain instruments) shall be amended as follows.

(2) In subsection (2), after paragraph (ab) there shall be inserted—
"(ac) any accredited person drawing or preparing any instrument—
(i) which creates, or which he believes on reasonable grounds will create, a farm business tenancy (within the meaning of the Agricultural Tenancies Act 1995), or
(ii) which relates to an existing tenancy which is, or which he believes on reasonable grounds to be, such a tenancy;".

(3) In subsection (3A), immediately before the definition of "registered trade mark agent" there shall be inserted—
"'accredited person' means any person who is—
(a) a Full Member of the Central Association of Agricultural Valuers,
(b) an Associate or Fellow of the Incorporated Society of Valuers and Auctioneers, or
(c) an Associate or Fellow of the Royal Institution of Chartered Surveyors;".

GENERAL NOTE

The likely increase in fixed-term tenancies as a result of this legislation will lead to an increase in the number of agricultural tenancies which will need to be executed by deed. Section 52 of the Law of Property Act 1925 requires all conveyances of land or of any interest in land to be by deed. Failure to comply with s.52 renders the conveyance void for the purposes of conveying or creating a legal estate. As a result of exceptions in s.54 of the Law of Property Act 1925, if the lease is to take effect in possession for a term not exceeding three years and at the best rent, it can be in writing or oral and need not be executed by deed.

Prior to the coming into force of this Act it was common for land agents and surveyors to prepare tenancy agreements for the grant of tenancies protected by the 1986 Act, giving effectively lifetime security, and this section recognises that expertise.

Under s.22 of the Solicitors Act 1974 it is a criminal offence for persons who are not solicitors to prepare deeds relating to real property if done for a fee, or for gain or reward. Section 22(2) sets out a list of exceptions for certain classes of accredited persons to enable them to prepare certain classes of documents. This amendment extends that list to enable those persons listed in the amendment set out in subs. (3) to prepare deeds relating to farm business tenancies, whether creating such a tenancy or dealing with surrenders or assignments.

Supplemental

Service of notices

36.—(1) This section applies to any notice or other document required or authorised to be given under this Act.

(2) A notice or other document to which this section applies is duly given to a person if—
(a) it is delivered to him,
(b) it is left at his proper address, or
(c) it is given to him in a manner authorised by a written agreement made, at any time before the giving of the notice, between him and the person giving the notice.

(3) A notice or other document to which this section applies is not duly given to a person if its text is transmitted to him by facsimile or other electronic means otherwise than by virtue of subsection (2)(c) above.

(4) Where a notice or other document to which this section applies is to be given to a body corporate, the notice or document is duly given if it is given to the secretary or clerk of that body.

(5) Where—
(a) a notice or other document to which this section applies is to be given to a landlord under a farm business tenancy and an agent or servant of his is responsible for the control of the management of the holding, or
(b) such a document is to be given to a tenant under a farm business tenancy and an agent or servant of his is responsible for the carrying on of a business on the holding,

the notice or document is duly given if it is given to that agent or servant.

(6) For the purposes of this section, the proper address of any person to whom a notice or other document to which this section applies is to be given is—

(a) in the case of the secretary or clerk of a body corporate, the registered or principal office of that body, and

(b) in any other case, the last known address of the person in question.

(7) Unless or until the tenant under a farm business tenancy has received—

(a) notice that the person who before that time was entitled to receive the rents and profits of the holding ("the original landlord") has ceased to be so entitled, and

(b) notice of the name and address of the person who has become entitled to receive the rents and profits,

any notice or other document given to the original landlord by the tenant shall be deemed for the purposes of this Act to have been given to the landlord under the tenancy.

DEFINITIONS
"farm business tenancy": s.1.
"holding": s.38(1).
"landlord": s.38(1), (5).
"original landlord, the": subs. (7).
"proper address": subs. (6).
"tenancy": s.38(1).
"tenant": s.38(1), (5).

GENERAL NOTE

Subs. (2)
A notice may presumably be "delivered" or "left" even if sent through in the postal system. Any agreement for service by a different method must be in writing. Such an agreement can be included in the tenancy agreement itself but, if the notices are preliminary notices to comply with the notice conditions (see s.1(4) above) the agreement will have to precede the tenancy agreement.

Subs. (3)
Electronic means of communication will mean, in addition to facsimile, e-mail or telex. Where service is to take effect between agents in accordance with subs. (5) below, an agreement to allow such methods of service may be useful although care will have to be taken to ensure that evidential safeguards are built into the agreement so that receipt of a notice by these means has to be acknowledged within a specified timescale.

Subs. (5)
If subs. (5) is to be relied upon, it will be prudent to ensure that there is agreement between the parties at the outset, updated as necessary, as to whether a particular agent falls within the description set out in paras. (a) or (b).

Subs. (7)
Note also that ss.47 and 48 of the Landlord and Tenant Act 1987 (c. 31) apply to agricultural holdings (see *Dallhold Estates (U.K.) Pty (In Administration) v. Lindsey Trading Properties* [1994] 17 E.G. 148).

Crown land

37.—(1) This Act shall apply in relation to land in which there subsists, or has at any material time subsisted, a Crown interest as it applies in relation to land in which no such interest subsists or has ever subsisted.

(2) For the purposes of this Act—

(a) where an interest belongs to Her Majesty in right of the Crown and forms part of the Crown Estate, the Crown Estate Commissioners shall be treated as the owner of the interest,

(b) where an interest belongs to Her Majesty in right of the Crown and does not form part of the Crown Estate, the government department having the management of the land or, if there is no such department, such person as Her Majesty may appoint in writing under the Royal Sign Manual shall be treated as the owner of the interest,

(c) where an interest belongs to Her Majesty in right of the Duchy of Lancaster, the Chancellor of the Duchy shall be treated as the owner of the interest,

(d) where an interest belongs to a government department or is held in trust for Her Majesty for the purposes of a government department, that department shall be treated as the owner of the interest, and

(e) where an interest belongs to the Duchy of Cornwall, such person as the Duke of Cornwall or the possessor for the time being of the Duchy of Cornwall appoints shall be treated as the owner of the interest and, in the case where the interest is that of landlord, may do any act or thing which a landlord is authorised or required to do under this Act.

(3) If any question arises as to who is to be treated as the owner of a Crown interest, that question shall be referred to the Treasury, whose decision shall be final.

(4) In subsections (1) and (3) above "Crown interest" means an interest which belongs to Her Majesty in right of the Crown or of the Duchy of Lancaster or to the Duchy of Cornwall, or to a government department, or which is held in trust for Her Majesty for the purposes of a government department.

(5) Any compensation payable under section 16 of this Act by the Chancellor of the Duchy of Lancaster may be raised and paid under section 25 of the Duchy of Lancaster Act 1817 (application of monies) as an expense incurred in improvement of land belonging to Her Majesty in right of the Duchy.

(6) In the case of land belonging to the Duchy of Cornwall, the purposes authorised by section 8 of the Duchy of Cornwall Management Act 1863 (application of monies) for the advancement of parts of such gross sums as are there mentioned shall include the payment of compensation under section 16 of this Act.

(7) Nothing in subsection (6) above shall be taken as prejudicing the operation of the Duchy of Cornwall Management Act 1982.

DEFINITIONS
"Crown interest": subs. (4).
"landlord": s.38(1), (5).

Interpretation

38.—(1) In this Act, unless the context otherwise requires—
"agriculture" includes horticulture, fruit growing, seed growing, dairy farming and livestock breeding and keeping, the use of land as grazing land, meadow land, osier land, market gardens and nursery grounds, and the use of land for woodlands where that use is ancillary to the farming of land for other agricultural purposes, and "agricultural" shall be construed accordingly;
"building" includes any part of a building;
"fixed term tenancy" means any tenancy other than a periodic tenancy;
"holding", in relation to a farm business tenancy, means the aggregate of the land comprised in the tenancy;
"landlord" includes any person from time to time deriving title from the original landlord;
"livestock" includes any creature kept for the production of food, wool, skins or fur or for the purpose of its use in the farming of land;
"the RICS" means the Royal Institution of Chartered Surveyors;
"tenancy" means any tenancy other than a tenancy at will, and includes a sub-tenancy and an agreement for a tenancy or sub-tenancy;

"tenant" includes a sub-tenant and any person deriving title from the original tenant or sub-tenant;

"termination", in relation to a tenancy, means the cesser of the tenancy by reason of effluxion of time or from any other cause.

(2) References in this Act to the farming of land include references to the carrying on in relation to land of any agricultural activity.

(3) A tenancy granted pursuant to a contract shall be taken for the purposes of this Act to have been granted when the contract was entered into.

(4) For the purposes of this Act a tenancy begins on the day on which, under the terms of the tenancy, the tenant is entitled to possession under that tenancy; and references in this Act to the beginning of the tenancy are references to that day.

(5) The designations of landlord and tenant shall continue to apply until the conclusion of any proceedings taken under this Act in respect of compensation.

GENERAL NOTE

Definitions have been considered where the words or phrases appear in the Act and, therefore, a detailed annotation of this section is unnecessary. One or two things ought, however, to be noted.

Agriculture. This definition is the same definition as is contained in s.96 of the 1986 Act and reference should be made to Scammell & Denshams, *Law of Agricultural Holdings*, 7th Edition (Butterworths) and Muir Watt, *Agricultural Holdings*, 13th Edition (Sweet & Maxwell) for a detailed analysis.

Livestock. This definition is different from the definition in the 1986 Act which also includes any creature kept for the carrying on in relation to land of any agricultural activity. It is arguable that those words in the 1986 Act were superfluous, as they would be in this Act, as the farming of land includes references to the carrying on in relation to land of any agricultural activity in any event (see subs. (2)).

Index of defined expressions

39. In this Act the expressions listed below are defined by or otherwise fall to be construed in accordance with the provisions indicated—

agriculture, agricultural	section 38(1)
begins, beginning (in relation to a tenancy)	section 38(4)
building	section 38(1)
farm business tenancy	section 1
farming (of land)	section 38(2)
fixed term tenancy	section 38(1)
grant (of a tenancy)	section 38(3)
holding (in relation to a farm business tenancy)	section 38(1)
landlord	section 38(1) and (5)
livestock	section 38(1)
planning permission (in Part III)	section 27
provision (of a tenant's improvement) (in Part III)	section 15
the review date (in Part II)	section 10(2)
the RICS	section 38(1)
statutory review notice (in Part II)	section 10(1)
tenancy	section 38(1)
tenant	section 38(1) and (5)
tenant's improvement (in Part III)	section 15
termination (of a tenancy)	section 38(1).

Consequential amendments

40. The Schedule to this Act (which contains consequential amendments) shall have effect.

Short title, commencement and extent

41.—(1) This Act may be cited as the Agricultural Tenancies Act 1995.

(2) This Act shall come into force on 1st September 1995.

(3) Subject to subsection (4) below, this Act extends to England and Wales only.

(4) The amendment by a provision of the Schedule to this Act of an enactment which extends to Scotland or Northern Ireland also extends there, except that paragraph 9 of the Schedule does not extend to Northern Ireland.

Section 40   SCHEDULE

CONSEQUENTIAL AMENDMENTS

The Small Holdings and Allotments Act 1908 (c. 36)

1.—(1) Section 47 of the Small Holdings and Allotments Act 1908 (compensation for improvements) shall be amended as follows.

(2) In subsection (1), after "to any tenant" there shall be inserted "otherwise than under a farm business tenancy".

(3) In subsection (2), after "small holdings or allotments" there shall be inserted "otherwise than under a farm business tenancy".

(4) In subsection (3), after "if" there shall be inserted "he is not a tenant under a farm business tenancy and".

(5) In subsection (4), after "allotment" there shall be inserted "who is not a tenant under a farm business tenancy".

(6) After that subsection, there shall be inserted—

"(5) In this section, 'farm business tenancy' has the same meaning as in the Agricultural Tenancies Act 1995."

The Law of Distress Amendment Act 1908 (c. 53)

2. In section 4(1) of the Law of Distress Amendment Act 1908 (exclusion of certain goods), for "to which that section applies" there shall be substituted "on land comprised in a tenancy to which that Act applies".

The Allotments Act 1922 (c. 51)

3. In section 3(7) of the Allotments Act 1922 (provision as to cottage holdings and certain allotments), after "landlord" there shall be inserted "otherwise than under a farm business tenancy (within the meaning of the Agricultural Tenancies Act 1995)".

4. In section 6(1) of that Act (assessment and recovery of compensation), after "contract of tenancy" there shall be inserted "(not being a farm business tenancy within the meaning of the Agricultural Tenancies Act 1995)".

The Landlord and Tenant Act 1927 (c. 36)

5. In section 17(1) of the Landlord and Tenant Act 1927 (holdings to which Part I applies), for the words from "not being" to the end there is substituted "not being—

(a) agricultural holdings within the meaning of the Agricultural Holdings Act 1986 held under leases in relation to which that Act applies, or

(b) holdings held under farm business tenancies within the meaning of the Agricultural Tenancies Act 1995."

6. In section 19(4) of that Act (provisions as to covenants not to assign etc. without licence or consent), after "the Agricultural Holdings Act 1986" there shall be inserted "which are leases in relation to which that Act applies, or to farm business tenancies within the meaning of the Agricultural Tenancies Act 1995".

The Agricultural Credits Act 1928 (c. 43)

7. In section 5(7) of the Agricultural Credits Act 1928 (agricultural charges on farming stock and assets) in the definition of "other agricultural assets", after "otherwise" there shall be inserted "a tenant's right to compensation under section 16 of the Agricultural Tenancies Act 1995,".

The Leasehold Property (Repairs) Act 1938 (c. 34)

8. In section 7(1) of the Leasehold Property (Repairs) Act 1938 (interpretation), at the end there shall be added "which is a lease in relation to which that Act applies and not being a farm business tenancy within the meaning of the Agricultural Tenancies Act 1995".

The Reserve and Auxiliary Forces (Protection of Civil Interests) Act 1951 (c. 65)

9.—(1) Section 27 of the Reserve and Auxiliary Forces (Protection of Civil Interests) Act 1951 (renewal of tenancy expiring during period of service or within two months thereafter) shall be amended as follows.

(2) In subsection (1), for the words from "are an agricultural holding" onwards there shall be substituted—

"(a) are an agricultural holding (within the meaning of the Agricultural Holdings Act 1986) held under a tenancy in relation to which that Act applies,

(b) are a holding (other than a holding excepted from this provision) held under a farm business tenancy, or

(c) consist of or comprise premises (other than premises excepted from this provision) licensed for the sale of intoxicating liquor for consumption on the premises."

(3) In subsection (5), after paragraph (b) there shall be inserted—

"(bb) the expressions 'farm business tenancy' and 'holding', in relation to such a tenancy, have the same meaning as in the Agricultural Tenancies Act 1995;".

(4) After that subsection, there shall be inserted—

"(5A) In paragraph (b) of the proviso to subsection (1) of this section the reference to a holding excepted from the provision is a reference to a holding held under a farm business tenancy in which there is comprised a dwelling-house occupied by the person responsible for the control (whether as tenant or servant or agent of the tenant) of the management of the holding."

(5) In subsection (6), for the words from the beginning to "liquor" there shall be substituted "In paragraph (c) of the proviso to subsection (1) of this section, the reference to premises excepted from the provision".

The Landlord and Tenant Act 1954 (c. 56)

10. In section 43(1) of the Landlord and Tenant Act 1954 (tenancies excluded from Part II)—

(a) in paragraph (a), for the words from "or a tenancy" to "1986" there shall be substituted "which is a tenancy in relation to which the Agricultural Holdings Act 1986 applies or a tenancy which would be a tenancy of an agricultural holding in relation to which that Act applied if subsection (3) of section 2 of that Act", and

(b) after that paragraph there shall be inserted—

"(aa) to a farm business tenancy;".

11. In section 51(1) of that Act (extension of Leasehold Property (Repairs) Act 1938), for paragraph (c) there shall be substituted—

"(c) that the tenancy is neither a tenancy of an agricultural holding in relation to which the Agricultural Holdings Act 1986 applies nor a farm business tenancy".

12. In section 69(1) of that Act (interpretation), after the definition of "development corporation" there shall be inserted—

"'farm business tenancy' has the same meaning as in the Agricultural Tenancies Act 1995;".

The Opencast Coal Act 1958 (c. 69)

13.—(1) Section 14 of the Opencast Coal Act 1958 (provisions as to agricultural tenancies in England and Wales) shall be amended as follows.

(2) In subsection (1)(b), for "or part of an agricultural holding" there shall be substituted "held under a tenancy in relation to which the Agricultural Holdings Act 1986 (in this Act referred to as 'the Act of 1986') applies or part of such an agricultural holding".

(3) In subsection (2), for the words from "Agricultural" to "of 1986")" there shall be substituted "Act of 1986".

14. After section 14A of that Act, there shall be inserted—

"Provisions as to farm business tenancies

14B.—(1) Without prejudice to the provisions of Part III of this Act as to matters arising between landlords and tenants in consequence of compulsory rights orders, the provisions of this section shall have effect where—

(a) opencast planning permission has been granted subject to a restoration condition, and

(b) immediately before that permission is granted, any of the land comprised therein consists of the holding or part of the holding held under a farm business tenancy,

whether any of that land is comprised in a compulsory rights order or not.

(2) For the purposes of section 1 of the Agricultural Tenancies Act 1995 (in this Act referred to as 'the Act of 1995'), the land shall be taken, while it is occupied or used for the permitted activities, to be used for the purposes for which it was used immediately before it was occupied or used for the permitted activities.

(3) For the purposes of the Act of 1995, nothing done or omitted by the tenant or by the landlord under the tenancy by way of permitting any of the land in respect of which opencast planning permission has been granted to be occupied for the purpose of carrying on any of the permitted activities, or by way of facilitating the use of any of that land for that purpose, shall be taken to be a breach of any term or condition of the tenancy, either on the part of the tenant or on the part of the landlord.

(4) In determining under subsections (1) and (2) of section 13 of the Act of 1995 the rent which should be properly payable for the holding, in respect of any period for which the person with the benefit of the opencast planning permission is in occupation of the holding, or of any part thereof, for the purpose of carrying on any of the permitted activities, the arbitrator shall disregard any increase or diminution in the rental value of the holding in so far as that increase or diminution is attributable to the occupation of the holding, or of that part of the holding, by that person for the purpose of carrying on any of the permitted activities.

(5) In this section 'holding', in relation to a farm business tenancy, has the same meaning as in the Act of 1995.

(6) This section does not extend to Scotland."

15.—(1) Section 24 of that Act (tenant's right to compensation for improvements and other matters) shall be amended as follows.

(2) In subsection (1)(a), after "holding" there shall be inserted "held under a tenancy in relation to which the Act of 1986 applies".

(3) In subsection (10), after "Scotland" there shall be inserted "the words 'held under a tenancy in relation to which the Act of 1986 applies' in subsection (1)(a) of this section shall be omitted and".

16. After section 25 of that Act, there shall be inserted—

"Tenant's right to compensation for improvements etc.: farm business tenancies

25A.—(1) The provisions of this section shall have effect where—

(a) any part of the land comprised in a compulsory rights order is held, immediately before the date of entry, under a farm business tenancy;

(b) there have been provided in relation to the land which is both so comprised and so held ('the tenant's land') tenant's improvements in respect of which, immediately before that date, the tenant had a prospective right to compensation under section 16 of the Act of 1995 on quitting the holding on the termination of the tenancy;

(c) at the end of the period of occupation, the tenant's land has lost the benefit of any such improvement; and

(d) immediately after the end of that period, the tenant's land is comprised in the same tenancy as immediately before the date of entry, or is comprised in a subsequent farm business tenancy at the end of which the tenant is not deprived, by virtue of section 23(3) of that Act, of his right to compensation under section 16 of that Act in respect of any tenant's improvement provided during the earlier tenancy in relation to the tenant's land.

(2) For the purposes of subsection (1) of this section, subsection (2) of section 22 of the Act of 1995 (which requires notice to be given of the intention to make a claim) shall be disregarded.

(3) Subject to subsection (4) of this section, Part III of the Act of 1995 shall apply as if—

(a) the tenant's land were in the state in which it was immediately before the date of entry, and

(b) the tenancy under which that land is held at the end of the period of occupation had terminated immediately after the end of that period and the tenant had then quitted the holding.

(4) Where the tenant's land has lost the benefit of some tenant's improvements but has not lost the benefit of all of them, Part III of the Act of 1995 shall apply as mentioned in subsection (3) above, but as if the improvements of which the tenant's land has not lost the benefit had not been tenant's improvements.

(5) For the purposes of subsections (1) and (4) of this section, the tenant's land shall be taken to have lost the benefit of a tenant's improvement if the benefit of that improvement has been lost (wholly or in part) without being replaced by another improvement of comparable benefit to the land.

(6) In this section 'holding', in relation to a farm business tenancy, 'tenant's improvement', 'termination', in relation to a tenancy, and references to the provision of a tenant's improvement have the same meaning as in the Act of 1995.

(7) This section does not extend to Scotland."

17.—(1) Section 26 of that Act (compensation for short-term improvements and related matters) shall be amended as follows.

(2) In subsection (1), after "agricultural land" there shall be inserted "and was not comprised in a farm business tenancy".

(3) In subsection (6), after "Scotland" there shall be inserted—

"(za) in subsection (1) of this section, the words 'and was not comprised in a farm business tenancy' shall be omitted;".

18.—(1) Section 28 of that Act (special provision as to market gardens) shall be amended as follows.

(2) In subsection (1), after "market garden" there shall be inserted "and was not comprised in a farm business tenancy."

(3) In subsection (6), after "Scotland" there shall be inserted "in subsection (1) of this section, the words 'and was not comprised in a farm business tenancy' shall be omitted; and".

19. In section 51 of that Act (interpretation) in subsection (1)—

(a) after the definition of "the Act of 1986" there shall be inserted—

"'the Act of 1995' means the Agricultural Tenancies Act 1995;" and

(b) after the definition of "emergency powers" there shall be inserted—

"'farm business tenancy' has the same meaning as in the Act of 1995;".

20.—(1) Schedule 7 to that Act (adjustments between landlords and tenants and in respect of mortgages and mining leases and orders) shall be amended as follows.

(2) After paragraph 1, there shall be inserted—

"1A.—(1) The provisions of this paragraph shall have effect where—

(a) paragraphs (a) and (b) of subsection (1) of section 25A of this Act apply, and

(b) the farm business tenancy at the end of which the tenant could have claimed compensation for tenant's improvements terminates on or after the date of entry, but before the end of the period of occupation, without being succeeded by another such subsequent tenancy.

(2) In the circumstances specified in sub-paragraph (1) of this paragraph, the provisions of Part III of the Act of 1995—

(a) shall apply, in relation to the tenancy mentioned in that sub-paragraph, as if, at the termination of that tenancy, the land in question were in the state in which it was immediately before the date of entry, and

(b) if the tenant under that tenancy quitted the holding before the termination of his tenancy, shall so apply as if he had quitted the holding on the termination of his tenancy.

(3) In sub-paragraph (2) of this paragraph, 'holding', in relation to a farm business tenancy, and 'termination', in relation to a tenancy, have the same meaning as in the Act of 1995."

(3) In paragraph 2, in sub-paragraph (1), after "agricultural holding" there shall be inserted "held under a tenancy in relation to which the Act of 1986 applies".

(4) After that paragraph there shall be inserted—

"2A.—(1) The provisions of this paragraph shall have effect where land comprised in a farm business tenancy is comprised in a compulsory rights order (whether any other land is comprised in the holding, or comprised in the order, or not), and—

(a) before the date of entry there had been provided in relation to the land in question tenant's improvements (in this paragraph referred to as 'the former tenant's improvements') in respect of which, immediately before that date, the tenant had a prospective right to compensation under section 16 of the Act of 1995 on quitting the holding on the termination of the tenancy, and

(b) at the end of the period of occupation the circumstances are such that Part III of that Act would have applied as mentioned in subsections (3) and (4) of section 25A of this Act, but for the fact that the benefit of the former tenant's improvements has been replaced, on the restoration of the land, by other improvements (in this paragraph referred to as 'the new improvements') of comparable benefit to the land.

(2) In the circumstances specified in sub-paragraph (1) of this paragraph, Part III of the Act of 1995 shall have effect in relation to the new improvements as if those improvements were tenant's improvements.

(3) Subsections (2) and (6) of section 25A of this Act shall apply for the purposes of this paragraph as they apply for the purposes of that section."

(5) After paragraph 3 there shall be inserted—

"3A. Where by virtue of section 25A of this Act a tenant is entitled to compensation for tenant's improvements as mentioned in that section and—

(a) after the end of the period of occupation expenses are incurred in replacing the benefit of the tenant's improvements by other improvements of comparable benefit to the land, and

(b) the person incurring those expenses (whether he is the landlord or not) is entitled to compensation in respect of those expenses under section 22 of this Act,

section 13 of the Act of 1995 shall apply as if the works in respect of which those expenses are incurred were not tenant's improvements, if apart from this paragraph they would constitute such improvements."

(6) At the end of paragraph 4, there shall be added—

"(7) In this paragraph 'agricultural holding' does not include an agricultural holding held under a farm business tenancy."

(7) After that paragraph there shall be inserted—

"4A.—(1) The provisions of this paragraph shall apply where—

(a) immediately before the operative date of a compulsory rights order, any of the land comprised in the order is subject to a farm business tenancy, and

(b) that tenancy continues until after the end of the period of occupation.

(2) The landlord or tenant under the tenancy may, by notice in writing served on his tenant or landlord, demand a reference to arbitration of the question whether any of the terms and conditions of the tenancy (including any term or condition relating to rent) should be varied in consequence of any change in the state of the land resulting from the occupation or use of the land in the exercise of rights conferred by the order; and subsection (3) of section 28 of the Act of 1995 shall apply in relation to a notice under this sub-paragraph as it applies in relation to a notice under subsection (2) of that section.

(3) On a reference by virtue of this paragraph, the arbitrator shall determine what variations (if any) should be made in the terms and conditions of the tenancy, and the date (not being earlier than the end of the period of occupation) from which any such variations are to take effect or to be treated as having taken effect; and as from that date the tenancy shall have effect, or, as the case may be, shall be treated as having had effect, subject to any variations determined by the arbitrator under this paragraph.

(4) The provisions of this paragraph shall not affect any right of the landlord or the tenant, or the jurisdiction of the arbitrator, under Part II of the Act of 1995; but where—

(a) there is a reference by virtue of this paragraph and a reference under Part II of that Act in respect of the same tenancy, and

(b) it appears to the arbitrator that the reference under Part II of that Act relates wholly or mainly to the consequences of the occupation or use of the land in the exercise of rights conferred by the order,

he may direct that proceedings on the two references shall be taken concurrently."

(8) In paragraph 5(1), after "agricultural holding" there shall be inserted "held under a tenancy in relation to which the Act of 1986 applies".

(9) In paragraph 6—
(a) in sub-paragraph (1), for "an agricultural holding" there shall be substituted "—
(a) an agricultural holding held under a tenancy in relation to which the Act of 1986 applies, or
(b) a holding under a farm business tenancy,"; and
(b) after sub-paragraph (2) there shall be added—
"(2A) In sub-paragraph (1) of this paragraph, 'holding', in relation to a farm business tenancy, has the same meaning as in the Act of 1995."
(10) In paragraph 7—
(a) after "The provisions of" there shall be inserted "sub-paragraphs (1) to (6) of";
(b) for "that paragraph" there shall be substituted "those sub-paragraphs"; and
(c) after "subject to a mortgage" there shall be inserted "but not comprised in a farm business tenancy".
(11) After that paragraph there shall be inserted—
"7A. The provisions of paragraph 4A of this Schedule shall apply in relation to mortgages of land comprised in farm business tenancies as they apply in relation to such tenancies, as if any reference in that paragraph to such a tenancy were a reference to such a mortgage, and any reference to a landlord or to a tenant were a reference to a mortgagee or to a mortgagor, as the case may be."
(12) In paragraph 12(1)(a), for the words from "did" to "holding" there shall be substituted "was not comprised in a tenancy in relation to which the Act of 1986 applies or in a farm business tenancy".
(13) In paragraph 13, after "or to a tenancy" there shall be inserted "(other than a reference to a tenancy in relation to which the Act of 1986 applies or a farm business tenancy)".
(14) In paragraph 25—
(a) in sub-paragraph (a), at the beginning there shall be inserted "subject to sub-paragraphs (ba), (bc), (bd)(i) and (be) of this paragraph,";
(b) after sub-paragraph (b), there shall be inserted—
"(ba) in sub-paragraph (1) of paragraph 2, the words 'held under a tenancy in relation to which the Act of 1986 applies' shall be omitted;
(bb) sub-paragraph (7) of paragraph 4 shall be omitted;
(bc) in sub-paragraph (1) of paragraph 5, the words 'held under a tenancy in relation to which the Act of 1986 applies' shall be omitted;
(bd) in paragraph (6)—
(i) for paragraphs (a) and (b) of sub-paragraph (1) there shall be substituted the words 'an agricultural holding'; and
(ii) sub-paragraph (2A) shall be omitted;
(be) in sub-paragraph (1)(a) of paragraph 12, for the words 'was not comprised in a tenancy in relation to which the Act of 1986 applies or in a farm business tenancy' there shall be substituted the words 'did not constitute or form part of an agricultural holding';" and
(c) in sub-paragraph (c), for "7" there shall be substituted "1A, 2A, 3A, 4A, 7, 7A".

The Agriculture (Miscellaneous Provisions) Act 1963 (c. 11)

21.—(1) Section 22 of the Agriculture (Miscellaneous Provisions) Act 1963 (allowances to persons displaced from agricultural land) shall be amended as follows.
(2) In subsection (1), for paragraph (a) there shall be substituted—
"(a) the land—
(i) is used for the purposes of agriculture (within the meaning of the Agricultural Tenancies Act 1995) and is so used by way of a trade or business, or
(ii) is not so used but is comprised in a farm business tenancy (within the meaning of the Agricultural Tenancies Act 1995) and used for the purposes of a trade or business,".
(3) In subsection (6)(c), for "the Agricultural Holdings Act 1986" there shall be substituted ", the Agricultural Tenancies Act 1995".

The Leasehold Reform Act 1967 (c. 88)

22. In section 1(3) of the Leasehold Reform Act 1967 (tenants entitled to enfranchisement or extension), for paragraph (b) there shall be substituted—

"(b) it is comprised in—
(i) an agricultural holding within the meaning of the Agricultural Holdings Act 1986 held under a tenancy in relation to which that Act applies, or
(ii) the holding held under a farm business tenancy within the meaning of the Agricultural Tenancies Act 1995."

The Agriculture (Miscellaneous Provisions) Act 1968 (c. 34)

23. In section 12 of the Agriculture (Miscellaneous Provisions) Act 1968 (additional payments in consequence of compulsory acquisition etc of agricultural holdings), after subsection (1) there shall be inserted—
"(1A) No sum shall be payable by virtue of subsection (1) of this section in respect of any land comprised in a farm business tenancy within the meaning of the Agricultural Tenancies Act 1995."

The Land Compensation Act 1973 (c. 26)

24. In section 48 of the Land Compensation Act 1973 (compensation in respect of agricultural holdings) at the beginning of subsection (1) there shall be inserted "Subject to subsection (1A) below" and after subsection (1) there shall be inserted—
"(1A) This section does not have effect where the tenancy of the agricultural holding is a tenancy to which, by virtue of section 4 of the Agricultural Tenancies Act 1995, the Agricultural Holdings Act 1986 does not apply."

The Rent (Agriculture) Act 1976 (c. 80)

25.—(1) Section 9 of the Rent (Agriculture) Act 1976 (effect of determination of superior tenancy, etc) shall be amended as follows.
(2) In subsection (3), after "the Agricultural Holdings Act 1986" there shall be inserted "held under a tenancy in relation to which that Act applies and land comprised in a farm business tenancy within the meaning of the Agricultural Tenancies Act 1995."
(3) In subsection (4), for the words from "or" at the end of paragraph (b) onwards there shall be substituted—
"(c) a tenancy of an agricultural holding within the meaning of the Agricultural Holdings Act 1986 which is a tenancy in relation to which that Act applies; or
(d) a farm business tenancy within the meaning of the Agricultural Tenancies Act 1995."
26. In Schedule 2 to that Act (meaning of "relevant licence" and "relevant tenancy"), in paragraph 2 for the words from "and a tenancy" to the end there shall be substituted ", a tenancy of an agricultural holding within the meaning of the Agricultural Holdings Act 1986 which is a tenancy in relation to which that Act applies, and a farm business tenancy within the meaning of the Agricultural Tenancies Act 1995."

The Rent Act 1977 (c. 42)

27. For section 10 of the Rent Act 1977 there shall be substituted—

"**Agricultural holdings etc.**
10.—(1) A tenancy is not a protected tenancy if—
(a) the dwelling-house is comprised in an agricultural holding and is occupied by the person responsible for the control (whether as tenant or as servant or agent of the tenant) of the farming of the holding, or
(b) the dwelling-house is comprised in the holding held under a farm business tenancy and is occupied by the person responsible for the control (whether as tenant or as servant or agent of the tenant) of the management of the holding.
(2) In subsection (1) above—
'agricultural holding' means any agricultural holding within the meaning of the Agricultural Holdings Act 1986 held under a tenancy in relation to which that Act applies, and
'farm business tenancy', and 'holding' in relation to such a tenancy, have the same meaning as in the Agricultural Tenancies Act 1995."
28.—(1) Section 137 of that Act (effect on sub-tenancy of determination of superior tenancy) shall be amended as follows.
(2) In subsection (3), after "the Agricultural Holdings Act 1986" there shall be inserted "held under a tenancy to which that Act applies and land comprised in a farm business tenancy within the meaning of the Agricultural Tenancies Act 1995."

(3) In subsection (4), in paragraph (c), for the words from "applies" onwards there shall be substituted "applies—
> (i) a tenancy of an agricultural holding within the meaning of the Agricultural Holdings Act 1986 which is a tenancy in relation to which that Act applies, or
> (ii) a farm business tenancy within the meaning of the Agricultural Tenancies Act 1995."

The Protection from Eviction Act 1977 (c. 43)

29. In section 8(1) of the Protection from Eviction Act 1977 (interpretation)—
(a) in paragraph (d), after "Agricultural Holdings Act 1986" there shall be inserted "which is a tenancy in relation to which that Act applies", and
(b) at the end there shall be added—
"(g) a farm business tenancy within the meaning of the Agricultural Tenancies Act 1995."

The Housing Act 1985 (c. 68)

30. In Schedule 1 to the Housing Act 1985 (tenancies which are not secure tenancies), for paragraph 8 there shall be substituted—

"Agricultural holdings etc.

8.—(1) A tenancy is not a secure tenancy if—
(a) the dwelling-house is comprised in an agricultural holding and is occupied by the person responsible for the control (whether as tenant or as servant or agent of the tenant) of the farming of the holding, or
(b) the dwelling-house is comprised in the holding held under a farm business tenancy and is occupied by the person responsible for the control (whether as tenant or as servant or agent of the tenant) of the management of the holding.
(2) In sub-paragraph (1) above—
'agricultural holding' means any agricultural holding within the meaning of the Agricultural Holdings Act 1986 held under a tenancy in relation to which that Act applies, and
'farm business tenancy', and 'holding' in relation to such a tenancy, have the same meaning as in the Agricultural Tenancies Act 1995."

The Landlord and Tenant Act 1985 (c. 70)

31. In section 14(3) of the Landlord and Tenant Act 1985 (leases to which section 11 does not apply), at the end there shall be added "and in relation to which that Act applies or to a farm business tenancy within the meaning of the Agricultural Tenancies Act 1995."

The Agricultural Holdings Act 1986 (c. 5)

32. In Schedule 6 to the Agricultural Holdings Act 1986 (eligibility to apply for a new tenancy under Part IV of that Act), in paragraph 6 (occupation to be disregarded for purposes of occupancy condition), in sub-paragraph (1) after paragraph (d) there shall be inserted—
"(dd) under a farm business tenancy, within the meaning of the Agricultural Tenancies Act 1995, for less than five years (including a farm business tenancy which is a periodic tenancy),".

The Housing Act 1988 (c. 50)

33. In section 101(2) of the Housing Act 1988 (which relates to tenancies and licences affecting property proposed to be acquired under Part IV of that Act), after "smallholdings)" there shall be inserted "nor the Agricultural Tenancies Act 1995 (farm business tenancies)".
34. In Schedule 1 to that Act (tenancies which cannot be assured tenancies), for paragraph 7 there shall be substituted—

"Tenancies of agricultural holdings etc

7.—(1) A tenancy under which the dwelling-house—
(a) is comprised in an agricultural holding, and
(b) is occupied by the person responsible for the control (whether as tenant or as servant or agent of the tenant) of the farming of the holding.
(2) A tenancy under which the dwelling-house—
(a) is comprised in the holding held under a farm business tenancy, and

(b) is occupied by the person responsible for the control (whether as tenant or as servant or agent of the tenant) of the management of the holding.

(3) In this paragraph—

'agricultural holding' means any agricultural holding within the meaning of the Agricultural Holdings Act 1986 held under a tenancy in relation to which that Act applies, and

'farm business tenancy' and 'holding', in relation to such a tenancy, have the same meaning as in the Agricultural Tenancies Act 1995."

The Town and Country Planning Act 1990 (c. 8)

35.—(1) Section 65 of the Town and Country Planning Act 1990 (notice etc. of applications for planning permissions) shall be amended as follows.

(2) In subsection (2), for "a tenant of any agricultural holding any part of which is comprised in that land" there shall be substituted "an agricultural tenant of that land".

(3) In subsection (8), for the definition of "agricultural holding" there shall be substituted—

"'agricultural tenant', in relation to any land, means any person who—

(a) is the tenant, under a tenancy in relation to which the Agricultural Holdings Act 1986 applies, of an agricultural holding within the meaning of that Act any part of which is comprised in that land; or

(b) is the tenant, under a farm business tenancy (within the meaning of the Agricultural Tenancies Act 1995), of land any part of which is comprised in that land;".

The Coal Mining Subsidence Act 1991 (c. 45)

36. In section 21 of the Coal Mining Subsidence Act 1991 (property belonging to protected tenants) in subsection (3), after paragraph (a) there shall be inserted—

"(aa) a tenant under a farm business tenancy within the meaning of the Agricultural Tenancies Act 1995;".

37. In Schedule 3 to that Act (property belonging to protected tenants) in paragraph 1(2), after paragraph (b) there shall be inserted—

"(bb) section 20 of the Agricultural Tenancies Act 1995;".

INDEX

COMMONWEALTH DEVELOPMENT CORPORATION ACT 1995

(1995 c. 9)

An Act to alter the limits under sections 9A and 10 of the Commonwealth Development Corporation Act 1978; to make provision in relation to interest on advances to the Commonwealth Development Corporation; and to make provision in relation to the remuneration, pensions and compensation ·of members of the Corporation.   [28th June 1995]

PARLIAMENTARY DEBATES
Hansard, H.C. Vol. 256, col. 1039. H.L. Vol. 562, col. 1456, Vol. 563, col. 1510, Vol. 564, col. 1048.

INTRODUCTION
This Act alters the limits on the amounts which may be borrowed or guaranteed by the Commonwealth Development Corporation, and makes provision in relation to the interest on advances to the Corporation and in relation to the remuneration, allowances and pensions of the members of the Corporation. This Act came into force on June 28, 1995.

Alteration of limits on borrowing etc.

1.—(1) In section 9A(2) of the Commonwealth Development Corporation Act 1978 (which imposes a limit of £750 million, or such larger sum not exceeding £850 million as may be specified by order, on the total amount outstanding in respect of sums borrowed or guaranteed by the Corporation or any of its subsidiaries)—

(a) for "£750 million" there shall be substituted "£1,100 million"; and

(b) for "£850 million" there shall be substituted "£1,500 million".

(2) In subsection (1) of section 10 of that Act (which provides for the making of advances by the Secretary of State to the Corporation up to a certain limit), the words "up to" onwards shall cease to have effect.

Interest on advances

2.—(1) In section 12 of the Commonwealth Development Corporation Act 1978 (repayment of, and interest on, advances and sums issued to meet guarantees), in subsection (1) after the words "Subject to" there shall be inserted "subsection (3A) and".

(2) After subsection (3) of that section there shall be inserted the following subsection—

"(3A) Nothing in this section shall be taken to prevent the Secretary of State, if he has the approval of the Treasury, from making interest-free advances to the Corporation under section 10(1) above."

(3) For section 13 of that Act (power of Secretary of State to remit certain debts of the Corporation) there shall be substituted—

"Power to remit interest on advances

13. The Secretary of State may, with the consent of the Treasury, remit the payment by the Corporation under section 12(1) above of interest on the whole or any part of the amount outstanding in respect of an advance under section 10(1) above, being interest for such period (beginning after the commencement of the Commonwealth Development Corporation Act 1995) as he may with the consent of the Treasury determine."

Remuneration etc. of members of the Corporation

3.—(1) Schedule 1 to the Commonwealth Development Corporation Act 1978 (supplementary provisions relating to the constitution etc. of the Corporation) shall be amended as follows.

(2) For paragraph 3 (which makes provision in relation to the remuneration and allowances of members of the Corporation) there shall be substituted the following paragraph—

"3. The Corporation shall pay to the members of the Corporation such remuneration and allowances as may be determined by the Secretary of State."

(3) In paragraph 4 (which makes provision in relation to the pensions etc. of members of the Corporation), for the words from "it is determined" to "make provision" there shall be substituted "it is determined by the Secretary of State to make provision".

(4) Paragraph 5 (which makes provision in relation to the remuneration and allowances of members of the Corporation who are employed about the affairs of the Corporation) shall cease to have effect.

(5) Before paragraph 6 there shall be inserted the following paragraph—

"5A. If, when a person ceases to be a member of the Corporation, the Secretary of State determines that there are special circumstances which make it right that he should receive compensation, the Corporation shall pay to him a sum by way of compensation of such amount as the Secretary of State may determine."

Repeals

4. The enactments mentioned in the Schedule to this Act are hereby repealed to the extent specified in the third column of that Schedule.

Short title and extent

5.—(1) This Act may be cited as the Commonwealth Development Corporation Act 1995.

(2) This Act extends to Northern Ireland.

Section 4   SCHEDULE

REPEALS

Chapter	Short title	Extent of repeal
1978 c. 2.	The Commonwealth Development Corporation Act 1978.	In section 10(1) the words "up to" onwards. Section 10(2). Section 18(3). In Schedule 1, paragraph 5.
1982 c. 54.	The Commonwealth Development Corporation Act 1982.	Section 3.

INDEX

References are to sections and the Schedule

HOME ENERGY CONSERVATION ACT 1995*

(1995 c. 10)

An Act to make provision for the drawing up of local energy conservation reports in relation to residential accommodation; to give the Secretary of State functions in connection therewith; and for related purposes.

[28th June 1995]

PARLIAMENTARY DEBATES
Hansard, H.C. Vol. 256, col. 1131. H.L. Vol. 563, col. 434, Vol. 564, col. 899.
This Bill was considered in Standing Committee C on February 8 and 15, 1995.

INTRODUCTION AND GENERAL NOTE
This Act provides a framework for local authorities with housing responsibilities to promote energy efficiency in residential premises in their areas. Its arrival on the statute book marks the end of a long and tortuous parliamentary process.

Since 1993 there have been two attempts by backbenchers to get a similar measure enacted, both of which were unsuccessful. This private members bill, sponsored by Diana Maddock MP (Christchurch), had a relatively smooth passage through parliament, reflecting strong back-bench support and the fact that the new Parliamentary Under-Secretary of State for the Environment with responsibility for energy efficiency, Robert Jones, had been a sponsor of one of the previous unsuccessful Bills.

The main purpose of the Act is to require each local authority to assess the energy efficiency of homes in its area and to draw up a local energy conservation report (ECR). The particular focus of this effort will be to extend "energy conservation measures" defined in s.1 to the privately rented and owner-occupied residential sectors.

Originally the Bill required ECRs to identify measures likely to achieve a 30 per cent energy saving. This was rejected by the government and replaced with a requirement on authorities to set out measures likely to result in "significant improvement" (s.2(2)). The meaning of this phrase is to be clarified in guidance to be produced by the Secretary of State (s.4), and is to be "along the lines" of the 30 per cent originally proposed, according to the Parliamentary Under-Secretary of State for the Environment (Standing Committee C, col. 60, February 15, 1995).

The ECR produced by each local authority will be published and submitted to the Secretary of State, by a date directed by him. The Secretary of State will then give the authority a timetable for the preparation of a progress report on the implementation of the measures contained in the report.

An amendment supported by the promoters to require annual reporting to Parliament by the Secretary of State, setting out progress made by authorities in implementation, was rejected by the government in favour of a duty to report to parliament "from time to time" (s.3(4)). Authorities are required to have regard to guidance produced by the Secretary of State (s.4(3)). It is understood that such guidance will be published by early 1996.

COMMENCEMENT
The Act comes into force on such day as the Secretary of State may, by order, appoint and different days may be appointed for different purposes, different energy conservation authorities, different description of energy conservation authority and different areas (s.9). It has been indicated by the Minister Robert Jones (Standing Committee C, col. 72, February 15, 1995) that for authorities where local government reorganisation is not a factor, the Act will be brought into force on April 1, 1996. For newly formed authorities, a date one year later is anticipated.

EXTENT
England, Wales, Scotland and Northern Ireland.

Interpretation

1.—(1) In this Act—
    "energy conservation authority" means—
    (a) in England and Wales, a local housing authority within the meaning of the Housing Act 1985,

---

*Annotations by Richard Stein, LLM, Leigh, Day & Co., Solicitors.

(b) in Scotland, a local authority within the meaning of the Housing (Scotland) Act 1987, and

(c) in Northern Ireland, the Northern Ireland Housing Executive;
"energy conservation measures" includes information, advice, education, promotion, making grants and loans and carrying out works;
"residential accommodation" means—

(a) premises occupied or intended to be occupied as a separate dwelling and forming the whole or part of a building, or

(b) a mobile home, that is—

(i) in England and Wales or Scotland, a caravan within the meaning of Part I of the Caravan Sites and Control of Development Act 1960 (disregarding the amendment made by section 13(2) of the Caravan Sites Act 1968) which is a dwelling for the purposes of Part I or II of the Local Government Finance Act 1992,

(ii) in Northern Ireland, a caravan within the meaning of the Caravans Act (Northern Ireland) 1963 which is a dwelling-house for the purposes of the Rates (Northern Ireland) Order 1977.

(2) Any reference in this Act to the area of an energy conservation authority is—

(a) in the case of a local housing authority in England and Wales, to the area of that authority within the meaning of the Housing Act 1985,

(b) in the case of a local authority in Scotland, to the area of that authority, and

(c) in the case of the Northern Ireland Housing Executive, to Northern Ireland.

Energy conservation reports

2.—(1) It shall be the duty of every energy conservation authority to prepare a report in accordance with this section.

(2) The report shall set out energy conservation measures that the authority considers practicable, cost-effective and likely to result in significant improvement in the energy efficiency of residential accommodation in its area.

(3) The report shall include—

(a) an assessment of the cost of the energy conservation measures set out in it;

(b) an assessment of the extent to which carbon dioxide emissions into the atmosphere would be decreased as a result of those measures; and

(c) a statement of any policy of the authority for taking into account, in deciding whether to exercise any power in connection with those measures, the personal circumstances of any person.

Nothing in this subsection shall be taken as requiring the authority to set out in the report energy conservation measures to be taken in relation to any particular dwelling or building.

(4) The report may, if the energy conservation authority considers it desirable, include—

(a) an assessment of the extent of decreases in emissions into the atmosphere of oxides of nitrogen and sulphur dioxide which would result from the implementation of the measures set out in the report;

(b) an assessment of the number of jobs which would result from the implementation of those measures;

(c) an assessment of the average savings in fuel bills and in kilowatt hours of fuel used that might be expected to result from the measures by different types of household in different types of accommodation;

(d) such other matters as it considers appropriate.

(5) An energy conservation authority may in preparing the report consult such persons as it considers appropriate.

(6) When an energy conservation authority has prepared a report in accordance with this section, it shall publish it and send a copy to the Secretary of State.

Functions of the Secretary of State in relation to reports

3.—(1) The Secretary of State shall give directions as to the date by which reports under section 2 are to be sent to him by energy conservation authorities.

The directions may set different dates for different authorities, different descriptions of authority and different areas.

(2) Where the Secretary of State has received a report under section 2 from an energy conservation authority, and it appears to him that the report has been duly prepared in accordance with this Act, he shall—

(a) notify the authority of a timetable in accordance with which the authority shall prepare, publish and send to the Secretary of State reports on the progress made in implementing the measures set out in the report, and

(b) take such steps as he considers desirable in order to assist with and to encourage other persons to assist with the measures set out in any such report.

(3) The Secretary of State may vary any timetable set by him under subsection (2).

(4) The Secretary of State shall from time to time prepare a report on—

(a) the progress made by energy conservation authorities in implementing the measures set out in reports prepared under section 2, and

(b) any steps he has taken pursuant to subsection (2)(b) above, and shall lay any such report before Parliament.

Guidance by the Secretary of State

4.—(1) The Secretary of State may, from time to time, give to energy conservation authorities such guidance as he considers appropriate in relation to the preparation of reports under section 2 or reports under section 3(2)(a).

(2) The Secretary of State may, in particular, give guidance as to what improvements in energy efficiency are to be regarded as significant.

(3) An energy conservation authority shall have regard to any guidance given by the Secretary of State under this section.

Modification of report and further reports

5.—(1) An energy conservation authority may, and if so directed by the Secretary of State shall—

(a) modify the report prepared under section 2; or

(b) prepare further reports setting out additional or modified energy conservation measures.

(2) The provisions of subsections (2) to (6) of section 2, subsections (2) to (4) of section 3, section 4 and subsection (1) of this section apply in relation to any such modified or further report.

Supplementary provisions

6.—(1) Nothing in this Act shall be taken as conferring—

(a) any power to make grants or loans;

(b) any power of entry; or

(c) any power to carry out works, or require any person to carry out works.

(2) Nothing in this Act requires an energy conservation authority to inspect any premises or requires any person to give any information to an energy conservation authority.

Expenses

7. There shall be paid out of moneys provided by Parliament—

(a) any expenses of the Secretary of State under this Act; and

(b) any increase attributable to this Act in the sums payable out of such moneys under any other Act.

Northern Ireland

8.—(1) This Act extends to Northern Ireland.

(2) In the application of this Act to Northern Ireland—

(a) the references to the Secretary of State (except in section 7) shall be construed as references to the Department of the Environment for Northern Ireland;

(b) the reference in section 3(4) to laying before Parliament shall be construed as a reference to laying before the Northern Ireland Assembly; and

(c) the reference in section 9(2) to an order made by statutory instrument shall be construed as a reference to an order which is a statutory rule for the purposes of the Statutory Rules (Northern Ireland) Order 1979.

Citation and commencement

9.—(1) This Act may be cited as the Home Energy Conservation Act 1995.

(2) This Act shall come into force on such day as may be appointed by order made by statutory instrument by the Secretary of State.

(3) Different days may be appointed under subsection (2) for different purposes, different energy conservation authorities, different descriptions of energy conservation authority and different areas.

INDEX

References are to sections

PROCEEDS OF CRIME ACT 1995*

(1995 c. 11)

An Act to make further provision for and in relation to the recovery of the proceeds of criminal conduct; to make further provision for facilitating the enforcement of overseas forfeiture and restraint orders; and for connected purposes.   [28th June 1995]

PARLIAMENTARY DEBATES
    Hansard, H.C. Vol. 253, col. 1322, Vol. 257, col. 1290. H.L. Vol. 563, col. 1011, Vol. 564, cols. 1184, 1541.

INTRODUCTION AND GENERAL NOTE

The Proceeds of Crime Act 1995 amends Pt. VI of the Criminal Justice Act 1988 (c. 33) (hereafter "the 1988 Act"), which empowers the courts to confiscate from defendants in certain criminal cases the proceeds of indictable offences and a limited range of summary offences, committed by them. The Act does not apply to confiscation of the proceeds of drug trafficking offences (on which see the Drug Trafficking Act 1994 (c. 37), hereafter "the 1994 Act") nor to certain terrorist offences (on which see Pt. III of the Prevention of Terrorism (Temporary Provisions) Act 1989 (c. 4)). While comments made during the passage through Parliament of the Proceeds of Crime Bill suggest that the Bill is designed to remove the proceeds of a limited range of non-drug-related lucrative offending, such as dealing in arms, trafficking in stolen art and antiques, organised car theft and large-scale dealing in pornography, the potential reach of the 1988 Act, as now amended, is much wider. There is no reason why persistent (and financially successful) robbers, burglars, thieves, or tax fraudsters could not be brought within its terms.

The origins of this Act may be found in the Second Report of the Home Office Working Group on Confiscation, which was published in 1992. It can properly be seen as part of a process

---

*Annotations by Professor Martin Wasik, University of Manchester.

of development in this area of the law, following the recommendations of the Hodgson Committee on *Forfeiture of the Proceeds of Crime* in 1984. Subsequent to that Report there have developed broadly parallel legislative schemes in respect of removal of the proceeds of drug trafficking (in the Drug Trafficking Offences Act 1986 (c. 32), as amended by the Criminal Justice Act 1993 (c. 36) and consolidated into the 1994 Act), removal of the proceeds of offences of terrorism (most recently in the Prevention of Terrorism (Temporary Provisions) Act 1989) and in respect of other lucrative offending (the 1988 Act, as amended by the Criminal Justice Act 1993). Further reform to this last branch of the powers was seen as being necessary in view of the hitherto infrequent use made by the courts of their powers to order confiscation under the 1988 Act. Only 13 orders for confiscation were made under that Act during the year 1993–1994, realising the total (and rather modest) sum of £265,000. This may be compared with a total of £5.3 million confiscated during the equivalent period under the drug trafficking powers. The Home Office Working Group made clear its view that there had been a number of cases where courts had failed to make a confiscation order under the 1988 Act even though the defendant had clearly benefited from crime, or had made an order for a sum which was clearly substantially less than the extent of the defendant's benefit. The government predicts "a moderate increase in the number of cases annually" as a result of the changes to the 1988 Act brought about by the Proceeds of Crime Act 1995.

The legislation was sponsored as a Private Member's Bill by Sir John Hannan (Exeter), but in reality it had full government support, having been drawn up by Home Office lawyers (see further the comments of Lord Harris of Greenwich, *Hansard*, H.L. Vol. 563, col. 1016 and the response by Baroness Blatch, *ibid*, col. 1019). The Bill also had the full support of the Opposition, and hence enjoyed a swift and smooth passage through Parliament. There were only minor amendments to the Bill during the Committee Stage in the Commons and no amendments in the Lords. The Bill received Royal Assent on June 28, 1995.

ABBREVIATIONS

1988 Act: Criminal Justice Act 1988.
1994 Act: Drug Trafficking Act 1994.

Making of confiscation orders

Duty to make confiscation orders

1.—(1) Section 71 of the Criminal Justice Act 1988 ("the 1988 Act") shall be amended as follows.

(2) For subsections (1) to (3) (orders confiscating the proceeds of an offence) there shall be substituted the following subsections—

"(1) Where an offender is convicted, in any proceedings before the Crown Court or a magistrates' court, of an offence of a relevant description, it shall be the duty of the court—

(a) if the prosecutor has given written notice to the court that he considers that it would be appropriate for the court to proceed under this section, or

(b) if the court considers, even though it has not been given such notice, that it would be appropriate for it so to proceed,

to act as follows before sentencing or otherwise dealing with the offender in respect of that offence or any other relevant criminal conduct.

(1A) The court shall first determine whether the offender has benefited from any relevant criminal conduct.

(1B) Subject to subsection (1C) below, if the court determines that the offender has benefited from any relevant criminal conduct, it shall then—

(a) determine in accordance with subsection (6) below the amount to be recovered in his case by virtue of this section, and

(b) make an order under this section ordering the offender to pay that amount.

(1C) If, in a case falling within subsection (1B) above, the court is satisfied that a victim of any relevant criminal conduct has instituted, or intends to institute, civil proceedings against the defendant in respect of loss, injury or damage sustained in connection with that conduct—

(a) the court shall have a power, instead of a duty, to make an order under this section;

(b) subsection (6) below shall not apply for determining the amount to be recovered in that case by virtue of this section; and

(c) where the court makes an order in exercise of that power, the sum required to be paid under that order shall be of such amount, not exceeding the amount which (but for paragraph (b) above) would apply by virtue of subsection (6) below, as the court thinks fit.

(1D) In this Part of this Act 'relevant criminal conduct', in relation to a person convicted of an offence in any proceedings before a court, means (subject to section 72AA(6) below) that offence taken together with any other offences of a relevant description which are either—

(a) offences of which he is convicted in the same proceedings, or

(b) offences which the court will be taking into consideration in determining his sentence for the offence in question.

(1E) For the purposes of this Part of this Act an offence is an offence of a relevant description—

(a) in the case of an offence of which a person is convicted in any proceedings before the Crown Court or which is or will be taken into consideration by the Crown Court in determining any sentence, if it is an offence to which this Part of this Act applies; and

(b) in the case of an offence of which a person is convicted in any proceedings before a magistrates' court or which is or will be taken into consideration by a magistrates' court in determining any sentence, if it is an offence listed in Schedule 4 to this Act."

(3) In subsection (6) (amount to be paid under a confiscation order)—

(a) at the beginning there shall be inserted "Subject to subsection (1C) above"; and

(b) for "must be at least the minimum amount, but must not exceed" there shall be substituted "shall be equal to".

(4) Subsections (7) and (8) (minimum amount of confiscation order) shall cease to have effect.

(5) In subsection (7A) (standard of proof required to determine matters under Part VI)—

(a) in paragraph (a), for "as mentioned in subsection (2)(b)(i) above" there shall be substituted "from any offence", and at the end there shall be inserted "or";

(b) paragraph (b) shall be omitted; and

(c) in paragraph (c), the words "by virtue of section 72 below" shall be omitted.

GENERAL NOTE

Section 1 makes two significant changes to the earlier law. First, it places a duty upon the court to exercise its powers to order confiscation in every case in which written notice has been given by the prosecutor. This brings the law into line with the change made in respect of orders made under the 1994 Act (see s.2(1)(a) of that Act). Formerly, while the court might in any appropriate case have exercised its powers, it was never placed under a specific duty to do so. Clearly, the legislative intention is that the courts should make more such orders, and it gives the prosecutor the prime role in encouraging this. Apart from cases where the prosecutor has served such a notice, the court retains its power to pursue the matter and to make a confiscation order of its own volition. This is also in line with the drug trafficking provisions (see s.2(1)(b) of the 1994 Act).

The second change is the abolition of the former rule which restricted the making of orders to cases in which at least £10,000 was expected to be recovered. There is now *no* minimum figure. This is in line with the equivalent provision in the 1994 Act, where there has never been a minimum figure prescribed by statute. During the course of Parliamentary debate on the Proceeds of Crime Bill it was pointed out that to pursue the making of orders for sums of substantially less than £10,000 might well not be cost effective (Lord Harris of Greenwich, for example, said that it would be "foolish in the extreme" to spend large sums of public money to seize a few hundred pounds' worth of assets). The government explained that guidelines were being drawn up by the Crown Prosecution Service in consultation with other prosecuting authorities to ensure that confiscation cases would be pursued only where this would involve recovery of assets clearly in excess of the expense involved in obtaining them. Baroness Blatch indicated (see *Hansard*, H.L. Vol. 563, col. 1020) that the £10,000 figure might well continue to be the ceiling for most practical cases. It may be noted in passing that in *R. v. Crutchley (Deborah) and Tonks (Trevor Reginald)* (1994) 15 Cr.App.R.(S.) 627 the trial judge erroneously imposed a confiscation order upon one of the defendants in the sum of £5,000 (*i.e.* less than the then minimum of £10,000). On discovery of this error the confiscation order was amended by the judge to a fine in the equivalent sum. The Court of Appeal said that in the circumstances of the case that was appropriate.

While the power to order confiscation applies to all indictable offences, it also extends to a limited range of summary offences, as set out in Pt. I of Sched. 4 to the 1988 Act. Currently the offences so listed are: the Local Government (Miscellaneous Provisions) Act 1982, Sched. 3, paras. 20 and 21 (offences relating to sex establishments); the Video Recordings Act 1984, s.9 (supplying video recording of unclassified work) and s.10 (possession of video recording of unclassified work for the purposes of supply); and the Cinemas Act 1985, s.10(1)(a) (use of unlicensed premises for exhibition which requires a licence). During the course of the passage of the Bill through Parliament, Mr John Greenaway moved an amendment to the Bill which would have added to the list of summary offences certain counterfeiting and copyright offences, *viz*: the Copyright, Designs and Patents Act 1988, s.107 (offences relating to the infringement of copyright) and s.198 (making, dealing with or using illicit recordings); the Trade Descriptions Act 1968, s.1 (offences relating to false trade descriptions); and the Trade Marks Act 1994, s.92 (offences relating to the unauthorised use of trade marks *etc.*). The amendment was withdrawn in light of a government undertaking to investigate whether such changes could better be incorporated by way of statutory instrument, rather than by amendment to the Bill. When the Bill completed its passage through Parliament (with its Third Reading in the House of Lords on June 12, 1995) this outstanding matter was returned to. At that time the government was still involved in "interdepartmental consultation" on the question, but the Minister of State Baroness Blatch expected a decision on whether to incorporate the new offences into the Schedule to be taken in the near future (*Hansard*, H.L. Vol. 264, col. 1541).

Section 1 does not apply in the case of proceedings against a person in which that person is convicted of an offence committed before the commencement of s.1 (s.16(5)).

Confiscation relating to a course of criminal conduct

2. The following section shall be inserted in the 1988 Act after section 72—

"Confiscation relating to a course of criminal conduct

72AA.—(1) This section applies in a case where an offender is convicted, in any proceedings before the Crown Court or a magistrates' court, of a qualifying offence which is an offence of a relevant description, if—

(a) the prosecutor gives written notice for the purposes of subsection (1)(a) of section 71 above;

(b) that notice contains a declaration that it is the prosecutor's opinion that the case is one in which it is appropriate for the provisions of this section to be applied; and

(c) the offender—

(i) is convicted in those proceedings of at least two qualifying offences (including the offence in question); or

(ii) has been convicted of a qualifying offence on at least one previous occasion during the relevant period.

(2) In this section 'qualifying offence', in relation to proceedings before the Crown Court or a magistrates' court, means any offence in relation to which all the following conditions are satisfied, that is to say—

(a) it is an offence to which this Part of this Act applies;

(b) it is an offence which was committed after the commencement of section 2 of the Proceeds of Crime Act 1995; and

(c) that court is satisfied that it is an offence from which the defendant has benefited.

(3) When proceeding under section 71 above in pursuance of the notice mentioned in subsection (1)(a) above, the court may, if it thinks fit, determine that (subject to subsection (5) below) the assumptions specified in subsection (4) below are to be made for the purpose—

(a) of determining whether the defendant has benefited from relevant criminal conduct; and

(b) if he has, of assessing the value of the defendant's benefit from such conduct.

(4) Those assumptions are—

(a) that any property appearing to the court—

(i) to be held by the defendant at the date of conviction or at any time in the period between that date and the determination in question, or

(ii) to have been transferred to him at any time since the beginning of the relevant period,

was received by him, at the earliest time when he appears to the court to have held it, as a result of or in connection with the commission of offences to which this Part of this Act applies;

(b) that any expenditure of his since the beginning of the relevant period was met out of payments received by him as a result of or in connection with the commission of offences to which this Part of this Act applies; and

(c) that, for the purposes of valuing any benefit which he had or which he is assumed to have had at any time, he received the benefit free of any other interests in it.

(5) Where the court has determined that the assumptions specified in subsection (4) above are to be made in any case it shall not in that case make any such assumption in relation to any particular property or expenditure if—

(a) that assumption, so far as it relates to that property or expenditure, is shown to be incorrect in the defendant's case;

(b) that assumption, so far as it so relates, is shown to be correct in relation to an offence the defendant's benefit from which has been the subject of a previous confiscation order; or

(c) the court is satisfied that there would (for any other reason) be a serious risk of injustice in the defendant's case if the assumption were to be made in relation to that property or expenditure.

(6) Where the assumptions specified in subsection (4) above are made in any case, the offences from which, in accordance with those assumptions, the defendant is assumed to have benefited shall be treated as if they were comprised, for the purposes of this Part of this Act, in the conduct which is to be treated, in that case, as relevant criminal conduct in relation to the defendant.

(7) In this section 'the date of conviction' means—

(a) in a case not falling within paragraph (b) below, the date on which the defendant is convicted of the offence in question, or

(b) where he is convicted of that offence and one or more other offences in the proceedings in question and those convictions are not all on the same date, the date of the latest of those convictions; and

'the relevant period' means the period of six years ending when the proceedings in question were instituted against the defendant."

GENERAL NOTE

Prior to the 1995 Act amendments, confiscation orders under the 1988 Act could only be made in respect of the offence (or offences) of conviction and any offence (or offences) which the defendant specifically requested the court to take into consideration. This point is clear from the wording of the Act, but was (in effect) confirmed by the Court of Appeal in *R. v. Crutchley (Deborah) and Tonks (Trevor Reginald)* (1994) 15 Cr.App.R.(S). 627. The Court there was mainly concerned to stress the unavailability of compensation orders in respect of offences not charged or formally taken into consideration, but that proposition was equally applicable to confiscation orders under the 1988 Act (see further the commentary on that case by Dr David Thomas at [1994] Crim.L.R. 309). It is clearly a central aim of the 1995 Act to relax these requirements in respect of confiscation orders. As Sir John Hannan explained in the House of Commons (*Hansard*, H.C. Vol. 253, col. 1323):

"[T]he 1988 Act has had little effect on criminals who amass large profits by repeating similar offences over a period of years. The best example of that is the difficulty illustrated by pornographic videos. A criminal may copy and distribute thousands of videos a month, but the production of each video will constitute a separate offence. For the entire proceeds of that criminal enterprise to be confiscated under the 1988 Act, every offence would have to be charged and convicted separately or taken into consideration by the court".

Section 2, therefore, empowers the court to make either or both of two assumptions relating to the defendant. The first assumption is that all property held by the defendant at the date of his conviction or at any time between that date and the making of the order, is assumed to be the proceeds of his criminal activity. The second assumption is that any property which has passed through the defendant's hands in the six years prior to the institution of the current proceedings against him is also assumed to represent the proceeds of his criminal activity.

These changes bring the law more closely into line with the equivalent provisions under the 1994 Act, but there will continue to be some significant differences between the two legislative schemes. These differences rest on a distinction between the 1994 Act, which is concerned with a relatively narrowly focused set of drug trafficking offences, and the 1988 Act as amended which, as we have seen, extends to all indictable offences and a clutch of summary ones. The first difference is that in the present context the court can make the relevant assumptions only where the prosecutor has given the appropriate written notice asking it to make a confiscation order, and where the notice contains a declaration that it would be appropriate, in the view of the prosecutor, for the court to make the said assumption. The court cannot make the assumptions where it has proceeded of its own motion to assess the issue. There is an important further restriction in that the assumptions may be made only where the defendant has been convicted of a relevant offence in previous proceedings within the last six years, or where the defendant is convicted of at least two relevant offences in the present proceedings. This last provision seems to be an attempt by the legislature to restrict the use of the assumptions to cases where the defendant betrays a "pattern" of offending. The Bill, as originally drafted, had required that the defendant be convicted of at least four relevant offences in the present proceedings, but the requirement of four was changed to two at the Committee Stage of the Bill in its passage through the Commons. So while under s.4 of the 1994 Act, the court must almost always make the relevant assumptions, under the 1988 Act, as now amended, they have a discretion whether to do so, and may do so only where the prosecutor has tendered relevant notice. A proposal at Commons Committee stage that the Bill should be amended so as to require courts to make these assumptions in all cases was not adopted. Further, under the 1994 Act an offender convicted of a single "drug trafficking offence" (as defined in s.1(3) of the 1994 Act) becomes subject to the confiscation powers; under the 1988 Act, as amended by the current Act, only offenders convicted of two or more relevant offences on the present occasion, or those who have a previous conviction for a relevant offence, will come within the range of the powers.

Incidental provisions relating to confiscation

Provision of information by prosecutor

3.—(1) For subsection (1) of section 73 of the 1988 Act (effect of provision of statement by prosecutor) there shall be substituted the following subsections—

"(1) Subsection (1A) below applies in a case where a person has been convicted of an offence of a relevant description if—

 (a) the prosecutor has given written notice to the court for the purposes of subsection (1)(a) of section 71 above; or

(b) the court is proceeding in pursuance of subsection (1)(b) of that section and requires a statement under this section from the prosecutor.

(1A) Where this subsection applies, the prosecutor shall, within such period as the court may direct, tender to the court a statement as to any matters relevant—

(a) to determining whether the defendant has benefited from any relevant criminal conduct; or

(b) to an assessment of the value of the defendant's benefit from that conduct;

and, where such a statement is tendered in a case in which a declaration has been made for the purposes of subsection (1)(b) of section 72AA above, that statement shall also set out all such information available to the prosecutor as may be relevant for the purposes of subsections (4) and (5)(b) or (c) of that section.

(1B) Where a statement is tendered to the court under this section—

(a) the prosecutor may at any time tender to the court a further statement as to the matters mentioned in subsection (1A) above; and

(b) the court may at any time require the prosecutor to tender a further such statement within such period as it may direct.

(1C) Where—

(a) any statement has been tendered to any court by the prosecutor under this section, and

(b) the defendant accepts to any extent any allegation in the statement,

the court may, for the purpose of determining whether the defendant has benefited from any relevant criminal conduct or of assessing the value of the defendant's benefit from such conduct, treat his acceptance as conclusive of the matters to which it relates."

(2) In subsection (2)(a) of that section (power of court to require defendant to indicate extent of acceptance of allegations), for "under subsection (1)(a) above" there shall be substituted "by the prosecutor under this section".

(3) In subsection (6) of that section (issue of certificate by court), for the words from "the offence" onwards there shall be substituted "any relevant criminal conduct".

(4) After subsection (6) of that section, there shall be inserted the following subsection—

"(7) Where the court has given a direction under this section, it may at any time vary the direction by giving a further direction."

General Note

This section requires the prosecutor to tender to the court a statement containing information relevant to whether the defendant has benefited from relevant criminal conduct and the value of any such benefit. It substitutes for subs. (1) of s.73 of the 1988 Act, new subsections (1), (1A), (1B) and (1C), and it echoes the 1994 Act, s.11. It may be noted that in *R. v. Crutchley (Deborah) and Tonks (Trevor Reginald)* (1994) 15 Cr.App.R.(S). 627 it was established that where the prosecution tenders such a statement the defendant should be asked specifically whether he admits the allegations contained therein. If he does, that admission is conclusive for the purposes of the Crown Court proceedings and for the purposes of any appeal against the confiscation order.

Provision of information by defendant

4. The following section shall be inserted in the 1988 Act after section 73—

"Provision of information by defendant

73A.—(1) This section applies in a case where a person has been convicted of an offence of a relevant description if—

    (a) the prosecutor has given written notice to the court for the pur-
poses of subsection (1)(a) of section 71 above; or

    (b) the court is proceeding in pursuance of subsection (1)(b) of that
section or is considering whether so to proceed.

    (2) For the purpose of obtaining information to assist it in carrying out
its functions under this Part of this Act, the court may at any time order
the defendant to give it such information as may be specified in the
order.

    (3) An order under subsection (2) above may require all, or any speci-
fied part, of the required information to be given to the court in such
manner, and before such date, as may be specified in the order.

    (4) Rules of court may make provision as to the maximum or mini-
mum period that may be allowed under subsection (3) above.

    (5) If the defendant fails, without reasonable excuse, to comply with
any order under this section, the court may draw such inference from
that failure as it considers appropriate.

    (6) Where the prosecutor accepts to any extent any allegation made
by the defendant—

    (a) in giving to the court information required by an order under this
section, or

    (b) in any other statement tendered to the court for the purposes of
this Part of this Act,

the court may treat that acceptance as conclusive of the matters to which
it relates.

    (7) For the purposes of this section an allegation may be accepted in
such manner as may be prescribed by rules of court or as the court may
direct."

GENERAL NOTE

    This section empowers the court to order the defendant to give it information to assist it in
carrying out its functions under Pt. VI of the 1988 Act. It creates a new s.73A in the 1988 Act, and
it echoes the 1994 Act, s.12. A failure to comply with such an order would be punishable as
a contempt of court. It may be noted that in *R. v. Crutchley (Deborah) and Tonks (Trevor
Reginald)* (1994) 15 Cr.App.R.(S). 627 it was clearly established that the offender's home may
properly form part of his realisable assets.

Review of cases where proceeds of crime not assessed

    5. The following section shall be inserted in the 1988 Act after section 74—

    "Review and revision of certain questions and determinations

Review of cases where proceeds of crime not assessed
    74A.—(1) This section applies in any case where—

    (a) a person has been convicted, in any proceedings before the
Crown Court or a magistrates' court, of an offence of a relevant
description;

    (b) the prosecutor did not give written notice for the purposes of sub-
section (1)(a) of section 71 above; and

    (c) a determination was made for the purposes of subsection (1)(b)
of that section not to proceed under that section or no determination was made for those purposes.

    (2) If the prosecutor has evidence—

    (a) which, at the date of conviction or, if later, when any determi-
nation not to proceed under section 71 above was made, was not
available to the prosecutor (and, accordingly, was not considered
by the court); but

    (b) which the prosecutor believes would have led the court to deter-
mine, if—

(i) the prosecutor had given written notice for the purposes of subsection (1)(a) of that section, and

(ii) the evidence had been considered by the court,

that the defendant had benefited from relevant criminal conduct, the prosecutor may apply to the relevant court for it to consider the evidence.

(3) If, having considered the evidence, the relevant court is satisfied that it is appropriate to do so, it shall proceed under section 71 above as if it were doing so before sentencing or otherwise dealing with the defendant in respect of any relevant criminal conduct, and section 72A above shall apply accordingly.

(4) In considering whether it is appropriate to proceed under section 71 above in accordance with subsection (3) above, the court shall have regard to all the circumstances of the case.

(5) Where, having decided in pursuance of subsection (3) above to proceed under section 71 above, the relevant court determines that the defendant did benefit from relevant criminal conduct—

(a) subsection (1B)(b) of that section shall not apply and subsection (6) of that section shall not apply for determining the amount to be recovered in that case;

(b) that court shall have a power, instead of a duty, to make a confiscation order; and

(c) if the court makes an order in exercise of that power, the sum required to be paid by that order shall be of such amount, not exceeding the amount which (but for paragraph (a) above) would apply by virtue of subsection (6) of that section, as the court thinks fit.

(6) In considering the circumstances of any case either under subsection (4) above or for the purposes of subsection (5)(b) and (c) above, the relevant court shall have regard, in particular, to—

(a) any fine imposed on the defendant in respect of any relevant criminal conduct; and

(b) any order made in connection with any such conduct under section 35 of the Powers of Criminal Courts Act 1973 (compensation orders).

(7) In making any determination under or for the purposes of this section the relevant court may take into account, to the extent that they represent respects in which the defendant has benefited from any relevant criminal conduct, any payments or other rewards which were not received by him until after the time when he was sentenced or otherwise dealt with in the case in question.

(8) Where an application under this section contains such a declaration as is mentioned in paragraph (b) of subsection (1) of section 72AA above, that section shall apply (subject to subsection (9) below) in the case of any determination on the application as if it were a determination in a case in which the requirements of paragraphs (a) and (b) of that subsection had been satisfied.

(9) For the purposes of any determination to which section 72AA above applies by virtue of subsection (8) above, none of the assumptions specified in subsection (4) of that section shall be made in relation to any property unless it is property held by or transferred to the defendant before the time when he was sentenced or otherwise dealt with in the case in question.

(10) No application shall be entertained by the court under this section if it is made after the end of the period of six years beginning with the date of conviction.

(11) Sections 73 and 73A above shall apply where the prosecutor makes an application under this section as they apply in a case where the

prosecutor has given written notice to the court for the purposes of sub-section (1)(a) of section 71 above, but as if the reference in section 73(1A) to a declaration made for the purposes of subsection (1)(b) of section 72AA above were a reference to a declaration for the purposes of subsection (8) above.

(12) In this section—

'the date of conviction' means—

    (a) in a case not falling within paragraph (b) below, the date on which the defendant was convicted of the offence in question, or

    (b) where he was convicted of that offence and one or more other offences in the same proceedings and those con-victions were not all on the same date, the date of the latest of those convictions;

    and

'the relevant court' means—

    (a) where the defendant was convicted in proceedings before the Crown Court, that Court; and

    (b) where he was convicted in proceedings before a magis-trates' court, any magistrates' court for the same area."

GENERAL NOTE

This section, which inserts a new s.74A into the 1988 Act, allows for questions relating to confiscation orders to be reopened in the Crown Court in cases where the court did not proceed against the defendant for the making of a confiscation order, but where further and contrary evidence comes to light within a period of time not exceeding six years from the date of the relevant conviction. This provision echoes s.13 of the 1994 Act.

Revision of assessment of proceeds of crime

6. The following section shall be inserted in the 1988 Act after the section 74A inserted by section 5 above—

"Revision of assessment of proceeds of crime

74B.—(1) This section applies where in any case there has been a determination under subsection (1A) of section 71 above ('the original determination') that the defendant in that case had not benefited from any relevant criminal conduct.

(2) If the prosecutor has evidence—

(a) which was not considered by the court which made the original determination, but

(b) which the prosecutor believes would have led that court (if it had been considered) to determine that the defendant had benefited from relevant criminal conduct,

the prosecutor may apply to the relevant court for it to consider that evidence.

(3) If, having considered the evidence, the relevant court is satisfied that (if that evidence had been available to it) it would have determined that the defendant had benefited from relevant criminal conduct, that court—

(a) shall proceed, as if it were proceeding under section 71 above before sentencing or otherwise dealing with the defendant in respect of any relevant criminal conduct—

    (i) to make a fresh determination of whether the defendant has benefited from any relevant criminal conduct; and

    (ii) then to make such a determination as is mentioned in subsection (1B)(a) of that section;

and

(b) subject to subsection (4) below, shall have a power, after making those determinations, to make an order requiring the payment of such sum as it thinks fit;

and an order under paragraph (b) above shall be deemed for all purposes to be a confiscation order.

(4) The court shall not, in exercise of the power conferred by paragraph (b) of subsection (3) above, make any order for the payment of a sum which is more than the amount determined in pursuance of paragraph (a)(ii) of that subsection.

(5) In making any determination under or for the purposes of subsection (3) above the relevant court may take into account, to the extent that they represent respects in which the defendant has benefited from any relevant criminal conduct, any payments or other rewards which were not received by him until after the making of the original determination.

(6) Where, in a case in which section 72AA above does not otherwise apply, an application under this section contains such a declaration as is mentioned in paragraph (b) of subsection (1) of that section, that section shall apply (subject to subsection (7) below) in the case of any determination on the application as if it were a determination in a case in which the requirements of paragraphs (a) and (b) of that subsection had been satisfied.

(7) For the purposes of any determination under or for the purposes of subsection (3) above to which section 72AA above applies, none of the assumptions specified in subsection (4) of that section shall be made in relation to any property unless it is property held by or transferred to the defendant before the time when he was sentenced or otherwise dealt with in the case in question.

(8) No application shall be entertained by the court under this section if it is made after the end of the period of six years beginning with the date of conviction.

(9) Section 72A above shall apply where the court is acting under this section as it applies where the court is acting under section 71 above.

(10) Sections 73 and 73A above shall apply where the prosecutor makes an application under this section as they apply in a case where the prosecutor has given written notice to the court for the purposes of subsection (1)(a) of section 71 above but—

(a) as if the reference in section 73(1A) to a declaration made for the purposes of subsection (1)(b) of section 72AA above included a reference to a declaration for the purposes of subsection (6) above; and

(b) as if any reference in section 73(6) to the time the confiscation order is made were a reference to the time the order is made on that application.

(11) In this section—

'the date of conviction' has the same meaning as in section 74A above; and

'the relevant court' means—

(a) where the conviction by reference to which the original determination was made was in proceedings before the Crown Court, that Court; and

(b) where that conviction was in proceedings before a magistrates' court, any magistrates' court for the same area.''

GENERAL NOTE

This section, which inserts a new s.74B into the 1988 Act, allows for questions relating to confiscation orders to be reopened in the Crown Court in cases where the court made an original determination that the defendant had not benefited from his offending, but where further and contrary evidence comes to light within a period of time not exceeding six years from the date of the relevant conviction. This provision echoes s.14 of the 1994 Act.

Revision of assessment of amount to be recovered

7. The following section shall be inserted in the 1988 Act after the section 74B inserted by section 6 above—

> ### "Revision of assessment of amount to be recovered
>
> 74C.—(1) This section applies where, in the case of a person convicted of any offence, there has been a determination under this Part of this Act ('the current determination') of any sum required to be paid in his case under any confiscation order.
>
> (2) Where the prosecutor is of the opinion that the value of any benefit to the defendant from any relevant criminal conduct was greater than the value at which that benefit was assessed by the court on the current determination, the prosecutor may apply to the relevant court for the evidence on which the prosecutor has formed his opinion to be considered by the court.
>
> (3) If, having considered the evidence, the relevant court is satisfied that the value of the benefit from any relevant criminal conduct is greater than the value so assessed by the court (whether because its real value was higher at the time of the current determination than was thought or because the value of the benefit in question has subsequently increased), the relevant court—
>
> > (a) subject to subsection (4) below, shall make a fresh determination, as if it were proceeding under section 71 above before sentencing or otherwise dealing with the defendant in respect of any relevant criminal conduct, of the following amounts, that is to say—
> >
> > > (i) the amount by which the defendant has benefited from such conduct; and
> > >
> > > (ii) the amount appearing to be the amount that might be realised at the time of the fresh determination;
> >
> > and
> >
> > (b) subject to subsection (5) below, shall have a power to increase, to such extent as it thinks just in all the circumstances of the case, the amount to be recovered by virtue of that section and to vary accordingly any confiscation order made by reference to the current determination.
>
> (4) Where—
>
> > (a) the court is under a duty to make a fresh determination for the purposes of subsection (3)(a) above in any case, and
> >
> > (b) that case is a case to which section 72AA above applies,
>
> the court shall not have power, in determining any amounts for those purposes, to make any of the assumptions specified in subsection (4) of that section in relation to any property unless it is property held by or transferred to the defendant before the time when he was sentenced or otherwise dealt with in the case in question.
>
> (5) The court shall not, in exercise of the power conferred by paragraph (b) of subsection (3) above, vary any order so as to make it an order requiring the payment of any sum which is more than the lesser of the two amounts determined in pursuance of paragraph (a) of that subsection.
>
> (6) In making any determination under or for the purposes of subsection (3) above the relevant court may take into account, to the extent that they represent respects in which the defendant has benefited from any relevant criminal conduct, any payments or other rewards which

were not received by him until after the making of the original determination.

(7) Where the Crown Court varies a confiscation order under subsection (3) above, it shall substitute for the term of imprisonment or of detention fixed under subsection (2) of section 31 of the Powers of Criminal Courts Act 1973 in respect of the amount to be recovered under the order a longer term determined in accordance with that section (as it has effect by virtue of section 75 below) in respect of any greater amount substituted under subsection (3) above.

(8) Subsection (7) above shall apply only if the effect of the substitution is to increase the maximum period applicable in relation to the order under section 31(3A) of that Act of 1973.

(9) No application shall be entertained by a court under this section if it is made after the end of the period of six years beginning with the date of conviction.

(10) Section 72A above shall apply where the court is acting under this section as it applies where the court is acting under section 71 above.

(11) Sections 73 and 73A above shall apply where the prosecutor makes an application under this section as they apply in a case where the prosecutor has given written notice to the court for the purposes of subsection (1)(a) of section 71 above, but as if any reference in section 73(6) to the time the confiscation order is made were a reference to the time of the determination to be made on that application.

(12) In this section—

'the date of conviction' has the same meaning as in section 74A above; and

'the relevant court' means—

(a) where the court which made the current determination is the Crown Court, that Court; and

(b) where the court which made that determination is a magistrates' court, any magistrates' court for the same area."

<small>GENERAL NOTE</small>

This section, which inserts a new s.74C into the 1988 Act, allows for a revision of an earlier assessment of the amount to be recovered from the defendant under a confiscation order. The matter may be reopened in the Crown Court, where further evidence of the true extent of that benefit comes to light within a period of time not exceeding six years from the date of the relevant conviction. This provision echoes s.15 of the 1994 Act.

Enforcement etc. of confiscation orders

8.—(1) In section 75 of the 1988 Act (application of procedure for enforcing fines), the following subsection shall be inserted after subsection (5)—

"(5A) Where the defendant serves a term of imprisonment or detention in default of paying any amount due under a confiscation order, his serving that term does not prevent the confiscation order from continuing to have effect, so far as any other method of enforcement is concerned."

(2) The following subsections shall be substituted for subsections (1) and (2) of section 76 of that Act (cases in which restraint or charging order may be made)—

"(1) The powers conferred on the High Court by sections 77(1) and 78(1) below are exercisable where—

(a) proceedings have been instituted in England and Wales against any person for an offence to which this Part of this Act applies;

   (b) the proceedings have not been concluded or (if they have) an application that has not been concluded has been made under section 74A, 74B or 74C above in respect of the defendant in those proceedings; and

   (c) the court is satisfied that there is reasonable cause to believe—

       (i) in a case where there is an application under section 74C above, that the court will be satisfied as mentioned in subsection (3) of that section;

      (ii) in any other case, that the proceedings may result or have resulted in, or that the application is made by reference to, a conviction of the defendant for an offence of a relevant description from which he may be, or has been, shown to have benefited.

  (1A) The court shall not exercise those powers by virtue of subsection (1) above if it is satisfied—

   (a) that there has been undue delay in continuing the proceedings or application in question; or

   (b) that the person who appears to the court to be the person who has or will have the conduct of the prosecution or, as the case may be, who made that application does not intend to proceed with it.

  (2) The powers conferred on the High Court by sections 77(1) and 78(1) below are also exercisable where—

   (a) the court is satisfied that a person is to be charged (whether by the laying of an information or otherwise) with an offence to which this Part of this Act applies or that an application of a kind mentioned in subsection (1)(b) above is to be made; and

   (b) the court is satisfied that the making or variation of a confiscation order may result from proceedings for that offence or, as the case may be, from the application."

  (3) In subsection (4) of section 76 of that Act—

  (a) after "otherwise)" there shall be inserted ", or (as the case may be) no application is made,"; and

  (b) at the end there shall be inserted "or if the court is satisfied that the case has become a case in which, in pursuance of subsection (1A) above, it would be unable to exercise the powers conferred by virtue of subsection (1) above."

  (4) In section 77(6) of that Act (discharge of restraint orders), the following paragraph shall be substituted for paragraph (b)—

    "(b) shall be discharged on the conclusion of the proceedings or application in question."

  (5) In section 78 of that Act (charging orders), the following subsection shall be substituted for subsection (7)—

    "(7) In relation to a charging order, the court—

   (a) may at any time make an order discharging or varying it; and

   (b) shall make an order discharging it on the occurrence of whichever of the following first occurs, that is to say—

       (i) the conclusion of the proceedings or application in question; and

      (ii) the payment into court of the amount payment of which is secured by the charge."

  (6) In section 80(1) of that Act (circumstances in which High Court may exercise powers relating to realisation of property), the following paragraphs shall be substituted for paragraphs (a) to (c)—

    "(a) a confiscation order is made in proceedings instituted for an offence to which this Part of this Act applies or an order is made or varied on an application under section 74A, 74B or 74C above;

   (b) the proceedings in question have not, or the application in question has not, been concluded; and

(c) the order or variation is not subject to appeal;".

(7) In section 84(6) of that Act (bankruptcy of defendant), the following paragraphs shall be substituted for paragraphs (a) and (b)—

"(a) no order shall be made under section 339 or 423 of that Act (avoidance of certain transactions) in respect of the making of the gift at any time when—

(i) proceedings for an offence to which this Part of this Act applies have been instituted against him and have not been concluded;

(ii) an application has been made under section 74A, 74B or 74C above in respect of the defendant in any such proceedings and has not been concluded; or

(iii) property of the person to whom the gift was made is subject to a restraint order or charging order; and

(b) any order made under section 339 or 423 of that Act after the conclusion of the proceedings or application shall take into account any realisation under this Part of this Act of property held by the person to whom the gift was made."

(8) In section 102 of that Act (interpretation of Part VI), the following subsections shall be substituted for subsection (12)—

"(12) Proceedings for an offence are concluded—

(a) when the defendant is acquitted on all counts or, as the case may be, every charge against him is dismissed;

(b) if he is convicted on one or more counts or charges but the court decides not to make a confiscation order against him, when the court makes that decision;

(c) if he is sentenced without the court having considered whether or not to proceed under section 71 above in his case, when he is sentenced; and

(d) if a confiscation order is made against him in those proceedings, when the order is satisfied.

(12A) An application under section 74A, 74B or 74C above is concluded—

(a) if the court decides not to make or, as the case may be, not to vary any order against the defendant on that application, when it makes that decision;

(b) if an order against the defendant is made or varied on that application, when the order is satisfied; and

(c) if the application is withdrawn, when the prosecutor notifies the withdrawal of the application to the court to which it was made.

(12B) For the purposes of this Part of this Act, a confiscation order is satisfied when no amount is due under it.

(12C) For the purposes only of section 84 above, a confiscation order shall be treated as satisfied when the defendant in respect of whom it was made has served a term of imprisonment or detention in default of payment of the amount due under the order."

GENERAL NOTE

Subsection (1) amends the earlier law by providing that where a defendant serves a term of imprisonment or detention in default of payment of a confiscation order, the serving of that term shall not expunge the obligation to pay the full sum which is due under the order. This brings the 1988 Act into line with the equivalent provisions under the 1994 Act (see s.9(5) of that Act), but the law stands in contrast with the position in relation to fines, where the serving of a term of imprisonment or detention in default of payment of a fine has the effect of wiping out the fine.

Subsection (1) shall not apply where the offence, or any of the offences, in respect of which the confiscation order was made was committed before the commencement of s.1 of this Act: see s.16(6).

Payment of interest on sums unpaid

9. The following section shall be inserted in the 1988 Act after section 75—

"Interest on sums unpaid under confiscation orders

75A.—(1) If any sum required to be paid by a person under a confiscation order is not paid when it is required to be paid (whether forthwith
on the making of the order or at a time specified under section 31(1) of
the Powers of Criminal Courts Act 1973 or for the purposes of section
75(1) or (2) of the Magistrates' Courts Act 1980)—

    (a) that person shall be liable to pay interest on that sum for the
period for which it remains unpaid, and

    (b) the amount of the interest shall, for the purposes of enforcement,
be treated as part of the amount to be recovered from him under
the confiscation order.

(2) The Crown Court may, on the application of the prosecutor,
increase the term of imprisonment or detention fixed in respect of the
confiscation order under section 31(2) of that Act of 1973 (as it has effect
by virtue of section 75 above) if the effect of subsection (1) above is to
increase the maximum period applicable in relation to the order under
section 31(3A) of that Act of 1973.

(3) The rate of interest under subsection (1) above shall be that for the
time being applying to a civil judgment debt under section 17 of the
Judgments Act 1838."

GENERAL NOTE

Section 9 makes it clear that whenever a sum required to be paid under a confiscation order is
not paid forthwith, or at the date specified by the court, the court may charge interest upon the
outstanding sum. The equivalent provision in the 1994 Act is s.10.

Section 9 shall not apply where the offence, or any of the offences, in respect of which the
confiscation order was made was committed before the commencement of s.1 of this Act: see
s.16(6).

Variation of confiscation order on receiver's application

10.—(1) Section 83 of the 1988 Act (variation of confiscation orders) shall
be amended as follows.

(2) In subsection (1) (variation on application of defendant), for "by the
defendant in respect of a confiscation order, the" there shall be substituted
"made in respect of a confiscation order—

    (a) by the defendant, or

    (b) by a receiver appointed under section 77 or 80 above, or in pursu-
ance of a charging order,

  the".

(3) In subsection (3), for "defendant" there shall be substituted "person
who applied for it".

(4) The following subsection shall be inserted after subsection (5)—

    "(6) Rules of court may make provision—

    (a) for the giving of notice of any application under this section; and

    (b) for any person appearing to the court to be likely to be affected by
any exercise of its powers under this section to be given an opportunity to make representations to the court."

GENERAL NOTE

This section amends the earlier provisions in s.83 of the 1988 Act for the variation of a confiscation order upon application by a receiver. Section 10 brings the law on the 1988 Act into line
with the equivalent provisions under the 1994 Act: see s.17 of that Act.

Order to make material available

11. The following section shall be inserted in the 1988 Act after section 93G—

"Investigations into the proceeds of criminal conduct

Order to make material available
93H.—(1) A constable may, for the purposes of an investigation into whether any person has benefited from any criminal conduct or into the extent or whereabouts of the proceeds of any criminal conduct, apply to a Circuit judge for an order under subsection (2) below in relation to particular material or material of a particular description.

(2) If, on such an application, the judge is satisfied that the conditions in subsection (4) below are fulfilled, he may make an order that the person who appears to him to be in possession of the material to which the application relates shall—
(a) produce it to a constable for him to take away, or
(b) give a constable access to it,
within such period as the order may specify.
This subsection has effect subject to section 93J(11) below.

(3) The period to be specified in an order under subsection (2) above shall be seven days unless it appears to the judge that a longer or shorter period would be appropriate in the particular circumstances of the application.

(4) The conditions referred to in subsection (2) above are—
(a) that there are reasonable grounds for suspecting that a specified person has benefited from any criminal conduct;
(b) that there are reasonable grounds for suspecting that the material to which the application relates—
(i) is likely to be of substantial value (whether by itself or together with other material) to the investigation for the purposes of which the application is made; and
(ii) does not consist of or include items subject to legal privilege or excluded material;
and
(c) that there are reasonable grounds for believing that it is in the public interest, having regard—
(i) to the benefit likely to accrue to the investigation if the material is obtained, and
(ii) to the circumstances under which the person in possession of the material holds it,
that the material should be produced or that access to it should be given.

(5) Where the judge makes an order under subsection (2)(b) above in relation to material on any premises he may, on the application of a constable, order any person who appears to him to be entitled to grant entry to the premises to allow a constable to enter the premises to obtain access to the material.

(6) An application under subsection (1) or (5) above may be made ex parte to a judge in chambers.

(7) Provision may be made by Crown Court Rules as to—
(a) the discharge and variation of orders under this section; and
(b) proceedings relating to such orders.

(8) An order of a Circuit judge under this section shall have effect as if it were an order of the Crown Court.

(9) Where the material to which an application under subsection (1) above relates consists of information contained in a computer—

(a) an order under subsection (2)(a) above shall have effect as an order to produce the material in a form in which it can be taken away and in which it is visible and legible; and

(b) an order under subsection (2)(b) above shall have effect as an order to give access to the material in a form in which it is visible and legible.

(10) An order under subsection (2) above—

(a) shall not confer any right to production of, or access to, items subject to legal privilege or excluded material;

(b) shall have effect notwithstanding any obligation as to secrecy or other restriction upon the disclosure of information imposed by statute or otherwise; and

(c) may be made in relation to material in the possession of an authorised government department;

and in this subsection 'authorised government department' means a government department which is an authorised department for the purposes of the Crown Proceedings Act 1947.

(11) For the purposes of sections 21 and 22 of the Police and Criminal Evidence Act 1984 (access to, and copying and retention of, seized material) material produced in pursuance of an order under subsection (2)(a) above shall be treated as if it were material seized by a constable.

(12) In this section—

(a) 'excluded material', 'items subject to legal privilege' and 'premises' have the same meanings as in the Police and Criminal Evidence Act 1984; and

(b) references to a person benefiting from any criminal conduct, in relation to conduct which is not an offence to which this Part of this Act applies but would be if it had occurred in England and Wales, shall be construed in accordance with section 71(4) and (5) above as if it had so occurred."

GENERAL NOTE

This section inserts a new s.93H into the 1988 Act. Its purpose, according to the government, is to permit the police and customs and excise officials to make an application to a Circuit judge for an order to permit the obtaining of any relevant materials (including information from bank accounts) relevant for use in making an assessment for a confiscation order. The equivalent provision in the 1994 Act is s.27.

Authority for search

12. The following section shall be inserted in the 1988 Act after the section 93H inserted by section 11 above—

"Authority for search

93I.—(1) A constable may, for the purposes of an investigation into whether any person has benefited from any criminal conduct or into the extent or whereabouts of the proceeds of any criminal conduct apply to a Circuit judge for a warrant under this section in relation to specified premises.

(2) On such application the judge may issue a warrant authorising a constable to enter and search the premises if the judge is satisfied—

(a) that an order made under section 93H above in relation to material on the premises has not been complied with;

(b) that the conditions in subsection (3) below are fulfilled; or
(c) that the conditions in subsection (4) below are fulfilled.
(3) The conditions referred to in subsection (2)(b) above are—
(a) that there are reasonable grounds for suspecting that a specified person has benefited from criminal conduct;
(b) that the conditions in subsection (4)(b) and (c) of section 93H above are fulfilled in relation to any material on the premises; and
(c) that it would not be appropriate to make an order under that section in relation to the material because—
    (i) it is not practicable to communicate with any person entitled to produce the material;
    (ii) it is not practicable to communicate with any person entitled to grant access to the material or entitled to grant entry to the premises on which the material is situated; or
    (iii) the investigation for the purposes of which the application is made might be seriously prejudiced unless a constable could secure immediate access to the material.
(4) The conditions referred to in subsection (2)(c) above are—
(a) that there are reasonable grounds for suspecting that a specified person has benefited from any criminal conduct;
(b) that there are reasonable grounds for suspecting that there is on the premises any such material relating—
    (i) to the specified person, or
    (ii) to the question whether that person has benefited from any criminal conduct or to any question as to the extent or whereabouts of the proceeds of any criminal conduct,
as is likely to be of substantial value (whether by itself or together with other material) to the investigation for the purposes of which the application is made, but that the material cannot at the time of the application be particularised; and
(c) that—
    (i) it is not practicable to communicate with any person entitled to grant entry to the premises;
    (ii) entry to the premises will not be granted unless a warrant is produced; or
    (iii) the investigation for the purposes of which the application is made might be seriously prejudiced unless a constable arriving at the premises could secure immediate entry to them.
(5) Where a constable has entered premises in the execution of a warrant issued under this section, he may seize and retain any material, other than items subject to legal privilege and excluded material, which is likely to be of substantial value (whether by itself or together with other material) to the investigation for the purposes of which the warrant was issued.
(6) Subsection (12) of section 93H above shall apply for the purposes of this section as it applies for the purposes of that section."

GENERAL NOTE
    This section inserts a new s.93I into the 1988 Act, and it allows for the issuing of a search warrant on application by the relevant investigating authority to a Circuit judge in pursuance of the powers under s.93H (see s.11 of the 1995 Act, above). The equivalent provision in the 1994 Act is s.28.

Disclosure of information held by government departments

    13. The following section shall be inserted in the 1988 Act after the section 93I inserted by section 12 above—

"Disclosure of information held by government departments
93J.—(1) Subject to subsection (4) below, the High Court may, on an application by the person appearing to the court to have the conduct of any prosecution, order any material mentioned in subsection (3) below which is in the possession of an authorised government department to be produced to the court within such period as the court may specify.

(2) The power to make an order under subsection (1) above is exercisable if—

(a) the powers conferred on the court by sections 77(1) and 78(1) above are exercisable by virtue of subsection (1) of section 76 above; or

(b) those powers are exercisable by virtue of subsection (2) of that section and the court has made a restraint order or a charging order which (in either case) has not been discharged;

but where the power to make an order under subsection (1) above is exercisable by virtue only of paragraph (b) above, subsection (3) of section 76 above shall apply for the purposes of this section as it applies for the purposes of sections 77 and 78 above.

(3) The material referred to in subsection (1) above is any material which—

(a) has been submitted to an officer of an authorised government department by the defendant or by a person who has at any time held property which was realisable property;

(b) has been made by an officer of an authorised government department in relation to the defendant or such a person; or

(c) is correspondence which passed between an officer of an authorised government department and the defendant or such a person;

and an order under that subsection may require the production of all such material or of a particular description of such material, being material in the possession of the department concerned.

(4) An order under subsection (1) above shall not require the production of any material unless it appears to the High Court that the material is likely to contain information that would facilitate the exercise of the powers conferred either—

(a) on the court by sections 77 to 80 above; or

(b) on a receiver appointed under section 77 or 80 above or in pursuance of a charging order.

(5) The court may by order authorise the disclosure to such a receiver of any material produced under subsection (1) above or any part of such material; but the court shall not make an order under this subsection unless a reasonable opportunity has been given for an officer of the department to make representations to the court.

(6) Material disclosed in pursuance of an order under subsection (5) above may, subject to any conditions contained in the order, be further disclosed for the purposes of the functions by virtue of any provision of this Part of this Act of the receiver, of the Crown Court or of any magistrates' court.

(7) The court may by order authorise the disclosure to a person mentioned in subsection (8) below of any material produced under subsection (1) above or any part of such material; but the court shall not make an order under this subsection unless—

(a) a reasonable opportunity has been given for an officer of the department to make representations to the court; and

(b) it appears to the court that the material is likely to be of substantial value in exercising functions relating to the investigation of crime.

(8) The persons referred to in subsection (7) above are—

(a) any member of a police force;

(b) any member of the Crown Prosecution Service; and

(c) any officer within the meaning of the Customs and Excise Management Act 1979.

(9) Material disclosed in pursuance of an order under subsection (7) above may, subject to any conditions contained in the order, be further disclosed for the purposes of functions relating to the investigation of crime, of whether any person has benefited from any criminal conduct or of the extent or whereabouts of the proceeds of any such conduct.

(10) Material may be produced or disclosed in pursuance of this section notwithstanding any obligation as to secrecy or other restriction upon the disclosure of information imposed by statute or otherwise.

(11) An order under subsection (1) above and, in the case of material in the possession of an authorised government department, an order under section 93H above may require any officer of the department (whether named in the order or not) who may for the time being be in possession of the material concerned to comply with it; and an order containing any requirement by virtue of this subsection shall be served as if the proceedings were civil proceedings against the department.

(12) Where any requirement is included in any order by virtue of subsection (11) above, the person on whom the order is served—

(a) shall take all reasonable steps to bring it to the attention of the officer concerned; and

(b) if the order is not brought to that officer's attention within the period referred to in subsection (1) above, shall report the reasons for the failure to the court;

and it shall also be the duty of any other officer of the department in receipt of the order to take such steps as are mentioned in paragraph (a) above.

(13) In this section 'authorised government department' means a government department which is an authorised department for the purposes of the Crown Proceedings Act 1947; and subsection (12)(b) of section 93H above shall apply for the purposes of this section as it applies for the purposes of that section."

GENERAL NOTE

This section inserts a new s.93J into the 1988 Act, and it allows for the making of an order by a High Court judge, on application by the prosecutor, requiring production of any document currently in the possession of a government department, where the document appears to the High Court judge to be relevant to the exercise of powers under the 1988 Act pursuant to the making of a confiscation order. The equivalent provision in the 1994 Act is s.29.

Enforcement of overseas forfeiture and restraint orders

Enforcement in UK of overseas forfeiture and restraint orders

14.—(1) In each of the following paragraphs of Schedule 4 to the Prevention of Terrorism (Temporary Provisions) Act 1989 (enforcement or overseas orders providing for the forfeiture or restraint of terrorist funds), namely—

(a) paragraph 10 (which relates to enforcement in England and Wales),

(b) paragraph 20 (which relates to enforcement in Scotland), and

(c) paragraph 30 (which relates to enforcement in Northern Ireland),

there shall be inserted, after sub-paragraph (2), the sub-paragraph set out in subsection (2) below.

(2) That sub-paragraph is—

"(2A) Without prejudice to the generality of sub-paragraph (1) above, the provision that may be made by virtue of that sub-paragraph includes provision which, for the purpose of facilitating the enforcement of any external order that may be made, has effect at times before there is an external order to be enforced."

(3) Section 9 of the Criminal Justice (International Co-operation) Act 1990 (enforcement of overseas forfeiture orders) shall have effect, and be deemed always to have had effect, with the insertion, after subsection (1), of the following subsection—

"(1A) Without prejudice to the generality of subsection (1) above the provision that may be made by virtue of that subsection includes provision which, for the purpose of facilitating the enforcement of any order that may be made, has effect at times before there is an order to be enforced."

GENERAL NOTE

Section 14 was added to the Proceeds of Crime Bill during the Commons stage. It is designed to remedy a possible defect in the Prevention of Terrorism (Temporary Provisions) Act 1989 and the Criminal Justice (International Co-operation) Act 1990. By amendment to both those statutes, s.14 makes it clear that a restraint order may be obtained from the High Court in advance of the enforcement of any equivalent order overseas.

Section 14 came into force on the passing of the Act (s.16(4)) and s.14 is the only part of the Act which is applicable to Scotland and to Northern Ireland, as well as to England and Wales (s.16(7)).

Supplemental

Consequential and transitional amendments and repeals

15.—(1) The 1988 Act shall have effect with the further amendments specified in Schedule 1 to this Act, being amendments consequential on the provisions of this Act.

(2) For the purposes of sections 21 and 22 of the Police and Criminal Evidence Act 1984 (access to, and copying and retention of, seized material) an investigation into whether any person has benefited from any criminal conduct or into the extent or whereabouts of the proceeds of any criminal conduct shall be treated (so far as that would not otherwise be the case) as if it were an investigation of, or in connection with, an offence.

(3) Expressions used in subsection (2) above and in Part VI of the 1988 Act have the same meanings in that subsection as in that Part.

(4) The enactments mentioned in Schedule 2 to this Act are hereby repealed to the extent specified in the third column of that Schedule.

Short title, interpretation, commencement and extent

16.—(1) This Act may be cited as the Proceeds of Crime Act 1995.

(2) In this Act "the 1988 Act" means the Criminal Justice Act 1988.

(3) Subject to subsections (4) to (6) below, this Act shall come into force on such day as the Secretary of State may by order made by statutory instrument appoint, and different days may be appointed under this subsection for different purposes.

(4) Section 14 above and this section come into force on the passing of this Act.

(5) Section 1 above shall not apply in the case of any proceedings against any person where that person is convicted in those proceedings of an offence which was committed before the commencement of that section.

(6) Sections 8(1) and 9 above shall not apply where the offence, or any of the offences, in respect of which the confiscation order was made was committed before the commencement of section 1 above.

(7) This Act, except for section 14 above and this section, does not extend to Scotland or Northern Ireland.

SCHEDULES

Section 15　　　　　　　SCHEDULE 1

CONSEQUENTIAL AMENDMENTS OF THE 1988 ACT

1. In section 72 of the 1988 Act (making of confiscation orders) subsections (1) to (4) shall cease to have effect.

2.—(1) Section 72A of that Act (postponed determinations of benefit and amount to be recovered) shall be amended as follows.

(2) In subsection (1)—

(a) in paragraph (a), for "as mentioned in section 71(2)(b)(i) above" there shall be substituted "from any relevant criminal conduct", and at the end there shall be inserted "or";

(b) paragraph (b) shall be omitted; and

(c) in paragraph (c), the words "by virtue of section 72 above" shall be omitted.

(3) For subsection (8) there shall be substituted the following subsection—

　"(8) Where the court has so proceeded—

　　(a) subsection (1) of section 71 above shall have effect as if the words from 'before sentencing' onwards were omitted;

　　(b) that section shall further have effect as if references to an offence that will be taken into consideration in determining any sentence included references to an offence that has been so taken into account; and

　　(c) section 72(5) above shall have effect as if after 'determining' there were inserted 'in relation to any offence in respect of which he has not been sentenced or otherwise dealt with'."

(4) In subsection (11)(b), for the words from "may be taken together" to "section 71 above" there shall be substituted "are comprised in relevant criminal conduct".

3. In the table in section 102(2) of that Act (table of defined expressions) the following entries shall be inserted in the appropriate places in the alphabetical order, that is to say—

Expression	Relevant provision
Offence of a relevant description	Section 71(1E)
Relevant criminal conduct	Section 71(1D)

Section 15　　　　　　　SCHEDULE 2

REPEALS

Chapter	Short Title	Extent of repeal
1988 c. 33.	The Criminal Justice Act 1988.	In section 71— (a) subsection (7); (b) in subsection (7A), paragraph (b) and, in paragraph (c), the words "by virtue of section 72 below"; and (c) subsection (8). In section 72, subsections (1) to (4). In section 72A(1), paragraph (b) and, in paragraph (c), the words "by virtue of section 72 above". In section 73, subsection (4).

INDEX

References are to sections and Schedules

CARERS (RECOGNITION AND SERVICES) ACT 1995*

(1995 c. 12)

An Act to provide for the assessment of the ability of carers to provide care; and for connected purposes. [28th June 1995]

PARLIAMENTARY DEBATES

Hansard, H.C. Vol. 255, col. 1369, Vol. 257, col. 1280, Vol. 258, col. 422. H.L. Vol. 564, cols. 628, 1467, 1895.

INTRODUCTION AND GENERAL NOTE

This Act has been welcomed by the Association of Directors of Social Services and the Carers National Association as "a major step forward in recognising both the invaluable and irreplaceable rôle of carers as well as establishing their rights to assessment". Originating as a Private Member's Bill sponsored by Mr Malcolm Wicks MP, it received Government support at Second Reading. Although it was heavily amended at Committee stage the basic philosophy behind the measure remained unchanged. This was described by Mr Wicks in the following terms: "it is crucial to ensure that local authorities take proper account of carers' circumstances when carrying out an assessment of the need for community care services of the person being cared for" (*Hansard*, H.C. Vol. 258, col. 430).

The White Paper *Caring for People* (Cm. 849) published in 1989, contained six key objectives on community care reform, one of which related to carers. It was "to ensure that service providers make practical support for carers a high priority" (para. 1.11). This objective was not given effect in the National Health Service and Community Care Act 1990 (c. 19), although Government guidance which was issued to local authorities stated that:

"carers who feel they need community care services in their own right can ask for a separate assessment. This can arise if the care plan of the person for whom they care does not, in their view, adequately address the carer's own needs".

It appears from evidence cited by Mr Wicks that many local authorities have not followed this guidance. Particular reference was made to a report sponsored by the Carers National Association, *Community Care: Just a Fairy Tale*, May 1994, which found that "only 13 per cent of carers received a separate assessment and nearly 80 per cent felt that community care reforms had made no difference to their lives" (*Hansard*, H.C. Vol. 258, col. 426).

The statistics behind the Act were graphically described by Mr Wicks as follows:

"we are dealing with a formidable number of people. According to the general household survey data, which are now somewhat out of date and therefore probably understate the numbers, there are some 6.8 million carers throughout Great Britain. At one end of the continuum, they may care for a few hours a week. At the other extreme, I have met people who care literally around the clock for a loved one – for someone with dementia or someone with a major physical handicap. I am particularly struck by the fact that an estimated 1.5 million carers provide care for 20 hours a week or more. It is often considerably more ... That caring army of 1.5 million people is a larger labour force of the national health service and social services combined" (*ibid.*).

The Institute of Actuaries has put the annual value of this unpaid care at £33.9 billion (*per* Lord Carter, *Hansard*, H.L. Vol. 564, col. 649).

Northern Ireland

Although this Act does not extend to Northern Ireland, the Under-Secretary at the Northern Ireland Office with responsibility for health and social services wrote to Mr Wicks on April 17, 1995, following a meeting that had been held with officials from the Carers National Association. In his letter the Under-Secretary said:

"I promised them that I would write to you confirming the Government's commitment to ensuring that Northern Ireland will keep in step with the rest of the United Kingdom on the assessment of the need of carers ... I can assure you that without resort to further legislation

---

* Annotations by Richard Jones, M.A., Solicitor.

should, hopefully, your Bill complete its Parliamentary stages the [Health and Social Services] Boards can be directed, and will be, to carry out assessments of carers' needs ... I can also assure you that in this context carers will include parents of disabled children" (*Hansard*, H.C. Vol. 258, col. 471).

Assessment of ability of carers to provide care: England and Wales

1.—(1) Subject to subsection (3) below, in any case where—

(a) a local authority carry out an assessment under section 47(1)(a) of the National Health Service and Community Care Act 1990 of the needs of a person ("the relevant person") for community care services, and

(b) an individual ("the carer") provides or intends to provide a substantial amount of care on a regular basis for the relevant person,

the carer may request the local authority, before they make their decision as to whether the needs of the relevant person call for the provision of any services, to carry out an assessment of his ability to provide and to continue to provide care for the relevant person; and if he makes such a request, the local authority shall carry out such an assessment and shall take into account the results of that assessment in making that decision.

(2) Subject to subsection (3) below, in any case where—

(a) a local authority assess the needs of a disabled child for the purposes of Part III of the Children Act 1989 or section 2 of the Chronically Sick and Disabled Persons Act 1970, and

(b) an individual ("the carer") provides or intends to provide a substantial amount of care on a regular basis for the disabled child,

the carer may request the local authority, before they make their decision as to whether the needs of the disabled child call for the provision of any services, to carry out an assessment of his ability to provide and to continue to provide care for the disabled child; and if he makes such a request, the local authority shall carry out such an assessment and shall take into account the results of that assessment in making that decision.

(3) No request may be made under subsection (1) or (2) above by an individual who provides or will provide the care in question—

(a) by virtue of a contract of employment or other contract with any person; or

(b) as a volunteer for a voluntary organisation.

(4) The Secretary of State may give directions as to the manner in which an assessment under subsection (1) or (2) above is to be carried out or the form it is to take but, subject to any such directions, it shall be carried out in such manner and take such form as the local authority consider appropriate.

(5) Section 8 of the Disabled Persons (Services, Consultation and Representation) Act 1986 (duty of local authority to take into account ability of carers) shall not apply in any case where—

(a) an assessment is made under subsection (1) above in respect of an individual who provides the care in question for a disabled person; or

(b) an assessment is made under subsection (2) above.

(6) In this section—

"community care services" has the meaning given by section 46(3) of the National Health Service and Community Care Act 1990;

"child" means a person under the age of eighteen:

"disabled child" means a child who is disabled within the meaning of Part III of the Children Act 1989;

"disabled person" means a person to whom section 29 of the National Assistance Act 1948 applies;

"local authority" has the meaning given by section 46(3) of the National Health Service and Community Care Act 1990; and

"voluntary organisation" has the same meaning as in the National Assistance Act 1948.

(7) In Schedule 1 to the Local Authority Social Services Act 1970 (enactments conferring functions assigned to social services committees) at the end there shall be inserted—

> "Carers (Recognition and Services)
>   Act 1995 (c.12)

Section 1	Assessment of ability of carers to provide care.".

DEFINITIONS
   "child": subs. (6).
   "community care services": subs. (6).
   "disabled child": subs. (6).
   "local authority": subs. (6).
   "voluntary organisation": subs. (6).

GENERAL NOTE
   This section, which applies to England and Wales, gives a person (the carer) who provides or intends to provide a substantial amount of care on a regular and unpaid (subs. (3)) basis to a person (the client) who is the subject of a community care assessment by a local authority, a right to request the local authority to assess his ability to provide and continue to provide such care. If such a request is made the authority must carry out the assessment and take into account the results of the assesssment when making a decision as to whether the needs of the client call for the provision of any community care services.

Subs. (1)
Assessment. This would include any reassessment of a client's needs.

The carers. All categories of carers are included: young and old, and the carers of children and adults. Malcolm Wicks MP made the following comments about child carers: "None of us knows how many children play the role of carers. Estimates vary; early estimates suggested 10,000 to 20,000, while recent research suggests up to 40,000. We need better research in that area to establish the facts, not least so that local authorities can plan properly ... We have to grapple with the complexity of relating the needs of the child-carer both to community care objectives and, perhaps more important, to objectives of enhancing children's welfare" (*Hansard*, H.C. Vol. 258, cols. 428, 429).
   A letter from the Chief Inspector of the Social Services Inspectorate to Directors of Social Services dated April 28, 1995, under the reference C1 (95) 12, outlines the relevant legislation relating to young carers and sets out guiding principles for the development of practice. Parent carers and other carers of children are dealt with in subs. (2).

Intends to provide. "It is particularly important that we assure those about to assume a caring rôle, for example, when someone is being discharged from hospital, that they are covered by [this section]", *per* Malcolm Wicks, MP, *Hansard*, H.C. Vol. 258, col. 430.

Substantial amount of care on a regular basis. A significant and sustained contact between the carer and the client would be required. A person who calls in to "keep an eye" on the client would not qualify under this provision.

May request. Child carers in particular should be encouraged to make requests. "Some carers who look after those they love will not want anything as formal as an assessment. The Bill makes that an option and local authorities should continue to follow our guidance and take due account of the informal care that is provided to a person who is receiving community care services, irrespective of whether the carer asks for a formal assessment", *per* the Parliamentary Under-Secretary of State for Health, *Hansard*, H.C. Vol. 258, col. 466.

Before they make their decision. "We do not want the carers' needs to be considered only in the last resort. The local authorities must be able to respond to the needs of carers and those who receive community care service in advance of any difficulties", *per* Lord Carter, *Hansard*, H.L. Vol. 564, col. 631.

Assessment. This Act "does not seek to separate the needs of the carer and the person being cared for. Assessment must look at the circumstances of the whole family or the whole situation in which a person will be cared for. The services provided must reflect that holistic approach and avoid the possibility of two assessment procedures running in parallel", *per* Lord Carter, *ibid.*, col. 630.

Ability to provide. The assessment should not assume a carer's willingness to continue to provide care.

Take into account the results of that assessment. Services for the client and the carer should complement each other, with the client being the centre of concern. Malcolm Wicks MP gave the following illustration of how services under this Act might be provided: "it would enable the social services department to say, 'Although the elderly person did not mention respite care, the carer is crying out for it, and among the services that we will provide, albeit to the cared-for person, respite care will be there regularly'" (*Hansard*, H.C. Vol. 258, col. 432).

Subs. (2)

As local authority functions in respect of children with disabilities are covered by the Children Act 1989 (c. 41) this subsection gives parents or other carers of disabled children the right to an assessment when the child is being assessed under that Act or under s.2 of the Chronically Sick and Disabled Persons Act 1970 (c. 44).

The carer. Subsection (3) excludes paid and volunteer carers from this section.

Person. This includes a corporation (see the Interpretation Act 1978 (c. 30), s.5, Sched.1).

Assessment of ability of carers to provide care: Scotland

2.—(1) Section 12A of the Social Work (Scotland) Act 1968 (duty of local authority to assess needs for certain services) shall be amended as follows.

(2) After subsection (3) there shall be inserted—

"(3A) Subject to subsection (3B) below, in any case where—

    (a) a local authority make an assessment of the needs of any person ('the relevant person') under subsection (1)(a) above, and

    (b) a person ('the carer') provides or intends to provide a substantial amount of care on a regular basis for the relevant person,

the carer may request the local authority, before they make their decision under subsection (1)(b) above, to make an assessment of his ability to provide and to continue to provide care for the relevant person; and if he makes such a request, the local authority shall make such an assessment and shall have regard to the results of that assessment in making that decision.

(3B) No request may be made under subsection (3A) above by a person who provides or will provide the care in question—

    (a) by virtue of a contract of employment or other contract; or

    (b) as a volunteer for a voluntary organisation.

(3C) Section 8 of the Disabled Persons (Services, Consultation and Representation) Act 1986 (duty of local authority to take into account ability of carers) shall not apply in any case where an assessment is made under subsection (3A) above in respect of a person who provides the care in question for a disabled person.".

(3) In subsection (8), after the definition of "medical practitioner" there shall be inserted—

" 'person' means a natural person.".

Definitions

"person": subs. (3).

General Note

This section deals with the Act's application to Scotland. Although the section mirrors s.1 in relation to those caring for adults (and reference should be made to the General Note to that section), it was not possible to give people who are caring for children in Scotland a right of assessment because the Children Act 1989 is not applicable there. The Government's intention for Scotland "is to achieve maximum consistency with the reforms south of the border" (*per* the Under-Secretary of State for Scotland, *Hansard*, H.C. Vol. 258, col. 443). With this intention in mind the Minister of State at the Scottish Office wrote to Malcolm Wicks MP on April 11, 1995, to confirm that the Government would table amendments to the Children (Scotland) Bill to "provide for the same intention as that reflected for England and Wales in [s.1(2)]" (*ibid.*, col. 434).

Isles of Scilly

3.—(1) The Secretary of State may by order provide that section 1 shall apply, with such modifications (if any) as may be specified in the order, as if the Council of the Isles of Scilly were a local authority within the meaning of that section.

(2) The power of the Secretary of State to make an order under this section shall be exercisable by statutory instrument; and a statutory instrument containing such an order shall be subject to annulment in pursuance of a resolution of either House of Parliament.

Financial provision

4. There shall be paid out of money provided by Parliament any increase attributable to this Act in the sums payable out of money so provided under any other enactment.

Short title, commencement and extent

5.—(1) This Act may be cited as the Carers (Recognition and Services) Act 1995.

(2) This Act shall come into force on 1st April 1996.

(3) Sections 1 and 3 do not extend to Scotland.

(4) Section 2 does not extend to England and Wales.

(5) This Act does not extend to Northern Ireland.

INDEX

References are to sections

ROAD TRAFFIC (NEW DRIVERS) ACT 1995*

(1995 c. 13)

An Act to make provision about newly qualified drivers who commit certain offences, including provision with respect to tests of competence to drive. [28th June 1995]

PARLIAMENTARY DEBATES
Hansard, H.C. Vol. 253, col. 1340, Vol. 258, col. 1131. H.L. Vol. 564, cols. 763, 1441, Vol. 565, col. 16.

INTRODUCTION AND GENERAL NOTE

This Act provides for the retesting of those drivers who commit offences during the first two years of driving after passing a driving test. Although the age of new drivers varies, the vast majority of them are young. Statistics show that young drivers account for 10 per cent of the drivers on the road, that they are involved in 20 per cent of road accidents and 25 per cent of road fatalities. By retesting those newly qualified drivers who commit offences and fall within the ambit of the Act it is hoped that these figures will improve (*Hansard*, H.L. Vol. 564, cols. 763–765).

The basic structure of the Act is as follows.

From the implementation of this Act a driver passing a driving test in any class of vehicle becomes a "qualified driver". From that date a two-year probationary period starts. If during the probationary period the driver is convicted of an offence involving obligatory endorsement, and the penalty points to be endorsed on the driver's licence number six or more, then the licence has to be surrendered. The court or the fixed penalty clerk must send to the Secretary of State the licence and a notice setting out the details of the matters to be endorsed on the licence.

The Act applies to all holders of British licences. It will not matter whether the test was taken here, or in a country where reciprocal arrangements apply. Where the date of passing a driving test outside this country is known then this will be recorded on the licence and will define the start of the probationary period.

Once the licence is received by the Secretary of State, he must issue a notice revoking the licence. The driver can then no longer drive as a full licence holder. The driver is allowed to apply

---

* Annotations by Mark Lucraft, Barrister.

for a provisional licence and to drive under the conditions applying to a learner driver. Before the driver can hold a full driving licence again he must pass a driving test. Where a person appeals against a conviction that causes his licence to be revoked then, providing that the Secretary of State is notified of the appeal, he must issue a licence to allow the driver to continue to drive whilst his appeal is pending.

In situations where a person holds a test certificate but has not yet applied for a full driving licence (the current law provides for a two-year period in which the pass certificate can be exchanged), he cannot avoid the provisions of the Act by not claiming his licence. Where a driver is the subject of an order under s.36 of the Road Traffic Offenders Act 1988 (c.53) (an order that he be disqualified until passing a driving test) within the two-year probationary period then the probationary period comes to an end. Additionally where a person has his licence revoked under this Act and is granted a full licence after passing a retest, then he is no longer subject to the provisions of this Act. The effect of this is to prevent a driver being caught in a vicious circle of retesting. The normal rules will apply to the penalty points endorsed on the licence which lead to the order revoking the licence, so there will be the risk of a "totting-up" disqualification where 12 or more penalty points are endorsed on the driver's licence within a three-year period.

COMMENCEMENT

The Act comes into force on such day as the Secretary of State may by order made by statutory instrument appoint and different days may be so appointed for different provisions. The indications are that commencement of the provisions of this Act will be flexible so as to allow for the scheme to be well publicised and for the courts and police to have time to make necessary arrangements (*Hansard*, H.L. Vol. 564, col. 767). Section 10 also makes it clear that the provisions will not apply to anyone who becomes a qualified driver before the Act comes into force.

ABBREVIATIONS
  RTA 1988:   Road Traffic Act 1988.
  RTOA 1988:   Road Traffic Offenders Act 1988.

Introductory

Probationary period for newly qualified drivers

1.—(1) For the purposes of this Act, a person's probationary period is, subject to section 7, the period of two years beginning with the day on which he becomes a qualified driver.

(2) For the purposes of this Act, a person becomes a qualified driver on the first occasion on which he passes—

  (a) any test of competence to drive mentioned in paragraph (a) or (c) of section 89(1) of the Road Traffic Act 1988;

  (b) any test of competence to drive conducted under the law of another EEA State or Gibraltar.

(3) In subsection (2) "EEA State" means a State which is a contracting party to the EEA Agreement but until the EEA Agreement comes into force in relation to Liechtenstein does not include the State of Liechtenstein.

(4) In subsection (3) "EEA Agreement" means the Agreement on the European Economic Area signed at Oporto on 2nd May 1992 as adjusted by the Protocol signed at Brussels on 17th March 1993.

DEFINITIONS
  "EEA Agreement": s.1.
  "EEA State": s.1.
  "probationary period": s.1.
  "qualified driver": s.1.
  "test of competence to drive": s.1 and RTA 1988, s.108.

GENERAL NOTE
   This section defines the probationary period for new drivers. A two-year period begins with the passing of a driving test. It is important to note that this period will only occur for each driver once: there will not be a new probationary period if an order for retesting is made.

Subss. (2), (3) and (4)
   The test passed can be a test passed in Great Britain under the provisions of the RTA 1988, Gibraltar or those States which are signatories to the European Economic Area which was signed on May 2, 1992 and amended by the Protocol signed on March 17, 1993.

Revocation of licences and re-testing

Surrender of licences

   2.—(1) Subsection (2) applies where—
   (a) a person is the holder of a licence;
   (b) he is convicted of an offence involving obligatory endorsement;
   (c) the penalty points to be taken into account under section 29 of the Road Traffic Offenders Act 1988 on that occasion number six or more;
   (d) the court makes an order falling within section 44(1)(b) of that Act in respect of the offence;
   (e) the person's licence shows the date on which he became a qualified driver, or that date has been shown by other evidence in the proceedings; and
   (f) it appears to the court, in the light of the order and the date so shown, that the offence was committed during the person's probationary period.
   (2) Where this subsection applies, the court must send to the Secretary of State—
   (a) a notice containing the particulars required to be endorsed on the counterpart of the person's licence in accordance with the order referred to in subsection (1)(d); and
   (b) on their production to the court, the person's licence and its counterpart.
   (3) Subsection (4) applies where—
   (a) a person's licence and its counterpart have been sent to the fixed penalty clerk under section 54(7) of the Road Traffic Offenders Act 1988 or delivered to the fixed penalty clerk in response to a conditional offer issued under section 75 of that Act;
   (b) the offence to which the fixed penalty notice or the conditional offer relates is one involving obligatory endorsement;
   (c) the fixed penalty clerk endorses the number of penalty points to be attributed to the offence on the counterpart of the licence;
   (d) the penalty points to be taken into account by the fixed penalty clerk in respect of the offence number six or more;
   (e) the licence shows the date on which the person became a qualified driver; and
   (f) it appears to the fixed penalty clerk, in the light of the particulars of the offence endorsed on the counterpart of the licence and the date so shown, that the offence was committed during the person's probationary period.
   (4) Where this subsection applies, the fixed penalty clerk—
   (a) may not return the licence and its counterpart under section 57(3) or (4) or 77(1) of the Road Traffic Offenders Act 1988; but
   (b) must send them to the Secretary of State.
   (5) For the purposes of subsection (3)(d) the penalty points to be taken into account by the fixed penalty clerk in respect of the offence are the penalty points which would have been taken into account under section 29 of the Road Traffic Offenders Act 1988 if—

(a) the person in question had been convicted of the offence; and
(b) the number of penalty points to be attributed to the offence on that occasion had been determined in accordance with section 28(3) of that Act.

DEFINITIONS
   "licence": RTA 1988, s.108.
   "notice": s.9(3).

GENERAL NOTE
   This section outlines the circumstances in which a licence for a driver who commits an offence during the probationary period will have to be sent to the Secretary of State.

Subss. (1) and (2)
   These two subsections deal with a conviction by a court. Where a driver is convicted of a driving offence during the probationary period which involves obligatory endorsement and carries six or more penalty points, the court must send a notice setting out the particulars of the present offence which are required to be endorsed on the driver's licence and the driver's licence and counterpart if it is produced to the court. It is important to note that s.27 of the RTOA 1988 requires that the licence is produced to the court for endorsement at the time of conviction. A failure to produce the licence to the court, unless the driver can show that he has applied for a new one, is an offence in itself with a maximum fine of level 3.

Subss. (3), (4) and (5)
   These three subsections deal with fixed penalty offences. Where a driver has been issued with a fixed penalty notice in respect of an offence committed within the probationary period and the offence is one which carries with it obligatory endorsement and six penalty points, then the fixed penalty clerk on receipt of the licence must send it to the Secretary of State together with the counterpart. Subsection (3)(e) states that the licence received by the fixed penalty clerk must show the date on which the person became a qualified driver, otherwise subs. (4) will not apply.

Revocation of licences

   3.—(1) Where the Secretary of State receives—
   (a) a notice sent to him under section 2(2)(a) of particulars required to be endorsed on the counterpart of a person's licence, or
   (b) a person's licence and its counterpart sent to him in accordance with section 2(2)(b) or (4),
the Secretary of State must by notice served on that person revoke the licence.
   (2) A revocation under subsection (1) shall have effect from a date specified in the notice of revocation which may not be earlier than the date of service of that notice.

DEFINITIONS
   "notice": s.9(3).

GENERAL NOTE
   This section sets out the next stage in the procedure. The Secretary of State on receipt of the notice of particulars from the court, or the licence and counterpart sent from the court or the fixed penalty clerk, must revoke the driver's licence by serving on him a notice to that effect. The Secretary of State is only able to revoke a British licence, not non-British licences (see Standing Committee C., April 5, 1995, col. 20).

Subs. (2)
   The notice must state the date from which it takes effect. That date cannot be before the notice is served.

Re-testing

   4.—(1) Subject to subsection (5) and section 5, the Secretary of State may not under Part III of the Road Traffic Act 1988 grant a person whose licence has been revoked under section 3(1) a full licence to drive any class of vehicles in relation to which the revoked licence was issued as a full licence unless he satisfies the Secretary of State that within the relevant period he has passed a relevant driving test.

(2) In this section "relevant driving test" means, in relation to a person whose licence has been revoked, any test which—

(a) falls within paragraph (a) or (b) of section 1(2); and

(b) is a test of competence to drive any vehicle included in any class of vehicles in relation to which the revoked licence was issued as a full licence.

(3) If the Secretary of State grants a full licence to a person who is required to pass a relevant driving test in order to be granted that licence, the licence granted must (subject to section 92 and Part IV of the Road Traffic Act 1988) be one authorising that person to drive all the classes of vehicles in relation to which the revoked licence was issued as a full licence.

(4) In subsection (1) "the relevant period" means the period beginning—

(a) after the date of the revocation of the licence; and

(b) not more than two years before the date on which the application for the full licence is made.

(5) Subsection (1) does not apply to a person whose licence has been revoked under section 3(1) if, before he passes a relevant driving test, an order is made in relation to him under section 36 of the Road Traffic Offenders Act 1988 (disqualification until test is passed).

General Note
  Once the notice has been served and is effective, the driver is in the position of a learner driver. Before a further full driving licence can be issued to the driver, he must pass a test: either a test under the RTA 1988, or a test under the law of Gibraltar or an EEA State. The test in Great Britain will be the standard test. It should be noted that the test must be passed within two years of applying for a full licence after the order of revocation.

Restoration of licence without re-testing in certain cases

5.—(1) If the Secretary of State receives notice that a person whose licence has been revoked under section 3(1) is appealing against a conviction or endorsement which was the basis or formed part of the basis for the revocation, he must grant that person free of charge a full licence for a period prescribed by regulations.

(2) Regulations under subsection (1) may in particular prescribe—

(a) a period expiring when the appeal is finally determined or abandoned; or

(b) a period expiring on the date on which the revoked licence would have expired if it had not been revoked.

(3) If the regulations prescribe a period other than that mentioned in subsection (2)(a), a licence granted under subsection (1) shall be treated as revoked if—

(a) following the appeal, the penalty points taken into account for the purposes of section 2 are not reduced to a number smaller than six; or

(b) the appeal is abandoned.

(4) If, in the case of a person whose licence has been revoked under section 3(1), the Secretary of State receives notice that a court—

    (a) has quashed a conviction which was the basis or formed part of the basis for the revocation of the licence,

    (b) has quashed an endorsement which was the basis or formed part of the basis for the revocation of the licence and has not on doing so ordered him to be disqualified, or

    (c) has made an order which has the effect of reducing the penalty points taken into account for the purposes of section 2 to a number smaller than six,

then, subject to subsection (5), the Secretary of State must grant that person free of charge a full licence for a period expiring on the date on which the revoked licence would have expired if it had not been revoked.

(5) Subsection (4) does not require the Secretary of State to grant a licence to a person who has been granted a previous licence which has not been surrendered unless that person provides the Secretary of State with an explanation for not surrendering the previous licence that the Secretary of State considers adequate.

(6) If, in accordance with subsection (1) or (4), the Secretary of State grants a full licence to a person whose licence has been revoked under section 3(1), the licence granted must be one authorising that person to drive all the classes of vehicles in relation to which the revoked licence was issued as a full licence.

(7) Any licence granted in accordance with subsection (1) or (4) shall have effect for the purposes of the Road Traffic Acts as if it were a licence granted under Part III of the Road Traffic Act 1988.

(8) Regulations may make provision for requiring such courts as may be prescribed to give notice to the Secretary of State—

    (a) that a person whose licence has been or is due to be revoked under section 3(1) is appealing against a conviction or endorsement which is the basis or forms part of the basis for the revocation;

    (b) that such an appeal has been abandoned.

(9) Regulations under this section may—

    (a) include such incidental or supplementary provision as appears to the Secretary of State to be expedient;

    (b) make different provision for different cases.

(10) Any regulations made under this section shall be made by the Secretary of State by statutory instrument which shall be subject to annulment in pursuance of a resolution of either House of Parliament.

DEFINITIONS
    "licence": RTA 1988, s.108.

GENERAL NOTE
    This section deals with those circumstances where there is an appeal against the conviction or the endorsement which has led to the issuing of a notice revoking a driver's licence. There is an obligation upon the Secretary of State to grant a full licence to the appellant driver pending his appeal. The duration of the licence granted to the driver is to be determined by regulation. It is clear that should the appeal fail or be abandoned, any licence granted to the driver as a result of the appeal will be revoked. Equally where an appeal is successful in either quashing the conviction or quashing the endorsement which formed the basis of the revocation or in reducing the penalty points to be attributed to the driver's licence, then the Secretary of State has to grant to the successful appellant a full licence permitting the driver to drive those classes of vehicles he was permitted to drive before the order was made.

Subs. (5)
    This is of interest as it excludes the Secretary of State from granting a full licence to a successful appellant where the appellant's licence was not surrendered to the court, unless there is an explanation which is considered adequate.

Subss. (8), (9) and (10)
    Regulations covering the full position on appeals, time periods and other matters made by the Secretary of State by statutory instrument are subject to annulment by resolution by either

House of Parliament. As it is clear that the date of implementation of the Act is still to be decided, no date is given for any regulations. The options for time periods are kept open (see Standing Committee C., April 19, 1995, col. 49).

Miscellaneous and general

Newly qualified drivers holding test certificates

6. Schedule 1 (which makes provision about newly qualified drivers who hold test certificates) shall have effect.

DEFINITIONS
"licence": RTA 1988, s.108.
"prescribed conditions": Sched. 1 and RTA 1988, ss.1(2), 97(3).
"provisional licence": RTA 1988, s.108.
"test certificate": Sched. 1 and RTA 1988, ss.1(1), 108.

GENERAL NOTE
This section and Sched. 1 largely replicate ss.2, 3, 4 and 5 of the Act. Section 6 and Sched. 1 apply to those cases where a driver has passed a test, but has yet to surrender the test certificate and be given a full driving licence. On passing a test there is a two-year period during which the test certificate can be exchanged for a full driving licence.

Where the driver commits an offence which involves obligatory endorsement during the two-year period from the passing of the test, then upon conviction he must produce the test certificate to the court, or to the fixed penalty clerk where the fixed penalty notice procedure is being followed. The very detailed provisions of Sched. 1 are important as they close potential loopholes which might allow the retesting procedure to be evaded by people with unclaimed test certificates (*Hansard*, H.L. Vol. 564, col. 766).

Early termination of probationary period

7. For the purposes of this Act a person's probationary period comes to an end if—
   (a) an order is made in relation to him under section 36 of the Road Traffic Offenders Act 1988 (order that a person be disqualified until he passes the appropriate driving test);
   (b) after his licence is revoked under section 3(1), he is granted a full licence following the passing of a test which is a relevant driving test for the purposes of section 4; or
   (c) after his test certificate is revoked under paragraph 5(1) of Schedule 1, or his licence and test certificate are revoked under paragraph 8(1) of that Schedule, he is granted a full licence following the passing of a test which is a relevant driving test for the purposes of paragraph 6 or 9 of that Schedule.

DEFINITIONS
"licence": RTA 1988, s.108.
"probationary period": s.1.
"test certificate": Sched. 1 and RTA 1988, ss.1(1), 108.

GENERAL NOTE
The provisions of s.7 prevent a driver facing a double penalty. If during the course of the probationary period a driver is convicted of an offence and the court makes an order that he be

retested under s.36 of the RTOA 1988, then his probationary period is at an end. Equally where an order of revocation is made in respect of a licence or test certificate under this Act, and the driver passes his subsequent test, the probationary period will be at an end.

Although the probationary period might in each of these circumstances be shorter than two years, the driver will still retain the penalty points endorsed on his licence as a result of the conviction and therefore be at risk of a "totting" disqualification if further points are endorsed.

The Crown

8. This Act applies to persons in the public service of the Crown.

Interpretation etc.

9.—(1) Expressions used in this Act which are also used in Part III of the Road Traffic Act 1988 shall be construed in the same way as in that Act.

(2) Expressions used in this Act which are also used in the Road Traffic Offenders Act 1988 shall be construed in the same way as in that Act.

(3) In this Act "notice" means notice in writing.

(4) Section 107 of the Road Traffic Act 1988 (service of notices) applies to a notice served under section 3 or paragraph 5 or 8 of Schedule 1 as it applies to a notice served under any of the sections referred to in that section.

(5) Any requirement under any provision of this Act that a licence and its counterpart, a test certificate or a notice must be sent to the Secretary of State is a requirement that the licence and its counterpart, the test certificate or the notice must be sent to the Secretary of State at such address as the Secretary of State may determine.

GENERAL NOTE

The notices required by the provisions of this Act must be in writing. The notice (subs. (4)) may be served on the driver by delivering it to him, by leaving it at his proper address (his latest address as known to the person serving it), or by sending it to him by post (see s.107 of the RTA 1988).

Short title, commencement, extent etc.

10.—(1) This Act may be cited as the Road Traffic (New Drivers) Act 1995.

(2) The provisions of this Act shall come into force on such day as the Secretary of State may by order made by statutory instrument appoint and different days may be so appointed for different provisions.

(3) Nothing in any provision of this Act applies to a person who becomes a qualified driver before the day on which the provision comes into force.

(4) The consequential amendments set out in Schedule 2 shall have effect.

(5) This Act does not extend to Northern Ireland.

GENERAL NOTE

The consequential amendments are set out in Sched. 2.

The Act does not apply to Northern Ireland (subs. (5)). During the debate in committee, reference was made to the system in Northern Ireland where a system of "R" plates is used for those drivers who have recently passed a test. The "R" or "Restricted" plate restricts the speed of a newly qualified driver to 45 mph (Standing Committee C., April 5, 1995, cols. 17–18).

SCHEDULES

Section 6　　　　　　　　　　SCHEDULE 1

NEWLY QUALIFIED DRIVERS HOLDING TEST CERTIFICATES

PART I

GENERAL

Interpretation

1.—(1) In this Schedule "test certificate" means a certificate or other document which by virtue of regulations under section 89 of the Road Traffic Act 1988 is evidence that a person has not more than two years previously passed a test of competence to drive prescribed by virtue of such regulations.

(2) In this Schedule "prescribed conditions" means the prescribed conditions referred to in section 97(3) of the 1988 Act (subject to which provisional licences are granted).

Application of Schedule

2.—(1) Part II of this Schedule applies to any person to whom Part III or IV of this Schedule applies.

(2) Part III of this Schedule applies to a person who holds—

(a) a licence issued as a provisional licence; and

(b) a test certificate.

(3) Part IV of this Schedule applies to a person who falls within sub-paragraph (4) or (5).

(4) A person falls within this sub-paragraph if—

(a) he holds a licence issued as a full licence in relation to a class or certain classes of vehicles;

(b) he is treated under section 98(2) of the Road Traffic Act 1988 as authorised by a provisional licence to drive another class or other classes of vehicles; and

(c) he holds a test certificate which relates to that other class of vehicles or any of those other classes of vehicles.

(5) A person falls within this sub-paragraph if he holds—

(a) a licence issued as a full licence in relation to a class or certain classes of vehicles and as a provisional licence in relation to another class or other classes of vehicles; and

(b) a test certificate which relates to that other class of vehicles or any of those other classes of vehicles.

PART II

DUTY TO PROVIDE TEST CERTIFICATE

3.—(1) Sub-paragraph (2) applies where—

(a) a person to whom this Part of this Schedule applies is prosecuted for an offence involving obligatory endorsement; and

(b) the time at which the offence for which he is prosecuted is alleged to have occurred is a time during his probationary period.

(2) Any obligations imposed on the person under section 7 of the Road Traffic Offenders Act 1988 as respects his licence and its counterpart shall also apply as respects his test certificate.

(3) If, in a case where sub-paragraph (2) applies—

(a) the person is convicted in the proceedings in question of an offence involving obligatory endorsement, and

(b) he has not previously caused his test certificate to be delivered or posted it to the clerk of the court,

he must produce his test certificate to the court.

(4) In a case where—

(a) the licence of a person to whom this Part of this Schedule applies has (with its counterpart) been sent to the fixed penalty clerk under section 54(7) of the Road Traffic Offenders Act 1988 or delivered to the fixed penalty clerk in response to a conditional offer issued under section 75 of that Act,

(b) the offence to which the fixed penalty notice or the conditional offer relates is one involving obligatory endorsement and occurring during his probationary period, and

(c) the person proposes to pay the fixed penalty to the fixed penalty clerk,

the person must ensure that when the fixed penalty is paid his test certificate is sent to the fixed penalty clerk to whom the payment is made.

(5) A person who without reasonable excuse fails to comply with sub-paragraph (3) or (4) is guilty of an offence and shall be liable on summary conviction to a fine not exceeding level 3 on the standard scale.

PART III

NEWLY QUALIFIED DRIVER WITH PROVISIONAL LICENCE AND TEST CERTIFICATE

Surrender of test certificate

4.—(1) Where the circumstances mentioned in section 2(1) exist with respect to a person to whom this Part of this Schedule applies, sub-paragraph (2) applies instead of section 2(2).

(2) The court must send to the Secretary of State—
(a) a notice containing the particulars required to be endorsed on the counterpart of the person's licence in accordance with the order referred to in section 2(1)(d); and
(b) on its production to the court, the person's test certificate.

(3) Where—
(a) the circumstances mentioned in section 2(3)(a) to (d) and (f) exist with respect to a person to whom this Part of this Schedule applies,
(b) the fixed penalty clerk has received the person's test certificate in accordance with paragraph 3(4), and
(c) the test certificate shows the date on which the person became a qualified driver, sub-paragraph (4) applies instead of section 2(4).

(4) The fixed penalty clerk must send to the Secretary of State—
(a) a notice containing the particulars endorsed on the counterpart of the person's licence; and
(b) the person's test certificate.

Revocation of test certificate

5.—(1) Where the Secretary of State—
(a) has received a notice sent to him under paragraph 4 of particulars required to be endorsed or endorsed on the counterpart of a person's licence, and
(b) has received the person's test certificate sent to him under paragraph 4(2)(b) or (4)(b) or is satisfied that the person has been issued with a test certificate,
the Secretary of State must by notice served on that person revoke the test certificate.

(2) A revocation under sub-paragraph (1) shall have effect from a date specified in the notice of revocation which may not be earlier than the date of service of that notice.

(3) The effect of the revocation of a person's test certificate is that any prescribed conditions to which his provisional licence ceased to be subject when he became a qualified driver shall again apply.

Re-testing

6.—(1) Subject to Part V of this Schedule, the Secretary of State may not under Part III of the Road Traffic Act 1988 grant a person whose test certificate has been revoked under paragraph 5(1) a full licence to drive any class of vehicles that, immediately before his test certificate was revoked, he was permitted to drive without observing prescribed conditions, unless he satisfies the Secretary of State that within the relevant period he has passed a relevant driving test.

(2) In this paragraph "relevant driving test" means, in relation to a person whose test certificate has been revoked, any test which—
(a) falls within paragraph (a) or (b) of section 1(2); and
(b) is a test of competence to drive any vehicle included in any class of vehicles that, immediately before his test certificate was revoked, he was permitted to drive without observing prescribed conditions.

(3) If the Secretary of State grants a full licence to a person who is required to pass a relevant driving test in order to be granted that licence, the licence granted must (subject to section 92 and Part IV of the Road Traffic Act 1988) be one authorising that person to drive all the classes of

vehicles that, immediately before his test certificate was revoked, he was permitted to drive without observing prescribed conditions.

(4) In sub-paragraph (1) "the relevant period" means the period beginning—

(a) after the date of the revocation of the test certificate; and

(b) not more than two years before the date on which the application for the full licence is made.

PART IV

Newly qualified driver with full and provisional entitlements and test certificate

Surrender of licence and test certificate

7.—(1) Where the circumstances mentioned in section 2(1) exist with respect to a person to whom this Part of this Schedule applies, sub-paragraph (2) applies instead of section 2(2).

(2) The court must send to the Secretary of State—

(a) a notice containing the particulars required to be endorsed on the counterpart of the person's licence in accordance with the order referred to in section 2(1)(d);

(b) on their production to the court, the person's licence and its counterpart; and

(c) on its production to the court, the person's test certificate.

(3) Where—

(a) the circumstances mentioned in section 2(3) exist with respect to a person to whom this Part of this Schedule applies, and

(b) the fixed penalty clerk has received the person's test certificate in accordance with paragraph 3(4),

sub-paragraph (4) applies instead of section 2(4).

(4) The fixed penalty clerk—

(a) may not return the person's licence and its counterpart under section 57(3) or (4) or 77(1) of the Road Traffic Offenders Act 1988; but

(b) must send them and the person's test certificate to the Secretary of State.

Revocation of licence and test certificate

8.—(1) Where the Secretary of State—

(a) has received a notice sent to him under paragraph 7(2)(a) of particulars required to be endorsed on the counterpart of a person's licence or has received the licence and its counterpart under paragraph 7(2)(b) or (4)(b), and

(b) has received the person's test certificate sent to him under paragraph 7(2)(b) or (4)(b) or is satisfied that the person has been issued with a test certificate,

the Secretary of State must by notice served on that person revoke the licence and the test certificate.

(2) A revocation under sub-paragraph (1) shall have effect from a date specified in the notice of revocation which may not be earlier than the date of service of that notice.

Re-testing

9.—(1) Subject to Part V of this Schedule, the Secretary of State may not under Part III of the Road Traffic Act 1988 grant a person whose licence and test certificate have been revoked under paragraph 8(1) a full licence to drive any class of vehicles mentioned in sub-paragraph (4), unless he satisfies the Secretary of State that within the relevant period he has passed a relevant driving test.

(2) In this paragraph "relevant driving test" means any test which—

(a) falls within paragraph (a) or (b) of section 1(2); and

(b) is a test of competence to drive any vehicle included in any class of vehicles mentioned in sub-paragraph (4).

(3) If the Secretary of State grants a full licence to a person who is required to pass a relevant driving test in order to be granted that licence, the licence granted must (subject to section 92 and Part IV of the Road Traffic Act 1988) be one authorising that person to drive all the classes of vehicles mentioned in sub-paragraph (4).

(4) The classes of vehicles are—

(a) any class of vehicles in relation to which the revoked licence was issued as a full licence; and

(b) any class of vehicles—

(i) that he was treated under section 98(2) of the Road Traffic Act 1988 as authorised to drive under a provisional licence, or

(ii) in relation to which the revoked licence was issued as a provisional licence, and that, immediately before the test certificate was revoked, he was permitted to drive without observing prescribed conditions.

(5) In sub-paragraph (1) "the relevant period" means the period beginning—

(a) after the date of the revocation of the licence and the test certificate; and

(b) not more than two years before the date on which the application for the full licence is made.

PART V

SUPPLEMENTARY

Effect of disqualification until test is passed on re-testing rule

10. Where—

(a) a person's test certificate has been revoked under paragraph 5(1) or his licence and test certificate have been revoked under paragraph 8(1), but

(b) before he passes a relevant driving test, an order is made in relation to him under section 36 of the Road Traffic Offenders Act 1988 (disqualification until test is passed),

paragraph 6(1) or, as the case may be, paragraph 9(1) shall not apply to him.

Regulations

11.—(1) The Secretary of State may by regulations make provision for cases where, after the Secretary of State has revoked a person's test certificate under paragraph 5(1), or a person's licence and test certificate under paragraph 8(1), he receives notice—

(a) that the person is appealing against a conviction or endorsement which was the basis or formed part of the basis for the revocation;

(b) that a court has quashed a conviction which was the basis or formed part of the basis for the revocation;

(c) that a court has quashed an endorsement which was the basis or formed part of the basis for the revocation and has not on doing so ordered that person to be disqualified;

(d) that a court has made an order which has the effect of reducing the penalty points taken into account for the purposes of section 2 to a number smaller than six.

(2) Regulations under sub-paragraph (1) may in particular make provision for—

(a) issuing licences for such period as may be prescribed;

(b) licences issued under the regulations to be treated as revoked in such circumstances as may be prescribed;

(c) re-issuing a test certificate which has been revoked under paragraph 5(1) or 8(1);

(d) suspending or terminating any prescribed conditions applied by virtue of paragraph 5(3);

(e) requiring such courts as may be prescribed to give notice to the Secretary of State of the matters mentioned in sub-paragraph (3).

(3) The matters referred to are—

(a) that a person whose certificate has been or is due to be revoked under paragraph 5(1) or whose licence and certificate have been or are due to be revoked under paragraph 8(1) is appealing against a conviction or endorsement which is the basis or forms part of the basis for the revocation;

(b) that such an appeal has been abandoned.

(4) Any regulations under this paragraph may—

(a) include such incidental or supplementary provision as appears to the Secretary of State to be expedient;

(b) make different provision for different cases.

(5) Any regulations under this paragraph shall be made by statutory instrument which shall be subject to annulment in pursuance of a resolution of either House of Parliament.

Section 10(4)   SCHEDULE 2

CONSEQUENTIAL AMENDMENTS

The Road Traffic Act 1988 (c.52)

1. The Road Traffic Act 1988 shall be amended as follows.

2.—(1) In the provisions mentioned in sub-paragraph (2) after "section 89 of this Act" insert "or section 4(1) of or paragraph 6(1) or 9(1) of Schedule 1 to the Road Traffic (New Drivers) Act 1995".

(2) The provisions are—

(a) section 88(1A)(b)(ii) (meaning of "qualifying application" for purposes of exception to requirement that driver must have a licence);

(b) section 97(1)(d) (person to whom licence must be granted must be a person who is not prevented from obtaining it by section 89 of the Act).

The Road Traffic Offenders Act 1988 (c.53)

3. The Road Traffic Offenders Act 1988 shall be amended as follows.

4. In section 47 (supplementary provisions as to disqualifications and endorsements) after subsection (2) (cases where the court may or must send licence and its counterpart to the Secretary of State) insert—

"(2A) Subsection (2) above is subject to section 2(2) of and paragraph 7(2) of Schedule 1 to the Road Traffic (New Drivers) Act 1995 (obligation of court to send licence and its counterpart to the Secretary of State)."

5. In section 57 (endorsement of licences without hearings) after subsection (6) insert—

"(7) Subsections (3) and (4) above are subject to section 2(4)(a) of and paragraph 7(4)(a) of Schedule 1 to the Road Traffic (New Drivers) Act 1995; and the fixed penalty clerk need not comply with subsection (6) above in a case where he sends a person's licence and its counterpart to the Secretary of State under section 2(4)(b) of or paragraph 7(4)(b) of Schedule 1 to that Act."

6. In section 77 (endorsement where penalty paid) after subsection (9) insert—

"(10) Subsection (1) above is subject to section 2(4)(a) of and paragraph 7(4)(a) of Schedule 1 to the Road Traffic (New Drivers) Act 1995; and the fixed penalty clerk need not send a notice falling within subsection (6)(a) above in a case where he sends a person's licence and its counterpart to the Secretary of State under section 2(4)(b) of or paragraph 7(4)(b) of Schedule 1 to that Act."

7. In Schedule 1 (offences to which various sections of the Act apply), in paragraph 2 (offences to which section 6 applies) omit the word "and" immediately preceding paragraph (c) and after that paragraph insert "and

(d) to an offence under paragraph 3(5) of Schedule 1 to the Road Traffic (New Drivers) Act 1995."

INDEX

References are to sections and Schedules

LAND REGISTERS (SCOTLAND) ACT 1995

(1995 c. 14)

An Act to make prepayment of the appropriate statutory fees a condition of acceptance of writs for recording in the Register of Sasines and of applications for registration in the Land Register of Scotland.

[28th June 1995]

PARLIAMENTARY DEBATES
Hansard, H.C. Vol. 254, col. 1011. H.L. Vol. 564, col. 995.

INTRODUCTION
This Act provides that prepayment of the appropriate statutory fees, payable under s.25 of the Land Registers (Scotland) Act 1868 (c. 64), is a condition of acceptance of writs for recording in the Register of Sasines and of applications for registration in the Land Register of Scotland.

Prepayment of recording and registration fees

1.—(1) No writ shall be accepted for recording in the Register of Sasines unless payment of the fee payable in that respect under section 25 of the Land Registers (Scotland) Act 1868 has been tendered.

(2) Accordingly, in section 6 of that Act (procedure where writs sent by post for recording in Register of Sasines) the words from "intimation" to "effect", where secondly occurring, are repealed.

(3) In section 4(2) of the Land Registration (Scotland) Act 1979 (circumstances where applications for registration are not to be accepted) after paragraph (d) there shall be added the following paragraph—

"(e) payment of the fee payable in respect of such registration under section 25 of the Land Registers (Scotland) Act 1868 has not been tendered.".

Short title, commencement and extent

2.—(1) This Act may be cited as the Land Registers (Scotland) Act 1995.

(2) This Act shall come into force on such date as the Secretary of State may, by order made by statutory instrument, appoint.

(3) This Act extends to Scotland only.

INDEX

References are to sections

ACTIVITY CENTRES (YOUNG PERSONS' SAFETY) ACT 1995*

(1995 c. 15)

An Act to make provision for the regulation of centres and providers of facilities where children and young persons under the age of 18 engage in adventure activities, including provision for the imposition of requirements relating to safety.   [28th June 1995]

PARLIAMENTARY DEBATES

Hansard, H.C. Vol. 253, col. 590, Vol. 254, col. 903, Vol. 257, col. 600. H.L. Vol. 563, col. 445, Vol. 564, col. 1265, Vol. 565, col. 154.

This Bill was discussed in Standing Committee C on February 22 and March 1 and 8, 1995.

INTRODUCTION AND GENERAL NOTE

This Act was introduced as a Private Member's Bill following concerns arising from the Lyme Bay tragedy when four teenagers died in a canoeing accident. They had attended the St. Albans Activity Centre and subsequently the managing director of the company running the centre and the company itself were convicted of manslaughter.

The Act is an enabling Act and provides a general framework for detailed regulations to be made by the Secretary of State for Education after consultations with interested bodies. Draft regulations are being prepared by the Health and Safety Executive and, following a consultation period, the formal regulations are likely to come into force in the early part of 1996.

There are four main elements to the Act:

(1) the setting up of a licensing authority for such centres;

(2) the setting up of an inspectorate;

(3) a complaints procedure for consumers or others who have reservations about the safety of activity centres; and

(4) provision for the licensing authority to charge fees and any shortfall in financing to be met by central government.

Activity centres are, of course, already subject to the general requirements for health and safety under the HSAWA 1974 and the Management of Health and Safety at Work Regulations 1992 (S.I. 1992 No. 2051) which apply generally to employers and employees. This Act, however, will require those activity centres specified in the regulations, catering for young persons up to the age of 17 years, to apply for and obtain a licence to be issued by a new licensing authority. Operating without a licence or in breach of licence conditions will be a criminal offence. The object will be to ensure that activity centres have properly trained and qualified staff, have proper equipment and maintain high and safe standards of operation.

The provisions for licensing will apply to centres providing "facilities for adventure activities" which include sporting, recreational or outdoor activities. The precise scope of the activities to be covered will be specified in the detailed regulations but specifically excluded are facilities which provide exclusively for those aged 18 and over or facilities which do not include some element of instruction or leadership.

COMMENCEMENT

The Act will come into force on August 28, 1995 (see s.5).

ABBREVIATIONS

HSAWA 1974: Health and Safety at Work etc. Act 1974.

Adventure activities: licensing

1.—(1) The Secretary of State shall by order designate a person ("the licensing authority") to exercise such functions as may be prescribed by regulations relating to the licensing of persons providing facilities for adventure activities.

(2) The Secretary of State shall not make an order under subsection (1) designating a person other than one nominated by the Health and Safety Commission.

(3) In this section "facilities for adventure activities" means such facilities, for such sporting, recreational or outdoor activities, as may be prescribed by regulations; but the expression does not include—

---

*Annotations by M.E. Cowell, Solicitor, Dibb Lupton Broomhead

(a) facilities which are provided exclusively for persons who have attained the age of 18; or

(b) facilities which do not consist of, or include some element of, instruction or leadership.

(4) Regulations may make provision as to—

(a) the cases or circumstances in which persons providing facilities for adventure activities are, or are not, required to hold a licence;

(b) any requirements relating to safety (whether applying to facilities for adventure activities or to other facilities) which must be satisfied by an applicant for a licence;

(c) the conditions subject to which licences are granted (which may include conditions relating to inspection by the licensing authority and conditions imposing requirements of the kind referred to in paragraph (b));

(d) the variation of such conditions;

(e) the renewal, variation, transfer and revocation of licences by the licensing authority;

(f) the charging by the licensing authority of such fees in connection with licences as may be specified in the regulations;

(g) the making of payments by the licensing authority into the Consolidated Fund;

(h) the investigation by the licensing authority of complaints concerning licence-holders;

(i) the exercise of functions of the licensing authority by persons authorised by them;

(j) the keeping, and availability for inspection by the public, of a register of licences;

(k) the bringing of appeals to the Secretary of State against such decisions of the licensing authority as may be specified in the regulations; and

(l) the procedure to be followed on, and the orders which may be made on determination of, such appeals.

(5) In exercising their functions under regulations made under this section the licensing authority shall have regard to any guidance given to them from time to time by the Health and Safety Commission; and before giving guidance under this subsection the Commission shall consult such persons (if any) as they consider it appropriate to consult.

DEFINITIONS

"Secretary of State": The Secretary of State for Education.
"The Health and Safety Commission": s.10 of the HSAWA 1974.

GENERAL NOTE

Subss. (1) and (2)
These subsections provide for the Secretary of State to designate a person nominated by the Health and Safety Commission to act as the "licensing authority". During parliamentary debate it was indicated that it was the intention that the licensing authority would not be the Health and Safety Executive or local authorities, which currently have responsibility for enforcing the HSAWA 1974.

Subs. (3)
The exact type of "facilities for adventure activities" will be defined in detailed regulations but expressly excluded are facilities provided exclusively for those aged 18 or over or facilities which do not include some element of instruction or leadership.

Subs. (4)
This subsection lists the provisions to be covered under the proposed regulations.

Subs. (5)
This subsection requires the licensing authority to have regard to guidance given by the Health and Safety Commission and for the Commission to consult other persons.

Offences

2.—(1) Regulations may provide for it to be an offence—

(a) to do anything for which a licence is required under the regulations, otherwise than in accordance with a licence; or

(b) for the purposes of obtaining or holding a licence—

(i) to make a statement to the licensing authority (or someone acting on their behalf) knowing it to be false in a material particular, or

(ii) recklessly to make a statement to the licensing authority (or someone acting on their behalf) which is false in a material particular.

(2) A person convicted of an offence under regulations made under subsection (1) shall be liable—

(a) on summary conviction, to a fine not exceeding the statutory maximum;

(b) on conviction on indictment—

(i) for an offence under regulations made under subsection (1)(a), to imprisonment for a term not exceeding two years, or a fine, or both;

(ii) for an offence under regulations made under subsection (1)(b), to a fine.

(3) Regulations under subsection (1)—

(a) may provide defences to be available in proceedings for an offence under the regulations either generally or in specified circumstances;

(b) may make, in relation to provisions of the regulations, provision which applies (with or without modifications), or has a similar purpose to that of, any of the provisions of the Health and Safety at Work etc. Act 1974 set out in subsection (4).

(4) The provisions mentioned in subsection (3)(b) are:

(a) sections 15(7) and 35 (venue);

(b) sections 18 to 20 and 26 (enforcement authorities and inspectors);

(c) sections 21 to 24 (improvement and prohibition notices);

(d) sections 25 (power to deal with cause of imminent danger);

(e) sections 27 and 28 (obtaining and disclosure of information);

(f) section 33(1)(e) to (j), (n) and (o), and (2) to (4) (ancillary offences);

(g) section 34(2) to (6) (extension of time for bringing summary proceedings);

(h) sections 36(1) and 37 (offences due to fault of other person and offences by bodies corporate);

(i) sections 38 and 39 (prosecutions in England and Wales only by inspectors or by or with the consent of the Director of Public Prosecutions);

(j) sections 40 and 41 (onus of proving limits of what is practicable, and evidence);

(k) section 42 (power of court to order cause of offence to be remedied); and

(l) section 46 (service of notices).

DEFINITIONS
"statutory maximum": £5,000.

Subss. (1), (2) and (3)(a)
These subsections enable regulations to provide criminal sanctions against those operating without a licence where one is required, for making a false statement to obtain a licence or recklessly making a false statement to the licensing authority. The maximum penalty for conviction on indictment would be two years' imprisonment or an unlimited fine.

The offence under subs. (1)(a) is apparently an offence of strict liability whereas those under subs. (1)(b) would require proof of knowledge or recklessness.

The regulations may provide a defence and it was certainly contemplated during parliamentary debate that the regulations would provide what is commonly referred to as the "due diligence" defence found in many statutes imposing strict liability. See, for example, the Local Government (Miscellaneous Provisions) Act 1982 (c.30), Sched. I, para. 12(3) which deals with public entertainment licences.

Subss. (3)(b) and (4)

It is envisaged that the detailed regulations will adopt identical or similar provisions to those already contained in the HSAWA 1974 as listed in these subsections. These provisions will effectively give powers to the licensing authority and its inspectorate similar to those given to those charged with the enforcement of the HSAWA 1974.

Supplementary provisions

3.—(1) An order under section 1(1) shall be made by statutory instrument; and an order revoking a previous order may include transitional or incidental provision (including provision for the transfer of property, rights and liabilities from the old licensing authority to the new).

(2) Regulations under section 1 or 2—

(a) shall be made by the Secretary of State by statutory instrument;

(b) may make different provision for different cases; and

(c) may include transitional provisions.

(3) Before making regulations under section 1 or 2 the Secretary of State shall consult the Health and Safety Commission and such other persons (if any) as he considers it appropriate to consult.

(4) The Health and Safety Commission may from time to time submit to the Secretary of State such proposals as the Commission considers appropriate for the making of regulations under section 1 or 2; and where the Secretary of State proposes to make regulations in the form submitted under this subsection, the requirement under subsection (3) to consult the Commission shall not apply.

(5) Nothing in, or done by virtue of, this Act or regulations under it shall prejudice any of the relevant statutory provisions (whenever made) as defined in Part I of the Health and Safety at Work etc. Act 1974 or anything done by virtue of any of those provisions.

(6) A statutory instrument containing an order or regulations under section 1 or 2 shall be subject to annulment in pursuance of a resolution of either House of Parliament.

(7) The Secretary of State may make grants to the licensing authority in respect of such of their expenses under this Act as are not met by fees; and grants under this subsection may be made subject to such conditions, including conditions as to repayment, as the Secretary of State may determine.

DEFINITIONS

"Secretary of State": The Secretary of State for Education.

"Health and Safety Commission": s.10 of the HSAWA 1974.

Subss. (1) and (2)

The order appointing the licensing authority and regulations made under ss.1 and 2 of the Act are to be made by statutory instrument. In particular they are likely to include transitional provisions to give those affected by the regulations time to obtain licences.

Subs. (5)

This makes it clear that the HSAWA 1974 and any regulations made under it will continue to apply to those activity centres that are required to be licensed.

Subs. (7)

By virtue of s.1(4)(f) regulations will enable the licensing authority to charge fees to those applying for licences. During parliamentary debate it was anticipated that the level of fees would be such that once the scheme was up and running it would be self-financing. Start up costs and any shortfall, however, are to be made up by central government.

Expenses

4. There shall be paid out of money provided by Parliament any expenditure incurred by the Secretary of State under or by virtue of this Act.

Commencement

5. This Act shall come into force at the end of the period of two months beginning with the date on which it is passed.

Short title and extent

6.—(1) This Act may be cited as the Activity Centres (Young Persons' Safety) Act 1995.

(2) This Act shall not extend to Northern Ireland.

INDEX

References are to sections

PRISONERS (RETURN TO CUSTODY) ACT 1995

(1995 c. 16)

An Act to make provision, by the creation of an offence and the conferring of powers of entry, for the punishment and return to lawful custody of persons unlawfully at large.   [28th June 1995]

PARLIAMENTARY DEBATES
Hansard, H.C. Vol. 251, col. 946. H.L. Vol. 564, col. 488.

INTRODUCTION
    This Act creates a summary offence of remaining unlawfully at large, without reasonable excuse, after being temporarily released from a prison, remand centre or young offender institution. Provision is made for the police to enter and search premises without a warrant for the purpose of arresting persons unlawfully at large.

Remaining at large after temporary release

1.—(1) Subject to subsection (2) below, a person who has been temporarily released in pursuance of rules made under section 47(5) of the Prison Act 1952 (rules for temporary release) is guilty of an offence if—
    (a) without reasonable excuse, he remains unlawfully at large at any time after becoming so at large by virtue of the expiry of the period for which he was temporarily released; or
    (b) knowing or believing an order recalling him to have been made and while unlawfully at large by virtue of such an order, he fails, without reasonable excuse, to take all necessary steps for complying as soon as reasonably practicable with that order.
    (2) Subsection (1) above shall not apply in the case of a person temporarily released from a secure training centre.
    (3) A person guilty of any offence under this section shall be liable, on summary conviction, to imprisonment for a term not exceeding six months or to a fine not exceeding level 5 on the standard scale, or to both.
    (4) An offence under this section shall be taken to be committed at the place where the offender was required to be detained immediately before being temporarily released.
    (5) A person shall be deemed for the purposes of this section to be unlawfully at large whenever he is deemed to be so at large for the purposes of section 49 of the Prison Act 1952 (which confers powers of arrest).
    (6) This section shall not apply where the period of temporary release expired, or the order of recall was made, before the commencement of this section.

Entry to arrest a person unlawfully at large

2.—(1) In subsection (1) of section 17 of the Police and Criminal Evidence Act 1984 (entry for the purpose of arrest), after paragraph (c) there shall be inserted the following paragraphs—

"(ca) of arresting, in pursuance of section 32(1A) of the Children and Young Persons Act 1969, any child or young person who has been remanded or committed to local authority accommodation under section 23(1) of that Act;
(cb) of recapturing any person who is, or is deemed for any purpose to be, unlawfully at large while liable to be detained—
    (i) in a prison, remand centre, young offender institution or secure training centre, or
    (ii) in pursuance of section 53 of the Children and Young Persons Act 1933 (dealing with children and young persons guilty of grave crimes), in any other place;"
and in paragraph (d) of that subsection, for "a person" there shall be substituted "any person whatever".

(2) In section 32 of the Children and Young Persons Act 1969 (detention of absentees)—
(a) in paragraph (b) of subsection (1A), for the words from "or 23(1)" to the end of the paragraph there shall be substituted "of this Act; or
    (iii) to which he has been remanded or committed under section 23(1) of this Act"; and
(b) in subsection (2A), for "(1A)" there shall be substituted "(1A)(a) or (b)(i) or (ii)".

Short title, commencement and extent

3.—(1) This Act may be cited as the Prisoners (Return to Custody) Act 1995.

(2) This Act shall come into force on such day as the Secretary of State may by order made by statutory instrument appoint, and different days may be appointed under this subsection for different purposes.

(3) This Act extends to England and Wales only.

INDEX

References are to sections

HEALTH AUTHORITIES ACT 1995*

(1995 c. 17)

An Act to abolish Regional Health Authorities, District Health Authorities and Family Health Services Authorities, require the establishment of Health Authorities and make provision in relation to Health Authorities and Special Health Authorities and for connected purposes.

[28th June 1995]

PARLIAMENTARY DEBATES
 Hansard, H.C. Vol. 251, cols. 632, 716; Vol. 255, col. 165; Vol. 262, col. 569. H.L. Vol. 562, cols. 11, 272, 1504, 1588, 1712; Vol. 563, cols. 186, 706, 1482.

INTRODUCTION AND GENERAL NOTE

This Act has two main effects. The first is to abolish one level of health authorities in the National Health Service, the Regional Health Authorities. The second is to merge two classes of health authorities, both of which currently cover similar geographical areas, but play different functions. District Health Authorities are responsible for purchasing hospital and community health services on behalf of the local population. Family Health Services Authorities are responsible for primary medical (provided by general practitioners) and dental care, and for general pharmaceutical services. From April 1, 1996, DHAs and FHSAs will no longer exist, and their functions will be carried out by the new Health Authorities established under this Act.

This reorganisation will be less disruptive than might be thought, because in many ways it has been pre-empted by restructuring within the existing legal framework. Although FHSAs and DHAs currently retain separate statutory powers and duties, in a number of areas the two authorities have effectively already been united under a single chief executive and management team. The statutory authorities still meet separately to exercise their functions, but the executive work to implement decisions and manage day-to-day issues is carried out by a single set of officers. The Health Authorities Act 1995 will legitimise and formalise this arrangement for the whole of England and Wales.

The abolition of Regional Health Authorities will be the continuation of a process that has already been set in train. The number of RHAs was reduced from 14 to eight with effect from April 1, 1994. The eight remaining RHAs already have a joint management structure with the regional offices of the NHS Executive. The NHSE offices have already taken over the non-statutory functions of RHAs, and from April 1, 1996 those offices will continue to exist as the only remaining regional level of NHS management. Consequently, many of the day-to-day functions of regional officers will remain the same.

---

* Annotations by Jonathan Montgomery, B.A., LL.M., Senior Lecturer in Law, University of Southampton, Non-executive Director, Southampton Community Health Services NHS Trust.

The abolition of RHAs and the merger of FHSAs and DHAs is regarded by the Government and the NHSE as the final stage in the implementation of the NHS "market" introduced by the National Health Service and Community Care Act 1990 (c.19). From April 1, 1996, when the new Act takes effect, 98 per cent of NHS services will be managed by NHS Trusts, and the residual function of DHAs of directly managing services will effectively be at an end. The new Health Authorities will be concerned with planning and contracting for services, not delivering them. It is thought that the transitional phase of the move towards a market structure, which required management through a regional tier has now been passed. The reforms introduced by this Act ensure that the main force that shapes the provision of publicly funded health services will be the contracting between the new local purchasing HAs and providers.

The way in which the NHS is expected to operate under the new system is set out in two important documents. An overall statement of who is responsible for what can be found in the Department of Health's *Statement of Responsibilities and Accountabilities: public health, the NHS and social care* issued in May 1995. Within this framework, the core functions of the new HAs will be to evaluate the health and healthcare needs of the local population, establish a strategy to meet those needs and national priorities, and implement that strategy by purchasing the necessary services. The functions of the regional NHSE offices will include performance management of HAs, some monitoring of the performance of NHS Trusts (so far as it cannot be achieved by HAs through the contracting process), advising on and approving capital investments by NHS Trusts, and ensuring the NHS market functions effectively. A fuller discussion of the implication of this new structure can be found in *Managing the new NHS: functions and responsibilities in the new NHS* issued by the NHSE in July 1994. (Copies of the NHSE report can be obtained from Oonagh Whitehead, Functions and Manpower Implementation Team, NHS Executive, Quarry House, Quarry Hill, Leeds LS2 7UE. Copies of the Department of Health's statement are available from The Policy Management Unit, Department of Health, Richmond House, 79 Whitehall, London SW1A 2NS.)

The abolition of RHAs will require the reallocation of a number of functions currently carried out by those Authorities. Indications were given by Ministers as to how some of those functions would be distributed (and in some cases this Act effects those intentions through the amendment of existing provisions). Some will be devolved to the new HAs. These will include the supervision of midwives under the Nurses, Midwives and Health Visitors Act 1979 (c. 36), s.16 (as amended by Sched. 1, para. 104 of this Act), and reporting on the incidence of and services for people with AIDS (AIDS (Control) Act 1987 (c. 33), as amended by Sched. 1, para. 113 of this Act). In some cases HAs will act as a lead for other Authorities, for example in work associated with confidential inquiries into stillbirths and deaths in infancy, cancer registry services, quality assurance for breast and cancer screening services, and the approval of doctors for the purposes of s.12 of the Mental Health Act 1983 (c. 20) (see *Hansard*, H.L. Vol. 562, col. 1606). HAs may also combine to form purchasing consortia. It was suggested that this would happen in the case of regional specialist services such as neurosurgery (*Hansard*, H.L. Vol. 562, col. 1518). Such delegation and co-operation will be permitted by regulations to be made under the new s.16 of the 1977 Act, which is introduced by Sched. 1, para. 7 of this Act. Initially, the regional offices of the NHSE will support purchasing on lead and consortia bases, until HAs develop the necessary expertise.

The regional offices of the NHSE will take over some of the current functions of RHAs. These will include establishing and supporting Community Health Councils (Standing Committee A, February 14, 1995, col. 216). The monitoring of the purchasing of specialist services will initially be quite tight, for example a standard contract will be drawn up for cancer registration by the NHSE pending their satisfaction that other arrangements would maintain standards (Standing Committee A, February 7, 1995, col. 144). The regional offices of the NHSE will perform a general co-ordinating role in relation to information needed for public health functions (Standing Committee A, February 7, 1995, col. 142). They will also be responsible for emergency planning, public consultation on the establishment of NHS Trusts, the implementation of information management and technology strategy, medical workforce planning, and GP vocational training (Standing Committee A, February 7, 1995, col. 142).

Membership of the regional offices of the NHSE will be determined by the NHSE, and not by regulation. The Government has indicated that each regional office will have a director of public health who will ensure that public health programmes such as breast cancer screening and immunisation programmes are properly co-ordinated. It argues that such directors will be more influential than before because they will be centrally involved with policy making (*Hansard*, H.L. Vol. 562, col. 16). The Opposition has pointed out that they will become civil servants, and has expressed concern regarding the consequent effect on their ability to criticise policy in public. The Government position is that the function of officers of the NHSE will be to advise

Ministers, and that they are therefore properly governed by the Armstrong code for relationships between civil servants and Ministers (Standing Committee A, February 14, 1995, col. 227).

The scheme of the Act
Section 1 of the Act abolishes the RHAs, and provides for new HAs combining the functions of the existing DHAs and FHSAs. Much of the substance of the Act is to be found in the Schedules. These introduce amendments to the existing legislation (see s.2, which introduces Sched. 1), and effect revocations (s.5, which brings in Sched. 3). Transitional provisions are made by s.3 (preparations for the reorganisation) and Sched. 2 (which is introduced by s.4). Changes of significance introduced by the Schedules are discussed in the General Notes to the sections that give effect to them.

Extent
The main provisions of the Act extend to England and Wales only (s.9(1)). It may be applied, by order, to the Isles of Scilly (s.9(3)). The consequential provisions of the Act, and the amendments and revocations made, have the same extent as the provisions they replace (s.9(2)).

Commencement
The changes introduced by the Act come into force on April 1, 1996 (ss.1(2), 2(3), 4(2), 5(2)). The powers to prepare for the change take effect from the date of Royal Assent, which was June 28, 1995 (ss.3, 8). The Secretary of State has the power to make transitional provisions, waiving the effect of any amendment or repeal made by the Act (Sched. 2, para. 20). These would have to be made by statutory instrument (s.6).

Abbreviations
DHA: District Health Authority
FHSA: Family Health Services Authority
HA: Health Authority
NHSE: National Health Service Executive
RHA: Regional Health Authority
1977 Act: National Health Service Act 1977
1990 Act: National Health Service and Community Care Act 1990

Abolition of RHAs, DHAs and FHSAs and duty to establish HAs

1.—(1) For sections 8 and 10 of the National Health Service Act 1977 (Secretary of State's duty to establish Regional Health Authorities, District Health Authorities and Family Health Services Authorities) substitute—

"Health Authorities
8.—(1) It is the duty of the Secretary of State by order to establish, in accordance with Part I of Schedule 5 to this Act, authorities to be called Health Authorities.

(2) Subject to subsection (4) below, a Health Authority shall act for such area of England or of Wales as is specified in the order establishing the authority.

(3) A Health Authority shall be known by such name, in addition to the title 'Health Authority', as—
(a) appears to the Secretary of State appropriately to signify the connection of the Health Authority with the area for which the authority are to act; and
(b) is specified in the order establishing the authority.

(4) The Secretary of State may by order—
(a) vary a Health Authority's area;
(b) abolish a Health Authority; or
(c) establish a new Health Authority.

(5) The Secretary of State shall act under this section so as to secure—
(a) that the areas for which Health Authorities are at any time acting together comprise the whole of England and Wales; but
(b) that no area for which a Health Authority act extends both into England and into Wales.

(6) The power to make incidental or supplemental provision conferred by section 126(4) below includes in particular, in its application to

orders made under this section, power to make provision for the transfer of staff, property, rights and liabilities."

(2) Subject to section 8, subsection (1) shall not come into force until 1st April 1996.

GENERAL NOTE

This section replaces two provisions from the 1977 Act. Section 8 of that Act provided for the creation of Regional and District Health Authorities. Section 10 established the power to set up Family Health Services Authorities. They are now replaced by the power to set up a single type of authority, to be known as a Health Authority. Such authorities are to be set up by order, and will be subject to the negative resolution procedure in Parliament (s.126 of the 1977 Act). There continues to be provision for the establishment of Special Health Authorities in s.11 of the 1977 Act.

Subs. (1) of the new s.8

A new Pt. I of Sched. 5 to the 1977 Act is introduced by Sched. 1, para. 59 to this Act. It provides that a HA shall consist of an equal number of executive and non-executive members, plus a chairman. The latter two categories of member are to be appointed by the Secretary of State. Regulations will provide for certain prescribed posts and designations. The Government has indicated that the prescribed executive posts will be the chief executive, director of finance, and director of public health (*Hansard*, H.C. Vol. 251, col. 641; Standing Committee A, February 9, 1995, col. 176). Non-executives will be selected for their "personal qualities" not "sectional interests" (*Hansard*, H.C. Vol. 251, col. 642). There will usually be five non-executives, but provision will be made for up to seven to be appointed where circumstances warrant it (Standing Committee A, February 7, 1995, col. 160). Where a Health Authority's area includes a university with a medical or dental school, there will be a prescribed non-executive position for someone holding a post in that university (Standing Committee A, February 9, 1995, col. 180). These provisions are similar to the current provisions.

Subs. (6) of the new s.8

Section 126 of the 1977 Act provides for the making of orders and regulations. Section 126(4) concerns the making of general provision for classes of HAs rather than specific directions to individual health authorities.

Related amendments

2.—(1) Schedule 1 shall have effect for making—
  (a) amendments consequential on, or otherwise connected with, the provision made by section 1(1), and
  (b) other amendments relating to Health Authorities and Special Health Authorities.

(2) The Secretary of State may by order make in any local Act such amendments as appear appropriate in consequence of, or otherwise in connection with, the provision made by section 1(1) or by subsection (1) (and Schedule 1).

(3) Subject to section 8, subsection (1) (and Schedule 1) shall not come into force until 1st April 1996.

GENERAL NOTE

Section 2 gives effect to Sched. 1. Most of the amendments introduced by Sched. 1 concern the changing of references to the now defunct DHAs and FHSAs to the new terminology, and the removing of references to RHAs. The substantive changes relating to the constitution of the new HAs (introduced by Sched. 1, para. 59) have been discussed in the General Note to s.1. Other significant changes are noted below.

Sched. 1, para. 3; new s.12 of the 1977 Act (see p. 17–9, below)

This new section ensures that Health Authorities make arrangements to secure advice from health professionals to enable them effectively to perform their functions. It differs from the provision it replaces (the old s.19(3) of the 1977 Act) in that the onus is on the Authority to take steps to secure advice, not merely for the Secretary of State to give recognition to representative committees of health professionals. Health Authorities must obtain such advice, but they have more control over its source than was previously the case. The Government has said that professionals will be able to tender unsolicited advice to Health Authorities. However it is unclear whether any legal force lies behind that expectation. Guidance has already been issued to explain how Health Authorities will be expected to secure professional advice; see *Ensuring the Effective Involvement of Professionals in Health Authority Work* HSG(95)11. It leaves Health Authorities with considerable discretion as to what steps they take. The recognition of local committees representing those who provide general medical, dental, ophthalmic and pharmaceutical services continues under s.44 of the 1977 Act, as amended by Sched. 1, para. 32 of this Act.

Sched. 1, para. 7; new s.16 of the 1977 Act (see p. 17–10, below)
The new section removes the saving of a general power to act through agents, which was contained in the old s.16(3). However, that power probably remains available under the general law of agency. Otherwise the new s.16 provides for similar powers for Health Authorities to authorise other authorities to perform statutory functions on their behalf. This enables consortia of Health Authorities to be set up to purchase specialist services, or for one lead Authority to do so on behalf of a group.

Sched. 1, para. 10; amendments to s.19 of the 1977 Act (see p. 17–11, below)
This repeals the provision for the recognition of professional advisory committees with respect to England, although it remains in force for Wales. Consequential amendments are made to Sched. 6 to the 1977 Act, which deals with local advisory committees, by para. 61 of Sched. 1. The Government argued that professional advice was already available for the new regional office through the NHSE, and that this reform would not mean that professional advice would be excluded. Professional advice to Health Authorities is to be given under the provisions of the new s.12 of the 1977 Act introduced by Sched. 1, para. 3 to the 1995 Act (see above).

Sched. 1, para. 61; amendments to Sched. 6 to the 1977 Act (see p. 17–19, below)
These amendments are consequential on the abolition of regional advisory committees (see the annotation to para. 10 of Sched. 1, above).

Sched. 1, para. 69; amendments to s.5 of the 1990 Act (see p. 17–20, below)
A new s.5(2) replaces s.5(2)–(4) of the 1990 Act. This has the effect of removing the rights of Community Health Councils to be consulted about the establishment of NHS Trusts. It was previously the responsibility of the RHAs to undertake such consultation. The new subsection provides for consultation to be prescribed by regulations rather than in the statute itself. The Government has indicated that Community Health Councils will continue to be one of the bodies that must be consulted when those regulations are made (*Hansard*, H.C. Vol. 251, col. 709).

Sched. 1, para. 73; amendments to s.14 of the 1990 Act (see p. 17–21, below)
The effect of these amendments is to make the decision to recognise new fund-holding general practices the responsibility of the Secretary of State rather than the RHAs. This will, in fact, be a task undertaken by the regional offices of the NHSE (Standing Committee A, February 7, 1995, col. 146).

Sched. 1, para. 74; amendments to s.15 of the 1990 Act (see p. 17–21, below)
These amendments make the determination of budgets for fund-holding general practices the responsibility of the Secretary of State and not the RHAs. However, this will in fact be done by the regional offices of the NHSE (Standing Committee A, February 7, 1995, col. 146).

Sched. 1, para. 75; amendments to s.16 of the 1990 Act (see p. 17–21, below)
The effect of these amendments is to make the decision to remove recognition, or withhold funds, from fund-holding general practices the responsibility of the Secretary of State instead of the RHAs. This will in fact be a task undertaken by the regional offices of the NHSE (Standing Committee A, February 7, 1995, col. 146).

Sched. 1, para. 91; amendments to Public Bodies (Admission to Meetings) Act 1960 (see p. 17–23, below)
These amendments ensure that Health Authority meetings will generally be held in public, although the provision whereby complaints hearings against general practitioners are held in private remains in effect.

Sched. 1, para. 95; amendments to the Health Services and Public Health Act 1968 (see p. 17–24, below)
This paragraph amends s.63 of the 1968 Act, which concerns professional training. The new subs. (5A) permits regulations to be made allowing Health Authorities and NHS Trusts to operate jointly to provide such training. Concerns were voiced in debate about the potential for fragmentation of training once the RHAs were abolished. The Government has indicated that

there will be national strategic bodies (*Hansard*, H.L. Vol. 562, cols. 1718–1719), and regional education and development groups, on which HAs, general practitioners, NHS Trusts and non-NHS providers will be represented (*Hansard*, H.L. Vol. 562, col. 71). Training contracts for junior doctors' education will probably be held by the postgraduate medical deans, but their employment contracts will be held by NHS Trusts (who will also be parties to the education contracts). See *Hansard*, H.C. Vol. 162, col. 573; H.L. Vol. 562, cols. 1520, 1603.

Sched. 1, para. 103; amendments to the Employment Protection (Consolidation) Act 1978 (see p. 17–26, below)

Under the current system, the employment contracts of some NHS staff are held by the RHAs because they are undertaking training programmes that require them to rotate amongst different NHS employers. Those contracts will now be held by the individual NHS Trusts, or other provider. Rotation would then normally constitute a break in employment and rob them of the protection that continuity of employment gives under the 1978 Act. The amendments made by this paragraph ensure that staff on such schemes will be deemed to have continuous service with the same employer. The staff involved are medical registrars and senior registrars, clinical psychology trainees, finance and general management trainees, and pharmacy and scientist training grades (*Hansard*, H.L. Vol. 563, col. 1500).

Sched. 1, para. 107; amendments to the Mental Health Act 1983 (see p. 17–26, below)

Some of the existing responsibilities of RHAs are transferred to HAs by these amendments. These are the provision of information to courts minded to make hospital orders (subpara. (5)) and the notification to social services of arrangements for emergency admissions (subpara. (12)). Subparagraph (6) provides that Mental Health Review Tribunals will continue to be organised on a regional basis. Up until now, Tribunals have been established for each of the NHS regions. As this Act abolishes such regions, it will be necessary for new regions to be defined purely for the purposes of the Mental Health Review Tribunals. The transitional provisions of Sched. 2, para. 15 provide that there is deemed to be an order providing that the regions are to be the same as those currently in place.

Sched. 1, para. 109; amendments to the Hospital Complaints Procedure Act 1985 (see p. 17–28, below)

The amendments introduced by this paragraph do not significantly alter the provisions of the 1985 Act. However, the Government has stated that it will be issuing directions to introduce a new scheme of NHS complaints procedures. It has indicated that this will take effect on April 1, 1996 (see *Acting on Complaints*, Department of Health, 1995 issued with EL(95)37). The terms of the 1985 Act remain directed at complaints about service provision, and do not provide a mechanism for complaining about purchasing decisions. The Government's document acknowledges this weakness, but does not contain concrete proposals for remedying it.

Preparations for reorganisation of authorities

3.—(1) The functions of Regional Health Authorities, District Health Authorities and Family Health Services Authorities shall include the power to do anything which appears appropriate for facilitating the implementation of any provision made by or by virtue of this Act.

(2) The Secretary of State may by regulations provide for functions exercisable by a Family Health Services Authority to be exercisable—

    (a) on their behalf—

        (i) by a District Health Authority or two or more District Health Authorities jointly, or

        (ii) by a joint DHA/FHSA committee, or

    (b) by them jointly with one or more District Health Authorities.

(3) The Secretary of State may by regulations provide for functions exercisable by a District Health Authority to be exercisable—

    (a) on their behalf—

        (i) by two or more Family Health Services Authorities jointly, or

        (ii) by a joint DHA/FHSA committee, or

    (b) by them jointly with one or more Family Health Services Authorities.

(4) Regulations made under this section in respect of any function shall not, except in prescribed cases, preclude an authority by whom the function is exercisable apart from the regulations from exercising the function.

(5) In this section—

    "District Health Authority" and "functions" have the same meanings as in the National Health Service Act 1977,

"joint DHA/FHSA committee" means a joint committee, or joint sub-committee, of—
  (a) one or more District Health Authorities, and
  (b) one or more Family Health Services Authorities, and
"prescribed" means prescribed by regulations made under this section.
  (6) The powers to make regulations conferred by this section are in addition to the power conferred by section 16 of the National Health Service Act 1977 (which, in particular, permits the making of regulations providing for functions exercisable by a District Health Authority to be exercisable on their behalf by a Family Health Services Authority).
  (7) Section 17 of the National Health Service Act 1977 (directions as to exercise of functions) applies in relation to functions exercisable under or by virtue of this section as if they were exercisable by virtue of section 16 of that Act; and the provisions of that Act relating to directions given in pursuance of section 17 apply accordingly.
  (8) In the National Health Service Act 1977, in section 18(3), the words following paragraph (b) (which would preclude functions of a Family Health Services Authority under section 15 of that Act from being exercisable by a District Health Authority) shall cease to have effect.
  (9) Section 125 of the National Health Service Act 1977 (protection of members and officers of authorities) applies as if this section were contained in that Act.
  (10) This section (apart from subsection (8)) shall cease to have effect on 1st April 1996.

GENERAL NOTE
  This section creates a power to make regulations enabling DHAs and FHSAs to act together, or to ask other Authorities to carry out functions on their behalf, even before their formal amalgamation on April 1, 1996. The Government has indicated that such regulations will be produced at an early stage (Standing Committee A, February 14, 1995, col. 212). The need for these regulations was presented as a means for arranging the smooth transition through collaborative preparatory work such as the transfer of staff, computer and management systems (Standing Committee A, February 14, 1995, cols. 211–212). It also has the effect of providing powers for those FHSAs and DHAs who have already combined their work for most practical purposes to do so legally.

Transitional provisions and savings

  4.—(1) Schedule 2 shall have effect for making, and conferring powers to make, transitional provisions and savings in connection with the provisions of this Act.
  (2) Subject to section 8, subsection (1) (and Schedule 2) shall not come into force until 1st April 1996.

GENERAL NOTE
  This section gives effect to Sched. 2, which contains transitional provisions. It includes the power to make further transitional provisions, including saving from the effect of any amendment or repeal made by the Act (see Sched. 2, para. 20).
  The property, rights and liabilities of RHAs are vested in the Secretary of State, who may then transfer them to Health Authorities and NHS Trusts by order. The property, rights and liabilities of DHAs and FHSAs will also be transferred by order. Such orders would usually be by statutory instrument, see s.6. These transfers of property will bind third party lessors even without consent (although compensation may be paid), and will not attract stamp duty (Sched. 2, para. 5).
  Provision is also made for the transfer of staff to the new Authorities, after consultation, by order of the Secretary of State. To ensure that staff transferring between authorities as a result of the restructuring are not disadvantaged, their contracts of employment are not terminated by the transfer and employees are entitled to terminate their contracts if their working conditions are significantly worse (Sched. 2, para. 9). These provisions are intended to mirror the effect of the Transfer of Undertakings (Protection of Employment) Regulations 1981 (S.I. 1981 No. 1794), which the Government has accepted will apply (Standing Committee A, February 14, 1995, cols. 219, 235–236). They are placed in the Act in order to ensure that those staff to whom

the TUPE regulations may not apply have similar protection. Those who remain NHS employees will retain their pension arrangements. However, those who join the NHSE regional offices will become civil servants and will not be able to continue to contribute to the NHS superannuation scheme.

Repeals and revocations

5.—(1) The enactments and instruments specified in Schedule 3 (which include spent provisions) are repealed or revoked to the extent specified in the third column of that Schedule.

(2) Except so far as relating to the repeal in section 18(3) of the National Health Service Act 1977, subsection (1) (and Schedule 3) shall not come into force until 1st April 1996.

GENERAL NOTE

Subsection (2) amends s.18(3) of the 1977 Act to remove the prohibition on the exercise by DHAs of the powers of FHSAs under s.15 of the 1977 Act. The repeal of this prohibition from the Royal Assent rather than April 1, 1996 enables the provisions of s.3 of this Act to have full effect.

Subordinate instruments

6.—(1) Subject to subsection (2), any power to make an order or regulations under this Act shall be exercisable by statutory instrument.

(2) Subsection (1)—

(a) does not apply to the power conferred by paragraph 2 of Schedule 2, and

(b) does not apply to the power conferred by paragraph 4 of that Schedule unless it is exercised in relation to property which consists of or includes trust property.

(3) A statutory instrument containing an order or regulations made under this Act, other than a statutory instrument containing only an order made under section 9(3), shall be subject to annulment in pursuance of a resolution of either House of Parliament.

(4) Where any provision of this Act confers power to make an order or a scheme, the provision includes power to vary or revoke any order or scheme previously made under the provision.

(5) Subsection (4) is without prejudice to the operation of section 14 of the Interpretation Act 1978 (implied power to amend regulations, orders made by statutory instrument etc.) in relation to this Act.

(6) Subsections (4) and (5) of section 126 of the National Health Service Act 1977 (supplementary provisions about orders etc. made under that Act) apply in relation to orders, regulations and schemes made under this Act as if the provisions of this Act were contained in that Act.

GENERAL NOTE

The majority of rule-making powers created by this Act concern transitional provisions. Three powers to make regulations will exist after the transitional period expires. These are the powers created by Sched. 1, paras. 69, 95, and 107. Those powers are discussed in the General Note to s.2.

Financial provisions

7.—(1) There shall be paid out of money provided by Parliament—

(a) any expenditure of the Secretary of State under this Act, and

(b) any increase attributable to this Act in the sums payable out of money so provided under any other Act.

(2) Any sums received by the Secretary of State by virtue of this Act shall be paid into the Consolidated Fund.

GENERAL NOTE
The Government expects considerable savings to result from the implementation of the Act.

Commencement of provisions conferring functions

8.—(1) Section 1(1), section 2(1) (and Schedule 1) and section 4(1) (and Schedule 2) shall come into force on the passing of this Act so far as is necessary for enabling the making of any regulations, orders, directions, schemes or appointments for which they provide.

(2) Subsection (1) is without prejudice to the operation of section 13 of the Interpretation Act 1978 (anticipatory exercise of powers) in relation to this Act.

Extent

9.—(1) Sections 1 and 3, and paragraphs 1 to 15 of Schedule 2, extend to England and Wales only.

(2) The amendment of any enactment made by section 2(1) (and Schedule 1), and the repeal or revocation of any enactment or instrument made by section 5(1) (and Schedule 3), has the same extent as the provision amended, repealed or revoked.

(3) The Secretary of State may by order provide that this Act shall apply in relation to the Isles of Scilly subject to such modifications as are specified in the order.

Short title

10. This Act may be cited as the Health Authorities Act 1995.

SCHEDULES

Section 2(1)   SCHEDULE 1

AMENDMENTS

PART I

AMENDMENTS OF THE NATIONAL HEALTH SERVICE ACT 1977

1. The National Health Service Act 1977 shall be amended as follows.
2. In section 11 (special health authorities)—
(a) in subsection (1), for "a District Health Authority or a Family Practitioner Committee" substitute "a Health Authority",
(b) in subsection (3), for "special health authority" substitute "Special Health Authority", and
(c) for the sidenote substitute "Special Health Authorities".
3. Section 12 (supplementary provisions about health authorities) shall be renumbered as subsection (2) of that section and—
(a) before that subsection as so renumbered insert—
"(1) Every Health Authority shall make arrangements for securing that they receive from—
(a) medical practitioners, registered nurses and registered midwives; and
(b) other persons with professional expertise in and experience of health care, advice appropriate for enabling the Health Authority effectively to exercise the functions conferred or imposed on them under or by virtue of this or any other Act.",
(b) in that subsection as so renumbered, for paragraphs (a) to (c) substitute—
"(a) Health Authorities established under section 8 above; and
(b) any Special Health Authority established under section 11 above.", and
(c) in the sidenote, for "to" substitute "and".
4. In section 13 (Secretary of State's directions)—

(a) in subsection (1)—
　　　　(i) for the words from "Regional" to "authority" substitute "Health Authority or Special Health Authority",
　　　　(ii) omit "(subject to section 14 below)", and
　　　　(iii) for "body in question" substitute "Health Authority or Special Health Authority", and
(b) in subsection (2), omit paragraph (b) and the word "but" immediately preceding it.
5. Omit section 14 (Regional Health Authority's directions).
6. In section 15 (duty of Family Health Services Authority)—
(a) in subsection (1)—
　　　　(i) for the words from "each" to "Regional Health Authority" substitute "each Health Authority, in accordance with regulations", and
　　　　(ii) for "locality" substitute "area",
(b) omit subsection (1A),
(c) in subsection (1B)—
　　　　(i) for "practices" substitute "practises",
　　　　(ii) for "Family Health Services Authority" substitute "Health Authority",
　　　　(iii) for "Authority", in each other place, substitute "Health Authority",
　　　　(iv) for "Authority's" substitute "Health Authority's",
　　　　(v) for "Authorities" substitute "Health Authorities", and
　　　　(vi) for "locality" (in both places) substitute "area",
(d) after that subsection insert—
　　　　"(1C) In relation to the operation of a fund-holding practice by medical practitioners the relevant Health Authority in respect of one or more of whom would (apart from this subsection) be different from that in respect of the other or others, the relevant Health Authority for each of them shall be determined for the purposes of the application of any provision relating to fund-holding practices as if they were all practising in a single partnership.", and
(e) for the sidenote substitute "Duty of Health Authority in relation to family health services."
7. For section 16 substitute—

"Exercise of functions
16.—(1) Regulations may provide for functions exercisable by a Health Authority under or by virtue of this Act or the National Health Service and Community Care Act 1990, or under or by virtue of any prescribed provision of any other Act, to be exercisable—
　(a) on behalf of the Health Authority—
　　　　(i) by another Health Authority;
　　　　(ii) by a committee or sub-committee, or an officer, of the Health Authority or another Health Authority;
　　　　(iii) by a joint committee, or joint sub-committee, of the Health Authority and one or more other Health Authorities;
　　　　(iv) by a Special Health Authority; or
　　　　(v) by an officer of a Special Health Authority; or
　(b) by the Health Authority jointly with one or more other Health Authorities.
(2) Regulations may provide for functions exercisable by a Special Health Authority by virtue of section 11 or 13 above to be exercisable—
　(a) on behalf of the Special Health Authority—
　　　　(i) by another Special Health Authority;
　　　　(ii) by a committee or sub-committee, or an officer, of the Special Health Authority or another Special Health Authority; or
　　　　(iii) by a joint committee, or joint sub-committee, of the Special Health Authority and one or more other Special Health Authorities; or
　(b) by the Special Health Authority jointly with one or more other Special Health Authorities."
8. For section 17 substitute—

"Directions as to exercise of functions
17.—(1) The Secretary of State may give directions with respect to the exercise—
　(a) by Health Authorities of any functions exercisable by them under or by virtue of this or any other Act; and
　(b) by Special Health Authorities of any functions exercisable by them by virtue of section 11 or 13 above or under the National Health Service and Community Care Act 1990.

(2) It shall be the duty of a Health Authority or Special Health Authority to whom directions are given under subsection (1) above to comply with the directions."

9. In section 18 (general provisions about directions)—

(a) in subsection (1), for "13 to 17" substitute "11 to 17",

(b) omit subsection (2),

(c) in subsection (3)—

(i) for "13" substitute "11", and

(ii) for "a body or" substitute "an authority or a", and

(d) for the sidenote substitute "Directions and regulations under ss.11 to 17".

10. In section 19 (local advisory committees)—

(a) in subsection (1), omit—

(i) ", or for the region of a Regional Health Authority,", and

(ii) "or of the region",

(b) in subsection (2), omit paragraph (b),

(c) omit subsection (3),

(d) in subsection (4), for "subsections (1) and (3)" substitute "subsection (1)", and

(e) in the sidenote and the heading immediately preceding that section, for "Local advisory committees" substitute "Advisory committees for Wales".

11. In section 20 (Community Health Councils)—

(a) in subsection (1), for the words from "section" to "those Authorities" substitute "section, in the case of the area of each Health Authority, a council for the area, or separate councils for such separate parts of the area", and

(b) in subsection (2)—

(i) in paragraph (a), for the words from "Area Health Authorities" to "District Health Authorities" substitute "Health Authorities", and

(ii) in paragraph (b), for "an Area Health Authority or of the district of a District Health Authority" substitute "a Health Authority".

12. In section 22 (co-operation between health authorities and local authorities)—

(a) in subsection (1), for "health authorities, Family Practitioner Committees and local authorities" substitute "Health Authorities and Special Health Authorities (on the one hand) and local authorities (on the other)",

(b) in subsection (2), after "who shall" insert "advise",

(c) omit the Table,

(d) for subsection (3) substitute—

"(3) Except as provided by an order under the following provisions of this section, each joint consultative committee shall represent one or more Health Authorities together with, in the case of each, one or more associated local authorities; and a Health Authority shall be represented together with each of the local authorities associated with that Health Authority in one or other of the committees (but not necessarily the same committee).

(3ZA) For the purposes of subsection (3) above a local authority is associated with a Health Authority if it is a local authority whose area is wholly or partly within the area of the Health Authority.", and

(e) in subsection (4)(b), for the words from "an Area" to the end substitute "a Health Authority to be represented on a joint consultative committee together with a local authority none of whose area is within the area of the Health Authority;".

13. In section 23 (voluntary organisations and other bodies), in subsection (2), for "health authority" substitute "Health Authority or Special Health Authority".

14. In section 26 (supply of goods and services by Secretary of State)—

(a) for "health authority" (in each place) substitute "Health Authority or Special Health Authority", and

(b) in subsection (4)(b), for "health authorities" substitute "Health Authorities or Special Health Authorities".

15. In section 27 (conditions of supply under section 26)—

(a) in subsection (1), for "health authority" (in both places) substitute "Health Authority or Special Health Authority", and

(b) in subsection (3)—

(i) for "health authorities" substitute "Health Authorities and Special Health Authorities", and

(ii) for "health authority's duty" substitute "duty of Health Authorities and Special Health Authorities".

16. In section 28 (supply of goods and services by local authorities)—

(a) in subsection (1), for "health authority" substitute "Health Authority and any Special Health Authority", and

(b) in subsection (3), for "health authorities" (in both places) substitute "Health Authorities, Special Health Authorities".

17. In section 28A (power to make payments towards expenditure on community services)—

(a) in subsection (1), for the words from "authorities" to "established" substitute "authorities—

    (a) a Health Authority; and

    (b) a Special Health Authority established", and

(b) in subsection (7)(a), for "districts" substitute "areas".

18. In section 29 (arrangements and regulations for general medical services)—

(a) in subsection (1)—

    (i) for "Family Practitioner Committee" substitute "Health Authority", and

    (ii) for "locality" (in both places) substitute "area",

(b) in subsection (2)—

    (i) in paragraph (e), for "locality" (in both places) substitute "area", and

    (ii) in paragraph (f), for "in the locality of a Family Practitioner Committee" substitute "in the area of a Health Authority", and

(c) in subsection (6)—

    (i) for "a locality" substitute "an area", and

    (ii) for "the locality" substitute "the area".

19. In section 30 (applications to provide general medical services)—

(a) in subsection (1)—

    (i) for "Family Practitioner Committee" substitute "Health Authority",

    (ii) for "that Committee of" substitute "the Health Authority of",

    (iii) for "Committee's locality" substitute "Health Authority's area",

    (iv) for "the Committee" substitute "the Health Authority", and

    (v) for "that Committee shall" substitute "the Committee shall", and

(b) in subsection (1A)—

    (i) for "Family Practitioner Committee" (in each place) substitute "Health Authority", and

    (ii) for "Committee's locality" substitute "Health Authority's area".

20. In section 31 (requirement of suitable experience), in subsection (1)(b)—

(a) for "Family Practitioner Committee" (in both places) substitute "Health Authority",

(b) for "Committee's locality" substitute "Health Authority's area", and

(c) for "their locality" substitute "their area".

21. In section 32 (regulations as to section 31), in subsection (3)(a), for "localities" substitute "areas".

22. In section 33 (distribution of general medical services)—

(a) in subsection (1), for "locality of the Family Practitioner Committee concerned or in the relevant part of that locality" substitute "area of the Health Authority concerned or in the relevant part of that area",

(b) in subsection (1A), for "Family Health Services Authorities for localities" (in both places) substitute "Health Authorities for areas",

(c) in subsection (2), for "locality or part of a locality" substitute "area or part of an area",

(d) in subsection (2A)—

    (i) for "locality of a Family Health Services Authority" substitute "area of a Health Authority", and

    (ii) for "the Authority" (in both places) substitute "the Health Authority",

(e) in subsection (3)—

    (i) for "Family Practitioner Committee" (in both places) substitute "Health Authority", and

    (ii) for "locality" substitute "area",

(f) in subsection (4)(b), for "Family Practitioner Committee's locality" substitute "Health Authority's area", and

(g) in subsection (8)—

    (i) for "Family Health Services Authority" substitute "Health Authority", and

    (ii) for "locality" substitute "area".

23. In section 34 (regulations for Medical Practices Committee)—

(a) the provisions preceding subsection (2) shall be renumbered as subsection (1) of that section, and

(b) in that subsection as so renumbered—

    (i) for "Family Practitioner Committees" (in both places) substitute "Health Authorities", and

    (ii) for "localities" (in both places) substitute "areas".

24. In section 35 (arrangements for general dental services), in subsection (1)—
(a) for "Family Practitioner Committee" substitute "Health Authority", and
(b) for "locality" (in both places) substitute "area".

25. In section 36 (regulations as to section 35)—
(a) in subsection (1)(d), for "locality" (in both places) substitute "area", and
(b) in subsection (2)—
  (i) for "Family Practitioner Committee" substitute "Health Authority",
  (ii) for "the Committee" substitute "the Health Authority", and
  (iii) for "Committee's locality" substitute "Health Authority's area".

26. In section 37 (Dental Practice Board), in subsection (1)(b), for "an Area or District Health Authority" substitute "a Health Authority".

27. In section 38 (arrangements for general ophthalmic services), in subsection (1)—
(a) for "Family Practitioner Committee" substitute "Health Authority", and
(b) for "locality" substitute "area".

28. In section 39 (regulations as to section 38), in paragraph (d), for "locality" (in both places) substitute "area".

29. In section 41 (arrangements for pharmaceutical services)—
(a) for "Family Practitioner Committee" substitute "Health Authority",
(b) for "locality" (in both places) substitute "area", and
(c) for "by a health authority or an NHS trust of dental services" substitute "of dental services by a Health Authority, a Special Health Authority or an NHS trust".

30. In section 42 (regulations as to pharmaceutical services)—
(a) in subsection (1)—
  (i) for "Family Practitioner Committee" substitute "Health Authority", and
  (ii) for "Committee's locality" substitute "Health Authority's area",
(b) in subsection (2)—
  (i) for "a Committee" (in both places) substitute "a Health Authority", and
  (ii) for "Committee's locality" substitute "Health Authority's area", and
  (iii) for "Committee is" substitute "Health Authority are", and
(c) in subsection (3)—
  (i) for "Committee" (in each place) substitute "Health Authority",
  (ii) for "Committee's locality." substitute "Health Authority's area;",
  (iii) for "Family Health Services Authority in whose locality" substitute "Health Authority in whose area", and
  (iv) for "that Family Health Services Authority may give its" substitute "that Health Authority may give their".

31. In section 43 (persons authorised to provide pharmaceutical services), in subsection (1), for "a Family Practitioner Committee" substitute "a Health Authority".

32. In section 44 (recognition of local representative committees)—
(a) in subsection (1)—
  (i) for "Family Health Services Authority is satisfied" substitute "Health Authority are satisfied",
  (ii) for "its locality" substitute "their area",
  (iii) for "locality", in each other place, substitute "area", and
  (iv) for "the Family Health Services Authority" substitute "the Health Authority", and
(b) in subsection (2), for "Family Health Services Authority" substitute "Health Authority".

33. In section 45 (functions of local representative committees)—
(a) for "Family Practitioner Committee" (in each place) substitute "Health Authority",
(b) in subsection (1), for "a locality" substitute "an area", and
(c) in subsection (2), for "locality" substitute "area".

34. In section 46 (disqualification of practitioners)—
(a) in subsections (1) and (2), for "a Family Practitioner Committee" substitute "a Health Authority",
(b) in subsection (2), for "other Family Practitioner Committee" substitute "other Health Authority", and
(c) in subsection (4), for "Family Practitioner Committee or Committees" substitute "Health Authority or Health Authorities".

35. Section 51 (university clinical teaching and research) shall be renumbered as subsection (1) of that section and—
(a) in that subsection as so renumbered, for "make available, in premises provided by him by virtue of this Act," substitute "exercise his functions under this Act and Part I of the National Health Service and Community Care Act 1990 so as to secure that there are made available", and

(b) after that subsection insert—

"(2) Regulations may provide for any functions exercisable by a Health Authority or Special Health Authority in relation to the provision of facilities such as are mentioned in subsection (1) above to be exercisable by the Health Authority or Special Health Authority jointly with one or more other relevant health service bodies.

(3) For the purposes of subsection (2) above the following are relevant health service bodies—

(a) Health Authorities;

(b) Special Health Authorities; and

(c) NHS trusts."

36. In section 54 (prohibition on sale of medical practices), for subsections (2) to (4) substitute—

"(2) Subsection (1) above does not render unlawful the sale by a medical practitioner of the whole or part of the goodwill of a medical practice (or part of a medical practice) if—

(a) his name has ceased to be entered on any list of medical practitioners undertaking to provide general medical services; and

(b) he has not at any time carried on the practice (or the part of the practice) anywhere which was, at a time when he provided services pursuant to arrangements with any Council, Committee or Authority, within the area, district or locality of the Council, Committee or Authority.

(3) Subsection (1) above does not render unlawful the sale of, or of any part of, the goodwill of a medical practice by a medical practitioner by reason only that the goodwill, or any part of the goodwill, to be sold is attributable to a practice previously carried on by a person whose name was entered on a list of medical practitioners undertaking to provide general medical services.

In this section "general medical services" includes the services so described provided pursuant to the provisions of the National Health Service Act 1946, the National Health Service Reorganisation Act 1973 or this Act by arrangement with any Council, Committee or Authority."

37. In section 56 (inadequate services)—

(a) for "the locality of a Family Practitioner Committee or part of the locality of such a Committee" substitute "the area, or part of the area, of a Health Authority",

(b) for the words from "in question" to "are not" substitute "in question in that area or part, or that for any other reason any considerable number of persons in any such area or part are not", and

(c) for "the Family Practitioner Committee" substitute "the Health Authority".

38. In section 65 (accommodation and services for private patients)—

(a) in subsection (1)—

(i) for "District or Special Health Authority" substitute "Health Authority or Special Health Authority",

(ii) for the words from "available, such charges" to "satisfied" substitute "available, such charges as the Health Authority or Special Health Authority may determine and may make and recover such charges as they may determine in respect of such accommodation and services and calculate those charges on any basis that they consider to be the appropriate commercial basis; but they shall do so only if and to the extent that they are satisfied", and

(iii) for "the Authority of any function conferred on the Authority under" substitute "the Health Authority or Special Health Authority of any function conferred on them under",

(b) in subsection (1A), for "District or Special Health Authority" substitute "Health Authority or Special Health Authority",

(c) in subsection (2), for "A District or Special Health Authority" substitute "A Health Authority or Special Health Authority", and

(d) in subsection (3)—

(i) for "District or Special Health Authority" substitute "Health Authority or Special Health Authority", and

(ii) for "an authority" substitute "a Health Authority or Special Health Authority".

39. In section 83 (sums payable to persons providing services), for—

(a) the words in paragraph (a) from "a Regional" to "Committee", and

(b) the words in paragraph (b) from "an Area" to "Committee",

substitute "a Health Authority or Special Health Authority".

40. In section 83A (remission and repayment of charges and payment of travelling expenses), in subsection (1)(c), for "District Health Authority" (in both places) substitute "Health Authority".

41. In section 85 (default powers), in subsection (1), for paragraphs (a) to (g) substitute—
  "(a) a Health Authority;
  (b) a Special Health Authority;
  (c) an NHS trust;
  (d) the Medical Practices Committee; or
  (e) the Dental Practice Board;".
42. In section 90 (gifts on trust), for "health authority" substitute "Health Authority or Special Health Authority".
43. In section 91 (private trusts for hospitals), in subsection (3)(b), for "District Health Authority" substitute "Health Authority".
44. In section 92 (further transfers of trust property)—
  (a) in subsection (1)—
        (i) for "health authority", in the first place, substitute "Health Authority or Special Health Authority", and
        (ii) for the words from "from any health authority" to the end substitute "from any relevant health service body to any other relevant health service body.",
  (b) after that subsection insert—
  "(1A) In this section "relevant health service body" means—
  (a) a Health Authority;
  (b) a Special Health Authority;
  (c) an NHS trust;
  (d) special trustees; or
  (e) trustees for an NHS trust.",
  (c) in subsection (2)—
        (i) for "one or more health authorities or NHS trusts" substitute "one or more bodies which are relevant health service bodies by virtue of subsection (1A)(a) to (c) above", and
        (ii) for the words from "health authority" to the end substitute "body or, in such proportions as may be specified in the order, to those bodies.",
  (d) in subsection (3), for "health authorities or NHS trusts and special trustees" substitute "special trustees and other bodies", and
  (e) in subsection (4), for "authorities or NHS trusts" substitute "bodies".
45. In section 96 (trusts: supplementary provisions), in subsection (1A), for "health authority" substitute "Health Authority or Special Health Authority".
46. In section 96A (power to raise money by appeals, collections etc.)—
  (a) in subsection (1), for—
        (i) "health authority", and
        (ii) "authority",
    substitute "Health Authority, Special Health Authority",
  (b) in subsections (3) and (4), for "health authority, NHS trust or Board" substitute "Health Authority, Special Health Authority or NHS trust",
  (c) in subsection (5), for "District Health Authority" substitute "Health Authority",
  (d) in subsection (6), omit the words from "to another" to "for an NHS trust",
  (e) in subsections (7) to (9), for—
        (i) "health authority, NHS trust or Board" (in each place), and
        (ii) "authority", NHS trust or Board" (in each place),
    substitute "Health Authority, Special Health Authority or NHS trust", and
  (f) in subsection (8), omit—
        (i) "or by a Regional Health Authority", and
        (ii) "or that Authority".
47. For section 97 substitute—

"Means of meeting expenditure of Health Authorities and Special Health Authorities out of public funds
97.—(1) It is the duty of the Secretary of State to pay to each Health Authority sums equal to expenditure of the Health Authority which—
  (a) is attributable to the payment of remuneration to persons providing services in pursuance of Part II of this Act; but
  (b) is not expenditure within subsection (2) below.
(2) It is also the duty of the Secretary of State to pay in respect of each financial year to each Health Authority sums not exceeding the amount allotted for that year by the Secretary of State to the Health Authority towards meeting the expenditure of the Health Authority which is attributable to the reimbursement of expenses of persons providing services in pursuance of Part II of this Act which are expenses—

(a) incurred in connection with the provision of the services (or in giving instruction in matters relating to the services); and

(b) of a description specified in the allotment.

(3) It is also the duty of the Secretary of State to pay in respect of each financial year to each Health Authority sums not exceeding the amount allotted for that year by the Secretary of State to the Health Authority towards meeting the expenditure of the Health Authority which—

(a) is attributable to the performance by the Health Authority of their functions in that year; but

(b) is not expenditure within subsection (1) or (2) above.

(4) It is the duty of the Secretary of State to pay in respect of each financial year to each Special Health Authority sums not exceeding the amount allotted for that year by the Secretary of State to the Special Health Authority towards meeting the expenditure of the Special Health Authority which is attributable to the performance by the Special Health Authority of their functions in that year.

(5) An amount is allotted to a Health Authority or Special Health Authority for a year under this section when they are notified by the Secretary of State that it is allotted to them for that year; and the Secretary of State may make an allotment under this section increasing or reducing an allotment previously so made.

(6) The Secretary of State may give directions to a Health Authority or Special Health Authority with respect to—

(a) the application of sums paid to them under subsections (1) to (3), or subsection (4), above;

(b) the payment of sums by them to the Secretary of State in respect of charges or other sums referable to the valuation or disposal of assets; or

(c) the application by them of sums received by them by virtue of section 15(7)(a) of the National Health Service and Community Care Act 1990.

(7) Where directions have been given to a Health Authority or Special Health Authority under subsection (6) above it is the duty of the Health Authority or Special Health Authority to comply with the directions.

(8) Where an order establishing a Special Health Authority provides for any expenditure of the Special Health Authority to be met by a Health Authority or by two or more Health Authorities in portions determined by or in accordance with the order, it is the duty of the Health Authority, or each of the Health Authorities, to pay to the Special Health Authority sums equal to, or to the appropriate portion of, that expenditure.

(9) Sums falling to be paid under this section shall be payable subject to compliance with such conditions as to records, certificates or otherwise as the Secretary of State may determine."

48. For section 97A substitute—

"Financial duties of Health Authorities and Special Health Authorities

97A.—(1) It is the duty of every Health Authority, in respect of each financial year, to perform their functions so as to secure that the expenditure of the Health Authority which is attributable to the performance by them of their functions in that year (not including expenditure within subsection (1) of section 97 above) does not exceed the aggregate of—

(a) the amounts allotted to them for that year under subsections (2) and (3) of that section;

(b) any sums received by them in that year under any provision of this Act (other than sums received by them under that section); and

(c) any sums received by them in that year otherwise than under this Act for the purpose of enabling them to defray any such expenditure.

(2) It is the duty of every Special Health Authority, in respect of each financial year, to perform their functions so as to secure that the expenditure of the Special Health Authority which is attributable to the performance by them of their functions in that year does not exceed the aggregate of—

(a) the amount allotted to them for that year under subsection (4) of section 97 above;

(b) any sums received by them in that year under any provision of this Act (other than sums received by them under that subsection); and

(c) any sums received by them in that year otherwise than under this Act for the purpose of enabling them to defray any such expenditure.

(3) The Secretary of State may give such directions to a Health Authority or Special Health Authority as appear to be requisite to secure that the Health Authority or Special Health Authority comply with the duty imposed on them by subsection (1) or (2) above.

(4) Directions under subsection (3) above may be specific in character.

(5) Where directions have been given to a Health Authority or Special Health Authority under subsection (3) above it is the duty of the Health Authority or Special Health Authority to comply with the directions.

(6) To the extent to which—

(a) any expenditure is defrayed by a Health Authority or Special Health Authority as trustee or on behalf of a Health Authority or Special Health Authority by special trustees; or

(b) any sums are received by a Health Authority or Special Health Authority as trustee or under section 96A above,

that expenditure and, subject to subsection (8) below, those sums shall be disregarded for the purposes of this section.

(7) For the purposes of this section sums which, in the hands of a Health Authority or Special Health Authority, cease to be trust funds and become applicable by the Health Authority or Special Health Authority otherwise than as trustee shall be treated, on their becoming so applicable, as having been received by the Health Authority or Special Health Authority otherwise than as trustee.

(8) Of the sums received by a Health Authority or Special Health Authority under section 96A above so much only as accrues to the Health Authority or Special Health Authority after defraying any expenses incurred in obtaining them shall be disregarded under subsection (6) above.

(9) Subject to subsection (6) above, the Secretary of State may by directions determine—

(a) whether sums of a description specified in the directions are, or are not, to be treated for the purposes of this section as received under this Act by a Health Authority or Special Health Authority of a description specified in the directions;

(b) whether expenditure of a description specified in the directions is, or is not, to be treated for those purposes as—

(i) expenditure within subsection (1) above of a Health Authority of a description so specified; or

(ii) expenditure within subsection (2) above of a Special Health Authority of a description so specified; or

(c) the extent to which, and the circumstances in which, sums received—

(i) by a Health Authority under subsections (1) to (3) of section 97 above; or

(ii) by a Special Health Authority under subsection (4) of that section,

but not yet spent are to be treated for the purposes of this section as part of the expenditure of the Health Authority or Special Health Authority and to which financial year's expenditure they are to be attributed."

49. Omit section 97B (financial duties of Family Health Services Authorities in Wales).

50. In section 98 (accounts and audit)—

(a) in subsection (1), for paragraphs (a) to (cc) substitute—

"(a) every Health Authority;

(b) every Special Health Authority;

(c) every NHS trust;",

(b) in subsection (2A)—

(i) for "District Health Authority" substitute "Health Authority",

(ii) for "Authority's district" substitute "Health Authority's area", and

(iii) for "Authority is the prescribed Authority" substitute "Health Authority is prescribed for the purposes of this subsection",

(c) in the subsection numbered (2B) which was inserted by section 20(2)(b) of the National Health Service and Community Care Act 1990—

(i) after "paid" insert "under section 15 of the National Health Service and Community Care Act 1990",

(ii) for "Family Health Services Authority" (in both places) substitute "Health Authority", and

(iii) for "the Authority" substitute "the Health Authority", and

(d) omit subsection (5).

51. In section 99 (regulation of financial arrangements), in subsection (1), for paragraphs (a) to (d) substitute—

"(a) Health Authorities,

(b) Special Health Authorities,".

52. In section 103 (special arrangement as to payment of remuneration), in subsection (3), for "Family Health Services Authority which, under Part II of this Act, has" substitute "Health Authority which, under Part II of this Act, have".

53. In section 104 (superannuation of officers of certain hospitals), in subsection (1)(a), for "Area or District Health Authorities" substitute "Health Authorities".

54. In section 105 (payments for certain medical examinations), in subsection (2)(b), for "health authority" substitute "Health Authority or Special Health Authority".

55. In section 124 (special notices of births and deaths)—

(a) in subsection (2)—
> (i) for the words from "prescribed" to "includes" substitute "Health Authority the area of which includes", and
> (ii) for "Authority's area or district as are entered (on and after 1st April 1974)" substitute "Health Authority's area as are entered",

(b) in subsection (4), for the words from "prescribed" to "district" substitute "Health Authority for the area",

(c) in subsection (5)—
> (i) for the words from "prescribed" to "office" substitute "Health Authority at their offices",
> (ii) for "that officer's office" substitute "the Health Authority's offices",
> (iii) for "an Area or District Health Authority" substitute "a Health Authority", and
> (iv) omit "or district",

(d) in subsection (6), for "Area or District Health Authority" substitute "Health Authority", and

(e) in subsection (7), for "medical officer" substitute "Health Authority".

56. In section 125 (protection of members and officers of authorities), for paragraphs (a) to (d) substitute—

"(a) a Health Authority,
(b) A Special Health Authority, and
(c) an NHS trust,".

57. In section 126 (regulations and directions: general provisions), for the second sentence of subsection (3) substitute—

"(3A) Directions given by the Secretary of State in pursuance of any provision of this Act or Part I of the National Health Service and Community Care Act 1990 shall be given by an instrument in writing.

(3B) In relation to directions given in pursuance of sections 11 to 17 above section 18 above applies in place of subsections (3) and (3A) above."

58. In section 128 (interpretation), in subsection (1)—

(a) omit the definitions of "District Health Authority" and "health authority", and

(b) after the definition of "functions" insert—
> " "fund-holding practice" shall be construed in accordance with section 14 of the National Health Service and Community Care Act 1990;".

59. In Schedule 5 (authorities), insert as Part I (and in substitution for the existing heading of the Schedule)—

"HEALTH AUTHORITIES AND SPECIAL HEALTH AUTHORITIES

PART I

MEMBERSHIP OF HEALTH AUTHORITIES

1. A Health Authority shall consist of—
(a) a chairman appointed by the Secretary of State;
(b) not more than a prescribed number of persons (not being officers of the Health Authority) appointed by the Secretary of State; and
(c) a prescribed number of officers of the Health Authority.

2. Regulations may provide that all or any of the persons appointed as members of a Health Authority under paragraph 1(b) above—
(a) must hold posts of a prescribed description; or
(b) must fulfil any other prescribed conditions.

3. Regulations shall provide that each of the persons who is a member of a Health Authority under paragraph 1(c) above must either—
(a) hold an office of the Health Authority of a prescribed description; or
(b) be appointed by the chairman of the Health Authority and the persons appointed as members of the Health Authority under paragraph 1(b) above.

4. Regulations may provide for a person of a prescribed description who is not an officer of a Health Authority to be treated for the purposes of this Part of this Schedule, and any

other prescribed provision relating to members of (or of committees or sub-committees of) Health Authorities, as if he were such an officer."

60. In Part III of that Schedule (supplementary provisions about authorities)—

(a) in paragraph 8, for the words from "Regional" to "Committee" substitute "Health Authority and each Special Health Authority",

(b) in paragraph 9—

(i) in sub-paragraph (1), omit "or a Regional Health Authority", and

(ii) in sub-paragraph (7), for the words from "means" to "which is specified" substitute "means—

(a) a Health Authority; or

(b) any Special Health Authority which is specified",

(c) in paragraph 10—

(i) in sub-paragraph (1)(b), after "employ" insert "a chief officer and officers of such other descriptions as may be prescribed and to employ", and

(ii) in sub-paragraph (3), omit paragraphs (b) and (d),

(d) in paragraph 11, omit—

(i) in sub-paragraph (2), "or, as the case may be, a Regional Health Authority's,", "or the Authority" (in both places), "or itself" and "or paragraph (d)", and

(ii) in sub-paragraph (3), "or Regional Health Authority" and "or paragraph (b)" and "or the Authority" (in both places),

(e) in paragraph 12(b), omit ", and the exercise of functions by,",

(f) in paragraph 12A, for the words from "or Schedule 1" to "those Schedules)" substitute "may make provision (including provision modifying this Schedule)", and

(g) omit paragraph 15(3).

61. In Schedule 6 (local advisory committees)—

(a) in paragraph 1(1), omit ", or for the region of a Regional Health Authority, or the area or district of an Area or District Health Authority,",

(b) in paragraph 2, omit "or (3)",

(c) omit paragraph 4,

(d) in paragraph 5—

(i) for "An Authority" substitute "The Secretary of State",

(ii) for "paragraphs 3 or 4" substitute "paragraph 3",

(iii) for "the Authority" substitute "the Secretary of State", and

(iv) omit the second sentence, and

(e) in the heading, for "Local Advisory Committees" substitute "Advisory Committees for Wales".

62. In Schedule 7 (Community Health Councils)—

(a) in paragraph 2—

(i) in paragraph (d), for the words from "Regional" to "Committees" substitute "Health Authorities and NHS trusts",

(ii) in paragraph (e), for the words from "Regional" to "Services Authorities" substitute "Health Authorities and NHS trusts" and for "such health authorities" substitute "Health Authorities",

(iii) in paragraph (f), for "such Authorities and Committees" substitute "Health Authorities", and

(iv) in paragraph (g), for "such Authorities or Committees" substitute "Health Authorities",

(b) in paragraph 3(d), for the words from "Regional" to the end substitute "Health Authority.",

(c) in paragraph 7, in the definition of "district", for the words from "the locality" to "District Health Authorities" substitute "the district for which it is established, whether the district consists of the whole or part of the area of a Health Authority or of the whole or part of the area of one Health Authority together with the whole or part of the area of one or more others,", and

(d) omit paragraph 8.

63. In Schedule 9 (tribunal for purposes of section 46), in paragraph 3, for "Family Practitioner Committees" (in both places) substitute "Health Authorities".

64. In Schedule 14 (transitional provisions and savings), in paragraph 13—

(a) in sub-paragraph (1)(b), for the words from "paragraphs" to "152" substitute "paragraphs 2, 7 to 9, 40, 68, 82, 109, 111, 123, 124(2) and (3), 125(2), 128, 130, 131(2), 132, 133, 151 and 152", and

(b) in sub-paragraph (2)—

(i) after "this Act" insert "or the Health Authorities Act 1995", and

(ii) for "131" substitute "131(2)".

AMENDMENTS OF THE NATIONAL HEALTH SERVICE AND COMMUNITY CARE ACT 1990

65. The National Health Service and Community Care Act 1990 shall be amended as follows.

66. In section 1 (regional and district health authorities), in subsection (3), for "Part III of Schedule 5 to the principal Act" substitute "In the National Health Service Act 1977 (in this Part of this Act referred to as "the principal Act"), Part III of Schedule 5".

67. In section 3 (primary and other functions of health authorities etc. and exercise of functions)—

(a) for subsection (1) substitute—

"(1) Any reference in this Act to the primary functions of a Health Authority or Special Health Authority is a reference to those functions for the time being exercisable by the Health Authority or Special Health Authority by virtue of—

(a) directions under section 11 or 13 of the principal Act;

(b) section 15 or Part II of the principal Act; or

(c) any provision of this Act (apart from subsection (2) below).",

(b) in subsection (2), for—

(i) "Regional, District or Special Health Authority or a Family Health Services Authority", and

(ii) "authority",

substitute "Health Authority or Special Health Authority",

(c) in subsection (5), for—

(i) "Regional, District or Special Health Authority", and

(ii) "authority",

substitute "Health Authority or Special Health Authority",

(d) in subsection (6)—

(i) in paragraph (a), for "Regional, District or Special Health Authority" substitute "Health Authority or Special Health Authority",

(ii) in paragraph (b), for "health authority" substitute "authority which is a Health Authority or Special Health Authority", and

(iii) in the words following that paragraph, for "the authority" substitute "the Health Authority or Special Health Authority" and for "other health authority" substitute "other authority", and

(e) in subsection (8), for—

(i) "Regional, District or Special Health Authority", and

(ii) "authority",

substitute "Health Authority or Special Health Authority".

68. In section 4 (NHS contracts), in subsection (2)—

(a) for paragraph (a) substitute—

"(a) a Health Authority;

(aa) a Special Health Authority;", and

(b) omit paragraph (d).

69. In section 5 (NHS trusts)—

(a) in subsection (1), for "Regional, District or Special Health Authorities" substitute "Health Authorities or Special Health Authorities",

(b) for subsections (2) to (4) substitute—

"(2) No order shall be made under subsection (1) above until after the completion of such consultation as may be prescribed.",

(c) in subsection (6), for "health authorities" substitute "Health Authorities or Special Health Authorities", and

(d) in subsection (7), the words from "and, without prejudice" onwards shall follow (rather than form part of) paragraph (f).

70. In section 6 (transfer of staff to NHS trusts)—

(a) for "health authority" (in each place) substitute "Health Authority or Special Health Authority", and

(b) in subsection (4)(a), for "health authority's rights, powers, duties and liabilities" substitute "rights, powers, duties and liabilities of the Health Authority or Special Health Authority".

71. In section 7 (supplementary provisions as to transfer of staff), in subsection (1)(b), for "health authority" substitute "Health Authority or Special Health Authority".

72. In section 8 (transfer of property, rights and liabilities to NHS trusts), for "health authority" (in each place) substitute "Health Authority or Special Health Authority".

73. In section 14 (recognition of fund-holding practices of doctors)—
(a) in subsections (1) and (2), for "relevant Regional Health Authority" substitute "Secretary of State",
(b) omit subsections (3) to (5), and
(c) in subsection (6), omit paragraph (d).
74. In section 15 (payments to recognised fund-holding practices)—
(a) for subsection (1) substitute—
"(1) In respect of each financial year, every Health Authority shall be liable to pay to the members of each recognised fund-holding practice in relation to which they are the relevant Health Authority a sum determined by the Secretary of State in such manner and by reference to such factors as the Secretary of State may direct (in this section referred to as an "allotted sum").",
(b) omit subsection (2),
(c) in subsection (3), omit "or subsection (2)",
(d) for subsection (4) substitute—
"(4) In any case where—
(a) a Health Authority make a payment of, or of any part of, an allotted sum to the members of a recognised fund-holding practice, and
(b) some of the individuals on the list of patients of any of the members of the practice reside in the area of another Health Authority, or in the area of a Health Board,
the Health Authority making the payment shall be entitled to recover from that other Health Authority, or from that Health Board, an amount equal to such portion of the payment as may be determined in accordance with directions given by the Secretary of State.",
(e) omit subsection (5),
(f) in subsection (7)—
(i) in paragraph (a), for "Regional Health Authority", and
(ii) in paragraph (c), for "District Health Authority",
substitute "Health Authority",
(g) omit subsection (8), and
(h) in subsection (9), for—
(i) "Family Health Services Authority", and
(ii) "Authority", in the other place,
substitute "Health Authority".
75. In section 16 (renunciation and removal of recognition as a fund-holding practice and withholding of funds)—
(a) in subsection (2), omit—
(i) "the relevant Regional Health Authority or, as the case may be,", and
(ii) "the Regional Health Authority or, as the case may be,",
(b) in subsection (3)(b), omit the words from the beginning to "Authority;",
(c) in subsection (4)—
(i) for "District Health Authorities" substitute "Health Authorities", and
(ii) omit "the Regional Health Authority or, as the case may be,",
(d) omit subsection (5),
(e) in subsection (6), for the words from "Regional" to the end substitute "Health Authority of an amount equal to that determined by the Secretary of State as having been so applied.", and
(f) omit subsection (7).
76. In section 17 (transfer of functions relating to recognised fund-holding practices)—
(a) in subsection (1)—
(i) omit "a Regional Health Authority or, in Wales,", and
(ii) for "Family Health Services Authority" substitute "Health Authority",
(b) in subsection (2), for "Family Health Services Authority" substitute "Health Authority", and
(c) after that subsection insert—
"(2A) Where regulations under this section provide for any function of the Secretary of State to become a function of a Health Authority, the regulations may make provision for and in connection with appeals against any decision made, or other thing done, in exercise of the function."
77. In section 18 (indicative amounts)—
(a) in subsection (1), for—
(i) "Family Health Services Authority" (in both places), and
(ii) "Authority",
substitute "Health Authority", and

(b) in subsections (4), (5) and (7), for "Family Health Services Authority" substitute "Health Authority".

78. In section 20 (extension of functions of Audit Commission to cover health service), in subsection (1)(a), for "health authorities" substitute "Health Authorities, Special Health Authorities".

79. In section 21 (schemes for meeting losses and liabilities etc. of certain health service bodies)—

(a) in subsection (2), for paragraph (a) substitute—

"(a) Health Authorities;"

(aa) Special Health Authorities;", and

(b) in subsections (3)(a), (4)(b) and (5), for "health authority" substitute "Health Authority, Special Health Authority".

80. In section 46 (local authority plans for community care services), in subsection (2)—

(a) in paragraph (a), for "District Health Authority the whole or any part of whose district" substitute "Health Authority the whole or any part of whose area", and

(b) omit paragraph (b).

81. In section 47 (assessment of needs for community care services), in subsection (3), for "District Health Authority" (in each place) substitute "Health Authority".

82. In section 49 (regulations for the transfer of staff from the health service to local authorities), in subsection (4)(b), for "Regional, District or Special Health Authority" substitute "Health Authority or Special Health Authority".

83. In section 60 (removal of Crown immunities), in subsection (7)—

(a) for paragraph (a) substitute—

"(a) a Health Authority established under section 8 of the National Health Service Act 1977;

(aa) a Special Health Authority established under section 11 of that Act;", and

(b) omit paragraph (d).

84. In section 62 (Clinical Standards Advisory Group), in subsection (7)—

(a) in the definition of "health service body"—

(i) for paragraph (i) substitute—

"(i) a Health Authority established under section 8 of the National Health Service Act 1977;

(ia) a Special Health Authority established under section 11 of that Act;",

(ii) at the end of paragraph (iv) insert "and", and

(iii) omit paragraph (vi) and the word "and" immediately preceding it, and

(b) in the definition of "services", for paragraph (a) substitute—

"(a) in England and Wales by virtue of—

(i) directions under section 13 of the National Health Service Act 1977;

(ii) Part II of that Act; or

(iii) section 5 of this Act; or".

85. In Schedule 2 (NHS trusts)—

(a) in paragraph 3(1)(f), for "health authority which is" substitute "Health Authority or Special Health Authority which are",

(b) in paragraph 4—

(i) in sub-paragraph (1), for "Regional, District or Special Health Authority" substitute "Health Authority or Special Health Authority", and

(ii) in sub-paragraph (2), for "Regional, District or Special Health Authority's functions" substitute "functions of the Health Authority or Special Health Authority",

(c) in paragraph 5(3), for "Regional, District or Special Health Authority" substitute "Health Authority or Special Health Authority",

(d) in paragraph 6(2)—

(i) in paragraph (e), for "health authorities" (in both places) substitute "Health Authorities or Special Health Authorities", and

(ii) at the end (but not as part of paragraph (f)) insert "and with any directions given to it under section 1(1A) of the Hospital Complaints Procedure Act 1985",

(e) in paragraph 13, for "Regional, District or Special Health Authority" substitute "Health Authority or Special Health Authority",

(f) in paragraph 19(1)—

(i) in paragraph (c), for "District Health Authority", and

(ii) for "Authority", in the other place,

substitute "Health Authority",

(g) in paragraph 30, in sub-paragraph (1), for paragraph (b) substitute—

"(b) a Health Authority, or

(bb) a Special Health Authority, or",

and, in sub-paragraph (2), for "health authority" substitute "Health Authority, Special Health Authority", and

(h) in paragraph 31, for "or health authority" substitute ", or such Health Authority or Special Health Authority,".

PART III

AMENDMENTS OF OTHER ENACTMENTS

The Polish Resettlement Act 1947

86. In section 4 of the Polish Resettlement Act 1947 (provision of health services), in subsection (1), for "Area Health Authorities District Health Authorities" substitute "Health Authorities".

The National Assistance Act 1948

87.—(1) The National Assistance Act 1948 shall be amended as follows.

(2) In section 26 (provision of accommodation in premises maintained by voluntary organisations), in subsection (1C), for "District Health Authority" substitute "Health Authority".

(3) In the sixth Schedule (transitional provisions), omit paragraphs 7 to 9.

The Reserve and Auxiliary Forces (Protection of Civil Interests) Act 1951

88. In the second Schedule to the Reserve and Auxiliary Forces (Protection of Civil Interests) Act 1951 (paying authorities), in Part I, for paragraph 15 substitute—

"15. Officer of a Health Authority, a Special Health Authority or any other body constituted under the National Health Service Act 1977 or the National Health Service and Community Care Act 1990	The Health Authority, Special Health Authority or other body.
15A. Officer of a Health Board, the Common Services Agency for the Scottish Health Service or any other body constituted under the National Health Service (Scotland) Act 1978	The Health Board, Agency or other body.",

and, in paragraph 16, for the entry in the second column substitute "The Health Authority or Health Board for the area for which the services are provided.".

The Landlord and Tenant Act 1954

89. In section 57 of the Landlord and Tenant Act 1954 (modification on grounds of public interest of rights under Part II of that Act), in subsection (6), for the words from "Regional" to "special health authority" substitute "Health Authority or Special Health Authority".

The Public Records Act 1958

90. In the first Schedule to the Public Records Act 1958 (definition of public records), in the Table at the end of paragraph 3, in Part I, in the second column, at the end of the entry relating to health service hospitals insert—

"records of trust property passing to a Health Authority or Special Health Authority by virtue of the Health Authorities Act 1995 or under section 92 of the National Health Service Act 1977 or held by a Health Authority under section 90 or 91 of that Act."

The Public Bodies (Admission to Meetings) Act 1960

91. In the Schedule to the Public Bodies (Admission to Meetings) Act 1960 (bodies to which that Act applies), for paragraph 1(f) and (g) substitute—

"(f) Health Authorities, except as regards the exercise of functions under the National Health Service (Service Committees and Tribunal) Regulations 1992 or any regulations amending or replacing those Regulations;

(g) if the order establishing a Special Health Authority so provides, the Special Health Authority;".

The Human Tissue Act 1961

92. In section 1 of the Human Tissue Act 1961 (removal of parts of bodies for medical purposes), in subsection (10)(a), for "has the meaning given by section 128(1) of the National Health Service Act 1977" substitute "means a Health Authority established under section 8 of the National Health Service Act 1977 or a Special Health Authority established under section 11 of that Act".

The Parliamentary Commissioner Act 1967

93. In Schedule 3 to the Parliamentary Commissioner Act 1967 (matters not subject to investigation), in paragraph 8—
(a) for the words from "Regional" to "special health authority" substitute "Health Authority, a Special Health Authority", and
(b) omit "a Family Practitioner Committee,".

The Leasehold Reform Act 1967

94. In section 28 of the Leasehold Reform Act 1967 (retention or resumption of land required for public purposes)—
(a) in subsection (5)(d), for the words from "Regional" to "special health authority" substitute "Health Authority, any Special Health Authority", and
(b) in subsection (6), in the second sentence, in paragraph (c), for the words from "Regional" to "special health authority" substitute "Health Authority, Special Health Authority".

The Health Services and Public Health Act 1968

95.—(1) The Health Services and Public Health Act 1968 shall be amended as follows.
(2) In section 63 (provision of instruction for officers of hospital authorities etc.)—
(a) in subsection (1)(a), for the words from "Regional" to "special health authority" substitute "Health Authority or Special Health Authority or a Health Board",
(b) in subsection (2)(b), for "a Family Practitioner Committee" substitute "a Health Authority",
(c) after subsection (5) insert—
    "(5A) The Secretary of State may by regulations provide for any functions exercisable by a Health Authority or Special Health Authority under or in relation to arrangements made under subsection (1) above to be exercisable by the Health Authority or Special Health Authority jointly with one or more other relevant health service bodies; and section 126 of the 1977 Act shall apply in relation to regulations made under this subsection as if this subsection were contained in that Act.
    (5B) For the purposes of subsection (5A) above the following are relevant health service bodies—
      (a) Health Authorities;
      (b) Special Health Authorities; and
      (c) NHS trusts.", and
(d) after subsection (8) insert—
    "(8A) Expressions used in both this section and the 1977 Act have the same meaning in this section as in that Act.".
(3) In section 64 (financial assistance to voluntary organisations), in subsection (3)(b), for "a Family Practitioner Committee is, by virtue of Part IV of the National Health Service Act 1946," substitute "a Health Authority are, by virtue of Part II of the National Health Service Act 1977,".

The Post Office Act 1969

96. In section 86 of the Post Office Act 1969 (interpretation of Part III of that Act), in subsection (1), in paragraph (a) of the definition of "national health service authority", for the words from "Regional" to the end substitute "Health Authority or a Special Health Authority;".

The Local Government Act 1972

97.—(1) The Local Government Act 1972 shall be amended as follows.
(2) In section 113 (placing of staff of local authorities at disposal of other authorities), in subsection (1A), for—

(a) "Regional Health Authority, Area Health Authority District Health Authority or special health authority",
(b) "Regional Area or District Health Authority or special health authority", and
(c) "Regional Area or District Health Authority or the special health authority",
substitute "Health Authority, Special Health Authority".

(3) In section 261 (remuneration of certain employees), in subsection (7), for the words from "the National" to "section 24" substitute "section 44 of the National Health Service Reorganisation Act 1973 and section 24".

The National Health Service Reorganisation Act 1973

98. The National Health Service Reorganisation Act 1973 shall cease to have effect.

The Health and Safety at Work etc. Act 1974

99. In section 60 of the Health and Safety at Work etc. Act 1974 (employment medical advisory service: supplementary), in subsection (1), for "Area Health Authority and each District Health Authority arranges for one of its officers who is" substitute "Health Authority arranges for".

The House of Commons Disqualification Act 1975

100. In Schedule 1 to the House of Commons Disqualification Act 1975 (offices disqualifying for membership of the House of Commons), in Part III, for the entry beginning "Chairman or any member, not being also an employee, of any Regional Health Authority" substitute—
"Chairman or any member, not being also an employee, of any Health Authority or Special Health Authority which is a relevant authority for the purposes of paragraph 9(1) of Schedule 5 to the National Health Service Act 1977.".

The Adoption Act 1976

101. In section 2 of the Adoption Act 1976 (local authorities' social services), for "health authorities" substitute "Health Authorities, Special Health Authorities,".

The National Health Service (Scotland) Act 1978

102.—(1) The National Health Service (Scotland) Act 1978 shall be amended as follows.
(2) In section 17A (NHS contracts), in subsection (2)—
(a) for paragraph (f) substitute—
"(f) Health Authorities established under section 8 of the National Health Service Act 1977;
(ff) Special Health Authorities established under section 11 of the National Health Service Act 1977;", and
(b) omit paragraph (i).
(3) In section 17B (reimbursement of Health Boards' costs), in subsection (1), for "District or Special Health Authority" substitute "Health Authority or Special Health Authority".
(4) In section 87A (recognition of fund-holding practices of doctors), in subsection (4)(g), for "Family Health Services Authority established under section 10" substitute "Health Authority established under section 8".
(5) In section 87B (payments to recognised fund-holding practices), in subsection (3)—
(a) in paragraph (b), for "region of a Regional Health Authority" substitute "area of a Health Authority", and
(b) for "the Authority" substitute "the Health Authority".
(6) In section 87D (indicative amounts for doctors' practices), in subsection (7), for "Family Health Services Authority established under section 10" substitute "Health Authority established under section 8".
(7) In Schedule 7A (NHS trusts)—
(a) in paragraph 6(2), at the end (but not as part of paragraph (f)) insert "and with any directions given to it under section 1(1A) of the Hospital Complaints Procedure Act 1985", and
(b) in paragraph 22(1)—
(i) in paragraph (c), for "District Health Authority within the meaning" substitute "Health Authority established under section 8", and
(ii) for "or Authority" substitute "or Health Authority".
(8) In Schedule 15 (transitional provisions and savings), in paragraph 10(b)—
(a) omit "94(b),", and
(b) for "135(a) to (c)" substitute "135(b) and (c)".

The Employment Protection (Consolidation) Act 1978

103.—(1) The Employment Protection (Consolidation) Act 1978 shall be amended as follows.

(2) In section 29 (time off for public duties)—

(a) in subsection (1)(d), for the words from "Regional" to "Committee" substitute "Health Authority or Special Health Authority", and

(b) in subsection (2)(b), for the words preceding " "Health Board" " substitute " "Health Authority" means a Health Authority established under section 8 of the National Health Service Act 1977 and "Special Health Authority" means a Special Health Authority established under section 11 of that Act, and".

(3) In Schedule 13 (computation of period of employment)—

(a) in paragraph 17(1) (provisions of Schedule to relate only to employment with the one employer unless any of paragraphs 17(2) to (5), 18 and 18A apply), for "and 18A" substitute "to 18B", and

(b) after paragraph 18A insert—

"18B.—(1) If a person employed in relevant employment by a health service employer is taken into relevant employment by another such employer, his period of employment at the time of the change of employer shall count as a period of employment with the second employer and the change shall not break the continuity of the period of employment.

(2) For the purposes of sub-paragraph (1) employment is relevant employment if it is employment of a description—

(a) in which persons are engaged while undergoing professional training which involves their being employed successively by a number of different health service employers, and

(b) which is specified in an order made by the Secretary of State.

(3) The following are health service employers for the purposes of this paragraph—

(a) Health Authorities established under section 8 of the National Health Service Act 1977,

(b) Special Health Authorities established under section 11 of that Act,

(c) National Health Service trusts established under Part I of the National Health Service and Community Care Act 1990,

(d) the Dental Practice Board, and

(e) the Public Health Laboratory Service Board.".

The Nurses, Midwives and Health Visitors Act 1979

104. In section 16 of the Nurses, Midwives and Health Visitors Act 1979 (local supervision of midwifery practice), in subsection (1), for paragraphs (a) and (b) substitute—
  "(a) in England and Wales, Health Authorities;".

The Overseas Development and Co-operation Act 1980

105. In Schedule 1 to the Overseas Development and Co-operation Act 1980 (statutory bodies with powers under section 2(1) of that Act), in Part II, after "A Health Authority" insert—
  "A Special Health Authority".

The Local Government Finance Act 1982

106. In section 12 of the Local Government Finance Act 1982 (accounts subject to audit by Audit Commission), in subsection (3B)—

(a) for "Family Health Services Authority" substitute "Health Authority", and

(b) for "Authority's" substitute "Health Authority's".

The Mental Health Act 1983

107.—(1) The Mental Health Act 1983 shall be amended as follows.

(2) In section 23 (discharge of patients)—

(a) in subsection (3), for the words from "Regional" to the end substitute ", Health Authority or Special Health Authority, by that National Health Service trust, Health Authority or Special Health Authority.", and

(b) in subsection (5)(a), for—
        (i) "a District or Special Health Authority", and
        (ii) "such an authority",
  substitute "a Health Authority or Special Health Authority".

(3) In section 24 (visiting and examination of patients), in subsection (3)—

(a) for "Regional Health Authority, District Health Authority National Health Service trust or special health authority" substitute "Health Authority, Special Health Authority or National Health Service trust", and

(b) for "authority or trust" substitute "Health Authority, Special Health Authority or National Health Service trust".

(4) In section 32 (regulations), in subsection (3), for "Regional Health Authorities, District Health Authorities National Health Service trusts or special health authorities" substitute "Health Authorities, Special Health Authorities or National Health Service trusts".

(5) In section 39 (information as to hospitals)—

(a) in subsection (1)—

(i) for "Regional Health Authority" (in both places) substitute "Health Authority",

(ii) for "the region" substitute "the area",

(iii) for "that Authority has" substitute "that Health Authority have",

(iv) for "its region" substitute "their area", and

(v) for "that Authority shall" substitute "that Health Authority shall", and

(b) omit subsection (2).

(6) In section 65 (Mental Health Review Tribunals), for subsection (1) substitute—

"(1) There shall be tribunals, known as Mental Health Review Tribunals, for the purpose of dealing with applications and references by and in respect of patients under the provisions of this Act.

(1A) There shall be—

(a) one tribunal for each region of England, and

(b) one tribunal for Wales.

(1B) The Secretary of State—

(a) shall by order determine regions for the purpose of subsection (1A)(a) above; and

(b) may by order vary a region determined for that purpose;

and the Secretary of State shall act under this subsection so as to secure that the regions together comprise the whole of England.

(1C) Any order made under subsection (1B) above may make such transitional, consequential, incidental or supplemental provision as the Secretary of State considers appropriate.".

(7) In section 79 (interpretation of Part V), after subsection (6) insert—

"(7) In this Part of this Act any reference to the area of a tribunal is—

(a) in relation to a tribunal for a region of England, a reference to that region; and

(b) in relation to the tribunal for Wales, a reference to Wales.".

(8) In section 117 (after-care)—

(a) in subsection (2), for "District Health Authority" (in both places) substitute "Health Authority", and

(b) in subsection (3), for the words from "section" to "for the area" substitute "section 'the Health Authority' means the Health Authority, and 'the local social services authority' means the local social services authority, for the area".

(9) In section 121 (Mental Health Act Commission)—

(a) in subsection (1), for "special health authority" substitute "Special Health Authority", and

(b) in subsection (11), for "health authorities" substitute "Special Health Authorities".

(10) In section 134 (correspondence of patients), in subsection (3)(e), for "health authority within the meaning of the National Health Service Act 1977" substitute "Health Authority or Special Health Authority".

(11) In section 139 (protection for acts done in pursuance of that Act), in subsection (4), for "health authority within the meaning of the National Health Service Act 1977" substitute "Health Authority or Special Health Authority".

(12) In section 140 (notification of hospitals having arrangements for reception of urgent cases)—

(a) for "Regional Health Authority and in Wales every District Health Authority" substitute "Health Authority",

(b) for "region or district, as the case may be, of the Authority" substitute "Health Authority's area", and

(c) for "to the Authority" substitute "to the Health Authority".

(13) In section 143 (regulations, orders and rules), in subsection (2), after "54A" insert "or 65".

(14) In section 145 (interpretation), in subsection (1)—

(a) after the definition of "approved social worker" insert—

" "Health Authority" means a Health Authority established under section 8 of the
National Health Service Act 1977;",
(b) in paragraph (a) of the definition of "the managers", for "District Health Authority or
special health authority" substitute "Health Authority or Special Health Authority", and
(c) after the definition of "restriction order" insert—
" "Special Health Authority" means a Special Health Authority established under section 11 of the National Health Service Act 1977;".

The Public Health (Control of Disease) Act 1984

108.—(1) The Public Health (Control of Disease) Act 1984 shall be amended as follows.
(2) In section 1 (authorities administering that Act), in subsection (4), for paragraph (b)
substitute—
"(b) Health Authorities or Special Health Authorities,".
(3) In section 11 (cases of notifiable disease and food poisoning to be reported), in subsection
(3)—
(a) in paragraph (a), for "District Health Authority within whose district" substitute "Health
Authority within whose area", and
(b) in paragraph (b)(ii)—
(i) for "District Health Authority for the district" substitute "Health Authority for
the area", and
(ii) for "that Authority is" substitute "that Health Authority are".
(4) In section 12 (fees for certificates under section 11), in subsection (1), for "District Health
Authority" substitute "Health Authority".
(5) In section 13 (regulations for control of certain diseases), in subsection (4)(a), for the
words from "Regional Health Authorities" to "special health authorities" substitute "Health
Authorities, Special Health Authorities or National Health Service trusts".
(6) In section 37 (removal to hospital of person with notifiable disease), in subsection (1)—
(a) in paragraph (c), for "District Health Authority" substitute "Health Authority", and
(b) in the words following that paragraph, for "District Health Authority in whose district"
substitute "Health Authority in whose area".
(7) In section 39 (keeper of common lodging-house to notify case of infectious disease), in
subsection (3), for "Area Health Authority within whose area, or the District Health Authority
within whose district," substitute "Health Authority within whose area".
(8) In section 41 (removal to hospital of inmate of common lodging-house with notifiable
disease), in subsection (1)—
(a) in paragraph (c), for "District Health Authority" substitute "Health Authority", and
(b) in the words following that paragraph, for "District Health Authority in whose district"
substitute "Health Authority in whose area".

The Hospital Complaints Procedure Act 1985

109.—(1) The Hospital Complaints Procedure Act 1985 shall be amended as follows.
(2) In section 1 (hospital complaints procedure)—
(a) in subsection (1)—
(i) for "health authority" substitute "Health Authority and Special Health Authority", and
(ii) for "authority or Board is" substitute "Health Authority, Special Health Authority or Board are", and
(b) after that subsection insert—
"(1A) It shall also be the duty of the Secretary of State to give to each NHS trust
which is responsible for the management of a hospital such directions as appear necessary for the purpose of securing that, as respects each hospital for the management of
which that NHS trust is responsible—
(a) such arrangements are made for dealing with complaints made by or on behalf
of persons who are or have been patients at that hospital; and
(b) such steps are taken for publicising the arrangements so made,
as (in each case) are specified or described in the directions.".
(3) Omit section 1A (NHS trust hospitals).

The Health Service Joint Consultative Committees (Access to Information) Act 1986

110. In section 1 of the Health Service Joint Consultative Committees (Access to Information) Act 1986 (interpretation), in subsection (2), for "District Health Authority, Family
Practitioner Committee" substitute "Health Authority".

The Disabled Persons (Services, Consultation and Representation) Act 1986

111.—(1) The Disabled Persons (Services, Consultation and Representation) Act 1986 shall be amended as follows.

(2) In section 2 (rights of authorised representatives of disabled persons), in subsection (9), in the definition of "health authority", for "has the meaning given by section 128(1) of the 1977 Act" substitute "means a Health Authority or a Special Health Authority".

(3) In section 7 (persons discharged from hospital)—

(a) in subsection (1)(a), omit "district or", and

(b) in subsection (9)—

(i) in the definition of "health authority", for "District Health Authority" substitute "Health Authority", and

(ii) in the definition of "the managers", after "(other than a special hospital" and after "(other than a State hospital" insert "or a hospital vested in a National Health Service trust" and for "District Health Authority or special health authority" substitute "Health Authority or Special Health Authority".

(4) In section 16 (interpretation), in subsection (1)—

(a) after the definition of "guardian" insert—

" "Health Authority" means a Health Authority established under section 8 of the 1977 Act;", and

(b) after the definition of "services" insert—

" "Special Health Authority" means a Special Health Authority established under section 11 of the 1977 Act;".

The Education (No. 2) Act 1986

112. In section 7 of the Education (No. 2) Act 1986 (appointment of representative governors in place of co-opted governors), in subsection (2)(a), for "District Health Authority" substitute "Health Authority".

The AIDS (Control) Act 1987

113.—(1) The AIDS (Control) Act 1987 shall be amended as follows.

(2) In section 1 (periodical reports on matters relating to AIDS and HIV)—

(a) in subsection (1)—

(i) omit paragraph (a), and

(ii) in paragraph (b), for sub-paragraphs (i) and (ii) substitute—

"(i) each Health Authority in England and Wales;",

(b) for subsections (2) and (3) substitute—

"(2) Any report under this section—

(a) shall contain the information specified in the Schedule to this Act and such other relevant information as the Secretary of State may direct; and

(b) shall be published by the Health Authority, Health Board or NHS trust by which it is made.",

(c) in subsection (5)—

(i) for "special health authority" substitute "Special Health Authority", and

(ii) for "that authority" substitute "that Special Health Authority", and

(d) in subsection (9), for the words from " "Regional" to "1977" substitute " "Health Authority" means a Health Authority established under section 8 of the National Health Service Act 1977 and "Special Health Authority" means a Special Health Authority established under section 11 of that Act".

(3) In the Schedule (contents of reports), in paragraphs 4 and 7, omit "district or".

The Income and Corporation Taxes Act 1988

114. In section 519A of the Income and Corporation Taxes Act 1988 (health service bodies), in subsection (2)—

(a) for paragraph (a) substitute—

"(a) a Health Authority established under section 8 of the National Health Service Act 1977;

(aa) a Special Health Authority established under section 11 of that Act;", and

(b) omit paragraph (c).

The Dartford-Thurrock Crossing Act 1988

115. In section 19 of the Dartford-Thurrock Crossing Act 1988 (exemption from tolls), in paragraph (b), for "health authority (as defined in the National Health Service Act 1977)" substitute "Health Authority established under section 8 of the National Health Service Act 1977 or a Special Health Authority established under section 11 of that Act".

The Community Health Councils (Access to Information) Act 1988

116. In section 1 of the Community Health Councils (Access to Information) Act 1988 (access to Council meetings and documents), in subsection (6)(a), for the words from "regional" to "region or district" substitute "Health Authority within whose area".

The Road Traffic Act 1988

117. In section 159 of the Road Traffic Act 1988 (payments for treatment)—
(a) in subsection (1)(a), for—
 (i) "Area Health Authority, District Health Authority or special health authority", and
 (ii) "such authority",
 substitute "Health Authority or Special Health Authority", and
(b) in subsection (3), for "Authority (in Scotland, Board)" substitute "Health Authority or Special Health Authority (or, in Scotland, Health Board)".

The Children Act 1989

118.—(1) The Children Act 1989 shall be amended as follows.
(2) In section 19 (review of provision for day care, child minding etc.), in subsection (7)(a), for "health authority" substitute "Health Authority, Special Health Authority".
(3) In section 21 (provision of accommodation for children in police protection or detention or on remand etc.), in subsection (3), for "District Health Authority" substitute "Health Authority".
(4) In section 24 (advice and assistance for certain children), in—
(a) subsection (2)(d), and
(b) subsection (12)(b),
for "health authority" substitute "Health Authority, Special Health Authority".
(5) In section 27 (co-operation between authorities), in subsection (3)(d), for "health authority" substitute "Health Authority, Special Health Authority".
(6) In section 29 (recoupment of cost of providing services etc.), in subsection (8)(c), for "District Health Authority" substitute "Health Authority".
(7) In section 47 (local authority's duty to investigate), in subsection (11)(d), for "health authority" substitute "Health Authority, Special Health Authority".
(8) In section 80 (inspection of children's homes by persons authorised by Secretary of State)—
(a) in subsection (1)(d), for "health authority" substitute "Health Authority, Special Health Authority", and
(b) in subsection (5)(e), for "health authority" substitute "Health Authority, Special Health Authority,".
(9) In section 85 (children accommodated by health authorities and local education authorities), in subsection (1), for "health authority" substitute "Health Authority, Special Health Authority,".
(10) In section 105 (interpretation), in subsection (1)—
(a) omit the definition of "district health authority",
(b) for the definition of "health authority" substitute—
 " "Health Authority" means a Health Authority established under section 8 of the National Health Service Act 1977;", and
(c) for the definition of "special health authority" substitute—
 " "Special Health Authority" means a Special Health Authority established under section 11 of the National Health Service Act 1977;".

The Access to Health Records Act 1990

119.—(1) The Access to Health Records Act 1990 shall be amended as follows.
(2) In section 1 (definitions), in subsection (2), for "Family Practitioner Committee" substitute "Health Authority".
(3) In section 7 (duty of health service bodies etc. to take advice)—
(a) in subsection (1), omit "or Family Practitioner Committee",
(b) in subsection (2), after "(other than a" insert "Health Authority or", and
(c) in subsection (3)—
 (i) for "Family Practitioner Committee or a" substitute "Health Authority or", and
 (ii) for "Committee or Board" substitute "Health Authority or Health Board".
(4) In section 11 (interpretation)—
(a) after the definition of "general practitioner" insert—

" "Health Authority" means a Health Authority established under section 8 of the National Health Service Act 1977;",
(b) in the definition of "health service body", for paragraph (a) substitute—
"(a) a Health Authority or Special Health Authority;", and
(c) after the definition of "parental responsibility" insert—
"Special Health Authority" means a Special Health Authority established under section 11 of the National Health Service Act 1977.".

The Water Industry Act 1991

120.—(1) The Water Industry Act 1991 shall be amended as follows.
(2) In section 87 (fluoridation of water supplies at request of health authorities)—
(a) in subsection (1), for "District Health Authority" substitute "Health Authority",
(b) in subsection (3), for "district of the authority" substitute "area of the Health Authority",
(c) in subsection (5), for "District Health Authority" substitute "Health Authority", and
(d) in subsection (9), for the words from "District" to the end substitute "Health Authority are references to any Health Authority established under section 8 of the National Health Service Act 1977.".
(3) In section 89 (publicity and consultation)—
(a) for "District Health Authority" (in each place), and
(b) in subsection (7), for "authority",
substitute "Health Authority".
(4) In Schedule 7 (pre-1985 fluoridation schemes)—
(a) in paragraph 2(2), for "Regional or District Health Authority" substitute "Health Authority", and
(b) in paragraph 3(1)—
(i) for "District Health Authority" substitute "Health Authority", and
(ii) for "such an authority" substitute "a Health Authority".

The Health and Personal Social Services (Northern Ireland) Order 1991

121.—(1) The Health and Personal Social Services (Northern Ireland) Order 1991 shall be amended as follows.
(2) In Article 8 (HSS contracts), in paragraph (2)(g), for paragraphs (i) and (ii) substitute—
"(i) Health Authorities;
(ii) Special Health Authorities;".
(3) In Article 9 (primary and other functions of boards)—
(a) in paragraph (2)—
(i) for "a health authority" substitute "a Health Authority or Special Health Authority", and
(ii) for "health authority", in the other place, substitute "Health Authority, Special Health Authority", and
(b) in paragraph (5)(c), for "health authority" substitute "Health Authority or Special Health Authority".
(4) In Schedule 3 (HSS trusts), in paragraph 19(1)—
(a) for "a health authority" substitute "a Health Authority or Special Health Authority", and
(b) for "health authority", in the other place, substitute "Health Authority, Special Health Authority".

The Trade Union and Labour Relations (Consolidation) Act 1992

122. In section 279 of the Trade Union and Labour Relations (Consolidation) Act 1992 (health service practitioners), in paragraph (a), for "Family Health Services Authority" substitute "Health Authority".

The Tribunals and Inquiries Act 1992

123. In Schedule 1 to the Tribunals and Inquiries Act 1992 (tribunals under general supervision of Council on Tribunals), in Part I, for paragraph 33 substitute—

"National Health Service	33. (a) Health Authorities established under section 8 of the National Health Service Act 1977 (c. 49) in respect of their functions under the National Health Service (Service Committees and Tribunal) Regulations 1992 or any regulations amending or replacing those Regulations;

      (b) the tribunal constituted under section 46 of that Act;

      (c) committees of Health Authorities established under regulation 3 of those Regulations or any provision amending or replacing that regulation."

The Education Act 1993

124.—(1) The Education Act 1993 shall be amended as follows.

(2) In section 166 (duty of District Health Authority or local authority to help local education authority), for "District Health Authority" (in each place, including the sidenote) substitute "Health Authority".

(3) In section 176 (duty of District Health Authority or NHS trust to notify parent etc.)—

    (a) in subsection (1) and in the sidenote, for "District Health Authority", and

    (b) in subsections (2) and (3), for "health authority" (in each place),

substitute "Health Authority".

The Welsh Language Act 1993

125. In section 6 of the Welsh Language Act 1993 (meaning of "public body"), in subsection (1)—

    (a) for paragraph (f) substitute—

      "(f) a Health Authority established under section 8 of the National Health Service Act 1977 or a Special Health Authority established under section 11 of that Act;", and

    (b) omit paragraph (h).

The Health Service Commissioners Act 1993

126.—(1) The Health Service Commissioners Act 1993 shall be amended as follows.

(2) In section 2 (health service bodies subject to investigation)—

    (a) in subsection (1), for paragraphs (a) and (b) substitute—

      "(a) Health Authorities whose areas are in England,",

    and omit paragraph (e), and

    (b) in subsection (2), for paragraph (a) substitute—

      "(a) Health Authorities whose areas are in Wales,",

    in paragraph (b), after "Wales," insert "and" and omit paragraph (d) and the word "and" immediately preceding it.

(3) In section 6 (restrictions on certain investigations), in subsection (3), for "Family Health Services Authority" substitute "Health Authority".

(4) In section 14 (reports by Commissioners), in subsection (1)—

    (a) in paragraph (d), after "of," insert "and", and

    (b) for paragraphs (e) and (f) substitute—

      "(e) to the Secretary of State.".

The Value Added Tax Act 1994

127. In Schedule 8 to the Value Added Tax Act 1994 (zero-rating), in Part II, in Group 15, in Note (4)(a), for "Regional, District or Special Health Authority" substitute "Health Authority or Special Health Authority".

GENERAL NOTE

The effect of the provisions of this Schedule is discussed in the General Note to s.2 above.

Section 4(1)   SCHEDULE 2

TRANSITIONAL PROVISIONS AND SAVINGS

Property, rights and liabilities of RHAs, DHAs, FHSAs and SHAs

1.—(1) On 1st April 1996—

    (a) all property held by a Regional Health Authority immediately before that date, and

    (b) all rights and liabilities to which a Regional Health Authority are entitled or subject immediately before that date,

shall by virtue of this sub-paragraph be transferred to and vest in the Secretary of State.

(2) Sub-paragraph (1) has effect in relation to any rights and liabilities which immediately before 1st April 1996 are (by or by virtue of any enactment) enforceable by or against a Regional Health Authority so that on and after that date they are enforceable by or against the Secretary of State.

(3) Sub-paragraph (1) does not apply to—

(a) property, rights or liabilities transferred to an NHS trust on 1st April 1996,

(b) property, rights or liabilities transferred by virtue of paragraph 3 of this Schedule or section 92 of the National Health Service Act 1977 (transfers of trust property and rights and liabilities arising from trust property) on that date, or

(c) rights or liabilities which are transferred by paragraph 9 of this Schedule (or would be so transferred but for sub-paragraph (5) or (8) of that paragraph) or to which paragraph 14 of this Schedule applies.

2.—(1) The Secretary of State may, where it appears appropriate to do so, by order transfer to a specified Health Authority or Special Health Authority any specified property, rights or liabilities which have been transferred by paragraph 1(1).

(2) An order may be made under sub-paragraph (1) to have effect in relation to any specified rights or liabilities such as are mentioned in paragraph 1(2) so that they are enforceable by or against (or only by or against) a specified Health Authority or Special Health Authority.

(3) An order made under sub-paragraph (1) may take effect immediately after paragraph 1 takes effect or on a later specified date.

(4) An order made under sub-paragraph (1) may, in particular, specify any Special Health Authority administering a scheme under section 21 of the National Health Service and Community Care Act 1990 (schemes for meeting liabilities of health service bodies).

(5) An order made under sub-paragraph (1) may create or impose such new rights or liabilities in respect of what is transferred, or what is retained by the Secretary of State, as appear appropriate.

(6) In the case of any transfer made by an order under sub-paragraph (1), a certificate issued by the Secretary of State that—

(a) any property described in the certificate,

(b) any interest in or right over property so described, or

(c) any right or liability so described,

is vested in the specified Health Authority or Special Health Authority shall be conclusive evidence of that fact for all purposes.

(7) Sub-paragraph (1) does not affect any power of the Secretary of State to transfer any property, rights or liabilities to a Health Authority or Special Health Authority otherwise than under this paragraph.

3.—(1) The Secretary of State may by order transfer on 1st April 1996 to a specified health service body any specified property held on trust by a Regional Health Authority immediately before that date.

(2) In sub-paragraph (1) "health service body" means—

(a) a Health Authority,

(b) a Special Health Authority,

(c) an NHS trust,

(d) special trustees, or

(e) trustees for an NHS trust.

(3) Sub-paragraph (1) does not apply to property transferred by virtue of section 92 of the National Health Service Act 1977 on 1st April 1996.

(4) The Secretary of State shall exercise the power conferred by sub-paragraph (1) so as to secure that all property to which that sub-paragraph applies is dealt with in exercise of the power.

(5) In this paragraph references to property include references to any rights and liabilities arising from the property.

4.—(1) The Secretary of State may by order transfer on 1st April 1996 to a specified Health Authority—

(a) any specified property held by a District Health Authority or a Family Health Services Authority immediately before that date, or

(b) any specified rights or liabilities to which a District Health Authority or a Family Health Services Authority are entitled or subject immediately before that date.

(2) An order may be made under sub-paragraph (1) to have effect in relation to any specified rights or liabilities which immediately before 1st April 1996 are (by or by virtue of any enactment) enforceable by or against a District Health Authority or a Family Health Services Authority so that on and after that date they are enforceable by or against (or only by or against) a specified Health Authority.

(3) Sub-paragraph (1) does not apply to—

(a) property, rights or liabilities transferred to an NHS trust on 1st April 1996,

(b) property transferred by virtue of section 92 of the National Health Service Act 1977 on that date, or

(c) rights or liabilities which are transferred by paragraph 9 of this Schedule (or would be so transferred but for sub-paragraph (5) or (8) of that paragraph) or to which paragraph 14 of this Schedule applies.

(4) The Secretary of State shall exercise the power conferred by sub-paragraph (1) so as to secure that all property to which that sub-paragraph applies is, and all rights and liabilities to which that sub-paragraph applies are, dealt with in exercise of the power.

(5) In this paragraph references to property include trust property; and, for the purposes of this paragraph, rights and liabilities arising from trust property shall be treated as being part of the property (so that references in this paragraph to rights and liabilities do not include rights and liabilities arising from trust property).

5.—(1) Where an order made under paragraph 2, 3 or 4 transfers—

(a) land held on lease from a third party, or

(b) any other asset leased or hired from a third party or in which a third party has an interest,

the transfer shall be binding on the third party even if, apart from this sub-paragraph, it would have required his consent or concurrence; and the order may contain such provisions as appear appropriate to safeguard the interests of the third party, including (where appropriate) provision for the payment of compensation of an amount to be determined in accordance with the order.

(2) Stamp duty is not chargeable in respect of any transfer effected by or by virtue of any of paragraphs 1 to 4.

(3) The references in sections 93(1), 94(1) and (3) and 96A(10) of the National Health Service Act 1977 (provisions about trust property) to section 92 of that Act include references to paragraphs 3 and 4 of this Schedule; and the reference in section 93(2) of that Act to Part IV of that Act includes a reference to those paragraphs.

6. Nothing in this Act prevents any rights or liabilities which immediately before 1st April 1996 are (by or by virtue of any enactment repealed by this Act) enforceable by or against a Special Health Authority from continuing on and after that date to be enforceable by or against the Special Health Authority.

Staff of RHAs, DHAs and FHSAs

7.—(1) The Secretary of State may—

(a) by order made in relation to any specified description of relevant health authority employees specify the health service body to which they are to be transferred on 1st April 1996, and

(b) by scheme made in relation to relevant health authority employees designated by the scheme (either individually or as members of a class) designate the health service body to which they are to be transferred on 1st April 1996.

(2) In this paragraph and paragraphs 8 to 10 references to relevant health authority employees are to persons who immediately before 1st April 1996 are employees of—

(a) a Regional Health Authority,

(b) a District Health Authority, or

(c) a Family Health Services Authority,

other than persons to whom sub-paragraph (3) applies.

(3) This sub-paragraph applies to persons to whom section 6 of the National Health Service and Community Care Act 1990 (transfers of staff to an NHS trust) applies if the operational date of the trust in question (or, in the case of employees within subsection (5) of that section, the date on which they take up employment) is 1st April 1996.

(4) In this paragraph and paragraphs 8 to 11 references to a health service body are to—

(a) the Secretary of State,

(b) a Health Authority,

(c) a Special Health Authority, or

(d) an NHS trust.

(5) The Secretary of State shall exercise the power conferred by this paragraph so as to secure that all relevant health authority employees are dealt with in exercise of the power.

(6) A scheme may be made under this paragraph only if sub-paragraph (7) is satisfied in relation to each of the employees to be designated by the scheme.

(7) This sub-paragraph is satisfied in relation to an employee if—

(a) the employee, or such body as the Secretary of State may recognise as representing the employee, has been consulted about the scheme by the Secretary of State, or

(b) the Secretary of State is satisfied that the employee, or such body as the authority from which the employee would be transferred by the scheme may recognise as representing the employee, has been consulted about the scheme by that authority.

8.—(1) This paragraph applies where, at any time during the period beginning with 1st April 1996 and ending with 30th September 1996, it appears to the Secretary of State appropriate for any relevant health authority employees to be transferred from the health service body to which they were transferred on 1st April 1996 to another health service body.

(2) The Secretary of State may at any time during that period make, in relation to any of the employees who (in the opinion of the Secretary of State) ought to be transferred and are designated by the scheme (either individually or as members of a class), a scheme designating the body to which they are to be transferred on a date during that period designated by the scheme.

(3) A scheme may be made under this paragraph only if sub-paragraph (4) is satisfied in relation to each of the employees to be designated by the scheme.

(4) This sub-paragraph is satisfied in relation to an employee if—

(a) the employee, or such body as the Secretary of State may recognise as representing the employee, has been consulted about the scheme by the Secretary of State, or

(b) the Secretary of State is satisfied that the employee, or such body as the body from which the employee would be transferred by the scheme may recognise as representing the employee, has been consulted about the scheme by that body.

9.—(1) The abolition on 1st April 1996 of the authority by which a relevant health authority employee was employed immediately before that date does not operate to terminate his contract of employment.

(2) Subject to sub-paragraph (3), the contract of employment of a relevant health authority employee shall have effect on and after that date as if originally made between the employee and the health service body to which he is transferred on that date.

(3) Where a scheme is made in relation to a relevant health authority employee under paragraph 8 his contract of employment shall have effect on and after the date designated by the scheme as if originally made between the employee and the health service body to which he is transferred on that date.

(4) Without prejudice to sub-paragraphs (2) and (3)—

(a) all the rights, powers, duties and liabilities of the authority or body from which an employee is transferred in accordance with an order or scheme made under paragraph 7 or 8 under or in connection with his contract of employment shall by virtue of this sub-paragraph be transferred to the body to which the employee is transferred in accordance with the order or scheme, and

(b) anything done before the date of the transfer by or in relation to the authority or body from which he is so transferred in respect of the employee or the contract of employment shall be deemed from that date to have been done by or in relation to the body to which he is so transferred.

(5) Sub-paragraphs (2) and (4) do not transfer an employee's contract of employment, or the rights, powers, duties and liabilities under or in connection with it, if he informs the authority or body from which they would be transferred, or the body to which they would be transferred, that he objects to the transfer.

(6) Where an employee objects as mentioned in sub-paragraph (5) his contract of employment with the authority or body from which he would be transferred shall be terminated immediately before the date on which the transfer would occur; but he shall not be treated, for any purpose, as having been dismissed by that authority or body.

(7) This paragraph is without prejudice to any right of a relevant health authority employee to terminate his contract of employment if a substantial change is made to his detriment in his working conditions; but no such right shall arise by reason only that, under this paragraph, the identity of his employer changes unless the employee shows that, in all the circumstances, the change is a significant change and is to his detriment.

(8) This paragraph does not apply—

(a) to so much of a contract of employment as relates to an occupational pension scheme (within the meaning of section 1 of the Pension Schemes Act 1993), or

(b) to any rights, powers, duties or liabilities under or in connection with a contract of employment, or otherwise arising in connection with a person's employment, and relating to such a scheme,

other than any provisions of the scheme which do not relate to benefits for old age, invalidity or survivors.

10.—(1) A scheme made under paragraph 7 or 8 may provide that the contract of employment of a relevant health authority employee designated by the scheme shall, on 1st April 1996 (in the case of a scheme made under paragraph 7) or the date designated by the scheme (in the case of a scheme made under paragraph 8), be divided so as to constitute two separate contracts of employment with two health service bodies designated by the scheme.

(2) Where a scheme makes such provision it shall provide for paragraph 9 to have effect in the case of the employee and his contract of employment subject to appropriate modifications.

11. Where as a result of the operation of paragraph 9 an employee has both—

(a) a contractual right against any health service body to benefits in the event of his redundancy, and

(b) a statutory right against the body to a redundancy payment,
any benefits provided to him by virtue of the contractual right shall be taken as satisfying the statutory right.

Early retirements on reorganisation under 1973 Act

12. The repeal by this Act of the National Health Service Reorganisation Act 1973 does not prevent the continuing operation on and after 1st April 1996 of section 44 of that Act (provision for early retirement in lieu of compensation for loss of office) or regulations made under that section (or of any other provision relating to that section or such regulations).

Accounts and winding up of affairs of RHAs, DHAs and FHSAs

13.—(1) The Secretary of State—
(a) shall keep, or prepare, any accounts which (but for this Act) would have been required by section 98 of the National Health Service Act 1977 (accounts and audit) to be kept, or prepared and transmitted, by a Regional Health Authority, and
(b) may do any other thing which appears appropriate in connection with the winding up of the affairs of a Regional Health Authority.
(2) The Secretary of State—
(a) shall by order provide that any accounts which (but for this Act) would have been required by that section to be kept, or prepared and transmitted, by a District Health Authority or Family Health Services Authority shall be kept, or prepared and transmitted, by a specified Health Authority, and
(b) may by order provide that any other thing which appears appropriate in connection with the winding up of the affairs of a specified District Health Authority or Family Health Services Authority shall be done by a specified Health Authority.
(3) An order made under sub-paragraph (2) may provide that the Health Authority keeping, or preparing and transmitting, accounts or doing any other thing shall be assisted by any other specified Health Authority.
(4) The provisions of subsection (1) of section 98 of the National Health Service Act 1977 relating to audit and examination shall apply in relation to accounts kept under or by virtue of this paragraph and related records and reports.
(5) Subsection (2B)(c) of that section shall apply, in relation to accounts of the members of a fund-holding practice in respect of the financial year ending with 31st March 1996, as if the reference to the relevant Health Authority were a reference to the Health Authority specified by virtue of sub-paragraph (2)(a) of this paragraph in relation to the Family Health Services Authority which was the relevant Family Health Services Authority in relation to the members in that financial year.
(6) Subsection (4) of that section shall apply in relation to accounts relating to Regional Health Authorities, District Health Authorities and Family Health Services Authorities in respect of the financial year ending with 31st March 1996.

Trustees etc.

14.—(1) The Secretary of State may by order provide that a power to make any appointment (including an appointment of a trustee) which, immediately before 1st April 1996, is exercisable by—
(a) a Regional Health Authority,
(b) a District Health Authority, or
(c) a Family Health Services Authority,
shall be exercisable on and after that date by a specified Health Authority or Special Health Authority.
(2) The Secretary of State may by order provide that any qualification for holding any office (including office as a trustee) which, immediately before 1st April 1996, consists of being a member or officer of—
(a) a Regional Health Authority,
(b) a District Health Authority, or
(c) a Family Health Services Authority,
shall, on and after that date, consist of being a member or officer of a specified Health Authority or Special Health Authority.
(3) An order under this paragraph may include provision for the appointment of a person holding any office to which it relates immediately before 1st April 1996 to continue, or not to continue, on and after that date.

Mental Health Review Tribunals

15.—(1) On 1st April 1996 the Secretary of State shall be deemed to have determined by an order made under subsection (1B)(a) of section 65 of the Mental Health Act 1983 (Mental Health Review Tribunals) as regions for the purposes of subsection (1A)(a) of that section each of the regions for which, immediately before that date, a Regional Health Authority is established in pursuance of the National Health Service Act 1977.

(2) Each Mental Health Review Tribunal in existence immediately before that date shall, subject to the provisions of that section and of Schedule 2 to that Act (provisions about Tribunals), continue on and after that date to be the Tribunal for the area for which it was the Tribunal immediately before that date.

Complaints and appeals

16.—(1) Nothing in this Act—
(a) prevents a complaint or appeal made (but not disposed of) before 1st April 1996 from being continued on and after that date, or
(b) prevents the exercise of any right to make a complaint or appeal which has arisen (but not been exercised) before that date at any time on or after that date when it would have been exercisable but for this Act.

(2) The Secretary of State may by order make such provision as appears appropriate in relation to complaints and appeals which may be continued, or any right which may be exercised, by virtue of sub-paragraph (1).

(3) Sub-paragraph (1) applies in particular—
(a) to complaints to the Health Service Commissioner for England or (except in relation to a Regional Health Authority) the Health Service Commissioner for Wales, and
(b) (except in relation to a Family Health Services Authority) to complaints in relation to which section 1 of the Hospital Complaints Procedure Act 1985 (directions as to hospital complaints procedure) applies.

Arrangements about certain hospital premises etc.

17. The Secretary of State may by order make provision for and in connection with continuing in effect on and after 1st April 1996 any arrangements under paragraph 7 or 8 of the sixth Schedule to the National Assistance Act 1948 (transitional provisions) which are in force immediately before that date.

Continuity

18.—(1) The abolition by this Act of Regional Health Authorities, District Health Authorities and Family Health Services Authorities on 1st April 1996 does not affect the validity of anything done by any of those authorities before that date.

(2) The Secretary of State may by order provide—
(a) for anything which immediately before 1st April 1996 is in the process of being done by or in relation to a Regional Health Authority, District Health Authority or Family Health Services Authority (or a particular such Authority) to be continued, and
(b) for anything done by or in relation to such an authority (or a particular such authority) before 1st April 1996 to be treated on and after that date as if done,
by or in relation to the Secretary of State or by or in relation to a Health Authority or Special Health Authority (or a specified such Authority).

(3) Sub-paragraph (2)(b) applies in particular to—
(a) allotments, applications, appointments, arrangements, determinations, records and representations made,
(b) approvals, directions and notices given,
(c) conditions and disqualifications imposed,
(d) consultations undertaken,
(e) contracts (including NHS contracts) entered into,
(f) information recorded,
(g) facilities, goods, materials and services made available, provided or supplied,
(h) payments made,
(i) proceedings (including appeals) begun, and
(j) recognitions granted or removed.

Instruments and other documents

19.—(1) The Secretary of State may by order provide that any instrument (including an instrument made under any enactment) made by or in relation to a Regional Health Authority, District Health Authority or Family Health Services Authority shall continue in force on and after 1st April 1996.

(2) The Secretary of State may by order—

(a) provide that any reference in any instrument (including any instrument made under an enactment) or any other document to a Regional Health Authority, District Health Authority or Family Health Services Authority (or a particular such Authority) shall be construed on and after 1st April 1996 as being, or as including, a reference to the Secretary of State or to a Health Authority or Special Health Authority (or a specified such Authority), and

(b) make any other provision amending or otherwise modifying any such instrument or other document which appears appropriate in consequence of, or otherwise in connection with, any provision of this Act.

General

20.—(1) The Secretary of State may by order make any transitional provision which appears appropriate in connection with any provision of this Act.

(2) Nothing in any other provision of this Act prejudices the generality of the power conferred by sub-paragraph (1).

(3) An order made under sub-paragraph (1) may, in particular, include any saving from the effect of any amendment or repeal made by this Act.

21. Nothing in any provision made by or by virtue of this Schedule prejudices the operation of sections 16 and 17 of the Interpretation Act 1978 (effect of repeals).

Interpretation

22.—(1) In this Schedule "specified" means specified in an order made under this Schedule.

(2) Expressions used in both this Schedule and the National Health Service Act 1977 have the same meaning in this Schedule as in that Act.

GENERAL NOTE

This schedule is discussed in the General Note to s.4, above.

Section 5(1)　　　　　　　　　SCHEDULE 3

REPEALS AND REVOCATIONS

Reference	Short title or title	Extent of repeal or revocation
11 & 12 Geo. 6 c. 29.	The National Assistance Act 1948.	In the sixth Schedule, paragraphs 7 to 9.
14 & 15 Geo. 6 c. 65.	The Reserve and Auxiliary Forces (Protection of Civil Interests) Act 1951.	In section 61, the proviso to subsection (5).
1967 c. 13.	The Parliamentary Commissioner Act 1967.	In Schedule 3, in paragraph 8, the words "a Family Practitioner Committee,".
1971 c. 40.	The Fire Precautions Act 1971.	Section 40(10A).
1973 c. 32.	The National Health Service Reorganisation Act 1973.	The whole Act.
1974 c. 37.	The Health and Safety at Work etc. Act 1974.	Section 78(8)(d).
1976 c. 71.	The Supplementary Benefits Act 1976.	In Schedule 6, in Part II, in paragraph 4, the words "the National Assistance Act 1948". In Schedule 7, paragraph 6(b).
1977 c. 49.	The National Health Service Act 1977.	In section 13, in subsection (1), the words "(subject to section 14 below)" and, in subsection (2), paragraph (b) and the word "but" immediately preceding it. Section 14. Section 15(1A). In section 18, subsection (2) and, in subsection (3), the words following paragraph (b).

Reference	Short title or title	Extent of repeal or revocation
		In section 19, in subsection (1), the words ", or for the region of a Regional Health Authority," and "or of the region" and subsections (2)(b) and (3).
		In section 22, the Table.
		In section 93(2), the words ", or Part II of that Act of 1973".
		In section 96A, subsection (2), in subsection (6), the words from "to another" to "for an NHS trust" and, in subsection (8), the words "or by a Regional Health Authority" and "or that Authority".
		Section 97B.
		Section 98(5).
		In section 124(5), the words "or district".
		Section 126(1)(a).
		In section 128(1), the definitions of "District Health Authority" and "health authority" and, in the definition of "local authority", the words "and includes the King Edward VII Welsh National Memorial Association;".
		In Schedule 5, in Part III, in paragraph 9(1), the words "or a Regional Health Authority", paragraph 10(3)(b) and (d), in paragraph 11, in sub-paragraph (2), the words "or, as the case may be, a Regional Health Authority's", "or the Authority" (in both places), "or itself" and "or paragraph (d)" and, in sub-paragraph (3), the words "or Regional Health Authority", "or paragraph (b)" and "or the Authority" (in both places), in paragraph 12(b), the words ", and the exercise of functions by," and paragraph 15(3).
		In Schedule 6, in paragraph 1(1), the words ", or for the region of a Regional Health Authority, or the area or district of an Area or District Health Authority,", in paragraph 2, the words "or (3)", paragraph 4 and, in paragraph 5, the second sentence.
		In Schedule 7, paragraph 8.
		In Schedule 14, paragraph 16.
		In Schedule 15, in paragraph 12, paragraph (a) and, in paragraph (b), the words from "and" to the end and paragraphs 58 and 59.
1978 c. 29.	The National Health Service (Scotland) Act 1978.	Section 17(A)(2)(i).
		In Schedule 15, in paragraph 10(b), the words "94(b),".
		In Schedule 16, paragraphs 3(3) and 8.
1978 c. 30.	The Interpretation Act 1978.	In Schedule 2, in Part I, in paragraph 4(6), the words "the National Health Service Reorganisation Act 1973 and".
1980 c. 30.	The Social Security Act 1980.	In Schedule 4, paragraph 2(3).
1980 c. 53.	The Health Services Act 1980.	Section 1(1) to (6) and (8) to (10).
		Section 6(1) and (2).
		In Schedule 1, in Part I, paragraphs 4, 6, 9 to 11, 14, 16, 18, 19(1), (3) and (4), 20, 22, 23, 24, 26, 28, 31 to 34, 36, 38 to 41, 43(b), 50,

Reference	Short title or title	Extent of repeal or revocation
		62 to 65, 67, 69(a), 70, 71, 75, 76, 77(a), 78(1), 80, 81, 82(1) and (4) and 84 to 86.
1982 c. 32.	The Local Government Finance Act 1982.	Section 28A.
1983 c. 20.	The Mental Health Act 1983.	Section 39(2). In Schedule 4, paragraph 47(f). In Schedule 5, paragraph 46.
1983 c. 41.	The Health and Social Services and Social Security Adjudications Act 1983.	In Schedule 5, paragraph 3(a). In Schedule 6, paragraph 4. In Schedule 9, in Part I, paragraphs 7 and 28.
1984 c. 22.	The Public Health (Control of Disease) Act 1984.	In Schedule 2, paragraph 7.
1984 c. 24.	The Dentists Act 1984.	In Schedule 5, paragraph 11.
1984 c. 48.	The Health and Social Security Act 1984.	Section 5(1), (3), (5) and (6). Section 6(1). In Schedule 3, paragraphs 2, 3(a), (c) and (d), 6(b), 7, 9 to 11, 13, 14, 16 and 17.
1985 c. 42.	The Hospital Complaints Procedure Act 1985.	Section 1A.
S.I. 1985/39.	The Family Practitioner Committees (Consequential Modifications) Order 1985.	Articles 2, 3, 5, 6, 7(2), (3)(b) and (c), (6), (7)(b), (10), (12), (13)(b), (14) to (21) and (22)(a), 8 and 9.
1986 c. 33.	The Disabled Persons (Services, Consultation and Representation) Act 1986.	In section 7(1)(a), the words "district or".
1987 c. 33.	The AIDS (Control) Act 1987.	Section 1(1)(a). In the Schedule, in paragraphs 4 and 7, the words "district or".
1988 c. 1.	The Income and Corporation Taxes Act 1988.	Section 519A(2)(c).
1988 c. 24.	The Community Health Councils (Access to Information) Act 1988.	Section 1(7).
1988 c. 49.	The Health and Medicines Act 1988.	Section 16(1) and (2).
1989 c. 41.	The Children Act 1989.	In section 105(1), the definition of "district health authority".
1989 c. 44.	The Opticians Act 1989.	Section 37(2).
1990 c. 19.	The National Health Service and Community Care Act 1990.	Section 1(1), (2), (4) and (5). Section 2. Section 3(3) and (4). Section 4(2)(d). In section 11(5), in paragraph (a), the words from "and for the words" to the end and paragraphs (b) and (c). In section 12, subsections (1)(a) and (2), in subsections (3) and (4), paragraph (b) and the word "and" immediately preceding it and subsection (5). Section 13. Section 14(3) to (5) and (6)(d). In section 15, subsection (2), in subsection (3), the words "or subsection (2)" and subsections (5) and (8). In section 16, in subsection (2), the words "the relevant Regional Health Authority or, as the case may be," and "the Regional Health Authority or, as the case may be,",

Reference	Short title or title	Extent of repeal or revocation
		in subsection (3)(b), the words from the beginning to "Authority;", in subsection (4)(c), the words "the Regional Health Authority or, as the case may be," and subsections (5) and (7).
		In section 17(1), the words "a Regional Health Authority or, in Wales,".
		Section 19.
		Section 20(2)(c) and (d).
		Section 23(5).
		Section 25(2)(b) and (c) and (4)(a).
		Section 26(2)(b).
		Section 46(2)(b).
		Section 59(1).
		Section 60(7)(d).
		In section 62(7), in the definition of "health service body", paragraph (vi) and the word "and" immediately preceding it.
		In Schedule 1, Parts I and II and, in Part III, paragraph 6.
		In Schedule 2, in Part III, in paragraph 23, in sub-paragraph (1), the words "of health authorities etc." and sub-paragraphs (2) and (5) and paragraphs 24(1) and 25(a).
		In Schedule 9, in paragraph 18, sub-paragraph (1)(b), in sub-paragraph (7), in paragraph (a), the words from "for paragraph (e)" to "and" and paragraph (c) and sub-paragraph (13)(a), in paragraph 24, in sub-paragraph (3)(a), the words from ", and after" to " "trust or"", sub-paragraph (4), in sub-paragraph (5), the words from "after" to "trusts" and" and sub-paragraph (6), paragraph 26(1), paragraph 29 and, in paragraph 32(1), in paragraph (a), the words "the word "and" at the end of sub-paragraph (ii) shall be deleted and" and paragraphs (b) and (c).
1990 c. 23.	The Access to Health Records Act 1990.	In section 7(1), the words "or Family Practitioner Committee".
1990 c. 44.	The Caldey Island Act 1990.	In section 3, the words "and the district of the Pembrokeshire Health Authority".
		In section 4(1), paragraph (d) and the word "and" immediately preceding it.
1993 c. 38.	The Welsh Language Act 1993.	Section 6(1)(h).
1993 c. 46.	The Health Service Commissioners Act 1993.	In section 2, subsection (1)(e) and, in subsection (2), paragraph (d) and the word "and" immediately preceding it.
1994 c. 19.	The Local Government (Wales) Act 1994.	In Schedule 10, paragraph 11(1).

INDEX

References are to sections and Schedules

JOBSEEKERS ACT 1995*

(1995 c. 18)

---

* Annotations by Professor N. J. Wikeley, M.A. (Cantab.), Barrister, Faculty of Law, University of Southampton.

28. Expedited claims for housing benefit and council tax benefit.
29. Pilot schemes.

An Act to provide for a jobseeker's allowance and to make other provision to promote the employment of the unemployed and the assistance of persons without a settled way of life.　　　　　　　　　　　　　　[28th June 1995]

PARLIAMENTARY DEBATES
　Hansard. H.C. Vol. 252, col. 47; Vol. 257, cols. 354, 504; Vol. 262, col. 578. H.L. Vol. 563, cols. 11, 321, 584, 646, 794, 1030, 1095, 1377, 1482; Vol. 564, cols. 195, 297, 330, 414, 494, 922, 943, 997.
　The Bill was discussed in Standing Committee B between January 24, 1995 and March 7, 1995.

INTRODUCTION AND GENERAL NOTE
　The Jobseekers Act 1995 abolishes unemployment benefit (UB). It replaces UB with a new and less generous benefit, jobseeker's allowance (JSA), which also assumes the function of providing means-tested assistance for the unemployed, a role currently performed by income support. Its significance therefore surpasses that of last year's Social Security (Incapacity for Work) Act 1994 (c. 18), which was itself described by this annotator as "arguably the single most important piece of social security legislation since the Social Security Act 1986" (*Current Law Statutes 1994*, Vol. 1, c. 18, at p. 18–1).

The objectives of the Act
　The 1994 White Paper *Jobseeker's Allowance* (Cm. 2687, para. 1.5) described the three aims of JSA as:
　(1) to improve the operation of the labour market by helping people in their search for work, while ensuring that they understand and fulfil the conditions for receipt of benefit;
　(2) to secure better value for money for the taxpayer by a streamlined administration, closer targeting on those who need financial support and a regime which more effectively helps people back to work;
　(3) to improve the service to unemployed people themselves by a simpler, clearer, more consistent benefit structure, and by better service delivery.
　Each of these objectives warrants further examination. The first aim reflects a continuing concern with the personal motivation of unemployed people. This has been a characteristic feature of government policy in recent years, manifested most notably by the introduction in the Social Security Act 1989 (c. 24) of the requirement that claimants *actively* seek employment, in addition to being available for work. Thus a central theme of the Act is the perception that a substantial cause of high long-term unemployment is the failure of unemployed people to take advantage of the opportunities available in today's more flexible labour market. The Parliamentary Under-Secretary of State for Social Security declared that "the work-shy are an unknown quantity, but they are thought to be one in six claimants" (*per* Mr R Evans, *Hansard*, H.C. Vol. 252, col. 119). According to the White Paper, jobseeker's allowance, "as its title makes clear, will be a means of support while an unemployed person looks for work, not an income for a lifestyle divorced from work" (see para. 2.5). The Act therefore presages an administrative regime which will place yet more emphasis on the responsibility of claimants actively to seek work. Such

activity will be monitored by periodic reviews of the jobseeker's agreement which all unemployed people will be required to enter as a condition for receipt of benefit.

The second rationale for JSA is phrased in the familiar terms of targeting resources more effectively. JSA is therefore a less generous benefit than its predecessor, most notably in that the maximum duration of contribution-based JSA is six months, rather than 12 months, as is the case currently with UB. There are a number of other important differences between the scope of JSA and UB, which are discussed further below (see *The key differences between unemployment benefit and contribution-based jobseeker's allowance* at p. 18–4). The associated policy goal of helping people more effectively back into work is reflected in the introduction of the jobseeker's agreement (see above) and in a number of work-incentive measures designed to assist the long-term unemployed contained in Pt. II of the Act.

The third reason for introducing JSA is in order to improve service delivery by rationalising the existing parallel system of benefits (contributory UB and means-tested income support). The inefficiency inherent in this dual structure has been a matter of concern to official policy-makers since Mrs Thatcher's first administration (see Rayner Scrutiny, *Payment of Benefits to Unemployed People*, DE/DHSS, 1980). The introduction of a single benefit in the form of JSA offers the potential for a significant improvement in terms of the simplification and clarification of the rules of entitlement. The rules for JSA are to be broadly aligned with those for income support, on the basis that income support is the "more modern benefit" (White Paper, para. 3.7). Whilst there is undoubtedly some force in the argument that JSA represents a rationalisation of the existing arrangements, its limits should be recognised. In the first place, JSA is a single benefit in name only. It comprises two distinct elements, a contribution-based jobseeker's allowance (replacing UB) and an income-based jobseeker's allowance (replacing income support for the unemployed). Although there are some common conditions for JSA (s.1), these two components are the subject of separate rules of entitlement in ss.2 and 3 respectively. Secondly, JSA does not follow income support in all respects: for example, JSA cannot be paid for the first three waiting days of a claim, a concept imported from UB and alien to the income support regime. Thirdly, responsibility for JSA remains divided between two government departments. UB has been administered by the Employment Service and its predecessors as agent for the Department of Social Security, which is primarily responsible for policy development. This division of functions will remain under JSA, although the Employment Department disappeared in the government reshuffle of July 1995, a matter of days after the Act received the Royal Assent. The Employment Service now falls within the orbit of the Department for Education and Employment (DFEE). The precise administrative arrangements for JSA are still unclear, but it appears that Benefits Agency staff will be placed in Jobcentres run by the Employment Service in order to give a full range of benefits advice.

Given the controversy surrounding JSA, it is not surprising that the debates on the Act in Parliament divided along party lines. There was one notable exception: Mr A Howarth M.P., a Conservative backbencher and former minister, made a series of highly critical interventions at various stages of the Bill's passage, declaring that "the Bill widens inequality and deepens impoverishment" (*Hansard*, H.C. Vol. 252, col. 77) and that the powers it vested in the Employment Service were "profoundly illiberal" (*ibid.*, col. 80).

The introduction of JSA can only be understood in the context of the changes to UB which have taken place in the last 15 years. Accordingly a brief historical survey is appropriate before the provisions of the Act are considered in more detail.

The history of unemployment benefit

Great Britain was the first developed state to introduce a national unemployment insurance system (National Insurance Act 1911 (c. 55)). In the 1920s and early 1930s the scheme underwent frequent changes in the face of repeated fiscal crises. The concept of UB as a daily benefit for those out of work is still recognisably based on the structure laid down by the Unemployment Act 1934 (c. 29), albeit that there have been modifications both as a result of the Beveridge reforms and more recently.

Since the election of Mrs Thatcher's first administration in 1979, successive Conservative governments have introduced a number of important changes to the rules governing entitlement to UB. The overall thrust of these reforms has been to reduce both the number of eligible claimants and to reduce the value of the benefit itself. Thus the earnings-related supplement to UB was abolished in 1982, and the lower rates for those with inadequate contributions records followed in 1986. The contributions conditions themselves were narrowed in 1988. The administrative arrangements for checking on claimants' availability for work were tightened up in the mid-1980s, while the Social Security Act 1989 introduced the additional requirement that claimants must actively seek employment. A further significant change in 1989, made by regulations, was the introduction of a rule precluding entitlement to UB where the claimant earned more than the national insurance lower earnings limit for the week in question. The maximum disqualification for cases of "voluntary unemployment", originally set at six weeks in 1911, was increased to 13 weeks in October 1986 and then to 26 weeks in April 1988. Finally, the rights of students and occupational pensioners to claim UB have been extensively curtailed. The consequence of this process of attrition is that today the U.K. has one of the least generous forms of unemployment insurance in the European Union, at 23 per cent of previous earnings, compared to an EU average of 61 per cent (Commission of the European Communities, *Social Protection in Europe 1993*, 1994, p. 57).

On the other side of the equation, there have been very few extensions in the scope of UB. The complex additional requirements for seasonal workers were abolished in 1989, and in the same year the worst excesses of the "full extent normal" rule were tempered for those in minimal part-time work. Overall, however, the trend has been to pare down the contributory scheme, so increasing dependence on means-tested income support. In 1980/81, 59 per cent of unemployed claimants received UB, either alone or with supplementary benefit. By 1993/94, this proportion had fallen to 22 per cent.

The key differences between unemployment benefit and contribution-based jobseeker's allowance
There are four differences which are of particular significance in the transition from UB to JSA. The single most important change is the reduction in the duration of entitlement to contributory unemployment insurance. Although formally UB is a daily benefit, entitlement in any one period of unemployment lasts for a maximum of 312 days (*i.e.* 12 months, excluding Sundays). The maximum duration of contribution-based JSA is 182 days, *i.e.* six months (s.5(1)). The Government justified halving the duration of the maximum entitlement by reference to the fact that about two-thirds of all unemployed people leave the register within six months of becoming unemployed. The restriction of contribution-based JSA to six months will have an especially adverse effect on two groups of claimants. These are, first, unemployed people with savings in excess of £8,000 (*e.g.* from a redundancy payment), who will be precluded from claiming income-based JSA. Those with capital between £3,000 and £8,000 will be eligible for the means-tested benefit but will be subject to the tariff income rules, which will reduce any entitlement to benefit. The second group are those with partners in work, who will similarly be excluded from income-based JSA. However, the Government has announced that the threshold for "remunerative work" will be raised from 16 to 24 hours for partners of unemployed claimants, in order to preserve work incentives. It has been estimated that the six-month rule could result in 165,000 people losing entitlement to benefit (*Hansard*, H.C. Vol. 251, col. 537w).

The second major change concerns the introduction into contribution-based JSA of different age bands for benefit rates. The standard rate of UB is paid at one of two rates, depending on whether or not the claimant is under or over pensionable age. Contribution-based JSA will follow the model of income support, with a lower rate of benefit paid to 18–24 year olds, although they remain liable to pay the same contributions under the national insurance scheme. This change does not appear on the face of the Act, but will be implemented by regulations made under s.4(2).

The third significant change is the introduction of the concept of a jobseeker's agreement by s.9. All JSA claimants (for both contribution-based and income-based components) will be required, as a condition of entitlement to benefit, to enter into such an agreement with an officer of the Employment Service. The jobseeker's agreement is principally concerned with setting out the steps which the claimant should be taking in order to secure employment. These compulsory agreements (a paradox which is indicative of the underlying philosophy of the Act) will be subject to periodic reviews and can be varied by the parties. Disputes over their contents can be referred for determination to the social security adjudicating authorities.

The fourth change concerns the sanctions for voluntary unemployment and the availability of hardship payments (ss.19–20). Claimants who may have lost their employment because of misconduct, or who possibly left voluntarily without just cause, will not be suspended pending determination of that issue by an adjudication officer. This represents an improvement on the existing arrangements. However, once a sanction is imposed, they will have no automatic right to reduced payments of income-based JSA, but will have to demonstrate hardship. The Act also brings in a system of fixed two-week disqualifications for failure to attend compulsory courses or to comply with a jobseeker's direction issued by an employment officer.

There are a number of further changes consequential to the introduction of JSA. At present UB claimants may qualify for an allowance for an adult dependant; these will not exist under contribution-based JSA, although of course the calculation of entitlement to income-based JSA will be based in part on family composition. The earnings rules for UB and income support are rationalised, with a standard disregard of £5 for single people and £10 for couples being applied to both forms of JSA. The rules on occupational and personal pensions will be revised. Under the existing rules UB for those aged over 55 is reduced in line with any such pension over £35 per week which they receive. Under contributory-based JSA, the threshold will be increased to £50 a week, but will affect all claimants, regardless of age (subject to transitional protection). JSA, unlike UB, will only be available to those under state pension age. Finally, JSA (like income support) is a weekly benefit, unlike UB, which is formally assessed on a daily basis.

It will be clear from the discussion above that the abolition of UB and the introduction of JSA represents a significant cut in the value of the main short-term contributory benefit. Approximately 250,000 claimants will lose some benefit entitlement as a result (*Hansard*, H.C. Vol. 248, col. 1135w). In this respect the Jobseekers Act 1995 follows the pattern set by the Social Security (Incapacity for Work) Act 1994, which replaced invalidity benefit with the less generous incapacity benefit. Whilst the benefits available under the National Insurance Fund have been restricted, the levy payable by most contributors has actually increased. The standard primary Class 1 contribution rate, payable by non-contracted out employees, was raised in 1994 from 9 per cent to 10 per cent, the first increase in a decade (Social Security (Contributions) Act 1994 (c. 1), s.1).

On the other side of the equation, Pt. II of the Act introduces a number of work incentive measures which are designed to help long-term unemployed people get back into work. It has been estimated that the most significant of these, the back to work bonus (s.26), will benefit 150,000 people each year who take on part-time work while on benefit. Participants stand to receive a tax-free lump sum of up to £1,000 when they leave benefit for full-time work.

The scheme of the Act

The Jobseekers Act 1995 comprises three Parts. In many respects the Act is deficient in terms of both principle and detail, and so it will not be possible to form a full understanding of the nature and scope of JSA until the relevant secondary legislation has been issued (see further *The use of powers to make delegated legislation* at p. 18–6). Nonetheless, Pt. I is clearly the core of the Act and sets out the bare legislative framework for JSA. Sections 1–5 are concerned with entitlement. Section 1 lists the essential conditions of eligibility for JSA, while ss.2 and 3 set out the further conditions as regards entitlement to the contribution-based and income-based forms of JSA respectively. Section 4 lays down the broad principles governing the calculation of the amount of JSA, while s.5 deals with the duration of entitlement and requalification. Sections 6–11 cover various aspects of "jobseeking", a word which does not appear in this annotator's *Shorter OED* but may be the Employment Department's legacy to the English language. Sections 6 and 7 go some way to defining what is meant by availability for employment and actively seeking employment respectively, while s.8 makes provision for rules governing attendance, information and evidence, and so carries forward the "signing on" procedures. A claim for JSA cannot subsist unless the claimant has entered into a current jobseeker's agreement (s.1(2)(b)), and ss.9–11 deal with the nature of such an agreement, its variation and review and appeals procedures. Sections 12 and 13 consist of enabling powers to make regulations covering the assessment of income and capital. Sections 14 and 15 carry forward into JSA the existing provisions as regards disqualification for involvement in a trade dispute, and the consequences thereof for other claimants in the same family. Sections 16–18 are all concerned with special rules relating to persons under 18, as regards severe hardship provision (s.16), reduced payments (s.17) and recovery of overpayments (s.18). Sections 19 and 20 re-enact and modify the rules about disqualification from benefit (the "voluntary unemployment" sanctions) and the associated exceptions. Finally, ss.21–25 concern various miscellaneous provisions.

Part II of the Act, entitled "Back to Work Schemes", consists of four provisions designed to assist long-term unemployed people back into employment. Section 26 introduces the "back to work bonus" scheme, under which unemployed claimants who have part-time earnings can accumulate credits up to a maximum lump sum of £1,000, payable when they leave JSA and return to full-time work. Section 27 makes provision for a national insurance "holiday" from the payment of contributions for employers who take on long-term unemployed people. Section 28 enables the Secretary of State to require local authorities to give priority, when assessing claims to housing benefit and council tax benefit, to people coming off JSA or income support. Section 29 allows the Secretary of State to introduce pilot schemes, subject to various safeguards, to test the effect of certain changes to the benefit rules on work incentives.

Part III of the Act consists of miscellaneous and supplemental powers. Section 30 has nothing to do with JSA and is included simply because this is a DSS statute. It is concerned with changes to the arrangements for the provision of resettlement units for people without a settled way of life. Section 31 deals with the termination of awards and is designed to prevent confusion when claimants transfer from JSA to income support (or vice versa). Section 32 amends the law on personal insolvency as it relates to certain social security benefits. Sections 33 and 34 makes provision for inspectors and offences under the Act. Section 35 is the general definitions section, while ss.36–41 concern the other genuinely supplemental provisions, governing regulations and orders (s.36), Parliamentary control (s.37), general financial arrangements (s.38), Northern Ireland (s.39), transitional provisions (s.40) and short title, commencement and extent (s.41).

There are also three Schedules. Schedule 1 comprises supplementary provisions for JSA, which are yet more regulation-making powers. Schedule 2 consists of consequential amendments, some two-thirds of which are to the two 1992 social security consolidation statutes (Social Security Contributions and Benefits Act 1992 (c. 4) and the Social Security Administration Act 1992 (c. 5)). Schedule 3 lists various repeals, most of which again relate to earlier social security legislation.

The use of powers to make delegated legislation

The Jobseekers Act 1995, as with much social security legislation, sets little more than the framework for the new benefit. By the time the Bill had completed the Committee stage in the House of Lords, the Bill had 87 subsections and 17 paragraphs in Schedule 1 which contained powers to create delegated legislation. This caused considerable concern to the House of Lords Select Committee on the Scrutiny of Delegated Powers. The Select Committee issued both an interim report (*Fifth Report*, H.L. 50, 1994–95) and a further report (*Sixth Report*, H.L. 54, 1994–95). The Government's argument in favour of this high degree of delegation was that "the degree of detail involved in specifying entitlement and financial structure, the desire to incorporate sensitivity to the labour market, and the need to maintain coherence with changes in other benefits, all point up the importance of a degree of legislative flexibility" (*Fifth Report*, Annex I, para. 7).

The Select Committee concluded that, notwithstanding this argument, there was "a strong argument that the bill is no more than a skeleton bill" (*Sixth Report*, para. 4), and accordingly drew the attention of the House of Lords to the extent of the powers which Parliament was being asked to delegate to Ministers. The Government's response was to table amendments which subsequently became ss.6–8 of the Act, dealing with the scope of the powers relating to the requirements that claimants be available for employment, be actively seeking employment and provide sufficient evidence and information. These replaced the original cl. 6 of the Bill, which was skeletal in the extreme.

Considerable information on the projected use of the regulation-making powers enshrined in the Act is to be found in the joint Employment Department/Department of Social Security Memorandum to the Select Committee, published as Annex I to the *Fifth Report*.

Impact on other benefits

When the Act is implemented, income support will become a residual benefit for people who are not expected to seek work as a condition of receiving benefit. The four main groups who will continue to receive income support are disabled people, lone parents, those with significant caring responsibilities and men aged 60–64. Pensioners will also still qualify for income support. The necessary consequential amendments to the conditions of entitlement to income support are made by Sched. 2, para. 30. Thus the minimum age of entitlement is reduced to 16 and the requirement that income support claimants be both available for and actively seeking employment (except where otherwise prescribed) is abolished. Entitlement to JSA and income support are made mutually exclusive.

The interface between JSA and the new incapacity benefit is more problematic. Disability pressure groups have expressed concern that some disabled people will fail the new test for determining incapacity for work, and so not qualify for incapacity benefit, and yet still be disadvantaged in the labour market. There is the added risk that they may be found to be not available for work, or not actively seeking work, and so also fail to qualify for JSA. During the debates on the Act, Ministers were anxious to give reassurances that disabled people would be able to place reasonable restrictions on their availability for employment without jeopardising their JSA entitlement.

Other labour market reforms

As part of the reforms announced in the 1994 Budget Statement, although not included in this Act, three parallel changes to the social security system should be noted, all of which are designed to make low-paid work more attractive. First, employers' secondary Class 1 national insurance contributions were cut by 0.6 per cent from April 1, 1995 for all employees earning less than £205 a week (Social Security (Contributions) (Re-Rating and National Insurance Fund Payments) Order 1995 (S.I. 1995 No. 561)). Secondly, recipients of family credit or disability working allowance working for more than 30 hours a week qualify for an extra £10 a week as from July 1995 (Income-Related Benefits Schemes (Miscellaneous Amendments) (No. 2) Regulations 1995 (S.I. 1995 No. 1339)). Thirdly, the rules governing national insurance credits are to be liberalised. As at present, JSA claimants will receive credits for the duration of their claim. The existing regulations permit an unemployed person working eight hours or less a week to receive a Class 1 national insurance credit, but those working more than eight but less than 16 hours a week do not receive an automatic credit. Credits will be extended to this latter group from April 1996 (White Paper, para. 4.34).

The 1994 Budget Statement also included a number of further measures designed to help long-term unemployed people back into work. The provision of Work Trials has been extended; these allow an employer to take on people unemployed for six months or more for a trial period of up to three weeks while they receive benefit plus expenses. Community Action, under which participants receive an allowance equivalent to their benefit entitlement plus £10 per week, has also been extended for a further three years until 1997–1998. The scheme is open to people who have been unemployed for more than 12 months. Two other much smaller programmes are being piloted for claimants unemployed for two years or more. Jobstart pays a weekly allowance of £50 for six months for an unemployed person who takes up part-time or self-employed work. Workstart pays a subsidy (currently £60 a week for six months, then £30 per week for six months) to employers who take on long-term unemployed people.

Other changes include the extension of Workwise and 1–2–1 interviews, two Employment Service programmes specifically directed at the 18–24 year old group, which replace Jobplan Workshops. These are essentially "re-motivation" programmes for the younger long-term unemployed. Jobfinder's Grants, averaging £200, have also been available since April 1995. These are designed to assist with the transitional costs of returning to work for people unemployed for more than two years. The job must pay below £150 a week gross and be expected to be permanent in order for the claimant to qualify.

COMMENCEMENT

The Act received Royal Assent on June 28, 1995. The original target date for full implementation was April 1996. At the Report stage in the House of Lords, however, it was announced that JSA would not be introduced until October 1996. The reason given for this delay was the need to ensure that the relevant computer software and staff training programmes were in place before the new benefit came on stream. This indicates an awareness in official circles of the need to avoid the problems surrounding the launch of the Child Support Agency.

However, a number of changes will be introduced in April 1996. These include: the restriction of entitlement to contributory UB to six months (by regulations to be made under s.40); the one-year national insurance holiday for employers taking on people who have been unemployed for the previous two years (s.27); and the run-on of housing benefit at the full rate for people who take a job after six months of unemployment (s.28). In nearly all respects, the Act is to come into force on such days as the Secretary of State may appoint (s.41(2)).

ABBREVIATIONS

Bonner	: *Non-Means Tested Benefits: The Legislation*, commentary by D. Bonner, I. Hooker and R. White (1994, Sweet & Maxwell)
BTWP	: Back To Work Plan
Fifth Report	: House of Lords Select Committee on the Scrutiny of Delegated Powers, Interim Report (*Fifth Report*, H.L. 50, 1994–95)
JSA	: jobseeker's allowance
Mesher and Wood	: *Income-Related Benefits: The Legislation*, commentary by J. Mesher and P. Wood (Sweet & Maxwell)
Ogus, Barendt and Wikeley	: *The Law of Social Security* (4th ed, 1995, Butterworths)
SSAA 1992	: Social Security Administration Act 1992
SSAT	: Social Security Appeal Tribunal
SSCBA 1992	: Social Security Contributions and Benefits Act 1992
SS (USI) Regulations 1983	Social Security (Unemployment, Sickness and Invalidity Benefit) Regulations 1983 (S.I. 1983 No. 1598)
UB	: unemployment benefit
White Paper	: *Jobseeker's Allowance* (Cm. 2687, 1994)

PART I

THE JOBSEEKER'S ALLOWANCE

Entitlement

The jobseeker's allowance

1.—(1) An allowance, to be known as a jobseeker's allowance, shall be payable in accordance with the provisions of this Act.

(2) Subject to the provisions of this Act, a claimant is entitled to a jobseeker's allowance if he—

(a) is available for employment;

(b) has entered into a jobseeker's agreement which remains in force;

(c) is actively seeking employment;

(d) satisfies either—

      (i) the conditions set out in section 2; or

      (ii) the conditions set out in section 3;

(e) is not engaged in remunerative work;

(f) is capable of work;

(g) is not receiving relevant education;

(h) is under pensionable age; and

(i) is in Great Britain.

(3) A jobseeker's allowance is payable in respect of a week.

(4) In this Act—

"a contribution-based jobseeker's allowance" means a jobseeker's allowance entitlement to which is based on the claimant's satisfying conditions which include those set out in section 2; and

"an income-based jobseeker's allowance" means a jobseeker's allowance entitlement to which is based on the claimant's satisfying conditions which include those set out in section 3.

DEFINITIONS

"actively seeking employment": s.7(1).

"availability for employment": s.6(1).

"capable of work": s.35(2) and Sched. 1, para. 2.

"claimant": s.35(1).

"contribution-based jobseeker's allowance": subs. (4).

"employment": s.35(1).

"Great Britain": s.35(1).

"income-based jobseeker's allowance": subs. (4).

"jobseeker's agreement": ss.9(1) and 35(1).

"pensionable age": s.35(1).

"relevant education": s.35(2) and Sched. 1, para. 14.

"remunerative work": s.35(2) and Sched. 1, para. 1.

"week": s.35(1).

"work": s.35(1).

GENERAL NOTE

This section provides the statutory authority for the payment of jobseeker's allowance (subs. (1)) and sets out the basic conditions of entitlement (subs. (2)). The new benefit is payable on a weekly basis (subs. (3)), as is the case with income support, but unlike UB, which is calculated on a daily basis. JSA actually consists of two possible components (subs. (4)), a "contribution-based jobseeker's allowance", which essentially replaces UB, and an "income-based jobseeker's allowance", which supersedes income support so far as unemployed people are concerned.

Subs. (2)

These conditions of entitlement to JSA are modelled on those for UB and income support for unemployed people, with one important exception. An essential precondition for title to the new benefit is that the claimant "has entered into a jobseeker's agreement which remains in force" (subs. (2)(b)). The references in subs. (2)(d) to ss.2 and 3 are to the separate contribution-based and income-based conditions respectively for JSA. Most of the conditions listed here are subject to modification in regulations.

Available for employment. See further s.6 and the annotations in *Bonner* to SSCBA 1992, s.57(1)(a)(i).

Jobseeker's agreement. See further s.9.

Actively seeking employment. See further s.7 and the annotations in *Bonner* to SSCBA 1992, s.57(1)(a)(i).

Not engaged in remunerative work. See further the enabling power in Sched. 1, para. 1, and the annotations to the Income Support (General) Regulations 1987 (S.I. 1987 No. 1967), regs. 5 and 6, in *Mesher and Wood.* A welcome consequence of the application of the exclusion from both contributory and income-related JSA of persons in remunerative work is that the old "full extent normal" rule has been abolished (SS (USI) Regulations 1983, reg. 7(1)(e)).

Capable of work. See further the enabling power in Sched. 1, para. 2, and the annotations in *Bonner* to SSCBA 1992, s.57(1)(a)(ii). Notwithstanding this provision, claimants will be able to remain in receipt of JSA for short periods of up to two weeks when they experience a short spell of illness. This is a welcome reform which will reduce the potential for the complications which can occur when people transfer from one benefit to another. People unable to work for a longer period because of sickness will need to claim incapacity benefit (see SSCBA 1992, ss.30A–30E and 171A–171G, inserted by the Social Security (Incapacity for Work) Act 1994 (c.18)).

Not receiving relevant education. See further the enabling power in Sched. 1, para. 14, and the annotations to the Income Support (General) Regulations 1987 (S.I. 1987 No. 1967), regs. 12 and 13, in *Mesher and Wood.*

Is under pensionable age. Under the UB scheme it is possible for certain people over pensionable age who have deferred their retirement pension or elected to "de-retire" to claim benefit. It is thought that as few as 200 claimants avail themselves of this possibility. JSA will only be payable to persons under pensionable age.

In Great Britain. See further the enabling power in Sched. 1, para. 11. This rule is, of course, subject to the provisions of EC Regulation 1408/71.

Subs. (3)

See further the enabling power in Sched. 1, para. 5 to make provision for periods of less than a week.

Subs. (4)

A claimant for JSA must, as a prerequisite, satisfy the conditions of entitlement in subs. (2). The claimant must then meet the criteria for the award of the contribution-based JSA (see s.2) and/or the income-based JSA (see s.3), depending on the circumstances. The provisions for dealing with the actual calculation of JSA entitlement are contained in s.4.

The contribution-based conditions

2.—(1) The conditions referred to in section 1(2)(d)(i) are that the claimant—

(a) has actually paid Class 1 contributions in respect of one ("the base year") of the last two complete years before the beginning of the relevant benefit year and satisfies the additional conditions set out in subsection (2);

(b) has, in respect of the last two complete years before the beginning of the relevant benefit year, either paid Class 1 contributions or been credited with earnings and satisfies the additional condition set out in subsection (3);

(c) does not have earnings in excess of the prescribed amount; and

(d) is not entitled to income support.

(2) The additional conditions mentioned in subsection (1)(a) are that—

(a) the contributions have been paid before the week for which the jobseeker's allowance is claimed;

(b) the earnings factor derived from earnings upon which primary Class 1 contributions have been paid or treated as paid is not less than the base year's lower earnings limit multiplied by 25.

(3) The additional condition mentioned in subsection (1)(b) is that the earnings factor derived from earnings upon which primary Class 1 contributions have been paid or treated as paid or from earnings credited is not less, in each of the two complete years, than the lower earnings limit for the year multiplied by 50.

(4) For the purposes of this section—

(a) "benefit year" means a period which is a benefit year for the purposes of Part II of the Benefits Act or such other period as may be prescribed for the purposes of this section;

(b) "the relevant benefit year" is the benefit year which includes—

(i) the beginning of the jobseeking period which includes the week for which a jobseeker's allowance is claimed, or

(ii) (if earlier) the beginning of any linked period; and

(c) other expressions which are used in this section and the Benefits Act have the same meaning in this section as they have in that Act.

DEFINITIONS

"base year": subs. (1)(a).
"Benefits Act": s.35(1).
"benefit year": subs. (4)(a) and s.35(1).
"claimant": s.35(1).
"earnings": s.35(3).
"earnings factor": SSCBA 1992: ss.22, 23.
"jobseeking period": s.35(1).
"linked period": s.35(2) and Sched. 1, para. 3.
"lower earnings limit": SSCBA 1992, s.5(1)(a).
"prescribed": s.35(1).
"primary Class 1 contributions": SSCBA 1992, ss.6, 8.
"relevant benefit year": subs. 4(b).
"week": s.35(1).
"year": s.35(1).

GENERAL NOTE

A person claiming a contribution-based JSA must satisfy the conditions laid down in this section, as well as those in s.1. The contribution conditions set out in subss. (1)(a) and (b), (2) and (3) essentially replicate the existing insurance test for entitlement to UB (SSCBA 1992, Sched. 3, Pt. I, para. 1). These require payment of the requisite amount of Class 1 contributions in one of the last two full tax years (subss. (1)(a) and (2)) and either payment of or crediting with the appropriate Class 1 contributions in *both* of those two years (subss. (1)(b) and (3)). There are, however, two further conditions which must be satisfied for contribution-based JSA; these are considered separately.

Subs. (1)(c)

First, there is now a fundamental rule that the claimant must "not have earnings in excess of the prescribed amount". The Government's view is that this "is designed to protect claimants of a contribution-based jobseeker's allowance whose earnings, after account is taken of any disregarded amount, would exceed their contributory entitlement. In these circumstances a person would have entitlement to benefit but not receive any payment. The provision ensures that this is treated as a period of disentitlement and does not count towards the claimant's 182 days' entitlement to a contribution-based JSA. It is intended that regulations will set a level equal to the personal rate plus the appropriate disregard minus one penny in order to achieve this" (*Fifth Report*, Annex I, para. 18). One wonders how this provision will be explained in plain English to claimants. The fact is that the combined effect of this provision and s.4(1)(b) is that there is now an explicit means-test for contribution-based JSA. No such express provision applies in relation to UB, although the same end result is achieved by a number of provisions precluding certain days of unemployment from counting for purposes of entitlement to UB. Thus no benefit is payable for a week in which the claimant has earnings equal to or in excess of the weekly lower earnings limit (SS (USI) Regulations 1983, reg. 7(1)(o)); any day on which the claimant earns more than £2 does not rank as a day of unemployment (*ibid.*, reg. 7(1)(g)); and the notorious "full extent normal rule" (*ibid.*, reg. 7(1)(e) may also have the effect of excluding entitlement once a regular level of earnings has been reached. In addition, a person aged 55 or over in receipt of an occupational pension loses £1 in UB for every £1 that such a pension exceeds £35 per week (*ibid.*, reg. 24, and SSCBA 1992, s.30). The new provision at least has the advantage of being relatively straightforward, and does not arbitrarily distinguish between different sources of income or claimants of different ages.

Subs. (1)(d)
The second new condition is that the claimant must not be entitled to residual income support. There may, of course, be an entitlement to income-based JSA, which will follow the same principles as income support. Section 4 specifies the rules governing the amount of JSA payable, whether one or both components are payable.

The income-based conditions

3.—(1) The conditions referred to in section 1(2)(d)(ii) are that the claimant—

(a) has an income which does not exceed the applicable amount (determined in accordance with regulations under section 4) or has no income;
(b) is not entitled to income support;
(c) is not a member of a family one of whose members is entitled to income support;
(d) is not a member of a family one of whose members is entitled to an income-based jobseeker's allowance;
(e) is not a member of a married or unmarried couple the other member of which is engaged in remunerative work; and
(f) is a person—
(i) who has reached the age of 18; or
(ii) in respect of whom a direction under section 16 is in force; or
(iii) who has, in prescribed circumstances to be taken into account for a prescribed period, reached the age of 16 but not the age of 18.

(2) Regulations may provide for one or both of the following conditions to be included in the income-based conditions, in the case of a person to whom subsection (1)(f)(ii) or (iii) applies—
(a) a condition that the claimant must register for employment;
(b) a condition that the claimant must register for training.
(3) In subsection (1)(f)(iii) "period" includes—
(a) a period of a determinate length;
(b) a period defined by reference to the happening of a future event; and
(c) a period of a determinate length but subject to earlier determination upon the happening of a future event.
(4) Regulations under subsection (2) may, in particular, make provision by reference to persons designated by the Secretary of State for the purpose of the regulations.

DEFINITIONS
"applicable amount": s.35(1).
"claimant": s.35(1).
"employment": s.35(1).
"family": s.35(1).
"income-based conditions": s.35(1).
"income-based jobseeker's allowance": ss.1(4) and 35(1).
"married couple": s.35(1).
"period": subs. (3).
"prescribed": s.35(1).
"regulations": s.35(1).
"remunerative work": s.35(2) and Sched. 1, para. 1.
"training": s.35(1).
"unmarried couple": s.35(1).

GENERAL NOTE

A person claiming an income-based JSA must satisfy the conditions laid down in this section, as well as those in s.1. The six conditions set out in subs. (1) are broadly modelled on the existing criteria for income support for unemployed people.

Subs. (1)(a)

This imports the standard income support means-test into income-based JSA. "Income" will be defined by regulations made under s.12, as under income support; the "applicable amount", determined under s.4(5), is also a concept taken from the income support scheme, and consists of the aggregate of a number of set amounts appropriate to the person's age and status (*e.g.* a weekly personal allowance together with any appropriate premiums and housing costs, if an owner-occupier).

Subs. (1)(b)

This confirms the residual status of income support for people outside the labour market. Means-tested JSA is not payable to anyone to whom income support is payable. See the corresponding amendment to SSCBA 1992, s.124(1) in Sched. 2, para. 30(5) as regards the grounds of entitlement to income support itself.

Subs. (1)(c) and (d)

Family. This has the conventional social security meaning of a married or unmarried couple, with or without dependent children, or a lone parent (s.35(1)). Thus an unemployed 20-year-old living at home with her parents, who are also unemployed and on income support, will remain entitled to income support in her own right. This is because for social security purposes she is a non-dependant and not a member of the same family as her parents.

Subs. (1)(e)

Remunerative work. It is currently a condition of entitlement to income support that neither the claimant nor any partner is engaged in remunerative work (SSCBA 1992, s.124(1)(c)). For income support purposes the threshold is set at 16 hours per week (Income Support (General) Regulations 1987 (S.I. 1987 No. 1967), reg. 5(1)). The concept of remunerative work is to be defined for the purposes of JSA in regulations made under Sched. 1, para. 1. The Government has made it clear that its intention is to enable partners of unemployed claimants to work for up to 24 hours a week before losing entitlement to income-based JSA. This reform is clearly designed as a work incentive.

Subs. (1)(f)

As with income support, there are special provisions for young people aged 16 or 17 who seek to claim income-based JSA. The general principle is that the minimum age of entitlement to income-based JSA is 18, the Government's thinking being that young people under that age should be in education, in work or in receipt of training. However, a minority of 16 and 17 year olds will receive benefit if the Secretary of State directs that they would otherwise suffer severe hardship (subs. (1)(f)(ii) and s.16) or where they fall into specified vulnerable groups (subs. (1)(f)(iii)). The latter will include the following groups: couples with at least one child, young people leaving care, ex-prisoners, temporarily-stopped workers, childless married couples and those living away from home because of the threat of physical or sexual abuse (*Fifth Report*, Annex I, para. 21). Such 16 and 17 year olds may be required to register for employment and/or training (subs. (2)).

Subs. (2)

The requirement that 16 and 17 year olds may be required to register for employment replicates existing legislation (SSCBA 1992, s.124(3)), but the provision as regards registration for training is new. It has been included "to ensure that (young people) receive the assistance of those who are delivering careers guidance" (*Fifth Report*, Annex I, para. 22).

Subs. (4)

This allows the Secretary of State flexibility in determining the appropriate registration procedures for young people. It is linked with the transfer from local education authorities to the Secretary of State of the responsibility to provide careers services (see Trade Union Reform and Employment Rights Act 1993 (c. 19), ss.45 and 46).

Amount payable by way of a jobseeker's allowance

4.—(1) In the case of a contribution-based jobseeker's allowance, the amount payable in respect of a claimant ("his personal rate") shall be calculated by—

(a) determining the age-related amount applicable to him; and

(b) making prescribed deductions in respect of earnings and pension payments.

(2) The age-related amount applicable to a claimant, for the purposes of subsection (1)(a), shall be determined in accordance with regulations.

(3) In the case of an income-based jobseeker's allowance, the amount payable shall be—

(a) if a claimant has no income, the applicable amount;

(b) if a claimant has an income, the amount by which the applicable amount exceeds his income.

(4) Except in prescribed circumstances, a jobseeker's allowance shall not be payable where the amount otherwise payable would be less than a prescribed minimum.

(5) The applicable amount shall be such amount or the aggregate of such amounts as may be determined in accordance with regulations.

(6) Where a claimant satisfies both the contribution-based conditions and the income-based conditions but has no income, the amount payable shall be—

(a) the applicable amount, if that is greater than his personal rate; and

(b) his personal rate, if it is not.

(7) Where the amount payable to a claimant to whom subsection (6) applies is the applicable amount, the amount payable to him by way of a jobseeker's allowance shall be taken to consist of two elements—

(a) one being an amount equal to his personal rate; and

(b) the other being an amount equal to the excess of the applicable amount over his personal rate.

(8) Where a claimant satisfies both the contribution-based conditions and the income-based conditions and has an income, the amount payable shall be—

(a) the amount by which the applicable amount exceeds his income, if the amount of that excess is greater than his personal rate; and

(b) his personal rate, if it is not.

(9) Where the amount payable to a claimant to whom subsection (8) applies is the amount by which the applicable amount exceeds his income, the amount payable to him by way of a jobseeker's allowance shall be taken to consist of two elements—

(a) one being an amount equal to his personal rate; and

(b) the other being an amount equal to the amount by which the difference between the applicable amount and his income exceeds his personal rate.

(10) The element of a jobseeker's allowance mentioned in subsection (7)(a) and that mentioned in subsection (9)(a) shall be treated, for the purpose of identifying the source of the allowance, as attributable to the claimant's entitlement to a contribution-based jobseeker's allowance.

(11) The element of a jobseeker's allowance mentioned in subsection (7)(b) and that mentioned in subsection (9)(b) shall be treated, for the purpose of identifying the source of the allowance, as attributable to the claimant's entitlement to an income-based jobseeker's allowance.

(12) Regulations under subsection (5) may provide that, in prescribed cases, an applicable amount is to be nil.

DEFINITIONS

"claimant": s.35(1).

"contribution-based conditions": s.35(1).

"contribution-based jobseeker's allowance": ss.1(4) and 35(1).
"earnings": s.35(3).
"income-based conditions": s.35(1).
"income-based jobseeker's allowance": ss.1(4) and 35(1).
"pension payments": s.35(1).
"personal rate": subs. (1).
"prescribed": s.35(1).

GENERAL NOTE

This section sets out how the amount payable by way of jobseeker's allowance is to be calculated. Its maze-like complexity is principally due to the fact that JSA is an amalgam of two benefits, one contributory (UB) and one means-tested (income support for unemployed people). Subsections (1) to (5) establish the basic principles for calculating JSA, while subss. (6) to (11) govern the position where a claimant is entitled to both forms of JSA.

The House of Lords Select Committee on the Scrutiny of Delegated Powers (see Introduction and General Note, above) drew attention to this provision as it allows the calculation of the amount of JSA to be governed by delegated legislation. Notwithstanding the precedent of the income support scheme, the Committee reported that "The House may wish to consider with care whether regulations under this Clause should not always be subject to the affirmative procedure regardless of when they are made" (*Sixth Report*, para. 8). An amendment to give effect to this recommendation was defeated in the House of Lords at the Report stage (*Hansard*, H.L. Vol. 564, cols. 399–404).

Subss. (1)–(5)

Where a claimant is entitled to *contribution-based* JSA, by virtue of ss.1 and 2, the amount of benefit is calculated by determining the relevant age-related amount and then making deductions for earnings and pension payments, as prescribed in regulations (subs. (1); see also s.2(1)(c)). This is known as the "personal rate". The age-related amounts are also to be set out in regulations (subs. (2)), but it is known that there will be different rates for claimants of different ages, *i.e.* those aged 18–24, and those aged 25 or over. This follows the age structure currently used for income support, but is a major departure from principle for a contributory benefit.

Where a claimant is entitled to *income-based* JSA, by virtue of ss.1 and 3, and has no income, the amount of benefit will be calculated simply by determining the appropriate applicable amount (subs. (3)(a)). The applicable amount will be set out in regulations (subs. (5); see to similar effect SSCBA 1992, s.135(1)), and will follow the pattern of income support. It will therefore comprise the aggregate of the relevant personal allowances for the claimant and any members of their family, appropriate premiums and housing costs for mortgage interest (if relevant). There will be some modifications to the rules governing premiums to reflect the different nature of JSA (*e.g.* income support, but not JSA, can be paid to people over pensionable age).

In the event that the claimant has some income, the income-based JSA will be a sum equal to the amount by which the applicable amount exceeds the income (subs. (3)(b)). This is the standard method of assessment for income support (SSCBA 1992, s.124(4)).

Regulations will enable a minimum level of JSA (whether contribution-based or income-based) to be prescribed for the purposes of payment of benefit (subs. (4)). This will be 10p per week, as is the case with income support. Amounts of less than 10p will be paid if the payment is for arrears or for part weeks when the weekly entitlement is more than 10p (*Fifth Report*, Annex I, para. 28).

Subss. (6)–(11)

The remaining subsections provide for the calculation of JSA in more complex situations. By virtue of subs. (6)(a), if the claimant is entitled to both forms of JSA but has no income, then the amount of benefit payable is the applicable amount, if greater than the personal rate (*i.e.* the standard contribution-based JSA). In such a case the individual's JSA is deemed to consist of the contribution-based component plus a top-up from income-based JSA (subs. (7)). The end result is very similar to that which applies at present to claimants entitled to both UB and income support. If the claimant's applicable amount is equal to or less than the personal rate, then the latter is payable by way of JSA (subs. (6)(b)). The purpose of these provisions is to give priority and recognition to the contribution-based element of JSA.

Similar provisions are made for claimants who are entitled to both forms of JSA but do have some income, with the necessary modifications to reflect that fact (subss. (8) and (9)).

Subsection (10) makes further express provision for the recognition of the contribution-based component of JSA where both forms are payable. This will enable an amount equivalent to the contribution-based element to be attributed to the National Insurance Fund for accounting purposes, and also for the purposes of counting towards the maximum 182 days' entitlement to contribution-based JSA (see s.5(1)). Subsection (11) ensures that the top-up element of income-based JSA in such cases is attributed to the Consolidated Fund for accounting purposes.

Subs. (12)

Finally, subs. (12) enables regulations to provide that in prescribed cases a person's applicable amount may be nil, so that benefit is not payable even though the conditions of entitlement are met. This repeats an existing power under the income support scheme (SSCBA 1992, s.135(2)), and may apply to persons in religious orders, some prisoners and certain persons from abroad (see *e.g.* Income Support (General) Regulations (S.I. 1987 No. 1967), Sched. 7).

Duration of a contribution-based jobseeker's allowance

5.—(1) The period for which a person is entitled to a contribution-based jobseeker's allowance shall not exceed, in the aggregate, 182 days in any period for which his entitlement is established by reference (under section 2(1)(b)) to the same two years.

(2) The fact that a person's entitlement to a contribution-based jobseeker's allowance ("his previous entitlement") has ceased as a result of subsection (1), does not prevent his being entitled to a further contribution-based jobseeker's allowance if—

(a) he satisfies the contribution-based conditions; and

(b) the two years by reference to which he satisfies those conditions includes at least one year which is later than the second of the two years by reference to which his previous entitlement was established.

(3) Regulations may provide that a person who would be entitled to a contribution-based jobseeker's allowance but for the operation of prescribed provisions of, or made under, this Act shall be treated as if entitled to the allowance for the purposes of this section.

DEFINITIONS

"contribution-based jobseeker's allowance": ss.1(4) and 35(1).
"entitled": s.35(1).
"his previous entitlement": subs. (2).
"prescribed": s.35(1).
"regulations": s.35(1).
"year": s.35(1).

GENERAL NOTE

This short section embodies one of the most fundamental differences between UB and the contribution-based JSA. It limits entitlement to the latter to six months, and lays down the criteria for requalifying for benefit.

Subs. (1)

A person's entitlement to UB ceases after 312 days in any one period of interruption of employment (SSCBA 1992, s.26(1)); effectively this means that UB lasts for a maximum of one year in any one spell, given that UB is calculated on a six-day week, as Sundays do not count (SSCBA 1992, s.57(1)(e)). In contrast, the maximum entitlement to contribution-based JSA is 182 days, *i.e.* 26 weeks, as JSA operates on a full week basis (s.1(3)). Although the duration of JSA is half that of UB, the contribution conditions test is the same (s.1(1)(a) and (b), (2) and (3)).

Subs. (2)

Under the current scheme, a claimant can requalify for UB by working for at least 16 hours a week for a minimum of 13 weeks in the 26 weeks before the subsequent claim (SSCBA 1992, s.26(2)). The requalification rule for contribution-based JSA is tied in more closely with contributions records. The claimant will have to satisfy the contributions conditions specified in s.2, and will not be able to base such a further claim on the same two tax years as were used to give title to benefit on the first occasion. However, it would be possible for the second tax year in the initial claim to be used as the first in a fresh pair of tax years for the second claim (subs. (2)(b)). Thus a person might receive contribution-based JSA in respect of contributions paid in 1995–1996 and 1996–1997. Once the 182 days of entitlement have been exhausted, a fresh claim could not be based on the 1995–1996 and 1996–1997 tax years, but could be grounded on the 1996–1997 and 1997–1998 tax years.

Subs. (3)

This enables regulations to provide that any period in which entitlement to benefit has been withdrawn may still count towards the maximum entitlement of 182 days. This follows the existing power under SSCBA 1992, s.26(6); see further SS (USI) Regulations 1983, regs. 16 and 28. This power will be used to ensure that claimants who are receiving payments of an income-based JSA under Sched. 1, paras. 8 and 9 (claimants who fail to meet certain conditions for JSA but receive reduced payments on grounds of severe hardship) have their contributory entitlement of 182 days eroded, where a contributory entitlement would otherwise have existed (*Fifth Report*, Annex I, para. 31). It should be noted that the current power has not, to date, been exercised so as to provide that days when a person is subject to a period of disqualification for voluntary unemployment should count for these purposes. The White Paper, however, indicated that such periods of disqualification will cut into the period of entitlement for contribution-based JSA (para. 4.38). Yet during the passage of the Bill, the Under-Secretary of State for Social Security indicated that he had "no plans at present to use the power" (Standing Committee B, col. 296, February 9, 1995).

Jobseeking

Availability for employment

6.—(1) For the purposes of this Act, a person is available for employment if he is willing and able to take up immediately any employed earner's employment.

(2) Subsection (1) is subject to such provisions as may be made by regulations; and those regulations may, in particular, provide that a person—

(a) may restrict his availability for employment in any week in such ways as may be prescribed; or

(b) may restrict his availability for employment in any week in such circumstances as may be prescribed (for example, on grounds of conscience, religious conviction or physical or mental condition or because he is caring for another person) and in such ways as may be prescribed.

(3) The following are examples of restrictions for which provision may be made by the regulations—

(a) restrictions on the nature of the employment for which a person is available;

(b) restrictions on the periods for which he is available;

(c) restrictions on the terms or conditions of employment for which he is available;

(d) restrictions on the locality or localities within which he is available.

(4) Regulations may prescribe circumstances in which, for the purposes of this Act, a person is or is not to be treated as available for employment.

(5) Regulations under subsection (4) may, in particular, provide for a person who is available for employment—

(a) only in his usual occupation,

(b) only at a level of remuneration not lower than that which he is accustomed to receive, or

(c) only in his usual occupation and at a level of remuneration not lower than that which he is accustomed to receive,

to be treated, for a permitted period, as available for employment.

(6) Where it has been determined ("the first determination") that a person is to be treated, for the purposes of this Act, as available for employment in any week, the question whether he is available for employment in that week may be subsequently determined on a review of the first determination.

(7) In this section "permitted period", in relation to any person, means such period as may be determined in accordance with the regulations made under subsection (4).

(8) Regulations under subsection (4) may prescribe, in relation to permitted periods—

    (a) the day on which any such period is to be regarded as having begun in any case;

    (b) the shortest and longest periods which may be determined in any case;

    (c) factors which an adjudication officer may take into account in determining the period in any case.

(9) For the purposes of this section "employed earner's employment" has the same meaning as in the Benefits Act.

DEFINITIONS

"Benefits Act": s.35(1).
"claimant": s.35(1).
"employed earner's employment": subs. (9) and SSCBA 1992, ss.2(1) and 122(1).
"employment": s.35(1).
"the first determination": subs. (6).
"permitted period": subs. (7).
"prescribed": s.35(1).
"regulations": s.35(1).
"week": s.35(1).

GENERAL NOTE

The requirement that claimants be "available for employment" is fundamental to entitlement to UB and to income support for unemployed people, and is naturally carried forward into JSA. As originally drafted, the Bill simply left the meaning of this term and that of "actively seeking employment" to be prescribed in regulations. Following criticism from the House of Lords Select Committee on the Scrutiny of Delegated Powers (see Introduction and General Note, above), the Government introduced amendments (now ss.6 and 7) which have put more detail into the primary legislation. Regulations made under this section are subject to the affirmative procedure, following a further Government concession (s.37(1)(c)). Note also that additional conditions as regards availability for work for special groups may be imposed under regulations made under Sched. 1, para. 17.

There was much Parliamentary debate on the question of the availability for work rules and the position of part-time students, although this problem is not specifically addressed by this section. At present claimants can be treated as available for work and eligible for income support where they are pursuing a course lasting less than 21 hours a week, providing certain other criteria are also met (Income Support (General) Regulations 1987 (S.I. 1987 No. 1967), reg. 9). Changes in the further education system, and in particular the advent of modularisation, have made it increasingly difficult to determine whether a course is full-time or part time. In response the Government announced that the upper limit for JSA entitlement purposes would be 16 "guided learning" hours, rather than 21 "supervised" hours. This change will be implemented via regulations.

Finally, changes in the consequences of non-compliance should be noted. Under the current arrangements, where there is an unresolved issue as to an existing claimant's availability for work, UB remains in payment until the matter is decided by an adjudication officer. Any entitlement to income support is suspended pending such a determination, although hardship payments may be made. Under JSA there will be no entitlement to benefit while the outcome of the adjudication officer's decision is awaited, subject to the provision of hardship payments. On the penalties for non-compliance with the requirements of this section, see s.20(4)–(6).

Subs. (1)

This effectively puts into statutory language the traditional case law understanding of the expression "available for employment". Thus in *R(U) 1/53* the Commissioner held that claimants "must be prepared to accept at once any offers of suitable employment brought to their notice" (para. 7). This principle is subject to regulations made under the enabling provisions of the rest of the section. For discussion of the existing case law, see the annotations in *Bonner* to SSCBA 1992, s.57(1)(a)(i).

Able to take up. Case law demonstrates that a person will not be able to take up employment, and so not be available for employment, if he, *e.g.* is subject to immigration rules prohibiting him from working (*Shaukat Ali v. Chief Adjudication Officer*, reported as Appendix to *R(U) 1/85*

[1985] C.L.Y. 3339), or is still contractually bound to another employer (*R(U) 11/51*), or is about to go abroad (*R(U) 1/90(T)*).

Immediately. The full rigour of this rule is marginally relaxed for certain categories of claimants who are deemed to be available providing they are ready on 24 or 48 hours' notice (*Ogus, Barendt and Wikeley*, pp. 110–111).

Employed earner's employment. This carries the same meaning as under SSCBA 1992, ss.2(1) and 122(1) (see subs. (9)). It follows that, in order to qualify for JSA, the claimant must be available for *employment*. Availability for *self-employment* is not sufficient (see *R(U) 14/51*), whereas steps taken to establish oneself as self-employed *may* satisfy the parallel condition of actively seeking employment (s.7(8)). Under the UB rules, availability for part-time work could be enough, providing this did not adversely affect the claimant's overall availability and prospects of finding work (*CU 109/48(KL)*). Under JSA, on the other hand, claimants will be expected to be available for a minimum of 40 hours a week. A claimant will be able to agree any pattern of 40 hours' availability across the week, providing it "does not limit unreasonably his prospect of securing work" (*per* Lord Mackay of Ardbrecknish, *Hansard*, H.L. vol 564, col. 215). Yet although claimants will be expected to be available to work a full week, they will be expected to accept part-time employment: "People will be expected to be *willing* to work those hours to receive benefit even if they would prefer to work fewer hours. But people who are offered suitable work of fewer hours will be expected to accept it" (White Paper, para. 4.4, original emphasis). However, "people who refuse work of less than 24 hours a week will not normally be subject to sanctions" (*per* Lord Inglewood, *Hansard*, H.L. Vol. 563, col. 1131).

Subss. (2) and (3)

These provisions enable regulations to be made which permit claimants to restrict their availability for employment in various ways without jeopardising entitlement to benefit. These regulations will build on the model set by reg. 7B of the SS (USI) Regulations 1983; see further annotations in *Bonner* to SSCBA 1992, s.57(1)(a)(i) and to reg. 7B.

Government spokesmen made it clear during the debates that disabled people will be able to restrict their availability in accordance with their physical or mental condition, as will people with sincerely held religious or conscientious objections (*per* Lord Inglewood, *Hansard*, H.L. Vol. 563, col. 822). Carers will also be able to limit the number of hours' work for which they are available, below the minimum of 40 hours, in line with their caring responsibilities.

Subs. (4)

Existing legislation provides for claimants in certain circumstances to be deemed to be available for employment. Volunteers and others are treated as being so available for the purposes of entitlement to UB (SS (USI) Regulations 1983, regs. 9–12A), whilst others are deemed to be available for the purpose of reckoning periods of interruption of employment (*ibid.*, regs. 13 and 14). There are no express provisions in the UB legislation deeming persons *not* to be available for employment. However, there are rules under the income support scheme which both deem some claimants to be available and treat others as not being available for employment: Income Support (General) Regulations 1987 (S.I. 1987 No. 1967), regs. 9 and 10.

Subs. (5)

This reflects current legislation enabling claimants to protect job skills and the general level of remuneration to which they are accustomed, for a limited period at least (see SSCBA 1992, s.29(1)(b) and SS (USI) Regulations 1983, regs. 7B(4)(c)–(6) and 12F). This period, known as the "permitted period", lasts for a maximum of 13 weeks, after which claimants are expected to widen their horizons so far as job opportunities are concerned. There are further regulation-making powers as regards permitted periods in subss. (7) and (8).

Subs. (6)

This is in the same terms as SSCBA 1992, s.57(4) and (5). Where a question arises as to whether a claimant is available for employment, that person is deemed to satisfy the relevant condition until such time as a decision on the matter is taken (SS (USI) Regulations 1983, reg. 12A). This provision enables the claimant's actual availability to be determined subsequently on review.

Actively seeking employment

7.—(1) For the purposes of this Act, a person is actively seeking employment in any week if he takes in that week such steps as he can reasonably be

expected to have to take in order to have the best prospects of securing employment.

(2) Regulations may make provision—

(a) with respect to steps which it is reasonable, for the purposes of subsection (1), for a person to be expected to have to take in any week;

(b) as to circumstances (for example, his skills, qualifications, abilities and physical or mental limitations) which, in particular, are to be taken into account in determining whether, in relation to any steps taken by a person, the requirements of subsection (1) are satisfied in any week.

(3) Regulations may make provision for acts of a person which would otherwise be relevant for purposes of this section to be disregarded in such circumstances (including circumstances constituted by, or connected with, his behaviour or appearance) as may be prescribed.

(4) Regulations may prescribe circumstances in which, for the purposes of this Act, a person is to be treated as actively seeking employment.

(5) Regulations under subsection (4) may, in particular, provide for a person who is actively seeking employment—

(a) only in his usual occupation,

(b) only at a level or remuneration not lower than that which he is accustomed to receive, or

(c) only in his usual occupation and at a level of remuneration not lower than that which he is accustomed to receive,

to be treated, for the permitted period determined in his case for the purposes of section 6(5), as actively seeking employment during that period.

(6) Regulations may provide for this section, and any regulations made under it, to have effect in relation to a person who has reached the age of 16 but not the age of 18 as if "employment" included "training".

(7) Where it has been determined ("the first determination") that a person is to be treated, for the purposes of this Act, as actively seeking employment in any week, the question whether he is actively seeking employment in that week may subsequently be determined on a review of the first determination.

(8) For the purposes of this section—

"employment" means employed earner's employment or, in prescribed circumstances—

(a) self-employed earner's employment; or

(b) employed earner's employment and self-employed earner's employment; and

"employed earner's employment" and "self-employed earner's employment" have the same meaning as in the Benefits Act.

DEFINITIONS

"Benefits Act": s.35(1).

"employed earner's employment": subs. (8) and SSCBA 1992, ss.2(1), 122(1).

"employment": subs. (8).

"the first determination": subs. (7).

"prescribed": s.35(1).

"regulations": s.35(1).

"self-employed earner's employment": subs. (8) and the SSCBA 1992, ss.2(1), 122(1).

"training": s.35(1).

"week": s.35(1).

GENERAL NOTE

Unlike the requirement that a claimant be available for employment, the condition that an unemployed person be "actively seeking employment" is relatively new. This latter requirement was introduced by the Social Security Act 1989, s.10 and has generated considerable controversy. It has inevitably been carried forward from UB and income support into JSA. As originally drafted, the Bill simply left the meaning both of this term and that of "availability for employment" as matters entirely to be prescribed in regulations. Following criticism from the House of Lords Select Committee on the Scrutiny of Delegated Powers (see Introduction and General Note), the Government introduced amendments (now ss.6 and 7) which now provide more of a definitional framework in the primary legislation. Regulations made under this section are also subject to the affirmative procedure, following a further Government concession (s.37(1)(c)).

Finally, changes in the consequences of non-compliance should be noted. Under the current arrangements, where there is an unresolved issue as to whether an existing claimant is actively seeking employment, payment of UB is suspended until the matter is decided by an adjudication officer. Any entitlement to income support is also suspended pending such a determination, although hardship payments may be made. Under JSA there will similarly be no entitlement to benefit while the outcome of the adjudication officer's decision is awaited, subject to the provision of hardship payments. However, the actual amount of these hardship payments will be restricted: on the penalties for non-compliance with the requirements of this section, see s.20(4)–(6).

Subs. (1)

This attempt to define in primary legislation what is meant by "actively seeking employment" is modelled on the definition which presently exists in subordinate legislation (SS (USI) Regulations 1983, reg. 12B(1), made under SSCBA 1992, s.57(3)(b)(i)). There is one potentially significant difference: the present regulation refers to those reasonable steps which "offer [the claimant] his best prospects of *receiving offers of* employment". The new statutory reformulation refers merely to "the best prospects of *securing* employment". At one level this may simply be a matter of tidying up the drafting. However, it may also be symptomatic of the expectation in the Act as a whole that claimants are meant to be positive actors in the labour market, and not passive recipients of possible offers of employment. Note also that the term "employment" is used here in a wider sense to that in s.6, as potentially encompassing self-employed work (subs. (8)).

Subs. (2)

This enables regulations to be made specifying in more detail what precisely constitutes "actively seeking employment". These regulations will presumably build on the existing provisions in the SS (USI) Regulations 1983, reg. 12B.

Subs. (3)

This is a remarkable provision. It is one thing for the Secretary of State to reserve the power to prescribe what types of steps are to count for determining whether a person is "actively seeking employment" (subs. (2)). These might include, as they currently do, making oral or written applications for work, seeking information about employment openings, registering with an employment agency, *etc.* It is quite another matter to provide for such steps, which would otherwise be relevant, "to be disregarded in such circumstances (*including circumstances constituted by, or connected with, his behaviour or appearance*) as may be prescribed" (emphasis added).

One might well wonder what is the justification for this power. According to the DSS's *Notes on Clauses*, "regulations will enable a person's jobseeking activity to be disregarded if he behaves or presents himself in such a way as deliberately to reduce or extinguish his chance of receiving offers of employment". This was reinforced by the Minister of State in the House of Lords, who stated that a sanction was needed for "people who will try to avoid work by deliberately making a poor impression to a prospective employer" (*per* Lord Mackay of Ardbrecknish, *Hansard*, H.L. Vol. 563, col. 13). Another Government spokesman stressed that "dress codes will not be established ... The regulations will not go into detail about specific actions which will negate jobsearch" (*per* Lord Inglewood, *Hansard*, H.L. Vol. 563, col. 857). The specific example was given in debate of a bearded claimant telling a potential employer in the food processing industry that he would not wear a face mask (*Hansard*, H.L. Vol. 564, col. 279). This might suggest that the provision has a fairly narrow remit. However, at the Committee stage in the House of Commons, the Minister of State indicated that a jobseeker's direction might be issued where "someone's appearance was militating against him." The Department would effectively be saying " 'We think that there is something you can do to enhance your employability. We ask you to take reasonable steps' – which does not include the person doing something that he cannot afford to do – 'to approve (sic) your appearance and attitude' " (*Standing Committee B*, col. 129, January 31, 1995).

Two obvious points may be made in this regard. First, the regulations will have to be carefully constructed in such a way that they do not permit the rules to be applied in a discriminatory fashion, either on the grounds of gender or race (*e.g. vis-à-vis* men with long hair or dreadlocks). Secondly, the social security scheme already contains a sanction for some forms of such behaviour, although there is little evidence that it is ever used nowadays. A person can be disqualified from receiving UB if "he has without good cause neglected to avail himself of a reasonable opportunity of employment" (SSCBA 1992, s.28(1)(c)). This provision was used in one case to disqualify a man who attended for an interview as a job as a parcel porter in a "dirty and unshaven state" (*R(U) 28/55*).

Subs. (4)
For the current provision deeming certain persons to be actively seeking employment, see SS (USI) Regulations 1983, reg. 12D. Unlike under s.6(4), which deals with deeming provisions for availability for employment, there is no power to make regulations treating certain persons as *not* actively seeking employment.

Subs. (5)
See General Note to s.6(5), the equivalent provision as regards availability for employment.

Subs. (6)
This is clearly designed to reinforce the Government's intention to highlight the importance of training for 16 and 17 year olds.

Subs. (7)
See General Note to s.6(6), the equivalent provision as regards availability for employment.

Subs. (8)
In the context of availability for employment, "employment" refers to work as an employee. In this section, however, dealing with actively seeking employment, the relevant steps can (subject to regulations) be with a view to securing work as a self-employed person.

Attendance, information and evidence

8.—(1) Regulations may make provision for requiring a claimant—
(a) to attend at such place and at such time as the Secretary of State may specify; and
(b) to provide information and such evidence as may be prescribed as to his circumstances, his availability for employment and the extent to which he is actively seeking employment.
(2) Regulations under subsection (1) may, in particular—
(a) prescribe circumstances in which entitlement to a jobseeker's allowance is to cease in the case of a claimant who fails to comply with any regulations made under that subsection;
(b) provide for entitlement to cease at such time (after he last attended in compliance with requirements of the kind mentioned in subsection (1)(a)) as may be determined in accordance with any such regulations;
(c) provide for entitlement not to cease if the claimant shows, within a prescribed period of his failure to comply, that he had good cause for that failure; and
(d) prescribe—
(i) matters which are, or are not, to be taken into account in determining whether a person has, or does not have, good cause for failing to comply with any such regulations; and
(ii) circumstances in which a person is, or is not, to be regarded as having, or not having, good cause for failing to comply with any such regulations.

DEFINITIONS
"claimant": s.35(1).
"employment": s.35(1).
"prescribed": s.35(1).
"regulations": s.35(1).

GENERAL NOTE
The Secretary of State already enjoys a general power to require claimants to produce "certificates, documents, information and evidence in connection with the claim" (Social Security (Claims and Payments) Regulations 1987 (S.I. 1987 No. 1968), reg. 7; on the scope of this provision, see *R(IS) 4/93*). In addition, so far as both UB and income support for unemployed people are concerned, there is a provision enabling the Secretary of

State to direct the attendance of claimants at an unemployment benefit office (Social Security (Claims and Payments) Regulations 1987 (S.I. No. 1968 of 1987), reg. 8). This is the basis of the requirement placed upon claimants to "sign on" to demonstrate their availability for work, and that they are actively seeking work. The enabling power in subs. (1)(a) largely replicates these existing powers, but subs. (1)(b) enables more detailed provision to be made. According to the DSS's *Notes on Clauses*, "regulations will enable local offices to monitor whether people continue to meet the conditions of entitlement". A failure to sign on, as at present, can lead to withdrawal of benefit, and subs. (2) also includes provisions allowing good cause to be used in appropriate cases where it is not possible to sign on at the allotted time.

The jobseeker's agreement

9.—(1) An agreement which is entered into by a claimant and an employment officer and which complies with the prescribed requirements in force at the time when the agreement is made is referred to in this Act as "a jobseeker's agreement".

(2) A jobseeker's agreement shall have effect only for the purposes of section 1.

(3) A jobseeker's agreement shall be in writing and be signed by both parties.

(4) A copy of the agreement shall be given to the claimant.

(5) An employment officer shall not enter into a jobseeker's agreement with a claimant unless, in the officer's opinion, the conditions mentioned in section 1(2)(a) and (c) would be satisfied with respect to the claimant if he were to comply with, or be treated as complying with, the proposed agreement.

(6) The employment officer may, and if asked to do so by the claimant shall forthwith, refer a proposed jobseeker's agreement to an adjudication officer for him to determine—

    (a) whether, if the claimant concerned were to comply with the proposed agreement, he would satisfy—

        (i) the condition mentioned in section 1(2)(a), or

        (ii) the condition mentioned in section 1(2)(c); and

    (b) whether it is reasonable to expect the claimant to have to comply with the proposed agreement.

(7) An adjudication officer to whom a reference is made under subsection (6)—

    (a) shall, so far as practicable, dispose of it in accordance with this section before the end of the period of 14 days from the date of the reference;

    (b) may give such directions, with respect to the terms on which the employment officer is to enter into a jobseeker's agreement with the claimant, as the adjudication officer considers appropriate;

    (c) may direct that, if such conditions as he considers appropriate are satisfied, the proposed jobseeker's agreement is to be treated (if entered into) as having effect on such date, before it would otherwise have effect, as may be specified in the direction.

(8) Regulations may provide—

    (a) for such matters as may be prescribed to be taken into account by an adjudication officer in giving a direction under subsection (7)(c); and

    (b) for such persons as may be prescribed to be notified of—

        (i) any determination of an adjudication officer under this section;

        (ii) any direction given by an adjudication officer under this section.

(9) Any determination of an adjudication officer under this section shall be binding.

(10) Regulations may provide that, in prescribed circumstances, a claimant is to be treated as having satisfied the condition mentioned in section 1(2)(b).

(11) Regulations may provide that, in prescribed circumstances, a job-seeker's agreement is to be treated as having effect on a date, to be determined in accordance with the regulations, before it would otherwise have effect.

(12) Except in such circumstances as may be prescribed, a jobseeker's agreement entered into by a claimant shall cease to have effect on the coming to an end of an award of a jobseeker's allowance made to him.

(13) In this section and section 10 "employment officer" means an officer of the Secretary of State or such other person as may be designated for the purposes of this section by an order made by the Secretary of State.

DEFINITIONS
  "adjudication officer": s.35(1).
  "claimant": s.35(1).
  "employment": s.35(1).
  "employment officer": subs. (13).
  "jobseeker's agreement": subs. (1).
  "prescribed": s.35(1).
  "regulations": s.35(1).

GENERAL NOTE
   This section governs the jobseeker's agreement, a feature of the JSA which has no parallel under the UB system. The notion of a jobseeker's agreement builds on the existing arrangements (introduced in 1990) for claimants to agree a "Back to Work Plan" (BTWP).
   The BTWP is a proforma document on which claimants are asked, at the end of a Restart or other review interview, to agree appropriate job search steps. The BTWP is, in principle, a purely voluntary matter; but even under the present arrangements a failure to match the steps agreed can be used as grounds for the withdrawal of benefit on the basis that it provides evidence that the claimant is not actively seeking work. The jobseeker's agreement, in contrast, is expressly stated to be a mandatory requirement for entitlement to JSA. Thus it is an essential condition of eligibility for JSA that the claimant "has entered into a jobseeker's agreement which remains in force" (s.1(2)(b)). The rationale for the jobseeker's agreement was explained in the White Paper (para. 4.16):
   "It will help jobseekers to identify with the Employment Service the steps back to work most appropriate for them and will enable their activities to be monitored effectively. The longer people stay on benefit the more their motivation and skills may decline. It is essential that all action possible is taken at an early stage of the period of unemployment and then regularly reviewed and monitored. The Jobseeker's Agreement is integral to that process".
   The jobseeker's agreement will also contain information about the facilities provided by the Employment Service and the standard of service which claimants can expect to receive, as set out in the Jobseeker's Charter (*ibid.*, para. 4.17).
   The original clause, which subsequently became this section, vested considerable power in the Secretary of State in terms of the legal framework involved. Following the criticisms of the House of Lords Select Committee on the Scrutiny of Delegated Powers (see Introduction and General Note, above), the Government brought forward amendments including what is now this section. Although an improvement on the clause in the Bill, this section still provides little more than an outline of the nature of the jobseeker's agreement, as subss. (1), (8), (10) and (11) include important enabling powers.
   A jobseeker's agreement is an agreement entered into by an employment officer (defined by subs. (13)) and the claimant, which satisfies prescribed conditions (subs. (1)). Regulations will specify that the agreement should cover certain matters such as the claimant's name, the type of work sought and any agreed restrictions on availability (*Fifth Report*, Annex I, para. 39). A special version of the agreement will be tailored for 16 and 17 year olds. A jobseeker's agreement exists only for the purpose of establishing title to benefit under s.1 (subs. (2)). It does not, therefore, create any contractual or other private law relationship. It must be in writing and signed by both parties (subs. (3)). A copy of the agreement must be given to the claimant (subs. (4)). The employment officer can only enter the agreement if the conditions in subs. (5) are met. If there is a disagreement between the employment officer and the claimant as to the appropriateness of the terms of the agreement, the issue may be referred for determination to an adjudication officer under subs. (6). The powers of the adjudication officer, whose decision is binding (subs. (9)), are dealt with in subs. (7). A jobseeker's agreement may be varied under s.10 and

review and appellate procedures are provided under s.11. Doubtless a key part of the six-monthly Restart interview for unemployed people will involve a review of the existing job-seeker's agreement.

Only time will tell how far jobseeker's agreements genuinely reflect a claimant's individual circumstances, and how far they will effectively be standard form contracts. There is undoubtedly some conceptual difficulty in characterising such a document as an "agreement", given that a person will not be able to establish entitlement to a basic form of income (JSA) in the absence of compliance. The point was put most forcefully by a Conservative backbencher: "I have never heard, however, of an agreement or contract that falls to be arbitrated by one of the parties to it and under which one party may impose penalties. In such circumstances, to talk of a jobseeker's agreement is an abuse of language in an abuse of power" (*per* Mr A. Howarth, *Hansard*, H.C. Vol. 262, col. 600).

For the quite separate provisions dealing with non-compliance by a claimant with a "jobseeker's direction" issued by an employment officer, see s.19(5)(a) and (10)(b).

Subs. (3)
Presumably where claimants are illiterate, then their mark will suffice (*R. v. Kent Justices* (1873) L.R. 8 Q.B. 305). In addition, for claimants who do not speak English, there is the moot question of what facilities will be available for interpretation where they do not have a relative or friend who can assist.

Subs. (5)
This provides that an employment officer "*shall* not enter" (emphasis added) into a job-seeker's agreement if the terms of the agreement are such that, were the claimant to act in accordance with them, the availability or actively seeking employment conditions would not be met. This appears to place the onus squarely on Employment Service staff to police claimants' compliance with the conditions of eligibility for JSA.

Subs. (6)
This provision enables proposed jobseeker's agreements to be referred by either the employment officer or the claimant for consideration by an adjudication officer. Further provisions for this process of referral are contained in subss. (7)–(9).

Subs. (7)(a)
This is in accordance with the standard statutory duty imposed on adjudication officers when dealing with claims (SSAA 1992, s.21(1)).

Subs. (7)(b)
Regulations made under this power will ensure that the employment officer may not refuse to sign an agreement which the adjudication officer considers appropriate (*Fifth Report*, Annex I, para. 42).

Subs. (7)(c)
Regulations made under this power will ensure that the agreement can be backdated to, *e.g.* the date of claim, if the adjudication officer decides that the claimant's proposals were satisfactory and reasonable (*Fifth Report*, Annex I, para. 42).

Subs. (9)
The adjudication officer's decision is binding but not final, so will be susceptible to formal review and appeal under the procedures specified in s.11.

Subs. (10)
This power enables regulations to be made so that claimants can be treated as having entered into a jobseeker's agreement which remains in force even when they have not done so. This power might be needed where a backlog of agreements arise because of a mass redundancy which stretches the resources of the local Employment Service in dealing with claimants (*Fifth Report*, Annex I, para. 44).

Subs. (11)
This will enable regulations to make provision for the backdating of jobseeker's agreements, *e.g.* where there is a gap between the date of claim and the date on which entitlement is decided.

This is essentially a technical matter, distinct from the similar power vested in adjudication officers under subs. (7)(c).

Subs. (12)
The normal position is that a jobseeker's agreement will not continue after a claim has been terminated. However, the Government wished to include this power to cover cases "in which it is desirable to allow an agreement to stand, for example, if a claimant disentitled himself to jobseeker's allowance for a short period during a claim" (*Fifth Report*, Annex I, para. 46).

Subs. (13)
Presumably this should read "In this section and sections 10 and 11 ...", as the term "employment officer" also appears in s.11, although it is not defined by that section or s.35.

Variation of jobseeker's agreement

10.—(1) A jobseeker's agreement may be varied, in the prescribed manner, by agreement between the claimant and any employment officer.

(2) Any agreement to vary a jobseeker's agreement shall be in writing and be signed by both parties.

(3) A copy of the agreement, as varied, shall be given to the claimant.

(4) An employment officer shall not agree to a variation of a jobseeker's agreement, unless, in the officer's opinion, the conditions mentioned in section 1(2)(a) and (c) would continue to be satisfied with respect to the claimant if he were to comply with, or be treated as complying with, the agreement as proposed to be varied.

(5) The employment officer may, and if asked to do so by the claimant shall forthwith, refer a proposed variation of a jobseeker's agreement to an adjudication officer for him to determine—

(a) whether, if the claimant concerned were to comply with the agreement as proposed to be varied, he would satisfy—
    (i) the condition mentioned in section 1(2)(a), or
    (ii) the condition mentioned in section 1(2)(c); and
(b) whether it is reasonable to expect the claimant to have to comply with the agreement as proposed to be varied.

(6) An adjudication officer to whom a reference is made under subsection (5)—

(a) shall, so far as practicable, dispose of it in accordance with this section before the end of the period of 14 days from the date of the reference;
(b) shall give such directions as he considers appropriate as to—
    (i) whether the jobseeker's agreement should be varied, and
    (ii) if so, the terms on which the claimant and the employment officer are to enter into an agreement to vary it;
(c) may bring the jobseeker's agreement to an end where the claimant fails, within a prescribed period, to comply with a direction given under paragraph (b)(ii);
(d) may direct that, if—
    (i) the jobseeker's agreement is varied, and
    (ii) such conditions as he considers appropriate are satisfied,
the agreement as varied is to be treated as having effect on such date, before it would otherwise have effect, as may be specified in the direction.

(7) Regulations may provide—

(a) for such matters as may be prescribed to be taken into account by an adjudication officer in giving a direction under subsection (6)(b) or (d); and
(b) for such persons as may be prescribed to be notified of—
    (i) any determination of an adjudication officer under this section;
    (ii) any direction given by an adjudication officer under this section.

(8) Any determination of an adjudication officer under this section shall be binding.

DEFINITIONS
   "adjudication officer": s.35(1).
   "claimant": s.35(1).
   "employment officer": s.9(13).
   "jobseeker's agreement": s.35(1).
   "prescribed": s.35(1).
   "regulations": s.35(1).

GENERAL NOTE
   This section makes provision for the variation of jobseekers' agreements and for the necessary adjudication arrangements. The jobseeker's agreement "is not a binding contract and it must not become a straitjacket" (*per* Lord Inglewood, *Hansard*, H.L. Vol. 563, col. 813). As one might expect, the statutory requirements for variation follow closely those for the creation of a jobseeker's agreement in the first instance. The purpose of this provision is to ensure that the agreement keeps pace with changes in the claimant's circumstances or with the labour market (*Fifth Report*, Annex I, para. 49). Reviews and appeals are dealt with in s.11.
   Variation can only take place by agreement of the claimant and the employment officer (subs. (1)). As with the original agreement, the varied agreement must be in writing and signed by both parties (subs. (2)), and a copy given to the claimant (subs. (3)). Subsections (4), (5), (7) and (8) replicate the provisions of s.9(5), (6), (8) and (9). The adjudication officer's powers under subs. (6) are based on those in s.9(7), but are modified to take account of the specific context of variation of an existing agreement.

Jobseeker's agreement: reviews and appeals

11.—(1) Any determination of, or direction given by, an adjudication officer under section 9 or 10 may be reviewed (by a different adjudication officer) on the application of the claimant or of an employment officer.

(2) Regulations may make provision with respect to the procedure to be followed on a review under this section.

(3) The claimant may appeal to a social security appeal tribunal against any determination of, or direction given by, an adjudication officer on a review under this section.

(4) A social security appeal tribunal determining an appeal under this section may give a direction of a kind which an adjudication officer may give under section 9(7)(b) or (c) or (as the case may be) section 10(6)(b) or (d).

(5) Where a social security appeal tribunal gives a direction under subsection (4) of a kind which may be given by an adjudication officer under section 10(6)(b)(ii), an adjudication officer may bring the jobseeker's agreement to an end if the claimant fails to comply with the direction within a prescribed period.

(6) An appropriate person may, on the ground that it was erroneous in point of law, appeal to a Commissioner against the decision of a social security appeal tribunal on an appeal under this section.

(7) Any of the following is an appropriate person for the purposes of subsection (6)—
   (a) the claimant;
   (b) an adjudication officer;
   (c) in prescribed circumstances, a trade union;
   (d) in prescribed circumstances, any other association which exists to promote the interests and welfare of its members.

(8) Subsections (7) to (10) of section 23 of the Administration Act (appeals to Commissioners) shall apply in relation to appeals under this section as they apply in relation to appeals under that section.

(9) In this section "Commissioner" has the same meaning as in the Administration Act.

  "adjudication officer": s.35(1).
  "Administration Act": s.35(1).
  "an appropriate person": subs. (7).
  "claimant": s.35(1).
  "Commissioner": subs. (9).
  "jobseeker's agreement": s.35(1).
  "regulations": s.35(1).

GENERAL NOTE

This section introduces a system of review and appeals following a referral of a jobseeker's agreement. The appeal arrangements proper, to a SSAT on any ground and then to a Social Security Commissioner on a point of law only, broadly follow those for mainstream social security matters (SSAA 1992, ss.22 and 23). There are, however, two important modifications. First, there is no *automatic* right of appeal; a claimant who is dissatisfied with an adjudication officer's decision following a referral under ss.9 or 10 must first seek a *review* by a different adjudication officer (subs. (1)). It is only thereafter that the claimant can appeal to a SSAT (subs. (3)). This interpolation of a mandatory internal review procedure follows the precedent set by appeals relating to disability living allowance and to child support maintenance assessments. There is a risk that such an arrangement discourages some claimants from exercising their right of appeal and merely prolongs the appeals process for those who do pursue the matter to a SSAT. Secondly, whereas either the employment officer or the claimant can seek an internal review (subs. (1)), only the claimant can lodge an appeal to a SSAT (subs. (3)). The SSAT has a similar power to issue directions as the adjudication officer (subs. (4)). Either the claimant or the adjudication officer, or indeed other interested parties, can appeal to the Commissioner (subss. (6) and (7)) on a point of law.

Subs. (1)

The expression "employment officer" is not defined in this section or in s.35. Presumably this is a drafting error, and it should be understood in the same sense as in s.9(13).

Subs. (6)

Erroneous in point of law. A decision may be erroneous in law if (1) it contains an incorrect proposition of law, (2) there has been a breach of the requirements of natural justice, (3) the tribunal's decision is supported by no evidence, (4) the facts found by the tribunal are such that no reasonable tribunal, properly directing itself on the law and relevant facts, could have come to the decision in question, and (5) there has been a failure to record adequately the reasons for the tribunal's decision (*R(SB) 11/83* ([1983] C.L.Y. 3542) and *R(SB) 18/83* ([1983] C.L.Y. 3573)).

Subs. (8)

This incorporates SSAA 1992, s.23(7)–(10) into this appeals system. Those provisions are concerned with the procedure for obtaining leave to appeal to the Commissioner and the Commissioner's powers on finding a tribunal decision to be erroneous in point of law.

Subs. (9)

On the appointment of Social Security Commissioners, see SSAA 1992, s.52.

Income and capital

Income and capital: general

12.—(1) In relation to a claim for a jobseeker's allowance, the income and capital of a person shall be calculated or estimated in such manner as may be prescribed.

(2) A person's income in respect of a week shall be calculated in accordance with prescribed rules.

(3) The rules may provide for the calculation to be made by reference to an average over a period (which need not include the week concerned).

(4) Circumstances may be prescribed in which—

(a) a person is treated as possessing capital or income which he does not possess;

(b) capital or income which a person does possess is to be disregarded;

(c) income is to be treated as capital;
(d) capital is to be treated as income.

DEFINITIONS
"prescribed": s.35(1).
"week": s.35(1).

GENERAL NOTE

This section enables regulations to prescribe the manner in which a claimant's income and capital should be calculated or estimated for the purposes of JSA. This is principally important in relation to the income-based JSA, but is also relevant to the contribution-based form of the benefit (see *e.g.* ss.2(1)(c) and 4(1)(b)). These wide enabling powers follow the model of SSCBA 1992, s.136 in relation to income support, and it is anticipated that the content of the substantive rules will be substantially the same for JSA. Thus under subs. (4), in assessing entitlement to benefit, certain forms of income will be disregarded (*e.g.* some benefits, such as disability living allowance) together with some types of capital (*e.g.* the claimant's home). See further Income Support (General) Regulations 1987 (S.I. 1987 No. 1967), regs. 40–51 and Scheds. 9 and 10. Further provision as regards the effect of income and capital is made by s.13.

Income and capital: income-based jobseeker's allowance

13.—(1) No person shall be entitled to an income-based jobseeker's allowance if his capital, or a prescribed part of it, exceeds the prescribed amount.

(2) Where a person claiming an income-based jobseeker's allowance is a member of a family, the income and capital of any member of that family shall, except in prescribed circumstances, be treated as the income and capital of the claimant.

(3) Regulations may provide that capital not exceeding the amount prescribed under subsection (1), but exceeding a prescribed lower amount, shall be treated, to a prescribed extent, as if it were income of a prescribed amount.

DEFINITIONS
"claimant": s.35(1).
"family": s.35(1).
"income-based jobseeker's allowance": ss.1(4) and 35(1).
"prescribed": s.35(1).
"regulations": s.35(1).

GENERAL NOTE

This section makes further provision for the treatment of a claimant's income and capital in determining whether an income-based JSA is payable. Subsection (1) enables a capital cut-off to be set by regulation, as under SSCBA 1992, s.135(1). The intention is to prescribe £8,000 as the capital limit for income-based JSA, as is the case with income support. The existing rules for aggregation of resources within a family are carried forward by subs. (2) (see SSCBA 1992, s.136(1)). There will continue to be exceptions to this principle, *e.g.* with the treatment of income and capital of children and young persons. Subsection (3) similarly allows the income support rules as regards deemed tariff income from capital (currently between £3,000 and £8,000) to be applied to JSA (see also SSCBA 1992, s.136(2)).

Trade disputes

Trade disputes

14.—(1) Where—
(a) there is a stoppage of work which causes a person not to be employed on any day, and
(b) the stoppage is due to a trade dispute at his place of work,
that person is not entitled to a jobseeker's allowance for the week which includes that day unless he proves that he is not directly interested in the dispute.

(2) A person who withdraws his labour on any day in furtherance of a trade dispute, but to whom subsection (1) does not apply, is not entitled to a jobseeker's allowance for the week which includes that day.

(3) If a person who is prevented by subsection (1) from being entitled to a jobseeker's allowance proves that during the stoppage—

(a) he became bona fide employed elsewhere;

(b) his employment was terminated by reason of redundancy within the meaning of section 81(2) of the Employment Protection (Consolidation) Act 1978, or

(c) he bona fide resumed employment with his employer but subsequently left for a reason other than the trade dispute,

subsection (1) shall be taken to have ceased to apply to him on the occurrence of the event referred to in paragraph (a) or (b) or (as the case may be) the first event referred to in paragraph (c).

(4) In this section "place of work", in relation to any person, means the premises or place at which he was employed.

(5) Where separate branches of work which are commonly carried on as separate businesses in separate premises or at separate places are in any case carried on in separate departments on the same premises or at the same place, each of those departments shall, for the purposes of subsection (4), be deemed to be separate premises or (as the case may be) a separate place.

DEFINITIONS

"employment": s.35(1).
"entitled": s.35(1).
"place of work": subs. (4).
"trade dispute": s.35(1).
"week": s.35(1).

GENERAL NOTE

This section essentially reproduces the existing UB trade dispute disqualification, currently in SSCBA 1992, s.27, and applies it to JSA. As at present, the disqualification applies in two situations. The first is where claimants are unemployed as a result of a stoppage of work due to a trade dispute at their place of work, unless they have no direct interest in the dispute (subs. (1)). The other traditional "escape routes" from disqualification under this head still apply (subs. (3)). The second is where claimants have withdrawn their labour in furtherance of a trade dispute (subs. (2)). In some respects the statutory language has been simplified, but presumably with no intention of changing its meaning (*e.g.* the use of the term "place of work" rather than "place of employment", although the complex dispensation for persons in separate branches of work is retained (subs. (5)). The considerable body of Commissioners' case law on the trade dispute disqualification will therefore remain important: see *Ogus, Barendt and Wikeley*, pp. 135–142, and the annotations to SSCBA 1992, s.27 in *Bonner*.

There are, however, two changes in the impact of these rules. First, where the disqualification bites, the claimant loses benefit for the whole week, given the nature of JSA (see s.1(3)), rather than for the individual days affected, as was the case with UB. The significance of the second change is less clear. Under SSCBA 1992, ss.27 and 126, a person involved in a trade dispute is *disqualified* for receiving UB and income support respectively. In other words, this period remains one of underlying entitlement but benefit is taken away. Under the new provision, such a person is simply *not entitled* to JSA at all. The practical significance of this change in terminology will only become evident when regulations are issued under the Act.

Effect on other claimants

15.—(1) Except in prescribed circumstances, subsection (2) applies in relation to a claimant for an income-based jobseeker's allowance where a member of his family "A") is, or would be, prevented by section 14 from being entitled to a jobseeker's allowance.

(2) For the purposes of calculating the claimant's entitlement to an income-based jobseeker's allowance—

(a) any portion of the applicable amount which is included in respect of A shall be disregarded for the period for which this subsection applies to the claimant;

(b) where the claimant and A are a married or unmarried couple, any portion of the applicable amount which is included in respect of them shall be reduced to one half for the period for which this subsection applies to the claimant;

(c) except so far as regulations provide otherwise, there shall be treated as the claimant's income—

(i) any amount which becomes, or would on an application duly made become, available to A in relation to that period by way of repayment of income tax deducted from A's emoluments in pursuance of section 203 of the Income and Corporation Taxes Act 1988 (PAYE); and

(ii) any other payment which the claimant or any member of his family receives or is entitled to obtain because A is without employment for that period; and

(d) any payment by way of a jobseeker's allowance for that period or any part of it which apart from this paragraph would be made to the claimant—

(i) shall not be made, if the weekly rate of payment ("the rate") would be equal to or less than the prescribed sum; and

(ii) shall be at a weekly rate equal to the difference between the rate and the prescribed sum, if the rate would be more than the prescribed sum.

(3) Where a reduction under subsection (2)(b) would not produce a sum which is a multiple of 5p, the reduction shall be to the nearest lower sum which is such a multiple.

(4) Where A returns to work with the same employer after a period during which subsection (2) applied to the claimant (whether or not his return is before the end of any stoppage of work in relation to which he is, or would be, prevented from being entitled to a jobseeker's allowance), subsection (2) shall cease to apply to the claimant at the commencement of the day on which A returns to work.

(5) In relation to any period of less than a week, subsection (2) shall have effect subject to such modifications as may be prescribed.

(6) Subsections (7) to (9) apply where an order made under section 150 of the Administration Act (annual up-rating of benefits) has the effect of increasing the sum prescribed in regulations made under section 4(5) as the personal allowance for a single person aged not less than 25 ("the personal allowance").

(7) For the sum prescribed in regulations made under subsection (2)(d) there shall be substituted, from the time when the order comes into force, a sum arrived at by increasing the prescribed sum by the percentage by which the personal allowance has been increased by the order.

(8) If the sum arrived at under subsection (7) is not a multiple of 50p—

(a) any remainder of 25p or less shall be disregarded;

(b) any remainder of more than 25p shall be rounded up to the nearest 50p.

(9) The order shall state the sum substituted for the sum prescribed in regulations made under subsection (2)(d).

(10) Nothing in subsection (7) prevents the making of further regulations under subsection (2)(d) varying the prescribed sum.

DEFINITIONS

"applicable amount": s.35(1).
"claimant": s.35(1).
"employment": s.35(1).
"entitled": s.35(1).
"family": s.35(1).
"income-based jobseeker's allowance": ss.1(4) and 35(1).
"prescribed": s.35(1).
"the rate": subs. (2)(d)(i).
"regulations": s.35(1).

General Note

This convoluted provision governs the amount of income-based JSA payable where a member of the claimant's family is involved in a trade dispute. The underlying principle is that where the partner of a person involved in a trade dispute makes a claim for JSA, then no benefit is payable in respect of the person involved in the dispute. Equally, it is designed to ensure that the claimant or a member of the family cannot benefit from any income received, or available, due to the dispute. The section accordingly follows the existing rules for income support contained in SSCBA 1992, s.126: see further the annotations in *Mesher and Wood*.

Subs. (1)

Where one member of a family is involved in a trade dispute, the family's reduced amount of income-based JSA is to be calculated in accordance with the principles in subs. (2). The Government intends to provide that entitlement to benefit is not affected by subs. (2) where a partner involved in a trade dispute falls ill or is within the maternity period (*Fifth Report* Annex I, para. 63).

Subs. (2)

The general principle in assessing entitlement to income-based JSA when one partner is involved in a trade dispute is that the rules governing the calculation of the applicable amount and the assessment of the claimant's income are much stricter than in the normal case. These less generous provisions are set out in this subsection (especially subss. (2)(a) and (b)).

Subsection (2)(c) contains a power to prescribe exceptions to the way in which various payments are taken into account. This is in similar terms to the power at SSCBA 1992, s.126(5)(a) which has never been exercised. The Government has stated it has no current intentions to utilise the power, but wishes to retain the flexibility to do so if appropriate: "any such exceptions would be beneficial to the claimant" (*Fifth Report*, Annex I, para. 64).

Subsection (2)(d) applies the deemed strike pay rule contained in SSCBA 1992, s.126(5)(b). See further subss. (6)–(10).

Subs. (3)

This is a rounding provision which simply ensures that parts of the applicable amount modified under subs. (2)(b) are expressed in terms of a multiple of 5p, in order to avoid awkward fractions.

Subs. (4)

In plain(er) English, the rules imposing reduced amounts of income-based JSA cease to apply as from the day the person involved in the trade dispute returns to work, whether or not there is a continuing stoppage of work.

Subs. (5)

This mirrors SSCBA 1992, s.126(6), a power which is used to enable part-weeks of benefit to be reduced by a proportion of the relevant sum appropriate to the number of days in the part-week: see Income Support (General) Regulations 1987 (S.I. 1987 No. 1967), reg. 77.

Subss. (6)–(10)

These provisions replicate those contained in SSCBA 1992, s.126(8), and are concerned with the impact of up-rating statements on the amount of deemed strike pay for the purposes of subs. (2)(d).

Persons under 18

Severe hardship

16.—(1) If it appears to the Secretary of State—
(a) that a person—
      (i) has reached the age of 16 but not the age of 18,
      (ii) is not entitled to a jobseeker's allowance or to income support, and
      (iii) is registered for training but is not being provided with any training, and
(b) that severe hardship will result to him unless a jobseeker's allowance is paid to him,
the Secretary of State may direct that this section is to apply to him.

(2) A direction may be given so as to have effect for a specified period.

(3) The Secretary of State may revoke a direction if—

(a) it appears to him that there has been a change of circumstances as a result of which failure to receive a jobseeker's allowance need no longer result in severe hardship to the person concerned;

(b) it appears to him that the person concerned has—

(i) failed to pursue an opportunity of obtaining training; or

(ii) rejected an offer of training,

and has not shown good cause for doing so; or

(c) he is satisfied that it was given in ignorance of some material fact or was based on a mistake as to some material fact and considers that, but for that ignorance or mistake, he would not have given the direction.

(4) In this section "period" includes—

(a) a period of a determinate length;

(b) a period defined by reference to the happening of a future event; and

(c) a period of a determinate length but subject to earlier determination upon the happening of a future event.

DEFINITIONS
  "employment": s.35(1).
  "period": subs. (4).
  "training": s.35(1).

GENERAL NOTE
  This is yet another provision which is carried over from the income support scheme (see SSCBA 1992, s.125). It deals with a residual category of entitlement to JSA for some 16 and 17 year olds. The basic rule is that entitlement to JSA does not arise until the age of 18 (s.3(1)(f)(i)), reflecting the Government's view that there is no need for 16 and 17 year olds to be unemployed and claiming benefit in view of the youth training guarantee. There are, however, three exceptions to this rule.
  First, certain 16 and 17 year olds, *e.g.* disabled young people and lone parents, are able to claim income support without having to be available for employment, actively seeking employment or registering for employment or training. Secondly, some other 16 and 17 year olds may claim JSA in their own right by virtue of s.3(1)(f)(iii). These include couples with children and young people leaving care. Thirdly, under this section, other 16 and 17 year olds may claim JSA if they can show that they would otherwise suffer severe hardship. For the most comprehensive guide to the law relating to the benefit entitlement of young people, see Ball and Maclagan, *Youthaid's Guide to Training and Benefits for Young People* (revised ed., 1995).
  Thus under subs. (1) the Secretary of State may issue a direction enabling a 16 or 17 year old to be paid benefit if failure to do so would result in severe hardship. The criteria for determining severe hardship include such matters as the young person's personal and financial circumstances, health, vulnerability, financial commitments and the prospect of postponing payments, the threat of or actually experienced homelessness and the family's ability to help. Such a direction is for a specified period (subs. (2)) and may be revoked on any one of the grounds set out in subs. (3). Revocation may lead to reduced payments under s.17.

Reduced payments

17.—(1) Regulations may provide for the amount of an income-based job-seeker's allowance payable to any young person to whom this section applies to be reduced—

(a) in such circumstances,

(b) by such a percentage, and

(c) for such a period,

as may be prescribed.

(2) This section applies to any young person in respect of whom—

(a) a direction is in force under section 16; and

(b) either of the conditions mentioned in subsection (3) is satisfied.

(3) The conditions are that—

(a) the young person was previously entitled to an income-based job-seeker's allowance and that entitlement ceased by virtue of the revocation of a direction under section 16;

(b) he has failed to complete a course of training and no certificate has been issued to him under subsection (4) with respect to that failure.

(4) Where a young person who has failed to complete a course of training—

(a) claims that there was good cause for the failure, and

(b) applies to the Secretary of State for a certificate under this subsection,

the Secretary of State shall, if he is satisfied that there was good cause for the failure, issue a certificate to that effect and give a copy of it to the young person.

(5) In this section "young person" means a person who has reached the age of 16 but not the age of 18.

DEFINITIONS

"income-based jobseeker's allowance": ss.1(4) and 35(1).
"prescribed": s.35(1).
"regulations": s.35(1).
"training": s.35(1).
"young person": subs. (5).

GENERAL NOTE

This provision did not appear in the White Paper or the original Bill, but was tabled as an amendment at the Report stage in the House of Commons (*Hansard*, H.C. Vol. 257, cols. 504–539). The changes are designed "to reflect the Government's opinion that young people who are offered suitable training should both accept it and complete it" (*per* Miss A. Widdecombe, Standing Committee B, col. 453, February 21, 1995). The Government has expressed particular concern about those young people who leave youth training courses without giving reasons. The amendments do not seek to address complaints that have been made about the quality of some training places.

This section accordingly provides for the amount of an income-based JSA payable to a young person subject to a s.16 direction to be reduced where specified circumstances are satisfied (subs. (2)). The amount of benefit otherwise payable can be reduced in two types of situation. The first is where entitlement to an income-based JSA is lost through revocation of the severe hardship direction (subs. (3)(a)). The second is where the young person has failed to complete a course of training and has not secured a certificate from the Secretary of State to the effect that there was good cause for that failure (subss. (3)(b) and (4)).

The changes to be introduced under this section represent both an easing and a tightening of the existing rules. The rules will be eased in that it will be justifiable for a young person to refuse a job offer if the job has no reasonable training element. More significantly, however, the rules will be narrowed as regards refusals of training offers. Under the new system, if young people reject two suitable training offers (or leave two places early without good cause, or a combination of the two), three consequences will flow from that decision. First, they will have taken themselves outside the youth training guarantee and will have to re-register for it. Secondly, they will no longer be able to refuse jobs on the grounds that they contain an insufficient training element. Thirdly, they will be subject to a penalty of 40 per cent in their income support for two weeks.

Recovery of overpayments

18. In the Administration Act, insert after section 71—

"Jobseeker's allowance

Recovery of jobseeker's allowance: severe hardship cases

71A.—(1) Where—

(a) a severe hardship direction is revoked; and

(b) it is determined by an adjudication officer that—

(i) whether fraudulently or otherwise, any person has mis-represented, or failed to disclose, any material fact; and

(ii) in consequence of the failure or misrepresentation, payment of a jobseeker's allowance has been made during the relevant period to the person to whom the direction related,

an adjudication officer may determine that the Secretary of State is entitled to recover the amount of the payment.

(2) In this section—

"severe hardship direction" means a direction given under section 16 of the Jobseekers Act 1995; and

"the relevant period" means—

(a) if the revocation is under section 16(3)(a) of that Act, the period beginning with the date of the change of circumstances and ending with the date of the revocation; and

(b) if the revocation is under section 16(3)(b) or (c) of that Act, the period during which the direction was in force.

(3) Where a severe hardship direction is revoked, the Secretary of State may certify whether there has been misrepresentation of a material fact or failure to disclose a material fact.

(4) If the Secretary of State certifies that there has been such misrepresentation or failure to disclose, he may certify—

(a) who made the misrepresentation or failed to make the disclosure; and

(b) whether or not a payment of jobseeker's allowance has been made in consequence of the misrepresentation or failure.

(5) If the Secretary of State certifies that a payment has been made, he may certify the period during which a jobseeker's allowance would not have been paid but for the misrepresentation or failure to disclose.

(6) A certificate under this section shall be conclusive as to any matter certified.

(7) Subsections (3) and (6) to (10) of section 71 above apply to a jobseeker's allowance recoverable under subsection (1) above as they apply to a jobseeker's allowance recoverable under subsection 71(1) above.

(8) The other provisions of section 71 above do not apply to a jobseeker's allowance recoverable under subsection (1) above."

DEFINITIONS
"adjudication officer": s.35(1).
"Administration Act": s.35(1).
"the relevant period": SSAA 1992, s.71A(2).
"severe hardship direction": SSAA 1992, s.71A(2).

GENERAL NOTE
This section, inserting a new SSAA 1992, s.71A, provides for the recovery of a jobseeker's allowance in specified circumstances where a severe hardship direction made under s.16 is revoked. This follows the existing rules under SSAA 1992, s.72.

Denial of jobseeker's allowance

Circumstances in which a jobseeker's allowance is not payable

19.—(1) Even though the conditions for entitlement to a jobseeker's allowance are satisfied with respect to a person, the allowance shall not be payable in any of the circumstances mentioned in subsection (5) or (6).

(2) If the circumstances are any of those mentioned in subsection (5), the period for which the allowance is not to be payable shall be such period (of at least one week but not more than 26 weeks) as may be prescribed.

(3) If the circumstances are any of those mentioned in subsection (6), the period for which the allowance is not to be payable shall be such period (of at least one week but not more than 26 weeks) as may be determined by the adjudication officer.

(4) Regulations pay prescribe—

(a) circumstances which an adjudication officer is to take into account, and

(b) circumstances which he is not to take into account,

in determining a period under subsection (3).

(5) The circumstances referred to in subsections (1) and (2) are that the claimant—

(a) has, without good cause, refused or failed to carry out any jobseeker's direction which was reasonable, having regard to his circumstances;

(b) has, without good cause—

(i) neglected to avail himself of a reasonable opportunity of a place on a training scheme or employment programme;

(ii) after a place on such a scheme or programme has been notified to him by an employment officer as vacant or about to become vacant, refused or failed to apply for it or to accept it when offered to him;

(iii) given up a place on such a scheme or programme; or

(iv) failed to attend such a scheme or programme on which he has been given a place; or

(c) has lost his place on such a scheme or programme through misconduct.

(6) The circumstances referred to in subsections (1) and (3) are that the claimant—

(a) has lost his employment as an employed earner through misconduct;

(b) has voluntarily left such employment without just cause;

(c) has, without good cause, after a situation in any employment has been notified to him by an employment officer as vacant or about to become vacant, refused or failed to apply for it or to accept it when offered to him; or

(d) has, without good cause, neglected to avail himself of a reasonable opportunity of employment.

(7) In such circumstances as may be prescribed, including in particular where he has been dismissed by his employer by reason of redundancy within the meaning of section 81(2) of the Employment Protection (Consolidation) Act 1978 after volunteering or agreeing to be so dismissed, a person who might otherwise be regarded as having left his employment voluntarily is to be treated as not having left voluntarily.

(8) Regulations may—

(a) prescribe matters which are, or are not, to be taken into account in determining whether a person—

(i) has, or does not have, good cause for any act or omission; or

(ii) has, or does not have, just cause for any act or omission; or

(b) prescribe circumstances in which a person—

(i) is, or is not, to be regarded as having, or not having, good cause for any act or omission; or

(ii) is, or is not, to be regarded as having, or not having, just cause for any act or omission.

(9) Subject to any regulations under subsection (8), in determining whether a person has, or does not have, good cause or (as the case may be) just cause for any act or omission, any matter relating to the level of remuneration in the employment in question shall be disregarded.

(10) In this section—

(a) "employment officer" means an officer of the Secretary of State or such other person as may be designated for the purposes of this section by an order made by the Secretary of State;

  (b) "jobseeker's direction" means a direction in writing given by an employment officer with a view to achieving one or both of the following—
     (i) assisting the claimant to find employment;
     (ii) improving the claimant's prospects of being employed; and
  (c) "training scheme" and "employment programme" have such meaning as may be prescribed.

DEFINITIONS
  "adjudication officer": s.35(1).
  "claimant": s.35(1).
  "employment": s.35(1).
  "employment officer": subs. (10).
  "employment programme": subs. (10).
  "jobseeker's direction": subs. (10).
  "prescribed": s.35(1).
  "regulations": s.35(1).
  "training scheme": subs. (10).
  "week": s.35(1).

GENERAL NOTE
  This section carries forward into the JSA scheme the sanctions which provide for claimants to be disqualified in cases of "voluntary unemployment" (SSCBA 1992, s.28), but with some important modifications. There are essentially two different types of disqualification from benefit involved. The first and less significant category comprises grounds for withdrawing benefit which are concerned with the claimant's failure to comply with official directions or with avoidable loss or refusal of a training scheme opportunity (subs. (5)). The second and more important group consists of those heads of disqualification listed in subs. (6), dealing with the avoidable loss or refusal of employment. The Secretary of State has increased his control over the use of these sanctions in four ways. First, he has reserved the power to specify a fixed period of disqualification for breaches of subs. (5) (see subs. (2)). Secondly, he may prescribe factors relevant to setting the period of disqualification under subs. (6) (see subs. (4)). Thirdly, he may define the circumstances which come within the redundancy exemption to the sanction for voluntarily leaving without just cause (subs. (7)). Finally, he has reserved the power to define what is and is not "good cause" and "just cause" for the purpose of these penalties (subs. (8)).

Subs. (2)
  Where the claimant is subject to a penalty under subs. (5), the period of disqualification will be for a fixed, prescribed period of between one week and 26 weeks. The Government's intention is to specify a period of two weeks, with four weeks for a second infringement. The justification for this system of fixed sanctions is that these types of cases are qualitatively different from those under subs. (6) (which are dealt with on a discretionary basis under subs. (3)), and lend themselves to readily understandable sanctions for non-compliance (*Fifth Report*, Annex I, para. 73).
  It should be noted that under subs. (2) and (5) there is no express reference to the decision-making machinery for determination of such issues. This should be contrasted with subs. (3), which specifically provides for the period of disqualification for voluntary unemployment cases to be such period "as may be determined by the adjudication officer". The omission of such a requirement in subs. (2) would enable the development of a two-tier system of benefit sanctions, as envisaged in an Employment Department internal memorandum, *Submission on moving labour market adjudication to the front line under JSA* (unpublished, December 1, 1994). If this policy is adopted, adjudication officers would continue to deal with cases of voluntary leaving and misconduct, while Employment Service Client Advisers would make decisions in relation to refusals or failures to attend training programmes. However, during the passage of the Bill the Minister of State indicated that adjudication officers would decide whether sanctions should be imposed for non-compliance with a jobseeker's direction under subs. (5)(a) (*per* Miss A. Widdecombe, Standing Committee B, col. 513, February 21, 1995).

Subs. (3)
  Where the claimant is subject to a penalty under subs. (6), the period of disqualification will be for a period of between one week and 26 weeks, at the discretion of the adjudication officer. The current disqualification period may be for as little as one day, but the move to a one-week mini-

mum period is in keeping with the general shift towards JSA as a weekly benefit (s.1(3)). For the power to prescribe relevant factors in determining the appropriate period, see subs. (4).

Subs. (4)

For the first time the Secretary of State has, in this provision, assumed the power to prescribe what matters are (and are not) to be taken into account in assessing the appropriate period of disqualification under subs. (3). It is unclear how extensive this guidance will be; on the existing body of Commissioners' case law, see further the annotations to SSCBA 1992, s.28 in *Bonner*). The Government has indicated that guidelines will be made as regards sanctions for refusal of temporary work (*Fifth Report*, Annex I, para. 74).

Subs. (5)

The common theme between these various grounds for disqualification is that they are all concerned with a claimant's failure to follow out official directions or to complete satisfactorily an official training programme. For the length of any penalty, see subs. (2).

Para. (a). This is a reformulation of the existing rather convoluted head of disqualification under SSCBA 1992, s.28(1)(d), dealing with refusals or failures to carry out official recommendations given with a view to assisting the person to find employment. That provision had effectively fallen into desuetude, and it remains to be seen how often the new sanction is invoked. The new provision is wider than its predecessor in that a jobseeker's direction may be designed to improve "the claimant's prospects of being employed" (subs. (10)(b)(ii)). Thus an employment officer might direct a claimant to enhance such employability by "attending a course to improve jobseeking skills or motivation, or taking steps to present themselves acceptably to employers. This Jobseeker's Direction will be an important means of ensuring that jobseekers are taking the right steps to get back to work" (White Paper, para. 4.18). The jobseeker's direction may therefore be deployed to enforce compulsory attendance at various Government training or "re-motivation" courses, involvement in which has in most instances been voluntary to date.

Para. (b). The first two of these grounds are essentially the same as the existing heads of disqualification under SSCBA 1992, s.28(1)(f) and (g). The latter two heads, subs. (5)(b)(iii) and (iv), appear to replace in part s.28(1)(e) insofar as that penalises claimants who "voluntarily left such a place without good cause".

The heads of disqualification under both paras. (5)(b) and (c) all refer to a "training scheme" or "employment programme". These terms are to have such meanings as are prescribed in regulations (subs. (10)(c)). The existing grounds in SSCBA 1992, s.28 refer to "approved training schemes", an expression which was expressly defined under s.28(6)(c). *Bonner* suggests that at present SSATs enjoy the power to determine whether a scheme does in fact fall within the criteria specified in s.28(6)(c). That possibility, albeit a rather remote one, is excluded under the new regime, where the question is simply whether the scheme or programme is "prescribed" (subs. (10)(c)).

Para. (c). This partly replicates the existing head of disqualification under SSCBA 1992, s.28(1)(e).

Subs. (6)

These are long standing grounds for disqualification from UB (SSCBA 1992, s.28(1)(a)–(c)). They are all concerned with avoidable loss or refusal of employment, and must therefore be distinguished from those under subs. (5) in connection with failures to carry out official directions or to complete training programmes. On the existing body of Commissioners' case law, see further the annotations in *Bonner* to SSCBA 1992, s.28. For the length of any penalty, see subs. (3).

Two important changes to the practical arrangements for such cases were announced during the passage of the Bill (Standing Committee B, cols. 762–764, March 7, 1995). At present, the procedure is that, where a voluntary unemployment question arises, the claimant is automatically suspended from UB (if otherwise eligible) and (again, if eligible) receives reduced payments of income support pending determination of the question by an adjudication officer. The reduction is 20 per cent or 40 per cent of the income support personal allowance, depending on the circumstances. If the decision is in the claimant's favour, either at first instance or on appeal, then arrears of benefit are paid. The JSA arrangements adopt a different approach. First, full payment of JSA will be made, pending the outcome of the adjudication officer's decision, with any sanction being imposed from the date of that determination. However, where a sanction is imposed, there will be no automatic entitlement to reduced income-based JSA. Claimants will have to demonstrate hardship under the restrictive rules which currently apply to those who have breached the requirements of availability for, and actively seeking, employment (see s.20(4)–(6)). Those whose compliance with the latter requirements is doubtful will remain suspended until a decision is made.

Subs. (7)

This provision follows the precedent set by SSCBA 1992, s.28(4), and is designed to remove the threat of disqualification from persons who volunteer for or agree to redundancy. There is a considerable body of case law from the Commissioners on the proper interpretation of s.28(4), not all of it entirely mutually consistent (see *R(U) 3/91* and the unreported decisions on this point discussed in *Bonner*). The new provision is different in two respects. First, this subsection is technically more accurate in that it deems such persons "as not having left voluntarily". Section 28(4) at present declares that such a person "shall not be deemed to have left his employment voluntarily", when there are in fact no such "deeming" provisions. Secondly, and more significantly, the new subsection reserves to the Secretary of State the right to specify in regulations the circumstances in which a person is to be treated as not having left voluntarily. The Government has indicated that regulations will provide that "provided there is a genuine redundancy situation, the exact manner of the termination of employment is not to affect the protection provided by the power" (*Fifth Report*, Annex I, para. 75).

Subs. (8)

The notion of "good cause" is an important safeguard so far as disqualifications under subss. (5)(a) and (b) and (6)(c) and (d) are concerned. This provision in part enables the Secretary of State to specify what can and cannot constitute good cause. This follows the precedent set in the SS (USI) Regulations 183, reg. 12E. However, the Secretary of State also now has the power to prescribe what is (and is not) relevant in determining "just cause", which applies to cases of voluntary leaving under subs. (6)(b). This has been the subject of a considerable body of case law (see *e.g. Crewe v. Anderson (National Insurance Officer), sub nom. Crewe v. Social Security Commissioner (R(U) 3/81)* [1982] 2 All E.R. 745 and *R(U) 4/87*) but no statutory guidance to date. Presumably the new regulations will seek to codify the existing body of case law (on which see the analysis in the annotations to SSCBA 1992, s.28(1)(a) in *Bonner*). The Government's argument is that "it is preferable for adjudication officers to make their decision on the basis of regulation, rather than on a complex body of case law, in order to introduce greater clarity and transparency into the process of making decisions" (*Fifth Report*, Annex I, para. 76). Yet it remains questionable whether the use of regulations is a sufficiently sensitive way for dealing with issues such as this which embody a considerable discretionary element. Clarity and transparency are certainly not attributes that are commonly associated with social security legislation.

Subs. (9)

This replaces the existing law to some extent (see SSCBA 1992, s.28(5)), but is wider in that it applies the principle that the level of remuneration is to be disregarded in cases where "just cause" rather than "good cause" is in issue. At present this principle governs only the latter type of case. There is clear authority in the current case law which demonstrates that workers may have "just cause" for leaving a job where they are expected to suffer a drop in wages (*R(U) 15/53*). It remains to be seen how far this protection is preserved under the JSA scheme, although it should be noted that this subsection is made expressly subject to regulations made under subs. (8).

Exemptions from section 19

20.—(1) Nothing in section 19, or in regulations under that section, shall be taken to prevent payment of a jobseeker's allowance merely because the claimant refuses to seek or accept employment in a situation which is vacant in consequence of a stoppage of work due to a trade dispute.

(2) Section 19 does not apply, in the circumstances mentioned in subsection (5) of that section, if—

    (a) a direction is in force under section 16 with respect to the claimant; and

    (b) he has acted in such a way as to risk—

        (i) having that direction revoked under subsection (3)(b) of section 16; or

(ii) having the amount of his jobseeker's allowance reduced by virtue of section 17, because he has failed to complete a course of training.

(3) Regulations shall make provision for the purpose of enabling any person of a prescribed description to accept any employed earner's employment without falling within section 19(6)(b) or (d) should he leave that employment voluntarily and without just cause at any time during a trial period.

(4) In such circumstances as may be prescribed, an income-based jobseeker's allowance shall be payable to a claimant even though section 19 prevents payment of a jobseeker's allowance to him.

(5) A jobseeker's allowance shall be payable by virtue of subsection (4) only if the claimant has complied with such requirements as to the provision of information as may be prescribed for the purposes of this subsection.

(6) Regulations under subsection (4) may, in particular, provide for a jobseeker's allowance payable by virtue of that subsection to be—

(a) payable at a prescribed rate;

(b) payable for a prescribed period (which may differ from the period fixed under section 19(2) or (3)).

(7) In subsection (3), "trial period" has such meaning as may be prescribed.

(8) Regulations may make provision for determining, for the purposes of this section, the day on which a person's employment is to be regarded as commencing.

DEFINITIONS

"adjudication officer": s.35(1).
"claimant": s.35(1).
"employment": s.35(1).
"income-based jobseeker's allowance": ss.1(4) and 35(1).
"jobseeker's agreement": ss.9(1) and 35(1).
"regulations": s.35(1).
"trade dispute": s.35(1).
"trial period": subs. (7).

GENERAL NOTE

This section is consequential upon s.19 and makes further provision for the sanctions to be applied in cases of voluntary unemployment, and as such is modelled in part on SSCBA 1992, s.29. The section contains three exemptions from the sanctions contained in s.19 (subss. (1)–(3)) as well as provision for hardship payments where JSA is not payable because of the operation of s.19 (subss. (4)–(6)).

Subs. (1)

This provision re-enacts a long standing principle of social security law that a claimant should not be penalised for declining to act as a strike-breaker (see also SSCBA 1992, s.29(1)(a)).

Subs. (2)

This essentially avoids the position whereby certain 16 or 17 year olds might face the risk of double jeopardy. It makes it clear that a young person who is the subject of a severe hardship direction and who faces the revocation of that direction or a reduction in JSA should be dealt with under ss.16 or 17 as appropriate, and not under s.19.

Subs. (3)

Regulations made under this subsection will allow a claimant to accept a job and then leave it within a trial period (as defined in regulations under subs. (7)) without incurring the voluntary unemployment sanction. The intention is that claimants will have to be unemployed for 13 weeks in order to qualify for this safeguard, a reduction in the present 26-week qualifying period (see SS (USI) Regulations 1983, reg. 12G(1)).

Subs. (4)

This subsection enables regulations to define the situations in which claimants subject to a s.19 sanction can nonetheless receive hardship payments of JSA at a reduced rate. Under the existing rules, non-attendance on a mandatory course is penalised by a reduction of 40 per cent in the personal allowance for a single income support claimant for the week in question. This will be replaced by a disqualification from all benefit entitlement for two weeks, rising to four weeks for a further breach. See further subs. (6).

Subs. (5)
The standard powers relating to the provision of information exist in relation to details necessary to decide a claim. In these hardship cases the claim will already have been determined, hence the need for this enabling power to ensure that information can be required where the claim has already been determined, but benefit is not payable because of the sanction.

Subs. (6)
The Government's intention is that certain vulnerable groups will be able to claim hardship payments from the beginning of the period in which the sanction operates. These will include claimants with children, those who are sick, disabled or pregnant, and those with caring responsibilities. Other claimants will only qualify for hardship payments after the first two weeks. The necessary corollary of this is that some claimants will have no means of subsistence for four weeks, as JSA is payable fortnightly in arrears.

Subs. (7)
Regulations will define a trial period as the period between the end of the fourth week and the end of the twelfth week of a claimant's employment (*Fifth Report* Annex I, para. 83). This is rather more generous than the existing definition of 6 to 12 weeks (SSCBA 1992, s.29(2)). For the difficulties in determining when precisely the relevant week ends, see *R(U) 1/92*.

Subs. (8)
Regulations will, as at present, specify that a person's employment is to be regarded as commencing for the purposes of the trial period on the Sunday of the week in which the work starts, so allowing the rule to be administered in calendar weeks (*Fifth Report*, Annex I, para. 84). See also SS (USI) Regulations 1983, ret. 12G.

Miscellaneous

Supplementary provisions

21. Further provisions in relation to a jobseeker's allowance are set out in Schedule 1.

GENERAL NOTE
This section introduces Sched. 1 which contains miscellaneous supplementary powers.

Members of the forces

22.—(1) Regulations may modify any provision of this Act, in such manner as the Secretary of State thinks proper, in its application to persons who are or have been members of Her Majesty's forces.

(2) The regulations may, in particular, provide for section 19(6)(b) not to apply in relation to a person who is discharged from Her Majesty's forces at his own request.

(3) For the purposes of this section, Her Majesty's forces shall be taken to consist of such establishments and organisations in which persons serve under the control of the Defence Council as may be prescribed.

DEFINITIONS
"Her Majesty's forces": subs. (3).
"prescribed": s.35(1).
"regulations": s.35(1).

GENERAL NOTE
This section enables regulations to be made modifying the provisions of the Act in relation to members of the armed forces, especially as regards the sanction for leaving employment voluntarily. It reflects the existing position under SSCBA 1992, s.116; see further *Ogus, Barendt and Wikeley*, p. 143. The current regulations exclude serving members of HM Forces from unem-

ployment benefit except, in appropriate circumstances, members of territorial or reserve forces and members of the Ulster Defence Regiment. It is intended that regulations made under subs. (2) will also carry forward the existing rule, namely that persons who are discharged from HM Forces at their own request may not be subject to a sanction for leaving their employment voluntarily.

Recovery of sums in respect of maintenance

23.—(1) Regulations may make provision for the court to have power to make a recovery order against any person where an award of income-based jobseeker's allowance has been made to that person's spouse.

(2) In this section "recovery order" means an order requiring the person against whom it is made to make payments to the Secretary of State or to such other person or persons as the court may determine.

(3) Regulations under this section may make provision for the transfer by the Secretary of State of the right to receive payments under, and to exercise rights in relation to, a recovery order.

(4) Regulations made under this section may, in particular, include provision—

(a) as to the matters to which the court is, or is not, to have regard in determining any application under the regulations; and

(b) as to the enforcement of recovery orders.

(5) In this section, "the court" means—

(a) in relation to England and Wales, a magistrates' court; and

(b) in relation to Scotland, the sheriff.

DEFINITIONS
"court, the": subs. (5).
"income-based jobseeker's allowance": ss.1(4) and 35(1).
"recovery order": subs. (2).
"regulations": s.35(1).

GENERAL NOTE
This section is concerned with the liability of individuals to maintain their spouses. It provides for regulations to be made enabling (i) the court to make a recovery order where a spouse of a liable person has received income-based JSA (subs. (2)), and (ii) the Secretary of State to transfer the right to receive payment under, and to exercise rights in relation to, that order (subs. (3)). The section therefore carries forward powers which currently exist under the income support scheme so far as spousal maintenance is concerned (SSAA 1992, ss.106 and 107). How far these powers are used in practice remains to be seen, given the emphasis on securing child support maintenance under the Child Support Act 1991 (c. 48).

Effect of alteration of rates

24. In the Administration Act, insert after section 159—

"Effect of alteration of rates of a jobseeker's allowance

159A.—(1) This section applies where—

(a) an award of a jobseeker's allowance is in force in favour of any person ("the recipient"); and

(b) an alteration—

(i) in any component of the allowance, or

(ii) in the recipient's benefit income,

affects the amount of the jobseeker's allowance to which he is entitled.

(2) Subsection (3) applies where, as a result of the alteration, the amount of the jobseeker's allowance to which the recipient is entitled is increased or reduced.

(3) As from the commencing date, the amount of the jobseeker's allowance payable to or for the recipient under the award shall be the increased or reduced amount, without any further decision of an adjudication officer; and the award shall have effect accordingly.

(4) In any case where—

(a) there is an alteration of a kind mentioned in subsection (1)(b); and

(b) before the commencing date (but after that date is fixed) an award of a jobseeker's allowance is made in favour of a person,

the award may provide for the jobseeker's allowance to be paid as from the commencing date, in which case the amount of the jobseeker's allowance shall be determined by reference to the components applicable on that date, or may provide for an amount determined by reference to the components applicable at the date of the award.

(5) In this section—

"alteration" means—

(a) in relation to any component of a jobseeker's allowance, its alteration by or under any enactment; and

(b) in relation to a person's benefit income, the alteration of any of the sums referred to in section 150 above by any enactment or by an order under section 150 above, to the extent that any such alteration affects the amount of the recipient's benefit income;

"benefit income", in relation to a recipient, means so much of his income as consists of—

(a) benefit under the Contributions and Benefits Act; or

(b) a war disablement pension or war widow's pension;

"the commencing date" in relation to an alteration, means the date on which the alteration comes into force in relation to the recipient;

"component", in relation to a jobseeker's allowance, means any of the sums specified in regulations under the Jobseekers Act 1995 which are relevant in calculating the amount payable by way of a jobseeker's allowance."

DEFINITIONS

"adjudication officer": s.35(1).
"Administration Act": s.35(1).
"alteration": SSAA 1992, s.159(A)(5).
"benefit income": SSAA 1992, s.159A(5).
"commencing date, the": SSAA 1992, s.159(5).
"component": SSAA 1992, s.159(5).
"entitled": s.35(1).
"recipient, the" SSAA 1992, s.159A(1)(a).

GENERAL NOTE

This section inserts a new s.159A into the SSAA 1992 and is concerned with the computation of benefit, principally at the time of the annual uprating. The general rule is that where there is any change in benefit rates, as specified in s.159A(1)(b), then any consequential change in the amount of JSA payable takes effect without the need for a formal decision by an adjudication officer (s.159A(3)). This follows the existing provision governing the effect of an alteration in the component rates of income support (SSAA 1992, s.159). As there is no decision by an adjudication officer, it follows that there is no right of appeal in relation to such a change. As regards the possibility of a request for a review, see the annotations to reg. 69(3) and (3A) of the Social Security (Adjudication) Regulations 1986 (S.I. 1986 No. 2218) in *Mesher and Wood* (now Social Security (Adjudication) Regulations 1995 (S.I. No. 1801 of 1995), reg. 63(3)).

Age increases

25. In the Administration Act, insert after section 160—

"Implementation of increases in income-based jobseeker's allowance due to attainment of particular ages

160A.—(1) This section applies where—

(a) an award of an income-based jobseeker's allowance is in force in favour of a person ("the recipient"); and

(b) a component has become applicable, or applicable at a particular rate, because he or some other person has reached a particular age ("the qualifying age").

(2) If, as a result of the recipient or other person reaching the qualifying age, the recipient becomes entitled to an income-based jobseeker's allowance of an increased amount, the amount payable to or for him under the award shall, as from the day on which he becomes so entitled, be that increased amount, without any further decision of an adjudication officer; and the award shall have effect accordingly.

(3) Subsection (2) above does not apply where, in consequence of the recipient or other person reaching the qualifying age, a question arises in relation to the recipient's entitlement to—

(a) a benefit under the Contributions and Benefits Act; or

(b) a jobseeker's allowance.

(4) Subsection (3)(b) above does not apply to the question—

(a) whether the component concerned, or any other component, becomes or ceases to be applicable, or applicable at a particular rate, in the recipient's case; and

(b) whether, in consequence, the amount of his income-based jobseeker's allowance falls to be varied.

(5) In this section "component", in relation to a recipient and his jobseeker's allowance, means any of the amounts determined in accordance with regulations made under section 4(5) of the Jobseekers Act 1995."

DEFINITIONS

"adjudication officer": s.35(1).
"Administration Act": s.35(1).
"component": SSAA 1992, s.160A(5).
"Contributions and Benefits Act, the": SSAA 1992, s.191.
"entitled": s.35(1).
"income-based jobseeker's allowance": ss.1(4) and 35(1).
"qualifying age, the": SSAA 1992, s.160A(1)(b).
"recipient, the": SSAA 1992, s.160A(1)(a).

GENERAL NOTE

This section, which inserts a new s.160A into the SSAA 1992, is concerned with making routine adjustments to the amount of income-based JSA consequential upon the claimant, or a relevant member of the family, attaining a particular age. For example, under s.160A(1), a pensioner premium will become payable to a male jobseeker at 60, who chooses to continue claiming JSA rather than income support. Equally a child in the claimant's family may reach the age at which a higher personal allowance is payable. Such increases are made without the need for a decision by an adjudication officer. This section therefore follows the pattern set by SSAA 1992, ss.159, 159A and 160.

PART II

BACK TO WORK SCHEMES

The back to work bonus

26.—(1) Regulations may make provision for the payment, in prescribed circumstances, of sums to or in respect of persons who are or have been entitled to a jobseeker's allowance or to income support.

(2) A sum payable under the regulations shall be known as a "back to work bonus".

(3) Subject to section 617 of the Income and Corporation Taxes Act 1988 (which, as amended by paragraph 16 of Schedule 2, provides for a back to work bonus not to be taxable), a back to work bonus shall be treated for all purposes as payable by way of a jobseeker's allowance or (as the case may be) income support.

(4) The regulations may, in particular, provide for—

(a) a back to work bonus to be payable only on the occurrence of a prescribed event;
(b) a bonus not to be payable unless a claim is made before the end of the
prescribed period;
(c) the amount of a bonus (subject to any maximum prescribed by virtue
of paragraph (g)) to be determined in accordance with the regulations;
(d) enabling amounts to be calculated by reference to periods of entitlement to a jobseeker's allowance and periods of entitlement to income
support;
(e) treating a bonus as payable wholly by way of income support or wholly
by way of a jobseeker's allowance, in a case where amounts have been
calculated in accordance with provision made by virtue of paragraph
(d);
(f) keeping persons who may be entitled to a bonus informed of the
amounts calculated in accordance with any provision of the regulations made by virtue of paragraph (c);
(g) the amount of a bonus not to exceed a prescribed maximum;
(h) a bonus not to be payable if the amount of the bonus which would
otherwise be payable is less than the prescribed minimum;
(i) prescribed periods to be disregarded for prescribed purposes;
(j) a bonus which has been paid to a person to be treated, in prescribed
circumstances and for prescribed purposes, as income or capital of his
or of any other member of his family;
(k) treating the whole or a prescribed part of an amount which has
accrued towards a person's bonus—
(i) as not having accrued towards his bonus; but
(ii) as having accrued towards the bonus of another person;
(l) the whole or a prescribed part of a back to work bonus to be payable,
in such circumstances as may be prescribed, to such person, other than
the person who is or had been entitled to a jobseeker's allowance or to
income support, as may be determined in accordance with the
regulations.

DEFINITIONS
"a back to work bonus": subs. (2).
"family": s.35(1).
"prescribed": s.35(1).
"regulations": s.35(1).

GENERAL NOTE
This section introduces one of the central proposals of the White Paper. The purpose of the
back to work bonus scheme is to enable claimants who take on part-time work and so lose some
entitlement to benefit to build up entitlement to a lump sum payment. This lump sum payment
will then be paid to them when they move off benefit completely. As with much of the Act, this
section essentially provides little more than a regulation-making framework for the new scheme.
The existing rules governing UB and income support are undoubtedly both complex and a
disincentive to take up work. Under the UB scheme, unemployed people are not entitled to
benefit for any day on which they earn more than £2, or for any week in which they earn in excess
of the lower earnings limit (currently £58 per week). For income support purposes, unemployed
people can retain the first £5 per week that they earn, but any earnings thereafter reduce their
benefit entitlement pound for pound. A couple who are both under 60 and have been continuously entitled to income support for at least two years are entitled to the higher disregard of £15
(this group will no longer be able to claim this higher disregard once JSA is introduced: White
Paper, para. 4.30).
The position with JSA will be different. Unemployed people and their partners will still keep
the first £5 per week of their earnings (£10 in the case of couples) but lose benefit pound for
pound thereafter. However, for every pound that they earn above that level, they will build up
entitlement to a credit of 50p. This will then be paid in a lump sum when the claimant moves into
employment of 16 hours or more a week (24 hours or more for partners). The Government's
intention is to prescribe a maximum lump sum of £1,000 (by regulations made under subs.
(4)(g)). For example, people earning £30 a week will have their JSA reduced by £25 a week,

given the operation of the £5 disregard. However, £12.50 a week will be accrued under the back to work bonus. If they then return to full-time work 10 weeks later, they will receive a lump sum of £125; if they move off benefit 20 weeks later, they will be paid a lump sum of £250. The Government anticipates that 150,000 bonuses will be paid in a full year to JSA claimants.

It might be argued that the difficulty with the back to work bonus is that it does not provide claimants with the money when they most need it, *i.e.* when living on a low income consisting of benefit plus disregarded part-time earnings. It also presupposes compliance with the rules governing such earnings and benefit entitlement. The new scheme is quite distinct from the Jobfinder's Grant, designed to meet the transitional costs of unemployed people taking up jobs, which was introduced on a national basis in April 1995 (see Introduction and General Note).

Subs. (1)

The important wording here is "persons who *are or have been* entitled to" (emphasis added) JSA or income support. This enables payments to be claimed by a person either before or after leaving benefit. The groups eligible for the bonus will be all claimants of JSA and income support claimants aged under 60.

Subs. (3)

The back to work bonus, unlike other elements of JSA, will not be taxable.

Subs. (4)

The variety and breadth of these enabling powers demonstrates the extent to which the detail of the back to work bonus is to be determined by the Secretary of State. The first regulations under this section are subject to the affirmative procedure (s.37(1)(b)). The Government's view is that this approach is necessary in order to "retain a discretion to adapt the detailed rules in the light of experience of the scheme's operation, and to reflect changing labour-market conditions" (*Fifth Report*, Annex, para. 95). The following information about the Government's intentions is drawn from that same source.

Para. (a). The principal event in which the bonus will become payable is when claimants terminate their claim to JSA or income support as a result of moving into remunerative work (or their partner doing so). The bonus will also be paid to claimants when they reach the age of 60 on income support, or when they move off JSA at retirement age.

Para. (b). The prescribed time-limit will normally be 12 weeks after leaving benefit. There will be a standard "good cause" provision for late claims.

Para. (c). An amount equal to half of the amount by which benefit is reduced as a result of the claimant (or partner) receiving part-time earnings will count towards the build-up of the bonus. It is said that adjudication officers will decide on a weekly basis the amount which will count towards the bonus, and will determine both eligibility and the amount of any bonus when a claim is made. In practice the success of this reform will depend greatly on the quality of the computer systems involved.

Para. (d). This will enable separate periods in receipt of JSA and income support to be aggregated for the purposes of establishing entitlement to the bonus. This would benefit a lone parent who, over a period of time, might move from JSA to income support (or vice versa).

Para. (e). Where aggregation has taken place under subs. (4)(d), this provision enables the resulting bonus to be treated as one derived wholly from JSA or income support. By concentrating on the benefit currently in payment, this should ease potential administrative complications.

Para. (f). The intention is to notify claimants on a quarterly basis of the document of bonus accrued in their name. This is clearly designed as an incentive measure.

Para. (g). The basic rule will be a maximum bonus of £1,000 per benefit claim unit. Thus where two partners are involved in a single claim, the maximum bonus will still be £1,000. An exception will be where two previously single people become a couple for social security purposes and the aggregated total of their accrued bonuses exceeds £1,000: in such a situation the accrued amount will be frozen at that figure over £1,000. So two individuals with accrued bonuses of £900 each would be well advised to delay becoming a couple until their bonuses have been cashed in. This therefore represents another good reason for claimants to seek to avoid the impact of the so-called cohabitation rule. Similarly, it might also operate as a rather perverse disincentive against marriage.

Para. (h). The lower limit will be set at £5, in order to avoid undue administrative costs. This is arguably a very generous lower threshold for payment, as it will presumably cost considerably more to process a claim for a bonus at this level than the amount of the bonus itself.

Para (i). Claimants will be required to have been in receipt of JSA or income support for 13 weeks before they begin accruing the bonus. No earnings will count towards the back to work bonus between April and October 1996, but people unemployed in October for three months will qualify at once for the new scheme.

Where a person has claimed the bonus and subsequently makes a fresh claim for benefit, the 13 weeks' qualifying period will have to be served again. The Government also intends to introduce a linking rule protecting people who take spells out of the labour market because of ill-health. Thus a person who has accrued a bonus and then falls sick and has to claim incapacity benefit, or has to care for another person and claim invalid care allowance, will have the bonus protected for up to two years.

Para. (j). The intention is to treat payments of the bonus as capital, the effect of which will almost always be to the advantage of claimants. The Government also indicated that receipt of a back to work bonus will be disregarded for 52 weeks for people moving off JSA or income support and on to family credit, housing benefit or council tax benefit (*i.e.* the three main income-related in-work benefits). However, if a recipient of a bonus later returns to JSA or income support, the normal capital rules will apply. This is unlikely to constitute much of a problem, given that the maximum bonus is £1,000 and capital below £3,000 is disregarded for income support purposes anyway.

Para. (k). Regulations will provide that, where a couple separate, partners may receive the benefit of any contributions which they have made to the accrued amount. They will, accordingly, be able to carry with them what might be best described as a benefit dowry, *i.e.* their portion of the accrued amount, when making a future benefit claim. Accrued amounts will be divided pro rata in line with each partner's earnings level. The practical ramifications of this procedure hardly bear thinking about, given the extent to which separating partners either become reconciled or find a new partner.

Para. (l). Regulations will be made under this power to ensure that amounts can be allocated to another party (*e.g.* a partner), and can be paid to that person even if they are not the income support or JSA claimant. Thus where a couple separate and the female partner moves directly into work, she will be able to receive a payment of that part of the bonus to which her earnings have contributed.

Employment of long-term unemployed: deductions by employers

27.—(1) An employee is a "qualifying employee" in relation to his employer for the purposes of this section if, immediately before beginning his employment with that employer, he had been entitled to a jobseeker's allowance for a continuous period of not less than two years.

(2) An employee is also a "qualifying employee" in relation to his employer for the purposes of this section if—

(a) immediately before beginning his employment with that employer, he had been unemployed for a continuous period of not less than two years;

(b) he is under pensionable age; and

(c) he falls within a prescribed description of person.

(3) Regulations may make provision for any employer who employs a person who is a qualifying employee in relation to him, to make deductions from the employer's contributions payments in accordance with the regulations and in prescribed circumstances.

(4) Those regulations may, in particular, make provision as to the period for which deductions may be made by an employer.

(5) Regulations may provide, in relation to cases where an employee is a qualifying employee in relation to more than one employer at the same time, for the right to make deductions to be confined to one employer—

(a) determined in accordance with the regulations; and

(b) certified by the Secretary of State, in accordance with the regulations, to be the employer entitled to make those deductions.

(6) Regulations may—

(a) provide that, in prescribed circumstances, a person who would not otherwise satisfy the condition in subsection (1) is to be treated as satisfying it;

(b) provide that, in prescribed circumstances, a person who would not otherwise satisfy the condition in subsection (2)(a) is to be treated as satisfying it;

(c) prescribe circumstances in which, for prescribed purposes, two or more employers are to be treated as one;

(d) make provision for the payment, in prescribed circumstances, by the Secretary of State or by the Commissioners of Inland Revenue on behalf of the Secretary of State, of sums to employers who are unable to make the whole or part of any deductions which they are entitled to make;

(e) require persons to maintain such records in connection with deductions made by them as may be prescribed;

(f) require persons who have made deductions to furnish to the Secretary of State such documents and information, at such time, as may be prescribed.

(7) Where, in accordance with any provision of regulations made under this section, an amount has been deducted from an employer's contributions payments, the amount so deducted shall (except in such cases as may be prescribed) be treated for the purposes of any provision made by or under any enactment in relation to primary or secondary Class 1 contributions as having been—

(a) paid (on such date as may be determined in accordance with the regulations); and

(b) received by the Secretary of State,

towards discharging the employer's liability in respect of such contributions.

(8) In this section—

"contributions payments", in relation to an employer, means the aggregate of the payments which he is required to make by way of primary or secondary Class 1 contributions;

"deductions" means deductions made in accordance with regulations under subsection (3); and

"employee" and "employer" have such meaning as may be prescribed.

DEFINITIONS

"contributions payments": subs. (8).
"deductions": subs. (8).
"employee": subs. (8).
"employer": subs. (8).
"employment": s.35(1).
"pensionable age": s.35(1).
"prescribed": s.35(1).
"qualifying employee": subss. (1) and (2).
"regulations": s.35(1).
"year": s.35(1).

GENERAL NOTE

This section introduces the contribution holiday, which represents a further measure intended to improve job prospects for long-term unemployed people. (Curiously the marginal note uses the conventional terminology of "long-term unemployed", rather than the voguish expression of "jobseekers"). Only the most general outline of the scheme is at present available, as, yet again, the section operates largely by way of investing the Secretary of State with regulation-making powers. The section thus enables regulations to be made allowing employers to make deductions from their Class 1 national insurance contributions in respect of any person employed by them who was previously entitled to JSA for at least two years (subs. (1)) or who was unemployed for at least two years and falls within prescribed criteria (subs. (2)). The Government's intention is that this contribution holiday should last for up to 12 months.

The remainder of the section consists of the necessary enabling powers (see *Fifth Report*, Annex I, paras. 96–103), which give the Secretary of State considerable latitude in devising the scheme, and the power to make any modifications deemed expedient with experience. Note also that regulations will create offences to deal with fraud in respect of contribution holiday payments. Such offences will be punishable on summary conviction to a fine not exceeding level 3 on the standard scale: see s.34(3) and (5).

Subss. (1) and (2)

The definition of the principal group of qualifying employees – those continuously entitled to JSA for at least two years – is set out in subs. (1). Other workers may also count as qualifying employees, even if they have not actually been in receipt of JSA, providing that they have been continuously unemployed for at least two years before starting work with that employer and meet the other conditions specified in subs. (2). Regulations under this power will enable lone parents who have been receiving income support immediately before starting work to be qualifying employees.

Subs. (3)

This is a technical provision permitting regulations to specify how employers are to calculate the amount they may reclaim. The intention is that this sum should represent a complete refund on contributions for up to 12 months. Employers will save on average £300 for each unemployed person taken on.

Regulations are likely to provide that employers who operate an occupational pension scheme will be able to claim an amount equal to their gross national insurance liability, *i.e.* the actual amounted of contracted-out contributions paid, plus an amount equal to the employers' three per cent contracted-out rebate (*per* Mr R Evans, *Hansard*, H.C. Vol. 257, col. 445).

Subs. (4)

Regulations will specify that an employer may not reclaim any payments until the qualifying employee has worked for a qualifying period. Once this period has expired, it is intended that the employer may reclaim payments for this period, and can continue to do so for a period of one year from the start of the employee's employment.

Subs. (5)

The Government's intention is that the contribution holiday will apply only to one employer in cases where a person starts more than one job. This will normally be the first employer with whom the qualifying employee starts work. However, where the employee earns less than the national insurance lower earnings limit in one job but not the other, regulations will enable the Secretary of State to certify that it is the employer from whom contributions are due that will be able to reclaim.

Subs. (6)

Paras. (a) and (b). These powers enable regulations to be made deeming persons to be qualifying employees even where they do not meet the criteria in subss. (1) and (2). These could cover cases where there is a small gap between the employee coming off benefit and starting work. They will also allow people previously in receipt of UB or income support to be treated as if they were in receipt of JSA for the purposes of subs. (1).

Para. (c). This might be appropriate where the ownership of a company changes hands but the employee remains continuously employed throughout.

Para. (d). This measure will be welcomed by small employers. It permits the Secretary of State, either directly or via the Commissioners of Inland Revenue, to make payments *to* employers of sums representing in whole or in part the deductions which they are entitled to make. This will enable employers to receive payment promptly where the deduction to which they are entitled exceeds the total amount which they are required to pay by way of national insurance and tax payments to the Inland Revenue each month.

Paras. (e) and (f). These powers are similar to those which exist under the national insurance scheme for the purposes of monitoring.

Subs. (7)

This provision deems employers to have met their statutory liabilities to make contribution payments where they have in fact made deductions in respect of their entitlement to contribution holidays.

Subs. (8)

The definitions of "employee" and "employer" to be made in regulations will correspond with the meanings they bear in the context of liability for Class 1 national insurance contributions.

Expedited claims for housing benefit and council tax benefit

28.—(1) This section provides for the making of regulations to enable—

(a) information to be passed between authorities, and

(b) priority to be given to certain persons,

with a view to claims for housing or council tax benefit made by or in respect of persons who cease to be entitled to a jobseeker's allowance or income support being dealt with quickly.

(2) In the Administration Act, insert after section 128—

"Expedited claims for housing and council tax benefit

Disclosure of information by authorities

128A.—(1) Regulations may make provision requiring the disclosure by one authority ("the disclosing authority") to another authority ("the receiving authority"), in prescribed circumstances, of information of a prescribed description obtained by the disclosing authority in respect of persons who have been entitled to a jobseeker's allowance or to income support.

(2) The regulations may in particular provide for—

(a) information to be disclosed—

(i) at the request of the receiving authority;

(ii) at the request of any person who falls within a prescribed category; or

(iii) otherwise than in response to such a request;

(b) the period within which information is to be disclosed; and

(c) information to be disclosed only if it has been obtained by the disclosing authority in the exercise of any of their functions in relation to housing benefit or council tax benefit."

(3) In section 63 of the Administration Act (adjudication of claims for housing benefit or council tax benefit), insert after subsection (2)—

"(2A) Regulations may make provision requiring authorities to whom claims for housing benefit or council tax benefit are made by, or in respect of, persons who have been entitled to a jobseeker's allowance or to income support to give priority, in prescribed circumstances, to those claims over other claims for any such benefit.".

DEFINITIONS

"the Administration Act": s.35(1).

"the disclosing authority": SSAA 1992, s.128A(1).

"the receiving authority": SSAA 1992, s.128A(1).

"prescribed": s.35(1).

"regulations": s.35(1).

GENERAL NOTE

This measure was introduced as a Government amendment at the Report stage of the Bill in the House of Commons (*Hansard*, H.C. Vol. 257, col. 354) and received the support of the Opposition. It implements the commitment made by the Secretary of State in the November 1994 uprating statement that entitlement to housing benefit and council tax benefit would run on for four weeks after returning to work for those unemployed persons or lone parents who have been on JSA or income support for six months or more. According to the Under-Secretary of State, this reform "is designed to deal with the major concern of those who are moving off benefits and on to work as to whether they will be able to pay the rent in the initial period of their return to work" (*Hansard*, H.C. Vol. 257, col. 355).

The general purpose of the new provision is set out in subs. (1). Subsection (2) inserts a new s.128A into the SSAA 1992 to achieve this end. It deals with the situation where an unemployed person moves from one local authority area in which housing benefit has been in payment to another local authority area to obtain work. The new provision includes enabling powers allowing regulations to require information to be exchanged between local authorities. Subsection (3) contains the regulatory power requiring authorities to give priority to jobseekers in determining claims.

Local authorities are already under an obligation to determine claims for housing benefit and council tax benefit within 14 days of receipt of the necessary information, or as soon as reasonably practicable thereafter (Housing Benefit (General) Regulations 1987 (S.I. 1987 No. 1971), reg. 76(3)). This section does not affect that duty, which is as much honoured in the breach as the observance. The Government also intend to introduce a financial incentive and penalty scheme to encourage all local authorities to process quickly claims from persons starting work and claiming this "run-on" period of benefit. The Government's intention is that entitlement to the run-on should commence in April 1996, with six months' receipt of UB or income support prior to April 1996 counting for these purposes.

Pilot schemes

29.—(1) Any regulations to which this subsection applies may be made so as to have effect for a specified period not exceeding 12 months.

(2) Any regulations which, by virtue of subsection (1), are to have effect for a limited period are referred to in this section as "a pilot scheme".

(3) A pilot scheme may provide that its provisions are to apply only in relation to—

(a) one or more specified areas or localities;

(b) one or more specified classes of person;

(c) persons selected—

(i) by reference to prescribed criteria; or

(ii) on a sampling basis.

(4) A pilot scheme may make consequential or transitional provision with respect to the cessation of the scheme on the expiry of the specified period.

(5) A pilot scheme ("the previous scheme") may be replaced by a further pilot scheme making the same, or similar, provision (apart from the specified period) to that made by the previous scheme.

(6) Subject to subsection (8), subsection (1) applies to—

(a) regulations made under this Act, other than—

(i) regulations made under section 4(2) or (5) which have the effect of reducing any age-related amount or applicable amount; or

(ii) regulations made under section 27;

(b) regulations made under the Administration Act, so far as they relate to a jobseeker's allowance;

(c) regulations made under Part VII of the Benefits Act (income-related benefits), other than any mentioned in subsection (7); and

(d) regulations made under the Administration Act, so far as they relate to income-related benefits payable under Part VII of the Benefits Act.

(7) The regulations referred to in subsection (6)(c) are—

(a) regulations under section 128(5) of the Benefits Act which have the effect of reducing the appropriate maximum family credit;

(b) regulations under section 129(8) of that Act which have the effect of reducing the appropriate maximum disability working allowance;

(c) regulations under section 130(4) of that Act which have the effect of reducing the appropriate maximum housing benefit;

(d) regulations under section 131(10)(a) of that Act which have the effect of reducing the appropriate maximum council tax benefit; and

(e) regulations reducing any of the sums prescribed under section 135(1) of that Act.

(8) Subsection (1) applies only if the regulations are made with a view to ascertaining whether their provisions will, or will be likely to, encourage persons to obtain or remain in work or will, or will be likely to, facilitate the obtaining by persons of work or their remaining in work.

DEFINITIONS

"adjudication officer": s.35(1).

"Administration Act, the": s.35(1).

"pilot scheme, a": subs. (2).

"applicable amount": s.35(1).

"Benefits Act, the": s.35(1).
"prescribed": s.35(1).
"previous scheme, the": subs. (5).
"regulations": s.35(1).
"work": s.35(1).

GENERAL NOTE
This novel and important provision allows for changes in regulations to be made on an experimental or "pilot" basis, in order to assess the likely success of such modifications to the existing system of benefits. Piloted changes to the benefit rules can only be made with a view to assessing their effectiveness in terms of work incentives (subs. (8); a provision which will doubtless be welcomed by the research community). Such changes are also limited to the types of regulations specified in subs. (6). The piloting may be across a particular geographical area or across a specified category of claimants (subs. (3)). Transitional protection may apply when a pilot terminates (subs. (4)).

There are three safeguards governing the exercise of this power to pilot benefit changes. First, regulations made under this section are subject to the affirmative resolution procedure (s.37(1)(c)). Secondly, pilot schemes are limited to 12 months in duration (subs. (1)), although they can effectively be extended, subject to further Parliamentary approval (subs. (5)). Thirdly, the actual rate of benefit itself cannot be reduced (subss. (6)(a)(i), 6(c) and (7)).

It would clearly be open to the Government to vary the availability rules and those relating to earnings disregards in such pilots (White Paper, para. 3.12). The first pilot will be in relation to a modified form of family credit. The Department of Social Security has announced plans for a three-year pilot project providing new benefit assistance for single people and couples without children, to be known as "earnings top-up", on similar lines to family credit (DSS Consultation Paper, *Piloting change in Social Security – Helping people into work*, July 1995).

PART III

MISCELLANEOUS AND SUPPLEMENTAL

Grants for resettlement places

30.—(1) The Secretary of State may pay such grants, to such persons, as he considers appropriate in relation to expenditure in connection with the provision or maintenance of resettlement places.

(2) In this section "resettlement places" means places at which persons without a settled way of life are afforded temporary accommodation with a view to assisting them to lead a more settled life.

(3) Any grant under this section may be made on such terms and subject to such conditions as the Secretary of State considers appropriate.

(4) Section 30 of, and Schedule 5 to, the Supplementary Benefits Act 1976 (provision of resettlement units) shall cease to have effect.

(5) Any grants made by the Secretary of State under this section shall be paid out of money provided by Parliament.

(6) Any sums received by the Secretary of State by way of the repayment of any such grant shall be paid by him into the Consolidated Fund.

DEFINITIONS
"resettlement places": subs. (1).

GENERAL NOTE
This section is rather out of keeping with the contents of the remainder of the Act, hence the specific reference in the long title to "Provide for ... the assistance of persons without a settled way of life". The section deals with one of the less well-publicised successes of the Government's Next Steps Agencies programme. The Resettlement Agency was established in 1989 as the first DSS executive agency. It has two principal tasks; first, to operate hostels for single homeless people with an unsettled way of life, and, secondly, to arrange for the gradual replacement of these hostels by more appropriate accommodation, run by local authorities and voluntary bodies. It was originally envisaged that the Agency would not disengage from the direct running of its remaining hostels until the next century. However, the speed of this disengagement programme is such that it is anticipated that the Agency will withdraw from the administration of the last remaining hostels by April 1996.

This section makes the necessary consequential statutory changes. The Secretary of State's power to make direct provision of resettlement units is removed by subs. (4). However, subs. (3) enables the Secretary of State to continue making grants to meet expenditure incurred in connection with the provision or maintenance of such places. There is no restriction on the types of recipients for such grants, so they could be local authorities, voluntary agencies or private providers.

Termination of awards

31.—(1) Regulations may make provision allowing, in prescribed circumstances, an award of income support to be brought to an end by an adjudication officer where the person to whom it was made, or where he is a member of a married or unmarried couple his partner, will be entitled to a jobseeker's allowance if the award is brought to an end.

(2) Regulations may make provision allowing, in prescribed circumstances, an award of a jobseeker's allowance to be brought to an end by an adjudication officer where the person to whom it was made, or where he is a member of a married or unmarried couple his partner, will be entitled to income support if the award is brought to an end.

(3) In this section "partner" means the other member of the couple concerned.

DEFINITIONS
 "adjudication officer": s.35(1).
 "partner": subs. (3).
 "prescribed": s.35(1).
 "regulations": s.35(1).

GENERAL NOTE
 This section enables the Secretary of State to make regulations terminating awards of income support or jobseeker's allowance where the claimant, or any partner, would be entitled to the other benefit. The purpose of this power is to allow claimants to exercise their option of choice in such matters, and to ensure a smooth transition between the two benefits.

Subs. (1)
 Regulations will enable a person who would normally have an award of income support (*e.g.* a lone parent with a child under 16) to choose to make herself available for work, and so claim JSA. If so, the award of income support would need to end before the JSA award commenced. It is envisaged that a single adjudication officer will terminate one benefit while awarding the second, so avoiding any gaps in provision.

Subs. (2)
 This provides for the reverse eventuality to that under subs. (1). This might be appropriate where the partner of a JSA claimant becomes incapable of work; it may suit the couple better if the partner becomes an income support claimant with the former JSA claimant (and now carer) becoming the dependent partner in an award of income support.

Insolvency

32.—(1) In section 71 of the Administration Act (overpayments), after subsection (10) insert—
  "(10A) Where—
  (a) a jobseeker's allowance is payable to a person from whom any amount is recoverable as mentioned in subsection (8) above; and
  (b) that person is subject to a bankruptcy order,
  a sum deducted from that benefit under that subsection shall not be treated as income of his for the purposes of the Insolvency Act 1986.
   (10B) Where—
  (a) a jobseeker's allowance is payable to a person from whom any amount is recoverable as mentioned in subsection (8) above; and

(b) the estate of that person is sequestrated,

a sum deducted from that benefit under that subsection shall not be treated as income of his for the purposes of the Bankruptcy (Scotland) Act 1985."

(2) In section 78 of the Administration Act (recovery of social fund awards), after subsection (3) insert—

"(3A) Where—

(a) a jobseeker's allowance is payable to a person from whom an award is recoverable under subsection (3) above; and

(b) that person is subject to a bankruptcy order,

a sum deducted from that benefit under subsection (2) above shall not be treated as income of his for the purposes of the Insolvency Act 1986.

(3B) Where—

(a) a jobseeker's allowance is payable to a person from whom an award is recoverable under subsection (3) above; and

(b) the estate of that person is sequestrated,

a sum deducted from that benefit under subsection (2) above shall not be treated as income of his for the purposes of the Bankruptcy (Scotland) Act 1985."

DEFINITIONS
"Administration Act, the": s.35(1).

GENERAL NOTE
The purpose of this measure, introduced at the Committee stage in the House of Lords (*Hansard*, H.L. Vol. 563, col. 1144), is to enable recovery of overpayments of social security benefits from JSA paid to bankrupt people. The section applies both to recovery of overpaid benefit under s.71 of the SSAA 1992 and recovery of social fund awards under s.78 of that Act. The amendments provide that any such amounts deducted from JSA payable to a bankrupt person are not treated as income for the purposes of the Insolvency Act 1986 (c. 45) and the Bankruptcy (Scotland) Act 1985 (c. 66). The effect of this is that creditors would be unable to obtain access to such sums; equally, however, it means that so far as overpayments of benefit are concerned, the Department of Social Security will effectively be in the position of a preferential creditor.

These amendments appear to be designed to reverse the effect of *R. v. Secretary of State for Social Security, ex p. Mulvey* (Court of Session, SCOLAG Journal, December 1994, p. 187). In that case the petitioner, Mrs Mulvey, had been sequestrated (*i.e.* made bankrupt), her debts including social fund loans. The Benefits Agency made deductions from her weekly income support after sequestration in repayment of these loans. Lord Abernethy held that the Secretary of State had no power to recover the petitioner's pre-sequestration social fund loans by deduction from her post-sequestration income support. "Were it otherwise one creditor, the respondent [the Secretary of State], would in effect obtain an unfair preference to the prejudice of the general body of creditors and, moreover, would in effect be overriding the provisions of section 35(5) of the 1985 Act [Bankruptcy (Scotland) Act 1985]".

A consequential amendment has been made to the Bankruptcy (Scotland) Act 1985 by Sched. 2, para. 8, but rather unhelpfully no parallel consequential amendment has been made to the relevant English legislation in the Insolvency Act 1986.

Inspectors

33.—(1) An inspector appointed under section 110 of the Administration Act (appointment and powers of inspectors) shall have power, for purposes of this Act—

(a) to enter at all reasonable times any premises liable to inspection under this section;

(b) to make such examination and inquiry there as may be necessary for ascertaining whether the provisions of this Act are being, or have been, complied with;

(c) to examine, either alone or (if he thinks fit) in the presence of any other person, in relation to any matters arising under this Act on which he may reasonably require information, any person whom he finds there;

(d) to exercise such other powers as may be necessary for carrying this Act into effect.

(2) The premises liable to inspection under this section are any where an inspector has reasonable grounds for supposing that—

(a) one or more persons are employed;

(b) a trade or business is being carried on;

(c) a personal or occupational pension scheme is being administered; or

(d) information relating to the carrying on of any trade or business is kept by the person carrying on that trade or business,

but do not include a private dwelling-house unless the inspector has reasonable grounds for supposing that the dwelling-house is being used for the purposes of a trade or business.

(3) An inspector applying for admission to any premises, in the exercise of his powers under this section, shall produce his certificate of appointment if asked to do so.

(4) Where any premises—

(a) are liable to be inspected by an inspector or officer appointed or employed by another government department, or

(b) are under the control of another government department,

the Secretary of State may make arrangements with that department for any of the powers or duties of inspectors under this section to be exercised or discharged by an inspector or officer employed by that department.

(5) A person to whom this subsection applies shall—

(a) furnish to an inspector all such information, and

(b) produce for his inspection all such documents,

as the inspector may reasonably require for purposes of this Act.

(6) Subsection (5) applies to—

(a) any licensing authority;

(b) any person carrying on an agency or other business for the introduction or supply to persons requiring them of persons available to do work or to perform services.

(7) Except where subsection (5) applies, subsections (6) and (7) of section 110 of the Administration Act (furnishing of information about contributions etc.) shall have effect as if this Act were among those mentioned in subsection (8) of that section.

(8) In the application of subsection (7) of section 110 in relation to this Act, the reference in paragraph (a) to section 110 of that Act shall be read as a reference to this section.

(9) No person shall be required under this section to answer any questions or to give evidence tending to incriminate himself, or in the case of a person who is married, his or her spouse.

(10) In this section—

"licensing authority" means a local authority acting in its capacity as an authority responsible for granting any licence; and

"local authority" means any of the following—

(i) a county council;

(ii) any county borough council;

(iii) any district council;

(iv) any council constituted under section 2 of the Local Government etc. (Scotland) Act 1994;

(v) any London borough council;

(vi) the Common Council of the City of London;

(vii) the Council of the Isles of Scilly.

(11) In this section, and in subsection (7) of section 110 of the Administration Act, as it applies in relation to this Act, "premises" includes any—

(a) place;

(b) movable structure or tent;

(c) vehicle, vessel, aircraft or hovercraft;

(d) installation which is an offshore installation for the purposes of the Mineral Workings (Offshore Installations) Act 1971.

<small>DEFINITIONS</small>
"Administration Act": s.35(1).
"licensing authority": subs. (10).
"local authority": subs. (10).
"occupational pension scheme": s.35(1).
"personal pension scheme": s.35(1).
"premises": subs. (11).

<small>GENERAL NOTE</small>
This section, on the face of it rather alarming, is simply designed to give DSS fraud investigators and national insurance inspectors the necessary powers to obtain information from employers about their employees in circumstances where fraud or non-compliance with the national insurance scheme is suspected. It makes similar provision as regards entry to premises to that which already exists under SSAA 1992, s.110. Moreover, the duties on persons specified in SSA 1992, s.110(7) to furnish information under s.110(6) is expressly incorporated by subs. (7). Inspectors must, of course, produce their certificate of appointment if so asked (subs. (3)), and the protection against self-incrimination (or incrimination of a spouse, but not an unmarried partner) is retained (subs. (9)).

Offences

34.—(1) A person is guilty of an offence if, for the purpose of obtaining a jobseeker's allowance (whether for himself or for some other person) or for any other purpose connected with this Act, he—
  (a) makes a statement or representation which he knows to be false; or
  (b) produces or furnishes, or knowingly causes or knowingly allows to be produced or furnished, any document or information which he knows to be false in a material particular.
(2) A person is guilty of an offence if he—
  (a) intentionally delays or obstructs an inspector in the exercise of any power under section 33; or
  (b) refuses or neglects to answer any question or to furnish any information or to produce any document when required to do so under that section.
(3) Regulations under section 27 may provide for contravention of, or failure to comply with, any of their provisions to be an offence.
(4) A person guilty of an offence under subsection (1) shall be liable on summary conviction to a fine not exceeding level 5 on the standard scale, or to imprisonment for a term not exceeding three months, or to both.
(5) A person guilty of an offence under subsection (2), or under any regulations made under section 27, shall be liable on summary conviction to a fine not exceeding level 3 on the standard scale.
(6) A person who is convicted of an offence under subsection (2)(b)—
  (a) is guilty of a further offence if the refusal or neglect is continued by him after his conviction; and
  (b) shall be liable on summary conviction to a fine not exceeding £40 for each day on which it is continued.
(7) A person who is convicted of an offence of contravening or failing to comply with any regulations under section 27 ("the original offence")—
  (a) is guilty of a further offence if the contravention or failure is continued by him after his conviction, and
  (b) shall be liable to a fine not exceeding £40 for each day on which the contravention or failure is continued,
if regulations provide for this subsection to apply in relation to the original offence.

DEFINITIONS
    "original offence, the": subs. (7).
    "regulations": s.35(1).

GENERAL NOTE
    This section sets out the offences which may be committed under the Act. The provisions of
this section replicate similar offences under the SSAA 1992. Thus subs. (1) is in the same terms
as SSAA 1992, s.112(1) and subs. (2) follows SSAA 1992, s.111(1). Subsection (3) enables regulations to be made covering offences in respect of the contribution holiday provisions: this power
is in regulations because the arrangements for the contribution holiday scheme are themselves
to be specified in regulations. The continuing offences in subss. (6) and (7) have a precedent in
SSAA 1992, s.111(2).

Interpretation

35.—(1) In This Act—
    "adjudication officer" means an adjudication officer appointed under
        section 38 of the Administration Act;
    "the Administration Act" means the Social Security Administration
        Act 1992;
    "applicable amount" means the applicable amount determined in
        accordance with regulations under section 4;
    "benefit year" has the meaning given by section 2(4);
    "the Benefits Act" means the Social Security Contributions and Bene-
        fits Act 1992;
    "child" means a person under the age of 16;
    "claimant" means a person who claims a jobseeker's allowance;
    "continental shelf operations" has the same meaning as in section 120 of
        the Benefits Act;
    "contribution-based conditions" means the conditions set out in section
        2;
    "contribution-based jobseeker's allowance" has the meaning given in
        section 1(4);
    "employed earner" has the meaning prescribed for the purposes of this
        Act;
    "employment", except in section 7, has the meaning prescribed for the
        purposes of this Act;
    "entitled", in relation to a jobseeker's allowance, is to be construed in
        accordance with—
                (a) the provisions of this Act relating to entitlement; and
                (b) sections 1 and 68 of the Administration Act;
    "family" means—
                (a) a married or unmarried couple;
                (b) a married or unmarried couple and a member of the same
        household for whom one of them is, or both are, responsible and
        who is a child or a person of a prescribed description;
                (c) except in prescribed circumstances, a person who is not a
        member of a married or unmarried couple and a member of the
        same household for whom that person is responsible and who is a
        child or a person of a prescribed description;
    "Great Britain" includes the territorial waters of the United Kingdom
        adjacent to Great Britain;
    "income-based conditions" means the conditions set out in section 3;
    "income-based jobseeker's allowance" has the meaning given in section
        1(4);
    "jobseeker's agreement" has the meaning given by section 9(1);
    "jobseeking period" has the meaning prescribed for the purposes of this
        Act;

"married couple" means a man and woman who are married to each other and are members of the same household;

"occupational pension scheme" has the same meaning as it has in the Pension Schemes Act 1993 by virtue of section 1 of that Act;

"pensionable age" has the meaning prescribed for the purposes of this Act;

"pension payments" means—

(a) periodical payments made in relation to a person, under a personal pension scheme or, in connection with the coming to an end of an employment of his, under an occupational pension scheme or a public service pension scheme; and

(b) such other payments as may be prescribed;

"personal pension scheme" means—

(a) a personal pension scheme as defined by section 1 of the Pension Schemes Act 1993;

(b) a contract or trust scheme approved under Chapter III of Part XIV of the Income and Corporation Taxes Act 1988; and

(c) a personal pension scheme approved under Chapter IV of that Part of that Act;

"prescribed" means specified in or determined in accordance with regulations;

"public service pension scheme" has the same meaning as it has in the Pension Schemes Act 1993 by virtue of section 1 of that Act;

"regulations" means regulations made by the Secretary of State;

"tax year" means the 12 months beginning with 6th April in any year;

"trade dispute" means any dispute between employers and employees, or between employees and employees, which is connected with the employment or non-employment or the terms of employment or the conditions of employment of any persons, whether employees in the employment of the employer with whom the dispute arises, or not;

"training" has the meaning prescribed for the purposes of this Act and, in relation to prescribed provisions of this Act, if regulations so provide, includes assistance to find training or employment, or to improve a person's prospects of being employed, of such a kind as may be prescribed;

"unmarried couple" means a man and woman who are not married to each other but are living together as husband and wife otherwise than in prescribed circumstances;

"week" means a period of seven days beginning with a Sunday or such other period of seven days as may be prescribed;

"work" has the meaning prescribed for the purposes of this Act;

"year", except in the expression "benefit year", means a tax year.

(2) The expressions "capable of work", "linked period", "relevant education" and "remunerative work" are to be read with paragraphs 2, 3, 14 and 1 of Schedule 1.

(3) Subject to any regulations made for the purposes of this subsection, "earnings" is to be construed for the purposes of this Act in accordance with section 3 of the Benefits Act and paragraph 6 of Schedule 1 to this Act.

GENERAL NOTE

This definition section is not exhaustive, in that it provides for several terms to be defined by regulations. The affirmative procedure applies to regulations defining "pension payments" under para. (b) of that definition. Note also the supplementary powers in Sched. 1.

Regulations and orders

36.—(1) Any power under this Act to make regulations or orders, other than an order under section 9(13) or 19(10)(a), shall be exercisable by statutory instrument.

(2) Any such power may be exercised—

(a) either in relation to all cases to which it extends, or in relation to those cases subject to specified exceptions, or in relation to any specified cases or classes of case;

(b) so as to make, as respects the cases in relation to which it is exercised—

(i) the full provision to which the power extends or any less provision (whether by way of exception or otherwise),

(ii) the same provision for all cases in relation to which it is exercised, or different provision for different cases or different classes of case or different provision as respects the same case or class of case for different purposes of this Act,

(iii) any such provision either unconditionally or subject to any specified condition.

(3) Where any such power is expressed to be exercisable for alternative purposes it may be exercised in relation to the same case for any or all of those purposes.

(4) Any such power includes power—

(a) to make such incidental, supplemental, consequential or transitional provision as appears to the Secretary of State to be expedient; and

(b) to provide for a person to exercise a discretion in dealing with any matter.

(5) Any power to make regulations or an order for the purposes of any provision of this Act is without prejudice to any power to make regulations or an order for the purposes of any other provision.

DEFINITIONS
"regulations": s.35(1).

GENERAL NOTE
This section is a general provision governing the power to make regulations and orders. It is in essentially identical terms to the parallel provisions in SSAA 1992, s.189 and SSCBA 1992, s.175. Section 37 deals specifically with those regulations which must be approved under the affirmative resolution procedure.

Parliamentary control

37.—(1) Subsection (2) applies in relation to the following regulations (whether made alone or with other regulations)—

(a) regulations made under, or by virtue of, any provision of this Act other than—

(i) section 6, 7, 26, 29 or 40,

(ii) paragraph (b) of the definition of "pension payments" in section 35(1), or

(iii) paragraph 17 of Schedule 1,

before the date on which jobseeker's allowances first become payable;

(b) the first regulations to be made under section 26;

(c) regulations made under section 6, 7, 29, paragraph (b) of the definition of "pension payments" in section 35(1) or paragraph 17 of Schedule 1.

(2) No regulations to which this subsection applies shall be made unless a draft of the statutory instrument containing the regulations has been laid before Parliament and approved by a resolution of each House.

(3) Any other statutory instrument made under this Act, other than one made under section 41(2), shall be subject to annulment in pursuance of a resolution of either House of Parliament.

DEFINITIONS
"pension payments": s.35(1).
"regulations": s.35(1).

GENERAL NOTE
This section sets out which regulations must be approved in draft by both Houses of Parliament before the Secretary of State can issue the relevant statutory instrument. This effectively applies to all regulations made before JSA first becomes payable (subss. (1)(a) and (c)), to the first back to work bonus regulations (subs. (1)(b)) and at any time to those governing availability for employment, actively seeking employment, pilot schemes and the other matters mentioned in subs. (1)(c).

General financial arrangements

38.—(1) There shall be paid out of money provided by Parliament—
(a) any sums paid by the Secretary of State by way of jobseeker's allowance; and
(b) any expenditure incurred by the Secretary of State under or by virtue of this Act.

(2) The expenditure mentioned in subsection (1)(b) includes expenditure incurred in connection with any inquiry undertaken on behalf of the Secretary of State with a view to obtaining statistics relating to the operation of any provision of this Act relating to a jobseeker's allowance.

(3) There shall be paid out of the National Insurance Fund and into the Consolidated Fund sums estimated by the Secretary of State to balance payments made by him by way of contribution-based jobseeker's allowance.

(4) The Secretary of State shall pay into the National Insurance Fund sums estimated by him to balance sums recovered by him in connection with payments of contribution-based jobseeker's allowance.

(5) The Secretary of State shall pay into the National Insurance Fund sums estimated by him to be equal to the aggregate of the amounts deducted by employers in accordance with regulations under section 27.

(6) The Secretary of State shall pay into the Consolidated Fund sums estimated by him to balance sums recovered by him in connection with payments made by way of income-based jobseeker's allowance.

(7) Estimates under this section shall be made by the Secretary of State—
(a) in any manner which, after consulting the Government Actuary or the Deputy Government Actuary, he considers appropriate and the Treasury has approved; and
(b) at such times as he considers appropriate and the Treasury has approved.

(8) Payments which are required to be made by this section shall be made at such times and in such manner as the Secretary of State considers appropriate and the Treasury has approved.

DEFINITIONS
"contribution-based jobseeker's allowance": ss.1(4) and 35(1).
"income-based jobseeker's allowance": ss.1(4) and 35(1).

GENERAL NOTE
This section deals with the financial arrangements for jobseeker's allowance. In particular, monies will be paid from the National Insurance Fund into the Consolidated Fund to reflect the proportion of payments of contributions-based JSA (subs. (3)). This preserves the contributory principle in accounting terms. However, the arrangements differ from those for UB in that the administrative costs involved in paying contributory-based JSA will be a charge on the Consolidated Fund and not the National Insurance Fund (subs. (1)(b)). The other provision of note concerns the financial arrangements for the "contribution holiday" under s.27. The Secretary of State is required to estimate such sums deducted by employers from their Class 1 national insurance payments. These amounts will then be met from the Consolidated Fund as an expense under subs. (1)(b) and paid into the National Insurance Fund (subs. (5)).

Provision for Northern Ireland

39. An Order in Council under paragraph 1(1)(b) of Schedule 1 to the Northern Ireland Act 1974 (legislation for Northern Ireland in the interim period) which states that it is made only for purposes corresponding to those of this Act—

(a) shall not be subject to paragraph 1(4) and (5) of that Schedule (affirmative resolution of both Houses of Parliament); but

(b) shall be subject to annulment in pursuance of a resolution of either House of Parliament.

This Act itself does not apply to Northern Ireland, with the exceptions specified in s.41(6). As is customary with social security legislation, corresponding provision will be made under the Northern Ireland Act 1974 (c.28) by an Order in Council. As this will be identical in all material respects to the legislation on the mainland, this section provides for such an Order to be subject to the negative resolution procedure.

Transitional provisions

40.—(1) The Secretary of State may by regulations make such transitional provision, consequential provision or savings as he considers necessary or expedient for the purposes of or in connection with—

(a) the coming into force of any provision of this Act; or

(b) the operation of any enactment repealed or amended by any such provision during any period when the repeal or amendment is not wholly in force.

(2) Regulations under this section may in particular make provision—

(a) for the termination or cancellation of awards of unemployment benefit or income support;

(b) for a person whose award of unemployment benefit or income support has been terminated or cancelled under regulations made by virtue of paragraph (a) to be treated as having been awarded a jobseeker's allowance (a "transitional allowance")—

(i) of such a kind,

(ii) for such period,

(iii) of such an amount, and

(iv) subject to such conditions,

as may be determined in accordance with the regulations;

(c) for a person's continuing entitlement to a transitional allowance to be determined by reference to such provision as may be made by the regulations;

(d) for the termination of an award of a transitional allowance;

(e) for the review of an award of a transitional allowance;

(f) for a contribution-based jobseeker's allowance not to be payable for a prescribed period where a person is disqualified for receiving unemployment benefit;

(g) that days which were days of unemployment for the purposes of entitlement to unemployment benefit, and such other days as may be prescribed, are to be treated as having been days during which a person was, or would have been, entitled to a jobseeker's allowance;

(h) that days which were days of entitlement to unemployment benefit, and such other days as may be prescribed, are to be treated as having been days of entitlement to a contribution-based jobseeker's allowance;

(i) that the rate of a contribution-based transitional allowance is to be calculated by reference to the rate of unemployment benefit paid or payable.

DEFINITIONS
"contribution-based jobseeker's allowance": ss.1(4) and 35(1).
"prescribed": s.35(1).
"regulations": s.35(1).

GENERAL NOTE
This section enables regulations to be made to cover the transitional arrangements at the point of change in October 1996. The Government's intention is that existing recipients of UB and income support at that point will not lose as a result of the change. Such transitional protection will extend to those under 25 years of age, those with an adult dependency increase and those with an occupational or personal pension. The rationale for the regulation-making powers in subs. (2) is explained more fully in the *Fifth Report*, Annex I, para. 133.

The Government's intentions were also set out by the Minister of State on the Third Reading in the House of Lords (*per* Lord Mackay of Ardbrecknish, *Hansard*, H.L. Vol. 564, cols. 925–926). When the Jobseekers Act comes fully into force in October 1996, the relevant parts of the SSCBA 1992 will be repealed (see Sched. 3). Existing awards of UB and income support will be terminated under the powers contained in subs. (2) and claimants transferred to JSA. Days of unemployment prior to October 1996 will count towards the 182 days' maximum entitlement to contribution-based JSA. Where a person's period of unemployment began before April 8, 1996, the full entitlement of up to 12 months' contributory benefit remains. Such transitional protection will thus end in April 1997.

Short title, commencement, extent etc.

41.—(1) This Act may be cited as the Jobseekers Act 1995.

(2) Section 39 and this section (apart from subsections (4) and (5)) come into force on the passing of this Act, but otherwise the provisions of this Act come into force on such day as the Secretary of State may by order appoint.

(3) Different days may be appointed for different purposes.

(4) Schedule 2 makes consequential amendments.

(5) The repeals set out in Schedule 3 shall have effect.

(6) Apart from this section, section 39 and paragraphs 11 to 16, 28, 67 and 68 of Schedule 2, this Act does not extend to Northern Ireland.

GENERAL NOTE
Subject to the exceptions specified in subs. (6), this Act does not apply to Northern Ireland (subs. (6)). However, corresponding provision will be made for Northern Ireland under the powers contained in the Northern Ireland Act 1974 (s.39).

SCHEDULES

Section 21   SCHEDULE 1

SUPPLEMENTARY PROVISIONS

Remunerative work

1.—(1) For the purposes of this Act, "remunerative work" has such meaning as may be prescribed.

(2) Regulations may prescribe circumstances in which, for the purposes of this Act—

(a) a person who is not engaged in remunerative work is to be treated as engaged in remunerative work; or

(b) a person who is engaged in remunerative work is to be treated as not engaged in remunerative work.

GENERAL NOTE
The enabling power in para. 1(1) will allow regulations to define what will normally constitute "remunerative work" for the purposes of s.1(2)(e). This will generally mean 16 hours per week, but in the context of the income-based JSA will be 24 hours for the claimant's partner. Paragraph 1(2) mirrors SSCBA 1992, s.137(2)(c) and (d). Regulations under para. 1(2)(a) will deal with the averaging of hours where a person works fluctuating hours or for intermittent periods. Regulations under para. 1(2)(b) will cover special categories (*e.g.* unpaid volunteers, some trainees) who may work for more than 16 hours but are deemed not to be in remunerative work.

Capacity for work

2.—(1) The question whether a person is capable or incapable of work shall be determined, for the purposes of this Act, in accordance with the provisions of Part XIIA of the Benefits Act.

(2) References in Part XIIA of the Benefits Act to the purposes of that Act shall be construed, where those provisions have effect for the purposes of this Act by virtue of sub-paragraph (1), as references to the purposes of this Act.

(3) Section 171B of the Benefits Act (incapacity for work: the own occupation test) shall have effect, as applied by sub-paragraph (1) for the purposes of this Act, as if for the references in subsections (3) and (4)(a) to any purpose of the Benefits Act there were substituted references to any purpose of this Act.

GENERAL NOTE

This provision is intended to ensure that the assessment of capacity or incapacity for work for the purposes of this Act (see s.1(2)(f)) is to be determined according to Pt. XIA of the SSCBA 1992, inserted by the Social Security (Incapacity for Work) Act 1994 (c.18).

Linking periods

3. Regulations may provide—
(a) for jobseeking periods which are separated by not more than a prescribed number of weeks to be treated, for purposes of this Act, as one jobseeking period;
(b) for prescribed periods ("linked periods") to be linked, for purposes of this Act, to any jobseeking period.

GENERAL NOTE

This provision enables the existing linking rules for UB to be carried forward into JSA. However, the linking period will be 12 weeks for JSA, and not eight weeks as with UB. It is intended that the linking rules will apply to income-based JSA in order to avoid waiting days on each claim. Periods in which the claimant has been in receipt of invalid care allowance will also be included in the linking provisions for JSA (*per* Mr R. Evans, Standing Committee B, col. 160, February 2, 1995).

Waiting days

4. Except in prescribed circumstances, a person is not entitled to a jobseeker's allowance in respect of a prescribed number of days at the beginning of a jobseeking period.

GENERAL NOTE

This provision allows regulations to be made specifying the number of days at the beginning of a jobseeking period for which there will be no entitlement to JSA ("waiting days"), and detailing exceptions to this rule. The intention is to operate the same three waiting days rule as applies to UB (however, as that period is not enshrined in primary legislation, as at present (SSCBA 1992, s.25(3)), there is nothing to prevent the period being extended by regulation). The three waiting days rule will apply across JSA; however, the following groups will be exempt: persons transferring from income support, incapacity benefit or invalid care allowance to JSA, and 16 and 17 year olds who qualify for an income-based JSA under a severe hardship direction (*Fifth Report*, Annex I, para. 140).

Periods of less than a week

5. Regulations may make provision in relation to—
(a) entitlement to a jobseeker's allowance, or
(b) the amount payable by way of such an allowance,
in respect of any period of less than a week.

Employment protection sums

6.—(1) In relation to any contribution-based jobseeker's allowance, regulations may make provision—
(a) for any employment protection sum to be treated as earnings payable by such person, to such person and for such period as may be determined in accordance with the regulations; and

(b) for any such period, so far as it is not a period of employment, to be treated as a period of employment.

(2) In this paragraph "employment protection sum" means—

(a) any sum, or a prescribed part of any sum—

(i) payable, in respect of arrears of pay, under an order for reinstatement or re-engagement made under the Employment Protection (Consolidation) Act 1978;

(ii) payable, by way of pay, under an order made under that Act for the continuation of a contract of employment;

(iii) payable, by way of remuneration, under a protective award made under section 189 of the Trade Union and Labour Relations (Consolidation) Act 1992; and

(b) any prescribed sum which the regulations provide is to be treated as related to any sum within paragraph (a).

Pension payments

7. Regulations may make provision, for the purposes of any provision of, or made under, this Act—

(a) for such sums by way of pension payments to be disregarded for prescribed purposes;

(b) as to the week in which any pension payments are to be treated as having begun;

(c) for treating, in a case where—

(i) a lump sum is paid to a person in connection with a former employment of his or arrangements are made for a lump sum to be so paid; or

(ii) benefits of any description are made available to a person in connection with a former employment of his or arrangements are made for them to be made so available; or

(iii) pension payments to a person are assigned, reduced or postponed or are made otherwise than weekly,

such payments as being made to that person by way of weekly pension payments as are specified in or determined under the regulations;

(d) for the method of determining whether pension payments are made to a person for any week and their amount.

GENERAL NOTE

Pension payments will be taken into account for the purposes of contribution-based JSA if they are over £50 per week, regardless of the claimant's age. Regulations made under subpara. (2) will provide that a period in which a person's benefit entitlement is reduced to nil by the operation of this rule will nonetheless count towards the 182 days of entitlement to the contribution-based JSA. This reflects the existing position (SS (USI) Regulations 1983, reg. 28).

Exemptions

8. Regulations may prescribe circumstances in which a person may be entitled to an income-based jobseeker's allowance without—

(a) being available for employment;

(b) having entered into a jobseeker's agreement; or

(c) actively seeking employment.

9. Regulations may provide—

(a) for an income-based jobseeker's allowance to which a person is entitled by virtue of regulations under paragraph 8 to be payable at a prescribed rate;

(b) for it to be payable for a prescribed period.

GENERAL NOTE

Paragraphs 8 and 9 will be used to make reduced payments to claimants in certain vulnerable categories who fail to meet the conditions for receipt of JSA specified in para. 8 but would otherwise suffer hardship.

Claims yet to be determined and suspended payments

10.—(1) In such circumstances as may be prescribed, a claimant may be treated as being entitled to an income-based jobseeker's allowance before his claim for a jobseeker's allowance has been determined.

(2) In such circumstances as may be prescribed, an income-based jobseeker's allowance shall be payable to a claimant even though payment to him of a jobseeker's allowance has been suspended by virtue of regulations under section 5(1)(n) of the Administration Act.

(3) A jobseeker's allowance shall be payable by virtue of sub-paragraph (1) or (2) only if the claimant has complied with such requirements as to the provision of information as may be prescribed for the purposes of this paragraph.

(4) Regulations may make provision for a jobseeker's allowance payable by virtue of sub-paragraph (1) or (2) to be—

(a) payable at a prescribed rate;

(b) payable for a prescribed period;

(c) treated as being a contribution-based jobseeker's allowance for the purposes of section 5 of this Act.

(5) Regulations may make provision—

(a) for the recovery, by prescribed means and in prescribed circumstances, of the whole or part of any amount paid by virtue of sub-paragraph (1) or (2);

(b) for the whole or part of any amount paid by virtue of sub-paragraph (1) to be treated, if an award is made on the claim referred to there, as having been paid on account of the jobseeker's allowance awarded;

(c) for the whole or part of any amount paid by virtue of sub-paragraph (2) to be treated, if the suspension referred to there is lifted, as having been paid on account of the suspended allowance.

Presence in and absence from Great Britain

11.—(1) Regulations may provide that in prescribed circumstances a claimant who is not in Great Britain may nevertheless be entitled to a contribution-based jobseeker's allowance.

(2) Regulations may make provision for the purposes of this Act as to the circumstances in which a person is to be treated as being or not being in Great Britain.

Households

12. Regulations may make provision for the purposes of this Act as to the circumstances in which persons are to be treated as being or not being members of the same household.

GENERAL NOTE

This reflects an existing enabling power in relation to income support. It will allow regulations to provide that persons can still be treated as members of the same household even though, *e.g.* one partner is working away from home (see SSCBA 1992, s.137(2)(l)).

Responsibility for another person

13. Regulations may make provision for the purposes of this Act as to the circumstances in which one person is to be treated as responsible or not responsible for another.

GENERAL NOTE

This similarly carries forward a provision relating to income support. Thus a person will be treated as responsible for a child if in receipt of child benefit for that child (see SSCBA 1992, s.137(2)(m) and Income Support (General) Regulations 1987 (S.I. 1987 No. 1967), reg. 15(1)).

Relevant education

14. Regulations may make provision for the purposes of this Act—

(a) as to what is or is not to be treated as relevant education; and

(b) as to the circumstances in which a person is or is not to be treated as receiving relevant education.

GENERAL NOTE

Again, this has its parallel in the existing rules governing entitlement to income support (SSCBA 1992, s.124(1)(d)(ii)).

Calculation of periods

15. Regulations may make provision for calculating periods for any purpose of this Act.

Employment on ships etc.

16.—(1) Regulations may modify any provision of this Act in its application to any person who is, has been, or is to be—

(a) employed on board any ship, vessel, hovercraft or aircraft,

(b) outside Great Britain at any prescribed time or in any prescribed circumstances, or

(c) in prescribed employment in connection with continental shelf operations,

so far as that provision relates to a contribution-based jobseeker's allowance.

(2) The regulations may in particular provide—

(a) for any such provision to apply even though it would not otherwise apply;

(b) for any such provision not to apply even though it would otherwise apply;

(c) for the taking of evidence, in a country or territory outside Great Britain, by a British consular official or other prescribed person;

(d) for enabling payment of the whole, or any part of a contribution-based jobseeker's allowance to be paid to such of the claimant's dependants as may be prescribed.

GENERAL NOTE

Few major pieces of social security legislation are complete without some reference to the position of share fishermen and other maritime workers. This provides the necessary enabling power to make modifying regulations for these and other special groups.

Additional conditions

17. Regulations may require additional conditions to be satisfied with respect to the payment of a jobseeker's allowance to any person who is, has been, or is to be, in employment which falls within a prescribed description.

GENERAL NOTE

This provision carries forward, albeit in rather broader language, the power currently found in SSCBA 1992, s.28(3). Regulations under this power are subject to the affirmative procedure (s.37(1)(c)). The Government's intention is to use it to place additional availability requirements on share fishermen claiming contribution-based JSA and special availability conditions for those who have been temporarily laid off or put on short-time working. Share fishermen will be subject to special provisions as under the UB regime. However, new rules will be introduced for those who are temporarily laid off or working short-time. Claimants in these categories will be able to look for temporary or part-time work as appropriate for up to 13 weeks. After that time, they will be expected to take a full-time job even if it means giving up the existing job (*per* Lord Mackay of Ardbrecknish, *Hansard*, Vol. 564, cols. 533–534; see also the White Paper, para. 4.9).

Benefits Act purposes

18. Regulations may provide for—

(a) a jobseeker's allowance;

(b) a contribution-based jobseeker's allowance; or

(c) an income-based jobseeker's allowance,

to be treated, for prescribed purposes of the Benefits Act, as a benefit, or a benefit of a prescribed description.

Section 41(4)   SCHEDULE 2

CONSEQUENTIAL AMENDMENTS

The Social Work (Scotland) Act 1968 (c. 49)

1. In section 78(2A) of the Social Work (Scotland) Act 1968 (relief from payment of contributions in respect of children subject to supervision requirements etc.), after "income support" insert ", an income-based jobseeker's allowance (payable under the Jobseekers Act 1995)".

The Employment Protection (Consolidation) Act 1978 (c. 44)

2.—(1) Section 132 of the Employment Protection (Consolidation) Act 1978 (recoupment of certain benefits) is amended as follows.

(2) For "unemployment benefit", in each case, substitute "jobseeker's allowance".

(3) In subsection (3)(e), after "recoupment of" insert "an income-based jobseeker's allowance or of".

(4) In subsection (4), after "reference to the " insert "jobseeker's allowance or".

(5) In subsection (6), in the appropriate place insert—

" "income-based jobseeker's allowanc" has the same meaning as in the Jobseekers Act 1995;".

The Education Act 1980 (c. 20)

3. In section 22(3) of the Education Act 1980 (school meals), after "income support" insert "or of an income-based jobseeker's allowance (payable under the Jobseekers Act 1995)" and for "it" substitute "that benefit".

The Magistrates' Courts Act 1980 (c. 43)

4. In Part I of Schedule 6 to the Magistrates' Courts Act 1980 (fees to be taken by clerks to justices), in paragraph (a) of the Note at the end, after "1992" insert "or of an income-based jobseeker's allowance (payable under the Jobseekers Act 1995)".

The Education (Scotland) Act 1980 (c. 44)

5. In section 53(3) of the Education (Scotland) Act 1980 (school meals), after "income support" insert "or of an income-based jobseeker's allowance (payable under the Jobseekers Act 1995)" and for "it" substitute "that benefit".

The Administration of Justice Act 1982 (c. 53)

6. In section 10 of the Administration of Justice Act 1982 (assessment of damages for personal injuries), in paragraph (ii), for "unemployment benefit" substitute "contribution-based jobseeker's allowance (payable under the Jobseekers Act 1995)".

The Transport Act 1982 (c. 49)

7. In section 70(2)(b) of the Transport Act 1982 (payments in relation to exemption from wearing seat belts), after "income support" insert "or an income-based jobseeker's allowance (payable under the Jobseekers Act 1995)".

The Bankruptcy (Scotland) Act 1985 (c. 66)

8. In section 31(8) of the Bankruptcy (Scotland) Act 1985 (definition of "whole estate of the debtor"), for "section 89(2)" substitute "sections 71(10B), 78(3B) and 89(2)".

The Legal Aid (Scotland) Act 1986 (c. 47)

9.—(1) The Legal Aid (Scotland) Act 1986 is amended as follows.
(2) In section 8(b) (availability of advice and assistance), after "income support" insert ", an income-based jobseeker's allowance (payable under the Jobseekers Act 1995)".
(3) In section 11(2)(b) (contributions in respect of advice and assistance), after "income support" insert ", an income-based jobseeker's allowance (payable under the Jobseekers Act 1995)".

The Abolition of Domestic Rates Etc. (Scotland) Act 1987 (c. 47)

10. Paragraph 7A of Schedule 2 to the Abolition of Domestic Rates Etc. (Scotland) Act 1987 (recovery of outstanding community charge by deduction from income support) shall, so far as it continues to have effect by virtue of Article 2 of the Local Government Finance Act 1992 (Recovery of Community Charge) Saving Order 1993, apply as if there were inserted at the end—
"(3) This paragraph applies to a jobseeker's allowance as it applies to income support.".

The Income and Corporation Taxes Act 1988 (c. 1)

11. The Income and Corporation Taxes Act 1988 is amended as follows.
12. After section 151, insert—

"Jobseeker's allowance
151A.—(1) Subject to the following provisions of this section, payments to any person of a jobseeker's allowance in respect of any period shall be charged to income tax under Schedule E.
(2) Where the amount of a jobseeker's allowance paid to any person in respect of any week or part of a week exceeds the taxable maximum for that period as defined below, the excess shall not be taxable.
(3) For the purposes of subsection (2) above, the taxable maximum in respect of a week shall be determined in accordance with subsections (4) to (8) below and the taxable maximum in respect of part of a week shall be equal to one-seventh of the taxable maximum in respect of a week multiplied by the number of days in the part.

(4) Where an income-based jobseeker's allowance is paid to one of a married or unmarried couple, in a case which does not fall within subsection (8) below, the taxable maximum in respect of a week shall be equal to the portion of the applicable amount which is included in respect of them for that week.

(5) Where a contribution-based jobseeker's allowance is paid to a person ("the claimant") who is a member of a married or unmarried couple, the taxable maximum in respect of a week shall be equal to the portion of the applicable amount which would be included in respect of them if an income-based jobseeker's allowance was payable to the claimant for that week.

(6) Where an income-based jobseeker's allowance is paid to a person who is not a member of a married or unmarried couple, the taxable maximum in respect of a week shall be equal to the age-related amount which would be applicable to him if a contribution-based jobseeker's allowance was payable to him for that week.

(7) Where a contribution-based jobseeker's allowance is paid to a person who is not a member of a married or unmarried couple, the taxable maximum in respect of a week shall be equal to the age-related amount which is applicable to him for that week.

(8) Where an income-based jobseeker's allowance is paid to a person ("the claimant") who is a member of a married or unmarried couple, the other member of which is prevented by section 14 of the Jobseekers Act 1995 (trade disputes) or any corresponding enactment in Northern Ireland from being entitled to a jobseeker's allowance, the taxable maximum in respect of a week shall be equal to half the portion of the applicable amount which is included in respect of them for that week.

(9) In this section—

"age-related amount" and "applicable amount" mean the amounts determined as such in accordance with regulations made under section 4 of the Jobseekers Act 1995 or, for Northern Ireland, regulations made under any corresponding enactment in Northern Ireland; and

"contribution-based jobseeker's allowance", "income-based jobseeker's allowance", "married couple" and "unmarried couple" have the same meanings as in the Jobseekers Act 1995 or, for Northern Ireland, the same meanings as in any corresponding enactment in Northern Ireland."

13. In section 152 (notification of amount taxable), in subsection (1), after "unemployment benefit" insert ", jobseeker's allowance".

14.—(1) Section 204 (PAYE repayments) is amended as follows.

(2) After paragraph (a) insert—

"(aa) he has claimed a jobseeker's allowance in respect of a period including that time; or".

(3) After paragraph (c) insert—

"or

(d) he is prevented at the time from being entitled to a jobseeker's allowance by section 14 of the Jobseekers Act 1995 (trade disputes) or any corresponding enactment in Northern Ireland or would be so prevented if he otherwise satisfies the conditions for entitlement;".

(4) After "paragraph (c)" insert "or (d)".

15.—(1) Section 347B (qualifying maintenance payments) is amended as follows.

(2) For subsection (12)(b) substitute—

"(b) under an order—

(i) made under section 106 of the Social Security Administration Act 1992 or section 101 of the Social Security Administration (Northern Ireland) Act 1992 (recovery of expenditure on benefit from person liable for maintenance) in respect of income support claimed by the other party to the marriage; or

(ii) made by virtue of section 23 of the Jobseekers Act 1995 (recovery of sums in respect of maintenance), or any corresponding enactment in Northern Ireland, in respect of an income-based jobseeker's allowance claimed by the other party to the marriage,".

(3) After subsection (12) insert—

"(13) In subsection (12) above, "income-based jobseeker's allowance" has the same meaning as in the Jobseekers Act 1995 or, for Northern Ireland, the same meaning as in any corresponding enactment in Northern Ireland.".

16. In section 617 (social security benefits and contributions), in subsection (2) insert after paragraph (aa)—

"(ab) payments of a jobseeker's allowance, other than payments which are taxable by virtue of section 151A;

(ac) payments of a back to work bonus;".

The Education Reform Act 1988 (c. 40)

17. In section 110(3)(b) of the Education Reform Act 1988 (charges and remissions: parents receiving benefit), after "family credit" insert "or an income-based jobseeker's allowance (payable under the Jobseekers Act 1995)".

The Local Government Finance Act 1988 (c. 41)

18. In paragraph 6 of Schedule 4 to the Local Government Finance Act 1988 (recovery of outstanding community charge by deduction from income support), insert at the end—
     "(3) This paragraph applies to a jobseeker's allowance as it applies to income support.".

The Children Act 1989 (c. 41)

19.—(1) The Children Act 1989 is amended as follows.
     (2) In section 17(9) (person receiving benefit not to be liable to repay assistance), add at the end "or of an income-based jobseeker's allowance".
     (3) In section 29(3) (person receiving benefit not to be liable to pay charges), add at the end "or of an income-based jobseeker's allowance".
     (4) In section 105 (interpretation), after the definition of "ill-treatment" insert—
        " "income-based jobseeker's allowance" has the same meaning as in the Jobseekers Act 1995;".
     (5) In paragraph 21(4) of Schedule 2 (person receiving benefit not to be liable to pay contributions), add at the end "or of an income-based jobseeker's allowance".

The Child Support Act 1991 (c. 48)

20.—(1) The Child Support Act 1991 is amended as follows.
     (2) In section 6(1) (applications by those receiving benefit), after "income support," insert "an income-based jobseeker's allowance,".
     (3) In section 14(2) (use by Secretary of State of information acquired under other enactments), after "benefit Acts" insert "or the Jobseekers Act 1995".
     (4) In section 46(11) (definitions), in the definition of "relevant benefit", after "income support," insert "an income-based jobseeker's allowance,".
     (5) In section 47(3) (regulations about fees), after "income support," insert "an income-based jobseeker's allowance,".
     (6) In section 54 (interpretation), after the definition of "income support" insert—
        " "income-based jobseeker's allowance" has the same meaning as in the Jobseekers Act 1995;".
     (7) In paragraph 5(4) of Schedule 1 (assessable income), after "income support" insert ", an income-based jobseeker's allowance".

The Criminal Justice Act 1991 (c. 53)

21.—(1) Section 24 of the Criminal Justice Act 1991 (recovery of fines etc. by deductions from income support) is amended as follows.
     (2) In subsection (1), before paragraph (a), after "income support" insert "or a jobseeker's allowance".
     (3) In subsection (1)(a), for "income support" substitute "that benefit".
     (4) In subsection (2)(d), after "income support" insert "or a jobseeker's allowance".

The Social Security Contributions and Benefits Act 1992 (c. 4)

22. In section 22 of the Benefits Act (earnings factors), in subsections (2)(a) and (5), after "entitlement to" insert, in each case, "a contribution-based jobseeker's allowance or to".
23. In section 61 of the Benefits Act (exclusion of increase of benefit for failure to satisfy contribution condition), for subsection (2) substitute—
     "(2) Where a person is entitled to short-term incapacity benefit at a rate determined under section 30B(3) above and the retirement pension by reference to which the rate of the benefit is determined—
        (a) would have been payable only by virtue of section 60 above, and
        (b) would, in consequence of a failure to satisfy a contribution condition, have contained no basic pension,

the benefit shall not be increased under section 47(1) above or under Part IV below on account of a child or an adult.".

24. In section 82 of the Benefits Act (short-term benefit: increase for adult dependants), for subsection (2) substitute—

"(2) Subject, in particular, to subsection (5) and section 87 below, the weekly rate of a maternity allowance shall be increased by the amount specified in relation to that benefit in Schedule 4, Part IV, column (3) ("the amount of the relevant increase") for any period to which this subsection applies by virtue of subsection (3) or (4) below.".

25. In section 84 of the Benefits Act (pension increase for dependent husband), for subsection (1)(a) substitute—

"(a) which began immediately on the termination of a period for which the pensioner was entitled to an increase in incapacity benefit by virtue of any provision of regulations under section 86A below prescribed for the purposes of this paragraph, and".

26. In section 87 of the Benefits Act (rate of increase where associated retirement pension is attributable to reduced contributions), for subsection (1)(a) substitute—

"(a) is entitled to short-term incapacity benefit under section 30A(2)(b) above; and".

27. In section 91 of the Benefits Act (effect of trade disputes on entitlement to dependency increases), for subsection (2) substitute—

"(2) A person falls within this subsection if—

(a) he is prevented from being entitled to a jobseeker's allowance by section 14 of the Jobseekers Act 1995 (trade disputes); or

(b) he would be so prevented if he were otherwise entitled to that benefit.".

28. In section 116 (application to Her Majesty's forces), in subsection (2), for the words following "provide" substitute—

", in the case of persons who are employed earners in respect of their membership of those forces, for reducing the rate of the contributions payable in respect of their employment and for determining—

(a) the amounts payable on account of those contributions by the Secretary of State and the time and manner of payment, and

(b) the deduction (if any) to be made on account of those contributions from the pay of those persons.".

29. In section 122(1) of the Benefits Act (interpretation of Parts I to VI of that Act), after the definition of "contract of service" insert—

" "contribution-based jobseeker's allowance" has the same meaning as in the Jobseekers Act 1995;".

30.—(1) Section 124 of the Benefits Act (entitlement to income support) is amended as follows.

(2) For subsection (1)(a) substitute—

"(a) he is of or over the age of 16;".

(3) Omit "and" at the end of subsection (1)(c).

(4) For subsection (1)(d) substitute—

"(d) except in such circumstances as may be prescribed, he is not receiving relevant education;".

(5) In subsection (1), after paragraph (d) insert—

"(e) he falls within a prescribed category of person; and

(f) he is not entitled to a jobseeker's allowance and, if he is a member of a married or unmarried couple, the other member of the couple is not entitled to an income-based jobseeker's allowance.".

31. In section 126 of the Benefits Act (income support: trade disputes)—

(a) in subsection (1)(a), for "is disqualified under section 27 above for receiving unemployment benefit" substitute "is prevented from being entitled to a jobseeker's allowance by section 14 of the Jobseekers Act 1995 (trade disputes)"; and

(b) in subsection (1)(b), for "disqualified" substitute "prevented".

32. In section 127 of the Benefits Act (effect of return to work), for "disqualified from receiving unemployment benefit" substitute "prevented from being entitled to a jobseeker's allowance".

33. In section 128 of the Benefits Act (family credit), in subsection (4)(b), after "income support" insert ", an income-based jobseeker's allowance".

34. In section 129 of the Benefits Act (disability working allowance), in subsections (2)(a)(iii) and (7)(b), in each case after "income support" insert ", an income-based jobseeker's allowance".

35.—(1) Section 137 of the Benefits Act (interpretation of Part VII and supplementary provisions) is amended as follows.

(2) In subsection (1), after the definition of "family" insert—

" "income-based jobseeker's allowance" has the same meaning as in the Jobseekers Act 1995;".

(3) In subsection (2), for paragraph (d) substitute—

"(d) as to circumstances in which a person is or is not to be treated as engaged or normally engaged in remunerative work;".

36.—(1) Schedule 7 to the Benefits Act (industrial injuries benefits) is amended as follows.

(2) In paragraph 3(10), for "it has for the purposes of unemployment benefit" substitute "a jobseeking period and any period linked to such a period has for the purposes of the Jobseekers Act 1995.".

(3) For paragraph 13(10) substitute—

"(10) "Day of interruption of employment" means a day which forms part of—

(a) a jobseeking period (as defined by the Jobseekers Act 1995), or

(b) a linked period (as defined by that Act).".

37. In Schedule 13 to the Benefits Act (relationship of statutory maternity pay with benefits and other payments), for paragraph 1 substitute—

"1. Except as may be prescribed, a day which falls within the maternity pay period shall not be treated as a day of incapacity for work for the purposes of determining, for this Act, whether it forms part of a period of incapacity for work for the purposes of incapacity benefit.".

The Social Security Administration Act 1992 (c. 5)

38. In section 1 of the Administration Act (entitlement to benefit dependent on claim), in the definition of "benefit" in subsection (4), after "Benefits Act;" insert—

"(aa) a jobseeker's allowance;".

39. In section 5 of the Administration Act (claims and payments regulations), in subsection (2) after paragraph (a) insert—

"(aa) a jobseeker's allowance;".

40.—(1) Section 15A of the Administration Act (payment out of benefit of sums in respect of mortgage interest etc.) is amended as follows.

(2) In subsection (1) after "income support" insert (in each place) "or an income-based jobseeker's allowance".

(3) In the definition of "qualifying associate", in subsection (4)—

(a) after "support" insert "or an income-based jobseeker's allowance"; and

(b) after "Act" insert "or (as the case may be) under the Jobseekers Act 1995,".

(4) In the definition of "relevant benefits" in subsection (4), after "Act;" insert—

"(aa) a jobseeker's allowance;".

41. In section 17(1) of the Administration Act (questions for adjudication by the Secretary of State), omit "and" at the end of paragraph (g) and after paragraph (h) insert—

"; and

(i) any question arising under section 27 of the Jobseekers Act 1995, or under any provision of regulations under that section, as to—

(i) whether a person is, or was, an employee or employer of another;

(ii) whether an employer is entitled to make any deduction from his contributions payments in accordance with regulations under section 27 of that Act;

(iii) whether a payment falls to be made to an employer in accordance with those regulations;

(iv) the amount that falls to be so deducted or paid; or

(v) whether two or more employers are, by virtue of regulations under section 27 of that Act, to be treated as one.".

42.—(1) Section 20 of the Administration Act (claims and questions to be submitted to adjudication officer) is amended as follows.

(2) In subsection (1), omit "and" at the end of paragraph (b) and after paragraph (c) insert—

"; and

(d) any question whether a jobseeker's allowance is not payable to a person by virtue of section 19 of the Jobseekers Act 1995.".

(3) In subsection (2), after "which", insert—

"—

(a) may be determined by an adjudication officer under section 9(6) or 10(5) of the Jobseekers Act 1995; or

(b)".

(4) In subsection (6), after paragraph (a) insert—

"(aa) a jobseeker's allowance;".

43. In section 25 of the Administration Act (review of decisions), in subsection (1)(e), for "25A(4) or (5) of the Contributions and Benefits Act" substitute " 6(6) or 7(7) of the Jobseekers Act 1995".

44.—(1) In section 58 of the Administration Act (determination of questions and matters arising out of, or pending, reviews and appeals)—

(a) in subsection (1), after "Benefits Act" insert ", the Jobseekers Act 1995"; and

(b) in subsection (4), after "unemployment benefit" insert "or a jobseeker's allowance".

45. In section 61 of the Administration Act (supplementary matters relating to determinations), in subsection (4), after paragraph (a) insert—

"(aa) to a jobseeker's allowance;".

46. In section 68 of the Administration Act (restrictions on entitlement to benefit in certain cases of error), in the definition of "benefit" in subsection (4), after "Act;" insert—

"(aa) a jobseeker's allowance;".

47. In section 70 of the Administration Act (correction of errors and setting aside of decisions), in subsection (3), omit "or" at the end of paragraph (i) and after paragraph (j) insert—

"; or

(k) the Jobseekers Act 1995.".

48. In section 71 of the Administration Act (recovery of overpayments), in subsection (11), after paragraph (a) insert—

"(aa) subject to section 71A below, a jobseeker's allowance;".

49.—(1) Section 73 of the Administration Act (adjustment of benefits) is amended as follows.

(2) In subsection (1)—

(a) after "Act" insert ", or a contribution-based jobseeker's allowance,"; and

(b) for "its receipt" substitute "receipt of that benefit".

(3) For subsection (4) substitute—

"(4) Regulations may provide for adjusting—

(a) benefit as defined in section 122 of the Contributions and Benefits Act; or

(b) a contribution-based jobseeker's allowance,

payable to or in respect of any person where there is payable in his case any such benefit as is described in subsection (5) below.".

50. In section 74 (recovery and abatement of income support), in subsections (1), (2) and (3) after "support" insert, in each place, "or an income-based jobseeker's allowance".

51. In section 78 of the Administration Act (recovery of social fund awards), in subsection (6)(d), after "support" insert "or an income-based jobseeker's allowance".

52. In section 81(1) of the Administration Act (interpretation of Part IV), in the definition of "benefit" after "means" insert "a jobseeker's allowance or,".

53.—(1) Section 105 of the Administration Act (failure to maintain) is amended as follows.

(2) In subsection (1)(b), after "support" insert "or an income-based jobseeker's allowance".

(3) In subsection (3), at the beginning insert "subject to subsection (4) below,".

(4) After subsection (3) insert—

"(4) For the purposes of this section, in its application to an income-based jobseeker's allowance, a person is liable to maintain another if that other person is his or her spouse.".

54. In section 110 of the Administration Act (appointment and powers of inspectors), add at the end of subsection (9) "; but "relevant benefit" does not include a jobseeker's allowance".

55. In section 115 of the Administration Act (offences by bodies corporate), in subsection (1), after "Act" insert ", or under the Jobseekers Act 1995,".

56.—(1) Section 116 of the Administration Act (legal proceedings) is amended as follows.

(2) In subsection (1), after "Act" insert "or the Jobseekers Act 1995".

(3) In subsection (2)(a), after "council tax benefit" insert ", or for an offence under the Jobseekers Act 1995,".

(4) In subsection (7)(a), after "this Act" insert "or the Jobseekers Act 1995".

57. In section 117 of the Administration Act (questions arising in proceedings), in subsection (1)(a), after "Act" insert "or the Jobseekers Act 1995".

58.—(1) Section 122 of the Administration Act (disclosure of information by Inland Revenue) is amended as follows.

(2) In subsection (1)(c)—

(a) after "Benefits Act" insert ", the Jobseekers Act 1995"; and

(b) for "to either of them" substitute "to any of those Acts".

(3) In subsection (3)(b)—

(a) after "Benefits Act" insert ", the Jobseekers Act 1995"; and

(b) for "either of them" substitute "any of those Acts".

59. In section 124 of the Administration Act (provisions relating to age, death and marriage), in subsection (1), after "applies;" insert—

"(aa) of the provisions of Parts I and II of the Jobseekers Act 1995;".

60. In section 125 of the Administration Act (notifications of deaths), in subsection (1)—

(a) after "Benefits Act" insert ", the Jobseekers Act 1995"; and

(b) for "either of them" substitute "any of those Acts".

61. In section 126 of the Administration Act (information to be provided by personal representatives in certain cases), in subsection (1), after "support" insert ", an income-based jobseeker's allowance".

62. In section 127 of the Administration Act (information for purposes of housing benefit), in subsections (1) and (2), after "Benefits Act" insert, in each case, ", the Jobseekers Act 1995".

63. In section 128 of the Administration Act (information for purposes of council tax benefits), in subsection (1), after "Benefits Act" insert ", the Jobseekers Act 1995".

64.—(1) Section 150 of the Administration Act (annual up-rating of benefits) is amended as follows.

(2) In subsection (1), after paragraph (j) insert—

"(k) specified in regulations under section 4(2) or (5) of the Jobseekers Act 1995;".

(3) In subsection (7), after "Benefits Act" insert "or under the Jobseekers Act 1995,".

65. In section 164(1) of the Administration Act (destination of repayments), after "Subject to" insert "section 38 of the Jobseekers Act 1995 and to".

66.—(1) Section 166 of the Administration Act (financial review and report) is amended as follows.

(2) In subsection (1), for the words from "the 1975 Act" to the end substitute—
"—

(a) the 1975 Act;

(b) Parts I to VI of the Contributions and Benefits Act (except Part I of Schedule 8);

(c) the provisions of the Jobseekers Act 1995 relating to a contribution-based jobseeker's allowance; and

(d) this Act so far as it relates to the provisions specified in paragraphs (b) and (c) above.".

(3) In subsection (2), for the words from "Parts I" to the end substitute—
"—

(a) Parts I to VI of the Contributions and Benefits Act (except Part I of Schedule 8);

(b) the provisions of the Jobseekers Act 1995 relating to a contribution-based jobseeker's allowance; and

(c) this Act so far as it relates to the provisions specified in paragraphs (a) and (b) above.".

67. In section 170 of the Administration Act (the Social Security Advisory Committee), in subsection (5)—

(a) in the definition of "the relevant enactments", after "payments;" insert—

"(aa) the provisions of the Jobseekers Act 1995;" and

(b) in the definition of "the relevant Northern Ireland enactments", after paragraph (a) insert—

"(aa) any provisions in Northern Ireland which correspond to provisions of the Jobseekers Act 1995; and".

68.—(1) Section 177(5) of the Administration Act (co-ordination with Northern Ireland) is amended as follows.

(2) In paragraph (a), after "Benefits Act" insert ", the Jobseekers Act 1995".

(3) In paragraph (b), after "Benefits Act" insert ", any enactment in Northern Ireland corresponding to the Jobseekers Act 1995".

(4) After "income support;" insert—

"(ia) income-based jobseeker's allowance;".

69.—(1) Section 178 of the Administration Act (reciprocal arrangements with Northern Ireland) is amended as follows.

(2) In subsection (1), after "Benefits Act" insert ", the Jobseekers Act 1995".

(3) In subsection (2), after paragraph (a) insert—

"(aa) income-based jobseeker's allowance;".

(4) In subsection (3), after "this Act" insert (in each place) ", the Jobseekers Act 1995".

70.—(1) Section 179 of the Administration Act (reciprocal agreements with countries outside the United Kingdom) is amended as follows.

(2) In subsection (3), after "this Act" insert ", the Jobseekers Act 1995".

(3) In subsection (4), after "Benefits Act;" insert—

"(aa) to the Jobseekers Act 1995;".

(4) In subsection (5), after paragraph (a) insert—

"(aa) jobseeker's allowance;".

71. In section 180 of the Administration Act (payment of travelling expenses by Secretary of State), after "Benefits Act" (in both places) insert ", the Jobseekers Act 1995".

72. In section 187 of the Administration Act (certain benefit to be inalienable), in subsection (1), after paragraph (a) insert—

"(aa) a jobseeker's allowance;".

73.—(1) Section 191 of the Administration Act (interpretation) is amended as follows.

(2) In the definition of "benefit", after "Act" insert "and includes a jobseeker's allowance".

(3) After the definition of "the Consequential Provisions Act" insert—

" "contribution-based jobseeker's allowance" has the same meaning as in the Jobseekers Act 1995;".

(4) After the definition of "housing benefit scheme" insert—

" "income-based jobseeker's allowance" has the same meaning as in the Jobseekers Act 1995;".

74. In Schedule 4 to the Administration Act (persons employed in social security administration or adjudication), in paragraph 2 of Part II, after "relate to" insert "a jobseeker's allowance or to".

The Local Government Finance Act 1992 (c. 14)

75.—(1) Paragraph 6 of Schedule 4 to the Local Government Finance Act 1992 (deductions from income support) is amended as follows.

(2) In sub-paragraph (1)—

(a) after first "income support" insert "or a jobseeker's allowance";

(b) omit "within the meaning of the Social Security Contributions and Benefits Act 1992"; and

(c) in paragraph (a), for "income support" substitute "that benefit".

(3) In sub-paragraph (2)(b) after "income support" insert "or a jobseeker's allowance".

76.—(1) Paragraph 6 of Schedule 8 to the Local Government Finance Act 1992 (enforcement in Scotland) is amended as follows.

(2) In sub-paragraph (1)—

(a) after first "income support" insert "or a jobseeker's allowance";

(b) omit "within the meaning of the Social Security Contributions and Benefits Act 1992"; and

(c) in paragraph (a), for "income support" substitute "that benefit".

(3) In sub-paragraph (2)(b) after "income support" insert "or a jobseeker's allowance".

Section 41(5)   SCHEDULE 3

REPEALS

Chapter	Short title	Extent of repeal
1976 c. 71.	Supplementary Benefits Act 1976.	Section 30. Schedule 5.
1991 c. 53.	Criminal Justice Act 1991.	In section 24(4), in the definition of "income support", the words "unemployment, or".
1992 c. 4.	Social Security Contributions and Benefits Act 1992.	In section 20, subsection (1)(a) and in the definition of "short-term benefit", in subsection (2), paragraph (a). In section 21(2), in the Table relating to short-term benefits, the entry relating to unemployment benefit. Section 25. Section 25A. Section 25B. Section 26. Section 27. Section 28. Section 29. Section 30. Section 80(2)(a). Section 82(1). In section 124, the word "and", at the end of subsection (1)(c) and subsections (2) and (3). Section 125.

Chapter	Short title	Extent of repeal
1992 c. 5.	Social Security Administration Act 1992.	In section 163(1), the definition of "period of interruption of employment". In Schedule 3, paragraph 1. In Schedule 4, paragraph 1 of Part I and paragraph 1 of Part IV. In Schedule 11, in paragraph 2(g), the words ", within the meaning of section 27 above,". In Schedule 12, in paragraph 1, the words "a period of interruption of employment for the purposes of unemployment benefit or". In section 17(1)(g), the word "and" at the end. In section 20(1)(b), the word "and" at the end. In section 70(3)(i), the word "or". In section 71(11)(b), the words "subject to section 72 below". Section 72.
1992 c. 14.	Local Government Finance Act 1992.	In paragraph 6(1) of Schedule 4, the words "within the meaning of the Social Security Contributions and Benefits Act 1992.". In paragraph 6(1) of Schedule 8, the words "within the meaning of the Social Security Contributions and Benefits Act 1992."
1994 c. 18.	Social Security (Incapacity for Work) Act 1994.	In Schedule 1, paragraphs 4, 5, 6, 19, 21, 24(2) and (3), 30, 35, 36, 37, sub-paragraph (b) of paragraph 39, 41(3), 45(2) and 47.

INDEX

References are to sections and Schedules

APPROPRIATION ACT 1995

(1995 c. 19)

An Act to apply a sum out of the Consolidated Fund to the service of the year ending on 31st March 1996; to appropriate the supplies granted in this Session of Parliament; and to repeal certain Consolidated Fund and Appropriation Acts.   [19th July 1995]

PARLIAMENTARY DEBATES
Hansard, H.C. Vol. 263, col. 1339. H.L. Vol. 566, col. 344.

INTRODUCTION
This is the annual measure which provides for certain sums to be applied out of the Consolidated Funds for the year ending March 31, 1996.

GRANT OUT OF THE CONSOLIDATED FUND

Issue out of the Consolidated Fund for the year ending 31st March 1996

1. The Treasury may issue out of the Consolidated Fund of the United Kingdom and apply towards making good the supply granted to Her Majesty for the service of the year ending on 31st March 1996 the sum of £112,783,415,000.

APPROPRIATION OF GRANTS

Appropriation of sums voted for supply services

2. All sums granted by this Act and the other Acts mentioned in Schedule (A) annexed to this Act out of the said Consolidated Fund towards making good the supply granted to Her Majesty amounting, as appears by the said schedule, in the aggregate, to the sum of £210,796,770,897·35 are appropriated, and shall be deemed to have been appropriated as from the date of the passing of the Acts mentioned in the said Schedule (A), for the services and purposes expressed in Schedule (B) annexed hereto.

The abstract of schedules and schedules annexed hereto, with the notes (if any) to such schedules, shall be deemed to be part of this Act in the same manner as if they had been contained in the body thereof.

In addition to the said sums granted out of the Consolidated Fund, there may be applied out of any money directed, under section 2 of the Public Accounts and Charges Act 1891, to be applied as appropriations in aid of the grants for the services and purposes specified in Schedule (B) annexed hereto the sums respectively set forth in the last column of the said schedule.

Repeals

3. The enactments mentioned in Schedule (C) annexed to this Act are hereby repealed.

Short title

4. This Act may be cited as the Appropriation Act 1994.

ABSTRACT
OF
SCHEDULES (A) and (B) to which this Act refers

Section 2   SCHEDULE (A)

Grants out of the Consolidated Fund .... £210,796,770,897·35

Section 2   SCHEDULE (B)—APPROPRIATION OF GRANTS

	Supply Grants	Appropriations in Aid
	£	£
1993–94 and 1994–95		
Part 1. Civil (Excesses), 1993–94	167,222,897·35	−16,569,725·82
Part 2. Supplementary, 1994–95	2,448,182,000	88,905,000
1995–96		
Part 3. Class I	22,559,371,000	3,328,940,000
Part 4. Class II	3,090,715,000	132,453,000
Part 5. Class III	860,236,000	3,106,558,000
Part 6. Class IV	1,811,690,000	1,357,930,000
Part 7. Class V	3,240,058,000	673,472,000
Part 8. Class VI	5,813,826,000	244,297,000
Part 9. Class VII	39,043,481,000	1,110,859,000
Part 10. Class VIII	6,303,172,000	133,178,000
Part 11. Class IX	2,734,732,000	354,282,000
Part 12. Class X	11,679,573,000	3,439,450,000
Part 13. Class XI	2,850,773,000	43,361,000
Part 14. Class XII	30,322,983,000	7,542,054,000
Part 15. Class XIII	48,549,001,000	1,524,631,000
Part 16. Class XIV	13,303,445,000	1,146,504,000
Part 17. Class XV	6,079,651,000	368,008,000
Part 18. Class XVI	2,888,655,000	8,257,000
Part 19. Class XVII	3,133,103,000	1,088,604,000
Part 20. Class XVIII	2,790,146,000	1,396,093,000
Part 21. Class XIX	956,925,000	26,531,000
Part 22. Class XIX, A	123,230,000	4,838,000
Part 23. Class XIX, B	37,600,000	6,000,000
TOTAL	208,181,366,000	27,036,300,000
GRAND TOTAL	210,796,770,897·35	27,108,635,274·18

SCHEDULE (A)

GRANTS OUT OF THE CONSOLIDATED FUND

	£
For the service of the year ended 31st March 1994—	
Under Act 1995 c. 2	167,222,897·35
For the service of the year ended 31st March 1995—	
Under Act 1994 c. 41	1,276,707,000·00
Under Act 1995 c. 2	1,171,475,000·00
For the service of the year ending on 31st March 1996—	
Under Act 1994 c. 41	95,397,951,000·00
Under this Act	112,783,415,000·00
TOTAL	210,796,770,897·35

SCHEDULE (B).—PART 1   Civil (Excesses),
1993–94

CIVIL (EXCESSES), 1993–94

SUMS granted, and sums which may be applied as appropriations in addition thereto, to make good excesses on certain grants for civil services, for the year ended 31st March 1994, viz.:—

	Supply Grants	Surplus receipts available to be applied as Appropriations in Aid
	£	£
Vote		
Class III		
1 Central Government administered social security benefits and other payments	141,339,391·28	*–7,658,293·53
Class XIV		
13 Family health services (part) and NHS Trusts external financing etc., Scotland	20,660,804·07	*–8,911,432·29
Class XVII		
8 Inland Revenue: payments in lieu of tax relief	5,222,702·00	—
TOTAL, CIVIL (EXCESSES), 1993–94.................................	167,222,897·35	*–16,569,725·82

Deficit

SCHEDULE (B).—PART 2   Supplementary,
1994–95

SUPPLEMENTARY, 1994–95

SCHEDULE OF SUPPLEMENTARY SUMS granted, and of the sums which may be applied as appropriations in aid in addition thereto, to defray the charges for the Services herein particularly mentioned, for the year ending 31st March 1995, viz.:—

	Supply Grants	Appropriations in Aid
	£	£
Vote		
CLASS I		
1. For expenditure by the Ministry of Defence on personnel costs etc. of the armed forces and their reserves and cadet forces etc., personnel costs etc. of Defence Ministers and of certain civilian staff employed by the Ministry of Defence, movements, certain stores, supplies and services, certain spares and maintenance, plant and machinery, charter of ships, certain research, lands and buildings, works services, certain contingent liabilities, sundry grants, other payments, including those abroad, and assistance to Russia in the resettlement of military personnel	1,000	—
2. For expenditure by the Ministry of Defence on logistics services for the armed forces and the related per-		

	Supply Grants	Appropriations in Aid
	£	£
sonnel costs; for spares, repair, maintenance, stores and supply services; for associated capital facilities and works, contractors' redundancy costs; for some works costs for visiting forces and sundry services, subscriptions and grants	1,000	*–14,764,000
3. For expenditure by the Procurement Executive of the Ministry of Defence in operating its Headquarters and Establishments and for its other common services; for research etc. by contract; for development by contract, production and purchases for sale abroad of sea systems, land systems, air systems and associated equipment; for certain contingent liabilities, and for sundry other Procurement Executive services including those on repayment terms to non-exchequer customers	1,000	—

CLASS II

	Supply Grants	Appropriations in Aid
1. For expenditure by the Foreign and Commonwealth Office on its salaries, building and other accommodation services, and administration, and those of HM Diplomatic Service, official information services, sundry services and loans and payments in connection with catering services	1,000	5,750,000
2. For expenditure by the Foreign and Commonwealth Office on grants and subscriptions etc. to certain international organisations, contributions in respect of international peacekeeping forces, special payments and assistance, scholarships, military aid and sundry other grants and services	41,334,000	23,843,000
3. For expenditure by the Foreign and Commonwealth Office as payments to the British Broadcasting Corporation for external broadcasting and monitoring services	2,749,000	—
4. For expenditure by the Foreign and Commonwealth Office on the British Council	2,119,000	—
5. For expenditure by the Foreign and Commonwealth Office: Overseas Development Administration under the Overseas Development and Co-operation Act 1980 on the United Kingdom overseas aid budget, including financial and technical assistance to governments, institutions, voluntary agencies and individuals; capital and other subscriptions and contributions, including payments under guarantee, to multilateral development banks and other international and regional bodies; emergency, refugee and other relief assistance; pensions, and allowances in respect of overseas service including contributions to pension funds (including payments under the Overseas Pensions Act 1973, and grants in lieu of pensions); and on global environment assistance; loans to the Commonwealth Development Corporation under the Commonwealth Development Corporation Acts 1978–1986; expenditure on the Turkey Ankara Metro and the Botswana Flight Information Region mixed credit Aid and Trade Provision projects; costs in connection with the privatisation of the Crown Agents; and running costs, related capital expenditure and other administrative costs including		

	Supply Grants	Appropriations in Aid
	£	£
for the Natural Resources Institute (an executive agency)	11,069,000	1,971,000

CLASS III

1. For expenditure by the Intervention Board—Executive Agency in giving effect in the United Kingdom to the agricultural support provisions of the Common Agricultural Policy of the European Community and for other services	34,645,000	*–43,076,000
3. For expenditure by the Ministry of Agriculture, Fisheries and Food on market support; miscellaneous payments and loan guarantees; support for agriculture in special areas and compensation to sheep producers; and animal health	9,306,000	—
4. For expenditure by the Ministry of Agriculture, Fisheries and Food on commissioned research and development; advice, education and training services; botanical services; assistance to production, marketing and processing; support for the fishing industry; flood and coast protection and arterial drainage; emergency and strategic food services; protective, agency, administrative, scientific and policy advice services; grants and loans for capital and other improvements and alternative land uses and other services	1,213,000	1,530,000
5. For expenditure by the Ministry of Agriculture, Fisheries and Food on departmental research, advisory services and administration and certain other services	6,392,000	25,000

CLASS IV

1. For expenditure by the Department of Trade and Industry on support for business, research and development; consumer protection and the regulation of trade, energy related programmes, including research and development, and residual privatisation expenses; departmental administration, central and miscellaneous services; security of oil and gas supplies; the operational costs of departmental executive agencies and associated research laboratory privatisation expenses; the provision of land and buildings; loans, grants and other payments	12,526,000	3,187,000
2. For expenditure by the Department of Trade and Industry on regional development grants, exchange risk and other losses, selective assistance to individual industries and firms, UK contributions arising from its commitments under the International Natural Rubber Agreement, a strategic mineral stockpile, support for the aerospace and shipbuilding industries, assistance to redundant coal and steel workers, for expenditure related to petroleum licensing and royalty, for other payments and for loans to trading funds	1,000	8,821,000
4. For expenditure by the Department of Trade and Industry in connection with the privatisation of the coal industry	5,402,000	1,037,000
5. For expenditure by the Department of Trade and Industry on grants and loans to the British Coal Corpor-		

	Supply Grants	Appropriations in Aid
	£	£
ation; on grants to operators of licensed mines; on setting up and running of the Coal Authority; on the costs to the Coal Authority of subsidence claims and other physical liabilities; on liabilities in respect of former employees of British Coal Corporation and their dependants; and on costs of the subsidence adviser	151,981,000	*–177,960,000
7. For expenditure by the Export Credits Guarantee Department in connection with interest support to banks and other lenders of export finance, cover under the tender to contract/forward exchange supplement scheme, grants towards financing of exports to match foreign competition, residual commitments under discontinued guarantees offered to banks and external trade agencies, and cost escalation	1,000	33,092,000
10. For expenditure by the Office of Telecommunications on administrative and operational costs	299,000	22,000
11. For expenditure by the Office of Gas Supply on administrative costs	100,000	—

CLASS V

| 1. For expenditure by the Department of Employment including expenditure via Training and Enterprise Councils and local enterprise companies and amounts retained by them as surpluses and spent by them on training and other initiatives within Training and Enterprise Councils' articles and memoranda of association, including the provision of training and assessment programmes for young people and adults and initiatives, programmes within education and careers guidance and services; on the promotion of enterprise and the encouragement of self-employment; payments for training and employment projects assisted by the EC; on help for unemployed people; the improvement of industrial relations; the promotion of equal opportunities and coordination of certain issues of particular importance to women; industrial tribunals; compensation for persons disabled by certain industrial diseases; payments towards expenses of trade union ballots; on residual liabilities and disposal of the remaining assets of the former National Dock Labour Board; on the costs of maintaining and disposing of the former Skills Training Agency; administration, central and miscellaneous services, including assistance on employment issues to Eastern Europe in cooperation with the Foreign and Commonwealth Office and on research and publicity .... | 28,549,000 | 690,000 |

CLASS VI

| 1. For expenditure by the Department of Transport on the construction, improvement and maintenance of motorways and trunk roads, including the acquisition of land, scheme design and preparation, archaeological survey and rescue work, compensation, the purchase of maintenance vehicles and equipment, administration costs of the Highways Agency and research and development in support of Highways Agency operations .... | 44,374,000 | 1,558,000 |

	Supply Grants	Appropriations in Aid
	£	£
2. For expenditure by the Department of Transport on central administration and miscellaneous services; shipping services; civil aviation services; the Marine Safety, Coastguard, Transport Research Laboratory and Vehicle Certification Agencies; grants for freight and travel concessions; and certain other transport services including research and development; civil defence; transport security; residual expenses associated with the privatisation of transport industries and expenses associated with the sale of the Trust Ports, Transport Research Laboratory Agency, DVOIT and London Buses Limited subsidiaries	15,621,000	200,000
3. For expenditure by the Department of Transport on support to Nationalised Transport Industries, grants to European Passenger Services, capital expenditure by transport industries funded by EC grants, National Freight Company pension funds, rebate of fuel duty to bus operators, loans to the Vehicle Inspectorate and costs of driver testing and training	167,477,000	282,000
5. For expenditure by the Department of Transport on transport supplementary grants to Highway Authorities in England; special grants to Passenger Transport Authorities for the additional costs of supporting rail services resulting from the restructuring of the railways; and certain other grants and payments in support of roads and local transport expenditure; a grant to the Traffic Director for London and other expenditure on priority routes in London; highways expenditure; government office expenditure; vehicle and traffic enforcement; road safety, publicity, censuses, surveys and studies; licence refunds; the maintenance of the Woolwich Ferry and grants to the Humber Bridge Board to cover the Board's liabilities	59,669,000	—
7. For expenditure by the Office of Passenger Rail Franchising on the franchising of passenger rail services; the provision of, and support for, passenger rail services; the formation and financing of companies formed to facilitate the Franchising Director's functions; and administration and miscellaneous services	115,131,000	525,000
8. For expenditure by the Office of Rail Regulator on administration and associated capital and other expenditure and on costs of the Rail Users' Consultative Committees	2,794,000	70,000

CLASS VII

| 1. For expenditure by the Department of the Environment on subsidies, improvements and investments, payments to the Housing Corporation, payments to commute loan charges on grants to local authorities including the urban programme and urban development grant, and other sundry services .... | 1,000 | 2,204,000 |
| 2. For expenditure by the Department of the Environment on housing administration, including housing, urban, construction and EC programme research and rent officers and Rent Assessment Panels; grants for housing for the single homeless and special needs accommodation; housing management and mobility; | | |

	Supply Grants	Appropriations in Aid
	£	£
the provision of gypsy sites; home improvement agencies; and for sundry housing services and projects	1,000	333,000
3. For expenditure by the Department of the Environment on Single Regeneration Budget payments to support urban and other regeneration, regeneration projects in Manchester, coalfield areas fund grant and special grants to the voluntary sector	23,420,000	11,757,000
5. For expenditure by the Department of the Environment on countryside and the environment, including research and support to the environmental protection industry; on disposal of radioactive waste; on the promotion of environmental issues and awareness; on energy efficiency; on grant in aid to the Development Commission, National Rivers Authority, UK Ecolabelling Board and British Waterways Board; on other water supply and sewerage services including civil defence; on agency payments on behalf of the European Community from the European Regional Development Fund; on the National Parks; on grants to the Broads Authority and to voluntary bodies; on contributions to the Local Government Management Board; on subscriptions and contributions to international organisations and on residual services in connection with the privatisation of the water supply industry	2,000	3,627,000
6. For expenditure by the Department of the Environment (Property Holdings and Other Services to Government) on acquisitions, public building work, accommodation services, administration and certain other services for civil purposes in the United Kingdom, for Ministry of Defence and for civil purposes required in connection with the Channel Fixed Link and for loans to The Buying Agency	2,000	*–24,445,000
7. For expenditure by the Department of the Environment and its agencies on administration including research, royal commissioners, committees, etc., and by the Planning Inspectorate Executive Agency on appeals, and by the Building Research Establishment Executive Agency on buildings research and surveys	1,000	1,413,000
8. For expenditure by the Department of the Environment on revenue support grant, on payment of non-domestic rates to receiving authorities in England, on a special transitional grant to those receiving authorities most affected by changes in their Standard Spending Assessments, on payments to specified bodies and the Commission for Local Administration in England, on payments for Valuation Officer Agency rating and valuation services, on payments to meet the expenses of valuation tribunals, and on payments in respect of expenditure by the Local Government Commission	2,166,000	—
10. For expenditure by the Ordnance Survey in the Survey of Great Britain and other mapping services	1,357,000	—
12. For expenditure by the Department of the Environment on payments under the council tax transitional reduction scheme, on residual payments of community charge grant, on payments of rate rebate grants, on emergency financial assistance to local		

	Supply Grants	Appropriations in Aid
	£	£
authorities, on grants to local authorities in respect of certain costs incurred in relation to displaced persons from the former Yugoslavia and unaccompanied refugee and asylum-seeking children, on residual payments under the community charge reduction scheme, and on repayments of excess contributions made by local authorities and other bodies in respect of non-domestic rates in 1993–94 and previous years	50,865,000	—
13. For expenditure by the Department of the Environment: PSA Services on the sale of PSAS Businesses	2,000	—

CLASS VIII

	Supply Grants	Appropriations in Aid
1. For expenditure by the Home Office on compensation for criminal injuries, probation, police and superannuation payments for police and fire services	2,000	*–2,750,000
3. For expenditure by the Home Office on police, the forensic science service, emergency planning, fire, the Fire Service College, administration of justice, other services related to crime, diversion from custody, prevention of drugs abuse, control of immigration and nationality, issue of passports etc., equal opportunities and general services, and the National Lottery Charities Board; on administration (excluding the provision made for prisons administration carried on Class VIII, Vote 2); on residual payments associated with the privatisation of Directorate of Telecommunications; and on agency payments on behalf of the Department of the Environment	20,481,000	7,083,000
4. For expenditure of the Charity Commission for England and Wales on administrative costs	1,220,000	—

CLASS IX

	Supply Grants	Appropriations in Aid
1. For expenditure by the Lord Chancellor's Department on the Court Service, magistrates' courts, legal aid administration, tribunals, the court building programme and certain other legal services	18,175,000	*–71,100,000
3. For expenditure by the Northern Ireland Court Service on court services, legal aid administration, tribunals, the court building programme and certain other legal services	758,000	—
11. For expenditure by the Department of the Procurator General and Treasury Solicitor, and the Government Property Lawyers' Agency, on costs and fees for legal services	1,000	8,859,000

CLASS X

	Supply Grants	Appropriations in Aid
1. For expenditure by the Department for Education in respect of the assisted places scheme, voluntary and special agreement schools, City Technology Colleges, grant maintained schools, education associations, the Funding Agency for Schools, music and ballet schools, direct grant schools, the youth service, grants for miscellaneous international and other educational services, administrative costs of the Student Loans Company, research, information and central government grants to local authorities	3,527,000	239,000
2. For expenditure by the Department for Education on payments to the Higher Education Funding Council (England) and the Further Education Funding Coun-		

	Supply Grants	Appropriations in Aid
	£	£
cil (England), for teacher training, other payments for higher and further education, and payment of certain licence fees to the Home Office	3,415,000	600,000
3. For expenditure by the Department for Education on student awards and fees; provision of loans to students; reimbursement of fees for qualifying European Community students; compensation payments to redundant teachers and staff of certain institutions; and payments to the Further Education Funding Council	117,500,000	—
4. For expenditure by the Department for Education on administration	1,890,000	28,000

CLASS XI

	Supply Grants	Appropriations in Aid
1. For expenditure by the Department of National Heritage on payments to the national and other museums and galleries, to the Museums and Galleries Commission, to the Inland Revenue for assets accepted in lieu of tax; and for improvements and for related research, surveys and other services	4,326,000	—
2. For expenditure by the Department of National Heritage on payments to the Arts Council and other bodies; on the Government Art Collection; and for research, surveys and other services for the benefit of the arts	605,000	—
3. For expenditure by the Department of National Heritage on payments to the British Library and the Royal Geographical Society; on the British Library St Pancras project; the Royal Commission on Historical Manuscripts; on payments in respect of Public Lending Right; for a development incentive scheme; and for the Royal National Institute for the Blind Embossed Literature Service	6,430,000	—
4. For expenditure by the Department of National Heritage on payments to the British Broadcasting Corporation for home broadcasting and for licence fee reimbursements, and payments to the Independent Television Commission and to the Welsh Fourth Channel Authority	8,853,000	—
5. For expenditure by the Department of National Heritage on payments to film bodies and projects, sport and certain broadcasting services, the promotion of and assistance to tourism, and for commemorative services	3,122,000	670,000
6. For expenditure by the Department of National Heritage on Royal Palaces, Historic Royal Palaces Agency, Royal Parks Agency, Royal Armouries etc. (including administration), historic buildings, ancient monuments and certain public buildings, the national heritage, on the inspection of historic wreck sites and on the assessment of possible listed buildings; a contribution to the Incentive Award Scheme for Arts and Architecture; grants to voluntary bodies and research and consultancies in connection with Heritage conservation	2,054,000	109,000
7. For expenditure by the Department of National Heritage and the Royal Fine Art Commission on administration, and on payments to the Millennium Commission	283,000	—

	Supply Grants	Appropriations in Aid
	£	£
8. For expenditure by the Office of the National Lottery on capital and administrative costs	500,000	95,000
CLASS XII		
1. For expenditure by the Department of Health on hospital, community health, family health and family health service administration services, National Health Service trusts, and on related services	2,000	229,325,000
3. For expenditure by the Department of Health on administration, including certain expenditure on behalf of the Department of Social Security, on the National Health Service in England, on family health administration and related services, on miscellaneous health, personal social and other services (some of which are administered on a United Kingdom basis), including mental health, medical, scientific and technical services, services for disabled persons, grants to voluntary organisations, etc., payments in respect of Home Office inspection of public health laboratories services, grants in aid and subscriptions to international organisations, a contribution to the International Peto Institute and payment on behalf of the European Medicines Evaluation Agency	1,000	8,216,000
4. For expenditure by the Department of Health on family health services	206,620,000	*–84,085,000*
5. For expenditure by the NHS Pensions Agency on pensions, allowances, gratuities etc., to or in respect of persons engaged in health services or in other approved employment	6,103,000	*–15,478,000*
6. For the expenditure of the Office of Population Censuses and Surveys on administrative and operational costs	1,833,000	931,000
CLASS XIII		
1. For expenditure by the Department of Social Security on non-contributory retirement pensions, Christmas bonus payments to pensioners, pensions etc., for disablement or death arising out of war, or service in the armed forces after 2 September 1939 and on sundry other services, on attendance allowances, invalid care allowance, severe disablement allowance, mobility allowances; disability living allowance; disability working allowance; on pensions, gratuities and sundry allowances for disablement and specified deaths arising from industrial causes; on income support, child benefit, one parent benefit, family credit, the vaccine damage payment scheme and payments in respect of spousal and child maintenance	395,365,000	26,429,000
2. For expenditure by the Department of Social Security on rent rebate, rent allowance, council tax benefit, community charge benefit, community charge rebate and rate rebate subsidies and on sums payable in respect of anti-fraud measures to housing, charging, levying and local authorities; on transitional payments to help certain housing benefit claimants significantly affected by the changes to the housing benefit scheme and certain supplementary benefit		

	Supply Grants	Appropriations in Aid
	£	£
claimants not entitled to benefit under the income support scheme; on sums payable into the National Insurance Fund to increase its income and on compensation payments in respect of statutory sick pay and statutory maternity pay and on sums payable into the Social Fund for expenditure on maternity expenses, funeral expenses and heating expenses in exceptionally cold weather	527,238,000	*–6,000,000
4. For expenditure by the Department of Social Security on administration, for agency payments, the promotion of Government policy on disability issues, and for certain other services including grants to local authorities and voluntary organisations	45,825,000	75,564,000

CLASS XIV

	Supply Grants	Appropriations in Aid
3. For expenditure by the Scottish Office Industry Department on Scottish Enterprise and Highlands and Islands Enterprise; on innovation and technology support; on regional enterprise grants; on technical and vocational education; on the promotion of tourism; on financial assistance for training and employment; on roads and certain associated services, including the acquisition of land, lighting, road safety and related services; on assistance to local transport; on grants to Strathclyde Passenger Transport Authority for the additional costs of supporting rail services resulting from the restructuring of the railways; on support for transport services in the highlands and islands; on piers and harbours, and on certain other transport services and grants; on fees relating to the privatisation of the Scottish Bus Group; and on other sundry services in connection with trade and industry, etc.	29,735,000	1,500,000
7. For expenditure by the Scottish Office Environment Department on housing subsidies, financial support for Scottish Homes, other expenditure, contributions and grants relating to housing; on historic buildings and monuments (including administration); on natural heritage; on other central and environmental services; and on the Water Authorities in Scotland	1,748,000	904,000
8. For expenditure by the Scottish Office Environment Department on water and sewerage, flood and storm emergencies, other environmental services, sites for travelling people and residual grants to housing associations	1,000,000	—
11. For expenditure by the Scottish Office Home and Health Department on legal aid, criminal injuries compensation (excluding administration), police, police and fire services superannuation and welfare food	2,875,000	—
12. For expenditure by the Scottish Office Home and Health Department on legal aid administration; certain services relating to crime including the Parole Board for Scotland, the Scottish Prison Service (an Executive Agency), police services (excluding grants to local authorities and superannuation); fire, the Scottish Office Pensions Agency, civil defence (including grants) and other protective and miscellaneous services; miscellaneous health services; social work services including the Scottish Chil-		

	Supply Grants	Appropriations in Aid
	£	£
dren's Reporters Administration, the provision of residential and secure accommodation for children; services for offenders including probation and supervised attendance orders; grants to voluntary organisations; training and research; unemployed voluntary action fund; other grants to local authorities	5,822,000	89,000
13. For expenditure by the Scottish Office Home and Health Department on the provision of family health services under the National Health Service in Scotland and certain other services	25,055,000	*−13,555,000
14. For expenditure by the Scottish Office Home and Health Department on hospital, community health, family health and other health services, including National Health Service trusts, central health services and civil emergency planning.............................	23,893,000	*−304,000
15. For expenditure by the Scottish Office Pensions Agency on superannuation allowances and gratuities etc., in respect of teachers, and the widows, widowers and dependants of deceased teachers	3,843,000	*−525,000
16. For expenditure by the Scottish Office Pensions Agency on pensions, allowances, gratuities, etc., to or in respect of persons engaged in health service or in other approved employment	25,076,000	*−15,014,000
17. For expenditure by the Scottish Office Education Department on schools, including self-governing schools; special educational needs; higher education and research, including the Scottish Higher Education Funding Council; the Scottish Office Student Awards Agency, compensation payments; further education, including payments to further education colleges, curriculum development, international and other educational services, including support for School Boards, and the careers service, and training and research; sport, Gaelic broadcasting; arts, libraries, museums and galleries, including purchase grants; cultural activities and organisations including the Royal Society of Edinburgh, Royal Scottish Geographical Society; Scottish Film Production Fund; publicity; indemnities; administration; central government grants to local authorities	434,000	—
18. For expenditure by the Scottish Office Education Department on student loans including administration, access funds, student awards, fees and reimbursement of fees for the qualifying European Community students	11,116,000	—
21. For expenditure by the Scottish Office on administration and operational costs	470,000	1,524,000
22. For expenditure by the Scottish Record Office on administrative and operational costs	1,588,000	30,000
23. For expenditure by the General Register Office for Scotland on administrative and operational costs	545,000	94,000
24. For the expenditure of Registers of Scotland on administrative costs	1,000	610,000

CLASS XV

1. For expenditure by the Welsh Office on market support, support for agriculture in special areas and compensation to sheep producers, and animal health	7,300,000	101,000
2. For expenditure by the Welsh Office on assistance to agricultural production, marketing and processing,		

	Supply Grants	Appropriations in Aid
	£	£
grants for capital and other improvements, and certain alternative land uses, support for the fishing industry, fisheries protection, and agency payments for fishing projects, and other miscellaneous agricultural services; arterial drainage, flood and coast protection; on regional selective assistance, regional development grants, small firms measures, small firms merit award for research and technology, support for products under research, regional enterprise grants, industrial support services; industrial development and other activities undertaken by the Welsh Development Agency and the Development Board for Rural Wales; support for medium and small sized firms and certain other services and expenses	1,000	148,000
3. For expenditure by the Welsh Office on Regional Selective Assistance, European Investment Bank and European Coal and Steel Community guarantees and on housing subsidy for the Development Board for Rural Wales	1,700,000	150,000
4. For expenditure by the Welsh Office including expenditure via Training and Enterprise Councils and amounts retained by them as surpluses on training, including the provision of training programmes for young people and adults and initiatives and programmes within education; on the promotion of enterprise, and the encouragement of self-employed and small firms; on help for unemployed people; on Careers Service, publicity and research; education and certain other services	11,544,000	5,000
5. For expenditure by the Welsh Office on tourism, roads and transport and certain associated services, housing, historic buildings and ancient monuments, Cadw Agency, other environmental services (including civil defence, national parks, Planning Inspectorate Agency and certain payments related to EC matters), arts, libraries and museums, health and personal social services, and other grants and certain other services, including research	10,133,000	200,000
7. For expenditure by the Welsh Office on the family health services under the National Health Service ...	24,836,000	*–5,122,000*
8. For expenditure by the Welsh Office on hospital, community health, family health (part), family health service administration services, National Health Service trusts and on related services	10,409,000	21,416,000
9. For expenditure by the Welsh Office on central administration and other services	819,000	87,000
11. For expenditure by the Welsh Office on grants to local authorities in Wales in respect of the community charge, on special grants to local authorities following natural emergencies, on rate rebates for disabled people, and on repayments of excess contributions made by billing authorities and adjustments for shortfalls in receipts made by the Secretary of State in respect of non-domestic rates in previous years	1,000	—
12. For expenditure by the Office of Her Majesty's Chief Inspector of Schools in Wales on administration, publicity, inspections, training, grants for courses for teachers and associated capital, etc.	203,000	13,000

	Supply Grants	Appropriations in Aid
	£	£
CLASS XVII		
1. For expenditure by Her Majesty's Treasury on economic, financial and related administration; including debt management, payments to certain parliamentary bodies and certain other services including general expenses of certain pay review bodies, expenses in connection with Honours and Dignities and a grant in aid to the Private Finance Panel Executive; and residual costs in connection with Foward: Civil Service Catering	1,000	*–831,000
3. For expenditure by Her Majesty's Treasury on the superannuation of civil servants; pensions, etc., in respect of former members of the Royal Irish Constabulary and other pensions and non-recurrent payments, and for certain other services	30,000,000	—
4. For expenditure by the Customs and Excise Department on the administration of taxation, the operation of customs and revenue controls and other customs and excise work. It also includes payments in respect of the Customs and Excise National Museum and a gift to the Vigilant Trust	1,000	—
5. For expenditure by the Inland Revenue Department on the management and collection of the direct taxes and services provided for the Department's information technology partner and for other departments	695,000	—
8. For rates and contributions in lieu of rates paid by Inland Revenue in respect of property occupied by the Crown and premises occupied by representatives of Commonwealth and foreign countries and international organisations	34,586,000	—
10. For expenditure on administrative costs by the Registry of Friendly Societies on behalf of the Building Societies Commission, the Friendly Societies Commission and the Central Office of the Registry	172,000	157,000
11. For expenditure by the National Debt Office and Public Works Loan Board on administrative costs ..	199,000	*–224,000
12. For expenditure by Paymaster on administrative costs	1,023,000	1,791,000
13. For expenditure by the Central Statistical Office on the provision of national accounts and other statistics and on departmental administration	3,281,000	*–560,000
14. For the expenditure of the Department of the Government Actuary on administrative costs	132,000	—
16. For the expenditure by Her Majesty's Treasury in connection with the sales of residual Government shareholdings and the sales of privatised companies' debt	1,000	70,998,000
CLASS XVIII		
1. For expenditure by the Office of Public Service and Science on the central management of the civil service and certain other services	7,000,000	—
2. For expenditure by the Cabinet Office: Office of Public Service and Science on payments to the Science Research Councils, the Royal Society, the Royal Academy of Engineering and the Centre for the Exploitation of Science and Technology; and on other sundry services	840,000	2,551,000

	Supply Grants	Appropriations in Aid
	£	£
4. For expenditure by the Controller of Her Majesty's Stationery Office to compensate the HMSO Trading Fund for the price concessions to public libraries; to meet the cost of goods and services provided on repayment to public sector bodies within the European Union, and elsewhere; and to meet the cost of government and other publications supplied to United Kingdom members of the European Parliament	59,000	—
CLASS XIX		
1. For the expenditure by the Cabinet Office on administrative costs, the Offices of the Prime Minister, the Parliamentary Counsel and the Government Chief Whip, payments to the Chequers Trust and the British National Committee for the History of the Second World War, and certain other services	2,952,000	*–365,000
2. For the expenditure by Her Majesty's security and intelligence services on administration and operational costs, works and equipment, pensions and other payments	1,000	3,000,000
3. For expenditure of the Department of Her Majesty's Privy Council on administrative costs and for the financing of a Central Drugs Coordination Unit	390,000	*–390,000
TOTAL, SUPPLEMENTARY, 1994–95 .... £	2,448,182,000	88,905,000

*Deficit

Class I
1995–96

SCHEDULE (B).—PART 3

CLASS I

SCHEDULE OF SUMS granted, and of the sums which may be applied as appropriations in aid in addition thereto, to defray the charges of the several Services herein particularly mentioned, which will come in course of payment during the year ending on 31st March 1996, including provision for numbers of personnel as set out hereunder, viz.:—

	Sums not exceeding	
	Supply Grants	Appropriations in Aid
	£	£
Vote 1. For expenditure by the Ministry of Defence on personnel costs etc. of the armed forces and their reserves and cadet forces etc., (including provision for Naval Service to a number not exceeding 53,500; provision for Army Service to a number not exceeding 142,990; for the Individual Reserves to a number not exceeding 131,000 and for the Territorial Army to a number not exceeding 63,950; and provision for Air Force Service to a number not exceeding 73,860, for the Royal Air Force Reserve to a number not exceeding 18,150, and for the Royal Auxiliary Air Force to a number not exceeding 2,050); personnel costs etc. of Defence Ministers and of certain civilian staff		

	Sums not exceeding	
	Supply Grants	Appropriations in Aid
	£	£
employed by the Ministry of Defence, movements, certain stores, supplies and services, certain spares and maintenance, plant and machinery, charter of ships, certain research, lands and buildings, works services, certain contingent liabilities, sundry grants, other payments, including those abroad, some works costs for visiting forces, assistance to the former Soviet Union in the resettlement of military personnel, and VE/VJ Day commemoration	10,616,956,000	1,391,785,000
2. For expenditure by the Ministry of Defence on logistics services for the armed forces and the related personnel costs; for spares, repair, maintenance, stores and supply services; for associated capital facilities and works, contractors' redundancy costs; for some works costs for visiting forces and sundry services, subscriptions and grants; and VE/VJ Day commemoration	4,957,988,000	516,585,000
3. For expenditure by the Procurement Executive of the Ministry of Defence in operating its Headquarters and Establishments and for its other common services; for research etc. by contract; for development by contract, production and purchases for sale abroad of sea systems, land systems, air systems and associated equipment; for certain contingent liabilities; for sundry other Procurement Executive services including those on repayment terms to non-exchequer customers and interest support for certain defence export sales	6,145,325,000	396,407,000
4. For expenditure by the Ministry of Defence on retired pay, pensions and other payments, etc.	839,102,000	1,024,163,000
TOTAL, CLASS I .... £	22,559,371,000	3,328,940,000

SCHEDULE (B).—PART 4   Class II
                                                     1995–96
_____

CLASS II

SCHEDULE OF SUMS granted, and of the sums which may be applied as appropriations in aid in addition thereto, to defray the charges of the several Services herein particularly mentioned, which will come in course of payment during the year ending on 31st March 1996, viz.:—

	Sums not exceeding	
	Supply Grants	Appropriations in Aid
	£	£
Vote		
1. For expenditure by the Foreign and Commonwealth Office on its salaries, building and other accommodation services, and administration, and those of HM Diplomatic Service, official information services, sundry services and loans and payments in connection with catering services	709,165,000	37,473,000
2. For expenditure by the Foreign and Commonwealth		

	Sums not exceeding	
	Supply Grants	Appropriations in Aid
	£	£
Office on grants and subscriptions etc. to certain international organisations, contributions in respect of international peacekeeping forces, special payments and assistance, scholarships, military aid and sundry other grants and services	211,632,000	19,553,000
3. For expenditure by the Foreign and Commonwealth Office on payments to the British Broadcasting Corporation for external radio broadcasting and monitoring services and for contractual services in connection with FCO relay stations	175,039,000	3,721,000
4. For expenditure by the Foreign and Commonwealth Office on the British Council	98,496,000	—
5. For expenditure by the Foreign and Commonwealth Office: Overseas Development Administration under the Overseas Development and Co-operation Act 1980 on the United Kingdom's overseas aid; including financial and technical assistance to governments, institutions, voluntary agencies and individuals; capital and other subscriptions and contributions including payments under guarantee, to multilateral development banks and other international and regional bodies; emergency, refugee and other relief assistance; pensions and allowances in respect of overseas service including contributions to pension funds (including payments under the Overseas Pensions Act 1973, and grants in lieu of pensions); and on global environment assistance; loans to the Commonwealth Development Corporation under the Commonwealth Development Corporation Acts 1978–1986; expenditure on the Turkey Ankara Metro and Botswana Flight Information Region mixed credit Aid and Trade Provision projects; costs in connection with privatising the Crown Agents and the Natural Resources Institute; and running costs, related capital expenditure and other administrative costs including for the Natural Resources Institute (an executive agency); and payments (under the Authority of the European Communities Act 1972) to certain beneficiaries of the Gibraltar Social Insurance Fund (Revised sum)	1,759,358,000	71,447,000
6. For expenditure by the Foreign and Commonwealth Office (Overseas Development Administration) on pension and superannuation payments etc. in respect of overseas service and sundry other services and expenses	137,025,000	259,000
TOTAL, CLASS II .... £	3,090,715,000	132,453,000

SCHEDULE (B).—PART 5   Class III
1995–96

CLASS III

SCHEDULE OF SUMS granted, and of the sums which may be applied as appropriations in aid in addition thereto, to defray the charges of the several Services herein particularly mentioned, which will come in course of payment during the year ending on 31st March 1996, viz.:—

	Sums not exceeding	
	Supply Grants	Appropriations in Aid
	£	£
Vote		
1. For expenditure by the Intervention Board—Executive Agency in giving effect in the United Kingdom to the agricultural support provisions of the Common Agricultural Policy of the European Community and for other services	27,235,000	2,957,071,000
2. For expenditure by the Intervention Board—Executive Agency on central administration and agents' services	49,238,000	2,865,000
3. For cash limited and demand led operational expenditure by the Ministry of Agriculture, Fisheries and Food to: promote food safety, take action against diseases with implications for human health, safeguard essential supplies in an emergency, and promote action to alleviate flooding and coastal erosion; to encourage action to reduce water and other pollution and by other measures to safeguard the aquatic environment including its fauna and flora, to improve the attractiveness and bio-diversity of the rural environment and protect the rural economy; implement MAFF's CAP obligations efficiently and seek a more economically rational CAP while avoiding discrimination against UK businesses (including expenditure on existing CAP measures and schemes), to create the conditions in which efficient and sustainable agriculture, fishing and food industries can flourish, take action against animal and plant diseases and pests, encourage high animal welfare standards; provide specialist support services and allocate resources where they are most needed; provide for some inter-agency payments and undertake research and development	461,693,000	33,847,000
4. For expenditure by the Ministry of Agriculture, Fisheries and Food on departmental research, advisory services and administration, executive agencies and certain other services	322,070,000	112,775,000
TOTAL, CLASS III .... £	860,236,000	3,106,558,000

Appropriation Act 1995

CLASS IV

SCHEDULE OF SUMS granted, and of the sums which may be applied as appropriations in aid in addition thereto, to defray the charges of the several Services herein particularly mentioned, which will come in course of payment during the year ending on 31st March 1996, viz.:—

	Sums not exceeding	
	Supply Grants	Appropriations in Aid
	£	£
Vote		
1. For expenditure by the Department of Trade and Industry on and related to; support for business research and development; consumer protection and the regulation of trade; regional and selective assistance; the aerospace and shipbuilding industries; exchange risk and other losses; international subscriptions including those arising from commitments under the International Rubber Agreement; energy-related programmes including research and development and security of oil and gas supplies; assistance to redundant steel workers; departmental administration including a share in the running costs of the Government Offices for the Regions; central and miscellaneous services; the operational costs of departmental executive agencies; privatisation expenses; loans to trading funds; petroleum licensing and royalty; provision of land and buildings; loans, grants and other payments (Including a Supplementary sum of £13,962,000)	1,220,873,000	307,815,000
2. For payment of pensions, etc., to members of the United Kingdom Atomic Energy Authority's superannuation schemes and other related expenditure ...	98,884,000	47,313,000
3. For expenditure by the Department of Trade and Industry in connection with the privatisation of the coal industry (Including a Supplementary sum of £10,499,000)	14,128,000	999,000
4. For assistance to the coal industry including expenditure on: grants and loans to the British Coal Corporation; grants to operators of licensed mines; grant in aid to the Coal Authority; payments to redundant workers and other liabilities in respect of former employees of British Coal Corporation and their dependants and on the costs of the subsidence adviser and statutory subsidence arbitration arrangements .	374,129,000	420,041,000
5. For expenditure by the Export Credits Guarantee Department on administration	24,982,000	1,559,000
6. For expenditure by the Export Credits Guarantee Department in connection with interest support to banks and other lenders of export finance, cover under the tender to contract/forward exchange supplement scheme, grants towards financing of exports to match foreign competition, residual commitments under discontinued guarantees offered to banks and external trade agencies, and cost escalation	9,331,000	170,435,000
7. For expenditure by the Export Credits Guarantee Department in connection with export credit guaran-		

	Sums not exceeding	
	Supply Grants	Appropriations in Aid
	£	£
tees, other guarantees given in the national interest or to render economic assistance to overseas countries, overseas investment, insurance and trading expenses	1,000	408,078,000
8. For expenditure by the Office of Fair Trading on administrative and operational costs	19,050,000	185,000
9. For expenditure by the Office of Telecommunications on administrative and operational costs	9,464,000	279,000
10. For expenditure by the Office of Gas Supply on administrative costs	5,352,000	—
11. For expenditure by the Office of Electricity Regulation on administrative and operational costs	10,567,000	1,155,000
12. For expenditure by the Department of Trade and Industry in connection with the privatisation of the nuclear power industry (New Estimate)	24,929,000	71,000
TOTAL, CLASS IV .... £	1,811,690,000	1,357,930,000

SCHEDULE (B).—PART 7   Class V
                                        1995–96

CLASS V

SCHEDULE OF SUMS granted, and of the sums which may be applied as appropriations in aid in addition thereto, to defray the charges of the several Services herein particularly mentioned, which will come in course of payment during the year ending on 31st March 1996, viz.:—

	Sums not exceeding	
	Supply Grants	Appropriations in Aid
	£	£
Vote		
1. For expenditure by the Department of Employment, including expenditure via Training and Enterprise Councils and local enterprise companies and amounts retained by them as surpluses and spent by them on training and other initiatives within Training and Enterprise Councils' articles and memoranda of association, including the provision of training and assessment programmes for young people and adults and initiatives, programmes within education and careers guidance and services; on the promotion of enterprise and the encouragement of self-employment; payments for training and employment projects including those assisted by the EC; on help for unemployed people; the improvement of industrial relations; the promotion of equal opportunities and coordination of certain issues of particular importance to women; industrial tribunals; compensation for persons disabled by certain industrial diseases; payments towards expenses of trade union ballots; on the cost of maintaining and disposing of the remaining assets of the former Skills Training Agency; transfer expenses for surplus staff taking up posts in other		

	Sums not exceeding	
	Supply Grants	Appropriations in Aid
	£	£
Departments; administration, central and miscellaneous services including assistance on employment issues to eastern Europe in cooperation with the Foreign and Commonwealth Office; on research, publicity and on costs associated with marking the 50th anniversary of VE day (including a Supplementary sum of £9,465,000)	2,121,711,000	65,626,000
2. For expenditure by the Employment Service of the Department of Employment on help for people seeking work, particularly unemployed people; on support for people with disabilities, including a grant in aid to Remploy Ltd; on assistance to eastern Europe on labour market issues, in cooperation with the Foreign and Commonwealth Office and other agencies; and on research, publicity and administration	907,800,000	607,845,000
3. For expenditure by the Department of Employment on grants in aid to the Health and Safety Commission, and to the Advisory, Conciliation and Arbitration Service	210,547,000	1,000
TOTAL, CLASS V .... £	3,240,058,000	673,472,000

SCHEDULE (B).—PART 8   Class VI
1995–96

CLASS VI

SCHEDULE OF SUMS granted, and of the sums which may be applied as appropriations in aid in addition thereto, to defray the charges of the several Services herein particularly mentioned, which will come in course of payment during the year ending on 31st March 1996, viz.:—

	Sums not exceeding	
	Supply Grants	Appropriations in Aid
	£	£
Vote		
1. For expenditure by the Department of Transport's Highways Agency on the construction, improvement and maintenance of motorways and trunk roads, including the acquisition of land, scheme design and preparation, archaeological survey and rescue work, compensation, the purchase of maintenance vehicles and equipment, administration costs of the Highways Agency and research and development in support of Highways Agency operations	1,863,279,000	146,849,000
2. For expenditure by the Department of Transport on central administration and miscellaneous services; shipping services; civil aviation services; grants for freight and travel concessions; and certain other transport services including research and development; civil defence; transport security; residual expenses associated with the privatisation of transport industries and expenses associated with the sale		

	Sums not exceeding	
	Supply Grants	Appropriations in Aid
	£	£
of the Trust Ports, Transport Research Laboratory Agency and London Buses Limited subsidiaries	165,054,000	46,302,000
3. For expenditure by the Department of Transport on support to nationalised transport industries, grants to Railtrack, European Passenger Services, Union Railways, expenditure connected with the privatisation of British Rail businesses and Railtrack, capital expenditure by transport industries funded by EU grants, railway industry and National Freight Company pension funds, Royal travel by rail, audit of Government grants and rebate of fuel duty to bus operators	1,332,298,000	5,500,000
4. For expenditure by the Department of Transport in connection with driver and vehicle registration and licensing, the collection of revenue, compensation and payments towards the pension of Local Authority staff employed on driver and vehicle licensing before the setting up of DVLC; and the development and operation of other registration and licensing systems and the provision of miscellaneous services to other parts of the Department	176,549,000	15,505,000
5. For expenditure by the Department of Transport on transport supplementary grants to Highways Authorities in England; special grants to Passenger Transport Authorities for the additional costs of supporting rail services resulting from the restructuring of the railways; other grants and payments for consultancies in respect of various roads and transport projects, and in support of maintenance and operations of Woolwich Ferry, and payments in support of roads on priority routes in London; vehicle and traffic enforcement; road safety, publicity, census, surveys and studies; licence refunds; grants to the Humber Bridge Board to cover the Board's liabilities, Agency payments on behalf of the European Community and Government Office Programme Expenditure	513,157,000	16,234,000
6. For expenditure by the Department of Transport on the Marine Safety, Coastguard, Transport Research Laboratory, Vehicle Certification and Driving Standards agencies and loans to the Vehicle Inspectorate (Revised Sum)	134,256,000	12,283,000
7. For expenditure by the Office of Passenger Rail Franchising on the franchising of passenger rail services; the provision of, and support for, passenger rail services; the formation and financing of companies formed to facilitate the Franchising Director's functions; and administration and miscellaneous services	1,620,604,000	1,324,000
8. For expenditure by the Office of the Rail Regulator on administration and associated capital and other expenditure and on costs of the Rail Users Consultative Committees	8,629,000	300,000
TOTAL, CLASS VI .... £	5,813,826,000	244,297,000

Appropriation Act 1995

CLASS VII

SCHEDULE OF SUMS granted, and of the sums which may be applied as appropriations in aid in addition thereto, to defray the charges of the several Services herein particularly mentioned, which will come in course of payment during the year ending on 31st March 1996, viz.:—

	Sums not exceeding	
	Supply Grants	Appropriations in Aid
	£	£
Vote		
1. For expenditure by the Department of the Environment on Housing Revenue Account Subsidy; slum clearance, repairs and other improvements to housing; payments to the Housing Corporation; housing for the single homeless and special needs accommodation; housing management and mobility; Rent Officers and Rent Assessment Panels; grants for the provision of gypsy sites; grants to home improvement agencies; for research projects, including European Community programmes; publicity; payments to local authorities to commute loan charge grants; and for sundry other housing and construction services and projects (Revised sum)	6,266,127,000	1,275,000
2. For expenditure by the Department of the Environment on Single Regeneration Budget payments to support urban and other regeneration; for special grants to the voluntary sector; on countryside grants in aid; on support for the Groundwork Trusts and Foundation; on grants to the Broads Authority and for grants to voluntary bodies; central government grants to local authorities for the Single Regeneration Budget; National Parks, regeneration projects in Manchester and the coalfield areas fund; for payments to commute loan charges; for EC Agency payments; and on grants to the Commission for the New Towns for road infrastructure; on support for the National Forest strategy; and on publicity payments related to the promotion of the Department's regeneration and countryside policies and programmes and the private finance initiative (Including a Supplementary sum of £450,000)	1,504,948,000	12,172,000
3. For expenditure by the Department of the Environment on the environment, including research and support to the environmental protection industry; on the promotion of environmental issues and awareness; on grants to improve energy efficiency generally and environmental practice in industry; on disposal of radioactive waste; on support of the aims and implementation of the Convention on Biological Diversity; on support for the Tidy Britain Group and for the National Environmental Technology Centre; on recycling; on smoke control; on environmental publicity and promotion; on grant-in-aid to the National Rivers Authority, the UK Ecolabelling Board, Environmental Agency and British Waterways Board; on water supply and sewerage services including civil defence; on grants to voluntary bodies;		

	Sums not exceeding	
	Supply Grants	Appropriations in Aid
	£	£
on subscriptions and contributions to international organisations; on planning redevelopment and on residual services in connection with privatisation of the water supply industry (Including a Supplementary sum of £140,214,000)	316,734,000	5,706,000
4. For expenditure by the Department of the Environment on revenue support grant, on payment of non-domestic rates to receiving authorities in England, on payments to specified bodies and the Commission for Local Administration in England, on payments for Valuation Office Agency rating and valuation services, on payments to meet the expenses of valuation tribunals, on payments in respect of expenditure by the Local Government Commission, on residual payments of community charge grant, on payments under the council tax transitional reduction scheme, on payments of rate rebate grants, on emergency financial assistance to local authorities, residual payments of grants to local authorities in respect of certain costs incurred in relation to unaccompanied refugee and asylum seeking children, on repayment of excess contributions made by local authorities and other bodies in respect of non-domestic rates in 1994–95 and previous years, and on planning and minerals research and local government research and surveys, including contributions to the Local Government Management Board (Revised sum)	30,670,143,000	686,000
5. For expenditure by the Department of the Environment and its agencies on administration including research, royal commissioners, committees, etc., and by the Planning Inspectorate Executive Agency on appeals, and by the Building Research Establishment Executive Agency on building research and surveys	226,009,000	67,241,000
6. For expenditure for the Office of Water Services on administrative, and operational costs, and the provision of customer representation	8,146,000	19,000
7. For expenditure by the Ordnance Survey on the survey of Great Britain and other mapping services	14,952,000	66,071,000
8. For expenditure by the Department of the Environment (Property Holdings and Other Services to Government) on acquisitions, public building work, accommodation services, administration and certain other services for civil purposes in the United Kingdom, for Ministry of Defence and for civil purposes required in connection with the Channel Fixed Link and for loans to The Buying Agency	1,000	941,339,000
9. For expenditure by the Department of the Environment: PSA Services on central and residual functions (Revised sum)	36,371,000	7,750,000
10. For expenditure by the Department of the Environment: PSA Services on the sale of the PSAS businesses	50,000	8,600,000
TOTAL, CLASS VII .... £	39,043,481,000	1,110,859,000

Class VIII

Schedule of Sums granted, and of the sums which may be applied as appropriations in aid in addition thereto, to defray the charges of the several Services herein particularly mentioned, which will come in course of payment during the year ending on 31st March 1996, viz.:—

	Sums not exceeding	
	Supply Grants	Appropriations in Aid
	£	£
Vote		
1. For expenditure by the Home Office on police, the forensic science service, emergency planning, fire services, the Fire Service College, administration of justice, other services related to crime (including criminal injuries compensation and offender programmes), diversion from custody, prevention of drugs abuse, control of immigration and nationality, issue of passports etc., equal opportunities (including grants relating to ethnic minorities) and general services, and on administration (excluding the provision for prisons administration carried on Class VIII, Vote 2) (Revised sum)	4,620,055,000	102,632,000
2. For expenditure by the Home Office in England and Wales on prisons (including central administration and other costs arising from the detention of prisoners), placements in secure accommodation under Section 53 of the Children and Young Persons Act 1933, Prison Service colleges, the Parole Board, the storage and maintenance of equipment, transport management and grants to "Prisoners Abroad"	1,660,160,000	30,501,000
3. For expenditure of the Charity Commission for England and Wales on administrative costs	22,957,000	45,000
Total, Class VIII .... £	6,303,172,000	133,178,000

Class IX

Schedule of Sums granted, and of the sums which may be applied as appropriations in aid in addition thereto, to defray the charges of the several Services herein particularly mentioned, which will come in course of payment during the year ending on 31st March 1996, viz.:—

	Sums not exceeding	
	Supply Grants	Appropriations in Aid
	£	£
Vote		
1. For expenditure by the Lord Chancellor's Department on the Lord Chancellor's Department HQ and Associated Offices, payments in support of marriage		

	Sums not exceeding	
	Supply Grants	Appropriations in Aid
	£	£
guidance, conciliation and mediation, the Court Service, the Public Trust Office, legal aid in criminal cases, grants to the Legal Aid Fund, costs paid from central funds, grants to the magistrates' courts and other legal services (including a Supplementary sum of £1,694,000)	2,275,266,000	281,503,000
2. For expenditure by the Northern Ireland Court Service on court services, other legal services, accommodation services and legal aid	51,659,000	9,762,000
3. For expenditure by the Public Record Office on administrative and operational costs	40,396,000	1,440,000
4. For expenditure by the Crown Prosecution Service on administrative costs (including the hire of private prosecuting agents), Crown Prosecutions and in connection with the confiscation of the proceeds of crime	295,236,000	19,081,000
5. For expenditure by the Serious Fraud Office on administrative costs, investigations and prosecutions	17,376,000	101,000
6. For expenditure by the Department of the Procurator General and Treasury Solicitor, the Government Property Lawyers' Agency and the Legal Secretariat to the Law Offices on administration and on costs and fees for legal services (Revised sum) ...	8,509,000	42,225,000
7. For expenditure by the Crown Office and Lord Advocate's Department on administrative costs (including fees paid to temporary Procurators Fiscal), witnesses' expenses and other costs associated with Crown prosecutions	46,290,000	170,000
TOTAL, CLASS IX .... £	2,734,732,000	354,282,000

SCHEDULE (B).—PART 12   Class X
                                1995–96

CLASS X

SCHEDULE OF SUMS granted, and of the sums which may be applied as appropriations in aid in addition thereto, to defray the charges of the several Services herein particularly mentioned, which will come in course of payment during the year ending on 31st March 1996, viz.:—

	Sums not exceeding	
	Supply Grants	Appropriations in Aid
	£	£
Vote		
1. For expenditure by the Department for Education on the assisted places scheme, voluntary and special schools, City Colleges and other specialist schools, grant-maintained schools, the Funding Agency for Schools, education associations, music and ballet schools, direct grant schools, the youth service, grants for miscellaneous international and other educational services, research, information, and central government grants to local authorities	722,844,000	1,702,196,000
2. For expenditure by the Department for Education on		

	Sums not exceeding	
	Supply Grants	Appropriations in Aid
	£	£
payments to the Higher Education Funding Council (England) and the Further Education Funding Council (England), for teacher training, other payments for higher and further education, and payment of certain licence fees to the Home Office (Revised sum)	9,663,242,000	608,000
3. For expenditure by the Department for Education on administration and associated services	90,340,000	4,454,000
4. For expenditure by the Department for Education (Teachers' Pensions Agency) on superannuation allowances and gratuities, etc., in respect of teachers, and the widows, widowers, children and dependants of deceased teachers, and for premature retirement compensation payments made to members of the Teachers' Superannuation Scheme on behalf of their employers	1,104,995,000	1,731,390,000
5. For expenditure by the Office of Her Majesty's Chief Inspector of Schools in England for administration and programme costs	98,152,000	802,000
TOTAL, CLASS X .... £	11,679,573,000	3,439,450,000

SCHEDULE (B).—PART 13　　　　　Class XI
1995–96

CLASS XI

SCHEDULE OF SUMS granted, and of the sums which may be applied as appropriations in aid in addition thereto, to defray the charges of the several Services herein particularly mentioned, which will come in course of payment during the year ending on 31st March 1996, viz.:—

	Sums not exceeding	
	Supply Grants	Appropriations in Aid
	£	£
Vote		
1. For expenditure by the Department of National Heritage on payments in the support of national and other museums and galleries; for the Government Indemnity Scheme, to the Inland Revenue for assets accepted in lieu of tax; in the support of the British Library and other library institutions and services; to the Arts and Sports Councils and for other arts and sports bodies and schemes; to Royal Palaces and Parks; to the Royal Armouries, for historic buildings, ancient monuments, certain public buildings and the national heritage; for the promotion of tourism; to film bodies and projects; to the Welsh Fourth Channel Authority and for certain broadcasting services and schemes; for related research, surveys and other services; for central administration costs; for commemorative services; and for agency payments on behalf of the European Community (Revised sum)	993,273,000	43,261,000
2. For expenditure by the Department of National Heritage on payments to the British Broadcasting		

	Sums not exceeding	
	Supply Grants	Appropriations in Aid
	£	£
Corporation for home broadcasting, and payments to the Independent Television Commission	1,855,000,000	—
3. For expenditure by the Office of the National Lottery on administrative and operational costs	2,500,000	100,000
TOTAL, CLASS XI .... £	2,850,773,000	43,361,000

SCHEDULE (B).—PART 14   Class XII
                                         1995–96

CLASS XII

SCHEDULE OF SUMS granted, and of the sums which may be applied as appropriations in aid in addition thereto, to defray the charges of the several Services herein particularly mentioned, which will come in course of payment during the year ending on 31st March 1996, viz.:—

	Sums not exceeding	
	Supply Grants	Appropriations in Aid
	£	£
Vote		
1. For expenditure by the Department of Health on hospital, community health, mental health, family health and family health service administration services, National Health Service trusts, and on related services	27,897,305,000	6,135,582,000
2. For expenditure by the Department of Health on administration, including certain expenditure on behalf of the Department of Social Security, on miscellaneous health, personal social and other services (some of which are administered on a United Kingdom basis), including mental health, medical, scientific and technical services, medical treatment given to people from the UK in other countries of the EEA, welfare food, services for disabled persons, grants to voluntary organisations etc., payments in respect of Home Office inspection of public health laboratories services, grants in aid and subscriptions to international organisations and a contribution to the International Peto Institute	1,557,192,000	95,920,000
3. For expenditure by the NHS Pensions Agency on pensions, allowances, gratuities, etc., to or in respect of persons engaged in health services or in other approved employment	832,711,000	1,275,474,000
4. For expenditure of the Office of Population Censuses and Surveys on administrative and operational costs	35,775,000	35,078,000
TOTAL, CLASS XII .... £	30,322,983,000	7,542,054,000

Appropriation Act 1995

CLASS XIII

SCHEDULE OF SUMS granted, and of the sums which may be applied as appropriations in aid in addition thereto, to defray the charges of the several Services herein particularly mentioned, which will come in course of payment during the year ending on 31st March 1996, viz.:—

	Sums not exceeding	
	Supply Grants	Appropriations in Aid
Vote	£	£
1. For expenditure by the Department of Social Security on non-contributory retirement pensions, Christmas bonus payments to pensioners, pensions etc., for disablement or death arising out of war or service in the armed forces after 2 September 1939 and on sundry other services, on attendance allowances, invalid care allowance, severe disablement allowance, disability living allowance; disability working allowance; on pensions, gratuities and sundry allowances for disablement and specified deaths arising from industrial causes; on income support, payments of spousal and child maintenance, child benefit, one parent benefit, family credit, and on the vaccine damage payment scheme (Revised sum)	33,232,636,000	286,065,000
2. For expenditure by the Department of Social Security on rent rebate, rent allowance, council tax benefit, community charge benefit, community charge rebate and rate rebate subsidies and on sums payable in respect of anti-fraud measures to housing, charging, levying and local authorities; on transitional payments to help certain housing benefit claimants significantly affected by the changes to the housing benefit scheme and certain supplementary benefit claimants not entitled to benefit under the income support scheme; on sums payable into the National Insurance Fund to increase its income and as compensation payments in respect of statutory sick pay and statutory maternity pay and on sums payable into the Social Fund for expenditure on maternity expenses, funeral expenses and heating expenses in exceptionally cold weather	12,236,830,000	16,020,000
3. For expenditure by the Department of Social Security on sums payable as grants to the Independent Living; on subsidies to housing and local authorities towards the cost of administering the housing benefit scheme and to charging and levying authorities towards the costs of administering the council tax benefit scheme, as grants to Motability towards their administrative costs and to enable them to assist invalid vehicle users and others to have adapted and/or to purchase or lease cars from them, as grants to the British Limbless Ex-Servicemen's Association to enable them to assist certain other disabled vehicle users to have cars adapted, and on sums payable to the Social Fund to finance budgeting loans, crisis loans and community care grants	403,139,000	59,000

	Sums not exceeding	
	Supply Grants	Appropriations in Aid
	£	£
4. For expenditure by the Department of Social Security on administration, for agency payments, the promotion of Government policy on disability issues, and for certain other services including grants to local authorities and voluntary organisations	2,676,396,000	1,222,487,000
TOTAL, CLASS XIII .... £	48,549,001,000	1,524,631,000

SCHEDULE (B).—PART 16   Class XIV
1995–96

CLASS XIV

SCHEDULE OF SUMS granted, and of the sums which may be applied as appropriations in aid in addition thereto, to defray the charges of the several Services herein particularly mentioned, which will come in course of payment during the year ending on 31st March 1996, viz.:—

	Sums not exceeding	
	Supply Grants	Appropriations in Aid
	£	£
Vote		
1. For expenditure by the Scottish Office Agriculture and Fisheries Department on market support, support for agriculture in special areas including crofting communities; for structural measures (including agri-environmental measures); compensation to sheep producers and animal health; agricultural education, advisory, research and development services; botanical and scientific services; assistance to production marketing and processing; administration, land management and other agricultural services; assistance to the Scottish fishing industry; fishery protection; and certain other services including fisheries research and development and special services	165,027,000	20,455,000
2. For expenditure by the Scottish Office Industry Department on Scottish Enterprise and Highlands and Islands Enterprise; on innovation and technology support; on regional selective assistance; on regional enterprise grants; on regional development grants; on technical and vocational education; on the promotion of tourism; on roads and certain associated services, including the acquisition of land, lighting, road safety and related services; on assistance to local transport; on grants to Strathclyde Passenger Transport Authority for the additional costs of supporting rail services resulting from the restructuring of the railways; on support for transport services in the highlands and islands; on piers and harbours, and on certain other transport services and grants; on expenditure relating to the privatisation of Scottish Nuclear Ltd, the Scottish Bus Group and the		

	Sums not exceeding	
	Supply Grants	Appropriations in Aid
	£	£
electricity supply industry, Scotland; and on other sundry services in connection with trade and industry, etc. (Including a supplementary sum of £1,038,000)	941,222,000	14,945,000
3. For expenditure by the Scottish Office Industry Department on assistance to local transport, piers and harbours, on grants to new town development corporations in connection with housing and other services on the urban programme, on other urban regeneration initiatives, on expenses connected with the new towns' wind-up, on grants for ethnic minority groups and redemption of new towns National Loan Fund Debt	247,523,000	—
4. For expenditure by the Scottish Office Industry Department on European Regional Development Fund, European Social Fund, community initiatives and third party FEOGA to non-departmental public bodies, local authorities and other bodies and organisations	2,000	—
5. For expenditure by the Scottish Office Environment Department on housing subsidies, financial support for Scottish Homes, other expenditure, contributions and grants relating to housing; on historic buildings and monuments (including administration); on natural heritage; on other central and environmental services; on the Boards of the Water Authorities in Scotland; on the Scottish Water and Sewerage Customers Council; and on the Scottish Environment Protection Agency (Including a supplementary sum of £420,000)	417,068,000	9,028,000
6. For expenditure by the Scottish Office Environment Department on water and sewerage, flood and storm emergencies, other environmental services, sites for travelling people and residual grants to housing associations	11,321,000	—
7. For expenditure by the Scottish Office Environment Department for revenue support grants and payments of non-domestic rates in Scotland	4,974,997,000	—
8. For expenditure by the Scottish Office Environment Department on rate rebate grants and payments in connection with the community charge grant, the council tax transitional relief scheme and grants to shadow local authorities in Scotland	46,948,000	—
9. For expenditure by the Scottish Office Home and Health Department on legal aid, criminal injuries compensation (excluding administration), police, police and fire services superannuation and welfare food	475,637,000	314,000
10. For expenditure by the Scottish Office Home and Health Department on legal aid administration; certain services relating to crime including the Parole Board for Scotland, the Scottish Prison Service (and Executive Agency), the Scottish Prison Complaints Commission, police services (excluding grants to local authorities and superannuation); fire, the Scottish Office Pensions Agency, civil defence (including grants) and other protective and miscellaneous ser-		

	Sums not exceeding	
	Supply Grants	Appropriations in Aid
	£	£
vices; miscellaneous health services; social work services including the Scottish Children's Reporters Administration; the provision of residential and secure accommodation for children; services for offenders including probation and supervised attendance orders; grants to voluntary organisations; training and research; unemployed voluntary action fund; other grants to local authorities	311,890,000	8,520,000
11. For expenditure by the Scottish Office Home and Health Department on the provision of family health services under the National Health Service in Scotland and certain other services	648,004,000	191,838,000
12. For expenditure by the Scottish Office Home and Health Department on hospital, community health, family health and other health services, including National Health Service trusts, central health services and civil emergency planning	3,131,164,000	467,553,000
13. For expenditure by the Scottish Office Pensions Agency on superannuation allowances and gratuities etc., in respect of teachers, and the widows, widowers and dependants of deceased teachers	110,125,000	192,570,000
14. For expenditure by the Scottish Office Pensions Agency on pensions, allowances, gratuities, etc., to or in respect of persons engaged in health service or in other approved employment	149,584,000	159,395,000
15. For expenditure by the Scottish Office Education Department on schools, including self-governing schools; special educational needs; higher education and research, including the Scottish Higher Education Funding Council; the Student Awards Agency, Scotland; compensation payments; further education, including payments to further education colleges; curriculum development, international and other educational services, including support for School Boards and the careers service, and training and research; sport; Gaelic broadcasting; arts, libraries, museums and galleries, including purchase grants; cultural activities and organisations including the Royal Society of Edinburgh, Royal Scottish Geographical Society; Scottish Film Production Fund; publicity; indemnities; administration; central government grants to local authorities	965,655,000	2,600,000
16. For expenditure by the Scottish Office Education Department on student loans including administration, access funds, student awards and fees and reimbursement of fees for qualifying European Community students	395,231,000	6,972,000
17. For expenditure by the Scottish Courts Administration and the Scottish Court Service on court services, the Scottish Law Commission, certain legal services, costs and fees in connection with legal proceedings .	67,821,000	18,695,000
18. For expenditure by the Scottish Office on administrative costs and operational costs	168,862,000	10,279,000
19. For expenditure by the Scottish Record Office on administrative costs, on acquiring record material, on construction and associated costs of a new purpose-built repository, on conservation grants to local archives and on a grant to the Business Archives Council of Scotland	4,463,000	709,000

	Sums not exceeding	
	Supply Grants	Appropriations in Aid
	£	£
20. For expenditure by the General Register Office for Scotland on administrative and operational costs	5,035,000	2,577,000
21. For the expenditure of Registers of Scotland on administrative costs	1,000	32,054,000
22. For payments to Forestry Fund	65,865,000	8,000,000
TOTAL, CLASS XIV .... £	13,303,445,000	1,146,504,000

SCHEDULE (B).—PART 17   Class XV
1995–96

CLASS XV

SCHEDULE OF SUMS granted, and of the sums which may be applied as appropriations in aid in addition thereto, to defray the charges of the several Services herein particularly mentioned, which will come in course of payment during the year ending on 31st March 1996, viz.:—

	Sums not exceeding	
	Supply Grants	Appropriations in Aid
	£	£
Vote		
1. For expenditure by the Welsh Office on market support, support for agriculture in special areas and compensation to sheep producers; animal health; assistance to agricultural production, marketing and processing; grants for capital and other improvements and certain alternative land uses; support for the fishing industry, fisheries protection and agency payments for fishing projects; other miscellaneous agricultural services; arterial drainage, flood and coast protection	52,637,000	7,587,000
2. For expenditure by the Welsh Office on regional assistance and other industry expenditure (including Welsh Development Agency and Development Board for Rural Wales), exchange risk guarantees, housing subsidy to the Development Board for Rural Wales, the Teaching Company Scheme; expenditure via Training and Enterprise Councils and amounts retained by them as surpluses on training, including the provision of training programmes for young people and adults, initiatives and programmes within education; on the promotion of enterprise, and encouragement of self-employed and small firms; on help for unemployed people; on Careers Service, publicity and research; education (including the Further Education Funding Council for Wales and the Higher Education Funding Council for Wales) and certain other services and expenses	690,484,000	34,831,000

	Sums not exceeding	
	Supply Grants	Appropriations in Aid
	£	£
3. For expenditure by the Welsh Office on roads transport and certain associated services, housing, historic buildings and ancient monuments, Cadw Agency, other environmental services (including tourism, civil defence, national parks, Planning Inspectorate Agency and certain payments related to EU matters), arts, libraries and museums, health and personal social services, Welsh Office administration and TEC management fees and other grants and services, including research	553,941,000	8,983,000
4. For expenditure by the Welsh Office on housing, other environmental services, welfare food, the commutation of loan charge grants to local authorities and certain other services	553,292,000	1,061,000
5. For expenditure by the Welsh Office on hospital, community health, family health services including administration, National Health Service trusts and on other health services (part)	1,941,286,000	314,707,000
6. For expenditure by the Welsh Office on revenue support grant and payment of non-domestic rates income to receiving authorities in Wales, on payments to specified bodies, on a special grant to fund the running costs of shadow unitary authorities, on council tax preparation grant, on grants to local authorities in Wales in respect of the community charge, on rate rebates for disabled people, on special grants to local authorities following natural emergencies, on payments for Valuation Office Agency rating and valuation services, on running costs of Valuation Tribunals, on publicity costs, on Treasury Solicitor legal services, and on repayments of excess contributions made by billing authorities and adjustments for shortfalls in receipts made by the Secretary of State in respect of non-domestic rates in previous years, etc.	2,279,537,000	501,000
7. For expenditure by the Office of Her Majesty's Chief Inspector of Schools in Wales on inspections, publicity, training, teachers' short courses and conferences, administration and associated capital etc.	8,471,000	338,000
8. For expenditure by the Welsh Office on European Regional Development Fund grants to public corporations, local authorities and other bodies and organisations	3,000	—
TOTAL, CLASS XV .... £	6,079,651,000	368,008,000

SCHEDULE (B).—PART 18   Class XVI
                                          1995–96
_____

CLASS XVI

SCHEDULE OF SUMS granted, and of the sums which may be applied as appropriations in aid in addition thereto, to defray the charges of the several Services herein particularly mentioned, which will come in course of payment during the year ending on 31st March 1996, viz.:—

	Sums not exceeding	
	Supply Grants	Appropriations in Aid
	£	£
Vote		
1. For expenditure by the Northern Ireland Office on the central and miscellaneous services, services related to crime, police, prisons, security, criminal justice, training schools, probation and after-care etc., compensation schemes, crown prosecutions and other legal services and certain other grants	888,655,000	8,257,000
2. For expenditure by the Northern Ireland Office on a grant-in-aid of the Northern Ireland Consolidated Fund and other transfers	2,000,000,000	—
TOTAL, CLASS XVI .... £	2,888,655,000	8,257,000

SCHEDULE (B).—PART 19   Class XVII
                                          1995–96
_____

CLASS XVII

SCHEDULE OF SUMS granted, and of the sums which may be applied as appropriations in aid in addition thereto, to defray the charges of the several Services herein particularly mentioned, which will come in course of payment during the year ending on 31st March 1996, viz.:—

	Sums not exceeding	
	Supply Grants	Appropriations in Aid
	£	£
Vote		
1. For expenditure by Her Majesty's Treasury on economic, financial and related administration including debt management; payments to certain parliamentary bodies and certain other services including expenses in connection with Honours and Dignities and a grant in aid to the Private Finance Panel Executive (Revised sum)	66,843,000	3,714,000
2. For expenditure by Her Majesty's Treasury in connection with the manufacture, storage and distribution of coinage for use in the United Kingdom	26,000,000	4,500,000
3. For expenditure by the Customs and Excise Department on the administration of taxation, the operation of customs and revenue controls and other customs and excise work, and payments in respect of the Customs and Excise National Museum	850,237,000	17,300,000

	Sums not exceeding	
	Supply Grants	Appropriations in Aid
	£	£
4. For expenditure by the Inland Revenue Department on the management and collection of the direct taxes and services provided for the Department's information technology partner and for other departments	1,630,358,000	188,144,000
5. For expenditure by the Inland Revenue Department Valuation Office (Executive Agency) on the provision of rating and valuation services for government departments and other public bodies	1,000	189,028,000
6. For expenditure by the Inland Revenue Department on life assurance premium relief, mortgage interest relief, private medical insurance premium relief, vocational training relief and transitional payments to charities	252,000,000	—
7. For rates and contributions in lieu of rates paid by the Inland Revenue in respect of property occupied by the Crown and premises occupied by representatives of Commonwealth and foreign countries and international organisations	59,500,000	604,200,000
8. For expenditure of the Department for National Savings on administration, publicity costs and certain other expenses	192,261,000	2,360,000
9. For expenditure on administrative costs by the Registry of Friendly Societies on behalf of the Building Societies Commission, the Friendly Societies Commission and the Central Office of the Registry	3,242,000	5,280,000
10. For expenditure by the National Debt Office and Public Works Loan Board on administrative costs ..	400,000	1,574,000
11. For expenditure by Paymaster on administrative costs	1,378,000	27,317,000
12. For expenditure by the Central Statistical Office on the provision of national accounts and other statistics and on departmental administration	48,400,000	2,745,000
13. For expenditure of the Department of the Government Actuary on administrative costs	636,000	5,719,000
14. For the salaries of the Crown Estate Commissioners and the expenses of their Office	1,569,000	—
15. For expenditure by Her Majesty's Treasury in connection with the sales of residual Government shareholdings and the sale of privatised companies' debt (Revised sum)	1,000	36,723,000
16. For expenditure by Her Majesty's Treasury to repay to the Contingencies Fund certain miscellaneous advances made during the year ended 31 March 1995 (New Estimate)	277,000	—
TOTAL, CLASS XVII .... £	3,133,103,000	1,088,604,000

Class XVIII

Schedule of Sums granted, and of the sums which may be applied as appropriations in aid in addition thereto, to defray the charges of the several Services herein particularly mentioned, which will come in course of payment during the year ending on 31st March 1996, viz.:—

	Sums not exceeding	
	Supply Grants	Appropriations in Aid
	£	£
Vote		
1. For expenditure of the Minister for Public Service and Science on the central management of the civil service, and certain other services (including a supplementary sum of £2,123,000)	52,713,000	73,803,000
2. For expenditure by the Cabinet Office: Office of Public Service and Science on payments to the Science Research Councils, the Royal Society, the Royal Academy of Engineering; OST initiatives; fees payable under the Animals (Scientific Procedures) Act 1986 and Research Council Pensions	1,284,246,000	5,950,000
3. For expenditure by the Cabinet Office: Office of Public Service and Science on the superannuation of civil servants; pensions, etc., in respect of former members of the Royal Irish Constabulary and other pensions and non-recurrent payments; and for certain other services	1,449,620,000	1,316,090,000
4. For expenditure by the Central Office of Information on allied service work	1,370,000	—
5. For expenditure by the Controller of Her Majesty's Stationery Office to compensate the HMSO Trading Fund for the price concessions to public libraries; to meet the cost of government and other publications supplied to United Kingdom members of the European Parliament; and to meet the costs of certain goods and services provided exceptionally to customers in the private sector	2,197,000	250,000
Total, Class XVIII .... £	2,790,146,000	1,396,093,000

SCHEDULE (B).—Part 21   Class XIX
                                         1995–96

Class XIX

Schedule of Sums granted, and of the sums which may be applied as appropriations in aid in addition thereto, to defray the charges of the several Services herein particularly mentioned, which will come in course of payment during the year ending on 31st March 1996, viz.:—

	Sums not exceeding	
	Supply Grants	Appropriations in Aid
	£	£
Vote		
1. For expenditure by the Cabinet Office on administrative costs, the Offices of the Prime Minister, the Parliamentary Counsel and the Government Chief Whip, payments to the Chequers Trust and the British National Committee for the History of the Second World War, and certain other services	37,749,000	7,106,000
2. For expenditure by Her Majesty's security and intelligence services on administration and operational costs, works and equipment, pensions and other payments	799,117,000	18,719,000
3. For expenditure of the Department of Her Majesty's Privy Council on administrative costs and for the financing of a Central Drugs Coordination Unit	2,605,000	28,000
4. For expenditure of the Office of the Parliamentary Commissioner for Administration and the Health Service Commissioners for England, Scotland and Wales on administrative costs	9,000,000	—
5. For expenditure of the House of Lords on Peers' expenses and administrative costs, including staff pensions, security, stationery and printing	27,961,000	—
6. For expenditure by the House of Lords on works services; including a payment to the House of Commons in respect of administration	15,995,000	678,000
7. For expenditure of the House of Commons on Members' salaries, allowances, pensions, etc., financial assistance to Opposition parties and an Exchequer contribution to the Members' Fund	73,498,000	—
Total, Class XIX .... £	965,925,000	26,531,000

SCHEDULE (B).—PART 22   Class XIX, A
1995–96

Class XIX, A

SCHEDULE OF SUMS granted, and of the sums which may be applied as appropriations in aid in addition thereto, to defray the charges of the several Services herein particularly mentioned, which will come in course of payment during the year ending on 31st March 1996, viz.:—

	Sums not exceeding	
	Supply Grants	Appropriations in Aid
	£	£
Vote		
1. For expenditure by the House of Commons Commission on administration; including security, broadcasting, publicity, stationery, printing and grant in aid to the History of Parliament Trust	73,330,000	2,823,000
2. For expenditure by the House of Commons Commission on accommodation services, including administration	49,900,000	2,015,000
TOTAL, CLASS XIX, A .... £	123,230,000	4,838,000

SCHEDULE (B).—PART 23   Class XIX, B
1995–96

CLASS XIX, B

SCHEDULE OF SUMS granted, and of the sums which may be applied as appropriations in aid in addition thereto, to defray the charges of the several Services herein particularly mentioned, which will come in course of payment during the year ending on 31st March 1996, viz.:—

	Sums not exceeding	
	Supply Grants	Appropriations in Aid
	£	£
Vote		
1. For expenditure of the National Audit Office	37,600,000	6,000,000
TOTAL, CLASS XIX, B .... £	37,600,000	6,000,000

SCHEDULE (C)

ENACTMENTS REPEALED

Chapter	Short title
1992 c. 59	Consolidated Fund (No. 3) Act 1992
1993 c. 4	Consolidated Fund Act 1993
1993 c. 7	Consolidated Fund (No. 2) Act 1993
1993 c. 52	Consolidated Fund (No. 3) Act 1993
1993 c. 33	Appropriation Act 1993

INDEX

References are to sections and Schedules

CRIMINAL JUSTICE (SCOTLAND) ACT 1995*

(1995 c. 20)

---

*Annotations by Robert S. Shiels, solicitor in the Supreme Courts of Scotland.

PART II

PROCEEDS OF CRIME AND PROPERTY USED IN CRIME

CHAPTER I

CONFISCATION OF THE PROCEEDS OF CRIME

Confiscation orders

Exercise of powers

Compensation

117. Minor and consequential amendments and repeals.
118. Short title, commencement and extent.

An Act to amend the criminal justice system of Scotland as respects criminal proceedings, the investigation of offences, the sentences and other disposals applicable in respect of certain offences, legal aid in relation to certain appeals, and the treatment of offenders; to amend the law of Scotland in relation to confiscation of the proceeds of, and forfeiture of property used in, crime; to make further provision as respects Scotland in relation to the preparation of jury lists for the purposes of criminal and civil trials; and for connected purposes. [19th July 1995]

PARLIAMENTARY DEBATES
Hansard, H.L. Vol. 559, cols. 545, 1373, Vol. 560, cols. 295, 363, 409, 1591, Vol. 561, cols. 11, 83, 577, Vol. 565, col. 1153. H.C. Vol. 255, col. 707, Vol. 261, col. 215.
The Bill was discussed in First Scottish Standing Committee on March 23, 28 and 30; April 4, 20 and 25, 1995.

INTRODUCTION AND GENERAL NOTE
The 1995 Act covers two quite distinct areas. Before considering these in some detail it is worth noting the words of the Minister of State at the Scottish Office, Lord Fraser of Carmyllie, on the second reading of the Bill in the House of Lords. The Minister said that the Bill had "two main objectives. The first is to enhance the effectiveness of our criminal justice system by strengthening the powers of the criminal justice agencies in the fight against crime. The second is to improve its efficiency and its capacity to deal with those who break the law" (*Hansard*, H.L. Vol. 559, col. 545). He added that while the Scottish criminal justice system commanded "widespread respect and confidence" no-one could be complacent (*Hansard*, H.L. Vol. 559, col. 551).
Much of the detail of many of the clauses passed through Parliament without comment or division, but a few aspects undoubtedly raised political temperatures and are likely to be watched closely in practice.

Part I—The Course of Justice
This Part is concerned essentially with the law of evidence and procedure in Scottish criminal courts. Some of the sections make slight alterations to the existing law, while others introduce a wholly new procedure. Dissent to the proposed changes was more often than not directed at those sections making a slight alteration rather than something entirely new.

Part II—Proceeds of Crime and Property Used In Crime
This Part represents a widening of the general realisation that crime on many occasions can be profitable. The fairly sophisticated powers in the Criminal Justice (Scotland) Act 1987 (c. 41) are

extended from controlled drugs cases to a far wider range of crimes. The potential for error and unfairness is balanced by new duties for compensation.

Part III—Supplementary
This Part is concerned with the technical aspects of the interpretation of the 1995 Act and its commencement.

COMMENCEMENT
The Criminal Justice (Scotland) Act 1995 received Royal Assent on July 19, 1995. The Act comes into force on such days as the Secretary of State appoints by statutory instrument, and different days may be so appointed for different areas or purposes: s.118(2).

It seems unlikely that much of the 1995 Act will be brought into force. The Criminal Procedure (Scotland) Bill is as the author writes proceeding through Parliament as a consolidating measure, and that Bill is intended to repeal the 1995 Act and re-enact it with other amendments to Scots criminal law.

However, ss.22, 35, 42, 43, 65, 117(1), 117(2) and 118 of this Act were brought into force on September 26, 1995 by the Criminal Justice (Scotland) (Commencement No. 1, Transitional Provisions and Savings) Order 1995 (S.I. 1995 No. 2295 (C.45) (S.171)).

ABBREVIATIONS
S.L.C. Report (147)	: Scottish Law Commission: Report on Confiscation and Forfeiture (No. 147) (Cmnd. 2622) HMSO (September, 1994).
S.L.C. Report (149)	: Scottish Law Commission: Report on Hearsay Evidence in Criminal Proceedings (No. 149) HMSO (February, 1995).
The Bail Act	: Bail etc. (Scotland) Act 1980.
The 1975 Act	: Criminal Procedure (Scotland) Act 1975.
The 1980 Act	: Criminal Justice (Scotland) Act 1980.
The 1987 Act	: Criminal Justice (Scotland) Act 1987.
The 1988 Act	: Criminal Justice Act 1988.
The 1993 Act	: Prisoners and Criminal Proceedings (Scotland) Act 1993.
The 1995 Act	: Criminal Justice (Scotland) Act 1995.

PART I

THE COURSE OF JUSTICE

Bail

Bail conditions

1. For subsection (2) of section 1 of the Bail etc. (Scotland) Act 1980 (release on bail subject to conditions) there shall be substituted the following subsections—

"(2) In granting bail the court or, as the case may be, the Lord Advocate shall impose on the accused—
  (a) the standard; conditions; and
  (b) such further conditions as the court or, as the case may be, the Lord Advocate considers necessary to secure—
      (i) that the standard conditions are observed; and
      (ii) that the accused makes himself available for the purpose of participating in an identification parade or of enabling any print, impression or sample to be taken from him.

(2A) The standard conditions referred to in subsection (2) above are conditions that the accused—
  (a) appears at the appointed time at every diet relating to the offence with which he is charged of which he is given due notice;
  (b) does not commit an offence while on bail;
  (c) does not interfere with witnesses or otherwise obstruct the course of justice whether in relation to himself or any other person; and
  (d) makes himself available for the purpose of enabling enquiries or a report to be made to assist the court in dealing with him for the offence with which he is charged.".

DEFINITIONS
"standard conditions": s.1(2A) of the Bail etc. (Scotland) Act 1980.

GENERAL NOTE
   This section provides for the court or the Lord Advocate to impose standard conditions when granting bail, and to impose special conditions on bail where these are considered necessary to ensure that the standard conditions are observed and that the accused makes himself available to participate in an identification parade or to allow samples to be taken. The section places on a statutory basis the current practice of imposing conditions derived from s.1(2) of the Bail Act, known as "standard" conditions.
   The Bail Act specifies that when granting bail the court or the Lord Advocate, as the case may be, may impose such conditions as are considered necessary to ensure that the accused: appears in court at the appointed diets; does not commit an offence while on bail; does not interfere with witnesses or otherwise obstruct the course of justice whether in relation to himself or any other person; and makes himself available for the purposes of enabling inquiries or a report to be made to assist the court in dealing with him for the offence with which he is charged.
   This power is in practice always used when granting bail to impose what have become known as the "standard conditions". These are set out in s.1(2A) of the Bail Act, to be inserted by this section.
   Under the Bail Act at present the court (or the Lord Advocate as the case may be) may impose such other conditions as it considers necessary to secure certain specified objectives. That power will not in every case permit the court or the Lord Advocate to require an accused to present himself for identification purposes or for the taking of prints etc. This section provides the court and the Lord Advocate with such a power.
   Section 1 amends s.1(2) of the Bail Act by introducing new subss. (2) and (2A). The combined effect of these new subsections is that the standard conditions must be imposed on bail, together with any other conditions required to secure compliance with the standard conditions. The standard conditions are defined in subs. (2A). Where it appears necessary, the court must also impose conditions which ensure that the accused is available to take part in identity parades and which allow for samples to be taken.

Breach of bail conditions

   2.—(1) Section 3 of the Bail etc. (Scotland) Act 1980 (breach of bail conditions) shall be amended as follows.
   (2) In subsection (1), after the word "shall" there shall be inserted ", subject to subsection (2A) below,".
   (3) In subsection (2)(a), for the words "£200" there shall be substituted "level 3 on the standard scale".
   (4) After subsection (2) there shall be inserted the following subsections—
      "(2A) Where, and to the extent that, the failure referred to in subsection (1)(b) above consists in the accused having committed an offence while on bail (in this section referred to as "the subsequent offence"), he shall not be guilty of an offence under that subsection but, subject to subsection (2B) below, the court which sentences him for the subsequent offence shall, in determining the appropriate sentence or disposal for that offence, have regard to—
      (a) the fact that the offence was committed by him while on bail and the number of bail orders to which he was subject when the offence was committed;
      (b) any previous conviction of the accused of an offence under subsection (1)(b) above; and
      (c) the extent to which the sentence or disposal in respect of any previous conviction of the accused differed, by virtue of this subsection, from that which the court would have imposed but for this subsection.
   (2B) The court shall not, under subsection (2A) above, have regard to the fact that the subsequent offence was committed while the accused was on bail unless that fact is libelled in the indictment or, as the case may be, specified in the complaint.

(2C) Where the maximum penalty in respect of the subsequent offence is specified by or by virtue of any enactment, that maximum penalty shall, for the purposes of the court's determination, by virtue of subsection (2A) above, of the appropriate sentence or disposal in respect of that offence, be increased—

 (a) where it is a fine, by the amount for the time being equivalent to level 3 on the standard scale; and

 (b) where it is a period of imprisonment—

  (i) as respects a conviction in the High Court or the sheriff court, by 6 months; and

  (ii) as respects a conviction in the district court, by 60 days,

notwithstanding that the maximum penalty as so increased exceeds the penalty which it would otherwise be competent for the court to impose.

(2D) Where the sentence or disposal in respect of the subsequent offence is, by virtue of subsection (2A) above, different from that which the court would have imposed but for that subsection, the court shall state the extent of and the reasons for that difference.".

GENERAL NOTE

This section introduces new measures to tackle offending on bail. Where an accused is convicted of an offence committed while on bail the court may increase the sentence for the offence, having regard to the fact that the accused was on bail at the time. Where a fine is involved the increase may be up to level 3 on the standard scale (currently £1,000), and where imprisonment is involved an increase of up to six months (60 days in the district court) may be imposed. The penalty so increased may exceed what would otherwise be the court's maximum sentencing powers.

The section maintains as an offence the breach of other conditions of bail and increases the penalty for such breach from £200 to a fine equivalent to level 3 on the standard scale (currently £1,000). The maximum period of imprisonment which may be imposed remains at three months (60 days in the district court).

Section 3 of the Bail Act provides that failure to comply with bail conditions is itself an offence. Under s.3 of the 1980 Act a person found guilty of such an offence may be liable to a fine not exceeding £200 and imprisonment for a period of up to 60 days (where a case is tried in the district court) or up to three months (where a case is tried in the sheriff court or the High Court). Section 1(2A) of the Bail Act, as amended by this Act in s.1, provides that certain standard conditions must be imposed by the court or the Lord Advocate when granting bail, including a condition that no further offences should be committed by the accused while liberated on bail. In order to focus on breach of this condition and to provide the courts with additional sentencing powers in respect of the offence committed on bail, changes to the courts' powers and handling of such offences are thought necessary.

Subsection (3) replaces the reference in s.3(2)(a) of the Bail Act to the fine of £200 for breaching bail conditions with a reference to level 3 (currently £1,000) on the standard scale as specified under s.289G of the 1975 Act (as amended by the Criminal Justice Act 1991).

Subsection (4) inserts new subsections into s.3 of the Bail Act, all dealing with the commission of offences while on bail. The new subs. (2A) provides that a breach of bail conditions by offending on bail is no longer a separate offence. Instead, where an offence has been committed by an accused while liberated on bail, the court may have regard to this fact when determining the sentence for the offence. The new subs. (2B) provides that the court shall take into account that an offence has been committed on bail only where this is referred to, in solemn proceedings, in the indictment, or, in summary proceedings, in the complaint. The new subs. (2C) specifies the extent to which the court may increase a sentence for an offence committed on bail. Where the sentence is a fine it may be increased by the amount for the time being equivalent to level 3 on the standard scale (currently £1,000); where the sentence is a term of imprisonment, it may be increased by six months in High Court and sheriff court cases and by 60 days in district court cases. The increase may be imposed even if the total sentence exceeds the maximum sentencing power of the court in which the case is heard. The new subs. (2D) provides that the court shall specify to what extent a sentence has been increased and the reasons for the increase.

No bail in homicide or rape proceedings after previous conviction of such offences

3. After section 28 of the Criminal Procedure (Scotland) Act 1975 (in this

Act referred to as "the 1975 Act") there shall be inserted the following section—

"No bail for persons charged with or convicted of homicide or rape after previous conviction of such offences

28A.—(1) Notwithstanding sections 26 to 33 and 238 of this Act, a person who in any proceedings has been charged with or convicted of—

(a) attempted murder;

(b) culpable homicide;

(c) rape; or

(d) attempted rape,

in circumstances where this section applies shall not be granted bail in those proceedings.

(2) This section applies where—

(a) the person has previously been convicted by or before a court in any part of the United Kingdom of any offence specified in sub-section (1) above or of murder or manslaughter; and

(b) in the case of a previous conviction of culpable homicide or of manslaughter—

(i) he was sentenced to imprisonment or, if he was then a child or young person, to detention under any of the relevant enactments;

(ii) a hospital order was imposed in respect of him;

(iii) an order having the same effect as a hospital order was made in respect of him under section 174ZC(2)(a) of this Act; or

(iv) an order having equivalent effect to an order referred to in sub-paragraph (ii) or (iii) above has been made in respect of him by a court in England and Wales.

(3) This section applies whether or not an appeal is pending against conviction or sentence or both.

(4) In this section—

"conviction" includes—

(a) a finding that a person is not guilty by reason of insanity;

(b) a finding under section 174ZA(2) of this Act;

(c) a finding under section 4A(3) of the Criminal Procedure (Insanity) Act 1964 (cases of unfitness to plead) that a person did the act or made the omission charged against him; and

(d) a conviction of an offence for which an order is made placing the offender on probation or discharging him absolutely or conditionally;

and "convicted" shall be construed accordingly; and

"the relevant enactments" means—

(a) as respects Scotland, sections 205 and 206 of this Act;

(b) as respects England and Wales, section 53(2) of the Children and Young Persons Act 1933; and

(c) as respects Northern Ireland, section 73(2) of the Children and Young Persons Act (Northern Ireland) 1968.".

GENERAL NOTE

Section 26(1) of the 1975 Act provides that all crimes except murder and treason are bailable. Where an accused is brought before a sheriff or justice of the peace on any charge other than murder or treason the sheriff or justice of the peace may release the accused on bail.

This section extends the list of crimes which are not bailable by introducing a new s.28A into the 1975 Act.

This section applies to bail applications in proceedings where an accused is charged with, or convicted of, one of four crimes, namely attempted murder, culpable homicide, rape or attempted rape. Bail must be refused in these proceedings if the accused already has a conviction for murder, manslaughter or one of the four abovementioned crimes.

The section does not amend s.35 of the 1975 Act which enables the Lord Advocate or the High Court to admit to bail any person charged with any crime or offence.

Right of prosecutor to seek review of grant of bail

4. After each of sections 30 and 299 of the 1975 Act there shall be inserted the following section as, respectively, section 30A and section 299A—

> "**Application by prosecutor for review of court's decision to grant bail**
> .—(1) On an application by the prosecutor at any time after a court has granted bail to a person the court may, where the prosecutor puts before the court material information which was not available to it when it granted bail to that person, review its decision.
>
> (2) On receipt of an application under subsection (1) above the court shall—
> (a) intimate the application to the person granted bail;
> (b) fix a diet for hearing the application and cite that person to attend the diet; and
> (c) where it considers that the interests of justice so require, grant warrant to arrest that person.
>
> (3) On hearing an application under subsection (1) above the court may—
> (a) withdraw the grant of bail and remand the person in question in custody; or
> (b) grant bail, or continue the grant of bail, either on the same or on different conditions.
>
> (4) Nothing in the foregoing provisions of this section shall affect any right of appeal against the decision of a court in relation to bail.".

GENERAL NOTE

This section enables the prosecutor to apply to the court to reconsider a decision to grant bail. Application must be made on the basis of information relevant to the decision to grant bail which was not available to the court when the decision was taken.

At present, there is no statutory provision for the prosecutor to request the court to reconsider a decision to grant bail. The prosecutor does have a right under s.26(2) of the 1975 Act to be heard against an application for bail, and, under s.31(2) of the same Act, a right to appeal against a decision to grant bail. Section 33 of that Act makes clear that such an appeal must be made within fixed time-limits. This section will effectively provide a further right of appeal where the prosecutor has new information regarding a case which was not available to the court when the decision to grant bail was taken.

This is achieved by the insertion of two new and identical sections into the 1975 Act, dealing with solemn proceedings (s.30A) and summary proceedings (s.299A) respectively.

Subsection (2) of each new section describes the procedure to be followed on receipt of an application, namely that the court shall inform the person granted bail of the prosecutor's application; fix a diet for hearing the application and cite that person to attend; and if it considers that it is in the interests of justice, grant a warrant to arrest that person.

Subsection (3) specifies the options available to the court on hearing the prosecutor's application. It may either withdraw bail and remand the accused in custody, or grant bail or continue bail either on the same or on different conditions. Subsection (4) provides that nothing in the section shall affect any right of appeal against the decision of a court in relation to bail.

Bail pending appeal

5.—(1) Section 238 of the 1975 Act (admission of appellant to bail) shall be amended as follows.

(2) In subsection (1), at the beginning there shall be inserted "Subject to subsection (1A) below,".

(3) After subsection (1) there shall be inserted the following subsection—
"(1A) The High Court shall not admit a convicted person to bail under subsection (1) above unless—
   (a) where he is the appellant and has not lodged a note of appeal in accordance with section 233(1)(a) of this Act, the application for bail states reasons why it should be granted and sets out the proposed grounds of appeal; or
   (b) where the Lord Advocate is the appellant, the application for bail states reasons why it should be granted;
and, in either case, the High Court considers there to be exceptional circumstances justifying admitting the convicted person to bail.".

GENERAL NOTE

This section provides that bail pending the outcome of an appeal against conviction, sentence, or both, in respect of which no note of appeal has been lodged, should be granted only where reasons for the appeal have been stated and where the court considers there to be exceptional circumstances justifying liberation on bail. This is to prevent bail being granted where the grounds of appeal, and hence the likelihood of success of the appeal, are unknown.

The High Court may, by s.238(1) of the 1975 Act, admit a convicted person to bail pending the determination of that person's appeal. The power under s.238(1) of the 1975 Act is exercisable in solemn cases as soon as intimation of intention to appeal is lodged. Section 231 of the 1975 Act provides that an intimation of intention to appeal, which does not contain the grounds of appeal, must be lodged within two weeks of the final determination of the proceedings.

In effect, immediately following conviction in solemn proceedings, an appellant may lodge an intimation of intent to appeal and apply for bail. The court must then consider the application for bail with no knowledge of the grounds of appeal and is therefore unable to assess its prospect of success. The grounds of appeal may not be known for a further six weeks. It is considered appropriate that appellants who have not lodged a note of appeal should be required to state reasons in support of the application for bail, and indicate the proposed grounds of appeal in such form as may be prescribed by an Act of Adjournal. The High Court should only grant bail on such an application where it considers there to be exceptional circumstances.

Subsection (3) inserts a new provision, s.238(1A) into the 1978 Act. This section requires the High Court not to admit to bail a person who has not lodged a note of appeal in accordance with s.233(1)(a) of the 1975 Act, unless the application for bail is made in such form as may be prescribed by Act of Adjournal, the appellant states reasons in support of the application, including the proposed grounds of appeal, and the High Court considers that there are exceptional circumstances justifying admitting that person to bail.

Juries

Lists of potential jurors

6. In section 3 of the Jurors (Scotland) Act 1825 (sheriff principal to maintain lists of potential jurors)—
   (a) the existing provision shall become subsection (1);
   (b) in that subsection, for the word "designations" there shall be substituted "addresses"; and
   (c) after that subsection there shall be inserted the following subsections—
"(2) For the purpose of maintaining lists of potential jurors under subsection (1) above, a sheriff principal may require any person in the sheriff court district in question who appears to him to be qualified and liable to serve as a juror to provide such information, and in such form, as the Secretary of State may by order prescribe.
(3) A statutory instrument containing an order by virtue of subsection (2) above shall be subject to annulment pursuant to a resolution of either House of Parliament.
(4) Any person who fails to comply with a requirement under subsection (2) above shall be guilty of an offence and liable on summary conviction to a fine not exceeding level 1 on the standard scale.

(5) In proceedings against a person for an offence under subsection (4) above it is a defence to prove that he had reasonable excuse for the failure.".

GENERAL NOTE

This section allows the Sheriff Principal to request from potential jurors information for the purpose of maintaining a list of potential jurors and makes it a criminal offence for any person to fail, without reasonable cause, to comply with such a request. It also removes the requirement that a potential juror's occupation should be included on the list of potential jurors.

Section 3 of the Jurors (Scotland) Act 1825 (c. 22) requires the Sheriff Principal to maintain for each sheriff court two "lists of potential jurors" containing the names of persons within the district who appear to him to be qualified and liable to serve as jurors. Nearly a quarter of those who are approached when the lists are being drawn up fail to respond to a request for confirmation of details. In consequence they effectively exclude themselves from the possibility of jury service. To ensure that persons reply to the request for information an offence is created punishable by a maximum fine of level 1 on the standard scale (currently £200). The new subs. (5) of s.3 of the 1825 Act provides that it is a defence to show that there was some reasonable excuse for the failure to comply with the request.

The term "designation" is held to include the address and occupation of the potential juror. Paragraph (6) of this section substitutes "address" for designation, thereby removing the need to disclose occupation. Removal of occupation from the list is designed to ensure that people of all occupations have an equal opportunity to serve on a jury.

Jury service

7.—(1) After subsection (5) of section 1 of the Law Reform (Miscellaneous Provisions) (Scotland) Act 1980 (persons excused from jury service for good reason) there shall be inserted the following subsection—

"(5A) Where the clerk of court has, under subsection (5) above, excused a person from jury service in any criminal proceedings he shall, unless he considers there to be exceptional circumstances which make it inappropriate to do so, within one year of the date of that excusal cite that person to attend for jury service in criminal proceedings.".

(2) In Schedule 1 to that Act (ineligibility for and disqualification and excusal from jury service)—

(a) in Part II (persons disqualified from jury service), at the end of paragraph (b) there shall be inserted—

"(c) in respect of jury service in any criminal proceedings, persons who are on bail in or in connection with criminal proceedings in any part of the United Kingdom."; and

(b) in Part III (persons excusable as of right), at the end of Group D there shall be inserted—

"GROUP DD

Members of certain religious bodies

In respect of jury service in any criminal proceedings, practising members of religious societies or orders the tenets or beliefs of which are incompatible with jury service.".

GENERAL NOTE

This section provides that where the clerk of court excuses a person from jury service, the person is to be cited to attend for jury service within one year of the excusal except in exceptional circumstances. In addition, those on bail are disqualified from jury service. The section gives practising members of religious bodies, the tenets and beliefs of which are incompatible with jury service, the right to be excused from such service.

Section 1(5) of the Law Reform (Miscellaneous Provisions) (Scotland) Act 1980 provides that a person cited to attend for jury service, and not excused as of right, may be excused by the clerk of court if the person cited shows to the clerk's satisfaction that there is good reason why he should be excused from so attending. The main reason for excusal under this section is inconvenience. The intention is that, in future, those excused for such reason would be cited again and, if necessary, again, for a date that was more convenient to them. At present, those who are excused jury service for a particular court sitting may, by random selection, be cited to attend for jury service on a subsequent occasion but there is no requirement that, nor time-limit within which, they must be cited again. This section provides a time-limit of one year within which an excused person should be cited again, except in exceptional circumstances.

Schedule 1 to the Law Reform (Miscellaneous Provisions) (Scotland) Act 1980 sets out the various categories of those who are ineligible (Pt. I), those disqualified (Pt. II) and those who are excusable as of right (Pt. III). Persons on bail, who have been accused of committing an offence and are still subject to criminal proceedings, are to be added to the list of persons who are disqualified by subs. (2)(a).

In the House of Lords the suggestion was made by Lord Macauley of Bragar that this amendment was unfair: "there was no reason why the mere fact that a person has been charged with an offence should deprive him of his rights in the community". However, the Minister of State pointed out that an event such as a charge might improperly affect such a juror's attitude to the proceedings in which he would be contributing to the verdict (*Hansard*, H.L. Vol. 560, cols. 333–334).

The tenets and beliefs of some religious bodies are not compatible with jury service, and practising members of such bodies are to be excused as of right from jury service by being added to the list of groups in Pt. III: subs. (2)(b).

Challenges to jurors

8. In section 130 of the 1975 Act (challenges and objections to jurors—
(a) subsections (1) to (3) shall cease to have effect; and
(b) after subsection (3) there shall be inserted—

"(3A) Where, before a juror is sworn to serve, the parties jointly apply for him to be excused the court shall, notwithstanding that no reason is given in the application, excuse that juror from service.".

GENERAL NOTE
This section removes the right of the prosecution and the accused each to challenge three jurors without giving any reasons, but requires the court to excuse a juror on joint application by both parties, notwithstanding that no reason is given. The intention of this section is that challenges should only be permissible where there is agreement or cause is shown.

Subsections 130(1) and (2) of the 1975 Act permit each accused and the prosecution to challenge up to three potential jurors at the time when the name of that juror is called. Subsection (3) provides that such challenge of itself disqualifies a person from serving as a juror at that trial. Subsection 130(4) of the 1975 Act maintains the right of each accused and the prosecution to object to any potential juror on cause shown.

This section repeals subss. (1) to (3) of s.130 of the 1975 Act and inserts a new subs. (3A).

There may be occasions when it is apparent to the court that a person balloted is unsuitable for jury service, but a challenge stated in open court would offend, embarrass or distress the juror. To cover this situation the section provides that, where the prosecution and defence agree that a juror is unsuitable to sit on the jury, the court is required to excuse a juror without the cause being stated in open court.

This is another example of a simple change that provoked some debate in Parliament (*Hansard*, H.L. Vol. 560, cols. 334–346). The history of peremptory challenge is narrated in Lord Thomson's Report (Cmd. 6218) October 1975 at para. 51.28.

Pre-trial procedure

Execution of warrants granted by sheriff, etc.

9. For each of sections 15 and 327 of the 1975 Act (certain warrants granted by sheriff may be executed throughout Scotland), there shall be substituted the following section—

"Warrants granted by justice may be executed throughout Scotland
. Any warrant granted by a justice may, without being backed or endorsed by any other justice, be executed throughout Scotland in the

same way as it may be executed within the jurisdiction of the justice who granted it.".

"justice": s.462 of the Criminal Procedure (Scotland) Act 1975.

GENERAL NOTE
Section 9 provides that any warrant granted by a justice may be executed throughout Scotland without the need for backing or endorsement. Sections 15 and 327 of the 1975 Act made provision in solemn and summary proceedings, respectively, for the execution of a warrant for arrest throughout Scotland. Other warrants could only be executed outwith the area of the issuing court if a judge of the other area added a warrant of concurrence (*i.e.* "backed" or "endorsed" the original warrant). This procedure is lengthy and cumbersome. Sections 15 and 327 of the 1975 Act are now replaced by new sections, providing that all types of warrant granted by a justice may be executed throughout Scotland without the need for endorsement by any other justice.

Judicial examination

10.—(1) Section 20A of the 1975 Act (examination of accused by prosecutor before sheriff) shall be amended as follows.

(2) In subsection (1)—

(a) after the words "eliciting any" there shall be inserted "admission,"; and

(b) in paragraph (i) of the proviso to paragraph (a), for the words from "category" to the end there shall be substituted "defence".

(3) After subsection (3) there shall be inserted the following subsection—

"(3A) The accused shall be told by the sheriff that if he answers any question put to him at the examination under this section in such a way as to disclose an ostensible defence, the prosecutor shall be under the duty imposed by subsection (7) below.".

(4) After subsection (6) there shall be inserted the following subsections—

"(7) Without prejudice to any rule of law, on the conclusion of an examination under this section the prosecutor shall secure the investigation, to such extent as is reasonably practicable, of any ostensible defence disclosed in the course of the examination.

(8) The duty imposed by subsection (7) above shall not apply as respects any ostensible defence which is not reasonably capable of being investigated.".

GENERAL NOTE
The purpose and effect of this section is expressly to allow questions, directed towards eliciting an admission, to be asked of an accused person at judicial examination. Section 20A of the 1975 Act makes provision as to the questioning of an accused person during a first or further examination before a sheriff (judicial examination). Subsection (1) of s.20A of the 1975 Act in particular provides that a prosecutor may ask questions directed towards eliciting any denial, explanation, justification or comment which the accused may have as regards matters averred in the charge and certain other matters specified in that subsection. This has been interpreted, by some courts at least, as implying a prohibition on the prosecutor asking the accused questions which are designed to seek admissions. This section is designed to ensure that the prosecutor can ask such questions (see subs. (2)).

Lord Macaulay of Bragar saw this change as one that would transform the judicial examination "into an inquisitorial procedure which is inappropriate to the adversarial system we have" (*Hansard*, H.L. Vol. 560, col. 363). Lord McCluskey of Churchill, on the cross-benches, thought that the provision did not expand the powers of the Procurator Fiscal and that it did not invade any part of the right of silence. His Lordship reminded the House that judicial examination was conceived originally as being a means to allow an accused person to state a defence at the earliest opportunity and, if investigations proved that to be a sound defence, to avoid a public trial. While a Procurator Fiscal ought to investigate such defences as were stated, this was not always done. Lord McCluskey sought amendments designed to place a statutory duty on Procurators Fiscal to investigate as necessary. These amendments were withdrawn on the Lord Advocate agreeing to the principle but seeking time to consider the drafting (*Hansard*, H.L. Vol. 560, cols. 365–390).

This section also imposes a duty on prosecutors to secure the investigation, to such extent as is reasonably practicable, of any ostensible defence disclosed in the course of the examination (see subs. (4)). The duty imposed to investigate does not apply as respects any ostensible defence which is not reasonably capable of being investigated (subs. (5)). The sheriff at judicial examination is required to tell an accused of the prosecutor's duty to investigate any ostensible defence revealed by the accused's answers to the examination (subs. (3)).

Requirement to give notice of defence of automatism or coercion

11. After subsection (1) of section 82 of the 1975 Act (requirement to give notice of plea of special defence, etc.) there shall be inserted the following subsection—
"(1A) Subsection (1) above shall apply to a defence of automatism or coercion as if it were a special defence.".

GENERAL NOTE
The genesis of part of this amendment is the case of *Ross v. H.M. Advocate* 1991 S.L.T. 564, in which it was held that automatism could in particular circumstances constitute a defence. A majority of the judges expressed the view that pre-trial notice of the defence should be required. Section 149A of the 1975 Act allows a trial judge to permit the Crown to lead further evidence in the light of defence evidence or argument which could not have been anticipated. However, as was recognised by the Lord Justice General in the *Ross* case, replication can be a somewhat unsatisfactory and inconvenient solution. The view was expressed in *Ross* that it would be preferable to make the defence of automatism one of the special defences (such as coercion) that require prior notification, presumably because of the manner in which it arises.

Agreement of evidence

12.—(1) After section 84 of the 1975 Act there shall be inserted the following section—

"**Agreement of evidence**
84A.—(1) Subject to subsection (2) below, the prosecutor and the accused (or each accused if more than one) shall each identify any facts which are facts—
    (a) which he would, apart from this section, be seeking to prove;
    (b) which he considers unlikely to be disputed by the other party (or by any of the other parties); and
    (c) in proof of which he does not wish to lead oral evidence,
and shall (without prejudice to section 16 of the Criminal Justice (Scotland) Act 1995 (procedure for proving uncontroversial evidence)) take all reasonable steps to secure the agreement of the other party (or each of the other parties) to them; and the other party (or each of the other parties) shall take all reasonable steps to reach such agreement.
(2) Subsection (1) above shall not apply in relation to proceedings as respects which the accused (or any of the accused if more than one) is not legally represented.
(3) The duty under subsection (1) above applies from the date of service of the indictment until the swearing of the jury or, where intimation is given under section 102 of this Act, the date of that intimation.".
(2) After section 333A of that Act there shall be inserted the following section—

"**Agreement of evidence**
333B.—(1) Subject to subsection (2) below, the prosecutor and the accused (or each accused if more than one) shall each identify any facts which are facts—

(a) which he would, apart from this section, be seeking to prove;
(b) which he considers unlikely to be disputed by the other party (or by any of the other parties); and
(c) in proof of which he does not wish to lead oral evidence,
and shall (without prejudice to section 16 of the Criminal Justice (Scotland) Act 1995 (procedure for proving uncontroversial evidence)) take all reasonable steps to secure the agreement of the other party (or each of the other parties) to them; and the other party (or each of the other parties) shall take all reasonable steps to reach such agreement.

(2) Subsection (1) above shall not apply in relation to proceedings as respects which the accused (or any of the accused if more than one) is not legally represented.

(3) The duty under subsection (1) above applies from the date on which the accused pleads not guilty until the swearing of the first witness or, where the accused tenders a plea of guilty at any time before the first witness is sworn, the date when he does so.".

DEFINITIONS
"accused": s.114(1).
"prosecutor": s.462 of the Criminal Procedure (Scotland) Act 1975.

GENERAL NOTE
This section requires the prosecutor and, where he is legally represented, the accused to identify factual matters which may be capable of agreement and to take all reasonable steps to agree those matters before the trial. Sections 150 and 154 of the 1975 Act provide for admissions and agreement of evidence by the parties. Section 16 of this Act, below, provides for parties to agree uncontroversial evidence by a statement of facts. The collective purpose of these provisions is to allow uncontroversial evidence to be led without the necessity of witnesses attending court and giving evidence orally.

At present there is no onus on any party to agree uncontroversial evidence, nor even to address the possibility of doing so. The duty imposed by this section strengthens the authority of the courts in enquiring, during preliminary procedures, as to the efforts which have been made to agree evidence. The purpose of this duty is to ensure that parties give due consideration to the agreement of evidence. The duty would apply to the accused only while he is legally represented.

This section operates by creating two new sections which apply in the case of solemn and summary procedure (ss.84A and 333B respectively). The period for which the duty applies depends on the procedure being followed. It would apply, in solemn cases, from the date of service of the indictment until the swearing of the jury, or until intimation of a plea of guilty is made under s.102 of the 1975 Act. The duty to seek agreement in summary cases runs from the date on which the accused pleads not guilty until the swearing of the first witness, or, if the accused pleads guilty, until the date when he does so.

First and preliminary diets in solemn proceedings

13.—(1) In section 75 of the 1975 Act (notice of trial diet), after the word "at" there shall be inserted—
"(a) where the case is to be tried in the sheriff court, a first diet not less than 15 clear days after the service of the indictment and not less than 10 clear days before the trial diet; and
(b)"
(2) After section 75 of that Act there shall be inserted the following section—

"First diet
75A.—(1) At a first diet the court shall, so far as is reasonably practicable, ascertain whether the case is likely to proceed to trial on the date assigned as the trial diet and, in particular—
(a) the state of preparation of the prosecutor and of the accused with respect to their cases; and

    (b) the extent to which the prosecutor and the accused have complied with the duty under section 84A(1) of this Act.

    (2) In addition to the matters mentioned in subsection (1) above the court shall, at a first diet, consider any matter mentioned in subsection (3) below of which a party has, not less than two clear days before the first diet, given notice to the court and to the other parties.

    (3) The matters referred to in subsection (2) above are—

    (a) that the party intends to raise a matter relating to the competency or relevancy of the indictment or to raise an objection such as is mentioned in section 108(1) of this Act;

    (b) that he intends to submit a plea in bar of trial or to apply for separation or conjunction of charges or trials or to raise a preliminary objection under section 67 of this Act or to make an application under section 151(2) of this Act;

    (c) that there are documents the truth of the contents of which ought in his view to be admitted, or that there is any other matter which in his view ought to be agreed; and

    (d) that there is some other matter which could in his opinion be resolved with advantage before the trial.

    (4) At a first diet the court may ask the prosecutor and the accused any question in connection with any matter which it is required to ascertain or consider under subsection (1) or (2) above.

    (5) The accused shall attend a first diet of which he has been given notice and the court may, if he fails to do so, grant a warrant to apprehend him.

    (6) A first diet may proceed notwithstanding the absence of the accused.

    (7) The accused shall, at the first diet, be required to state how he pleads to the indictment, and section 103 of this Act shall apply where he tenders a plea of guilty.

    (8) Where at a first diet the court concludes that the case is unlikely to proceed to trial on the date assigned for the trial diet, the court—

    (a) shall, unless having regard to previous proceedings in the case it considers it inappropriate to do so, postpone the trial diet; and

    (b) may fix a further first diet.

    (9) Subject to subsection (8) above, the court may, if it considers it appropriate to do so, adjourn a first diet.

    (10) In this section "the court" means the sheriff court.".

(3) In section 76 of that Act (preliminary diet)—

(a) in subsection (1)—

    (i) after the words "where a party" there shall be inserted "to a case which is to be tried in the High Court"; and

    (ii) for the words "court before which the trial is to take place" there shall be substituted "High Court"; and

(b) after subsection (6) there shall be inserted the following subsections—

"(6A) At a preliminary diet the court shall, in addition to disposing of any matter specified in a notice given under subsection (1) above or referred to in subsection (3) above, ascertain, so far as is reasonably practicable, whether the case is likely to proceed to trial on the date assigned as the trial diet and, in particular—

    (a) the state of preparation of the prosecutor and of the accused with respect to their cases; and

    (b) the extent to which the prosecutor and the accused have complied with the duty under section 84A(1) of this Act.

(6B) At a preliminary diet the court may ask the prosecutor and the accused any question in connection with any matter specified in a notice under subsection (1) above or referred to in subsection (3) above or which it is required to ascertain under subsection (6A) above.

(6C) Where at a preliminary diet the court concludes that the case is unlikely to proceed to trial on the date assigned for the trial diet, the court—

(a) shall, unless having regard to previous proceedings in the case it considers it inappropriate to do so, postpone the trial diet; and

(b) may fix a further preliminary diet.

(6D) Subject to subsection (6C) above, the court may, if it considers it appropriate to do so, adjourn a preliminary diet.".

(4) In section 76A(1) of that Act (appeal in connection with preliminary diet), for the words "preliminary diet" there shall be substituted "first diet or a preliminary diet, other than a decision to adjourn the diet or to postpone the trial diet".

DEFINITIONS

"accused": s.114(1).

"prosecutor": s.462 of the Criminal Procedure (Scotland) Act 1975.

GENERAL NOTE

This section introduces mandatory first diets for sheriff and jury cases, and confines preliminary diets to cases to be heard in the High Court. The purposes of a preliminary diet are widened.

In solemn procedure, at present, preliminary diets are called, on notice given by either party, in sheriff courts or the High Court, for purposes which are defined in s.76 of the 1975 Act, as amended by s.39 of the 1993 Act. These purposes are: to raise a matter relating to the competency or relevancy of the indictment or to raise an objection such as is mentioned in s.108(1) of the 1975 Act (objections to validity of citation etc.); to submit a plea in bar of trial or to apply for separation or conjunction of the charges or to raise a preliminary objection under s.67 of the 1975 Act (offence committed in special capacity) or to make an application under s.151(2) of the 1975 Act (refusal to allow record of judicial examination to be heard); to raise a matter relating to the truth of the content of proposed documentary evidence; or to raise any other matter which could be resolved with advantage before the trial.

The provision of mandatory first diets in sheriff courts is intended to reduce the incidence of the unforeseen cancellation and adjournment of trials, by identifying cases which are unlikely to go to trial on the date programmed. In the High Court, programming a preliminary diet in every case would be difficult, but the provisions of this section permit preliminary diets to fulfill the same additional purposes created for the new first diets.

Subsection (1) amends s.75 of the 1975 Act. It introduces the new "first diet" as a mandatory diet in the sheriff court to be held not less than 15 clear days after service of the indictment and not less than 10 clear days before the trial.

Subsection (2) inserts a new s.75A (First diet) into the 1975 Act, detailing the purposes of, and procedure to be followed at, a first diet. The sheriff is required to ascertain whether the case is likely to proceed to trial on the date assigned as the trial diet, having particular regard to the state of preparation of the prosecutor and the accused, and the extent to which they have complied with the new duty to seek agreement of evidence under s.84A(1) of the 1975 Act (created by s.12 of this Act). Under s.75A(2), the court is required, at a first diet, to consider any matter specified in subs. (3) of which notice has been given two clear days prior to the first diet. These are all matters which may under current law be the subject of a preliminary diet. The sheriff court may ask the prosecutor and the accused any question in connection with any of the matters to be ascertained or considered under subss. (1) or (2) (see s.74A(4)).

Subsection (3) amends s.76(1) of the 1975 Act to confine preliminary diets to cases heard in the High Court and inserts new subsections which give the court powers and duties similar to those of the sheriff court in the case of a first diet.

Subsection (4) extends s.76A(1) of the 1975 Act (appeal in connection with preliminary diet) to cover first diets and provides that there shall be no appeal against a decision to adjourn the first or preliminary diet or discharge the trial diet.

Intermediate diet in summary proceedings

14.—(1) Section 337A of the 1975 Act (intermediate diet) shall be amended as follows.

(2) In subsection (1)—

(a) after the word "ascertaining" there shall be inserted ", so far as is reasonably practicable, whether the case is likely to proceed to trial on the date assigned as the trial diet and, in particular";

(b) the word "and" immediately following paragraph (a) shall cease to have effect; and

(c) after paragraph (b) there shall be inserted—

"; and

(c) the extent to which the prosecutor and the accused have complied with the duty under section 333B(1) of this Act.".

(3) After subsection (1) there shall be inserted the following subsections—

"(1A) Where at an intermediate diet the court concludes that the case is unlikely to proceed to trial on the date assigned for the trial diet, the court—

(a) shall, unless having regard to previous proceedings in the case it considers it inappropriate to do so, postpone the trial diet; and

(b) may fix a further intermediate diet.

(1B) Subject to subsection (1A) above, the court may, if it considers it appropriate to do so, adjourn an intermediate diet.".

(4) At the end of subsection (3) there shall be inserted—

"unless—

(a) he is legally represented; and

(b) the court considers that there are exceptional circumstances justifying him not attending.

(4) The foregoing provisions of this section shall have effect as respects any court prescribed by the Secretary of State by order, in relation to proceedings commenced after such date as may be so prescribed, with the following modifications—

(a) in subsection (1), for the word "may" there shall be substituted "shall, subject to subsection (1C) below,"; and

(b) after subsection (1B) there shall be inserted the following subsections—

"(1C) If, on a joint application by the prosecutor and the accused made at any time before the commencement of the intermediate diet, the court considers it inappropriate to have such a diet, the duty under subsection (1) above shall not apply and the court shall discharge any such diet already fixed.

(1D) The court may consider an application under subsection (1C) above without hearing the parties.".

(5) An order under subsection (5) above shall be made by statutory instrument, which shall be subject to annulment in pursuance of a resolution of either House of Parliament.".

DEFINITIONS

"accused": s.114(1).

"prosecutor": s.462 of the Criminal Procedure (Scotland) Act 1975.

GENERAL NOTE

This section makes mandatory the existing intermediate diet procedure in summary proceedings, extends the purposes for which such diets are held, and makes new provision as to attendance at such diets and as to the powers and duties of the court at such diets. Section 337A of the 1975 Act makes provision for intermediate diets in summary cases. Such a diet can be set by the court at any time while the case is adjourned for trial. The purpose of such a diet is to ascertain the state of preparation of the prosecutor and the accused, and whether the accused intends to adhere to his plea of not guilty. Such a diet was introduced, in 1990, because a large proportion of trials set down do not proceed to trial on the date assigned, causing inconvenience to victims, witnesses and jurors, and avoidable waste of valuable court resources.

Subsection (2) amends s.337A(1) of the 1975 Act to make the intermediate diet a mandatory hearing, with one exception detailed below. This subsection also redefines the purpose of this diet. The court will be required to address the broader purpose of ascertaining whether the case is likely to proceed to trial on the date assigned as the trial diet, having particular regard to the matters which have to be ascertained at an intermediate diet under the present provision as well as the extent to which the parties have complied with the proposed new duty to agree evidence (see s.12 of this Act, above).

This section also inserts four new subsections into s.337A of the 1975 Act. The new subs. (1A) imposes a new duty on the court. Where the court concludes that the case is unlikely to proceed to trial on the date assigned it must discharge the trial diet unless, having regard to previous proceedings in the case, it considers it inappropriate to do so. If the trial diet is discharged the court may fix a new intermediate diet. Subsection (1B) allows the court to adjourn an intermediate diet. This power is subject to the duty imposed by subs. (1A). The new subs. (1C) makes provision for the court to dispense with an intermediate diet where there is a joint application by the parties to do so and the court considers it inappropriate in that case to hold such a diet. Subsection (1D) permits the court to consider an application under subs. (1C) without hearing the parties.

Subsection (4) also amends s.337A(3) which requires the accused to be present at an intermediate diet. In particular, the amendment will allow the accused not to attend, if the accused is legally represented and the court considers that there are exceptional circumstances justifying his non-attendance.

Delay in trial

Calculation of specified period where accused detained outside Scotland

15. In section 101 of the 1975 Act (prevention of delay in trials), after subsection (1) there shall be inserted the following subsection—

"(1A) In calculating the period of 12 months specified in subsection (1) above there shall be left out of account any period during which the accused is detained, other than while serving a sentence of imprisonment or detention, in any other part of the United Kingdom or in any of the Channel Islands or the Isle of Man in any prison or other institution or place mentioned in subsection (1) or (1A) of section 29 of the Criminal Justice Act 1961 (transfer of prisoners for certain judicial purposes).".

GENERAL NOTE

A number of appeals have arisen in relation to s.101(1) and (5) of the 1975 Act in recent years: *Lyle v. H.M. Advocate* 1992 S.L.T. 467, *Ferguson v. H.M. Advocate* 1992 S.C.C.R. 480 and *Stewart v. H.M. Advocate* 1994 S.L.T. 518, all of which involve error on the part of the prosecutor. In *Duffy v. H.M. Advocate* 1991 S.C.C.R. 685 circumstances were said to involve fault on the part of the Crown, although that was not held to be so by the court. In *Fleming v. H.M. Advocate* 1992 S.C.C.R. 575 the High Court declined to interfere with the exercise of a discretion of a sheriff, especially where the extension of time had been restricted. Fault on the part of the police is not fault on the part of the Crown: *H.M. Advocate v. Davies* 1993 S.C.C.R. 645.

However, in *H.M. Advocate v. Rowan* 1995 S.L.T. 434, the High Court of Justiciary in its appellate capacity considered a Crown appeal against a refusal of an application to extend further the 12-month period within which R could be brought to trial on the charge of fraud. The application had been made in terms of s.101(1) and (5) of the 1975 Act. R was in custody in England on other matters, and the English authorities had no authority to transfer R to Scotland. The Crown appeal was allowed and an extension granted. The Court observed that the reform of the law was urgently needed to avoid the risk of injustice due to delay. This section follows that judicial suggestion and allows for a discounting of time spent in detention elsewhere in the United Kingdom, or in any of the Channel Islands or the Isle of Man. This section is the result of an amendment at the Report Stage (*Hansard*, H.L. Vol. 561, col. 39).

Evidence

Uncontroversial evidence

16.—(1) This section applies where, in any criminal proceedings, a party (in this section referred to as "the first party") considers that facts which that party would otherwise be seeking to prove are unlikely to be disputed by the other parties to the proceedings.

(2) Where this section applies, the first party may prepare and sign a statement—

(a) specifying the facts concerned; or

(b) referring to such facts as set out in a document annexed to the statement, and shall, not less than 14 days before the trial diet, serve a copy of the statement and any such document on every other party.

(3) Unless any other party serves on the first party, not more than seven days after the date of service of the copy on him under subsection (2) above or by such later time as the court may in special circumstances allow, a notice that he challenges any fact specified or referred to in the statement, the facts so specified or referred to shall be deemed to have been conclusively proved.

(4) Where a notice is served under subsection (3) above, the facts specified or referred to in the statement shall be deemed to have been conclusively proved only in so far as unchallenged in the notice.

(5) Subsections (3) and (4) above shall not preclude a party from leading evidence of circumstances relevant to, or other evidence in explanation of, any fact specified or referred to in the statement.

(6) Notwithstanding subsections (3) and (4) above, the court—
(a) may, on the application of any party, where it is satisfied that there are special circumstances; and
(b) shall, on the joint application of all the parties,
direct that the presumptions in those subsections shall not apply in relation to such fact specified or referred to in the statement as is specified in the direction.

(7) An application under subsection (6) above may be made at any time after the commencement of the trial and before the commencement of the prosecutor's address to the court on the evidence.

(8) Where the court makes a direction under subsection (6) above it shall, unless all the parties otherwise agree, adjourn the trial and may, without prejudice to sections 149 and 350 of the 1975 Act, permit any party to lead evidence as to any such fact as is specified in the direction, notwithstanding that a witness or production concerned is not included in any list lodged by the parties and that the notice required by sections 81 and 82(2) of that Act has not been given.

(9) A copy of a statement or a notice required, under this section, to be served on any party shall be served in such manner as may be prescribed by Act of Adjournal; and a written execution purporting to be signed by the person who served such copy or notice together with, where appropriate, the relevant post office receipt shall be sufficient evidence of such service.

DEFINITIONS
"prosecutor": s.462 of the Criminal Procedure (Scotland) Act 1975.

GENERAL NOTE
This section introduces a new procedure for agreeing facts in advance of trial by service of a statement of facts which the serving party considers to be unlikely to be disputed. Unless the party on whom the statement of facts is served gives notice within the prescribed time that those facts are disputed, then the facts in the notice will be deemed to be sufficiently proved.

When the parties to criminal proceedings are able to agree facts in advance of a trial, they are able, under ss.150 and 354 of the 1975 Act, to enter into a joint minute of agreement and the facts covered by that agreement need not then be proved at the subsequent trial. The Scottish Law Commission in their Report No. 137 *Evidence: Report on Documentary Evidence and Proof of Undisputed Facts in Criminal Proceedings* suggested the introduction of a new procedure which would be available only to the prosecution.

Under this procedure the prosecutor could specify facts which he considered to be uncontroversial in a statement of facts which would be served on the defence in advance of trial and, in the absence of a timeous counter-notice, the facts contained in the statement would not require to be proved at the subsequent trial. This new procedure, it was considered, would provide a useful additional means of agreeing evidence in advance of trial in circumstances in which the existing certificate evidence and minute of agreement provisions would not be suitable. This section implements the Scottish Law Commission's recommendations with one or two minor amendments, and makes the procedure available to both prosecution and defence.

Exceptions to the rule that hearsay evidence is inadmissible

17.—(1) Subject to the following provisions of this section, evidence of a statement made by a person otherwise than while giving oral evidence in court in criminal proceedings shall be admissible in those proceedings as evidence of any matter contained in the statement where the judge is satisfied—
- (a) that the person who made the statement will not give evidence in the proceedings of such matter for any of the reasons mentioned in subsection (2) below;
- (b) that evidence of the matter would be admissible in the proceedings if that person gave direct oral evidence of it;
- (c) that the person who made the statement would have been, at the time the statement was made, a competent witness in such proceedings; and
- (d) that there is evidence which would entitle a jury properly directed, or in summary proceedings would entitle the judge, to find that the statement was made and that either—
    - (i) it is contained in a document; or
    - (ii) a person who gave oral evidence in the proceedings as to the statement has direct personal knowledge of the making of the statement.

(2) The reasons referred to in paragraph (a) of subsection (1) above are that the person who made the statement—
- (a) is dead or is, by reason of his bodily or mental condition, unfit or unable to give evidence in any competent manner;
- (b) is named and otherwise sufficiently identified, but is outwith the United Kingdom and it is not reasonably practicable to secure his attendance at the trial or to obtain his evidence in any other competent manner;
- (c) is named and otherwise sufficiently identified, but cannot be found and all reasonable steps which, in the circumstances, could have been taken to find him have been so taken;
- (d) having been authorised to do so by virtue of a ruling of the court in the proceedings that he is entitled to refuse to give evidence in connection with the subject matter of the statement on the grounds that such evidence might incriminate him, refuses to give such evidence; or
- (e) is called as a witness and either—
    - (i) refuses to take the oath or affirmation; or
    - (ii) having been sworn as a witness and directed by the judge to give evidence in connection with the subject matter of the statement refuses to do so,

    and in the application of this paragraph to a child, the reference to a witness refusing to take the oath or affirmation or, as the case may be, to having been sworn shall be construed as a reference to a child who has refused to accept an admonition to tell the truth or, having been so admonished, refuses to give evidence as mentioned above.

(3) Evidence of a statement shall not be admissible by virtue of subsection (1) above where the judge is satisfied that the occurrence of any of the circumstances mentioned in paragraphs (a) to (e) of subsection (2) above, by virtue of which the statement would otherwise be admissible, is caused by—
- (a) the person in support of whose case the evidence would be given; or
- (b) any other person acting on his behalf,

for the purpose of securing that the person who made the statement does not give evidence for the purposes of the proceedings either at all or in connection with the subject matter of the statement.

(4) Where in any proceedings evidence of a statement made by any person is admitted by reference to any of the reasons mentioned in paragraphs (a) to (c) and (e)(i) of subsection (2) above—

(a) any evidence which, if that person had given evidence in connection with the subject matter of the statement, would have been admissible as relevant to his credibility as a witness shall be admissible for that purpose in those proceedings;

(b) evidence may be given of any matter which, if that person had given evidence in connection with the subject matter of the statement, could have been put to him in cross-examination as relevant to his credibility as a witness but of which evidence could not have been adduced by the cross-examining party; and

(c) evidence tending to prove that that person, whether before or after making the statement, made in whatever manner some other statement which is inconsistent with it shall be admissible for the purpose of showing that he has contradicted himself.

(5) Subject to subsection (6) below, where a party intends to apply to have evidence of a statement admitted by virtue of subsection (1) above he shall, before the trial diet, give notice in writing of—

(a) that fact;

(b) the witnesses and productions to be adduced in connection with such evidence; and

(c) such other matters as may be prescribed by Act of Adjournal,

to every other party to the proceedings and, for the purposes of this subsection, such evidence may be led notwithstanding that a witness or production concerned is not included in any list lodged by the parties and that the notice required by sections 81 and 82(2) of the 1975 Act has not been given.

(6) A party shall not be required to give notice as mentioned in subsection (5) above where—

(a) the grounds for seeking to have evidence of a statement admitted are as mentioned in paragraph (d) or (e) of subsection (2) above; or

(b) he satisfies the judge that there was good reason for not giving such notice.

(7) If no other party to the proceedings objects to the admission of evidence of a statement by virtue subsection (1) above, the evidence shall be admitted without the judge requiring to be satisfied as mentioned in that subsection.

(8) For the purposes of the determination of any matter upon which the judge is required to be satisfied under subsection (1) above—

(a) except to the extent that any other party to the proceedings challenges them and insists in such challenge, it shall be presumed that the circumstances are as stated by the party seeking to introduce evidence of the statement; and

(b) where such a challenge is insisted in, the judge shall determine the matter on the balance of probabilities, and he may draw any reasonable inference—

(i) from the circumstances in which the statement was made or otherwise came into being; or

(ii) from any other circumstances, including, where the statement is contained in a document, the form and contents of the document.

(9) Where evidence of a statement has been admitted by virtue of subsection (1) above on the application of one party to the proceedings, without prejudice to anything in any enactment or rule of law, the judge may permit any party to lead additional evidence of such description as the judge may specify, notwithstanding that a witness or production concerned is not included in any list lodged by the parties and that the notice required by sections 81 and 82(2) of the 1975 Act has not been given.

(10) Any reference in subsections (5), (6) and (9) above to evidence shall include a reference to evidence led in connection with any determination required to be made for the purposes of subsection (1) above.

DEFINITIONS
    "criminal proceedings": s.20(3).
    "document": s.20(3).
    "film": s.20(3).
    "made": s.20(3).
    "statement": s.20(1).

GENERAL NOTE

This section was introduced, along with the next three sections, at the Lords' consideration of Commons amendments. The Lord Advocate explained that the Scottish Law Commission had reported on the use of hearsay evidence in criminal proceedings and that there was anxiety at the difficulty that arose from *Perrie v. H.M. Advocate* 1991 S.C.C.R. 255 and *McLay v. H.M. Advocate* 1994 S.C.C.R. 397 where, under the law then existing, it had not been possible to lead evidence of an admission by an incriminee (*Hansard*, H.L. Vol. 565, col. 1157).

The final form of this section represents what the Lord Advocate described as "a matter of balance". It is not a simple reproduction of the Scottish Law Commission recommendations, as procedural aspects have been considered afresh. However, this section follows broadly cl. 1 of the draft Bill in S.L.C. Report (149) and recommendations 3 to 12, 14 and 15.

In essence, subs. (1) provides that hearsay in criminal proceedings shall be admissible if the judge is satisfied that the maker of the statement is unavailable for any of the reasons set out in subs. (2), that the evidence would be admissible if the person was available, that the person would have been a competent witness and that there is documentary or oral evidence to the effect that a statement has been made. Subsection (2) provides that the types of witness unavailability which allow hearsay include death or incapacity, absence abroad, disappearance, a refusal to give evidence on the grounds of self-incrimination and a refusal to take the oath or affirm or refusal to give evidence.

The remaining subsections provide, *inter alia*, that anyone causing the unavailability of a witness cannot call hearsay (subs. (3)), that where hearsay evidence is heard, evidence of the maker's credibility or inconsistency is allowed (subs. (4)), and that, while notice in writing of such hearsay evidence must be given (subs. (5)), notice is not required on cause shown (subs. (6)) or if there is no objection (subs. (7)).

Admissibility of prior statements of witnesses

18.—(1) Subject to the following provisions of this section, where a witness gives evidence in criminal proceedings, any prior statement made by the witness shall be admissible as evidence of any matter stated in it of which direct oral evidence by him would be admissible if given in the course of those proceedings.

(2) A prior statement shall not be admissible under this section unless—
   (a) the statement is contained in a document;
   (b) the witness, in the course of giving evidence, indicates that the statement was made by him and that he adopts it as his evidence; and
   (c) at the time the statement was made, the person who made it would have been a competent witness in the proceedings.

(3) For the purposes of this section, any reference to a prior statement is a reference to a prior statement which, but for the provisions of this section, would not be admissible as evidence of any matter stated in it.

(4) Subsections (2) and (3) above do not apply to a prior statement—
   (a) contained in a precognition on oath; or
   (b) made in other proceedings, whether criminal or civil and whether taking place in the United Kingdom or elsewhere,
and, for the purposes of this section, any such statement shall not be admissible unless it is sufficiently authenticated.

DEFINITIONS
    "criminal proceedings": s.20(3).
    "document": s.20(3).
    "film": s.20(3).

"made": s.20(3).
"statement": s.20(1).

GENERAL NOTE

This section permits the introduction of prior statements by a witness in criminal proceedings, as evidence of any matter stated therein of which direct oral evidence by him would be admissible if given in the course of those proceedings. This section, which has constraints in subss. (2), (3) and (4), follows broadly cl. 2 of the draft Bill in S.L.C. Report (149) and Recommendations 16 to 18. The section is heavily influenced also by the decision of the High Court of Justiciary in *Jamieson v. H.M. Advocate* 1994 S.L.T. 537.

Statements by accused

19.—(1) Subject to the following provisions of this section, nothing in sections 17 and 18 of this Act shall apply to a statement made by the accused.

(2) Evidence of a statement made by an accused shall be admissible by virtue of the said section 17 at the instance of another accused in the same proceedings as evidence in relation to that other accused.

(3) For the purposes of subsection (2) above, the first mentioned accused shall be deemed—

(a) where he does not give evidence in the proceedings, to be a witness refusing to give evidence in connection with the subject matter of the statement as mentioned in paragraph (e) of subsection (2) of the said section 17; and

(b) to have been, at the time the statement was made, a competent witness in the proceedings.

(4) Evidence of a statement shall not be admissible as mentioned in subsection (2) above unless the accused at whose instance it is sought to be admitted has given notice of his intention to do so as mentioned in subsection (5) of the said section 17; but subsection (6) of that section shall not apply in the case of notice required to be given by virtue of this subsection.

DEFINITIONS

"accused": s.114(1).
"criminal proceedings": s.20(3).
"document": s.20(3).
"made": s.20(3).
"statement": s.20(1).

GENERAL NOTE

This section excludes a statement made by the accused from the provisions of ss.17 and 18 of this Act. The section follows, in some detail, cl. 3(6) of the draft Bill in S.L.C. Report (149) and Recommendation 11. Note that the statements of an accused may become admissible against that accused, by virtue of s.17, where introduced by another accused in the same proceedings (subs. (2)).

Construction of sections 17, 18 and 19

20.—(1) For the purposes of sections 17, 18 and 19 of this Act, a "statement" includes—

(a) any representation, however made or expressed, of fact or opinion; and

(b) any part of a statement,

but does not include a statement in a precognition other than a precognition on oath.

(2) For the purposes of the said sections 17, 18 and 19 a statement is contained in a document where the person who makes it—

(a) makes the statement in the document personally;

(b) makes a statement which is, with or without his knowledge, embodied in a document by whatever means or by any person who has direct personal knowledge of the making of the statement; or

(c) approves a document as embodying the statement.

(3) In the said sections 17, 18 and 19—
"criminal proceedings" include any hearing by the sheriff under section 42 of the Social Work (Scotland) Act 1968 of an application for a finding as to whether grounds for the referral of a child's case to a children's hearing are established, in so far as the application relates to the commission of an offence by the child;
"document" includes, in addition to a document in writing—
    (a) any map, plan, graph or drawing;
    (b) any photograph;
    (c) any disc, tape, sound track or other device in which sounds or other data (not being visual images) are recorded so as to be capable (with or without the aid of some other equipment) of being reproduced therefrom; and
    (d) any film, negative, tape, disc or other device in which one or more visual images are recorded so as to be capable (as aforesaid) of being reproduced therefrom;
"film" includes a microfilm;
"made" includes allegedly made.
(4) Nothing in the said sections 17, 18 and 19 shall prejudice the admissibility of a statement made by a person other than in the course of giving oral evidence in court which is admissible otherwise than by virtue of those sections.
(5) Nothing in the said sections 17, 18 and 19 shall apply to—
    (a) proceedings commenced; or
    (b) where the proceedings consist of an application to the sheriff by virtue of section 42(2)(c) of the Social Work (Scotland) Act 1968, an application made,
before those sections come into force; and for the purposes of paragraph (a) above, solemn proceedings are commenced when the indictment is served.

GENERAL NOTE
This section makes provision for the construction of ss.17, 18 and 19 of this Act. The section follows parts of cl. 3 of the draft Bill in S.L.C. Report (149) and recommendations 1, 2, 11 and 21. By subs. (4) this section does not prejudice any other rule allowing admissibility of statements in the course of giving oral evidence in court: see for example s.147 of the 1975 Act.

Evidence of biological material

21.—(1) Evidence as to the characteristics and composition of any biological material deriving from human beings or animals shall, in any criminal proceedings, be admissible notwithstanding that neither the material nor a sample of it is lodged as a production.
(2) A party wishing to lead such evidence as is referred to in subsection (1) above shall, where neither the material nor a sample of it is lodged as a production, make the material or a sample of it available for inspection by the other party unless the material constitutes a hazard to health or has been destroyed in the process of analysis.

GENERAL NOTE
This section dispenses with the need to produce in court certain biological material in respect of which evidence is led. This is essentially a matter of public health. This section constitutes an exception to the authority that allows an accused to see productions: see s.28 of the 1975 Act.

Routine evidence

22.—(1) Section 26 of and Schedule 1 to the Criminal Justice (Scotland) Act 1980 (routine evidence) shall be amended as follows.

(2) After subsection (1) there shall be inserted the following subsections—

"(1A) The Secretary of State may by order—

(a) amend or repeal the entry in Schedule 1 to this Act in respect of any enactment; or

(b) insert in that Schedule an entry in respect of a further enactment.

(1B) An order under subsection (1A) above may make such transitional, incidental or supplementary provision as the Secretary of State considers necessary or expedient in connection with the coming into force of the order.".

(3) In subsection (2), the word "summary" and the words from "In the foregoing" to the end of the subsection shall cease to have effect.

(4) After that subsection there shall be inserted the following subsection—

"(2A) A forensic scientist is authorised for the purposes of subsection (2) above if—

(a) he is authorised for those purposes by the Secretary of State; or

(b) he—

(i) is a constable or is employed by a police authority under section 9 of the Police (Scotland) Act 1967;

(ii) possesses such qualifications and experience as the Secretary of State may for the purposes of that subsection by order prescribe; and

(iii) is authorised for those purposes by the chief constable of the police force maintained for the police area of that authority.".

(5) In subsection (3)—

(a) for the words "the prosecution" there shall be substituted "the prosecutor or the accused";

(b) in paragraph (a)—

(i) for the words "accused" there shall be substituted "other party"; and

(ii) for the word "his" there shall be substituted "the"; and

(c) in paragraph (b)—

(i) for the word "accused" where it first occurs there shall be substituted "other party";

(ii) for the words from "less" to "trial" in the second place where it occurs there shall be substituted "more than seven days after the date of service of the copy on him under paragraph (a) above or by such later time"; and

(iii) for the words "prosecutor that the accused" there shall be substituted "first party that he".

(6) In subsection (4), after the word "accused" where it first occurs there shall be inserted "or the prosecutor".

(7) After subsection (4) there shall be inserted the following subsection—

"(4A) Where, following service of a notice under subsection (3)(b) above, evidence is given in relation to a report referred to in subsection (2) above by both of the forensic scientists purporting to have signed the report, the evidence of those forensic scientists shall be sufficient evidence of any fact (or conclusion as to fact) contained in the report.".

(8) In subsection (5), the words "under summary procedure" shall cease to have effect.

(9) After subsection (7) there shall be inserted the following subsections—

"(7A) Where, following service of a notice by the accused under subsection (7) above, evidence is given in relation to an autopsy or forensic science report by both of the pathologists or forensic scientists purporting to have signed the report, the evidence of those pathologists or forensic scientists shall be sufficient evidence of any fact (or conclusion as to fact) contained in the report.

(7B) An order made under subsection (1A) or (2A)(b)(ii) above shall be made by statutory instrument.

(7C) No order shall be made under subsection (1A) above unless a draft of the order has been laid before, and approved by a resolution of, each House of Parliament.

(7D) A statutory instrument containing an order under subsection (2A)(b)(ii) above shall be subject to annulment pursuant to a resolution of either House of Parliament.".

(10) Schedule 1 shall be amended in accordance with Schedule 1 to this Act.

GENERAL NOTE

This section makes amendments to s.26 of the 1980 Act, which is concerned with the service of certificates which are the means by which matters which are unlikely to be disputed can be agreed in advance of trial, thereby reducing the need for witnesses to attend court to speak to matters which are uncontroversial.

Section 26 has been the subject of interest in recent years with challenges to certificates: see *Normand v. Wotherspoon* 1993 S.C.C.R. 912; *Straker v. Orr* 1994 S.C.C.R. 251; *McCrindle v. Walkingham* 1994 S.C.C.R. 299 and *O'Brien v. McCreadie* 1994 S.C.C.R. 516.

One characteristic of most of the procedures contained in s.26 is that the prosecution is required, in advance of the trial, to serve on the defence a copy of the certificate or report containing the facts which it is considered may be agreed. If the defence does not notify the prosecution that it does not accept the facts within the prescribed time, those facts need not then be proved at the subsequent trial. This procedure has been found to work well in enabling routine matters to be agreed in advance of trial, leaving the court free to focus on the issues which remain in contention between the parties at the trial. Not all the procedures are available on an equal basis to both the prosecution and defence in both solemn and summary proceedings. It was considered that the procedures available under s.26 should be more widely available. This section extends these procedures to all criminal proceedings and makes them available to both prosecution and defence on an equal basis.

The section makes various other provisions which are also intended to reduce unnecessary attendance of witnesses at court. The Secretary of State may add to the list of matters which may be introduced into evidence by certificate by subordinate legislation. This will enable suitable matters to be added to the list as they are identified, without the need to wait for a suitable opportunity to add to the list by primary legislation.

Another matter covered by this section is the evidential status of facts contained in a report by a forensic scientist or pathologist and subsequently spoken to in court during the course of oral evidence given by the forensic scientist or pathologist. This section puts it beyond doubt that the facts and conclusions as to facts spoken to either in the report or in the subsequent oral evidence based on the report are sufficient for the purpose of proving those facts. This does not prevent the evidence from being attacked on the grounds of credibility or unreliability. It does, however, mean that in the absence of such an attack the party leading the evidence will not require to prove the facts by other means.

If a forensic scientist is authorised, he can present evidence to a court in written form, without having to speak to it. This is an efficient and cost-effective way of operating. Scientists can only be authorised by the Secretary of State, and only if their qualifications meet certain criteria.

Forensic scientists are employed by the police authorities, and the Act provides that in future they may be authorised by their Chief Constable, providing that they meet criteria which will be prescribed by the Secretary of State by order.

Proof of custody of productions

23. In section 84 of the 1975 Act (proof as to productions)—
(a) after the word "prove" there shall be inserted "(a)";
(b) after the word "police" in the second place where it occurs there shall be inserted—
  "or
 (b) that the production examined by him is that taken possession of by the procurator fiscal or the police,"; and
(c) at the end there shall be inserted the words "or, as the case may be, that it is that taken possession of as aforesaid".

GENERAL NOTE

At present, s.84 of the 1975 Act provides that the accused may dispute a presumption as to the condition of a production during the period in which the production was in the custody of either the procurator fiscal or the police, or in the custody of the person examining the production. This section extends the right to dispute a presumption that the production lodged is the item taken into possession by the police or procurator fiscal.

Section 23 amends s.84 of the 1975 Act to put it beyond doubt that it is not necessary to prove that a production examined by a witness who gives evidence about that examination is the production which was taken possession of by the procurator fiscal or police; unless the accused gives written notice, in accordance with the terms of s.84 of the 1975 Act, that he does not admit that the production was that taken possession of by the procurator fiscal or police.

Evidence of criminal record and character of accused

24.—(1) In section 141 of the 1975 Act (accused competent witness for defence in solemn proceedings)—

(a) in subsection (1), in paragraph (f)(ii) of the proviso—

(i) after the word "character" where it first occurs there shall be inserted "or impugning the character of the complainer"; and

(ii) after the word "prosecution" in the second place where it occurs there shall be inserted "or of the complainer"; and

(b) after that subsection there shall be inserted the following subsections—

"(1A) In a case to which sub-paragraph (ii) of paragraph (f) of the proviso to subsection (1) above applies, the prosecutor shall be entitled to ask the accused a question of a kind specified in that paragraph only if the court, on the application of the prosecutor, permits him to do so.

(1B) An application under subsection (1A) above shall be made in the course of the trial but in the absence of the jury.

(1C) In subsection (1) above, references to the complainer include references to a victim who is deceased.".

(2) After section 141 of that Act there shall be inserted the following section—

"Evidence of criminal record and character of accused

141ZA.—(1) This section applies where—

(a) evidence is led by the defence, or the defence asks questions of a witness for the prosecution, with a view to establishing the accused's good character or impugning the character of the prosecutor, of any witness for the prosecution or of the complainer; or

(b) the nature or conduct of the defence is such as to tend to establish the accused's good character or to involve imputations on the character of the prosecutor, of any witness for the prosecution or of the complainer.

(2) Where this section applies the court may, without prejudice to section 149 of this Act, on the application of the prosecutor, permit the prosecutor to lead evidence that the accused has committed, or has been convicted of, or has been charged with, offences other than that for which he is being tried, or is of bad character, notwithstanding that a witness or production concerned is not included in any list lodged by the prosecutor and that the notice required by sections 81 and 82(2) of this Act has not been given.

(3) An application under subsection (2) above shall be made in the course of the trial but in the absence of the jury.

(4) In subsection (1) above, references to the complainer include references to a victim who is deceased.".

(3) In section 160 of that Act (laying of previous convictions before jury), for subsection (2) there shall be substituted the following subsection—

"(2) Nothing in subsection (1) above shall prevent the prosecutor—

    (a) asking the accused questions tending to show that he has been convicted of an offence other than that with which he is charged, where he is entitled to do so under section 141 of this Act; or

    (b) leading evidence of previous convictions where it is competent to do so—

        (i) as evidence in support of a substantive charge; or

        (ii) under section 141ZA of this Act.".

(4) In section 346 of that Act (accused competent witness for defence in summary proceedings)—

    (a) in subsection (1), in paragraph (f)(ii) of the proviso—

        (i) after the word "character" where it first occurs there shall be inserted "or impugning the character of the complainer"; and

        (ii) after the word "prosecution" in the second place where it occurs there shall be inserted "or of the complainer"; and

    (b) after that subsection there shall be inserted the following subsections—

"(1A) In a case to which sub-paragraph (ii) of paragraph (f) of the proviso to subsection (1) above applies, the prosecutor shall be entitled to ask the accused a question of a kind specified in that paragraph only if the court, on the application of the prosecutor, permits him to do so.

(1B) In subsection (1) above, references to the complainer include references to a victim who is deceased.".

(5) After section 346 of that Act there shall be inserted the following section—

"Evidence of criminal record and character of accused

346ZA.—(1) This section applies where—

    (a) evidence is led by the defence, or the defence asks questions of a witness for the prosecution, with a view to establishing the accused's good character or impugning the character of the prosecutor, of any witness for the prosecution or of the complainer; or

    (b) the nature or conduct of the defence is such as to tend to establish the accused's good character or to involve imputations on the character of the prosecutor, of any witness for the prosecution or of the complainer.

(2) Where this section applies the court may, without prejudice to section 350 of this Act, on the application of the prosecutor, permit the prosecutor to lead evidence that the accused has committed, or has been convicted of, or has been charged with, offences other than that for which he is being tried, or is of bad character.

(3) In subsection (1) above, references to the complainer include references to a victim who is deceased.".

(6) In section 357 of that Act (laying of previous convictions before court), in subsection (5), for the words from "evidence" where it first occurs to the end there shall be substituted "the prosecutor—

    (a) asking the accused questions tending to show that the accused has been convicted of an offence other than that with which he is charged, where he is entitled to do so under section 346 of this Act; or

    (b) leading evidence of previous convictions where it is competent to do so—

        (i) as evidence in support of a substantive charge; or

        (ii) under section 346ZA of this Act.".

DEFINITIONS

"prosecutor": s.462 of the Criminal Procedure (Scotland) Act 1975.

GENERAL NOTE

This section was not well received in the House of Lords, where Lord McCluskey referred to it as "a giant step" away from established principle (*Hansard*, H.L. Vol. 560, col. 391). However, as the Lord Advocate pointed out, without this provision there were circumstances where as a matter of tactics the defence might present a jury with a picture of the accused as a person of good character, or might bring out the faults of various witnesses or of a deceased person, and the jury would then be left with a one-sided picture. Hearing these points for one side would make it appropriate to hear them for the other. Otherwise, there is a risk that the jury would be asked to reach its verdict on "a false and essentially distorted basis" (*Hansard*, H.L. Vol. 560, col. 394).

This section enables the prosecution to lead evidence of the previous misconduct or bad character of an accused in order to rebut evidence led on the accused's behalf as to the prosecutor's or another person's character or conduct. Under the present law such evidence cannot be laid before the court unless the accused gives evidence on his own behalf.

Evidence as to controlled drugs and medicinal products

25.—(1) For the purposes of any criminal proceedings, evidence given by an authorised forensic scientist, either orally or in a report purporting to be signed by him, that a substance which satisfies either of the conditions specified in subsection (2) below is—

(a) a particular controlled drug or medicinal product; or

(b) a particular product which is listed in the British Pharmacopoeia as containing a particular controlled drug or medicinal product,

shall, subject to subsection (3) below, be sufficient evidence of that fact notwithstanding that no analysis of the substance has been carried out.

(2) Those conditions are—

(a) that the substance is in a sealed container bearing a label identifying the contents of the container; or

(b) that the substance has a characteristic appearance having regard to its size, shape, colour and manufacturer's mark.

(3) A party proposing to rely on subsection (1) above ("the first party") shall, not less than 14 days before the trial diet, serve on the other party ("the second party")—

(a) a notice to that effect; and

(b) where the evidence is contained in a report, a copy of the report,

and if the second party serves on the first party, not more than seven days after the date of service of the notice on him, a notice that he does not accept the evidence as to the identity of the substance, subsection (1) above shall not apply in relation to that evidence.

(4) A notice or copy report served in accordance with subsection (3) above shall be served in such manner as may be prescribed by Act of Adjournal; and a written execution purporting to be signed by the person who served the notice or copy together with, where appropriate, the relevant post office receipt shall be sufficient evidence of such service.

(5) In this section—

"controlled drug" has the same meaning as in the Misuse of Drugs Act 1971; and

"medicinal product" has the same meaning as in the Medicines Act 1968.

DEFINITIONS

"controlled drug": s.25(5).
"medicinal product": s.25(5).

GENERAL NOTE

This section enables evidence to be given, in certain circumstances, by an authorised forensic scientist in any criminal proceedings to the effect that a substance is, or is listed in the British Pharmacopoeia as containing, a controlled drug or medicinal product without the need to produce an analysis of that substance. The party against whom such evidence is led is, however, entitled to rebut this evidence. This section will apply when evidence is given, either orally or by way of a written report, by an authorised forensic scientist as to the composition of certain substances which can readily be identified either by virtue of the characteristic appearance of the substance or by virtue of the fact that it is contained in a sealed container bearing a label identifying its contents.

Any party proposing to lead evidence in this manner is required to give the other party (against whom the evidence is to be led) notice of that intention at least 14 days before the trial. The other party has an opportunity to reject the evidence as to the identity of the substance within seven days. If the prosecution intends to rely on this procedure and there is more than one accused, each accused will be entitled to receive notice and to challenge that notice for his own interest.

Evidence as to time and place of video surveillance recordings

26.—(1) For the purposes of any criminal proceedings, a certificate purporting to be signed by a person responsible for the operation of a video surveillance system and certifying—

(a) the location of the camera;

(b) the nature and extent of the person's responsibility for the system; and

(c) that visual images recorded on a particular video tape are images, recorded by the system, of events which occurred at a place specified in the certificate at a time and date so specified,

shall, subject to subsection (2) below, be sufficient evidence of the matters contained in the certificate.

(2) A party proposing to rely on subsection (1) above ("the first party") shall, not less than 14 days before the trial diet, serve on the other party ("the second party") a copy of the certificate and, if the second party serves on the first party, not more than seven days after the date of service of the copy certificate on him, a notice that he does not accept the evidence contained in the certificate, subsection (1) above shall not apply in relation to that evidence.

(3) A copy certificate or notice served in accordance with subsection (2) above shall be served in such manner as may be prescribed by Act of Adjournal; and a written execution purporting to be signed by the person who served the copy or notice together with, where appropriate, the relevant post office receipt shall be sufficient evidence of such service.

(4) In this section, "video surveillance system" means apparatus consisting of a camera mounted in a fixed position and associated equipment for transmitting and recording visual images of events occurring in any place.

DEFINITIONS
"video surveillance system": s.26(4).

GENERAL NOTE
This section provides for evidence as to certain matters to be given by certificate by a person who is responsible for the operation of a video surveillance system. The evidentiary matters which may be dealt with in the certificate are the location of the camera; the nature and extent of the person's responsibility for the system; and that the events recorded on a particular video tape were recorded by the system and occurred at a specified place, time and date. That certificate will be sufficient evidence of the facts contained in it unless there is a challenge, in which case the facts will require to be proved in the usual manner. This certificate evidence provision will remove the need for, *inter alia*, the operators of city centre surveillance systems to attend court to give evidence as to what are essentially routine matters which are seldom challenged. If the accused disputes any of the facts stated in the certificate, the operator may still be called to give evidence.

Evidence in relation to fingerprints

27.—(1) For the purposes of any criminal proceedings, a certificate purporting to be signed by two constables and certifying that the fingerprints produced thereon were taken from a person designated in the certificate at a time, date and place specified therein shall, subject to subsection (2) below, be sufficient evidence of the facts contained in the certificate.

(2) A party proposing to rely on subsection (1) above ("the first party") shall, not less than 14 days before the trial diet, serve on the other party ("the second party") a copy of the certificate and, if the second party serves on the first party, not more than seven days after the date of service of the copy certificate on him, a notice that he does not accept the evidence contained in the certificate, subsection (1) above shall not apply in relation to that evidence.

(3) A copy certificate or notice served in accordance with subsection (2) above shall be served in such manner as may be prescribed by Act of Adjournal; and a written execution purporting to be signed by the person who served the copy or notice together with, where appropriate, the relevant post office receipt shall be sufficient evidence of such service.

GENERAL NOTE
This section is intended to remove the need for police officers to attend court to give evidence as to the taking of fingerprints from an accused by enabling that evidence to be given by certificate signed by two police officers, unless the accused disputes the facts contained in the certificate in advance of the trial. The provision should reduce the need for police officers to attend court to give evidence which is not disputed.

Evidence in relation to sexual offences

28.—(1) In section 141A(2) of the 1975 Act (sexual offences in relation to which restrictions on admissible evidence apply)—
  (a) after paragraph (b) there shall be inserted the following paragraph—
      "(ba) clandestine injury to women;";
  (b) after sub-paragraph (i) of paragraph (g) there shall be inserted the following sub-paragraphs—
          "(ia) section 2A (incest);
          (ib) section 2B (unlawful sexual intercourse with stepchild);
          (ic) section 2C (unlawful sexual intercourse of person in position of trust with child under 16);"; and
  (c) after sub-paragraph (iv) of that paragraph there shall be inserted the following sub-paragraph—
          "(iva) section 7 (gross indecency between males)".

(2) In section 346A(2) of that Act (corresponding provision in relation to summary proceedings)—
  (a) after paragraph (b) there shall be inserted the following paragraph—
      "(ba) clandestine injury to women;";
  (b) after sub-paragraph (i) of paragraph (f) there shall be inserted the following sub-paragraphs—
          "(ia) section 2A (incest);
          (ib) section 2B (unlawful sexual intercourse with stepchild);
          (ic) section 2C (unlawful sexual intercourse of person in position of trust with child under 16);"; and
  (c) after sub-paragraph (iv) of that paragraph there shall be inserted the following sub-paragraph—
          "(iva) section 7 (gross indecency between males)".

GENERAL NOTE
This section provides for the addition of the crimes of clandestine injury to women and incest to the list of sexual offences to which ss.141A and 346A of the 1975 Act apply. As a consequence, evidence in respect of these offences will be subject to the restrictions contained in these sections as to the extent to which evidence can be led about the previous sexual character or history of a complainer. This follows the recommendation made in the Report *Sexual History and Sexual Character Evidence in Scottish Sexual Offence Trials* published by the Scottish Office Central Research Unit in 1992. While the crime of clandestine injury to women (*i.e.* unlawful sexual

intercourse with a woman who is not conscious) is comparatively rare, the same is not the case with incest.

The Scottish Law Commission did not include these crimes in its original recommendations which led to the enactment of ss.141A and 346A. The Scottish Law Commission observed that there were essential differences between these crimes and those included in the 1975 Act sections referred to. Those differences are evidently no longer considered sufficient to warrant continued exclusion from the protection which these sections afford to complainers in cases of clandestine injury or incest.

Proof of previous convictions

29.—(1) In section 162 of the 1975 Act (admissibility and proof of extract convictions in solemn proceedings), after subsection (3) there shall be inserted the following subsections—

"(4) Without prejudice to subsections (1) to (3) above, where proof of a previous conviction is competent in support of a substantive charge, any such conviction or an extract of it shall, if—

   (a) it purports to relate to the accused and to be signed by the clerk of court having custody of the record containing the conviction; and

   (b) a copy of it has been served on the accused not less than 14 days before the trial diet,

be sufficient evidence of the application of the conviction to the accused unless, within seven days of the date of service of the copy on him, he serves notice on the prosecutor that he denies that it applies to him.

(5) A copy of a conviction or extract conviction served under subsection (4) above shall be served on the accused in such manner as may be prescribed by Act of Adjournal, and a written execution purporting to be signed by the person who served the copy together with, where appropriate, the relevant post office receipt shall be sufficient evidence of service of the copy.".

(2) In section 357 of that Act (previous convictions in summary proceedings), after subsection (5) there shall be inserted the following subsections—

"(6) Without prejudice to subsections (1) to (3) above, where proof of a previous conviction is competent in support of a substantive charge, any such conviction or an extract of it shall, if—

   (a) it purports to relate to the accused and to be signed by the clerk of court having custody of the record containing the conviction; and

   (b) a copy of it has been served on the accused not less than 14 days before the trial diet,

be sufficient evidence of the application of the conviction to the accused unless, within seven days of the date of service of the copy on him, he serves notice on the prosecutor that he denies that it applies to him.

(7) A copy of a conviction or extract conviction served under subsection (6) above shall be served on the accused in such manner as may be prescribed by Act of Adjournal, and a written execution purporting to be signed by the person who served the copy together with, where appropriate, the relevant post office receipt shall be sufficient evidence of service of the copy.".

DEFINITIONS
"accused": s.114(1).
"clerk of court": s.114(1).

GENERAL NOTE
The purpose of this section is to reduce the unnecessary leading of evidence, including the attendance of witnesses, to speak to the previous convictions of an accused when proof of those convictions is necessary in support of a substantive charge. Where a copy of such a previous conviction is served on, and not challenged by, an accused, it will be sufficient evidence both of the conviction and of its application to the accused.

At present when a previous conviction requires to be proved for the purposes of a substantive charge (such as driving while disqualified) it is necessary for the prosecution to lead evidence to prove the earlier conviction. This evidence is very rarely disputed and, accordingly, witnesses are often called to give evidence which is not challenged. Under the provisions of this section the prosecution will require to lead evidence to prove a previous conviction only in cases where there is a dispute, thereby avoiding the attendance of witnesses.

The trial

Death, illness or absence of trial judge

30.—(1) Section 128 of the 1975 Act (death or illness of judge in solemn proceedings) shall be amended in accordance with subsections (2) and (3) below.

(2) For subsection (1) of that section there shall be substituted the following subsections—

"(1) Where the court is unable to proceed owing to the death, illness or absence of the presiding judge, the clerk of court may convene the court (if necessary) and—

    (a) in a case where no evidence has been led, adjourn the diet and any other diet appointed for that sitting to—

        (i) a time later the same day, or a date not more than seven days later, when he believes a judge will be available; or

        (ii) a later sitting not more than two months after the date of the adjournment; or

    (b) in a case where evidence has been led—

        (i) adjourn the diet and any other diet appointed for that sitting to a time later the same day, or a date not more than seven days later, when he believes a judge will be available; or

        (ii) with the consent of the parties, desert the diet pro loco et tempore.

(1A) Where a diet has been adjourned under sub-paragraph (i) of either paragraph (a) or paragraph (b) of subsection (1) above the clerk of court may, where the conditions of that subsection continue to be satisfied, further adjourn the diet under that sub-paragraph; but the total period of such adjournments shall not exceed seven days.

(1B) Where a diet has been adjourned under subsection (1)(b)(i) above the court may, at the adjourned diet—

    (a) further adjourn the diet; or

    (b) desert the diet pro loco et tempore.".

(3) In subsection (2) of that section, for the words "(1)(c)" there shall be substituted "(1)(b)(ii) or (1B)(b)".

(4) After section 331A of that Act there shall be inserted the following section—

"Death, illness or absence of judge

331B.—(1) Where the court is unable to proceed owing to the death, illness or absence of the presiding judge, it shall be lawful for the clerk of court—

    (a) where the diet has not been called, to convene the court and adjourn the diet;

    (b) where the diet has been called but no evidence has been led, to adjourn the diet; and

    (c) where the diet has been called and evidence has been led—

        (i) with the agreement of the parties, to desert the diet pro loco et tempore; or

        (ii) to adjourn the diet.

(2) Where, under subsection (1)(c)(i) above, a diet has been deserted pro loco et tempore, any new prosecution charging the accused with the

same or any similar offence arising out of the same facts shall be brought within two months of the date on which the diet was deserted notwithstanding that any other time limit for the commencement of such prosecution has elapsed.

(3) For the purposes of subsection (2) above, a new prosecution shall be deemed to commence on the date on which a warrant to apprehend or to cite the accused is granted, if such warrant is executed without undue delay.".

DEFINITIONS
"clerk of court": s.114(1).
"judge": s.462 of the Criminal Procedure (Scotland) Act 1975.

GENERAL NOTE
The purpose of this section is to provide for the adjournment, or desertion *pro loco et tempore* in both summary and solemn proceedings, of trial diets where the court is unable to proceed because of the death, illness or absence of "the presiding judge", there being no reference in the section to a sheriff or stipendiary magistrate.

Section 128 of the 1975 Act makes provision for the procedure in the event of the death or illness of the presiding judge in solemn proceedings, but there is no provision for the procedure to be followed in the event of the absence of the presiding judge for other reasons.

In summary proceedings, a court has power at common law to fix a new diet when "a judge" is taken ill during the course of a trial, and the possibility of a trial being postponed due to the illness of a judge is also recognised in s.333A(2)(a) of the 1975 Act. However, there is no summary provision for the procedure in the event of the death of a judge or his absence for reasons other than death.

Removal of accused from court

31. After section 337A of the 1975 Act there shall be inserted the following section—

"Removal of accused from court

337B.—(1) Without prejudice to section 338 of this Act, and subject to subsection (2) below, no part of a trial shall take place outwith the presence of the accused.

(2) If during the course of his trial an accused so misconducts himself that in the view of the court a proper trial cannot take place unless he is removed, the court may order—

(a) that he is removed from the court for so long as his conduct makes it necessary; and

(b) that the trial proceeds in his absence,

but if he is not legally represented the court shall appoint counsel or a solicitor to represent his interests during such absence.".

DEFINITIONS
"accused": s.114(1).

GENERAL NOTE
This section allows the court in summary proceedings to order that an accused be removed from court during the course of his trial where his conduct is such that a proper trial cannot take place. The court may order that the trial should continue in the accused's absence, and if he is not legally represented the court shall appoint counsel or a solicitor to represent him while he is absent.

In *Aitken v. Wood* 1921 J.C. 94 it was held that criminal proceedings are not competent outwith the presence of the accused. Section 338(1)(b) of the 1975 Act allows for trial in summary proceedings in the absence of the accused in certain circumstances (where the accused is charged with any statutory offence for which a sentence of imprisonment cannot be imposed in the first instance, or where the statute confers power on the court to do so) but not, as in solemn proceedings (under s.145 of the 1975 Act), if a person's conduct is such that a proper trial cannot take place. In this situation, the court is empowered in solemn proceedings to have the accused removed, and the trial may proceed in his absence but in the presence of his legal representative. Should the accused not have legal representation, the court is required to appoint counsel or a solicitor.

Similar disruptions can occur in summary cases, for which as indicated above, there are no equivalent provisions. Section 31 now gives the court in summary proceedings equivalent powers to those already provided for in s.145 of the 1975 Act for solemn proceedings.

Comment by prosecutor on accused's failure to give evidence

32. Sections 141(1)(b) (prosecutor may not comment on failure of accused to give evidence in solemn proceedings) and 346(1)(b) (corresponding provision in relation to summary proceedings) of the 1975 Act shall cease to have effect.

DEFINITIONS
"prosecutor": s.462 of the Criminal Procedure (Scotland) Act 1975.

GENERAL NOTE
Section 141 (in respect of solemn procedure) and s.346 (in respect of summary procedure) of the 1975 Act provide that the accused is a competent witness for the defence and make supplementary provision as to the terms on which the accused gives evidence, and the scope of the questions which he may be asked. Sections 141(1)(b) and 346(1)(b) provide that the failure of the accused to give evidence shall not be commented upon by the prosecution.

It is well established in common law at least since 1918, and confirmed in numerous reported cases thereafter, that the judge may comment on the accused's failure to give evidence and that it is proper for the jury or the court to take the accused's failure to give evidence into account when deciding their verdict: *Brown v. Macpherson* 1918 J.C. 3. It is competent for the defence to comment on the accused's failure to give evidence. It is therefore only the prosecutor who is forbidden to comment on the accused's failure to give evidence. Section 32 provides that subs. (1)(b) of ss.141 and 346 will cease to have effect, thus removing the prohibition on the prosecution commenting on the accused's failure to give evidence, in solemn and summary procedures respectively.

The right of a prosecutor to comment on the accused's failure to give evidence gave rise to some of the most vocal concern in Parliament, concern being focused on the "prosecuting zealot" (*Hansard*, H.L. Vol. 261, col. 259). Despite the great forensic experience of some Scottish Members of Parliament and Peers no actual case involving alleged abuse was cited and the concern appears to relate to the theoretical dangers of this reform. Coincidentally, convictions were set aside in *Dempsey v. H.M. Advocate* 1995 S.C.C.R. 431 because of the comments by a prosecutor to a jury. It may be that those comments would have been permissible after this change in the law, although clearly not prior to it.

At the second reading of the Bill in the House of Lords the Minister of State at the Scottish Office, Lord Fraser of Carmyllie, said the Government considered it "wholly appropriate that the prosecution, when addressing the jury should be able to comment on a matter on which the court may comment and which the jury may take into account in reaching its verdict" (*Hansard*, H.L. Vol. 559, col. 550). Lord Macaulay of Bragar, for the Opposition, questioned why the absence of the accused from the witness box is often referred to as a "failure" on the part of the accused: semantically there may be a good point there for lawyers, for the matter sounds like a breach of duty. However, the "failure" is first mentioned in the 1975 Act and merely repeated in this Act. It is unlikely that a jury would think it a duty of an accused to give evidence having heard proper instructions from the trial judge (*Hansard*, H.L. Vol. 559, col. 553).

Lord Macaulay also asked how far the prosecutor would be entitled to go, commenting "Who is to control the forensic excesses of a prosecuting zealot—and there are plenty of them—whose idea of exercise of judgment is at least questionable? Whose guidelines are they to follow?" (*Hansard*, H.L. Vol. 559, col. 554). The legal and practical answer to Lord Macaulay's question is: the Lord Advocate. On the second day of the Committee Stage of the Bill in the House of Lords, Lord Rodger of Earlsferry observed that "the prosecutor will comment only with restraint because of course he must have regard to the fact that as the law has been laid down it is only with restraint that this can be said to a jury, and it is only in special circumstances that it can be said. If he goes further than that, if he says something which goes beyond that, it will be the judge's duty to correct what the prosecutor has said and to give the proper direction to the jury. If he should fail to do so, or, in certain circumstances, if the appeal court thought that what was said by the prosecutor was so outrageous, then presumably the matter could be the basis for a ground of appeal. Where the law itself only allows comment with restraint, and only for inferences to be drawn in narrow circumstances, it would be a foolish prosecutor indeed who went further than that" (*Hansard*, H.L. Vol. 560, col. 416).

Lord McCluskey, from the Cross-benches, supported the provision, believing it "deeply patronising", a phrase repeated thereafter, to imagine that unless a prosecutor pointed out that the accused had not gone into the witness box, the jury would not notice it for themselves. He did not regard the prosecutor's comment as "a serious invasion of some precious constitutional right" (*Hansard*, H.L. Vol. 659, col. 569).

No-one has argued for a review of first principles: it is still certain that every person charged with a criminal offence will be presumed to be innocent of the same, and this presumption can be overcome only by evidence relevant to guilt. The burden of proving that the accused committed the crime libelled rests on the Crown throughout the trial. The persuasive burden remains on the Crown: see generally Renton and Brown *Criminal Procedure* (5th ed.) para. 18–02. However, it has been recognised at common law for many years that cases may occur in which the proved facts raise a presumption that the accused has committed the crime libelled, and in which, if he fails to put forward an explanation sufficient to create in the minds of the jury (or the court in summary matters) a reasonable doubt as to his guilt, the jury will be entitled to draw an inference of guilt: the thread of authorities starts with *H.M. Advocate v. Hardy* 1983 J.C. 144, runs through *McIlhargey v. Herron* 1972 J.C. 38 and concludes, for the moment, with *Deacons v. H.M. Advocate* 1994 G.W.D. 11–636.

In *Deacons* the learned judge referred to the "pieces of the jigsaw puzzle" and that puts the importance of the prosecutor's right to comment into context. In itself the self-evident fact that the accused elects to say nothing in the presence of the jury is only one aspect to which a jury will have regard. A jury, properly instructed, will consider the whole evidence led in their presence and, depending very much on the facts and circumstances, they will either be deeply impressed by the silence of the accused in court or utterly indifferent to it.

The Lord Advocate's view of this reform suggests a discreet and sensitive, indeed, passing reference to a procedural event having occurred earlier in a trial. Whether Crown counsel and procurators fiscal take the necessary tactical decision to limit comment severely in the heat of the moment and in the expectation, or anticipation, of the end of a trial will be watched for anxiously by the defence. In the long run things balance out: defence lawyers will require in providing effective assistance to their clients, to think more deeply about the tactical decision on giving evidence.

Conviction and sentence

Sentence following guilty plea

33. After each of sections 217 and 430 of the 1975 Act there shall be inserted the following section as, respectively, section 217A and section 430A—

"Sentence following guilty plea
In determining what sentence to pass on, or what other disposal or order to make in relation to, an offender who has pled guilty to an offence, a court may take into account—
  (a) the stage in the proceedings for the offence at which the offender indicated his intention to plead guilty, and
  (b) the circumstances in which that indication was given.".

GENERAL NOTE
This section allows the court, when determining the appropriate sentence to pass, to take into account the stage in the proceedings at which the accused pleads guilty, and the circumstances of that indication. There is no statute governing the consideration of guilty pleas when sentencing: the existing law is stated in *Strawhorn v. McLeod* 1987 S.C.R. 413, in which the Appeal Court disapproved the practice of giving a discount on a sentence for a plea of guilty. Section 33 permits the court to have regard to the accused who has accepted responsibility early on and to adjust sentence accordingly.

Sentencing guidelines

34.—(1) After section 254 of the 1975 Act there shall be inserted the following section—

"Sentencing guidelines
254A.—(1) In disposing of an appeal under section 228(1)(b), (bb), (bc), (bd) or (c) or 228A of this Act the High Court may, without prejudice to any other power in that regard, pronounce an opinion on the sentence or other disposal or order which is appropriate in any similar case.

(2) Without prejudice to any rule of law, a court in passing sentence shall have regard to any relevant opinion pronounced under subsection (1) above.".

(2) After section 455 of the 1975 Act there shall be inserted the following section—

"Sentencing guidelines

455A.—(1) In disposing of an appeal under section 442(1)(a)(ii), (iia) or (iii), (b)(ii) or (c) of this Act the High Court may, without prejudice to any other power in that regard, pronounce an opinion on the sentence or other disposal or order which is appropriate in any similar case.

(2) Without prejudice to any rule of law, a court in passing sentence shall have regard to any relevant opinion pronounced under subsection (1) above.".

GENERAL NOTE

This section gives the High Court of Justiciary express powers to pronounce Opinions on the appropriateness of sentences or other disposals. Courts of first instance are then required to have regard to such Opinions. Hitherto, there has been only guidance but not guidelines: see D. Kelly *Criminal Sentences* (Edinburgh, 1992) at p.*v.* There is no existing legislation which provides for the High Court to establish guidelines for sentencing by courts of first instance. Such guidelines might indicate the appropriate level of sentence in different types of cases, and promote consistency and certainty in sentencing. They might also inform the expectations of victims, accused persons and legal advisers and provide benchmarks for appeals against sentence.

Supervised attendance orders

35.—(1) Section 62 of the Law Reform (Miscellaneous Provisions) (Scotland) Act 1990 (supervised attendance orders) shall be amended in accordance with subsections (2) to (7) below.

(2) In subsection (1), at the end there shall be inserted the words "and shall, subject to paragraph 1 of Schedule 6 to this Act, make such an order where subsection (3A) below applies".

(3) In subsection (2)—

(a) for the words "with the consent" there shall be substituted "in respect";

(b) in paragraph (a), for the words "time, being 10, 20, 30, 40, 50 or 60 hours" there shall be substituted "period, being a period of not less than 10 hours and not more than—
　　　(i) where the amount of the fine, part or instalment which the offender has failed to pay does not exceed level 1 on the standard scale, 50 hours; and
　　　(ii) in any other case, 100 hours"; and

(c) in paragraph (b), for the word "time" there shall be substituted "period".

(4) In subsection (3)(a), for the word "16" there shall be substituted "18".

(5) After subsection (3) there shall be inserted the following subsections—

"(3A) This subsection applies where—

(a) the court is a court prescribed for the purposes of this subsection by order made by the Secretary of State;

(b) the offender is of or over 18 years of age and is not serving a sentence of imprisonment;

(c) having been convicted of an offence, he has had imposed on him a fine which (or any part or instalment of which) he has failed to pay and the court, but for this section, would have imposed on him a period of imprisonment under section 407(1)(b) of the Criminal Procedure (Scotland) Act 1975 (power of court to impose imprisonment for non-payment of fine); and

(d) the fine, or as the case may be, the part or instalment, is of an amount not exceeding level 2 on the standard scale.

(3B) An order under subsection (3A)(a) above shall be made by statutory instrument, which shall be subject to annulment in pursuance of a resolution of either House of Parliament.".

(6) After subsection (4) there shall be inserted the following subsection—

"(4A) The coming into force of a supervised attendance order shall have the effect of discharging the fine referred to in subsection (3)(b) or (3A)(c) above or, as the case may be, section 412A(3)(a) or 412B(1) of the Criminal Procedure (Scotland) Act 1975.".

(7) In subsection (6), the following definition shall be inserted in the appropriate place in alphabetical order—

" "imprisonment" includes detention;".

(8) In Schedule 6 to that Act of 1990 (further provisions with respect to supervised attendance orders)—

  (a) in paragraph 1(1)(a), after the word "persons" there shall be inserted "of a class which includes the offender";

  (b) in paragraph 4(2)(a), for the words from "as" to "made" in the second place where it occurs there shall be substituted—

      "not exceeding—

          (i) in the case of a sheriff court, three months; and

          (ii) in the case of a district court, 60 days,

      as the court considers appropriate;"; and

  (c) in paragraph 5(1)(d), for the words from "as" to "made" in the second place where it occurs there shall be substituted—

      "not exceeding—

          (i) in the case of a sheriff court, three months; and

          (ii) in the case of a district court, 60 days,

      as the court considers appropriate;".

(9) In section 194(2) of the 1975 Act, after the entry in respect of section 411 there shall be inserted—

      "section 412A (supervised attendance orders in place of fines for 16 and 17 year olds);

      section 412B (supervised attendance orders where court allows further time to pay;".

(10) In section 407(1)(b) of that Act (imprisonment for non-payment of fine), after the word "may" there shall be inserted ", subject to section 62(1) of the Law Reform (Miscellaneous Provisions) (Scotland) Act 1990,".

(11) After section 412 of that Act there shall be inserted the following sections—

"Supervised attendance orders

Supervised attendance orders in place of fines for 16 and 17 year olds

412A.—(1) This section applies where a person of 16 or 17 years of age is convicted of an offence by a court of summary jurisdiction and the court considers that, but for this section, the appropriate sentence is a fine.

(2) Where this section applies, the court shall determine the amount of the fine and shall consider whether the person is likely to pay a fine of that amount within 28 days.

(3) If the court considers that the person is likely to pay the fine as mentioned in subsection (2) above, it shall—

  (a) impose the fine; and

  (b) subject to paragraph 1 of Schedule 6 to the Law Reform (Miscellaneous Provisions) (Scotland) Act 1990 ("the 1990 Act"), make a supervised attendance order in default of payment of the fine within 28 days.

(4) A supervised attendance order made under subsection (3)(b) above—

(a) shall come into force on such date, not earlier than 28 days after the making of the order, as may be specified in the order, unless the person pays the fine within that period;

(b) shall, for the purposes of Schedule 6 to the 1990 Act, be deemed to be made on the date when it comes into force.

(5) Where, before the coming into force of a supervised attendance order made under subsection (3)(b) above, the person pays part of the fine, the period specified in the order shall be reduced by the proportion which the part of the fine paid bears to the whole fine, the resulting figure being rounded up or down to the nearest 10 hours; but this subsection shall not operate to reduce the period to less than 10 hours.

(6) If the court considers that the person is not likely to pay the fine as mentioned in subsection (2) above, it shall, subject to paragraph 1 of Schedule 6 to the 1990 Act, make a supervised attendance order in respect of that person.

(7) Sections 395A to 398, 400 to 404 and 407 of this Act shall not apply in respect of a person to whom this section applies.

(8) For the purposes of any appeal or review, a supervised attendance order made under this section is a sentence.

(9) In this section "supervised attendance order" means an order made in accordance with section 62(2), (5) and (6) of the 1990 Act.

Supervised attendance orders where court allows further time to pay fine

412B.—(1) Where a court, on an application to it under section 397(1) of this Act, allows a person further time for payment of a fine or instalments thereof it may, in addition, subject to paragraph 1 of Schedule 6 to the Law Reform (Miscellaneous Provisions) (Scotland) Act 1990 ("the 1990 Act"), impose a supervised attendance order in default of payment of the fine or any instalment of it on the due date.

(2) A supervised attendance order made under subsection (1) above—

(a) shall, if the person fails to pay the fine or any instalment of it on the due date, come into force on the day after the due date; and

(b) shall, for the purposes of Schedule 6 to the 1990 Act, be deemed to be made on the date when it comes into force.

(3) Where, before the coming into force of a supervised attendance order under subsection (1) above, the person pays part of the fine, the period specified in the order shall be reduced by the proportion which the part of the fine paid bears to the whole fine, the resulting figure being rounded up or down to the nearest 10 hours; but this subsection shall not operate to reduce the period to less than 10 hours.

(4) In this section "supervised attendance order" means an order made in accordance with section 62(2), (5) and (6) of the 1990 Act.".

DEFINITIONS

"supervised attendance order": s.62(2), (5) and (6) of the Law Reform (Miscellaneous Provisions) (Scotland) Act 1990.

GENERAL NOTE

This section amends s.62 of, and Sched. 6 to, the Law Reform (Miscellaneous Provisions) (Scotland) Act 1990 (c. 40). Under the proposed legislation, the power to impose imprisonment for default is retained but supervised attendance orders (SAOs) may replace imprisonment as a means of dealing with the default in certain circumstances and in areas designated by Order of the Secretary of State.

Section 62 of, and Sched. 6 to, the Law Reform (Miscellaneous Provisions) (Scotland) Act 1990 introduced SAOs as an alternative to imprisonment for fine default. Under the provisions of the 1990 Act a court, with the consent of the offender, may impose an SAO where it would otherwise have imposed a term of imprisonment for fine default and where it has been notified by the Secretary of State that the appropriate arrangements exist in the area where the offender resides.

Section 35 extends the existing arrangements to provide that SAOs may be used as an alternative to, or replacement for, imprisonment for fine default, and for 16 and 17 year olds as a replacement for the sentence of a fine. Under this section a court prescribed by the Secretary of State would now be required to make an SAO for failure to pay a fine of less than the equivalent of level 2 on the standard scale (currently £500) instead of imposing a period of imprisonment. The consent of the offender would no longer be required. The court's discretion to impose an SAO for fine default above level 2 would remain unaffected as would the power under s.407 of the 1975 Act, of the court to impose a term of imprisonment (alongside the fine), which the offender is, without further inquiry into his means, liable to serve on default of the fine.

The section also amends certain aspects of the SAO scheme. The number of hours which may be imposed under an SAO will be increased from 60 to 100 and the court will be given wider discretion when determining the length of an SAO. The new legislation increases the maximum penalties available to the court where an SAO has been breached.

The section further provides that a court may make an SAO when giving an offender further time to pay under s.397(1) of the 1975 Act which will be activated automatically if the outstanding amount has not been paid fully the day after the due date. Where a part of the outstanding amount has been paid the number of hours specified on the SAO will be reduced accordingly, to a minimum of 10 hours. The fine will be discharged when the SAO is made.

Special provisions are introduced for offenders aged 16 and 17. A court will be able to make an SAO in respect of 16 and 17 year olds where it would otherwise consider a fine to be the appropriate disposal. The court will retain the power to impose a fine where it appears likely that the offender will pay. In these cases and if an appropriate order has been made, the court will impose an SAO alongside the fine which will be activated automatically if the full amount has not been paid within 28 days. Where part of the amount has been paid, the number of hours may be reduced accordingly, to a minimum of 10 hours.

Supervised release orders: requirement for local authority report

36. After subsection (1) of section 212A of the 1975 Act (supervised release orders) there shall be inserted the following subsection—

"(1A) A court shall, before making an order under subsection (1) above, consider a report by a relevant officer of a local authority about the offender and his circumstances and, if the court thinks it necessary, hear that officer.".

GENERAL NOTE

This section requires the court to consider a report about the offender and his circumstances before making a supervised release order. The supervised release order (SRO) was introduced by the Prisoners and Criminal Proceedings (Scotland) Act 1993 (c. 9) (the 1993 Act). An SRO may be made by the court when passing a custodial sentence of not less than 12 months but less than four years, where the court considers it necessary to do so to protect the public from serious harm. The effect of an SRO is to require supervision of the offender for up to 12 months after release.

Some offenders for whom the court may consider imposing an SRO will not be the subject of an up-to-date social enquiry report. While the court is not to be required to request such a report in all cases where an SRO would be an option, such a report must be obtained before making an SRO, so that the court has current information on the offender and his circumstances.

This section requires the court to consider a report from a relevant officer of the appropriate local authority about the offender and his circumstances in all cases before an SRO is made, and if the court thinks fit, to hear that officer. "Relevant officer", in relation to a local authority, is defined as an officer of the authority employed by them in the discharge of their functions under s.27(1) of the Social Work (Scotland) Act 1968 (supervision and care of persons put on probation or released from prison etc.).

Offences committed by persons under supervision etc.: provision of local authority report

37.—(1) After section 179 of the 1975 Act there shall be inserted the following section—

"Offence committed by person under supervision etc.: provision of local authority report

179A. Where a person specified in section 27(1)(b)(i) to (vi) of the Social Work (Scotland) Act 1968 commits an offence, the court shall not

dispose of the case without obtaining from the local authority in whose area the person resides a report as to—
    (a) the circumstances of the offence; and
    (b) the character of the offender, including his behaviour while under the supervision, or as the case may be subject to the order, so specified in relation to him.".

(2) After section 380 of that Act there shall be inserted the following section—

"Offence committed by person under supervision etc.: provision of local authority report

380A.—(1) Where a person specified in section 27(1)(b)(i) to (vi) of the Social Work (Scotland) Act 1968 commits an offence, the court shall not dispose of the case without obtaining from the local authority in whose area the person resides a report as to—
    (a) the circumstances of the offence; and
    (b) the character of the offender, including his behaviour while under the supervision, or as the case may be subject to the order, so specified in relation to him.
    (2) In subsection (1) above, "the court" does not include a district court.".

GENERAL NOTE

Where a person appears before a court having committed a turtner offence while under supervision, by virtue of an order of a court of criminal jurisdiction, or of an order or licence of the Secretary of State, this section requires the court to obtain a report on the circumstances of the offence and the character of the offender, including his offending behaviour while under supervision.

Probation orders to be made only after conviction

38.—(1) In section 183(5A) of the 1975 Act (probation order)—
    (a) after the word "where" there shall be inserted "an offender has been convicted of an offence punishable by imprisonment and"; and
    (b) in paragraph (a), the words "has committed an offence punishable by imprisonment and" shall cease to have effect.

(2) For paragraph (b) of subsection (2) of each of sections 186 and 387 of that Act (failure to comply with requirement of probation orders) there shall be substituted the following paragraph—
    "(b) sentence the offender for the offence for which the order was made;".

(3) In section 384 of that Act (probation)—
    (a) in subsection (1)—
        (i) for the words "charged before a court of summary jurisdiction with" there shall be substituted "convicted of";
        (ii) the words from "and", where it first occurs, to "offence", in the third place where it occurs, shall cease to have effect; and
        (iii) for the words from ", without" to "applies)," there shall be substituted "instead of sentencing him";
    (b) in subsection (5A)—
        (i) after the word "where" there shall be inserted "an offender has been convicted of an offence punishable by imprisonment and"; and
        (ii) in paragraph (a), the words "has committed an offence punishable by imprisonment and" shall cease to have effect; and
    (c) in subsection (6), the words "convicted of and" shall cease to have effect.

GENERAL NOTE
Section 38 provides for the making of a probation order in summary proceedings following conviction of the offender. Under s.183(1) of the 1975 Act (in relation to solemn proceedings) it is already the case that a probation order can be made following conviction and a probation order may be made instead of sentencing the offender. By contrast, under s.384 of the 1975 Act (in relation to summary procedure) the court could, without proceeding to conviction, make a probation order if satisfied that the offender committed the offence. Now probation orders can only be made after conviction in summary proceedings.

Probation orders requiring treatment for mental condition

39.—(1) In each of sections 184 and 385 of the 1975 Act (probation orders requiring treatment for mental condition)—
  (a) in subsection (1), after the word "practitioner", in the second place where it occurs, there shall be inserted "or chartered psychologist"; and
  (b) in each of subsections (2)(c), (5) and (5B)(b), after the word "practitioner" there shall be inserted "or chartered psychologist".

(2) In section 462(1) of that Act (interpretation), at the appropriate place, there shall be inserted the following definition—
  " "chartered psychologist" means a person for the time being listed in the British Psychological Society's Register of Chartered Psychologists;".

DEFINITIONS
"chartered psychologist": s.462 of the Criminal Procedure (Scotland) Act 1975.

GENERAL NOTE
This section enables the court to make treatment by a chartered psychologist a condition of a probation order. An offender with a mental disorder which may be susceptible to treatment other than through detention under a hospital order under Pt. VI of the Mental Health (Scotland) Act 1984, and who may be subject to a probation order, may benefit from treatment by or under the direction of a chartered psychologist. Previous powers only allowed the court to require an offence to submit, for a period not exceeding 12 months, to treatment by or under the direction of a registered medical practitioner.

Sentence for offence committed while subject to requirement to perform unpaid work

40.—(1) After subsection (2) of section 187 of the 1975 Act (commission of further offence while on probation) there shall be inserted the following subsections—
  "(3) Where—
  (a) a court has, under section 183(5A) of this Act, included in a probation order a requirement that an offender shall perform unpaid work; and
  (b) the offender is convicted of an offence committed in the circumstances mentioned in subsection (4) below,
  the court which sentences him for the offence shall, in determining the appropriate sentence for that offence, have regard to the fact that the offence was committed in those circumstances.
  (4) The circumstances referred to in subsection (3) above are that the offence was committed—
  (a) during the period that the offender was subject to a requirement to perform unpaid work or within the period of three months following the expiry of that period; and

    (b) in any place where the unpaid work was being or had previously been performed.

    (5) The court shall not, under subsection (3) above, have regard to the fact that the offence was committed in the circumstances mentioned in subsection (4) above unless that fact is libelled in the indictment or, as the case may be, specified in the complaint.".

  (2) After subsection (2) of section 388 of that Act (commission of further offence while on probation) there shall be inserted the following subsections—

    "(3) Where—

    (a) a court has, under section 384(5A) of this Act, included in a probation order a requirement that an offender shall perform unpaid work; and

    (b) the offender is convicted of an offence committed in the circumstances mentioned in subsection (4) below,

the court which sentences him for the offence shall, in determining the appropriate sentence for that offence, have regard to the fact that the offence was committed in those circumstances.

    (4) The circumstances referred to in subsection (3) above are that the offence was committed—

    (a) during the period that the offender was subject to a requirement to perform unpaid work or within the period of three months following the expiry of that period; and

    (b) in any place where the unpaid work was being or had previously been performed.

    (5) The court shall not, under subsection (3) above, have regard to the fact that the offence was committed in the circumstances mentioned in subsection (4) above unless that fact is libelled in the indictment or, as the case may be, specified in the complaint.".

  (3) After section 5 of the Community Service by Offenders (Scotland) Act 1978 there shall be inserted the following section—

"Commission of offence while community service order in force

    5A.—(1) Where—

    (a) a court has made a community service order under section 1(1) of this Act in respect of an offender; and

    (b) the offender is convicted of an offence committed in the circumstances mentioned in subsection (2) below,

the court which sentences him for that offence shall, in determining the appropriate sentence for that offence, have regard to the fact that the offence was committed in those circumstances.

    (2) The circumstances referred to in subsection (1) above are that the offence was committed—

    (a) during the period when the community service order was in force or within the period of three months following the expiry of that order; and

    (b) in any place where unpaid work under the order was being or had previously been performed.

    (3) The court shall not, under subsection (1) above, have regard to the fact that the offence was committed in the circumstances mentioned in subsection (2) above unless that fact is libelled in the indictment or, as the case may be, specified in the complaint.".

GENERAL NOTE

    Section 40 requires the court to take into account, when sentencing, the fact that an offence has been committed in any place where an offender has undertaken community service or unpaid work, where the offence is committed during or within three months of the expiry of a requirement to perform unpaid work or of a community service order.

Cases have arisen where a person subject to an order commits an offence at premises where he performed a part of his unpaid work, either during the life of the order itself or shortly after the completion or termination of the order. This section enables courts, when sentencing for such an offence, to take into account the fact that the offender took advantage of the placement by imposing a sentence which reflects the circumstances and so strengthening public protection.

Amendment of records of conviction and sentence in summary proceedings

41. After section 439 of the 1975 Act there shall be inserted the following section—

"Amendment of records of conviction and sentence in summary proceedings

439A.—(1) Without prejudice to section 439 of this Act, where, on an application in accordance with subsection (2) below, the High Court is satisfied that a record of conviction or sentence in summary proceedings inaccurately records the identity of any person, it may authorise the clerk of the court which convicted or, as the case may be, sentenced the person to correct the record.

(2) An application under subsection (1) above shall be made after the determination of the summary prosecution and may be made by any party to the summary proceedings or any other person having an interest in the correction of the alleged inaccuracy.

(3) The High Court shall order intimation of an application under subsection (1) above to such persons as it considers appropriate and shall not determine the application without affording to the parties to the summary proceedings and to any other person having an interest in the correction of the alleged inaccuracy an opportunity to be heard.

(4) The power of the High Court under this section may be exercised by a single judge of the High Court in the same manner as it may be exercised by the High Court, and subject to the same provisions.".

DEFINITIONS
"clerk of court": s.114(1).

GENERAL NOTE
This section introduces further powers to amend records of conviction and sentence in summary proceedings. Section 439 of the 1975 Act permitted the correction of entries in the record of proceedings in a summary prosecution or the extract of a sentence passed or an order of court made in such proceedings "in so far as that entry constitutes an error of recording or is incomplete".

Section 439 proceeds on the basis that the matter to be corrected is the result of some sort of failing on the part of the clerk of court. The new section is necessary because of the comparatively widespread practice of the accused in summary proceedings giving false names, often of friends or relatives, so that the record of proceedings accurately reflects the crime or offence, but inaccurately states the name (and perhaps other details) of the accused.

Appeals

Leave to appeal

42.—(1) In section 228(1) of the 1975 Act (right of appeal), after the word "may" there shall be inserted ", with leave granted in accordance with section 230A of this Act,".

(2) After section 230 of that Act there shall be inserted the following section—

"Leave to appeal

230A.—(1) The decision whether to grant leave to appeal for the purposes of section 228(1) of this Act shall be made by a judge of the High Court who shall—

(a) if he considers that the documents mentioned in subsection (2) below disclose arguable grounds of appeal, grant leave to appeal and make such comments in writing as he considers appropriate; and

(b) in any other case—

(i) refuse leave to appeal and give reasons in writing for the refusal; and

(ii) where the appellant is on bail and the sentence imposed on his conviction is one of imprisonment, grant a warrant to apprehend and imprison him.

(2) The documents referred to in subsection (1) above are—

(a) the note of appeal lodged under section 233(1)(a) of this Act;

(b) in a case to which section 236 of this Act applies, the certified copy or, as the case may be, the record of the proceedings at the trial;

(c) where the judge who presided at the trial furnishes a report under section 236A of this Act, that report; and

(d) where, by virtue of section 275(1) of this Act, a transcript of the charge to the jury of the judge who presided at the trial is delivered to the Clerk of Justiciary, that transcript.

(3) A warrant granted under subsection (1)(b)(ii) above shall not take effect until the expiry of the period of 14 days mentioned in subsection (4) below without an application to the High Court for leave to appeal having been lodged by the appellant under that subsection.

(4) Where leave to appeal is refused under subsection (1) above the appellant may, within 14 days of intimation under subsection (10) below, apply to the High Court for leave to appeal.

(5) In deciding an application under subsection (4) above the High Court shall—

(a) if, after considering the documents mentioned in subsection (2) above and the reasons for the refusal, the court is of the opinion that there are arguable grounds of appeal, grant leave to appeal and make such comments in writing as the court considers appropriate; and

(b) in any other case—

(i) refuse leave to appeal and give reasons in writing for the refusal; and

(ii) where the appellant is on bail and the sentence imposed on his conviction is one of imprisonment, grant a warrant to apprehend and imprison him.

(6) Consideration whether to grant leave to appeal under subsection (1) or (5) above shall take place in chambers without the parties being present.

(7) Comments in writing made under subsection (1)(a) or (5)(a) above may, without prejudice to the generality of that provision, specify the arguable grounds of appeal (whether or not they are contained in the note of appeal) on the basis of which leave to appeal is granted.

(8) Where the arguable grounds of appeal are specified by virtue of subsection (7) above it shall not, except by leave of the High Court on cause shown, be competent for the appellant to found any aspect of his appeal on any ground of appeal contained in the note of appeal but not so specified.

(9) Any application by the appellant for the leave of the High Court under subsection (8) above—

(a) shall be made not less than seven days before the date fixed for the hearing of the appeal; and

(b) shall, not less than seven days before that date, be intimated by the appellant to the Crown Agent.

(10) The Clerk of Justiciary shall forthwith intimate—

(a) a decision under subsection (1) or (5) above; and

(b) in the case of a refusal of leave to appeal, the reasons for the decision,

to the appellant or his solicitor and to the Crown Agent.".

(3) After subsection (3) of section 233 of that Act (restriction on arguing ground not in note of appeal) there shall be inserted the following subsection—

"(3A) Subsection (3) above shall not apply as respects any ground of appeal specified as an arguable ground of appeal by virtue of subsection (7) of section 230A of this Act.".

(4) In section 442(1)(a) of that Act (right of appeal), after the word "may" there shall be inserted ", with leave granted in accordance with section 442ZA or, as the case may be, 453AA of this Act,".

(5) After section 442 of that Act there shall be inserted the following section—

"Leave to appeal against conviction etc.

442ZA.—(1) The decision whether to grant leave to appeal for the purposes of section 442(1)(a)(i) or (iii) of this Act shall be made by a judge of the High Court who shall—

(a) if he considers that the documents mentioned in subsection (2) below disclose arguable grounds of appeal, grant leave to appeal and make such comments in writing as he considers appropriate; and

(b) in any other case—

(i) refuse leave to appeal and give reasons in writing for the refusal; and

(ii) where the appellant is on bail and the sentence imposed on his conviction is one of imprisonment, grant a warrant to apprehend and imprison him.

(2) The documents referred to in subsection (1) above are—

(a) the stated case lodged under subsection (4) of section 448 of this Act; and

(b) the documents transmitted to the Clerk of Justiciary under subsection (3)(b) of that section.

(3) A warrant granted under subsection (1)(b)(ii) above shall not take effect until the expiry of the period of 14 days mentioned in subsection (4) below without an application to the High Court for leave to appeal having been lodged by the appellant under that subsection.

(4) Where leave to appeal is refused under subsection (1) above the appellant may, within 14 days of intimation under subsection (10) below, apply to the High Court for leave to appeal.

(5) In deciding an application under subsection (4) above the High Court shall—

(a) if, after considering the documents mentioned in subsection (2) above and the reasons for the refusal, the court is of the opinion that there are arguable grounds of appeal, grant leave to appeal and make such comments in writing as the court considers appropriate; and

(b) in any other case—

(i) refuse leave to appeal and give reasons in writing for the refusal; and

(ii) where the appellant is on bail and the sentence imposed on his conviction is one of imprisonment, grant a warrant to apprehend and imprison him.

(6) Consideration whether to grant leave to appeal under subsection (1) or (5) above shall take place in chambers without the parties being present.

(7) Comments in writing made under subsection (1)(a) or (5)(a) above may, without prejudice to the generality of that provision, specify the arguable grounds of appeal (whether or not they are contained in the stated case) on the basis of which leave to appeal is granted.

(8) Where the arguable grounds of appeal are specified by virtue of subsection (7) above it shall not, except by leave of the High Court on cause shown, be competent for the appellant to found any aspect of his appeal on any ground of appeal contained in the stated case but not so specified.

(9) Any application by the appellant for the leave of the High Court under subsection (8) above—

(a) shall be made not less than seven days before the date fixed for the hearing of the appeal; and

(b) shall, not less than seven days before that date, be intimated by the appellant to the Crown Agent.

(10) The Clerk of Justiciary shall forthwith intimate—

(a) a decision under subsection (1) or (5) above; and

(b) in the case of a refusal of leave to appeal, the reasons for the decision,

to the appellant or his solicitor and to the Crown Agent.".

(6) After subsection (3) of section 452 of that Act (restriction on arguing ground not in stated case) there shall be inserted the following subsection—

"(3A) Subsection (3) above shall not apply as respects any ground of appeal specified as an arguable ground of appeal by virtue of subsection (7) of section 442ZA of this Act.".

(7) After section 453A of that Act there shall be inserted the following section—

"Leave to appeal against sentence

453AA.—(1) The decision whether to grant leave to appeal for the purposes of section 442(1)(a)(ii) or (iia) of this Act shall be made by a judge of the High Court who shall—

(a) if he considers that the note of appeal and other documents sent to the Clerk of Justiciary under section 453B(4)(a) of this Act disclose arguable grounds of appeal, grant leave to appeal; and

(b) in any other case—

(i) refuse leave to appeal and give reasons in writing for the refusal; and

(ii) where the appellant is on bail and the sentence imposed on his conviction is one of imprisonment, grant a warrant to apprehend and imprison him.

(2) A warrant granted under subsection (1)(b)(ii) above shall not take effect until the expiry of the period of 14 days mentioned in subsection (3) below without an application to the High Court for leave to appeal having been lodged by the appellant under that subsection.

(3) Where leave to appeal is refused under subsection (1) above the appellant may, within 14 days of intimation under subsection (9) below, apply to the High Court for leave to appeal.

(4) In deciding an application under subsection (3) above the High Court shall—

(a) if, after considering the note of appeal and other documents mentioned in subsection (1) above and the reasons for the refusal, the court is of the opinion that there are arguable grounds of appeal, grant leave to appeal; and

(b) in any other case—

(i) refuse leave to appeal and give reasons in writing for the refusal; and

(ii) where the appellant is on bail and the sentence imposed on his conviction is one of imprisonment, grant a warrant to apprehend and imprison him.

(5) Consideration whether to grant leave to appeal under subsection (1) or (4) above shall take place in chambers without the parties being present.

(6) Comments in writing made under subsection (1)(a) or (4)(a) above may, without prejudice to the generality of that provision, specify the arguable grounds of appeal (whether or not they are contained in the note of appeal) on the basis of which leave to appeal is granted.

(7) Where the arguable grounds of appeal are specified by virtue of subsection (6) above it shall not, except by leave of the High Court on cause shown, be competent for the appellant to found any aspect of his appeal on any ground of appeal contained in the note of appeal but not so specified.

(8) Any application by the appellant for the leave of the High Court under subsection (7) above—

  (a) shall be made not less than seven days before the date fixed for the hearing of the appeal; and

  (b) shall, not less than seven days before that date, be intimated by the appellant to the Crown Agent.

(9) The Clerk of Justiciary shall forthwith intimate—

  (a) a decision under subsection (1) or (4) above; and

  (b) in the case of a refusal of leave to appeal, the reasons for the decision,

to the appellant or his solicitor and to the Crown Agent.".

GENERAL NOTE

This introduces a requirement for leave to appeal against conviction, sentence or other disposal to be on the basis of arguable grounds. An application for leave to appeal is to be considered by a single judge sitting in chambers on the basis of papers and without oral argument. Leave to appeal will be granted if the application demonstrates arguable grounds of appeal, otherwise leave will be refused.

If leave is refused an appellant will have 14 days in which to renew the application to the High Court. The renewed application will be considered by the High Court, again sitting in chambers, on the basis of the same papers that were before the single judge and the reasons for the refusal of leave given by the single judge. Leave to appeal will be granted only if the court considers that the application demonstrates arguable grounds of appeal.

Where an appellant is on bail pending appeal, the sentence is one of imprisonment and leave to appeal is refused, the single judge or the High Court must grant a warrant to apprehend and imprison the appellant. Where the warrant is issued by the single judge it shall not take effect until 14 days have passed from the intimation of the decision to the appellant and the appellant has not renewed the application for leave to appeal in that time.

This section (when it was cl. 35 of the Bill) was debated at some length at the committee stage in the House of Lords. The Lord Advocate advised the House that the intention of the new procedure was to allow the High Court of Justiciary to filter out frivolous and unmeritorious appeals quickly and simply (*Hansard*, H.L. Vol. 560, col. 480). There was, he reassured the House, "no question of these new arrangements reducing the level of scrutiny of appeals in general since only appeals which are clearly without merit—those which are inarguable in the way it is expressed—would be refused leave to appeal. Any appeal which appeared to demonstrate arguable grounds would be granted leave and would proceed to appeal hearing in open court" (*Hansard*, H.L. Vol. 560, col. 481).

Lord McCluskey suggested that there was "a good deal of danger" in having a single judge decide the matter in chambers. He thought also that, standing *Granger v. United Kingdom* (1990) 12 E.H.R.R. 469, the new procedure might contravene Art. 6 of the European Convention on Human Rights (*Hansard*, H.L. Vol. 560, cols. 481–484).

The Lord Advocate was of the view that the essence of the *Granger* case was the infringement of the equality of arms, a matter that did not arise in the particular procedure envisaged in the new legislation (*Hansard*, H.L. Vol. 560, col. 485).

Section 228 of the 1975 Act provides that a person convicted on indictment may appeal against conviction, against sentence or other disposal, against conviction *and* sentence or other disposal, on the grounds of any alleged miscarriage of justice in the proceedings in which he was convicted.

Reduction in quorum of High Court for appeals against sentence etc.

43.—(1) In section 245 of the 1975 Act (quorum of High Court in relation to appeals)—

(a) at the beginning of subsection (1) there shall be inserted "Subject to subsection (1A) below,"; and

(b) after subsection (1) there shall be inserted the following subsection—

"(1A) For the purpose of hearing and determining any appeal under section 228(1)(b), (bb), (bc) or (bd) of this Act, or any proceeding connected therewith, two of the Lords Commissioners of Justiciary shall be a quorum of the High Court, and each judge shall be entitled to pronounce a separate opinion; but where the two Lords Commissioners of Justiciary are unable to reach agreement on the disposal of the appeal, or where they consider it appropriate, the appeal shall be heard and determined in accordance with subsection (1) above.".

(2) After section 451 of that Act there shall be inserted the following section—

"Quorum of High Court in relation to appeals

451A.—(1) For the purpose of hearing and determining any appeal under this Part of this Act, or any proceeding connected therewith, three of the Lords Commissioners of Justiciary shall be a quorum of the High Court, and the determination of any question under this Part of this Act by the court shall be according to the votes of the majority of the members of the court sitting, including the presiding judge, and each judge so sitting shall be entitled to pronounce a separate opinion.

(2) For the purpose of hearing and determining appeals under section 442(1)(a)(ii) or (iia) of this Act, or any proceeding connected therewith, two of the Lords Commissioners of Justiciary shall be a quorum of the High Court, and each judge shall be entitled to pronounce a separate opinion; but where the two Lords Commissioners of Justiciary are unable to reach agreement on the disposal of the appeal, or where they consider it appropriate, the appeal shall be heard and determined in accordance with subsection (1) above.".

GENERAL NOTE

The intention of this section is to provide a means of reducing the burden placed on the High Court of Justiciary in recent years by the increasing number of appeals being lodged, especially the increase in appeals against sentence.

Section 245(1) of the 1975 Act provides that for the purpose of hearing and determining any appeal under Pt. I of the 1975 Act (*i.e.* appeals arising from solemn proceedings) or any proceedings connected therewith, three of the Lords Commissioners of Justiciary shall be a quorum of the High Court of Justiciary. The quorum of the High Court of Justiciary for hearing appeals under Pt. II of the 1975 Act (*i.e.* appeals arising from summary proceedings) is not specified in statute. In practice a quorum of three is adopted.

Therefore all appeals, no matter how minor, must at present be heard by at least three of the Lords Commissioners of Justiciary. The section allows appeals against sentence or other disposal alone to be heard by two of the Lords Commissioners of Justiciary. The section also provides, however, for the appeal to be heard and determined by three or more Lords Commissioners of Justiciary should the two Lords Commissioners of Justiciary be unable to reach agreement, or if they consider it appropriate for any other reason. This is to allow for cases to be referred to larger benches where they raise issues of general application or of particular difficulty; and also to allow for the possibility of the two judges failing to reach agreement on the appropriate disposal of the appeal.

This section provides that two of the Lords Commissioners of Justiciary should be a quorum of the High Court of Justiciary in hearing appeals against sentence or other disposals under subss. 228(1)(b), (bb), (bc) or (bd) of the 1975 Act. The current practice that three of the Lords

Commissioners of Justiciary is the quorum of the High Court of Justiciary in hearing appeals under Pt. II of the 1975 Act is now subject to the new provision that two of the Lords Commissioners of Justiciary should be a quorum of the High Court of Justiciary in hearing appeals against sentence or other disposals alone under subss. 442(1)(a)(ii) and (iia) of the 1975 Act.

Trial judge's report

44.—(1) Without prejudice to sections 236A and 453B(3)(b) of the 1975 Act, the High Court may, in relation to any appeal—

(a) under section 228(1), 228A or 442(1) of the 1975 Act;

(b) by way of bill of suspension or advocation; or

(c) by way of petition to the nobile officium,

at any time before the appeal is finally determined, order the judge who presided at the trial, passed sentence or otherwise disposed of the case to provide to the Clerk of Justiciary a report in writing giving the judge's opinion on the case generally or in relation to any particular matter specified in the order.

(2) The Clerk of Justiciary shall send a copy of a report provided under subsection (1) above to the convicted person or his solicitor, the Crown Agent and, in relation to cases referred under section 263(1) of the 1975 Act, the Secretary of State.

(3) Subject to subsection (2) above, the report of the judge shall be available only to the High Court, the parties and, on such conditions as may be prescribed by Act of Adjournal, such other persons or classes of persons as may be so prescribed.

(4) Expressions used in this section and in the 1975 Act have the same meaning in this section as in that Act.

GENERAL NOTE

This section reinforces the statutory duty on judges at first instance to provide a report in the event of an appeal. This section is probably due to the difficult position of the High Court of Justiciary in *Brady v. Barbour* 1994 S.C.C.R. 890, where the High Court was required to hear an appeal without a sheriff's report.

Extension of certain time limits with respect to appeals

45.—(1) In section 451(2) of the 1975 Act (power of sheriff principal to extend certain time limits with respect to appeal by stated case), for the words from "taken" to "the sheriff" there shall be substituted "taken—

(a) is temporarily absent from duty for any cause;

(b) is a temporary sheriff; or

(c) is a justice of the peace,

the sheriff".

(2) In the proviso to subsection (4) of section 453B of that Act (power of sheriff principal to extend time limit with respect to appeal against sentence), for the words from "judge" to "extend" there shall be substituted "judge—

(a) is temporarily absent from duty for any cause;

(b) is a temporary sheriff; or

(c) is a justice of the peace,

extend".

GENERAL NOTE

This amends ss.451(2) and 453B of the 1975 Act which allow sheriffs principal to extend the time-limits prescribed for the preparation of stated cases and sentencing reports. The amendments deal with cases where the appeal is against the judgment of a temporary sheriff or a justice of the peace who, while not absent from their judicial duties, may be unable to adhere to time-limits. Section 447 of the 1975 Act requires the judge against whose judgment an appeal against conviction is taken to state a case for the opinion of the Appeal Court within three weeks of the completion of the proceedings.

In the district court it is the duty of the clerk of court to prepare such a stated case. Under s.453B of the 1975 Act the judge against whose judgment an appeal against sentence is taken must prepare a sentencing report stating the reasons for his sentencing decision within two weeks of passing the sentence.

Sections 451 and 453B provide that those time-limits may be extended by the Sheriff Principal where a judge is absent from duty. The sections currently do not make provision for temporary sheriffs and justices of the peace who may be unable to keep to time-limits due to other professional commitments or because they are sitting in a different court. Section 451 makes no provision to extend time-limits for a stated case where a Clerk of District Court is absent from duty.

This section clarifies the position with respect to temporary sheriffs, justices of the peace and Clerks of the District Court by inserting an express reference in the relevant sections of the 1975 Act.

New prosecution for same or similar offence

46.—(1) In section 255 of the 1975 Act (supplementary provisions where High Court authorises new prosecution)—

  (a) at the beginning of subsection (1) there shall be inserted "Subject to subsection (1A) below,";

  (b) after subsection (1) there shall be inserted the following subsections—

"(1A) In a new prosecution under this section the accused shall not be charged with an offence more serious than that of which he was convicted in the earlier proceedings.

(1B) In proceedings in a new prosecution under this section it shall, subject to subsection (1 C) below, be competent for either party to lead any evidence which it was competent for him to lead in the earlier proceedings.

(1C) The indictment in a new prosecution under this section shall identify any matters as respects which the prosecutor intends to lead evidence by virtue of subsection (1B) above which would not have been competent but for that subsection."; and

  (c) after subsection (4) there shall be inserted the following subsections—

"(5) On granting authority under section 254(1)(c) of this Act to bring a new prosecution, the High Court shall, after giving the parties an opportunity of being heard, order the detention of the accused person in custody or admit him to bail.

(6) Subsections (2)(b) and (4) to (6) of section 101 of this Act (prevention of delay in trials) shall apply to an accused person who is detained under subsection (5) above as they apply to an accused person detained by virtue of being committed until liberated in due course of law.".

(2) In section 452B of the 1975 Act (corresponding provision in relation to summary proceedings—

  (a) at the beginning of subsection (1) there shall be inserted "Subject to subsection (1A) below,";

  (b) after subsection (1) there shall be inserted the following subsections—

"(1A) In a new prosecution under this section the accused shall not be charged with an offence more serious than that of which he was convicted in the earlier proceedings.

(1B) In proceedings in a new prosecution under this section it shall, subject to subsection (1C) below, be competent for either party to lead any evidence which it was competent for him to lead in the earlier proceedings.

(1C) The complaint in a new prosecution under this section shall identify any matters as respects which the prosecutor intends to lead evidence by virtue of subsection (1B) above which would not have been competent but for that subsection."; and

  (c) after subsection (4) there shall be inserted the following subsection—

"(5) On granting authority under section 452A(1)(d) of this Act to bring a new prosecution, the High Court may, after giving the parties an opportunity of being heard, order the detention of the accused person in custody; but an accused person may not be detained by virtue of this subsection for a period of more than 40 days.".

DEFINITIONS
"accused": s.114(1).
"prosecutor": s.462(1) of the Criminal Procedure (Scotland) Act 1975.

GENERAL NOTE
This section explains and limits the power of the prosecutor in relation to a new prosecution which has been authorised by the High Court of Justiciary. It might be called Boyle's section because of the extraordinary circumstances arising out of the trials of Daniel Boyle. These circumstances gave rise to the various parts of the section.

Boyle was charged with murder and after trial in the High Court of Justiciary at Glasgow he was convicted of culpable homicide in November 1991. He was sentenced to 10 years' detention. He appealed against conviction and that verdict was set aside in July 1992: *Boyle v. H.M. Advocate* 1992 S.C.C.R. 824.

The High Court of Justiciary, in setting aside that verdict, granted authority to the Crown to bring a new prosecution in accordance with ss.254(1)(c) and 255 of the 1975 Act.

A fresh indictment containing a charge of murder was served on Boyle on July 30, 1992 for trial on August 31, but the trial diet was overtaken by an appeal by the Crown against a decision at a preliminary diet: see s.76A of the 1975 Act.

The Crown appeal arose in this way: at the preliminary diet the accused argued that, the jury having returned a verdict of culpable homicide, the Crown was thus barred from indicting him for the more serious crime of murder. The Crown argued otherwise. The trial judge held the action of the Crown to be competent in law but unfair in the circumstances and dismissed the indictment. The Crown appeal was allowed and the indictment was remitted to the trial court to proceed: *H.M. Advocate v. Boyle* 1992 S.C.C.R. 939.

Thereafter there was a petition from the accused to the *nobile officium* to the High Court of Justiciary. Boyle in effect complained that the High Court of Justiciary (to whom he appealed) had exceeded its own authority in setting aside on the indictment certain of the charges on the original indictment which the accused had not appealed against. The petition was refused: *Boyle, Petitioner* 1992 S.C.C.R. 949.

For the sake of completeness it should be added that a diet of trial in November 1992 was adjourned to January 1993 because of difficulties that the Crown had with witnesses. Boyle had been in custody since August 1991 and he again petitioned the *nobile officium* of the High Court of Justiciary, this time for bail which was granted in terms of s.35 of the 1975 Act: *Boyle, Petitioner* 1993 S.C.C.R. 251. Daniel Boyle was acquitted at his second trial for murder.

Mental disorder and criminal proceedings

Insanity in bar of trial

47.—(1) For subsection (1) of section 174 of the 1975 Act (finding of insanity in bar of trial in solemn proceedings) there shall be substituted the following subsections—

"(1) Where the court is satisfied, on the written or oral evidence of two medical practitioners, that a person charged on indictment with the commission of an offence is insane so that his trial cannot proceed or, if it has commenced, cannot continue, the court shall, subject to subsection (1A) below—

(a) make a finding to that effect and state the reasons for that finding;

(b) discharge the trial diet and order that a diet (in this Act referred to as an "an examination of facts") be held under section 174ZA of this Act; and

(c) remand the person in custody or on bail or, where the court is satisfied—

(i) on the written or oral evidence of two medical practitioners, that he is suffering from mental disorder of a nature or degree which warrants his admission to hospital under Part V of the Mental Health (Scotland) Act 1984; and

(ii) that a hospital is available for his admission and suitable for his detention,

make an order (in this section referred to as a "temporary hospital order") committing him to that hospital until the conclusion of the examination of facts.

(1A) Subsection (1) above is without prejudice to the power of the court, on an application by the prosecutor, to desert the diet pro loco et tempore.

(1B) The court may, before making a finding under subsection (1) above as to the insanity of a person, adjourn the case in order that investigation of his mental condition may be carried out.

(1C) The court which made a temporary hospital order may, at any time while the order is in force, review the order on the ground that there has been a change of circumstances since the order was made and, on such review—

    (a) where the court considers that such an order is no longer required in relation to a person, it shall revoke the order and may remand him in custody or on bail;

    (b) in any other case, the court may—

        (i) confirm or vary the order; or

        (ii) revoke the order and make such other order, under subsection (1)(c) above or any other provision of this Part of this Act, as the court considers appropriate.".

(2) For subsection (2) of section 375 of the 1975 Act (finding of insanity in bar of trial in summary proceedings) there shall be substituted the following subsections—

"(2) Where the court is satisfied, on the written or oral evidence of two medical practitioners, that a person charged summarily in the sheriff court with the commission of an offence is insane so that his trial cannot proceed or, if it has commenced, cannot continue, the court shall, subject to subsection (2A) below—

    (a) make a finding to that effect and state the reasons for that finding;

    (b) discharge the trial diet and order that a diet (in this Act referred to as an "examination of facts") be held in accordance with section 375ZA of this Act; and

    (c) remand the person in custody or on bail or, where the court is satisfied—

        (i) on the written or oral evidence of two medical practitioners, that he is suffering from mental disorder of a nature or degree which warrants his admission to hospital under Part V of the Mental Health (Scotland) Act 1984; and

        (ii) that a hospital is available for his admission and suitable for his detention,

    make an order (in this section referred to as a "temporary hospital order") committing him to that hospital until the conclusion of the examination of facts.

(2A) Subsection (2) above is without prejudice to the power of the court, on an application by the prosecutor, to desert the diet pro loco et tempore.

(2B) The court may, before making a finding under subsection (2) above as to the insanity of a person, adjourn the case in order that investigation of his mental condition may be carried out.

(2C) The court which made a temporary hospital order may, at any time while the order is in force, review the order on the ground that there has been a change of circumstances since the order was made and, on such review—

    (a) where the court considers that such an order is no longer required in relation to a person, it shall revoke the order and may remand him in custody or on bail;

    (b) in any other case, the court may—

        (i) confirm or vary the order; or

(ii) revoke the order and make such other order, under sub-section (2)(c) above or any other provision of this Part of this Act, as the court considers appropriate.".

GENERAL NOTE
This section requires a court, in both solemn and summary proceedings, to hold an examin-ation of the facts (EOF) relating to the charges, following a finding that a person is insane so that his trial cannot proceed or continue. The section further provides for the court to remand in custody or on bail, or to commit such a person to hospital under a temporary hospital order, until the conclusion of the EOF. The procedure to be followed in an EOF is dealt with in s.49 (below).

At present, when a person is found insane in bar of trial, no attempt is made by the court to examine the evidence as to whether or not the accused did the act with which he is charged. This section provides that there shall be an examination of the relevant facts. It gives effect to certain recommendations contained in the Second Thomson Report on Criminal Procedure of 1975 (Cmnd. 6218) and was supported by the great majority of consultees who responded to the Government's consultation paper issued in February 1993.

Under present procedures (specified in s.174(1) of the 1975 Act) there is no statutory mini-mum requirement as to the extent of medical evidence which a court must hear before making a finding of insanity in bar of trial.

There are powers in the 1975 Act for the remand in custody or on bail, or for the committal to hospital, of an accused person in the period leading up to a trial. However, once an accused has been found unfit to plead and a trial is no longer in prospect, those powers are no longer apt. Section 47 therefore provides powers to remand or commit an accused in the period leading up to an EOF.

Insanity as ground of acquittal in summary proceedings

48. After subsection (3) of section 375 of the 1975 Act (insanity in bar of trial) there shall be inserted the following subsection—

"(3A) Where, in the case of any person charged summarily in the sheriff court, evidence is brought before the court that the person was insane at the time of doing the act or making the omission constituting the offence with which he is charged and the person is acquitted, the court shall state whether the person was insane at that time and, if so, whether he was acquitted on that ground.".

GENERAL NOTE
This section inserts in s.375 of the 1975 Act a provision enabling a court of summary jurisdic-tion to deliver a verdict of acquittal on the ground of insanity at the time of commission of the offence charged. Section 174(2) of the 1975 Act enables a court in solemn proceedings to deliver a verdict of acquittal on the ground that the accused person was insane at the time of doing the act or making the omission constituting the offence with which he was charged. There is no express provision in Pt. II of the 1975 Act equivalent to s.174(2). This section remedies that.

This section inserts into s.375 of the 1975 Act a new subsection which parallels s.174(2) of the 1975 Act for solemn proceedings. Subsection (3A) provides that, in the case of any person charged summarily in the sheriff court, where evidence is brought before the court that the person was insane at the time of doing the act (or making the omission) constituting the offence charged, and the person is acquitted, the court shall state whether the person was insane at that time and, if so, whether the person was acquitted on that ground.

Examination of facts

49.—(1) After section 174 of the 1975 Act there shall be inserted the fol-lowing sections—

"**Examination of facts**

174ZA.—(1) At an examination of facts ordered under section 174(1)(b) of this Act the court shall, on the basis of the evidence (if any) already given in the trial and such evidence, or further evidence, as may be led by either party, determine whether it is satisfied—

(a) beyond reasonable doubt, as respects any charge on indictment in respect of which the accused was being or was to be tried, that he did the act or made the omission constituting the offence; and

(b) on the balance of probabilities, that there are no grounds for acquitting him.

(2) Where the court is satisfied as mentioned in subsection (1) above, it shall make a finding to that effect.

(3) Where the court is not so satisfied it shall, subject to subsection (4) below, acquit the person of the charge.

(4) Where, as respects a person acquitted under subsection (3) above, the court is satisfied as to the matter mentioned in subsection (1)(a) above but it appears to the court that the person was insane at the time of doing the act or making the omission constituting the offence, the court shall state whether the acquittal is on the ground of such insanity.

(5) Where it appears to the court that it is not practicable or appropriate for the accused to attend an examination of facts the court may, if no objection is taken by or on behalf of the accused, order that the examination of facts shall proceed in his absence.

(6) Subject to the provisions of this section, section 174ZB of this Act and any Act of Adjournal, the rules of evidence and procedure and the powers of the court shall, in respect of an examination of facts, be as nearly as possible those applicable in respect of a trial.

(7) For the purposes of the application to an examination of facts of the rules and powers mentioned in subsection (6) above, an examination of facts—

(a) commences when the indictment is called; and

(b) concludes when the court—

    (i) acquits the person under subsection (3) above;

    (ii) makes an order under subsection (2) of section 174ZC of this Act; or

    (iii) decides, under paragraph (e) of that subsection, not to make an order.

Examination of facts: supplementary provisions

174ZB.—(1) An examination of facts ordered under section 174(1)(b) of this Act may, where the order is made at the trial diet, be held immediately following the making of the order and, where it is so held, the citation of the accused and any witness to the trial diet shall be a valid citation to the examination of facts.

(2) A warrant for citation of an accused and witnesses under section 69 of this Act shall be sufficient warrant for citation to an examination of facts.

(3) Where an accused person is not legally represented at an examination of facts the court shall appoint counsel or a solicitor to represent his interests.

(4) The court may, on the motion of the prosecutor and after hearing the accused, order that the examination of facts shall proceed in relation to a particular charge, or particular charges, in the indictment in priority to other such charges.

(5) The court may, on the motion of the prosecutor and after hearing the accused, at any time desert the examination of facts pro loco et tempore as respects either the whole indictment or any charge therein.

(6) Where, and to the extent that, an examination of facts has, under subsection (5) above, been deserted pro loco et tempore, the Lord Advocate may, at any time, raise and insist in a new indictment notwithstanding any time limit which would otherwise apply in respect of prosecution of the alleged offence.

(7) If, in a case where a court has made a finding under subsection (2) of section 174ZA above, a person is subsequently charged, whether on indictment or on a complaint, with an offence arising out of the same act or omission as is referred to in subsection (1) of that section, any order

made under section 174ZC(2) of this Act shall, with effect from the commencement of the later proceedings, cease to have effect.

(8) For the purposes of subsection (7) above, the later proceedings are commenced when the indictment or, as the case may be, the complaint is served.".

(2) After section 375 of the 1975 Act there shall be inserted the following sections—

"Examination of facts

375ZA.—(1) At an examination of facts ordered under section 375(2)(b) of this Act the court shall, on the basis of the evidence (if any) already given in the trial and such evidence, or further evidence, as may be led by either party, determine whether it is satisfied—

(a) beyond reasonable doubt, as respects any charge in a complaint in respect of which the accused was being or was to be tried, that he did the act or made the omission constituting the offence; and

(b) on the balance of probabilities, that there are no grounds for acquitting him.

(2) Where the court is satisfied as mentioned in subsection (1) above, it shall make a finding to that effect.

(3) Where the court is not so satisfied it shall, subject to subsection (4) below, acquit the person of the charge.

(4) Where, as respects a person acquitted under subsection (3) above, the court is satisfied as to the matter mentioned in subsection (1)(a) above but it appears to the court that the person was insane at the time of doing the act or making the omission constituting the offence, the court shall state whether the acquittal is on the ground of such insanity.

(5) Where it appears to the court that it is not practicable or appropriate for the accused to attend an examination of facts the court may, if no objection is taken by or on behalf of the accused, order that the examination of facts shall proceed in his absence.

(6) Subject to the provisions of this section, section 375ZB of this Act and any Act of Adjournal, the rules of evidence and procedure and the powers of the court in respect of an examination of facts shall be as nearly as possible those applicable in respect of a trial.

(7) For the purposes of the application to an examination of facts of the rules and powers mentioned in subsection (6) above, an examination of facts—

(a) commences when the diet is called; and

(b) concludes when the court—

(i) acquits the person under subsection (3) above;

(ii) makes an order under subsection (2) of section 375ZC of this Act; or

(iii) decides, under paragraph (e) of that subsection, not to make an order.

Examination of facts: supplementary provisions

375ZB.—(1) An examination of facts ordered under section 375(2)(b) of this Act may, where the order is made at the trial diet, be held immediately following the making of the order and, where it is so held, the citation of the accused and any witness to the trial diet shall be a valid citation to the examination of facts.

(2) Where an accused person is not legally represented at an examination of facts the court shall appoint counsel or a solicitor to represent his interests.

(3) The court may, on the motion of the prosecutor and after hearing the accused, order that the examination of facts shall proceed in relation to a particular charge, or particular charges, in the complaint in priority to other such charges.

(4) The court may, on the motion of the prosecutor and after hearing the accused, at any time desert the examination of facts pro loco et tempore as respects the whole complaint or any charge in the complaint.

(5) Where, and to the extent that, an examination of facts has, under subsection (4) above, been deserted pro loco et tempore, the prosecutor may, at any time, raise a fresh libel notwithstanding any time limit which would otherwise apply in respect of prosecution of the alleged offence.

(6) If, in a case where a court has made a finding under subsection (2) of section 375ZA of this Act, a person is subsequently charged, whether on indictment or on a complaint, with an offence arising out of the same act or omission as is referred to in subsection (1) of that section, any order made under section 375ZC(2) of this Act shall, with effect from the commencement of the later proceedings, cease to have effect.

(7) For the purposes of subsection (6) above, the later proceedings are commenced when the indictment or, as the case may be, the complaint is served.".

GENERAL NOTE

This section inserts new sections after ss.175 and 375 of the 1975 Act providing for a new diet, which is to be called an examination of facts (EOF), and which may be ordered to be held under the new provisions contained in s.47. The section specifies the procedures and powers of the court, its findings, and a number of detailed ancillary matters. The holding of an EOF will be a novel procedure in Scotland. It is necessary to specify what its remit will be and how it is to operate and be conducted.

Subsection (1) inserts two new sections (ss.174ZA and 174ZB) after s.174 of the 1975 Act, *i.e.* into that part of the Act which covers solemn proceedings.

Section 174ZA(1) provides that an EOF shall consider both any evidence already given in the trial (*i.e.* where the issue and finding of unfitness to plead arises part way through a trial) and the evidence led at the EOF itself, by either party. In light of that evidence the court must determine whether it is satisfied not only that (a) the accused did the act (or made the omission) constituting the offence, but also that (b) there are no grounds for his acquittal. The court must consider these matters in relation to any (*i.e.* each) charge on the indictment. As to standard of proof, the court must be satisfied beyond reasonable doubt that the accused did the act, and the court requires to be satisfied on the balance of probabilities that there are no grounds for acquittal. If the court is satisfied that the accused did the act or made the omission constituting the offence and that there are no grounds for acquitting him it must make a finding to that effect. As the court is required (under subs. (1)) to consider any (*i.e.* each) charge on the indictment, it follows that there will be a finding under s.174ZA(2) or an acquittal under s.174ZA(3) for each charge on the indictment. Section 174ZA(3) provides that where the court is not so satisfied as to (1)(a) and (b) it shall acquit the accused of the charge.

Section 174ZA(4) provides for the special case where the court is satisfied as to (1)(a) above, *i.e.* that the accused did the act, but is not satisfied as to (1)(b), *i.e.* it concludes that there are grounds for acquitting him. If that acquittal is on the ground that at the time of doing the act the accused was insane, the court is required to state that the finding of acquittal under subs. (3) above is on the ground of such insanity.

Section 174ZA(7) sets out the commencement and conclusion of an EOF. This is relevant in relation to s.101 of the 1975 Act which specifies that a trial under solemn proceedings (and therefore an EOF by virtue of s.174ZA(5)) shall commence within 110 days of any date on which an accused is committed, *i.e.* remanded in custody or committed to hospital. This subsection provides that the "commencement" of the EOF is the calling of the indictment. The "conclusion" is when the EOF delivers a finding of acquittal or, having delivered a finding to the effect that the accused did the act and that there are no grounds for acquitting him, either imposes one of the orders available under s.174ZC of the 1975 Act (inserted by s.50) or decides to make no order. As the EOF must examine the facts in relation to any charge on the indictment, it will not conclude until each charge on the indictment has been considered and has resulted in an acquittal or disposal.

Section 174ZB makes supplementary provisions as regards EOFs. Section 174ZB(1) provides that where an EOF is ordered under new s.174(1)(b) of the 1975 Act (inserted by s.47, above) at a trial diet, the EOF may be held immediately following the making of the order. Citation of the accused and the witnesses to appear at the trial shall be valid citation to appear at the EOF. The EOF may therefore follow on from the abandoned trial as all the necessary administrative arrangements will already be in place. Section 174ZB(2) provides, for the avoidance of doubt, that a warrant for citation of an accused and witnesses under s.69 of the 1975 Act, *i.e.* to appear at a trial diet, shall be sufficient warrant for citation to appear at an EOF.

Section 174ZB(4) provides that the court may grant a motion for the prosecutor for desertion of the EOF diet *pro loco et tempore* either as regards the whole of the indictment or any charge therein. The accused (*i.e.* his representative) must be given an opportunity to be heard. This procedure could, for example, be used where the indictment contains several charges, a main one and a number of lesser ones. If the EOF delivers a finding that the accused did the act charged as the main offence, *i.e.* paving the way for the EOF to make a disposal, the Crown may not wish to prolong the EOF and the defence may agree to that. If the Crown does not wish to desert the remaining charges *simpliciter* in case the accused recovers his sanity sufficiently to stand trial, it may seek desertion *pro loco et tempore*, terminating the present proceedings but allowing future re-indictment should the accused recover sufficiently to stand trial.

Subsection (2) of s.49 inserts two new sections, 375ZA and 375ZB, into that part of the 1975 Act which covers summary proceedings, and which have the same effect in relation to summary proceedings as ss.174ZA and 174ZB described above have for solemn proceedings.

Disposal of case where accused found to be insane

50.—(1) After section 174ZB of the 1975 Act (inserted by section 49(1) of this Act) there shall be inserted the following section—

"Disposal of case where accused found to be insane

174ZC.—(1) This section applies where—
- (a) a person is, by virtue of section 174(2) or 174ZA(3) of this Act, acquitted on the ground of his insanity at the time of the act or omission; or
- (b) following an examination of facts under section 174ZA, a court makes a finding under subsection (2) of that section.

(2) Subject to subsection (3) below, where this section applies the court may, as it thinks fit—
- (a) make an order (which shall have the same effect as a hospital order) that the person be detained in such hospital as the court may specify;
- (b) in addition to making an order under paragraph (a) above, make an order (which shall have the same effect as a restriction order) that the person shall, without limit of time, be subject to the special restrictions set out in section 62(1) of the Mental Health (Scotland) Act 1984;
- (c) make an order (which shall have the same effect as a guardianship order) placing the person under the guardianship of a local authority or of a person approved by a local authority;
- (d) make a supervision and treatment order (within the meaning of paragraph 1(1) of Schedule 5A to this Act); or
- (e) make no order.

(3) Where the offence with which the person was charged is murder, the court shall make orders under both paragraphs (a) and (b) of subsection (2) above in respect of that person.

(4) Sections 175(1) and (3) to (6) and 176 to 178 of this Act shall have effect in relation to the making, terms and effect of an order under paragraph (a), (b) or (c) of subsection (2) above as those provisions have effect in relation to the making, terms and effect of, respectively, a hospital order, a restriction order and a guardianship order as respects a person convicted of an offence, other than an offence the sentence for which is fixed by law, punishable by imprisonment.".

(2) After section 375ZB of the 1975 Act (inserted by section 49(2) of this Act) there shall be inserted the following section—

"Disposal of case where accused found to be insane

375ZC.—(1) This section applies where—

    (a) a person is, by virtue of section 375(3A) or 375ZA(3) of this Act, acquitted on the ground of his insanity at the time of the act or omission; or

    (b) following an examination of facts under section 375ZA, a court makes a finding under subsection (2) of that section.

    (2) Where this section applies the court may, as it thinks fit—

    (a) make an order (which shall have the same effect as a hospital order) that the person be detained in such hospital as the court may specify;

    (b) in addition to making an order under paragraph (a) above, make an order (which shall have the same effect as a restriction order) that the person shall, without limit of time, be subject to the special restrictions set out in section 62(1) of the Mental Health (Scotland) Act 1984;

    (c) make an order (which shall have the same effect as a guardianship order) placing the person under the guardianship of a local authority or of a person approved by a local authority;

    (d) make a supervision and treatment order (within the meaning of paragraph 1(1) of Schedule 5A to this Act); or

    (e) make no order.

    (3) Sections 376(1) and (6) to (9) and 377 to 379 of this Act shall have effect in relation to the making, terms and effect of an order under paragraph (a), (b) or (c) of subsection (2) above as those provisions have effect in relation to the making, terms and effect of, respectively, a hospital order, a restriction order and a guardianship order as respects a person convicted of an offence, other than an offence the sentence for which is fixed by law, punishable by imprisonment.".

    (3) The Schedule set out in Schedule 2 to this Act (which makes provision as respects supervision and treatment orders) shall be inserted in the 1975 Act as Schedule 5A to that Act.

GENERAL NOTE

    This section provides a court with a wider range of disposals than is presently available when dealing with an accused who is unfit to plead. At present, if an accused is found insane and unfit to stand trial in solemn proceedings, s.174(3) of the 1975 Act requires that he be detained either in a state hospital or such other hospital as the court may specify under a hospital order and a restriction order without limit of time. There is no examination of the charges, *i.e.* the case against him. The same position applies in summary proceedings, except that under s.376(2) of the 1975 Act a hospital order is obligatory, but a restriction order is optional.

    This section retains the court's power to make a hospital order, and the making of a restriction order becomes optional in both solemn and summary proceedings (and the requirements for making the order are the same as at present specified in ss.178 and 379 of the 1975 Act).

    This section provides the courts with three further options. First, the court may make a "guardianship order", placing the accused under the guardianship of a local authority, as under existing provisions in ss.175 and 376 of the 1975 Act. Secondly, the court may make a Supervision and Treatment Order. This is a new disposal for Scotland (but is provided by the Criminal Procedure (Insanity and Unfitness to Plead) Act 1991 for England and Wales). The accused is placed under the supervision of a local social work department for a specified period of up to three years with a condition that the person undergoes treatment for his mental condition. Thirdly, the court has the option of making no order. Only in one circumstance is the court's discretion circumscribed. When the charge is one of murder the court must impose a hospital order and a restriction order without limit of time (s.174ZC(3)).

    Subsection (1) inserts a new section (s.174ZC) into that part of the 1975 Act which covers solemn proceedings. Section 174ZC(1) specifies the application of the new s.174ZC. It will apply in three circumstances, namely where a person is acquitted on the ground of his insanity at the time of the act or omission charged, either by a court under s.174(2) of the 1975 Act or an EOF under s.174ZA(3) (provided for in s.49) or where an EOF makes a finding under s.174ZA(2) that the person did the act or made the omission constituting the offence.

    Section 174ZC(2) specifies (for the three circumstances in s.174ZC(1) above), the disposal options available to the court, as follows:

(a) an order having the same effect as a hospital order, that the person be detained in a State hospital or such other hospital as the court may, for special reasons, specify;

(b) in addition to making a hospital order, the court may also make an order having the same effect as a restriction order without limit of time. The order imposes the special restrictions in s.62(1) of the Mental Health (Scotland) Act 1984, which reserves certain powers to the Secretary of State;

(c) an order having the same effect as a guardianship order, the details of which are specified in s.175 of the 1975 Act placing the person under the guardianship of a local authority or a person approved by a local authority;

(d) a Supervision and Treatment Order, the details of which are specified in Sched. 2 to the Act, inserted as Sched. 5A in the 1975 Act, and which broadly parallel the details of the identically-named order in Sched. 2 to the Criminal Procedure (Insanity and Unfitness to Plead) Act 1991, which applies in England and Wales; or

(e) no order at all.

Subsection (2) of s.50 inserts a new section, s.375ZC, into that part of the 1975 Act which covers summary proceedings. Subsections 375ZC(1), (2) and (3) replicate for summary proceedings subss. 174ZC(1), (2) and (4) described above for solemn proceedings.

Appeal by accused in case involving insanity

51.—(1) After section 174ZC of the 1975 Act (inserted by section 50(1) of this Act) there shall be inserted the following section—

"Appeal by accused in case involving insanity

174ZD.—(1) A person may appeal to the High Court against—

(a) a finding made under section 174(1) of this Act that he is insane so that his trial cannot proceed or continue, or the refusal of the court to make such a finding;

(b) a finding under section 174ZA(2) of this Act; or

(c) an order made under section 174ZC(2) of this Act.

(2) An appeal under subsection (1) above shall be—

(a) in writing; and

(b) lodged—

(i) in the case of an appeal under paragraph (a) of that subsection, not later than seven days after the date of the finding or refusal which is the subject of the appeal;

(ii) in the case of an appeal under paragraph (b), or both paragraphs (b) and (c), of that subsection, not later than 28 days after the conclusion of the examination of facts;

(iii) in the case of an appeal under paragraph (c) of that subsection against an order made on an acquittal, by virtue of section 174(2) or 174ZA(3) of this Act, on the ground of insanity at the time of the act or omission, not later than 14 days after the date of the acquittal;

(iv) in the case of an appeal under that paragraph against an order made on a finding under section 174ZA(2), not later than 14 days after the conclusion of the examination of facts, or within such longer period as the High Court may, on cause shown, allow.

(3) Subsections (1)(a) and (2)(b)(i) above are without prejudice to section 76A(1) of this Act.

(4) Where an appeal is taken under subsection (1) above, the period from the date on which the appeal was lodged until it is withdrawn or disposed of shall not count towards any time limit applying in respect of the case.

(5) An appellant in an appeal under this section shall be entitled to be present at the hearing of the appeal unless the High Court determines that his presence is not practicable or appropriate.

(6) In disposing of an appeal under subsection (1) above the High Court may—

(a) affirm the decision of the court of first instance;

(b) make any other finding or order which that court could have made at the time when it made the finding or order which is the subject of the appeal; or

(c) remit the case to that court with such directions in the matter as the High Court thinks fit.

(7) Section 280 of this Act shall not apply in relation to any order as respects which a person has a right of appeal under subsection (1)(c) above.".

(2) After section 375ZC of that Act (inserted by section 50(2) of this Act) there shall be inserted the following section—

"Appeal by accused in case involving insanity

375ZD.—(1) A person may appeal to the High Court against—

(a) a finding made under section 375(2) of this Act that he is insane so that his trial cannot proceed or continue, or the refusal of the court to make such a finding;

(b) a finding under section 375ZA(2) of this Act; or

(c) an order made under section 375ZC(2) of this Act.

(2) An appeal under subsection (1) above shall be—

(a) in writing; and

(b) lodged—

(i) in the case of an appeal under paragraph (a) of that subsection, not later than seven days after the date of the finding or refusal which is the subject of the appeal;

(ii) in the case of an appeal under paragraph (b), or both paragraphs (b) and (c), of that subsection, not later than 28 days after the conclusion of the examination of facts;

(iii) in the case of an appeal under paragraph (c) of that subsection against an order made on an acquittal, by virtue of section 375(3A) or 375ZA(3) of this Act, on the ground of insanity at the time of the act or omission, not later than 14 days after the date of the acquittal;

(iv) in the case of an appeal under that paragraph against an order made on a finding under section 375ZA(2), not later than 14 days after the conclusion of the examination of facts,

or within such longer period as the High Court may, on cause shown, allow.

(3) Where an appeal is taken under subsection (1) above, the period from the date on which the appeal was lodged until it is withdrawn or disposed of shall not count towards any time limit applying in respect of the case.

(4) An appellant in an appeal under this section shall be entitled to be present at the hearing of the appeal unless the High Court determines that his presence is not practicable or appropriate.

(5) In disposing of an appeal under subsection (1) above the High Court may—

(a) affirm the decision of the court of first instance;

(b) make any other finding or order which that court could have made at the time when it made the finding or order which is the subject of the appeal; or

(c) remit the case to that court with such directions in the matter as the High Court thinks fit.

(6) Section 443 of this Act shall not apply in relation to any order as respects which a person has a right of appeal under subsection (1)(c) above.".

GENERAL NOTE

This section provides the accused with rights of appeal in relation to any finding (or refusal to make a finding) under s.174(1) or s.375(2) of the 1975 Act that the accused is insane in bar of trial, and against findings made by, and orders made at, examinations of facts (EOFs). Without this change an accused person had no right of appeal against a finding of insanity in bar of trial or against the refusal of any plea or motion that such a finding should be made. The only exception was where the finding was made at a preliminary diet in solemn proceedings, in which case the accused has a right of appeal under s.76A(1) of the 1975 Act.

By s.51(1) a new section (s.174ZD) is inserted into the part of the 1975 Act which covers solemn proceedings. Section 174ZD provides that an accused person may appeal to the High Court against a finding, or a refusal to make a finding, of insanity in bar of trial, against an EOF finding that he did the act constituting the offence (and that there are no grounds for his acquittal) and against any order made at an EOF.

The remaining subsections make various provisions in relation to the mode of making an appeal and the computation of time. In particular, s.174ZD specifies the disposals open to the High Court. It may affirm the decision of the original court, make any other finding or order which the original court could have made, or remit the case back to the original court with such directions as are thought fit.

By s.51(2) a new section (s.375ZD) is inserted into the part of the 1975 Act which covers summary proceedings. Appeals in respect of summary proceedings are made to the High Court. Generally, the summary provisions replicate the solemn proceedings, although the absence of a summary right of appeal that equates to a solemn appeal under s.76A(1) of the 1975 Act means that there is one difference.

Appeal by prosecutor in case involving insanity

52.—(1) After section 174ZD of the 1975 Act (inserted by section 51(1) of this Act) there shall be inserted the following section—

"Appeal by Lord Advocate in case involving insanity

174ZE.—(1) The Lord Advocate may appeal to the High Court on a point of law against—
  (a) a finding under subsection (1) of section 174 of this Act that an accused is insane so that his trial cannot proceed or continue;
  (b) an acquittal on the ground of insanity at the time of the act or omission by virtue of subsection (2) of that section;
  (c) an acquittal under section 174ZA(3) of this Act (whether or not on the ground of insanity at the time of the act or omission); or
  (d) any order made under section 174ZC(2) of this Act.
(2) An appeal under subsection (1) above shall be—
  (a) in writing; and
  (b) lodged—
        (i) in the case of an appeal under paragraph (a) or (b) of that subsection, not later than seven days after the finding or, as the case may be, the acquittal which is the subject of the appeal;
        (ii) in the case of an appeal under paragraph (c) or (d) of that subsection, not later than seven days after the conclusion of the examination of facts,
     or within such longer period as the High Court may, on cause shown, allow.
(3) Subsection (1)(a) and (2)(b)(i) above are without prejudice to section 76A(1) of this Act.
(4) A respondent in an appeal under this section shall be entitled to be present at the hearing of the appeal unless the High Court determines that his presence is not practicable or appropriate.
(5) In disposing of an appeal under subsection (1) above the High Court may—
  (a) affirm the decision of the court of first instance;
  (b) make any other finding or order which that court could have made at the time when it made the finding or order which is the subject of the appeal; or
  (c) remit the case to that court with such directions in the matter as the High Court thinks fit.".

(2) After section 375ZD of that Act (inserted by section 51(2) of this Act) there shall be inserted the following section—

"Appeal by prosecutor in case involving insanity

375ZE.—(1) The prosecutor may appeal to the High Court on a point of law against—

(a) a finding under subsection (2) of section 375 of this Act that an accused is insane so that his trial cannot proceed or continue;

(b) an acquittal on the ground of insanity at the time of the act or omission by virtue of subsection (3A) of that section;

(c) an acquittal under section 375ZA(3) of this Act (whether or not on the ground of insanity at the time of the act or omission); or

(d) any order made under section 375ZC(2) of this Act.

(2) An appeal under subsection (1) above shall be—

(a) in writing; and

(b) lodged—

(i) in the case of an appeal under paragraph (a) or (b) of that subsection, not later than seven days after the finding or, as the case may be, the acquittal which is the subject of the appeal;

(ii) in the case of an appeal under paragraph (c) or (d) of that subsection, not later than seven days after the conclusion of the examination of facts,

or within such longer period as the High Court may, on cause shown, allow.

(3) A respondent in an appeal under this section shall be entitled to be present at the hearing of the appeal unless the High Court determines that his presence is not practicable or appropriate.

(4) In disposing of an appeal under subsection (1) above the High Court may—

(a) affirm the decision of the court of first instance;

(b) make any other finding or order which that court could have made at the time when it made the finding or order which is the subject of the appeal; or

(c) remit the case to that court with such directions in the matter as the High Court thinks fit.".

GENERAL NOTE

This section provides the Crown with rights of appeal against a finding of insanity in bar of trial, against a trial verdict of acquittal on ground of insanity, against any acquittal at an examination of facts (EOF) and against an order made at an EOF. Such appeals may be only on a point of law.

Sections 174(1) and 375(2) of the 1975 Act enable a court to make a finding that an accused is insane in bar of trial. There was no Crown right of appeal against such a finding unless it was made at a preliminary diet in solemn proceedings, in which case either party had a right of appeal under s.76A of the 1975 Act. This section provides the Crown with rights of appeal, but only on a point of law, broadly parallel to the accused's rights of appeal provided for in s.52.

Review of committal of mentally disordered accused to hospital

53. In each of sections 25 and 330 of the 1975 Act (power of court to commit to hospital person suffering from mental disorder), after subsection (4) there shall be inserted the following subsections—

"(5) Without prejudice to subsection (3) above, the court may review an order under subsection (1) above on the ground that there has been a change of circumstances since the order was made and, on such review—

(a) where the court considers that such an order is no longer required in relation to a person, it shall revoke the order and may deal with him in such way mentioned in subsection (3) above as the court thinks appropriate;

(b) in any other case, the court may—
    (i) confirm or vary the order; or
    (ii) revoke the order and deal with him in such way mentioned in subsection (3) above as the court considers appropriate.

(6) Subsections (1) to (4) above shall apply to the review of an order under subsection (5) above as they apply to the making of an order under subsection (1) above.".

GENERAL NOTE

This section adds to the provisions in ss.25 and 330 of the 1975 Act which permit the court to commit to a specified hospital at the pre-trial stage an accused who appears to be suffering from a mental disorder. This section makes express provision for review of that committal.

Sections 25 and 330 of the 1975 Act enable a court, in solemn and summary proceedings respectively, to commit an accused who appears to be suffering from a mental disorder to a specified hospital at the pre-trial stage, provided that a hospital is available for his admission and suitable for his detention. No such committal may be made except on the written or oral evidence of a medical practitioner.

Subsection (2) of each of the two sections mentioned provides that if, on examination, the responsible medical officer at the specified hospital is satisfied that the accused is suffering from a mental disorder which warrants admission to hospital under Pt. V of the Mental Health (Scotland) Act 1984, that is where he shall be detained for the period of remand or committal or until he is liberated in due course of law. The accused may be recommitted to prison under subs. (3) if, on re-examination, he is found not to be suffering from a mental disorder.

Prior to these changes there was no express provision to permit any variation of the committal to hospital or for its revocation except in the circumstances identified in subs. (3) of each of the two sections mentioned, *i.e.* immediately following examination. That did not permit a response to changing circumstances. Thus, s.53 provides that an order of committal under ss.25 and 330 may be reviewed and confirmed, varied or revoked by the court at any time. Section 53 inserts into both ss.25 and 330 of the 1975 Act two new subsections ((5) and (6)) making these changes.

Restriction orders to be without limit of time

54.—(1) In subsection (1) of each of sections 178 and 379 of the 1975 Act (power of court to impose restriction order in addition to hospital order), the words "either" and "or during such period as may be specified in the order" shall cease to have effect.

(2) The amendments made by subsection (1) above shall not have effect in relation to any restriction order made before the coming into force of this section.

GENERAL NOTE

This section removes the possibility that a court may impose on a convicted mentally disordered offender a restriction order for a fixed period only. Where a court chooses to apply special restrictions to a patient these will be without limit of time.

For a convicted mentally disordered person, the court may impose a hospital order under ss.175 or 376 of the 1975 Act in order to detain that person in hospital for treatment. The court may, additionally, consider imposing a restriction order under ss.178 or 379 of the 1975 Act. The effect of the restriction order is to make the Secretary of State ultimately responsible for the leave, transfer and discharge arrangements for the person concerned. Patients subject to restriction orders are sometimes known as "Secretary of State" or "state" patients.

Fixed-term restriction orders are a serious constraint on an individual and an open restriction order even more so. However, the Secretary of State has a statutory duty under s.68 of the Mental Health (Scotland) Act 1984 to remove special restrictions from patients whose condition no longer warrants them.

Committal to hospital for inquiry into mental condition

55.—(1) Each of sections 180 and 381 of the 1975 Act (remand for inquiry into physical or mental condition) shall be amended as follows.

(2) In subsection (1) for the words "shall remand him in custody or on bail for" there shall be substituted—
    "shall—

(a) for the purpose of inquiry solely into his physical condition, remand him in custody or on bail;

(b) for the purpose of inquiry into his mental condition (whether or not in addition to his physical condition), remand him in custody or on bail or, where the court is satisfied—

(i) on the written or oral evidence of a medical practitioner, that the person appears to be suffering from a mental disorder; and

(ii) that a hospital is available for his admission and suitable for his detention,

make an order committing him to that hospital,

for".

(3) After subsection (1) there shall be inserted the following subsections—

"(1A) Where the court is of the opinion that a person ought to continue to be committed to hospital for the purpose of inquiry into his mental condition following the expiry of the period specified in an order for committal to hospital under paragraph (b) of subsection (1) above, the court may—

(a) if the condition in sub-paragraph (i) of that paragraph continues to be satisfied and a suitable hospital is available for his continued detention, renew the order for such further period not exceeding three weeks as the court thinks necessary to enable a medical examination and report to be made; and

(b) in any other case, remand the person in custody or on bail in accordance with subsection (1) above.

(1B) An order under subsection (1A)(a) above may, unless objection is made by or on behalf of the person to whom it relates, be made in his absence.

(1C) Where, before the expiry of the period specified in an order for committal to hospital under subsection (1)(b) above, the court considers, on an application made to it, that committal to hospital is no longer required in relation to the person, the court shall revoke the order and may make such other order, under subsection (1)(a) above or any other provision of this Part of this Act, as the court considers appropriate.".

(4) In subsection (4), after the word "section" there shall be inserted "to remand in custody or on bail".

(5) After subsection (4) there shall be inserted the following subsection—

"(4A) On making an order of committal to hospital under subsection (1)(b) above the court shall send to the hospital specified in the order a statement of the reasons for which the court is of the opinion that an inquiry ought to be made into the mental condition of the person to whom it relates, and of any information before the court about his mental condition.".

(6) In subsection (5)—

(a) after the word "imposed" there shall be inserted ", and a person committed to hospital under this section may appeal against the order of committal,";

(b) after the word "remand" there shall be inserted "or, as the case may be, committal"; and

(c) at the end of paragraph (b) there shall be inserted—

"; or

(c) in the case of an appeal against an order of committal to hospital, revoke the order and remand the person in custody.".

(7) After subsection (5) there shall be inserted the following subsections—

"(6) The court may, on cause shown, vary an order for committal to hospital under subsection (1)(b) above by substituting another hospital for the hospital specified in the order.

(7) Subsection (1)(b) above shall apply to the variation of an order under subsection (6) above as it applies to the making of an order for committal to hospital.".

GENERAL NOTE

This section amends ss.180 and 381 of the 1975 Act, which enable a court to remand a person found to have committed an imprisonable offence in custody or on bail, in order that inquiries may be made into his physical or mental condition prior to disposal of the case. The section provides for the court to commit someone to hospital for the purpose of inquiry into his mental condition.

The court may, under s.180 or s.381 of the 1975 Act (in solemn and summary proceedings respectively), seek to obtain medical information on the physical or mental condition of the accused, once the court is satisfied that he did the act or made the omission charged and before final disposal of the case. The offence that the accused is charged with must be punishable with imprisonment. Under subs. (1) of each section, a court may remand such an accused in custody or on bail for periods of up to three weeks at a time to enable a medical examination and report to be made. Under subs. (2), where the inquiry is made into the medical condition of the accused, and if arrangements have been made for his reception, it may be a condition of a bail order that the accused shall reside in a hospital. There is no power available to the court under ss.180 or 381 to commit the accused direct to hospital for the purpose of inquiry into his mental condition.

Miscellaneous

Criminal Courts Rules Council

56.—(1) There shall be established a body, to be known as the Criminal Courts Rules Council (in this section referred to as "the Council") which shall have the functions conferred on it by subsection (9) below.

(2) The Council shall consist of—

(a) the Lord Justice General, the Lord Justice Clerk and the Clerk of Justiciary;

(b) a further Lord Commissioner of Justiciary appointed by the Lord Justice General;

(c) the following persons appointed by the Lord Justice General after such consultation as he considers appropriate—

(i) two sheriffs;

(ii) two members of the Faculty of Advocates;

(iii) two solicitors;

(iv) one sheriff clerk; and

(v) one person appearing to him to have a knowledge of the procedures and practices of the district court;

(d) two persons appointed by the Lord Justice General after consultation with the Lord Advocate, at least one of whom must be a procurator fiscal;

(e) two persons appointed by the Lord Justice General after consultation with the Secretary of State, at least one of whom must be a person appearing to the Lord Justice General to have—

(i) a knowledge of the procedures and practices of the courts exercising criminal jurisdiction in Scotland; and

(ii) an awareness of the interests of victims of crime and of witnesses in criminal proceedings; and

(f) any persons appointed under subsection (3) below.

(3) The Lord Justice General may appoint not more than two further persons, and the Secretary of State may appoint one person, to membership of the Council.

(4) The chairman of the Council shall be the Lord Justice General or such other member of the Council, being a Lord Commissioner of Justiciary, as the Lord Justice General may nominate.

(5) The members of the Council appointed under paragraphs (b) to (f) of subsection (2) above shall, so long as they retain the respective qualifications (if any) mentioned in those paragraphs, hold office for three years and be eligible for reappointment.

(6) Any vacancy in the membership of the Council by reason of the death or demission of office, prior to the expiry of the period for which he was appointed, of a member appointed under any of paragraphs (b) to (f) of sub-section (2) above shall be filled by the appointment by the Lord Justice General or, as the case may be, the Secretary of State, after such consultation (if any) as is required by the paragraph in question, of another person having the qualifications (if any) required by that paragraph, and a person so appointed shall hold office only until the expiry of that period.

(7) The Council shall meet—

(a) at intervals of not more than 12 months; and

(b) at any time when summoned by the chairman or by three members of the Council,

but shall, subject to the foregoing, have power to regulate the summoning of its meetings and the procedure at such meetings.

(8) At any meeting of the Council six members shall be a quorum.

(9) The functions of the Council shall be—

(a) to keep under general review the procedures and practices of the courts exercising criminal jurisdiction in Scotland (including any matters incidental or relating to those procedures or practices); and

(b) to consider and comment on any draft Act of Adjournal submitted to it by the High Court, which shall, in making the Act of Adjournal, take account to such extent as it considers appropriate of any comments made by the Council under this paragraph.

(10) In the discharge of its functions under subsection (9) above the Council may invite representations on any aspect of the procedures and practices of the courts exercising criminal jurisdiction in Scotland (including any matters incidental or relating to those procedures or practices) and shall consider any such representations received by it, whether or not submitted in response to such an invitation.

(11) Except where the context otherwise requires, expressions used in this section and in the 1975 Act have the same meaning in this section as in that Act.

GENERAL NOTE

This section established the Criminal Courts Rules Council and sets out the statutory functions of the new council. These are generally to keep under review the procedure and practices of the Scottish criminal courts and to consider and comment on any draft Act of Adjournal submitted to it by the High Court of Justiciary. The council will assist the High Court of Justiciary in the discharge of its existing court procedure rule-making functions, primarily by providing a structured consultative forum for considering and commenting on proposals to court rules.

In the course of the debate before the First Scottish Standing Committee there appeared to be some criticism of the council on the basis that the lay representatives were to be "greatly overwhelmed" by professional representatives. However, it is difficult to know the true extent of the criticism as the Member of Parliament for Glasgow, Govan also asked why the Government was proposing such an example of "workers' control", when the Government was "not known for their interest in syndicalism" (Sixth sitting, April 4, 1995 col. 189).

Information for financial and other purposes

57.—(1) The Secretary of State shall in each year publish such information as he considers expedient for the purpose of—

(a) enabling persons engaged in the administration of criminal justice to become aware of the financial implications of their decisions; or

(b) facilitating the performance by such persons of their duty to avoid discriminating against any persons on the ground of race or sex or any other improper ground.

(2) Publication under subsection (1) above shall be effected in such manner as the Secretary of State considers appropriate for the purpose of bringing the information to the attention of the persons concerned.

GENERAL NOTE

This section permits the Secretary of State, though does not require him, to provide financial information relating to the criminal justice system.

Prints, samples etc. in criminal investigations

58.—(1) Section 28 of the Prisoners and Criminal Proceedings (Scotland) Act 1993 (prints, samples etc. in criminal investigations) shall be amended in accordance with subsections (2) to (4) below.

(2) In subsection (3)—

(a) at the beginning there shall be inserted the words "Subject to subsection (3A) below,";

(b) after the words "subsection (2) above" there shall be inserted ", all samples taken under subsection (4) below and all information derived from such samples"; and

(c) for the word "immediately" there shall be substituted "as soon as possible".

(3) After subsection (3) there shall be inserted the following subsections—

"(3A) The duty under subsection (3) above to destroy samples taken under subsection (4) below and information derived from such samples shall not apply where the destruction of the sample or the information could have the effect of destroying any sample, or any information derived therefrom, lawfully held in relation to a person other than the person from whom the sample was taken.

(3B) No sample, or information derived from a sample, retained by virtue of subsection (3A) above shall be used—

(a) in evidence against the person from whom the sample was taken; or

(b) for the purposes of the investigation of any offence.

(3C) The duty under subsection (3) above shall not apply where the record, sample or information in question is of the same kind as a record, a sample or, as the case may be, information lawfully held by or on behalf of any police force in relation to the person.".

(4) In subsection (4)—

(a) in paragraph (a)—

(i) after the word "body" there shall be inserted ", other than pubic hair,"; and

(ii) for the words "or combing" there shall be substituted ", combing or plucking"; and

(b) at the end there shall be inserted the following paragraph—

"(d) from the inside of the mouth, by means of swabbing, a sample of saliva or other material".

(5) After section 28 of that Act of 1993 there shall be inserted the following sections—

"Prints, samples etc. in criminal investigations: supplementary provisions

28A.—(1) This section applies where a person convicted of an offence—

(a) has not, since the conviction, had a sample, print or impression taken from him; or

(b) has (whether before or after the conviction) had a sample, print or impression taken from him but it was not suitable for the means of analysis for which it was taken or, though suitable, was insufficient (either in quantity or in quality) to enable information to be obtained by that means of analysis.

(2) Where this section applies, a constable may, within the permitted period—

(a) take from the convicted person fingerprints, palmprints and such other prints and impressions of an external part of the body as the constable reasonably considers it appropriate to take; and

(b) with the authority of an officer of a rank no lower than inspector, take from the person any sample mentioned in any of paragraphs (a) to (d) of subsection (4) of section 28 of this Act by the means specified in that paragraph in relation to that sample.

(3) A constable—

(a) may require the convicted person to attend a police station for the purposes of subsection (2) above;

(b) may, where the convicted person is in legal custody within the meaning of the 1975 Act, exercise the powers conferred by subsection (2) above in relation to the person in the place where he is for the time being.

(4) In subsection (2) above, "the permitted period" means—

(a) in a case to which paragraph (a) of subsection (1) above applies, the period of one month beginning with the date of the conviction;

(b) in a case to which paragraph (b) of that subsection applies, the period of one month beginning with the date on which a constable of the police force which instructed the analysis receives written intimation that the sample, print or impression was unsuitable or, as the case may be, insufficient as mentioned in that paragraph.

(5) A requirement under subsection (3)(a) above—

(a) shall give the person at least seven days' notice of the date on which he is required to attend;

(b) may direct him to attend at a specified time of day or between specified times of day.

(6) Any constable may arrest without warrant a person who fails to comply with a requirement under subsection (3)(a) above.

Use of prints, samples etc.

28B. Without prejudice to any power to do so apart from this section, prints, impressions and samples lawfully held by or on behalf of any police force or in connection with or as a result of an investigation of an offence and information derived therefrom may be checked against other such prints, impressions, samples and information.".

<small>Definitions</small>

"permitted period": s.28A(4) of the Prisoners and Criminal Proceedings (Scotland) Act 1993.

<small>General Note</small>

This section extends s.28 of the 1993 Act so as to enable constables, on the authority of an officer of a rank no lower than inspector, to pluck hair (excluding pubic hair) from an arrested or detained person, and to take a sample of fluid by means of swabbing from inside the mouth, without a warrant. It also provides that the provisions relating to the destruction of prints and impressions predicated in s.28(3) of the 1993 Act will be applied to samples taken by virtue of s.28(4) as amended, which will include samples taken by virtue of the new power, except in certain limited circumstances.

These circumstances are that a sample (and information about a person's DNA which is derived from such a sample) need not be destroyed where, in consequence of the destruction, a sample from another person (or information about that person's DNA) which can be lawfully retained would, in whole or in part, be destroyed. This can arise because of the limitations in some methods of processing samples: in some cases when samples are analysed together it is not possible to destroy the samples from the innocent person without also affecting the sample from a convicted person. Any sample or information therefrom retained by virtue of this exception, however, will not be used in evidence against the person from whom it was taken or for the purposes of any investigation of an offence.

This section further provides that the provision in s.28(3) of the 1993 Act, which requires that certain records should be destroyed "immediately", will be amended to "as soon as possible". This reflects practicalities in that it is not possible for records to be destroyed immediately due to the time taken for relevant information to be passed to the Scottish Criminal Record Office where records are held.

Section 58 also enables a constable to require a convicted person to attend the police station within a specified time to have samples taken. It also enables a constable to do this at a place where the person is in custody. This power is desirable because it will ensure that where prints or samples are deficient they may be replaced, thus providing an accurate record.

The section provides express authority for searches to be carried out by comparing existing prints and samples with other samples and prints which are lawfully held.

The power of the police to take certain samples without warrant is codified in s.28 of the 1993 Act. The power applies both to suspects detained under s.2 of the 1980 Act and to arrested persons. Section 28 of the 1993 Act enables an officer to use reasonable force to obtain a sample or print but extends only to external samples. Any sample which requires invasion of orifices or piercing of the skin must be taken under warrant if the suspect/accused refuses to provide the sample voluntarily. The position in Scotland, therefore, is that samples which are considered suitable for DNA analysis, such as hair roots and cells from inside the mouth, are deemed to be invasive or internal samples, and the taking of them requires a warrant if the police are unable to obtain them voluntarily.

The report of the Royal Commission on Criminal Justice, whose remit covered England and Wales but not Scotland, recommended that the police in England and Wales should have powers to take hair root samples and swabs from inside the mouth. This recommendation was implemented in the Criminal Justice and Public Order Act 1994, which also provides for the retention of samples in England and Wales under certain circumstances where they would otherwise be required to be destroyed.

The Government considered it appropriate to make similar provision in Scotland. Proposals were set out in the White Paper, *Firm and Fair: Improving the Delivery of Justice in Scotland* (Cm. 2600). At the same time the opportunity is being taken to provide expressly that any prints, samples, impressions or information derived therefrom which are lawfully retained by the police may be checked against any other prints and so forth.

Calculation of period of detention at police station where person previously detained under another enactment etc.

59. In section 2(3A) of the Criminal Justice (Scotland) Act 1980 (detention and questioning at police station)—

(a) for the words from "he" to "be" there shall be substituted "and is"; and

(b) after the word "detention" there shall be inserted ", the period of six hours mentioned in subsection (2) above shall be reduced by the length of that earlier detention".

GENERAL NOTE

This section provides that any person who has been detained under any enactment other than s.2(1) of the 1980 Act may subsequently be detained under s.2(1) where the grounds are the same or arise from the same circumstances. The section provides that any period during which the person was detained under any other enactment prior to detention under s.2(1) shall count towards the six hour maximum period of detention under that section.

Section 2(3A) of the 1980 Act places a prohibition on detention under s.2(1) of the 1980 Act in respect of persons detained in pursuance of any other enactment "on the same grounds or on grounds arising from the same circumstances as those which led to his earlier detention". This has the effect of preventing the police from detaining under s.2 of the 1980 Act people who have immediately beforehand been detained on the same grounds under some other statutory provision, for example, s.23 of the Misuse of Drugs Act 1971.

This section amends s.2(3A) of the 1980 Act by providing that, where a person has previously been detained in pursuance of any other enactment or subordinate instrument and is detained under s.2(1) of the 1980 Act, on the same grounds or on grounds arising from the same circumstances as those which led to his earlier detention, the maximum period of six hours detention mentioned in s.2(2) of the 1980 Act shall be reduced by the length of the earlier detention.

Jurisdiction of district court in relation to statutory offences

60. For subsection (1) of section 7 of the Criminal Justice (Scotland) Act 1980 (jurisdiction of district courts in relation to statutory offences) there shall be substituted the following subsections—

"(1) Except in so far as any enactment (including this Act and an enactment passed after this Act) otherwise provides, it shall be competent for a district court to try any statutory offence which is triable summarily.

(1A) Without prejudice to any other or wider power conferred by any enactment, it shall not be competent for a district court, as respects any statutory offence—

(a) to impose a sentence of imprisonment for a period exceeding 60 days;

(b) to impose a fine of an amount exceeding level 4 on the standard scale; or

(c) to ordain an accused person to find caution for any period exceeding six months or to an amount exceeding level 4 on the standard scale.".

GENERAL NOTE

This extends the jurisdiction of the district court to cover all statutory offences which are triable by summary procedure. The jurisdiction of the district court in respect of statutory offences was set out in s.7(1) of the Criminal Justice (Scotland) Act 1980. It provided that it was competent for a district court to try statutory offences in respect of which the maximum penalty which might be imposed did not exceed 60 days imprisonment or a fine of level 4 on the standard scale, or both.

There were in consequence many offences against statutory provisions which the district court could not try, even though specific examples of those offences would often be comparatively trivial. It also excluded many offences from the application of the "fiscal fine" procedure provided for in s.56 of the Criminal Justice (Scotland) Act 1987. The section extends the jurisdiction of the district court but does not alter any of the existing sentencing powers of that court.

At the committee stage of the Bill the Lord Advocate said that there was "no intention to drive cases down into the district court" (*Hansard*, H.L. Vol. 560, col. 503).

Conditional offer of fixed penalty by procurator fiscal

61.—(1) Section 56 of the Criminal Justice (Scotland) Act 1987 (conditional offer of fixed penalty by procurator fiscal) shall be amended as follows.

(2) After subsection (2) there shall be inserted the following subsection—

"(2A) In this section "the appropriate fixed penalty" means such fixed penalty on the scale prescribed under subsection (7) below as the procurator fiscal thinks fit having regard to the circumstances of the case.".

(3) In subsection (3)(b)(i), after the word "the" in the second place where it occurs there shall be inserted "appropriate".

(4) After subsection (3) there shall be inserted the following subsection—

"(3A) A conditional offer may be made in respect of more than one relevant offence and shall, in such a case, state the amount of the appropriate fixed penalty for all the offences in respect of which it is made.".

(5) In each of subsections (4) and (6), after the words "payment of the" there shall be inserted "appropriate".

(6) For subsection (7) there shall be substituted the following subsections—

"(7) The Secretary of State shall, by order, prescribe a scale of fixed penalties for the purposes of this section, the amount of the maximum penalty on the scale being a sum not exceeding level 1 on the standard scale.

(7A) An order under subsection (7) above—

(a) may contain provision as to the payment of fixed penalties by instalments; and

(b) shall be made by statutory instrument, which shall be subject to annulment in pursuance of a resolution of either House of Parliament.".

(7) In subsection (8), after the words "instalment of the" there shall be inserted "appropriate".

GENERAL NOTE

This allows the Secretary of State to set a range of fixed penalties from which the procurator fiscal can choose, according to the circumstances of the case, when offering the option of paying a fiscal fine.

Section 56 of the 1987 Act enables procurators fiscal to offer, in suitable cases, an accused the option of accepting a fiscal fine instead of being prosecuted. Subsection (7) of that section defines the fixed penalty payable under this section as "such sum, not exceeding level 1 on the standard scale, as the Secretary of State may, by order made by statutory instrument subject to annulment in pursuance of a resolution of either House of Parliament, determine". The current fixed fine of £25 was fixed by statutory instrument in 1987 when that sum represented half of level 1 on the standard scale. Level 1 is now £200. A system of set points of fixed monetary value on a scale will give flexibility, allowing fines to be offered in a wider range of cases and thus reflecting more closely the severity of the alleged offences.

Time limit for summary prosecution of statutory offences

62.—(1) Section 331 of the 1975 Act (time limit for summary prosecution of statutory offences) shall be amended as follows.

(2) In subsection (1), after the words "in respect of" there shall be inserted "any offence triable only summarily and consisting of".

(3) Subsection (2) shall cease to have effect.

DEFINITIONS

"offence": s.462 of the Criminal Procedure (Scotland) Act 1975.
"triable only summarily": s.457A(1) of the Criminal Procedure (Scotland) Act 1975.

GENERAL NOTE

This section in effect limits the six-month time-bar on summary prosecutions to a very narrow group of cases, namely those regulatory matters of a minor nature that can only be dealt with summarily.

Section 333(1) of the 1975 Act required summary prosecutions to be commenced within six months after the contravention occurred. That rule was not invariable, for other statutes could and did provide for their own limits: see, for example, s.25(5) of the Misuse of Drugs Act 1971.

On the amendment being brought into force, procurators fiscal will be able to prosecute cases which could otherwise have been incompetent prosecutions. This latitude in time is not unbounded for the common law plea of mora is likely to be available for extraordinary periods of time. The rigidity of the summary prosecution is likely to be changed somewhat by this amendment and also by the removal of the requirement for service and a note of penalty: see s.117(1) and Sched. 6, para. 109(b).

Abolition of private summary prosecutions

63. After section 310 of the 1975 Act there shall be inserted the following section—

"Abolition of private summary prosecutions

310A. Except where any enactment otherwise expressly provides, all prosecutions under this Part of this Act shall be brought at the instance of the procurator fiscal.".

DEFINITIONS

"procurator fiscal": s.462 of the Criminal Procedure (Scotland) Act 1975.

GENERAL NOTE

This section provides for the abolition of private summary prosecution unless permitted by statute. The title to prosecute criminal cases has rested with the Lord Advocate since the sixteenth century, and has since developed in practice into a virtually exclusive title to prosecute criminal matters. Only in exceptional circumstances has the High Court of Justiciary allowed private prosecutions by private individuals, and then only in solemn proceedings: see *J. & P. Coats v. Brown* (1909) 6 Adam 19 and *X. v. Sweeney* 1982 S.C.C.R. 161. In contrast, there is no record in living memory of any application to have a prosecution conducted privately in a summary court. As the Minister said to the First Scottish Standing Committee "provision for private summary prosecution is a hangover from the past" (First Scottish Standing Committee Debates, April 20, 1995, Seventh Sitting at col. 206).

Legal aid in case involving insanity in bar of trial

64. In subsection (1) of section 22 of the Legal Aid (Scotland) Act 1986 (circumstances in which criminal legal aid automatically available), after paragraph (d) there shall be inserted the following paragraphs—
"(da) in relation to any proceedings under solemn or summary procedure whereby the court determines (whether or not on a plea by the accused person) whether he is insane so that his trial cannot proceed or continue;
(db) in relation to an examination of facts held under section 174ZA or 375ZA of the Criminal Procedure (Scotland) Act 1975 and the disposal of the case following such examination of facts;
(dc) in relation to any appeal under section 174ZD (appeal by accused in case involving insanity) or 174ZE (appeal by Lord Advocate in case involving insanity) or section 375ZD or 375ZE (equivalent provisions as respects summary procedure) of that Act of 1975;".

GENERAL NOTE
This provides that criminal legal aid will be automatically available for proceedings where a court is required to decide whether an accused is insane in bar of trial, for the proposed examination of the facts for those who are found insane in bar of trial, and for appeals arising from either of these proceedings.
Section 22 of the Legal Aid (Scotland) Act 1986 provides for criminal legal aid to be automatically available in specified circumstances. This section extends those circumstances to proceedings, including appeal proceedings, relating to determination of the question of insanity in bar of trial or involving an accused found to be insane.

Legal aid in criminal appeals

65.—(1) Section 25 of the Legal Aid (Scotland) Act 1986 (legal aid in criminal appeals) shall be amended in accordance with subsections (2) to (5) below.
(2) In subsection (1)—
(a) after the word "sentence" there shall be inserted ", other disposal"; and
(b) at the end there shall be inserted the words "other than an appeal in relation to which section 22(1)(dc) of this Act applies.".
(3) In subsection (2)—
(a) the words "the Board is satisfied" shall cease to have effect;
(b) in paragraph (a), after the word "below," there shall be inserted "the Board is satisfied"; and
(c) for paragraph (b) and the preceding "and" there shall be substituted—
"(b) in the case of an appeal under section 228(1) or 442(1)(a) of the Criminal Procedure (Scotland) Act 1975, leave to appeal is granted; and
(c) in the case of an appeal under any provision of that Act other than sections 228(1) and 442(1)(a), where the applicant is the appellant, the Board is satisfied that in all the circumstances of the case it is in the interests of justice that the applicant should receive criminal legal aid.".
(4) After subsection (2) there shall be inserted the following subsection—
"(2A) Where the Board has refused an application for criminal legal aid on the ground that it is not satisfied as mentioned in subsection (2)(c)

above the High Court may, at any time prior to the disposal of an appeal, whether or not on application made to it, notwithstanding such refusal determine that it is in the interests of justice that the applicant should receive criminal legal aid in connection with the appeal, and the Board shall forthwith make such legal aid available to him.".

(5) For subsection (5) there shall be substituted the following subsections—

"(5) Subsections (2)(a), (3) and (4) above shall apply to an application for criminal legal aid in connection with consideration under section 230A, 442ZA or 453AA of the Criminal Procedure (Scotland) Act 1975 whether to grant leave to appeal as if—

(a) in subsection (2)(a), for the words "of the appeal" there were substituted "in connection with consideration whether to grant leave to appeal"; and

(b) in subsection (4), after the word "is" there were inserted ", subject to leave being granted,".

(6) Subsections (2)(a) and (c) and (2A) to (4) above shall apply to an application for criminal legal aid in connection with a petition to the nobile officium of the High Court of Justiciary (whether arising in the course of any proceedings or otherwise) as they apply for the purposes of subsection (1) above.

(7) Subsections (2)(a), (3) and (4) above shall apply to an application for criminal legal aid in connection with a reference by the Secretary of State under section 263 of the Criminal Procedure (Scotland) Act 1975 as they apply for the purposes of subsection (1) above.".

(6) In section 30(3) of that Act (application of section 25 of that Act to legal aid in contempt proceedings)—

(a) before the words "Section 25" there shall be inserted "Subsections (2)(a) and (c), (2A) to (4) and (6) of";

(b) for the words "it applies" there shall be substituted "they apply";

(c) after the word "sentence" there shall be inserted ", other disposal";

(d) after the word "application" there shall be inserted the following paragraph—

"(za) in subsection (2A) of that section, the reference to the High Court shall include a reference to the Court of Session;"; and

(e) in paragraph (b), for the word "(5)" there shall be substituted "(6)".

GENERAL NOTE
This section contains provisions to amend the availability of legal aid for criminal appeals. It extends legal aid to appeals against disposals other than conviction, sentence or acquittal; provides for legal aid in connection with the preparation of applications for leave to appeal; sets out provisions on eligibility for legal aid where leave to appeal has been granted; and where such leave is not necessary, provides that legal aid be granted where an applicant meets the test of financial eligibility and where the grant of legal aid is in the interests of justice.
Section 23 of the Legal Aid (Scotland) Act 1986 provides for criminal legal aid in connection with appeals against conviction, sentence or acquittal in criminal proceedings. This section provides for legal aid in connection with appeals against other disposals. Grants for such appeals are currently dealt with administratively as arising from conviction. The section makes further changes to the provisions for legal aid in criminal appeals in the light of recent judgments of the European Court of Human Rights.

Supervision and care of persons diverted from prosecution or subject to supervision requirement etc.

66. In section 27(1) of the Social Work (Scotland) Act 1968 (supervision and care of persons put on probation or released from prisons etc.)—

(a) after paragraph (a) there shall be inserted—

"(aa) making available to any children's hearing such reports relating to persons aged 16 and 17 years in relation to the commission of an offence, as the hearing may require for the disposal of a case;

> (ab) making available to any procurator fiscal or the Lord Advocate such reports as the procurator fiscal or the Lord Advocate may request in relation to persons who are charged with an offence;"; and
>
> (b) after sub-paragraph (iv) of paragraph (b) there shall be inserted the following sub-paragraphs—
>
>> "(v) without prejudice to sub-paragraphs (i) to (iv) above, persons in their area who are subject to a supervision and treatment order made under section 174ZC(2)(d) or 375ZC(2)(d) of the Criminal Procedure (Scotland) Act 1975; and
>>
>> (vi) persons in their area aged 16 and 17 years who are subject to a supervision requirement imposed in relation to the commission of any offence by that person; and
>>
>> (vii) persons in their area who are charged with, but not prosecuted for, any offence and are referred to the local authority by the procurator fiscal or the Lord Advocate; and".

GENERAL NOTE

This section requires the local authority to provide reports in relation to (a) persons who may be subject to schemes for diversion of offenders from prosecution, and (b) 16 and 17 year olds subject to a supervision requirement of a children's hearing imposed in relation to the commission of an offence by that person. The imposing of these functions in turn will enable the Secretary of State to give grants to the local authority under s.27A of the Social Work (Scotland) Act 1988 in respect of expenditure by the local authority on such services.

Transfer of fine orders

67.—(1) Section 403 of the 1975 Act (transfer of fine orders), shall be amended as follows.

(2) In subsection (3), at the beginning there shall be inserted the words "Subject to subsections (3A) and (3B) below,".

(3) After subsection (3) there shall be inserted the following subsections—
> "(3A) Where
>> (a) the court specified in a transfer of fine order is satisfied, after inquiry, that the offender is not residing within the jurisdiction of that court; and
>>
>> (b) the clerk of that court, within 14 days of receiving the notice required by section 404(1) of this Act, sends to the clerk of the court which made the order notice to that effect,
>
> the order shall cease to have effect.
>
> (3B) Where a transfer of fine order ceases to have effect by virtue of subsection (3A) above, the functions referred to in subsection (3) above shall again be exercisable by the court which made the order or, as the case may be, by the clerk of that court.".

GENERAL NOTE

This section contains provisions to permit the return of a transfer of fine order to the originating court where the receiving court has ascertained that the offender does not reside within its district.

Section 403(1) of the 1975 Act provides that where a court of summary jurisdiction has imposed a fine on a person convicted of an offence and it appears to the court that he is residing (a) within the jurisdiction of another court of summary jurisdiction in Scotland, or (b) in a petty sessions area or petty sessions district in England and Wales, or (c) in a petty sessions district in Northern Ireland, the court may order that payment of the fine shall be enforceable by that other court of summary jurisdiction or in that petty session area or district as the case may be.

Section 403(3) of the 1975 Act provides that where such an order is made with respect to any fine, any functions under any enactment relating to that fine which, if no such order had been made, would have been exercisable by the court which made the order or by the clerk of the court shall cease to be so exercisable.

The situation frequently arises in which a court makes an order under s.403 on the basis of erroneous information as to the offender's whereabouts. The receiving court will usually ascertain fairly rapidly that the offender is not residing within its district and, in practice, in such cases the papers will simply be returned to the originating court. This section provides for a period during which the receiving court can ascertain whether the offender is residing within its jurisdiction and, if he is not, can give notice to the originating court to that effect, in which case the transfer of fine order shall cease to have effect.

Liability of bankrupt to pay fines and compensation orders

68. In section 55(2) of the Bankruptcy (Scotland) Act 1985 (effect of discharge of bankrupt on certain liabilities), after paragraph (a) there shall be inserted the following paragraphs—
   "(aa) any liability to pay a fine imposed in a district court;
    (ab) any liability under a compensation order within the meaning of section 58 of the Criminal Justice (Scotland) Act 1980;".

GENERAL NOTE
   One of the unsatisfactory features of the law prior to the Bankruptcy (Scotland) Act 1985 was that many bankrupts remained undischarged: see *Bankruptcy and Related Aspects of Insolvency and Liquidation* Scottish Law Commission Report (No. 68) at para. 19.7 and Appendix 2.
   One of the reforms intended by the 1985 Act was the automatic discharge of the debtor. This occurs after three years: s.54(1). The effect is to discharge the debtor of all debts and obligations contracted by him, or for which he is liable, at the date of sequestration: s.55(1).
   The 1985 Act, however, specifically removed certain liabilities and obligations from which the debtor is not discharged merely by the passage of time: s.55(2).
   This section adds to the list of reserved liabilities and obligations by inserting in s.55(2) two new categories of liability. Subsection (aa) adds any liability to a fine imposed in a district court, and subs. (ab) adds any liability under a compensation order within the meaning of s.58 of the Criminal Justice (Scotland) Act 1980.

Child detainees unlawfully at large

69. For subsection (3) of section 40 of the Prisons (Scotland) Act 1989 (persons unlawfully at large) there shall be substituted the following subsection—
   "(3) In this section—
    (a) any reference to a person sentenced to imprisonment shall be construed as including a reference to any person sentenced or ordered to be detained under section 205, 206 or 413 of the 1975 Act;
    (b) any reference to a prison shall be construed as including a reference to a place where the person is liable to be detained under the sentence or order; and
    (c) any reference to a sentence shall be construed as including a reference to an order under section 413 of that Act.".

GENERAL NOTE
   This section clarifies the law relating to the position of children who were detained and have absconded.
   The provisions governing persons unlawfully at large are contained in s.40 of the Prisons (Scotland) Act 1989. While this covers adult prisoners and young offenders, it does not extend to children sentenced by the courts under s.205 of the 1975 Act to be detained in such place and under such conditions as the Secretary of State may determine, and to children who are sentenced in summary procedure to be detained in local authority residential care under s.413 of the same Act. Section 40(3) covers children detained under s.206 of the 1975 Act but provides only for the discounting of time spent unlawfully at large by such children.
   This section replaces the existing subs. (3) of s.40 of the Prisons (Scotland) Act 1989 with a new subs. (3), ensuring that subss. 40(1) and 40(2) clearly apply to persons sentenced or ordered

to be detained under s.205, 206 or 413 of the 1975 Act. The effect of this is that under s.40(1) a child detainee who is unlawfully at large may be arrested without warrant and returned to a place in which he may properly be detained. The power of arrest would be exercisable only by a police officer or a prison officer.

Under s.40(2) the period of unlawful absence would not count in the calculation of release dates.

PART II

PROCEEDS OF CRIME AND PROPERTY USED IN CRIME

CHAPTER I

CONFISCATION OF THE PROCEEDS OF CRIME

Confiscation orders

General provision

70.—(1) Subject to the provisions of this Chapter, where in respect of any offence to which this Chapter applies—
(a) the accused is convicted, whether in solemn or summary proceedings; or
(b) in the case of summary proceedings (without proceeding to conviction) an order is made discharging him absolutely,
the court, on the application of the prosecutor, may make an order (a "confiscation order") requiring the accused to pay such sum as the court thinks fit.
(2) This Chapter applies to any offence which has been prosecuted—
(a) on indictment; or
(b) on summary complaint if the offence is punishable by a fine of an amount greater than the amount corresponding to level 5 on the standard scale or by imprisonment for a period longer than 3 months or by both such fine and imprisonment,
but it does not apply to an offence to which section 1 of the 1987 Act (offences relating to drug trafficking) relates or to an offence under Part III of the 1989 Act (financial assistance for terrorism).
(3) A confiscation order shall not be made unless the court orders some other disposal (including an absolute discharge) in respect of the accused.
(4) The court may make a confiscation order against an accused only if it is satisfied that he has benefited from the commission of the offence concerned.
(5) The sum which a confiscation order requires an accused to pay must not exceed the lesser of—
(a) the amount of the benefit—
    (i) from the commission of the offence; or
    (ii) where section 71(4) of this Act applies, from the commission of the offence and any other offence to which this Chapter applies; or
(b) the amount that might be realised at the time the order is made.
(6) Any application under this section shall be made—
(a) in proceedings on indictment, when the prosecutor moves for sentence or, if the accused is remitted for sentence under section 104 of the 1975 Act, before sentence is pronounced; and
(b) in summary proceedings, following the conviction of the accused.
(7) For the purposes of any appeal or review, a confiscation order is a sentence.

DEFINITIONS
"accused": s.114(1).
"benefit": s.71(1).
"confiscation order": s.114(1).

"discount that might be realisable": s.72(3).

GENERAL NOTE

This section specifies the circumstances in which a confiscation order is competent and the maximum sum the accused may be required to pay. This section implements Recommendations 1, 2 (in part), 3, 4, 5, 21(1), 27 and 28 of S.L.C. Report (147).

Subsection (1) provides that a confiscation order is an order of court requiring the accused to pay a sum of money. The court has a discretion both as to whether to make the order and, subject to subs. (5), as to its amount. The court may make the order only on the application of the prosecutor, made after the accused is convicted or discharged absolutely. Subsection (2) specifies the nature of the offences in respect of which a confiscation order may be made. Offences relating to drug trafficking and financial assistance for terrorism are not included, as separate provision for confiscation in these cases is made in the Acts mentioned in the subsection. A confiscation order may be made in respect of any offence prosecuted on indictment, or in summary proceedings where the maximum penalty is a fine in excess of level 5 (currently £5,000) or imprisonment for longer than three months. The effect of the latter provision is that a confiscation order may *not* be imposed in the district court. Subsection (3) provides that a confiscation order should be imposed only in addition to another order or sentence.

Subsection (4) makes it a condition of the making of a confiscation order that the accused should have "benefited" from the commission of the offence. Subsection (5) prescribes the upper financial limit within which a confiscation order may be made. There is no lower limit. The upper limit is the lesser of the amount of "benefit" (s.71(1)) and "the amount that might be realised" (s.72(3)). Subsection (6) defines the time at which the prosecutor's application for a confiscation order is to be made. In solemn proceedings he is to apply when he moves for sentence or, in a remit to the High Court for sentence, before sentence is pronounced. In summary proceedings he is to apply after conviction. Subsection (7) provides that for the purpose of any appeal or review, a confiscation order is a sentence. It therefore allows an offender to challenge by appeal either the amount of the order or the fact that it has been made.

Benefit from commission of offence

71.—(1) For the purposes of this Chapter, an accused shall be held to have benefited from the commission of an offence if in connection with its commission he has obtained, directly or indirectly, any property or other economic advantage.

(2) Subject to subsection (4) below, in determining whether an accused has benefited from the commission of an offence and, if he has, the amount referred to in section 70(5)(a)(i) of this Act, the court may make the following assumptions, except in so far as he proves either of them, on the balance of probabilities, to be incorrect—

(a) that any property or other economic advantage which has been obtained by him since the relevant date has been obtained in connection with the commission of the offence; and

(b) that any expenditure by him since the relevant date was met out of property or other economic advantage obtained in connection with the commission of the offence.

(3) In subsection (2) above "the relevant date" means—

(a) the date of the offence; or

(b) if the offence is found to have been committed over a period of time, the date occurring at the beginning of that period.

(4) Where—

(a) the application for the confiscation order has been made in respect of two or more offences; or

(b) during the relevant period the accused has been convicted of at least one other offence to which this Chapter applies, being an offence committed after the coming into force of this Chapter,

the court may, in determining the amount referred to in section 70(5)(a)(ii) of this Act, make the assumptions set out in subsection (5) below, except in so far as the accused proves either of those assumptions, on the balance of probabilities, to be incorrect.

(5) Those assumptions are—
(a) that any property or economic advantage which has been obtained by the accused during the relevant period has been obtained in connection with the commission of an offence to which this Chapter applies; and
(b) that any expenditure by him during the relevant period was met out of property or other economic advantage obtained in connection with the commission of such an offence.
(6) In subsections (4) and (5) above, "the relevant period" means the period of six years ending with the date on which proceedings were instituted against the accused for the offence in respect of which the application for the confiscation order has been made.
(7) In this Part of this Act, "property" means any property wherever situated, whether heritable or moveable or whether corporeal or incorporeal.

DEFINITIONS
"accused": s.114(1).
"benefit": s.71(1).
"confiscation order": s.114(1).
"property": s.71(7).
"relevant date": s.71(3).
"relevant period": s.71(6).

GENERAL NOTE
This section sets out the criteria by which the court is to assess whether an offender has benefited from the commission of an offence. In particular, under subs. (2) the court may make two rebuttable assumptions. This section implements Recommendations 6(1), 6(2) and 30 of S.L.C. Report (147). The first presumption provides that an accused shall be held to have benefited from the commission of an offence if he has obtained, directly or indirectly, any property or other economic advantage (subs. (1)). It therefore enables the court to take a broad approach when assessing "benefit". Subsection (2) entitles the court to make two assumptions about the advantage obtained, and the expenditure made, since "the relevant date". The accused is entitled to prove on the balance of probabilities that either assumption is incorrect. Subsection (3) defines "the relevant date" and confines the assumptions to the period since the date of the offence. Subsection (4) defines "property".

Realisable property

72.—(1) In this Part of this Act "realisable property" means, subject to subsection (2) below—
(a) the whole estate wherever situated of a person—
(i) against whom proceedings have been instituted for an offence to which this Chapter applies; or
(ii) in respect of whom a restraint order has been made by virtue of section 95(3) of this Act;
(b) the whole estate wherever situated of a person to whom any person whose whole estate is realisable by virtue of paragraph (a) above has (directly or indirectly and whether in one transaction or in a series of transactions) made a gift caught by this Chapter;
(c) any other property in the possession or under the control of a person mentioned in paragraph (a) or (b) above; and
(d) any income or estate vesting in a person mentioned in paragraph (a) or (b) above.
(2) Property is not realisable if—
(a) held on trust by a person mentioned in subsection (1)(a) or (b) above for a person not so mentioned;
(b) a suspended forfeiture order is in force in respect of the property; or
(c) it is, for the time being, subject to a restraint order made in respect of other proceedings.
(3) Subject to section 73(4) of this Act, for the purposes of this Chapter, the amount that might be realised at the time a confiscation order is made in

respect of a person is the total value at that time of all his realisable property, and of all gifts caught by this Chapter which have been made by him, less any amount due by him at that time in respect of any compensation order under section 58 of the Criminal Justice (Scotland) Act 1980 made before the confiscation order.

(4) In assessing the value of realisable property (other than money) of a person in respect of whom it proposes to make a confiscation order, the court shall have regard to the likely market value of the property at the date on which the order would be made; but it may also have regard to any security or real burden which would require to be discharged in realising the property or to any other factors which might reduce the amount recoverable by such realisation.

(5) In assessing the value of realisable property of a person whose estate has been sequestrated, or who has been adjudged bankrupt in England and Wales or Northern Ireland, the court shall take into account the extent to which the property is subject to, as the case may be, sequestration or bankruptcy procedure by virtue of paragraph 1 or 2 of Schedule 4 to this Act.

(6) In subsection (4) above, "money" includes cheques, banknotes, postal orders, money orders and foreign currency.

DEFINITIONS
"amount that might be realisable": s.72(3).
"money": s.72(6).
"realisable property": s.72(1).

GENERAL NOTE
This section defines "realisable property" and specifies how it is to be valued. This section implements Recommendations 7, 8, 9, 12 and 13(1) to (3) of S.L.C. Report (147).
The term "realisable property" is defined as including:
(a) the whole estate of a person against whom proceedings have been instituted for an offence to which Chapter I of Pt. II applies (see s.70(2)) or in respect of whom a restraint order has been made before the institution of proceedings;
(b) the whole estate of anyone to whom such a person has made a gift which is "caught" (as mentioned in s.73(1));
(c) any other property in the possession of or under the control of a person mentioned in para. (a) or (b); and
(d) any income or estate vesting in such a person.
Subsection (2) specifies three types of property which are not realisable: first, property held on a trust for a third person by an accused or the recipient of a gift; second, property subject to a suspended forfeiture order (see s.87(2)), and third, property subject to a restraint order made in respect of any other offence.
Subsection (3) defines "the amount that might be realised" as:
(a) all the realisable property of the person concerned; and
(b) the value of all gifts "caught" by this Chapter of the Act which have been made by him (see s.73).
Subsection (4) deals with the valuation of realisable property (other than money). The value of the property is its likely market value at the date on which the order would be made. However, the court is to have regard also to (i) any security or real burden which may have to be discharged before the property may be realised and (ii) any other factors which might reduce the amount recoverable. The term "money" is defined in subs. (6).
Subsection (5) requires the court to take into account in assessing the value of realisable property of a person who has been sequestrated or made bankrupt the extent to which the property is subject to such insolvency proceedings.

Gifts

73.—(1) A gift is caught by this Chapter if—
(a) it was made by the accused in contemplation of, or after, the commission of the offence or, if more than one, in contemplation of any of the offences or after the commission of the earlier or the earliest of the offences to which the proceedings mentioned in section 72(1)(a)(i) of this Act for the time being relate; or

(b) where subsection (4) of section 71 of this Act applies, it was made by the accused within the relevant period within the meaning of subsection (6) of that section.

(2) In assessing the value of a gift caught by this Chapter, the court shall, subject to subsections (3) to (5) below, take it to be the greater of—

(a) the value of the gift when received adjusted to take account of subsequent changes in the value of money; or

(b) both of the following—

    (i) the likely market value, on the date on which the confiscation order is to be made, of—

        (A) the gift, if retained; or

        (B) where the recipient of the gift retains only part of it, the retained part, and any property or part of any property which, directly or indirectly, represents the gift; or

        (C) where the recipient of the gift retains no part of it, any property or part of any property which, directly or indirectly, represents the gift; and

    (ii) the value of any other property and any other economic advantage which by reason of the making of the gift the recipient of the gift has obtained, directly or indirectly, prior to the date on which the confiscation order is to be made, adjusted to take account of subsequent changes in the value of money.

(3) The circumstances in which the accused is to be treated as making a gift include those where he transfers an interest in property to another person directly or indirectly for a consideration the value of which is significantly less than the value of that interest at the time of transfer; and in those circumstances the value of the gift shall be the difference between the value of that consideration and the value of that interest at the time of transfer adjusted to take account of subsequent changes in the value of money.

(4) Where a gift caught by this Chapter was in the form of money and the recipient of the gift shows ʰthat, on the balance of probabilities, the money or any of it has not been used to purchase goods or services or to earn interest or any other return, the value of the gift or such part of it as has not been so used shall be taken to be the face value of the money or, as the case may be, unused amount of the money; and in this subsection, "money" includes cheques, banknotes, postal orders, money orders and foreign currency.

(5) The court may, notwithstanding the foregoing provisions of this section, disregard the amount (or part of the amount) of a gift caught by this Chapter if it considers it improbable that such amount (or part) could be realised.

(6) At any time before the realisation of property which is or represents a gift caught by this Chapter, the recipient of the gift may apply to the court for an order under this subsection, and, if the court is satisfied, on the balance of probabilities—

(a) that the person received the gift not knowing, not suspecting and not having reasonable grounds to suspect that the gift was made in contemplation of, or after, the commission of the offence or, if more than one, in contemplation of any of the offences or after the commission of the earlier or the earliest of the offences to which the proceedings for the time being relate; and

(b) that he was not associated with the giver in the commission of the offence; and

(c) that he would suffer hardship if the application were not granted,

it may make an order declaring that the gift or a part of the gift shall not be caught by this Chapter and that the property or part of the property of the recipient of the gift shall not be, or shall cease to be, realisable for the purposes of this Chapter and, if a confiscation order has already been made, varying that order accordingly, where necessary.

(7) An appeal shall lie to the High Court at the instance of—

(a) the applicant against the refusal;

(b) the prosecutor against the granting,

of an application under subsection (6) above, and the High Court in determining such an appeal may make such order as could have been made by the court on an application under subsection (6) above.

(8) The procedure in an appeal under this section shall be the same as the procedure in an appeal against sentence.

DEFINITIONS

"accused": s.114(1).
"caught": s.73(1).
"money": s.73(4).

GENERAL NOTE

This section specifies the circumstances in which a gift is "caught", prescribes rules for the assessment of its value and provides for the protection of the interests of an innocent recipient. Such a recipient may appeal the refusal or the granting of an application in relation to gifts.

This section implements Recommendations 15, 16(1), 17(1) and (2), 18, 19(1)–(4) of S.L.C. Report (147).

Making of confiscation orders

74.—(1) If the court decides to make a confiscation order, it shall determine the amount to be payable thereunder before making any decision as to—

(a) imposing a fine on the accused;

(b) making any order involving any payment by him.

(2) Where a court makes a confiscation order against an accused in any proceedings, it shall, in respect of any offence of which he is convicted in those proceedings, take account of the order before—

(a) imposing any fine on him;

(b) making any order involving any other payment by him,

but subject to that, the court shall leave the order out of account in determining the appropriate sentence or other manner of dealing with the accused.

(3) No enactment restricting the power of a court which deals with an accused in a particular way from dealing with him also in any other way shall, by reason only of the making of a confiscation order (or the postponement of a decision as regards making such an order), have the effect of restricting the court in dealing with the accused in any way it considers appropriate in respect of an offence.

(4) Where a court makes both a confiscation order and a compensation order under section 58 of the Criminal Justice (Scotland) Act 1980 against the same person in the same proceedings in relation to the same offence and the offence involves the misappropriation of property, it shall direct that the compensation shall be paid first out of any sums applied towards the satisfaction of the confiscation order.

DEFINITIONS

"accused": s.114(1).
"confiscation order": s.114(1).

GENERAL NOTE

This section is concerned with the relationship between a confiscation order and other orders the court may make when dealing with the offender. The confiscation order should be the first in the range of disposals to deprive the accused of his assets. The court is required to determine the amount payable under the order before making any decision as to other such disposals. When making a confiscation order the court is directed: first, to take the order into account if it goes on to make a further order depriving the accused of money or property; but second, not to take the order into account when it is imposing any other type of sentence, including a custodial sentence. This section implements Recommendations 22, 23(1), 24(1), 25(1) and 26(1) of S.L.C. Report (147).

Statements relevant to making confiscation orders

75.—(1) Where the prosecutor applies for the making of a confiscation order, the prosecutor may lodge with the clerk of court a statement as to any matters relevant—
    (a) to determining whether the accused has benefited from the commission of the offence; or
    (b) to an assessment of the value of the accused's benefit for the purposes of section 70(5)(a) of this Act.

(2) Without prejudice to section 150 (or as the case may be section 354) of the 1975 Act, if the accused accepts to any extent any allegation in the statement lodged under subsection (1) above, the court may, for the purpose of such determination or assessment as is mentioned in paragraph (a) or (b) of that subsection, treat his acceptance as conclusive of the matters to which it relates.

(3) Where—
    (a) a statement is lodged under subsection (1) above; and
    (b) the court is satisfied that a copy of that statement has been served on the accused,
the court may require the accused to indicate, within such period as the court may specify, to what extent he accepts each allegation in the statement and, in so far as he does not accept any such allegation, to indicate the basis of such non-acceptance.

(4) If the accused fails in any respect to comply with a requirement under subsection (3) above, he may be treated for the purposes of this section as accepting every allegation in the statement apart from any allegation in respect of which he has complied with the requirement.

(5) Without prejudice to section 150 (or as the case may be section 354) of the 1975 Act, where—
    (a) there is lodged with the clerk of court by the accused a statement as to any matters relevant to determining the amount that might be realised at the time the confiscation order is made; and
    (b) the prosecutor accepts to any extent any allegation in the statement,
the court may, for the purposes of that determination, treat that acceptance as conclusive of the matters to which it relates.

(6) Without prejudice to section 76(1) of this Act, where—
    (a) any allegation in the statement lodged under subsection (1) above is challenged by the accused, or
    (b) the basis of the non-acceptance by the accused of any such allegation is challenged by the prosecutor,
the court shall consider the matters being challenged at a hearing.

(7) Where the judge presiding at a hearing held under subsection (6) above is not the trial judge he may, on the application of either party, if he considers that it would be in the interests of justice to do so, adjourn the hearing to a date when the trial judge is available.

DEFINITIONS
    "accused": s.114(1).
    "benefit": s.71(1).
    "clerk of court": s.114(1).
    "confiscation order": s.114(1).

"prosecutor": s.462 of the Criminal Procedure (Scotland) Act 1975.

GENERAL NOTE
  This makes provision for the use of written statements in the procedure prior to the making of a confiscation order. First, subss. (1) to (4) provide for the lodging by the Crown of a statement relevant either to the determination of whether the accused has benefited from the commission of the offence or to the assessment of the value of his benefit. Secondly, subs. (5) provides for the lodging by the accused of a statement relevant to determining the amount that might be realised. Subsections (6) and (7) provide for a hearing on certain disputed issues. This section implements Recommendations 32, 33 and 34 of S.L.C. Report (147).

Postponed confiscation orders

  76.—(1) If the court considers that it has some, but not sufficient, relevant information for the purpose of enabling it to come to a decision as to whether to make a confiscation order or that it does not have sufficient relevant information to enable it to come to a decision as to the amount to be payable under the confiscation order, it may, subject as the case may be to subsection (6) or (10) below, postpone that decision for a period not exceeding 6 months after the date of conviction for the purpose of enabling further information to be obtained.
  (2) Without prejudice to sections 179 and 219 (or as the case may be sections 380 and 432) of the 1975 Act, the court may, notwithstanding postponement under subsection (1) above and subject to subsection (3) below, proceed, on the prosecutor's motion therefor, to sentence or to otherwise deal with the accused in respect of the conviction.
  (3) Where the court proceeds as mentioned in subsection (2) above—
  (a) no fine shall be imposed on the accused; and
  (b) no order shall be made involving any other payment by him,
in relation to the conviction before the decision whether to make a confiscation order is taken.
  (4) Where in the case of conviction on indictment a decision has been postponed under subsection (1) above for a period, any intention to appeal under section 228 of the 1975 Act against conviction or against both conviction and any sentence passed during that period in respect of the conviction, shall be intimated under section 231(1) of the 1975 Act not within 2 weeks of the final determination of the proceedings but within 2 weeks of—
  (a) in the case of an appeal against conviction where there has been no such sentence, the day on which the period of postponement commences;
  (b) in any other case, the day on which such sentence is passed in open court.
  (5) Notwithstanding any appeal of which intimation has been given by virtue of subsection (4) above, a person may appeal under section 228 of the 1975 Act against the confiscation order (if the decision is to make one) or against any other sentence passed, after the period of postponement, in respect of the conviction.
  (6) If during the period of postponement intimation is given by virtue of subsection (4) above by the person, the High Court may, on the application of the prosecutor, extend that period to a date up to 3 months after the date of disposal of the appeal.
  (7) This subsection applies where in the case of summary conviction a decision has been postponed under subsection (1) above for a period.
  (8) Where subsection (7) above applies and the offender appeals under section 442 of the 1975 Act against conviction or against both conviction and any sentence passed during the period of postponement—
  (a) his application for a stated case shall be made not within one week of the final determination of the proceedings but within one week of the day mentioned in paragraph (a) or (b) of subsection (4) above;

(b) his draft stated case shall be prepared and issued not within 3 weeks of the final determination of the proceedings but within 3 weeks of the said day.

(9) Where subsection (7) above applies, then, notwithstanding any appeal against conviction or sentence or both the offender may appeal under section 442(1)(a)(ii), and the prosecutor may appeal under section 442(1)(b)(ii), of the 1975 Act against any confiscation order or against any other sentence passed, after the period of postponement, in respect of the conviction.

(10) Where subsection (7) above applies, then, if during the period of postponement the offender applies for a stated case or lodges a note of appeal, the High Court may, on the application of the prosecutor, extend the period of postponement to a date up to 3 months after the date of disposal of the appeal.

DEFINITIONS
    "confiscation order": s.114(1).
    "prosecutor": s.462 of the Criminal Procedure (Scotland) Act 1975.

GENERAL NOTE
    This section enables the court to postpone a decision to make a confiscation order or to determine the amount payable because it requires further information. Notwithstanding such postponement, the court may impose a custodial sentence. The section also regulates appeals: subss. (4) to (6) deal with conviction on indictment, while subss. (7) to (10) deal with summary convictions. The section broadly follows the scheme of s.2 of the Criminal Justice (Scotland) Act 1987. This section implements Recommendation 36 of S.L.C. Report (147).

Increase in benefit or realisable property

77.—(1) This section applies where the court which made a confiscation order is satisfied, on an application made by the prosecutor, that at the time the application is made the benefit for the purposes of section 70(5)(a) of this Act, or the amount that might be realised, is greater than—
    (a) the benefit; or, as the case may be,
    (b) the amount that might be realised,
which was taken into account when the order was made.

(2) The considerations by reference to which the court may be satisfied as mentioned in subsection (1) above shall include—
    (a) the benefit was greater than was taken into account when the confiscation order was made or has increased in value since the confiscation order was made; or
    (b) further benefit has been obtained since the confiscation order was made; or
    (c) the value of realisable property was greater than was taken into account when the confiscation order was made; or
    (d) any realisable property taken into account at the time when the confiscation order was made has subsequently increased in value; or
    (e) that the amount, or part of the amount, of a gift which was disregarded under section 73(5) of this Act could now be realised.

(3) An application under subsection (1) above shall be made as soon as is reasonably practicable after the relevant information becomes available to the prosecutor but in any event within 6 years commencing with the date when the person was convicted of the offence.

(4) Where this section applies, and notwithstanding that any matters in relation to the making of the confiscation order are, by virtue of section 75(2) or (5) of this Act, to be treated as conclusive—
    (a) the court may make a new confiscation order for the payment of such sum as appears to the court to be appropriate having regard to what is now shown to be the benefit or the amount that might be realised; and
    (b) if the earlier confiscation order has not been satisfied then the court, in making the new confiscation order, shall recall the earlier order and

may take into account the amount unpaid (including any interest payable by virtue of section 81(1) of this Act) under the earlier order.

(5) Section 75 of this Act shall, subject to any necessary modifications, apply in relation to the making of a new confiscation order in pursuance of this section as it applies where the prosecutor has applied for the making of a confiscation order under section 70 of this Act.

(6) The assumptions mentioned in section 71(2) and (5) of this Act shall not apply for the purposes of this section.

DEFINITIONS
"accused": s.114(1).
"benefit": s.114(1).
"confiscation order": s.114(1).
"prosecutor": s.462 of the Criminal Procedure (Scotland) Act 1975.
"realisable property": s.72(1).

GENERAL NOTE
This is the first of three sections (ss.77, 78 and 79) providing for the variation of confiscation orders. This section provides for the case where it becomes apparent that there has been an increase in the benefit or the realisable property after the confiscation order was made. This section implements Recommendation 38 of S.L.C. Report (147).

Realisable property inadequate to meet payments under confiscation order

78.—(1) This section applies where the court which made a confiscation order is satisfied on the balance of probabilities, on an application made to it by the accused or the prosecutor, that the value of the realisable property is inadequate to meet any amount unpaid (including any interest payable by virtue of section 81(1) of this Act) under the confiscation order.

(2) When considering whether the value of the realisable property is inadequate the court—

(a) shall, unless already taken into account under section 72(5) of this Act, take into account the extent to which property of a person whose estate has been sequestrated or who has been adjudged bankrupt is or has been included in the bankrupt's estate for the purposes of the Bankruptcy (Scotland) Act 1985 or Part IX of the Insolvency Act 1986; and

(b) may disregard any inadequacy which appears to it to be attributable, wholly or partly, to anything done by the accused for the purpose of protecting the realisable property from realisation.

(3) Where this section applies, the court shall recall the confiscation order and make a new confiscation order for the payment of such sum of a lesser amount than that for which the original order was made which appears to the court to be appropriate having regard to—

(a) the value of the realisable property as determined under subsection (1) above; and

(b) any amount paid in pursuance of the original order.

(4) Section 75 of this Act shall, subject to any necessary modifications, apply in relation to an application under this section as it applies where the prosecutor has applied for the making of a confiscation order under section 70 of this Act.

DEFINITIONS
"accused": s.114(1).
"benefit": s.114(1).
"confiscation order": s.462 of the Criminal Procedure (Scotland) Act 1975.
"realisable property": s.72(1).

GENERAL NOTE
This section deals with the circumstances in which a new confiscation order may be substituted requiring a smaller amount to be paid because there is inadequate realisable property to satisfy

the original order. This section implements Recommendations 41(1) to (4) of S.L.C. Report (147).

Confiscation orders where proceeds of crime discovered at later date

79.—(1) This section applies where no confiscation order has been made in relation to an offence under section 70 or 76 of this Act.

(2) Where the court, on an application made to it by the prosecutor under this section, is satisfied—

- (a) that a person convicted of an offence to which this Chapter applies has benefited in connection with the commission of the offence concerned;
- (b) that the information necessary to enable a confiscation order to be made on the date on which an application under section 70 of this Act was or could have been made was not available to the prosecutor,

it may make a confiscation order in relation to that person.

(3) An application under this section shall be made as soon as is reasonably practicable after the relevant information becomes available to the prosecutor but in any event not later than 6 years after the date when the person was convicted of the offence.

(4) In determining the sum to be payable under a confiscation order made in pursuance of this section, the court shall take into account—

- (a) any order involving any payment by the offender;
- (b) any suspended forfeiture order or an order for forfeiture under any other enactment made in respect of the offender,

which forms part of the sentence already imposed for the offence concerned.

(5) Sections 70(3) and 74(1), (2) and (4) of this Act shall not apply in relation to a confiscation order made in pursuance of this section.

(6) Section 75 of this Act shall, subject to any necessary modifications, apply in relation to the making of a confiscation order in pursuance of this section as it applies where the prosecutor has moved for a confiscation order under section 70 of this Act.

(7) Where the court makes a confiscation order in pursuance of this section and a compensation order has been made under section 58 of the Criminal Justice (Scotland) Act 1980 in respect of misappropriation of property by the offender, the court shall direct that compensation shall first be paid out of any sums applied towards the satisfaction of the confiscation order to the extent of any sums outstanding in respect of the compensation order.

(8) The assumptions mentioned in section 71(2) and (5) of this Act shall not apply for the purposes of this section.

(9) In this section "the court" means the court which had jurisdiction in respect of the offence concerned to make a confiscation order under section 70 of this Act.

DEFINITIONS
    "confiscation order": s.114(1).
    "prosecutor": s.462 of the Criminal Procedure (Scotland) Act 1975.
    "the court": s.79(9).

GENERAL NOTE
    This applies where a confiscation order has not been made and the proceeds of crime are discovered at a later date. It implements Recommendations 42(1) to (4) of S.L.C. Report (147).
    Subsection (2) enables the court to make a confiscation order on an application by the prosecutor where it is satisfied (a) that the person convicted has benefited in connection with the commission of the offence and (b) that the information necessary to make a confiscation order

was not available to the prosecutor when the accused was convicted. Subsection (3) provides that the prosecutor must apply as soon as reasonably practicable after the relevant information becomes available and in any event within six years of the date of conviction.

Application of provisions relating to fines to enforcement of confiscation orders

80.—(1) Sections 196 and 203, or sections 402 and 412, of the 1975 Act and the provisions of that Act specified in subsection (2) below (or those provisions as applied by section 194 of that Act) shall, subject to the qualifications mentioned in subsection (2) below, apply in relation to confiscation orders as they apply in relation to fines; and section 91 of the Magistrates' Courts Act 1980 and Article 96 of the Magistrates' Courts (Northern Ireland) Order 1981 (provisions relating to transfer of fines from Scotland etc.) shall be construed accordingly.

(2) The provisions mentioned in subsection (1) above are—

(a) section 396, provided that any allowance under that section of time (or further time) for payment shall be without prejudice to the exercise by any administrator appointed in relation to the confiscation order of his powers and duties under this Act; and the court may, pending such exercise, postpone any decision as to refusing or allowing time (or further time) for payment;

(b) section 397, subject to the like proviso as in paragraph (a) above;

(c) section 398, but as if subsection (1)—

(i) gave the prosecutor an opportunity to be heard at any enquiry thereunder; and

(ii) applied whether the offender was in prison or not;

(d) section 399, provided that any order of payment by instalments shall be without prejudice to such exercise as is mentioned in paragraph (a) above;

(e) section 400;

(f) section 401(2) and (3);

(g) section 403;

(h) section 404;

(i) section 406;

(j) section 407, provided that—

(i) where a court imposes a period of imprisonment both in respect of a fine and of a confiscation order the amounts in respect of which the period is imposed shall, for the purposes of subsection (1A) of that section, be aggregated; and

(ii) before imposing a period of imprisonment to which there is a liability by virtue of that section the court shall, if an administrator has been appointed in relation to the confiscation order, require a report from him as to whether and in what way he is likely to exercise his powers and duties under this Act and shall take that report into account; and the court may, pending such exercise, postpone any decision as to such imposition;

(k) section 408;

(l) section 409, except that the reference in subsection (1) of that section to the person paying a sum to the governor of the prison under conditions prescribed by rules made under the Prisons (Scotland) Act 1989 shall be construed as including a reference to an administrator appointed in relation to the confiscation order making such payment under this Act in respect of the person;

(m) section 411, provided that an order of recovery by civil diligence shall not be made under the section where an administrator is appointed in relation to the confiscation order;

(n) Schedule 7.

(3) Where a court, by virtue of subsection (1) above, orders the sum due under a confiscation order to be recovered by civil diligence under section 411 of the 1975 Act, any arrestment executed by a prosecutor under subsection (2) of section 99 of this Act shall be deemed to have been executed by the court as if that subsection authorised such execution.

(4) Where in any proceedings a confiscation order has been made as regards a person and a period of imprisonment or detention is imposed on him in default of payment of its amount (or as the case may be of an instalment thereof), that period shall run from the expiry of any other period of imprisonment or detention (not being one of life imprisonment or detention for life) imposed on him in the proceedings.

(5) The reference in subsection (4) above to "any other period of imprisonment or detention imposed" includes (without prejudice to the generality of the expression) a reference to such a period on default of payment of a fine (or instalment thereof); but only where that default had occurred before the warrant for imprisonment is issued for the default in relation to the order.

DEFINITIONS
"confiscation order": s.114(1).
"prosecutor": s.462 of the Criminal Procedure (Scotland) Act 1975.

GENERAL NOTE
This section applies to the enforcement of confiscation orders, various provisions of the 1975 Act relating to fines. It applies two sets of statutory provisions: first, the fines enforcement and payment provisions of the 1975 Act with regard to solemn (ss.196 and 203) and summary (ss.402 and 412) procedure; and second, those provisions of the 1975 Act which are listed in subs. (2), as qualified in that subsection. The statutory provisions for the transfer of fines from Scotland to England and Wales and to Northern Ireland are to be construed accordingly. This section, by subs. (2) lists the provisions of the 1975 Act which, as qualified by the provisos in that subsection, are to apply to confiscation orders as they apply to fines. This section implements Recommendation 43 of S.L.C. Report (147).

Interest on sums unpaid under confiscation orders

81.—(1) If any sum required to be paid by a person under a confiscation order is not paid when it is required to be paid (whether forthwith on the making of the order or at a time specified under section 396(1) of the 1975 Act) that person shall be liable to pay interest on that sum for the period for which it remains unpaid and the amount of the interest shall for the purposes of enforcement be treated as part of the amount to be recovered from him under the confiscation order.

(2) The sheriff may, on the application of the prosecutor, increase the term of imprisonment or detention fixed in respect of the confiscation order under section 396(2) of the 1975 Act if the effect of subsection (1) above is to increase the maximum period applicable in relation to the order under section 407(1A) of the 1975 Act.

(3) The rate of interest under subsection (1) above shall be the rate payable under a decree of the Court of Session.

DEFINITIONS
"confiscation orders": s.114(1).
"prosecutor": s.462 of the Criminal Procedure (Scotland) Act 1975.

GENERAL NOTE
This section, which implements Recommendation 44 of S.L.C. Report (147), provides for the payment of interest on sums unpaid under confiscation orders.

Exercise of powers

Exercise of powers by court or administrator

82.—(1) This section applies to the powers as regards realisable property conferred on the court by sections 94, 95, 97, 98 and 99 of and paragraphs 1, 4 and 12 of Schedule 3 to this Act in relation to confiscation orders and on an administrator by that Schedule.

(2) Subject to the following provisions of this section, the powers shall be exercised with a view to making available for satisfying the confiscation order or, as the case may be, any confiscation order that may be made in the case of a person mentioned in section 72(1)(a) of this Act, the value for the time being of realisable property held by any person by the realisation of such property.

(3) In the case of realisable property held by a person by virtue only of having received a gift made directly or indirectly by the accused which is caught by this Chapter, the powers shall be exercised with a view to realising no more than the value of the gift as assessed under subsection (2), (3) or (4) of section 73 of this Act.

(4) The powers shall be exercised with a view to allowing any person other than a person mentioned in section 72(1)(a) of this Act or the recipient of any such gift to retain or recover the value of any property held by him.

(5) An order may be made or other action taken in respect of a debt owed by the Crown.

(6) In exercising those powers, no account shall be taken of any obligations of such a person or of the recipient of any such gift which conflict with the obligation to satisfy the confiscation order.

DEFINITIONS
"confiscation order": s.114(1).
"gift": s.73(1).
"realisable property": s.72.

GENERAL NOTE
This section sets out the general principles governing the exercise of the powers conferred by the Act on the court and on the administrator with regard to realisable property and confiscation orders. This section implements Recommendation 43 of S.L.C. Report (147). Subsection (2) sets out the first principle: that the powers are to be exercised with a view to the satisfaction of the confiscation order by making available the value for the time being of the realisable property. Subsection (3) provides that where realisable property is held by the recipient of a gift caught by the Act, the powers are to be exercised with a view to realising no more than the value of the gift. The powers are to be exercised to allow any person (other than the accused or the recipient of a caught gift) to retain or recover the value of any property held by him (subs. (4)). Subsection (5) provides that an order may be made, or other action taken, in respect of a debt owed by the Crown. The obligation to satisfy the confiscation order is to take priority over any other obligations (subs. (6)).

Compensation

Compensation

83.—(1) Subject to subsection (3) below, if proceedings are instituted against a person for an offence to which this Chapter applies and either—

(a) the proceedings do not result in his conviction for any such offence, or
(b) where he is convicted of one or more such offences—
　　(i) the conviction or convictions concerned are quashed (and no conviction for any such offence is substituted); or
　　(ii) he is pardoned by Her Majesty in respect of the conviction or convictions concerned,

the court may, on an application by a person who held property which was realisable property, order compensation to be paid to the applicant if, having regard to all the circumstances, it considers it appropriate to do so.

(2) Subsection (1) above is without prejudice to any right which may otherwise exist to institute proceedings in respect of delictual liability disclosed by such circumstances as are mentioned in paragraphs (a) and (b) of subsection (3) below.

(3) The court shall not order compensation to be paid under subsection (1) above in any case unless satisfied—

(a) that there has been some serious default on the part of a person concerned in the investigation of the offence or offences concerned, being a person mentioned in subsection (5) below, and that, but for that default, the proceedings would not have been instituted or continued; and

(b) that the applicant has suffered loss or damage in consequence of anything done in relation to the property under section 94, 95, 97, 98, 99 or 108 of or Schedule 3 to this Act.

(4) The amount of compensation to be paid under this section shall be such as the court thinks just in all the circumstances of the case.

(5) Compensation payable under this section shall be paid, where the person in default was—

(a) a constable of a police force within the meaning of the Police (Scotland) Act 1967, by the police authority or joint police board for the police area for which that force is maintained;

(b) a constable other than is mentioned in paragraph (a) above, but with the powers of such a constable, by the body under whose authority he acts;

(c) a procurator fiscal or was acting on behalf of the Lord Advocate, by the Lord Advocate;

(d) a person commissioned by the Commissioners of Customs and Excise, by those Commissioners; and

(e) an officer of the Commissioners of Inland Revenue, by those Commissioners.

(6) An application for compensation under this section shall be made not later than three years after the conclusion of the proceedings in respect of which the confiscation order was made; and subsection (6) of section 95 of this Act shall apply for the purpose of determining when proceedings are concluded for the purposes of this subsection as it applies for the purposes of that section.

(7) In this section, "the court" means the Court of Session or the sheriff exercising his civil jurisdiction.

(8) Until the date on which paragraph 71 of Schedule 13 to the Local Government etc. (Scotland) Act 1994 comes into force, the reference in subsection (5)(a) above to a joint police board shall be construed as a reference to a joint police committee.

DEFINITIONS
"Court, the": s.83(7).
"proceedings": s.114(3).
"procurator fiscal": s.462 of the Criminal Procedure (Scotland) Act 1975.
"property": s.114(1).
"realisable property": s.72.

GENERAL NOTE
This sets out the circumstances in which compensation may be payable to a holder of realisable property who has suffered loss or damage as a result of the exercise of the powers of the court or an administrator. This section implements Recommendations 59(2) to (6) of S.L.C. Report (147).

Investigations and disclosure of information

Order to make material available

84.—(1) The procurator fiscal may, for the purpose of an investigation into whether a person has benefited from the commission of an offence to which this Chapter applies and as to the amount of that benefit, apply to the sheriff for an order under subsection (2) below in relation to particular material or material of a particular description.

(2) If on such an application the sheriff is satisfied that the conditions in subsection (4) below are fulfilled, he may make an order that the person who appears to him to be in possession of the material to which the application relates shall—

(a) produce it to a constable for him to take away; or

(b) give a constable access to it,

within such period as the order may specify.

This subsection is subject to section 86(11) of this Act.

(3) The period to be specified in an order under subsection (2) above shall be seven days unless it appears to the sheriff that a longer or shorter period would be appropriate in the particular circumstances of the application.

(4) The conditions referred to in subsection (2) above are—

(a) that there are reasonable grounds for suspecting that a specified person has benefited from the commission of an offence to which this Chapter applies;

(b) that there are reasonable grounds for suspecting that the material to which the application relates—

(i) is likely to be of substantial value (whether by itself or together with other material) to the investigation for the purpose of which the application is made; and

(ii) does not consist of or include items subject to legal privilege; and

(c) that there are reasonable grounds for believing that it is in the public interest, having regard—

(i) to the benefit likely to accrue to the investigation if the material is obtained; and

(ii) to the circumstances under which the person in possession of the material holds it,

that the material should be produced or that access to it should be given.

(5) Where the sheriff makes an order under subsection (2)(b) above in relation to material on any premises he may, on the application of the procurator fiscal, order any person who appears to him to be entitled to grant entry to the premises to allow a constable to enter the premises to obtain access to the material.

(6) An application under subsection (1) or (5) above may be made ex parte in chambers.

(7) Provision may be made by rules of court as to—

(a) the discharge and variation of orders under this section, and

(b) proceedings relating to such orders.

(8) Where the material to which an application under this section relates consists of information contained in a computer—

(a) an order under subsection (2)(a) above shall have effect as an order to produce the material in a form in which it can be taken away and in which it is visible and legible; and

(b) an order under subsection (2)(b) above shall have effect as an order to give access to the material in a form in which it is visible and legible.

(9) An order under subsection (2) above—

(a) shall not confer any right to production of, or access to, items subject to legal privilege;

(b) shall have effect notwithstanding any obligation as to secrecy or other restriction upon the disclosure of information imposed by statute or otherwise; and

(c) may be made in relation to material in the possession of an authorised government department;

and in this subsection "authorised government department" means a government department which is an authorised department for the purposes of the Crown Proceedings Act 1947.

(10) In this section—

(a) "items subject to legal privilege" and "premises" have the same meanings as in section 40 of the Criminal Justice (Scotland) Act 1987; and

(b) references to a person benefiting from the commission of an offence to which this Chapter applies, in relation to conduct which is not such an offence but which would have been if it had occurred in Scotland, shall be construed in accordance with section 71 of this Act as if that conduct had so occurred.

DEFINITIONS

"authorised government department": s.84(9).

"benefit": s.114(1).

"constable": s.51(1) of the Police (Scotland) Act 1967.

"items subject to legal privilege": s.40 of the Criminal Justice (Scotland) Act 1987.

"premises": s.40 of the Criminal Justice (Scotland) Act 1987.

"procurator fiscal": s.462 of the Criminal Procedure (Scotland) Act 1975.

GENERAL NOTE

This section and the next two were introduced during the Third Reading of the Bill in the House of Commons. The Minister said that the powers provided by these sections were not new. Similar powers already existed under the 1987 Act, for the purpose of investigation into drug trafficking, to cover investigations into whether a person has benefited from the commission of any other offence. These new sections were inserted at the request of chief police officers (*Hansard*, H.C. Vol. 261, col. 216).

By s.84 a procurator fiscal may apply to the sheriff for an order in relation to particular material or material of a particular description. Subsections (2) and (3) allow a sheriff to make an order, for the production of material to a constable or to allow the constable access to it within a specified time if there are reasonable grounds for suspecting that a named person has benefited from the commission of a relevant offence and that the material is likely to be of substantial value and excludes items of legal privilege. Such an order must also be in the public interest having regard to likely benefit and the whole circumstance of possession.

Authority for search

85.—(1) The procurator fiscal may, for the purpose of an investigation into whether a person has benefited from the commission of an offence to which this Chapter applies and as to the amount of that benefit, apply to the sheriff for a warrant under this section in relation to specified premises.

(2) On such application the sheriff may issue a warrant authorising a constable to enter and search the premises if the sheriff is satisfied—

(a) that an order made under section 84 of this Act in relation to material on the premises has not been complied with; or

(b) that the conditions in subsection (3) below are fulfilled; or

(c) that the conditions in subsection (4) below are fulfilled.

(3) The conditions referred to in subsection (2)(b) above are—

(a) that there are reasonable grounds for suspecting that a specified person has benefited from the commission of an offence to which this Chapter applies; and

(b) that the conditions in section 84(4)(b) and (c) of this Act are fulfilled in relation to any material on the premises; and

(c) that it would not be appropriate to make an order under that section in relation to the material because—

(i) it is not practicable to communicate with any person entitled to produce the material; or

(ii) it is not practicable to communicate with any person entitled to grant access to the material or entitled to grant entry to the premises on which the material is situated; or

(iii) the investigation for the purposes of which the application is made might be seriously prejudiced unless a constable could secure immediate access to the material.

(4) The conditions referred to in subsection (2)(c) above are—

(a) that there are reasonable grounds for suspecting that a specified person has benefited from the commission of an offence to which this Chapter applies; and

(b) that there are reasonable grounds for suspecting that there is on the premises material relating to the specified person, or to the question whether that person has so benefited or the amount of that benefit, which is likely to be of substantial value (whether by itself or together with other material) to the investigation for the purpose of which the application is made, but that the material cannot at the time of the application be particularised; and

(c) that—

(i) it is not practicable to communicate with any person entitled to grant entry to the premises; or

(ii) entry to the premises will not be granted unless a warrant is produced; or

(iii) the investigation for the purpose of which the application is made might be seriously prejudiced unless a constable arriving at the premises could secure immediate entry to them.

(5) Where a constable has entered premises in the execution of a warrant issued under this section, he may seize and retain any material, other than items subject to legal privilege, which is likely to be of substantial value (whether by itself or together with other material) to the investigation for the purpose of which the warrant was issued.

(6) Subsection (10) of section 84 of this Act shall apply for the purposes of this section as it applies for the purposes of that section.

DEFINITIONS

"benefit": s.114(1).

"items subject to legal privilege": s.40 of the Criminal Justice (Scotland) Act 1987.

"premises": s.40 of the Criminal Justice (Scotland) Act 1987.

"procurator fiscal": s.462 of the Criminal Procedure (Scotland) Act 1975.

GENERAL NOTE

This section provides for a sheriff's warrant to search for material bearing on whether a person has benefited from the commission of an offence. The essential difference between s.84 and s.85 is that the former amounted to an order to co-operate in the production of material, whereas the latter does not necessarily presume or require co-operation.

Disclosure of information held by government departments

86.—(1) Subject to subsection (4) below, the Court of Session may on an application by the Lord Advocate order any material mentioned in subsection (3) below which is in the possession of an authorised government department to be produced to the Court within such period as the Court may specify.

(2) The power to make an order under subsection (1) above is exercisable if—

  (a) the powers conferred on the Court by section 94(1)(a) of this Act are exercisable by virtue of section 95(2) of this Act; or

  (b) those powers are exercisable by virtue of section 95(3) of this Act and the Court has made a restraint order which has not been recalled.

(3) The material referred to in subsection (1) above is any material which—

  (a) has been submitted to an officer of an authorised government department by a person who holds, or has at any time held, realisable property;

  (b) has been made by an officer of an authorised government department in relation to such a person; or

  (c) is correspondence which passed between an officer of an authorised government department and such a person;

and an order under that subsection may require the production of all such material or of a particular description of such material, being material in the possession of the department concerned.

(4) An order under subsection (1) above shall not require the production of any material unless it appears to the Court of Session that the material is likely to contain information that would facilitate the exercise of the powers conferred on the Court by section 94(1)(a) of or paragraph 1 or 12 of Schedule 3 to this Act or on an administrator appointed under paragraph 1(1) of that Schedule.

(5) The Court may by order authorise the disclosure to such an administrator of any material produced under subsection (1) above or any part of such material; but the Court shall not make an order under this subsection unless a reasonable opportunity has been given for an officer of the department to make representations to the Court.

(6) Material disclosed in pursuance of an order under subsection (5) above may, subject to any conditions contained in the order, be further disclosed for the purposes of the functions under Part II of this Act of the administrator or the High Court.

(7) The Court of Session may by order authorise the disclosure to a person mentioned in subsection (8) below of any material produced under subsection (1) above or any part of such material; but the Court shall not make an order under this subsection unless—

  (a) a reasonable opportunity has been given for an officer of the department to make representations to the Court; and

  (b) it appears to the Court that the material is likely to be of substantial value in exercising functions relating to the investigation of crime.

(8) The persons referred to in subsection (7) above are—

  (a) a constable;

  (b) the Lord Advocate or any procurator fiscal; and

  (c) an officer within the meaning of the Customs and Excise Management Act 1979.

(9) Material disclosed in pursuance of an order under subsection (7) above may, subject to any conditions contained in the order, be further disclosed for the purposes of functions relating to the investigation of crime or whether any person has benefited from the commission of an offence to which this Chapter applies or the amount of that benefit.

(10) Material may be produced or disclosed in pursuance of this section notwithstanding any obligation as to secrecy or other restriction upon the disclosure of information imposed by statute or otherwise.

(11) An order under subsection (1) above and, in the case of material in the possession of an authorised government department, an order under section 84(2) of this Act may require any officer of the department (whether named in the order or not) who may for the time being be in possession of the material concerned to comply with such order; and any such order shall be served as if the proceedings were civil proceedings against the department.

(12) Where any requirement is included in any order by virtue of subsection (11) above, the person on whom the order is served—
(a) shall take all reasonable steps to bring it to the attention of the officer concerned; and
(b) if the order is not brought to that officer's attention within the period referred to in subsection (1) above, shall report the reasons for the failure to the Court of Session,
and it shall also be the duty of any other officer of the department in receipt of the order to take such steps as are mentioned in paragraph (a) above.

(13) In this section "authorised government department" means a government department which is an authorised department for the purposes of the Crown Proceedings Act 1947; and subsection (10) of section 84 of this Act shall apply for the purposes of this section as it applies for the purposes of that section.

DEFINITIONS
"administrator": s.100 and Sched. 3, para. 1(1).
"authorised government department": s.86(13).
"realisable property": s.72.

GENERAL NOTE
This section permits the recovery of certain materials by the Lord Advocate if an order to that effect is granted by the Court of Session.
In particular, subs. (1) provides that the Court of Session may on the application of the Lord Advocate order relevant material which is in the possession of an authorised government department to be produced within a specified period of time. Subsection (2) provides that the court may make such an order if proceedings have been instituted, proceedings have not been concluded or a confiscation order has been made. Alternatively, such an order may be made if the court is satisfied that proceedings are about to commence.
Subsection (3) defines the material which may be the subject of an order as material that has been submitted to the authorised government department or has been made by an officer of that department or is correspondence between an officer of that department and the person holding realisable property.
Subsection (4) requires that the material sought be likely to assist the court, or an administrator appointed under this Act, in the exercise of their powers.

CHAPTER II

FORFEITURE OF PROPERTY USED IN CRIME

Suspended forfeiture order

87.—(1) This section applies where in respect of any offence—
(a) the accused is convicted, whether in solemn or summary proceedings; or
(b) in the case of summary proceedings, (without proceeding to conviction) an order is made discharging him absolutely.
(2) Where this section applies, the court may, if it is satisfied on the application of the prosecutor that any property which was at the time of the offence or of the accused's apprehension in his ownership or possession or under his control—
(a) has been used for the purpose of committing, or facilitating the commission of, any offence; or
(b) was intended to be used for that purpose,
make an order (a "suspended forfeiture order") in respect of that property.

(3) Any application under this section shall be made—

(a) in proceedings on indictment, when the prosecutor moves for sentence or if the accused is remitted for sentence under section 104 of the 1975 Act, before sentence is pronounced; and

(b) in summary proceedings, following upon the conviction of the accused or, as the case may be, the finding that he committed the offence with which he was charged.

(4) If the prosecutor knows or reasonably suspects the identity of a person (other than the accused) as being the owner of, or otherwise having an interest in, the property to which the suspended forfeiture order relates, he shall intimate that fact to the court on making the application and the order shall name that person as a person having an interest or suspected of having an interest in the property.

(5) Any reference in this Chapter to facilitating the commission of an offence shall include a reference to the taking of any steps after it has been committed for the purpose of disposing of any property to which it relates or of avoiding apprehension or detection.

(6) Where, by itself, the use of property constitutes an offence in whole or in part, that property shall be regarded for the purpose of subsection (2)(a) above as used for the purpose of committing the offence, unless the enactment which created the offence expressly excludes the application of this section.

(7) Subject to subsection (8) below, where the accused is convicted of an offence under any enactment, the court shall not be precluded from making a suspended forfeiture order in respect of any property by reason only that the property would not be liable to forfeiture under that enactment.

(8) Subsection (7) shall not apply—

(a) if the enactment concerned expressly excludes the application of this section; or

(b) to any property which has been used or has been intended to be used as mentioned in subsection (2)(a) or (b) above in relation to the offence of which the accused has been convicted, if the enactment concerned specifies the category of property which is to be liable to forfeiture thereunder, and the category so specified does not include the category of property which has been used or has been intended to be used as aforesaid.

(9) Where the court makes both a suspended forfeiture order and a compensation order under section 58 of the Criminal Justice (Scotland) Act 1980 against the same accused in the same proceedings, it may order that, in the event of the property subject to the suspended forfeiture order being forfeited under section 90 of this Act, the proceeds of sale of that property shall be first directed towards satisfaction of the compensation order.

(10) As soon as may be after a suspended forfeiture order has been made, the prosecutor—

(a) shall notify in writing any person named in the order in pursuance of subsection (4) above that the order has been made, and that the person so notified may be entitled to apply to the court for—

   (i) the order to be recalled under section 91 of this Act; or

   (ii) a direction under section 92 of this Act; and

(b) if the property in respect of which the order has been made includes heritable property in Scotland, shall cause a certified copy of the order to be recorded in the General Register of Sasines or as the case may be registered in the Land Register of Scotland; and

(c) if the court directs him to do so, shall insert a notice in the Edinburgh Gazette or in such other newspaper or journal as appears to the court to be appropriate specifying the terms of the suspended forfeiture order.

(11) Any property in respect of which a suspended forfeiture order is made shall be taken into the possession of or placed under the control of the clerk of court until—

(a) the order is recalled; or

(b) the property is forfeited to the Crown and disposed of under section 90 of this Act or forfeited to another person under that section.

(12) For the purposes of any appeal or review a suspended forfeiture order is a sentence.

(13) Where, in disposing of an appeal, the High Court makes an order the effect of which is to release from liability to forfeiture any heritable property in Scotland in respect of which a suspended forfeiture order was made, the prosecutor shall, as soon as may be after the appeal has been disposed of, cause a certified copy of the order of the court to be recorded in the General Register of Sasines or, as the case may be, registered in the Land Register of Scotland.

(14) In this section "the court" does not include a district court, whether or not constituted by a stipendiary magistrate.

DEFINITIONS
"accused": s.114(1).
"court, the": s.87(14).
"property": s.71(4).
"prosecutor": s.462 of the Criminal Procedure (Scotland) Act 1975.
"suspended forfeiture order": s.87(2).

GENERAL NOTE
This section prescribes the circumstances in which a suspended forfeiture order may be made and what the prosecutor must do after an order has been made. A suspended forfeiture order may be made where a person is convicted of any offence in solemn or summary proceedings or where, in summary proceedings, the court grants an absolute discharge.

This section implements Recommendations 60, 62, 63(1) and (2), 64, 67, 69, 70(1) and (2), 71, 76(1) and (2), 77, 78, 79, 80 and 85 of S.L.C. Report (147).

Forfeiture: district court

88.—(1) Where, in respect of any offence tried in the district court, the accused is convicted or (without proceeding to conviction) an order is made discharging him absolutely the court may, if it is satisfied on the application of the prosecutor that any moveable property which was at the time of the offence or of the accused's apprehension in his ownership or possession or under his control—

(a) has been used for the purpose of committing, or facilitating the commission of, any offence; or

(b) was intended to be used for that purpose,

order that the property shall be forfeited to and vest in the Crown or such other person as the court may direct.

(2) Any application under subsection (1) above shall be made following upon the conviction of the accused or, as the case may be, the finding that he committed the offence with which he was charged.

(3) Where, by itself, the use of property constitutes an offence in whole or in part, that property shall be regarded for the purpose of subsection (1)(a) above as used for the purpose of committing the offence, unless the enactment which created the offence expressly excludes the application of this section.

(4) Subject to subsection (5) below, where the accused is convicted of an offence under any enactment, the court shall not be precluded from making

an order under subsection (1) above in respect of any property by reason only that the property would not be liable to forfeiture under that enactment.

(5) Subsection (4) above shall not apply—

(a) if the enactment concerned expressly excludes the application of this section; or

(b) to any property which has been used or has been intended to be used as mentioned in subsection (1)(a) or (b) above in relation to the offence of which the accused has been convicted, if the enactment concerned specifies the category of property which is to be liable to forfeiture thereunder, and the category so specified does not include the category of property which has been used or has been intended to be used as aforesaid.

(6) Where the court makes—

(a) an order under subsection (1) above that property shall be forfeited to the Crown; and

(b) a compensation order under section 58 of the Criminal Justice (Scotland) Act 1980,

against the same accused in the same proceedings, it may order that the proceeds of sale of the property forfeited by virtue of subsection (1) above shall be first directed towards satisfaction of the compensation order.

(7) For the purposes of any appeal or review an order under subsection (1) above is a sentence.

(8) In this section "the court" means the district court.

DEFINITIONS
"court, the": s.88(8).
"offence": s.462 of the Criminal Procedure (Scotland) Act 1975.
"sentence": s.462 of the Criminal Procedure (Scotland) Act 1975.

GENERAL NOTE
This section makes provision specifically for the power of forfeiture, following a conviction in the district court, of any moveable property which was at the time of the offence or the accused's apprehension owned, possessed or controlled by the accused and likely to be used, or actually used, in the commission of the offence. This power is in addition to the power of forfeiture in s.436 of the 1975 Act, although there are differences between the two powers.

Warrant to search for and seize property

89.—(1) Where—

(a) the sheriff is satisfied, on an application being made to him by the prosecutor—

    (i) that proceedings have been, or are likely to be, instituted against a person in Scotland for an offence; and

    (ii) that there is reasonable cause to believe that property specified in the application is to be found in a place or in premises specified in the application; and

(b) it appears to him that there are reasonable grounds for thinking that in the event of the person being convicted of the offence a suspended forfeiture order might be made in relation to the property,

he may grant a warrant authorising a person named therein to enter and search the place or premises and seize the property.

(2) Where a court has made a suspended forfeiture order in respect of any property, if it is satisfied on the application of the prosecutor—

(a) that there is reasonable cause to believe that the property is to be found in any place or premises; and

(b) that admission to the place or premises has been refused or that it is reasonably believed that such admission will be refused, it may grant a warrant authorising a person named therein to enter and search the place or premises and seize the property.

(3) An application for a warrant under subsection (2) above may be made at the same time as an application for a suspended forfeiture order.

DEFINITIONS
    "premises": s.40 of the Criminal Justice (Scotland) Act 1987.
    "proceedings": s.114(3).
    "property": s.71.
    "suspended forfeiture order": s.87(2).

GENERAL NOTE
    This section makes provision for the granting of warrants to search for and seize property both before and after the making of a suspended forfeiture order. This section implements Recommendations 74 and 93 of S.L.C. Report (147).

Forfeiture of property subject to suspended forfeiture order

90.—(1) Subject to the following provisions of this section, property in respect of which a suspended forfeiture order has been made shall be forfeited to and vest in the Crown, or such other person as the court may direct, as follows—

(a) heritable property situated in Scotland shall be forfeited at the end of the period of six months commencing with the date on which a certified copy of the suspended forfeiture order is recorded in the General Register of Sasines or, as the case may be, registered in the Land Register of Scotland;

(b) heritable property situated outside Scotland shall be forfeited at the end of the period of six months commencing with the date of the making of the suspended forfeiture order;

(c) moveable property shall be forfeited at the end of the period of 60 days commencing with the date of the making of the suspended forfeiture order.

(2) Notwithstanding subsection (1)(c) above, moveable property which is certified by the prosecutor as being—

(a) of a perishable or dangerous nature;

(b) of no commercial value; or

(c) property which cannot lawfully be sold, supplied or possessed,

shall be forfeited immediately after the making of the suspended forfeiture order.

(3) If an application for recall or variation of the suspended forfeiture order concerned has been made under section 91 of this Act, there shall be no forfeiture of property mentioned in paragraph (a), (b) or (c) of subsection (1) above unless and until whichever is the later of the following occurs—

(a) the application is finally disposed of in favour of the prosecutor, or

(b) the period mentioned in that paragraph has expired.

(4) Without prejudice to subsection (2) above, in the event of an appeal against conviction or sentence, there shall be no forfeiture of property until whichever is the later of the following occurs—

(a) the appeal, if it is proceeded with, is determined in favour of the prosecutor, or

(b) the period mentioned in paragraph (a) or, as the case may be, (b) or (c) of subsection (1) above has expired.

(5) Property which has been forfeited to the Crown under this section shall be dealt with by the Crown in such manner as seems to it to be appropriate.

(6) A certificate by the clerk of court that property was forfeited to and vested in the Crown, or another person, under this section on the date specified in the certificate shall be conclusive evidence of that fact; and, in the case of a certificate in respect of heritable property situated in Scotland, the prosecutor shall, forthwith, cause a certified copy of the certificate to be recorded

in the General Register of Sasines or, as the case may be, registered in the Land Register of Scotland.

<small>DEFINITIONS</small>
    "clerk of court": s.114(1).
    "property": s.71.
    "prosecutor": s.462 of the Criminal Procedure (Scotland) Act 1975.
    "suspended forfeiture order": s.87(2).

<small>GENERAL NOTE</small>
    This specifies the time when property subject to a suspended forfeiture order is forfeited. This section implements Recommendations 81, 83(1) to (6), 84 and 86 of S.L.C. Report (147).

Recall or variation of suspended forfeiture order

91.—(1) The court shall, on an application being made to it under this section by a person other than the accused, make an order (a "recalling order") recalling a suspended forfeiture order in relation to any property or an interest in property if—

    (a) it is satisfied by the applicant on the balance of probabilities that he is the owner of the property or otherwise has an interest in it; and

    (b) subsection (2) or subsection (3) below is applicable.

(2) This subsection applies if the court is not satisfied by the prosecutor that—

    (a) where the applicant was the owner of or otherwise had an interest in the property before the commission of the offence in connection with which the suspended forfeiture order was made, he—

        (i) knew or ought to have known that the property was intended to be used for the purpose of committing, or facilitating the commission of, the offence, and

        (ii) did not take all the steps which were reasonable for him to take to prevent such intended use; or

    (b) where he has become the owner of, or has otherwise acquired an interest in, the property after the commission of the offence, the applicant knew or ought to have known that the property had been intended to be, or had been, so used.

(3) This subsection applies if the court is satisfied as mentioned in subsection (2) above, but it appears to the court that, in all the circumstances of the case, forfeiture of the property would be excessive or inappropriate.

(4) Where a recalling order relates to heritable property situated in Scotland, the prosecutor shall, as soon as may be after—

    (a) the expiry of the period within which the prosecutor may appeal under section 93(1)(b) of this Act against the making of the order without such an appeal being lodged; or

    (b) where such an appeal is lodged within that period, the determination of the appeal in favour of the recalling order,

cause a certified copy of the recalling order to be recorded in the General Register of Sasines or, as the case may be, registered in the Land Register of Scotland.

(5) Where the prosecutor believes that the person named in the suspended forfeiture order in pursuance of section 87(4) of this Act is not the owner of, or does not otherwise have an interest in, the property concerned then—

    (a) if he does not know who the true owner is, or who otherwise truly has the interest, he may apply to the court under this section for an order varying the suspended forfeiture order by deleting that name from it;

    (b) if he does know or reasonably suspects the identity of the true owner or the person who otherwise truly has the interest ("the correct person"), he may apply to the court under this section for an order varying the suspended forfeiture order by substituting the name of the correct person for that of the person so named.

(6) Where no person is named in the suspended forfeiture order in pursuance of section 87(4) of this Act but the prosecutor later comes to believe that a person is, or may be, the owner of, or otherwise has or may have an interest in, the property concerned, he may apply to the court for an order varying the suspended forfeiture order by naming that person as a person having or being suspected of having such an interest.

(7) The court shall grant any application made in pursuance of subsection (5) or (6) above; and sections 87(10) and 90 of this Act shall apply in relation to an order varying a suspended forfeiture order in accordance with an application under subsection (5) or (6) above as they apply in relation to a suspended forfeiture order.

(8) An application under this section may be made at any time before the property concerned is forfeited to the Crown or another person under section 90 of this Act.

(9) The court shall not be entitled in considering any application under this section to review the sentence passed, or any probation order or order of discharge made, in respect of the offence concerned otherwise than as provided by this section.

(10) In this section "the court" means the court which made the suspended forfeiture order.

DEFINITIONS
"accused": s.114(1).
"court, the": s.91(10).
"interest": s.114(1).
"property": s.71.
"prosecutor": s.462 of the Criminal Procedure (Scotland) Act 1975.
"recalling order": s.91(1).
"suspended forfeiture order": s.87(2).

GENERAL NOTE
This section provides for the recall or variation of a suspended forfeiture order, and implements Recommendations 87, 88, 89, 90 and 91 of S.L.C. Report (147). Appeals against decisions on applications made under this section are dealt with under s.93, below.

Property wrongly forfeited: return or compensation

92.—(1) Where the court, on an application being made to it by a person other than the accused—

(a) is satisfied by the applicant on the balance of probabilities that in relation to any property forfeited to the Crown or another person under section 90 of this Act or by virtue of an order for forfeiture made under any other enactment he was the owner of, or a person otherwise having an interest in, the property immediately before such forfeiture; and

(b) subsection (3) or (4) below is applicable,

it shall make an order under subsection (2) below.

(2) An order under this subsection shall direct the Crown or, as the case may be, the other person, if the applicant—

(a) was the owner of the property, to return it to him if reasonably practicable to do so or, if not, to pay compensation to him of an amount determined under subsection (5) below; or

(b) otherwise had an interest in the property, to pay compensation to him of an amount corresponding to the value of such interest.

(3) This subsection applies if the court is not satisfied that—

(a) where the applicant was the owner of or otherwise had an interest in the property before the commission of the offence in connection with which the suspended forfeiture order or order for forfeiture was made, he knew or ought to have known that the property was intended to be used for the purpose of committing, or facilitating the commission of, the offence, and did not take all the steps which were reasonable for him to take to prevent such intended use; or

(b) where the applicant has become the owner of, or has otherwise acquired an interest in, the property after the commission of the offence, he knew or ought to have known that the property had been intended to be, or had been, so used.

(4) This subsection applies if the court is satisfied as mentioned in subsection (3) above, but it appears to the court that, in all the circumstances of the case, forfeiture of the property would be excessive or inappropriate.

(5) For the purposes of subsection (2) above, the amount determined under this subsection shall be an amount equal to the amount of any consideration received for the property or the value of any such consideration at the time of the disposal, or, if no consideration was received, an amount equal to the value of the property at the time of the disposal.

(6) An application under subsection (1) shall be made not later than three years after the date on which the property was forfeited as mentioned in subsection (1)(a) above.

(7) Where, after property has been forfeited by virtue of section 90 of this Act, the prosecutor comes to believe that the person named in the suspended forfeiture order in pursuance of section 87(4) of this Act is not the owner of, or a person otherwise having an interest in, the property concerned, then—

(a) whether he knows who the true owner was, or who the person truly with the interest was, or not, he shall forthwith notify the court in writing of that belief; and

(b) if he does know or reasonably suspects the identity of the person who was the true owner or who truly had the interest, he shall forthwith notify that person in writing that he may be entitled to apply to the court for a direction under this section.

(8) Where no person has been named in the suspended forfeiture order in pursuance of section 87(4) of this Act or in a variation order under section 91(5) of this Act but, after the property concerned has been forfeited under section 90 of this Act, the prosecutor comes to believe that a person was or might have been the owner of, or otherwise had or might have had an interest in, the property concerned, he shall forthwith notify—

(a) the court of his belief; and

(b) that person in writing that he may be entitled to apply to the court for a direction under this section.

(9) The court shall not be entitled in considering any application under this section to review the sentence passed, or any probation order or order of discharge made, in respect of the offence concerned otherwise than as provided by this section.

(10) In this section "the court" means the court which made the suspended forfeiture order or order for forfeiture.

DEFINITIONS

"accused": s.114(1).
"court, the": s.91(10).
"interest": s.114(1).
"property": s.71.

GENERAL NOTE

This section deals with the protection of a third party's rights where property he owned or in which he had an interest has been wrongly forfeited, whether under this Act or another statute. This section entitles him to apply for the return of the property or for compensation. This section implements Recommendations 99(3), 100, 101, 102 and 103 of S.L.C. Report (147). Appeals against decisions on applications made under s.92(2) are dealt with under s.93, below.

Appeal against court decision under section 91(1) or 92(2)

93.—(1) An appeal shall lie to the High Court of Justiciary at the instance of—

(a) the applicant against the refusal to make;

(b) the prosecutor against the making of,

an order under section 91(1) or 92(2) of this Act, and the High Court in determining such an appeal may make such order as could have been made by the court on an application under that section.

(2) The procedure in an appeal under this section shall be the same as the procedure in an appeal against sentence.

(3) Where a suspended forfeiture order relating to heritable property situated in Scotland is recalled on appeal to the High Court of Justiciary, the prosecutor shall, as soon as may be after the appeal has been disposed of, cause a certified copy of the interlocutor of the Court to be recorded in the General Register of Sasines or, as the case may be, registered in the Land Register of Scotland.

DEFINITIONS
  "prosecutor": s.462 of the Criminal Procedure (Scotland) Act 1975.
  "suspended forfeiture order": s.87(2).

GENERAL NOTE
  This section provides for appeals against decisions on applications under ss.91(1) or 92(2), and it implements Recommendation 104 of S.L.C. Report (147).

CHAPTER III

RESTRAINT ORDERS

Restraint orders

94.—(1) The court may, on the application of the prosecutor, make an order (in this Chapter referred to as a "restraint order") in the circumstances mentioned in—

(a) section 95(2) or (3) of this Act interdicting—

    (i) any person named in the order from dealing with his realisable property; or

    (ii) that person and any person named in the order as appearing to the court to have received from him a gift caught by Chapter I of this Part from dealing with their own, or the other's, realisable property,

(whenever that property was acquired and whether it is described in the order or not); and

(b) section 96(1) of this Act interdicting any person named in the order from dealing with any property which is, or is liable to be, the subject of a suspended forfeiture order.

(2) A restraint order made under subsection (1)(a) above may contain conditions and exceptions to which the interdict shall be subject and in particular—

(a) may provide for the release to the person named in the order of such reasonable living expenses as the court thinks fit; and

(b) shall provide for the release of property in so far as it is required to meet reasonable legal expenses payable or likely to be payable in relation to proceedings—

    (i) as regards the offence by virtue of which the restraint order has been made; or

    (ii) as regards a confiscation order made on conviction of the offence.

(3) A restraint order shall—

(a) be made on an ex parte application which shall be heard in chambers; and

   (b) without prejudice to the time when it becomes effective, be intimated
     to each person affected by it.
  (4) For the purposes of this Chapter, dealing with property includes (without prejudice to the generality of the expression)—
   (a) making a payment to any person in reduction of the amount of a debt;
   (b) removing the property from the jurisdiction of the court; and
   (c) transferring or disposing of the property.
  (5) Where the court has made a restraint order, a constable or a person commissioned by the Commissioners of Customs and Excise may, for the purpose of preventing any property subject to the order being removed from the jurisdiction of the court, seize that property.
  (6) Property seized under subsection (5) above shall be dealt with in accordance with the court's directions.
  (7) In this Chapter "the court" means where, as regards the criminal proceedings in question, a trial diet or a diet fixed for the purposes of section 102 of the 1975 Act is intended to be held, is being or has been held—
   (a) in the High Court of Justiciary, the Court of Session;
   (b) in the sheriff court, a sheriff of that court exercising his civil
     jurisdiction.
  (8) The court may, where it has granted a restraint order, interdict a person not subject to that order from dealing with property affected by it while it is in force.
  (9) Subsections (2)(a) and (3)(a) above shall apply in relation to subsection (8) above as they apply in relation to subsection (1) above; and subsections (1), (2), (4) and (5) of section 97 of this Act shall apply in relation to an interdict under subsection (8) above as they apply in relation to a restraint order.
  (10) Without prejudice to the time when it becomes effective, an interdict under subsection (8) above shall be intimated to each person affected by it.

DEFINITIONS
  "court, the": s.94(7).
  "dealing with property": s.94(4).
  "gift": s.73(1).
  "property": s.71.
  "prosecutor": s.462 of the Criminal Procedure (Scotland) Act 1975.
  "realisable property": s.114(1).
  "suspended forfeiture order": s.87(2).

GENERAL NOTE
  This section contains general provisions as to the making by the appropriate civil court of restraint orders relative to confiscation or forfeiture proceedings. This is an order interdicting (a) a person named in the order from dealing with his realisable property or (b) that person and any person named in the order from dealing with his or the other's realisable property, or (c) a person named in the order from dealing with property which is, or may be, subject to a suspended forfeiture order. This section implements Recommendations 46(1) to (4), 50(1) and (2), 53 and 94(1) and (2) of S.L.C. Report (147).

Restraint orders in relation to realisable property

  95.—(1) A restraint order under section 94(1)(a) of this Act may be made in the circumstances mentioned in either subsection (2) or (3) below.
  (2) For the purposes of this subsection, the circumstances are—
   (a) proceedings have been instituted against an accused in Scotland for an
     offence to which Chapter I of this Part applies;
   (b) the proceedings have not been concluded; and
   (c) either a confiscation order has been made or it appears to the court
     that, in the event of his conviction of the offence, there are reasonable
     grounds for thinking that a confiscation order may be made in those
     proceedings.

(3) For the purposes of this subsection, the circumstances are that the court is satisfied that—

    (a) it is proposed to institute proceedings within 28 days against a person suspected of such an offence and it appears to the court that, in the event of his conviction of the offence, there are reasonable grounds for thinking that a confiscation order may be made in those proceedings; or

    (b) the prosecutor has made, or proposes within 28 days to make, an application under section 77 or, as the case may be, section 79 of this Act in relation to that person in respect of the offence, and it appears to the court that there are reasonable grounds for thinking that the application may be granted.

(4) Where the court has made a restraint order in the circumstances mentioned in subsection (3)(a) or (b) above and no proceedings have been instituted or application made within 28 days as mentioned in that subsection, the prosecutor shall forthwith apply to the court for the recall of the order and the court shall grant the application.

(5) When proceedings for the offence or, as the case may be, proceedings on an application under section 77 or 79 of this Act are concluded, the prosecutor shall forthwith apply to the court for recall of the order and the court shall grant the application.

(6) For the purposes of this section, proceedings are concluded as regards an offence where—

    (a) the trial diet is deserted simpliciter;

    (b) the accused is acquitted or, under section 101 or 331A of the 1975 Act, discharged or liberated;

    (c) the High Court of Justiciary or, as the case may be, the sheriff sentences or otherwise deals with him without making a confiscation order and without postponing a decision as regards making such an order;

    (d) after such postponement as is mentioned in paragraph (c) above, the High Court of Justiciary or, as the case may be, the sheriff decides not to make a confiscation order;

    (e) his conviction is quashed; or

    (f) a confiscation order made in the proceedings is satisfied (whether by payment of the amount due under the order or by the accused serving imprisonment in default).

(7) For the purposes of this section, proceedings on an application under section 77 or 79 of this Act are concluded—

    (a) when the application is refused; or

    (b) where the application is granted, when a confiscation order made in the proceedings is satisfied (whether by payment of the amount due under the order or by the accused serving imprisonment in default).

DEFINITIONS

    "proceedings not concluded": s.95(6) and (7).
    "proceedings not instituted": s.114(3).
    "prosecutor": s.462 of the Criminal Procedure (Scotland) Act 1975.
    "restraint order": s.114(1).

GENERAL NOTE

    This section is concerned with the making of a restraint order in relation to property which may be realised to satisfy a confiscation order (see also the General Note to s.94, above). It implements Recommendations 47(1) and (3), 48(1) and (2), 49(1) and (2), 51(5), (6) and (7) of S.L.C. Report (147).

Restraint orders in relation to forfeitable property

96.—(1) A restraint order may be made in respect of a person under section 94(1)(b) where—
  (a) proceedings have been instituted against him in Scotland for an offence;
  (b) the proceedings have not been concluded; and
  (c) a suspended forfeiture order has been made in respect of the property concerned or it appears to the court that, in the event of his conviction of the offence, there are reasonable grounds for thinking that a suspended forfeiture order may be made in those proceedings.

(2) A restraint order may also be made where the court is satisfied that it is proposed to institute proceedings in respect of an offence within 28 days and it appears to the court that, in the event of his conviction of the offence, there are reasonable grounds for thinking that a suspended forfeiture order may be made in those proceedings.

(3) Where the court has made a restraint order by virtue of subsection (2) above, and no proceedings have been instituted within 28 days as mentioned in that subsection, the prosecutor shall forthwith apply to the court for the recall of the order and the court shall grant the application.

(4) When proceedings for the offence are concluded, the prosecutor shall forthwith apply to the court for recall of the order and the court shall grant the application.

(5) For the purposes of this section, proceedings are concluded as regards an offence where—
  (a) the trial is deserted simpliciter;
  (b) the accused is acquitted or, under section 101 or 331A of the 1975 Act, discharged or liberated;
  (c) the High Court of Justiciary or (as the case may be) the sheriff sentences or otherwise deals with him without making a suspended forfeiture order;
  (d) his conviction is quashed;
  (e) a suspended forfeiture order made in the proceedings is recalled, or varied so as to exclude from forfeiture any property to which the restraint order relates; or
  (f) the property, or part of the property, to which the restraint order relates is forfeited.

DEFINITIONS
  "proceedings not instituted": s.114(3).
  "restraint order": s.114(1).
  "suspended forfeiture order": s.87(2).

GENERAL NOTE
  This section is concerned with the making of a restraint order in relation to property which is, or is liable to be, subject to a suspended forfeiture order. This section implements Recommendations 94 and 95 of S.L.C. Report (147).

Variation and recall of restraint orders

97.—(1) Subject to subsections (2) and (3) below, the court may, at the instance of—
  (a) the prosecutor, at any time vary or recall a restraint order in relation to any person or to any property;
  (b) any person having an interest, at any time vary or recall a restraint order in relation to the person or to any property.

(2) On an application made under subsection (1)(b) above by a person named in a restraint order as having received a gift caught by Chapter I of this

Part, the court may recall the order in relation to that person if it is satisfied on the balance of probabilities—

    (a) that he received the gift not knowing, not suspecting and not having reasonable grounds to suspect that the gift was made in contemplation of, or after, the commission of the offence or if more than one, in contemplation of any of the offences or after the commission of the earlier or the earliest of the offences to which the proceedings for the time being relate; and

    (b) that he was not associated with the giver in the commission of the offence; and

    (c) that he would suffer hardship if the order were not recalled.

(3) Where an application has been made under subsection (1) above for the variation or recall of a restraint order, any property in relation to which the restraint order was made shall not be realised during the period beginning with the making of the application and ending with the determination of the application by the court.

(4) The court may, where it has recalled a restraint order as mentioned in subsection (1)(b) or (2) above, order that property of the person at whose instance it was recalled shall cease to be realisable or, as the case may be, liable to forfeiture.

(5) The prosecutor or any person having an interest may reclaim or appeal to the Court of Session against an interlocutor refusing, varying or recalling or refusing to vary or recall a restraint order, within such period as may be prescribed by Act of Sederunt.

(6) Where, in relation to a restraint order which is recalled, interdict has been granted under section 94(8) of this Act, the clerk of court shall, on the restraint order being recalled, forthwith so inform each person so interdicted.

DEFINITIONS
    "clerk of court": s.114(1).
    "gift": s.73(1).
    "prosecutor": s.462 of the Criminal Procedure (Scotland) Act 1975.
    "restraint order": s.114(1).

GENERAL NOTE
    This section makes further general provisions about restraint orders, in addition to those contained in s.94. It provides for applications for their variation and recall and for appeals against decisions on such applications. It implements Recommendations 51(2) to (4), 52(1), 54(3), 55(1) and 95(1) of S.L.C. Report (147).

Inhibition of property affected by restraint order or by interdict

98.—(1) On the application of the Lord Advocate, the Court of Session may in respect of heritable realisable property in Scotland affected by a restraint order (whether such property generally or particular such property) grant warrant for inhibition against any person interdicted by the order or, in relation to that property, under section 94(8) of this Act; and subject to the provisions of this Part of this Act, the warrant—

    (a) shall have effect as if granted on the dependence of an action for debt at the instance of the Lord Advocate against the person and may be executed, recalled, loosed or restricted accordingly; and

    (b) shall have the effect of letters of inhibition and shall forthwith be registered by the Lord Advocate in the Register of Inhibitions and Adjudications.

(2) Section 155 of the Titles to Land Consolidation (Scotland) Act 1868 (effective date of inhibition) shall apply in relation to an inhibition for which warrant has been granted under subsection (1) above as that section applies to an inhibition by separate letters or contained in a summons.

(3) In the application of section 158 of that Act of 1868 (recall of inhibition) to such an inhibition as is mentioned in subsection (2) above, references in that section to a particular Lord Ordinary shall be construed as references to any Lord Ordinary.

(4) The fact that an inhibition has been executed under subsection (1) above in respect of property shall not prejudice the exercise of an administrator's powers under or for the purposes of this Part of this Act in respect of that property.

(5) No inhibition executed under subsection (1) above shall have effect once, or in so far as, the restraint order affecting the property in respect of which the warrant for the inhibition has been granted has ceased to have effect in respect of that property; and the Lord Advocate shall—

    (a) apply for the recall, or as the case may be restriction, of the inhibition; and

    (b) ensure that the recall, or restriction, of an inhibition on such application is reflected in the Register of Inhibitions and Adjudications.

DEFINITIONS
    "property": s.71(3).
    "restraint order": s.114(1).

GENERAL NOTE
    This gives the court ancillary powers in relation to heritable property affected by a restraint order; (1) to order inhibition for heritable property in Scotland, (2) to grant warrant for the assessment of moveable property. It implements Recommendations 54, 55(1) and 95(2) of S.L.C. Report (147).

Arrestment of property affected by restraint order

99.—(1) On the application of the prosecutor, the court may, in respect of moveable property affected by a restraint order (whether such property generally or particular such property), grant warrant for arrestment if the property would be arrestable if the person entitled to it were a debtor.

(2) A warrant under subsection (1) above shall have effect as if granted on the dependence of an action for debt at the instance of the prosecutor against the person and may be executed, recalled, loosed or restricted accordingly.

(3) The fact that an arrestment has been executed under subsection (2) above in respect of property shall not prejudice the exercise of an administrator's powers under or for the purposes of this Part of this Act in respect of that property.

(4) No arrestment executed under subsection (2) above shall have effect once, or in so far as, the restraint order affecting the property in respect of which the warrant for such arrestment has been granted has ceased to have effect in respect of that property; and the prosecutor shall apply to the court for an order recalling, or as the case may be, restricting the arrestment accordingly.

DEFINITIONS
    "property": s.71(3).
    "prosecutor": s.462 of the Criminal Procedure (Scotland) Act 1975.
    "restraint order": s.114(1).

GENERAL NOTE
    This section gives the court ancillary powers in relation to moveable property affected by a restraint order. It implements Recommendations 54, 55(1) and 95(2) of S.L.C. Report (147).

Administrators

100. Schedule 3 to this Act shall have effect as regards the appointment of administrators under this Part of this Act.

DEFINITIONS
"administrator": Sched. 3, para. 1.

GENERAL NOTE

This section introduces Sched. 3 which makes provision as to administrators appointed in relation to realisable or forfeitable property. This section and Sched. 3 implement Recommendations 56(2) and 96 of S.L.C. Report (147).

CHAPTER IV

RECIPROCAL ARRANGEMENTS FOR ENFORCEMENT ORDERS

Recognition and enforcement of orders made in England and Wales

101.—(1) An order to which this section applies shall, subject to this section and section 102 of this Act, have effect in the law of Scotland but shall be enforced in Scotland only in accordance with this section and that section.

(2) A receiver's functions under or for the purposes of section 77, 80 or 81 of the 1988 Act shall, subject to this section and section 102 of this Act, have effect in the law of Scotland.

(3) If an order to which this section applies is registered under this section—

(a) the Court of Session shall have, in relation to its enforcement, the same power;

(b) proceedings for or with respect to its enforcement may be taken, and

(c) proceedings for or with respect to any contravention of such an order (whether before or after such registration) may be taken,

as if the order had originally been made in that Court.

(4) Nothing in this section enables any provision of an order which empowers a receiver to do anything in Scotland under section 80(3)(a) of the 1988 Act to have effect in the law of Scotland.

(5) The orders to which this section applies are orders of the High Court—

(a) made under section 77, 78 or 81 of the 1988 Act;

(b) relating to the exercise by that Court of its powers under those sections; or

(c) relating to receivers in the performance of their functions under the said section 77, 78 or 81,

but not including an order in proceedings for enforcement of any such order.

(6) References in this section to an order under section 77 of the 1988 Act include references to a discharge under section 76(4) of that Act of such an order.

(7) In this section and in section 102 of this Act, "order" means any order, direction or judgment (by whatever name called).

(8) Nothing in any order of the High Court under section 80(6) of the 1988 Act prejudices any enactment or rule of law in respect of the recording of deeds relating to heritable property in Scotland or the registration of interests in such property.

(9) In this Chapter, "High Court" means the High Court of England and Wales.

DEFINITIONS
"High Court": s.101(9).
"order": s.101(7).

GENERAL NOTE

This deals with the enforcement in Scotland of orders made in England and Wales under Part VI of the 1988 Act, which is concerned with the confiscation of the proceeds of an offence to which that Part applies. This section replaces ss.90 to 93 of the 1988 Act, and implements Recommendation 108 of S.L.C. Report (147).

Provisions supplementary to section 101

102.—(1) The Court of Session shall, on application made to it in accordance with rules of court for registration of an order to which section 101 of this Act applies, direct that the order shall, in accordance with such rules, be registered in that Court.

(2) Subsections (1) and (3) of section 101 of this Act and subsection (1) above are subject to any provision made by rules of court—

(a) as to the manner in which and conditions subject to which that section applies are to be enforced in Scotland;

(b) for the sisting of proceedings for enforcement of such an order;

(c) for the modification or cancellation of the registration of such an order if the order is modified or revoked or ceases to have effect.

(3) This section and section 101 of this Act are without prejudice to any enactment or rule of law as to the effect of notice or the want of it in relation to orders of the High Court.

(4) The Court of Session shall have the like power to make an order under section 1 of the Administration of Justice (Scotland) Act 1972 (extended power to order inspection of documents etc.) in relation to proceedings brought or likely to be brought under Part VI of the 1988 Act in the High Court as if those proceedings were brought or were likely to be brought in the Court of Session.

(5) The Court of Session may, additionally, for the purpose of—

(a) assisting the achievement in Scotland of the purposes of orders to which section 101 of this Act applies;

(b) assisting receivers performing functions thereunder or for the purposes of section 77, 80 or 81 of the 1988 Act,

make such orders and do otherwise as seems to it appropriate.

(6) A document purporting to be a copy of an order under or for the purposes of Part VI of the 1988 Act by the High Court and to be certified as such by a proper officer of that Court shall, in Scotland, be sufficient evidence of the order.

DEFINITIONS
"High Court": s.101(9).

GENERAL NOTE
This section restates, with modifications, ss.91 and 93 of the 1988 Act. This section, together with s.101 and s.103, implements Recommendation 108 of S.L.C. Report (147).

Inhibition of Scottish property affected by order registered under section 101

103.—(1) On the application of the Lord Advocate, the Court of Session may in respect of heritable realisable property in Scotland affected by a restraint order registered under section 101 of this Act (whether such property generally or particular such property) grant warrant for inhibition against any person with an interest in that property; and the warrant—

(a) shall have effect as if granted on the dependence of an action for debt at the instance of the Lord Advocate against the person and may be executed, recalled, loosed or restricted accordingly;

(b) shall have the effect of letters of inhibition and shall forthwith be registered by the Lord Advocate in the Register of Inhibitions and Adjudications.

(2) Section 155 of the Titles to Land Consolidation (Scotland) Act 1868 (effective date of inhibition) shall apply in relation to an inhibition for which warrant has been granted under subsection (1) above as that section applies to an inhibition by separate letters or contained in a summons.

(3) In the application of section 158 of that Act of 1868 (recall of inhibition) to such an inhibition as is mentioned in subsection (2) above, references in that section to a particular Lord Ordinary shall be construed as references to any Lord Ordinary.

(4) The fact that an inhibition has been executed under subsection (1) above in respect of property shall not prejudice the exercise of a receiver's

powers under or for the purposes of section 77, 80 or 81 of the 1988 Act in respect of that property.

(5) No inhibition executed under subsection (1) above shall have effect once, or in so far as, the restraint order affecting the property in respect of which the warrant for the inhibition has been granted has ceased to have effect in respect of that property; and the Lord Advocate shall—

(a) apply for the recall, or as the case may be restriction, of the inhibition; and

(b) ensure that the recall, or restriction, of an inhibition on such application is reflected in the Register of Inhibitions and Adjudications.

(6) Any power of the Court of Session to recall, loose or restrict inhibitions shall, in relation to an order containing an inhibition under subsection (1) above and without prejudice to any other consideration lawfully applying to the exercise of the power, be exercised with a view to achieving the purposes specified in section 80 of the 1988 Act.

DEFINITIONS
 "property": s.71.
 "restraint order": s.114(1).

GENERAL NOTE
 This section restates, with modifications, s.92 of the 1988 Act. It makes supplementary provision for the enforcement of restraint orders registered in Scotland under s.101 by giving the Court of Session additional powers to order inhibitions and arrestment. This section is consequential to s.101 and Recommendation 108 of S.L.C. Report (147).

Arrestment of Scottish property affected by order registered under section 101

104.—(1) On the application of the Lord Advocate, the Court of Session may, in respect of moveable property affected by a restraint order registered under section 101 of this Act (whether such property generally or particular such property), grant warrant for arrestment if the property would be arrestable if the person entitled to it were a debtor.

(2) A warrant under subsection (1) above shall have effect as if granted on the dependence of an action for debt at the instance of the Lord Advocate against the person and may be executed, recalled, loosed or restricted accordingly.

(3) The fact that an arrestment has been executed under subsection (2) above in respect of property shall not prejudice the exercise of a receiver's powers under or for the purposes of section 77, 80 or 81 of the 1988 Act in respect of that property.

(4) No arrestment executed under subsection (2) above shall have effect once, or in so far as, the restraint order affecting the property in respect of which the warrant for such arrestment has been granted has ceased to have effect in respect of that property; and the Lord Advocate shall apply to the Court of Session for an order recalling, or as the case may be, restricting the arrestment accordingly.

(5) Any power of the Court of Session to recall, loose or restrict arrestments shall, in relation to an arrestment proceeding upon a warrant under subsection (1) above and without prejudice to any other consideration lawfully applying to the exercise of the power, be exercised with a view to achieving the purposes specified in section 80 of the 1988 Act.

DEFINITIONS
 "restraint order": s.94.
 "the 1988 Act": s.114(1).

GENERAL NOTE
Section 101 of this Act makes provision for the reciprocal recognition and enforcement of orders made in England and Wales. Section 104 makes provision for the taking or attaching of the Scottish property of another in the hands of a third party.

Enforcement of Northern Ireland orders

105.—(1) Her Majesty may by Order in Council provide that, for the purposes of Chapter III of Part II of and Schedules 3 and 4 to this Act, this Part of this Act shall have effect as if—

(a) references to confiscation orders included a reference to orders made by courts in Northern Ireland which appear to Her Majesty to correspond to confiscation orders;

(b) references to offences to which Chapter I of this Part applies included a reference to any offence under the law of Northern Ireland (not being an offence to which that Chapter applies) which appears to Her Majesty to correspond to such an offence; and

(c) such other modifications were made as may be specified in the Order in Council, being modifications which appear to Her Majesty to be requisite or desirable having regard to procedural differences which may for the time being exist between Scotland and Northern Ireland; and without prejudice to the generality of this paragraph modifications may include provision as to the circumstances in which proceedings in Northern Ireland are to be treated for the purposes of those sections as instituted or as concluded.

(2) An Order in Council under this section may provide for the provisions mentioned in subsection (1) above to have effect in relation to anything done or to be done in Northern Ireland subject to such further modifications as may be specified in the Order.

(3) An Order in Council under this section may contain such incidental, consequential and transitional provisions as Her Majesty considers expedient.

(4) An Order in Council under this section shall be subject to annulment in pursuance of a resolution of either House of Parliament.

DEFINITIONS
"confiscation orders": s.114(1).

GENERAL NOTE
This section restates, with modifications, s.94 of the 1988 Act which provides for the introduction by delegated legislation of arrangements for enforcing, in Scotland, that legislation in Northern Ireland which is equivalent to Part VI of the 1988 Act.
This section implements Recommendation 109 of S.L.C. Report (147).

Enforcement of orders made outside United Kingdom

106.—(1) Her Majesty may by Order in Council—

(a) direct in relation to a country or territory outside the United Kingdom designated by the Order that, subject to such modifications as may be specified, Chapter I of this Part and Chapter III of this Part so far as it relates to realisable property shall apply in relation to external confiscation orders and to proceedings which have been or are to be instituted in the designated country and may result in an external confiscation order being made there;

(b) make—
    (i) such provision as to evidence or proof of any matter for the purposes of this section and section 107 of this Act; and
    (ii) such incidental, consequential and transitional provision,
as appears to Her Majesty to be expedient.

(2) In this Chapter—
    "designated country" means a country or territory designated by an Order in Council made under this section; and

"external confiscation order" means an order made by a court in a designated country for the purpose of recovering payments or other rewards or property or other economic advantage received in connection with an offence corresponding with or similar to an offence to which Chapter I of this Part applies or the value of such payments, property, reward or economic advantage.

(3) An Order in Council under this section may make different provision for different cases or classes of case.

(4) The power to make an Order in Council under this section includes power to modify Chapter I of this Part or Chapter III of this Part so far as it relates to realisable property in such a way as to confer power on a person to exercise a discretion.

(5) An Order in Council under this section shall be subject to annulment in pursuance of a resolution of either House of Parliament.

DEFINITIONS
"designated country": s.106(2).
"external confiscation order": s.106(2).
"property": s.71.
"realisable property": s.114(1).

GENERAL NOTE
This section is concerned with the enforcement in Scotland of actual and potential confiscation and ancillary orders made outside the United Kingdom relative to offences similar to, or corresponding with, offences to which Chapter I of Pt. II applies (confiscation orders) and provides for an Order in Council to apply in respect of such orders under Chapters I and III (restraint orders) of this Part. This section and s.107 implement Recommendation 113 of S.L.C. Report (147).

Registration of external confiscation orders

107.—(1) On an application made by or on behalf of the Government of a designated country, the Court of Session may register an external confiscation order made there if—
(a) it is satisfied that at the time of registration the order is in force and not subject to appeal;
(b) it is satisfied, where the person against whom the order is made did not appear in the proceedings, that he received notice of the proceedings in sufficient time to enable him to defend them; and
(c) it is of the opinion that enforcing the order in Scotland would not be contrary to the interests of justice.

(2) In subsection (1) above "appeal" includes—
(a) any proceedings by way of discharging or setting aside a judgment; and
(b) an application for a new trial or a stay of execution.

(3) The Court of Session shall cancel the registration of an external confiscation order if it appears to the court that the order has been satisfied by payment of the amount due under it or by the person against whom it was made serving imprisonment in default of payment or by any other means.

DEFINITIONS
"appeal": s.107(2).
"external confiscation order": s.106(2).

GENERAL NOTE
This section provides for the registration in Scotland of "external confiscation orders" as defined in s.106(2). It allows the Court of Session to register an external confiscation order if the

specified conditions are met. It further implements Recommendation 113 of S.L.C. Report (147).

Enforcement of Scottish orders in England and Wales

108.—(1) Her Majesty may by Order in Council make such provision as Her Majesty considers expedient for the purpose—

(a) of enabling property in England and Wales which is realisable property to be used or realised for the payment of any amount payable under a confiscation order;

(b) of securing that, where no confiscation order has been made, property in England and Wales which is realisable property is available, in the event that such an order is so made, to be used or realised for the payment of any amount payable under it; and

(c) of enabling the enforcement in England and Wales of restraint orders, suspended forfeiture orders and forfeiture orders under any enactment other than the 1989 Act.

(2) Without prejudice to the generality of the power conferred by subsection (1) above, an Order in Council under this section may—

(a) provide that, subject to any specific conditions, such description of orders made under or for the purposes of Chapter I, II or III of this Part so far as it relates to realisable property shall have effect in the law of England and Wales;

(b) provide that, subject to any specified conditions, the functions of a person appointed under Schedule 3 to this Act shall have effect in the law of England and Wales;

(c) make provision—

(i) for the registration in the High Court of such descriptions of orders made under or for the purposes of Chapter I, II or III of this Part so far as it relates to realisable property as may be specified; and

(ii) for the High Court to have, in relation to the enforcement of orders made under or for the purposes of Chapter I, II or III of this Part so far as it so relates which are so registered, such powers as may be specified; and

(d) make provision as to the proof in England and Wales of orders made under or for the purposes of Chapter I, II or III of this Part so far as it so relates.

(3) In subsection (2) above "specified" means specified in an Order in Council under this section.

(4) An Order in Council under this section may amend or apply, with or without modifications, any enactment.

(5) An Order in Council under this section may contain such incidental, consequential and transitional provisions as Her Majesty considers expedient.

(6) An Order in Council under this section shall be subject to annulment in pursuance of a resolution of either House of Parliament.

DEFINITIONS
"confiscation order": s.114(1).
"realisable property": s.114(1).
"specified": s.108(3).
"suspended forfeiture order": s.87(2).

GENERAL NOTE
This section provides for the recognition and enforcement in England and Wales of orders and functions under Chapters I, II and III of Pt. II of the Act and of forfeiture orders made in Scotland under any enactment other than the Prevention of Terrorism (Temporary Provisions) Act 1989. The section is in substantially the same terms as the enforcement arrangements for drug trafficking confiscation orders (see s.37 of the Drug Trafficking Act 1994).

This section implements Recommendations 106 and 116 of S.L.C. Report (147).

Order in Council as regards taking of action in designated country

109.—(1) Her Majesty may by Order in Council make such provision in connection with the taking of action in a designated country in consequence of the making of a restraint order, confiscation order or suspended forfeiture order under this Act or a forfeiture order under any other enactment as appears to Her Majesty to be expedient.

(2) Without prejudice to the generality of subsection (1) above, the provision contained in an Order in Council made under this section may include a direction that in such circumstances as may be specified proceeds arising out of action taken in a designated country with a view to satisfying a confiscation order which are retained there shall nevertheless be treated as reducing the amount payable under the confiscation order to such extent as may be specified.

(3) An Order in Council under this section may amend or apply, with or without modifications, any enactment.

(4) Subsections (1)(b), (3) and (5) of section 106 of this Act shall apply in respect of Orders in Council under this section as they apply in respect of Orders in Council under that section.

DEFINITIONS
    "confiscation order": s.114(1).
    "designated country": s.106(2).
    "forfeiture order": s.109(1).
    "restraint order": s.114(1).
    "suspended forfeiture order": s.87(2).

GENERAL NOTE
    This section enables provision to be made by Order in Council for the taking of action outside the United Kingdom in consequence of the making of a restraint order, confiscation order, suspended forfeiture order or forfeiture order. It implements Recommendations 115 and 119 of S.L.C. Report (147).

CHAPTER V

MISCELLANEOUS AND GENERAL

Sequestration etc. of person holding realisable or forfeitable property

110.—(1) Schedule 4 to this Act shall have effect in relation to the sequestration, bankruptcy, winding up or receivership of persons or, as the case may be, companies holding realisable or forfeitable property.

(2) In this section and in that Schedule "forfeitable property" means property which is or is liable to be the subject of a suspended forfeiture order.

DEFINITIONS
    "forfeitable property": s.110(2).
    "realisable property": s.72(1).
    "suspended forfeiture order": s.87(2).

GENERAL NOTE
    This section introduces Sched. 4 which makes provision with regard to the sequestration, bankruptcy, winding up or receivership of persons or companies holding realisable or forfeitable property. It also defines "forfeitable property" for the purposes of this section and Sched. 4. This section implements Recommendations 57(2) and 98 of S.L.C. Report (147).

Disposal of family home under Chapter I or II

111.—(1) This section applies where—
(a) a confiscation order has been made in relation to any person and the

prosecutor has not satisfied the court that the person's interest in his family home has been acquired by means of the benefit derived from the commission of the offence concerned; or

(b) a person's family home has been forfeited to the Crown under section 90 of this Act.

(2) Where this section applies, then, before the Crown disposes of any right or interest in the person's family home it shall—

(a) obtain the relevant consent; or

(b) where it is unable to do so, apply to the court for authority to carry out the disposal.

(3) On an application being made to it under subsection (2)(b) above, the court, after having regard to all the circumstances of the case including—

(a) the needs and financial resources of the spouse or former spouse of the person concerned;

(b) the needs and financial resources of any child of the family;

(c) the length of the period during which the family home has been used as a residence by any of the persons referred to in paragraph (a) or (b) above,

may refuse to grant the application or may postpone the granting of the application for such period (not exceeding 12 months) as it may consider reasonable in the circumstances or may grant the application subject to such conditions as it may prescribe.

(4) Subsection (3) above shall apply—

(a) to an action for division and sale of the family home of the person concerned; or

(b) to an action for the purpose of obtaining vacant possession of that home,

brought by the Crown as it applies to an application under subsection (2)(b) above and, for the purposes of this subsection, any reference in the said subsection (3) to the granting of the application shall be construed as a reference to the granting of decree in the action.

(5) In this section—

"family home", in relation to any person (in this subsection referred to as "the relevant person") means any property in which the relevant person has or had (whether alone or in common with any other person) a right or interest, being property which is occupied as a residence by the relevant person and his or her spouse or by the relevant person's spouse or former spouse (in any case with or without a child of the family) or by the relevant person with a child of the family;

"child of the family" includes any child or grandchild of either the relevant person or his or her spouse or former spouse, and any person who has been treated by either the relevant person or his or her spouse or former spouse as if he or she were a child of the relevant person, spouse or former spouse, whatever the age of such a child, grandchild or person may be; and

"relevant consent" means in relation to the disposal of any right or interest in a family home—

(a) in a case where the family home is occupied by the spouse or former spouse of the relevant person, the consent of the spouse or, as the case may be, of the former spouse, whether or not the family home is also occupied by the relevant person;

(b) where paragraph (a) above does not apply, in a case where the family home is occupied by the relevant person with a child of the family, the consent of the relevant person.

DEFINITIONS
    "child of the family": s.111(5).
    "confiscation order": s.114(1).
    "family home": s.111(5).
    "prosecutor": s.462 of the Criminal Procedure (Scotland) Act 1975.
    "relevant consent": s.111(5).

GENERAL NOTE
    This section provides that in certain circumstances where a confiscation order has been made or where a person's family home has been forfeited under the Act, the Crown is not entitled to dispose of any right or interest in the family home without either the consent of the family members involved or the authority of the court. This section implements Recommendations 14(1) and 105 of S.L.C. Report (147).

Forfeiture of property where accused has died

112.—(1) This section applies where at any time after criminal proceedings have been instituted against an accused for an offence to which Chapter I of this Part applies and before the accused has been sentenced or otherwise dealt with in the proceedings he dies.

(2) The Court of Session, if it is satisfied beyond reasonable doubt on an application being made to it by the Lord Advocate—

(a) that the accused committed the offence; and

(b) that there is property—

(i) which the accused had obtained, directly or indirectly, in connection with the commission of the offence; or

(ii) which is a gift caught by Chapter I of this Part,

may, subject to subsection (5) below, make an order which shall have the effect of forfeiting that property.

(3) The Court of Session may, without prejudice to any other power available to it, at any time before the determination of the case, allow an amendment of the application under subsection (2) above if the amendment is of a type which could competently have been made in an indictment or complaint under section 123 or 335 of the 1975 Act in the criminal proceedings.

(4) An application under subsection (2) above shall be made as soon as is reasonably practicable after the relevant information becomes available to the Lord Advocate, but, in any event, within 6 years commencing with the date of death of the accused.

(5) An application under subsection (2) above in relation to property such as is mentioned in paragraph (b)(ii) of that subsection shall be served on the recipient of the gift and, if he satisfies the Court on the balance of probabilities—

(a) that he received the gift not knowing, not suspecting and not having reasonable grounds to suspect that the gift was made in contemplation of, or after, the commission of the offence or, if more than one, in contemplation of any of the offences or after the commission of the earlier or the earliest of the offences to which the proceedings for the time being relate; and

(b) that he was not associated with the giver in the commission of the offence; and

(c) that he would suffer hardship if the application were granted,

the Court may refuse to make an order as mentioned in that subsection.

(6) Where property has been forfeited under this section, then, if the Court of Session, on an application being made to it is satisfied by the applicant on the balance of probabilities that he was the owner of, or otherwise had an interest in, the property immediately before such forfeiture, it shall make an order under subsection (7) below.

(7) An order under this subsection shall direct the Crown, if the applicant—

(a) was the owner of the property, to return it to him if it is reasonably practicable to do so or, if not, to pay compensation to him of an amount determined under subsection (8) below; or

(b) otherwise had an interest in the property, to pay compensation to him of an amount corresponding to the value of such interest.

(8) For the purposes of subsection (7) above, the amount determined under this subsection shall be an amount equal to the amount of any consideration received for the property or the value of any such consideration at the time of the disposal, or, if no consideration was received, an amount equal to the value of the property at the time of the disposal.

(9) Property which has been forfeited under this section shall be dealt with by the Crown in such manner as seems to it to be appropriate.

(10) Where a restraint order is not in force in respect of a person when he dies in the circumstances mentioned in subsection (1) above, the Court of Session may, on the application of the Lord Advocate, in so far as the property concerned is—

(a) heritable property in Scotland, make an order inhibiting any person; and

(b) moveable property, grant warrant for arrestment if the property would be arrestable if the person entitled to it were a debtor.

(11) Paragraphs (a) and (b) of subsection (1) and subsections (2) to (5) of section 98 of this Act shall, subject to any necessary modifications, apply for the purposes of subsection (10)(a) above as they apply for the purposes of that section.

(12) Subsections (2) to (4) of section 99 of this Act shall, subject to any necessary modifications, apply for the purposes of subsection (10)(b) above as they apply for the purposes of that section.

(13) Proceedings under this section are civil proceedings for the purposes of section 10 of the Law Reform (Miscellaneous Provisions) (Scotland) Act 1968.

DEFINITIONS
"gift": s.73.
"proceedings instituted": s.114(3).
"property": s.71(1).
"restraint order": s.94.

GENERAL NOTE
This section enables the Crown to apply to the Court of Session for the forfeiture of property in a case where proceedings have been instituted against an accused for an offence to which Chapter I of Pt. II of the Act applies, but he has died before being sentenced. In contrast to confiscation proceedings, this procedure is competent only in a civil court, the Court of Session. In contrast to other forfeiture proceedings, a forfeiture order made in these proceedings relates to property which has been obtained in connection with the commission of an offence or which is a gift caught by Chapter I of Pt. II of the Act. Protection is afforded to an innocent recipient of a caught gift and to a third party with an interest in property which has been forfeited in error. This section implements Recommendations 120 to 124 of S.L.C. Report (147).

Transitional provision, amendment of 1987 Act, etc.

113.—(1) Where a person is charged with an offence in relation to which provision is made by Chapter I of this Part, being an offence committed before the coming into force of the said Chapter I, that Chapter shall not affect the powers of the court in the event of his being convicted of the offence.

(2) Where a person is charged with an offence committed before the coming into force of Chapter II of this Part, in the event of his being convicted of the offence, the court shall be entitled to exercise the powers conferred by section 223 or section 436 of the 1975 Act, but not the powers conferred by that Chapter.

(3) The 1987 Act shall be amended as specified in Schedule 5 to this Act.

(4) Section 28 of the Bankruptcy Act 1914 (effect of order of discharge) shall have effect as if amounts payable under confiscation orders were debts excepted under subsection (1)(a) of that section.

(5) In section 1(2)(a) of the Rehabilitation of Offenders Act 1974 (failure to pay fines etc. not to prevent person becoming rehabilitated) the reference to a fine or other sum adjudged to be paid by or on a conviction does not include a reference to an amount payable under a confiscation order.

(6) Section 281(4) of the Insolvency Act 1986 (discharge of bankrupt not to release him from liabilities in respect of fines, etc.) shall have effect as if the reference to a fine included a reference to a confiscation order.

(7) Section 55(2) of the Bankruptcy (Scotland) Act 1985 (discharge of debtor not to release him from liabilities in respect of fines, etc.) shall have effect as if the reference to a fine included a reference to a confiscation order.

DEFINITIONS
"confiscation order": s.114(1).

GENERAL NOTE
This section provides for the transitional provisions and minor and consequential amendments. It implements Recommendations 126(1) and (2) of S.L.C. Report (147).

Interpretation of Part II

114.—(1) In this Part of this Act, unless the context otherwise requires—
"the 1987 Act" means the Criminal Justice (Scotland) Act 1987;
"the 1988 Act" means the Criminal Justice Act 1988;
"the 1989 Act" means the Prevention of Terrorism (Temporary Provisions) Act 1989;
"accused" includes a person against whom criminal proceedings have been instituted in relation to the commission of an offence and a person convicted of an offence;
"clerk of court" includes the sheriff clerk;
"confiscation order" means an order made under section 70(1), 77(4), 78(3) or 79 of this Act;
"interest", in relation to property, includes right;
"property" has the meaning assigned by section 71 of this Act;
"realisable property" has the meaning assigned by section 72 of this Act;
"restraint order" means an order made under section 94 of this Act;
"suspended forfeiture order" means an order made under section 87(2) of this Act.

(2) This Part of this Act shall (except where the context otherwise requires) be construed as one with the 1975 Act.

(3) For the purposes of this Part of this Act proceedings for an offence are instituted against a person—
(a) on his arrest without warrant;
(b) when he is charged with the offence without being arrested;
(c) when a warrant to arrest him is granted;
(d) when a warrant to cite him is granted;
(e) in summary proceedings, on the first calling of the case; or
(f) when a petition is intimated to him or an indictment or a complaint is served on him,
and, where the application of this subsection would result in there being more than one time for the institution of proceedings, they shall be taken to be instituted at the earliest of those times.

(4) Any reference in this Part of this Act to a conviction of an offence includes a reference to a finding that the offence has been committed.

PART III

SUPPLEMENTARY

Interpretation

115. In this Act, "the 1975 Act" means the Criminal Procedure (Scotland) Act 1975.

Expenses

116. There shall be paid out of money provided by Parliament—
(a) any amount payable—
  (i) as compensation under section 83 or 92 of this Act; or
  (ii) under paragraph 6 of Schedule 3 to this Act in respect of remuneration or expenses of administrators;
(b) any administrative expenses incurred by the Secretary of State or the Lord Advocate under this Act; and
(c) any increase attributable to this Act in the sums payable out of money so provided under any other Act.

Minor and consequential amendments and repeals

117.—(1) The enactments mentioned in Schedule 6 to this Act shall have effect subject to the amendments there specified, being minor amendments and amendments consequential on the foregoing provisions of this Act.
(2) The enactments mentioned in Schedule 7 to this Act (which include enactments which are spent) are hereby repealed to the extent specified in the third column of that Schedule.

Short title, commencement and extent

118.—(1) This Act may be cited as the Criminal Justice (Scotland) Act 1995.
(2) This Act shall come into force on such day as the Secretary of State may by order made by statutory instrument appoint, and different days may be so appointed for different areas or different purposes.
(3) An order under subsection (2) above may make such transitional provisions and savings as appear to the Secretary of State to be necessary or expedient in connection with any provision brought into force by the order.
(4) Subject to subsections (5) to (7) below, this Act extends only to Scotland.
(5) Section 110 of and Schedule 4 to this Act extend to England and Wales as well as to Scotland.
(6) Section 108 of this Act extends only to England and Wales.
(7) The amendment or repeal of any enactment by Schedule 6 or 7 to this Act has the same extent as the enactment amended or repealed.

GENERAL NOTE
  This section provides principally for the extent of this Act namely that it extends only to Scotland except that s.110 and Sched. 4 apply to England and Wales as well as Scotland. Section 108 applies only to England and Wales.

SCHEDULES

SCHEDULE 1

CERTIFICATES AS TO PROOF OF CERTAIN MATTERS

1. Schedule 1 to the Criminal Justice (Scotland) Act 1980 (which makes a provision as regards the sufficiency of evidence by certificate in certain routine matters) shall be amended as follows.

2. Before the entry relating to the Wireless Telegraphy Act 1949 there shall be inserted—

"THE PARKS REGULATION ACTS 1872 to 1974	An officer authorised to do so by the Secretary of State.	That, on a date specified in the certificate— (a) copies of regulations made under those Acts, prohibiting such activity as may be so specified, were displayed at a location so specified; (b) in so far as those regulations prohibited persons from carrying out a specified activity in the park without written permission, such permission had not been given to a person so specified.".

3. After the entry relating to the Wireless Telegraphy Act 1949 there shall be inserted—

"THE BUILDING SCOTLAND) ACT 1959 (c. 24) Section 6(1) (prohibition of construction, demolition or change of use of building without warrant).	An officer of a local authority authorised to do so by the authority.	In relation to a building specified in the certificate, that on a date so specified, there had not been obtained a warrant under section 6 of that Act for construction, demolition or, as the case may be, change of use.
Section 9(5) (offence of occupying or using a building before certificate of completion issued).	An officer of a local authority authorised to do so by the authority.	That, on a date specified in the certificate— (a) a certificate of completion under section 9 of that Act had not been issued in respect of a building so specified; and (b) written permission for occupation or use of the building so specified, had not been granted under subsection (6) of that section by the local authority.".

4. In the entry relating to the Firearms Act 1968, for the words in column 2 there shall be substituted "As respects the matters specified in paragraph (a) of column 3, a constable or a person employed by a police authority, if the constable or person is authorised to do so by the chief constable of the police force maintained for the authority's area; and as respects the matters specified in paragraph (b) of column 3, an officer authorised to do so by the Secretary of State.'.

5. After the entry relating to the Social Security Act 1975 there shall be inserted—

"THE CRIMINAL PRO-CEDURE (SCOTLAND) ACT 1975 (c. 21) Section 338(2) (offence of failure of accused to appear at diet after due notice).	The clerk of court.	That, on a date specified in the certificate, he gave a person so specified, in a manner so specified, notice of the time and place appointed for a diet so specified.".

6. In the entry relating to the Bail etc. (Scotland) Act 1980, for the words in column 3 there shall be substituted—

"In relation to a person specified in the certificate, that—

(a) an order granting bail under that Act was made on a date so specified by a court so specified;

(b) the order or a condition of it so specified was in force on a date so specified;

(c) notice of the time and place apppointed for a diet so specified was given to him in a manner so specified;

(d) as respects a diet so specified, he failed to appear.".

7. After the entry relating to the Forgery and Counterfeiting Act 1981 there shall be inserted—

"THE WILDLIFE AND COUNTRYSIDE ACT 1981 (c. 69) Sections 1, 5, 6(1) to (3), 7, 8, 9(1), (2), (4) and (5), 11(1) and (2), 13(1) and (2) and 14 (certain offences relating to protection of wild animals or wild plants).	An officer of the appropriate authority (within the meaning of section 16(9) of that Act) authorised to do so by the authority.	In relation to a person specified in the certificate that, on a date so specified, he held, or as the case may be did not hold, a licence under section 16 of that Act and, where he held such a licence— (a) the purpose for which the licence was granted; and (b) the terms and conditions of the licence.".

8. After the entry relating to the Video Recordings Act 1984 there shall be inserted the following entries—

"THE ROAD TRAFFIC ACT 1988 (c. 52) Section 165(3) (offence of failure to give name and address and to produce vehicle documents when required by constable).	A constable.	In relation to a person specified in the certificate, that he failed, by such date as may be so specified, to produce such documents as may be so specified at a police station so specified.

THE CONTROL OF POL-LUTION (AMEND-MENT) ACT 1989 (c. 14) Section 1 (offence of transporting controlled waste without registering).	An officer of a regulation authority within the meaning of that Act authorised to do so by the authority.	In relation to a person specified in the certificate, that on a date so specified he was not a registered carrier of controlled waste within the meaning of that Act.
THE ENVIRONMENTAL PROTECTION ACT 1990 (c. 43) Section 33(1)(a) and (b) (prohibition on harmful depositing, treatment or disposal of waste).	An officer of a waste regulation authority within the meaning of that Act authorised to do so by the authority.	In relation to a person specified in the certificate that, on a date so specified, he held, or as the case may be he did not hold, a waste management licence.
Section 34(1)(c) (duty of care as respects transfer of waste).	An officer of a waste regulation authority within the meaning of that Act authorised to do so by the authority.	In relation to a person specified in the certificate, that on a date so specified he was not an authorised person within the meaning of section 34(3)(b) or (d) of that Act.".

9. After the entry relating to the Social Security Administration Act 1992 there shall be inserted—

"THE CRIMINAL JUSTICE AND PUBLIC ORDER ACT 1994 (c. 33) Paragraph 5 of Schedule 6 (offence of making false statements to obtain certification as prisoner custody officer).	An officer authorised to do so by the Secretary of State.	That— (a) on a date specified in the certificate, an application for a certificate under section 114 of that Act was received from a person so specified; (b) the application contained a statement so specified; (c) a person so specified made, on a date so specified, a statement in writing in terms so specified.".

Section 50   SCHEDULE 2

SUPERVISION AND TREATMENT ORDERS: SCHEDULE TO BE INSERTED IN THE 1975 ACT

"SCHEDULE 5A

SUPERVISION AND TREATMENT ORDERS

PART I

PRELIMINARY

1.—(1) In this Schedule "supervision and treatment order" means an order requiring the person in respect of whom it is made ("the supervised person")—
  (a) to be under the supervision of a social worker who is an officer of the local authority for the area where the supervised person resides or is to reside (in this Schedule referred to as

"the supervising officer") for such period, not being more than three years, as is specified in the order;

(b) to comply during that period with instructions given to him by the supervising officer regarding his supervision; and

(c) to submit during that period to treatment by or under the direction of a medical practitioner with a view to the improvement of his mental condition.

(2) The Secretary of State may by order amend sub-paragraph (1) above by substituting, for the period for the time being specified in that sub-paragraph, such period as may be specified in the order.

(3) An order under sub-paragraph (2) above may make any amendment to paragraph 8(2) below which the Secretary of State considers necessary in consequence of the order.

(4) The power of the Secretary of State to make orders under sub-paragraph (2) above shall be exercisable by statutory instrument subject to annulment in pursuance of a resolution of either House of Parliament.

PART II

MAKING AND EFFECT OF ORDERS

Circumstances in which orders may be made

2.—(1) The court shall not make a supervision and treatment order unless it is satisfied—

(a) that, having regard to all the circumstances of the case, the making of such an order is the most suitable means of dealing with the person; and

(b) on the written or oral evidence of two or more medical practitioners approved for the purposes of section 20 or 39 of the Mental Health (Scotland) Act 1984, that the mental condition of the person—

    (i) is such as requires and may be susceptible to treatment; but

    (ii) is not such as to warrant the making of an order under paragraph (a) of subsection (2) of section 174ZC or, as the case may be, 375ZC of this Act (whether with or without an order under paragraph (b) of that subsection) or an order under paragraph (c) of that subsection.

(2) The court shall not make a supervision and treatment order unless it is also satisfied—

(a) that the supervising officer intended to be specified in the order is willing to undertake the supervision; and

(b) that arrangements have been made for the treatment intended to be specified in the order.

(3) Subsection (2) to (4) of section 176, and subsections (2) to (4) of section 377, of this Act shall have effect with respect to proof of a person's mental condition for the purposes of sub-paragraph (1) above in solemn and summary proceedings respectively as they have effect with respect to proof of an offender's mental condition for the purposes of, respectively, sections 175(1)(a) and 376(1)(a) of this Act.

Making of orders and general requirements

3.—(1) A supervision and treatment order shall specify the local authority area in which the supervised person resides or will reside.

(2) Before making such an order, the court shall explain to the supervised person in ordinary language—

(a) the effect of the order (including any requirements proposed to be included in the order in accordance with paragraph 5 below); and

(b) that the sheriff court for the area in which the supervised person resides or will reside (in this Schedule referred to as "the relevant sheriff court") has power under paragraphs 6 to 8 below to review the order on the application either of the supervised person or of the supervising officer.

(3) After making such an order, the court shall forthwith give a copy of the order to—

(a) the supervised person;

(b) the supervising officer; and

(c) the person in charge of any institution in which the supervised person is required by the order to reside.

(4) After making such an order, the court shall also send to the relevant sheriff court—

(a) a copy of the order, and

(b) such documents and information relating to the case as it considers likely to be of assistance to that court in the exercise of its functions in relation to the order.

(5) Where such an order is made, the supervised person shall comply with such instructions as he may from time to time be given by the supervising officer regarding his supervision and shall keep in touch with that officer and notify him of any change of address.

Obligatory requirements as to medical treatment

4.—(1) A supervision and treatment order shall include a requirement that the supervised person shall submit, during the period specified in the order, to treatment by or under the direction of a medical practitioner with a view to the improvement of his mental condition.

(2) The treatment required by the order shall be such one of the following kinds of treatment as may be specified in the order, that is to say—

(a) treatment as a non-resident patient at such institution or place as may be specified in the order; and

(b) treatment by or under the direction of such medical practitioner as may be so specified; but the nature of the treatment shall not be specified in the order except as mentioned in paragraph (a) or (b) above.

(3) Where the medical practitioner by whom or under whose direction the supervised person is being treated for his mental condition in pursuance of a supervision and treatment order is of the opinion that part of the treatment can be better or more conveniently given at an institution or place which—

(a) is not specified in the order; and

(b) is one at which the treatment of the supervised person will be given by or under the direction of a medical practitioner,

he may, with the consent of the supervised person, make arrangements for him to be treated accordingly.

(4) Where any such arrangements as are mentioned in sub-paragraph (3) above are made for the treatment of a supervised person—

(a) the medical practitioner by whom the arrangements are made shall give notice in writing to the supervising officer, specifying the institution or place at which the treatment is to be carried out; and

(b) the treatment provided for by the arrangements shall be deemed to be treatment to which he is required to submit in pursuance of the supervision and treatment order.

Optional requirements as to residence

5.—(1) Subject to sub-paragraphs (2) to (4) below, a supervision and treatment order may include requirements as to the residence of the supervised person.

(2) Such an order may not require the supervised person to reside as a resident patient in a hospital.

(3) Before making such an order containing any such requirement, the court shall consider the home surroundings of the supervised person.

(4) Where such an order requires the supervised person to reside in any institution, the period for which he is so required to reside shall be specified in the order.

PART III

REVOCATION AND AMENDMENT OF ORDERS

Revocation of order in interests of health or welfare

6. Where a supervision and treatment order is in force in respect of any person and, on the application of the supervised person or the supervising officer, it appears to the relevant sheriff court that, having regard to circumstances which have arisen since the order was made, it would be in the interests of the health or welfare of the supervised person that the order should be revoked, the court may revoke the order.

Amendment of order by reason of change of residence

7.—(1) This paragraph applies where, at any time while a supervision and treatment order is in force in respect of any person, the relevant sheriff court is satisfied that—

(a) the supervised person proposes to change, or has changed, his residence from the area specified in the order to the area of another local authority;

(b) a social worker who is an officer of the other local authority ("the new supervising officer") is willing to undertake the supervision; and

(c) the requirements of the order as respects treatment will continue to be complied with.

(2) Subject to sub-paragraph (3) below the court may, and on the application of the supervising officer shall, amend the supervision and treatment order by substituting the other area for the area specified in the order and the new supervising officer for the supervising officer specified in the order.

(3) Where a supervision and treatment order contains requirements which, in the opinion of the court, can be complied with only if the supervised person continues to reside in the area

specified in the order, the court shall not amend the order under this paragraph unless it also, in accordance with paragraph 8 below, either—

(a) cancels those requirements; or

(b) substitutes for those requirements other requirements which can be complied with if the supervised person ceases to reside in that area.

Amendment of requirements of order

8.—(1) Without prejudice to the provisions of paragraph 7 above, but subject to sub-paragraph (2) below, the relevant sheriff court may, on the application of the supervised person or the supervising officer, by order amend a supervision and treatment order—

(a) by cancelling any of the requirements of the order; or

(b) by inserting in the order (either in addition to or in substitution for any such requirement) any requirement which the court could include if it were the court by which the order was made and were then making it.

(2) The power of the court under sub-paragraph (1) above shall not include power to amend an order by extending the period specified in it beyond the end of three years from the date of the original order.

Amendment of requirements in pursuance of medical report

9.—(1) Where the medical practitioner by whom or under whose direction the supervised person is being treated for his mental condition in pursuance of any requirement of a supervision and treatment order—

(a) is of the opinion mentioned in sub-paragraph (2) below; or

(b) is for any reason unwilling to continue to treat or direct the treatment of the supervised person,

he shall make a report in writing to that effect to the supervising officer and that officer shall apply under paragraph 8 above to the relevant sheriff court for the variation or cancellation of the requirement.

(2) The opinion referred to in sub-paragraph (1) above is—

(a) that the treatment of the supervised person should be continued beyond the period specified in the supervision and treatment order;

(b) that the supervised person needs different treatment, being treatment of a kind to which he could be required to submit in pursuance of such an order;

(c) that the supervised person is not susceptible to treatment; or

(d) that the supervised person does not require further treatment.

Supplemental

10.—(1) On the making under paragraph 6 above of an order revoking a supervision and treatment order, the sheriff clerk shall forthwith give a copy of the revoking order to the supervising officer.

(2) On receipt of a copy of the revoking order the supervising officer shall give a copy to the supervised person and to the person in charge of any institution in which the supervised person was required by the order to reside.

11.—(1) On the making under paragraph 7 or 8 above of an order amending a supervision and treatment order, the sheriff clerk shall forthwith—

(a) if the order amends the supervision and treatment order otherwise than by substituting a new area or a new place for the one specified in that order, give a copy of the amending order to the supervising officer;

(b) if the order amends the supervision and treatment order in the manner excepted by paragraph (a) above, send to the new relevant sheriff court—

(i) a copy of the amending order; and

(ii) such documents and information relating to the case as he considers likely to be of assistance to that court in exercising its functions in relation to the order;

and in a case falling within paragraph (b) above, the sheriff clerk shall give a copy of the amending order to the supervising officer.

(2) On receipt of a copy of an amending order the supervising officer shall give a copy to the supervised person and to the person in charge of any institution in which the supervised person is or was required by the order to reside.

12. On the making, revocation or amendment of a supervision and treatment order the supervising officer shall give a copy of the order or, as the case may be, of the order revoking or amending it, to the Mental Welfare Commission for Scotland.".

Section 100   SCHEDULE 3

ADMINISTRATORS

Appointment of administrators

1.—(1) On the application of the prosecutor the court may as regards property—
(a) affected by a restraint order or a suspended forfeiture order, appoint a person to manage, or otherwise deal with, the property; or
(b) where a suspended forfeiture order or a confiscation order has been made, appoint a person (or empower an appointee under paragraph (a) above) to realise the property,
in accordance with the court's directions and may (whether on making the appointment or from time to time) require any person having possession of the property to give possession of it to the appointee (any such appointee being in this Act referred to as an "administrator").
(2) A requirement under sub-paragraph (1) above—
(a) subject to paragraph (b) below, may relate to the property generally or to particular such property and may be subject to such exceptions and conditions as may be specified by the court;
(b) shall relate to property mentioned in paragraph (b) of section 72(1) of this Act only if expressly stated so to do and then only in so far as the person in whom such property is vested is named in the requirement as being subject to it.
(3) On a requirement being imposed under sub-paragraph (1) above—
(a) the clerk of court shall forthwith notify—
(i) the person in respect of whom the restraint order, or as the case may be the suspended forfeiture order or confiscation order, has been made; and
(ii) any other person named in the requirement as being subject to it; and
(b) any dealing of or with such person in relation to the property shall be of no effect in a question with the administrator unless whoever dealt with the person had, at the time when the dealing occurred, no knowledge of the appointment.
(4) The court, at the instance of any person having an interest, may at any time—
(a) vary or withdraw a requirement imposed under sub-paragraph (1) above; or
(b) without prejudice to paragraph 4 below or to the powers and duties of an administrator pending a decision under this sub-sub-paragraph, on cause shown, remove the administrator from office.
(5) On the death or resignation of the administrator, or on his removal from office under sub-paragraph (4)(b) above or paragraph 5 below, the court shall appoint a new administrator.
(6) Such of the property (if any) as was, by virtue of paragraph 2(3) below, vested in the administrator who has died, resigned or been removed shall forthwith vest in the new administrator; and any requirement imposed under sub-paragraph (1) above shall, on the person subject to the requirement being notified in writing of the appointment by the appointee, apply in relation to the appointee instead of in relation to his predecessor.
(7) The administration of property by an administrator shall be deemed continuous notwithstanding any temporary vacancy in that office.
(8) Any appointment under this paragraph shall be on such conditions as to caution as the accountant of court may think fit to impose; but the premium of any bond of caution or other security thereby required of the administrator shall be treated as part of his outlays in his actings as such.
(9) Without prejudice to paragraph 5 below, section 6 of the Judicial Factors (Scotland) Act 1889 (supervision of judicial factors) shall not apply in relation to an appointment under this section.

Functions of administrators

2.—(1) Subject to paragraph 5 below, an administrator—
(a) shall be entitled to take possession of, and if appointed (or empowered) under paragraph 1(1)(b) above where a confiscation order has been made shall as soon as practicable take possession of, the property as regards which he has been appointed and of any document which both—
(i) is in the possession or control of the person (in this paragraph referred to as "A") in whom the property is vested (or would be vested but for an order made under sub-paragraph (3) below); and

      (ii) relates to the property or to A's assets, business or financial affairs;

(b) shall be entitled to have access to, and to copy, any document relating to the property or to A's assets, business or financial affairs and not in such possession or control as is mentioned in paragraph (a) above;

(c) may bring, defend or continue any legal proceedings relating to the property;

(d) may borrow money in so far as it is necessary to do so to safeguard the property and may for the purposes of such borrowing create a security over any part of the property;

(e) may, if the administrator considers that to do so would be beneficial for the management or realisation of the property—

      (i) carry on any business of A;

      (ii) exercise any right of A as holder of securities in a company;

      (iii) grant a lease of the property or take on lease any other property; or

      (iv) enter into any contract, or execute any deed, as regards the property or as regards A's business;

(f) may, where any right, option or other power forms part of A's estate, make payments or incur liabilities with a view to—

      (i) obtaining property which is the subject of; or

      (ii) maintaining,

the right, option or power;

(g) may effect or maintain insurance policies as regards the property on A's business;

(h) where he has been appointed under paragraph 1(1)(b) above may, where A has an uncompleted title to any heritable estate, complete title thereto;

Provided that completion of title in A's name shall not validate by accretion any unperfected right in favour of any person other than the administrator;

(j) may sell, purchase or exchange property or discharge any security for an obligation due to A:

Provided that it shall be incompetent for the administrator or an associate of his (within the meaning of section 74 of the Bankruptcy (Scotland) Act 1985) to purchase any of A's property in pursuance of this paragraph;

(k) may claim, vote and draw dividends in the sequestration of the estate (or bankruptcy or liquidation) of a debtor of A and may accede to a voluntary trust deed for creditors of such a debtor;

(l) may discharge any of his functions through agents or employees;

Provided that the administrator shall be personally liable to meet the fees and expenses of any such agent or employee out of such remuneration as is payable to the administrator by virtue of paragraph 6(1) and (3) below;

(m) may take such professional advice as he may consider requisite for the proper discharge of his functions;

(n) may at any time apply to the court for directions as regards the discharge of his functions;

(o) may exercise any power specifically conferred on him by the court, whether such conferral was at the time of his appointment or on his subsequent application to the court in that regard; and

(p) may do anything incidental to the above powers and duties.

(2) Subject to the proviso to sub-paragraph (1)(j) above—

(a) a person dealing with an administrator in good faith and for value shall not require to determine whether the administrator is acting within the powers mentioned in that subsection; and

(b) the validity of any title shall not be challengeable by reason only of the administrator having acted outwith those powers.

(3) The exercise of a power mentioned in any of sub-paragraphs (1)(c) to (k) above shall be in A's name except where and in so far as an order made by the court under this sub-paragraph (either on its own motion or on the application of the administrator) has vested the property in the administrator (or in his predecessor in that office).

Money received by administrator

3.—(1) Subject to sub-paragraph (2) below, all money received by an administrator in the exercise of his functions shall be deposited by him, in the name (unless vested in the administrator by virtue of paragraph 2(3) above) of the holder of the property realised, in an appropriate bank or institution.

(2) The administrator may at any time retain in his hands a sum not exceeding £200 or such other sum as may be prescribed by the Secretary of State by regulations made by statutory instrument.

(3) In sub-paragraph (1) above, "appropriate bank or institution" means a bank or institution mentioned in section 2(1) of the Banking Act 1979 or for the time being specified in Schedule 1 to that Act.

Application of proceeds of realisation and other sums

4.—(1) This paragraph applies only to an administrator appointed to realise property where a confiscation order has been made.

(2) Subject to sub-paragraph (3) below, sums in the hands of an administrator which are—

(a) proceeds of a realisation of property under paragraph 1 above, and

(b) other property held by the person in respect of whom the confiscation order was made,

shall first be applied in payment of any expenses to the payment of which a person is entitled under paragraph 5(2) of Schedule 4 to this Act and then shall after such payments (if any) as the court may direct have been made out of those proceeds and sums, be applied on the person's behalf towards the satisfaction of the confiscation order.

(3) If, after the amount payable under the confiscation order has been fully paid, any such proceeds and sums remain in the hands of the administrator, he shall distribute them—

(a) among such of those who held property which has been realised under this Act, and

(b) in such proportions,

as the court may, after giving such persons an opportunity to be heard as regards the matter, direct.

(4) The receipt of any sum by a sheriff clerk on account of an amount payable under a confiscation order shall reduce the amount so payable, but the sheriff clerk shall apply the money—

(a) first, in payment of any expenses to the payment of which a person is entitled under paragraph 5(2) of Schedule 4 to this Act but which were not paid to him under sub-paragraph (2) above;

(b) next, in payment of the administrator's remuneration and expenses;

(c) next, in reimbursement of any sums paid by the Lord Advocate under paragraph 8(2) below;

(d) next, in accordance with any direction given by the court under section 74(4) or 79(7) of this Act,

and the balance shall be payable and recoverable (or as the case may be disposed of) under section 203 or 412 of the 1975 Act (destination of fines) as applied by section 80 of this Act.

Supervision of administrators

5.—(1) The accountant of court shall supervise the performance by administrators of the functions conferred on them by Part II of this Act; and in particular an administrator proposing to exercise functions conferred by any of paragraphs 2(1)(c) to (p) above shall first obtain the consent of the accountant of court to such exercise.

(2) If it appears to the accountant of court that an administrator has, without reasonable cause, failed to perform a duty imposed on him by any provision of section 82 of this Act or of this Schedule, he shall report the matter to the court which, after giving the administrator an opportunity to be heard as regards the matter, may remove the administrator from office, censure him or make such other order as the circumstances of the case may appear to the court to require.

Accounts and remuneration of administrator

6.—(1) The administrator shall keep such accounts in relation to his intromissions with the property as regards which he is appointed as the court may require and shall lodge these accounts with the accountant of court at such times as may be fixed by the court in that regard; and the accountant of court shall audit the accounts and issue a determination as to the amount of outlays and, on the basis mentioned in sub-paragraph (3) below, remuneration payable to the administrator in respect of those intromissions.

(2) Not later than two weeks after the issuing of a determination under sub-paragraph (1) above, the administrator or the Lord Advocate may appeal against it to the court.

(3) The basis for determining the amount of remuneration payable to the administrator shall be the value of the work reasonably undertaken by him, regard being had to the extent of the responsibilities involved.

(4) The accountant of court may authorise the administrator to pay without taxation an account in respect of legal services incurred by the administrator.

Effect of appointment of administrator on diligence

7. Without prejudice to sections 98 and 99 of this Act—

(a) no arrestment or poinding of property executed on or after an appointment as regards the property under paragraph 1 above shall be effectual to create a preference for the arrester or poinder and any such property so arrested or poinded, or the proceeds of sale thereof, shall be handed over to the administrator;

(b) no poinding of the ground in respect of property on or after such appointment shall be effectual in a question with the administrator except for the interest on the debt of a secured creditor, being interest for the current half-yearly term and arrears of interest for one year immediately before the commencement of that term;

(c) it shall be incompetent on or after such appointment for any other person to raise or insist in an adjudication against the property or to be confirmed as executor-creditor on that property; and

(d) no inhibition on property which takes effect on or after such appointment shall be effectual to create a preference for the inhibitor in a question with the administrator.

Further provision as to administrators

8.—(1) Where an administrator takes any action—

(a) in relation to property as regards which he has not been appointed, being action which he would be entitled to take if he had been so appointed,

(b) believing, and having reasonable grounds for believing, that he is entitled to take that action in relation to that property,

he shall not be liable to any person in respect of any loss or damage resulting from his action except in so far as the loss or damage is caused by his negligence.

(2) Any amount due in respect of the remuneration and expenses of an administrator appointed under this Schedule shall, unless in a case where a confiscation order has been made there are sums available to be applied in payment of it under paragraph 4(4)(b) above, be paid by the Lord Advocate.

(3) Any disposal of property under paragraph 1 above to a person taking in good faith shall vest the ownership of the property in that person.

Discharge of administrator

9. After an administrator has lodged his final accounts under paragraph 6(1) above, he may apply to the accountant of court to be discharged from office; and such discharge, if granted, shall have the effect of freeing him from all liability (other than liability arising from fraud) in respect of any act or omission of his in exercising the functions conferred on him by this Act.

Compensation

10.—(1) Where the court, on an application made to it by a person other than the accused or the recipient of a gift caught by Chapter I of Part II of this Act, is satisfied on the balance of probabilities that in relation to any property realised under paragraph 1 above he was the owner of, or a person otherwise having an interest in, the property immediately before such realisation, it shall make an order directing the Crown to pay to that person compensation of an amount equal to the consideration received for the property or, as the case may be interest or the value of any such consideration at the time of such realisation, or, if no consideration was received, an amount equal to the value of the property or interest at the time of the realisation.

(2) An application under this paragraph shall be made not later than three years after the conclusion of the proceedings in respect of which the confiscation order was made.

(3) Subsection (6) of section 95 of this Act shall apply for the purpose of determining for the purposes of this paragraph whether proceedings are concluded as it applies for the purposes of that section.

Rules of court as regards accountant of court's supervision etc of administrators

11. Without prejudice to section 5 of the Court of Session Act 1988 (power to regulate procedure etc. by Act of Sederunt), provision may be made by rules of court as regards (or as regards any matter incidental to) the accountant of court's powers and duties under Part II of this Act in relation to the functions of administrators.

Power to facilitate realisation

12.—(1) Without prejudice to any enactment or rule of law in respect of the recording of deeds relating to heritable property or the registration of interests therein, the court, to facilitate realisation under paragraph 1 above, may—

(a) order any person (in this paragraph referred to as "A") holding an interest in property, not being such person (in this paragraph referred to as "B") as is mentioned in paragraph (a) or (b) of section 72(1) or section 87 of this Act, to make such payment to an adminis-

trator appointed to realise estate comprising an interest of B in that property as the court may direct and may, subject to such payment being made—
      (i) authorise the administrator to transfer B's interest to A or to discharge it in favour of A; or
      (ii) itself by order transfer or discharge B's interest; or
(b) by order—
      (i) transfer A's interest to B; or
      (ii) discharge it in favour of B,
on the administrator making such payment to A out of that estate in respect of A's interest as the court may direct.

(2) The court may make such incidental provision in relation to any exercise of powers conferred on it by sub-paragraph (1) above as it considers appropriate; but it shall not exercise those powers without giving such persons as hold an interest in the property reasonable opportunity to make representations to it in that regard.

Section 110   SCHEDULE 4

SEQUESTRATION ETC. OF PERSONS HOLDING REALISABLE OR FORFEITABLE PROPERTY

Sequestration of person holding realisable or forfeitable property

1.—(1) Where the estate of a person who holds realisable or forfeitable property is sequestrated—
(a) property, other than heritable property situated in Scotland, for the time being subject to a restraint order made before the date of sequestration (within the meaning of section 12(4) of the 1985 Act) and heritable property situated in Scotland for the time being subject to a restraint order recorded in the General Register of Sasines or, as the case may be, registered in the Land Register of Scotland before such date of sequestration; and
(b) any proceeds of property realised by virtue of paragraph 1 of Schedule 3 to this Act for the time being in the hands of an administrator appointed under that paragraph,
is excluded from the debtor's estate for the purposes of that Act.

(2) Where an award of sequestration has been made, the powers conferred on the court by sections 94 to 99 and 101 to 104 of this Act or on an administrator appointed under paragraph 1 of the said Schedule 3 shall not be exercised in relation to—
(a) property comprised in the whole estate of the debtor (within the meaning of section 31(8) of the 1985 Act); or
(b) any income of the debtor which has been ordered, under subsection (2) of section 32 of that Act, to be paid to the permanent trustee or any estate which, under subsection (10) of section 31 of that Act or subsection (6) of the said section 32 of that Act, vests in the permanent trustee,
and it shall not be competent to submit a claim in relation to the confiscation order to the permanent trustee in accordance with section 48 of that Act.

(3) Nothing in the 1985 Act shall be taken as restricting, or enabling the restriction of, the exercise of the powers so conferred.

(4) Where, during the period before sequestration is awarded, an interim trustee stands appointed under section 2(5) of the 1985 Act and any property in the debtor's estate is subject to a restraint order, the powers conferred on the interim trustee by virtue of that Act do not apply to property for the time being subject to the restraint order.

(5) Where the estate of a person is sequestrated and he has directly or indirectly made a gift caught by Chapter I of Part II of this Act—
(a) no decree shall, at any time when proceedings as regards an offence to which Chapter I of Part II of this Act applies have been instituted against him and have not been concluded or when property of the person to whom the gift was made is subject to a restraint order, be granted under section 34 or 36 of the 1985 Act (gratuitous alienations and unfair preferences) in respect of the making of the gift; and
(b) any decree granted under either of the said sections 34 and 36 after the conclusion of the proceedings shall take into account any realisation under this Act of property held by the person to whom the gift was made.

(6) In any case in which, notwithstanding the coming into force of the 1985 Act, the Bankruptcy (Scotland) Act 1913 applies to a sequestration, sub-paragraph (2) above shall have effect as if for paragraphs (a) and (b) thereof there were substituted the following paragraphs—

"(a) property comprised in the whole property of the debtor which vests in the trustee under section 97 of the Bankruptcy (Scotland) Act 1913,

(b) any income of the bankrupt which has been ordered, under subsection (2) of section 98 of that Act, to be paid to the trustee or any estate which, under subsection (1) of that section, vests in the trustee,",

and sub-paragraph (3) above shall have effect as if, for the reference in it to the 1985 Act, there were substituted a reference to the said Act of 1913.

Bankruptcy in England and Wales of person holding realisable or forfeitable property

2.—(1) Where a person who holds realisable or forfeitable property is adjudged bankrupt—

(a) property, other than heritable property situated in Scotland, for the time being subject to a restraint order made before the order adjudging him bankrupt and heritable property situated in Scotland for the time being subject to a restraint order recorded in the General Register of Sasines or, as the case may be, registered in the Land Register of Scotland before the order adjudging him bankrupt was made; and

(b) any proceeds of property realised by virtue of paragraph 1 of Schedule 3 to this Act for the time being in the hands of an administrator appointed under that paragraph,

is excluded from the bankrupt's estate for the purposes of Part IX of the Insolvency Act 1986.

(2) Where a person has been adjudged bankrupt, the powers conferred on the court by sections 94 to 99 and 101 to 104 of this Act or on an administrator appointed under paragraph 1 of the said Schedule 3 shall not be exercised in relation to—

(a) property for the time being comprised in the bankrupt's estate for the purposes of the said Part IX;

(b) property in respect of which his trustee in bankruptcy may (without leave of the court) serve a notice under section 307, 308 or 308A of the Insolvency Act 1986 (after-acquired property and tools, clothes, etc. exceeding value of reasonable replacement and certain tenancies); and

(c) property which is to be applied for the benefit of creditors of the bankrupt by virtue of a condition imposed under section 280(2)(c) of the Insolvency Act 1986.

(3) Nothing in the Insolvency Act 1986 shall be taken as restricting, or enabling the restriction of, the exercise of the powers so conferred.

(4) Where, in the case of a debtor, an interim receiver stands appointed under section 286 of the Insolvency Act 1986 and any property of the debtor is subject to a restraint order the powers conferred on the receiver by virtue of that Act do not apply to property for the time being subject to the restraint order.

(5) Where a person is adjudged bankrupt and has directly or indirectly made a gift caught by Chapter I of Part II of this Act—

(a) no order shall, at any time when proceedings for an offence to which Part VI of the Criminal Justice Act 1988 applies have been instituted against him and have not been concluded or when property of the person to whom the gift was made is subject to a restraint order, be made under section 339 or 423 of the Insolvency Act 1986 (avoidance of certain transactions) in respect of the making of the gift, and

(b) any order made under either of those sections after the conclusion of the proceedings shall take into account any realisation under this Act of property held by the person to whom the gift was made.

(6) In any case in which a petition in bankruptcy was presented, or a receiving order or adjudication in bankruptcy was made, before the date on which the Insolvency Act 1986 came into force, sub-paragraphs (2) to (5) above have effect with the following modifications—

(a) for references to the bankrupt's estate for the purposes of Part IX of that Act there are substituted references to the property of the bankrupt for the purposes of the Bankruptcy Act 1914;

(b) for references to the said Act of 1986 and to sections 280(2)(c), 286, 339, and 423 of that Act there are respectively substituted references to the said Act of 1914 and to sections 26(2), 8, 27 and 42 of that Act;

(c) the references in subsection (4) to an interim receiver appointed as there mentioned include, where a receiving order has been made, a reference to the receiver constituted by virtue of section 7 of the said Act of 1914, and

(d) subsection (2)(b) is omitted.

Winding up of company holding realisable or forfeitable property

3.—(1) Where realisable or forfeitable property is held by a company and an order for the winding up of the company has been made or a resolution has been passed by the company for the voluntary winding up, the functions of the liquidator (or any provisional liquidator) shall not be exercisable in relation to—

(a) property, other than heritable property situated in Scotland, for the time being subject to a restraint order made before the relevant time and heritable property situated in Scotland for the time being subject to a restraint order recorded in the General Register of Sasines or, as the case may be, registered in the Land Register of Scotland before the relevant time; and

(b) any proceeds of property realised by virtue of paragraph 1 of Schedule 3 to this Act for the time being in the hands of an administrator appointed under that paragraph.

(2) Where, in the case of a company, such an order has been made or such a resolution has been passed, the powers conferred on the court by sections 94 to 99 and 101 to 104 of this Act or on an administrator appointed under paragraph 1 of the said Schedule 3 shall not be exercised in relation to any realisable or forfeitable property held by the company in relation to which the functions of the liquidator are exercisable—

(a) so as to inhibit the liquidator from exercising those functions for the purpose of distributing any property held by the company to the company's creditors; or

(b) so as to prevent the payment out of any property of expenses (including the remuneration of the liquidator or any provisional liquidator) properly incurred in the winding up in respect of the property.

(3) Nothing in the Insolvency Act 1986 shall be taken as restricting, or enabling the restriction of, the exercise of the powers so conferred.

(4) For the purposes of the application of Parts IV and V of the Insolvency Act 1986 (winding up of registered companies and winding up of unregistered companies) to a company which the court has jurisdiction to wind up, a person is not a creditor in so far as any sum due to him by the company is due in respect of a confiscation order (whether under this Act or under and within the meaning of section 2 of the Drug Trafficking Act 1994 or section 1 of the 1987 Act or any corresponding provision in Northern Ireland).

(5) Where an order for the winding up of a company has been made or a resolution has been passed by a company for its voluntary winding up and before the relevant time the company has directly or indirectly made a gift caught by Chapter I of Part II of this Act—

(a) no order or, as the case may be, decree shall, at any time when proceedings as regards an offence to which that Chapter applies have been instituted against the company and have not been concluded or when property of the person to whom the gift was made is subject to a restraint order, be made under section 238 or 239 of the Insolvency Act 1986 (transactions at an undervalue and preferences) or granted under section 242 or 243 of that Act (gratuitous alienations and unfair preferences) in respect of the making of the gift; and

(b) any order made under either of the said sections 242 and 243 or decree granted under either of the said sections 242 or 243 after the conclusion of the proceedings shall take into account any realisation under Part II of this Act of property held by the person to whom the gift was made.

(6) In this paragraph—

"company" means any company which may be wound up under the Insolvency Act 1986; and

"the relevant time" means—

(a) where no order for the winding up of the company has been made, the time of the passing of the resolution for voluntary winding up;

(b) where such an order has been made and, before the presentation of the petition for the winding up of the company by the court, such a resolution had been passed by the company, the time of the passing of the resolution; and

(c) in any other case where such an order has been made, the time of the making of the order.

(7) In any case in which a winding up of a company commenced, or is treated as having commenced, before the date on which the Insolvency Act 1986 came into force, sub-paragraphs (2) to (6) above have effect with the substitution for references to that Act of references to the Companies Act 1985.

Property subject to floating charge

4.—(1) Where any property held subject to a floating charge by a company is realisable or forfeitable property and a receiver has been appointed by, or on the application of, the holder of the charge, the powers of the receiver in relation to the property so held shall not be exercisable in relation to—

(a) so much of it, not being heritable property situated in Scotland, as is for the time being subject to a restraint order made before the appointment of the receiver and so much of it, being heritable property situated in Scotland, as is for the time being subject to a restraint order recorded in the General Register of Sasines or, as the case may be, registered in the Land Register of Scotland before the such appointment; and

(b) any proceeds of property realised by virtue of paragraph 1 of Schedule 3 to this Act for the time being in the hands of an administrator appointed under that paragraph.

(2) Where, in the case of a company, such an appointment has been made, the powers conferred on the court by sections 94 to 99 and 101 to 104 of this Act or on an administrator appointed under paragraph 1 of the said Schedule 3 shall not be exercised in relation to any realisable property held by the company in relation to which the powers of the receiver are exercisable—

(a) so as to inhibit the receiver from exercising his powers for the purpose of distributing any property held by the company to the company's creditors; or

(b) so as to prevent the payment out of any property of expenses (including the remuneration of the receiver) properly incurred in the exercise of the receiver's powers in respect of the property.

(3) Nothing in the Insolvency Act 1986, shall be taken as restricting, or enabling the restriction of, the exercise of the powers so conferred.

(4) In this paragraph—

"company" has the same meaning as in paragraph 3 above; and

"floating charge" includes a floating charge within the meaning given by section 462 of the Companies Act 1985 (power of incorporated company to create floating charge).

(5) In any case in which a receiver was appointed as is mentioned in sub-paragraph (1) above before the date on which the Insolvency Act 1986 came into force, sub-paragraphs (2) to (4) above have effect with the substitution for references to that Act of references to the Companies Act 1985.

Insolvency practitioners dealing with property subject to restraint order

5.—(1) Without prejudice to the generality of any enactment contained in the Insolvency Act 1986 or in the 1985 Act, where—

(a) any person acting as an insolvency practitioner seizes or disposes of any property in relation to which his functions are, because that property is for the time being subject to a restraint order, not exercisable; and

(b) at the time of the seizure or disposal he believes, and has reasonable grounds for believing, that he is entitled (whether in pursuance of a court order or otherwise) to seize or dispose of that property,

he shall not be liable to any person in respect of any loss or damage resulting from the seizure or disposal except in so far as the loss or damage is caused by the insolvency practitioner's negligence; and the insolvency practitioner shall have a lien on the property, or the proceeds of its sale, for such of his expenses as were incurred in connection with the liquidation, sequestration or other proceedings in relation to which the seizure or disposal purported to take place and for so much of his remuneration as may reasonably be assigned for his actings in connection with those proceedings.

(2) Any person who, acting as an insolvency practitioner, incurs expenses—

(a) in respect of such realisable property as is mentioned in sub-paragraph (1)(a) above and in so doing does not know and has no reasonable grounds to believe that the property is for the time being subject to a restraint order; or

(b) other than in respect of such realisable property as is so mentioned, being expenses which, but for the effect of a restraint order, might have been met by taking possession of and realising the property,

shall be entitled (whether or not he has seized or disposed of that property so as to have a lien under sub-paragraph (1) above) to payment of those expenses under paragraph 4(2) or (4)(a) of Schedule 3 to this Act.

(3) In the foregoing provisions of this paragraph, the expression "acting as an insolvency practitioner" shall be construed in accordance with section 388 (interpretation) of the said Act of 1986 except that for the purposes of such construction the reference in subsection (2)(a) of that section to a permanent or interim trustee in a sequestration shall be taken to include a reference to a trustee in a sequestration and subsection (5) of that section shall be disregarded; and the expression shall also comprehend the official receiver acting as receiver or manager of the property.

Interpretation

6.—(1) In this Schedule "the 1985 Act" means the Bankruptcy (Scotland) Act 1985.

(2) References in this Schedule to the conclusion of proceedings, except for the purposes of paragraph 2(5) above, shall be construed—

(a) as regards property subject to a restraint order under section 94(1)(a) of this Act, in accordance with section 95(6) of this Act; and

(b) as regards property subject to a restraint order under section 94(1)(b) of this Act, in accordance with section 96(5) of this Act.

(3) References in this Schedule to property held by a person include a reference to property vested in the interim or permanent trustee in his sequestration or in his trustee in bankruptcy or liquidation.

Section 113(3) SCHEDULE 5

AMENDMENTS TO THE CRIMINAL JUSTICE (SCOTLAND) ACT 1987 RELATING TO PART II

1. The Criminal Justice (Scotland) Act 1987 shall be amended as follows.

2. In section 1 (confiscation orders)—

(a) in subsection (1)—

(i) for the words from "High Court" to "pronounced)" there shall be substituted the words "High Court or sheriff court (in this section and sections 2 to 7A of this Act referred to as "the court") of an offence to which this section relates the court, on the application of the prosecutor, may", and in the remainder of that subsection for the word "Court" where it appears there shall be substituted the word "court"; and

(ii) in paragraph (b), for the word "property" where it first appears there shall be substituted the word "amount" and for the words "the value of that property" there shall be substituted the words "that amount";

(b) in subsection (2), after the word "following" there shall be inserted the words "offences when prosecuted either on indictment or on summary complaint before the sheriff if the offence is punishable by a fine in excess of level 5 or by imprisonment for a period of more than 3 months or by both such fine and imprisonment";

(c) after subsection (2) there shall be inserted the following subsections—

"(2A) Any application under this section shall be made—

(a) in proceedings on indictment, when the prosecutor moves for sentence or, if the offender is remitted for sentence under section 104 of the 1975 Act, before sentence is pronounced; and

(b) in summary proceedings following the conviction of the accused.

(2B) A confiscation order shall not be made unless the court orders some other disposal (including an absolute discharge) in respect of the offender.

(2C) If the court decides to make a confiscation order, it shall determine the amount to be payable thereunder before making any decision as to—

(a) imposing a fine on the person;

(b) making any order involving any other payment by him.

(2D) Where a court makes a confiscation order against an accused in any proceedings, it shall, in respect of any offence of which he is convicted in those proceedings, take account of the order before—

(a) imposing any fine on him;

(b) making any order involving any other payment by him,

but subject to that, the court shall leave the order out of account in determining the appropriate sentence or other manner of dealing with the accused.

(2E) Where a court makes both a confiscation order and a compensation order under section 58 of the Criminal Justice (Scotland) Act 1980 against the same person in the same proceedings in relation to the same offence and the offence involves the misappropriation of property, it shall direct that the compensation shall be paid first out of any sums applied towards the satisfaction of the confiscation order.";

(d) subsection (3) shall cease to have effect; and

(e) in subsection (5) for the words "High Court" and "Court" where they occur there shall be substituted the word "court".

3. For section 2 (postponed confiscation orders) there shall be substituted the following section—

"2.—(1) If the court considers that it has some, but not sufficient, relevant information for the purpose of enabling it to come to a decision as to whether to make a confiscation order or that it does not have sufficient relevant information to enable it to come to a decision as to the amount to be payable under the confiscation order, it may, subject as the case may be to subsection (6) or (10) below, postpone that decision for a period not exceeding 6 months after the date of conviction for the purpose of enabling further information to be obtained.

(2) Without prejudice to sections 179 and 219 (or as the case may be sections 380 and 432) of the 1975 Act, the court may notwithstanding postponement under subsection (1) above and subject to subsection (3) below, proceed, on the prosecutor's motion therefor, to sentence or to otherwise deal with the accused in respect of the conviction.

(3) Where the court proceeds as mentioned in subsection (2) above—

(a) no fine shall be imposed on the accused; and

(b) no order shall be made involving any other payment by him,

in relation to the conviction before the decision whether to make a confiscation order is taken.

(4) Where in the case of conviction on indictment a decision has been postponed under subsection (1) above for a period, any intention to appeal under section 228 of the 1975 Act against conviction or against both conviction and any sentence passed during that period in respect of the conviction, shall be intimated under section 231(1) of the 1975 Act not within 2 weeks of the final determination of the proceedings but within 2 weeks of—

(a) in the case of an appeal against conviction where there has been no such sentence, the day on which the period of postponement commences;

(b) in any other case, the day on which such sentence is passed in open court.

(5) Notwithstanding any appeal of which intimation has been given by virtue of subsection (4) above, a person may appeal under section 228 of the 1975 Act against the confiscation order (if the decision is to make one) or against any other sentence passed, after the period of postponement, in respect of the conviction.

(6) If during the period of postponement intimation is given by virtue of subsection (4) above by the person, the High Court may, on the application of the prosecutor, extend that period to a date up to 3 months after the date of disposal of the appeal.

(7) This subsection applies where in the case of summary conviction a decision has been postponed under subsection (1) above for a period.

(8) Where subsection (7) above applies and the offender appeals under section 442 of the 1975 Act against conviction or against both conviction and any sentence passed during the period of postponement—

(a) his application for a stated case shall be made not within one week of the final determination of the proceedings but within one week of the day mentioned in paragraph (a) or (b) of subsection (4) above;

(b) his draft stated case shall be prepared and issued not within 3 weeks of the final determination of the proceedings but within 3 weeks of the said day.

(9) Where subsection (7) above applies, then, notwithstanding any appeal against conviction or sentence or both the offender may appeal under section 442(1)(a)(ii), and the prosecutor may appeal under section 442(1)(b)(ii), of the 1975 Act against any confiscation order or against any other sentence passed, after the period of postponement, in respect of the conviction.

(10) Where subsection (7) above applies, then, if during the period of postponement the offender applies for a stated case or lodges a note of appeal, the High Court may, on the application of the prosecutor, extend the period of postponement to a date up to 3 months after the date of disposal of the appeal.".

4. In section 3 (assessing the proceeds of drug trafficking—

(a) in each of subsections (2) and (4) for the word "Court" where it appears there shall be substituted the word "court";

(b) at the end of paragraph (a)(ii) of subsection (2) there shall be added the words "or being served with the complaint (as the case may be)"; and

(c) subsection (5) shall cease to have effect.

5. In section 4 (statements relating to drug trafficking)—

(a) in each of subsections (1), (2) and (4) for the word "Court" where it appears there shall be substituted the word "court";

(b) in each of subsections (1) and (4) after the words "section 150" there shall be inserted the words "or, as the case may be, section 354";

(c) at the end there shall be added the following subsections—

"(6) Without prejudice to section 2(1) of this Act, where—

(a) any allegation in the statement lodged under subsection (1) above is challenged by the accused; or

(b) the basis of the non-acceptance by the accused of any such allegation is challenged by the prosecutor,

the court shall consider the matters being challenged at a hearing.

(7) Where the judge presiding at a hearing held under subsection (6) above is not the trial judge he may, on the application of either party, if he considers that it would be in the interests of justice to do so, adjourn the hearing to a date when the trial judge is available.".

6. In section 5 (realisable property)—
(a) for subsections (1) to (3) there shall be substituted the following—
"(1) In this Part of this Act "realisable property" means, subject to subsection (2) below—
(a) the whole estate wherever situated of a person—
(i) against whom proceedings have been instituted for an offence to which section 1 of this Act relates; or
(ii) in respect of whom a restraint order has been made by virtue of section 8(4) of this Act;
(b) the whole estate wherever situated of a person to whom any person whose whole estate is realisable by virtue of paragraph (a) above has (directly or indirectly and whether in one transaction or in a series of transactions) made an implicative gift;
(c) any other property in the possession or under the control of a person mentioned in paragraph (a) or (b) above; and
(d) any income or estate vesting in a person mentioned in paragraph (a) or (b) above.
(2) Property is not realisable if—
(a) held on trust by a person mentioned in subsection (1)(a) or (b) above for a person not so mentioned;
(b) a suspended forfeiture order is in force in respect of the property; or
(c) it is, for the time being, subject to a restraint order made in respect of other proceedings.
(3) For the purposes of this section proceedings for an offence are instituted against a person—
(a) on his arrest without warrant;
(b) when he is charged with the offence without being arrested;
(c) when a warrant to arrest him is granted;
(d) when a warrant to cite him is granted;
(e) in summary proceedings, on the first calling of the case; or
(f) when a petition is intimated to him or an indictment or a complaint is served on him,
and, where the application of this subsection would result in there being more than one time for the institution of proceedings, they shall be taken to be instituted at the earliest of those times.";
(b) in subsection (4)—
(i) for the words "realisable property owned" there shall be substituted the words "his realisable property"; and
(ii) for the words from "except that" to the end there shall be substituted ", less any amount due by him at that time in respect of any compensation order under section 58 of the Criminal Justice (Scotland) Act 1980 made before the confiscation order.";
(c) in subsection (5)—
(i) for the words "High Court" there shall be substituted the word "court";,
(ii) after the words "regard to the" there shall be inserted the word "likely";
(iii) after paragraph (a) there shall be inserted the following paragraph—
"(aa) of realisable property held by a person whose estate has been sequestrated, or who has been adjudged bankrupt in England and Wales or Northern Ireland, the court shall take into account the extent to which the property is subject to, as the case may be sequestration or bankruptcy procedure by virtue of section 33 or 34 of this Act;";
(iv) paragraph (b) shall cease to have effect; and
(v) at the end there shall be added the words "and in this subsection, "money" includes cheques, banknotes, postal orders, money orders and foreign currency";
(d) subsection (6) shall cease to have effect;
(e) in subsection (7)
(i) for the word "Court" there shall be substituted the word "court"; and
(ii) the words "notwithstanding subsections (5)(b) and (6) above" shall cease to have effect;
(f) after subsection (7) there shall be inserted the following subsections—
"(7A) Where the court is satisfied, on the application of a person in receipt of an implicative gift made before or after a confiscation order has been made—
(a) that the person received the gift not knowing, not suspecting and not having reasonable grounds to suspect that the giver was in any way concerned in drug trafficking; and
(b) that he is not, and has never been, associated with the giver in drug trafficking; and
(c) that he would suffer hardship if the application were not granted,

it may make an order declaring that the gift or a part of the gift shall not be an implicative gift and that the property or part of the property of the recipient of the gift shall not be, or shall cease to be, realisable for the purposes of this Part of this Act and, if a confiscation order has already been made, varying that order accordingly, where necessary.

(7B) An appeal shall lie to the High Court at the instance of—

(a) the applicant against the refusal;

(b) the prosecutor against the granting,

of an application under subsection (7A) above.

(7C) The procedure in an appeal under this section shall be the same as the procedure in an appeal against sentence."; and

(g) subsection (8) shall cease to have effect.

7. In section 6 (implicative gifts)

(a) in subsection (1), in paragraph (a) for the words "the warrant to arrest and commit was granted" there shall be substituted the words "the proceedings were commenced within the meaning of section 5(3) of this Act";

(b) for subsections (2) and (3) there shall be substituted the following—

"(2) In assessing the value of an implicative gift, the court shall, subject to subsections (3) and (3A) below, take it to be the greater of—

(a) the value of the gift when received adjusted to take account of subsequent changes in the value of money; or

(b) both of the following—

(i) the likely market value, on the date on which the confiscation order is to be made, of—

(A) the gift, if retained; or

(B) where the recipient of the gift retains only part of it, the retained part, and any property or part of any property which, directly or indirectly, represents the gift; or

(C) where the recipient of the gift retains no part of it, any property or part of any property which, directly or indirectly, represents the gift; and

(ii) the value of any other property and any other economic advantage which by reason of the making of the gift the recipient of the gift has obtained, directly or indirectly, prior to the date on which the confiscation order is to be made, adjusted to take account of subsequent changes in the value of money.

(3) The circumstances in which the accused is to be treated as making a gift include those where he transfers an interest in property to another person directly or indirectly for a consideration the value of which is significantly less than the value of that interest at the time of transfer; and in those circumstances the value of the gift shall be the difference between the value of that consideration and the value of that interest at the time of transfer adjusted to take account of subsequent changes in the value of money.

(3A) Where an implicative gift was in the form of money and the recipient of the gift shows that, on the balance of probabilities, the money or any of it has not been used to purchase goods or services or to earn interest or any other return, the value of the gift or such part of it as has not been so used shall be taken to be the face value of the money or, as the case may be, unused amount of the money.

(3B) In subsection (3A) above, "money" includes cheques, banknotes, postal orders, money orders and foreign currency."; and

(c) subsections (4) and (5) shall cease to have effect.

8. After section 6 (implicative gifts) there shall be inserted the following sections—

"Increase in value of proceeds of drug trafficking or realisable property

6A.—(1) This section applies where the court which made a confiscation order is satisfied, on an application made by the prosecutor, that at the time the application is made the value of the proceeds of the person's drug trafficking, or the amount that might be realised, is greater than—

(a) the value of the proceeds of the person's drug trafficking; or, as the case may be,

(b) the amount that might be realised,

which was taken into account when the order was made.

(2) The considerations by reference to which to court may be satisfied as mentioned in subsection (1) above shall include—

(a) the value of the proceeds of the person's drug trafficking was greater than was taken into account when the confiscation order was made or has increased since the order was made; or

(b) further proceeds of drug trafficking have been obtained since the confiscation order was made; or

   (c) the value of realisable property was greater than was taken into account when the confiscation order was made; or

   (d) any realisable property taken into account at the time when the confiscation order was made has subsequently increased in value; or

   (e) the amount, or part of the amount, of a gift which was disregarded under section 5(7) of this Act could now be realised.

(3) An application under subsection (1) above shall be made as soon as is reasonably practicable after the relevant information becomes available to the prosecutor but in any event within 6 years commencing with the date when the person was convicted of the offence.

(4) Where this section applies—

   (a) the court may make a new confiscation order for the payment of such sum as appears to the court to be appropriate having regard to what is now shown to be the value of the proceeds of drug trafficking or the amount that might be realised; and

   (b) if the earlier confiscation order has not been satisfied, then the court, in making the new confiscation order shall recall the earlier order and may take into account the amount unpaid (including any interest payable by virtue of section 15(1) of the Criminal Justice (International Co-operation) Act 1990) under the earlier order.

(5) Section 4 of this Act shall, subject to any necessary modifications, apply in relation to the making of a new confiscation order in pursuance of this section as it applies where the prosecutor has moved for a confiscation order under section 1 of this Act.

(6) The assumptions mentioned in section 3(2) of this Act shall not apply for the purposes of this section.

Confiscation orders where proceeds of crime discovered at later date

6B.—(1) This section applies where no confiscation order has been made in relation to an offence under section 1 or 2 of this Act.

(2) Where the court, on an application made to it by the prosecutor under this section, is satisfied—

   (a) that a person convicted of an offence to which this Part of this Act relates was in receipt of the proceeds of drug trafficking in respect of that offence;

   (b) that the information necessary to enable a confiscation order to be made on the date on which an application under section 1 of this Act was or could have been made was not available to the prosecutor,

it may make a confiscation order in relation to that person.

(3) An application under this section shall be made as soon as is reasonably practicable after the relevant information becomes available to the prosecutor but in any event within 6 years commencing with the date when the person was convicted of the offence.

(4) In determining the sum to be payable under a confiscation order made in pursuance of this section, the court shall take into account—

   (a) any order involving any payment by the offender;

   (b) any order under section 87 of the Criminal Justice (Scotland) Act 1995 or an order for forfeiture under any other enactment made in respect of the offender,

which forms part of the sentence already imposed for the offence concerned.

(5) In determining such sum the court may take into account any payment or other reward received by the offender on or after the date of conviction, but only if the prosecutor satisfies the court that it was received by the offender in connection with drug trafficking carried on by the offender or another on or before that date.

(6) Section 4 of this Act shall, subject to any necessary modifications, apply in relation to the making of a confiscation order in pursuance of this section as it applies where the prosecutor has moved for a confiscation order under section 1 of this Act.

(7) Section 1(2B), (2C), (2D) and (2E) of this Act shall not apply in relation to a confiscation order made in pursuance of this section.

(8) The assumptions mentioned in section 3(2) of this Act shall not apply for the purposes of this section.

(9) Where the court makes a confiscation order in pursuance of this section and a compensation order has been made under section 58 of the Criminal Justice (Scotland) Act 1980 in respect of misappropriation of property by the offender, the court shall direct that compensation shall first be paid out of any sums applied towards the satisfaction of the confiscation order to the extent of any sums outstanding in respect of the compensation order.

(10) In this section "the court" means the court which had jurisdiction in respect of the offence concerned to make a confiscation order under section 1 of this Act.".

9. In section 7 (application of provisions relating to fines to enforcement of confiscation orders)—

   (a) in subsection (1)—

(i) after "203" there shall be inserted the words "or, as the case may be, 402 and 412";
(ii) for the words from "as applied" to "below shall" there shall be substituted the words "the provisions of that Act specified in subsection (2) below (or those provisions as applied by section 194 of that Act) shall";
(b) in subsection (2)—
(i) in the entry relating to section 398, at the end there shall be inserted the words "but as if subsection (1)—
(a) gave the prosecutor an opportunity to be heard at any enquiry thereunder; and
(b) applied whether the offender was in prison or not;"; and
(ii) in the entry relating to section 411, the words "except the proviso to subsection (3)" shall cease to have effect;
(c) after subsection (2) there shall be inserted the following subsection—
"(2A) Where a court, by virtue of subsection (1) above, orders the sum due under a confiscation order to be recovered by civil diligence under section 411 of the Criminal Procedure (Scotland) Act 1975, any arrestment executed by a prosecutor under subsection (2) of section 11A of this Act shall be deemed to have been executed by the court as if that subsection authorised such execution.".

10. After section 7 (application of provisions relating to fines to enforcement of confiscation orders) there shall be inserted the following section—

"Disposal of family home
7A. Section 111 of the Criminal Justice (Scotland) Act 1995 shall apply in respect of a person's family home if a confiscation order has been made in relation to that person as it applies in respect of a person's family home if a confiscation order has been made in relation to that person under section 70(1) of that Act but as if for subsection (1) there were substituted the following subsection—
"(1) This section applies where a confiscation order has been made in relation to any person and the prosecutor has not satisfied the court that the person's interest in his family home has been acquired by means of the proceeds of drug trafficking.".".

11. For sections 8 (cases in which restraint orders may be made) and 9 (restraint orders) there shall be substituted the following sections—

"Restraint orders
8.—(1) The court may, on the application of the prosecutor, make an order (in this Part of this Act referred to as a "restraint order") in the circumstances mentioned in either subsection (3) or (4) below interdicting—
(a) any person named in the order from dealing with his realisable property; or
(b) that person and any person named in the order as appearing to the court to have received from him an implicative gift from dealing with their own, or the other's, realisable property,
(whenever that property was acquired and whether it is described in the order or not).
(2) A restraint order may contain conditions and exceptions to which the interdict shall be subject and in particular—
(a) may make provision for the release to the person named in the order of such reasonable living expenses as the court thinks fit; and
(b) shall provide for the release of property in so far as it is required to meet reasonable legal expenses payable or likely to be payable in relation to proceedings—
(i) as regards the offence by virtue of which the restraint order has been made; or
(ii) as regards a confiscation order made on conviction of the offence.
(3) For the purposes of this subsection, the circumstances are—
(a) proceedings have been instituted against an accused in Scotland for an offence to which section 1 of this Act relates;
(b) the proceedings have not been concluded; and
(c) either a confiscation order has been made or it appears to the court that, in the event of his conviction of the offence, there are reasonable grounds for thinking that a confiscation order may be made in those proceedings.
(4) For the purposes of this subsection, the circumstances are that the court is satisfied that—
(a) it is proposed to institute proceedings within 28 days against a person suspected of such an offence and it appears to the court that, in the event of his conviction of the offence, there are reasonable grounds for thinking that a confiscation order may be made in those proceedings; or
(b) the prosecutor has made, or proposes within 28 days to make, an application under section 6A or, as the case may be, section 6B of this Act in relation to that person in

respect of the offence and it appears to the court that there are reasonable grounds for thinking that the application may be granted.

(5) Where the court has made a restraint order in the circumstances mentioned in subsection (4)(a) or (b) above and no proceedings have been instituted or application made within 28 days as mentioned in that subsection, the prosecutor shall forthwith apply to the court for the recall of the order and the court shall grant the application.

(6) When proceedings for the offence or, as the case may be proceedings on an application under section 6A or 6B of this Act are concluded, the prosecutor shall forthwith apply to the court for recall of the order and the court shall grant the application.

(7) A restraint order shall—

(a) be made on an ex parte application which shall be heard in chambers; and

(b) without prejudice to the time when it becomes effective, be intimated to each person affected by it.

(8) For the purposes of this Part of this Act, dealing with property includes (without prejudice to the generality of the expression)—

(a) making a payment to any person in reduction of the amount of a debt;

(b) removing the property from the jurisdiction of the court; and

(c) transferring or disposing of the property.

(9) In this section and sections 9 to 12 of this Act, "the court" means where, as regards the criminal proceedings in question, a trial diet or a diet fixed for the purposes of section 102 of the 1975 Act is intended to be held, is being or has been held—

(a) in the High Court of Justiciary, the Court of Session;

(b) in the sheriff court, a sheriff of that court exercising his civil jurisdiction.

(10) For the purposes of this section, proceedings on an application under section 6A or 6B of this Act are concluded—

(a) when the application is refused; or

(b) where the application is granted, when a confiscation order made in the proceedings is satisfied (whether by payment of the amount due under the order or by the accused serving imprisonment in default).

(11) References in this section to the institution of proceedings for an offence against a person shall be construed in accordance with section 5(3) of this Act.

Variation and recall of restraint orders

9.—(1) Subject to subsections (2) and (3) below, the court nt may, at the instance of—

(a) the prosecutor, at any time vary or recall a restraint order in relation to any person or to any property;

(b) any person having an interest, at any time vary or recall a restraint order in relation to the person or to any property.

(2) On an application made under subsection (1)(b) above of a person named in a restraint order as having received an implicative gift, the court may recall the order in relation to that person if it is satisfied on the balance of probabilities—

(a) that he received the gift not knowing, not suspecting and not having reasonable grounds to suspect that the gift was made in contemplation of, or after, the commission of the offence or if more than one, in contemplation of any of the offences or after the commission of the earlier or the earliest of the offences to which the proceedings for the time being relate; and

(b) that he was not associated with the giver in the commission of the offence; and

(c) that he would suffer hardship if the order were not recalled.

(3) Where an application has been made under subsection (1) above for the variation or recall of a restraint order, any property in relation to which the restraint order was made shall not be realised during the period beginning with the making of the application and ending with the determination of the application by the court.

(4) The court may where it has recalled a restraint order as mentioned in subsection (1)(b) or (2) above, order that property of the person at whose instance it was recalled shall cease to be realisable.

(5) The prosecutor or any person having an interest may reclaim or appeal to the Court of Session against an interlocutor refusing, varying or recalling or refusing to vary or recall a restraint order, within such period as may be prescribed by act of sederunt.

(6) Where, in relation to a restraint order which is recalled, interdict has been granted under section 12(1) of this Act, the clerk of court shall, on the restraint order being recalled, forthwith so inform each person so interdicted.".

12. In section 11 (inhibition and arrestment of property affected by restraint order or by interdict under section 12)—

(a) in subsection (1), in paragraph (ii), the words "where granted under subsection (1)(a) above," shall cease to have effect;

(b) in subsection (2), for the words "(1)(a)" there shall be substituted "(1)";
(c) in subsections (4) and (5), the words "or arrestment", in each place where they occur, shall cease to have effect; and
(d) subsection (6) shall cease to have effect.

13. After section 11 there shall be inserted the following section—

"Arrestment of property affected by restraint order

11A.—(1) On the application of the prosecutor, the court may, in respect of moveable property affected by a restraint order (whether such property generally or particular such property), grant warrant for arrestment if the property would be arrestable if the person entitled to it were a debtor.

(2) A warrant under subsection (1) above shall have effect as if granted on the dependence of an action for debt at the instance of the prosecutor against the person and may be executed, recalled, loosed or restricted accordingly.

(3) The fact that an arrestment has been executed under subsection (2) above in respect of property shall not prejudice the exercise of an administrator's powers under or for the purposes of this Part of this Act in respect of that property.

(4) No arrestment executed under subsection (2) above shall have effect once, or in so far as, the restraint order affecting the property in respect of which the warrant for such arrestment has been granted has ceased to have effect in respect of that property; and the prosecutor shall apply to the court for an order recalling, or as the case may be, restricting the arrestment accordingly.".

14. In section 12 (interdict of person not subject to a restraint order)—
(a) in subsection (1)—
        (i) for the words "Court of Session" there shall be substituted the word "court"; and
        (ii) the words from "and the clerk of court" to the end shall cease to have effect;
(b) for subsection (2) there shall be substituted the following subsection—
    "(2) Subsections (2)(a) and (7)(a) of section 8 of this Act shall apply in relation to an interdict under subsection (1) above as they apply in relation to a restraint order; and subsections (1) (2), (4) and (5) of section 9 thereof shall apply in relation to subsection (1) above as they apply in relation to subsection (1) of the said section 9."; and
(c) for subsection (3) there shall be substituted the following—
    "(3) Without prejudice to the time when it becomes effective, an interdict under subsection (1) above shall be intimated to every person affected by it.".

15. In section 13 (administrators)—
(a) for the words "Lord Advocate" there shall be substituted the word "prosecutor";
(b) for the words "Court of Session" where they appear there shall be substituted the word "court"; and
(c) for the word "Court" where it appears other than as mentioned in paragraph (b) above there shall be substituted the word "court".

16. In section 14 (functions of administrators)—
(a) in subsection (1)—
        (i) in paragraph (c) the words from "and, without" to the end of the paragraph shall cease to have effect;
        (ii) in the proviso to paragraph (j) after the words "of his" there shall be inserted the words "(within the meaning of section 74 of the 1985 Act)"; and
        (iii) in paragraphs (n) and (o) for the words "Court of Session" and "Court" where they occur there shall be substituted the word "court"; and
(b) in subsection (3), for the words "Court of Session" there shall be substituted the word "court".

17. In section 16 (application of proceeds of realisation and other sums)—
(a) in subsections (1) and (2) for the words "Court of Session" where they occur there shall be substituted the word "court";
(b) in subsection (1) for the words "such expenses as are payable" there shall be substituted the words "any expenses to the payment of which a person is entitled"; and
(c) in subsection (3)—
        (i) after paragraph (c) there shall be inserted the following paragraph—
        "(d) next, in accordance with any direction given by the court under section 1(2E) or 6B(9) of this Act,";
        (ii) for the words "of the 1975 Act (fines payable to H.M. Exchequer)" there shall be substituted the words "or 412 of the 1975 Act (destination of fines)".

18. In section 17 (supervision of administrators), in subsection (2), for the words "Court of Session" and "Court" where they occur there shall be substituted the word "court".

19. In section 18 (accounts and remuneration of administrator), for the words "Court of Session" and "Court" where they occur there shall be substituted the word "court".

20. In section 19 (effect of appointment under section 13 of that Act on diligence) for the words "section 11" there shall be substituted "sections 11 and 11A".

21. In section 20 (further provision as to administrators), at the end there shall be added the following subsection—

"(3) Any disposal of property under section 13 of this Act to a person taking in good faith shall vest the ownership of the property in that person.".

22. In section 23 (exercise of powers by Court of Session or administrator)—

(a) for the words "Court of Session" where they appear there shall be substituted the word "court";

(b) in subsection (1) for the words "11(1) to (5)" there shall be substituted "9, 11, 11A";

(c) in subsection (3) for the words from ", so far as" to the end there shall be substituted "be exercised with a view to realising no more than the value of the gift as assessed in pursuance of section 6(2), (3) or (3A) of this Act";

(d) in subsection (6) the words from "and without" to "family" and the words "(other than an obligation having priority, within the meaning of section 5(8) of this Act)" shall cease to have effect; and

(e) in subsection (7) for the words from "and" to "11(6)" there shall be substituted "28, 28A and 28B".

23. In section 24 (power to facilitate realisation), for the words "Court of Session" there shall be substituted the word "court" and thereafter for the word "Court" where it appears there shall be substituted the word "court".

24. For section 25 (variation of confiscation order), there shall be substituted the following section—

"Realisable property inadequate to meet payments under confiscation order

25.—(1) This section applies where the court which made a confiscation order is satisfied on the balance of probabilities, on an application made to it by the offender or the prosecutor, that the value of the realisable property is inadequate to meet any outstanding amount payable (including any interest payable by virtue of section 15(1) of the Criminal Justice (International Co-operation) Act 1990) under the confiscation order.

(2) When considering whether the value of the realisable property is inadequate the court—

(a) shall, unless already taken into account under section 5(5)(aa) of this Act, take into account the extent to which property held by a person whose estate has been sequestrated or who has been adjudged bankrupt is subject to, as the case may be, sequestration or bankruptcy procedure by virtue of section 33 or 34 of this Act; and

(b) may disregard any inadequacy which appears to it to be attributable, wholly or partly, to anything done by the offender for the purpose of protecting the realisable property from realisation.

(3) Where this section applies, the court shall recall the confiscation order and make a new confiscation order for the payment of such sum of a lesser amount than that for which the original order was made which appears to the court to be appropriate having regard to—

(a) the value of the realisable property as determined under subsection (1) above; and

(b) any amount paid in pursuance of the original order.

(4) Section 4 of this Act shall, subject to any necessary modifications, apply in relation to the making of a new confiscation order in pursuance of this section as it applies where the prosecutor has moved for a confiscation order under section 1 of this Act.".

25. In section 26 (compensation)—

(a) in subsection (1)—

(i) for paragraph (b) there shall be substituted the following paragraph—

"(b) where he is convicted of one or more such offences—

(i) the conviction or convictions concerned are quashed (and no conviction for any such offence is substituted); or

(ii) he is pardoned by Her Majesty in respect of the conviction or convictions concerned,";

(ii) for the words "Court of Session" there shall be substituted the word "court"; and

(iii) for the words from "; but this subsection" to the end there shall be substituted the words "if, having regard to all the circumstances, it considers it appropriate to do so.";

(b) after subsection (1) there shall be inserted the following—

"(1A) Subsection (1) above is without prejudice to any right which may otherwise exist to institute proceedings in respect of delictual liability disclosed by such circumstances as are mentioned in paragraphs (a) and (b) of subsection (2) below.";

(c) in subsections (2) and (3) for the words "Court of Session" where they occur there shall be substituted the word "court";

(d) in subsection (2)(b)—

    (i) the word "substantial" shall cease to have effect; and

    (ii) for the word "11" there shall be substituted "9, 11, 1 1A";

(e) in subsection (4)

    (i) for the words "this section" there shall be substituted the words "subsection (1) above";

    (ii) after paragraph (c) the word "and" shall cease to have effect; and

    (iii) at the end there shall be added "; and

      (e) an officer of the Commissioners of Inland Revenue, by those Commissioners."; and

(f) after subsection (4) there shall be added the following subsections—

"(5) Where the court, on an application made to it by a person other than the accused or the recipient of an implicative gift is satisfied on the balance of probabilities that in relation to any property realised under section 13 of this Act he was the owner of, or a person otherwise having an interest in, the property immediately before such realisation, it shall make an order directing the Crown to pay to that person compensation of an amount equal to the consideration received for the property or, as the case may be, interest or the value of any such consideration at the time of such realisation, or, if no consideration was received, an amount equal to the value of the property or interest at the time of the realisation.

(6) An application for compensation under this section shall be made not later than three years after the conclusion of the proceedings in respect of which the confiscation order was made.".

26. After section 28 (provisions supplementary to section 27), there shall be inserted the following sections—

"Inhibition of Scottish property affected by order registered under section 27

28A.—(1) On the application of the Lord Advocate, the Court of Session may in respect of heritable realisable property in Scotland affected by a restraint order registered under section 27 of this Act (whether such property generally or particular such property) grant warrant for inhibition against any person with an interest in that property; and the warrant—

(a) shall have effect as if granted on the dependence of an action for debt at the instance of the Lord Advocate against the person and may be executed, recalled, loosed or restricted accordingly;

(b) shall have the effect of letters of inhibition and shall forthwith be registered by the Lord Advocate in the Register of Inhibitions and Adjudications.

(2) Section 155 of the Titles to Land Consolidation (Scotland) Act 1868 (effective date of inhibition) shall apply in relation to an inhibition for which warrant has been granted under subsection (1) above as that section applies to an inhibition by separate letters or contained in a summons.

(3) In the application of section 158 of that Act of 1868 (recall of inhibition) to such an inhibition as is mentioned in subsection (2) above, references in that section to a particular Lord Ordinary shall be construed as references to any Lord Ordinary.

(4) The fact that an inhibition has been executed under subsection (1) above in respect of property shall not prejudice the exercise of a receiver's powers under or for the purposes of section 26, 29 or 30 of the Drug Trafficking Act 1994 in respect of that property.

(5) No inhibition executed under subsection (1) above shall have effect once, or in so far as, the restraint order affecting the property in respect of which the warrant for the inhibition has been granted has ceased to have effect in respect of that property; and the Lord Advocate shall—

(a) apply for the recall, or as the case may be restriction, of the inhibition; and

(b) ensure that the recall, or restriction, of an inhibition on such application is reflected in the Register of Inhibitions and Adjudications.

(6) Any power of the Court of Session to recall, loose or restrict inhibitions shall, in relation to an order containing an inhibition under subsection (1) above and without prejudice to any other consideration lawfully applying to the exercise of the power, be exercised with a view to achieving the purposes specified in section 31 of the Drug Trafficking Act 1994.

Arrestment of Scottish property affected by order registered under section 27

28B.—(1) On the application of the Lord Advocate, the Court of Session may, in respect of moveable property affected by a restraint order registered under section 27 of this Act (whether such property generally or particular such property), grant warrant for arrestment if the property would be arrestable if the person entitled to it were a debtor.

(2) A warrant under subsection (1) above shall have effect as if granted on the dependence of an action for debt at the instance of the Lord Advocate against the person and may be executed, recalled, loosed or restricted accordingly.

(3) The fact that an arrestment has been executed under subsection (2) above in respect of property shall not prejudice the exercise of a receiver's powers under or for the purposes of section 26, 29 or 30 of the Drug Trafficking Act 1994 in respect of that property.

(4) No arrestment executed under subsection (2) above shall have effect once, or in so far as, the restraint order affecting the property in respect of which the warrant for such arrestment has been granted has ceased to have effect in respect of that property; and the Lord Advocate shall apply to the Court of Session for an order recalling, or as the case may be, restricting the arrestment accordingly.

(5) Any power of the Court of Session to recall, loose or restrict arrestments shall, in relation to an arrestment proceeding upon a warrant under subsection (1) above and without prejudice to any other consideration lawfully applying to the exercise of the power, be exercised with a view to achieving the purposes specified in section 31 of the Drug Trafficking Act 1994.".

27. In section 30 (enforcement of other external orders)—
(a) in subsection (1), paragraph (b)(i) and paragraph (c) and the word "and" immediately preceding paragraph (c) shall cease to have effect; and
(b) in subsection (2), in the definition of "external confiscation order" after the word "rewards" there shall be inserted the words "or property or other economic advantage".

28. In section 32 (Orders in Council as regards taking action in designated country)—
(a) in subsection (2), for the words "(9)(a), (10), (11) and (12)" there shall be substituted the words "(1)(b)(ii) and (iii), (3) and (5)"; and
(b) after subsection (2) there shall be inserted the following subsection—
"(3) An Order in Council under this section may amend or apply, with or without modifications, any enactment.".

29. In section 33 (sequestration of person holding realisable property)—
(a) in subsection (1), for paragraph (a) there shall be substituted the following paragraph—
"(a) property, other than heritable property situated in Scotland, for the time being subject to a restraint order made before the date of sequestration (within the meaning of section 12(4) of the 1985 Act) and heritable property situated in Scotland for the time being subject to a restraint order recorded in the General Register of Sasines or, as the case may be, registered in the Land Register of Scotland before such date of sequestration;"; and
(b) in subsection (2)—
(i) for the words "Court of Session" there shall be substituted the word "court"; and
(ii) for the words from "sections 8" to "27 and 28" there shall be substituted the words "sections 8, 9, 11 to 13, 16 and 24 and on the Court of Session by sections 27, 28, 28A and 28B".

30. In section 34 (bankruptcy in England and Wales of person holding realisable property)—
(a) in subsection (1), for paragraph (a) there shall be substituted the following paragraph—
"(a) property, other than heritable property situated in Scotland, for the time being subject to a restraint order made before the order adjudging him bankrupt and heritable property situated in Scotland for the time being subject to a restraint order recorded in the General Register of Sasines or, as the case may be, registered in the Land Register of Scotland before the order adjudging him bankrupt was made;"; and
(b) in subsection (2)—
(i) for the words "Court of Session" there shall be substituted the word "court"; and
(ii) for the words from "sections 8" to "27 and 28" there shall be substituted the words "sections 8, 9, 11 to 13, 16 and 24 and on the Court of Session by sections 27, 28, 28A and 28B".

31. In section 35 (winding up company holding realisable property)—
(a) in subsection (1), for paragraph (a) there shall be substituted the following—
"(a) property, other than heritable property situated in Scotland, for the time being subject to a restraint order made before the relevant time and heritable property situated in Scotland for the time being subject to a restraint order recorded in the General Register of Sasines or, as the case may be, registered in the Land Register of Scotland before the relevant time;";
(b) in subsection (2)—
(i) for the words "Court of Session" there shall be substituted the word "court"; and

(ii) for the words from "sections 8" to "27 and 28" there shall be substituted the words "sections 8, 9, 11 to 13, 16 and 24 and on the Court of Session by sections 27, 28, 28A and 28B"; and

(c) after subsection (4) there shall be inserted the following subsection—

"(4A) Where an order for the winding up of a company has been made or a resolution has been passed by a company for its voluntary winding up and before the relevant time the company has directly or indirectly made an implicative gift—

(a) no order or, as the case may be, decree shall, at any time when proceedings as regards an offence to which section 1 of this Act relates have been instituted against the company and have not been concluded or when property of the person to whom the gift was made is subject to a restraint order, be made under section 238 or 239 of the Insolvency Act 1986 (transactions at an undervalue and preferences) or granted under section 242 or 243 of that Act (gratuitous alienations and unfair preferences) in respect of the making of the gift; and

(b) any order made under either of the said sections 238 or 239 or decree granted under either of the said sections 242 and 243 after the conclusion of the proceedings shall take into account any realisation under this Act of property held by the person to whom the gift was made.".

32. In section 36 (property subject to floating charge)—

(a) in subsection (1) for paragraph (a) there shall be substituted the following paragraph—

"(a) so much of it, not being heritable property situated in Scotland, as is for the time being subject to a restraint order made before the appointment of the receiver and so much of it, being heritable property situated in Scotland, as is for the time being subject to a restraint order recorded in the General Register of Sasines or, as the case may be, registered in the Land Register of Scotland before the such appointment;"; and

(b) in subsection (2) for the words for the words from "Court of Session" to "16 and 24" there shall be substituted the words "court by sections 8, 9, 11 to 13, 16 and 24 and on the Court of Session by sections 27, 28, 28A and 28B".

33. After section 37 (insolvency practitioners dealing with property subject to restraint order), there shall be inserted the following section—

"Forfeiture of property where accused has died

Forfeiture of property where accused has died

37A.—(1) Section 112 of the Criminal Justice (Scotland) Act 1995 shall, subject to any necessary modifications, apply in respect of an offence to which Part I of this Act relates as it applies to an offence to which Chapter I of Part II of that Act applies.

(2) Without prejudice to subsection (1) above, in the application of subsection (2) of that section, in paragraph (b)(i) for the words "in connection with the commission of the offence" there shall be substituted the words "in connection with drug trafficking"."

34. In section 41(2) (disclosure of information held by government departments)—

(a) in paragraph (a), for the words "paragraph (a) thereof" there shall be substituted "subsection (3) of that section";

(b) in paragraph (b), for the words "paragraph (b) of subsection (1)" there shall be substituted "subsection (4)"; and

(c) the words from the end of paragraph (b) to the end of the subsection shall cease to have effect.

35. In section 44(1) (offences relating to controlled drugs: fines), for the words "the proviso to subsection (1)" there shall be substituted "subsection (3)(a)".

36. In section 47 (interpretation of Part I)—

(a) in subsection (1)—

(i) the definition of "associate" shall cease to have effect;

(ii) for the definition of "confiscation order" there shall be substituted the following definition—

" "confiscation order" means an order under section 1(1), 6A, 6B or 25 of this Act;"; and

(iii) after the definition of "confiscation order" there shall be inserted the following definition—

" "the court" means—

(a) for the purpose of sections 1 to 7A, the High Court of Justiciary or sheriff court;

(b) for the purposes of sections 8 to 26 and 33 to 37, the Court of Session or the sheriff court;";

(b) in subsection (5), in each of paragraphs (c) and (d) after the words "High Court" there shall be inserted the words "or, as the case may be, the sheriff"; and

(c) at the end there shall be added the following subsection—

"(6) Any reference in this Part of this Act to a conviction of an offence includes a reference to a finding that the offence has been committed.".

Section 117   SCHEDULE 6

Minor and Consequential Amendments

Part I

Amendments Relating to Part I

The Criminal Procedure (Scotland) Act 1887 (c. 35)

1. Section 3 of and Schedules D (form of execution of citation of witnesses), E (form of execution of citation of jurors), N (form of notice of further diet) and O (form of notice of postponed second diet) to the Criminal Procedure (Scotland) Act 1887 shall cease to have effect.

The Criminal Justice (Scotland) Act 1949 (c. 94)

2. Schedule 7 to the Criminal Justice (Scotland) Act 1949 (forms of notices to accused in proceedings on indictment) shall cease to have effect.

The Summary Jurisdiction (Scotland) Act 1954 (c. 48)

3. Parts I and III to VI of Schedule 2 (forms of procedure) and Schedule 3 (table of fees) to the Summary Jurisdiction (Scotland) Act 1954 shall cease to have effect.

The Backing of Warrants (Republic of Ireland) Act 1965 (c.45)

4. In section 8(1)(b) of the Backing of Warrants (Republic of Ireland) Act 1965 (rules of court), for the words "457(a)" there shall be substituted "457ZA".

The Criminal Justice Act 1967 (c. 80)

5. In section 69(2) of the Criminal Justice Act 1967 (extension of enactments relating to persons sentenced to imprisonment or detention to young offenders), the words ", section 40 of the Prisons (Scotland) Act 1989" shall cease to have effect.

The Criminal Procedure (Scotland) Act 1975 (c. 21)

6. The Criminal Procedure (Scotland) Act 1975 shall be amended as follows.

7. In section 6(3) (jurisdiction and procedure in respect of certain indictable offences committed abroad)—

(a) after the word "section" there shall be inserted "—(a)"; and

(b) for the words "as if" there shall be substituted—

"; or

(b) in such sheriff court district as the Lord Advocate may determine, as if".

8. Sections 14(3) and 323(3) (warrant to search for or remove any person accused of an offence in respect of a child) shall cease to have effect.

9. After section 15 there shall be inserted the following section—

"Warrants for search and apprehension to be signed by judge

15A. Any warrant for search or apprehension granted under this Part of this Act shall be signed by the judge granting it, and execution upon any such warrant may proceed either upon the warrant itself or upon an extract of the warrant issued and signed by the clerk of court.".

10. In section 18(3) (penalty for breach of undertaking to appear), for the words "£200" there shall be substituted "level 3 on the standard scale".

11. In section 19(1)(a) (intimation to a solicitor), for the words from "of" to the end there shall be substituted—

"(i) of the place where the person is being detained;

(ii) whether the person is to be liberated; and

(iii) if the person is not to be liberated, the date on which he is to be taken to court and the court to which he is to be taken;".

12. Section 20(2) (record where accused does not emit declaration) shall cease to have effect.

13. In section 20B(9) (service of transcript of record of proceedings at examination)—

(a) for the words from "may", where it first occurs, to "service", where it first occurs, there shall be substituted "shall be served in such manner as may be prescribed by Act of Adjournal"; and

(b) for the words from "a post" to "letter" there shall be substituted "the relevant post office receipt".

14. In each of sections 23 and 329 (remand and committal of persons under 21)—

(a) in paragraph (a) of subsection (1), for the words from "commit" to the end there shall be substituted ", instead of committing him to prison, commit him to the local authority in whose area the court is situated to be detained—

(i) where the court so requires, in secure accommodation within the meaning of the Social Work (Scotland) Act 1968; and

(ii) in any other case, in a suitable place of safety chosen by the authority;"; and

(b) in subsection (4), for the words from "and" in the second place where it occurs to the end there shall be substituted "to be detained—

(a) where the court so requires, in secure accommodation within the meaning of the Social Work (Scotland) Act 1968; and

(b) in any other case, in a suitable place of safety chosen by the authority.".

15. In section 26 (bail before committal)—

(a) in subsection (2), for the words from "immediately" to "or" there shall be substituted ", on any occasion on which he is brought before the sheriff prior to his committal until liberated in due course of law, to apply"; and

(b) in subsection (3), the words "or justice" shall cease to have effect.

16. In section 31 (appeal in respect of bail), after subsection (4) there shall be inserted the following subsection—

"(4A) Where an applicant in an appeal under this section is under 21 years of age, section 23 of this Act shall apply to the High Court or, as the case may be, the Lord Commissioner of Justiciary when disposing of the appeal as it applies to a court when remanding or committing a person of the applicant's age for trial or sentence.".

17. In section 33 (liberation of applicant when appeal by public prosecutor)—

(a) in subsection (1), the words from ", or where" to "ninety-six hours,"; and

(b) in subsection (2), the words "by telegraph",

shall cease to have effect.

18. For section 42 (procedure on resignation, death or removal of Lord Advocate) there shall be substituted the following section—

"Resignation, death or demission of office of Lord Advocate

42.—(1) All indictments which have been raised by a Lord Advocate shall remain effective notwithstanding his subsequently having died or demitted office and may be taken up and proceeded with by his successor.

(2) During any period when the office of Lord Advocate is vacant it shall be lawful to indict accused persons in the name of the Solicitor General then in office.

(3) The advocates depute shall not demit office when a Lord Advocate dies or demits office but shall continue in office until their successors receive commissions.

(4) The advocates depute and procurators fiscal shall have power, notwithstanding any vacancy in the office of Lord Advocate, to take up and proceed with any indictment which—

(a) by virtue of subsection (1) above, remains effective; or

(b) by virtue of subsection (2) above, is in the name of the Solicitor General.

(5) For the purposes of this Act, where, but for this subsection, demission of office by one Law Officer would result in the offices of both being vacant, he or, where both demit office on the same day, the person demitting the office of Lord Advocate shall be deemed to continue in office until the warrant of appointment of the person succeeding to the office of Lord Advocate is granted.

(6) The Lord Advocate shall enter upon the duties of his office immediately upon the grant of his warrant of appointment; and he shall as soon as is practicable thereafter take the oaths of office before any Secretary of State or any Lord Commissioner of Justiciary.".

19. After section 48 there shall be inserted the following sections—

"Common law and statutory offences in same indictment

48A. It shall be competent to include in one indictment both common law and statutory charges.

Description of offence in words of statute or order

48B. In an indictment the description of any offence in the words of the statute or order contravened, or in similar words, shall be sufficient.".

20. In section 50 (latitude as to time and place), after subsection (3) there shall be inserted the following subsection—

"(4) Notwithstanding subsection (3) above, nothing in any rule of law shall prohibit the amendment of an indictment to include a time outwith the exceptional latitude if it appears to the court that the amendment would not prejudice the accused.".

21. In section 54 ("money" to include coin, bank notes and post office orders), for the words from "all" to the end there shall be substituted "cheques, banknotes, postal orders, money orders and foreign currency".

22. In subsection (2) of section 58 (authentication of deletion or correction on service copy of indictment etc.), for the word "or" in the fourth place where it occurs there shall be substituted—

"shall be sufficiently authenticated by the initials of any procurator fiscal or of the person serving the same.

(3) Any deletion or correction made".

23. After section 60 there shall be inserted the following section—

"Proceedings under the Merchant Shipping Acts

60A. In any proceedings under the Merchant Shipping Acts it shall not be necessary to produce the official register of the ship referred to in the proceedings in order to prove the nationality of the ship, but the nationality of the ship as stated in the indictment shall, in the absence of evidence to the contrary, be presumed.".

24. Sections 62 and 313 (mode of charging certain offences committed against two or more children under 17) shall cease to have effect.

25. In section 68 (notice of previous convictions), in each of subsections (2) and (4), the words "of Form No. 1 of Schedule 7 to the Criminal Justice (Scotland) Act 1949 or in the form" shall cease to have effect.

26. In section 69 (warrants for citation)—
(a) the existing provision shall become subsection (1);
(b) in that subsection—
(i) after the words "accused persons" there shall be inserted ", witnesses or jurors";
(ii) the words from "and" in the third place where it occurs to "Act" in the fourth place where it occurs shall cease to have effect; and
(iii) the words from "The executions" to the end shall cease to have effect; and
(c) after that subsection there shall be inserted—

"(2) A witness may be cited by sending the citation to the witness by ordinary or registered post or by the recorded delivery service and a written execution in the form prescribed by Act of Adjournal or as nearly as may be in such form, purporting to be signed by the person who served such citation together with, where appropriate, the relevant post office receipt shall be sufficient evidence of such citation.".

27. In section 72 (citation of jurors and witnesses)—
(a) the existing provision shall become subsection (1);
(b) in that subsection, after the word "shall" in the second place where it occurs there shall be inserted ", subject to subsection (2) below,"; and
(c) after that subsection there shall be inserted the following subsection—

"(2) A court shall not issue a warrant to apprehend a witness who fails to appear at a diet to which he has been duly cited unless the court is satisfied that the witness received the citation or that its contents came to his knowledge.".

28. In section 73(1) (execution of citation of indictment), the words from ", unless" to the end shall cease to have effect.

29. In section 77 (alteration of trial diet), for paragraphs (a) and (b) there shall be substituted the words "two months".

30. In section 78(1) (lodging of record copy of indictment and list of witnesses) for the words from "record" to the end there shall be substituted "prosecutor shall on or before the date of service of the indictment lodge the record copy of the indictment with the clerk of court before which the trial is to take place, together with a copy of the list of witnesses and a copy of the list of productions.".

31. In section 79(1) (description of witnesses), for the words from ", with" to the end there shall be substituted "together with an address at which they can be contacted for the purposes of precognition.".

32. In section 80(1) (objection to witnesses), after the word "accused" there shall be inserted ", where the case is to be tried in the sheriff court, at or before the first diet and, where the case is to be tried in the High Court,".

33. In section 81 (examination by prosecutor of witnesses, etc. not included in lists lodged) after the word "address" there shall be inserted "as mentioned in section 79(1) above,".

34. In section 82 (notice of special defence, incrimination etc.)—
(a) in subsection (1)—
      (i) in paragraph (a), after the word "lodged" there shall be inserted ", where the case is to be tried in the sheriff court, at or before the first diet and, where the case is to be tried in the High Court,"; and
      (ii) for paragraph (b) there shall be substituted—
        "(b) the court, on cause shown, otherwise directs."; and
(b) in subsection (2), for the words from "written notice" to "the court" there shall be substituted—
      "(a) written notice of the names and addresses of such witnesses and of such productions shall have been given—
        (i) where the case is to be tried in the sheriff court, to the procurator fiscal of the district of the trial diet at or before the first diet; and
        (ii) where the case is to be tried in the High Court, to the Crown Agent at least ten clear days before the day on which the jury is sworn; or
      (b) the court, on cause shown, otherwise directs, in which case it".

35. For section 85 (45 jurors to be returned for trials), there shall be substituted the following section—

"Number of jurors to be returned for trial
85. For the purposes of a trial, the sheriff principal shall return such number of jurors as he thinks fit or, in relation to a trial in the High Court, such other number as the Lord Justice Clerk or any Lord Commissioner of Justiciary may direct.".

36. In section 93 (names of jurors to be inserted in one roll), for the word "designations" there shall be substituted "addresses".

37. In section 100 (no exemptions by sex or marriage from liability to serve as juror), in subsection (1) the words from "but" to the end of the subsection, and subsections (2) and (3), shall cease to have effect.

38. In section 103(1) (pleas of guilty), after the word "he" where it first occurs there shall be inserted "shall do so in open court and".

39. In section 108 (certain objections competent only at preliminary diet)—
(a) in subsection (1), after the word "section" there shall be inserted "75A(2) or"; and
(b) in subsection (2), after the word "section" in the second place where it occurs there shall be inserted "75A(2) or".

40. Section 110 (where sentence delayed, original warrant of commitment stands) shall cease to have effect.

41. After section 114 there shall be inserted the following section—

"Transfer of sheriff court solemn proceedings
114A.—(1) Where an accused person has been cited to attend a sitting of the sheriff court the prosecutor may, at any time before the commencement of his trial, apply to the sheriff to transfer the case to a sheriff court in any other district in that sheriffdom.
(2) On an application under subsection (1) above the sheriff may—
(a) after giving the accused or his counsel or solicitor an opportunity to be heard; or
(b) on the joint application of the parties,
make an order for the transfer of the case.".

42. In section 124 (plea of guilty at trial diet), the proviso shall cease to have effect.

43. For section 125 (on plea of not guilty, jury to be balloted and sworn) there shall be substituted the following section—

"On plea of not guilty, plea to be recorded and jury balloted
125. Where the accused pleads not guilty, the clerk of court shall record that fact and proceed to ballot the jury."

44. In section 127 (procedure where trial does not take place)—
(a) in subsection (1), for the words "date of such trial diet" there shall be substituted "last day of the sitting in which the trial diet was to be held";
(b) after subsection (1) there shall be inserted the following subsection—
      "(1ZA) Without prejudice to subsection (1) above, where a trial diet has been deserted pro loco et tempore and the court has appointed a further trial diet to be held on a subsequent date at the same sitting the accused shall require to appear and answer the indictment at that further diet.";
(c) in subsection (2), the words "Schedule N to the Criminal Procedure (Scotland) Act 1887 or in" shall cease to have effect; and
(d) after subsection (4) there shall be inserted the following subsection—
      "(5) The warrant issued under section 69 of this Act shall be sufficient warrant for the citation of the accused and witnesses to any further diet appointed under this section.".

45. In section 129 (procedure for selection of jurors), for the words from "which" to the end there shall be substituted "in such manner as shall be prescribed by Act of Adjournal, and the persons so chosen shall be the jury to try the accused, and their names shall be recorded in the minutes of the proceedings.".

46. Section 132(2) (procedure in High Court trials where jurors chosen for one trial may continue to serve) shall cease to have effect.

47. In section 134 (provision for death or illness of jurors)—

(a) for the words "any juror is, through illness or for any other reason, unfit" there shall be substituted "it is for any reason inappropriate for any juror"; and

(b) for the words "or on behalf of the Lord Advocate" there shall be substituted "the prosecutor".

48. In section 135 (clerk to state charge and swear jury)—

(a) the existing provision shall become subsection (1);

(b) in subsection (1), for the words from "it", where it first occurs, to the end there shall be substituted "copies of the indictment shall be provided for each member of the jury without lists of witnesses or productions"; and

(c) at the end of subsection (1) there shall be inserted the following subsections—

"(2) Subject to subsection (3) below, where the accused has lodged a plea of special defence, the clerk of court shall, after informing the jury, in accordance with subsection (1) above, of the charge against the accused, and before administering the oath, read to the jury the plea of special defence.

(3) Where the presiding judge on cause shown so directs, the plea of special defence shall not be read over to the jury in accordance with subsection (2) above; and in any such case the judge shall inform the jury of the lodging of the plea and of the general nature of the special defence.

(4) Copies of a plea of special defence shall be provided for each member of the jury.".

49. In section 140A(1)(b) (no case to answer), the words "were the offence charged the only offence so charged" shall cease to have effect.

50. For section 142 (evidence of the accused) there shall be substituted the following section—

"142. Where, in any trial, the accused is to be called as a witness he shall be so called as the first witness for the defence unless the court, on cause shown, otherwise directs.".

51. Section 144 (notice of spouse as witness) shall cease to have effect.

52. Section 145(4) (interruption of trial) shall cease to have effect.

53. Section 146 (sheriff's notes of evidence) shall cease to have effect.

54. In each of sections 148 and 340 (examination of witnesses)—

(a) the existing provision shall become subsection (1); and

(b) after that subsection there shall be inserted the following subsections—

"(2) The judge may, on the motion of either party, on cause shown order that the examination of a witness for that party ("the first witness") shall be interrupted to permit the examination of another witness for that party.

(3) Where the judge makes an order under subsection (2) above he shall, after the examination of the other witness, permit the recall of the first witness.".

55. In section 150 (admissions and agreements as to evidence in solemn proceedings)—

(a) in subsection (1), the words ", where the accused is legally represented," shall cease to have effect; and

(b) in subsection (2), for paragraphs (a) and (b) there shall be substituted the following paragraphs—

"(a) in the case of an admission, by the party making the admission or, if that party is the accused and he is legally represented, his counsel or solicitor; and

(b) in the case of an agreement, by the prosecutor and by the accused or, if he is legally represented, his counsel or solicitor".

56. In section 151(2) (application to have all or part of record of proceedings at judicial examination withheld from jury)—

(a) after the words "competent for" there shall be inserted "the prosecutor or"; and

(b) for the words "the defence and for the prosecutor" there shall be substituted "either party".

57. In section 153 (seclusion of jury, etc, after retiral)—

(a) subsection (1) shall cease to have effect; and

(b) in subsection (3)(b)(ii), the words from "(as" to the end shall cease to have effect.

58. In section 156 (interruption of trial to give direction to jury in preceding trial)—

(a) in subsection (1)(b), the words from ", as" to the end; and

(b) subsections (4) and (5),

shall cease to have effect.

59. In section 157 (interruption of trial for plea or sentence in another cause)—
(a) in subsection (1) the words "through his counsel", "in which the panel has pleaded guilty under section 102 of this Act" and "(other than a trial for murder)"; and
(b) subsection (2),
shall cease to have effect.

60. Section 159(1) (previous convictions libelled as aggravations) and (3) (passing of sentence on second or subsequent conviction) and section 356(1) and (3) (equivalent provisions in relation to summary procedure) shall cease to have effect.

61. Section 160(3) (verdict as to whether previous convictions proved) shall cease to have effect.

62. In section 162(3) proof of convictions), for the words "An official" there shall be substituted "A prison officer".

63. Section 163 (extract conviction to be issued by clerk having record copy of indictment) shall cease to have effect.

64. In each of sections 166 and 362 (power to clear court while child giving evidence), in subsection (1) for the words from "members" to the end there shall be substituted—
"(a) members or officers of the court
(b) parties to the case before the court, their counsel or solicitors or persons otherwise directly concerned in the case;
(c) bona fide representatives of news gathering or reporting organisations present for the purpose of the preparation of contemporaneous reports of the proceedings; or
(d) such other persons as the court may specify authorise to be present,
shall be excluded from the court during the taking of the evidence of that witness.".

65. In section 174 (insanity in bar of trial or as ground of acquittal)—
(a) in subsection (2)—
(i) for the words "as aforesaid" in the first place where they occur there shall be substituted "on indictment with the commission of the offence"; and
(ii) after the word "and" in the second place where it occurs there shall be inserted ", if so,"; and
(b) subsections (3) and (4) shall cease to have effect.

66. In section 176 (requirements as to medical evidence)—
(a) in subsection (1), after the word "sections" there shall be inserted "174(1),";
(b) in subsection (2), for the word "section" where it first occurs there shall be substituted "sections 174(1) and"; and
(c) in subsection (4), after the word "hospital" there shall be inserted "or, as respects a report for the purposes of section 174(1), remanded in custody".

67. In section 178(3) (restriction orders), for the words "section 60(4)" there shall be substituted "section 60(3)".

68. In each of sections 179(1) and 380(1) (power of court to adjourn case before sentence)—
(a) for the words "so adjourns the case" there shall be substituted "adjourns the case solely for that purpose"; and
(b) after the words "shall not" there shall be inserted "solely".

69. After section 182 there shall be inserted the following—

"Caution

Caution
182A. Where a person is convicted of an offence (other than an offence the sentence for which is fixed by law) the court may, instead of or in addition to imposing a fine or a period of imprisonment, ordain the accused to find caution for good behaviour for a period not exceeding 12 months and to such amount as the court considers appropriate.".

70. In subsection (7) of each of sections 183 and 384 (notification of probation order)—
(a) after the word "shall" there shall be inserted "(a)";
(b) the words ", to the probationer," shall cease to have effect; and
(c) at the end there shall be inserted—
"; and
(b) cause a copy thereof to be given to the probationer or sent to him by registered post or by the recorded delivery service; and an acknowledgement or certificate of delivery of a letter containing such copy order issued by the Post Office shall be sufficient evidence of the delivery of the letter on the day specified in such acknowledgement or certificate.".

71. In each of sections 186(1) and 387(1) (failure to comply with requirement of probation order), the words "on oath" shall cease to have effect.

72. Sections 190 and 391 (supplementary provisions as to probation: security for good behaviour) shall cease to have effect.

73. In section 191(4) (effect of probation and absolute discharge) the words "placed on probation or" and "probation order or" shall cease to have effect.

74. In each of sections 192 and 393 (probation reports), the words from "(other than" to "Act)" and the proviso shall cease to have effect.

75. In each of sections 196(1) and 402 (fines, etc. may be enforced in another district), the proviso shall cease to have effect.

76. Sections 225 (interlocutors to be signed by clerk), 226 (record copies to be inserted in books of adjournal of High Court) and 227 (indictment to be inserted in record book in sheriff court) shall cease to have effect.

77. In section 235 (applications in connection with appeals may be made orally or in writing), the words from "but in regard" to the end shall cease to have effect.

78. In section 236A(3) (judge's report), for the words "and the parties" there shall be substituted ", the parties and, on such conditions as may be prescribed by Act of Adjournal, such other persons or classes of persons as may be so prescribed".

79. Section 236C (signing of appeal documents) shall cease to have effect.

80. Section 237 (note of proceedings) shall cease to have effect.

81. In section 238 (bail pending appeal), in subsection (2), the words "or of any application for leave to appeal" and, in paragraphs (a)(i) and (b)(i), the words "or application" shall cease to have effect.

82. In section 239 (clerk to give notice of date of hearing)—

(a) in subsection (1), the words from "and" in the second place where it occurs to the end; and

(b) subsection (2),

shall cease to have effect.

83. In section 240 (appellant may be present at hearing), the words from "except" where it first occurs to the end shall cease to have effect.

84. Section 246 (sittings of the High Court to be arranged by Lord Justice General) shall cease to have effect.

85. In section 254 (disposal of appeals)—

(a) in subsection (4)(b), for the words "and ordering" to the end there shall be substituted "and—

(i) making, in respect of the appellant, any order mentioned in section 174ZC(2) (a) to (d) of this Act; or

(ii) making no order."; and

(b) for subsection (5) there shall be substituted the following subsection—

"(5) Subsections (3) and (4) of section 174ZC of this Act shall apply to an order made under subsection (4)(b)(i) above as they apply to an order made under subsection (2) of that section.".

86. After section 254A there shall be inserted the following section—

"Convictions not to be quashed on certain grounds

254B. No conviction, sentence, judgment, order of court or other proceeding whatsoever in or for the purposes of solemn proceedings under this Act—

(a) shall be quashed for want of form; or

(b) where the accused had legal assistance in his defence shall be suspended or set aside in respect of any objections to—

(i) the relevancy of the indictment, or the want of specification therein; or

(ii) the competency or admission or rejection of evidence at the trial in the inferior court, unless such objections were timeously stated.".

87. Section 256 (summary dismissal of frivolous or vexatious appeals) shall cease to have effect.

88. In section 257 (failure to appear at hearing), for the words from the beginning to "where" in the second place where it occurs there shall be substituted—

"Where—

(a) intimation of the diet appointed for the hearing of an appeal has been made to the appellant;

(b) no appearance is made by or on behalf of the appellant at the diet; and

(c)".

89. Section 259 (continuation of hearing) shall cease to have effect.

90. In section 263 (prerogative of mercy), after subsection (2) there shall be inserted the following subsection—

"(3) This section shall apply in relation to a finding under section 174ZA(2) and an order under section 174ZC(2) of this Act as it applies, respectively, in relation to a conviction and a sentence.".

91. In section 263A (power of Lord Advocate to refer point of law for opinion of High Court)—

(a) in subsection (1), after the word "acquitted" there shall be inserted "or convicted"; and

(b) in subsection (5), after the word "acquittal" there shall be inserted "or, as the case may be, conviction".

92. In section 264 (disqualification, forfeiture etc.)—

(a) in each of subsections (1) and (2), after the words "section 228(1)(b)" there shall be inserted ", (bb), (bc) or (bd)"; and

(b) after subsection (3) there shall be inserted the following subsection—

"(4) Where, upon conviction, a fine has been imposed on a person or a compensation order has been made against him under section 58 of the Criminal Justice (Scotland) Act 1980, then, for a period of four weeks from the date of the verdict against such person or, in the event of an intimation of intention to appeal (or in the case of an appeal under section 228(1)(b), (bb), (bc) or (bd) or 228A of this Act a note of appeal) being lodged under this Part of this Act, until such appeal, if it is proceeded with, is determined,—

(a) the fine or compensation order shall not be enforced against that person and he shall not be liable to make any payment in respect of the fine or compensation order; and

(b) any money paid by that person under the compensation order shall not be paid by the clerk of court to the person entitled to it under section 60(1) of the Act of 1980.".

93. In section 265 (fines and caution)—

(a) in subsection (1), for the word "thereto" there shall be substituted "to the conviction or sentence"; and

(b) subsections (3) and (5) shall cease to have effect.

94. In section 268 (reckoning of time spent on bail pending appeal), in subsection (4)—

(a) after the word "safety" in the first place where it occurs there shall be inserted "or, as respects a child sentenced to be detained under section 206 of this Act, the place directed by the Secretary of State"; and

(b) after the word "safety" in the second place where it occurs there shall be inserted "or, as respects such a child, place directed by the Secretary of State".

95. In section 269 (extract convictions), after the words "section 228(1)(b)" there shall be inserted ", (bb), (bc), or (bd)".

96. In section 270 (release of documents, productions etc. after trial), the following provisions shall cease to have effect—

(a) in subsection (2), the words from "(or any" to "note of appeal)" where first occurring and from "(or in the case" to "note of appeal)" where second occurring;

(b) in subsection (3), the words from "(or in the case" to "note of appeal)"; and

(c) in subsection (4), the words from "(or in the case" to "note of appeal)".

97. Sections 272 (note to be kept of appeal) and 273 (register of appeals) shall cease to have effect.

98. In section 274(5)(e) (record of proceedings at trial), for the words "summing up by the judge" there shall be substituted "judge's charge to the jury".

99. Section 276 (declaration administered to shorthand writer) shall cease to have effect.

100. In section 277(2) (non-compliance with certain provisions may be waived), the words "section 236C", "section 237", "section 246", "section 259", "section 272" and "section 273" shall cease to have effect.

101. Section 282 (power to make Acts of Adjournal: solemn procedure) shall cease to have effect.

102. For subsection (1) of section 283 (application of Part II of that Act) there shall be substituted the following subsections—

"(1) This Part of this Act applies to summary proceedings in respect of any offence which might prior to the passing of this Act, or which may under the provisions of this or any Act, whether passed before or after this Act, be tried summarily.

(1A) Without prejudice to subsection (1) above, this Part of this Act also applies to procedure in all courts of summary jurisdiction in so far as they have jurisdiction in respect of—

(a) any offence or the recovery of a penalty under any enactment or rule of law which does not exclude summary procedure as well as, in accordance with section 196 of this Act, to the enforcement of a fine imposed in solemn proceedings; and

(b) any order ad factum praestandum, or other order of court or warrant competent to a court of summary jurisdiction.".

103. Section 289D(1A)(d) (power to alter sums specified in section 435(e) of that Act) shall cease to have effect.

104. In section 296 (police liberation or detention of children arrested), in subsections (1) and (2), the words "sitting summarily" in each place where they occur shall cease to have effect.

105. In section 300 (appeal in respect of bail)—

(a) after subsection (3) there shall be inserted the following subsection—

"(3A) Where an applicant in an appeal under this section is under 21 years of age, section 329 of this Act shall apply to the High Court or, as the case may be, the Lord Commissioner of Justiciary when disposing of the appeal as it applies to a court when remanding or committing a person of the applicant's age for trial or sentence."; and

(b) in subsection (4)—

    (i) the words from ", or where" to "96 hours" shall cease to have effect; and

    (ii) for the word "periods" there shall be substituted "period".

106. For section 305 (intimation to a solicitor) there shall be substituted the following section—

"Right of accused to have access to solicitor

305.—(1) Where any person has been arrested on any criminal charge, such person shall be entitled immediately upon such arrest—

(a) to have intimation sent to a solicitor that his professional assistance is required by such a person and informing him—

    (i) of the place where the person is being detained;

    (ii) whether the person is to be liberated; and

    (iii) if the person is not to be liberated, the date on which he is to be taken to court and the court to which he is to be taken;

(b) to be told what rights there are under paragraph (a) above and subsections (2) and (3) below.

(2) Such solicitor shall be entitled to have a private interview with the person accused before he is examined on declaration, and to be present at such examination.

(3) It shall be in the power of the sheriff or justice to delay such examination for a period not exceeding 48 hours from and after the time of such person's arrest, in order to allow time for the attendance of such solicitor.".

107. In section 309(1) (forms of procedure in summary proceedings), the words "Schedule 2 to the Summary Jurisdiction (Scotland) Act 1954 or in" shall cease to have effect.

108. In section 310 (incidental applications)—

(a) the words "Part I of Schedule 2 to the Summary Jurisdiction (Scotland) Act 1954 or in" shall cease to have effect; and

(b) after the word "open" there shall be inserted "shut and".

109. In section 311 (complaint)—

(a) in subsection (1), the words from "in" where it first occurs to the end shall cease to have effect; and

(b) subsections (4) and (5) shall cease to have effect.

110. In section 312 (form of charge in complaint)—

(a) in paragraph (f), at the end there shall be inserted the words "provided also that nothing in the foregoing provisions of this paragraph or in any rule of law shall prohibit the amendment of a complaint to include a time outwith the exceptional latitude if it appears to the court that the amendment would not prejudice the accused;"; and

(b) in paragraph (j), for the words from "all" to the end there shall be substituted "cheques, banknotes, postal orders, money orders and foreign currency;".

111. In section 314 (orders of court on complaint)—

(a) in subsection (1)(d), the words "or interim order" shall cease to have effect; and

(b) after subsection (4) there shall be inserted the following subsection—

"(4A) Where all the parties join in an application under subsection (4) above, the court may proceed under that subsection without hearing the parties.".

112. In section 315(2) (citation), the words "Part IV of Schedule 2 to the Summary Jurisdiction (Scotland) Act 1954 or in" shall cease to have effect.

113. In section 316(3) (manner of citation of accused)—

(a) after the word "accused" in the first place where it occurs there shall be inserted "or a witness";

(b) after the words "prosecutor and" there shall be inserted—

"(a) in the case of the accused,";

(c) after the word "service" there shall be inserted—

"; and

(b) in the case of a witness, sent by ordinary post,"; and

(d) after the word "accused" in the second place where it occurs there shall be inserted "or witness".

114. In section 318(2) (citation of offender) the words "Part IV of Schedule 2 to the Summary Jurisdiction (Scotland) Act 1954 and the corresponding forms contained in" shall cease to have effect.

115. In section 319(1) (citation by post), the words "other than a witness" shall cease to have effect.

116. In section 320 (apprehension of witness), after the word "may" where it first occurs there shall be inserted ", if it is satisfied that he received the citation or that its contents came to his knowledge,".

117. In section 321 (warrants of apprehension and search)—
(a) in subsection (1), the words "Part IV of Schedule 2 to the Summary Jurisdiction (Scotland) Act 1954 or in" shall cease to have effect;
(b) in subsection (3), the words "either by way of trial or by way of remit to another court" shall cease to have effect;
(c) in subsection (5), for the words from "the date" to the end there shall be substituted—
    "(a) the date fixed for the hearing of the case; or
       (b) the date when security to the amount fixed under subsection (6) below is found,
    whichever is the earlier."; and
(d) after subsection (5), there shall be inserted the following subsection—
    "(6) A witness apprehended under a warrant under section 320 of this Act shall, wherever practicable, be brought immediately by the officer of law who executed that warrant before a justice, who shall fix such sum as he considers appropriate as security for the appearance of the witness at all diets.".

118. In section 335(1) (amendment of complaint), the words "penalty or" shall cease to have effect.

119. Section 336 (record of plea of guilty) shall cease to have effect.

120. In section 338(1) (failure of accused to appear), after the word "cited" where it first occurs there shall be inserted "(other than a diet which, by virtue of section 337A(3) of this Act, he is not required to attend)".

121. In section 339 (alibi), for the words "prior to the examination of the first witness for the prosecution" there shall be substituted "at any time before the first witness is sworn".

122. In section 344(1) (punishment of witness for contempt), the words "or to produce documents in his possession when required by the court," shall cease to have effect.

123. Section 345 (administration of oath to same witness in case at same diet) shall cease to have effect.

124. For section 347 (evidence of the accused) there shall be substituted the following section—

"**Evidence of the accused**
347. Where, in any trial, the accused is to be called as a witness he shall be so called as the first witness for the defence unless the court, on cause shown, otherwise directs.".

125. In section 352(2) (application to have all or part of record of proceedings at judicial examination not admitted as evidence)—
(a) after the words "competent for" there shall be inserted "the prosecutor or"; and
(b) for the words "the defence and for the prosecutor" there shall be substituted "either party".

126. In section 354(1) (admissions and agreements as to evidence in summary proceedings), the proviso shall cease to have effect.

127. In section 357 (proof of convictions)—
(a) in subsection (1)(a), the words "Form No. 2 or 3 of Part III of Schedule 2 to the Summary Jurisdiction (Scotland) Act 1954 or of" shall cease to have effect;
(b) in subsection (2)—
      (i) for the words "An official" there shall be substituted "A prison officer"; and
      (ii) for the word "official" in the second place where it occurs there shall be substituted "prison officer"; and
(c) subsection (4) shall cease to have effect.

128. In section 359 (record of summary proceedings), after the words "than the complaint" there shall be inserted ", or a copy of the complaint certified as true by a procurator fiscal".

129. Section 360 (proceedings written or printed) shall cease to have effect.

130. In section 360A (interruption of summary proceedings for verdict in earlier trial)—
(a) in subsection (1)(b), the words from "as" to the end of the paragraph; and
(b) subsection (2),
shall cease to have effect.

131. In section 366 (procedure where sheriff sits summarily in respect of offence by child)—
(a) in subsection (1)(c), for the words "newspapers or news agencies" there shall be substituted "news gathering or reporting organisations present for the purpose of contemporaneous reports of the proceedings"; and
(b) subsection (2) shall cease to have effect.

132. In section 375(3) (insanity in bar of trial), for the word "called" there shall be substituted "sworn".

133. In section 376 (power of court to order hospital admission or guardianship)—

(a) subsection (2) shall cease to have effect; and

(b) in subsection (3), for the words "as aforesaid" there shall be substituted "summarily in the sheriff court with an act or omission constituting an offence".

134. In section 377 (requirements as to medical evidence)—

(a) in subsection (1), after the word "sections" there shall be inserted "375(2),";

(b) in subsection (2), for the word "section" in the first place where it occurs there shall be substituted "sections 375(2) and"; and

(c) in subsection (4), after the word "hospital" there shall be inserted "or, as respects a report for the purposes of section 375(2), remanded in custody".

135. In section 379(3) (restriction orders), for the words "section 62(1)" there shall be substituted "section 60(3)".

136. In section 392 (effects of probation and absolute discharge on right to appeal)—

(a) in subsection (4), the words "placed on probation or" shall cease to have effect; and

(b) in subsection (5), the words "placed on probation or" and "probation order or" shall cease to have effect.

137. In section 396(7) (time for payment of fine), the words ", subject to any rules under this Part of this Act" shall cease to have effect.

138. In section 398(1) (restriction on imprisonment after fine or caution)—

(a) after the word "fine" in the second place where it occurs there shall be inserted "or, as the case may be, to find caution"; and

(b) after the word "paid" there shall be inserted "or, as the case may be, caution has not been found".

139. In section 406 (substitution of custody for imprisonment where a child defaults on fine), the words "damages or expenses," shall cease to have effect.

140. In section 408 (discharge from imprisonment to be specified), for the words "for payment of a fine or for finding of" there shall be substituted "in default of payment of a fine or on failure to find".

141. In section 413(1) (detention of children in residential care)—

(a) after the word "authority" in the first place where it occurs there shall be inserted "for such period not exceeding one year as may be specified in the order"; and

(b) the words from "and shall" to the end shall cease to have effect.

142. In section 430 (consecutive sentences)—

(a) in subsection (1), the words "Part V of Schedule 2 to the Summary Jurisdiction (Scotland) Act 1954 or in" shall cease to have effect; and

(b) for subsection (4) there shall be substituted the following subsection—

"(4) A court of summary jurisdiction may frame—

(a) a sentence following on conviction; or

(b) an order for committal in default of payment of any sum of money or for contempt of court,

so as to take effect on the expiry of any previous sentence or order which, at the date of the later conviction or order, the accused is undergoing.".

143. In section 432(1) (deferred sentence), the words from "and", where it second occurs, to the end shall cease to have effect.

144. Section 435 (expenses) shall cease to have effect.

145. In section 440 (extract sufficient warrant for imprisonment), the words "Part V of Schedule 2 to the Summary Jurisdiction (Scotland) Act 1954 or in" shall cease to have effect.

146. In section 441 (provision for court comprising more than one judge), the words from ", although" to "place," shall cease to have effect.

147. In section 443A (disqualification, forfeiture etc.), after subsection (2) there shall be inserted the following subsection—

"(3) Where, upon conviction, a fine has been imposed upon a person or a compensation order has been made against him under section 58 of the Criminal Justice (Scotland) Act 1980—

(a) the fine or compensation order shall not be enforced against him and he shall not be liable to make any payment in respect of the fine or compensation order; and

(b) any money paid under the compensation order shall not be paid by the clerk of court to the entitled person under section 60(1) of the Act of 1980,

pending the determination of any appeal against conviction or sentence (or disposal or order).".

148. In section 444(1)(b) (contents of application for stated case), for the words "a statement of that fact" there shall be substituted "the ground of appeal against that sentence or disposal or order".

149. In section 446 (procedure in relation to appeal by stated case where appellant in custody)—

(a) in subsection (4), at the end there shall be inserted the words "or, on the application of the appellant, such earlier date as the court thinks fit, not being a date later than the date of expiry of any term or terms of imprisonment imposed subsequently to the conviction appealed against";

(b) in subsection (5)—

(i) after the words "person is" there shall be inserted "in custody or"; and

(ii) for the words "the term" there shall be substituted "any term"; and

(c) after subsection (5) there shall be inserted the following subsection—

"(6) The court shall not make an order under subsection (5) above to the effect that the sentence or, as the case may be, unexpired portion of the sentence shall run other than concurrently with the subsequently imposed term of imprisonment without first notifying the appellant of its intention to do so and considering any representations made by him or on his behalf.".

150. In section 451(3) (computation of time) after the words "442(1)(a)(i)" there shall be inserted "or (in so far as it is against conviction) (iii)".

151.—(1) Section 453 (prosecutor's consent to or application for setting aside of conviction) shall be amended as follows.

(2) In subsection (1)—

(a) at the beginning there shall be inserted "Without prejudice to section 442(1)(b) or (c) of this Act,";

(b) in paragraph (a)—

(i) for the words "442(1)(a)(i) or (iii)" there shall be substituted "442(1)(a)"; and

(ii) after the word "conviction" there shall be inserted "or sentence or, as the case may be, conviction and sentence ("sentence" being construed in this section as including disposal or order)"; and

(c) in paragraph (b)—

(i) after the word "founded" there shall be inserted "or the sentence imposed following such conviction"; and

(ii) after the word "conviction" in the second place where it occurs there shall be inserted "or sentence or, as the case may be, conviction and sentence".

(3) In subsection (4)—

(a) in paragraph (a)—

(i) after the word "conviction" where it first occurs, there shall be inserted "or the sentence, or both,";

(ii) the word "and" at the end of sub-paragraph (i) shall cease to have effect;

(iii) at the end of sub-paragraph (ii) there shall be inserted—

"; and

(iii) where the sentence is set aside, pass another (but not more severe) sentence;"; and

(b) in paragraph (b), after the word "conviction" there shall be inserted "or sentence, or, as the case may be conviction and sentence,".

152. In section 453B (appeals against sentence only), after subsection (4) there shall be inserted the following subsection—

"(4A) Subject to subsection (4) above, the report mentioned in subsection (3)(b) above shall be available only to the High Court, the parties and, on such conditions as may be prescribed by Act of Adjournal, such other persons or classes of persons as may be so prescribed.".

153. In section 453D (disposal of appeal where appellant insane)—

(a) in subsection (1)(b), for the words "and ordering" to the end there shall be substituted "and—

(i) making, in respect of the appellant, any order mentioned in section 375ZC(2)(a) to (d) of this Act; or

(ii) making no order."; and

(b) for subsection (2) there shall be substituted the following subsection—

"(2) Subsection (3) of section 375ZC of this Act shall apply to an order made under subsection (1)(b)(i) above as it applies to an order made under subsection (2) of that section."

154. In section 454(1) (convictions not to be quashed on certain grounds), the words "at the trial by the solicitor of the accused" shall cease to have effect.

155. Section 457 (power to make Acts of Adjournal: summary procedure) shall cease to have effect.

156. Before section 457A there shall be inserted the following section—

"**Acts of Adjournal**

457ZA.—(1) The High Court may by Act of Adjournal—

(a) regulate the practice and procedure in relation to criminal procedure; and

(b) make such rules and regulations as may be necessary or expedient to carry out the purposes and accomplish the objects of any enactment (including an enactment in this Act) in so far as it relates to criminal procedure,

provided that no rule, regulation or provision which affects the governor or any other officer of a prison shall be made by any such Act of Adjournal except with the consent of the Secretary of State.

(2) The High Court may by Act of Adjournal modify, amend or repeal any enactment (including an enactment in this Act) in so far as that enactment relates to matters with respect to which an Act of Adjournal may be made under subsection (1) above.".

157.—(1) Section 462 (interpretation) shall be amended as follows.

(2) In subsection (1)—

(a) at the appropriate places, there shall be inserted the following definitions—

" "examination of facts" means an examination of facts held under section 174ZA or 375ZA of this Act;";

" "governor" means, in relation to a contracted out prison within the meaning of section 106(4) of the Criminal Justice and Public Order Act 1994, the director of the prison;"; and

" "prison officer" and "officer of a prison" means, in relation to a contracted out prison within the meaning of section 106(4) of the Criminal Justice and Public Order Act 1994, a prisoner custody officer within the meaning of section 114(1) of that Act;"; and

(b) in the definition of "officer of law", after paragraph (ii) there shall be inserted the following paragraph—

"(iia) any person who is employed under section 9 of the Police (Scotland) Act 1967 for the assistance of the constables of a police force and who is authorised by the chief constable of that police force in relation to service and execution as mentioned above;"; and

(c) in the definition of "prosecutor", the words "private prosecutor," in the second place where they occur shall cease to have effect.

(3) In subsection (6), for the words "Great Britain" there shall be substituted "the United Kingdom".

(4) Subsection (10) shall cease to have effect.

158. In Schedule 5 (discharge and amendment of probation orders), in paragraph 4—

(a) after the word "practitioner" where it first occurs there shall be inserted "or chartered psychologist"; and

(b) after the word "practitioner" where it second occurs there shall be inserted "or psychologist".

The Sexual Offences (Scotland) Act 1976 (c. 67)

159. In section 4 of the Sexual Offences (Scotland) Act 1976 (unlawful sexual intercourse with girl between 13 and 16)—

(a) in the proviso to subsection (1), the words "on indictment" shall cease to have effect; and

(b) after subsection (2) there shall be inserted the following subsection—

"(3) For the purposes of the proviso to subsection (1) above, a prosecution shall be deemed to commence on the date on which a warrant to apprehend or to cite the accused is granted, if such warrant is executed without undue delay.".

The Community Service by Offenders (Scotland) Act 1978 (c. 49)

160. The Community Service by Offenders (Scotland) Act 1978 shall be amended as follows.

161. In section 2 (offender to be provided with copy order)—

(a) in subsection (3)(a), after the word "give" there shall be inserted ", or send by registered post or the recorded delivery service,"; and

(b) after subsection (3) there shall be inserted the following subsection—

"(4) Where a copy of a community service order has, under subsection (3)(a) above, been sent by registered post or by the recorded delivery service, an acknowledgement or certificate of delivery of a letter containing the copy order issued by the Post Office shall be sufficient evidence of the delivery of the letter on the day specified in such acknowledgement or certificate.".

162. In section 4(1) (failure to comply with requirements of community service orders), for the words "evidence on oath" there shall be substituted "information".

The Criminal Justice (Scotland) Act 1980 (c. 62)

163. In section 26(4) of the Criminal Justice (Scotland) Act 1980 (service of certificates, reports etc.)—
(a) for the words "either of those subsections" there shall be substituted "that subsection";
(b) for the words from "may", where it second occurs, to "service", where it first occurs, there shall be substituted "shall be served in such manner as may be prescribed by Act of Adjournal"; and
(c) for the words from "a post" to "letter" there shall be substituted "the relevant post office receipt".

The Mental Health (Scotland) Act 1984 (c. 36)

164. The Mental Health (Scotland) Act 1984 shall be amended as follows.
165. In section 67(1) (application of sections 63 to 66 to certain persons treated as restricted patients)—
(a) paragraph (a)(ii) and the preceding "or"; and
(b) the words from "or the order" to the end,
shall cease to have effect.
166. In section 69(3) (persons ordered to be kept in custody during Her Majesty's pleasure), for the words from "an order" to the end there shall be substituted "a hospital order together with a restriction order".
167. In section 71(7)(a) (removal to hospital of persons serving sentences of imprisonment etc.), for the words "or 255" there shall be substituted ", 174ZC, 254, 375, 375ZC or 453D".
168. In section 73(1) (transfer order to cease to have effect where proceedings dropped or case disposed of)—
(a) after the word "section" in the third place where it occurs there shall be inserted "174ZC"; and
(b) after "178," there shall be inserted "375ZC,".
169. In section 125(4) interpretation)—
(a) after "174," there shall be inserted "174ZC,"; and
(b) after "375," there shall be inserted "375ZC,".

The Criminal Justice (Scotland) Act 1987 (c. 41)

170. In section 60(3) of the Criminal Justice (Scotland) Act 1987 (service of documents relating to police interview)—
(a) for the words from "may" to "service", where it first occurs, there shall be substituted "shall be served in such manner as may be prescribed by Act of Adjournal"; and
(b) for the words from "a post" to "letter" there shall be substituted "the relevant post office receipt".

The Road Traffic Offenders Act 1988 (c. 53)

171. In section 19 of the Road Traffic Offenders Act 1988 (evidence of disqualification in Scotland)—
(a) the existing provision shall become subsection (1);
(b) in that subsection for the words "less than six days before his trial" there shall be substituted "more than seven days after the date of service of the copy"; and
(c) after that subsection there shall be inserted—
"(2) A copy of a conviction or extract conviction served on the accused under subsection (1) above shall be served in such manner as may be prescribed by Act of Adjournal, and a written execution purporting to be signed by the person who served such copy conviction or extract conviction together with, where appropriate, the relevant post office receipt shall be sufficient evidence of service of such a copy.".
172. In section 20 of that Act (admissibility of certain evidence regarding speeding offences etc.), after subsection (8) there shall be inserted the following subsection—
"(8A) As respects proceedings in Scotland, a copy of a document served on a person under subsection (8) above shall be served in such manner as may be prescribed by Act of Adjournal, and a written execution purporting to be signed by the person who served such copy document together with, where appropriate, the relevant post office receipt shall be sufficient evidence of service of such a copy.".
173. In sections 31(2) (court may take account of particulars endorsed on licence) and 32(6) (court may take account of extract from licensing records) of that Act—
(a) for the words "sections 311(5) and" there shall be substituted "section"; and
(b) the words "penalties and" shall cease to have effect.

The Law Reform (Miscellaneous Provisions) (Scotland) Act 1990 (c. 40)

174. The Law Reform (Miscellaneous Provisions) (Scotland) Act 1990 shall be amended as follows.

175. In section 56 (evidence of children through television link in criminal trials)—

(a) in subsection (1), after the word "been" there shall be inserted "or is likely to be"; and

(b) in subsection (2)—

    (i) the word "and" immediately following paragraph (a) shall cease to have effect; and

    (ii) after paragraph (b) there shall be inserted "; and

(c) the views of the child.".

176. In section 58 (prior identification of accused by child witness), the words "cited to give evidence in a trial" shall cease to have effect.

177. In Schedule 6 (supervised attendance orders)—

(a) in paragraph 2—

    (i) in sub-paragraph (3)(a), after the word "give" there shall be inserted ", or send by registered post or by the recorded delivery service,"; and

    (ii) after sub-paragraph (3) there shall be inserted the following sub-paragraph—

"(4) Where a copy of a supervised attendance order has, under sub-paragraph (3)(a) above, been sent by registered post or by the recorded delivery service, an acknowledgement or certificate of delivery of a letter containing the copy order issued by the Post Office shall be sufficient evidence of the delivery of the letter on the day specified in such acknowledgement or certificate."; and

(b) in paragraph 4(1) (failure to comply with supervised attendance orders), for the words "evidence on oath" there shall be substituted "information".

The Criminal Justice Act 1991 (c. 53)

178. In Schedule 3 to the Criminal Justice Act 1991 (reciprocal enforcement of certain orders), in paragraph 6(5)(a)(i), for the words "evidence on oath" there shall be substituted "information".

The Prisoners and Criminal Proceedings (Scotland) Act 1993 (c. 9)

179.—(1) The Prisoners and Criminal Proceedings (Scotland) Act 1993 shall be amended as follows.

(2) In section 11(3)(b) (duration of licence), for the words from "the" in the second place where it occurs to the end there shall be substituted—

"there has elapsed—

    (i) a period (reckoned from the date on which he was ordered to be returned to prison under or by virtue of subsection (2)(a) of that section) equal in length to the period between the date on which the new offence was committed and the date on which he would (but for his release) have served the original sentence in full; or

    (ii) subject to subsection (4) below, a total period equal in length to the period for which he was so ordered to be returned to prison together with, so far as not concurrent with that period, any term of imprisonment to which he was sentenced in respect of the new offence,

whichever results in the later date.

(4) In subsection (3)(b) above, "the original sentence" and "the new offence" have the same meanings as in section 16 of this Act.".

(3) For section 16(7) (application of early release provisions where further offence committed by released prisoner) there shall be substituted the following subsection—

"(7) Where an order under subsection (2) or (4) above is made in respect of a person released on licence—

(a) the making of the order shall have the effect of revoking the licence; and

(b) if the sentence comprising—

    (i) the period for which the person is ordered to be returned to prison; and

    (ii) so far as not concurrent with that period, any term of imprisonment to which he is sentenced in respect of the new offence,

is six months or more but less than four years, section 1(1) of this Act shall apply in respect of that sentence as if for the word "unconditionally" there were substituted the words "on licence".".

(4) In section 18(1) (breach of supervised release order), for the words from the beginning to "by" where it second occurs, there shall be substituted "Where it appears to the court which imposed a supervised release order on a person, on information from".

(5) In section 28(3) (destruction of prints and impressions), the words "or 384(1) (probation)" shall cease to have effect.

(6) In section 33 (evidence of children on commission)—

(a) in subsection (1), the words from the beginning to "and" where it first occurs shall cease to have effect; and

(b) after subsection (3) there shall be inserted the following subsection—

"(4) Subsections (2) to (4), (5A) and (6) of section 32 of the 1980 Act (evidence by letter of request or on commission) shall apply to an application under subsection (1) above and evidence taken by a commissioner appointed under that subsection as those subsections apply to an application under subsection (1) of that section and evidence taken by a commissioner appointed on such an application.".

(7) In section 34 (concealment by screen of accused from child giving evidence), after the word "been" there shall be inserted "or is likely to be".

(8) In Schedule 3 (documentary evidence in criminal proceedings), in paragraph 6(4), for the words "after the close of that party's evidence and" there shall be substituted "at any time".

PART II

AMENDMENTS RELATING TO PART II

The Trade Marks Act 1938 (c. 22)

180. In section 58B of the Trade Marks Act 1938 (delivery up of offending goods and material), in subsection (6) for the words "section 223 or 436 of the Criminal Procedure (Scotland) Act 1975" there shall be substituted the words "Chapter II of Part II of the Criminal Justice (Scotland) Act 1995".

The Criminal Procedure (Scotland) Act 1975 (c. 21)

181.—(1) The Criminal Procedure (Scotland) Act 1975 shall be amended as follows.

(2) Sections 223 and 436 (forfeiture of property) shall cease to have effect.

(3) In section 231 (intimation of intention of appeal)—

(a) in subsection (1) after "1987" there shall be inserted the words "and section 76(4) of the Criminal Justice (Scotland) Act 1995"; and

(b) in subsection (5) after "1987" there shall be inserted the words "and subsection (4) of section 76 of the said Act of 1995" and for the words "that section" there shall be substituted the words "the said section 2 or 76".

(4) In section 444 (manner and time of appeal), in subsection (1) at the beginning there shall be inserted the words "Subject to section 76(8) of the Criminal Justice (Scotland) Act 1995,".

The Community Service by Offenders (Scotland) Act 1978 (c. 49)

182. In section 1(7) of the Community Service by Offenders (Scotland) Act 1978 (making of community service orders not to restrict making of certain other orders), at the end there shall be added the following paragraph—

"(d) making a suspended forfeiture order under section 87 of the Criminal Justice (Scotland) Act 1995 in respect of the offence.".

The Civil Jurisdiction and Judgments Act 1982 (c. 27)

183. In subsection (4A) of section 18 of the Civil Jurisdiction and Judgments Act 1982 (enforcement of U.K. judgments in other parts of U.K.)—

(a) after the words "Court of Session" there shall be inserted the words "or by the sheriff"; and

(b) at the end there shall be added "or Part II of the Criminal Justice (Scotland) Act 1995".

The Telecommunications Act 1984 (c. 12)

184. In Schedule 3 to the Telecommunications Act 1984 (penalties and mode of trial under the Wireless Telegraphy Act 1949), in paragraph 3(b) for the words "sections 223 and 436 of the Criminal Procedure (Scotland) Act 1975" there shall be substituted the words "Chapter II of Part II of the Criminal Justice (Scotland) Act 1995".

The Bankruptcy (Scotland) Act 1985 (c. 66)

185.—(1) The Bankruptcy (Scotland) Act 1985 shall be amended as follows.

(2) In section 5(4) (meaning of qualified creditor), for the words "or by section 2(9) of the Drug Trafficking Act 1994" there shall be substituted the words "by section 2(9) of the Drug Trafficking Act 1994 or by section 114(1) of the Criminal Justice (Scotland) Act 1995".

(3) In section 7(1) (meaning of apparent insolvency), in the definition of "confiscation order", for the words "or by section 2(9) of the said Act of 1994" there shall be substituted the words "by section 2(9) of the Drug Trafficking Act 1994 or by section 114(1) of the Criminal Justice (Scotland) Act 1995".

The Criminal Justice Act 1988 (c. 33)

186.—(1) The Criminal Justice Act 1988 shall be amended as follows.

(2) In section 74(2)(c) (meaning of realisable property) after the word "property)" there shall be inserted the words "or Chapter II of Part II of the Criminal Justice (Scotland) Act 1995 (suspended forfeiture orders)".

(3) In section 77 (restraint orders)—

(a) in subsection (10) for the words "the High Court has made a restraint order" there shall be substituted the words "a restraint order has been made" and at the end of that subsection there shall be added the words—

"In this subsection, the reference to a restraint order includes a reference to a restraint order within the meaning of Part II of the Criminal Justice (Scotland) Act 1995 and, in relation to such an order, "realisable property" has the same meaning as in that Part"; and

(b) in subsection (11), for the words "court's directions" there shall be substituted the words "directions of the court which made the order".

(4) In section 89(2)(b) (compensation), for the words "an order under this Part of this Act" there shall be substituted the following paragraphs—

"(i) an order under this Part of this Act; or

(ii) an order of the Court of Session under section 101, 102, 103 or 104 of the Criminal Justice (Scotland) Act 1995."

(5) Sections 90 (recognition and enforcement of orders in Scotland), 91 (supplementary provision to section 90), 92 (inhibition and arrestment of property in Scotland), 93 (proof in Scotland of High Court orders) and 95 (enforcement of Northern Ireland order in Scotland) shall cease to have effect.

(6) In section 93E (applications of provisions relating to money laundering and other offences to Scotland), after the word "summarily)" there shall be inserted the words "or an offence punishable on summary conviction by a fine of an amount greater than the amount corresponding to level 5 on the standard scale or by imprisonment for a period exceeding 3 months or by both such fine and imprisonment".

The Copyright, Designs and Patents Act 1988 (c. 48)

187.—(1) The Copyright, Designs and Patents Act 1988 shall be amended as follows.

(2) In section 108(6) (order for delivery up in criminal proceedings) for the words "section 223 or 436 of the Criminal Procedure (Scotland) Act 1975" there shall be substituted the words "Chapter II of Part II of the Criminal Justice (Scotland) Act 1995".

(3) In section 199(6) (order for delivery up in criminal proceedings) for the words "section 223 or 436 of the Criminal Procedure (Scotland) Act 1975" there shall be substituted the words "Chapter II of Part II of the Criminal Justice (Scotland) Act 1995".

The Road Traffic Offenders Act 1988 (c. 53)

188. After section 33 of the Road Traffic Offenders Act 1988 (fine and imprisonment), there shall be inserted the following section—

"Forfeiture of vehicles: Scotland

33A.—(1) Where a person commits an offence to which this subsection applies by—

    (a) driving, attempting to drive, or being in charge of a vehicle; or

    (b) failing to comply with a requirement made under section 7 of the Road Traffic Act 1988 (failure to provide specimen for analysis or laboratory test) in the course of an investigation into whether the offender had committed an offence while driving, attempting to drive or being in charge of a vehicle, or

    (c) failing, as the driver of a vehicle, to comply with subsections (2) and (3) of section 170 of the Road Traffic Act 1988 (duty to stop and give information or report accident),

the court may, on an application under this subsection make an order forfeiting the vehicle concerned; and any vehicle forfeited under this subsection shall be disposed of as the court may direct.

    (2) Subsection (1) above applies—

    (a) to an offence under the Road Traffic Act 1988 which is punishable with imprisonment; and

    (b) to an offence of culpable homicide.

    (3) An application under subsection (1) above shall be at the instance of the prosecutor made when he moves for sentence or (if the person has been remitted for sentence under section 104 of the Criminal Procedure (Scotland) Act 1975) made before sentence is pronounced.

    (4) Where—

    (a) the court is satisfied, on an application under this subsection by the prosecutor—

        (i) that proceedings have been, or are likely to be, instituted against a person in Scotland for an offence to which subsection (1) above applies allegedly committed in the manner specified in paragraph (a), (b) or (c) of that subsection; and

        (ii) that there is reasonable cause to believe that a vehicle specified in the application is to be found in a place or in premises so specified; and

    (b) it appears to the court that there are reasonable grounds for thinking that in the event of the person being convicted of the offence an order under subsection (1) above might be made in relation to the vehicle,

the court may grant a warrant authorising a person named therein to enter and search the place or premises and seize the vehicle,

    (5) Where the court has made an order under subsection (1) above for the forfeiture of a vehicle, the court or any justice may, if satisfied on evidence on oath—

    (a) that there is reasonable cause to believe that the vehicle is to be found in any place or premises; and

    (b) that admission to the place or premises has been refused or that a refusal of such admission is apprehended,

issue a warrant of search which may be executed according to law.

    (6) In relation to summary proceedings, the reference in subsection (5) above to a justice includes a reference to the sheriff and to a magistrate.

    (7) Chapter II of Part II of the Criminal Justice (Scotland) Act 1995 shall not apply in respect of a vehicle in relation to which this section applies.

    (8) This section extends to Scotland only.".

The Prevention of Terrorism (Temporary Provisions) Act 1989 (c. 4)

189.—(1) Schedule 4 to the Prevention of Terrorism (Temporary Provisions) Act 1989 (forfeiture orders) shall be amended as follows.

    (2) In paragraph 16—

    (a) in sub-paragraph (1), paragraph (b) shall cease to have effect;

    (b) in sub-paragraph (2)(b), the words "where granted under sub-paragraph (1)(a) above," shall cease to have effect; and

    (c) in sub-paragraphs (5) and (6), the words "or arrestment", in each place where they occur, shall cease to have effect.

    (3) After paragraph 16 there shall be inserted the following paragraph—

    "16A.—(1) On the application of the prosecutor, the court may, in respect of moveable property affected by a restraint order (whether such property generally or particular such property), grant warrant for arrestment if the property would be arrestable if the person entitled to it were a debtor.

    (2) A warrant under sub-paragraph (1) above shall have effect as if granted on the dependence of an action for debt at the instance of the prosecutor against the person and may be executed, recalled, loosed or restricted accordingly.

    (3) The fact that an arrestment has been executed under sub-paragraph (2) above in respect of property shall not prejudice the exercise of an administrator's powers under or for the purposes of this Part of this Schedule in respect of that property.

(4) No arrestment executed under sub-paragraph (2) above shall have effect once, or in so far as, the restraint order affecting the property in respect of which the warrant for such arrestment has been granted has ceased to have effect in respect of that property; and the prosecutor shall apply to the court for an order recalling, or as the case may be, restricting the arrestment accordingly.".

(4) In paragraph 19 (enforcement in Scotland of orders made elsewhere in the British Isles—

(a) in sub-paragraph (5), for the words "and 16" there shall be substituted ", 16 and (subject to sub-paragraph (5A) below) 16A"; and

(b) after sub-paragraph (5) there shall be inserted the following sub-paragraph—

"(5A) In its application by virtue of sub-paragraph (5) above paragraph 16A above shall have effect with the following modifications—

(a) for the references to the prosecutor there shall be substituted references to the Lord Advocate; and

(b) for the references to the court there shall be substituted references to the Court of Session.".

The Criminal Justice (International Co-operation) Act 1990 (c. 5)

190.—(1) In section 9(6) of the Criminal Justice (International Co-operation) Act 1990 (enforcement of overseas forfeiture orders), for the words from "or an" to the end there shall be substituted the words "an offence to which Part VI of the Criminal Justice Act 1988 applies, an offence to which Chapter I of Part II of the Criminal Justice (Scotland) Act 1995 applies or an offence in respect of which a suspended forfeiture order may be made under section 87 of the said Act of 1995.".

(2) In section 15(3) of that Act (interest on sums unpaid under confiscation orders), for the words "applicable to an award of damages in" there shall be substituted "payable under a decree of".

(3) Section 17 (increase in realisable property: Scotland) of that Act shall cease to have effect.

The Northern Ireland (Emergency Provisions) Act 1991 (c. 24)

191. In section 50(2) of the Northern Ireland (Emergency Provisions) Act 1991 (realisable property, value and gifts), for paragraph (e) there shall be substituted the following paragraph—

"(e) Chapter II of Part II of the Criminal Justice (Scotland) Act 1995".

The Road Traffic Act 1991 (c. 40)

192. Section 37 of the Road Traffic Act 1991 (forfeiture of vehicles: Scotland) shall cease to have effect.

The Drug Trafficking Act 1994 (c. 37)

193.—(1) The Drug Trafficking Act 1994 shall be amended as follows.

(2) In section 4(7) (assessing the proceeds of drug trafficking), after paragraph (b) there shall be inserted—

"; or

(c) Part II of the Criminal Justice (Scotland) Act 1995.".

(3) In section 6(3) (meaning of realisable property), after paragraph (d) there shall be inserted the following paragraph—

"(e) Chapter II of Part II of the Criminal Justice (Scotland) Act 1995 (suspended forfeiture orders);".

(4) In section 18(2)(b)(ii) (compensation), for the words from "11" to "28" there shall be substituted "27, 28, 28A or 28B".

(5) In section 26(10) (restraint orders), after the words "1987" there shall be inserted "or Part II of the Criminal Justice (Scotland) Act 1995".

SCHEDULE 7

REPEALS

PART I

REPEALS RELATING TO PART I

Chapter	Short Title	Extent of repeal
1887 c. 35.	The Criminal Procedure (Scotland) Act 1887.	Section 3. Schedule D. Schedule E. Schedule N. Schedule O.
1949 c. 94.	The Criminal Justice (Scotland) Act 1949.	Schedule 7.
1954 c. 48.	The Summary Jurisdiction (Scotland) Act 1954.	In Schedule 2, Parts I and III to VI. Schedule 3.
1967 c. 80.	The Criminal Justice Act 1967.	In section 69((2), the words ", section 40 of the Prisons (Scotland) Act 1989".
1975 c. 21.	The Criminal Procedure (Scotland) Act 1975.	Section 14(3). Section 20(2). In section 26(3), the words "or justice". In section 33, in subsection (1), the words from "or where" to "application,"; and in subsection (2), the words "by telegraph". Section 62. In section 68, in each of subsections (2) and (4), the words "of Form No. 1 of Schedule 7 to the Criminal Justice (Scotland) Act 1949 or in the form". In section 69, the words from "and" in the third place where it occurs to "Act" in the fourth place where it occurs, and the words from "The executions" to the end. In section 73(1), the words from ", unless" to the end. In section 100, in subsection (1), the words from "but" to the end; and subsections (2) and (3). Section 110. In section 124, the proviso. In section 127(2), the words "Schedule N to the Criminal Procedure (Scotland) Act 1887 or in". Section 130(1) to (3). Section 132(2). In section 140A(1)(b), the words "were the offence charged the only offence so charged". Section 141(1)(b). Section 144. Section 145(4). Section 146. In section 150(1), the words ", where the accused is legally represented,". In section 153, subsection (1) and, in subsection (3)(b)(ii), the words from "(as" to the end. In section 156, in subsection (1)(b), the words from ", as" to the end; and subsections (4) and (5).

Chapter	Short Title	Extent of repeal
		In section 157, in subsection (1), the words "through his counsel", "in which the panel has pleaded guilty under section 102 of this Act" and "(other than a trial for murder)"; and subsection (2).
		Section 159(1) and (3).
		Section 160(3).
		Section 163.
		In section 174, subsections (3) and (4).
		In section 178(1), the words "either" and "or during such period as may be specified in the order".
		In section 183, in subsection (5A)(a), the words "has committed an offence punishable by imprisonment and"; and in subsection (7) the words "to the probationer".
		In section 186(1), the words "on oath".
		Section 190.
		In section 191(4), the words "placed on probation or" and "probation order or".
		In section 192, the words from "(other than" to "Act)" and the proviso.
		In section 196(1), the proviso.
		Section 225.
		Section 226.
		Section 227.
		In section 235, the words from "but in regard" to the end.
		Section 236C.
		Section 237.
		In section 238, in subsection (2), the words "or of any application for leave to appeal" and, in paragraphs (a)(i) and (b)(i), the words "or application".
		In section 239, in subsection (1), the words from "and" in the second place where it occurs to the end; and subsection (2).
		In section 240, the words from "except" where it first occurs to the end.
		Section 246.
		Section 256.
		Section 259.
		Section 265(3) and (5).
		In section 270, in subsection (2) the words from "(or any" to "note of appeal)" where first occurring and from "(or in the case" to "note of appeal)" where second occurring; in subsection (3), the words from "(or in the case" to "note of appeal)"; and in subsection (4), the words from "(or in the case" to "note of appeal)".
		Section 272.
		Section 273.
		Section 276.
		In section 277, in subsection (2), the words "section 236C", "section 237", "section 246", "section 259", "section 272" and "section 273".
		Section 282.

Chapter	Short Title	Extent of repeal
		Section 289D(1A)(d).
		In section 296, in subsections (1) and (2), the words "sitting summarily" in each place where they occur.
		In section 300(4), the words from ", or where" to "96 hours,".
		In section 309(1), the words "Schedule 2 to the Summary Jurisdiction (Scotland) Act 1954 or in".
		In section 310, the words "Part I of Schedule 2 to the Summary Jurisdiction (Scotland) Act 1954 or in".
		In section 311, in subsection (1), the words from "in" where it first occurs to the end; and subsections (4) and (5).
		Section 313.
		In section 314(1)(d), the words "or interim order".
		In section 315(2), the words "Part IV of Schedule 2 to the Summary Jurisdiction (Scotland) Act 1954 or in".
		In section 318(2), the words "Part IV of Schedule 2 to the Summary Jurisdiction (Scotland) Act 1954 and the corresponding forms contained in".
		In section 319(1), the words "other than a witness".
		In section 321, in subsection (1), the words "Part IV of Schedule 2 to the Summary Jurisdiction (Scotland) Act 1954 or in"; and in subsection (3), the words "either by way of trial or by way of remit to another court".
		Section 323(3).
		Section 331(2).
		In section 335(1), the words "penalty or".
		Section 336.
		In section 337A(1), the word "and" immediately following paragraph (a).
		In section 344(1), the words "or to produce documents in his possession when required by the court,".
		Section 345.
		Section 346(1)(b).
		In section 354(1), the proviso.
		Section 356(1) and (3).
		In section 357, in subsection (1)(a), the words "Form No. 2 or 3 of Part III of Schedule 2 to the Summary Jurisdiction (Scotland) Act 1954 or of"; and subsection (4).
		Section 360.
		In section 360A, in subsection (1)(b), the words from "as" to the end; and subsection (2).
		Section 366(2).
		Section 376(2).
		In section 379(1), the words "either" and "or during such period as may be specified in the order".

Chapter	Short Title	Extent of repeal
		In section 384, in subsection (1), the words from "and", where it first occurs, to "offence" in the third place where it occurs; in subsection (5A)(a), the words "has committed an offence punishable by imprisonment and"; in subsection (6), the words "convicted of and"; and in subsection (7) the words "to the probationer".
		In section 387(1), the words "on oath".
		Section 391.
		In section 392, in subsection (4), the words "placed on probation or"; and in subsection (5), the words "placed on probation or" and "probation order or".
		In section 393, the words from "(other than" to "Act)" and the proviso.
		In section 396(7), the words ", subject to any rules under this Part of this Act".
		In section 402, the proviso.
		In section 406, the words "damages or expenses,".
		In section 413(1), the words from "and shall" to the end.
		In section 430(1), the words "Part V of Schedule 2 to the Summary Jurisdiction (Scotland) Act 1954 or in".
		In section 432(1), the words from "and", where it second occurs, to the end.
		Section 435.
		In section 440, the words "Part V of Schedule 2 to the Summary Jurisdiction (Scotland) Act 1954 or in".
		In section 441, the words from ", although" to "place,".
		In section 453(4)(a)(i), the word "and".
		In section 454(1), the words "at the trial by the solicitor of the accused".
		Section 457.
		In section 462, in subsection (1), in the definition of "prosecutor", the words "private prosecutor," in the second place where they occur; and subsection (10).
		Schedule 3.
1976 c. 67.	The Sexual Offences (Scotland) Act 1976.	In section 4(1), in the proviso, the words "on indictment".
1980 c. 62.	The Criminal Justice (Scotland) Act 1980.	In section 26, in subsection (2), the word "summary" and the words from "In the foregoing" to the end; in subsection (4), the words from "or of a conviction" to "(8) below,"; and in subsection (5), the words "under summary procedure". In Schedule 4, paragraph 20.
1984 c. 36.	The Mental Health (Scotland) Act 1984.	In section 67(1), paragraph (a)(ii) and the preceding "or", and the words from "or the order" to the end.
1986 c. 36.	The Incest and Related Offences (Scotland) Act 1986.	In Schedule 1, paragraph 2.
1986 c. 47.	The Legal Aid (Scotland) Act 1986.	In section 25(2), the words "the Board is satisfied".
1988 c. 53.	The Road Traffic Offenders Act 1988.	In section 31(2), the words "penalties and". In section 32(6), the words "penalties and".

Chapter	Short Title	Extent of repeal
1990 c. 40.	The Law Reform (Miscellaneous Provisions) (Scotland) Act 1990.	In section 56(2), the word "and" immediately following paragraph (a). In section 58, the words "cited to give evidence in a trial".
1993 c. 9.	The Prisoners and Criminal Proceedings (Scotland) Act 1993.	In section 28(3), the words "or 384(1) (probation)". In section 33(1), the words from the beginning to "and" where it first occurs. In Schedule 5, paragraph 1(25)(a)(ii), (b)(i) and (c)(i), (26) and (28).
1994 c. 33.	The Criminal Justice and Public Order Act 1994.	In Schedule 10, paragraph 47.

PART II

REPEALS RELATING TO PART II

Chapter	Short Title	Extent of repeal
1975 c. 21.	The Criminal Procedure (Scotland) Act 1975.	Section 223. Section 436.
1987 c. 41.	The Criminal Justice (Scotland) Act 1987.	Section 1(3). Section 3(5). In section 5, in subsection (5), paragraph (b); subsection (6); in subsection (7) the words "notwithstanding subsections (5)(b) and (6) above", and subsection (8). In section 6, subsections (4) and (5). In section 7(2), in the entry relating to section 411, the words "except the proviso to subsection (3)". In section 11, in subsection (1), in paragraph (ii), the words "where granted under subsection (1)(a) above,"; in subsections (4) and (5), the words "or arrestment" in each place where they occur; and subsection (6). In section 12, in subsection (1), the words from "and the clerk of the court" to the end. In section 14(1)(c) the words from "and, without" to the end of the paragraph. In section 23(6) the words from "and without" to "family" and the words "(other than an obligation having priority, within the meaning of section 5(8) of this Act)". In section 26, in subsection (2)(b), the word "substantial"; and in subsection (4), after paragraph (c) the word "and". In section 30, in subsection (1), paragraphs (b)(i) and (c) and the word "and" immediately preceding paragraph (c). In section 41(2), the words from the end of paragraph (b) to the end of the subsection.

Chapter	Short Title	Extent of repeal
		In section 47(1) the definition of "associate".
1988 c. 33.	The Criminal Justice Act 1988.	Sections 90 to 93. Section 95.
1989 c. 4.	The Prevention of Terrorism (Temporary Provisions) Act 1989.	In Schedule 4, in paragraph 16, sub-paragraph (1)(b); in sub-paragraph (2)(b) the words "where granted under sub-paragraph (1)(a) above,"; and in sub-paragraphs (5) and (6), the words "or arrestment", in each place where they occur.
1990 c. 5.	The Criminal Justice (International Co-operation) Act 1990.	Section 17.
1991 c. 40.	The Road Traffic Act 1991.	Section 37.

INDEX

References are to sections and Schedules